The Cultural Context of Aging

WORLDWIDE PERSPECTIVES

Third Edition

EDITED BY

Jay Sokolovsky

Westport, Connecticut
London

Library of Congress Cataloging-in-Publication Data

The cultural context of aging : worldwide perspectives / edited by Jay Sokolovsky — 3rd ed.
    p. cm.
  Includes bibliographical references and index.
  ISBN 978-0-275-99288-0 (alk. paper) — ISBN 978-0-275-99302-3 ((pbk) : alk. paper)
    1. Older people—Cross-cultural studies. 2. Aging—Cross-cultural studies. I. Sokolovsky, Jay.
  HQ1061.C79   2009
  305.26—dc22   2008027348

British Library Cataloguing in Publication Data is available.

Library of Congress Catalog Card Number: 2008027348
ISBN: 978-0-275-99288-0
    978-0-275-99302-3 (pbk.)

First published in 2009

Praeger Publishers, 88 Post Road West, Westport, CT 06881
An imprint of Greenwood Publishing Group, Inc.
www.praeger.com

Printed in the United States of America

The paper used in this book complies with the Permanent Paper Standard issued by the National Information Standards Organization (Z39.48–1984).

10 9 8 7 6 5 4 3 2 1

To my beloved grandchildren Josephine, Alex, Natalie and Zemanel, who have made my life more complete by enrolling in "Grandpa Jay's Summer Playschool" for the past twelve summers. They are my enduring legacy.

Contents

Preface

I approached the latest edition of this book as I was beginning my sixth decade of life. This has caused me to reflect and comment in places throughout
the introductory text materials about my own encounter with the edges of late
adulthood. In one aspect this has involved learning to live with and adjust to
bodily changes, such as the growth of cataracts or arthritis beginning to appear
in my joints. Unlike a number of the book's authors, I did not have to cope
with prolonged eldercare, as my own parents died very quickly from rapidly
advancing cancers before their mid-seventies. As the eldest child of these
parents, their passing did elevate me into the very senior rank of my siblings
and their grown children. Yet, a sense of my own changing place in the generational scheme of things has been most influenced by the birth and maturation of four grandchildren, two of whom are now teenagers.

When I first taught a course on the anthropology of aging in fall 1976, there
was a mere scattering of substantial writings on aging in diverse societies
around the world. However, this has dramatically changed as readers will find
in this third edition. Since that time, there has been an explosion of research
undertaken not only by anthropologists, but by scholars in other social and behavioral sciences. It has grown far beyond what can be contained in any one,
even quite large, volume. Because of this, I first developed for the second edition a large Web site to expand readers' connections to the enormous body of
knowledge emerging in the global study of aging. I hope students and faculty
will take the time to explore these additional paths of knowledge.

NEW TO THE THIRD EDITION

This latest edition is almost completely new. It substantially expands upon
the broad thematic focus of cultural context to explore the dual themes of the

"cultural scripts" and "cultural spaces" in which aging is experienced. This new volume continues the emphasis on seeking out cutting-edge research on aging from around the world. It includes an expanded geographical reach with new original articles dealing with China, India, Italy, Indonesia, Okinawa, Peru, Amazonia and suburban and small-city America. Since the second edition was completed in 1996, there have developed exciting new directions and topics in gerontological research and a growth of long-term and cross-cultural projects. In the first instance, there are now articles dealing with the new topics such as: the "grandmother hypothesis" and the bioevolution of late life; "conscious" aging; the "age-friendly" community movement; menopause in comparative context; globalization; custodial grandparenting; the long-term care "culture change" movement; and urban aging. I have also drawn upon the latest work from major global projects such as: The World Cities Project; The Okinawa Centenarian Study; Tsimane Health and Life History Project; the Ageing in Indonesia Project; and Project AGE, Generation and Experience.

Crucial additions take advantage of the Internet. Most important is the inclusion of a "Web book" drawn mostly from key articles in the previous edition. This literally provides readers with two books in one. These ten Web book chapters are listed in the print table of contents, but can only be accessed on the Internet at www.stpt.usf.edu/~jsokolov/webbook. The book is supported by a huge Cultural Context of Aging Web site (www.stpt.usf.edu/~jsokolov) with resources keyed to the different sections and chapters of the new book. A special feature is the inclusion of PowerPoints developed by many of the book's authors.

This book would not have been possible without the constant support of my wife, anthropologist Maria Vesperi, who not only provided invaluable editing help, but also sustained me during very long hours spent over the past two years trying to get everything right. I especially want to thank Marianne Gillogly, who, as my assistant in the final stages of this book, made its completion possible. She literally helped me put it together with fine editing, masterful file organization and image processing. There are many other people who made this book possible. Important among them are Pat Draper, Juliana McDonald, Meridith Uttley, Janelle Christensen and Paulo Saad, who took the time to provide insightful comments on some of the book chapters. I would also like to thank Dan Kaufman, former student and now computer professional, who helped design the book's Web site and continues to provide support in this arena. Also much appreciated was the help in typing parts of this manuscript by Harriet Fletcher. Finally, I would like to thank my editors at Greenwood, Debora Carvalko and Elizabeth Potenza, who supported my efforts with a steady hand and sage advice.

Introduction: Human Maturity and Global Aging in Cultural Context

Jay Sokolovsky

The real voyage of discovery consists in not seeking new landscapes but in having new eyes.

Marcel Proust

Elder competitive biker in Tokyo, Japan 2007. Photo by Jay Sokolovsky.

The first decade of the twenty-first century has been marked by a dramatic interest and growing concern over an unprecedented human transformation, the global aging of human populations. As suggested by the French poet Marcel Proust, in understanding the older Japanese competitive biker seen in the photo above and his contemporaries around the world, we indeed will need new eyes focused on dynamic elderscapes emerging in the most unlikely places. In China, India, Mexico, Italy and Japan, with unanticipated rapid fertility declines and large population cohorts surviving into late adulthood, a whole new matrix of generational relations and late-life possibilities is emerging. As Kevin Kinsella will detail in this book's first section, over the past century there has been both a doubling in average human longevity and the near prospect of our planet having more seniors than young children (see Figure 01.1). These facts have brought many societies to the shores of uncharted social waters, promising transformations in almost every aspect of our lives. Fully, 85 percent of all children born in postindustrial nations can now expect to reach age sixty-five and many will experience two more decades of relatively healthy life. This is creating expectations and perceptions of older adulthood that never before existed for our species (Butler 2008).

Perceptions of aging itself seem to be maturing in many places with the creation of a whole new stage of late adulthood, identified not so much with closeness to death, but with productive and creative engagement with life

Figure 01.1
Young Children and Older People as a Percentage of the Global Population

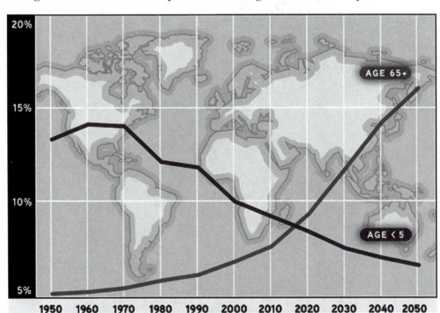

Source: Figure adapted from National Institute on Aging. 2007. "Why Population Aging Matters: A Global Perspective," page 6, Washington: National Institute on Aging.

Figure 01.2
Probability of 50-Year-Old-Living to 90, 1900 to 2002

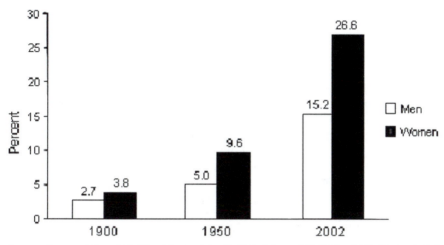

Source: Computed from U.S. life tables in: Arias E. *United States Life Tables, 2002*. National vital statistics reports; vol. 53. no. 6. Hyattsville, MD: National Center for Health Statistics, 2004.

(Smith and Clurman 2007). The early manifestation of this shift came in the 1990s with Western Europe realizing the need to mount a public campaign to promote "Active Aging" (Ney 2005). The rapid aging of its workforce has added a new focus on remaining economically competitive by opening up high-tech educational opportunities to older adults and discouraging early retirement. The European Union's new 2007 action plan "Ageing Well in the Information Society" is targeted at improving the life of older people at home, in the workplace and in society in general.[1] Such ideas have reverberated in some unlikely places, like China, where the collapse of the communal system and reduced availability of filial support have pushed elders to promote self-care as the key to healthy aging. When anthropologist Hong Zhang returned to her homeland in 2007 (this volume Part III), she did not find elders waiting to be cared for by doting relatives. Instead she encountered mass groups of aged, flocking to urban parks doing Tai Chi, the waltz and various other forms of exercise to avoid what they saw as a newly problematic dependence on the family and state.

IT'S NOT YOUR GRANDMA'S OLD AGE ANYMORE!

Some of the dramatic implications of this new millennium of aging are seen in Figure 01.2. We see here that in the United States at the mid-point of the twentieth century a middle-aged woman had almost a one-in-ten chance of living until age ninety. But, by the twenty-first century, the odds of a similarly aged person still living into their ninth decade had almost tripled! Even more impressive, the Society of Actuaries estimates that in 2006, if you are part of a couple, both aged sixty-five, at least one of you had a 50–50 chance of reaching beyond age ninety-two and a 25 percent chance of living past your ninety-seventh birthday (Society of Actuaries 2006). And listen up, students: if you were born between 1980 and 1990, you have a 50–50 chance of living to age 100! You can even improve your odds of living a long and healthy life by carefully reading the chapter by Willcox et al. in Part VI of this book. It details the research of the Okinawa Centenarian Project, documenting the life of elders who on average live the longest and also have the planet's highest healthy longevity.

A handful of nations such as Japan and Italy lead the global aging pack, having grandly ushered in this new millennium with more elders than youths. As will be seen through new original research in this volume, these countries are struggling to both understand their unique situation and to find culturally appropriate answers to their all-too-rapidly maturing societies.

It is the goal of this book to pull together research addressing such concerns from a global, cross-cultural perspective. In doing so, the chapters that follow explore two broad, interrelated facets of late adulthood: (1) how older adults function as social actors in the setting of diverse societies; and (2) how the intersection of culture and globalizing contexts creates increasingly varied ways of experiencing late adulthood. In every corner of the world this is becoming the new reality of what elderhood means and how it connects to the broader society. This new global age of aging is catching the world's attention (United Nations 2007c).

GLOBAL AGING BECOMES TOPIC "A"

From Problem to Catastrophe to Hero

Western thinking about elders and aging has changed over the last several decades, from images of dependent frailty and impending disaster to second life, new opportunities and perhaps saviors of society (Freedman 2007). Documentation on the social support provided by older adults to their families and communities is simply staggering. In the early twenty-first century, adults age fifty-five and older in the United States contributed $161.7 billion worth of volunteering and unpaid caregiving in caring for family members, helping friends and neighbors and volunteering for nonprofit organizations. The value of help provided by older family caregivers alone reached nearly $100 billion (Johnson and Schaner 2005). This is dramatically observed in the rapid rise of custodial child care by grandparents, reaching across ethnic and class lines in North America (see Hayslip Part IV and Weibel-Orlando Part II Web book). William Thomas even had the audacity to subtitle a book *How Elders Can Save the World* (2004) and this sentiment has been echoed more recently by Caroline Van Dullemen who sees Africa's elders as one of the keys to productive development of that continent (2006; see also Makoni 2008). We will see in Box III.1, "The Grandmother Project," the powerful function of older women in enhancing the health and well-being of younger community members in West

Africa. Gradually, the global community has come to embrace this new vision of aging. This was reflected in 1999, when the United Nations celebrated the "International Year of Older Persons." More substantially, in 2002, the United Nations developed an International Consensus on Aging in its meetings in Spain, where it laid out the central premise of the Madrid Plan in developing a "Society for All Ages" (Sidorenko 2007).[2] As documented by Shenk and Mahon in Part III, such actions have inspired grass roots and governmental action within impoverished countries like Peru, which had previously done its best to ignore the dire situation of many older citizens.

These efforts of the United Nations consolidated almost two decades of a global focus to appraise the needs and potential of the aged through two world assemblies, numerous commissions, experts meetings, reports and publications (www.un.org/esa/socdev/ageing).[3] Importantly, the UN's World Health Organization has just launched an ambitious international project called SAGE—The Study of Global Ageing and Adult Health—in China, Ghana, India, Mexico and Russia, with more in-depth studies being planned in Asia and Africa.[4] Nations around the globe are finally beginning to take late life seriously.

The maturing of our planet's citizens is a topic generating heated discussion and "action plans" from Washington, DC, to Mexico City and especially throughout Asia where the largest number of elders now live (Mujahid 2006). Suddenly the phrase "Global Aging" is topic "A." We see this in new university centers such as Harvard's Global Generations Policy Institute (www.genpolicy.com); non-governmental organizations (NGOs) such as the Global Aging Initiative (http://www.csis.org/gai); international research networks such as NICE, National Initiative for the Care of the Elderly (www.nicenet.ca); and venture capital companies selling advise on making a killing by catching the "Age Wave" (www.agewave.com). Some large corporations like insurance giants HSBC and MetLife, along with technology focused Intel, view global aging as the millennium's golden business opportunity. Each of these companies has begun to invest in both substantial international research on retirement planning, the creation of healthy "livable" communities and the role of technology in allowing older adults to age well in their own neighborhoods. HSBC Insurance in conjunction with Oxford University is carrying out "The Future of Retirement" project, the world's largest investigation of attitudes towards aging, longevity and retirement. Their latest survey was undertaken in twenty-one countries and territories across five continents (HSBC Insurance 2007).

In the case of Intel, in 2006 it initiated the "Global Aging Experience Study" to look at how older adults in various parts of the world use their local environment to experience a positive old age. Much of this work is being done by anthropologists applying the kind of qualitative focus elaborated on in this volume. One of this book's authors, anthropologist Athena McLean (Part VI), was working in Ireland in 2008 with an offshoot of this effort called the TRIL Project, Technology Research for Independent Living. Here interdisciplinary teams of engineers, physicians, neuroscientists and other social and behavioral scientists work together to develop technologies that will enable elders to remain in their own homes. The initial phase of their European field research was completed in 2006 and Intel social scientists are now analyzing the results and planning the next phase of this project, which will also take Intel researchers to Asia. Such applied studies are strongly connected to a growing international movement to promote life-span and elder friendly communities, an issue that is directly addressed by Philip Stafford in Part V.[5] Laid out in Box 01.1 are the parameters of the Intel project and some basic findings from the research.

BOX 01.1 INTEL'S GLOBAL AGING EXPERIENCE STUDY

Intel believes that new technologies, designed with an explicit focus on the needs of older adults and their clinicians and care providers, can help to meet those challenges, easing the burden on strained health-care systems and providing peace of mind and meaningful engagement for the aging. In support of that goal, the Product Research and Innovation (PRI) group within Intel's Digital Health Group launched a multiyear project called the Global Aging Experience Study. The objective of the research project is to gain an understanding of the social and cultural differences in people's experiences of aging and health and to identify the types of technologies and services that could empower people to be more proactive in managing their health and wellness.

Since data shows that western European countries are experiencing the effects of this aging demographic shift most acutely, we focused initially on seven European nations: France, Germany, Ireland, Italy, Spain, Sweden and the United Kingdom. We utilized ethnographic research techniques such as open-ended interviews, observations and multiday visits to dozens of households. Following are the key findings of the field research.

KEY FINDINGS: In the seven European countries we studied, we found a range of differences in people's experiences of aging and health. However, we also uncovered several common themes that help us to determine what technology might be useful to an aging population.

People want to focus on what they CAN do, not what they can't. Few people self-identify as either sick or old. Many people seek out challenges in order to keep themselves mentally sharp and choose not to use canes or other assistive devices. Still, many people will need assistance. The key is to provide technology that people recognize as helping them to do what they want, rather than reminding them that they are no longer capable.

Aging in place means more than staying at home. The ability to take care of one's own home maintenance or gardening, to buy groceries and prepare meals, to move about the neighborhood or town—all of these factors can seriously impact an aging person's ability to live a desired life. Technology can play a major role here, for instance, by helping communities to identify and enable trusted providers of home services, to enable mobility and to provide increased peace of mind, both within and outside the home.

Health is not an objective quality; it's defined collaboratively and culturally. Health is defined through interactions and negotiations among various people,

continued

including informal caregivers, family members, hired in-home and medical caregivers and the elderly themselves—all of whom may differ in their assessments of the elders' health. Cultural, social and political systems also shape attitudes and behaviors related to health. People mark the progression of aging by watershed events such as falls, change of residence or loss of a loved one. Monitoring and early intervention are useful, but people often are in a state of healthy denial about aging and thus may not embrace such solutions. Our technologies must enable people to understand the state of their own health through active daily monitoring, but to do so in a way that aligns with their preferred ways of living.

Healthy aging is inextricably linked to social participation. People of all ages aspire to have a sense of belonging, a legitimate role in the lives of their families and communities. Aging adults want to continue to feel useful, productive and engaged with family and community, without feeling they are a burden.

Related Resources

"Aging-in-Place: Advanced Smart-Home Systems" is a related ongoing Intel project in Seattle, which seeks to enable elders with severe cognitive and physical impairment to being moved into a hospital or institution: www.intel.com/research/prohealth/cs-aging_in_place.htm.

CAST (Center for Aging Services Technologies): www.agingtech.org/index.aspx.

Journal of the International Society for Gerontechnology. This is the first international scientific journal devoted to gerontechnology. It contains articles that juxtapose research in aging and technology with the broader categories of housing, mobility, health, communication, leisure and work: www.gerontechnology.info/Journal.

The TRIL Project (Technology Research for Independent Living) is a coordinated collection of research projects addressing the physical, cognitive and social consequences of aging, all informed by ethnographic research and supported by a shared pool of knowledge and engineering resources: www.trilcentre.org.

Adapted from: Intel Web site, www.intel.com/healthcare/hri/pdf/gaexperience.pdf.

THE CULTURAL CONTEXT OF AGING

As explored by Gurven and Kaplan in Part I, the evolutionary legacy of aging involves both a substantial postreproductive survival and a powerful biological dimension of senescence. Yet a global perspective on aging yields a wondrous array of social responses to the physical imperatives of growing old.[6] The chapters in this volume will explore the fabric of values, perceptions, human relationships and socially engineered behavior that clothes people as they pass through the older adult years. Such varied patterns of created ideology, social organization and the ways people produce and distribute valued objects constitute the cultural systems into which all humans grow. Each cultural system creates a perceptual lens composed of potent symbols and meanings through which a particular version of reality is developed. A powerful example is provided in the study of East Asian Indian transplants to America who appreciate the availability of high-tech health care but find unbearable, end-of-life norms in hospitals or nursing homes. Likewise, in such settings, well-meaning and compassionate caregiving professionals reject as irrational and unhealthy the behavior of Indian families toward a relative in the last moments of life. This transcultural misunderstanding flows from the Hindu cultural practice of placing the dying person on the floor to sever their link to material things and thereby make it easier for the soul to leave at the moment of death (Lamb 2006; see also Lamb this volume).

Yet, people are not just passive recipients of culture. We will see that at every turn and in far-flung cultural venues. In globalizing urban India, as Sarah Lamb shows in Part V, new social inventions such as "Laughing Clubs" mark an age-peer alternative to traditional paths to contentment and health in old age (See also Box V.1). In the United States, more than thirty years ago, J. Scott Francher suggested that the symbolic themes represented in the glorification of the youthful, competitively self-reliant and action-oriented "Pepsi Generation" presented a set of core values contradictory and harmful to the self-esteem of the old (1973). The continuation of this advertising sentiment through the Nike corporation's "Just Do It" campaign reflects key elements of American culture that have not been ignored by the elderly (See Featherstone and Hepworth Part II this volume). As I write this introduction, older adults in the United States are harnessing elements of cultural ideals such as independence, personal initiative and civic responsibility in the process of reshaping the very meaning of mid-and-late life (Harvard School of Public Health 2004; Wilson and Simson 2006; Freedman 2007). As will be further discussed in Parts I, II and V, this involves both a powerful ethos of community engagement through groups and organizations such as the "Raging Grannies," "Civic Ventures" or the "Gray Panthers" (Sanjek 2009), but also a more introspective turn toward what has come to be called "Conscious Aging" (see Moody Part I).

Culture exists in relation to the contextual framework in which human actors find themselves (Fry 2006). Such "background" factors can be relevant at various levels of analysis. On the personal level, this might involve looking at how childlessness or poor health affect the chances for aging well or the nature of support in one's later years (Kreager and Schröder-Butterfill 2005). Alternatively, on a societal scale one could examine how differential access to wealth and status through kinship, or even structural differences between communities in the same society, alter culturally based premises about how one grows old. This will be seen dramatically in Part V with a study of aging among the women-centered Mingakabau of Indonesia, where older females control land wealth, homes and the marriage system, reversing many Western assumptions about gender and the life course. Likewise in Zhang's work in China, she shows that there are dire consequences for elders depending on whether late life is experienced in rural or urban communities (see Garrett 1998 for the United States).

Situational factors can be strong enough to completely reverse patterns of respect and support linked to cultural traditions. As we will see in this chapter's discussion of the Tiwi of Australia and in Anthony Glascock's chapter in Part I, "death hastening" of the aged can take place in societies that, in general, claim to revere old people (see also Barker Part VI). The decision to quicken the demise of an elderly person is vitally connected to situational conditions, such as very low levels of functioning by an elder or a lack of close kin. Similarly, in Part IV, my own research examines how the clash of ethnic cultures and contextual realities in the United States can dramatically transform the traditional meaning of "filial devotion" toward the elderly in some Asian groups.

Cultural systems are in fact highly adaptable, although they tend to craft lifestyles within broad patterns of values and ideal behavior (Fry 2006). This will be encountered in the day-to-day realities of the Iranian immigrants living in the Silicon Valley area of Northern California, who strive to retain a sense of Iranian identity without the densely kin-enmeshed neighborhoods of Iran (Hegland Part IV). Here the ethnic mix of the United States' social landscape greatly complicates any simple analysis of "American" culture. Everywhere we look at the ways in which people grow old, one encounters increasingly varied *scripts* for the life course, new *cultural spaces* and emergent *elderscapes*.

CULTURAL SCRIPTS, CULTURAL SPACES AND ELDERSCAPES

My use of the term *cultural scripts* comes from work in Asia by Kalyani Mehta (1997) and Susan Long (2005). In studying ethnic Chinese, Malays and Indians in the multiethnic city-state of Singapore, Mehta shows that enactment of broadly similar scripts for the life course and late adulthood are impacted by both situational contexts and specific cultural dictates. For example, late-life migration to the city places kinship ties in a new cultural space and usually means that while one might have a married son and perhaps grandchildren in the local environment, one would not have siblings or many other age-peer relatives around for support. Within a seemingly similar cultural perspective there are different implications among Hindu Indians and Islamic Malaysians in the script of late-life women who experienced the death of a spouse. In the first instance, widowhood was stigmatized and such women were strongly discouraged from remarrying, while the widows practicing Islam were not stigmatized and remarriage of females was strongly encouraged (see also Cattell Part I). Here the comingling of the situational and the cultural can be particularly powerful for older women, especially in the urban immigrant situation where supportive homegrown institutions and networks may not be in full flower or even exist.

Susan Long's recent research in Japan focuses on how people, through the use of varied cultural scripts, navigate the changing cultural landscape of death and end-of-life decision-making (Long 2005). Part of the difficulty for many Japanese is adjusting to a dramatic shift of dying at home versus the cultural space where it almost always happens now, in hospitals. In Part III, Brenda Jenike and John Traphagan also look at Japan and examine the broader new cultural spaces and emergent cultural scripts by which elder care is being transformed. Elsewhere is Asia, in both urban China (Zhang Part III) and India (Lamb Part V), cultural scripts focused on filial devotion enacted in multigenerational households are being short-circuited by "outsourced" sons and the competing demands of educating children. Expanding the space for experiencing older life has meant seeking age-peer communion in urban parks with dance groups and laughing clubs and in seeking residential refuge in Hindu temples and new kinds of elder residences.

In certain countries there has developed a dramatic connection of emergent scripts for aging with new interconnected sets of cultural spaces for experiencing late adulthood. One of the best places to observe this is Charlotte County, Florida, home to the nation's highest proportion of older adults, with 35 percent of its residents over age sixty-five. In this setting, sociologist Stephen Katz (Part V) uses innovative methods to take readers into the heart of what he calls the "Elderscapes" of this elderly dense area. The notions of cultural spaces and elderscapes overlap with a construct Gene Cohen calls "Landscapes for Aging" to describe the growing number of sites described by Katz in Florida where older persons reside, create active social lives and receive care (www.gwumc.edu/cahh/rsch/index.htm). These new Landscapes for Aging include the growing diversity of retirement, life-care, continuing-care and "active-living" communities, congregate housing, assisted living facilities, senior hotels, foster care, group homes, day care, respite care and nomadic mobile home communities. What is particularly important about the elderscapes and new cultural spaces created within them is the continuing engagement of old adults in shaping the very context of their lives (see especially Counts and Counts 2001 and Part V Web book).

ANTHROPOLOGY AND THE QUALITATIVE SEARCH FOR MEANING

Typically, cultural anthropologists have chosen to study such human variation by establishing themselves for long-term stays in locales where people carry out their everyday lives. Called "ethnography," this prolonged, very personal encounter of an anthropologist with individuals in their community can provide a special insight into how people confront and deal with the cultural contexts life has dealt them (Keith 1988; Sokolovsky 2001). The aim of this approach is to acquire a holistic understanding of cultural systems through "participant observation," enabled by engaging in daily life and recording in the native language the meanings of things, persons and actions.

Participant observation is critical in understanding the cultural context of old age and even in learning appropriate questions to ask (Sokolovsky 2006). This applies as much to studying aging in small villages in the South Pacific as it does to research in American nursing homes, ethnic enclaves, rural Japan, or neighborhoods in four "world cities." Jane Peterson, in trying to understand Seattle's black aged, entered into the midst of their cultural world by working as a nurse for a church group that provided important services to the elderly

(Part IV Web book). In my own work with the older homeless population, I found that asking seemingly straightforward questions without a clear understanding of the lifestyle of long-term homelessness resulted in almost worthless data and frequent hostility. It was necessary not only to learn the colorful argot of the streets—such as "carrying the banner" (sleeping outdoors)—and to travel with people on their daily rounds, but also to work in a soup kitchens and drop-in centers that sustained many of the older homeless adults with whom I worked (Part V Web book).

Several of the authors in this volume have had long-term research connections—upwards of three decades—to the people they write about. We shall see the advantages of this approach in the articles in Part I by Rosenberg and Cattell and later on with my work in Mexico (Part III). Such temporal perspectives provide a unique opportunity to scrutinize how well the implications of gerontological theory stand up to longitudinal testing within whole communities. This is an indispensable way to examine the roles of aged citizens and the support directed toward elderly people within the context of sweeping global changes.

The Rise of "Ethnogerontology"

Despite the early seminal book by Leo Simmons, *The Role of the Aged in Primitive Society* (1945), concern for a worldwide, cross-cultural analysis of aging has developed slowly.[7] In the 1950s and 1960s, a serious ethnographic gaze was first directed, not within the non-Western world, but at frail elders interacting with the U.S. medical system. In the late 1950s, Otto von Mering conducted fieldwork in the geriatric wards of psychiatric hospitals, illustrating how cultural devaluing of old age led to a withdrawal of psychosocial care for older patients (1957). This was followed by Jules Henry's *Culture Against Man* (1963), a searing ethnographic account of life in three American nursing homes and Clark and Anderson's *Culture and Aging* (1967), exploring the dynamics of San Francisco's community-based care of mentally impaired older citizens.[8] The serious issues explored in these pioneering works are far from resolved in the twenty-first century. They will be explored in this book's final section, where the modern quest for what Thomas calls "Eldertopia" is being sought, in part, through the powerful "Culture Change Movement" seeking to radically reform elder care (see especially Baker 2007; McLean; Polivka; and Thomas Part VI).

From a global perspective, it was not until the publication of the volume *Aging and Modernization*, edited by Cowgill and Holmes in 1972, that knowledge from modern ethnographic studies was employed to test gerontological theory. Here, detailed studies of fourteen different societies were compared to examine the impact of industrialization, urbanization and Westernization on the status of the aged. Although now superseded by the framework of globalization, the theoretical propositions developed by Cowgill and Holmes in *Aging and Modernization* and in their later works have served as a most controversial stimulus to subsequent work on aging done around the world (Cowgill 1986; Rhoads and Holmes 1995; see also Part III).

The maturing of an anthropological specialty in aging has unfolded through gerontologically focused ethnographies and edited books, texts and special issues of journals (see Sokolovsky 2009; this volume's Web site). Books such as *New Methods for Old Age Research* (Fry and Keith 1986), *Age and Anthropological Theory* (Kertzer and Keith 1984), *Old Age in Global Perspective* (Albert and Cattell 1994), *The Aging Experience* (Keith et al. 1994), *Other Cultures, Elder Years* (Rhoads and Holmes 1995) and *Ageing Societies* (Harper 2006) have finally brought to bear the distinct realm of anthropological methods and theory on questions of aging and the aged (see also Fry 2008a, Fry 2008b; Sokolovsky 2009). Out of this scholarship there has emerged, over the last two decades, an important new specialty variously referred to as "comparative sociocultural gerontology," "ethnogerontology," or "anthropology of aging" (Sokolovsky 2009).[9]

Qualitative Gerontology

The importance of this perspective has spilled over into other disciplines often focused on developing cultural competence among social workers, psychologists and physicians who serve ethnically varied communities (Crewe 2004; Tanabe 2007). For example, some medical schools, such as Stanford and Florida State University, are developing what they call "ethnogeriatrics" as a specialty exploring the interface of late-life health with culture and ethnicity.[10] From a broader perspective, a multidisciplinary movement sometimes referred to as "Qualitative Gerontology," has also been seeking to establish in-depth modes of analysis as an equal partner to more quantitative methods (Rowles and Schoenberg 2002). While many of this volume's authors come from my own discipline of anthropology, there are also contributions from social work, psychology, medicine, philosophy, sociology and public health. Nevertheless, these contributions are framed by a twenty-first century paradigm of cultural anthropology, which gathers data on cultural systems via community-based, long-term qualitatively oriented research and then tries to understand this information within broader regional and global settings.

Outside of anthropology, one of the strongest advocates of this approach is sociologist Jaber Gubrium, who, in an editorial in *The Gerontologist*, argues that qualitative approaches should not be viewed solely as a second-class precursor to more "powerful" statistical analysis (1992). According to Gubrium, good qualitative research is scientific in striving to generate theoretically informed findings. Such work attempts to represent the "native complexity" of behavior and how that complexity is organized within an existing community (Schoenberg and McAuley 2007; Traphagan 2007). Most of the articles in this volume follow this approach and seek to deeply enter the world of meaning by viewing how the lives of real people intersect with the reality of cultural systems and community settings. We will see the importance of the approach in Part I where Harriet Rosenberg shows how narratives of elder complaints can be part of a positive system of care. Later, in Part VI, Athena McLean shows that much disruptive behavior of cognitively impaired seniors lies outside the disease process and is better explained by how the care system interacts with personhood.

ANTHROPOLOGICAL ENCOUNTERS WITH AGING AND LATE LIFE

While gerontological research as an anthropological specialty spans barely three decades, studies conducted earlier in this century can provide revealing, yet tantalizingly incomplete, glimpses of the elderly in non-Western cultural settings (see especially Warner 1937; Arensberg and Kimball 1940; Spencer 1965). For example, in 1928 anthropologist C. W. Hart encountered the cultural context of frail old age among a preliterate people called the Tiwi, who generally accorded the healthy elderly high levels of support. As seen in these diary passages from his early fieldwork, the severe physical and cognitive decline of a particular Tiwi woman set in motion a dramatic ritual for dealing with this situation.

After a few weeks on the islands I also became aware that [the Tiwi] were often uneasy with me because I had no kinship linkage to them. This was shown in many ways, among others in their dissatisfaction with the negative reply they always got to their question, "What clan does he belong to?" Around the Mission, to answer it by saying, "White men have no clans," was at least a possible answer, but among the pagan bands like the Malauila and Munupula such an answer was incomprehensible—to them everybody must have a clan, just as everybody must have an age. If I had a clan I would be inside the kinship system, everybody would know how to act toward me, I would know how to act toward everybody else and life would be easier and smoother for all.

How to get myself into the clan and kinship system was quite a problem. Even Mariano, [Hart's native guide], while admitting the desirability, saw no way of getting me in. There did not seem much hope and then suddenly the problem was solved entirely by a lucky accident. I was in a camp where there was an old woman who had been making herself a terrible nuisance. Toothless, almost blind, withered and stumbling around, she was physically quite revolting and mentally rather senile. She kept hanging round me asking for tobacco, whining, wheedling, sniveling, until I got thoroughly fed up with her. As I had by now learned the Tiwi equivalents of "Go to hell" and "Get lost," I rather enjoyed being rude to her and telling her where she ought to go. Listening to my swearing in Tiwi, the rest of the camp thought it a great joke and no doubt egged her on so that they could listen to my attempts to get rid of her. This had been going on for some time when one day the old hag used a new approach. "Oh, my son," she said, "please give me tobacco." Unthinkingly I replied, "Oh, my mother, go jump in the ocean." Immediately a howl of delight arose from everybody within earshot and they all gathered round me patting me on the shoulder and calling me by a kinship term. She was my mother and I was her son. This gave a handle to everybody else to address me by a kinship term. Her other sons from then on called me brother, her brothers called me "sister's son"; and so on. I was now in the kinship system; my clan was Jabijabui (a bird) because my mother was Jabijabui.

From then on the change in the atmosphere between me and the tribe at large was remarkable. Strangers were now told that I was Jabijabui and that my mother was the old so-and-so and when told this, stern old men would relax, smile and say "then you are my brother" (or my son, or my sister's son, or whatever category was appropriate) and I would struggle to respond properly by addressing them by the proper term.

How seriously they took my presence in their kinship system is something I never will be sure about. However, toward the end of my time on the islands an incident occurred that surprised me because it suggested that some of them had been taking my presence in the kinship system much more seriously than I had thought. I was approached by a group of about eight or nine senior men all of whom I knew. They were all senior members of the Jabijabui clan and they had decided among themselves that the time had come to get rid of the decrepit old woman who had first called me son and whom I now called mother. As I knew, they said, it was Tiwi custom, when an old woman became too feeble to look after herself, to "cover her up." This could only be done by her sons and her brothers and all of them had to agree beforehand, since once it was done they did not want any dissension among the brothers or clansmen, as that might lead to a feud. My "mother" was now completely blind, she was constantly falling over logs or into fires and they, her senior clansmen, were in agreement that she would be better out of the way. Did I agree? I already knew about "covering up." The Tiwi, like many other hunting and gathering peoples, sometimes got rid of their ancient and decrepit females. The method was to dig a hole in the ground in some lonely place, put the old woman in the hole and fill it in with earth until only her head was showing. Everybody went away for a day or two and then went back to the hole to discover to their surprise, that the old woman was dead, having been too feeble to raise her arms from the earth. Nobody had "killed" her, her death in Tiwi eyes was a natural one. She had been alive when her relatives last saw her. I had never seen it done, though I knew it was the custom, so I asked my brothers if it was necessary for me to attend the "covering up." They said no and they would do it, but only after they had my agreement. Of course I agreed and a week or two later we heard in our camp that my "mother" was dead and we all wailed and put on the trimmings of mourning. (Hart 1970:149–54)

AGING AND THE ANTHROPOLOGICAL PARADIGM

This brief encounter with aging among the Tiwi can help introduce students to the way in which an anthropological approach can help us understand the late phases of adulthood in cross-cultural context. Such an anthropological paradigm has a dual lens: an internal focus (called an *emic* perspective), which seeks to comprehend the "native's" view of why certain behaviors are performed or images about the world are held; and an external, comparative focus (called an *etic* perspective), which uses the world's societies as a natural laboratory to separate the universal from the particular.

The "Native" View of Aging

The *emic* component of the anthropological paradigm seeks to behold the world through the eyes of the people being studied. Hart's research on the Tiwi was a classic example of ethnographic fieldwork. The Tiwi incorporated Hart into their kinship system and made use of him in a difficult situation, just as he used his designation as "son" and clan member to study their society on an intimate basis. When Hart first lived with the Tiwi, they were a foraging, semi-nomadic, small-scale society where kin-based groups (clans) named after myth-ological ancestors controlled key elements of the life cycle. How one entered adulthood, whom one married and the consequences of frailty in old age were largely determined by the cluster of elder males who had membership in a given clan. The Tiwi represent one of the few actual cases of gerontocracy—rule by the eldest group of males—and an exaggerated case of what has been called "gerontogamy." This latter term denotes a case in which a society not only practices polygyny (men can have more than one spouse at the same time) but where the older adult males have greater access than the younger men to the youngest women. Typically, Tiwi men older than middle age already have several wives, including very young teenagers, while a man marrying for the first time after age twenty-five might be wed to a forty-five-year-old widow.

While not controlling material wealth as might be the case in an agrarian tribal society, groups of elder males cautiously dole out esoteric wisdom to younger persons. Without this knowledge, they cannot relate to spiritual forces or function as culturally competent adults. Regarded with a mixture of fear and reverence, the oldest males sit at the top of a generational pyramid, authorita-tively dominating society by the exclusive possession of key cultural knowl-edge. These elders, as a group, also dominate the dramatic life-cycle rituals that mark the transition from status to status as one goes from birth to death. Unlike the Western linear view of the life cycle, which sees death as a discon-tinuity from life, the Tiwi have a cyclical, mythologically linked notion of time and the passage of life forms through it. From this perspective, ancestors can have a powerful influence on the fate of the living and can be reborn in a future generation. As Judith Barker shows in her article dealing with another Pacific Island people (Part VI), an *emic* understanding of belief systems is nec-essary to comprehend the radical change in behavior that can accompany the shift from healthy old age to severe senescence.

While females among the Tiwi had fewer formal bases of power, one must not assume from the very limited segment of Hart's research that women in old age are a totally repressed lot. Subsequent work among the Tiwi by Jane Good-ale (1971) shows the impressive amount of de facto power women could accu-mulate by middle age, especially through their ability to control conflict in the community. Other ethnographic studies have demonstrated how, even in quite "male chauvinistic" cultural contexts, older women can acquire an impor-tance and power far beyond the normative societal constraints placed on females (see especially Kerns and Brown 1992; Putnam-Dickerson and Brown 1998).

The Comparative View of Aging

How are we to apply the second, transcultural part of the anthropological paradigm? The treatment of the frail and possibly demented older woman in

Hart's narrative must not only be examined through an *emic* understanding of the process of "covering up," but also by applying an *etic* comparative perspective. One way of doing this is to translate the insider's "folk" view into comparable categories, such as "abandoning" or "forsaking," that can be used to construct theories ánd test hypotheses. The broadest such research design, called "holocultural analysis," makes use of the major anthropological data bank, the Human Relations Area Files (HRAF), which house ethnographic data representing over 1,000 societies. The intent of this approach is to statistically measure "the relationship between two or more theoretically defined and operationalized variables in a world sample of human societies" (Rohner et al. 1978:128). In this way it is hoped that we may eventually comprehend what aspects of aging are universal, as opposed to those factors that are largely shaped by a specific sociocultural system.

As demonstrated by Anthony Glascock in Part I, carefully defining types of "death hastening" behaviors allows us to make powerful use of the holocultural method. Using this approach, Glascock's research demonstrates that counter to what one might expect, about half of his worldwide sample act out variants of behavior that lead to the death of older citizens. As the case of Hart's Tiwi "mother" exemplifies, this is seldom a simple matter and is usually predicated on severe physical and cognitive decline and the redefinition of the person from a functional to a nonfunctional individual (see also Barker Part VI).[11]

CROSS-NATIONAL VERSUS CROSS-CULTURAL

Cross-National Research

It is important to distinguish *cross-national* from *cross-cultural* studies in gerontological research (Fry 1988).[12] The first type of study takes as the unit of analysis the nation-state, or a major portion of that entity and compares whole countries by measuring, through survey questionnaires, a large array of primarily demographic, interactional and health-related variables (Andrews et al. 1986; Altergott 1988; Commission on Behavioral and Social Sciences and Education 2001; Eyetsemitan et al. 2003; Lee 2007).[13]

Over the past three decades, there has been a dramatic growth of cross-national studies spanning most regions of the globe (Lee 2007). Early projects such as a seven nation study within Asia, Africa and the Middle East (Kendig, Hashimoto and Coppard 1992) and the United Nations Fertility Survey Among Six Latin American Nations (De Vos 1990) have provided important demographic sources of information, although their mass survey approach often obscured crucial cultural differences within and between the nations sampled (Sokolovsky 2002). Subsequently, a number of more sophisticated cross-national projects have emerged, which integrate more qualitative case materials into the research design. We see this in Part V where Michael Gusmano pulls together the results of the ongoing World Cities Project. Here he examines the national contexts of four major urban places and the role played by environment, neighborhood and city support systems in sustaining older citizens (Rodwin and Gusmano 2006). Other key examples include a study of "Rapid Demographic Change and the Welfare of the Elderly" in East Asia (Hermalin 2002); the SABE Project in Latin America and the Caribbean (Palloni, Peláez and Wong 2006) and the OASIS and SHARE studies throughout Europe (Lowenstein and Daatland 2006; Ogg and Renaut 2006).

Cross-Cultural Studies

In contrast to cross-national studies, *cross-cultural* studies of aging tend to focus on small-scale societies or individual communities of industrial states. The lead chapter in Part V reports on research from the *Ageing in Indonesia 1999–2007 Project,* which is a longitudinal anthropological and demographic study of three Indonesian communities. Here the authors focus on a West Sumatran village of the Minangkabau people, who live in one of the world's largest matrilineal societies. The benefit of in-depth cultural analysis comes sharply into focus by contrasting the impact on the life course and aging of this "women-centered" society with that in the more male-dominated cultural settings of China (Zhang Part III), Mexico (Sokolovsky Part III), or India (Lamb Part V). This perspective permits comparisons to be made between the complex interwoven wholes of cultural systems. One approach centers on highly controlled comparisons, where the social units under study are similar except for one or two features. A classic example is S. F. Nadel's (1952) study of two African tribal societies, the Korongo and the Mesakin. While alike in terms of environment and economic, political and kinship organization, each society differed in the degree of intergenerational conflict and the attitude of males toward aging. The key difference seemed to lie in the greater number of age distinctions recognized by the Korongo and the smoother transition into old age characteristic of this society. As a consequence, there was not only a greater congruence between social and physical aging among the Korongo, but also an easier and more cheerful acceptance of old age itself. A very different use of this approach is seen in McLean's powerful documentation of how contrasting care philosophies in otherwise identical dementia units result in distinct outcomes for elder residents (Part VI).

Alternatively, the more typical approach to cross-cultural studies has been to maximize the difference between the societies, or ethnic communities, being contrasted. Researchers have either searched the available literature or conducted original research in different places to see what could be learned about a specific aspect of aging such as intergenerational relations, age as a basis of social organization, widowhood and general aspects of female aging.[14] Most parts of this volume have examples of this kind of approach such as: Beyene's bicultural comparison of menopause in Greece and Mexico (Part I); Akiyama, Antonucci and Cambell's contrast of intergenerational exchange in Japan and the United States (Part II Web book); Hayslip's cross-ethnic analysis of custodial grandparenting (Part IV); or the contrast by Counts and Counts of community engagement of older adults in mobile home parks and a village in Papua New Guinea (Part V Web book).

One of the significant problems with cross-cultural research, however, is the difficulty of gaining consistency in methods used to qualitatively study the intricate cultural phenomena observed in the societies being contrasted (Miedema and de Jong 2005). An attempt at confronting this issue directly is project AGE (Age, Generation and Experience), the most serious cross-cultural study of aging to date. Here a team of anthropologists carried out a comparison of aging in Hong Kong, Botswana, rural Ireland and two American communities, combining long-term fieldwork with a precise and consistent research protocol (see Keith et al. 1994; Fry et al. Part I Web book). This project has been especially important in detailing how intercommunity variation interacts with cultural systems to influence how people define successful aging.[15] In Part II, Jennie Keith, Project Age co-director, sets her study of suburban Swarthmore, Pennsylvania, within a cross-cultural framework to explore how residential instability intersects with the life course to hinder social relationships across age lines. It will be important to consider her findings in light of Stafford's discussion, in Part V, of factors promoting elder-friendly communities.

USING THE GLOBAL PERSPECTIVE

Whichever approach is taken, cross-cultural research on aging is important in at least three ways. First, it may suggest general hypotheses about the aging experience that can be tested by employing larger samples or conducting longitudinal studies. By using a relatively small number of cases, it is possible to retain a picture of the qualitative nature of sociocultural variables and thereby hopefully avoid overly simple theoretical models. A good example of this is found in Part I where Beyene undertakes a classic cross-cultural comparison of menopause. She shows how the complex biocultural interplay of the life course, nutrition and reproductive histories results in very different bodily responses to this universal experience for mid-life females. Her research clarifies the factors that either promote or inhibit what many North Americans mistakenly believe are universal physical symptoms associated with the end of a woman's reproductive capacity.

Secondly, intercultural comparisons can help us to understand in a detailed fashion how the response to aging in the United States varies from that experienced in other places. Such analysis can suggest alternative strategies for developing diverse environments in which to grow old. This is brought home clearly by the examination of Denmark's innovative long-term care system. As noted by Stuart and Hansen in Part III, a decade after this nation implemented its integrated home- and community-based services system, there is wide access to services and the growth of long-term care expenditures appears to be *decreasing* even for the over-eighty population. In the United States, opposite trends mark our long-term care system for elders.

In a related manner, a third use of global information is to create an interactive cultural laboratory where innovations are absorbed, transformed and sometimes improved as they pass into different societal settings (Weaver 2008). The last several decades have, in fact, seen a flowering of numerous cultural transplants in areas such as long-term care, service delivery and residential design. For example, the "Day Hospital" model was developed within the British health system as an alternative to traditional nursing homes. It was used as the archetype for the creation of the very successful "On Lok" community-based long-term care system in the United States (see Sokolovsky Part IV for more detail on On Lok). In another part of the world, Japan in 2002 initiated a national long-term care insurance system based on German and British models (see Jenike and Traphagan Part III).

Another good example of intercultural exchange comes from a residential and community design model called "co-housing," developed in Scandinavia. These innovative, resident-run "intentional" communities not only facilitate autonomous aging in place, but promote small-scale, age-integrated and sustainable/energy efficient neighborhoods. Pioneered in Denmark during the 1970s, they have been emulated elsewhere in Europe and developed with distinct local slants in the United States since the 1990s (Durrett 2005). By 2008 there were about one hundred such communities spread throughout North America, with innovations involving radically revamping older urban neighborhoods to the co-housing, multigenerational model. You can follow the progress of the co-housing movement at www.culturechangenow.com/stories/cohousing.html.

YOUR GLOBAL AGING FUTURE IS NOW

As will be discovered in the following parts of this book, the consequences of global aging will influence most areas of life to be encountered in the twenty-first century, including the biological limits of the human life span, the cultural construction of the life cycle, generational exchange and kinship, the makeup of households and community, symbolic representations of midlife and old age and attitudes toward disability and death. In the chapters that follow, you will encounter the laughing clubs of India, the Okinawan Centenarian diet plan, the waltzing elders of urban China, the elderscapes of Florida, Japan's robotic granny minders, elder-friendly communities, Denmark's "Flexicurity" system and the "Green House" model for dementia care. Welcome to your future!

Special Note on This Book's Web Site

There is now an amazing array of serious academic information available on the World Wide Web, including whole books, video and audio documentation, the latest statistical data and reports from governments, universities and research centers. Some of these key links are provided in the printed text or in endnotes for each part of the book. However, at "The Cultural Context of Aging" Web site (www.stpt.usf.edu/~jsokolov) click on the **Resources** menu—keyed to each part of the book—and you will have access to extensive supplemental resources expanding the text readings. This will sometimes include PowerPoint files and videos related to the specific chapters. Clicking on **Web Book** will bring you to digital chapters listed in the print Table of Contents, but only available on the Web.

NOTES

1. The details of this plan can be seen at: http://ec.europa.eu/information_society/activities/einclusion/policy/ageing/launch/index_en.htm. It should be noted, however, that the idea of promoting active aging is not the only answer to population aging and in Europe, to date, the push to get people to work longer has not been particularly effective. See the following for a report on this situation: http://www.euractiv.com/en/social europe/workers-unenthusiastic-active-ageing/article-164358.

2. You can follow the important developments on aging at the United Nations through the Web site: www.un.org/esa/socdev/ageing/impl_map.html.

3. In 1982, the United Nations convened a World Assembly on Ageing in Vienna, Austria and later that year, the UN General Assembly endorsed the International Plan of Action on Ageing. In 1990, the UN designated October 1 as the International Day of the Elderly and one year later adopted Principles for Older Persons.

4. For information about SAGE, see www.who.int/healthinfo/systems/sage/en/index.html. The SAGE questionnaire was piloted in over 1,500 respondents in three countries, Ghana, India and Tanzania, in 2005. Implementation of the full SAGE began in 2006, with completion anticipated in the first half of 2008 in all countries. Data sets will be available in the public domain by the second half of 2008.

5. For an important discussion of applied anthropology and aging, see Harmon (2005).

6. In the April 1996 edition of *Science*, it was reported that molecular biologists have discovered the gene associated with the accelerated aging of young adults, symptomatic of a very rare disorder called Werner's disease. This may provide important clues to dealing with many age-related diseases such as diabetes, arteriosclerosis and osteoporosis.

7. There were also short articles by such luminaries as Gregory Bateson (1950) and Margaret Mead (1951, 1967), but this did little to stimulate much interest in global aging.

8. In that same year, it was an article by Margaret Clark that laid out a model for developing an anthropology of aging in: 1967. "The Anthropology of Aging: A New Area of Studies for Culture and Personality." *The Gerontologist* 7:55–64.

9. The most important professional organization focusing on the anthropology of aging, the AAGE, The Association for Anthropology and Gerontology, which was established in 1978 as a multidisciplinary group dedicated to the exploration and understanding of aging within and across the diversity of human cultures. Their Web site is at: http://www.slu.edu/organizations/aage.

10. For information about these programs, see http://sgec.stanford.edu and http://med.fsu.edu/geriatrics/ethnogeriatric/links.asp.

11. For another kind of study on aging using the HRAF files, see Winn and Newton (1982).

12. Some of this research I have labeled "Cross-National" (e.g., Arnoff, Leon and Lorge 1964; and Seefeldt 1984) is described by the authors as cross-cultural. However,

the survey questionnaire approach of these studies places them in the methodological camp of what I call cross-national studies and perhaps explains why they find so few differences in the samples they examine. A good resource for this issue is: Preparing for an Aging World: The Case for Cross-National Research at www.nap.edu/catalog. php?record_id=10120#toc.

13. For some classic examples of such studies, see Arnoff, Leon and Lorge (1964); Heikkinen, Waters and Brzezinski (1983); Seefeldt (1984); Altergott (1988). During the 1990s, a good number of cross-national studies on aging were begun. The best source of information about this earlier research is contained in Nusberg and Sokolovsky (1994). There are a growing number of direct comparative studies of the United States with another nation. Two good examples are, Borsch-Supan (1994; U.S.-Germany) and Buss, Beres, Hofstetter and Pomidor (1994; U.S.-Hungary).

14. For comparative analysis of intergenerational relations, see Levine (1965); Rubinstein and Johnsen (1982); Simic (1990); Hashimoto (1996). For age as a basis of social organization, see Eisenstadt (1956); Stewart (1977); Foner and Kertzer (1978); Bernardi (1985); for widowhood, see Lopata (1972, 1987a, b, 1988); Cattell this volume. For general aspects of female aging, see Bart (1969); Datan et al. (1970); Dougherty (1978); Cool and McCabe (1987); Kerns and Brown (1992).

15. The methodologies employed in this project were developed in the early 1980s by a working group of anthropologists and other scholars concerned with cross-cultural gerontology. The book that resulted from this collaboration, *New Methods for Old Age Research* (Fry and Keith 1986), constitutes the most important guide available for conducting research on aging in different cultural contexts.

PART I

A Global Vision of Aging, Culture and Context

Jay Sokolovsky

In 2006, almost 500 million people worldwide were sixty-five and older. By 2030, that total is projected to increase to one billion—one in every eight of the earth's inhabitants. Significantly, the most rapid increases in the sixty-five and older population are occurring in industrializing countries, which will see a jump of 140 percent by 2030.

"Why Population Aging Matters: A Global Perspective," U.S. Department of State, 2006

THE NEW MILLENNIUM OF GLOBAL AGING

Over the next two decades, most industrializing world regions will still not have reached the level of societal aging now faced by North America, much of Europe and Japan; but currently "youthful" nations such as Indonesia, China and Mexico are starting to catch up. Already, by 2007, two-thirds of the globe's population past their sixth decade lives in the industrializing world (Weinberger 2007). Through the first half of this century, it is the East Asian region, fueled by dramatic drops in fertility levels and rapid urban industrialization, that will age fastest. Although in some areas, especially in sub-Saharan Africa and in Russia, populations have experienced recent "shortgevity," an overall drop in life expectancy, global trends are massively progressing in the opposite direction.[1]

Most Western countries and Japan already contain a sizable portion of older citizens within their boundaries. As of 2007 (see Figure I.1), several nations, Germany, Italy and Japan, had more than a fifth of their population age sixty-five or older. Also noticed here, is the dramatic, relative youth of the United States, which will continue for at least the next two decades. This provides a comparative framework for the ongoing debate in that country around such issues as generational equity and elder care, topics that will be explored later on in this volume.

Figure I.1
The World's Oldest Nations. Measured by the Percent over Age Sixty-Five

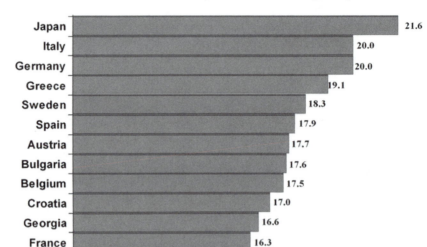

Source: U.S. Census Bureau, International Data Base, Available at: www.census.gov/ipc/www/idb/

The implications of these demographic trends have serious consequences for the functioning of societies around the globe (see Jackson and Howe 2008). The National Institute on Aging and the U.S. Bureau of the Census, in 1985, established an International Data Base and later an Aging Studies Branch to address the issue of global population *greying*. In this section's first article, Kevin Kinsella, Chief of this Census Bureau unit, discusses some of the key parameters that have caught the attention of those who study the demography of aging (see www.census.gov/ipc/www/idb/index.html). In a global survey, he lays out the critical social, medical and policy consequences of the numbers flowing from demographic reports.

A GLOBAL FRAMEWORK FOR CULTURALLY CONSTRUCTING AGING AND OLD AGE

Cultural perceptions of older adulthood, or old age, link changes in the person's physical being (reduction of work capacity, beginning of menopause) with social changes (such as the birth of grandchildren) to create a culturally defined sense of oldness (Ikels and Beall 2001). As will be elaborated upon in the next section, human cultural systems usually recognize the importance of this part of the life cycle by linguistically creating labels delineating a stage of late adulthood (Cattell and Albert this volume). The conception of being "old" is a *near* human universal and is differentially entered by a variety of measures.

As Cattell and Albert show in Part II, the socially constructed boundaries of oldness can have various gradations that even extend beyond the point of death into a category of ancestors (Kopytoff 1971). Many societies also recognize, as a different category of old, those truly ancient living adults who show sharp declines in functioning. For example, among the *Ju/'hoansi* people of Botswana, old age is perceived to begin relatively early and can start in a person's mid-forties when and if changes in physical capabilities begin to diminish functional ability. Here there are three levels of "old," a beginning early stage, a frail but functional stage and a physically disabled designation. Counterbalancing the *Ju/'hoansi* linkage of older adults with physical decline, is a powerful association with greater spiritual and emotional strength often put to use by the aged in healing rituals or in settling disputes (Rosenberg Part I).

Only one study to date has systematically used worldwide data, to examine the passage into old age. Anthropologists Anthony Glascock and Susan Feinman found that in a random sample of sixty societies there were three basic means of identifying a category of "old": change of social/economic role; chronology; and change in physical characteristics (1981). Their study produced the following conclusions:

1. A shift in social/economic roles was the common marker of being designated as old. Typical examples are: one's children having their own kids; changes in a person's productive activities; or beginning to receive more goods and services than one gives.

2. A change in physical capabilities is the least common marker. Severe frailty or dementia is quite rare as an initial indicator of being called old. This has happened because sampled societies typically create a category of old starting before people encounter many radical signs of physical decline.

3. About half of the societies use multiple definitions of being aged. Such varied markers of aging are commonly applied to distinct categories of "old" itself, which can include a phase of oldness linked to images associated with a movement toward death and the loss of normal functioning.

Table I.1
Percent Distribution of Old Age Definitional Classifications: From the Human Relations Area Files (Absolute Numbers in Parentheses)

How the beginning of old age is defined?	Single Definition of Aging	Multiple Definitions of Aging
Change in social role	71% (30)	46% (27)
Chronology	19% (08)	34% (20)
Change in capabilities	10% (04)	20% (12)
Total	100% (42)	100% (59)

Source: Glascock and Feinman 1981: 20.

This last item seems to add a component of both complexity and ambiguity to how societies fully articulate their images of aging. As we will see later on in this section, confronting an image of the old, tilted toward the dimensions of death and incapacity, can initiate drastic changes in the attitudes and behavior toward those so labeled (see also Barker Part VI).

GLOBAL PERSPECTIVES ON STATUS AND SUPPORT OF THE AGED

One of the promises of a truly cross-cultural comparative gerontology is to gain an understanding of aging, divorced from the narrow boundary of a single case such as the *Jul'hoansi*. In fact, it is among such types of society—nomadic, nonagricultural, lacking economic stratification, with bilateral descent—that one is statistically most likely to find the very frail elderly having their lives "hastened."

The first serious attempt to deal with such issues on a worldwide basis was the massive study by Leo Simmons, *The Role of the Aged in Primitive Society* (1945). Despite methodological problems with the very early use of the Human Relations Area Files (HRAF), this book has many insights that have served as a guidepost to more recent, controlled comparisons and holocultural studies.[2] Simmons shows the variety of ways elderly function in society including: knowledge bearing; child care; and ritual, judicial and political decision making. Numerous ethnographies have validated how a combination of deep knowledge held by older adults and their nurturative actions toward younger generations sustains human societies. Collins, for example, found that among contemporary Inuit in Canada, ideological rather than material contributions were central to their positive evaluation by younger community members. That is, successful elders were those who were willing to transmit their accumulated knowledge to junior members of their community (2001).

Working independently with small, cross-cultural samples, Cowgill (1974) and Press and McKool (1972) proposed similar variables that account for high status in traditional peasant societies. These involve four interrelated clusters of cultural phenomena: 1) an available role set emphasizing continuity and important responsibilities in community organization and public life; 2) integration into a residentially viable extended family organization; 3) control of some important material and informational resources; and 4) a value system praising a group-oriented ideology while de-emphasizing individual ego development.

In applying these variables to the *Jul'hoansi* people studied by Rosenberg, we can see that their cultural context does not fulfill all of the criteria listed above. This is especially the case in terms of their lack of a residentially stable extended-family organization, such as the families that Sokolovsky studied in rural Mexico (Part III). Yet, Rosenberg found that there is a powerful cumulative effect of the important roles the elderly play in kinship relations, control of knowledge and mastery of the dangerous spiritual force called *num*. When combined with the *Jul'hoansi*'s communal ideological orientation, there is created a cultural context in which the elderly are well supported.

A series of holocultural studies have corroborated, in many respects, the association of status and deference with the control of informational and administrative roles (Sheehan 1976; Silverman and Maxwell 1987) as well as valued activities and extended family integration (McArdle and Yeracaris 1981). In terms of resource and information control, Silverman and Maxwell have demonstrated that only certain types of control, particularly administrative and consultative, correlate with beneficent treatment of the elderly. Some forms of supernatural information control, especially transformational powers, were in fact a potential threat to the elderly. This is highly relevant to some historically known situations of massive societal change, such as in thirteenth-to-sixteenth-century Europe, colonial North America and contemporary Ghana. In Europe, the typical person burned at the stake for their "transformational knowledge" (witchcraft) was an older female between the ages of fifty-five and sixty-five (Bever 1982; Banner 1992). Similar demographics of witch accusations were found when John Demos studied those most likely to be condemned in seventeenth-century Puritan Massachusetts. Such female suspects were likely to be old and poor, either single or widowed and known as being unusual or irritating to neighbors (Haber 1997; Demos 1982). As seen in Box I.1 below, similar dynamics appear to be driving accusations of sorcery in northern Ghana over the past decade (see also Cattall Part II; Van der Geest 2002; and Adinkrah 2004 for broader perspectives on aging and witchcraft).

BOX I.1 OLDER WOMEN AS WITCHES IN GHANA

Although both men and women can practise witchcraft, it is only the women, especially the older ones, who are branded as witches and banished from the village while their male counterparts are treated with the greatest caution and are feared.

The witches' camps where the exiled women gather are found throughout northern Ghana but the "ambaga Witches camp" is widely known for accommodating most of the accused. The camp, about 160 kilometres from the regional capital of Tamale, was established in the late 18th century. But now Gambaraan, an exorcist and a custodian of the camp, says the number of witches is getting out of hand. Presently there are about 8,000 outcasts in camps in Ghana's Northern Region. About 80 percent of them are women between the ages of 45 and 90 years old and some of them have been there for over 30 years. Although living conditions are poor, most dare not go back to their respective communities since they have been stigmatized and are likely to be lynched. One of the outcasts says she was accused of causing a range of ills including polio and cerebro-spinal meningitis in her village and so was exiled. Most of the deaths that are attributed to the "witches" are not based on any spiritual dimension but on human activity—such as the overcrowding and poor sanitary conditions that often precipitate malaria, cholera, polio and meningitis.

Adapted from: "Witch's Curse: Poor Living Standards Banish Older Women from Their Communities," *New Internationalist*, March, 2001 by Samuel Wiafe.

"FIRST PEOPLES" AND AGING

Anthropologists have long been interested in examining life in societies that, in their traditional way of life, resemble the earliest forms of human cultural systems. While many tribal societies such as the Amazonian Yanomamo remain on the brink of extinction, the last decade has witnessed an unexpected resilience among indigenous, "first" peoples. These groups, which constitute about four percent of the earth's population, have sometimes managed to maintain their core cultural values in the face of ferocious onslaughts by industrial nations. Among the best studied examples fitting this description are the *Ju/'hoansi*, described in this section by Harriet Rosenberg. They are also part of the Project AGE sample discussed in this section's last Web article. The *Ju/'hoansi*, also known variously as the Bushmen, !Kung, or San peoples, are a formerly nomadic gathering and hunting group in Botswana. Despite the erroneous image created in the feature film *The Gods Must Be Crazy*, they are not an unchanged people, lacking contact with the outside world.[3] Instead, over the last three decades they at times have been a captive group, restricted to a reservation and forced to significantly alter their quite successful foraging lifestyle. Nonetheless, this harsh political context has not yet destroyed core cultural features of *Ju/'hoansi* family, community and ritual life, forums in which the elderly still perform valued roles. These cultural niches for the elderly include: being a knowledge repository about kin ties and natural resource management; transcendental curing and performance; entertainment through clowning and dancing; and being an emotional focus for community integration.

Here we clearly see the benefits of long-term ethnographic research combined with discourse and narrative analysis in understanding the cultural mechanisms of caring for the elderly (Randall and Kenyon 2004).[4] Without having lived with the group for an extended period or having had access to her husband's thirty years of experience with the *Ju/'hoansi*, Rosenberg might have mistaken the constant "kvetching" (sharp complaining) of most elderly as proof that this society habitually abandons its older citizens in need of care. Instead, her nuanced analysis linking the narrative of complaint discourse to the egalitarian and communal roots of *Ju/'hoansi* society shows that outspoken nagging is a part of their package of cultural devices that reinforce values of caring and extreme compassion for even the very frail elderly. Importantly, caregiving is carried out evenly by persons of both sexes, avoiding the overdependence on female caregivers typical for industrialized countries.

ARE WE HUMAN BECAUSE WE HAVE ELDERS?

Humans are the primate species with not only the longest life span, but also the greatest proportion of those years spent in social and biological maturity (Wachter and Finch 1997; Crews 2003, 2007). Clinical psychologist David Gutmann suggests that this evolved, not because of the developing capacities and moral imperative to keep the weak alive, but rather we are in fact human *because we have elders* (1987). This "strong face of aging," as Gutmann terms it, derives from the function of elders in our species' early history, as a vital link in the transmission of our socially learned systems of belief and behavior, which imbue children with the essence of humanity.[5] In other words, we attained our humanity through the very existence of elders and their enactment of post-parental roles. More recent life-span psychology research in a wide range of cultures also suggests that an adaptive advantage of long life to group survival is the greater integration of knowledge and socioemotional regulation observed in later years, despite decrements in some aspects of memory and other cognitive processes (Carstensen and Löckenhoff 2003).

One of the interesting issues emerging from both evolutionary anthropology and psychology is whether our species' long, post-reproductive life span is a modern artifact or an evolutionary mechanism long adapted through natural selection of our pre-modern ancestors (Caspari and Lee 2004).[6] The limited age-estimated data on our Paleolithic ancestors did not initially indicate very significant survival past the third decade of life, with life expectancy at birth hovering around the mid-twenties. However, as Harper summarizes the current available data, "Even in Stone Age populations, the life expectancy of females at age 45 was more than 10 years and probably in the range of 12–25 years; and up to 30 percent of the female population was post-reproductive (2006:86; see also Gurven and Kaplan 2007 for discussion of this data).

Since the mid-1990s, a very lively debate has emerged around the selective advantage of elder citizens to early human communities. Much of this was stimulated by the work of Kristen Hawkes and colleagues, based on her work in East Africa with the hunter-forager Hadza peoples (Hawkes and Jones 2005). They have focused on what has come to be known as the "grandmother hypothesis"—the notion that aging women gain an inclusive fitness advantage from investing in their grandchildren. This hypothesis has evolved from an explanation for menopause into an explanation for the exceptionally long post-reproductive lifespan in human females.

As detailed in the chapter by Gurven and Kaplan, other models of late-life importance to early human selective advantage have developed and are currently being explored through the Tsimane Health and Life History Project. Set in the Bolivian Amazon, this project examines over time the economic, demographic and developmental aspects of aging in eighteen communities of forager-horticultural peoples. In doing so, they are testing out their "Embodied Capital Model" linking human skill acquisition over long maturation with lowered mortality rates and greater longevity. Their model proposes that cross-generational contributions from both genders were critical to the evolution of longevity in our species.

CONSCIOUS AGING AND THE "POSTMODERN" EVOLUTION OF AGING

As upward transformations in longevity and healthy functioning of older adults are exceeding predictions made barely a decade ago (see Part VI), so too is the societally constructed image of aging being altered. One element here is the constructed reality of late life through language, popular culture and various forms of media. We will address this in Part II, especially in the chapter by Featherstone and Hepworth exploring the cultural representations of late life. Another perspective is the self-conscious effort to transform how individuals think about and seek to experience the aging process. Harry Moody notes in this section a shift toward perceiving older adults as "wellderly" rather than "illderly." This has stimulated the redefining of retired life and the promotion of a construct of "successful aging," keyed to active vitality and "productive aging" (Rowe and Kahn 1998; Martinson and Minkler 2006; Bowling 2007).

Moody suggests that models of both successful and productive aging are a post-modern strategy for turning old age into a "second middle age," in effect a strategy for an age-less old age (Katz 2005). Taking a critical eye to these perspectives, his chapter does two things: (1) it notes how the success and productive aging models narrowly and ethnocentrically enshrine Western ideology concerning success in adulthood; and (2) it shows how understanding cultural variation offers other inner-seeking alternatives that many people in North America are embracing (see Lamb and Myers 1999; Hsu 2007; and McFadden 2008). This latter focus seeks to move beyond loss and decline with a "conscious" aging approach nurtured by spirituality and transcendence. Moody suggests, in effect, adding a spiritual element of what Tornstam calls "gerotranscendence" to the developmental psychologies of Jung, Erickson and Maslow (Moody and Carroll 1998; Tornstam 2005). The introduction to Part II will further discuss the "conscious aging" movement and the new language and discourse it is trying to provoke about late life.

ASSISTED SUICIDE AND THE DARKER SIDE OF AGING

A special concern within the growing comparative perspective on being old is confronting the darker side of aging—various types of non-supportive and even "death-hastening" behaviors directed toward the elderly. In the United States and other countries, this has created a legal, ethical and medical battleground concerning euthanasia as an option for terminally ill aged (Norwood 2007). In 2007, "Dr. Death," Jack Kevorkian, was released after eight years in prison for assisting in over 100 assisted suicides. This event reignited a powerful debate that impacts people of all ages. The judicial dilemmas stemming from this issue are worthy of King Solomon. For example, in January 1996, a man from Petoskey, Michigan, won custody of his Alzheimer disease-stricken father in a court case against his own mother. The son had maintained that the mother and his siblings were conspiring to seek the help of Dr. Kevorkian to end the father's life.

As we have already seen in the discussion of the Tiwi, high-tech societies are not the only ones to grapple with this dilemma. Anthony Glascock in this section throws the question into historical and global relief and finds some disquieting results. A majority of the societies in his sample exhibited some form of "death-hastening" behavior, with less than one-third providing unconditional support. However, few societies enforce a single treatment of their elderly, and it was commonly found that both supportive as well as death-hastening behavior coexist in the same social setting.

The important and related issue of elder abuse is beginning to be investigated in diverse settings, such as among Native American tribes (Holkup et al. 2007), North American families (Fisher and Regan 2006) and in varied international settings (World Health Organization 2002b; Yan and Tang 2003; Daichman 2005; Malley-Morrison, Nolido and Chawla 2006).[7] In the book's final section, varied cultural responses to the oldest old will be more fully explored.

THE FEMINIZATION OF OLD AGE

As noted by Kinsella in this section, women constitute more than a majority of the older population in virtually all parts of the world. At birth, females in the United States have a life expectancy almost six years greater than males, and when they reach age sixty-five they can expect to survive three more years than their male counterparts. For third-world nations, there is typically about half this difference in life expectancies, and past the sixth decade there is a more even gender ratio than found in the post-industrial world. However, it is in the former type of societies that the worlds of males and females are found to be most socially and culturally divergent. As Ellickson notes for rural Bangladesh, this is especially the case in patrilineal societies with a good deal of social and gendered stratification, where distinct separate male and female subcultures emerge and men try to strongly control the sexuality and reproductive history of women in their family (1988; see also Dickerson-Putman 1996). It is here that one sees a clear divergence of cultural scripts in late life. In Bangladesh there may be rewards for an older woman if she manages to become the head of the domestic realm of an extended family, but this is typically brief, as she loses that role when her husband dies. The elder man, however, only relinquishes authority and economic control upon his own death.

The typical dominance of males in public arenas is linked to the divergent imagery of aging created on the basis of gender. Predominant in this difference is the common hydra-headed perception of older women in the same society, from the positive, nurturing matriarch/granny to the mystical shamaness and finally to the feared, evil witch. The ethnographic literature now abounds with this type of dramatic alternation between "Dear Old Thing" and "Scheming Hag" metaphors (Cool and McCabe 1987). In the United States, Carole Haber has documented the varied historical image of older women as witch, widow, wife and worker constructed through the agency of men (1997). It is noteworthy that in "woman-centered" societies, such as the Indonesian Minangkabu discussed in Part V, while aging women are seen as the virtual pillars of society, they seldom use their cultural dominance to replicate a negative and subordinate image of men that is promulgated toward the opposite sex in strongly male-dominated societies.

In this regard it is crucial to note the impact of colonial domination in Latin America and Africa and the imposition of forms of Christianity and Islam that have altered power relationships in communities as well as within family life, often reducing both the domestic and public roles of adult women. One recently discovered example comes from highland Ethiopia among the Gamo people, where the imposition of Christianity allowed the continuation of a powerful male community leadership role, but eliminated a parallel female position, of the *gimuwa* held by post-menopausal women. Such individuals had crucial roles in fertility rituals for crops and families, held feasts to help redistribute resources among households and settled disputes between men and women in the community (Kathy Weedman Personal Communication 2008).

It is unfortunate that until the 1990s the analysis of aging in such societies has largely portrayed the male perspective, despite the importance of older women to the functioning of society. Many authors have begun to document a common pattern in non-industrial societies of dramatic positive changes in role, power and status by women as they pass into the middle and latter adult years (Foner 1989; Kerns and Brown 1992; Brown, Subbaiah and Therese 1994).[8]

The past decade, however, has seen the publication of important ethnographic studies, especially in Africa, India and the Caribbean showing the complex interaction of culture, gender and aging. These include: *Contingent Lives, Fertility, Time and Aging in West Africa* (Bledsoe 2002); *Aging, Gender and Famine in Rural Africa* (Cliggett 2005); *The Poetics and Politics of Tuareg Aging* (Rasmussen 1997); *No Aging in India* (Cohen 1998); *White Saris and Sweet Mangoes* (Lamb 2000); and *Midlife and Older Women: Family Life, Work and Health in Jamaica* (Rawlins 2006).

MENOPAUSE: A KEY BIO-CULTURAL NEXUS

One of the universal imperatives of a woman's midlife biological transition is the eventual cessation of reproductive capacity. Various writers have noted that for women, the fourth and fifth decades of life, in their association with menopause, often provide a key turning point. Cross-cultural work in this area has shown the need for sophisticated research that takes a bio-cultural approach to this issue.[9] Beginning with Marsha Flint's research in India, during the 1970s, it was shown that the biological and social responses to a female's reproductive capacity were quite variable in different cultural settings and responsive to cultural scripts for mid and late life. As Kaufert and Lock note:

Most women know the script laid out in their particular society for the woman in midlife, including what symptoms she should expect from her body.... Women in California are told that a loss in libido is a medical problem to be treated by hormone therapy, whereas a Bengali woman in India knows very well that sexual activity is inappropriate for the postmenopausal woman.... Both the denial and the affirmation of sexuality are social phenomena, but for the California woman the responses of her body have been transformed into a medical problem to be medically managed.... Just as obstetricians and pediatricians would define how women should feel and behave when becoming mothers, gynecologists and psychiatrists tell women what it is to be menopausal. (1992:203)

How the complex interplay of biology, nutrition and culture shapes women's experience of menopause is nicely analyzed by Yewoubdar Beyene in *From Menarche to Menopause: Reproductive Lives of Peasant Women in Two Cultures* (1989). Beyene's chapter in this section is taken from her book and provides a comparison of rural Mayan and Greek women. She shows that, despite similar values and behaviors regarding menstruation and childbearing, their experience of menopause differed. She found that Greek women typically had a pattern of symptoms and a negative perception of menopause and aging not unlike that reported by many females in North America. In contrast, the Mayan women not only systematically lacked these same responses to menopause, but welcomed its new freedoms and saw it as a social passage to higher status in old age.

With the stimulation of such research, cross-cultural studies of menopause and aging have exploded in recent years and include both long-term focused comparisons (Sievert 2006) and massive cross-national works such as the Decisions At Menopause Study (DAMES) and the Study of Women Across the Nation (SWAN), the largest and most exhaustive comparative investigation of menopause across populations (see Obermeyer and Sievert 2007 for a discussion of this research).

"PROJECT AGE" LOOKS AT A GOOD OLD AGE

The focus of this section's concluding Web chapter, Project AGE, represents the most sophisticated cross-cultural approach to questions surrounding aging ever undertaken. Integrating both qualitative and quantitative approaches within a common methodology, complex ethnographies of age and aging were conducted at seven sites around the world between 1982 and 1990. The research shows how both "system wide" community features (such as social inequality) and "internal mechanisms" (such as values) create distinct contexts for conceptualizing the life cycle, establishing age norms and influencing the perception of well-being in old age (Keith et al. 1994). In their article presented here, the authors of Project AGE address this last vexing issue. Their focus is on how cultures create a sense of a "good old age" and the factors that shape this perception. It is particularly interesting to note that in one of the sites, Hong Kong, despite continuing ideals of filial concern, and actual intergenerational co-residence, old age receives the lowest status compared to other parts of the life course. In Part II, the chapter by Keith examines in detail the changing setting of another Project AGE site, suburban Swarthmore, Pennsylvania, and finds the options for a good old age to be dwindling.

NOTES

1. In sub-Saharan Africa, a major culprit in shortgevity is the AIDS epidemic, while in Russia it is a failed health care system combined with rampant alcoholism and other lifestyle-related unhealthy behavior patterns, especially for men.

2. The methodological flaws included a poorly drawn sample, inadequate statistical controls and imprecise definition of some key variables.

3. While quite popular with the general public, the 1982 film *The Gods Must Be Crazy* has evoked a storm of protest from scholars. They have criticized the film for depicting an erroneous, benign view of a South African political structure that protects the childlike *Ju/'hoansi* living in a pristine state of Stone Age existence. In reality, the *Ju/'hoansi* have been placed on a fenced-in reservation, their traditional lifestyle has been prohibited, and the men are often conscripted by the South African military to fight guerila forces in rural areas.

4. For connections to the emerging literature on narrative analysis, see McKim and Randall (2007). For an interesting Web blog on the subject, see http://narrativegerontology. blogspot.com/.

5. For a discussion of the broad biological implications of aging, see Crews and Garruto 1994; Crews 2003, 2007 and Ice 2006.

6. For new research on biological aspects of aging, see Ice (2006).

7. An increasing concern and awareness of elder abuse has developed in the past decade. Access to key information can be obtained from: The International Network for the Prevention of Elder Abuse (www.inpea.net); the World Health Organization (www .who.int/ageing/projects/elder_abuse/en/); and the Elder Justice Coalitions (www.elder justicecoalition.com), which is fighting to have the U.S. Congress pass an "Elder Justice Act." There is also a relatively new journal dealing with this subject, the *Journal of Elder Abuse & Neglect*.

8. While some theorists have stressed the cultural turning points linked to procreative and family cycles, others have suggested that universal intrapsychic personality development best explains the frequent reversals observed among older adults (Gutmann 1987). For other cross-cultural discussion of this issue, see especially Bart (1969); Brown (1982); Kerns (1983); Cool and McCabe (1987); Gutmann (1987):133–84; and Teitlebaum (1987).

9. For other classic works on mid-life women and menopause in various cultures, see du Toit (1990); Flint and Samil (1990); Kaufert and Lock (1992); Lock (1993); and Callahan (1995).

CHAPTER 1

Global Perspectives on the Demography of Aging

Kevin Kinsella

Population aging represents the triumph of public health, medical advancement and economic development over diseases and injuries that constrained human life expectancy for thousands of years. Accompanying this broad demographic process, however, are other changes—macroeconomic strains, emergent technologies, new disease patterns, changing social norms—that challenge policy planning. The interaction of such changes against an evolving demographic background may generate unforeseen problems for current and future generations. It is increasingly clear that societal aging affects economic growth and many other issues, among them national security, the sustainability of families and the ability of states and communities to provide resources for older citizens. In the early stages of the twenty-first century, nations need to recognize and understand the magnitude of the new demographic reality in order to plan accordingly.

HOW DO WE MEASURE POPULATION AGING?

Although nearly all populations are becoming older on average, the extent and pace of aging may vary enormously from society to society. Likewise, the meaning of the term *older population* varies as a result of wide national differences in average longevity and health status. Any chronological demarcation of age boundaries is arbitrary and open to dispute on grounds that it poorly represents biological, physiological, or even psychological dimensions of the human experience. Living to age eighty-five may be as extraordinary in one nation as it is commonplace in another. Nevertheless, the establishment of such boundaries is necessary for a descriptive comparison of international aging. In this chapter, the term *older population* refers to persons aged sixty-five or older, and the term *oldest old* refers to those who are at least eighty years old.

Proportions Aged Sixty-Five or Above

Human population aging refers most commonly to an increase over time in the percentage of all extant persons who have lived to or beyond a certain age. While the size of the world's older population has been increasing for centuries, only recently has the percentage caught the attention of researchers and policymakers. In 2007, the 495 million persons aged sixty-five or over constituted 7.5 percent of the earth's total population. Projections to the year 2030 suggest that nearly one out of eight of the earth's inhabitants (12 percent) will be aged sixty-five or above, with a further rise to 16 percent by the middle of this century. In absolute terms, today's older population will double in size to 1 billion by 2030, and likely reach 1.5 billion before 2050.[1]

Japan was the demographically oldest of the world's major[2] nations in 2007, with 20 percent of its population aged sixty-five or above. Other notably high levels are seen in Italy, Germany, and Greece (more than 19 percent each). The older share of total population is increasing only modestly in most industrialized nations today, a function of the relatively small cohorts born prior to and during World War II. After 2010, however, numbers and percentages of older population will increase rapidly in many countries as the large "Baby Boom" post-war birth cohorts begin to reach age sixty-five.

Sometimes lost amid the attention given to population aging in Europe and North America is the fact that older populations in developing countries typically are growing faster than their industrialized counterparts.[3] During the period 2002–2007, the net size of the world's older population increased by 925,000 persons each month; 75 percent of this change occurred in the developing world. Projections to the year 2030 suggest that the growth rate of older population in the developing world will remain significantly higher than in today's industrialized countries (Figure 1.1). Many nations will experience a boom in older population. In India, the sixty-five-or-over population in 2030 is projected to be 160 percent more numerous than in 2007. Other examples of growth during 2007–2030 are 146 percent in Brazil, 136 percent in Indonesia, 151 percent in Kenya and 123 percent in Tunisia.

As a result of past trends in fertility and current trends in mortality, age categories within the older aggregate may grow at different rates. An increasingly important feature of societal aging is the progressive aging of the older population itself. The fastest growing age segment in most countries is the "oldest old" (persons aged eighty or over). In 2007, ten developed and seven developing countries had oldest old populations in excess of one million. This age group constitutes 25 percent of the aggregate older population in industrialized countries, and approximately 5 percent of the *total* population in France, Sweden, and Norway. While proportions of oldest old are lower in developing countries, absolute numbers may be quite high. China had an estimated 16 million persons aged eighty or older in 2007, more than any other country.

The demands of the oldest old vis-à-vis policymaking should increase markedly in the twenty-first century due to levels of illness and disability that are

Figure 1.1
Average Annual Percent Growth of Older Population in Developed
and Developing Regions: 1950 to 2050

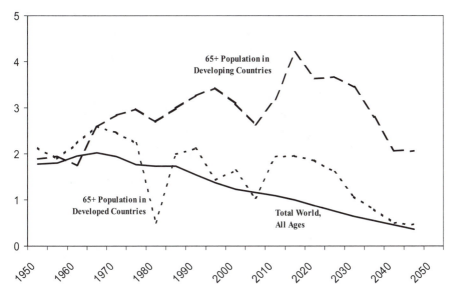

Source: United Nations Department of Economic and Social Affairs 2005.

much higher than in other population groups. Although population aging and rising health care expenditures seem to go hand in hand, it is too simplistic to equate cost increases with aging. While there is a relationship between health expenditure and aging in the Organization for Economic Cooperation and Development (OECD) nations, the relationship is fairly weak. A growing number of analyses now suggest that population aging is not the main driver of health care costs. Other factors—rising per capita incomes, health insurance coverage, new medical technology and workforce demographics that affect the unit cost of health care—may be more important (see, e.g., Reinhardt 2003; Zweifel, Felder and Werblow 2004; Bryant and Sonerson 2006).

Speed of Population Aging

The transition from a youthful to a more aged society has occurred gradually in some nations, but will be compressed in many others. For instance, it took about one-quarter of a century, from 1970 to 1996, for the percentage of population aged sixty-five and over in Japan to increase from 7 to 14 percent. A similarly short transition period is underway in China and several other East Asian nations. The pace of change in parts of Asia stands in stark contrast to some European countries, where the comparable change occurred over a period of 80 to 115 years (Figure 1.2). The rapid change in many developing countries is being driven by

Figure 1.2
**The Speed of Population Aging (Number of years required or expected for percent
of population aged 65 and over to rise from 7% to 14%)**

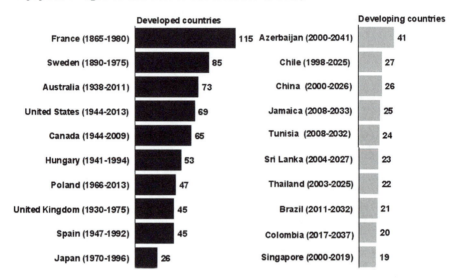

Sources: Kinsella and Gist 1995; U.S. Census Bureau 2006a.

precipitous declines in fertility levels. In South Korea, for example, the total fertility rate[4] plummeted from 5 children per woman in the late 1960s to 1.3 today.

Today's rapidly aging societies are likely to face the contentious issues related to health care costs, social security and intergenerational equity that have sparked public debate in Europe and North America. The speed of population aging already has prompted some developing countries to rethink their population policies. Singapore, once a prime advocate of fertility reduction, made such strides in this arena that its declining birth rate became a cause of political and economic concern, leading to policy changes in the late 1980s. More recently, the Chinese government has recognized that the success of its "one-child-per-couple" policy raises the prospect of having too few children to support a rapidly aging population (Kaneda 2006; Zhang this volume). However, as we know from the experience of developed countries, policies to increase fertility and attenuate population aging have had only minimal impact in most settings (Teitelbaum 2000; Sleebos 2003; Weibel-Orlando this volume).

Median Age

Another way to look at population aging is to consider a society's median age, the age that divides a population into numerically equal parts of younger and older persons. While nearly all industrialized countries are above the thirty-five-year level, the median age in a majority of developing nations is less than twenty-five.

In much of Africa and parts of the Middle East, median ages are below twenty, and high numbers of annual births are likely to keep these countries relatively young in the near future. Yet in developing countries such as Cuba, South Korea and Taiwan, where fertility rates have fallen precipitously, median ages are rising rapidly and are projected to approach or exceed forty-five by the year 2030.

The concept of median age encourages a broader view of population aging, one which is focused less on the older population per se. In many developing countries, the initial effects of population aging will be seen in the relative growth of young- and middle-aged adult populations, with accompanying changes in labor force characteristics, household/family structure and disease patterns. From a business or government-planning perspective, a pressing aspect of this trend is the growth in the working-age population that produces concern about available jobs. For example, the aggregate number of potential job seekers (people aged fifteen to sixty-four) in Africa is projected to double between 2000 and 2030. The percentage increase will be less in other developing regions, but the absolute growth will be substantial. In Asia alone, economies will need to generate more than 800 million additional jobs by 2030 simply to maintain levels of employment seen in the year 2000.

THE DEMOGRAPHIC TRANSITION

The process of population aging primarily involves change over time in levels of fertility and mortality. Populations with high fertility tend to have low proportions of older persons and vice versa. In Malawi, Niger and Yemen, for instance, current total fertility rates well in excess of six children per woman correlate with older population shares of 3 percent or less. Demographers use the term *demographic transition* to refer to a gradual process wherein a society moves from high rates of fertility and mortality to low rates of fertility and mortality. This transition is characterized first by declines in infant and childhood mortality as infectious and parasitic diseases are controlled. The resulting improvement in life expectancy at birth occurs while fertility tends to remain high, thereby producing large birth cohorts and an expanding proportion of children relative to adults.

Whole populations begin to age when fertility rates decline and mortality improvements occur more at older ages than at younger ages. Successive birth cohorts may eventually become smaller and smaller, although countries may experience a "Baby Boom echo" as women from large birth cohorts reach childbearing age. International migration usually does not play a major role in the demography of aging, but can be important in small nations. Certain Caribbean nations, such as Montserrat, Aruba and Martinique, have experienced a combination of working-age-adult emigration, immigration of older retirees from other countries and return migration of former emigrants who are above the average population age; all three factors contribute to population aging.

Figure 1.3 illustrates the historical and projected transition in population size and age structure in developed and developing countries. At one time, most if

Figure 1.3
Population Age Structure in Developed and Developing Countries,
by Age and Sex: 1950, 1990 and 2030 (in millions)

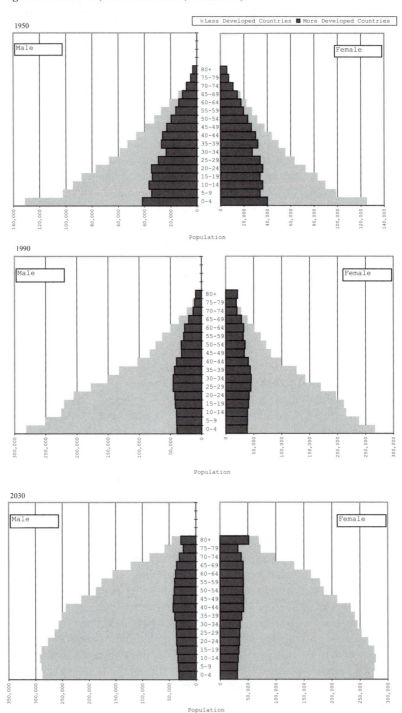

Source: United Nations, 2005. *World Population* Prospects. The 2004 Revision.

not all countries had a youthful age distribution similar to that of developing countries as a whole in 1950. A large percentage of the entire population was under the age of fifteen. Given the relatively high rates of fertility that prevailed in most developing countries from 1950 through the early 1970s, the overall pyramid shape had changed very little by 1990. However, the effects of fertility and mortality decline can be seen in the projected pyramid for 2030, which loses its strictly triangular shape as the older portion of the total population increases.

The picture in developed countries has been and will be quite different. In 1950, there was relatively little variation in the size of five-year groups between the ages of five and twenty-four. The beginnings of the post-World War II Baby Boom can be seen in the zero-to-five-year age group. By 1990, the Baby Boom cohorts were twenty-five to forty-four years old, and the cohorts under age twenty-five were becoming successively smaller. If fertility rates continue as projected through 2030, the pyramid will start to invert, with more weight on the top than on the bottom. The prominence of the oldest old, especially women, will increase, and persons aged eighty or over will outnumber any five-year age group. Because of persistent low fertility, some developed countries are now faced with an historically unprecedented phenomenon: simultaneous population aging and overall population decline. Total population size is projected to decline by at least 1 million in ten developed countries between 2002 and 2030, while the percentage sixty-five-or-over continues to increase (Kinsella and Phillips 2005). For a visual display of changing population age structure, readers can access a time series of dynamic population pyramids for any country at: www.census.gov/ipc/www/idb/pyramids.html.

Life Expectancy

Although the effect of fertility decline is usually the driving force behind changing population age structures, changes in mortality assume greater importance as countries reach lower levels of fertility (Gjonka, Brockmann and Maier 2000). Since the beginning of this century, industrialized countries have made great progress in extending life expectancy at birth (Table 1.1). Japan enjoys the highest life expectancy of the entire world's major countries today—the average Japanese person born in 2005 can expect to live nearly eighty-two years—and the level in several other developed nations is at least seventy-nine years. Three observations can be made concerning the trends in developed countries: (1) the relative difference among countries has narrowed with time; (2) the pace of improvement has not been linear, especially for males. From the early 1950s to the early 1970s, for example, there was little or no change in male life expectancy in Australia, the Netherlands, Norway and the United States, while in Eastern Europe and much of the former Soviet Union, male life expectancy declined in the 1970s and early 1980s; and (3) the difference in female versus male longevity, which universally has been in favor of women in this century, generally widened with time.

Table 1.1
Life Expectancy at Birth for Selected Developed Countries: 1900 to 2007 (In years)

	Circa 1900		Circa 1950		Circa 2007	
Region/Country	Male	Female	Male	Female	Male	Female
Northern and Western Europe						
Austria	37.8	39.9	63.2	68.4	76.9	82.6
Belgium	45.4	48.9	65.0	70.2	76.5	82.3
Denmark	51.6	54.8	69.6	72.4	76.0	80.6
France	45.3	48.7	63.7	69.5	77.1	84.1
Germany	43.8	46.6	65.3	69.6	76.5	82.1
Norway	52.3	55.8	70.9	74.5	77.8	82.5
Sweden	52.8	55.3	70.4	73.3	78.7	83.0
United Kingdom	46.4	50.1	66.7	71.8	77.2	81.6
Southern and Eastern Europe						
Czech Republic	38.9	41.7	64.5	70.3	73.4	79.5
Greece	38.1	39.7	64.3	67.5	77.1	81.9
Hungary	36.6	38.2	61.5	65.8	69.2	77.4
Italy	42.9	43.2	64.3	67.8	77.5	83.5
Spain	33.9	35.7	61.6	66.3	77.7	84.2
Other						
Australia	53.2	56.8	66.9	72.4	78.9	83.6
Japan	42.8	44.3	61.6	65.5	79.0	86.1
United States	48.3	51.1	66.1	72.0	75.6	80.8

Sources: Siampos 1990; United Nations Department of Economic and Social Affairs 2007a.

Changes in life expectancy in developing regions of the world have been more uniform (Table 1.2). Most nations have showed continued improvement, with some exceptions in Latin America and more recently in Africa, the latter due to the impact of the HIV/AIDS epidemic.

The most impressive gains have been achieved in East Asia, where regional life expectancy at birth increased from less than forty-five years in 1950 to seventy-four years in 2005. Extreme variations exist throughout the developing world, however. While Costa Rica, Hong Kong and numerous Caribbean island nations enjoy levels that match or exceed those in a majority of European nations, the average lifetime in other countries spans fewer than forty-five years. Aggregate life expectancy at birth in Latin America and the Caribbean (seventy-three years) is twenty-three years higher than in sub-Saharan Africa. On average, an individual born in an industrialized country in 2005 will outlive his/her counterpart in the developing world by eleven years according to current mortality schedules (United Nations 2007).

While global reductions in overall mortality levels have been the norm in recent decades, the HIV/AIDS epidemic has reversed life expectancy gains in some countries of Africa and Asia, and threatens to do so in other parts of the world.

Table 1.2
Life Expectancy at Birth for Selected Developing Countries:
1950 and 2007 (In years)

Region/Country	Circa 1950		Circa 2007	
	Male	Female	Male	Female
Africa				
Egypt	41.2	43.6	69.1	73.6
Ghana	41.8	44.6	59.6	60.5
Mali	31.2	32.4	52.1	56.6
Nigeria	34.8	37.9	46.6	47.3
South Africa	44.0	46.0	48.8	49.7
Uganda	38.5	41.6	50.8	52.2
Asia				
China	39.3	42.3	71.3	74.8
India	39.4	38.0	63.2	66.4
Kazakhstan	50.2	60.6	61.6	72.4
South Korea	46.0	49.0	75.0	82.2
Syria	44.8	47.2	72.3	76.1
Thailand	49.8	54.3	66.5	75.0
Latin America				
Argentina	60.4	65.1	71.6	79.1
Brazil	49.3	52.7	68.8	76.1
Chile	52.9	56.8	75.5	81.5
Cuba	57.8	61.3	76.2	80.4
Mexico	48.9	52.5	73.7	78.6
Venezuela	53.8	56.6	70.9	76.8

Source: United Nations Department of Economic and Social Affairs 2007a.

The impact of the epidemic on life expectancy at birth can be considerable, given that AIDS deaths often are concentrated in the childhood and middle adult (thirty to forty-five) ages. Projections to the year 2010 suggest that AIDS may reduce average life expectancy at birth by fourteen years or more from otherwise-expected levels in at least twenty countries, mostly in sub-Saharan Africa. The impact on future population age structure is less striking insofar as the effects of a long-term epidemic become more evenly distributed across age groups (Stanecki 2004).

Where infant mortality rates are still relatively high but declining, as in many developing countries, most of the improvement in life expectancy at birth results from infants surviving the high-risk initial years of life. But when infant and childhood mortality reach low levels, improvements in average life expectancy are achieved primarily by declines in mortality among older segments of the population. In Japan, life expectancy at age sixty-five rose 5.6 years for men and nearly 8 years for women during the period 1970–2005. Under the mortality conditions of 2005, the average Japanese woman aged sixty-five years could expect to live an additional twenty-three years, and the

Figure 1.4
Life Expectancy at Age 65 in Japan and the United States (Years of life remaining for those who reach age 65)

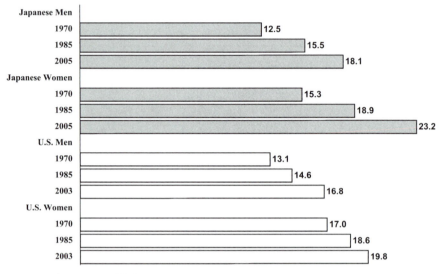

Source: National sources 2006a.

average Japanese man eighteen years. A similar though less pronounced trend is seen in the United States (Figure 1.4) and most other developed countries.

THE QUALITY OF LONGER LIFE

When individuals live longer, the quality of that longer life becomes a central issue. There is extensive debate about the relationship between increased life expectancy and disability status. Are we living healthier as well as longer lives, or are our additional years spent in poor health? Some researchers posit a "compression of morbidity" wherein improvements in survival are accompanied by a decrease in the prevalence of disability. Others argue that as mortality decreases, there is an "expansion of morbidity" wherein the proportion of life lived with disabilities increases. Yet others maintain that as advances in medicine slow the progression from chronic disease to disability, there is a decline in severe disability but perhaps a greater prevalence of milder chronic disease throughout a given population (see Robine and Jagger 2005 for more detail). There is a compelling need for definitive evidence and comparable cross-national measures to assess these possibilities. While the research consensus to date suggests that we are living healthier as well as longer, a recent cross-national analysis states that it is not possible to detect a general pattern of disability decline across member states of the OECD (Lafortune, Balestat and OECD 2007).

COROLLARIES OF DEMOGRAPHIC CHANGE

Epidemiologic Transition

The increases in human life expectancy that began in the mid-1800s and continued during the following century are often ascribed primarily to improvements in medicine. However, the major impact of improvements both in medicine and sanitation did not occur until the late nineteenth century. Earlier and more important factors in lowering mortality were innovations in industrial and agricultural production and distribution, which enabled nutritional diversity and consistency for large numbers of people. Researchers have come to attribute the gain in human longevity since the early 1800s to a complex interplay of advancements in medicine and sanitation coupled with new modes of familial, social, economic and political organization (Moore 1993; Riley 2001).

One correlate of this interplay of factors has been an epidemiologic transition, which is related to but has lagged behind the demographic transition. The initial mortality declines that characterize the demographic transition result largely from reductions of infectious diseases. As children survive and age, they increasingly are exposed to accidents and risk factors linked to chronic disease. And as fertility declines lead to population aging, growing numbers of older persons shift national health patterns in the direction of more continuous and degenerative ailments.

Recognition of this fundamental health transition has prompted considerable effort to quantify the impact of shifting disease epidemiology throughout the world. Survival itself is not a comprehensive indicator of health. The Global Burden of Disease (GBD) project conducted by the World Health Organization and the World Bank combines information about mortality and morbidity in order to assess the total loss of health from diseases and injuries (Lopez et al. 2006). GBD results dispel the myth that a high prevalence of noncommunicable disease is found only in higher-income countries. During the period 1990–2001, the global burden (all ages) of noncommunicable diseases increased by 10 percent, reflecting in part the rapidity of population aging in many developing countries. By 2002, the estimated burdens of communicable and noncommunicable disease were equal in low- and middle-income countries, setting the stage for the emerging primacy of noncommunicable diseases in these countries (Figure 1.5). The critical issue for low- and middle-income countries is how to mobilize and allocate scarce resources to deal with changing disease patterns, given that many such nations continue to struggle with a high incidence of communicable disease.

Gender Differences

Women live longer on average than men in virtually all countries. The difference may be slight, as in parts of South Asia, or as large as 13.5 years in parts of the former Soviet Union (Figure 1.6). Although human biology

Figure 1.5
The Increasing Burden of Chronic Noncommunicable Diseases: 2002–2030

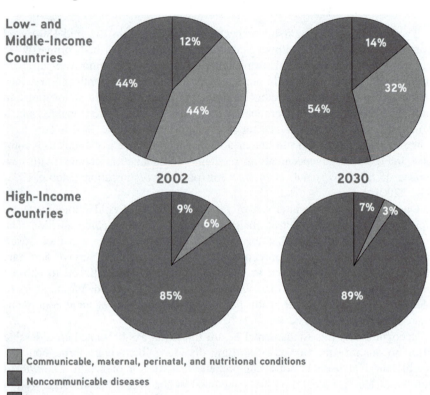

Low- and
Middle-Income
Countries

2002   2030

High-Income
Countries

Communicable, maternal, perinatal, and nutritional conditions

Noncommunicable diseases

Injuries

Source: Lopez AD, Mathers CD, Ezzati M, Jamison DT, Murray CJL, eds. *Global Burden of Disease and Risk Factors.* Washington, DC: The World Bank Group, 2006.

produces more male births than female births throughout the world, male mortality rates usually are higher than female rates at all ages. Therefore, the percent female increases and the numerical male advantage disappears as a birth cohort grows older: by age forty or forty-five, women start to outnumber men in many countries, and the absolute female advantage increases with age. The ratio of women to men among the oldest old may exceed two-to-one, as seen in Austria and Germany, and can, in Russia and Ukraine, reach more than three-to-one.

The gender difference in absolute numbers at older ages translates into a major difference in marital status. Most older men are married. But because women tend to live longer than men, marry males older than themselves, and remarry less frequently after the loss of a spouse, a majority of older women in many countries are widowed. In countries that lack a formal social safety net, older widows—often illiterate and without significant financial savings—represent an

Figure 1.6
Female-Male Difference in Life Expectancy at Birth: 2005 (Difference in years between females and males)

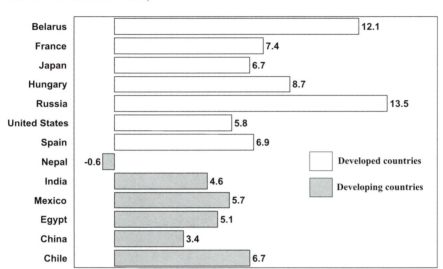

Source: U.S. Census Bureau 2006a.

especially vulnerable population that must rely on younger family members for economic support (see Cattell this volume).

Changing Family Structure

Declines in fertility and mortality affect family structures and influence social arrangements for providing care to older persons. Most older persons today have children, many have grandchildren, and many also have siblings. However, in countries with very low birthrates, future generations of adults may have few, if any, siblings. The global trend towards fewer children portends less familial care for older parents.

Lowered mortality has increased the odds of joint survival of different generations within a family. In developed countries, joint survival has manifested itself in the "beanpole family," a vertical extension of family structure characterized by an increase in the number of living generations within a lineage and a decrease in the number of members within each generation (see Bengtson et al. 1995). As mortality rates continue to improve, more and more people in their fifties and sixties are likely to have surviving parents, aunts and uncles. There is no historical precedent for a majority of middle-aged and older adults having living parents.

While the picture of the nuclear or extended family that stays together through life is still the norm in most nations, the picture is changing. Among Baby Boom generations in the West, for example, there is a wide variety of family forms and lifestyle. These reflect higher rates of divorce, remarriage, blended and step-family relations and never-married and voluntarily childless adults. Many couples and single mothers delay childbearing until their thirties and forties. Households increasingly have both adults working, and more children are being raised in single-parent households.

Persons currently divorced are a small proportion of older populations. This will soon change in many countries as younger cohorts with higher proportions of divorced/separated people move into older age. In the United States, for example, 9 percent of the sixty-five-or-over population were divorced or separated in 2005, compared with about 18 percent of people in the age groups fifty-five to sixty-four and forty-five to fifty-four. This trend has gender-specific implications: non-married women are less likely than non-married men to have accumulated assets and pension wealth for use in older age; older men are less likely to form and maintain supportive social networks (Antonucci and Akiyama 1995).

Childlessness is another important factor that will affect the nature of future caregiving, but has received relatively scant attention considering its potential impact. In some industrialized societies, 15 percent or more of women do not give birth, with unusually high levels of childlessness documented in Western Germany and Britain (Basu 2004; Simpson 2006;). Rising percentages of childless women are seen in Europe and North America, and we may anticipate a similar trend in Latin America and Southeast Asia. Attitudinal research among younger European adults (ages eighteen to thirty-nine) shows that more than one-third in some countries (Germany, the Netherlands, Finland, and Poland) either intend to remain, or are uncertain about remaining, childless (Sobotka and Testa 2006). Given the variation in family structure worldwide, it will be increasingly important to understand different types of childlessness (e.g., voluntary; involuntary "coerced"; involuntary "natural"; loss of children due to HIV/AIDS) and the implications for eventual care arrangements as current and future cohorts of middle-aged people reach older age (Kreager and Schröder-Butterfill 2004; Indrizal, Kreager, and Schröder-Butterfill this volume).

Living Arrangements and Social Support

Living arrangements of older people reflect both the nature of accommodation required (regular or specially built or adapted) and the need for community or institutional long-term care. Living arrangements also indicate sociocultural preferences, for example, living in nuclear households versus with extended families. The number and often the percentage of older people, especially women, living alone is rising in most countries. In earlier times, living alone in older age was often equated with social isolation or family abandonment. However, research in many cultural settings consistently shows that older persons, including those living alone, prefer to reside in their own homes and communities. This preference is reinforced by many factors, among them greater longevity, expansion of pension and other social benefits, increased levels of home ownership, elder-friendly housing and a greater emphasis in many nations on provision of community care (see Stafford this volume).

Figure 1.7
Percent of People Aged 60 and Over Living with Child and/or Grandchild,
Circa 2000

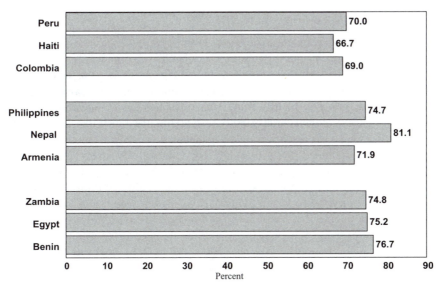

Source: United Nations Department of Economic and Social Affairs 2007a.

While the tendency has been for multigeneration households to become relatively fewer in the more developed world, two- and three-generation households are still the norm in most developing countries (Figure 1.7). In spite of the apparent robustness of such living arrangements for older persons, concerns are emerging. One relates to specific groups such as unmarried women or widows without children, who can be left with little support and nowhere to live if extended family members will not take them in. Another has to do with changes in household structures occurring in the face of large numbers of AIDS deaths in parts of Africa and Asia, which leave many orphans living with and supported by grandparents. There also are broader concerns surrounding young-adult migration to urban areas, levels of intrafamily remittances and return migration of adults after extended periods of employment in other countries (see Lamb; Sokolovsky; and Zhang this volume).

Long-term care for older persons has become a key issue throughout the West and also in many industrializing middle-income nations (Phillips and Chan 2002; Polivka this volume). Such care involves a range of support mechanisms, from home nursing and home helpers through various forms of community care and assisted living to residential care, long-stay hospitals and similar institutions. Beyond the obvious familial and social cost implications of such care, the manpower needs of caring for aging populations have increased the migration of health workers from lower-income to higher-income nations such as Weibel-Orlando describes in her chapter about elder care in Italy (see Stilwell et al. 2004; International Labour Organization 2006).

THOUGHTS ON FUTURE LONGEVITY

One of the most contentious debates in gerontology today centers around limits to life and the shape of the human survival curve (see Willcox and Willcox this volume). Is average life expectancy destined to peak around age eighty-five or ninety, as some have argued, or will we find new ways to sustain the dramatic increase in life expectancy that unfolded during the twentieth century? The epidemiological transition mentioned earlier shifts the human survival curve, which represents people's chances of surviving another year as they age. In a so-called "wild" survival curve that likely characterized early nonindustrial societies, the risk of death remains relatively constant throughout life, and only a small proportion of those born reach old age (Gurven this volume). Modern survival curves in industrialized societies are much more rectangular, as most people live past middle age and deaths are highly concentrated at older ages. Figure 1.8 depicts the evolution of survival for white females in the United States between 1901 and 2003. As in most countries, the curve moves to the right over time. The key issues for policy planning and service delivery are: (1) how far the curve will shift; and (2) the quality of life of these remaining years.

Figure 1.8
Survival Curve, U.S. White Females: 1901 and 2003

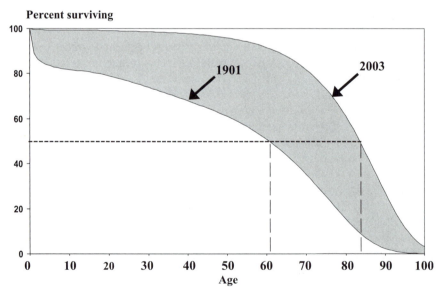

Sources: U.S. Census Bureau, 1936; Arias, 2006.

Increases in the probability of survival make us wonder about limits to average life expectancy, and the potential for human life span. Recent research has led to the questioning of many of the theoretical tenets of the aging process. Some scientists, for example, have made a strong case that certain species of fish, reptiles and birds experience negligible senescence (Finch and Austad 2001). More startling is the contention that *negative senescence*—a decline in death rates with advancing age—is not only theoretically possible, but can be observed in plants and some animals (Vaupel et al. 2004). And in spite of repeated assertions that human life expectancy must be approaching some limit, an examination of the highest reliable recorded national female life expectancies over the period 1840–2000 showed a steady increase of three months per year (Oeppen and Vaupel 2002). The country with the highest average life expectancy has varied over time—in 1840 it was Sweden, today it is Japan—but the linearity of the pattern (also seen for males) is remarkable. While HIV/AIDS, obesity, and other factors may temper future expectations of improvement in human survival, several positive factors suggest optimism, among them: studies showing that death rates at very old ages level off or decline; the explosion of centenarians worldwide; the finding that, even at older ages, mortality rates are plastic and amenable to social interventions; and empirical demonstrations of the positive impact of medical advances and new drugs on life expectancy.

NOTES

The views expressed in this chapter are those of the author and do not necessarily reflect those of the U.S. Census Bureau.

1. These and other demographic estimates and projections in this chapter are, unless otherwise noted, from the International Data Base maintained by the International Programs Center, U.S. Census Bureau and supported by the Behavioral and Social Research Program of the U.S. National Institute on Aging.

2. Some small nations or areas of special sovereignty have relatively high proportions of older population. Nearly 23 percent of people living in Monaco, for example, have reached age 65.

3. The country classification used in this chapter corresponds to that of the United Nations, wherein *industrialized* and its synonym *developed* comprise all nations in Europe and North America, plus Japan, Australia, and New Zealand. The remaining nations of the world are classified as *developing*.

4. The average number of children that would be born per woman if all women lived to the end of their childbearing years and bore children according to a given set of age-specific fertility rates.

CHAPTER 2

Complaint Discourse, Aging and Caregiving among the Ju/'hoansi of Botswana

Harriet G. Rosenberg

> Old people have long complained: it is an old thing. Even if the child did everything for them, they would complain.
>
> Koka, age eighty

This chapter explores the social basis of caregiving discourses among the Ju/'hoansi of southern Africa.[1] It looks at how a particular cultural system reproduces the social relations of care for elders, and examines the language through which care is negotiated. These forms of speech locate caregiving in gender, family and community relationships. They also reproduce the ideology of caring for elders in both its public and domestic realm, and legitimate this behavior so it is experienced as "natural."

Despite the changes in economic and social life that the Ju/'hoansi have experienced in the last twenty-five years, caring discourse appears to be autonomous in the Dobe area, in the sense that it is constructed within the culture itself, with very little influence from state agencies (legal, health, educational, military and social services) or non-Ju/'hoansi religious philosophies.[2]

THE JU/'HOANSI OF THE DOBE AREA

The Ju/'hoansi (an approximate English pronunciation would be "juntwasi") of Botswana and Namibia are one of the best known and documented gatherer-hunter peoples in the world. Although their history of contact has been a complex one, some lived as relatively isolated foragers[3] well into the 1960s. As gatherer-hunters, the Ju/'hoansi can provide insights into a way of life that was, until 10,000 years ago, a human universal.

Studies of the Ju/'hoansi have been carried out on a wide variety of topics by over a dozen investigators including Project AGE described by Fry et al.

Web book Part I. The Dobe area, where the majority of these studies were undertaken, is a line of eight waterholes in northern Botswana, which has as recently as 2005 supported a population of 1,000 to 1,200 people, of whom approximately 85 percent are Ju/'hoansi and the remainder pastoralists, mainly of the Herero ethnic group. Our more intensive studies in the mid-1980s of aging and caregiving covered both the Herero and the Ju/'hoansi, but the present chapter focuses on the latter people and is updated where possible with new information from brief field visits by Lee and others between 1999 and the present.[4]

During the 1960s, the majority of Ju/'hoansi lived in small camps of about fifteen to thirty people, often centered around a core of siblings, their spouses and children. The groups relied on wild food products for the bulk of their subsistence needs, and moved three to six times a year in search of food and water. These camps were characterized by egalitarian social relations and the widespread sharing of foodstuffs—the typical features of a small-scale communal social formation. The language and kinship system were intact and fully functioning.

Missionizing has had little influence in the Dobe area. Indigenous religious practices included belief in two major deities (a high god and a lesser, trickster god) and ghosts of ancestors called *gangwasi*. Trance dancing maintained the health of the community and was used to cure individual sicknesses. At some camps the all-night dances took place two or three times a week. A woman's drum dance was also prominent.[5]

After 1968, conditions began to change rapidly. The first store opened in 1968, followed by a school in 1973, and a health post and airstrip in 1978. During this period, the Ju/'hoansi began to shift over to small-scale livestock and crop production and settle into semipermanent villages. Cash became a common medium of exchange, coexisting with the traditional regional gift exchange system called *hxaro*.[6] Migrant labor, livestock sales and craft production became sources of cash income. In addition, some young men were drawn across the border into the South African military, where they earned high salaries as trackers in the war against the South West African People's Organization (SWAPO).[7]

While HIV/AIDS has had a devastating impact on Botswana and Namibia in the last decade, the Ju/'hoansi on both sides of the border have had very few cases, likely because of the high status of women that has empowered them to insist on condom use. As reported in research by Lee and colleagues, Ju/'hoansi women refuse sex to partners unwilling to comply (Lee 2006). Thus the tragic pattern of ill or dying parents cared for by grandmothers and young children is not evident among the Ju of Dobe or across the border.

By the mid-1980s, in their dress and economy, the Dobe Ju/'hoansi came to resemble the lifestyle of many impoverished southern African peasants. They received drought relief in the 1980s, and bags and containers from overseas countries littered their villages. Their children went to school, but the majority usually dropped out in the early grades. More recently, a few have gone on to high school and have become literate in other African languages and in

English. By 2007, Namibia had a Ju member of parliament, and strides have been made to create a written form of the Ju language, develop curricular material in that language and create a resource center and local schools with materials in Ju/'hoansi (Biesele 2007). In the Dobe area, people now seek health care at local clinics or from mobile health units, and they often spend their modest incomes on transistor radios, European-style clothing, tea, sugar, tobacco and beer.

On both sides of the border old-age pensions have been introduced, adding to the prestige of seniors who now have independent access to cash. But problems have also arisen as drinking establishments (*shebeens*) have sprung up, luring pensioners to spend their money while waiting for transport back to remote villages. Health workers in Namibia have expressed worries that the nexus of cash and alcohol may be especially dangerous for accompanying family members who may be having unprotected sex while under the influence of alcohol and risk bringing STDs or HIV into the local communities (Lee 2006).

Their transition to an agricultural way of life has been far from successful. In the mid-1980s, over half the families lacked livestock, and even the "affluent" herders numbered their stock in the range of ten to twenty head of cattle.[8] Foraging declined in the mid-1980s with the introduction of drought relief, but bow and arrow hunting has once again increased in Botswana, encouraged by the Game Department (Lee and Rosenberg 1993). Over the past two decades the knowledge of Dobe area elders about the environment, seasonal variation, and their technical advice about hunting and gathering became highly prized as younger community members intensified foraging activities (Lee and Biesele 1991; Biesele 2007).[9]

On a deeper level, the Dobe Ju/'hoansi are struggling—not without success—to adhere to the values and beliefs of their ancestral culture. It is this cultural context that has continued to generate the motifs, themes, and rationales about aging and caregiving that are explored in this chapter.

AGE AND CHANGE IN JU/'HOANSI SOCIETY

Like most foraging peoples, the Ju/'hoansi were not interested in and did not keep track of chronological age. Birthdays and anniversaries were not social markers, and age segregation has been noticeably absent. Major life transition hallmarks existed at the younger end of the age spectrum distinguishing among infants, children, adolescents and adults. No ceremonies marked the onset of old age or menopause, but all elders (including those without children) carry the honorific *na* in their names, which means "old," "big" or "great." No ritual occasion marks the moment when one becomes *na*, usually in one's mid to late forties; certainly, everyone fifty or over is called *na*.[10]

Old age is divided into three broad categories. All elders are *na*, while those who are very old but still functioning are called "old/dead" *da ki*, a term that designates extreme old age and one that is also a joking term. A sick or decrepit elder may be referred to as "old to the point of helplessness" *da kum*

kum. Da ki and *da kum kum* do not denote a sharp decline in social status. Unlike many societies described in this volume (see Glascock Part I and Barker Part VI), the frail elderly are not a particular butt of ridicule or a source of fear and anxiety.

It should be noted that growing old and the changes that accompany it are a constant topic of conversation and a source of humor. Linking sexuality and aging seem to make the best jokes, and much campfire discussion features endless stories about decline in sexual prowess, especially among men. Postmenopausal women also delight in engaging in broad sexual joking (Lee 1984).

Although the Ju/'hoansi do link old age with degeneration, elders are also associated with generative and life-giving activities, as Biesele and Howell have pointed out in their analysis of a beautiful folktale of a grandmother/granddaughter relationship (1981). Similarly, elders are felt to have special powers that permit them to eat certain foods (e.g., ostrich eggs) considered too dangerous for younger people to consume. Elders with physical infirmities have taken strong leadership roles, for example, the case of four blind seniors whose decision-making advice and curing roles were very influential in the political and social life of one water hole in the 1960s (Lee 1968:36). Death is not exclusively connected with old age. Historically, the Ju/'hoansi have had a high infant mortality rate, and now tuberculosis is prevalent in the Dobe area. Thus, death can and does occur at any age.

In the realm of sociopolitical power, Ju/'hoansi elders have had limited prerogatives. Traditionally, they commanded control over defining kinship relationships. A senior person, male or female, has the right to decide who fits where in the kinship system and to determine an avoidance or a joking framework for social interactions. This system of seniority gives elders power within the social universe, but it does not constitute a gerontocracy. Before settling down, the Ju/'hoansi were, for the most part, without property and could not wield the threat of disinheritance to encourage compliance. In 1995, an adult daughter of an elder with cows was asked how cattle ownership affects the quality of care, and she responded by saying that "it hasn't changed things. We took care of our elders then and we still take care of them" (Richard Lee field notes May 1995).

However, this mother of six children also indicated that at her passing her eldest child (female) would inherit her cattle, and that she alone among her siblings anticipated receiving her mother's property because she saw herself as the principal caregiver. But she also stated that she might decide to share her inheritance with her siblings (Lee *ibid*).

How property and inheritance will, in the long run, influence personal relationships including eldercare, is still very much in the process of being worked out. Sedentary life has brought changed patterns in subsistence and marriage customs, which may also create significant changes in the lives of Ju/'hoansi elders. In the past, old people, by dint of their personal authority, attempted to construct marriage alliances that seemed sensible to them, but young people often refused such arrangements, thwarting the intentions of their seniors. An emerging pattern of bride wealth[11] in lieu of bride service and an increase in informal interethnic liaisons has made marriage a contentious issue in the Dobe area.[12] At the same time, elders have argued that they see no real change in their own lives as a result of a movement away from bride service toward bride wealth, and that receiving a cow at the marriage of a daughter seems to be equivalent to having a son-in-law's hunting skill at their disposal.

Another arena of personal authority for elders has been their role as healers. Richard Katz, who had done fieldwork among healers in the Dobe area in the late 1980s, notes that the social status of certain elderly healers was very high (personal communication 1995). These old men are "the healers' healers," and it is their experience and their strength in not being overpowered by the forces with which they work that commands respect. In a culture where boasting of any kind is frowned upon, these senior healers are permitted to talk about their skill and achievements. Not all old people develop the power to heal—to sing, dance, go into a trance and "pull sickness" out of others. Those who do can often go on until they are quite old, teaching other healers and participating in healing the community at large. Katz has described the charismatic energy of some elderly healers and their aura of exceptional strength and spirituality (1982). Later research indicated that while some elders say that they are strengthened by their access to *num* (medicine), others have found that healing is very wearing and hastens the aging process (Katz, Biesele and St. Denis 1995). By 2007, a consensus among researchers was that Ju/'hoansi healers continue to be viewed with the respect described previously, but that the temptations of payment for services may complicate the situation (Katz, Biesele, Guenther and Lee personal communications 2007).

THE 1986/1987 PROJECT

The discussion that follows is based on field research (participant observation, formal questionnaires and open-ended, unstructured interviews) with the Ju/'hoansi in 1986, 1987[13] and updated as described previously. It also makes use of the accumulated work by anthropologists who have worked with them since 1963. We were, thus, often able to compare our informants' retrospective accounts with field descriptions of observed behavior over a period of three decades. Until recently, however, there has been very little systematic research on aging in Ju/'hoansi culture.

In 1964, 9 percent of the population was over sixty. By 1986, the figure was 12.5 percent, with 7.5 percent over age sixty-five. In addition, the birth rate has risen. As of 1986, almost 40 percent of the population was under fifteen years of age. Thus at the time of our field research, 48 percent of the population was between fifteen and forty-nine and supported both young and old. In stark contrast to the rest of southern Africa where the AIDS epidemic has shortened life expectancy, the Dobe area's rates have remained stable (Lee 2006.)

This project focused on the social experience of aging and caregiving as mediated by the following: (1) narratives of neglect and abandonment, (2) the concept of entitlement and (3) the social organization of care.

NARRATIVES OF NEGLECT AND ABANDONMENT

To the observer, Ju/'hoansi elders appear to be hale and hearty[14] and well integrated into the social life of their community. Frail[15] elders are embedded in caregiving networks of several on-site caregivers, who provide for their needs. Yet the discourse used by elders to describe their situation is often one of unrelenting complaint and blaming. In general, the most common response to the question, "Who looks after old people?" is "Their children." But when we stepped outside the normative system and asked elders, "Who looks after you?" the response was very frequently, "No one. Can't you see that I am starving and dressed in rags?"

Elders frequently complained about the neglected state they were in and told lengthy tales about the deficiencies of those who should be caring for them but were not. While neglect discourse took on a variety of forms, two common styles will be examined here. One is the nagging style and the other is broad melodrama.[16]

The first style is typified by Chuko, age seventy-two at the time of the interview. In the mid-1980s, Chuko lived with her husband, her daughter and her son-in-law, all of whom shared in the caregiving. Yet Chuko described herself as neglected because she stated that her three half-brothers and their children did not provide for her.

The care that she received from her daughter, son-in-law and husband was scarcely acknowledged. Chuko asserted that caregiving had deteriorated in the present. She maintained that in the past, children were collectively responsible for all elders.

When I say the past was better I mean this: before, the child listened to his/her parents.[17] When children went out to play and an adult who saw an elder ailing came upon them, he scolded them for letting the elder die of thirst and ordered them to attend to [the elder]. Today an adult will merely look and say or think: "Let his/her children take care of him/her." And even the children themselves are not caring by nature.

She then reiterated her complaints against her half-siblings.

Two of Chuko's brothers agreed to be interviewed, and they defined themselves as being caregivers to their sister and pointed out that they sent food and water to her via their children and grandchildren. Nevertheless, Chuko maintained a persistent patter of complaint. Far from not wishing to seem a burden or a dependent, she went out of her way to publicly blame her brothers and their families as being delinquent caregivers. Her form of expression was often a quiet oration to no one in particular.

Chuko's complaint discourse can be interpreted in a variety of ways. She may have been detecting changes in the distribution of social obligations that have accompanied settlement, and may indeed have picked up a drift away from sibling care towards a more nuclear pattern. Her family and her brothers had lived together in the past in a traditional sibling core unit, but at the time of the interview, the brothers lived on the other side of Dobe. Two of these brothers have many children, grandchildren and elders to care for and may well have been preoccupied with their immediate situations. The third sibling is often dismissed as a person with no sense who cannot be relied on. Thus, Chuko may be complaining about a new experience of social distance that has fractured horizontal sibling bonds and is delimiting caregiving responsibilities within the nuclear family. But while the Ju/'hoansi may talk constantly about the importance of adult children, they also mobilize other caregiving networks by means of eloquent complaint.[18]

Anthropologists consider the Ju/'hoansi to be "among the most talkative people in the world. Much of this talk verges on argument, often for its own sake, and usually ad hominem" (Lee 1979:372). Thus, Chuko's stream of complaints is not viewed within the culture as unusual or as a particular attribute of old age.[19]

Complaining is an important leveling discourse and a medium for the expression of a variety of complex feelings (Wiessner 1983). In describing the circumstances leading to and the aftermath of the deaths of three elders, Wiessner (1983) noted vociferous complaints about the adequacy of care in all cases, even in a family where adult children and more distant kin were doing everything they could, including purchasing and slaughtering goats, and holding healing ceremonies. "These accusations," according to Wiessner, are part of "the rhetoric of reciprocity which pervades San life" (1983:1). Guenther has called this discursive pattern "an expressive version of foraging," with a number of elements that include entertainment, rhetorical persuasion and acoustical bonding (2006). Complaining is a public exhortation to keep goods and services circulating: It warns against hording and is thus at the center of the foraging way of life.

Complaining rhetoric may also have been part of Chuko's individual efforts to keep herself visible. Just as Jewish elders in Barbara Myerhoff's study of a seniors' drop-in center used narration and "competitive complaining" (1978:146) as a performance strategy to mark their continued presence in the world, so Chuko's constant hum of words may well be her way of saying, "I'm still here."

No competing legitimate discourse to the ideology of sharing has thus far emerged among the Dobe Ju/'hoansi. There is no language yet that expresses a world of personal needs that might be at odds with obligations to others, and there is very little leniency shown to those who may have many conflicting obligations. Those who have attempted to limit the circle of reciprocity when they switched from foraging to agro-pastoralism have found it difficult to explain why they were not sharing their crops or killing their goats and cattle to meet the needs of their kinspeople (Lee 1979:412–14).

One woman in her early sixties, a very vociferous complainer, relished denouncing all and sundry for their failure to share. One day, while following one of the research team members who was packing up camp, she delivered a blistering tirade against his stinginess. Back and forth from tent to truck they trudged, the anthropologist silent, carrying bundles of goods, Nuhka on his heels, yelling at him. Suddenly, she stopped, and like a scene in a Brecht play, she stepped out of character, altered the tone of her voice, and calmly announced, "We have to talk this way. It's our custom." Then she stepped back into character and resumed her attack.

The Ju/'hoansi have a name for this type of discourse: It is called *hore hore* or *oba oba*, and can be translated as "yakity yak." In Nuhka's case, she stepped out of character to break the tension of the verbal assault she had mounted. In other cases, the tension can be broken by a joke that leaves "the participants rolling on the ground helpless with laughter" (Lee 1979:372). Neglect discourse is, thus, not peculiar to elders, but may be invoked by anyone at any time to decry real or potential stinginess. However, elders will frequently avail themselves of the opportunity to complain. In contrast to Chuko's nagging style, others recount their complaints with great theatrical flare.

Kasupe, age seventy-four, a skilled storyteller, responded to the question of who looked after him by denouncing his entire family. First, he attacked his children.

My own children do not look after me. See the clothes I am wearing—these rags I'm wearing—I get them from my own work, my own sweat. None of them have done anything for me. Because they do not look after me, I, their parent say they are "without sense."

He went on to discuss his future prospects:

I do not know who will take care of me when I am old and frail. Right now I can manage; I still have some strength. But as I grow old, I cannot point out a child—a person—about whom I can say, "This one will take care of me." Perhaps I will perish.

Warming up to his tale of woe, Kasupe also denounced his brothers and sisters. In fact, all of his relatives were dismissed as being uncaring. To illustrate the depths of their perfidy, he launched into the following story:

Here is proof of the uncaring nature of my children. I will tell you a story. I'd gone hunting with some Herero [men] and we had split up agreeing to meet later at a certain point. Those Herero warned me that they had set a trap in the direction I was headed. I went on but because it was dark, I could not see and was caught in the trap. It grabbed my ankle. I stayed there and my wife and children were following me. None of them came to see how I was. I was only helped by you Gakegkoshe [the Tswana/Herero translator] and Tontah [Richard Lee, an anthropologist]. You helped me heal and saw to it that I got better. None of [my family] came to see how I was doing. It was only you. Even my brothers and sisters in Southwest [Namibia] did not come to see how I was doing.

At this juncture, Gakegkoshe turned to me and said in English, "A big story." And indeed it was.

After the interview concluded, Richard Lee and I returned to camp, fetched a copy of the book *The Dobe !Kung* and returned to confront Kasupe. There on page 105 of the book was a photo of Kasupe "on the day of the crisis" lying on the ground surrounded by family and Ju/'hoansi healers. The text also included a lengthy account from Lee's field notes describing Kasupe's wife and children sobbing and wailing as community members worked on curing him. Lee administered some penicillin. The next day, Kasupe began to improve, and within three months he was hunting again (Lee 1984:104–106).

Feeling some glee in having caught Kasupe in a "lie," we laid the evidence out before him. Here was the story and photograph of his family and community making heroic efforts to save his life. Kasupe's only response was to break out into a loud, long, thigh-slapping laugh, which was immediately echoed by the Ju/'hoansi audience and the anthropologists.

Kasupe was completely unabashed and expressed no regret at having "accused" his relatives of neglect, abandonment and death-hastening behavior. Whether there was any "truth" to his narrative was quite irrelevant. His version of events made a good story. It was gripping and dramatic; he was impressive as he told it. The listener was captivated by "the utterance" (Eagleton 1983:115).

Kasupe expressed what "might" happen if caregivers were not to do their duty. He described aloud what the world would be like should the caring

Kasupe laughing after telling his story, with his friend Twi (seated).

system not be reproduced. His narrative allowed his audience to imagine the dire scene of family neglect. By negative example, he restated the social contract of caregiving obligations. His laughter, and the audience's laughter, did not mean that the complaint lacked seriousness, only perhaps that he had been topped by a better story this time. But the complaint was important: the Ju/'hoansi system of mutual responsibility and caregiving requires constant lubrication, and complaining greases the wheels.

TALES OF "REAL" ABANDONMENT

In a more serious vein, Xoma, a respected elder, who was not given to extravagant rhetoric, pointed out that there were indeed cases of real abandonment in the past. He explained the circumstances of an abandonment in a previous generation:

They'd leave him/her and go off, because they didn't know what to do with him/her. Naturally, they had no truck, no donkey, nothing. And they were also carrying her/his things on their bodies. Sometimes they'd try to carry him/her where they were going. Someone else would carry his/her things, if there were many people. But if the people were few, or if there was only one man, they didn't know what to do with the old person. They would admit defeat, leave him/her, and go.

It is likely that there have been cases of death-hastening among the Ju/'hoansi in the past. We do not have any sustained ethnographic account of such behavior comparable to Hart's encounter with the Tiwi custom of "covering up" (see Introduction, this volume[20]).

The Ju/'hoansi, themselves, use the equivocal term *na a tsi* (to leave in the bush), which implies abandonment. As Xoma's dispassionate analysis implies, "burden of care" was often not a metaphor, but a concrete description of physically carrying a frail elder on one's back. When this was the only means of transportation, there were likely to have been times when the coping skills of the caregivers were stretched to the breaking point, and the elder was abandoned in the bush.[21]

Settlement has made a difference in eldercare. In the mid-1980s, we found incapacitated elders being scrupulously cared for by kin and community. The conditions of a settled lifestyle, the availability of soft foods and access to vehicles in cases of medical emergencies all make it easier to care for frail elders today in comparison to thirty or more years ago. Furthermore, settlement has meant that Ju/'hoansi practices are now more closely scrutinized by the state than they were in the past. The presence of a legal apparatus and police in the Dobe district have likely influenced community thinking on abandonment of elders.

The question of what constitutes "real" abandonment was a thorny problem for the researchers, and we found no easy answers. About 90 percent of our informants said that they knew of no cases of elders being abandoned in the past. Many described cases of young people carrying frail elders on their backs from water hole to water hole until they died "in our hands." Many others said that they had never heard of old people being abandoned.

But a few informants recounted explicit stories describing elders being left intentionally to perish. A consistent element in these accounts was that those associated with death-hastening activities were always close relatives—a spouse or children. This finding is consistent with Glascock's discussion (in Part I) that the decision to abandon an old person is almost always made within the immediate family, although in the Ju/'hoansi case, elders do not appear to be part of the negotiations. What is unknown, but nevertheless very important, in these discussions of euthanasia is how long the elder was incapacitated before the decision to terminate life was made. It may be that among the Ju/'hoansi, if close family members have been seen to be caring for a decrepit elder for a very long period of time, a culturally acknowledged but unexpressed statute of limitations comes into play and abandonment is permitted, especially if it is *not* presented as a premeditated action.

The discourse of neglect is thus quite complicated.[22] It is used to describe cases in which "real" abandonment may have occurred. It is used as a social regulatory mechanism to reinforce sharing and caregiving. It is used as a vehicle to tell a good story. What is most apparent about this discourse is that it is words, and words alone, that have up until very recently been the main social regulators of behavior. The Ju/'hoansi themselves have no legal/police system with which to coerce behavior or punish offenders.

ENTITLEMENT

"Old people in this country are just brushed to one side, like rubbish, past our sell-by date," claims Alfie Carretta, lead singer of the Zimmers, a group of forty British pensioners. In 2007, the group created a sensation reinterpreting The Who's song "My Generation" from the perspective of seniors (*Toronto Star*, June 9, 2007:A3).

Ju/'hoansi elders do not see themselves as burdens. They are not apologetic if they are no longer able to produce enough to feed themselves. They expect others to care for them when they can no longer do so. Entitlement to care is naturalized within the culture: Elders do not have to negotiate care as if it were a favor, rather, it is perceived of as an unquestioned right.

The needs of elders are not defined as being markedly different from the needs of anyone else. The material aspects of caring for elders were uniformly defined by our informants as providing *da, gu* and *msi* (firewood, water and food). These are the basics of life, which are procured and shared among all members of the community. Obtaining these necessities in the past has not been especially onerous, requiring on average twenty hours of work a week in food gathering by the active population, but today those with herd animals work longer hours. Thus, elders have not been experienced as a particular economic burden or a category of people with "special needs."[23] In fact, in terms of health care, elders are both givers and receivers of care. Even with the arrival of government health workers in the district, healing dances continue to flourish, giving elders a prominent role in community life.

One rarely hears an old person express appreciation for the care that she or he receives, and one never hears elders express the desire to live alone in order not to burden the family with caregiving obligations. The desire to live alone is classified as a form of mental illness. "Only a crazy person would live alone," said one young informant.

The following story illustrates how old people make demands. In the middle of a hot afternoon in 1986, Gumi[24] was sleeping in her house next to a small fire. I had never met her before, but she was Tontah's (Richard Lee's) social mother and they had had a close relationship for over twenty-three years. At first sight, Gumi, age eighty-three, looked to be very frail, weighing perhaps sixty pounds. Her daughter Sagai spoke to her by cupping her hands and shouting about four inches from her ear. Although Gumi had awakened from a sound sleep and had not seen her "European" son for six years, she immediately tuned into the situation, greeted her visitors and established their place in the kinship system.

Throughout the interview, Gumi gave alert responses to our questions. At the same time, she launched her own demanding harangue for gifts: "Give me some medicine ... Well, I got some clothing ... Tontah, *hxaro*[25] *mi cosisi* (give me things). Give me beads.... Give me clothing."

At one point during the lengthy interview, her daughter interrupted the steady flow of demands and laughingly said, "Oh, stop going on and on about *hxaro*." Gumi was completely undeterred: "No! No! You tell Tontah that I want to still talk about *hxaro*. Hey, give me things."

When we returned to Dobe, we were asked how Gumi was faring. We described her situation and her persistent requests for gifts.[26] Two elders glanced at each other with knowing looks when we mentioned the demands for *hxaro*, and one said, "Even as old as she is, she still knows how to talk nicely. Her thoughts are still sound."

What I had experienced as demanding ingratitude was culturally interpreted as a sign that Gumi was in good mental health. She "talked nicely" in the sense that her words were considered to be appropriate to a gift exchange situation in which she was an active participant. The ability to make demands is a signal of social connectedness, and a symbol of entitlement. For some, entitlement to care flows directly from the parent/child relationship. Tasa, age sixty-five, described this process of socialization:

When a child is born you teach that child to care for her/his parents throughout the time the child is growing up, so that when the child is older s/he will willingly care for his/her parents. But if that child has a crippled heart, is a person with no sense, that will come from inside her/him and s/he will neglect the parents.

As Tasa pointed out, childrearing practices provide no guarantee of filial caregiving performance. Many of our informants felt that, ultimately, nothing could be done to compel a child with "no sense" to act appropriately.

The elderly Gumi Na clasping the hand of her visiting "European son," Richard Lee, as her daughter Sagai looks on.

Others, however, argued that direct sanctions from the spirit world would occur in cases of filial neglect. According to Gai Koma, fear of ancestors underlies elders' entitlement to care. "We feel under an obligation [to care for our parents] because they brought us up. We've drained all their energies. After they die, we would be left with bad luck if we had not cared for them. We could fall ill." Many concur that there is a link between elder care and the role of *gangwasi* (the ghosts of ancestors), but the relationship between the two worlds is not clear cut. *Gangwasi* have both a punitive side and a charitable side.

The *gangwasi* are not interested solely in elder care but in all phases of human interaction, and their messages to the living are remarkably contradictory. They visit misfortune and sickness on the living to punish, but they also "long for" the living and wish to take them with them to the villages of the dead simply because they are lonely for their loved ones (Wiessner 1983; Lee 1984:107–9). Thus, the reasons for a caregiver's illness or death may be explained either by negligence or devotion; their poor performance may have provoked ancestral anger or their good deeds may have unleashed yearnings among the *gangwasi* to be reunited with their loved one. This ambiguity about motives of the *gangwasi* ultimately lodges the obligation for caregiving in the land of the living.

THE SOCIAL ORGANIZATION OF CAREGIVING

Caregiving is normatively described as being the responsibility of all adult children. All but one informant said that the responsibility should be shared equally among all the children.[27] No elder thought the responsibility was linked to gender or that daughters should be or were doing more than sons. According to Nahka, a woman with many children and grandchildren, feminization of caregiving is not a social norm.

In my household, both my sons and daughters help me. The care they give balances so that I see no difference. I don't think girls are more caring than boys. [Is this the same for others at Dobe?] Yes. I give the example of Nai who has no daughters but the care that her sons give her is of the same quality as that which I get from my children.

Most caregivers subscribed to this version, but a few women felt they were doing more than men. Gumi's daughter, Sagai, was particularly angry with her brother Toma, and fought with him about his lack of attention to their mother. On the other hand, Toma felt that his sister had not been sufficiently attentive when their father was ill and dying.

For our informants it was not gender that divided the population between active caregivers and delinquents, but rather a personal quality or quirk. An elder noted that if you have a child and that child has a good heart, regardless of whether s/he is male or female, s/he will look after their parent.

Nothing can be done to force a child to be a good caregiver. If a child fails to do his/her duty, then others are expected to pitch in, especially if the old person has no children. The situation of Chwa is illustrative.

Chwa was in her late eighties at the time of the interview, had poor eyesight, good hearing and could still walk. She had no children and lived with her co-wife[28] Bau and their husband, both of whom were in their early eighties. Throughout our discussion, neighbors dropped by with food and water. Chwa entered a conversation that compared past caregiving of the elderly to the current situation. One of her neighbors commented that she had never heard of elders being left in the bush in the past. Chwa stated that she had "heard of people carrying those who were sick on their backs from village to village," but "today, people do not look after the old sufficiently." Two of her neighbors immediately disagreed and took turns affirming that the young do *nabe nabe* (care for) the old.

Chwa, however, was adamant. She pointed out that her nephew Tsau was derelict in his duty. (Tsau is her brother's son, a man of about sixty, married and living in another village.) "He wants to," she went on, "but his wife won't let him. But those who do take care of me are this Nisa here [an elderly neighbor] and that woman there, my co-wife [Bau], while our husband tends the cattle."

She then proceeded to recount this positive description of care, one of the very few, that I had ever heard from an elder:

Once, when I was very sick, I was burning with fever, she [Nisa] poured water on me, and then she held me in her arms. These women, Nisa, Tankae [an elderly neighbor], and my co-wife cared for me. I slept in their arms … my heart craved bush food and these women collected it for me.

I turned to one of the collectors and asked, "What made you think of doing that?" And Bau, Chwa's co-wife, using her hands for emphasis, responded: "What is there to think about? You see an old person. She is your person. She can't walk. She can't do it for herself, so you do it."

Thus, although Chwa has no children of her own, she was firmly anchored in a responsive caregiving network. These ties can be quite distant, in kinship terms, as in the case of Chwa's network. Chwa's neighbor, Nisa, calls Chwa "elder sister" although they have a very remote kinship connection. She and other caregivers use the word *ju* to express an affiliation that incorporates a mixture of sentiment based on ethnicity and residential proximity and is expressed in quasi-kinship terms.

The caregiving role for someone who is "your person" is naturalized and it is not feminized.[29] Caregiving is explained as a quality of human, not female, nature. We have observed male and female caregivers providing food, firewood and water, although the foods may represent a gendered division of labor, with men hunting and women gathering. Government drought relief food will be carried to elders who cannot manage to go to the relief trucks themselves by any of "their people." Both men and women also care in other ways. Massage is an important service rendered by caregivers. Both men and women will gather the plants and nuts used to prepare the ointments that are used during massage. Women are more likely to provide other, smaller services for female elders, like grooming hair, but both men and women spend time visiting, talking and drinking tea with elders. In the delicate area of toileting old people, there did seem to be a gender link. Male caregivers would take responsibility for guiding male elders in and out of the bush, and female caregivers would look after the needs of women elders.

Children, regardless of sex, were enlisted in caregiving as well. Sometimes the special relationship of grandparent/grandchild was used to mobilize care. This relationship is quite expandable into an inclusive kinship mode, which draws in distant kin. Elders, for example, may invoke the "name" relationship so children with the same name as the old person will be regarded as grandchildren and available to perform services like fetching water, if they are willing.[30]

The web of caregiving, thus, moves well beyond the limited confines of the nuclear family[31]—it is located in kinship/community ideology. It is not sentimentalized as a form of self-sacrifice.[32]

Dobe area elders have continued to be independent and autonomous (as are all members of the community) in the sense that they can do what they wish when they wish. Able-bodied elders forage, fetch water, visit, trade gifts, make crafts, dance, sleep and eat whenever they choose.[33] They still do not face fears of pauperization with old age or the struggles of living on a "fixed income." But on the Namibian side, the last decade has brought an era of greater anxiety about personal safety as non-Ju'/hoansi populations have move into the area (Biesele 2008, personal communication.). There has been a subsequent advent of homes with doors and locks as fears about unruly behavior and robbery associated with alcohol consumption affect that community.

It is generally thought among the Namibian Ju/'hoansi that their Botswana relatives are safer and that they are less likely to lock their house doors. People on both sides of the border with these concerns tend to lock their doors during the day when they are away, but do not lock themselves in at night (Lee 2008, personal communication.). Biesele (2008 personal communication) reports that the status of Namibian and Botswana elders has been enhanced by old age pensions, but that status may be negatively affected by the exclusion of seniors from access to drivers licenses and computers. Elders continue to be integrated into all other aspects of community life and the conversational theme of the "agony of loneliness" (Hillebrant 1980:408) remains absent. And unlike Western elders, they do not grapple with the difficult decision of whether to sell their homes and lose a whole way of life to take up a diminished but more secure living environment (Draper and Keith 1992).

Frail Ju/'hoansi elders are enmeshed in a network of caregiving. The eight frail elders we interviewed had between four and eight people looking after them, for a total of forty-four people undertaking frontline elder care responsibilities. In Canada, a recent estimate suggests a caregiver ratio of one personal support person to ten residents in a care facility, describing it as "laughably inadequate" within a context of caregiver "burn-out," leading to "substandard, uncaring service" (Bennett 2007).

In Dobe, even those who were extremely weak were not segregated from the social landscape. We observed a situation in which Dau, a very sick elder who slept almost all the time, was placed in the center of social life. Around him gathered family and neighbors who chatted, smoked and cooked together. Nearby, his son hacked up the carcass of a kudu, and the old man's wife, Koka, stirred the cooking pot, children played and an infant nursed. As the meat cooked, his wife lifted his head every few minutes and fed him a morsel of food. He chewed silently, his eyes shut. When he was done, he rested his head on the blanket. In the meantime, Dau's wife chatted with those at the fire. Both the old man and his caregivers were rooted in a social matrix that undoubtedly eased the burden of care and perhaps enhanced the quality of this very frail person's last days.

CONCLUSION: THE PARADOX OF SHARING AND COMPLAINING

By North American standards, the material situation of the Dobe Ju/'hoansi is poor, but the social circumstances of elders is quite positive (see also Draper and Keith 1992; Draper and Harpending 1994). They have personal autonomy, respect and a great deal of control over the immediate circumstances of their lives. They live in a culture that strongly values caregiving and support. Old people participate in social, political, economic and spiritual life. They may regret growing old and ask someone to pull out the first few grey hairs, but they are also equipped with rich cultural resources for articulating their concerns, fears and anxieties, and for ensuring support.

Yet the Ju/'hoansi complain all the time. They are cranky, funny and loud. They live in a moral universe of high caregiving standards, in which the ideal

Ju/'hoan trainees at work transcribing their "legacy collection." On the right is
Fridirick/ti!kae (Tikae) and on the left is Charlie/ui (Twi). Photo by Megan
Biesele.

seems to be that every person is directly obligated to meet the needs of every
other person all the time. But since such a perfect world is impossible to obtain,
they find ample justification for their complaints of inadequate caregiving. Furthermore, personal preferences, personality conflicts, and old unresolved grievan-
ces enter into the caregiving equation, making it far from an ideal universe.
There is always someone who is not doing enough. And there is always someone
ready to denounce that person in terms that are not pleasant or polite.

The cultural forms that reproduce respect and care for elders through complaint discourse reflect deep patterns in Ju/'hoansi culture. Boasting, self-
aggrandizement or displays of pride are strongly discouraged as behaviors that
impede sharing and may lead to violence. Thus, it is not polite etiquette but
"rough humor, back-handed compliments, put-downs and damning with faint
praise" (Lee 1979:458)—the rhetoric of complaint—that is in constant use to
constrain potentially dangerous behaviors. Complaining is the only social arena
in which the Ju/'hoansi are competitive, and it is hardly surprising that elders
are so good at it; they have been practicing their whole lives.

These discourses have not abruptly unraveled with changes in material culture like the appearance of transistor radios, cassette tape players and bicycles.
In other words, cultural formations are resilient, and contrary to the highly
romanticized myth presented in the South African film *The Gods Must Be
Crazy*, the world is not turned upside down by the introduction of a minor artifact of Western society.

In fact, in a collaborative project with the Ju/'hoansi of Namibia, Biesele is working with local youth to transcribe close to forty years of audio materials including folktales, hunting stories and healing narratives, much of it from elders, onto computers to create an archive of materials for the Ju/'hoan people and scholars around the world (2007). In a recent publication, she describes the trainees hard at work trying to transcribe a particularly complicated narrative from a healer. The trainee sighs aloud and says: "If only /Kunta Boo [the raconteur on the old sound file] were here to help explain all this to us so we could get it written down right." At that very moment, Biesele and the young trainees looked up to find that very elder and his wife standing in the doorway of the resource centre.

The couple stayed in the village of Tsumkwe and worked for two solid weeks in the resource center. As they were leaving to return to their remote village, one of the young trainees "was moved to read a speech he had written, which contained the words: 'We young people could never have done this work correctly without you, our elders'" (Biesele 2007).[34]

The Ju/'hoansi of the Kalahari drink soda pop and are learning how to use computers, and are still conducting trance dances, still complaining about those who do not share and still caring for their elders.

NOTES

The field research upon which the bulk of this chapter is based was carried on in Botswana between May and July 1986 and January and August 1987. The "we" used here refers to a team of investigators, research assistants and translators. The investigators included Richard B. Lee, who interviewed in the Ju language, and Meg Luxton and Harriet Rosenberg, who used translators. We gratefully acknowledge the assistance of Nandi Ngcongco, Dorothy Molokome and Leonard Ramatakwame of the University of Botswana; Makgolo Makgolo, M.A., of Gaborone; and Gakekgoshe Isaaka and Gai Koma of the Dobe region. In addition, Megan Biesele consulted on this project. We thank her for the careful translation/transcriptions she made of interviews she conducted in Ju/'hoanis in Namibia.

The investigators wish to thank the Social Science and Humanities Research Council of Canada for providing funding for this project, "Aging, Caregiving and Social Change in an African Population," file number 410-84-1298.

A version of this chapter was presented to the International Congress of Anthropological and Ethnological Sciences, Zagreb Yugoslavia, July 24–31, 1988. I appreciate the insightful comments made by Christine Gailey and Richard Lee at that time.

In addition, I would like to thank Patricia Draper, Mathias Guenther, Richard Katz, Robin Oakley and Polly Wiessner for their gracious assistance with this version. Finally, thanks go to Richard Lee for gathering additional information for this project while doing research in Namibia in the spring of 1995.

1. The Ju/'hoansi are also known by the terms *!Kung San*, or the *!Kung Bushman*, in anthropological and popular literature. The word *Ju/'hoansi* is the people's name for themselves and means "the real people." In the years since this article first appeared, the Ju/'hoansi like many other indigenous peoples of the world have come to political

consciousness and are engaged in a variety of political and economic struggles. The terms *!Kung*, *San* and *Bushmen* are moving into positions analogous to *Indian* and *Eskimo* in North America where they are often replaced by *First Nations* and *Inuit* as indicators of pride in cultural identity. The spelling "Ju/'hoansi" was worked out in collaborative efforts between the people themselves and the linguist Patrick Dickens in the late 1980s. The term *Ju* means person or people.

Their language contains clicking sounds that are unique to the Khoisan and neighboring languages of southern and eastern Africa. In addition, the language contains glottal stops and nasalizations. Anthropologists, in committing their words to writing, have developed an orthography, which has recently been revised, to approximate a rendering of these sounds in English.

There are four major clicks: dental, alveolar, alveopalatal and lateral. In this chapter, only one click is marked. This is the dental click indicated by a slash. In English it sounds like the mild reproach "tsk, tsk." Nasalization is indicated by an apostrophe. Thus the word *Ju/'hoansi* might be approximated in English as "juntwasi" with a soft "j" as in the French "je," a dental click on the "t" and a nasalization of the "a."

2. Influences from Herero practices have been observed among the Ju/'hoansi. The issue of burial practices is discussed in note 22.

3. By *foraging* I mean a mode of subsistence entirely based on wild food sources, without agriculture or domesticated animals, except for the dog.

4. In 1999 and 2002, Lee and colleague Ida Susser visited the region while doing research primarily on HIV/AIDs. Follow-up research on that topic was undertaken by Lee and others in 2005, 2007 and 2008.

5. See Katz 1982, Katz and Biesele 1987.

6. See note 25.

7. See John Marshall's film "Nai, the Story of a Kung Woman" for a vivid depiction of the effects of militarization on the Ju/'hoansi of Namibia.

8. In the mid-1990s, herd ownership amongst the Ju'/hoansi was set back by an outbreak of cattle disease that resulted in the slaughter of cattle in the district.

9. On the Namibian side of the border, some elders have fared less well with rapid social change. When the war ended in 1990 and Namibia became independent of South African rule, a group of approximately 4,000 Ju/'hoansi, including family members of those who had acted as scouts and soldiers for the South African military, were relocated to Schmidtsdrift, near Kimberley South Africa (Steyn 1994). This newly created community has had significant difficulties and the elderly have been particularly affected: Many were bored, dependent, marginalized and perceived themselves to be largely worthless within the framework of changed values and circumstances (Steyn 1994:37).

10. However, there is a social convention, not understood by the anthropologists, whereby some younger adults in their thirties are called *na*. It may be a combination of the personal magnetism and social stature of a particularly sober and thoughtful member of the community that earns this honorific or some other life experience that is significant to the community.

11. Bride wealth is a common part of marriage arrangements among pastoralist peoples in Africa. The bride's family is given cattle and/or other property to mark the marriage exchange. Customarily, bride wealth is related to the bride's residence with the groom's family, that is, virilocal residence. Should the betrothal or the marriage fail, the cattle are returned. Furthermore, if the relationship produced children, their custody would normally reside with the father and his family.

By contrast, bride service is associated with the groom's responsibility to move to the bride's family (uxorilocal residence) and to provide subsistence for his in-laws for a specified period of time, often several years. In marriage systems where the age at marriage for females can be very young, bride service offers a structure whereby the bride's parents can be assured that their daughter is being well treated and that their son-in-law is a good provider. If a divorce should occur, any children would normally remain with the mother and her family.

12. As some young women find themselves locked into restrictive arrangements (especially problematic is the new pattern of paternal child custody at divorce within bride wealth systems), many women have chosen to avoid marriage altogether (Lee and Rosenberg 1993; see also Draper 1992). The destruction of cattle herds in the mid-1990s undermined the trend toward bride wealth and thus the issue remains in flux (Lee 2007 personal communication).

13. Fieldwork was conducted at the three main villages of Dobe, Xai Xai and Kangwa, and to a lesser extent in the smaller villages of Mahopa and Goshe. The 1986 population of Ju/'hoansi in the region was 663, of whom 83 people were sixty or older. The research team interviewed 90 percent of the elders and about thirty caregivers.

14. The Ju/'hoansi themselves do not mark chronological age. The ages used in this essay represent estimates made by the demographer Nancy Howell during field work in 1968 (see Howell 1979) and revisions made according to census updates by Lee during field trips in 1973, 1983 and 1986–1987.

15. In 1967–68, Trusswell and Hansen (1976) conducted a health survey of the region. They found Ju/'hoansi elders to be remarkably fit and not suffering from high blood pressure or other stress-related illnesses. More recent research indicates that changed diet has produced elevated blood pressures in the population (Kent and Lee 1992; Hansen et al. 1993). We divided the elderly into five categories of functionality: one was the most fit and five represented those who were completely dependent. "Frail" refers to those in categories four and five, twelve people.

16. Readers interested in cross-cultural explorations of complaint discourse are directed to Michael Wex's historical/linguistic study of Yiddish (2005).

17. The third-person singular is not gendered in the Ju/'hoansi language. Thus, the English term *his/her* or *she/he* is used in the text to translate the speaker's usage. While *he/she* may seem awkward to some English speakers, it is consistent with the Ju/'hoansi language, which does not distinguish between male and female in the third-person singular, just as English does not in the third-person plural *they*, but French does in the forms *ils/elles*.

18. This trend may be what Pat Draper detected in 1987–1988 while doing research in the Dobe area for Project AGE (see Fry et al. Web book this section). She reported that the Ju/'hoansi seem to have an "extreme cultural preoccupation with parent-adult child relationships" (Draper and Buchanan 1992:1). Oakley, in a comparison of Draper and Rosenberg's research on eldercare, reviewed Rosenberg and Lee's field diaries and found that thirty-three of thirty-nine elders interviewed by Lee stated that without adult children "they would be as good as dead" (1992:29). Oakley distinguished between these normative responses and the empirical evidence collected by Rosenberg and Lee, which indicated that caregiving networks centerd on spouses, co-wives, siblings, name-sakes or more distant kin were significant sources of support. Oakley also noted that support networks play significant roles in eldercare in other cultures citing Wentowski (1981:600) among others who has argued that "the presence or absence of informal

support … [has] been recognized as a crucial predictor of the well-being and autonomy of older people." Nevertheless, these networks are not infallible as the work of Wiessner (1983) demonstrates.

19. Makoni and Stroeken (2002) in discussing complaint discourse in a South African township argue that it is seen as a linguistic signature of aging. But this is not the case amongst the Ju/'hoansi where complaining cuts across generational lines.

20. Simmons's (1945) accounts of abandonment, based on the work of Ratzel for South African populations (1894:ll:275) and Bleek for the Naron (1928:35), are unreliable, although often repeated in the literature. Bleek's account of rough treatment and abandonment is repeated almost verbatim by Schapera (1930:162) but is gentler in its moralizing tone. Versions of Bleek's account are also repeated by Hewitt (1986:31). Mathias Guenther, who has done extensive fieldwork with the Nharo or Naron (of the Central Kalahari) has noted that previous German sources (Hahn 1870:122) offer similar unreliable visions of abandonment; whereas, Almeida (1965) describes a very tender scene of eldercare among Angolan Bushmen (Guenther personal communication 1994). Ratzel's encyclopedic work is like many nineteenth century social evolutionary anthropological projects in casting the "less evolved" Bushmen in crude racist terms at the bottom of a social evolutionary ladder.

21. Wiessner (1983) has given the example of an old woman whose social position in the Xai Xai water hole was weak, in that she was from a distant area, had few relatives in the camp and her son was absent when she became ill. Xai Xai residents let loose a chorus of complaints about the inadequacy of her care, but no one in the community took direct responsibility to provide for her needs or mount a healing dance for her. The circumstances of her death were very painful: Old Bau became delirious, accused people of starving her, and she ran into the bush to gather for herself, where she died.

The accusations surrounding this death had a very different tone from the everyday discourse of complaining invoked in cases of impeccable care. This was a time when complaint did not generate the bonds of reciprocity as it was supposed to, and the community was shocked. While other deaths in the water hole were followed by a short cathartic mourning period, which included soon-forgotten charges of neglect, the impact of Old Bau's death on the community lingered in an unresolved fashion for months (Wiessner 1983). This was the kind of outcome that Kasupe may well have had in mind when he wove his tale of callous abandonment.

22. Acculturation to Herero beliefs about death and burial seem to have influenced Ju/'hoansi perceptions about death and abandonment. One traditional way has been to collapse the hut around the person who died in camp or to dig a shallow grave and leave it unmarked if someone dies on the trail. Wiessner (1983) describes a more complicated burial ritual including a deep grave, specific attention to the orientation of the corpse in the grave, ceremonial activities when the body is moved from the house, rituals for the mourners, eulogies and grave markers. The postmortem period is not marked by lengthy ritual grieving as it is among the Herero, but by complaint discourse as a way of reframing social relations and restructuring traditional trading relationships.

The Herero, by contrast, have elaborate funerary rituals (Vivelo 1977:127–29) and seem to have been particularly offended by what appeared to them as the casualness of some Ju/'hoansi practices. In discussion with the Ju/'hoansi in the mid-1980s, it seemed as if their own funeral customs were being viewed from the Herero perspective and that statements about the abandonment of elders might be referencing "improper burials."

Suicide among the elderly was treated by informants as an incomprehensible notion.

23. Nor have children been viewed as economic burdens. Until quite recently, children did not participate in subsistence activities until their teens. With settlement and the acquisition of goats and cattle, children now do more work.

24. Old women among the Ju/'hoansi are thus quite different from the passive "Dear Old Grans" described as commonplace among old women in a long-term geriatric ward "who cheerfully surrender [their] autonomy and ... potential to challenge" (Evers 1981:119–20).

25. *Hxaro* is a gift exchange system for "circulating goods, lubricating social relations, and maintaining ecological balance" (Lee 1984:97). Receiving hxaro implies that you will also give it. See also Wiessner (1977).

26. The term *demand sharing* has been used to describe this rhetorical/economic form of narrativity (Guenther 2006).

27. She said that it was the duty of the first born, "the one who cracked your bones," to look after an aging parent.

28. Polygyny occurred in about 5 percent of marriages among the Ju/'hoansi in the 1960s and 1970s. In most socially sanctioned forms, men will take two wives, although cases of more than two have been reported historically. Occasionally, irregular polyandrous unions have also been reported.

29. In Western societies, where elder care is predominantly done by unwaged women workers in the household and women in the waged workforce, expressing the experience of caregiving in ungendered language poses a problem (Finch and Groves 1983). For example, a young man, in trying to articulate his experience in caring for his lover with AIDS, found that: the closest model with which to compare my seven months with Paul is the experience of *mothering*. (My mother brought this home to me.) By this analogy I mean the cluster of activities, characteristics and emotions associated with the *social role* of motherhood. Whether performed by women or men, mothering—and its analogue within the health care system, nursing—involves intimate physical care of another being, the provision of unconditional care and love, the subordination of self to others, and an investment in separation (Interrante 1987:57–58). First emphasis (mothering) is mine, second emphasis (social role) is the author's.)

In this context, only the gendered term *mothering* was found to be able to convey the intensity of commitment Interrante had felt. Interestingly, his insight is substantiated by a footnote referencing three feminist theoreticians—Dinnerstein, Chowdorow and Eherensaft—all of whom have analyzed the social construction of female caregiving.

Mothering carries with it the meanings of long-term unconditional support. "Mothers" are people who do not abandon no matter how demanding the circumstance becomes. Mothering is thus not only a feminized metaphor for caregiving, it is also highly idealized and sentimentalized.

30. Draper (1976) and Shostak (1981) have pointed out that children are raised in a very nonauthoritarian manner and were normally not expected to work or do anything for adults that they did not wish to do. Even today, with settlement and the beginnings of a pastoralist economy, which often utilizes child labor, many parents say that they cannot make children perform work if the children refuse. Children are still seen as not owing any special deference to adults.

31. Gubrium (1987:31–35) describes the conflict that follows an elder's creation of a caregiving network that is perceived to be competing with the rightful caregivers—the adult children. Maida, the old person in question, is described as rejecting her "own" children, whom she has accused of not being her "real" children because they have placed her in a nursing home against her wishes. Maida formed close bonds with a

small group of coresidents who have constituted themselves as a "family," including the designated roles of "baby" and "grandma." Both Maida's children and the health professionals identified this alternate caring network as a "problem." The mother's actions were interpreted by the children as a repudiation and described as a sign of mental confusion. The health workers found the group to be cliquish and divisive to equitable caring on the floor. Thus, Maida's stepping outside the discourse of filial caregiving was construed as a contentious and threatening counter-discourse.

32. Self-sacrifice is not always considered admirable in caregivers in the North American context. Gubrium's 1987 account of a support group for the families of Alzheimer patients reveals a strong counter-discourse to expressions of wifely devotion. Caregivers are warned not to burn themselves out and to be "realistic" when assessing the burdens of caregiving. One pointed expression of this counter-discourse was: "Dear, you're not an old man's lover; you're an old man's slave" (Gubrium 1987:31).

33. Their old age is not filled with anxieties about personal security such as Sagner describes for those elders living in the region's townships (2002). The article by Draper and Keith (1992) elaborates on the contrast drawn here between the feelings of personal security among Ju/'hoansi elders and the fears and painful choices of elders within a North American community.

34. For a full description of the many facets of this project, see Biesele (2007), which includes a description of the projects, and materials already published or available online and those in development. Local people have been working collaboratively with scholars from North America and Europe to develop an authoritative "legacy collection" of curricular material in Ju for local schools, new materials elicited from elders and the transcription of older audio materials from Biesele's previous research.

CHAPTER 3

Beyond the Grandmother Hypothesis: Evolutionary Models of Human Longevity

Michael Gurven and Hillard Kaplan

The maximum life expectancy has risen steadily by more than two years every decade over the past two centuries, a dramatic improvement that suggests new answers to old questions about programmed senescence and the existence of biologically determined maximal life spans (Wachter and Finch 1997; Austad 1999; Oeppen and Vaupel 2003). Although much of the increase in life expectancy in the nineteenth century can be attributed to better sanitation, modern medicine and improved diets (Riley 2001), there is strong evidence that the general pattern of a long life span is not unique to the past century, and that current increases in life span may be a consequence of plasticity in our evolved human life history. Converging evidence shows that living into "old age" is not unique to modern populations or to even agriculturalists (cf. Lovejoy 1981; Washburn 1981). Data from extant foragers with little to no access to medical attention or modern foods, including the Ju/'hoansi (Rosenberg this volume), Ache and Hadza, show that women who survive to age forty-five can expect to live an additional twenty to twenty-two years, even though at birth mean life expectancies in these populations range from thirty to thirty-seven years of life (Blurton Jones K. Hawkes and J. O'Connell 2002; Gurven and Kaplan 2007). Extrapolations based on comparative analyses of brain weights and body sizes among nonhuman primates suggest a maximum life span between sixty-six and seventy-eight years for early *Homo sapiens* (Hammer and Foley 1996).[1] Existing paleontological evidence suggests that a postreproductive life span existed anywhere from 150,000–1.6 million years ago (Bogin and Smith 1996; Caspari and Lee 2004). A recent cross-cultural exploration of mortality patterns across the life course among hunter-gatherers and forager-horticulturalists shows survival into the sixth and seventh decades of life and depicts a unique life history characteristic of our species that cannot be explained as an artifact of modern conditions (Figure 3.1).

Figure 3.1
Age-Specific Life Expectancy: Expected Number of Years Remaining for Six Sample Human Populations, Sweden, 1751–1759, and Wild Chimps

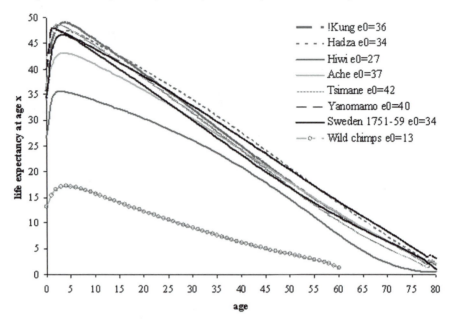

Note: All groups show roughly the same trajectory, with most differences concentrated in the first few years of life. The much shorter life expectancy for wild chimpanzees is given as a comparison. All curves are based on life-table estimates using the Siler model. Life expectancies at birth (e_0) are given in the legend. Figure adapted from Gurven and Kaplan (2007).

Elsewhere we have argued that sixty-five to seventy-five years is the closest equivalent of an adaptive human life span as this is the modal age range of many later adult deaths for hunter-gatherers (Gurven and Kaplan 2007). Figure 3.1 shows that much of the variation in age-specific life expectancies among preindustrial populations occurs in the first few years of life, and the subsequent age trajectories of mortality show a similar profile across the life course. The longevity of these societies is noteworthy, as an individual that survives to age fifteen can expect to live an additional thirty to forty-four years, and a survivor to age forty can expect to live an additional twenty to twenty-eight years. Departures from these patterns in the ethnographic and paleodemographic literature are likely due to high rates of contact-related infectious disease and violence, and methodological problems such as poor age estimates of older individuals, biased preservation of the skeletons of infants and older individuals, and improper usage of model life tables (Blurton Jones et al. 2002; Gurven and Kaplan 2007).[2] However, recent reestimation of several common paleo-mortality curves based on improved methods shows a life course pattern similar to that of the ethnographic sample (Konigsberg and Herrmann 2006).

Chimpanzees in both the wild and under favorable conditions in captivity show much higher rates of adult mortality and significantly shorter life spans.

A fundamental feature of the human life course of evolutionary significance is the substantial postreproductive period for women. Even men, while physiologically capable of producing viable offspring well until their eighties, show a similar age-specific decline in fertility, but the decline appears five to ten years later than for females, among the Ju/'hoansi, Ache and Yanomamo (Hill and Hurtado 1996). Initial enthusiasm for a theory that could explain menopause and more generally reproductive cessation (Hawkes, O'Connell and Blurton Jones 1989; Hill and Hurtado 1991; Rogers 1993) was met with some obstacles after theoretical modeling, and early empirical tests showed little support for the notion that reproduction should terminate early in the life span. Moreover, there is little evidence for any upward secular trend in the age at menopause over the past century, despite increases in life span, changes in the age at menarche and an estimated heritability in the age of menopause of 40 to 60 percent. Reproductive cessation exists in other closely related primate species, especially in captivity, although there is no evidence for a lengthy postreproductive life span among our primate cousins. It is now thought that menopause is the conserved ancestral condition, which thereby shifts the focus of explanation to the long life span after the termination of reproduction (Kaplan 1997; Hawkes et al. 1998; Judge and Carey 2000).

From the perspective of natural selection, the significant period of human life spent in a postreproductive state is a conundrum, because sterility is the evolutionary equivalent of death. Its occurrence in humans (and absence in most other mammals) is one of the most challenging puzzles of evolutionary biology today. As described previously, recent data from chimpanzees and other primates suggest that menopause itself is not unusual among mammals (and appears to occur roughly at the same age among chimpanzees and humans); rather it is the extended lifespan of humans after reproduction has ceased that is rare (Gould, Flint and Graham 1981; Treolar 1981).

EVOLUTION AND LONGEVITY

Several theories have been proposed to explain this remarkable extension of the human life span. The classic theory of senescence in evolutionary biology was first proposed by Medawar (1952), developed further by Williams (1957), and then formalized by Hamilton (1966). It proposes that as individuals age, they contribute less to biological fitness, or the future proliferation of their DNA in the gene pool, because less of their expected lifetime fertility remains. Consequently, natural selection acts more weakly to reduce mortality at older ages. The existence of substantial postreproductive life among humans therefore suggests that older individuals have "reproductive value" by increasing fitness through nonreproductive means.

George Williams was first to propose that beginning at ages forty-five to fifty, mothers may benefit more from investing their energy and resources in existing children rather than from producing new ones (1957). This idea became known thirty years later as the "Grandmother Hypothesis." A specific version of the Grandmother Hypothesis has been proposed by Hawkes, Blurton-Jones and O'Connell (1998) and explained more fully by Hawkes (2003). Their model focuses on intergenerational transfers among women and proposes that older women can increase their future genetic representation (i.e., inclusive fitness) by enhancing offspring fertility and survivorship of grandchildren through provisioning or providing support to younger generations. Among foragers, the resources acquired by women are strength-intensive, disadvantaging young children and thereby increasing the value of older women's labor contributions. According to this view, extensions in the human life span are driven by selection on women, and the value of resource transfers from grandmothers to grandchildren. Some of the initial inspiration for the Grandmother Hypothesis came from fieldwork done with Hadza foragers in Tanzania, where "hardworking" older women were observed to produce substantial quantities of food.

BEYOND THE GRANDMOTHER HYPOTHESIS

Peccei proposes an amendment to this view (2001). She points out that long-term juvenile dependence among humans implies that adults who cease reproducing in their forties will not finish parenting until they are sixty or older (see also Lancaster and King 1985). The notion that most of the benefits to longevity derive from helping offspring rather than grandchildren has been called the "Mother Hypothesis."

An alternative view focuses on men. Marlowe argues that the extension of the life span is driven by selection on men, stressing the fact that men do not experience menopause and can have children into the seventh and eighth decades of life (2000). His argument, called the "Patriarch Hypothesis," is that men accrue status and power as they age, which they use to obtain reproductive benefits. These benefits and the lack of a physiological menopause selects for their greater longevity. Formal demographic models of life history evolution typically focus only on females, but two-sex demographic models where men tend to be older than their spouses may also lead to a pattern of delayed senescence after the age of fifty (Tuljapurkar, Puleston and Gurven 2007).

A fourth view, the "Embodied Capital Model" proposes that timing of life events is best understood as an "embodied capital" investment process (Kaplan et al. 2000; Kaplan and Robson 2002; Gurven, Kaplan and Gutierrez 2006). Embodied capital is organized somatic tissue such as muscles, immune system components and brains. In a functional sense, embodied capital includes strength, skill, knowledge and other abilities. Humans are specialists in brain-based capital. High levels of knowledge and skill are required to exploit the suite of high-quality, difficult-to-acquire resources human foragers consume (Walker et al. 2002; Gurven, Kaplan and Gutierrez 2006). Those abilities require a large brain and a long time commitment to development. This extended learning phase during which productivity is low is compensated for by higher productivity during the adult period. Since productivity increases with age, the time investment in skill acquisition and knowledge leads to selection for lowered mortality rates and greater longevity, because the returns on the investments in development occur at older ages. Thus, the long human lifespan coevolved with the lengthening of the juvenile period, increased brain capacities for information processing and storage and intergenerational resource flows.

Embodied capital theory also proposes that meat acquisition and extractive foraging generate complementary roles for men and women in a sexual division of labor, where both invest directly in offspring and grandoffspring in long-term unions. Contributions from older men, in addition to that of women, are therefore expected, rather than the solitary pursuit of alternative mating opportunities as men's partners age. In fact, men often experience "effective menopause," because their last reproductive event is often tied to their wife's last reproduction (Gurven and Hill 1997).

EMPIRICAL STUDIES OF BENEFITS TO OLD AGE

The starting point for most evolutionary theories is the realization that successful reproduction is not only a matter of producing offspring (i.e., maximizing fertility). Among humans, it requires many years of assistance and nurturing. This includes common tasks like acquiring food and sharing it with offspring, protecting children from environmental dangers and other hazards and fostering education of productive and social skills necessary for successful adulthood. This perspective places the acquisition and distribution of food at the center of reproductive fitness, rather than fertility. These hypotheses have broad implications for understanding the evolution of distinct human life history traits, the organization of social communities and intergenerational social dynamics. Nonetheless, there have been few empirical investigations, and no studies where data were collected for the primary purpose of comparing the different hypotheses.

Existing attempts to measure the effects of older individuals on descendant kin have produced mixed results. Among foragers, Hawkes et al.'s initial report of "hardworking grandmothers" who produce more calories than younger women was an impetus for the growing interest in grandparental effects on life history (1989). These same researchers later showed that grandmothers who worked longer hours had grandchildren who experienced positive weight gain (Hawkes et al. 1998). In a rural farming population in the Gambia, Sear and colleagues (2000; 2002) showed that maternal, but not paternal, grandmothers had a positive effect on grandchild nutrition and on survivorship among children one to two years old, whereas only paternal grandparents had a positive effect on a daughter's fertility (Sear et al. 2003). Several historical studies reveal significant grandparental effects. Jamison et al. showed that maternal grandmother presence was associated with substantially higher grandoffspring survivorship in a Japanese village from 1671–1871 (2002). Voland and Beise

(2002) found significant positive effects of maternal grandmothers on grand-child survival, negative effects of paternal grandmothers and no effects of grandfathers (Beise and Voland 2002). Some evidence suggests that variation in child mortality may affect reproductive success more than variation in fertil-ity in populations not using modern birth control, and so grandparental effects may be concentrated on reducing child mortality (Strassmann and Gillespie 2003). Several survey studies also suggest that maternal grandmothers and grandfathers are more emotionally close, spend more time with and invest more resources in grandchildren than paternal grandparents (DeKay 1995; Euler and Weitzel 1996).[3]

However, among the Ache of Paraguay, grandparents had little to no effect on offspring fertility and grandoffspring survivorship (Hill and Hurtado, 1996). Additionally, analyses of forager food production where substantial quantita-tive data exist suggest that adult women, including postmenopausal women, of-ten consume more food than they produce (Kaplan and Gurven 2005). Despite the hard work of Hadza grandmothers, even these women supply only a small proportion of the total calories in the diet. Contrary to stereotypes that situate the Ju/'hoansi as the "typical forager," the majority of food in forager diets comes from hunting and fishing activities, and these are largely the domain of men (Cordain et al. 2000; Kaplan et al. 2000). Moreover, limited macronu-trients such as proteins and lipids are widely acquired almost exclusively by men in many forager groups. Thus, the strong evidence in support of male sub-sidization of female reproduction is inconsistent with the notion that older indi-viduals, particularly females, are important breadwinners who can significantly influence nutrition.

To date, most studies of grandparental effects have suffered from limited data, insufficient sample size or specific statistical problems.[4] More impor-tantly, no study has yet measured and linked the proximate ways in which grandparents exhibit the positive, negative, or neutral effects found in analyses of survival and fertility. Grandparental helping behavior is usually measured with proxies, such as the state of being alive or dead at the time of a grand-child's birth, during the study, or throughout early childhood. Behavioral stud-ies of older women in preindustrial contexts also consist of small samples and usually focus only on absolute food production rather than food transfers to kin or other noncaloric contributions. In an attempt to address these problems and advance the ecological study of longevity, we initiated the Tsimane Health and Life History Project in 2002.

TSIMANE HEALTH AND LIFE HISTORY PROJECT

Since 1999, we have conducted fieldwork with Tsimane Amerindians living in the Bolivian Amazon. In 2002, we began focusing on household economics, demography, growth, development, and aging with a large-scale project con-ducted in eighteen villages.[5] The underlying goal of our project has been to understand different physical and cultural dimensions of the aging process in a fairly remote, traditional population of forager-horticulturalists who live in a world without supermarkets, refrigerators, plumbing, health care and formalized social security benefits. Tsimane inhabit a highly infectious environment, with prevalence and incidence rates of respiratory and gastrointestinal disease and parasitic infection much higher than those experienced in the developed world. Mortality rates among Tsimane resemble those of Sweden and other European countries in the mid-nineteenth century and are indicative of a population in the beginning stages of an epidemiologic transition (Gurven, Kaplan and Zelada Supa 2007), where the causes of deaths shift from those due to infectious disease to chronic conditions such as heart disease and cancers (Omran 1971). Given the relatively large population of Tsimane (roughly 8,000 individuals), we have been fortunate to learn about the lives of a large sample (by anthropological standards) of older adults.

It is very rare for Tsimane to live beyond the age of eighty, and there is no reliable evidence that Tsimane have ever lived beyond the age of ninety. However, it must be remembered that even if mortality was low among older adults, there is still likely to be only a small percentage of older individuals present in small, high-fertility populations. Among high-fertility national populations in the year 2000, such as Botswana or Bolivia, only 0.3–0.9 percent were older than eighty years. If the Tsimane population pyramid were representative of these national patterns, the study sample of 2,500 individuals would show at most seven to twenty-three individuals older than eighty. Problems with age estimates aside, there have been few studies of the very elderly in foraging and small-scale horticultural societies for the simple reason that small foraging populations of (say) 150 individuals are unlikely to have even one individual over eighty, and perhaps only four people over the age of sixty-five (see Rosenberg in this volume).

Among the Tsimane, older adults are referred to as *isho' muntyi* (old people). No specific language terms connote different stages of older life (*p̂urdye'*), although certain physical descriptions such as *p̂ucruij jam mi'i aty jam ca've'* (white-haired, cannot walk and can no longer see well) have been used to describe very old adults in their seventh decade. Old age is often defined by the Tsimane themselves as severe physical decline such as frequent aches and pains over most of the body, an inability to walk far distances and when overall ability to perform common tasks is compromised.

As in many cultures, older adults are held in esteem in popular Tsimane ideology. Older adults are sometimes respectfully addressed as *jayej* (grandmother) or *via'* (grandfather) by nonrelatives and treated with respect. They are revered for their specialized knowledge of medicinal plants, animals, and navigation in the tropical rain forest that surrounds their thatch homes. They also possess greater knowledge about navigating the world of forest spirits that provoke sickness and bad luck if certain transgressions are made. It is widely recognized that older adults are often fearless speakers unafraid to voice their opinion, and they often resolve conflicts or reprimand the wayward. This is often expressed as literally "knowing how to speak" (*chij peyaqui*). Even

One of the oldest Tsimane women alive today, Francisca Temba, age 76, and her daughter Demecia, age 48, prepare the fermented beverage *shucdye* made from masticated manioc and mixed with maize.

with the institution of formal chiefs and bilingual Tsimane teachers over the past thirty years, older adults (who are mostly monolingual in Tsimane) still voice their opinion through the younger chiefs and teachers. Grandparents also sometimes help set up marriages for their grandchildren and are often used as babysitters and as foster parents, especially when parents undertake extended visits to other villages or the local market town. Older adults are frequently noted as experts in common manufacturing activities, such as handbag weaving and bow and arrow making, and named as skilled hunters and fishers. When queried, many people name their parents or other older adult relatives as key people who through example or close proximity have helped "train" them in a variety of important activities. These observations suggest that older people are motivated to help younger generations often and in critical ways that are not captured by solely focusing on daily caloric contribution to the diet.

Despite an ideology that highlights some strengths of older people and the sentiment often voiced that "it's good to have them around," the lives of older people are not carefree or without considerable difficulty. During informal conversations, we heard stories of siblings conflicting over who should care for their aged parents and complaints by older people that they are too frequently neglected by their kin.[6] It is our impression that with physical decline past age

Tsimane economic life is inherently social. Here members of an extended family composed of three generations from the remote riverine village of Catumare eat fish stew (*jo'na*) with plantains.

sixty, older Tsimane seem to be viewed more as net burdens, and especially so by the time they reach their seventies. Based on conversations and demographic interviews, parental abandonment, neglect and suicide (especially upon the death of a spouse) were probably not uncommon occurrences in the past. Living alone without kin support and visits by children is a haunting prospect for many older people and characterizes the essential fear of growing old among many Tsimane. It is a fear that should not be permitted to consume one's thoughts. As a forty-three-year-old man from a remote community on the upper Maniqui river remarked, "I am not afraid [of getting old]. It's dangerous to be afraid. Filled with fear we die."

IMPLICATIONS FOR NEW RESEARCH DIRECTIONS

Activities of Older Individuals

Most evolutionary hypotheses regarding lifespan extension focus on the benefits of living longer via the flow of resources from parents to children and from grandparents to grandchildren. On average, a Tsimane woman will be a mother by age eighteen, a grandmother by age thirty-six and a great-grand-mother by age fifty-four. She therefore has many opportunities to improve the health, survivorship, fertility, economic success and overall well-being of descendant kin. As mentioned previously, quantifying the types and magnitude of assistance made by older adults is a necessary first step in assessing whether postreproductive lifespan is adaptive, and for evaluating whether the separate forms of aid provided by women and by men can help differentiate among evolutionary models. Among Tsimane, for example, older men shift activities away from hunting and rely more heavily on farming, whereas older women spend much of their productive time processing, rather than directly acquiring food. At their peaks, both men (in their forties) and women (in their thirties) share over half of their production with their children. After these peaks, the proportion directed towards children declines as that toward grandchildren increases. By the sixties, women are directing much more of their production to grandchildren than to children, and no longer have any subadult children to invest in. Men provide comparable amounts to children and grandchildren in their sixties. Tsimane men and women in their seventies do not contribute many calories to their descendents (Figure 3.2). Figure 3.2 shows that both men and women make contributions to younger generations, consistent with the Embodied Capital Model, and that grandparental contributions decline sharply at late ages, which is consistent with the Mother Hypothesis. The fact that husbands, fathers and grandfathers contribute more than wives, mothers and grandmothers, respectively, also runs counter to the sole female focus of the Grandmother Hypothesis.

Figure 3.2
Net Contributions from Parents to Children, from Grandparents to Grandchildren, and Husband to Wife by Age for the Tsimane, 2002–2005

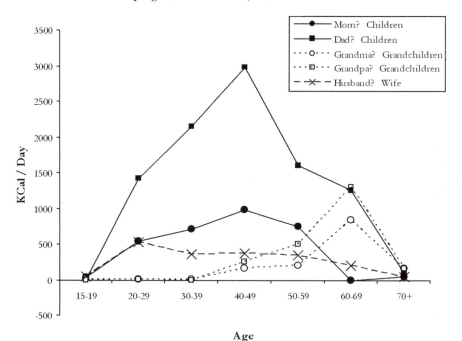

If older age is functionally designed to improve the fitness of descendant kin, then we should expect a wide range of psychological, motivational, cognitive, emotional and behavioral traits that focus attention on perceiving and responding to needs of particular kin. Life span psychological studies do seem to indicate that older adults acquire greater ability to integrate their knowledge and make efficient decisions as they age. This research also shows older adults to be more skilled problem solvers and negotiators, have a more positive outlook and show less emotional distress than their younger counterparts—features that are consistent with the caretaking role of older adults (Carstensen and Lockenhoff 2003). To the extent that older adults are helpful, younger kin should be motivated to maintain proximity to them and to help ensure that they are adequately cared for. The extent of grandmaternal or grandpaternal effects on fitness through noncaloric means, while difficult to quantify, requires much additional attention. It has been suggested that grandparents may provide protection, direct child care, useful skills and knowledge, and political leverage (Gutmann 1994), but no published study has systematically examined these possibilities. As described in the previous section, preliminary investigation of nonproductive roles among older Tsimane adults has shown that they are vocal advisors, mediators, and trainers of younger adults and children in more traditional and difficult skills.

Physiological Design

If we want to understand why the human lifespan seems to be about seventy years among preindustrial peoples, and not fifty, eighty or one hundred years, the costs of remaining alive and in good condition must be considered in addition to fitness benefits. The human immune and repair systems broadly defined appear to generate a lifespan in which many cells, organs and physiological processes show significant life-threatening changes in the seventh decade of life. Cancers, heart disease, decreased ability to work, cognitive decline and impaired immune function greatly increase in frequency at this time, as do mortality rates (see Willcox and Willcox this volume). These outcomes are not only caused by cumulative wear and tear and novel exposure to fatty diets and a sedentary lifestyle, but instead are the result of epigenetic processes that were set in motion at the beginning of life and potentially altered throughout early and late development (Gluckman and Hanson 2006).[7]

To examine changes in biological age (as opposed to chronological age), a growing number of biomarkers such as Apolipoprotein-E (ApoE) and interleukine-6 (IL-6) allelic variants, C-reactive protein (CRP), fibrinogen, telomere cap lengths, and several others are being measured in national longitudinal aging studies.[8] The markers are generally used as predictors of healthy function, morbidity and mortality among middle-aged and elderly populations, and can be useful for making objective cross-population comparisons in health status among elderly individuals. For example, Tsimane display higher levels of the inflammation-inducing CRP than do Americans at all ages, so a forty-year-old Tsimane may have similar cumulative levels of inflammation as Americans do in their mid-fifties (Gurven et al. 2008). The high levels of chronic inflammation among Tsimane are likely caused by the accumulated impacts of repeated exposure to acute infections over the life course.

Although there may be broad similarities in the order in which different physiological systems decline, differences in the timing and rates of decline may be widely variable within and among populations. It will be important to examine this variation in light of differences in early life exposure to disease and malnutrition, activity profiles, stress and social support. While life history theory has illuminated some patterns underlying physiological processes, the direct application of life history to physiology is still in its infancy, and its impact on our understanding of physiological processes is still rather limited, especially among humans.

Adaptive Aging?

Additional evidence suggests that life experiences can significantly impact rates of biological aging (see Epel et al. 2004). We propose that features of behavior, culture and physiology may be responses to the aging process itself and that behavioral adjustment can influence the rate of aging. Analysis of time budgets among the Tsimane, and the Machiguenga and Piro and Tsimane populations who inhabit the Amazonian rain forests of Peru, has revealed that people adjust their activities in relation to their physical condition (Gurven and Kaplan 2006). Work effort among small-scale subsistence populations peaks at about age forty and declines thereafter. If people worked as hard in their sixties as they did in their forties, they would likely age faster and die earlier. It is likely that the advent of agriculture provides a less intensive and less dangerous set of alternatives to hunting and gathering that may reduce morbidity in older individuals among farming and forager-farming populations independently of the nutritional supplements derived from having a predictable, storable resource base. In our medical surveys, Tsimane men over age sixty, for example, complained *less* about pains in the joints, getting lost and other problems while hunting than did men in their fifties, presumably because of the former's decreased effort and frequency in hunting activities. Older people may also differ in the size and composition of kinship and other social networks available to them, and the extent to which others in these networks act as a possible safety net or buffer during critical periods of disease or dysfunction. Research investigating characteristics of networks and their effects among Tsimane is currently underway.

As people age, deterioration in condition is likely to affect the fitness costs and benefits of alternative physiological and behavioral responses. The possibility that selection has acted on physiology in similar fashion suggests new research directions. Some age-related changes in hormone profiles, lean body mass, lipoproteins, blood hemoglobin levels and other biomarkers may themselves be adaptive responses to aging. At present, biomarkers of aging (such as those listed previously) are used as predictors of mortality in population research. It is often not well understood, either in terms of mechanism or functional design, why such markers correlate with biomedical risk factors and with outcomes such as morbidity and mortality. Aging and other forms of morbidity produce changes in physiological condition. Disentangling the direct deleterious effects of aging from intrinsic endogenous, and possibly adaptive, components of the aging process is a challenging task, but should lead the way to a more profound understanding of aging and its population-level manifestations.

CONCLUSION

The Grandmother Hypothesis has been historically influential for inspiring a generation of empirical and theoretical studies to better understand why longevity is a hallmark feature of the human life history. The current picture, however, is more complicated. As argued herein, grandmothers do not usually make substantial economic contributions to the diet among hunter-gatherers, while others, including fathers and grandfathers, can and do make substantial contributions. Men experience "effective" reproductive cessation and so their long period of postreproductive lifespan also merits explanation. The Grandmother Hypothesis also ignores the long, slow physical growth of children and the costly expansion of the human brain. The Embodied Capital Model instead includes these as evolved components of our life history related to the skills-intensive foraging and social niche of humans. The elongated lifespan is required to reap the gains of delayed productivity in adulthood given the sacrifices made early in life, such as slow growth, low productivity, and delayed maturation. Theoretical approaches should include contributions from both sexes, as well as any differences in fitness costs to maintaining the body. Empirical inquiries that integrate provision of calories with other fitness-relevant types of contributions from older adults, such as marriage negotiation, social transmission of knowledge, mediation during conflicts, and emotional support, will be important avenues for future research.

An ultimate goal in the biodemography of aging is to understand the processes linking genes to phenotypes, phenotypes to mortality and fertility outcomes, and those outcomes to gene distributions over generational time. This will require both mechanistic physical models and specific theories of how natural selection acts to order those processes, both within populations of a single species and among species in evolving ecosystems. "Bottom-up" research investigates the mechanisms by which genes translate into their products, and how those products interact with environmental inputs to result in physiological and, ultimately, demographic outcomes. It is bottom-up in the sense that knowledge about how those processes work provides the empirical facts that evolutionary theories must explain. Evolutionary modeling, of which the Grandmother Hypothesis and Embodied Capital Model are one component, is "top-down" in the sense that it provides the deductive logic and the organizing principles that bring order to organismal design. Any biological understanding of the aging process and longevity in humans—in the past, in the present and with a keen eye focused on the future—will require innovative research initiatives that integrate both bottom-up and top-down approaches.

NOTES

1. These analyses are based on estimations of allometric equations of the form $Y = aX^b$, where Y is one of many species-typical life-history characteristics such as life span, metabolic rate, age at first reproduction or gestation length; X is adult body size; b is the scaling exponent that describes how Y increases with changes in X; and a often adjusts for different orders or families. See Harvey, Martin and Clutton-Brock (1987).

2. Paleodemographic estimates of low child and high adult mortality for early humans does not match any modern pattern, and violates assumptions of uniformitarianism.

3. In urban societies, there is evidence that grandmothers positively impact cognitive and health outcomes and psychological and sociological well-being: Alawad and Sonugabarke (1992); Falk and Falk (2002); Hayslip and Kaminski (2005); Hayslip (this volume).

4. Of particular concern here are issues of "phenotypic correlation" and "unobserved heterogeneity." Phenotypic correlation in life history analyses refers to the situation where variation in physical condition or access to resources can lead to a spurious positive correlation between investments in two life history traits (e.g., growth and reproduction) when the true trade-off suggests a negative correlation. Only experimental manipulation or multivariate statistics can detect life history trade-offs in the face of phenotypic correlations. The problem of unobserved heterogeneity refers to the unexpected correlations between observed and omitted or unmeasured variables that can complicate the interpretation of cross-sectional analyses.

5. Research has been supported by grants from the National Science Foundation (NSF BCS-0422690, BCS-0136274) and from the National Institute of Aging (NIH/NIA 1R01AG024119-01). We are grateful to the Tsimane with whom we have worked for their generous hospitality, collaboration and support.

6. Others such as Sokolovsky (Introduction, this volume) and Rosenberg (this volume) have commented on the interpretation of claims of neglect among older people. We believe that while many Tsimane may complain about a lack of attention merely as a way of soliciting more kin support, other older Tsimane show clear physical signs of neglect, such as an inadequate diet and poor health.

7. Epigenetic processes are characterized by heritable and potentially reversible changes in genome function that occur without altering DNA sequences. For example, paternal grandsons of Swedish men from the nineteenth century who were exposed to an abundance of food during childhood in the nineteenth century were significantly more likely to die from cardiovascular disease and diabetes, which suggests epigenetic inheritance across multiple generations based perhaps on sex-linked nutritional cues (Kaati, Bygren and Edvinsson (2002).

8. Several of these influential long-term prospective studies include the Health and Retirement Study (HRS), http://hrsonline.isr.umich.edu/; Mexican Health and Aging Study (MHAS) [http://www.mhas.pop.upenn.edu/]; and English Longitudinal Study of Aging (ELSA), http://www.ifs.org.uk/elsa/index.htm.

CHAPTER 4

From Successful Aging to Conscious Aging

Harry Moody

A human being would certainly not grow to be seventy or eighty years old if this longevity had not meaning for the species. The afternoon of human life must also have a significance of its own and cannot be merely a pitiful appendage to life's morning.

Carl Jung

When we look at our globe from planetary perspective we recognize that population growth is slowing and that populations are aging. United Nations demographers estimate that by the middle of this current century global population will peak and then begin to decline, a process chiefly attributable to rapid decrease in fertility in both the industrialized and the developing world. Does this leveling of population mean the decline of humanity? On the contrary, it means an achievement of equilibrium, ecologically speaking, and the opening of a new chapter in the human story (Munford 1956). What does this new chapter entail? Specifically, what does a new planetary ecological balance involve in psychological or symbolic terms, in terms of how we think of ourselves and of the human future?

Within two decades, Americans over sixty-five years of age, instead of being one in eight (as of now) in the population, will be one in five—a dramatically larger proportion. In the nations of Japan and Western Europe, this shift is already further advanced. Developing countries will move in this direction as well. What will this shift mean for the economy, for family life, for the health care system? For those who unconsciously identify growth with sheer size or quantitative expansion, population aging provokes unease, even gloom (Moody 1988). An aging represents a shadow across the face of things to come and, psychologically speaking, it represents the shadow part or the unexamined dimension of our future selves. As a storm at sea approaches land, signs in the sky are evident before the storm reaches the shore. So, too, there are signs that this enormous transformation of population aging is already having its effect on our understanding of ourselves and on our image of the second half of life.

THE FACE OF AGING

The face of aging in America is changing. We are moving away from a negative image (the "ill-derly") toward a more positive image (the "well-derly"). The current sea change is prompted by rising longevity and health, by an exploding population of aging baby boomers, and by emerging deals of growth and development over the life span. A survey of periodical literature over the twentieth century confirms this shift away from managing problems of aging in favor of health promotion and contributions toward the well-being of society (Holkup 2001). This development is one chapter in an older story of ambivalence about aging, which historian Thomas Cole called "bipolar ageism" (Cole 1992). We vacillate between hope and fear, between negative stereotypes of old age and positive elixirs that promise the secret of overcoming time and aging itself (McHugh 2003).

The current shift can be summarized, in slogan form at least, by two phrases that redefine a shared understanding of what aging might mean:

• the first is Successful Aging (sometimes called "Vital Aging" or "Active Aging")
• the second is Productive Aging (often linked to "redefining retirement").

Successful aging is the expectation that later life can be a time of sustained health and vitality. Successful aging appeals to individual hopes and dreams: "You should live and be well." Productive aging is the expectation that later life should be a time not for disengagement but for a continued contribution to society, through worklife extension, volunteerism, or other contributive roles. Both ideals—sometimes subsumed under the label of "The New Gerontology"— amount to a new, more positive version of later life: rejection of familiar notions of old age as a social problem in favor of the idea of aging is an opportunity for the individual and society (Rowe 1997; Gergen and Gergen 2001). Both Successful aging and Productive aging represent the attraction of gerontology by the power of positive thinking, a hardy perennial in American life. But these deeply rooted cultural ideals of growth and expansion also may represent a refusal to face the "shadow" side of aging itself (Zweig and Abrams 1991).

SUCCESSFUL AGING: SCIENCE OR IDEOLOGY?

In this chapter, I want to look critically at the new positive image of aging—not so much to reject it, as some commentators have done (Holstein and Minkler 2003), but to understand what social and psychological conditions are required if the ideals are ever to become more than a slogan. Specifically, I want to look at the shadow elements neglected by our embrace of the new gerontology. I have elsewhere described Successful aging and Productive aging as different elements of an ideology: that is, a system of ideas that expresses and simultaneously conceals underlying human interests (Moody 2001). To grasp this point about ideology, it is enough to note that in the United States, anything that appeals to success and productivity is likely to prove decisive, because values of success and productivity are so deeply embedded in the national character.

Where does the agenda of Successful aging come from? How will it evolve in the future? First, note that the notion of Successful aging is not exactly a new idea. The hope that later life could be a period of vitality and activity was first expressed in Cicero's treatise, De Senectute. The outlines of Cicero's view are parallel to what Rowe and Kahn (1998) would develop in their book, *Successful Aging*. Apparently, it took the MacArthur Successful Aging project millions of dollars to discover what a Roman philosopher stumbled upon 2,000 years ago and expressed so eloquently in his classic treatise.

But, in all fairness, the MacArthur Foundation was not mistaken to undertake its project. The MacArthur researchers needed to justify their conclusions by science, not by philosophical speculation. That fact makes all the difference in terms of the credibility of Successful aging for Americans today. To be persuasive, an ideology must be accepted as true, not merely useful, to human interests of different kinds. Proponents of Successful aging want us to believe it is not mere opinion, still less an ideology (as I have suggested). Indeed, in the spirit of positivism, Successful aging is present as a fact, the way things are, in contrast to old-fashioned prejudice (i.e., ageism). This rhetorical foundation for Successful aging is based on rejecting myths: for example, the mistaken idea that the course of the later life is foreordained by fate or genetic determinism. To the contrary, Rowe and Kahn reassure us, if only we open our mind to the facts, we will see that our condition in old age is largely up to us.

Now, it would be unfair to criticize Successful aging simply as Horatio Alger in geriatric dress. But we do have to recognize an unmistakable appeal here to personal autonomy and individual responsibility ("A healthy old age is up to you!"), which is certainly a message Americans will respond to.

This characteristically American culture approach to Successful aging demands that we look more carefully at Rowe and Kahn's original formulation of the idea. They distinguish Successful aging from normal aging. Following their formulation, subsequent debate about Successful aging has tended to assume that success in coping with aging means delaying the features of normal aging. Thus, for someone gifted with Successful aging, to be eighty years old means looking and acting like a seventy year old, and so on. But, as Torres (1999) points out, this prevailing understanding of Successful aging enshrines an activity and future oriented set of values. "Managing on one's own becomes prized above all else. Refusal of dependency is understandable insofar as dependency in caregiving often leads to loss of dignity" (Lustbader 1991). But the result of uncritically accepting the prevailing version of Successful aging is that "dignity" becomes equated with independence, thus rectifying individualist values and neglecting cross-cultural variations in patterns of family caregiving. Not all situations of caregiving entail loss of dignity.

What is needed to correct this misunderstanding is both more refined empirical work and a more thoughtful critique of the atheoretical patterns of social gerontology, which has long been a problem in the field. For example, some recent empirical work in Sweden by Torres and colleagues has involved looking more closely at the relationship between cultural values and Successful aging: specifically, at value orientations around relational modes and social networks (Torres 1999). Whether dependency entails loss of dignity will be heavily influenced by such cultural differences, not by physical traits alone. In short, different cultures, even today, view self-sufficiency in ways that are profoundly different.

What is clear is that taking for granted our individualist, activity-oriented and future-oriented approach to Successful aging becomes an uncritical kind of cultural blindness (a kind of ethnocentrism) that will not be overcome by empirical investigation by itself. Empiricism alone will not correct the problem. Offering more precise correlations between locus of control and life-satisfaction and then extrapolating these findings to ideas about autonomy or Successful aging simply disregards the cultural context in which people live their lives. A genuinely critical gerontologist would attempt to bring such presuppositions to the surface, and Holstein and Minkler's critique is in the spirit of critical gerontology (Minkler and Estes 1999).

VARIETIES OF SUCCESSFUL AGING

A comprehensive review of the term Successful aging in the academic literature turned up a variety of definitions. But different uses of the term converge on key ideas such as life satisfaction, longevity, freedom from disability, mastery and growth, active engagement with life, and independence. The preponderant emphasis here is on maintaining positive functioning as long as possible (Phelan and Larson 2002). Against this progress-oriented version of Successful aging, this review also acknowledged a certain fluidity tied to a diversity of socioeconomic variables. Thus, individual progress is balanced by tolerance and relativism in characteristically American fashion.

By contrast, British gerontologist Alan Walker avoids the term Successful aging in favor of active aging, which he links to five policy domains: employment, pensions, retirement, health, and citizenship (Walker 2002). Focusing mainly on Europe, Walker believes that a policy strategy on behalf of active aging can be justified on both an ethical basis (greater equality) and an economic basis (reduced old age dependency). In contrast to American proponents of Successful aging, Walker's approach focuses on population and the life course: that is, he looks beyond individualism and emphasizes long-range consequences of habits of early life (Bower 2001). When we look at the new gerontology from a global, international perspective, it becomes clear why analysts in other countries outside the United States prefer the concept of active aging instead of Successful aging. The semantic difference suggests a deeper divergence between images of positive aging in America in contrast to the rest of the world (World Health Organization 2002a). Again, the ethnocentrism of the dominant version of Successful aging is apparent.

Finally, let us note that even critics of Rowe and Kahn's approach—for instance, those who favor a religious or spiritual view—seem to accept the premise that Successful aging represents happy and healthy aging. For example, Crowther and her colleagues have argued that spirituality is a forgotten factor in the Successful-aging paradigm (2002). But they end up arguing that spirituality or religiosity (the two are often conflated) is a factor that promotes better physical and mental health in old age. This line of argument—"Religion is good for your health"—will certainly have its appeal (Koenig 1999). But it amounts to accepting all too quickly the basic premise of Rowe and Kahn's initial formulation of Successful aging.

POWER OF POSITIVE THINKING

Before we too quickly dismiss Rowe and Kahn's formulation, we need, again to look carefully at their text. When we do look closely, we note that the book actually contains not one, but two different definitions of Successful aging. The first definition, the one discussed up to this point, is couched in terms of maximum wellness: avoidance of disease and disability and active engagement with life. A good old age, in this definition, is just an old age with minimum sickness or frailty, as much like youth or midlife as possible.

On this point, Rowe and Kahn bring forward the idea of "compression or morbidity" (Fries and Crapo 1995) originally articulated by Oliver Wendell Holmes in his poem "The Wonderful One-Horse Shay," which is cited in their book. Compression of morbidity is not exactly "prolongevity," but it is a descendent of the same progressivist spirit (Gruman 2003). We can think of compression of morbidity as a bit like political liberalism, in contrast to revolutionary political ideology. Political liberalism works the system to promote progress without challenging limits. By contrast, revolutionary ideology wants to overthrow the status quo. So, too, compression of morbidity doesn't promise we will live longer than the maximum life span in previous epochs, but incremental progress is still assured.

Compression of morbidity, and Successful aging, are mainstream, liberal ideologies, whereas appeals to so-called anti-aging medicine are revolutionary and reject the dogmas of mainstream biology and medicine. Even if their present claims are bogus, this goal of "uncapping" maximum life span may not be impossible. However, these prospects lie outside what Rowe and Kahn understand Successful aging to be. Their liberal incremental version of Successful aging means that, as far as we can, we postpone sickness (morbidity) until the very end of life and then die quickly, without lingering illness or debility. This is a hopeful, but realistic, version of progress in Successful aging, couched in terms of individual responsibility and initiative: the triumph of contemporary American values.

DECREMENT WITH COMPENSATION

Now, interestingly enough, a close reading of Rowe and Kahn's book turns up quite a different definition of Successful aging, a definition expressed by the phrase "decrement with compensation." Like compression of morbidity, decrement with compensation is easy enough to understand. In this case, the goal of positive aging is not to stay healthy longer and longer but, rather, to adapt, to make the best of our situation, even if it means chronic illness and decline. Instead of postponing decline, we recognize that decline is to be expected, and so we compensate for it and adapt to it.

Successful aging, in this second version, does not mean remaining healthy as long as possible but adapting to losses when they occur. For example, instead of downhill skiing, one takes up cross-country skiing. Instead of remaining a professional athlete, one becomes a coach; and so on. This definition of Successful aging is more realistic in acknowledging the limits of individual autonomy. No matter how vigorous one's efforts at health promotion, anyone can succumb to accidents and the failings of advanced age. In statistical terms there is steady increase of chronic illness and frailty in later life and Gompertz's law (first formulated in 1828) still confirms that the rate of mortality in human beings doubles every eight years.

Successful aging, then, comes in to two quite different versions. The first version stakes the whole meaning of success on avoiding bad outcomes and preserving health and vitality as long as possible. The second version looks for compensating factors and invites us to ask just what sorts of compensation might be possible, either individually or societally. I will come back to this point later, but for now it is enough to see that the two definitions of Successful aging are very different in their implications. Curiously, they are never quite reconciled by Rowe and Kahn. Most commentators, especially those who attack the idea of Successful aging, have concentrated their fire entirely on the first definition while ignoring the second.

The ideal of Successful aging—understood in its first version as indefinite prolongation of the values of middle age—is a prescription for remaining on a superficial level of life: "Hold on to what you've got as long as possible." By contrast, when losses demand a new approach—the second definition of Successful aging as "decrement with compensation"—we have the potential for going beyond, or below, that superficial level of life. Once we take seriously the second version of Successful aging, then age itself can be an opportunity for spiritual growth, as in the Sufi saying "When the heart grieves for what it has lost, the spirit rejoices for what it has found." It is this spiritual opportunity—what we may call "conscious aging"—that I turn to now.

MEETING THE SHADOW

Drew Leder accurately pinpoints the attractiveness of Successful aging in terms of a Western model of combating losses as best as we can (2000). He contrasts this with what he terms "spiritual aging" that involves embracing losses as a curriculum for developing the soul: "Age challenges us to see beyond the ego-self, now failing into disrepair. Who am I, if not just this wrinkled face in the mirror?" The advent of illness in later life sometimes proves to be the trigger for this call, or descent into the underworld," which is an encounter with a deeper level of living, as psychiatrist Jean Shinoda Bolen describes it:

When life is lived superficially or is almost entirely outer-directed, something has to happen that leads to soul-searching. Until then, there may be very little communication between the upperworld and the underworld, between the inner world of the personal and collective unconscious and the outer-world concerns of the ego. Layers of façade, of entitlement, and privilege that were built up over the years have no bearing on the occurrence or progression of an illness, and do not adequately prepare a person for the underworld descent. (1998:70)

If we can no longer sustain the midlife values of maximum wellness and productivity, then the descent will trigger troublesome questions not asked earlier in life:

Illness raises questions: Who are you when you stop doing? When you cannot be productive or are no longer indispensable to others? When you can no longer go on as before because you are sick, when you lose status? Who are you when you can't be a caretaker or a boss or do your job, whatever this might be? Do you matter?

If we listen to these questions—those posed in the second version of Successful aging as decrement with compensation—then we move along a different path from the prolongation of the values held supreme in the first half of life:

The truth that will set us free in the last half of our lives is not to be found in ego complexification. Consciousness has a developmental quality in the first half. In our old age, it grows through disenvelopment. It moves backward. It is regression in the service of transcendence. (Bouklas 1997:300)

Bouklas writes from his long experience as a geriatric psychotherapist. Yet his conclusions echo our second version of Successful aging. True, decrement with compensation rings like the jargon of abstract social science and the phrase "regression in the service of transcendence" does little to improve it. Yet, these ideas reflect a profound truth that the greatest artists have conveyed in their lives and works.

LATE FREEDOM

Take the case of Beethoven, who experienced an ultimate narcissistic wound with sensory disability that attacked the very core of his creative identity. In his Heiligenstadt testimony, Beethoven recorded his own descent into despair and soul-searching (Sullivan 1960). After he became totally deaf, he went on to produce the Ninth Symphony. His last years were a creative journey rooted in the solitude of inner silence. One could imagine a Beethoven who never lost his hearing but went on to produce more and more symphonic creations that pushed the limits of classical form, just as the first version of Successful aging would simply prolong the virtues of midlife. But Beethoven was forced to take the path of descent and solitude. He produced the Ninth Symphony and the last string quartets, and he burst the limits of conventional form in the service of musical transcendence (Solomon 2003).

Beethoven did not live into old age, but this pattern of creative response to disability—decrement with compensation—is recognized in other great artists. Some artists—Picasso is a great example—demonstrate the first version of Successful aging: productive engagement, activity, and prolongation of the values of youth and midlife (Schiff 1984). But others are forced to undergo descent and decrement.

One of the most brilliant examples is the late work of Matisse, produced when the old artist suffered physical infirmities that confined him to a wheelchair and prevented him from painting large canvases. Instead, Matisse turned to cutting out colored pieces of cardboard. These cut-outs represented a radical simplification of his lifelong style (Elderfield 1978). In keeping with the continuity theory of aging, Matisse never lost his passionate love of color. But in his later years, the evocation of color became simplified, purified, and transformed into that late freedom seen in so many artists in old age (Dormandy 2000). Matisse demonstrated not ego complexification but a sublime kind of regression, a simplicity that was the fruit of a lifetime's experience.

THE VIRTUES OF AGE

So we may wonder: is the dominant version of Successful aging an expression of our wider antiaging culture? In his critique of the contemporary ideology of Successful aging, Stephen Katz points to the ascendance of ideas grouped under categories such as postmodernism and posthumanism (2001). Katz notes that the appeal of timelessness and self-reliance is tied to the promise of technology and the mirage of overcoming all limits. As a marketing agenda, Successful aging tends to blend imperceptibly into antiaging (Katz 2001). From cosmetic surgery to lifelong learning, from virtual bodies to the prosthetic self, the appeal is always to turn away from outdated images of maturity in favor of a reinvented identity outside of time and finitude. By contrast, Katz urges us to reflect more deeply about the true resources of temporality— the resources of tradition, wisdom, narrative, memory and generativity—that affirm intrinsic values of aging instead of dwelling exclusively on risk and loss (Katz and Marshall 2003).

Let us push this matter of risk and loss to its ultimate extreme and ask the question: Is it possible to find Successful aging in a nursing home? If we adopt the first version of it (prolonged wellness), then evidently not. But what about the second version, decrement with compensation? Here it is appropriate to point out that Erik Erikson, modern-day prophet of the virtues of the life cycle, died in a nursing home, as did his wife Joan. We have no testimony about their final days in a long-term care facility and can only speculate about it. But we do have a remarkable record of Successful aging in a nursing home: the journal of Florida Scott-Maxwell (Berman 1986). Her powerful words give a new meaning to the idea of decrement with compensation:

Another secret we carry is that though drab outside—wreckage to the eye, mirrors a mortification—inside we flame with a wild life that is almost incommunicable.... It is a place of fierce energy. Perhaps passion would be a better word than energy, for the sad fact is that this vivid life cannot be used. If I try to transpose it into action, I am soon spent. It has to be accepted as passionate life, perhaps the life I never lived, never guessed I had it in me live. It feels other and more than that. It feels like the far side of precept and aim. It is just life, the natural intensity of life, and when old, we have it for our reward and undoing. (1968:32–33).

Rarely have we heard words that so vividly convey the dialectical truth of losses balanced by gains, physical decline compensated by spiritual insight. The message of Florida Scott-Maxwell's nursing home journal is not far from the spirit of Rembrandt's late self-portraits, the visual record of a long journey toward ego-integrity achieved in the midst of losses and tragedy. What Rembrandt's late-life portraits convey are the same qualities some psychologists have discerned in Successful aging: self-acceptance, inner mastery, purpose in life, and personal growth (Ryff 1989).

The testimony of great artists converges with life-span developmental theories and clinical concepts of personal growth. Whether in Matisse's cutouts, in Florida Scott-Maxwell's nursing home journal, or Rembrandt's self-portraits, we find the same recurring motif. Personal meaning is sustained through inner resources permitting continued growth even in the face of loss, pain, and physical decline. This compensation for decrement arises from a spiritual core that makes transcendence a genuine path in the last stage of life (Moody 2002). The inspiring account by Ram Dass of his struggle with a near-fatal stroke evokes the same message, the same decrement with compensation, that we have seen repeatedly in those who have made the descent and returned (Ram Dass 2001).

SHARED TRANSCENDENCE

Is this gero-transcendence limited to great artists or writers (Tornstam 1997)? Not at all. Collins conducted an empirical study of Successful aging among the Inuit people on Victoria Island in the Canadian Archipelago (2001). It turned out that the Inuit people understand elderhood in much the same way as our own society. But they do not share the first version of Successful aging (active engagement and good health). Instead, Successful old age was viewed as the ability to manage declines in health in a positive way. The key element was understood as a capacity to transmit accumulated wisdom to the next generation. Rabello de Castro and Rabello de Castro's case studies of Brazilian elders came to a similar conclusion: mechanisms of Successful aging reflect ways in which we constitute a sense of meaning in terms of a total life history, not gains or losses at a particular point in time (2001).

This entire line of ethnographic research underscores the way in which Successful aging—understood as decrement with compensation—depends in crucial ways on what Bourdieu would call social capital, especially the cultural and symbolic resources that provide a sense of meaning when the mask of midlife achievement slips away (Marin 2001). Even in the American environment, we know that social networks and social relationships are of enormous importance for sustaining cognitive function associated with Successful aging (Seeman et al. 2001). In contrast to the individualism (a la Horatio Alger) of the first version of Successful aging, these sources of compensation are correlated with the social capital and the resources of the wider society. Instead of looking to elders on the ski slopes, we need to look at elders in wheelchairs who can inspire us with examples of Successful aging in the face of chronic illness (Poon, Gueldner and Sprouse 2003).

With this wider perspective—society's instead of the individual's—we come, full circle, to the question with which I began this exploration: namely, how do we come to see human aging in the widest ecological, planetary perspective? The prophets of gloom see in population aging only a loss because they have not listened to the testimony of those who have gone through the descent and returned with a message of hope. Coming full circle means coming to recognize the circle of life, which is compensation for finitude and a glimpse of what lies beyond. As the Celtic proverb puts it: "Make time a circle, not a line." When we regain this vision, a vision of the great circle of life, Successful aging becomes conscious aging.

NOTE

CHAPTER 5

Is Killing Necessarily Murder? Moral Questions Surrounding Assisted Suicide and Death

Anthony Glascock

Although the key elements associated with assisted suicide have remained largely the same for the last two decades, the nature of the discussion within American society has changed dramatically. Twenty years ago discussions of assisted suicide were on the periphery of academic debate; today some of the most prominent scholars and legal experts in the United States are engaged in these discussions; interviews with political leaders two decades ago were rare and usually in non-prime time periods, whereas today, such debates among talking heads appear frequently on the twenty-four-hour-a-day cable networks; and issues that seemed uniquely American twenty years ago are now on the political agendas in a growing number of postindustrial countries. However, as much as the world appears to have changed, the main issue is still the central question: What is right and what is wrong and how do people in various societies determine the difference? In other words, the key issue is still a moral one.

However, before there is any further discussion of morality, it is necessary to explicitly state what I mean by assisted suicide. Assisted suicide, often termed physician-assisted suicide, is "making a means of suicide (such as a prescription for barbiturates) available to a patient who is otherwise physically capable of suicide and who subsequently acts on his or her own" (Quill, Cassel and Meier 1992:1381). This is different from voluntary euthanasia in which an individual actually administers the means of suicide or turns off the life support of a terminally ill individual.

As dramatic and important as much of this discussion in the United States and other industrial societies may be, it is interesting that it is taking place with two implied assumptions: (1) that this is the first time the issue of assisted suicide has been raised within advanced industrial societies, such as the United States; and (2) that twenty-first-century society is the first one that has ever had to face such a morally vexing dilemma. There are a variety of reasons for these assumptions, but in general there appear to be two main causes for this widely held view. The first explanation derives from the obvious advances in medical technology that allow for the prolongation of life beyond anything that has existed before in our own society or in any other society at any other point in time. Although the technology may be unique, the situation is not, either historically or cross-culturally. As I will show, even though medical technology allows us to prolong life, the same dilemma faced people in our own society prior to the late twentieth century, as well as in other societies; it only happened at an earlier stage in the dying process.

The second explanation is broader and more complex and is not as easily countered. It is hubris—the belief that we cannot learn from other societies and cultures, certainly not cultures that are less technologically advanced than we are. If we did turn to these societies for help in answering our own perplexing questions, this would be tacit recognition that we are not morally more advanced and that we could learn from other populations, many of which we would regard as primitive or backward. I will address both of these assumptions in the remainder of this chapter as I first discuss the role of assisted suicide, death-accelerating behavior and euthanasia in American society. I will continue by briefly considering a similar debate over these very same issues in nineteenth-century America, and conclude with a more detailed discussion of the nature of death-hastening behavior directed toward decrepit old people in many nonindustrial societies. It is my hope that this discussion will show that the ethical, moral and legal questions that surround these issues are not unique to twenty-first-century American society, and that people at other times and in other societies have had to struggle with them just as we have.

AMERICAN SOCIETY

Given the changes that have occurred in the level of discussion about assisted suicide over the last two decades, it appears that the best way to organize a discussion of the role of assisted suicide in American society is to examine the changes that have occurred by decade: the 1980s, 1990s and the 2000s. In this way, current beliefs, laws and behavior can be placed within both an historical perspective and a cultural context.

The 1980s

Three main events dominated the consideration of assisted suicide in the 1980s: (1) a 1984 New York Supreme Court ruling; (2) the case of Roswell Gilbert; and (3) the public outcry that followed statements by two prominent politicians that terminally ill people had a "duty to die." In 1984, the New York Supreme Court ruled that "a nursing home should not force-feed an eighty-five-year-old patient who was in poor health and had been fasting." The court decided that the man was "entitled to die of his own will [and] that the nursing home was not obliged to force-feed the man" (Hirsh 1985:9).

However, just across the Hudson River in New Jersey, an appellate court ruled that a hospital could not remove the nasogastric tube of an eighty-four-year-old man who wanted to die. In California, a hospitalized woman was prevented, through force-feeding, from starving herself to death (Hirsh 1985:10). Thus, in less than one year, three different courts in three different states had ruled differently in cases of terminally ill patients in nursing homes. Courtroom contradictions, however, were not limited to nursing home cases as, also in 1985, the issue that filled the tabloids was the Florida case of Roswell Gilbert, a seventy-six-year-old man who shot and killed his seventy-three-year-old wife who was suffering from Alzheimer's disease and osteoporosis. Gilbert was sentenced to twenty-five years to life for murder, even though an outcry was raised by a wide range of supporters and sympathizers. While Gilbert was sent to jail, two other men who violently killed close relatives went free. In an ironic twist, a seventy-nine-year-old man who shot and killed his wife, also suffering from Alzheimer's disease, had his case dismissed in the same courthouse in which Gilbert was sentenced.

The outcry over what many perceived as the inconsistency of state laws resulted in much activity over the last half of the 1980s as political leaders, editorialists, state legislatures, the American Medical Association and the general public were confronted by the moral, ethical, legal and religious issues surrounding euthanasia and assisted suicide. At the end of the decade, ex-Governor Richard Lamm of Colorado and ex-Senator Jacob Javits of New York raised the sensitive issue of the costs associated with the medical care of the terminally ill elderly and even suggested that terminally ill people may have the "duty to die." Although both politicians denied that they supported "mercy killing," both men called for a national debate on these topics and the development of national legislation that would "allow" the elderly to die when they desired. The challenge to debate these issues did not emerge on a national level as Lamm and Javits anticipated. Instead, the discussion was largely held at the level of individual states in both state legislatures and voting booths. The result was that by the beginning of the 1990s, thirty-six states had passed laws that explicitly prohibited assisted suicide, and in most of the other fourteen states, there was ambiguity as to the legal status of assisted suicide (Newman 1991).

The 1990s

A couple of brief examples illustrate this ambiguity quite nicely. In 1992, a referendum that would have legalized assisted suicide and voluntary euthanasia was narrowly defeated in the state of Washington. At almost the same time, the state legislature of Washington passed a law prohibiting assisted suicide, which was then declared unconstitutional in 1993 by a federal court because it interferes with individual liberty and privacy (Miller et al. 1994:120). In 1994, the people of Oregon approved by referendum "The Oregon Death with Dignity Act," which would, in very carefully defined situations, allow for assisted suicide. This law, although approved, could not be immediately enacted because a federal court, in response to a petition from individuals living in Oregon who opposed the Act, ordered a stay. The United States Supreme Court eventually ruled favorably on the law's constitutionality, and it went into effect in 1997. However, also in 1997, the Supreme Court ruled unanimously that both the New York and Washington laws banning assisted suicide were constitutional. The impact of these rulings will be discussed in detail in the next section.

As the political and legal processes have failed in their attempts to clarify these vexing issues, several individuals have taken a more direct, hands-on approach. The most famous, or notorious, depending on your point of view, is Dr. Jack Kevorkian, a retired pathologist who has acted on his beliefs by "assisting" in over thirty suicides. "Assisting" is in quotations because there was much debate in the 1990s as to whether Dr. Kevorkian had undertaken assisted suicide or voluntary euthanasia. It was unclear whether in each and every case he had only provided a means of suicide, or whether he had crossed the line to voluntary euthanasia by actually administering the means of suicide, such as turning on a machine attached to intravenous tubes filled with barbiturates. Although the details were somewhat muddled, the state of Michigan passed specific laws on several occasions to prevent Dr. Kevorkian from "assisting" in a person's suicide. He continued to assist, was prosecuted on three separate occasions, and was acquitted each time, after which he returned to his "practice." On November 22, 1998, CBS's "60 Minutes" aired a videotape showing Kevorkian giving a lethal injection to Thomas Youk, 52, who suffered from Lou Gehrig's disease. This broadcast triggered intense debate. Two days later, Dr. Kevorkian was charged by Michigan prosecutors with first-degree murder, for violating the assisted suicide law and delivering a controlled substance without a license in the death of Youk. In April 1999, Dr. Kevorkian was convicted of second-degree murder and delivery of a controlled substance in the death of Youk, and a Michigan judge sentenced him to ten to twenty-five years in prison. On June 1, 2007, Dr. Kevorkian, at the age of seventy-nine, was paroled from state prison in Michigan. His parole prohibits him from providing care to anyone over age sixty-two, giving counseling on how to commit suicide, or being present at any suicide or euthanasia. However, in a series of interviews after his release, Kevorkian reiterated his belief in both the right of individuals to end their own lives and the right of physicians to assist in these suicides (*Philadelphia Inquirer*, May 31, 2007).

The prosecutions and ultimate conviction of Dr. Kevorkian stimulated much debate about the extent and acceptability of assisted suicide in America. One study estimated that "(a)pproximately 6,000 deaths per day in the United States are said to be in some way planned or indirectly assisted" (Quill, Cassel and Meier 1992:1381). This is a surprisingly large number of cases, but one must take into consideration that the 6,000 include people who die because of "the discontinuation or failure to start life-prolonging treatments," in addition to those individuals who die because of the administering of pain relieving medication in dosages sufficient to hasten death (Quill et al. 1992:1381). In fact, there was sufficient discussion of the appropriate use of life-prolonging treatments within the medical profession in the 1990s to produce a "how-to" article. Angela Holder, writing in *Medical Economics*, advised physicians how to properly write "Do Not Resuscitate" (DNR) orders so that lawsuits are avoided. She suggested that the orders be explicit and that the family members and the patient be consulted, but the results of DNR orders are that elderly patients are allowed to die when they could technically be kept alive.

The attitudes of physicians toward assisted suicide is extremely variable, and even though the American Medical Association's Council on Ethical and Judicial Affairs has issued a report on "Decisions Near the End of Life" (Council of Ethical and Judicial Affairs, 1992:2229–33), there was far from a consensus in the 1990s as to the physician's role in suicides of terminally ill patients (Brody 1992; CeloCruz 1992). It is fair to say that the problems surrounding the desire of some terminally ill patients to actively end their lives had been "relatively unacknowledged and unexplored by the medical profession ... (and that) ... little is objectively known about the spectrum and prevalence of such requests or about the range of physicians' responses" (Quill et al. 1992:1380). Although it became clear that whatever position is finally taken by the American Medical Association, no physician would ever be compelled, as part of a treatment protocol, to assist in the suicide of a patient. However, there was a move in the 1990s toward a position that would support the right of a terminally ill patient to end his/her life and for physicians, by following very well-established guidelines, to assist in this action (Miller et al. 1994).

The Twenty-First Century

Although, at this writing, the new millennium is less than a decade old, there has been more activity and controversy centered on assisted suicide in this short period than during the past twenty years combined. It is impossible to go into detail about all of the various events that have occurred; instead, I will concentrate on two examples that represent the larger trends concerning assisted suicide and conclude with a summary of where things stand today.

The first example is the demise of the Hemlock Society. The Hemlock Society, founded in 1980, was an international organization that advocated voluntary physician aid-in-dying for the terminally ill. At its peak in the mid-1990s, the Hemlock Society had over 46,000 dues-paying members and over 80,000 supporters in the United States alone. The Hemlock Society promulgated the belief that all terminally ill people should have the right to self-determination for all end-of-life decisions, and it put this belief into action through a program of education and research. Members of the Hemlock Society helped draft the Oregon assisted suicide law and provided much of the labor and financing for referenda in Oregon, Washington, Maine, Michigan and California. However, by the beginning of the new century, membership had declined to less than 18,000. There were many reasons for the decline—including the growth of state level organizations with a focus on getting specific laws passed, and internal divisions within the society—but perhaps the biggest reason came from its overall success. The Hemlock Society succeeded in putting the issue of "death-with-dignity" in front of the American public and into both state legislatures and the United States Congress. Even though the only legislative and court-backed success was in Oregon, assisted suicide was no longer a hidden topic, and therefore, the Hemlock Society had accomplished its main goal. Although the Hemlock Society closed its doors in 2003, there are now at least four organizations—Compassions and Choices, the Death with Dignity National Center, the Euthanasia Research and Guidance Organization, and the Final Exit Network—that have taken up the death-with-dignity mandate.

The second example that encapsulates the events of the last half-decade is the consequences of Oregon's Death with Dignity Law that was upheld by the United States Supreme Court in 1997. This edict allows individuals to end their lives through the use of prescription medication after their terminal diagnosis has been confirmed by two physicians. Nevertheless, the legislation has not been without controversy and legal challenges. In 2001, the Bush administration, with then Attorney General John Ashcroft taking the lead, challenged the law by threatening to prosecute physicians if they prescribed medication for "euthanasia." The challenge ended when, in January 2006, the United States Supreme Court ruled 6–3 that the Oregon law was not superseded by the federal government. Two interesting facts emerge from the consequences of the Oregon law. First, on average, fewer than thirty individuals chose to end their lives each year under the procedure outlined by the Oregon law; and the average number of such individuals has been declining in the last several years. In fact, since the enactment of the law in 1997, only 292 Oregonians have died under its provisions (Crary 2007). Thus, the "rush-to-suicide" that many commentators had predicted has not come to pass. Second, even with the success of the law, both legally and practically, no other state has followed Oregon's lead.

This brings me to the brief summary of where things stand today in the United States on the issue of assisted suicide. Four states, Washington, New York, Michigan and Florida, had bills introduced into their legislatures concerning assisted suicide in the late 1990s; none of the bills were enacted into law. Likewise, between 2000 and 2004, four additional state legislatures debated laws allowing some form of assisted suicide: California, Colorado, Hawaii, and Maine. Once again, none of the bills became law.

In contrast, forty states have specific laws that criminalize assisted suicide. Some of these laws have been challenged in court, and the Ninth U.S. Circuit Court of Appeals declared the Washington State law unconstitutional for violating the equal protection clause of the U.S. Constitution. However, as of now, it does not appear that much will change over the remaining years of this decade. Even if the Ninth Circuit Court's ruling is extended to other circuits and ultimately upheld by the Supreme Court, it does not appear that over the next several years any state, in addition to Oregon, will pass laws legalizing assisted suicide. This state of affairs in America is matched, to a large extent, in the rest of the postindustrial world. There are only three countries that legally allow assisted suicide: Switzerland, Belgium and the Netherlands. In some other countries, most notably the Northern Territories of Australia, a specific province or state has legalized assisted suicide, but in the vast majority of countries, assisted suicide is illegal; and it appears that it will remain so for the foreseeable future.

HISTORICAL AND CROSS-CULTURAL PATTERNS

Historical Evidence

It is interesting to note that the controversy over whether it was moral for terminally ill individuals to take their own lives, what role, if any, should be played by physicians in such suicides, and whether active euthanasia should be allowed go back to at least Greek and Roman times (Carrick 1985). However, I am most interested in the similarity between the contemporary discussion of these issues in America and a comparable, intense debate in the mid- and late-nineteenth century, as a result of the discovery and use of anesthesia. Anesthesia, whether morphine, chloroform or ether, could not only alleviate pain, but, in sufficient dosages, end life. The debate became especially intense in 1872 when Samuel Williams, who was not a physician, published a book in England that argues it was the "duty of the medical attendant whenever so desired by the patient, to administer chloroform or such other anesthesia as may by-and-by supersede chloroform—so as to destroy consciousness at once, and put the sufferer to a quick and painless death" (Emanuel 1994:794). Publication of Williams's book generated considerable discussion on both sides of the Atlantic throughout the 1870s and 1890s. This discussion culminated in various attempts, both within the medical profession and within individual states, to codify various opinions into coherent policy and law. An editorial in the *Journal of the American Medical Association* in 1885 summarizes the position taken by the majority of physicians and certainly the medical establishment, arguing that the acceptance of Williams's position on euthanasia was really an attempt to make "the physician don the robes of an executioner" (Emanuel 1994:795). Responding to a growing demand for greater patients' rights, several state legislatures, in the 1890s, and for the first few years after the turn of the century, debated legislation that would have legalized some form of what today would be termed assisted suicide. None of these bills became law, and after the Ohio legislature rejected a bill in 1906 titled "An Act Concerning Administration of Drugs etc. to Mortally Injured and Diseased Persons," the clamor for patients' rights and euthanasia died down, only to reappear in the 1980s and 1990s.

Cross-Cultural Evidence

The previous discussion should help refute the assumption that this is the first time the issue of assisted suicide has been raised in American society. I will now turn my attention to refuting the second assumption, that we are the first society that has ever had to face such a morally vexing dilemma. To do this I will turn to ethnographic data collected on a wide variety of nonindustrial societies and employ a methodology—holocultural analysis—that allows for the systematic analysis of data collected from a very carefully selected sample of these societies.[1] As noted in Sokolovsky's discussion of "covering up" among the Tiwi (Introduction this volume), much anecdotal information is available concerning the killing of particular individuals within nonindustrial societies. For example, almost everyone has heard stories about the old Eskimo woman who is set adrift on an ice floe or the elderly man left behind to die alone because he is no longer able to walk when his relatives move to a new location. Holocultural analysis, on the other hand, allows for the systematic analysis and interpretation of ethnographic material in order to more reliably reach conclusions on human behavior. My research used data drawn from the Human Relations Area Files, which is a compilation of ethnographic information on over 1,000 societies. However, I did not utilize all societies in the Files, but instead examined a sample of societies that have been selected for very specific reasons to ensure geographical distribution, as well as relative independence from each other. The sample is the Probability Sample Files (PSF) and is comprised of sixty nonindustrial societies (Naroll, Michik and Naroll 1976). The focus of the study was on the treatment directed toward the elderly in these societies.

Definitions

Although the study examined all types of behavior, the most surprising and potentially important finding was that nonsupportive treatment, especially the killing, abandonment and forsaking of the elderly, was widespread. In order to describe these life-threatening behaviors in a coherent manner, I coined the term "death-hastening behavior," which is a broader concept than gerontocide or gericide, and includes killing, abandoning and forsaking of the elderly; it is defined as nonsupportive treatment that leads directly to the death of aged individuals. Four brief examples from the literature analyzed illustrate the type of data found in the Human Relations Area Files and the scope of the death-hastening concept.

Killing

Chukchee—reindeer-herding people who speak a Paleo-Siberian language and live in northeastern Siberia, principally on the Chukotsk Peninsula.

Few old Chuchi die a natural death. When an old person takes ill and becomes a burden to his surroundings, he or she asks one of the nearest relatives to be killed. The oldest son or daughter or son-in-law stabs the old one in the heart with a knife (Sverdrup 1938:133).

Abandoning

Lau—a horticultural and fishing people who speak a Malayo-Polynesian language and live in the Lau Islands off southern Fiji in the central Pacific Ocean.

Informants on Fulanga said that when the tui naro (headman) of the Vandra clan became old and feeble, he was taken to Taluma Islet in the lagoon and abandoned there in a cave filled with skeletal remains of old people who died there after having left the community (Thompson 1940:10).

Forsaking—Denial of Food

Bororo—a horticultural people who speak a Ge language and live in the Amazonian forest of Central Brazil.

It is the same for the old people; after a hunt or successful fishing trip, they are brought a piece of meat or a few fish. But also they sometimes are forgotten. The indigent person is then reduced to going without a meal and all night long, alone, utters ritual lamentations (Levi-Strauss 1936:276).

Forsaking—Denial of All Support

Yakut—Yak herders who speak a Turkic language and live in north-central Siberia in the former Soviet Union.

The position of older people who were decrepit and no longer able to work was also difficult. Little care was shown for them; they were given little to eat and were poorly clothed, sometimes even reduced to complete destitution (Tokarev and Gurvich 1964:277). Aged people are not in favor; they are beaten by their own children and are often forced to leave their dwellings and to beg from house to house (Jochelson 1933:134).

Each of these behaviors leads directly to the death of the elderly within the particular society. The example of killing is self-evident—the elderly are not left to die, but rather are dispatched directly by members of the social group. The abandoning example is also fairly clear-cut, and ranged from the elderly who are physically removed from a permanent community, to societal members leaving the elderly behind as the group moves to a different location. The two examples of forsaking behavior show some of the range of this behavior. Forsaking is the broadest of the three behaviors and includes the denial of sufficient food, medical care, clothing, and shelter (see Barker this volume for specific examples of this category).

These behaviors contrast with supportive treatment, which is defined as the active support of the elderly including the provision of food, shelter, medical care and transportation. Supportive treatment is more than the expression of deference or respect and must be accompanied by tangible actions that aid in the survival of the elderly individual. Behavior that falls between supportive and death-hastening is, for the present study, defined as nonsupportive, nonthreatening behavior, and includes such behavior as insulting the elderly, requiring them to give up certain property, and removing them from their normal residence. These behaviors can be unpleasant and may even have long-term detrimental effects on the well-being of the old person, but they do not directly threaten his or her life. Thus, nonthreatening behavior can be viewed as transitional between supportive and death-hastening, and may eventually lead to death. A definitional problem was raised by the type of data analyzed: how is elder suicide to be categorized? If an old person asks his sons to kill him, if an old woman wanders away from camp in order to die, or if an elderly individual gives away all of his or her possessions and then wanders from village to village, eventually to die of neglect and exposure, are these examples of suicide, and perhaps even assisted suicide, rather than death-hastening? To avoid the development of numerous coding categories that would prove too difficult and confusing to employ, the decision was made to include such behavior in the existing categories of killing, abandoning and forsaking. The issue as to who initiates the death-hastening behavior is considered as each of the particular categories is discussed.

FINDINGS

Data concerning the treatment of the elderly were available for forty-one of the sixty societies in the Probability Sample Files. In twenty-one of these societies, a slight majority, at least one type of death-hastening behavior was present (see Table 5.1). While twelve societies directed only support toward the aged, almost an equal number (eleven) displayed both death-hastening and supportive actions toward their elders. Examining the data more closely, ten societies have a single form of death-hastening behavior, while eleven societies have a combination of behaviors. Killing is the most frequent means of hastening the death of old people; it occurs in fourteen of the twenty-one societies. Forsaking is found in nine of the societies, and old people are abandoned in eight societies. The most frequent combination of behaviors, to both kill and abandon the elderly within the same social group, occurs in five instances. A combination of forsaking and killing is present in four societies, and forsaking and abandoning are present in only a single society. Interestingly, there is no difference in the treatment directed toward older males and older females.

Importantly, in all but one society in which multiple forms of death-hastening occur, supportive or nonthreatening treatment is also found. The most common pattern is for the killing, forsaking and abandoning to be present with supportive treatment. Intuitively, it would appear to be emotionally, cognitively and behaviorally inconsistent for such extremes of treatment—killing and support—to be present in the same society. This is resolved by answering the following questions: Who is to be supported? Who is to be denied food? Who is to be killed? A cultural contradiction is apparently avoided simply by directing different treatments toward different categories of the elderly within a given society (Barker this volume). The criteria upon which this differentiation is based are complex and will be discussed in detail in the analysis/discussion section.

The data on death-hastening provided additional details concerning the forsaking and killing of the elderly. In five of the nine societies in which old people are forsaken, there is total nonsupport. The elderly are denied food, shelter and treatment for illness. Most often, as the previous examples show, the elderly are driven from their homes and forced to either beg or scrounge for food. Interestingly,

Table 5.1
Treatments in Nonindustrial Societies

Treatment	Number of Societies	Percent
Only support	12	29
Support and nonthreatening	4	10
Only nonthreatening	4	10
Only death-hastening	6	14
Death-hastening and nonthreatening	4	10
Death-hastening and support	11	27
Total	41	100

societies in which the elderly are specifically denied sufficient or "desirable" food tend to be horticultural societies, whereas those that practice total forsaking tend to rely on hunting, fishing or animal husbandry. The existence of relatively frequent "hunger seasons" in horticultural societies appears to result in the elderly being denied food, or only being provided with foods that are low in nutritional value or not easily chewed and digested (Fortes 1978:9; Ogbu 1973:319–23). Even though these "hunger seasons" appear to occur more frequently than is commonly presumed, it is usually only by chance that a researcher is in a community during a period of a severe food shortage. Thus, the forsaking of the elderly through the denial of sufficient food or the substitution of undesirable food is perhaps underrepresented in the available ethnographic literature.

Details concerning the killing of the elderly are generally lacking in the ethnographic material. An outsider is just not going to easily collect specific information on the killing of societal members, regardless of the age of the people being killed. The available data, though, do indicate several interesting patterns. The elderly are killed violently: beaten to death (three societies), buried alive (three societies), stabbed (two societies) or strangled (one society); and no difference based on sex was uncovered. The decision to kill the elderly individual was made, in all but one instance, within the family. The common procedure was for the children and the elderly individual to decide jointly that the time was "right to die." In two societies, the elderly individual appears to decide on his or her own when it is the proper time to die. Among the Yanoama, a South American shifting horticultural society, the decision is removed from the family and placed in the hands of the village leaders. The actual killing of the old person is also a family affair. In six of the seven societies on which data were available, a son, usually the eldest, kills his parent. Once again there is no variation based on sex.

ANALYSIS/DISCUSSION

The findings presented above answer three of the main questions posed earlier. The killing of the elderly does occur in other societies, and when killing, forsaking and abandoning are combined into the broad category of death-hastening, the elderly are dispatched in 50 percent of the societies with data in the PSF. The sex of the individual does not appear to make a difference since both males and females have their deaths hastened. Children, after consultation with their parents, make the decision, and sons carry out the actual killing. Three questions still remain to be answered: Why are old people killed, forsaken or abandoned? In what type of societies is death-hastening found? How does this behavior compare to the killing of the elderly in our society?

Death-hastening is directed toward individuals who have passed from being active and productive to being inactive and nonproductive members of the social group. This transformation of the elderly from intact to decrepit has long been recognized within the anthropological literature, but the connection between it and death-hastening behavior has only recently been systematically analyzed (Rivers 1926; Simmons 1945, 1960; Maxwell, Silverman and Maxwell 1982; Glascock 1982; Kiemo 2004). Leo Simmons perhaps best described the results associated with the transformation when he stated: "Among all people a point is reached in aging at which any further usefulness appears to be over, and the incumbent is regarded as a living liability. "Senility" may be a suitable label for this. Other terms among primitive people are the "overaged," the "useless stage," the "sleeping period," the "age grade of the dying" and the "already dead" (1960:87). Thus, at least two categories of the elderly exist in nonindustrial societies: "normal old age" (the intact) and the "already dead" (the decrepit). In the most simple terms, it is when people are defined as decrepit that they have their deaths hastened.

In fourteen of the sixteen PSF societies in which a distinction is made between the intact and the decrepit elderly, some form of death-hastening behavior is present. In the majority of these cases, as Barker shows (Part VI this volume), both supportive and death-hastening treatments occur. The evidence clearly indicates that the intact elderly are supported and the decrepit elderly are killed, abandoned or forsaken. This dichotomization of treatment can be most easily seen in several ethnographic studies. D. Lee Guemple's research among the Eskimo documents well the change in behavior that accompanies the redefinition of an elderly individual as decrepit as his or her health declines: "They [the aged] suffer a marked reduction in both respect and affection when they are no longer able to make a useful contribution. As they grow older and are increasingly immobilized by age, disease, and the like, they are transformed into neglected dependents without influence and without consideration. In short, old age has become a crisis" (1969:69). At this point, "the practical bent of the Eskimo asserts itself forcefully. To alleviate the burden of infirmity, the old people are done away with" (Guemple 1969:69).

Finally, research in New Guinea and its neighboring islands shows the transition from intact to decrepit and the resultant change in behavior. "Van Baal reports that the Marind Amin elderly are respected and well treated as long as they are in good health. When they become helpless and senescent they may be buried alive by their children" (Counts and Counts 1985a:13). Research among the Kaliai of New Britain conducted by Dorothy and David Counts provides an example of an elderly man who, because he was suffering from physical disabilities and declining mental acuity, had, in the eyes of his sons, lived too long. The sons, therefore, conducted final mortuary ceremonies, distributed property, and essentially defined their father as socially dead (Counts and Counts 1985b:145).

Although drawn from widely different societies, the previous examples show that death-hastening behavior is directed toward a specific type of elderly individual—the decrepit who have experienced actual or perceived changes in their health to the degree that they are no longer able to contribute to the well-being of the social group. This inexorable journey is traveled by males and females alike, but there is some evidence in the ethnographic literature that females begin the journey at a slightly later age than males.[2]

Thus, death-hastening behavior is directed toward the decrepit elderly, but is this behavior found equally in all nonindustrial societies? To answer this question, a series of variables selected from the Ethnographic Atlas were correlated with the killing, forsaking and abandoning of the elderly (Murdock 1967). The results indicate that death-hastening tends to be present in societies that: (1) are located in areas with harsh climates, in particular, desert and tundra environments, (2) have no horticultural activity or only shifting horticulture in which grain crops predominate, and (3) lack systems of social stratification. Societies that lack death-hastening and instead have only supportive treatment tend to: (1) be located in areas with temperate climates, (2) have intensive agriculture, (3) have a system of social stratification, and (4) have a belief in active high gods. In other words, death-hastening tends to occur in societies that can be characterized as simple—hunting and gathering, pastoral and shifting horticultural—while societies with exclusively supportive treatment are more economically complex—sedentary agricultural.

Although death-hastening behavior tends to be found in more technologically simple societies, it is common for this treatment to be present in conjunction with support of older people and to be directed toward only the decrepit elderly. Likewise, the supportive behavior found in more technologically advanced societies can vary depending upon internal conditions, such as social stratification, residential location, and gender. In many ways it is more desirable to be old in Pygmy society, even if one faces being abandoned and killed, than in some advanced agricultural societies. As long as they are intact, older Pygmies can look forward to respect and supportive treatment, receiving the most desirable foods in an environment that provides abundantly for the general population. In advanced agricultural societies, even though supportive treatment for the elderly is present, it must be put in the context of often harsh environmental and societal conditions; isolated residences, frequent food shortages and exploitive state political systems can put the elderly in jeopardy even if they are generally supported.

CONCLUSION

The discussion of the cross-cultural material on death-hastening should refute the second assumption that we are the first society that has ever had to face such a morally vexing dilemma as assisted suicide. Death-hastening is a common occurrence in nonindustrial societies, and people in these societies have had to make decisions concerning the decrepit or terminally ill elderly that are morally complicated and emotionally painful. I want to continue with the comparison by briefly analyzing the way in which the killing, abandoning and forsaking of the elderly in these nonindustrial societies compares to assisted suicide in American culture. I also want to consider how we can learn from the similarities and differences that exist between these behavioral responses in nonindustrial and American society as we struggle to reach some type of societal consensus on what has become a significant moral dilemma. There are some clear similarities between death-hastening and assisted suicide:

1. The behaviors are directed toward people, often old, who have experienced a decline in physical or mental health and who are often terminally ill;

2. These individuals are considered burdens to themselves, their families and to the community;

3. The decision to hasten death is difficult and involves family members, the stricken individual and often other members of the social group, such as physicians in American society, political and/or religious figures in nonindustrial societies.

There are, however, some significant differences between the behaviors found in American and nonindustrial societies.

First, examples of overt, direct killing of the elderly in America are still relatively rare enough to produce sensational responses in news reports. However, as discussed previously, approximately 6,000 deaths per day in the United States appear likely to be in some way planned or indirectly assisted by the joint decision of family and medical personnel through the discontinuation of or failure to initiate life support, or overmedication. Thus, there is an important difference in American society between dramatic, overt assisted suicide (i.e., Dr. Kevorkian), and more subtle, covert assisted suicides (i.e., discontinuing life support). The behaviors present in many nonindustrial societies—killing, abandoning and forsaking—although emotionally demanding, resemble the less dramatic covert behavior found in American society. There appear to be some definite reasons for this response to death-hastening. Death-hastening is part of the culture of these nonindustrial societies; children have personally experienced the death of close relatives, and as they age they may be called upon to hasten the death of one of their parents, and they in turn may ask their children to do the same. As a result, death-hastening is open and socially approved in nonindustrial societies. In contrast, the covert nature of the vast majority of assisted suicides in American society indicates that there is not a society-wide acceptance of this behavior, and consequently it must be kept under cover and not open to discussion.

Second, the people who decide and undertake assisted suicide or death-hastening are quite different in the two types of societies. In nonindustrial societies, the decisions are made by the family, often with open discussions with the older person. As Maxwell et al. state, "Gerontocide is usually a family affair" (1982:77). The decision is made by family members and usually carried out by a son. In American society, it is often unclear as to who decides—children, spouse, the terminally ill person, medical staff, courts of law or some combination. Most often, the decisions appear to be made on an ad hoc basis, with the family brought in at the last minute and the stricken individual often not consulted at all. As the earlier examples of recent legal cases in America show, when the decision is made and implemented by a single person or undertaken in an overt fashion, the consequences can be severe—people can be charged with premeditated murder. Thus, it is not surprising that people, especially hospital and nursing home administrators and physicians, are reluctant to openly take responsibility for aiding in the termination of life to the point that decisions regarding the discontinuing of life support can end up in courts of law. Social sanctions in the form of prosecution and lawsuits are applied inconsistently, with the result being that most assisted suicide is done covertly and then covered up. In contrast, death-hastening in nonindustrial societies is open and direct and people are willing to take responsibility because the rules are known and accepted by the social group.

Perhaps the most significant difference between assisted suicide and death-hastening is the respective levels of technological sophistication of the two types of societies in which the behaviors are found. As has been shown, death-hastening is most prevalent in societies with simple subsistence/technological systems: hunting and gathering, pastoral or shifting horticultural. Even though the issues surrounding the killing, abandoning and forsaking are similar to those found in our society, the technological ability to maintain life is significantly different. In addition, the need for the social groups in these technologically simple societies to move frequently produces a threat to decrepit individuals as does the inability of most of these societies to store sufficient quantities of food to allow all members to survive severe food shortages.

American society is the most technologically sophisticated society that has ever existed. We have the ability not only to maintain life, but also to prolong life beyond the point many people think is reasonable. We are able to provide physically incapacitated individuals with many technological marvels, allowing these individuals to live, if not a productive life, one that certainly extends beyond that even imagined by members of nonindustrial societies. Yet we inarguably assist the deaths of large numbers of individuals every day and then struggle over the moral, ethical and legal questions revolving around these actions. We search for a societal consensus that seems to be further away today than a decade ago.

NOTES

1. For a more complete discussion of the methodology employed, please refer to Glascock and Feinman 1980, 1981.

2. In certain nonindustrial societies, especially foraging and horticultural, women are often defined as "old" at a later chronological age than men. This is the result of people

in these societies employing a definition of elderly/old based on a change in the tasks that a person can accomplish. Once a person can no longer accomplish normal adult tasks, for example, hunting for men and gathering for women in foraging societies, he or she is defined as old, regardless of the individual's chronological age. In fact, it is rare in these societies for people to be aware of their "age" or the number of years they have lived. Since in foraging societies gathering is generally less strenuous than hunting, a woman will be able to undertake normal adult tasks at an older chronological age than a man. Thus, women tend to be defined as "old" at a later chronological age than men.

CHAPTER 6

Menopause: A Biocultural Event

Yewoubdar Beyene

The few existing data on menopausal experiences of women in non-Western cultures suggest that menopausal women in Western cultures report more symptoms than women in non-Western cultures. In the cross-cultural literature, the rarity or complete absence of menopausal symptoms in non-Western cultures was thought to be due to the fact that menopause precipitates a positive role change for women in these cultures (Flint 1975; Griffin 1977, 1982). A change from high to low status is assumed to correlate with experience of menopause as negative and incapacitating, while improvement and freedom from cultural taboos associated with childbearing years at middle age correlate with positive or indifferent attitudes and thus reports of fewer symptoms (Flint 1975).

In comparing the menopausal experience of Mayan women with those of women in Western, industrialized cultures, however, one may mistakenly attribute the differences to different attitudinal factors and to gain or loss in status at middle age. In Mayan society, a woman's role change and gains in status do not correlate with menopausal age. As described earlier, a woman's status in Mayan society does not depend solely on her chronological age. Rather, it is a result of an interrelation of factors such as age and the marital status of her sons, both of which are independent of onset of menopause.

The data suggest the following hypothesis instead: the Mayans' positive attitude towards menopause and aging accounts for the lack of psychological symptoms in the Mayan women as compared to Western women. But the hypothesis does *not* explain the absence of hot flashes among Mayan women, a symptom said to be due to hormonal changes that are universal. This absence raises a question about the link between hormonal change and hot flashes.

Comparing the menopausal experiences of Western and non-Western women is difficult and gives rise to misleading conclusions if social, economic and cultural differences are not taken into account. Comparisons of menopausal experiences of women from different nonindustrial societies may provide us with the means for distinguishing the physiological, social and cultural manifestations of menopause.

COMPARISON OF THE REPRODUCTIVE HISTORIES OF MAYAN AND GREEK WOMEN

Comparisons of the data from these two groups indicate both similarities and some marked differences between women in the two cultures. The women seem to share similar cultural values regarding many beliefs and practices about menstruation and childbearing, but had differences in their childbearing patterns, experiences with menopause, as well as in their diets and the ecological niche in which they lived.

Similarities

The information indicates that women in both cultures were concerned much more with menstruation and factors related to child birth than with menopause. Like Mayan women, the Greeks also have taboos and restrictions related to menstruation and childbearing. For example, rural Greek women believe that menstruation is a curse as a result of Eve's sin. Consequently, among Greek peasants, a menstruating woman and a woman who just gave birth are not allowed to participate in religious activities because they are considered "unclean" and contaminated. Mayans believe that a menstruating woman can cause disaster and induce sickness in a newborn baby. Moreover, in both cultures, citrus fruit, cold drinks, and bathing are forbidden during menstruation because they were believed to stop the menstrual flow. Both groups use a variety of herbs to treat menstrual irregularities and different illnesses. Some of these herbs are used by both groups for similar ailments. For example, both Mayans and Greeks used oregano to treat menstrual irregularities.

Women in both cultures perceive menopause as a life stage free of taboos and restriction, which, consequently, offers increased freedom to participate in many activities. For example, Greek women could participate fully in church activities, and Mayan women moved freely without anxiety about inducing sickness in others. Because the risk of pregnancy was no longer present, both groups reported that they felt more relaxed about sexual activities, thereby improving their sexual relationships with their husbands. The women also stated that they felt relieved from the fear of unwanted pregnancies, as well as from the monthly menstrual flow, which was considered bothersome.

The data also indicate that in both cultures, the roles of good mother, housekeeper, and hard worker are highly valued. In both societies, old age is associated with increased power and respect. Particularly for a woman, status increases with age, as her sons marry and establish their own families. The mother-in-law, both in Mayan and Greek culture, occupies the most authoritative position as the head of the extended family households of her married sons. Moreover, older women are believed to possess special healing skills. Therefore, in both Mayan and Greek villages, the older woman of the family is the first to be consulted when a family member gets sick, particularly her grandchildren. In both cultures, healing is one of the older woman's nurturing roles as a mother and as a carrier of old traditions (Campbell 1964; Blum and Blum 1965; Elmendorf 1976; Steggerda 1941; Redfield 1941).

Differences

The data also indicate marked differences between the Mayan and Greek women in relation to menopausal experience and childbearing patterns. The average reported age for onset of menarche for both cultures was approximately the same: 13 for Mayan women and 14 for Greek women. However, the average age for onset of menopause was 42 for the Mayans and 47 for the Greeks. With regard to the age for onset of menopause (see Table 6.2), the age difference between the two groups is quite striking. The Mayan women clustered between the ages of 36 and 45, while the Greek women clustered between the ages of 46 and 55.

Moreover, Mayan women did not associate menopause with any physical or emotional symptomatology. The only recognized physiological event associated with menopause is the cessation of menstruation. Among the Mayan women, menopause is welcomed and expressed with such phrases as "being happy," "free like a young girl again," "content and good health." No Mayan woman reported having hot flashes or cold sweats. Anxiety, negative attitudes, health concerns, and stress for Mayan women were associated with the childbearing years, not with menopause. Menopause was not a negatively perceived concept. Women were pleased to get rid of their periods; thus, premenopausal women in the study looked forward to the onset of menopause.

On the other hand, menopausal experiences among rural Greek women seem to bear more resemblance to the experiences of women in Western, industrialized societies. Even though the postmenopausal and menopausal women reported being relieved from the taboos and restrictions of childbearing years at menopause, overall it was perceived negatively by the premenopausal women. The premenopausal women expressed anxiety and anticipated possible

Table 6.1
Comparison of the Distribution of Menstrual Stages of Mayan and Greek Women

Menstrual Stages	Mayan (N = 107)		Greek (N = 96)	
	N	Percent	N	Percent
Premenopausal	36	33.6	30	31.3
Menopausal	36	33.6	31	32.3
Postmenopausal	35	32.7	35	36.5

Table 6.2
Comparison of the Distribution of Age at Onset of Menopause
for Mayan and Greek Women

| | Mayan (N = 71) x = 42.0 | | Greek (N = 66) x = 47.0 | |
Age at Onset	N	Percent	N	Percent
30–35	5	7.0	2	3.3
36–40	25	35.3	6	9.0
41–45	30	42.3	19	28.8
46–50	8	11.3	25	37.8
51–55	3	4.2	14	21.1

health problems with menopause and were not looking forward to its onset.
There is respect and status gain for older women in Greek culture, but getting
old was perceived by some Greek women as tantamount to dropping out of the
main stream of life. Therefore, some Greek women, particularly the premenopausal group, associated menopause with growing old, diminution of energy,
and a general downhill course in life. In striking contrast to the Mayan women,
Greek premenopausal women reported anxiety and a negative affect in association with menopause.

Greek postmenopausal and menopausal women reported hot flashes and
some cold sweats similar to women in Western, industrialized societies (see
Table 6.3). Greek women, however, differed from women from Western,
industrialized countries in their perceptions and management of menopausal
hot flashes. Greek women did not perceive hot flashes as a disease symptom
and did not seek medical intervention. While they had a variety of herbs to
treat menstrual pain and discomfort, they had none for hot flashes. They felt
that it was a natural phenomenon causing a temporary discomfort that would

Table 6.3
Comparison of the Distribution of Menopausal Symptoms
for Mayan and Greek Women

| | Mayan (N = 71) | | Greek (N = 66) | |
Menopausal Symptoms	N	Percent	N	Percent
Headache	22	31.0	28	42.4
Dizziness	25	35.2	28	42.4
Hot Flashes	0	0	48	72.7
Cold Sweats	0	0	20	30.3
Hemorrhage	13	18.3	8	12.1
Insomnia	0	0	20	30.3
Irritable	0	0	10	15.2
Melancholia	0	0	3	3.0

stop with no intervention. Symptoms such as irritability, melancholia, and emotional problems were not expected in the normal process of menopause; these symptoms were said to appear only with premature menopause, that is, if it occurred before age 40.

CONCLUSIONS

This comparison suggests that the existence or lack of physiological symptoms cannot be explained in terms of role changes at midlife or by the removal of cultural taboos. Greek women and Mayan women in the study seemed to share similar cultural values regarding beliefs and practices of menstruation and childbearing, but have very different menopausal experiences. If menopausal hot flashes and osteoporosis are hormonally induced physiological phenomena, differences in their occurrence should be related to cultural and environmental factors that could affect the production of a hormone such as estrogen. Two such factors could be the diet and fertility patterns which showed such striking differences in the two cultures. In the following, I consider these two factors, diet and fertility patterns, as possible explanations for the variation between the Greek and Mayan women in the experiences of the physiological symptom of menopause, namely, hot flashes.

Hypothesis

Mayan and Greek women differed strikingly in their diet and in their childbearing patterns. Could the differences between their actual experience of menopause in the sense of physiological phenomena be related to these differences? The question is how do childbearing patterns and diet affect reproductive hormones, and in turn, how do such hormones affect the appearance of the physiological phenomena?

For Mayan women, pregnancy was a stressful experience. Because they did not use any birth control, many were pregnant at regular two-year intervals. They married early and continued to bear children until menopause. They all breast-fed their children until they attained age one and one-half or two. Mayan women rarely had a steady menstrual cycle because successive pregnancies and long periods of amenorrhea due to lactation were so common. Unlike Mayan women, Greek women had few pregnancies; they married in their late twenties or early thirties, used birth control and planned their family size. They breast-fed only six to nine months, and they tended to have steady menstrual cycles.

Moreover, these two cultures also differed in their ecology, which affects diet. The Mayans live in a semitropical environment, a lowland with poor soil, and used a slash-and-burn technique of farming. The climate in Chichimila is generally humid and hot, with temperatures sometimes reaching 110°F. On the other hand, the Greeks live in a rugged mountainous area. The climate in the Greek village varies among seasons: it has short, cold winters with temperatures at times below freezing; temperate, mild springs and falls; and summers with highs of only 80°F. Even though the land cannot be called fertile, the small plots of land that the Greeks use for farming have more top soil than that of the Mayans. Finally, the Greeks have draft animals and produce a greater variety of foods than do the Mayans.

Another striking difference between the two cultures is their diets. The Mayan diet consists of corn, beans, tomatoes, *chaya* (a green leafy plant), some radishes, squash, *camote* (sweet potatoes), very little animal protein and no milk products. The Mayans are reported to have a high incidence of vitamin deficiency and anemia (Balam 1981). Greeks, on the other hand, have a wide variety of nutrients: wheat, cheese, milk, eggs, olives, a variety of wild greens, legumes, plenty of meat and fish, fruit and wine.

Diet

The important role that diet plays in growth and development is well-documented. Poor nutrition allied with chronic infections before puberty is known to have a permanent affect on stature. Malnutrition during childhood slows down skeletal development and delays sexual maturity, such as the onset of menarche in girls. For example, menarche is reported to be earlier in women from well-off families than those from underprivileged families. The number of children in a family and the family's social class have also been related to the onset of menarche because these variables correlate with nutritional status (Frisch and McArthur 1974; Eveleth and Tanner 1976). It has been documented that nutrition plays a role in reproduction: it affects conception, fetal mortality, and health of the newborn and the length of postpartum susceptibility. As Frisch and McArthur (1974) assert, poor nutrition delays menarche, lengthens the period of adolescent sterility and postpartum amenorrhea, and lowers fecundity.

Not only is the onset of menarche related to a woman's nutritional status, but menstrual activity continues to be affected by nutritional factors throughout a woman's reproductive life. In premenopausal women, the regularity of the menstrual cycle is controlled by neurotransmitters and levels of biogenic amines. However, environmental changes such as fasting or excessive weight loss can inhibit cycling, ovulation and pituitary response to luteinizing-releasing hormone and thyrotropin-releasing hormone. Thus diet, through modification of brain function as measured by electro-encephalographic activity and sleep patterns or by direct action alters hormone metabolism (Hill et al. 1980; Merimee and Fineberg 1974; Akesode, Migeon and Kowarski 1977; Hurd, Palumbo and Gharib 1977).

Differences in hormone production between populations have been partly accounted for by differences in diet (MacMahon et al. 1974). It has also been reported that diet affects ovarian function and adrenal activity, which could be increased by a high protein diet. Hill and his associates (1977) compared Japanese women with Caucasian women and concluded that different populations of comparable age might also have different plasma levels of hormones and that dietary factors, such as dietary fat intake, influence the hormone profile in women.

In another study of diet and menstrual activity, Hill and his associates (1980) compared South African black women with North American white women and concluded that the groups had different hormonal balances during the menstrual cycle. These hormonal differences are assumed to be related to genetic or environmental factors or to both of them. The South African black women maintained a diet high in carbohydrates supplemented with vegetable protein with low fat content. They were shorter and heavier in stature than the white women and maintained greater physical activity in their daily lives. Because physical activities such as running and aerobic exercises are also known to modify androgen metabolism (Kuoppasalmi et al. 1976), Hill and his colleagues assumed that the differences in hormonal activity between the South African black women and North American white women could be partially explained by differences in their levels of activity. However, a study of premenopausal and postmenopausal black South African women on a Western-type diet indicated hormonal changes different from the pattern associated with the high carbohydrate diet, which suggests that diet has the primary effect on pituitary activity.

Another study (Hill et al. 1976) also indicates that urbanization and Westernization may also produce changes in the hormone secretion in women through changes in diet. These studies indicate that nutritional patterns and the amount of animal fat consumed and body weight (Frisch 1980) may influence hormone production.

Certainly, diet varies dramatically between the groups of Mayan and Greek women studied. Improvement in the diet of the rural Greek villages in the last two decades has resulted in the disappearance of marked nutritional deficiencies in Greece. For example, pellagra, which appeared before [World War II] in hundreds of cases yearly in Greece, is not seen now (May 1963). Protein malnutrition is seldom seen and severe cases of nutritional deficiency are rare in Greece.

The cultural practices of nutritional intake and ecological as well as economic limitations are major factors in the differences in diet between these two cultures. Although both groups are agrarian, differences exist in the ecological niches they inhabit and the types of food substances that they produce and consume. As discussed before, the Mayans live in a semitropical climate where the only method of farming is slash-and-burn. Their diet consists mainly of corn and beans. Overall, Yucatan is known to have poor soil and the few areas of land that are relatively arable are owned by the middle-class Ladinos who use the land to raise livestock for profit. In recent years, the Eastern part of Yucatan (Tizimin and Panaba), which was mainly a maize growing zone, has been affected by the expansion of private land ownership, *parvifundismo* (Balam 1981). The Mayan peasants have been pushed off their communal lands to farm on poor soil while the semirich soil is used to grow feed for livestock.

Nutritional research in Latin America indicates that the proportion of maize and beans typically used by Latin Americans for meal combinations provides optimum amino acid complementarity for the two grains when they are eaten together (Maffia 1974). A national nutritional survey in Mexico (May and Donna 1972) indicated that because of the large amount consumed by the rural communities, corn is responsible not only for 70 to 80 percent of the energy supplied, but also for a large percentage of proteins, fats, and vitamins, especially thiamine. This survey also concluded that meat is not very commonly eaten in the rural parts of Mexico. Therefore, animal protein accounts only for 22.9 grams of the total 71.9 grams of protein. Carbohydrates and starches provide 75.2 percent of the calories, protein 14.5 percent and fats 10.3 percent. The protein comes mainly from corn and beans. Animal protein is in short supply and of low quality. Moreover, nutritional anemia is common in rural Mexico, in spite of an adequate level of iron in the diet. This is believed to be the consequence of malabsorption or losses due to parasites. Chavez and Rosado (1967) also found that in Merida, the state capital of Yucatan, 50 percent of the children examined showed signs of malnutrition. Overall, the survey found that the most important clinically expressed nutritional deficiency problems in Mexico are the result of riboflavin, niacin and protein deficiencies.

Despite the balanced nutrient value of the average Mexican diet, the Mayans' social and economic position, together with the poor nature of the soil, an unpredictable ecosystem, the prevalence of parasites and the large family size, make it difficult to have enough corn and beans to meet the nutritional demands for an individual. In Chichimila, my observation was that people use few beans in their bean soup. Dishes such as *frijol colado* (mashed bean soup) were rarely prepared by most households because they require large amounts of beans. Most households eat their tortillas with a soup made from a few beans and water.

Because diet affects growth, development and hormone production, malnutrition should be one of the variables studied in relation to the relatively early onset of menopause for Mayan women. In addition, the effect of the Mayan diet on menopausal symptomatology in general needs further investigation.

Furthermore, information from physicians providing services to both Greek and Mayan villages indicates that in neither culture does osteoporosis appear to be a problem. The mineral contents of the nutrients that these people eat and their daily physical activities also must be studied in relation to osteoporosis. Even though the Mayan diet is deficient in protein, people get an adequate supply of calcium derived from tortillas and from drinking water. For example, the lime water used to soak maize before grinding it into *masa* for tortillas, a practice common to the Mayans and other Latin American peoples, provides the needed calcium in the diet. A Mexican gets more than 500 mg of calcium per day from tortillas alone (Cravioto et al. 1945). Mayans also obtain calcium from their drinking water because of the abundant lime in their soil.

Green vegetables are also a source of calcium. One of the prominent newspapers in Yucatan, *Diario de Yucatan* (1981), had a profile on *chaya:* "El Mal de Huesos y La Chaya" ("Bone Illness, Osteoporosis, and Chaya"). This article stated that a United States physician, Everett Smith, recommended that his readers eat *chaya,* a green leafy plant, as a means of preventing osteoporosis. *Chaya* is known to be a rich source of calcium and Vitamin A and it is one of the very few green vegetables that the Maya eat often.

The Greeks also have calcium in their diet from their use of milk and cheese, as well as from their drinking water. In the West, some physicians prescribe both high dietary intake of calcium and physical exercise as a way of preventing osteoporosis (Nordin 1982; Bachmann 1984). In addition to their dietary calcium intake, both Mayan and Greek village women of all ages maintain a high level of physical activity. They perform rigorous work at home and in the fields and walk long distances.

Fertility Patterns

A striking difference between the Mayan and Greek women is their fertility patterns. As discussed before, Mayan women marry early, have successive pregnancies, and experience long periods of amenorrhea (because of prolonged lactation coupled with malnutrition). Therefore, Mayan women rarely experience a regular menstrual cycle.

The Mayan fertility pattern is typical of most nonindustrialized, traditional societies. For example, data from the !Kung hunters and gatherers in the Kalahari Desert suggest that given the fertility patterns of traditional societies, a woman would experience about 15 years of lactational amenorrhoea and about 48 menstrual cycles during her entire reproductive life, equivalent to four years (Konner and Worthman 1980). On the other hand, a woman in an industrialized society with a family size of two children, little or no breast feeding, and a short period of postpartum amenorrhoea (McNeilly 1979), can expect 35 of her 37 reproductive years to have consistent menstrual cycles (Short 1978).

Short (1978) also suggests that the reproductive patterns of the traditional, simple societies, such as those of the hunter-gatherer, most likely represent the situation to which human genes are best adapted. Therefore, because no evidence is found of a fundamental change in the reproductive biology of humans in millions of years, there may be significant biological consequences of the present low fertility pattern of women in industrialized societies. The phenomenon of estrogen dependency or deficiency at menopause also may be a result of the change in the reproductive pattern of women in modern industrialized societies. One hypothesis is that decreased childbearing with short periods of lactation and postpartum amenorrhoea possibly expose the body to more estrogenic stimulation and its sudden decline could be manifested in both hot flashes and bone density loss, or in just one of these phenomena.

Furthermore, repeated pregnancies and lactation are known to lead to frequent interruption in cyclic ovarian function (Neville 1983). For example, during pregnancy, the serum concentration of estrogens and total progesterone

levels are high. However, during lactation basal prolactin levels are elevated
and progesterone and estrogens are suppressed (Martin and Hoffman 1983).
Studies on lactation and hormone levels also indicate that prolactin levels of
lactating women are high where breast milk forms all or a substantial portion
of infant's diet (Madden et al. 1978; Konner and Worthman 1980).

Women are usually infertile at least for four to eight weeks after the birth of
an infant. However, lactation is known to prolong the infertility period due to
the suppression of ovarian activity as a result of high levels of basal prolactin
brought about by frequent suckling (McNeilly 1979). The duration of lactational infertility varies considerably from one society to another, being as short
as two to three months in Western, industrialized societies, and as long as three
years in the !Kung hunters and gatherers (Simpson-Herbert and Huffman
1981). The existing evidence suggests that high levels of prolactin has direct
interference with ovarian steroid production (McNatty, Sawers and McNeilly
1974). Some believe that frequent suckling stimulus itself may be a factor in
lactational infertility; however, whether it is prolactin alone or suckling stimulation or both, the fact is that ovulation is suppressed during lactation. For
women in industrialized societies where the childbearing rate is low and breast
feeding of short duration, the chances of exposure to high levels of prolactin
and its biochemical effect is decreased.

The only biological effect of high levels of prolactin that we know about is
amenorrhea. However, the adverse effect of continuous exposure of the endometrium and other reproductive tissues of the body to estrogenic stimulation
has been documented. For example, estrogen is known to play a major role in
the genesis of breast cancer; also postmenopausal women treated with estrogen
replacement therapy have a high risk of endometrium carcinoma (Smith 1967;
Ziel and Finkle 1975). Moreover, studies on cancer rates in parous and nulliparous women (Cole, Brown and MacMahon 1976) suggest that parity and age
at first pregnancy may also alter the estrogen profile.

Although there are no cross-cultural studies specifically concerned with fertility patterns and their effect on bone density loss, some research has periph-
erally touched on the phenomenon. The few available data suggest that high
parity does not predispose to osteoporosis or hip fracture (Garn 1970; Smith
1967; Daniell 1976; Aloia et al. 1983; Wyshak 1981). Aloia and coworkers
(1983) suggest that relatively longer lactation also decreases the risk of osteo-
porotic fractures; although other studies have shown that lactation is associated with calcium depletion (Atkinson and West 1970; Wardlaw and Pike
1986). It has been proposed that reports of osteoporosis in lactating women
were probably due to inadequate intake of calcium and vitamin D (Daniell
1976).

This raises questions about the extent to which frequent interruption in
cyclic ovarian function due to successive childbearing, prolonged lactation,
and amenorrhoea affect the production of reproductive hormones and the
degree to which the latter may affect age at onset of menopause and the presence or absence of hot flashes or even osteoporosis.

CONCLUSION

This study has focused on the experience of menopause, its cultural significance and meaning and its physiological manifestation in peasant women. The findings from this study indicate that the perception and experience of menopause vary among cultures. However, the findings also suggest that cultural factors such as status gain and removal of menstrual taboos are inadequate explanations for cross-cultural variation in the menopausal experiences of women. Besides the social role restrictions and cultural taboos of menstruation, women in nonindustrialized societies have strong similarities in their fertility patterns which in turn may also have effects on the biochemical transformation of the reproductive system.

Like other human developmental events, menopause is a biocultural experience. Therefore, this study points to the fact that research on menopause should consider biocultural factors such as environment, diet, fertility patterns, and exercise levels which could also affect the production and equilibrium of hormones in a woman's body. To do so, more comparisons of menopausal experiences of women from different nonindustrialized societies, as well as within industrialized societies, are needed.

In addition, the data from this study raise significant questions regarding the effect of frequent childbearing patterns and long periods of lactational amenorrhea on postmenopausal bone mass. The effect of frequent lactational amenorrhea on bone mass needs to be investigated.

Research efforts to understand the role of estrogen in the etiology of osteoporosis have been limited to samples in industrialized societies who rarely experience frequent childbearing and long periods of lactational amenorrhea. Cross-cultural studies addressing the above mentioned issues will contribute new insights into the study of menopause and the etiology of osteoporosis.

NOTE

Reprinted from *Menarche to Menopause: Reproductive Lives of Peasant Women in Two Cultures*. Reprinted with permission of SUNY Press.

CHAPTER 7

Web Book: Culture and the Meaning of a Good Old Age

Christine L. Fry et al.

Available at www.stpt.usf.edu/~jsokolov/webbook/fry.htm.

This chapter details the work of Project AGE (Age, Generation and Experience), the most serious cross-cultural study of aging to date. Here a team of anthropologists carried out a comparison of aging in Hong Kong, Botswana, rural Ireland and two American communities, combining long-term fieldwork with a precise and consistent research protocol. In Part II, Keith discusses one of the other communities studied in Project AGE, Swarthmore, Pennsylvania.

RELATED RESOURCE

Draper, P. 2007. "Conducting Cross-Cultural Research in Teams and the Search for the 'Culture-proof' Variable." *Menopause* 14(4):680–87.

PART II

The Life Course and Intergenerational Ties in Cultural and Global Context

Jay Sokolovsky

GENERATIONS UNBOUND AND RECONNECTED

In *Boomsday*, Christopher Buckley's 2007 comedic best-seller novel set in the "not too distant future," angry mobs of youths storm gated senior commun-ities and deface golf courses. They are egged on by Ms. Cassandra Devine, a twenty-nine-year-old fictional "blogger" and central character in the book. She is perplexed and agitated about why someone her age should spend their entire life paying unfair taxes, just so the boomers can hit the golf course at age sixty-two and drink gin and tonics until their nineties. Certain that this grave social injustice is due to the coming mass retirement of 77 million baby boom-ers set to reach age sixty-five in 2011, she offers a neat solution to the national costs of aging. Ms. Devine proposes a national "transitioning ceremony," where volunteers at age seventy receive a wonderful vacation paid by the fed-eral government and then are required to commit suicide; in return, their heirs pay no inheritance tax.[1]

Buckley's book captures in exaggerated and dramatic terms one of the gen-erational narratives that emerged in the last decade of the twentieth century— the tyranny of the greedy geezer, or what market analysts call WHOOPIES, "well-off older people." At the beginning of the twenty-first century, associa-tions such as Americans for Generational Equity (www.age-usa.org) or the Concord Coalition (www.concordcoalition.org) have echoed these sentiments and premises underlying the novel *Boomsday*.

However, another narrative slant emerging in the United States is captured by the words on the fly jacket of another recent book, *The Boomer Century: 1942–2046*:

They didn't just date, they reinvented Western sexuality. They didn't just go to the doc-tor; they reinvented Health Care and are now reinventing retirement and aging. They are pioneers in a new stage spanning the decades between middle and late life. Neither young nor old, they represent an extraordinary pool of social and human capital. And, in large numbers, they want to do work that serves a greater good. (Croker 2007)[2]

These two seemingly irreconcilable perspectives frame the outer edges of the ongoing dynamics of a changing life course and the multiplying cultural spaces in which generations interact and new models of late life are being enacted (see especially Arber and Attias-Donfut 2000; Hudson 2008). In the center of all this are global efforts often situated in university centers, nonprofit organizations and governmental agencies promoting intergenerational cooperation and interdependence as a mechanism of finding solutions for common problems faced by society (see especially the Web site for Generations United, www.gu.org). One of the most interesting efforts in this direction is documented by Thang in her ethnographic study of Kotoen, a facility in Tokyo that combines housing and services for older people with a nursery for children under five years old (2001). A key goal at Kotoen is to produce a feeling of *fureai* between the generations, which means not only a coming together, but also seeking to promote spontaneous interaction involving feelings and emotions. Similar efforts, often under the rubric of developing life-span neighborhoods and communities, are underway in many nations (see Vanderbeck 2007; Stafford Part V).

IT'S NOT YOUR GRANDFATHER'S LIFE COURSE ANYMORE

As we grow older, many of us are recalling memories of our parents and grandparents at our current ages, but we are seldom experiencing our elder relatives' life courses. We can often expect to live longer, reach the boundaries of late adulthood in better health and have taken different passages through youth and adulthood. As Cattell and Albert tell us in this section's first chapter, the cultural reshaping of late life is part of a potent rethinking of aged-based social passages. They examine the life course in the broad cross-cultural contexts of elderhood, being aged, "ancient" and sometimes attaining ancestorhood. Their comprehensive chapter will help readers not only understand the kinds of dramatic changes taking place in North American society, but also the kinds of variations emerging globally (Biggs 2007; Seedsman 2007). Through this part of the book, chapters will explore the cultural construction of the life course and the intergenerational ties that connect people to the cultural spaces of family, work, gender and community (Motel-Klingebiel and Arber 2006; Bratter and Dennis 2008).[3]

LANGUAGE AND THE PERSISTENCE OF AGEISM

A universal feature of human cultural systems is having language categories that describe certain boundaries of the life course. This will vary considerably, but most languages have, at a minimum, words designating: infant, child, adult and elder. Importantly, existing words marking life cycle periods can show radical changes in meaning over time. For example, the word *hag* derives from the Greek root *hagia* or "holy one" and prior to the thirteenth century referred to a woman with positive supernatural capabilities. During the Middle Ages, the Catholic Church felt competition from literally hundreds of new religious movements. Independent older women, especially those working as midwives, came to be seen as a threat. In this context, the term *hag* became synonymous with evil, ugliness and witchcraft (Rhoads and Holmes 1995).

In Western society, how key points along the life span are evaluated, stereotyped and represented within a society has received a good deal of attention and study (Giles and Dorjee 2004). One of the more recent studies (see Box II.1 below) found that in the United States, the further along the life course one is, the more negative the associated words are and less congruence is found between older and younger samples. Both young and old adults use mostly positive adjectives to describe youth, while their words for describing mature adults are more disapproving. Additionally, a salient difference between younger and older respondents was that the under-fifty-five crowd used fewer positive words to describe aging itself.

BOX II.1 DO YOU KNOW THE DIRTY WORDS FOR OLD AGE?

PHILADELPHIA - Adriane Berg recently wrote a financial planning book she wanted to call How to Have a Great Old Age. The publisher wouldn't hear of it, the 53-year-old New Jersey author said this week. The title would contain no hint of "old." The book came out this year as *How Not to Go Broke at 102*.

What makes the concept of "old" or "old age" so radioactive? In a National Council on Aging study three years ago, half the people between 65 and 74 thought of themselves as middle-aged, as did a third of people over 75.

What's wrong with "old age"? Janice Wassel, gerontologist at the University of North Carolina at Greensboro, has no ready answer. But her linguistic research suggests that society's frequent avoidance of the word "old" leads to something worse: a contorted language that can anger the very people it is intended to soothe. Wassel, 54, looked up in a thesaurus all the words that apply to different age groups. Then she surveyed people, both young and old, about the images and emotions those words evoke.

Infants nearly got a free ride. Fifteen of 16 words describing them were deemed positive. Everyone liked "cherubs," "babies" and "bambinos." Only "preemie" fared poorly. Toddlers evoked more neutral images, though the six positive words, including "peewee" and "tyke," outdistanced the one negative: "brat." Even teenagers overcame "punk" and "teenaged juvenile" to score more positive words than negative.

But something changes in middle age. Only one of 10 phrases, "prime of life," was considered positive, vs. seven negative phrases, including "middle life." "I don't know what happens to us at middle age," Wassel said, speaking at a joint meeting of the National Council on Aging and American Society on Aging in Philadelphia. "But it's a sad statement of how we perceive people as they grow

continued

older." Words that applied to the oldest group took a different twist. With all other age groups, survey respondents generally agreed whether a term was positive, negative or neutral. When assessing the older group, though, opinions about words often split along generational lines.

OLD DOGS AND SPRING CHICKENS

Younger people, perhaps straining not to call older people "old," sometimes use surrogate words that older people can find offensive. Professor Janice Wassel of the University of North Carolina at Greensboro measured how two different age groups reacted to images of aging represented by different words. Here are some examples:

	55 OR OLDER	54 OR YOUNGER	
NEGATIVE			
Battleaxe		Battleaxe	Old man
Dirty Old Man		Codger	Old Maid
Elderly		Dirty Old Man	Old Timer
Geriatric		Geezer	Old Wife
Old Maid		Geriatric	Older Generation
Retiree		No spring chicken	Oldest
Senior citizen		Old Dog	Oldster
The Old		Old Duffer	Over the Hill Gang
		Old Granny	The Old
POSITIVE			
Eldest	Old Granny	Elderly	Golden-ager
Gramps	Old Timer	Eldest	Grandfather
Grandfather	Old Wife		Matron
Granny	Older Generation		Old chap
No spring chicken	Over the Hill Gang		Retiree
Old chap	Veteran		Senior
Old Dog			Veteran
NEUTRAL			
Codger	Old man		Gramps
Geezer	Oldest		Granny
Golden-ager	Oldster		Senior citizen
Matron	Senior		
Old Duffer			

Times art – TERESANNE COSSETTA

People age 54 or younger apparently saw "old" as a pejorative, Wassel said. Fourteen of 16 phrases containing the word "old" were deemed negative. Only "old gentleman" and "old person" evoked a neutral image. But respondents 55

continued

and older liked many of the images, such as "old chap," "old dog," "old granny," and "older generation." The only negatives containing the word "old" were "dirty old man," "old maid," "old woman" and "the old."

What older people really didn't like were the words society has created while trying not to call them old. Retiree? Nope. Elderly? Nope. Senior citizen? Not a chance. Meanwhile, younger people saw these surrogate words as either positive or neutral. Older and younger respondents could agree on only a third of the words describing older people. Younger people thought "no spring chicken" and "over-the-hill gang" were insults. Older people liked those phrases. "Young people and older people aren't speaking the same language. That's a problem," Wassel said. "This is important because of social changes that are coming. We will have people in their 70s in the work force, working with people in their 20s and 30s. "We have to come up with a language that works and is respectful to all of us."

AARP figured it out five years ago when it dropped "retired" from its name and became just AARP. What used to be senior citizen centers in Nebraska are now active adult centers. The Barnstable Senior Center in Massachusetts is about to become the Barnstable Center: A Center for Lifelong Learning. Language depends on the context, said Phyllis Rule, 76, who works for the National Council on Aging in Michigan. "When we go to breakfast, you see us sitting there with gray hair, we can call each other old and crack jokes. That doesn't mean I would appreciate someone many years younger than me saying I'm old. I prefer to be called mature or a work in progress."

Worse than words themselves, conference goers said, are the ways some younger people treat older people in misguided, condescending attempts to be sympathetic. A waitress calls someone "sweetie" or "honey" but doesn't use those terms to customers in their 30s or 40s. Or they refer to an older person as "young man" or "young lady." Or they dole out exuberant praise in response to a mundane task, like parents do when a picky-eating child cleans his or her plate.

To the extent that society sometimes needs labels, Wassel suggested "older adult" to describe someone in the later stages of life. As a role model, she recalled a telephone conversation a few years ago with her mother, who had just turned 77. Hearing her mother refer to herself as old, Wassel said she hemmed and hawed, trying to politely deflect the issue. Finally, her mother interrupted. "She said, 'Janice, it's okay that I'm old. I never thought I would be this old. I never thought that I would be this healthy. I never thought I would have this much fun. It's okay that I'm old. I wish it for you."

Adapted from: "Do You Know the Dirty Words for Old Age?" By Stephen Nohlgren, *St. Petersburg Times*, March 12, 2005. Reprinted with the permission of the St. Petersburg Times.

DERAILING THE NARRATIVE OF DECLINE—
REBRANDING AGING

Despite efforts to fight what Robert Butler, in 1976, termed *Ageism*, it is still deeply encoded in our language and pervasively transmitted by our youth-enamored media (Abramson and Silverstein 2006; Tornstam 2007; Vesperi 2008). For example, even among older adults, studies show that greater exposure to television is associated with more negative images of aging (Donlon, Ashman and Levy 2005).

However, as with the development of ideas such as "Conscious Aging" and "Gerotranscendence" (see Part I), the rapidly changing global landscape of late life is being altered through popular culture, language, discourse and imagery.[4] As noted by Featherstone and Hepworth in this section, some gerontological writers see the postmodern life course as characterized by a blurring of traditional age divisions and the integration of formerly segregated periods of life. New images of aging are being created where "elderhood has been constructed as a marketable lifestyle that connects the commodified values of youth with body care techniques for masking the appearance of age" (Katz 1995:70). This began in earnest during the 1990s with attempts to recast the life span in fantasy images of timelessness drawn from fountain-of-youth movies such as *Cocoon (1 and 2)* and self-help books such as Dr. Deepak Chopra's *Ageless Body, Timeless Mind* (1993).[5] In this new millennium with a seeming obsession of bodily makeovers, there are also books like *Don't Retire, Rewire* (Sedlar and Miners 2002), or Web sites such as www.secondjourney.org promoting tales of a reborn "second life" similar to the myths of rebirth, so prominent in many cultures (Hollis 2005; Smith and Clurman 2007).[6] There is even a company called *AfterLife* (www.afterlife. org) that offers, for a fee, to update your Web page after your death!

A more serious revisioning of aging has arisen, creating new vocabularies, turning aging into *saging* and *eldering*, proffering a positive, active embrace of nonmaterial gains from human maturity, especially in the creative and spiritual realms (Schachter-Shalomi and Miller 1995; Ram Das 2000). This seems more than just another kind of "rebranding" that readers might have noticed when their local "Retirement Community" became an "Active Living Adult Community." There has opened up an astonishing range of largely new cultural spaces involving social activism, electronic blogs and social networking, third-age niche magazines, senior-oriented cable TV networks and performance groups.[7] In this last category, many viewers of the Web video portal www.youtube.com have become enamored with the singing of octogenarian rock groups such as Britain's " Zimmers" and the United States' "Young@Heart," who belt out songs by OutKast and Nirvana and transform The Clash's "Should I Stay or Should I Go" into a drama about life and death.[8]

There are also new organizations developing such as "The Institute for Eldering Options" (http://elderingoptions.net), which is committed to shifting the aging paradigm by connecting personal living options to the emerging concepts of the age-friendly cities and communities to be discussed in Part V by Phil Stafford.

FAMILIES AND GENEALOGICAL GENERATIONS

A basic structural difference between kin-based, small-scale societies such as the Tiwi or the Ju/'hoansi and the United States is that elderly in the first type of society have continuous access over the life span to essential resources derived from membership in kinship groupings. In such cultural settings, the wide embrace of family frequently provide what Simic (1978) calls a "life term arena"—a stable setting for the engagement of an entire life. Even in the age-set societies discussed by Cattel and Albert (this section), the intense ties among age-mates or the ritual bonds across "social" generations do not destroy the links between "genealogical" generations, forged from the developmental cycle of family formation.

In capitalist, postindustrial societies, it is more typical that access to resources and status over the life span requires productive participation outside of one's kin group and the transition through numerous "short-term arenas." Careful historical research has shown that this pattern is not new in North America or Western Europe (Ruggles 2002). Various studies have decried any easy assumption that the elderly are socially divorced from their younger kin, but emphasize family networks in the United States have not been destroyed, but transformed along the following lines: (1) family support systems are becoming more "vertical," with more relationships that cross generational lines and have fewer links to siblings and cousins; (2) a shift toward "top heavy" family caregiving roles, with middle generation women now likely to spend more time dealing with dependent parents over age sixty-five than with children under eighteen; (3) the development of "reconstructed" or stepfamilies emerging out of increased divorce and single-parent families; (4) changing patterns in the timing of childbearing; and (5) extended potential ties across multiple generations as those in the oldest generation live longer (Lowenstein 2005; Stuifbergen, van Delden and Dykstra 2008).

Nevertheless, relatively little attention has been paid to understanding the cultural factors shaping such interaction. The remaining articles in this section seek to remedy this situation by examining cultural spaces along the globally altering life course.

PERSONHOOD AND COMMUNITY

As Jennie Keith notes in her chapter in this section, diverse ethnographic research has documented the emergent social ties and distinctive norms and practices that can create supportive new cultural spaces for older persons who live in age-homogeneous residential settings (see Part V, Counts and Counts Web book). Her chapter focuses on Swarthmore, a U.S. suburban community that was part of the cross-cultural, Project AGE (see Part I Web book, Fry et al.). In discussing community-situated personhood in late life, she found a dramatic tension between younger adults perceiving elder residents as mere symbolic icons of the good community and those in late life who actually experience a strong disconnect from the age-heterogeneous social life of a previous generation. This is important original research for exploring channels to create new cultural spaces for the aging in suburbs and small towns.

WIDOWHOOD AND CULTURAL CONTEXT

As will be noticed in many of the case studies presented within this book's chapters, loss of a spouse in late life, especially for women, provides important guideposts to how cultural systems provide options for surviving into old age. While not exclusively a late-life experience or female experience, widowhood does disproportionably relate to the lives of older women (Martin-Matthews and Davidson 2006). Globally, there is usually at least a three-to-one differential in the number of females versus males past age sixty-five who are widowed. As well, the consequences of becoming widowed can have dramatically varied economic and social impacts depending on culture and the broad context of community life (Burkhauser 2005). In this section, Maria Cattell combines a global examination of widowhood with her long-term research in rural Kenya to draw readers into the experience of older widows in Africa, Guatemala, India and the United States. From this perspective, she explores how the different vulnerabilities among widows intersect with the new cultural spaces in which widowhood is being experienced. Cattell shows how postmenopausal Samia women often see widowhood as a way of consolidating social and economic power and independence, which they have accrued slowly over a lifetime. Cattell's article shows that older women are not only crucial to the functioning of households and larger kin groupings, but can also act as initiators of changes that have broad importance to the community. In this regard, as we will see in Part III, while large proportions of older adults in industrializing nations live with or quite near to family, globalization and urbanization are rapidly altering the framework of kin support (see for example van Eeuwijk 2006).

GENERATIONS AND EXCHANGE

The relatively few attempts to conduct cross-cultural studies of family support systems for the aged have been marred by a lack of attention to the qualitative, internal mechanisms. This section's initial Web chapter seeks to avoid such a limited perspective. Using a variety of qualitative and quantitative approaches, from individual case studies to national surveys, Akiyama, Antonucci and Campbell provide a path-breaking study of intergenerational transactions between women in Japan and in the United States.[9] Drawing on exchange theory and Antonucci's concept of a life-long "Social Support Bank," the authors clearly delineate how the distinct cultural spaces in which reciprocity occurs regulates the flow of goods, services and emotions between adult daughters and their mothers. In Part III, the chapter by Jenike and Traphagan will expand on the caregiving role of women in Japan for their elderly relatives and discuss the dramatic changes that are altering these patterns.

IS NECESSITY THE GRANDMOTHER OF INVENTION?

In *The New American Grandparent*, Cherlin and Furstenberg noted that in the 1950s psychologists were talking about the appropriate distancing of grandparents from younger generations, and some even elaborated on a negative "grandparent syndrome," implying potential harm from meddlesome behavior to grandkids and adult children (1992:3). This perspective has certainly changed in a more positive direction, prompted by powerful changes in American family structures over the last three decades (Bengtson 2001; see Harper 2005 for a discussion of Europe and Ando 2005 for Japanese grandparents).

Grandparents increasingly occupy an "expanding position" in North American and European families and society at large, as many people are now grandparents for approximately a third of their life span, or about twenty-five years. This importance of grandparenthood within families is not only due to demographic changes, but also to the development of welfare states, resulting in greater resources for the elderly (in time and money), which in turn increased capacities of financial intergenerational transfers (Harper 2005; Hinterlong and Ryan 2008).

Within many non-Western cultures, the fostering of children by the grandparental generation is a well-established cultural mechanism and even a normative right that many older adults invoke. In fact, in some societies, such as among certain South Pacific Islanders, upwards of 40 percent of children get fostered by older adults who are not their biological parents (Dickerson-Putnam, forthcoming). As will be detailed by Hayslip in Part IV, for certain American ethnic groups a parenting role for grandparents has always been a normative, anticipated option. Joan Weibel-Orlando, in this section's second Web chapter focuses on Native American grandparents in urban California and at a reservation in South Dakota.[10] Compared to Euro-American background families, less-restricted boundaries between genealogical generations often provided the possibility for grandparents to have crucial roles as "cultural conservators" and even to request that they bring up as their own one or more of their offspring's children. However, in her sensitive portrayal of contemporary Native American life, Weibel-Orlando shows that there are a diverse variety of grandparenting models among the peoples she studied (Schweitzer 1987). These different ways of being an Indian grandparent reflect not only ancient, indigenous patterns, but also the needs generated by poverty-imposed stresses placed on the parenting generation. The lessons from her study can be profitably connected to Hayslip's discussion in Part IV on the growing custodial nature of grandparenthood stretching across culturally varied family formations (Schweitzer 1999; Mooradian, Cross and Stutzky 2007).

NOTES

1. At the end of the 1980s, ex-Governor Richard Lamm of Colorado raised the sensitive issue of the costs associated with the medical care of the terminally ill elderly and even suggested that terminally ill people may have the "duty to die."

2. To see the reaction to this book of a member of the younger generation see the self-published *Why Baby Boomers Suck!: (No Offense Mom)* by Finley Harrison. See also Kaskie et al. (2008).

3. A contribution to the qualitative discussion of legacy and intergenerational ties is found in Savishinsky 2006.

4. For an important study of popular culture and images of aging, see Blaikie (1999).

5. For a global view of the impact of postmodern aging, see Polivka (2000).

6. To take advantage of this trend, in North America especially, there have developed consulting and marketing organizations with names such as AgeWave, Primelife and Lifespan Communications.

7. Blogs for electronic elders include: "2young2retire" at http://2young2retire.com; virtual social networking is found at Eons, the Facebook for the over-fifty set; new third-age niche magazines include *Grand—The Magazine of Grandparents*; and senior-oriented cable TV can be found at "Retirement TV" (http://rl.tv/).

8. Walker George created in 2007 an award-winning documentary about the U.S. group, titled "Young@Heart."

9. For probably the best binational study of aging and generations between the United States and Japan, see Hashimoto (1996).

10. It should be noted that a transition is currently going on between the elder generation of respondents studied by Weibel-Orlando who refer to themselves as *Indians* and their children and grandchildren who are more apt to use the term *Native Americans*.

CHAPTER 8

Elders, Ancients, Ancestors and the Modern Life Course

Maria G. Cattell and Steven M. Albert

The life course perspective in aging research considers human lives in terms of person, place and time, and how the interactions of these factors provide shape or structure to experiences of aging from birth to death—or even beyond death into the ancestral realm. In the past quarter century, life course studies have expanded from a narrow focus on the temporal patterning of life stages to highlight more complex relationships between human development, cultural systems, demography and history. Bringing so many different perspectives to bear on the experience of aging is challenging, but, as Christine Fry tells us, "The study of lives is a messy business" (2003:271).

Messy as all these factors are, there is more to be considered when it comes to life course research. Until recently, most life course research, and even much gerontological research, has not considered the impacts of gender and other significant sources of inequality on individuals' experiences of aging and old age. In the mid-1990s, one of us found there was little published information on gender and health because most medical research in the United States was carried out on younger males, excluding women and older people (Cattell 1996). Researchers have often lumped "the elderly" into one undifferentiated category using chronological age as the defining characteristic. Feminist theory has not recognized age as a major factor producing inequality along with gender, class and race/ethnicity (Calasanti and Slevin 2006).

Such essentialist views are changing, however, and the complexly interwoven elements in the relations of power and inequality—gender, race/ethnicity, sexuality, social class and age itself—are receiving more attention from researchers. For example, medical research including women and elders has expanded greatly, and the role of race/ethnicity in elders' lives has been the focus of a good deal of research. Age is increasingly viewed as having subdivisions such as the terms in our title, *elders* and *ancients*, or the *young-old* (active, healthy) and the *old-old* (frail, decrepit). However, when it comes to life course research, gender is glaringly absent. In a recent review on aging and the life course, Richard Settersten did not consider gender at all (2006), though others have pointed out the need to take gender into account in life course research because of the enormous differences in female and male life patterns which are found everywhere (Rossi 1985; Calasanti and Slevin 2000; Moen 2001). Of course all this makes the study of lives an even messier business!

The burgeoning development of cumulative advantage/disadvantage theory is helping to sort out some of these complexities (Dannefer 2003a). For example, in the matter of health, females everywhere suffer lifelong cumulative disadvantages from cultural beliefs and practices such as parents favoring sons in the allocation of family resources (food, health care, education), female subordination to males and discrimination in economic opportunities, male violence against women, and the marginalization that often results from widowhood (Cattell 1996 this volume; see also Mirowsky and Ross 2005; Zarit and Pearlin 2005).

Defining the Life Course

We define the life course as *a patterned sequence of stages, defined by successive roles and statuses, through which individuals move during their lifetimes.* The life course is biologically based to the extent that it reflects psychobiological development (the "life cycle" or "lifespan") from birth to death. But, it is also powerfully nonbiological, constructed through cultural beliefs that can extend stages of life beyond death into ancestorhood, consider a similar stage of life to begin at very different ages, or assign quite different lengths of time to any particular stage. Elements of the life course are sometimes "chronologized" in the sense that transitions, such as movement from "youth" to "adulthood," are based on the number of years since birth (Settersten 1999). In many cultures chronological age is important for assuming or vacating roles and statuses, but in other cultures people either do not know their chronological age or other factors, such as birth of a grandchild or hosting key ritual events, can be equally or even more important. Among the Lak of New Ireland, Papua New Guinea, for example, hosting mortuary ritual for a deceased lineage member defines seniority and leadership capacity.

In this chapter, attention is first given to diverse perspectives on the life course from many disciplines. We then consider cultural distinctions in its definition, stressing cross-cultural variation in the stages of life and in particular, old age, which may have its own divisions such as young-old and old-old or ancients. This is followed by a look at explicit and implicit cultural models of the life course and its stages and transitions, followed by thoughts on old age as a "new" stage of life in the industrialized and postindustrial world.

Readers may wish to read this chapter in light of an earlier attempt to summarize the life course literature (Albert and Cattell 1994). To track changes in the now booming field of life course research, we begin with a brief review of the growing interest in the field and identify emerging principles that link different disciplines in their approach to the life course.

THE LIFE COURSE AS A MULTIDISCIPLINARY FIELD OF INVESTIGATION

The life course perspective has been embraced by scholars in many disciplines, including anthropology, history, developmental psychology, sociology, demography and epidemiology. Life course perspectives guide research on a wide range of topics, such as cognitive function, crime, disability, divorce, friendship, gender, health, identity and agency, intergenerational relations, migration, risk perception, spirituality, time use, violence and work.

The centrality of the life course perspective is evident in its prominent place in key handbooks in diverse disciplines. The life course has been the focus of chapters in all six editions of the *Handbook of Aging and the Social Sciences*, spanning thirty years, from 1976 to 2006. Early editions had only a single chapter on the life course; later editions have multiple chapters on the life course. In the newest edition, separate chapters are dedicated to particular facets of the life course, such as social stratification, health risks and disparities, and gender, and the overarching principle for the organization of the book is "aging and the life course" (Binstock and George 2006). The field has burgeoned to the point that the study of the life course now has its own handbook (Mortimer and Shanahan 2003) and volumes covering methodologies for life course research (e.g., Giele and Elder 1998; Heinz and Marshall 2003; Settersten 2003).

In our earlier global examination of the life course, we identified the following basic principles for study of the life course (Albert and Cattell 1994:59):

- The life course can be treated as a conceptual unit: aging "begins with birth and ends with death." At the same time, the life course is multidimensional in its elements, encompassing "interdependent biological, psychological, and social processes" (Riley and Abeles 1982:2).
- The life course is linked to a secular (time) context; that is, a specific social, environmental, and historical context.
- With increasing age, there is increasing variation among individuals in life course processes. Plasticity is a lifelong characteristic; that is, "behavior and personality are to some degree malleable throughout the life course" (Fry 1990).

Most researchers utilizing a life course perspective accept these premises, which have been very productive for investigation of life course transitions in American life. Following an early investigation of generational processes in an American industrial town (Hareven 1982), more recent research has applied the life course approach to transitions in rural American experience (Elder 1999; Elder and Conger 2000). An extensive array of longitudinal survey research, conducted primarily in the United States and other postindustrial nations, has demonstrated that the life course is more flexible, less standardized and more open to the possibility of change than earlier research indicated (O'Rand and Campbell 1999:61). A key illustration of this greater flexibility is evident in changes in labor force participation. Under pressure from increasingly older populations, Canada and the European OECD nations now seek policies that decouple age from work experience, or at least provide flexibility in work across the life span. The goal for this effort is "to develop a set of incentives that would allow parents to take extended leave during their 'prime' working years, while allowing older adults to work into their 70s" (Policy Research Initiative, Canada 2004). Thus, policy initiatives can recognize changes in life course patterning.

The power and challenges of life course research are well illustrated in ongoing cohorts that have been followed since high school graduation, as in the Wisconsin Longitudinal Survey (WLS), begun in 1957, or since birth, in the British Medical Research Council (MRC) National Survey of Health and Development that used a random sample of children born in 1946 (disc. wisc.edu/wls/; www.nshd.mrc.ac.uk/). The WLS enrolled over 10,000 people, and the MRC cohort includes over 16,000 people. Each cohort has been followed for nearly fifty years through periodic surveys, which in some cases include performance assessments of physical ability and cognition, biomarker studies and merged records from school assessments and medical contacts. The challenges of maintaining participation in these efforts over half a century are legion. People move. They change names and statuses. Likewise, investigator teams change. Researchers retire. Funding comes and goes. For all these reasons, true life course studies, in which people are followed over their entire lifetimes, are extremely difficult, and to this day there is no study that has followed a large cohort from birth to death. Thus, the half century of follow-up available in the WLS and MRC studies is an extraordinary resource.

The WLS, for example, seeks to answer a wide array of questions relevant to aging and life course processes including:

Which women and men will be "healthy, wealthy, and wise," and which will be less fortunate in their later years? ... How does the quality of life among the elderly depend on conditions and experiences in childhood, youth, and mid-life? ... What vocational or social activities lead to better cognitive and psychological functioning among the aging? ... When and how do the near elderly begin to prepare for their own deaths? How—and for how long—are the lives of parents disrupted by disability or death among their own children? How do family structure and history affect the transition to retirement? (Hauser and Rowan 2006:12).

These questions cannot be answered without the long view of lives lived in context, across many transitions, in which a common body of measures is obtained wave after wave. These studies suggest new complexities in the life course:

- Life course transitions are decreasingly tied to age: events in family, education, work, health and leisure domains occur across the life span at different (and many at increasingly later) ages than previously expected (Settersten 2006);
- Life transitions are not necessarily abrupt or irreversible events, but often gradual and even reversible processes. Such transitions as family formation, educational attainment, career entry and exit, and divorce and retirement are often more protracted and multidirectional than previously recognized (Hagestad 2002; O'Rand 2006);
- Specific life pathways in education, family, work, health and leisure are interdependent within and across lives; that is, trajectories develop simultaneously and reciprocally within and across individual lives (Angel and Angel 2006).

These aspects of the life course stress micro-level phenomena, occurrences related to individuals and families, evident in choices and life course patterns. Increased attention has also been paid to macro-level phenomena—social structure and economic and political contexts—and the linkages between micro and macro phenomena (Hagestad and Dannefer 2001). Still lacking, in our view, are cultural accounts of the life course that take into account the temporal perspective made possible by long-term fieldwork. Few anthropological investigations carry fieldwork forward over fifty or more years because such efforts are plagued by the same challenges as the WLS and MRC long-term follow-up of birth cohorts.

CULTURAL VARIATION IN DEFINITIONS OF THE LIFE COURSE

The life course is a broadly shared story of the ways lives unfold. Against the backdrop of chronologic time, maturational processes and age, shared models emerge to mark stages of development. This is the work of culture. Cultural conceptions of the life course always vary at least by gender and often by other factors, such as ethnicity and social class. Often these models involve implicit knowledge, what people know but do not ordinarily express, as in the American identification of frail old age with a return to infanthood, which is evident in speech forms—"infantilizing speech" and use of saccharine terms or "baby talk" to address the elderly—as well as preemptive control over decision making by relatives. But sometimes the models are culturally explicit, as among Maasai and Samburu pastoralists in Kenya who organize males into "age-sets" who enter and leave defined stages of life as a group, culminating in a "retired" state. We turn to these models of the life course as they apply to aging in more detail later in this chapter.

Across cultures and within a culture over time we often see variation in how "standardized" the life course is (Settersten 1999). Does everyone of the same gender (or ethnicity or social class) in a given time and place follow pretty much the same life pattern, with similar transitions from one role to another and similar timing of major life experiences? Is the life course seen as a fixed set of roles and statuses, or is it looked upon as a flexible set of options and opportunities from which individuals can construct identities as they age?

Cultures differ in where they stand along this continuum. Also, within any culture, we see variation in individual experiences of the life course. Individual agency and unpredictable events shape lives, even in age-set societies. These individual experiences are connected to historic or locally contingent factors, leading to flexibility in the timing, definition and sequencing of life stages.

Life Course Stages and Individual Agency

To illustrate how life course stages may govern a life, but also how a person may subvert or push the boundary of a cultural model, consider the life course of Maria Cattell, one of this chapter's authors. Her personal life course ran with, and then counter to, cultural definitions of the female life course. Born in 1934, she followed the normative path for middle-class women of her era: she went to college, worked for a few years, then was a stay-at-home mom with four children for almost a decade in the 1960s. Maria returned to the work force in 1969, but many of her friends and age peers did not. Eventually, in her forties, she became a "nontraditional" student. She went to graduate school, spent two years in Kenya doing dissertation research and earned a PhD in anthropology when she was nearly fifty-five, by which time she was a grandmother. Maria was "on time" as wife, mother and grandmother, but "late" in starting her career. The cultural norms of the 1950s that pushed women into the "housewife and mother" roles were powerful and hard to resist in this pre-women's movement era (Friedan 1963; Harvey 1993; Cattell and Schweitzer 2006). Today, in the twenty-first century, a majority of college students are "off-time" or nontraditional, suggesting that what was once nontraditional has become mainstream, and that the life course has become more flexible in America (National Center for Education Statistics 2002).

Most Americans would likely view the life course as a progression: from childhood and youth, marked by schooling; through adulthood, which is characterized by college or technical training, employment, parenthood and citizenship; to retirement and leisure-filled "golden years" followed by a decline into frailty. To this they might also add a "finding myself" period, a decade or so of wandering between adolescence and adulthood, which has been called the "odyssey years" (Brooks 2007). Whatever their view of the progression of a person's life, Americans would expect individual agency to play a big part in shaping a person's life course trajectory. But in many places, poverty, war and other forces limit individual agency. For example, among poor communities in South Asia, where child bondage and family migration for work are common, childhood has a different meaning, and formal education is unlikely to be part of this stage of life, and, for girls, prostitution may be normal (Dannefer 2001). Currently, in some African nations, children as young as ten or twelve are forced to become soldiers, surely a violation of our understanding of the separate spheres of childhood and adulthood, as it enforces a violent end to childhood and initiates adulthood at developmentally inappropriate ages. Even in the United States, a group's behavioral rules can limit individual agency, as among urban gangs that have their own markers for transitions from the lowest to the highest ranks in their gangs and the expectation of not living much past the age of thirty (Dannefer 2003b).

Old Age: Powerful Seniors, Declining Elders and Ambiguous Ancestors

A few examples (only a few among many possibilities) of cultural models of the life course follow. The Elizabethan and Thai models illustrate elaboration in the cultural organization of old age, with powerful seniors at the peak of their lives who then decline into "ancients" or frail elders. In some models, old age is not the final stage of the life course, as it is in many African societies where powerful seniors may decline into frailty and death but then become spiritually powerful as ancestors. Also, the boundary between very old person and ancestor may be porous, as in the case of Sukuma agropastoralists in Tanzania, among whom the very old live in an ambiguous zone between life and death, elderhood and ancestorhood. In this situation, death is not a sharp dividing line, and elders fade into an ancestral state in a gradual process that imbues those still living with the qualities and powers of ancestral spirits (Stroeken 2002).

Consider Shakespeare's "seven ages of man" (*As You Like It*, II, 7). This Elizabethan model of the life course has been rendered in a stained-glass composition (Figure 8.1). "One man in his time plays many parts, his acts being seven ages." The seven stages include infancy, "whining schoolboy … creeping unwillingly to school," lover, soldier ("seeking the bubble reputation even in the cannon's mouth"), judge or administrator, retirement based on frailty ("his big manly voice, turning again towards childish treble"), and finally "second childishness and mere oblivion … sans teeth, sans eyes, sans taste, sans everything." In this seven-stage model, the pinnacle is reached in middle age as the individual moves from the family to the civic sphere, and old age is a time of decline into childishness—a decline perhaps long accepted as inevitable, but that America's baby boomers are now currently resisting.

Compare the Elizabethan model to the nine-stage life course pictured in a Thai temple engraving (Figure 8.2). The same curvilinear shape appears, with the pinnacle again reached in middle age. The left side shows ascension through infancy, courtship, parenthood, and career, culminating in civic responsibility and statesmanship. The right side shows decline, indexed by use of a cane, increasingly stooped posture, and the shrinking of the body typical of old age frailty. A major difference between the Elizabethan and Buddhist models is the recycling of lives implied in the Thai conception, in which the infant emerges from, and the elder returns to, the same place. Asian systems stress decline, but also recycling, of lives into newborns (Thompson 1990; Albert and Cattell 1994; Lamb 2000).

Yet another model occurs in many African societies, where lives reach fullest potential not in middle age but in ancestorhood. In the worldview of many sub-Saharan African societies, the passage through death opens the door to a new life stage, that of ancestors, who—as the most senior members of their lineages—play an active role in the lives of their descendants.[1] For example, among mid-twentieth century Tallensi in Ghana, dead lineage elders were

Figure 8.1
Seven Ages of Man: An Elizabethan Model of the Life Course

Source: Nicola D'Ascenzo. *Seven Ages of Man* from *As You Like It*, 1932. Reproduced with permission from the Folger Shakespeare Library.

transformed into ancestor spirits with great power and authority, both mystical and worldly (Fortes 1961). Ancestors were fed at gravesites and crossroads and regularly consulted by their descendants. They were petitioned when crops failed or someone was sick, or when a lineage's fortunes declined. Ancestors' response could be to curse or to bless, to bring further disaster or good fortune. Junior lineage members were linked to clan ancestors through living elders who represented the ancestors. The living elders communicated with ancestors, spoke for them, and drew on ancestors' authority to enhance their own.

While Meyer Fortes was working with the Tallensi, a man named Teezien gave him a vivid account of the immediate, direct connection Tallensi saw between themselves and their ancestors: "We provide for them ... and beg crops.... If we deny him [ancestor], he will not provide for us, he will not give to us, neither wife nor child. It is he who rules over us so that we may live.... If you gave him nothing, will he give you anything? He is the master of

Figure 8.2
Thai Temple Engraving of a Buddhist Image of the Life Cycle

Source: Shinobu Kitayama, *The Aging Mind: Opportunities in Cognitive Research.* National Research Council. Washington, DC: National Academy Press, 2000, p. 222. Reprinted with permission from the National Academies Press, Copyright 2000, National Academy of Sciences.

everything. We brew beer for him and sacrifice fowls so that he may eat to satisfaction and then he will secure guinea corn and millet for us" (1961:186). Fortes challenged Teezien: "Ancestors ... are dead; how can they eat and do such material things as making crops thrive?" Imperturbable, Teezien responded: "It is exactly as with living people."

In her research in western Kenya in the mid-1980s, Maria Cattell found that for Samia people, as for Tallensi, Zulus and many other Africans, death marked the end of life, but not the end of a person's role in the family (Cattell 1989). Old women and men were closely associated with the ancestors and shared in the mystical powers of the spirits, especially in the power to curse (like Sukuma elders mentioned earlier). As spirits (*emisambwa* or *emisebe* in the Samia language), the dead used their spiritual powers to continue to affect their kin in various ways, for good or ill. This was true of women as well as men, for in this very patriarchal society where females were subordinated throughout life, ancestorhood brought equality. Ancestor spirits expected descendants to be named after them and appeared in dreams to their descendants. Such dreams could be interpreted by diviners, who advised their clients on sacrifices or other actions to be taken when an angry spirit was causing problems; and spirit mediums could communicate with the ancestors.

By the early twenty-first century, though Samia still speak of ancestors and even report being visited by ancestors in dreams, there seem to be few practicing diviners and spirit mediums. Beliefs about ancestors have been attenuated by influences such as Christianity and the Christian revivalist movement, formal education, and the increasingly cosmopolitan experiences and attitudes of rural Samia (Cattell 1992; 2008). The actions of individuals have also contributed to changed attitudes. For example, in the mid 1980s, Regina Makuda was caring for a grandchild who was named for her. In the indigenous belief system, to name a child after a living person would lead to problems when an ancestor became angry that the child was not named for her or him, and the angered ancestor would cause the child to become sick or even die. Some people criticized Regina for allowing the child to be named for her. But Regina, who as a born again (saved) Christian rejected many old beliefs and practices, was contemptuous of such criticism: "But is that child not doing well?" Customary Samia burial practices have given way to Christian burials, and for many, the belief that spirits of the dead hover around homesteads (where bodies are buried) and intervene in their descendants' lives is fading into the Christian belief that the souls of the dead go to heaven. Ancestorhood as a life stage has become even more ambiguous than it had been.

Among Samia, one of the conditions of being accepted into the community of the saved (which is not a church, but a cross-denominational revivalist movement) is that a person has to break the clay houses used for making sacrifices to ancestor spirits (Cattell 1992). While beliefs about ancestors may linger, it would seem that, like the broken clay houses, they have little power today among Samia and perhaps also in other African societies as they move into the modern world.

Progressive Loss of Competencies or Acquisition of New Capacities?

Some cultures conceive their lifetimes as a gradual loss of some vital quality that causes loss of function and social competencies. For example, the Bororo in Brazil see *raka* as a finite entity acquired at birth. The rapid loss of *raka* is tied to things such as too much sex or violation of food or other social taboos (Crocker 1977). This loss is directly tied to the physical markers of old age, such as wrinkled skin, loss of physical power and changed posture. It is believed one can stabilize the rate of decline in *raka* through control over sexuality and adherence to taboos.

In contrast, some cultures see the life course as a continuing acquisition of vital knowledge and spiritual power right through old age. Among many Australian aboriginal groups, a system of "sanctified keeping" allows the very oldest to keep the most important ritual and spiritual knowledge of their peoples (Maxwell 1986). As junior citizens graduate through elaborate age-set systems, they slowly acquire this secret knowledge of the "dreamtime," the period of creation in the world of ancestors. This is the privileged knowledge of older people, which makes them the bridge between society and its mystical origins and gives them spiritual power.

The Hua of the eastern highlands of Papua New Guinea link aging and changes in vitality to gender (Meigs 1984). Among the Hua, a person's gender status is determined by the amount of a substance called *nu* that he or she possesses. *Nu* is a life-giving substance that can be gained, lost, or transferred to others. Females generally have more than males, and that makes them dangerous to men; so men and women generally live apart, in men's houses and women's houses. Women transfer *nu* to men during intercourse and certain other interactions. Thus, during life men gain *nu* and women lose it. This transfer and rebalancing of *nu* allows people to reach a kind of gender equilibrium in old age, when they are no longer considered strictly male or female. Accordingly, old (postmenopausal) women can be included in men's house activities.

Curiously, the American model of aging is not so different from what might seem exotic ideas of gain and loss in old age. The Hua attribute the declining abilities of later life to loss of *nu*. We attribute the declines of later life to other kinds of losses, such as loss of physiological resilience, or, more simply, "strength" or "vitality." But the resemblance stops when we note that we isolate the elderly and consider this loss of resilience threatening and perhaps contagious. Think of the many people who refuse to set foot in a skilled-care facility or who are extremely uncomfortable there. Among the Hua, the very old dying elder is sought out to pass on her or his *nu*, and kinsmen may consume part of the deceased's body in order to incorporate into themselves the final gift of *nu* from their elder.

This brief review of cultural models of the life course suggests that the biological imperative of maturation and decline lends itself to a variety of cultural emphases. People everywhere age and die, but within African and other cultural systems personhood and agency are viewed as extending beyond death. Aging brings both decrements in physical strength and cognitive capacity and continuing accumulation of experience. Societies differ in whether they emphasize progressive loss or accumulated wisdom and power. Some consider middle age as the pinnacle of life and old age as a period of declining abilities and powers. Others focus on new, socially valued statuses in old age, such as Australian aboriginal elders who gain power from their close connection to the ancestral dreamtime and the Hua de-gendered powerful elders. Since the reality of senescence puts limits on conceptions of the life course in old age, the diversity of cultural models of old age speaks to the creative power of the human imagination.

EXPLICIT AND IMPLICIT MODELS OF THE LIFE COURSE

The stages of the life course may be explicitly articulated, as in East African age-set systems, or largely implicit. American ideas about the life course are largely implicit. Americans will tick off "childhood," "adulthood" and "old age" as stages of life, but will be hard pressed to say when these stages begin or end. For example, a National Council of Aging (NCOA) survey in 2000 determined that people dated the start of old age to vastly different ages, and that these ages depended most critically on the age of the interviewee. People in their teens thought old age began at age forty; people in their sixties thought it began in the seventies (Albert 2006). Men thought women were "old" at relatively young ages; women were more charitable about the start of old age in men. The implicit model of the life course in American culture is also evident in language, though Americans usually do not recognize that often the language they use to address or speak about the elderly is similar to that used for children (Albert and Brody 1996; Box II.1 this volume). Insight on the staging of life course transitions is best seen in African age-set systems, where elaborate rituals mark the transitions.

Formal Models of Life Stages and Transitions

Among Samburu of northern Kenya, each age-set is given a name, such as *Mekuri* or *Merisho*, and consists of males initiated since the last age-set formed some twelve to fourteen years previously. Each age-set moves up the ladder of life stages from *moran* (unmarried warriors) to elder (married men) in six stages: junior *moran*, senior *moran*, probationary elder (when a man may marry), junior (firestick) elder, senior (patron) elder, and father-of-*moran* elder (Spencer 1965). The fathers-of-*moran* stage, which may come around the chronological age of sixty and up (though chronological age is not the determinant for entry into age-sets), is followed by movement out of the formal system into the "declining elders" stage. Ceremonies mark the passage from one life stage to the next, thus making clear each individual's place in the system. There are clear expectations in regard to behavior in general and relations within and between age-set members.[2]

There is no similar system for Samburu women, who are either "girls" (unmarried) or "women" (wives or widows). Of twenty East African societies with male age-set systems, only three had a female equivalent, none of which was described by the ethnographers who reported on the men's systems (Kertzer and Madison 1981). In West Africa, women have various organizations through which they govern themselves and to some extent regulate relationships between women and men, including secret societies and political organizations paralleling those of men (Leith-Ross 1939; Okonjo 1976; MacCormack

1979) and at least three women's age-set systems (Gessain 1971; Ottenberg 1971; Kertzer and Madison 1981). Kertzer and Madison consider several possible explanations for the rarity of women's age-set systems, but it could also be that male ethnographers, following the bias of their times, were simply ignoring women or not allowed to observe their ritual.

Age-set systems, which were most highly developed in East Africa and native North America, represent an extreme form of age grading. Age-sets are lifelong identities that cut across kinship and residence and allow a group to assume statuses as a whole. Age-mates marry at the same time, are initiated into religious ritual as a group and generally take on social responsibilities collectively. Age grading, by contrast, is simply use of age (or indicators of plausible age) to assign both a social status and, most critically, senior or junior status. Thinking again of the American system, what does it take to be considered an adult? For some purposes, such as buying alcohol, voting or obtaining a driver's license, chronologic age is enough to establish "adulthood." But in other contexts, age twenty-one may not confer adult identity. Adults are expected to work to support themselves, buckle down and accept the responsibilities of marriage and parenthood, or serve in the military. Any of these social indicators may be used to assign status as an adult and serve an age-grading function. For example, today's Americans are ashamed of the high school graduate who stays home to play video games on the computer, as a sign that the gamer has refused to grow up. Until recently, the same was true for the college graduate who returned to the parental nest, though this has now become both common and acceptable.

Age grading is central for establishing deference relations between juniors and seniors. A wonderful illustration is given in Homer's *Iliad*. On the fields of Troy, young men defeat elders in a chariot race held by Agamemnon's army. But the victorious young men give their trophy to their elders. To do otherwise, the poet says, would be "unseemly." Similarly, in academic circles younger faculty are likely to use formal titles as terms of address in the case of senior scholars. Greater age implies seniority and a deference relationship, even though in practice these do not always work out in the manner of the Greek soldiers of the *Iliad*.

Life course patterns commonly change as new things, such as formal education and different economic opportunities, accompany shifts in social behavior and intergenerational relationships. A good example comes from Maria Cattell's long-term research on aging and social change among Samia farmers in rural western Kenya. One of her early research projects was to elicit Samia people's ideas about the male and female life courses, past and present, as well as events in their own lives (Cattell 1989). She found that the life patterns of females and males had been greatly altered in response to the many changes resulting from colonialism and incorporation into the global economy, processes that began in the early twentieth century. Transitions from one age status to another have changed, with some indigenous rituals completely gone, such as traditional wedding and infant naming ceremonies. Other ritualized components of the life course have also dropped out, for example, tests of a young man's strength (pulling grass to thatch a house, to see if he was ready for marriage) and of a bride's virginity.[3] Timing of some transitions has changed, with females marrying at later ages and males at younger ages.[4]

Wage employment and labor migration became part of the male pattern by the 1920s, and increasingly females are participating in it as well. With formal employment came formal retirement—something that did not exist in indigenous Samia society, except in the sense that a frail elder (an ancient, or in the Samia language, *omukofu muno*, literally "very old person") would withdraw from productive work and "just sit and eat." Family members would bring food to the old person who had no strength to work and who could do little more than sit all day on a stool or mat. Today, those who return from work outside Samia with a little pension money (often a lump sum rather than monthly payments) may have a very different experience of old age. They may resume the farming lifestyle and engage in other activities to generate income, utilize their work skills, have a social life and participate in community service. They are creating new lives for themselves in the new cultural space of retirement.

Governments, through laws and policies, can also be a powerful influence on the life course. For example, in Kenya, mandatory retirement age is fifty-five (for many years it was fifty-five for men, fifty for women), leading to retirement from employment by people who are still vigorous. We have already seen how, in the United States, chronologic age is a common criterion in legal requirements governing when someone can work in some settings (e.g., civil service) or drive, vote, inherit, receive pensions or state health insurance, or be accused of particular crimes. Age-based life course transitions can be "mandatory" (carry legal or financial penalties), as in the case of retirement at age sixty-five or the requirement that adolescents stay in school through age sixteen. Thus even where there are no formal or explicit models of the life course, as in age-set societies, there can be formal constraints on behavior that help to shape the life course.

Implicit Models of the Life Course

We have already seen how relatively unarticulated but shared ideas may govern thinking about the life course among Americans. Another example from American society is the May-December romance, the marriage between a woman and a man "old enough to be her father." This marriage is often socially condemned and implicitly likened to incest. This kind of age difference violates a model of the life course, where early adulthood and old age are viewed as distinct stages of life that should not be confounded. But wealth allows exceptions, as in the many African and Melanesian societies that allow older, wealthy men to take additional young wives. Think also of the many years that separate some American media personalities from their wives and the accusation of "gold-digger" sometimes applied to these younger wives.

The hallmark of implicit systems is the absence of ritual to mark life course transitions. Looking back to the example of when adulthood begins in American society, there is no common event or ritual. Entering old age is similarly unmarked, though it is commonly linked with retirement from employment. In this regard, Savishinsky (2000) has noted that retirement is often coupled with travel. He has convincingly argued that the long trip to a place one has always wanted to go may have begun to take on the function of a ritual transition, as it helps older people embrace a new freedom and articulate a new identity.

GLOBALIZATION AND THE MODERN LIFE COURSE: NEW CULTURAL SPACES IN OLD AGE AND RETIREMENT

The Samia of western Kenya illustrate how the life course can be impacted by historical processes such as globalization, the far-flung net of interdependencies created by communication technology, and an increasingly globalized economy of transnational commerce, capital and labor flows (see Fry this volume). Economic globalization manifests itself in our daily lives as voices in India responding to business calls made in the United States, "made in China" labels on almost anything (including "traditional" craft products), and "made in the U.S." cars produced by Japanese auto makers in American cities. This increasingly global economy will certainly affect labor force participation and retirement in profound ways.

In the United States, the civil rights and women's movements have greatly altered social and economic landscapes, and the American emphasis on independence and autonomy have encouraged individuals to shape their own life course. The simple "three box" structure of the life course (education, work, retirement) no longer describes the American model of age stratification (see Settersten 2006). We saw earlier how engagement with education and work often take various patterns, including concurrent as well as back-and-forth movement between activities. The rigid three boxes, which applied primarily to the white middle-class male life course, are being replaced by intertwined life trajectories. Formerly sharp transitions, such as college-to-work and work-to-retirement, have become processes that may go on for years. Marriage, which until recent decades almost always began with a wedding, appears to be shifting into a long process involving cohabitation and even childbirth before the wedding ceremony (if any) takes place. The situation is complicated further by new options for marriage and childbirth, such as greater acceptance of single parenthood, gay marriage, and very late pregnancies achieved through reproductive technologies.

Retirement as a New Stage of Life

Retirement in industrial nations involves exiting the work force and receiving a state pension, but this is not a universal phenomenon—and indeed, even in the industrial world such retirement is a fairly new phenomenon. Many societies have a variety of other practices that could be regarded as retirement, while some have none; and the social implications of retirement vary widely, from retired Fulani in West Africa being regarded as socially dead to Americans who look forward to retirement as an opportunity to embark on a new life (Luborsky and LeBlanc 2003). In many parts of the world, people, especially in rural areas, leave productive work only if their health forces them to do so, as was the case in the indigenous Samia model of frail elders "sitting and eating." The ancient Hindu life course model regards the ideal last phase of life to be retirement from the world to a spiritual life, with elders renouncing all social ties and becoming wandering ascetics with a begging bowl—though in practice, few Hindus follow this path (Savishinsky 2004; Lamb this volume).

In industrialized nations, retirement became a new stage of life in the twentieth century. It was invented by nations and businesses to reduce the number of older workers, who were presumed to be less efficient than younger workers (Quadagno and Hardy 1996). Retirement was made financially possible by government and corporate pension schemes. In the United States, for example, the first Social Security Act was passed by Congress in 1935, though initially few collected pensions because not many people lived to retirement age.

But life expectancies steadily increased in the twentieth century, from forty-seven years in 1900 to seventy-six years in 2000 in the United States. By the 1950s and 1960s, the life course of middle-class white males included education followed by steady employment, often with the same employer, until retirement at around age sixty to sixty-five (an age often mandated by law). The transition from employment to retirement was a single event, perhaps marked by a ceremony, perhaps not, and was followed by the start of pension payments. Retirement itself was a new cultural space, which the market quickly recognized and filled with senior discounts, senior centers, retirement communities and the lure of travel.

In recent decades, in a context of rapidly expanding globalization and corporate downsizing, mergers and job outsourcing, the nature of work has changed, and individuals must make many more decisions. No longer can a man expect to work for the same employer all his working life or to have a single career path. Middle-class white women, who once played homemaker to the husband's breadwinner family role, have entered the labor force in huge numbers, and they too undertake multiple careers, with multiple employers, and need to acquire many different job skills and from time to time retrain for new jobs (Merrill Lynch 2006). Along with these changes have come changes in benefits, from employer-managed pensions to those managed by individual employees, and changes in the way people retire and what they do in their retirement years.

Creating Meaningful Lives in Retirement

Individual choice also figures in what people do during retirement. Americans have many cultural stereotypes about retirement: being "over the hill," settling into a rocking chair, declining into senile dependence and then moving to a nursing home. For many retirees, retirement can amount to one-quarter of their lives. More and more of them are viewing "being retired" as a time for exploring and creating a meaningful life that is no longer largely defined by work (Savishinsky 2000; Katz this volume).

For example, for the hundreds of thousands of North Americans who call a recreational vehicle home, their nomadic lifestyle is a way to experience freedom and independence, explore new places and build community while living on wheels (Counts and Counts 1996, this volume Web book). These "RVing" seniors see themselves as living an adventurous lifestyle. As one woman who left RVing at age eighty-one said: "I was on the road for 15 years … [now] I am living in a senior complex.… Very lively here with tourists, but the seniors are not the same as 'traveling seniors.' Aches and pains and TV all day!" (Counts and Counts 1996:24). RVers have created a rootless, independent lifestyle of deep personal meaning and have become experts at building community over time and space and creating instant communities wherever they park their rigs.

For most retirees, home remains the place where they were living at the time they retired, though for them, as for RVing elders, retirement can be a time of exploration, personal transformation and service (also see Stafford this volume). Some retirees take up hobbies and/or use their expertise in volunteer or compensated activities in their communities. A long and active period of grandparenthood was another major life course change brought about by the longevity revolution. Today, for millions of grandparents (many of them retirees), grandparenthood includes primary responsibility for raising grandchildren (Szinovacz 1998; Hayslip and Patrick 2006; Hayslip this volume; Weibel-Orlando this volume Web book).

The baby boomer generation, now moving into retirement, has already begun shaping retirement into something very different from what their parents and grandparents created (Merrill Lynch 2006; Croker 2007). For example, rather than an abrupt transition, the shift from work to retirement is becoming a "blurred" status passage that may play out over a period of several decades, the "midcourse" between work and frailty (Moen 2003). This process of retiring may begin when individuals or couples (who tend to plan retirement jointly) are in their fifties or even younger, and involve a long period of planning for retirement income, activities and residence.

Boomers may leave their primary jobs and take on other employment in "encore careers" in order "to become a vital workforce for social change," as boomer Al Gore has done in regard to global climate change (www.encore.org; Wilson and Simson 2006; Freedman 2007). Indeed, columnist Ellen Goodman calls an encore career "an altogether new stage of life" (2007). Opportunities to recreate yourself and serve others abound—for example, at Civic Ventures you can join the Experience Corps, which offers "new adventures for service" (www.civicventures.org). Civic Ventures also makes awards such as the Purpose Prize, given to those over sixty "who are using their experience to transform our nation." The Senior Corps offers Foster Grandparent, Senior Companion and RSVP (retired senior volunteers) programs (www.seniorcorps. org). To qualify to serve in the RSVP program a person must be at least fifty-five years of age, a refreshing switch from the ageist attitude that older people have nothing to offer.

Another idea boomers are playing with is the "third age." Phyllis Moen sees it as the period from age forty through the sixties (2006). An enlarged notion of this period of life is being promoted by The Third Age Foundation, which envisions three stages of life: childhood followed by family and career, and then "the rest of your life" or the third age (www.thirdagefoundation.com). Here the third age covers the years from fifty to eighty and has four divisions: preparation, achievement, fulfillment and completion; and, it includes fulfillment and completion as "the last stage of life on this plane," apparently leaving room for postcompletion ancestral activity (www.thirdagecenter.com).

One thing is certain: Retirement "ain't what it used to be."

CONCLUSION: THE FUTURE OF THE LIFE COURSE AND LIFE COURSE RESEARCH

What does the future hold for research on the life course? Research on the life course matters because in today's fractured and fast-changing world, we need to understand globally interdependent lives and the ways people and institutions in different parts of the world affect each other (Settersten 2006). We need to understand history and social change in terms of the relationship between the "micro," or individual lives, and the "macro," that is, social institutions, the state and other structural components of the historical and contemporary settings in which individuals live. Such knowledge can contribute to policy formation, the development and implementation of programs, and individuals' search for a rewarding life.

Research on variables implicated in systems of inequality—gender, race/ethnicity, sexual preference, social class—will certainly continue to expand, enhanced by the idea of cumulative advantage/disadvantage across the life course. In the future, researchers are likely to do more linking of qualitative and quantitative data along the lines of the present authors' earlier work and engage in more cross-national and cross-cultural research projects (Albert and Cattell 1994; Furstenberg 2003). It also seems quite possible that life course principles will become the dominant paradigm for integrating sociology, life span psychology and history in the study of human lives over time (George 2003).

As for the future of the life course itself, Furstenberg makes the bold prediction that racial barriers will gradually disappear in the twenty-first century (2003). He also expects that ethnic differences will diminish as immigrants become more Americanized, social class will become more prominent in life course structuring, and greater longevity will bring about greater differentiation of stages within old age. We see gender inequities continuing to decline in coming decades, especially as women have greater opportunities to resolve life course quandaries regarding family and career conflicts and baby boomers explore old age as a time of opportunities and action.

The tendency for "deinstitutionalization" of the life course is likely to continue with risks and protections becoming increasingly individualized, for example, individuals making decisions about matters such as investing for retirement and choosing health insurance that had been a part of employment contracts (O'Rand 2003). In our crystal ball we see the forces of modernity and globalization continuing to bring about change, creating differences in life course patterns within societies, and, at the same time, making the life course more flexible and contingent everywhere.

NOTES

1. One of the most detailed discussions of ancestors ("shades") and their importance in everyday life is found in Berglund (1976). Berglund, not a Zulu himself, grew up with Zulu playmates and companions and became fluent in their language.

2. In practice the transitions are less abrupt than the definiteness of the ceremonies might suggest—senior moran, for example, may already behave much like elders and even be invited to join elders' gossip and discussions, or moran may be in conflict with the elders they hope soon to replace (for more on age-set transitions, see Gulliver 1963 and Foner and Kertzer 1978).

3. Today there are several ways to marry (customary, civil, church) but many people just start living together without a ceremony or wait until they have been "married" for some time and even have children before having a ceremony. Parents prefer to have a daughter's husband be well educated rather than strong enough to pull grass to thatch a house. Brides' virginity is a thing of the past: premarital pregnancies are common.

4. In indigenous Samia, girls usually were married (or forced to marry) when they were very young, but men had to wait until they could come up with bridewealth (cattle), often not until they were in their late twenties or even in their forties.

CHAPTER 9

Images of Aging: Cultural Representations of Later Life

Mike Featherstone and Mike Hepworth

INTRODUCTION: GLOBAL IMAGES

Why do we need to study images of aging? In part it is a result of living in societies in which images can be readily reproduced to circulate in public and private life. In many areas of the contemporary world, it is hard to avoid images of youthful, fit and beautiful bodies of ten associated with idealized representations of a consumer lifestyle. These images are now global as even a cursory glance at the Internet quickly reveals. At the same time these consumer lifestyle ideals are accompanied by negative images of overweight and sickly bodies, those people we encounter in public spaces in the mall and street whose bodies have somehow betrayed them. Older people are often included in the latter category and in ageist stereotypes are caricatured as frail, forgetful, shabby, out-of-date and on the edge of senility and death. In a number of countries, campaigns have recently been mounted to counteract such negative images of older people; in Denmark, for example, explicit efforts are being made to confront the caricature of the older people as negative and outdated. In Australia, the government of Victoria has provided $50,000 to promote positive images of older men and women not in terms of the youthfulness of their external appearance but in celebration of their continuing contribution to social life—one billboard in Melbourne, Australia, urged readers to "Look past the wrinkles." The Madrid International Plan of Action on Ageing (2002) included images of aging as part of the promotion of a new plan of action to promote more positive attitudes towards older people.

Such counter images of positive aging are increasingly evident, and it is also clear that the various attempts to redefine the meaning of old age over the last twenty years occur within a changing social context. We all live in a world growing older: in the United States it is expected that the proportion of people over sixty-five will double to 70 million by 2030 (Seabrook 2004:7). In Britain, the visibility of old people increased dramatically with the number of prisoners rising from 6 percent to 18 percent over the course of the twentieth century. Yet if we consider the question of aging on a global level, it is clear that globalization and the expansion of the neo-liberal market economy is producing a range of differential effects. We cannot assume that all countries and governments will have the resources to follow the same solutions proposed in the West. Will the image of the pensioner or senior citizen able to look forward to a consumer lifestyle retirement apply around the world? Images of aging cannot be easily detached from the politics and economics of aging.

SOCIAL GERONTOLOGY

In this changing and diverse social context there is an increasing tendency in gerontology to acknowledge the importance of images of aging. An indication of broader changes in the interpretation of the aging process can be found in Blaikie's analysis of representations of aging in popular culture (1999). In this text the author shows how evidence of significant transformations in social attitudes towards aging and retirement can be found in images of aging in photographs, films, popular fiction and the media.

It is therefore not surprising that the study of images of aging has gradually moved from a marginal position in social gerontology to occupy a more central position in discipline. Several examples can be cited: Shuichi Wada's study of the image and status of older people in Japan (1995); the analysis by Hummel, Rey and Lalive D'Epinay (1995) of the images produced by children in an international competition, "Draw your grandma," which involved children aged 6–14 years in thirty-three different countries; and Kaid and Garner's work (2004) on the portrayal of older adults in political advertising in America. In the United Kingdom, one of the key textbooks on aging by Bond, Coleman and Peace, includes a chapter by the authors of this article on "Images of Aging" (1993).

This tendency reflects the contemporary global understanding that the aging process cannot be adequately explained solely in biological and medical terms but is an interactive process involving social and cultural factors. From a biomedical perspective, the aging process after midlife is seen to be one of decline into a dependent old age, but the alternative view of aging as a complex process of interaction between biological, psychological and social factors has resulted in a more sustained interrogation of medical and policy-based models of aging, calling for an enlarged awareness of the aging process as lived experience which individuals and groups endow with specific meanings. If the quality of later life is to be improved, it is argued, not only are medical improvements necessary but people's attitudes towards the aging process and old age must be changed. This concern, as the examples briefly quoted above show, has directed attention to images used to represent the process of aging into old age.

WHAT ARE IMAGES?

How do we understand images? Who produces images and how are they disseminated? What is the relationship between images and the everyday world of lived experience? And how do we evaluate the potential for the reform of images in a more positive anti-ageist direction? What are the main directions of global flows of images around the world today?

On its most basic level an image is seen as a representation or copy of the original reality, as found, for example, in certain types of paintings, statues and photographs which aim to present an accurate likeness or "living image" of the human models. The impetus here is to produce valid documentary evidence of the person, as, for example, in a photograph of Queen Victoria in later life. Yet, as this reference to a royal and remote personage suggests, an image can also mean not so much an accurate copy or imitation of the actual individual but rather an impression, or incomplete rendition governed by interpretive and imaginative framing—something intended to reveal essential features of the persona, which are not evident in a superficial glance, or the preoccupation with an accurate recording of external appearance. A photograph of a famous older person may therefore be seen as an interpretation of the essential inner character of an individual which has been artfully constructed for public display. Other examples of such images of historical celebrities in later life include Gandhi, Albert Schweitzer, Einstein and Mother Theresa. It is the interplay between these two interpretations of the term "image" (copy and impression) which leads to disputes over the distortion of an image in which the accuracy, imaginative input and representativeness are subjected to close scrutiny as in the question: "what was Queen Victoria 'really' like in old age?" (Rennell 2001). A further interpretation of an image as a mental impression refers to a representation deriving from any of the senses, including sound impressions, touch and smell. But it is the impact of the visual which the phrase "images of aging most frequently connotes, and in the discussion in this chapter "images of aging" refers to the public representations of older people in a visually and age-conscious society.

IMAGES, THE BODY AND THE SELF

Behind the public image of aging are, of course, the "lived bodies" of individuals who carry embodied memories. As Rennell (2001) shows, the widely publicized image of Queen Victoria as the grandmother of her people was in sharp contrast to the lived reality of her later life where not even her closest physician was allowed access to her aging body. A similar example can be found in the concealment of the paralysis of the American President Franklin D. Roosevelt. The "lived body" of aging points to the way in which our identities are embodied and formed not just through internal biological and psychological changes, but through encounters with other bodies in direct face-to-face communication, or perceived more indirectly as when we look at someone across the street. As human beings, we experience a double aspect to our existence: our embodied identities work through both seeing (subjective perception) and also being seen by others.

In contemporary Western culture the dominant message is that a positive perception of the body is central to the way the body functions and performs. The perception of the body's functioning, health and outer appearance is formed in a social and cultural context which has two dimensions. It is firstly, predominantly, governed by the visual: a medium in which judgments (both positive and negative) are constantly made in the daily social interactions with others who can feed back positive and negative evaluations of the body. Secondly, it is a context in which we not only look at and are looked at by others, but in which we are confronted in our daily lives by countless images of the human body in the media and elsewhere.

In addition to the multitude of human images which can be found in paintings, drawings, statues, photographs, television, the cinema and the new digital media, there is the more fluid notion of body self-image (Ferguson 1997). This double sense of image—the image depicted and recorded in various visual media and the notion that our self-image is linked to our body images—suggests that the formation of our own body image and self-image take place in a cultural context in which images cannot be seen as transparent and neutral. Our perception of our own bodies is mediated by the direct and tacit judgments of others in interactions and our own reflexive judgments of their view, compounded by what we think we see in the mirror. Through this reflexive process we are guided by our culture to react emotionally and evaluate the relationship between public and self-images in ways which become habitual and taken for granted. In this way we learn different ways of seeing and assessing the repertoire of positive and negative body images and ways of looking at human bodies in different cultures. Every image of a human being is effectively an image of aging, given that it provides a representation of the face and body which is of a person at a particular point on a chronological time scale and therefore immediately marked in terms of linear age. But our bodies do not just age in time, in tune with the mechanisms of some inner biological clock, but are "aged by culture" (Gullette 2004). The fact that we have "cultured bodies," therefore, suggests that our bodies are never just biomedical entities but are perceived through a cultural matrix in which the visible signs of the aging of the body are not only externally displayed but have become regarded as manifestations of what is regarded in the Western tradition as a process of decline and loss.

IMAGES OF AGING IN SOCIAL GERONTOLOGY

Visual representations of later life occur widely in the history of Western art. David Lowenthal's study of memory, history and changing attitudes toward the past (1985) includes a chapter on "The look of age" where he discusses the tendency in Western culture to value the appearance of aging in objects (antique buildings, furniture, etc.) much more highly than the appearance of age in human beings. Antique objects age "gracefully" whilst human beings pass into a state of "decline." The idea that many people in Western culture find the external signs of human aging displeasing or a source of disgust (Elias 1985) is persistent and well documented, but it is not simply a question of the disgust provoked by the external appearance of age as such—negative attitudes toward aging extend beyond surface appearances to include attitudes toward the basic fact of chronological age. A good example is the celebration of the birthday in cards and other numerical markers of time passing.

As noted earlier, one of the central themes in the gerontological analysis of images of aging in Western culture is the pervasive nature of negative or ageist images and the importance of replacing this ageist tradition with more positive images celebrating old age as a valued period of the lifecourse. As Bytheway (1995) shows, ageism is closely associated with a particular form of collective social imagery which ignores the diversity of individual experiences of aging and lumps all older people together under a limited range of social categories. In his book, he compiles a record of visual and verbal images of ageism in order to show how deeply embedded they are in popular culture and their influence over our attitude towards older people. His examples include advertisements, cartoons, greeting cards and photographs of older people in care. Another striking example of the analysis of ageist imagery is detailed research by Warnes (1993) into the origins of the word "burden" and the ways in which it has become negatively associated with later life in the popular media and in political pronouncements about the "burden of old age" in contemporary society. As Warnes shows, this dismissive interpretation of old age is a social construction, reflecting negative beliefs and attitudes about old age rather than any valid objective evidence concerning the quality of life of older people or their ability to make a positive contribution to society. The experience of old age is thus shaped not simply by processes of biological change but through the power of the image of "burden" to shape our perceptions of growing older.

Ageism, then, refers to a process of collective stereotyping which emphasizes the negative features of aging which are ultimately traced back to biomedical "decline," rather than the culturally determined value placed on later life. This interpretation of growing older has been described by Gullette (1997), who has carried out extensive research into images of aging in fiction, as the "decline narrative." The decline narrative defines middle age (a period which begins around the age of fifty) as the point of "entrance" into a physical decline which continues relentlessly into old age and death. Gullette (1985) shows, in her detailed analysis of cultural intersections between fictional and non-fictional literature on aging, how this idea has become firmly fixed in the social imagination of later life.

Whilst the central concern of gerontologists with images of aging continues to involve a critical engagement with evidence of ageism, a number of recent developments have added a layer of theoretical sophistication to this area of study.

SOCIAL CONSTRUCTIONISM

Social constructionism provides a critique of the "decline narrative" and the ways in which old age is "naturalized" and fixed, by conceptualizing aging as a cultural category (Hockey and James 2003). It argues that the prejudice against later life, which the existing power balances operating in social and cultural life have helped to construct, can always be progressively reconstructed. A good example of this process is the effort which has been made to create active images of retirement as a dynamic phase of the lifecourse, in contrast to traditional images of retirement as a passive disengagement from social life and removal into a world represented by the "retirement uniform" prescribed for both women and men (Featherstone and Hepworth 1995).

Another example of the influence of images of aging on our interpretation of biomedical change is found in Gubrium's (1986) analysis of the processes involved in the social construction of Alzheimer's disease in America. In this research into the difficult issue of determining the origins of signs of confusion in older people, Gubrium shows how images of Alzheimer's disease in, for example, poetry written by caregivers (a popular image is that of Alzheimer's as a "thief" who steals self) are used by carers to make sense of the identity changes that have taken place in suffering relatives. The changes in social and verbal competence resulting from the biomedical changes associated with Alzheimer's disease have to be given meaning through the use of culturally prescribed imagery. On the level of everyday lived experience, Alzheimer's disease is not only a biomedical problem: it challenges the meaning of the self and of life. The problem is that Alzheimer's disease as a biomedical category is still imprecisely defined and there are serious gaps in the diagnosis of the origins of mental confusion in later life (see Traphagan Part VI). Gubrium argues that, faced with these problems, non-sufferers draw on visual and verbal images such as that of Alzheimer's as a "thief" to fill the knowledge vacuum. In this process "Alzheimer's disease" becomes a generalized label for all kinds of confusion associated with aging.

Hockey and James (1993) adopt a similar analytical perspective when they examine the role of images in the construction of old age as a process of infantilization. Older people are not, of course, children, but there is strong evidence that when in residential care they are often treated as if they are. Older people who have become dependent in some way on their carers are treated as having reduced claims on conventional adult status. Thus, when addressed by carers, they may lose the adult title "Miss," "Mrs." or "Mr." and be summoned like children by their Christian names or given anonymous diminutive titles like "dear" or "love." The use of the metaphor of old age as a childlike state or "second childhood" therefore justifies and supports certain forms of care in which older people are denied the status of being fully adult, and Hockey and James' analysis provides persuasive evidence of the power of images to influence the ways in which carers relate to older people.

Infantilization is, of course, regarded as a prime example of ageism and, as such, is damaging to the elderly's self-esteem. Self-esteem is regarded as a key factor in positive aging, and a crucial factor in the cultivation and maintenance of self-esteem is awareness of the approval of others. Self-esteem involves an affirmative interplay between the self and the external world; as described by Coleman (1993) it has two components: "self evaluation" (a comparative exercise) and "self worth" (1993:128). Self-worth arises out of positive interaction with others who perceive our value, and, if such positive evaluations are absent, then those older people who are directly affected are likely to experience a diminished sense of social worth (Coleman 1993:129).

The role of the approval of others in the maintenance of personal self-esteem raises another significant question concerning the influence of images of aging on the subjective experience of growing older. Images of aging create expectations in both younger and older people about how older people should speak and act. An important issue here is the discrepancy revealed in research between the subjective experience of aging and attitudes and expectations of others towards those they perceive as older. A useful way of conceptualizing the distance that may exist in everyday experience of aging between public images of aging and private experience is to think of aging as a kind of mask (Biggs 1993; Featherstone and Hepworth 1991, 1993). The image of aging as a mask is most commonly expressed in the words "I don't feel old." In this image, the body and the self do not closely correspond and the outward appearance and functioning of the aging body do not adequately represent the subjective experience of the inner self. The self, or the "I," in this model is usually experienced as "younger" than the body. The mask, as a sense of discrepancy between a "younger" subjective self and the outward appearance of the social category of "old person," is closely associated with ageist images. When images of old age are perceived to be negative then it is not surprising that older people may not wish to be identified as "old" or, as suggested above, may reluctantly enter into collaborative performance with others, during which they present themselves as old according to the conventional stereotypes. Old age thus becomes the performance of ageist stereotype and thereby perpetuates negative images of later life. As Coleman has indicated, a "culture's expectations of older people's roles within society have a vital place in encouraging or inhibiting personality change in later life" (Coleman 1993:96)—a judgment also supported in Kitwood's (1997) sociological analysis of the treatment of persons suffering from Alzheimer's disease. The difficulties in organizing speech and thought caused by neuropathology are aggravated by social interaction with those carers who refuse or are unable to help the sufferer maintain his or her former self. The self of the sufferer is thus masked not only by the disease but also by the social interaction of others. Negative and misleading images of Alzheimer's disease as "loss of self" thereby contribute reflexively towards the social construction of dementia.

CONSUMER CULTURE, POSTMODERN TENDENCIES
AND GLOBALIZATION

It has frequently been argued that a significant factor in the formation of cultural expectations of older people in society is the rapid expansion of consumer culture. This social development has played a crucial role in changing public attitudes toward aging and the experience of growing older. Not only does a greater part of social life revolve around leisure and the purchase and utilization of commodities, but the culture of consumption suggests a world of new opportunities of self-improvement, fulfillment and expanded possibilities as more and more activities are mediated through images of the good life (Featherstone 1991, 2001; Featherstone and Hepworth 1982). The imagery of consumer culture places a strong emphasis upon the body and body maintenance and the active cultivation of youthful lifestyles, including the potential to renew and transform the body through new technologies, and the integration into mechanic systems which makes possible cyborg and "posthuman" bodies. All of these present the body as renewable, and aging as something which can be held at bay and even "defeated" through purchase, hard work and dedication (Featherstone 1982).

The high value placed in consumer culture on visual imagery has been regarded as particularly influential by gerontologists, who are now beginning to explore the implications of consumer culture for the future of aging (Gilleard and Higgs 2000). But this is not to suggest that consumer culture only works through general stereotypes of idealized images of aging which everyone is persuaded to follow. Rather, consumer culture cannot today be seen as producing a unified dominant culture in which everyone follows the same pattern of behavior. Studies of media usage by older people and portrayals of older people in the media in America conclude that older people are "a diverse, heterogeneous group" (Robinson et al. 2004). In addition, what have been referred to as "postmodern" tendencies within consumer culture have become more evident since the 1980s, and are manifest in greater product differentiation and the exercise of personal choice, which can include the rejection of ageist imagery. As was noted in the anti-ageist examples from Australia, Denmark and Madrid (above), the struggle to promote alternative images of aging works directly against the youthful stereotyping of later life in consumer culture.

Consumer culture includes an expansion in the range of alternative and bohemian lifestyles, along with the growth of urban spaces of experimentation and identity exploration, especially in large cities. The traditional age-stereotypical dress styles are less in evidence and there has been a migration of more youthful and casual styles across the lifecourse. More positive images of aging and later life are evident, especially in retirement and self-help literature which seeks to blur the boundaries between middle and later life (Featherstone and Hepworth 1995), leading toward a less regulated and socially sanctioned "postmodern" lifecourse (Hockey and James 2003).

Under the impact of globalization, Western metropolises have become more diverse and multicultural with a wide range of ethnic styles and cultural forms evident. We are confronted by an expanding range of styles of dress, modes of adornment, body shapes and sizes and modes of self-presentation, which are more difficult "to read." There are therefore more varied and conflicting models of aging and later life in circulation, along with a diversity of family and lifestyle forms, ranging from traditional to extended families in which the grandparent role still operates, to single households in which older people have chosen to explore single lifestyles.

The direction of this change also has implications for gender distinctions in experiences of aging, which have also recently come to the forefront of gerontology. The emergence of feminist gerontology has focused attention on the important question of the difference gender makes to the process of aging (Arber and Ginn 1995; Bernard 2001; Woodward 1999). Feminist theorization of the body and aging has resulted in a number of studies of images of aging women, including representations of aging women examined in a historical context (Gullette 1985; Harper 1997; Mangum 1999; Woodward 1999). Since Sontag's pioneering article (1978), the negative impact of images has been seen to be greater on men than on women because of the relative importance of the appearance of women in a world divided into public and private spheres and with a gendered division of labor. But the global impact of consumer culture and the "postmodern turn" have, it is argued, destabilized the division of labor along lines of gender and this development has significant implications, at least as far as future generations of older people are concerned, for the experience of aging. As Fairhurst (1998) shows, men are now facing similar problems to women as far as the appearance of aging is concerned. Gullette (2004), too, has noted the merging of gender issues with regard to aging in response to changes in the occupational structuring of society.

While consumer culture offers body maintenance and fitness routines along with a more positive, active, energetic image of later life, it also provides fast food and the pleasures of the inactive life of the television viewer. Currently over 60 percent of people living in the United States are overweight, with around 20 percent of these defined as obese (Critser 2003). For the legions of "failed" dieters and gym-goers who cannot attain the body image ideals of consumer culture, there is the hope of the technological fix. The assumption of technological solutions to the problem of the aging process is also found in the treatment offered to women for the menopause, with hormone replacement therapy (HRT) widely advocated and used, despite evidence of cancer risk. The image of a "youth pill," of the desire to avoid the negative consequences of aging, is very much part of the publicity surrounding HRT. This now applies to men as well as women. While male menopause is clearly not a medical condition, the term has continued to resurface regularly in the media over the last 30 years, featuring a discourse of loss and decline with the usual consumer culture, medical and fitness remedies offered (Featherstone and Hepworth 1995; Hepworth and Featherstone 1982; Marshall and Katz 2002). With the help of the new "love drugs" such as Viagra, and a growing army of imitators (similar drugs are being designed for women), men are told they will be able to "enjoy sex forever." The problems of aging may well be featured negatively and ageist discourses may dominate, yet consumer culture always holds out new positive images of aging, exemplary profiles of the "heroes of aging" who fight decline, along with the "quick fix" solutions which are there to be purchased.

DIRECTIONS FOR FUTURE RESEARCH

As we have indicated, images are now accepted as an integral feature of the process of defining aging and old age which is the very basis of the discipline of social gerontology. Images shape and constitute both professional and lay conceptions of what it means to grow older, and therefore the treatment that older people receive. Not surprisingly, the study of the history of images of aging is the study of the history of our ideas about aging. And, on the level of practical everyday experience, the analysis of the care of older people and of patterns of social interaction in later life shows that verbal and visual images are regularly deployed and manipulated to produce aging and old age as a social activity. We cannot therefore escape the process through which images shape these definitions, but we can understand the context within which they constitute lived experience and enhance our awareness of the possibility of change. Images are always historical and therefore never eternally fixed. Nor are images neutral; they always carry a moral and political message concerning the value we place on older people and the distinctions we make between acceptable and unacceptable forms of aging (Hepworth 1995).

And yet serious gaps in our knowledge of images of aging remain. On the level of culture and history, we have only recently begun to collect and analyze the range of images available. On the level of lived experience, the sociological understanding of aging as a process of interaction through which older people compare themselves with others requires a great deal more research into how people perceive and respond to images—the role played by images in interpersonal relationships through which individuals make sense of growing older. There is also a significant gap in our knowledge of ethnic variations in images of aging (Wray 2003).

One of the most significant pointers to future research is a more nuanced sense of the process of globalization as generating both uniformities and differences [see Fry Part III]. The global postmodern, then, does not point to a new universal stage of postmodernity which supplants modernity, which everyone will have to go through; rather, it suggests a world of expanding differences which are also transmitted through the global media. The various economic, social and cultural power struggles evident globally open up the possibility that no single model of aging, such as the Westernized consumer culture image, will prevail. This possibility goes beyond recent gerontological concern with postmodern flexibility within a Western context (Gilleard and Higgs 2000) to prompt us to look more closely at alternative images of aging, for example in Chinese and Indian cultures, in the Middle East and Eastern Europe. Thus, the study of images of aging opens prospect of greater diversity in the future images of aging, reflecting wider shifts in the global distribution of power than have tended to predominate in the gerontological imagination.

NOTE

This chapter is from *The Cambridge Handbook of Age and Aging*, Malcolm Johnson, ed., 354–62. © Cambridge University Press, 2005. Reprinted with permission of Cambridge University Press.

CHAPTER 10

When Old Is New: Cultural Spaces and Symbolic Meaning in Late Life

Jennie Keith

Studies of old age and aging have often invoked the anthropological concept of culture in terms of loss. The loss of "traditional" cultural meanings, roles and practices has frequently been reported as undermining the position of the elderly. In this chapter, I regard the relationship between culture and age as more dynamic, more fluid and more reciprocal by exploring several ways age as a feature of social organization is defining new cultural spaces within which old age is experienced—such as new life stages, new norms, new communities. Exploration of these new cultural spaces highlights the role of older people as creators of culture, as well as tensions between age groups about new cultural space, and the influence of structural factors such as residential stability on the significance of age in social structure.[1]

THE LIFE COURSE AS A NEW CULTURAL SPACE

The life course itself exists within a dynamic cultural space delineated by age. In most postindustrial societies, it has become choreographed into a series of stages associated with normative expectations and schedules according to which we can be early, late or on time for universal human events such as becoming a parent, starting or stopping subsistence activity, being widowed or dying (Hagestad 1990; Settersten 2006; Cattell and Albert this volume). However, a staged life course is still not universally an elaborated or salient cultural feature (Fry 2003). For example, the cross-cultural research carried out by Project AGE found two sites—Clifden, Ireland, and the Ju/'hoansi villages of Botswana—in which there was no shared concept of life course or life stages. Neither individual persons, roles, norms nor expectations were categorized in terms of life stages. Our questions about these were perceived as puzzling, irrelevant or annoying (for a fuller description of Project AGE and its findings, see Keith et al. 1994 and Fry et al. this volume Web book).

Recognition that the staged life course is not a universal concept raises questions about the conditions that promote salience for the cultural concept of a life course, the forces that delineate its internal stages, transitions, and timelines, and the consequences such factors have on individual lives (Cattell and Albert this volume). These questions in turn connect to more specific queries about new cultural spaces created by and for old people (Sokolovsky volume introduction; Katz this volume).

Other researchers have pointed out that emergence of state-level political systems promoted institutionalization of a timetable for the life course, with many rights and obligations available or imposed at certain ages (e.g., Kohli 1986; Cattell and Albert this volume). This explains some of the differences across the Project AGE sites, but does not account for all of them, for example, the Irish town of Clifden. Even in the cases where some perceptions of the life course might be explained by state systems such as schools or pensions, it is also important to understand the *mechanisms* through which that influence reaches into individual lives. When we considered all seven of the research sites in Project AGE, the following community and individual characteristics appeared to give age or life stage greater cultural significance:

- Large and unstable social fields in which many individuals were not known to each other
- Higher predictability of life events, such as widowhood or loss of income from work
- More formal education
- Subsistence activity that is not primarily physical, but requires training.

In the settings where subsistence activity is not solely physical, and requires various levels of training, it defines life stages as part of a career. When work participation is directly related to physical capacity, for example among the Ju/'hoansi, that capacity is more significant than chronological age or an abstract notion of life stage or career. In Clifden, Ireland, for a different reason, work did not contribute to defining a series of life stages. In this community, very few people had formal employment. Because a high proportion of the population received welfare payments, or as they put it, "were on the dole," people of different ages were simply eligible for welfare payments from different government agencies.

AGE GROUPING, COMMUNITY CREATION
AND NEW CULTURAL SPACE

Where a staged life course *is* a cultural reality, there is the possibility of a new cultural space between work and death, often defined by chronological age, and given names such as retirement, young-old or *troisième* age. This is a relatively recent possibility because it requires an extended life expectancy, enhanced health and the economic resources to support individuals who no longer work. Within this new life stage, residential communities of older people have given "new cultural space" tangible form.

The emergence of communities within residential settings for the elderly can usefully be considered in the context of examples and explanations of community creation in other settings, as well as other examples and explanations of age as a basis of group formation. The comparison with examples of age-grouping at other points in the life span highlights the ways that non-congruence in perceptions and statuses of group insiders and outsiders affect the internal social relations of the age group.

Residential communities of older people, labeled villages, worlds or centers, appeared on the social landscape in the United States in the late 1950s and early 1960s. At first it was not obvious that any of these would become communities in any sense but marketing. However, in spite of negative stereotypes that were widespread at the time—waiting rooms for death, foyers for the tomb, geriatric ghettos—in many cases these age-homogeneous settings for older people did become communities. They provided a context for the emergence of new shared understandings, norms and practices that are significant cultural creations.

A number of anthropologists carried out ethnographic studies of the conditions and consequences of age-homogeneous communities, most of them sharing a fixed territory (e.g., Myerhoff 1978; Keith 1982; and see Silverman 1987 for a review),[2] but some traveling in nomadic groups of recreational vehicles (Counts and Counts 1992; Counts and Counts this volume Web book) or "snowbirding" seasonally between two locations, often one more and one less age homogeneous (see Katz this volume). Many of these studies have been in the anthropological genre of the voyage of discovery. We were reporting about what one writer called "the unexpected community" (Hochschild 1973). What we documented were both affective and structural dimensions of community, and patterns of social life that were not pale reflections of previous lives. In fact, frequently shared values included emphasis on commonalities, equality and reciprocity in the present tense, and rejection of efforts to translate past statuses into the new communities. "We're all old people here," was a common way for residents in one California residence I visited to express the sentiment, "Who does she think she is anyway?" In the same place, I observed other residents sanction a man who bought *two* units and combined them into one unusually large residence—they voted him off the elected governing committee.

Explanations for the development of community within age-homogeneous settings intersect with theory from many disciplines about community creation and also with anthropological theory about age as a feature of social organization. As creators of community within age-homogeneous settings, old people act like people. We do not need age-based explanations. Research in a wide range of settings has revealed factors that promote formation of community. Background factors—present when members of a potential community first come together—include such things as homogeneity in characteristics that are both visible and salient to the individual involved, lack of alternatives to the situation in which they find themselves and the extent and irreversibility of the investment they are required to make to be there. Emergent factors—which may or may not develop over time—include level of participation in group-wide activities, proportion of kinds of social contacts inside and outside the group, and extent of perceived interdependence among members of the potential community. These same principles that account for community creation among utopians, urban squatters, nation states or residents of total institutions effectively explain the ways that old people living together form, or do not form, the affective and structural bonds of community (Keith 1982).

Similarly, what anthropologists have learned about age-grouping in societies where age-grades are prominent features of social structure intersects with what we have observed in retirement villages, continuing care communities and public housing for the elderly. In both cases a strong influence on the internal relations of the age-group is the disjunction between the actual capabilities for social participation of the group members and the extent to which they are allowed to use those in the wider, mixed-age community.

The most prominent age-grade in most societies with age-grades, such as the Samburu, Masai, or some Plains Indians and Amazon groups, is the one in which late adolescent males find themselves (Cattell and Albert this volume).[3] These men encounter a strong disjunction between their physical maturity and their exclusion from social maturity. In spite of extensive symbolic elaboration of their life stage, they do not have full access to tangible resources. Although Masai or Samburu warriors, for example, have rights to special hair styles, costumes and rituals, they do not have the right to marry or take on central political roles. Ethnographers of communities in which these age structures exist have also reported very strong bonds of brotherhood within these grades, and a powerful emphasis on equality.

This comparison with retirement communities is informative. Although at the other end of the life course, again we see individuals who face a disjunction between their physical abilities and the social expectation that they not hold influential roles. Even without mandatory retirement laws, there are strong cultural expectations that older individuals "gracefully" step aside from many central roles, in spheres such as the workplace, the family and formal organizations in urban and suburban locations. Looked at this way, the emphasis on equality and mutual help that we find in the age-homogeneous communities of retired people parallels the brotherly bonds inside the late adolescent age-grades of Masai, Samburu or Plains Indians (Legesse 1973).

RESIDENTIAL STABILITY, SENIORITY AND OPPORTUNITIES FOR NEW CULTURAL SPACE

One of the questions Project AGE hoped to answer was about conditions and consequences of age-grouping among older people in our research communities. Would there be circumstances under which we would find

age-homogeneous groups offering the same kinds of opportunity for maintenance of personal identity and for peer support as we saw in the separate residential communities?

Age-homogeneous groups were most prominent as a way to channel social
interaction in the suburban U.S. community of Swarthmore, Pennsylvania.
Swarthmore is a suburb of Philadelphia, although its residents try hard to assert
an identity of "small town." In Swarthmore, we found that most community
organizations, including churches and leisure groups, were separated by age. In
Project AGE's other U.S. community, the Midwestern town of Momence, Illinois, some organizations were also subdivided internally into age groups, but
in sharp contrast to what we saw in Swarthmore, there was a seniority principle
operating in Momence. Long-term participation in various groups and public
arenas made it possible for individuals to move up a ladder of seniority, and
many community leaders were in fact older persons.

In Swarthmore, people talked to us about the seniority principle that had
existed in the past: the Junior Women's Club and the Senior Women's Club,
for example, were part of one organization, and people moved up a ladder of
seniority. By the time we did our research, however, there was only one Wom-
en's Club, and all its members were elderly. We observed other examples of
age-grouping within the churches, which had various labels for their internal
groups—Altar Guild, Bandage Group, Fellowship—but in fact were all separated by age. There were also bridge clubs, social gatherings and classes for
old people, all separate from those of younger ages. Age-separate channels for
both formal and informal social interaction appeared so natural to people in
this suburban community that the presence of older persons in a mixed-age
event, even a dinner party, was cause for a comment.

Although Momence and Swarthmore are differentiated by levels of income
and education, the salient factor most directly influencing the significance of
age as a social boundary was the difference in residential stability. The typical
adult in our study sample in Momence had lived two-thirds of their life in the
town. In Swarthmore, the most common answer to our query about years of
residence was five. Associated with these levels of movement in and out of
these communities is the dispersion of families. Two out of three people over
sixty in Momence had at least one child living in the town, and over half had
one or more grandchildren there. In Swarthmore, three out of four people over
sixty did not have a child living in town. For most of them the most basic unit
of multiage interaction, the family, was not part of their daily lives.

The mechanisms through which this difference in residential stability
seemed to affect the significance of age for channeling community life
included the presence or absence of the seniority principle in formal organizations and the strategies available to individuals for maintenance of personal
identity.

In Swarthmore, there was no stable audience to observe and validate movement up a seniority ladder. Neither was there a basis of legitimacy for younger
people to "wait their turn" or for older people to claim priority. A principle of

seniority, with its advantages for older people as social actors, is very difficult to maintain when individuals of all ages move in and out of a community. The exception we observed was among the Herero, nomadic herders, of Botswana. Here a lineal definition of kinship provided group membership, personal identity, and the benefits of a seniority principle even when individuals moved between villages. The lineage system gave them a portable identity and preserved their seniority. A partial parallel, available to some members of postindustrial societies, might be affiliations with national or international organizations, such as the Lions or Rotary clubs, which provide some "instant" membership and identity in a new location.

Another mechanism through which residential instability affects the lives of older people is the definition of personal identity or personhood. In Swarthmore, the most poignant comment I heard from older people, especially older women, was something like this: "No one knows who I was." Many older people living in Swarthmore had moved there as old persons, very often as widows, usually to live near a daughter. What they discovered was that their previous bases of personal identity—husband's job, volunteer work, career, recognition of skill in leisure activities—did not move with them. These sources of personal identity and value were like nonvested, nonportable pensions. Suddenly their identity in the eyes of others was reduced to being their daughter's mother, or possibly, a younger individual's grandmother.

The context in which older newcomers to Swarthmore found the possibility of re-creating an independent identity was in age-homogeneous groups and activities of various kinds. They joined these usually without much initial enthusiasm and usually with the strong encouragement of their children. However, like the residents of age-homogeneous residences, these older individuals often found friendships and strong support networks that helped them through illness, loneliness and bereavement. During the years of our research, we observed older people who were longer-term residents joining these groups and activities as well.

Once again, there is an interesting parallel with the late-adolescent men in the societies where age-grades are a prominent basis of social organization. The bonds among those age-mates also arise from a forced fraternity, and reflect a similar disjunction between actual capacity to perform more central social roles in a mixed-age community and exclusion from them.

RESIDENTIAL MOBILITY, RETIREMENT COMMUNITIES AND TENSIONS ABOUT NEW LIFE COURSE EXPECTATIONS

"I'm not ready to go!" I was once told by a widow in Swarthmore. She was in her early seventies, and telling me vehemently that she wasn't ready to move out of her home into a retirement community. Unlike many older residents of Swarthmore, she had been in the town for over forty years. What I heard from her was not only that she was not ready to go, but that she felt pressure from the expectation that at about her age she should be getting ready to go, or at the very least be making a considered decision about whether and when! As an ethnographer, I believe she is absolutely correct about this pressuring expectation. She is articulating the effects on older Swarthmore residents of an intersection between perceptions of a staged life course and a high level of residential mobility. The result is a definition of a life-stage transition at which older individuals, even those in good health and socially engaged, are expected to seriously consider moving away, and, in particular, moving into an age-homogeneous residence.

This life-stage transition brings together the new cultural space of the retirement communities, with emerging cultural norms promoting age-homogeneous channels for social life and personal identity in this suburb, and shows their influence on definition of life-stage expectations related to age.

In Swarthmore, there is an expectation, shared by residents of all ages, that at a certain point later in their lives, it is normal and appropriate for individuals to make a decision about moving away. For most, it's a decision about where to move—smaller home near a daughter? Retirement community? And if so, which one? Conversations about this are much like those that occur around an earlier life transition: Which college should I apply to? Will I get in, how much will it cost, and who else is going? The other major option for older persons in this suburb is to move nearer to adult children. And if so, whether to move to a retirement community there or into a smaller independent home?

For some the decision is about whether to move or stay. Those who don't move feel they are taking a major risk. As one older man said to me, "It's risky, it's a gamble, but we're going to give it a try." He was referring to their decision to stay in town, in the home where they had lived for many decades. Clearly, people do not all make the same decision. What they share is a response to a normative expectation that an appropriate event in this older life stage is decision-making about where to live. The enforcement strategy for this norm is much like that applied in this community to the family with a high school senior, with everyone asking, "Where is she going to go to college?" Older persons who do not visibly and audibly engage in decision-making about their residential future are nudged in that direction by frequent questions about what they are planning to do.

INCONGRUENT DEFINITIONS OF CULTURAL SPACE AND ACCESS TO SYMBOLIC AND TANGIBLE RESOURCES

There is a sharp contrast between the concerns older residents have about the risks of remaining in Swarthmore and the view expressed by many younger residents that the town is a superb place to grow old. They also enthusiastically value the presence of older people as a contribution to the "small town" atmosphere they treasure. However, little has been done in the community to address the perceived risks that push older people out of the town. (See Stafford this volume for examples of programs that make efforts to foster "elder-friendly communities.")

The most common reason older people gave for considering a move away from Swarthmore was their fear of becoming ill and being unable to stay in their own homes. Given that negative concern and the fact that many do move away, one might think that younger people in the town would have had a negative view of older residents. To the contrary, the younger people we interviewed emphasized their upbeat image of the town's older residents. They easily responded to our query about older individuals they knew who were doing well. There were many positive examples, sharing characteristics such as being optimistic, enjoying life, healthy, independent and above all "active." However, when we inquired about an older person they knew who was having problems, two out of three people under sixty could not even answer the question. They did not know any old person with problems. Probing further, we often discovered that they *had* once known such a person, but they had moved out of town. "She moved away from Swarthmore to a place where she could get medical care," or "she used to live here, but now she's in a nursing home."

Younger people often expressed their appreciation for the contribution older people living in Swarthmore made to the community. "You see wonderful old ladies tooling around the streets, digging in yards, all dolled up in town." More information about cross-age contacts emphasized the visual nature of the contribution younger residents saw the old people making. When we asked about what kinds of contacts people had with older residents, a prominent answer was, "I see her on the street."

For most older residents of Swarthmore who left to enter a retirement community, this was a strategy for meeting eventual health care needs in a way that preserved the most autonomy. Older people in Swarthmore saw the town as a place where it would be very problematic to grow even older. This view is strongly influenced by the emphasis on high-tech and institutional medical care in the United States. The contrast with the view of many younger Swarthmoreans that the town is special in part *because* of its lively older residents raised questions for me about why older individuals could not harness those perceptions to shape alternative strategies that would allow them to remain in town.

In fact, during the years of our research, there were efforts by elderly residents to create housing options or care networks that would make remaining in Swarthmore appear less risky. These usually dwindled, however, when several of the prime movers themselves moved out of town. The precipitating event for several moves was the occurrence of the kind of health episode they feared—an elderly widow suffering a stroke and lying undiscovered for several days.

I think the rosy view younger Swarthmoreans had of the elderly is in two ways an obstacle to their support for creation of facilities that would allow more older people to stay in town. The more benign interpretation is that the younger residents do not perceive the need for such facilities. A more pessimistic analysis would suggest that younger people enjoy the visual enhancement of vigorous old people "tooling around town," as a reinforcement of the desired definition of this suburb as a small town. Less vigorous old folks might not provide such a positive atmosphere. As long as social relationships across age lines are for the most part superficial, the turnover of individual elderly does not pose a threat to the symbolic presence of "wonderful old ladies" in the town. Acknowledgement of the actual needs and wishes of many elderly, on the other hand, would not only challenge their valued symbolic role, but might lead to calls for changes in policies, such as zoning, and use of funds, for example, for transportation.

Like other persons in a social category that carries potent symbolic significance for others—Native Americans and other indigenous groups, women in Mediterranean "honor-shame" societies[4]—older people in this suburb do not have strategies for translating their symbolic significance into tangible resources. In all of these cases, the positive symbolic characterization acts as both mask and obstacle. It conceals the true circumstances and needs of the persons behind it and creates a barrier to meeting those needs by impeding their access to authentic participation in the social setting.

One clue to what sustains the gap between symbolic significance and access to other forms of influence for older people in Swarthmore, as well as in the other cases, may be the separation of spheres of social activity for all of the groups mentioned. Like the older residents of Swarthmore, many indigenous groups, and women in many "honor-shame" societies, are restricted in their interactions with those who do not share the identity in question. From this perspective, Stafford's discussion in this volume about the wish of older people *not* to be separated from other ages takes on additional significance. The new "elder-friendly" community model, with its opportunities for cross-age social interaction, might offer the chance for the value placed on older residents to go beyond the symbolic. The lesson from Swarthmore, however, is that high residential instability, as an aspect of community, is quite difficult to prevent even by the most visionary planners. This undermines full personhood for individuals and creates barriers to nonsuperficial social relationships across age lines. Building opportunities for cross-age social relationships will require creativity and commitment.

CONCLUSION

Older people have been creative actors in the shaping of new life stages and new cultural spaces. In postindustrial societies, age-homogeneous settings have often offered the best opportunities for elders to maintain personhood, and to create new roles, even new communities. However, as many ethnographers have reported, separation from those of other ages is very seldom the initial wish of older individuals. A possible next step in cultural creativity that might reduce this tension is suggested by the organizational relationships between some residences for the elderly and neighboring colleges (Stafford this volume gives examples). Older people may find ways to use their age-bounded groups and communities as bases from which to open channels to other ages, first on the group level, and eventually for individuals.[5] Age-homogeneous bonds that have provided access to personhood and social participation not available in some mixed-age environments may eventually become a bridge back to fuller membership in communities that are truly "elder-friendly."

NOTES

1. I am grateful to the members of the Project AGE team whose research led to many of the findings discussed in this chapter. I also want to express special thanks to Christine Fry, codirector of the project, for our usual thought-provoking conversations when I was in the early stages of writing the chapter.

2. Landmark studies of age-homogeneous settings for the elderly include: Byrne (1974); Hochschild (1973); Fry (1979); Jonas (1979); Francis (1984).

3. Classic references for East African age groups include: Spencer (1965); Gulliver (1968); Legesse (1973); Stewart (1977); Almagor (1978); Kertzer (1978).

4. This term refers to societies in which the honor of women is a highly significant source of respect for the entire kin group. Loss of honor results in shaming of the kin group and may be punished in ways as severe as murder of the woman in order to restore lost honor. Peristiany (1964) is an important resource on this topic.

5. Examples of these opportunities on the individual level include cohousing that is intentionally multigenerational. My suggestion is that older people may be more able to promote such opportunities if they work from an age-group base.

CHAPTER 11

Global Perspectives on Widowhood and Aging

Maria G. Cattell

This chapter looks at widowhood from the perspectives of *variations in vulnerability* among widows, the *new cultural spaces* in which widowhood is being experienced and the *resilience and creativity of widows*. The focus here is on four places around the world: the United States, where widows tend to be relatively well off but have differing experiences related to education, race/ethnicity and other factors; Guatemala, where tens of thousands of women were widowed "unnaturally" during *la violencia*; India, famous or infamous for burning widows (actually very rare) and child widows (a very small proportion of widows); and sub-Saharan Africa, where AIDS has greatly increased the numbers of "unnatural" widows and the struggles of widows to survive.

Why focus on widows? What about widowers? Widowers are relatively scarce compared to widows. Women throughout the world tend to be younger than husbands, so relatively few men ever experience a spouse's death, whereas most women are likely to be widowed. Also, women are likely to live as widows for many years, since women live longer than men and are less likely to remarry, and they are more likely than widowers to be poor. Perhaps for these reasons, less research has been done on widowers than on widows, though in both cases much of the existing research has focused on the bereavement period rather than on long-term experiences of widowhood.

Around the world the proportions of widows and widowers vary, but the pattern is the same: much higher proportions of widows than widowers among older populations (over age sixty). Widows generally fall between 40 and 60 percent of the older population and widowers generally are under 15 percent, though China (with about one-sixth of the world's population) is a notable exception (Table 11.1). In terms of sheer numbers, the world's three most populous nations, China, India and the United States, have about 16 million widowers and about 51 million widows.[1]

Table 11.1

Proportions of Widowed Women and Men Age 60+ in Selected Countries

	Percent Widowed	
	Men	Women
Africa		
Egypt (1996)	11.8	65.4
Ethiopia (1994)	7.3	51.9
Nigeria (1991)	5.0	46.2
South Africa (1996)	12.2	48.6
Asia		
China (PRC)(1990)	23.5	51.4
India (1991)	11.0	54.0
Japan (2000)	9.1	38.5
Europe and North America		
Canada (2001)	9.7	37.3
France (1999)	9.9	39.8
Germany (2001)	10.5	39.0
Russia (2002)	15.6	51.5
United Kingdom (2001)	13.7	40.5
United States (2000)	11.2	38.9
Latin America		
Brazil (2000)	10.2	39.7
Mexico (2000)	14.2	41.3

Source: Calculations by Maria G. Cattell from United Nations Statistics Division Demographic Yearbooks (census dates in parentheses following country name).[2]

Not only are women around the world much more likely than men to be widowed, but as females they frequently suffer from the cumulative effects of lifelong gender inequities (Cattell 1996; Moen 2001). In most cultures, females, from infancy through old age, are less valued than males and have less access to resources such as food, education, health care, housing, employment and pensions. Females often have less secure rights to property such as land and livestock (for a rare exception, see Indrizal, Kreager and Schröder-Butterfill this volume, Part V). They are more likely to work in informal sectors of the economy, to earn less and to be poor. Women, more often than men, enter late life childless, yet economic inequalities make them more dependent on kin (especially their children if available). Ironically, they are also more likely to live long enough to the point of becoming frail.

Within this broad framework of female vulnerability, experiences of widowhood vary, with some widows better or worse off than others because of factors such as race/ethnicity, class, caste, education, income and living arrangements. Variations also arise from cultural and contextual factors including war, widespread poverty, behavior expected of widows and laws and customary practices favoring males. Even the definition of *widow* is not always clear-cut, as among

Guatemalan women whose husbands disappeared by state violence,[3] or African women, where questions may arise about whether they were in fact married even when they lived for many years with the late husband and had children with him. And in today's world, there are increasing numbers of "unnatural" widows—young women widowed by violence and AIDS.

With so many changes, new cultural spaces have opened up. They can be spaces in which widows experience intense poverty and powerlessness, heavy demands on their time and energy, stigma and ostracism. Yet in those same spaces, widows are creating new lives for themselves and engaging in collective action.

WIDOWS IN THE UNITED STATES: AN OVERVIEW

In 2003, among the nearly 36 million Americans aged sixty-five and over, 14.3 percent of men and 44.3 percent of women were widowed.[4] Among the "oldest old" (those aged eighty-five and over), only one-third (35 percent) of men were widowed compared to nearly all women (78 percent). These differences result from the greater age of husbands, greater longevity of women and the fact that widows are less likely than widowers to remarry, some because there is a "shortage" of eligible males, but many for a variety of other reasons, including loyalty to the deceased husband, family issues and a preference for their newly independent lives (Lopata 1996; van den Hoonard 2004; Youngblood 2005). Many widows move beyond grief and create meaningful and enjoyable new lives for themselves as single women (Lopata 1996).[5] In contrast, many widowers remarry and remarry quickly, even within the bereavement year, the first year following the wife's death. Of widowers who remain unmarried, some settle into their grief and become social isolates, while others are more resilient and learn necessary life skills (like cooking and cleaning), and develop a reasonably satisfying life as widowers (Rubinstein 1986[6]; Luborsky and Rubinstein 1997; Moore and Stratton 2003). It is possible that women tend to adjust better than men following the death of a spouse because women are likely to have domestic life skills and are better at maintaining social networks, though little research has adequately dealt with these issues (Martin-Matthews and Davidson 2006).

In the United States, older women are much more likely to be widowed than older men, and are twice as likely as older men to live alone (40 percent of women, 19 percent of men), but they are only slightly more likely to live in poverty (12.5 percent of women, 7.3 percent of men).[7] About 72 percent of older women and men completed high school or beyond (Table 11.2).

There are significant differences within the older population by racial/ethnic categories: those with high school or higher degrees include 76.1 percent of non-Hispanic whites and 70.3 percent of Asians, but only 51.6 percent of blacks and 36.3 percent of Hispanics (these statistics are not broken down by gender). Since education, in numerous studies throughout the world, has correlated positively with higher income and standard of living, such educational

Table 11.2
Selected Characteristics of Older Women and Men (Age 65+) in the United States in 2003

	Widowed	High School+	Living Alone	Living in Poverty
All age 65+	31.6%	71.5%	29.8%	9.9%
Women	44.3	72.0	40.0	12.5
Men	14.3	71.0	19.0	7.3

Sources: Federal Interagency Forum on Aging-Related Statistics 2004, 2006; He et al. 2005; Humes 2005.

differentials would predict that more black and Hispanic women live in poverty than white and Asian women, which is indeed the case (Table 11.3).

When a person is widowed, household income tends to drop, so older people who live alone are more likely to live in poverty than those living with a spouse. In 2003, only 5 percent of all older women and men living with a spouse were poor compared to 19 percent of those living alone. But in 2002, about 25 percent of black and Hispanic women were living in poverty compared to about 10 percent of white and Asian women, even though many of the latter lived alone (Table 11.3). These differences arise from lifelong economic disadvantages such as lower wages and less accumulation of material assets including Social Security and other pensions (Angel, Jiménez and Angel 2007).

The death of a spouse is an emotionally difficult experience for most people and widows often experience changes in their social networks such as becoming marginal to the social world of couples (van den Hoonard 1994; Youngblood 2005). But becoming a widow does not turn American women into social outcasts or second-class citizens, as can happen in some cultural settings. Many women's incomes drop when their husbands die, but most have at least a Social Security pension and Medicare health coverage to sustain them (though this is less true of black and Hispanic women). Such assets cannot be

Table 11.3
Proportions of Older Women and Men (Age 65+) in the United States Living Alone (in 2004) and Living in Poverty (2002)

	Living Alone		Living in Poverty	
	2004		2002	
	Women	Men	Women	Men
Non-Hispanic whites	41.1%	18.7%	10.1%	6.0%
Black	41.4	26.6	27.4	18.2
Asian	26.7	9.9	9.6	10.6
Hispanic (of any race)	24.8	15.7	23.0	19.8

Sources: Federal Interagency Forum on Aging-Related Statistics 2004, 2006.

taken away by in-laws and other kin, as occurs in many parts of the world where women (but not men) may lose property rights and access to productive resources when their spouses die. Nor have American widows had to deal with living in a war zone, like the Mayan widows described later, or in an AIDS-ravaged social system, like many African widows. Thus, many widows in the United States are healthy, financially comfortable, independent-minded, even "merry," while others struggle with problems such as low income or having to care for grandchildren.[8] Though there are disparities among American widows and suffering for some, most American widows enjoy a better lifestyle and have more freedom of action than widows in countries where the majority of the population lives in poverty and receives no government support and where women are subject to patriarchal rules that constrain their opportunities and actions.

WIDOWS IN GUATEMALA: VIOLENCE, AMBIGUITY AND TRANSFORMED LIVES

In Guatemala, conflict and violence have brought an "unnatural" widowhood to many women—unnatural because many would still have their husbands had it not been for their early deaths in war. Yet many widows in Guatemala, forced by circumstances to take on new roles, have managed to build new lives and, by exploring new cultural spaces, have created new identities and communities for themselves.

During Guatemala's thirty-six-year civil war, perhaps 150,000 to 200,000 Guatemalans (the majority being Mayan men) were murdered or disappeared, mostly by the army, though sometimes by leftist guerrillas. The number of Mayan widows increased dramatically from 1978 to 1985, the years of *la violencia* (the violence), a campaign of state terror aimed mostly at indigenous people. Today estimates of the number of "war widows" in Guatemala's population of about 12 million range from 40,000 to 75,000. Women whose husbands were disappeared may cling to the hope that their husbands will some day return. More commonly, the husbands are known to have been killed, because the widow herself or other family or community members witnessed the murder, though the bodies were buried by the death squads in clandestine graves. In either case, widows are unable to bury their husbands' bodies using traditional rituals, putting them in a permanent liminal state that is psychologically devastating and physically destructive, with much emotional pain and many bodily illnesses (Zur 1998; Green 1999).

These women have also experienced the collapse of the traditional Mayan system of widow support—a system of reciprocal aid and obligation founded on kin-based social relations, people's relationship with the land and the ancestors and a gendered division of labor in which men worked the *milpas* (land for growing corn, the staple food) and women cooked, cleaned, took care of children and wove cloth. Widows are "both mother and father now" and have to do the work of both (Green 1999:83). Under the traditional system, a widow's family would support her temporarily until she remarried. But that system requires having men in families. Now, because of the scarcity of men, most widows will never have the opportunity to remarry and consequently become long-term burdens on their families. To forestall this, widows' in-laws may chase them off their husbands' land, leaving the women with little ability to feed themselves and their families. Grown children often do not have the means to help widowed mothers because they themselves are struggling to survive. Zur found that many widows reject remarriage, some because of previous negative experiences or because they (especially older women) wish to preserve the psychological ties to their husbands (1998). Older widows with children to support them have less need to remarry and more authority to refuse offers of marriage.

This situation has created new cultural spaces in which widows have redefined their identities and taken on new roles as breadwinners—though this had already happened to a degree for women whose husbands had engaged in labor migration. Widows have become heads of families, the decision makers; they have become more confident in themselves. At the same time, they have experienced accusations and social isolation from other villagers and discord among themselves, including disagreements about how widows should behave in the presence of other widows and with other villagers. But many widows have come to like their new independence, being in control of the family economy, moving into new (male) spheres, acquiring new knowledge and having more freedom and autonomy. Some are questioning the old gender roles. The new cultural spaces opened up by the collapse of previously tight-knit communities have also led some widows to create alternative support networks and forms of community through development projects and participation in evangelical worship, both of which may help fill some of the social gaps left by *la violencia* (Green 1999). Some widows have become activists by forming or joining groups such as CONAVIGUA (National Coordination of Guatemalan Widows), which works to support widows and educate them about their rights.

While widows tend to be older, among Mayans many are relatively young. While older women have had to come to grips with a world gone radically awry from their once stable communities, younger widows (those under forty when they were widowed) have not experienced such stability. Though socialized into the same Mayan worldview as older women, younger widows have known only constant change (Zur 1998). And surely the repercussions from *la violencia* will follow them all the days of their lives. Their experiences of old age will be shaped by their memories of violence and the transformation of Mayan life ways wrought by violence. The civil war officially ended in 1996, but the violence continues. Widows are particular targets of violence, especially by village *jefes* (civil patrol chiefs) who make threats and foment discord among widows in order to strengthen their own positions of power (Zur 1998). Intimidation and rape are common. Widows may themselves be killed, especially if they join activist groups such as CONAVIGUA. Everyone continues to live in a state of fear (Green 1999). And the perpetrators continue to live among their victims—with impunity.

WIDOWS IN INDIA: POVERTY, PATRIARCHY AND THE VALUE OF SONS

India is famous for its widows—for *sati* (*suttee* in colonial texts), immolation of a widow on her husband's funeral pyre; for child widows; for ascetic widows devoting themselves to a spiritual life, but living miserably as beggars on the streets of India. These are stereotypes that do not match the real-life experiences of most Indian widows. *Sati*, always rare, was banned by the British colonial government in 1829, and today is so rare there may be only one instance in a decade (S. Lamb personal communication). Child widows—very young girls who were married to older men (sometimes much older men)—constitute a tiny minority (0.4 percent) of India's 34 million widows (Chen 2000). Some widows, abandoned by their families, turn to begging to eke out their days, perhaps making their way to the holy cities of Vrindavan and Varanasi in northern India, where they get meager meals and sleep in leaky huts in return for six hours of daily devotional chanting.[9] In reality, though, few widows are outcasts. In her 1991–1992 survey in seven states of India (both north and south), Martha Chen (2000) found that nearly 90 percent of the 562 widows she interviewed were living in the same village, and many in the same house, in which they had lived with their husbands. While it is true that millions of widows experience deprivation as a way of life, often it is because of preexisting and ongoing poverty (which affects a substantial proportion of India's 1.1 billion people). Being widowed in itself does not necessarily lead to impoverishment or social isolation.

Overall, variation characterizes the experiences of Indian widows, with dissimilarity deriving from differing state laws, customary laws and local variations in actual practices (Chen 1998, 2000). Upper caste Brahmans have the tightest restrictions on widows, while many lower castes place few or no restrictions on widows. Hindus consider widows to be inauspicious because of their association with the husband's death. Female sexuality, especially among upper caste Brahmans, is regarded as powerful and dangerous, to be controlled throughout a female's lifetime successively by fathers, husbands and sons. When Hindu women are widowed, they may undergo a social death and the loss of their status and identity as wives, through head-shaving, wearing only plain white saris and observing various dietary and other restrictions. However, there is a great deal of variation in these practices. For example, wearing plain white saris and dietary restrictions are practiced largely among the highest castes (often only Brahmans) and especially in West Bengal; head-shaving is almost never practiced any more (S. Lamb personal communication). In most middle and lower caste communities, widows are permitted to remarry, although in a different kind of ceremony that is not considered a full wedding. In practice, however, many widows with children have little freedom to remarry because they would not be able to keep their children with them in a second marriage (Chen 2000; Lamb 2000). As widows, they have limited or no employment opportunities; some lose their property rights.[10] A few are accused of being witches and some are even killed by in-laws who desire the widows' land.[11]

This contrasts with the experiences of Indian men, who are less likely to be widowed anyway and have no restrictions or limitations on remarriage and employment, do not lose property rights and, since men's sexuality is openly accepted, have no stigma, restrictions or taboos if they are widowed. But it also contrasts with the experiences of widows in India's matrilineal and Muslim communities and in southern India (where patriarchy is less intense than in the north). These widows are more likely to live among natal kin, have secure property rights, enjoy emotional and other support—and be allowed to remarry and work outside the home. A woman's position in the life course at the time she is widowed makes a big difference. Older widows (especially if post-menopausal and thus no longer regarded as sexually dangerous) have greater authority, personal freedom and autonomy, and are more likely to be secure in claims to land and other productive resources and support from married sons (Lamb Part V).

With a husband's death, sons become very important to a widow's well-being. A quarter of the 562 widows interviewed by Chen (2000) resided with another widow (usually a relative), 16 percent lived alone and about half lived with married sons in living arrangements that included shared living, "adjacent living,"[12] and alternating among sons—though no living arrangement guaranteed access to productive resources, food, other support or care and some widows without core-sident sons received financial support from sons working away from home.[13] Chen, calculating "vulnerability" as mortality risk, found that everywhere in India, the most vulnerable widows (23 percent) were living alone or in house-holds headed by persons other than adult sons (2000). Widows heading house-holds with no coresident adult son, or living in households headed by adult sons, were moderately vulnerable (59 percent). The least vulnerable widows (18 per-cent) were those who headed households and had adult sons living in them.

A great deal more could be said about Indian widows, but even this brief review indicates that few match the stereotypes of immolated widows, child widows and ascetic beggars. Rather, widows in India—like widows in many parts of the world—have varying experiences of widowhood and all too often their struggles are embedded in cultural systems favoring males and economic systems that keep them poor.

WIDOWS IN AFRICA: MODERNIZING TRADITION, TRANSFORMING OLD ROLES

In sub-Saharan Africa, about half of older women (aged sixty and above) are widows. A husband's death brings swift changes in a woman's life—emotional issues, loss of whatever support the husband provided and the question of remarriage. Remarriage is linked in many instances with the widow's housing and access to productive resources, especially land (Potash 1986; Cattell 2003). Land is important because the majority of Africans are farmers and grow much of their own food. In addition, widows often have dependents to support, perhaps with fewer resources than they had as wives. Some widows are even chased away from their homes by in-laws who want their land, though in many (probably most) cases widows retain rights of residence and access to land, or have alternatives such as rights with natal kin. But over the past century or so, modernization and development have wrought changes in informal support systems and the roles of widows and other older women, and women have had to be sensitive to these changes and creative in their responses.

For example, Kenda Mutongi describes how widows in Maragoli (a Kenyan Luyia community) responded to changing socioeconomic and political circumstances by using the language and gender roles intended to control them to appeal for assistance (2007). When harsh colonial policies made it difficult for children to meet their widowed mothers' needs and expectations, widows would take their "worries of the heart" to a public meeting of male elders and ask for the elders' protection. They presented themselves as dependent women and relied on cultural expectations regarding males as providers and protectors to get needed help. In the later colonial period and in the decades immediately following independence in 1963, widows turned to the courts and other legal bodies and used letter writing, lawsuits and the new "language of citizenship" to demand their rights as citizens. In both cases, the results were mixed: sometimes the widows got the help they asked for, and sometimes not.

Precolonial Africa was home to subsistence agriculturalists and herders. Africa's incorporation into the world political economy under European colonialism involved the introduction of money, a shift to cash crops, wage labor and labor migration, the growth of cities and slums and intensification of poverty. Christian missionaries brought new religions and female education for "domestic virtue," designed to teach domestic skills (by Euroamerican standards) and keep girls and women in the home and submissive to men (Kyomuhendo and McIntosh 2006; Mutongi 2007). In the past half century, the continent has experienced armed conflicts, genocides and famines resulting in widespread death, destruction and about 15 million people displaced from their homes. Sub-Saharan Africa also carries a heavy disease burden; for example, malaria kills 3,000 Africans (mostly young children) every day and reduces productivity among adults, thus contributing to increases in poverty. In 2007, Africa was the continent hardest hit by HIV/AIDS, with an estimated 22.5 million Africans infected and about 11.4 million children orphaned by AIDS (UNAIDS 2007).

Over the past quarter century, I have observed many transformations among Samia, a Luyia community in western Kenya (Cattell 2008).[14] In the mid-1980s, I lived for two years in Samia. The Samia region, then and now, is rural. Roads are dirt—mud or dust, as rains come and go—and most people are farmers. In the 1980s, houses with mud walls and grass-thatch roofs were common. Hardly anyone had electricity. Decades of labor migration created rural-urban and international connections and brought cosmopolitan influences such as newspapers and radios to Samia, but daily concerns and activities were local and rural. Today, more homes are "modern" (brick or cement with metal roofs) and many sport antennas for TVs powered by car batteries. At night, lights twinkle here and there across once-dark hills in homesteads with solar-generated electricity. In 1984, hardly anyone had a phone; during my 2004 visit everyone was giving me cell phone numbers and e-mail addresses (you can go online via satellite in post offices and private shops). There were many other indications of the influence of the wider world, including an AIDS warning poster at the entrance to Funyula trading center (Cattell 2008). One thing that had not changed in 2004: most people were still poor.[15]

Will She? Won't She? Marrying Again—Or Not

For a new widow, an issue that arises quickly is remarriage. Widows' freedom to make choices about remarriage varies. For Muslim women, divorce and remarriage are common throughout the life course and readily accepted, but seclusion can be an issue.[16] For example, among Nigeria's Muslim Hausa, younger widows are likely to remarry, reside with their new husbands and accept seclusion. But most Hausa women have in-home businesses and a woman in seclusion must depend on her children to carry out aspects of her business that involve leaving the house. Older widows may choose to remain single because it has business advantages—widows are not secluded. If such women do remarry, they are likely to arrange marriages that allow them either to maintain a separate residence or not be in seclusion in their marital home (Schildkrout 1986; Coles 1990). Among non-Muslims, some women choose to remain widows; others "marry" (often unwillingly) for ritual purposes only, to cleanse the pollution of death; and many are remarried (again, often unwillingly) through the levirate or widow inheritance.[17] The cultural rationale is that the new husband, levir or inheritor, will provide for the widow and her children—though in practice that may not happen, as women well know.

In the past, most Samia widows were inherited, but in recent decades some women are refusing it, preferring a widow's freedom (or even a widow's burdens) to what they see as the burden of another husband. By remaining widows, these women expect to be able to manage their own households and have more autonomy. Many times their refusal to be inherited occurs in new cultural spaces opened up by saved people, born again Christians who reject many local customs—including widow inheritance—as things of *Shaitani* (Satan).[18] Among the saved people's targets for change are burial customs and widow inheritance. While the rationale is religious, widows who reject being inherited are also rejecting patriarchal power and a husband's domination. Age also helps. Older women, at the top rung of the kinship ladder, have the confidence of age and experience and can be leaders in the politics of gender relations, bringing saved men along with them—as these men are supportive of widows' rejections of inheritance. Saved people have also brought conflicts to families and communities through their elitist assumptions and separatist behavior. At times the conflicts flare up; at other times they recede—a cycle that has continued for many years. In the mid-1980s, the conflicts were strong and often were expressed publicly at funerals, such as that of Oundo, an old man who died in December 1984. The conflict centered on the inheritance of Oundo's two widows.[19]

Case 1. Witness to Revolution: Samia Widows Say No to Men[20]

Many people are gathered in the home of Oundo, who left two widows, Anna, the elder wife, who is Catholic and saved, and Elizabeth, the younger wife, who is Protestant and not saved. Mourners at Oundo's funeral are divided in their religious persuasions. The divisions are physically obvious in seating arrangements and the presence of two choirs, Catholic and Protestant. The deepest divisions, however, are not interdenominational, but between the saved and the not-saved. Everyone is waiting for *obulori*, the "witness" (speeches) that are always part of a funeral. They are waiting for the widows to say whether they will be inherited and follow traditional burial customs. The tension is palpable.

Anna, the saved senior wife, speaks first. She tells the mourners that she had eleven children with Oundo and praises him as a good man who always took care of her. She does not speak to the matters everyone is waiting to hear about, although everyone expects her, as a saved woman, to refuse the customs. Then Elizabeth, the younger wife who is not saved, says she also had eleven children with Oundo and that Oundo spoke his last words to her. Oundo told her God was coming to take him on a journey. "The Lord relieved my husband of his problems. So there is no one who can say that any person did anything to Oundo." By these words Elizabeth is saying that Oundo's death was not caused by human agency (that is, witchcraft) but by God, so no purification rituals are necessary. "The second thing," Elizabeth continues, "is that there is no one who will bring here advice of inheritance of wives. Oundo refused. I am not saved nor am I Catholic but ... I cannot break his advice."[21] Thus Elizabeth calls on the authority of the dead husband to support his widows' refusal of funeral customs and widow inheritance. At her words some saved people say, "Thank you, thank you," and the Catholic choir (which is mostly saved people) sings a hymn. But the not-saved people are quiet.

The next speaker is Anjelina, sister-in-law to Anna and Elizabeth, a tough-minded woman in her sixties who refused to be inherited years ago. Anjelina is Catholic; she is saved. Anjelina recalls how she was forced to marry when she was a little girl, but says that is not how things are done today, for people have seen the light of God's new path. She condemns widow inheritance as incestuous.[22] The saved in the audience agree with her by clapping and shouting, "Let Jesus be praised!" The not-saved are very quiet. Anjelina continues: "I praise the Lord very much. When the inheritor comes and finds my son has brought me a kilo of sugar, he comes in and prepares tea for himself. And when I tell him to go out, he refuses." There is clapping and more praise of Jesus by the saved. Anjelina says: "We thank God who has given us light. He has really given us peace." The not-saved laugh at this, but Anjelina is undeterred: "God has made it that old women like us can control our own homes. May the Lord be praised!" Her saved colleagues echo the praises, but again, the not-saved are quiet.

Twenty years later, Anjelina remains saved—and a widow. And many women, some saved, some not, have followed the example of Anjelina and her sisters-in-law.

Case 2. Two Sisters-in-Law Who Refused Inheritance

"Is widow inheritance a good thing?" I asked Pamela Silingi (age seventy-one) in 1995. "It is useless, completely useless!" she spat out. She told me that when her husband died, he left three widows. One wife was inherited symbolically by a grandson, another was inherited by a son of the husband's brother, but Silingi, a woman who always knows her own mind, refused completely. "I have found that those who were inherited are just the same as me who was not inherited. We are all working hard and all surviving. So inheritance is useless." Today Silingi is still working hard, still surviving—and still a widow. In 2004, Silingi's sister-in-law Ndimu became a widow. Like Silingi, she refused to be inherited. Unlike Silingi, Ndimu was saved, so the saved people supported her decision—as did her family. Ndimu stayed in her house, caring for grandchildren and cultivating her husband's land, until her death in October 2007.

Where Widows Live: Home, Home Folks and Land Rights

Residence is not merely a matter of having a roof over one's head. Residence determines the people with whom a woman shares her daily social and work life and with whom she has conflicts and emotional bonds. It figures in rights to resources such as land and labor and is important for physical and emotional security.

In matrilineal societies, husbands often live in the wife's home—a plus for a woman as she has a stronger position with her maternal kin than among her husband's people. Among matrilineal Akan in Ghana, younger wives live in the husband's hometown or on his cocoa farm, but keep up lifelong ties with matrikin through gift giving and other forms of assistance. In their later years, many women (even some whose husbands are still living) return to their hometown, the village of their brothers, where they have rights in houses and farmland and, as older women, strong positions in their matrilineages—they can even become lineage elders (Vellenga 1986; Stucki 1992). In another matrilineal society, Gwembe Tonga in Zambia, a widow's best residential option is to live with a married son. Some still married women leave husbands to join a son. Perhaps they are anticipating challenges from in-laws to their rights to continue to farm the husband's land after his death, especially as the recent shift from matrilineality toward patrilineality has weakened the position of older women—though increasing poverty has also played a role (Cliggett 2005).[23]

Most African societies are patrilineal, with descent and property passing through and to males. Spouses usually live in the husband's home, so young wives are "strangers" with few rights and many duties. But by the time they become mothers-in-law and grandmothers, women have established themselves as persons with some authority and rights, including some rights to land. Usually the rights are to use the land, not to be outright owners, and often those rights are secured through the son or sons who are considered to be the owners.

Some reports have documented "landgrabbing," the dispossession of African widows from their land (White et al. 2002; Human Rights Watch 2003). Human Rights Watch (HRW) interviewed over 130 widows in Kenya who reported being chased from their marital homes and forced to undergo "remarriage" in the form of cleansing rituals (usually involving sexual intercourse). Awino Adipo: "I refused the ritual and then they [in-laws] physically attacked me. As a result of the attack I became blind in one eye" (p. 20). HRW reports that Kenyan legal experts and women's rights activists believe that "women's property rights abuses are widespread and increasing" (p. 6). Caroline Wanjiru: "My mother-in-law said that since my husband had died I could not stay there.... She told me to leave and took away all I had, including my clothes" (p. 23). Such anecdotal evidence conveys the anguish of the women and the resulting difficulties in supporting themselves and their children, but it is not enlightening about the extent of such abuses. Clearly some women have been dispossessed and some have suffered ritual rape or been forced to remarry—but how many or what proportion of widows have such experiences? As HRW says, these problems are "difficult to quantify" (p. 6).

In research on what happened to land whose male owners died of AIDS, Aliber et al. found little evidence of landgrabbing in more than 400 individual interviews and ten focus groups in three districts (counties) of Kenya (2004). They found many widows remaining on their late husband's land, just as I have found in Samia over the years and as Martha Chen found in India. Aliber's team found that, in spite of problems (especially stigma) associated with AIDS deaths, "most AIDS widows do not experience these challenges to their tenure status, and most of those that do are able to withstand them" (p. 155). These findings are radically at odds with the widespread perception that many widows are dispossessed of home and other property by their in-laws.

Another landgrabbing device is the use of witchcraft accusations (mentioned earlier in regard to Indian widows). Witchcraft beliefs are found everywhere in the world and throughout history. Much has been written about witchcraft in Africa as a system of beliefs to help people understand and explain events in everyday life and to assign blame for illness, death and other untoward events. So it is hardly surprising that witchcraft is sometimes invoked against a widow by in-laws eager to claim her dead husband's property. For example, in Tanzania some old widows have been accused of witchcraft and hacked to death with machetes so an in-law can seize their property (Kibuga and Dianga 2000). In Ghana, some widows are exiled to witches' villages, as described elsewhere in this volume (see Box I.1). As in the case of the HRW report on dispossession of Kenyan widows, the dramatic horror of such occurrences brings attention to them. But such reports overlook the fact that, in Kenya and Ghana and throughout sub-Saharan Africa, most widows are not dispossessed, are not accused of being witches and continue living with their families after the husband's death, like Ndimu, Silingi and Florence.

Case 3. Florence: A Widow Succeeds on Her Own

Florence, a saved woman widowed in 1994 when in her forties, was left with eight children to raise on her own. A hardworking farmer, she remained on her late husband's property and grew much of her own food. She also had a modest but regular cash income from employment. Her husband's parents, both saved and both opposed to widow inheritance, provided moral and spiritual support. In 1995, I asked Florence about widow inheritance. "I just chase the brothers-in-law away," she said. "Men would just eat me. They know I have a job and that is their aim. They would come and eat and contribute nothing." Her bitterness no doubt resulted from observing the experiences of other women who had been inherited and then abandoned by their "husbands." Florence carried on, seeing to it that her eight children had food and education. Now a grandmother, in 2004 Florence opened a chemist shop (pharmacy) in Funyula, the bustling trading center a few miles from her home. She remains a widow.

AIDS, Death and New Cultural Spaces: Old Roles Transformed

The forces of modernization have put enormous stress on Africans and their family systems of shared social support (Weisner, Bradley and Kilbride 1997). Ideally, persons in need are supported and cared for within their families. In practice many families suffering from illness, poverty, land scarcity and other constraints are overwhelmed in their struggles to care for all who are in need. There is just not enough—not enough money, not enough time, not enough energy—to go around. Even before AIDS, resources were limited and adults often had to make hard choices, such as paying their children's school fees *or* buying food and a blanket for a frail widowed mother. Now with many in the middle generation sick or dying of AIDS, the care of AIDS orphans often falls to grandparents, especially grandmothers[24] (Nhongo 2004). A critical issue here concerns shifts in family support that leave older women (many of them widows, nearly all grandmothers) with new burdens of responsibility caring for their dying adult children and orphaned grandchildren, new burdens of stigma and new worries about who will care for them when they themselves become too frail to work. However, media reports to the contrary, there is little evidence that extended families in Africa have rejected AIDS orphans on any scale; rather, they have taken responsibility "with remarkable generosity" (Iliffe 2006:117).

Historically, African grandmothers (who are often widows) have had important roles caring for and socializing grandchildren, including children born of premarital pregnancies (Cattell 1994a, 1997; Geissler, Alber and Whyte 2004). But the devastations of AIDS have transformed the grandmother roles of some women into sources of sorrow and stress, if not desperation, as they care for dying adult children and then find themselves the sole or chief support for orphaned grandchildren (e.g., Nyambedha, Wandibba and Aagaard-Hansen 2003). Unlike malaria victims, AIDS victims are stigmatized. Unlike malaria, which kills mostly children, the majority of AIDS deaths occur in the middle generation of working adults. So those who undertake to care for AIDS orphans must cope with stigma and the loss of the dead parent's income and labor.

As with widow dispossession, media accounts are heartrending: the frail old widow who is the sole support of ten or twelve grandchildren and has such great difficulty feeding them that she herself skips many meals. But how common is that experience? Over half of older African women (age sixty-five and over) live in multigenerational households with adult children and only 7 percent live alone, suggesting residential continuity for most women and that caring for grandchildren is done in extended family households (Bongaarts and Zimmer 2002). This is not to deny the extreme situations of some women. But the broader picture is that African families, and African widows, do as they have always done: they do their best to cope and, indeed, are resilient and creative even in the face of the AIDS pandemic.

LOOKING TOWARD THE FUTURE

In the United States, the future offers many hopeful and creative possibilities for widows. Lifelong inequities related to gender and race/ethnicity are slowly being remedied. In the long run, the effects of improvements in social justice will make widows less vulnerable to poverty and its companions such as poor nutrition and health. There will be a generational effect on widowhood, as more and more baby boomers join the ranks of widows. Will they follow the paths of their mothers and grandmothers, many of whom were "housewives and mothers" and, as widows, continue to do many of the same things they had done as wives? Boomers tend to be better educated and have more material assets than previous generations. They have followed career paths different from their parents and already are reshaping retirement (see Cattell and Albert this section). Boomer women are likely to be retiring from careers rather than continuing lifelong housewife roles. Will these women evolve different ways to cope with loss and develop social networks, two of the more critical issues of widowhood? Will boomer widowers, who have done more housework than their fathers, be better at self-maintenance?

Sarah Lamb (Part V) has written about old age homes as new cultural spaces being explored by older Indians, including widows living in large urban areas. In the United States, the new cultural spaces we call retirement communities have proliferated in recent decades (though most Americans "age in place," in the homes they were living in when they retired). Many such communities tout the security they offer and play on ideas of leisure and the golden years. Will baby boomers be more interested in retirement communities that promote livelier ideas such as "active living"? Some boomers in south-central Pennsylvania have formed a network called "Downtowners" and are working toward an intentional community in the city of Lancaster (lancasterdowntowners.org). Downtowners do not want to live in a conventional retirement community, but they do want to be part of a community. They like urban amenities and being able to walk to many destinations. Some already live in the city and others plan to move there within a few years. They buy their own homes and live independently, but have a network of friends to call on for information, advice and assistance, and with whom to share activities. It is too soon in this venture for many Downtowners to be widowed, but it is likely that when that happens, widows will have creative, community-oriented approaches to their lives.[25]

Elsewhere, the picture is not so rosy. In Guatemala, for instance, there has been a truth commission (the Historical Clarification Commission) that issued its report in 1999, but violence continues to make "unnatural" widows, while perpetrators continue to live with impunity and even hold high government positions. The Rigoberta Menchú Tum Foundation[26] and other NGOs are working toward peace and reconciliation, but it will be a long struggle. In India and sub-Saharan Africa, widows face patriarchal cultures and legal systems, poverty and disease as they struggle to achieve lives of dignity and provide for their children. Widows are being helped by their own local efforts such as Uganda's TASO,[27] the Women and Law in Southern Africa Project, and the Self-Employed Women's Association (SEWA) in India, and international efforts such as various UN agencies, the Gates Foundation and microcredit projects like Grameen Bank. Often change comes all too slowly while individuals continue to suffer. It would be foolish to predict any immediate end to poverty, disease and discrimination, but we most fervently hope for it.

NOTES

1. These figures come from censuses in 1990 (China), 1991 (India) and 2000 (United States); if more recent data were available from China and India, it is likely the numbers would increase considerably.

2. These data were calculated from the following source: http://unstats.un.org/unsd/demographic/products/dyb/dybcensus/V1_table2.xls.

3. *Disappeared* is used as a verb in regard to the disappearance of individuals primarily through state violence; the individual's fate usually remains unknown.

4. Statistics in this section are from *Older Americans 2004* unless otherwise stated. In the 65+ population, 75 percent of men and 43 percent of women are married; others are either divorced, never married or widowed.

5. Similar patterns have been described for widows in Australia, Canada and Europe (Byles, Feldman and Dobson 2007; Chambers 2005; Davidson and Fennell 2004).

6. Rubinstein's research included men living alone who were widowers, divorced and never married.

7. Overall poverty among those aged 65+ dropped from 35 percent in 1959 to 10 percent in 2002.

8. For a recent collection of articles about widows in the United States and elsewhere, see Jenkins (2003).

9. A few, the lucky ones, are accepted into Aamar Bari (My Home), a housing complex founded by Mohini Giri, where they eat well, learn skills and have decent shelter (Giri and Khanna n. d.).

10. Among patrilineal Hindus (80 percent of India's people), a bride leaves her natal village to live in her husband's village. Land inheritance usually is from father to sons or other male relatives (if no sons).

11. Though women rarely own land in their own names, they may have customary use rights to land and/or have it registered jointly with a son or sons. Even a young son with inheritance rights helps a widow's land claims. See Agarwal (1994) on women's property rights in India.

12. *Adjacent living*, a term coined by Drèze (1990), refers to living in the ancestral housing but separately from the rest of the family, with the separation sometimes marked by a physical barrier.

13. Of Chen's 562 widows, 62 percent had married sons. Many widows have young, unmarried sons. Drèze (1990) estimated that about 12 percent of rural Indian women were sonless.

14. Samia are a subgroup of Abaluyia, a Kenyan ethnic group (or tribe) of over 3 million people in 1999. In 1989 there were about 60,000 living in Samia Location (now Funyula Division); in 1999, there were 73,875.

15. My research among Abaluyia in Samia and also Bunyala (to the south of Samia) has focused on aging, older persons and their families and socioeconomic and cultural changes. Methods have included informal conversations, in-depth interviews, surveys, observations of daily life (Cattell 1989, 1994b). As always, I am grateful for the invaluable help of my Luyia coresearchers, especially John Barasa "JB" Owiti of Siwongo village and Frankline Mahaga of Port Victoria and Nairobi. Special thanks to Frankie, JB and their families for their love and hospitality over the past quarter century. Thanks also to Medical Mission Sisters (especially Sr. Marianna Hulshof), former administrators of Holy Family Hospital at Nangina and the many pupils and staff at Nangina Girls Primary School (now St. Catherine's) who have welcomed me over the years; and to Samia officials who supported my research, particularly my old friend, Fred Wandera Oseno, Chief of Funyula Division (Samia) since 1997. Above all, *mutio muno* to the many people in Samia and Bunyala who have let me share their lives in various ways. The research was funded by the National Science Foundation (grant BNS-8306802), Wenner-Gren Foundation for Anthropological Research (grant 4506), a Frederica de Laguna Fund grant from Bryn Mawr College and private sources, including my late husband, Bob Moss.

16. Seclusion or purdah is the Muslim custom that wives "do not leave their homes during the day except to attend ceremonies, visit relatives, or procure medical treatment" (Schildkrout 1986:135).

17. The levirate is marriage with a man (often the husband's brother) from the deceased husband's kin group; any children born are considered to be children of the

dead man. Widow inheritance is similar, except any children born are children of the inheritor.

18. The saved movement is an outgrowth of the Revival, a religious renewal movement that originated in Rwanda in the 1930s and spread rapidly in East Africa; its influence in Samia became apparent in the 1970s (Cattell 1992). It is not a church, but rather, a charismatic movement that crosscuts denominations.

19. Polygyny (often called polygamy), the practice of a man having two or more wives, is widespread in Samia.

20. For a fuller version of this case study and more on widows' resistance, see Cattell (1992; 1997:83–85).

21. Many saved Samia are Roman Catholics who form their own support groups ("tea groups"). The church has sometimes tolerated, sometimes rejected, the saved (Cattell 1992).

22. She says: "Is there any child in this world who takes the blanket shared by his father and mother and shares that blanket [sleeps with] his mother?" The real-life referent for her metaphor of incest is the fact that a widow can be inherited by her co-wife's son, who is also her son in Samia kinship.

23. Construction of Kariba dam in 1958 led to forced relocation of Tonga from fertile river lands into areas of uncertain rainfall, which have become places of environmental degradation and extreme poverty as Tonga strive to grow their crops in an unsuitable habitat (Cliggett 2005).

24. As is true around the world, African women are the primary family caregivers.

25. My interest in Downtowners is not remote—though I am not a boomer, but am the mother of boomers. I have been a Downtowner since its inception and have not yet moved back to Lancaster (where I raised my family many years ago). This is real life meeting social science—which happened to me previously in 1995, while I was writing about widows and became a widow myself (Cattell 1997).

26. Rigoberta Menchú Tum is a Mayan activist and 1992 Nobel Peace Prize winner.

27. AIDS has provoked many grassroots responses, one of the first and best known being TASO, The Aids Support Organization, tasouganda.org, founded in 1987 by an AIDS widow, Noerine Kaleeba. Through counseling and support groups, TASO teaches people to live positively with AIDS. TASO has supported over 100,000 people and become a model for many NGOs in Africa (Iliffe 2006).

CHAPTER 12

Web Book: Exchange and Reciprocity among Two Generations of Japanese and American Women

Hiroko Akiyama, Toni C. Antonucci and Ruth Campbell

Available at www.stpt.usf.edu/~jsokolov/webbook/akiyama.htm.

Using a variety of qualitative and quantitative approaches, from individual case studies to national surveys, Akiyama, Antonucci and Campbell provide a path-breaking study of intergenerational transactions between women in Japan and the United States. Drawing on exchange theory and Antonucci's concept of a life-long "Social Support Bank," the authors clearly delineate how the cultural construction of reciprocity regulates the flow of goods, services and emotions between adult daughters and their mothers. The comparison of these two societies is particularly important as it allows us to hold relatively constant the factor of urban-industrial development while comparing the effect of dramatically different cultures on the lives of the elderly. Here we see that in Japan the continuing pattern of high elderly coresidence with adult children is embedded within a cultural system with different values and perspectives on the nature of intergenerational reciprocity. Other key chapters dealing with Japan are found in Part III, by Jenike and Traphagan; and in Part VI, by Traphagan and by Willcox et al.

CHAPTER 13

Web Book: Grandparenting Styles: The Contemporary Native American Experience

Joan Weibel-Orlando

Available at: www.stpt.usf.edu/~jsokolov/webbook/weibel.htm.

Joan Weibel-Orlando, focusing in this section on Native Americans she studied in urban California and at a reservation in South Dakota, makes a strong contribution to our knowledge about how cultural context affects the grandparenting role. Here she finds a broad cultural space with fluid boundaries between genealogical generations that provides a context for cross-generational cultural transmission and fostering of grandchildren. The lessons from her study can be profitably added to the articles on the ethnic aged in Part IV.

PART III

Aging, Globalization and Societal Transformation

Jay Sokolovsky

The local is not transcended by globalization, but rather that the local is to be understood by global relationships.

> Savage, Bagnall and Longhurst (2005)

A famous Far Side cartoon shows a scene of tribally dressed natives, perhaps living along the Amazon, inside their simple thatch abode. They peer through a window at goofy looking, pith-helmeted first-world scholars arriving by canoe on their river bank. You notice the natives clutching a variety of fancy electronic gadgets in their arms. With panic in their eyes, they seek to hide these signs of modernity as someone shouts to his compatriots, "Anthropologists, Anthropologists!"

Such cartoons really hit home to anthropologists who must take into account the local-global nexus implied by the quote leading-off this section. Consider the implications of these kinds of changes. On the one hand, it jokingly illustrates a key point in Part III's first chapter by Chris Fry: the overly optimistic anticipated benefits for "less developed" peoples of an accelerated movement of consumer goods, people and capital across once inaccessible boundaries. On the other hand, it also obscures the fact that overall the enduring economic and social benefits from this explosion of "free" trade pacts, privatization of governmental functions and Internet accessibility end up helping small, affluent sectors of national citizenry—often those who needed it least. Along with VCRs and DVD players in Mexico or Kenya has come "Structural Adjustment," imposed by the IMF or World Bank to liberalize markets, end government support for basic commodities and services and stimulate foreign investment. Such imposed reforms have often resulted in loss of jobs to local citizens and in less effective and more expensive goods and services.

Until recently, the primary model for considering how massive worldwide change has impacted the elderly has been "modernization" theory. It tries to predict the impact of change from relatively undifferentiated rural-/traditional-based societies with limited technology to modern urban-based entities. This shift is marked by the use of complex industrial technology, inanimate energy sources and differentiated institutions to promote efficiency and progress. Third World countries are said to develop or progress as they adopt, through cultural diffusion, the modernized model of rational and efficient societal organization. While such a transformation is often viewed as an overall advance for such countries, a strong inverse relationship is suggested between the elements of modernization as an independent variable and the status of the aged as a dependent variable. Donald Cowgill, first by suggesting a number of discrete postulates and later in developing a more elaborate model, has been the most dominant writer on this subject (1974, 1986). The hypothesized decline in valued roles, resources and respect available to older persons in modernizing societies is said to stem from four main factors: modern health technology; economies based on scientific technology; urbanization; and mass education and literacy.

Validation of this paradigm has been uneven and has spurred a small industry of gerontological writings, which debate the proposed articulation of modernization and aging (see Rhoads and Holmes 1995:251–85; and Aboderin 2004 for excellent reviews). Historians have sharply questioned the model, saying it is not only ahistorical, but that by idealizing the past, an inappropriate "world we lost syndrome" has been created (Laslett 1976; Kertzer and Laslett 1994). For example, summing up research on the elderly living in Western Europe several hundred years ago, historian Andrejs Plakans states, "There is something like a consensus that the treatment of the old was harsh and decidedly pragmatic: dislike and suspicion, it is said, characterized the attitudes of both sides" (1989).

A good example of the complexity of this issue is seen in a study of three untouchable communities in India (Vincentnathan and Vincentnathan 1994). The authors show how in the poorest communities, the assumption of respect and high status as a prior condition did not hold. Here the elders had no resources to pass on. Modernization programs that included providing material resources for the elders became a new basis for binding together the young and old. However, increased education of the young led many children and young adults to feel superior to parents, fostering a distinct change in generational relations, closer to the predictions of modernization theory.[1]

BEYOND MODERNIZATION AND TOWARD GLOBALIZATION

The dramatic upsurge of older citizens remaining alive in Third World countries is a legacy of the last three decades. The demographic changes detailed by Kinsella (Part I) have been intertwined with alterations in economic production, wealth distribution and the often violent devolution of large states into smaller successor nations. Properly understood, such changes are but the latest wave of globalism emerging since the 1970s. Called "Super Capitalism" by Robert Reich, it features radical expansion of communication technology, multicountry agreements such as NAFTA to promote the unimpeded flow of capital across national borders, unprecedented population movement and shifts in the location and nature of production of goods and services (2007).

Globalization and the Moral Economy

Within this new "Culture of Wealth," despite the rise in numbers of billionaires, global inequality has dramatically accelerated. At the start of this new wave of globalization, in 1970, the difference in GNP wealth between the poorest and wealthiest nations was 88 to 1; in 2006 this differential had risen to 267. Such growing inequalities have had an impact on the United States. Despite impressive production of wealth from 1970 to 2000, there was a 7 percent *decline* in relative wages and benefits, a dramatic decline in employer-supported pension programs and a record number of Americans now lack health insurance (Henrickson 2007). As we will see in Part VI, it is the costs of Medicare and Medicaid that over the long-run will bankrupt the nation if our broken health care system is not mended. In the United States, a specific impact on the health of the most vulnerable elderly has been share-trading of nursing homes, as is done for entities like Dunkin Donuts, the *Wall Street Journal* or Wal-Mart. We will see in the book's last section how this has seriously worsened both the care of our impaired elders and the working conditions of those keeping them alive.

Beginning in the 1990s, neo-liberal economists began to expand their view of the "aging crisis" to a global arena. The basic argument as put forth by the World Bank in *Averting the Old Age Crisis* (1994) is that informal and public sector programs are incapable of handling the impending demographic imperatives brought about by aging in the developing world (see also Chawla et al. 2007). They stress allowing the private and voluntary sectors to fill the coming needs in social welfare and reducing state provision of support to only the most extreme cases of need. A presumption in such a model is that universal public pensions and other public support programs undercut "informal," family-based systems of support for the elderly. The work of Lloyd-Sherlock in Latin America (1997) and Briller in rural Mongolia (2000) provide a strong critique of this perspective. Briller for example showed that pensions can have a very positive effect on reinforcing the preexisting family-centered sentiments and practical support of the aged, while not "crowding out" traditional systems of filial devotion and assistance.

Others, such as Christine Fry in this section's first chapter, suggest that it is the actions of organizations such as the World Bank that substantially reduce the capacity of developing countries to provide for a "moral economy," that is to meet the educational, economic and health care needs of their growing populations (see also Polivka and Borrayo 2002; Harrison 2007; United Nations 2007c). Fry's chapter focuses discussion on the risks globalization imposes on the life of older adults. Her work sets the stage for examining this issue in diverse community—and national-based cultural settings—where, in essence, the globalized rubber hits the demographically aging road (see also Neilson 2003; Phillipson 2007).

FILIAL DEVOTION AND THE GOD OF WEALTH

While whole new social landscapes focusing on autonomous older adults are glaringly obvious to the casual visitor to Florida (see Katz Part V), this is also happening in the most unexpected societal contexts such as China, India, Japan and Italy. Here the plaintiff cry of "family is everything and will take care of the elders," often echoes off of empty rooms in closed elementary schools, especially in rural areas. East Asia is a global epicenter for considering the collision of unprecedented populations aging, with equally unrivaled engagement with capitalism (Choy 2006; Yun and Lachman 2006; Miller 2007; Powell and Cook 2009).[2] China, with a confluence of the globe's most rapid and massive urbanization and an exceptional rate of population aging, is just learning the limits of cultural scripts centered on son-dependent filial devotion (see Ikels 2004a; Hashimoto and Ikels 2005).

Zhang's chapter on China undertakes a monumental task, to understand the realities of aging in a nation with a fifth of the planet's citizens, a deeply rooted non-Western cultural heritage and a profoundly changing economic system. This has placed its elders at the leading edge of a globalizing world. Hong Zhang takes her experience of having grown up in Mao-era China, with her extensive anthropological research in both rural and urban areas, to capture the incredible dynamism of aging in the world's most populous nation. Since the 1980s and the end of the collectivist period, China has embraced what some have called the "God of Wealth" (Ikels 1996), while at the same time its population had begun to age at a pace equal to Japan. Most state efforts to support a rapidly growing older population have been concentrated in urban areas, where nonfamilial social and economic infrastructure supports are concentrated and are invoking new cultural constructions of aging and retirement. The new urban late-life script stresses age-peer mutual support and health, promoting outdoor activities. This is in competition with the more traditional late-life pattern of dependence on adult children and confinement to the home.

MULTILOCAL FAMILISM MEETS TWENTY-FIRST CENTURY REALITY

Aging in Translocal Communities

Among the most common processes to provoke local level change in the industrializing world is the delocalization of social and economic resources that sustain and connect families with their natal communities. Viewing this process in Africa, Weisner uses a construct of "multilocal" families to think more realistically about kin support (1997). In many of the rural places anthropologists have worked, economic necessity and desire and changed patterns of transportation and communication have created translocal and increasingly transnational communities (Baldassar, Baldock and Wilding 2007). Throughout Asia, Latin America and Africa, increasing numbers of a family's young adults must seek employment far from home communities (Torres 2006; Browne and Braun 2008). Zhang, in her chapter, finds that a combination of urban migration and neglect of rural areas has created dramatic hardships for elders in those areas. However, this has certainly not been a universal result of youthful urban migration, as recent work in Thailand clearly indicates (Knodel and Saegtienchai 2007; see also Indrizal, Kraeger and Schroder-Butterfill Part V).

Unlike for Asia, Latin America until very recently has received scant attention in terms of the social consequences of aging (Gomez and Zavala 2004; Palloni, Peláez and Wong 2006; Gasparini et al. 2007). The chapter by Sokolovsky, set in a Mexican indigenous village, examines how familial, work and public spaces in which people age have been transformed as the community has grown from a village to a town.

Here, a substantial portion of a community's citizens, while still residing in their home community, have almost daily reliance on nearby towns and cities for economic sustenance, social interaction and cultural ideas. In his work, Sokolovsky tries to understand the factors that have kept elders integrated in the heart of this rural community. This has occurred despite the replacement of the agrarian, campesino life-course script by a proletariat worker lifestyle surrounded by TVs, DVD players, cell phones and even an Internet café in the house compound where he resides while living in this community. One of the threads connecting Zhang's chapter with this work in Mexico is a shift toward a more equal relationship between generations over the past three decades. This has also been noted by Aboderin for urban Ghana (2006) and may represent a pervasive impact of globalization. Overall, Sokolovsky finds that global transformations are not necessarily a horrible thing for the aged if their locality has some control over key resources and older citizens are included in the process of figuring out what adaptations are best for the community. As seen in Box III.1, community development projects can also benefit from using the skills and knowledge of older women.

BOX III.1 THE GRANDMOTHER PROJECT

On mornings during farming season, Djina Sabaly cares for her granddaughter, brings food to her husband in the fields and gathers milk from the family cows. By lunchtime she has already walked eight kilometers. A long-time resident of the south Senegalese village of Darou Idjiratou, she takes great pride in her importance to the family. "We say that a family without a grandmother has no foundation because it has no guardian of traditional values." Sabaly, 68, provides daily child care for four grandchildren, assists her farmer husband, advises seven children and their spouses and works in the garden and fields. "In my village," she says, "elders always occupy the foremost position. They are consulted regarding the most important affairs."

continued

Grandmothers of Darou Idjiratou, a rural village of 700 inhabitants, are not unique in the developing world. Throughout Africa, Asia and Latin America, grandmothers provide primary child care, do domestic and farm work, act as family advisors and pass on cultural traditions. In areas without access to schools or health care, in countries where parents have fallen ill due to AIDS or other diseases, grandmothers frequently become the main parent and teacher. Despite grandmothers' importance, Western organizations that work in developing countries have been slow to incorporate elders into their activities. Fearing that grandmothers will be unwilling to accept new ideas, they offer young women training in health and nutrition while ignoring the grandmothers to whom these women turn for help. New mothers have to choose between the advice of a trusted family elder and the modern practices taught by an outside organization.

The Grandmother Project, a U.S. nonprofit, is working to redress this oversight (www.grandmotherproject.org). Founder Judi Aubel launched the organization in 2004 in order to strengthen the leadership of grandmothers in improving health for women and children. Since 1997, Aubel has been involved in community activities in Laos, Senegal, Mali, Uzbekistan and Albania that demonstrated the effectiveness of involving grandmothers in projects. Evaluations have documented greater confidence among grandmothers, increased community respect for elder women and improvements in advice to young women on pregnancy, infant feeding and neonatal health. In Senegal, the number of grandmothers advising women to give infants nutritious foods increased from 57 percent to 97 percent as a result of project efforts. Health improvements were greater in communities where grandmothers participated than where only younger women were involved.

The Grandmother Project's approach succeeds at introducing new practices by working with existing social structures and leaders. Using stories and songs, the Grandmother Project celebrates the traditional advisory role of grandmothers. Group training sessions teach health and nutrition to young and old alike–to women of childbearing age and to grandmothers who provide advice and care. Combining traditional practices and modern knowledge strengthens grandmothers' ability to promote good child care and increases the likelihood of lasting improvements in health.

These efforts enjoy widespread community support in Sabaly's rural village. Residents of Darou Idjaratou have noticed that fewer neighborhood children suffer from malnutrition and related illnesses than in the past. "In order for a development activity to work in the village, elders have to be included," says village leader Tidian Cisse. "We are thrilled that grandmothers are involved in nutrition activities because their role is to transmit knowledge to the younger generation."

Related Resource: Judi Aubel. 2006. "Grandmothers Promote Positive Child Health Practices: A Neglected Cultural and Communication Resource." Paper presented at the World Conference on Communication for Development, October 25–27, 2006, Rome. Available at: www.grandmotherproject.org/publications/ WCCD_2006.pdf.

Adapted from: Michael Gubser and Kristina Gryboski. 2006. "The Role of Grandmothers in Developing Countries." Available at: www.aarp.org/research/international/perspectives/ may_06_gubser_grandmother.html.

STANDING UP FOR OTHERS IN PERU

Part of the globalization picture that has emerged over the last two decades has been the massive and too-rapid growth of urban megacenters in such places as Mumbai, India, Lagos, Nigeria, Mexico City, Mexico, or Lima, Peru. In the interior and outskirts of such places, one too often sees the ugly side of globalization colliding with apathetic and ineffective governments that for too long have ignored the needs of their older citizens (Leinaweaver 2008). In their chapter, Dena Shenk and Joan Mahon examine such a situation in urban Peru, where, like many countries in the industrializing world, social policy toward older citizens has basically expected impoverished family systems to carry out all care functions for elders. It details the action research of one of the authors (Mahon) who lived for many years in Peru and returned to help implement some of the ideas of the UN's 2002 Madrid Plan on Aging. She helped bring together a volunteer group of local retired and underemployed social workers who formed a grassroots organization called AMIGOS. This group has been successful in not only galvanizing elders to collectively harness beneficial resources in their neighborhoods but to pressure the national government to implement already existing laws for the protection of older citizens.

The last two chapters in Part III shift attention from industrializing, developing nations where, numerically, most of the planet's elders live, to postindustrial countries in which a staggering proportion of persons survive past their seventh, eighth and ninth decades. In the cases of Japan and Denmark, we will see dramatic differences in public ideologies concerning the role of the family and the state in managing elder care.

MANAGING WARM CONTACT IN THE WORLD'S OLDEST SOCIETY

Japan is one of the best examples for looking at how a society adapts to the extremes of population aging. Its retention of the highest coresidence rates for any major, urban postindustrial society and a cultural system stressing prerogatives of senior status has collided with their unparalleled success in promoting exceptional longevity and the growing trend of adult women who desire to remain in the work force. This is the most central of several chapters that focus on Japan and sets the stage for discussions of women's intergenerational exchanges (Akiyama, Antonucci and Campbell Part II Web book), cultural responses to dementia (Traphagan Part VI) and unraveling the secrets of Okinawa's many centenarians (Willcox et al. Part VI). Here anthropologists Brenda Jenike and John Traphagan draw upon their extensive research in various regions of Japan to lay out the dimensions of changes in the cultural scripts for aging that are accelerating in the early twenty-first century.

Since the 1980s, there has begun a radical rethinking of the place of older citizens in Japanese society, countering the glowingly positive view presented in Erdman Palmore's *The Honorable Elders: A Cross-Cultural Analysis of*

Aging in Japan (1975). This work and a revised volume (1985), with Japanese gerontologist Daisaku Maeda, were largely based on statistical patterns of household organization and ideal cultural norms. They were criticized by scholars both in North America and Japan (Plath 1987; Koyano 1989). Asian scholars were also beginning to strongly question the continued reliance on family support systems as the best cultural medium to sustain the aged. A study in the 1990s by Tokyo's Metropolitan Institute of Gerontology found that almost half of the caregivers to the elderly were "burning out" from a combination of emotional and physical exhaustion, depersonalization and a decline in overall personal satisfaction with their lives. Almost 90 percent of these caregivers were women, most about sixty years of age, caring for elders averaging eighty years of age, two-thirds of whom were also female (Aging International 1994:8). At the same time, studies in East Asian industrial societies such as Japan, Singapore, Taiwan and Hong Kong showed that high levels of three-generation families, even in urban areas, were found in conjunction with exceedingly high rates of suicide by those over age sixty-five (Hu 1995). As Jenike and Traphagan note, in the twenty-first century for Japan these rates have not abated. Their paper gives a powerful voice to Japan's essential dilemma of its citizens aging beyond the familial mechanism of hands-on "warm contact" care, traditionally advocated by their cultural system. With so many people (especially women) surviving past age eighty-five, there has risen an essential conflict between principles of filial devotion and that of *meiwaku*—the shame of becoming an unsustainable burden.

Japan's societal response to such problems has been to undertake a succession of ambitious plans of public sector support for the social, economic and health needs of its oldest citizens. These efforts established widely arrayed, taxpayer-funded elder care services including adult day care, home visit nurses and short-term and long-term stays at public nursing homes. Importantly, as this is shifting responsibility onto individuals to pursue independent, healthy aging, the new environments for late-life care also attempt to mimic the cultural idea of *fureai*, or warm contact.[2]

REFINING THE "THE MIDDLE WAY": DENMARK'S FLEXICURITY SYSTEM

Europe's northern and western nations were, globally, the first to be demographically "mature." This was especially the case in Scandinavia, where, in the twentieth century, countries like Sweden and Denmark had developed a "middle way" between U.S.-style capitalism and centralized, planned socialism. However, by the 1970s and 1980s, policy makers in those nations saw that despite traditions of universal social welfare, policy toward older citizens was hampered by *overcare* in institutions and *undercare* within households (Zelkovitz 1997). Sweden initially took the lead by embarking on a national program to promote the independence, integrity and meaningful participation of the aged in community life (Sundström et al. 2008). It is important to note the clear difference here from the United States and Japan in that throughout Nordic countries, formal systems of social service have been considered a universal right. It is used to meet basic physical needs and enhance perceptions of autonomy, by avoiding over-dependence on one's close family and social network. Of the Scandinavian countries, Denmark seems the most successful in this area, replacing in various localities, traditional institutional care with sheltered housing in combination with flexible and generous home services (for a comparative European perspective see Billings and Leichsenring 2005).

In the final selection in Part III, Mary Stuart and E. B. Hansen present a comparative analysis of Denmark's Home Care Policy, which implemented a highly flexible but integrated system for home- and community-based services across its 275 municipalities. This approach to serving the needs of older citizens is called "flexicurity" by the Danes and is part of a larger flexible framework of health care, education and labor policy serving persons across the life course (Rasmussen 2007). Importantly, despite Denmark's growing population of citizens past age eighty, costs as a percentage of the gross domestic product are stable, as is access to quality long-term care services. This chapter provides an important bridge to the article by Polivka in Part VI, which explores the model of community-based care, initially pioneered in Florida, that has been adopted in Denmark and other postindustrial nations.

NOTES

1. A 1995 nationwide survey in India conducted by HelpAge India showed that almost 30 percent of India's aged have no family to live with or cannot live with the family they have.

2. For discussion of creative efforts under way in Japan to deal with their hyper-aging society problem, see Osako and Watanabe 2008.

3. See Canning 2007 for a broad discussion of aging and development in Asia.

CHAPTER 14

Globalization and the Risks of Aging

Christine L. Fry

Globalization has become a central focus of all the social sciences during the last three decades of the twentieth century. Yet globalization and aging are phenomena that have only recently been linked. Demographically the linkage is quite simple. As detailed by Kinsella in this volume, all populations are aging. The demographic transition is happening at a somewhat differential rate to all nations on the globe. More-developed nations have more aged populations, while the less-developed nations still have relatively youthful populations. Globalization and aging, however, are more complicated than demography. Globalization is an economic and political phenomenon that has and will continue to shape the life chances of all peoples around the globe.

Globalization is a part of and a product of urbanization triggered by economic growth associated with capitalism. Globalization, at the same time, is a little different in that it is a time, space compression that is a product of changes in transportation, communication and organizational technology. In this chapter, we will consider the following in exploring the linkages between globalization and aging from an anthropological perspective:

1. The phenomena of globalization.

2. The consequences of a globalized world for people of all ages.

3. The individualized risks and consequences of globalization for those who will become old in the twenty-first century.

GLOBALIZATION AND GROWTH

Within anthropology, globalization has become *the* major phenomena, process and context for understanding the communities we study. This reflects the times in which we live. It is much changed from the world that we studied in the early part of the twentieth century (Mintz 1998). By the 1970s, urban anthropology was invented in response to what was happening, under conditions of industrialization, to traditional communities abroad, and the increased need to study communities at home in the United States (Foster and Kemper 2002).

Globalization is both old and new. What makes globalization appear to be novel is that, since 1970, something quite profound has happened that has changed the lives of many people. The world has become a more complex and interdependent place in which to live. The more proximal political and economic roots of globalization appear in the eighteenth and nineteenth centuries. Politically, states, during this time, were transformed into nation states, which are different than the more traditional or archaic political entities that preceded them. Nation states coevolved with capitalism by creating the legal and financial institutions to accommodate and foster these emergent enterprises. As a result, nation states became major building blocks of the global economy (Wallerstein 1989). Their main role is: (1) to provide for an integrated division of labor; (2) to guarantee the flow of money, goods and people; and (3) to facilitate economic integration.

One rather obvious result of this new form of political and economic organization is the growth of population, which increasingly resides in urban areas. Since the industrial revolution, cities have become the key centers of production and exchange, as well as political power. In the past 200 years, urbanization has proceeded rather rapidly. Only 3 percent of the world's population was urbanized in 1800, and by 1900 had increased to 13 percent. Yet, by 2008 fully half of the globe's citizens will be living in urban areas (United Nations 2007a). The percentage of population living in cities differs by economic development. In the more-developed nations, three-quarters of the population is urbanized, while in the less-developed countries only 39 percent of the population is urban (United Nations Department of Economic and Social Affairs 2007). However, it is in these latter nations, such as India, Brazil and Mexico, where during the past two decades there has developed the greatest concentration of mega cities, with populations over 10 million inhabitants. Such an urbanized world is also a globalized world.

How did we become so globalized so fast? Most of the decisions that create new world orders are made at the conclusion of major wars. Following World War II, the international economic foundations for the present order were finalized in the Bretton Wood Conference, while the political foundations emerged in the creation of the United Nations.[1] However, by 1970, the post–World War II prosperity faced a crisis. The trigger was a crisis in Fordism and the oil shocks of the mid-1970s. Fordism is the vision of Henry Ford that involved a combination of mass production and a unionized labor force that had the purchasing power to consume manufactured goods. This was combined with state-sponsored consumerism and Keynesian fiscal management.[2] To partially resolve this crisis, then President Richard Nixon revoked the part of the Bretton Wood Agreement that anchored the world's currency to the U.S. dollar linked to gold. When the linkage was disassembled, the value of money became free floating, with the net result that the supply of money increased. To further stimulate profits, firms positioned themselves by creating a flexible labor force, one to which they were not committed to on a long-term basis. The declining profits, the increased supply of money and the flexible labor force resulted in all the things we associate with globalization, which include: offshore production; export production zones; out-sourcing of work, including international contracts; decrease in unionized labor; an increase in lowpaying jobs and the restructuring of the welfare state (Nash 1989). At the root of the changes of the past thirty years are political and economic arrangements with borders being opened through trade agreements. Nation states also altered tax laws to promote offshore production to encourage business and job creation by eliminating tariffs.

The net result is the phenomenon we identify as the globalized world. Most obvious are the stretching and deepening of social relations across national borders. People increasingly found that everyday activities were being influenced by events that happen at great distances (Hannerz 1992; Smith 2001). Social scientists noticed that phrases such as *globalized, transnational, translocal, delocalized, deterritorialized* and *the global village* crept into our vocabulary.

Much of the technology in transportation that makes this possible is not really new. For instance, the telegraph was invented in the nineteenth century. The stock market has been operating on real global time since its inception. The world was divided into twenty-four time zones in the 1880s because of railroads and the need to rationalize schedules. We do have some novel changes in social organization and technology. In the aftermath of World War II, supranational entities were invented such as the World Trade Organization, the World Bank, the International Monetary Fund, the United Nations, and more recently, NAFTA, the North American Free Trade Agreement, the European Economic Union and OPEC. New technologies were devised to facilitate exchange and communication, which include such things as container terminals and containerized cargo, jets (both passenger and cargo) and the Internet. This all makes it possible to more easily maintain relationships across state borders and has given birth to transnational communities.

CONSEQUENCES OF GLOBALIZATION

Globalization has brought with it consequences that are both good and bad for the social worlds in which we live. In a very real sense the cultural space everyone occupies is local. In this section we will examine a number of ways globalization impacts these spaces through economic and political forces.

Increased Cultural Homogeneity

One of the most obvious changes is the loss of cultural diversity. Where we see the spread of an economic form, we expect to observe some cultural transformation. Interestingly, the main factor in creating cultural homogeneity is the invention of nation states, not globalization (Weber 1976). To promote a potentially problematic integration, nation states require one official language. Males also share a common experience and acculturation through military service. Universal education, in providing basic skills and knowledge about the world, results in cultural uniformity. If cultural differences are too disruptive, nation states may promote programs of ethnocide and genocide.

On the other hand, the world may not become completely culturally homogenous. Anthropologically, the picture is quite complex, and not one of simple diffusion of markets. There is evidence of a creolization of cultural forms, which has been called glocalization (Hannerz 1992; Garcia Canclini 1997). In spite of electronic media and popular culture, much of the native cultural forms remain in modified form at the local level. Also, since the WorldWar II, the cities of Europe and the United States have seen the influx of migrants from impoverished countries seeking political asylum and economic opportunity. The net effect is the increase in heterogeneity at the core of capitalism. We also have evidence of cultural resistance. Fundamentalist movements, the revolt in Chiapas, Mexico, feminism, and ecological movements reject much of the changes being fostered in a globalized world, or attempt to transform it in what is seen as a more equitable direction.

Delocalization of Ordinary Life

Life in cities and many rural areas has produced cultural spaces that appear to have lost their territorial basis. The locale of where one lives becomes irrelevant other than as an indicator of social status (Durrschmidt 1997). Often in urban environments one does not know who lives next door, and personal networks are based on social factors and less likely grounded in attachment to the local neighborhood. With the prevalence of national electronic media (radio, television, the Internet), local spaces become interconnected to a larger world and boundaries vanish.

However, we have some evidence for a countertrend. This is perhaps a little counterintuitive since it goes in the opposite direction of globalization. There is evidence of increasing enclavement. Many people see disconnections with the larger world as not relevant to them. In the working class community of Momence, Illinois, I have had informants on their death beds tell me, "I have had a good life, a good wife, the kids are raised and that is all that counts." To date, the confident claims of global interconnectedness may be somewhat overblown. Only 2 to 5 percent of the world's population is *really* connected—super connected. These people have multiple phones and use the Internet several times a day. On the other hand, 60 percent of the world's population has never made a phone call (Graham 2002). A globalized planet has become a much more unequal one, and impoverished people are also excluded from the globalized world simply because they are unable to consume its products or live in safe, economically enriched environments (Phillipson 2007). As documented by Zhang in this volume, most of the rural elderly of China clearly are excluded from the advantages of globalization.

Deterritorialization or Erosion of the Sovereignty of Nations

Although nation states created the legal and financial institutions to foster capitalism, they face challenges in shaping and controlling the economic power structures. There are some concerns that nation states are becoming an archaic political form. In rationalizing their economies, nation states face many constraints. International aid is constraining because much of it is political in nature, while international trade agreements can alter internal economics. Nation states also face challenges from both transnational migration, and the power of transnational corporations. World migration intensified beginning around 1600, but after 1980 the pattern is very different (Kearney 1991; Basch, Schiller and Blanc 1994). About 2 percent of the world's population now lives and works in countries where they are not citizens and hope to return to their native country once they withdraw from the labor force. Most nations welcome the cheap labor, but not always the person providing it.

Transnational corporations have greatly profited from this situation and are possibly becoming the dominant governance institution on the global scene (Korton 1995; Reich 2007). Corporations are centered on private gain, but influence national policies. As of 2000, 51 of the top 100 global financial entities were corporations and 49 were nation states. Tops in the nation state category are the United States, Japan, Germany, France, United Kingdom, Italy, China, Brazil and Canada. A little lower in the list is General Motors (23), Wal-Mart (25), Exxon (26) and Ford (27). If money is power, then nation states may well be challenged.

Availability of Consumer Goods

With increased wealth, consumer goods and consumerism has increased over the past thirty years. What we see crowding the aisles of Wal-Mart would not be possible if China had not entered the global economy, dramatically increasing access of industrialized nations to cheap labor. Many of the products we consume such as lighting fixtures, coffeemakers, irons and computers are not only more readily available, but are often cheaper (in constant dollars) than they were twenty to thirty years ago. On the other hand, because of cheap labor, not everyone is able to consume equally.

Globalization of Production

Of all the consequences of globalization, this is the most directly economic and the force that has fueled the rapid increase in globalization (Rothstein and Blim 1992). Outsourcing of work moves production to less-developed countries. Manufacturing takes place in Export Production Zones where taxation on productive activities is avoided and often carried out in sweatshops with laborers working for very low wages. Women and children work in such places for less than $2.00 a day. This arrangement places workers all over the world in direct competition with each other. In this context, more-developed economies abandon manufacturing and shift to service provision.

Increased Segmentation of the Labor Market and Social Polarization

With the advent of capitalism, the labor market became segmented. This means there are good well-paying jobs and then there are menial jobs. Globalization has only increased this and the associated economic and social stratification that perhaps is the most significant consequence. A poignant example is the comparison of the wages of a CEO of a major corporation with those of ordinary workers in the same corporation. It can take the ordinary worker more than a year to earn the same wage the CEO earns in a day. The labor force is increasingly divided into two components: the knowledge workers and the manual workers (haves and have not's). Labor market dualism has resulted in a declining standard of living, especially as there is a reduction of opportunities for those without education (Levine 1995). There is even evidence that knowledge jobs are going overseas. Why pay a programmer $40,000 to $60,000 a year when you can get the same work for $20,000 a year in India? This is combined with changes in welfare systems shifting to privatization and workfare, which is resulting in depressed wages.

CONSEQUENCES OF GLOBALIZATION FOR OLDER PEOPLE

Global capitalism has transformed the economic world in a way that works to the disadvantage of older people. In family organized production, people of all ages were never divorced from units that controlled work activities. In rationalizing production, capitalism transformed work into wage labor, moving it into factories or places where it could be supervised and regulated. Wages are great as long as one earns enough to purchase goods and services on the market. However, when one no longer works or is temporarily out of work through unemployment or illness, the lack of wages becomes a problem. For older people who must withdraw from the labor force because of disability or who just may want to retire, the last phase of life must be adequately financed or one faces the risks of poverty. Because of the changes in families, work and increased longevity, by the early-twentieth century, capitalism had created the problem of old age. Nations, especially the wealthier nations of Europe and North America, have economically addressed some of the risks of old age to improve the welfare of older workers.

In being the economic building blocks of the global economy, nation states have organized their national economies into industrial complexes. Some of these receive state support in the form of corporate welfare, subsidies, tax breaks and by legislative stimulation for private interests. The most famous of these complexes is the "military industrial complex," first identified by Dwight Eisenhower back in the 1950s. There are lots of other industrial complexes such as an educational industrial complex, a financial industrial complex or a medical industrial complex and the like. And, yes, there is even a gerontological industrial complex. This complex has been identified as the "Aging Enterprise" by Carol Estes, and is also known as "The Aging Network." The legislative pillars for the gerontological industrial complex in the United States are: (1) the Social Security Act of 1935 that created a tax transfer program to address financial issues in old age; (2) the Medicare Act of 1965 that created a program to subsidize medical insurance for older people and a welfare program for those who cannot afford medical care (Medicaid); (3) The Older Americans Act of 1965 that created a network of agencies to improve access to services, and also programs such as "Meals on Wheels" and senior centers; and, finally, (4) the legislation that created the National Institute on Aging, within the National Institutes of Health to promote research on aging.

From a self-defined societal perspective, the risks of aging are promoted by changes in families, the financing of retirement and support services for older people. We will turn our attention to these risks and explore how globalization has increased potential problems both in wealthy and poorer countries.

Changes in Production and Transformed Families

The most profound change around the world in the past two centuries has been in the family. Work and productivity are no longer managed by families, thus changing the function of and reducing the power of domestic units. Individuals must earn wages to meet their needs. Initially families responded to industrial work by pooling the wages of all members, especially younger members, into a "family fund," but the real need for pooled resources largely vanished once Social Security stabilized the income of older members (Gratton 1993). Parents now find joy as children are launched into the world of work and are successful. In fact, a child returning to the family nest is often seen as a disappointment.

Also, the size and meaning of kindreds have changed. The effects of the Demographic Transition have created families where there are fewer children and much smaller kindreds (see Kinsella this volume). This is happening globally (Bengston and Lowenstein 2003; Durham 2006). With greater longevity, families are having longer shared lives at the end of the life course. This, combined with reduced fertility, has resulted in greater generational separation and marked age differentiation within a family unit. With the decrease in intergenerational economic interdependency, the meaning of kinship has changed. Kinship is not the descent and marriage defined in the law or what you see in genealogy software. At the beginning of the twenty-first century, descent and marriage have been replaced with a diversity of forms, and an emphasis on individualism rather than relatives (Strathern 1992). The implication is that descent groups, as flexible as they are, may entirely evaporate.

Wage Labor and the Financing of Retirement

Globalization has directly impacted the financing of retirement. In a capitalist economy, a wage laborer must defer and invest a significant portion of his/her income for support in what may be thirty years of retirement. As already noted, the international nature of labor markets and offshore production means that workers around the globe are placed in direct competition with each other. It is unclear if a sweatshop worker (usually a female) will be able to contribute much to an extended family and aging parents. Also, the working life in a sweatshop is remarkably short—a female textile worker or electronics worker is old by the age of twenty-four or twenty-seven. This is mostly because of the demands of the workplace (close work) and working conditions.

Facing international competition, the standard of living for all working people has declined. The growth in jobs during the 1990s was in the service industry and in minimum wage jobs. The net effect of unregulated global markets has been the creation of inequality and poverty. The World Bank estimates that over 70 percent of the world's older population relies on either their own labor or that of their family to support themselves in old age (HelpAge International 2004). Most of these older adults reside in developing nations. With the reduction of wages, many workers find themselves barely getting by with several jobs and facing a wage/time compression that makes it nearly impossible to do the work of kinship—caregiving. Making matters worse, since the 1980s pension plans have shifted from "defined benefit" plans where corporations defer wages and manage wealth for their employees to "defined contribution" plans where employees take responsibility for wealth management. The net result has not been positive. For instance, 40 percent of the Baby Boomer generation has less than $10,000 in retirement savings (Croker and Dychtwald 2007). With lower wages, that means less income to defer. Also, with high demands in the here and now (for major consumption needs), people are likely to borrow against the future, leaving even less in the future. In fact, the savings rate in the United States is the lowest it has been since the Great Depression.

Another consequence of globalized labor is the increased segmentation of an international labor market. The real dualism in globalized labor is the divide between: (1) the extremely rich who do little, but benefit from financial capitalism (investments), or own the productive organization at the international level; and (2) both the knowledge and manual workers who work for very low or relatively low wages. Predictable and stable life-long employment is increasingly being replaced by contingency labor (short term and less predictable). We are probably just beginning to see the effects of globalization among the old as Baby Boomers are nearing retirement. It is apparent that older women (about 50 percent of the Boomer generation) will be at greater risk since they hold lower-paying jobs, with no or minimal pensions and few health insurance packages (Estes 2004). When we look at labor markets in poorer countries and realize that nearly half of the world's workers are earning less than $2.00 a day, it is rather meaningless to discuss deferred income to finance retirement. With globalization of the economy, it is fairly certain that in the twenty-first century it will be much scarier to grow old. In many developing countries, the redistributive economy to support the welfare needs of a growing population including older people is sharply reduced by policies imposed by international financial institutions such as the International Monetary Fund and the World Bank. These nations find themselves in debt to finance development projects that sometimes exceed the gross national product of their nation. Even in the United States, the Baby Boomers are planning on working longer because of the decline of defined benefit pensions and unfavorable health care insurance offered by their employers (Mermin, Johnson and Murphy 2007).

Support of Older People

Gerontology has developed around the issue of the welfare of and quality of life of older adults. For the most part, both this research focus and older people themselves are dependent on the redistributive economy of the nation state. The redistributive taxation system is the part of the economy that supports the aging enterprise and what is sometimes referred to as the moral economy—that which works for the good of society and its citizens (Minkler and Estes 1999; Estes and Phillipson 2002).[3] It is the nation state that determines who gets what and when. In the United States, it is Medicare, Medicaid, Social Security, the Older Americans Act, NIA and so forth that shape the resource base for the support of the old. All have been under attack over the past five years, especially in the proposed revisions to Social Security and Medicare (see Polivka this volume). If the attack continues on these pillars, our foundations get shakier. European countries, especially in Scandinavia, have devised systems of old age security that are more flexible and are solidly funded through taxation (Stuart and Hansen this volume). This part of the economy has to compete with other industrial complexes supported by the state. For instance, military commitments in the Near East costing many billions of dollars a year leave other programs sharply competing for fewer dollars and under funded.

A globalized economy is an international political economy concerned with production, distribution, and exchange for private and corporate gain. During the past thirty years, we have seen tremendous expansion of this economy. At the same time, in many developing countries we have not yet seen the development of a moral economy. Within developing nations, the financing of globalization, often through the debt on loans from the World Bank or the International Monetary Fund, can severely limit the redistributive economy of poorer countries in the name of progress (see Shenk and Mahon this volume). Consequently, there is little left to invest in a moral economy. From the perspective of the twenty-first century, it is quite apparent that security in old age cannot be left up to families and voluntary social services. Also, recent schemes to privatize pensions do not seem like a good approach, as models such as that imposed under Chile's dictatorial rule in 1981 have failed to provide even a basic pension for more than half of its enrolled members (Riesco 2005). Somehow old age and its financing have to be built into a broad moral economy of nation states that work with capitalism and its infrastructure.

GLOBALIZATION, CULTURAL SPACES AND AGING

Capitalism, especially global capitalism, has not been completely negative. Capitalism is recognized for its creativity as entrepreneurs compete and create new culture to be sold on the market. New cultural spaces are not only of the material world, but include worlds of ideas marketed in the media and new social forms. For older people, one of the newest cultural spaces actually defines residential spaces through the invention of a more diversified housing market. This is the wide variety of senior housing ranging from luxurious gated communities with recreational amenities for seniors, to trailer parks catering to less wealthy seniors, to public housing, assisted living and nursing home facilities. The leisure and tourism industries have responded by marketing tours for seniors, and recreational vehicles that make their annual trek to RV parks in the sunshine states each winter. Educational institutions organize learning experiences for older people such as Elderhostel, which may also involve travel. As designated in the original Older Americans Act, the states have created senior centers to provide recreational space and congregate meals for their older adults (Tsuji Web book this volume). A wide variety of cultural spaces are not market driven, but more informal and self-generated and found at the local level. These occur in more ordinary spaces as seniors take over the local Burger King for coffee following the morning rush, or simply meet on the first Monday of the month for breakfast at a restaurant near the interstate. Certainly with the invention of retirement as an anticipated and positive stage of life, the possibility for new cultural spaces has expanded tremendously. In this volume, the chapter by Sarah Lamb demonstrates how middle-class Indians are negotiating a shift from reliance on the family in old age to new forms of aging in residences designed for the elderly. The chapter by Zhang in this volume illustrates how older people in urban areas in China can take advantage of state subsidies and specially designed public parks, while their rural counterparts are denied this new cultural space.

Old age itself can be seen as a new cultural space and a byproduct of the forces of globalization. Certainly with the expansion of the medical industrial complex and public health in the twentieth century old age is a phenomenon to be enjoyed by a majority of people. Old age can be a very positive experience for those who are included in the globalized economy at a fairly high level, and who can accumulate sufficient capital to finance this stage of life. These are the people who can travel, have second homes and enjoy leisure activities. For those who are excluded or who are included only at the lowest level with poorly paying jobs, old age is a much less desirable life stage. Since its inception, gerontology has addressed the issues of poverty in old age, but we are just beginning to see the effects of globalization on poverty around the world (Walker 2005).

Globalization has impacts that are not immediately financial, but which affect the communities in which people live. These are less obvious and not as well known, and consequently should be ethnographically investigated (Phillipson 2007). Real estate developments involving international flows of capital can result in regentrification projects that either displace long-term older residents from their neighborhoods or isolate them as younger and wealthier neighbors move in. Likewise, the policies of mortgage companies can shape the ease of selling a house. With no down payment on new construction, older people may find their older homes more difficult to sell and of lesser value if needed to finance their years in long-term care or assisted living. Even the way consumer goods are marketed has effects on the economy of localized communities. Discount merchandisers, such as Wal-Mart and K-Mart, and the developers of malls develop land at the edge of existing cities and along major traffic arteries. The former commercial districts that concentrated goods and services in a downtown district are now replaced by a dispersal of commercial establishments. For older people in suburban and rural areas, this means either prolonging the ability to drive a car or becoming dependent on others for shopping, especially in the frequent absence of public transportation.

Thirty years of transformation is hardly enough time to comprehend the process, much less to see how the consequences unfold in later life. Many people who grew old during this time had spent much of their adult lives when we were far less globalized. I think we see storm clouds on the horizon, if not right upon us, in the immediate future. It is time to start thinking about these issues to prepare ourselves for aging in a globalized world. It is happening in the here and now. It has consequences for the life chances of everyone, not only the young who are entering the labor force, but also the old who are retiring from the world of work. Most obvious is that we are going to see more people facing old age with less financial resources and more individualized risk. The Baby Boomers are among the first to face this world with pensions based primarily on their own savings and with under-funded health plans. In the underdeveloped world, older people either must continue to work or rely on the support of children.

By now it should be clear that the linkage between aging and globalization is more than demographic. In fact, without globalization, aging as we know it would be very different. The conditions that promoted the demographic transition would not have happened. Highly productive economies promoting consumerism and wage labor would not exist. People would grow old in families whose members did not face the competing demands of work and personal life. Social life would be based on proximity. Nation states would not have their sovereignty threatened by transnational corporate wealth. Moral economies promoting the welfare of citizenry would be the norm. But it did not turn out that way. Given this reality, I hope gerontology can remain one of the cultural responses working for the benefit of older people in a globalized world.

NOTES

1. The Bretton Wood Conference established the financial foundations to facilitate international trade. Among the institutions established were the International Monetary Fund and the World Bank.

2. Keynesian Economics is named after Lord Maynard Keynes, a British economist whose economic policies to reduce the effects of the economic booms and busts of capitalism were based on consumer confidence and state consumerism to make the necessary corrections.

3. For an important and classic treatment of this issue, see Estes (1979).

CHAPTER 15

The New Realities of Aging in Contemporary China: Coping with the Decline in Family Care

Hong Zhang

On December 3, 2006, *China Daily*, the official English newspaper of the state media, carried a rather disturbing news story that raised serious concerns about the plight of poor elderly in China today. On November 9, 2006, a seventy-one-year-old homeless man was detained after he deliberately set a forest fire on a mountainside in south China. Further investigation revealed that this same man was released from prison only a week previously after serving a five-year term in prison on charges of arson. In his self-defense, the old man insisted that he wanted to return to prison to spend his remaining years because it at least provided him with food and shelter (*China Daily* 2006).

On December 8, 2006, another news story concerning the Chinese elderly grabbed the headline, but in a rather different light. In the city of Shanghai, more than 8,000 senior citizens participated in a Web design contest and thirty contestants won various prizes in such categories as creativity and the best fine arts work (Xinhua News Agency 2006b). A seventy-nine-year-old female retiree was awarded an honorary title of "The Most Senior Participant." Upon receiving her award, she said, "Designing Web page enriches my life and makes me feel closer to the young people. This Web contest made me feel 20 years younger." Her words vividly captured a new attitude toward aging and old age among those urban retirees who have both the resources and the active mindset to broaden their horizon and enrich their life in later years.

On June 23, 2006, another mainstream newspaper reported the following story: Ms. Jin, a seventy-four-year-old widow moved into a retirement home against the wishes of her three sons (China News 2006). According to Ms. Jin, "the younger generations all have their own affairs to deal with. It would not be easy to schedule the lifestyles of two different generations under the same roof. Even though we may be next to each other we would have little to say." Now, at the retirement home, Ms. Jin was "quite happy" as she was able to be with people of her age, playing games or watching television together. However, her story did not end here. Apparently, since the early 2000s, her home city of Nanjing began a new experimental retirement home called "swap home for retirement." Under this plan, the retirees would turn over their apartments for the retirement home to rent out in exchange for care and services at the retirement home. When the retirees die, their apartments would become the retirement home's property. At the time, Ms. Jin's monthly rental income was 1,000 yuan (USD 125), more than enough to pay for the retirement home's monthly fee of 560 yuan. She felt proud that she could meet her retirement home expenses through this "swap home for retirement" plan and did not have to put a financial or caring burden on her children.

At the turn of the twenty-first century, old age in China has taken on new meanings and aging experiences have been greatly diversified and stratified as reform-era China embraces capitalism and focuses on rapid economic development. As the world's most populous country, China is also facing an unprecedented pace of population aging and demographic transition accelerated by both the stringent state population control policy and the rapid modernization and urbanization process that is now engulfing that nation. For example, over the next two decades, China is expected to complete the transition from a relatively young country to a demographically mature society, accomplishing this in less than thirty years, more than twice as fast as the United States (Kinsella this volume).[1] According to the latest data issued by the United Nations Population Division, China now contains more than one-fifth of the world's older population, with an estimated 147.8 million citizens aged sixty or older (United Nations Department of Economic and Social Affairs 2006). But in the years ahead, China will face an even more daunting reality of population aging, as by the year 2050, the percentage of China's elderly population aged sixty-five years and older is projected to triple from 8 percent in 2006 to 24 percent in 2050 to 322 million people (Kaneda 2006).

Advanced population aging is commonly associated with postindustrialized, highly urbanized countries in the West. Well-developed health care and social security systems have put these countries in a better position to cope with the attendant problems associated with the accelerated aging of their societies. However, China is becoming an aging society while its per capita income is still low, ranking 108 out of a total of 187 countries in the world as of 2004,[2] and over 60 percent of China's 1.3 billion people still live in rural areas. As a developing country with a large rural population, how will China cope with rapid population aging in the new millennium? How do the Chinese elderly fare as China moves from a closely knit rural society to a fast-paced industrial and consumer-oriented urban society, and from a state-planned economy to the capitalist market economy? Will drastic social changes affect their aging experiences and in what ways?

This chapter examines new aging experiences in light of rapid social transformations in contemporary China. More specifically, it focuses on how aging experiences shift and what new coping mechanisms have emerged among the elderly due to changes in government policies and social and economic contexts. The ethnographic data for this chapter is based on the author's fieldwork in a central Chinese village in the mid-1990s and early 2000s, elder homes in the city of Wuhan in 2001 and public parks in Guangzhou, Beijing and Shanghai in 2007.

DIFFERENTIAL AGING EXPERIENCES DUE TO THE DEEPENING RURAL-URBAN DIVIDE

China has been undergoing rapid social transformation from Mao's socialist revolution (1949–1978) to post-Mao's pro-market reform (1978–present). Social engineering and government policy have played a crucial role in reshaping the well-being of the Chinese elderly. In contemporary China, we can identify at least three emerging salient features concerning the lived experiences of old age that can be directly attributed to the consequences of government social policy and broad societal changes. One is the differential aging experience along the deepening rural-urban divide due to both the state-instituted household registration system and the government's market-reform agenda. The second is the increasing stratification in aging experiences as a result of the widening wealth gap as China repudiates its socialist egalitarian legacy to pursue a capitalist economy. The third feature is the declining family care accompanied by the rise of nonfamily and fee-based eldercare alternatives in post-Mao China.

Shortly after the Communist victory in 1949, the Chinese government began to implement a household registration system (the *hukou* system), which divided China's population into "agricultural" or "nonagricultural residents" according to both place of residence and entitlement to a wide range of state services and welfare benefits (Cheng and Selden 1994). The government provided urban residents and industrial workers with food rations, subsidized housing, free education, medical care and retirement pensions, while rural residents had no such state benefits, but had to depend on their local collectives for limited public services. During the collective economy of the Mao era, the *hukou* system served the purposes of ensuring resource distributions and controlling internal population migration. At that time, even though the *hukou* system accorded more advantages in terms of state welfare benefits to the urban population, and by extension to the urban elderly, it did not necessarily lead to a sharp divide in the general well-being between the urban and rural elderly for at least three reasons (Davis-Friedman 1991; Whyte and Parish 1984). First, because of enforcing socialist egalitarian principles and the practice of limited wages in the urban sector, the standard of living nationwide was generally low and did not differentiate greatly between the rural and the urban.[3] Second, even though rural elderly did not receive state pensions or the same level of health care as did their urban counterparts, they had access to a lower level of subsidized medical care and were guaranteed a basic livelihood by their collectives. Third, the *hukou* system that effectively restricted rural-to-urban migration also meant that most rural elderly parents had adult children living in the same villages who could provide prompt eldercare when needed.

But China's post-Mao market reform, the urban-centered developmental strategies China has subsequently pursued, and the legacy of the *hukou* system, have all disproportionately benefited the urban residents and have thus greatly enlarged the gap in the income and the living standards between the rural and the urban populations. In the early 1980s, the urban household income slightly exceeded that of rural households by a factor of 1.5 to 1.8, whereas by 2002 that figure had grown to 3.1 (Cai 2003). The collapse of the collective economy, coupled with urban-centered development strategies, not only caused a stagnation of farm incomes, but also led to a massive exodus of rural able-bodied men and women. As young adults left their aging parents behind in order to seek wage labor in cities, this has generated an especially detrimental impact on the welfare of rural elderly in China today.

In 2002, as a follow-up to earlier fieldwork in a central China village, I found that elderly parents living alone increased from 23 percent in 1994 to 54 percent in 2002. I also learned of three more suicides by the elderly since my last visit in 2000.[4] What is most tragic about these more recent three suicides is that two of the three elderly were a couple who ended their lives not out of the commonly encountered disputes with adult children over parental support,[5] but because they were afraid that caring for each of them would financially bankrupt their adult children.[6] Both in their early eighties, the elderly father was crippled for the previous five years and the elderly mother was his chief care provider, although the couple was living with their youngest daughter whose husband had married uxorilocally, moving in with his wife's natal family.[7] Then the mother's eyesight began to fail and she also developed some chest pains. Tensions flared among the older couple's children as to whom and how much each should pay for medicines needed by their mother. Finally, the mother got some medicine, but her chest pains continued. Feeling that there was no point wasting the money on her, the mother jumped over a bridge and killed herself in 2001. In less than a month, her husband followed suit and killed himself by jumping in the river. When relating this tragic story to me, the villagers claimed that it was the only alternative for a rural family caught in such a situation. They pointed out that the real motive for the elderly couple's suicides was that they did not want to incur too much financial burden, especially for their youngest daughter who had two school-age children. The collapse of the collective economy has not only meant higher medical costs, but also the costs are solely borne by individual families. Paying the medical bills for elderly parents is now often compromised as it is either too costly or competes with money put aside to pay for skyrocketing educational costs occurring since China's pro-market reform.

In his study of Xitucun in rural Hebei province of north China in 2004, Weiguo Zhang also observed a worsened welfare situation of childless elderly men in postreform China (Zhang 2007). Zhang began his observation also with the tragic death of an elderly in his seventies who was partially paralyzed, lived alone and died in his sleep when his clothes slipped over the coal stove and caused a fire. According to Zhang, despite the fact the village under study experienced overall prosperity in post-Mao reform, the condition of childless elderly actually deteriorated. Unlike in the collectivization period "when the childless elderly actively participated in community life, a time when being poor, childless and elderly was less stigmatized," in the market economy, being childless and elderly meant poverty and isolation from the community (p. 276). In the collective years, childless elderly would be provided with a localized welfare program called "wubao" (the "five-guarantee scheme"—food, clothing, medical care, housing and burial expenses). However, in China's market reform, "the dissolution of collective farming disrupted the financial basis of welfare assistance," and the village cadres in Xitucun claimed that "the village has no money to develop a welfare program" (p. 291). As a result, "the well-being of the childless is deteriorating, even with prosperity surrounding them" (p. 293).[8] That, as shown in the very beginning of this chapter, a homeless rural elder chose prison in order to find shelter and food highlights as well the bleak and precarious life faced by some elderly who lack family and community support.

Elsewhere, I have identified and discussed four unfavorable factors in post-Mao China that have contributed to the worsening eldercare situations in rural China (Zhang 2004). First, is the free-wheeling market economy in reform-era China, which intensifies competition among adult sons for limited family resources in order to maximize the benefits for their conjugal family, often at the expense of taking care of the needs of their aging parents. The second factor is the collapse of the socialist safety net for the rural elderly as a result of decollectivization and the subsequent disappearance of the collective-based, subsidized health care system in post-Mao China. A third problem concerns the limited economic autonomy among the rural elderly as they have no access to pensions or medical coverage available to their urban counterparts. Last, is the absence of effective intervention mechanisms in cases of parental neglect, due both to decollectivization and a weakened parental authority in Chinese family dynamics today.[9]

China's current urban-centered development strategies have further disadvantaged rural families in general, and compromised the well-being of the rural elderly in particular. China's post-Mao development strategies heavily favor urban centers where entire new industries and service sectors have emerged and have triggered an ongoing massive rural-to-urban labor migration. More than 200 million able-bodied rural men and women have left their home villages for urban employment, leaving behind their young children and elderly parents to fend for themselves. Moreover, while the Chinese government has loosened the *hukou* system to allow urban migration of rural men and women, it still denies them urban citizenship and limits their work to only certain industry sectors that are normally avoided by urban residents. These migrants have heavily concentrated in construction jobs, sanitation, service and labor-intensive manufacturing sectors. This work is low paid, onerous and requires long hours. In other words, urban labor migration can hardly serve as a strategy to enhance a rural family's economic situation since the low wages severely curtail their ability to send remittances home. In the meantime, rural families suffer severe disruptions and endure year-round geographic separations between husband and wife, parents and young children and aging parents and their adult children.

It is under this new, unrelenting mix of market forces and urban-centered development strategies that the aging experience of rural elderly has taken a severe downward turn. Not only do aging parents have to provide their own eldercare in late life, but they are also burdened with the care of grandchildren, and some have to toil in the fields despite being very old. The title of a recent study captures poignantly the plight of rural elderly in contemporary China: "Working Till You Drop: The Elderly of Rural China" (Pang, de Brauw and Rozelle 2004). Based on a survey conducted in 2000 of 1,199 households in sixty-six villages and involving six provinces, their research shows that the majority of rural elderly enjoy no retirement at all and have to continue working in the fields. On a daily basis, they must also perform numerous strenuous tasks such as fetching water, washing clothes, gathering wood for fuel and cooking. Indeed, in China today, rural elderly not only have no retirement to speak of, but large numbers have to struggle just to maintain a subsistence living. In a 2005 survey covering 10,400 peasants over sixty years old in 31 provinces, it finds, "45 percent were not living with their children; 5 percent did not know where their next meal would come [from]; 69 percent had just one set of clothes and 67 percent couldn't afford medicine ... 85 percent of them still toiled in the fields and 97 percent managed household chores" (*China Daily* 2006).

In contrast, their urban counterparts are in a better position to cope with China's market reform and rapid socioeconomic changes. Owing to the legacy of socialist institutions, most urban retirees receive pensions, medical care and subsidized housing. Such state-instituted benefits enable urban elderly to maintain a certain level of economic security in their old age and become less dependent upon their adult children for financial support.[10] Moreover, both the *hukou* system and China's urban-centered development strategies have meant that urban young people are more likely to stay in their hometown for their career, and as a result most urban elderly have adult children living in the same city and providing care when needed. Indeed, Martin Whyte's urban Baoding data reveals a high percentage (about 90 percent) of grown children living in the same city as their parents. Whyte further notes that this allows Baoding parents and their grown children to form "networked families" in which parents live "near several grown children who cooperate in providing support and assistance, but without the need to coreside with any one such child in order to find old-age security" (Whyte 2004:112).[11]

Certainly, China's market reform has also generated uncertainties for urban elderly. Due to health care reform, urban retirees have increasingly found themselves shouldering a larger share of their medical bills. Their limited pensions often fall behind soaring living costs and inflation in reform-era China. Charlotte Ikels's longitudinal study of urban elderly in Guangzhou shows some paradoxical effects of China's housing reform on the eldercare of urban elderly. While the housing construction boom in recent years has greatly increased living space for urban households, it has also led to "an exodus of married children from parental households" (Ikels 2004b:321). As a consequence, "the proportion of support delivered solely by household members dropped dramatically from 86.5% in 1987 to only 48.1% in 1999." No elders reported lacking support in her 1987 survey data, but by 1998, 7.4 percent of elders were not receiving needed support (pp. 347–349).

THE WIDENING WEALTH GAP AND A STRATIFIED AGING EXPERIENCE

Rising stratification along the socioeconomic scale characterizes another new salient feature of differential aging experiences in contemporary China. Prior to the Communist Revolution in 1949, the tradition of filial piety prescribed the norm of families living in large multigenerational households and the absolute obligation of the young to obey and serve their parents. In reality, however, few families were wealthy enough to reach that cultural ideal, and most families lived in conjugal and extended stem households with about five persons. According to Francis Hsu, "the poverty of the vast majority of the people of China may account for the statistical finding of a small family, for the large family tends to appear when the economic foundations of the family make such an expression practical" (1943:555). A typical scenario describing the livelihood of elderly men in the prerevolutionary era was that while a wealthy man could live in luxury and afford to have multiple wives (concubines) and household servants tending to his various needs, a poor man could only scavenge a living by toiling endlessly as a coolie and would remain a poor childless bachelor the rest of his life.[12]

Stratification in aging experiences was, however, greatly reduced during Mao's collective era from 1949 to the late 1970s. After the Communist victory in 1949, the Chinese government began to institute a socialist economy that eliminated private property and aimed at equity and redistribution of wealth and resources on egalitarian principles. In rural China, joint ownership of land and collective distribution of income and welfare on the basis of need ended the worst poverty and guaranteed a basic livelihood for rural families. In urban China, there essentially were two types of workers: state workers (about 80 percent) who labored in large state-owned enterprises and public institutions, and collective workers (20 percent) who were employed in the commerce and service sector or small neighborhood workshops. State workers received slightly higher wages and better fringe benefits than did collective workers. The National Labor Insurance Regulations implemented in 1951 "provided most urban workers with free medical care, disability pay and pensions" (Davis-Friedmann 1991:24). Although income disparity still existed between rural and urban populations, and even among urban workers, Maoist socialist economy was successful in ensuring an equitable redistribution of basic necessities and livelihood among all citizens. Consequently, the aging experiences of Chinese elderly under this era were rather homogenous as no new class of concentrated wealth emerged and the worst poverty was eliminated.

However, since launching pro-market reforms in the early 1980s, China has not only experienced the world's fastest economic growth, but also the largest increase in income inequality. The Gini coefficient ratio is often used as a measure of societal income stratification, with ratios in the 20s indicating low levels of inequality and those above 40 marking high levels of inequality. In 1981, China's Gini coefficient was 28.2, but by 2004, it had reached 47.3, ranking as the second highest inequality level in Asia (Yang 1999; Asia Development Bank 2007), and surpassing even the rapidly increasing level of economic difference in the United States.[13] Dramatic increases in inequality since China's market reform also have a direct impact on the changing livelihood of Chinese elderly and have given rise to greater stratification in their aging experiences. I have already mentioned the deepening rural-urban discrepancy in the aging experiences of contemporary Chinese elderly. However, China's market economy has not only increased the wealth gap between rural and urban, but also between regions and within rural and urban populations. In coastal areas of eastern and southern China, rural communities have seen the greatest economic gains through development of village/township enterprises and transfer of land resources for factory sites. Some of these rural communities have become prosperous enough to allocate monthly pensions for the elderly (Guo and Zhou 1997; Joseph and Phillips 1999). In contrast, in less-developed interior provinces, provision of formal support for the elderly is "effectively nonexistent," and "may even be far below that of even the modest provision possible in the collective period" (Joseph and Phillips 1999:165).

Even though urban elderly, in general, fare much better than rural counterparts in terms of financial security and economic independence, they are by no means a homogeneous group, and their standard of living and access to pensions and medical care has become increasingly differentiated. One major source of inequality in urban China lies in the rising differential of income distribution in different occupations and industries, and this income inequality has also directly stratified the life situations of Chinese urban elderly. In a recent survey on urban elderly in Guangzhou, Li found a sharp discrepancy in monthly pensions among urban retirees on the basis of their former occupations and social status. While "high-ranking cadres" (government officials) and "professionals" could receive an average of 1,929 yuan (USD 253) and 1,250 yuan (USD 164), respectively, retired blue-collar workers and staff workers in the commerce and service sectors received only 602 yuan (USD 79.2) and 656 yuan (USD 86.3).[14] Moreover, retired high-ranking cadres and professionals were further privileged with much better medical care and housing benefits. Here as the wealth gap widened in reform-era China, low-income urban retirees found themselves unable to maintain a basic livelihood, while more-privileged elderly were provided with substantial incomes and other generous fringe benefits (Li 2002). The increasing stratification in aging experiences among Chinese elderly can clearly be seen in the stark contrast between this chapter's first vignette where the poor homeless elderly person preferred prison for food and shelter and the second vignette where educated Shanghai elderly elites had the luxury of participating in the Web page design contest and acquiring modern technology skills to enrich their lives.

FAMILY CARE: A MYTH OR REALITY? ENGAGING THE LIMITATIONS OF FILIAL PIETY

It is generally assumed that in China and other East Asian countries as well, the cultural tradition of filial piety continues to exert a controlling influence on the eldercare patterns and old-age support despite rapid social and economic changes. Studies have shown that a high level of intergenerational coresidence and cooperation has persisted, and that family support and intergenerational reciprocity still play a major role in shaping the aging experiences for the elderly in these countries (Maeda and Ishikawa 2000; Whyte 2003, 2004; Ikels 2004; Takagi and Silverstein 2006; Jenike and Traphagan this volume). For example, Takagi and Silverstein note, "In 2002, about 30 percent of those 65 years and older in Japan lived with their married children, whereas equivalent figures in the United States and Germany were less than 5 percent" (p. 474). Based on his 1994 data in Baoding, a medium-size city in north China, Whyte noted that the coresidence rate was 64 percent and all the other measurements on filial attitudes and behaviors seem to "yield a picture that familial and filial obligations are robustly intact" (Whyte 2003:89).

However, despite the persistence of the cultural expectation for filial obligation, there are signs that new attitudes and practices have emerged regarding eldercare in contemporary China. According to the most recent report on the Chinese elderly population, the percentage of Chinese elderly living in "empty-nest" households increased from 42 percent in 2000 to 49.7 percent in 2006 for urban China, while it increased slightly from 37.9 percent to 38.3 percent in rural China (China National Committee on Aging 2007). In his study of Xiajia Village in northeastern China, Yunxiang Yan finds that for younger villagers, "unconditional filial piety which was based on the sacredness of parenthood no longer exists," and in its place is "a new logic of intergenerational exchange" in which "if the parents do not treat their children well or are otherwise not good parents, then the children have reason to reduce the scope and amount of generosity to their parents (Yan 2003:177–178). In my 2001 study of the elderly parent's motivation to live in elder homes, some told me frankly that residential care gave them more reliable eldercare than would their children (Zhang 2006). In several cases, rather than living with their children, parents either sold or rented their apartment to move into a residential home and saved the property proceeds or the rental fees for future residential care expenses. When I asked these parents why they felt they could not count on their children for eldercare, some said that their children had their own families and careers to worry about in China's new competitive economy, while others simply lamented that their children were unwilling to care for them.

Even by the early 1990s, a national survey on eldercare patterns showed that contrary to the general belief that adult children assume eldercare for aging parents, most elderly parents provided their own care or were cared for by their spouse: 77 percent among the urban elderly and 63 percent among rural elderly (Wang and Xia 2001:49–68). My 2001 study of elder homes in Wuhan showed that although an overwhelming 95.7 percent of the elderly in these homes had children, 58.8 percent of the parents cited "family care unavailable" and another 19.6 percent cited "strained relationship with children" as reasons for seeking residential care. Similarly, the study by Zhan, Liu and Bai of elder homes in Tianjin city also shows that despite the fact that more than 70.9 percent of the parents had more than two children (and of these more than half had more than three), 55.8 percent of the parents listed "having no children nearby or children being too busy" as the most common reason for moving into an institution (2005:179). Both this study and my elder home study in Wuhan revealed that loss of spouse very frequently preceded becoming an elder home resident (87.3 percent in Wuhan and 77 percent in Tianjin). My interviews with elder parents in these homes found that prior to moving to these institutional settings, many lived alone or with their spouse and provided eldercare for themselves or for their spouse. But once their spouse died, they decided to move into an elder home as many found it difficult to live alone and manage their daily routine by themselves.[15] Even though moving to live with their adult children was an option, some chose not to as they "claimed that they did not want to become a burden to their children while others simply stated that they did not get along with their children" (Zhang 2006:61–63).[16]

It appears that a new lifestyle that emphasizes autonomy and intergenerational independence has taken hold among both the rural and urban Chinese elderly. My village studies in the mid-1990s and early 2000s showed that despite physical difficulties in tending the vegetable gardens, gathering firewood for fuel and fetching water from the lake or river, rural elderly parents actively sought to live separately from their children because they now perceived separate living as giving them more "convenience," "freedom," and "better control of their lives" (Zhang 2004:63–87; Zhang 2005).[17] In a 2004 survey that involved 833 elderly who lived alone in Nanjing, a city with more than 6 million urban residents, it was found that while almost two-thirds had adult children in the city, only 14 percent claimed to be "willing" or "somewhat willing" to reside with these children (Zhang et al. 2006:218). When asked to list the reasons for "not willing to live with their adult children," the majority (63.2 percent) said that they chose separate living because it gave them "more freedom," and about one-third said that they did not want to "burden their children." Only 13.1 percent indicated that they lived alone because their adult children were unwilling to coreside with them.

We can identify several socioeconomic factors that may have contributed to this general trend of weakening family care for the elderly. One has to do with the pension system instituted in urban China since the 1950s. The 2006 national survey data shows that 78 percent of urban elderly received pensions (China National Committee on Aging 2007). With their pensions, urban elderly have not only become much less economically dependent upon their adult children, but they also tend to adopt a conscious choice of "not to burden" their adult children with eldercare tasks. As early as the mid-1980s, survey data found that parents with state pensions were four times more likely to live apart from their children than parents without pensions (Unger 1993). A 1997–1998 study in two Chinese cities by Zhan and Montgomery found that family caregivers "were much less likely to assist the elder if he or she has a pension" (Zhan and Montgomery 2003:222). In my recent interviews with the elderly parents on their motivations for seeking residential care, I was repeatedly told by some parents that since pensions were available that could help pay for their eldercare, they did not want to become a burden to their adult children financially or physically (Zhang 2006:66–69).

Another factor is the link between declining multigenerational coresidence and increased living space due to the housing construction boom since the mid-1980s. In her study of changing eldercare patterns in Guangzhou from 1987 to 1998, Charlotte Ikels noted that the proportion of support delivered by family members dropped dramatically from 86.5 percent in 1987 to only 48.1 percent in 1998. Over that same decade, the proportion of older people receiving paid care rose from a mere 3.8 percent 1987 to one-quarter of her sample in 1998. Ikels attributed such changes in the eldercare patterns to the city's recent housing boom: "first by making it less likely that family members are sharing the same household, and second, by freeing up space vacated by former household members that could now be utilized by a live-in domestic helper (Ikels 2004b:348).

Additionally, the decline in family care for the elderly has to do with the rapid expansion and increase in China's consumer culture and service sector since the mid-1980s. In Chinese cities, the household service sector has become a new industry, offering a wide range of fee-based services including providing care for the elderly. If their children or other family members are not available, elderly parents can purchase eldercare through hiring a helper who either lives in or gets paid by the hour. Fee-based residential care facilities, which did not exist in Mao's era, have mushroomed in many Chinese cities since the 1990s, offering another alternative for eldercare. With their pensions and savings, and housing property, more and more urban elderly are now turning to nonfamily-based alternatives to secure eldercare. As revealed in the third vignette opening this chapter, Ms. Jin's decision to move into a retirement home against the wishes of her three sons clearly demonstrates both the availability of this nontraditional eldercare form and the new autonomy among Chinese elderly. This is creating new conceptions of how to best meet one's needs in late life.

NEW CULTURAL SCRIPTS FOR OLD-AGE PROBLEMS: ACTIVE AGING AND PEER SOCIALIZING

On a January morning in 2007, I went to Xiaogang Park in Guangzhou, a city of 10 million people in southern China, and was immediately struck by the lively scenes there: on my left under a big tree, a group of thirty or so middle-aged and elderly men and women moved in unison practicing *Taichi*, following the music and instructions coming out of a portable tape-recorder, and toward my right, on the other side of the park, another group of fifty or so men and women danced in pairs and waltzed in circles; further along, a group of elderly women were moving to disco music, while another group (mostly middle-aged women) were dancing with red cloths in their hands.

As I walked further into the park, I saw more elderly people doing various exercises either individually or in small groups, playing chess or other board games, reading newspapers, or chatting with friends. By the time I reached the middle of the park, it was almost 10:30 A.M. and some groups began to disperse and wrap up their morning exercises. Then I came across a group of at least sixty men and women singing loudly to the music played by a band of elderly people. An even larger crowd gathered on a nearby sloping hill and sang vigorously as if they were in competition with the other singing group. Among the second singing group was an eighty-nine-year-old man who played "peng ling" (colliding bells) for the group. This man later told me that he came to the park every day and that he enjoyed doing so because playing music for the group

Doing group *Taichi* in Xiaogang Park, Guangzhou, 2007. Photo by Hong Zhang.

Practicing the waltz in Xiaogang Park, Guangzhou, 2007. Photo by Hong Zhang.

not only made him stay healthy and energetic, but also feel useful. He added, "I would probably be dead by now had I not been with the singing group."

Similar scenes of elderly and middle-aged men and women dancing, singing, exercising, playing chess or other board games (including mahjong), practicing calligraphy, chatting with friends and tending to grandchildren were repeated when in the summer of 2007 I visited four more parks, two in Beijing and two in Shanghai. In my interviews with some of these elderly, I learned that typically they are in the parks between two to three hours in the morning and then return for another period of time in late afternoon or after dinner. They all come in groups. Some are neighbors or former colleagues, while others are new acquaintances they have made in the parks. Almost all are urban retirees who have pensions and are thus economically independent. From my casual interviews, I also found that these urban retirees come from all walks of life, ranging from retired government officials, factory cadres and managers, school teachers and other professionals, to ordinary factory workers or service sector workers.

However, what I found even more important about these men and women who congregate daily in the parks for morning exercises and other leisure activities were the deep social bonds that developed among them through their collective exercises and other group activities. Many told me that besides the obvious health benefits, they were also drawn to the parks by the opportunity to chat with old pals, exchange tips and remedies about aging and health issues, seek advice on family/personal problems, share the recollections of their past, or simply gossip and have conversations on what is going on at their home, neighborhood, or former work unit. An eighty-two-year-old Beijing woman told me that she spent an average of four hours a day in the parks with friends, two-and-a-half hours in the morning and one-and-a-half hours in the late afternoon. She told me, "The parks are just like our home and my exercise pals are like my extended family of sisters. We exercise and chat together and give each other advice if we have any problems. You don't feel old or lonely this way." One of her exercise pals, a seventy-nine-year-old retired woman, added, "We always keep in contact. If one does not feel well and cannot come to the park, we will visit her and make sure she is okay." As they were speaking, many others in the group who gathered around us nodded in agreement.

Admittedly, the elderly people in the parks may comprise only a small fraction of China's elderly population who are not only healthy and mobile enough to go to the parks, but who are retired with state-assisted pensions and are thus free from the burden of eking out an income for daily subsistence. However, this new phenomenon is still worth further investigation and can shed some insight on new trends of aging among urban retirees in contemporary China. From my observation and interviews in the parks, I can identify four new trends of coping with aging in urban China.

First of all, contrary to conventional Chinese images linking old age to being dependent on family and home-bound,[18] these urban retirees are full of life and vitality as they actively seek outdoor activities to keep their bodies and minds healthy and young. Whether practicing *Taichi* or learning to dance the waltz or joining the chorus, these urban elderly take active aging to a new level. Although what we witness in China's parks may point to a new trend in aging among China's urban retirees, we also need to put this new fascination with active fitness exercises in the context of China's market reform and rapid social transformation. As far as urban workers and retirees are concerned, China's market reforms in the past two decades have also brought about a diminishment of social welfare benefits and an increased burden on families and individuals to shoulder soaring health care costs. In other words, knowing that they can no longer count on the state or their former work units during times of need, many urban retirees turn to self-reliance and physical exercise to keep themselves healthy so they can avoid or reduce hefty medical bills to themselves or their children.

Secondly, the middle-aged and elderly women are the most common, active participants in these group exercises and other activities in the parks. In fact, among the five parks I visited in 2007, women far outnumbered men. In Xiaogang Park, for example, among ten or so groups that had more than thirty people exercising or dancing together, four had both men and women, but the other six groups were almost exclusively female participants. In the Chinese tradition, leisure time and activities used to belong to elderly men almost exclusively; as they retired from work, elderly men would visit tea houses, playing chess, socializing with friends and colleagues or taking their birds out for a walk—still a popular hobby among elderly men in Beijing.

For middle-aged and elderly women, however, social mores confined them to the home and familial duties preoccupied them with time-consuming household chores such as cooking, cleaning and providing care for grandchildren or elderly parents-in-law. Several factors may be at play to account for this ubiquitous new trend of middle-aged and elderly women both finding leisure time and feeling it important to do morning exercises and other group activities in parks and other public places. First of all, reform-era China has brought great material progress to urban residents. In less than two decades, wide availability of modern household appliances such as washing machines, gas stoves, microwaves and refrigerators has greatly reduced the time and labor dedicated to household chores.[19]

Secondly, the almost universal enforcement of a one-child policy among urban families in the past thirty years means less child-care time for urban mothers and grandmothers. Finally, China's market reform has had a gendered impact on middle-aged women as they were disproportionately made "redundant" in the economic restructuring and many were forced to retire "early." In urban China, the legal retirement age is fifty for women workers and fifty-five for women cadres and professionals, and sixty for men. However, beginning in the mid-1990s, when state enterprises began massive lay-offs and mandatory retirement in the name of efficiency and competitiveness as China prepared to enter the World Trade Organization, women in their mid or late forties would even be let go or pressured into "accepting" early retirement (Wang 2000; Liu 2007). While "early" retirement may allow middle-aged women to have more free time, it also means a shorter working life, smaller pensions and reduced medical coverage. This is perhaps why we see middle-aged women far outnumbering middle-aged men doing group exercises in the parks. Sidelined by the market economy, they have to resort to such proactive measures as physical exercise to protect themselves against illness and disease.

Thirdly, in China's urban parks today there is a strong collective spirit of camaraderie among the middle-aged and elderly men and women who exercise together or participate in other group activities. As I discussed previously, many come to the parks not only for exercise to keep themselves physically healthy, but also for friendship and mutual help and to avoid feeling lonely and isolated at home. What seems to be emerging among urban Chinese retirees is the embracing of a new cultural construction of retirement and old age. It is manifested in a focus on age-peer sociability rather than dependence on their adult children and on active outdoor activities rather than confinement to the home. In my study on urban elderly parents spending their later years in elder homes, similar narratives such as "not wanting to burden the children," "seeking companionship with people of our own age," and "seeking independent living" (i.e., avoiding multigenerational living) were frequently mentioned by my elderly interviewees as the reasons why they chose to live in elder homes (Zhang 2006). While not necessarily abandoning the family centered support system of Chinese tradition, this new desire and practice of sharing the aging experience with peers and maintaining autonomy, among urban Chinese elderly, does indicate a new way of coping with aging that goes beyond the family domain. It prioritizes commonalities in shared work histories, life-cycle period and age-cohort experiences.

Finally, this new trend of active aging through outdoor fitness exercises and group socializing and friendship has been perceived as beneficial to society, family and the elderly themselves, because it is low cost, effective and socially contagious. The Chinese government has encouraged this new perception of aging. In 1995, the government issued "Outline of Nationwide Physical Fitness Program" and launched a public campaign calling for a nationwide movement toward self-health maintenance through physical fitness activities (State Council 1995). To facilitate this fitness program, the government has "stipulated that 60 percent of the proceeds from the sports lottery" will go to fund "the Nationwide Physical Fitness Program," and outdoor fitness centers "have been installed in urban communities, public parks, squares, roadside and other convenient locations, equipped with fitness equipment and facilities in various forms."[20] Indeed, by the year 2007, any cursory look would find fitness equipment that suit the exercise needs of the elderly conspicuously dotting residential areas, public parks and other open public spaces in Chinese cities. Here we find an interesting contrast between the U.S. parks, which are predominantly utilized by children and young adults, and similar areas in urban China, which mostly cater to elderly people.[21]

Moreover, since 2004, to further facilitate more elderly using public parks for physical exercises and other leisure activities, most Chinese cities have

Elders doing fitness exercises in Tiantan Park, Beijing, 2007. Photo by Hong Zhang.

either made their public parks free to the public, or instituted a reduced fare for retirees, or only charged fees at later hours after the elderly finish their morning exercises or activities in the parks. Clearly the Chinese government has a strong vested interest in facilitating this new trend of active aging among the elderly. China's market reform in the health sector has not only led to soaring medical costs, but also shifted the health care burden increasingly from the state to individuals and families. By encouraging and helping facilitate the elderly to engage in fitness activities, group exercises and other recreational activities, the government can reposition itself as working in the interest of the elderly people. A physically active and healthy retirement population will not only translate into fewer health costs for both the state and the retirees themselves and their families, but a more stable social order.

In 2001, the Chinese government also launched a "Starlight Project," which aimed at building more community-based recreational and service centers for elderly Chinese. Between 2001 and 2004, 13.5 billion yuan (USD 1.63 billion) from the welfare lottery proceeds were used to create "32,490 service stations, where elderly people can read books, play cards, do painting, practice calligraphy, have exercises and attend lessons specifically for aged people" (Xinhua News Agency 2005).[22] These community-based service centers not only provide another socializing venue for the elderly, but also "offer cleaning, laundry and medical care services" (Xinhua News Agency 2006a; Wu et al. 2005; Zhang 2007). Clearly, such newly emerging community service centers are increasingly fulfilling the role of caregiving that was traditionally provided at home and by family members. Here, again, as most of these newly emerging community-based service centers are being built in Chinese cities, we can only imagine that the rural/urban eldercare gap will only further widen as government resources continue to flow predominantly to cities.

CONCLUSION

In contemporary China, life situations and the standard of living for the elderly have become greatly differentiated along both the rural-urban divide and the widening wealth gap. While stratification in aging experiences existed in China before, its sharp rise in contemporary China is a more recent phenomenon and represents a reversal of the relatively homogenous aging experiences due to the government's prior commitment to a socialist egalitarian society during the Mao era. The three media vignettes, at the beginning of this chapter, attest to the increasingly diverse and stratified aging experiences of the elderly in China today. For most urban elderly who have access to state pensions and medical care, they are able to purchase eldercare services or pursue a more active late life through fitness, peer socializing and other recreational activities. For them, old-age support has increasingly extended beyond the family context and shifted more toward self-maintenance, peer socializing and paid care.

However, for the vast majority of rural elderly, life has become much more precarious, and for some, even destitute. According to the latest statistical data released by the China National Committee on Aging, at the end of 2006, China had 149 million people over age 60, of whom 38.6 million (or 26.3 percent) were urban elderly and 108.01 million (73.7 percent) were rural elderly (China National Committee on Aging 2007). However, despite their large numbers, rural elderly have been so marginalized by the consequences of China's market reform and socioeconomic changes that their dire situation has no end in sight. Despite China's impressive double-digit GDP growth in the past two decades, older people in rural China have been largely excluded from sharing the benefit of China's new-found prosperity. The government has yet to come up with a comprehensive national plan to protect millions of rural elderly against the vicissitudes of aging exacerbated by a competitive market economy, as well as a much weakened, if not disappearing, family support system.

NOTES

I would like to thank the Wenner-Gren Foundation for Anthropology Research, Colby College Humanities Travel Grants and ASIANetwork Freeman Foundation Student-Faculty Fellowship Grant for the financial support for this research. I am also grateful to Jay Sokolosky for his valuable suggestions and comments on an earlier draft of this chapter.

1. This "speed of aging" variable is usually measured as the time it takes a population to go from 7 percent of its population to 14 percent, sixty-five years or older.

2. According to the World Bank data, China's per capita income was USD 1,740 in 2004, ranking 108 out of a total of 187 countries in the world (World Bank 2006).

3. Although in general the standard of living was higher in urban areas than in rural areas during the Mao years, the rural elderly as a group were not singled out as being disadvantaged.

4. This is on top of nine elderly suicide cases that I documented in this village between 1991 and 2000 (Zhang 2004).

5. Studies have indicated that approximately 18 to 29 percent of parental suicides were caused by family conflict (He and Lester 2001). Lee and Kleinman note that suicide data collected from thirty-nine countries in the mid-1990s found that China had "the third highest suicide rate amongst the elderly (after Hungary and Sri Lanka)" (Lee and Kleinman 2000:224). As for the reasons leading to the elderly suicide, Lee and Kleinman cited "the decline of family solidarity, filial values and status of aging people" (p. 232).

6. The couple had two daughters and two sons, but their elder daughter moved out of the village through marriage and their elder son also transferred to work in the county seat. Only one son and a daughter still lived in the village at the time of their parents' death.

7. In a uxorilocal marriage, a daughter stayed in her natal home and her husband married in and joined her family. A uxorilocally married daughter would provide old-age support for her parents. Although considered less than ideal and practiced only under special circumstances, uxorilocal marriage has been common in this locality, side by side with the more culturally dominant patrilocal marriages (Zhang 1998).

8. Although the number of childless elder men was small at this time, Zhang's study of the marginalization of childless bachelors and their lack of access to welfare services from the state or the village in reform-era China raises a serious issue concerning the likely future facing millions of men who may not be able to find a wife and set up a family due to a severely skewed sex ratio as an unintended consequence of China's stringent birth control policy. The sex ratio in China has risen to 119:100 in 2005 (Reynolds 2007; Xinhua News Agency 2007). As Zhang points out, "the state cannot entirely dismiss the predicted 30 million unmarried men, a group created by the official population policy and society norms of son preference, and who, within the foreseeable future, will become elderly" (p. 293).

9. Yunxiang Yan has also provided an excellent analysis on various socioeconomic factors and changing intergenerational family dynamics behind the "crisis" in the old-age support for the elderly in rural China today (Yan 2003).

10. In fact, in his comparative study on the old-age support systems between urban China and Taiwan in the early 1990s, Martin Whyte found that even though Taiwan had a much higher level of economic development, urban elderly in Taiwan had "much more need to rely on their grown children or other family sources for old-age financial support than do their Baoding (a city in mainland China) counterparts" (Whyte 2004:118). Whyte's study shows that while only 27 percent of urban retirees receive pensions in Taiwan, in urban China the rate was 77 percent (p. 117).

11. Jonathan Unger made the same observation based on survey data on five Chinese cities in mid-1980s. See Unger 1993.

12. Looking at the demographic data from the 1640s to the 1940s, James Lee and Wang Feng note that "the shortage of women, exacerbated by the practice of polygyny and the discouragement of female remarriage, prevented a significant proportion of Chinese males in the past and some even today from ever marrying." According to Lee and Wang, "from the seventeenth through the late nineteenth centuries 10–20 percent of all men were unmarried" (Lee and Wang 2001:64–71). Lee and Wang further point out that "[a]ccess to marriage was determined by access to resources which were distributed unequally both by household positions and occupation" (p. 69, p. 80).

13. The United States' Gini coefficient was 46.9 in 2005. The speed at which China reached such a higher level of inequality is also astonishing, as its Gini coefficient rose from 28.6 in 1981 to 47.4 in 2004. In comparison, the Gini coefficient for the United States was 40.3 in 1980 and reached 46.9 in 2005 (from Wikipedia at http://en.wikipedia.org/wiki/Gini_coefficient).

14. As China does not have a uniform social security system, the pensions received by urban retirees thus vary greatly, based on one's association with a particular work unit. In general, government officials, professionals from big public institutions and workers in large, state-run enterprises receive much higher pensions and better fringe benefits than workers and staff members in smaller or collective-run enterprises. "High-ranking cadres" (*lixiu gangbu*), referring specifically to those officials who joined and worked for the Chinese Communist Party prior to 1949, stand out as a special category of retirees who receive far better retirement packages. As pointed out by Raymo and Xie, the huge preferential benefits for high-ranking elderly cadres could be seen as "an inducement to retirement for a highly privileged, yet redundant, group of cadres who were reluctant to retire. This 'buy-out' policy has resulted in a sizable number of urban elderly receiving huge returns to their political capital" (Raymo and Xie 2000:5–6).

15. Through my interviews, I can detect a gender difference among widowers and widows when they told me why they chose an elder home for residential care.

Widowers were much more likely to mention that they moved to an elder home because their spouse had died and they could not deal with daily life and manage their elder care alone. Although widows outnumber widowers in elder homes, they cited other reasons for going to elder homes such as advanced age, strained relationships, or avoiding boredom or loneliness, rather than their inability to manage self-care due to the loss of spouse.

16. Zhan et al.'s Tianjin data (2005) also shows that prior to institutional placement, "more than half (50.6 percent) of the elderly reported living alone or with a spouse" and presumably managed their own care (p. 179).

17. See also Yan 1997; Miller 2007.

18. The ideal old-age life encapsulated in Chinese sayings is "to live a happy family life surrounded by sons and grandsons" (*tianlun zhile, ersun raoqi*).

19. According to one study on the refrigerator market in China, in 1985, there were only 6.58 refrigerators per 100 urban households, but by 2001, the number increased to 82.3 refrigerators per 100 urban households (*Xiandai Jiadian* 2002).

20. This information is obtained from "China in Brief 2006" in the Chinese government's official sports site: http://www.china.org.cn/english/features/Brief/193374.htm.

21. Western-style theme parks and amusement parks have sprung up in reform-era urban China. But these parks are often very expensive (100 yuan to 150 yuan or more per person) and are very commercially oriented as they are owned and operated by private or joint ventures. These amusement parks are also a new phenomenon spurred by both the rising consumerism in China's market reform and the child-centered family trend as a result of China's one-child policy. Urban parents with newly found disposable income often compete to spend big money to indulge and pamper their only child through visiting such parks or eating at Western fast food restaurants.

22. It seems to have been a common practice for the state to raise money from the public through issuing lotteries nationwide for specific public causes such as a welfare lottery, a sports lottery and so on. A certain percentage from the proceeds raised through such lotteries funds the public programs set up by the state.

CHAPTER 16

Aging Proletariats in a Twenty-First-Century Indigenous Mexican Community

Jay Sokolovsky

It was a clear, February morning in 2006 as my wife and I drove from the Mexico City airport to an indigenous community two hours east of one of the planet's largest urban zones. We were returning to San Jeronimo Amatango to be part of the wedding ritual for our goddaughter, Rosalba Juarez, at the house compound called *Shalali*.[1] She is the twenty-two-year-old granddaughter of Jeronimo and Concha Juarez and the first child of their eldest son, Jose. In the mid-1990s my wife and I had been formally incorporated into the kin network centered in *Shalali* when we accepted the roles of *compadres* (coparents) to the family and *Padrinos* (godparents) to Rosalba, serving as the *patrons* or main ritual sponsors for her *Quinceañera* (fifteenth birthday celebration). As *compadres* our presence and support was also expected at all future major family rituals. Rosalba's lineage has been my anchor for long-term anthropological research in this Mexican village, which began with my PhD work in 1972.

Long gone are the nightmares that preceded my return to the community in 1989, to begin a study of aging and family dynamics. In these unsettling dreams, children from *Shalali* had succumbed to the high child mortality rate still prevalent in the early 1970s. In another dream, the passage up to the village, previously just mud and boulders, was nicely paved and the Aztec-era house mounds lining that road were covered with condominiums and American-style fast food restaurants.

Fortunately, my dreams were only slightly clairvoyant. I was relieved to find that it was no longer likely for a third of children born to die before age five and this new reality was starting to change how young adults and even the elderly felt about reproduction and intergenerational relations. Doña Concha Juarez,[2] the elder woman of *Shalali,* had lost four of six children prior to my first stay in the village in 1972. To my great relief, her surviving children, José and Lucia, who had been ages seven and two back then, and their two siblings born in the mid-1970s, were all alive and healthy.

Although a McDonald's was not yet within sight of village lands, global cultural influences were very much becoming part of daily life. The access road to the village had in fact been newly paved a month before my return in 1989. Although there were no fancy apartments atop the archeological ruins, Amatango's farmers had plowed under the ancient house lots and surrounding marginal lands to arduously reclaim the soils along the road, which overgrazing by the Spanish Conquistador's goats and sheep had ruined 200 years ago.

Driving through Amatango in 2006, one saw a former village grown into a globally connected town of more than 7,000 residents. Its young citizens were shifting their lives away from a cultural script centered on farm work that had dominated life for older generations. This was most glaringly noticed in a newly installed cell phone tower that sits on the edge of an uncultivated corn field across from the colonial-era church. Now almost all houses have a TV antenna on the roof, and inside, video and audio entertainment centers compete with saint's altars for the family's attention. Every few streets there are small general merchandise stores, selling everything from Coca-Cola and toilet paper to school supplies and cell phone cards. Previously, these items were available only in cities such as Mexico City or Texcoco. Along the smoothly paved central road taking cars and buses into the community's center, one passes an Internet/computer store (one of three now in the village), hair salon, a used CD and DVD store, kids on skateboards and a little store advertising "Pizza and Hamburger." The newest computer /Internet store was attached to the *Shalali* house compound and is run by twenty-one-year-old Anitita Mendez, the live-in girlfriend of José's brother, Angel.

This is indeed a community undergoing a profound transformation from an agrarian peasant village to a proletariat, wage-earning populace that is stretching the limits of a traditional cultural system to contain its globalizing circumstances. Yet, amidst newly installed speed bumps, ten teenage gangs, DVDs of pirated Hollywood movies, adolescents wearing "Metallica" tee-shirts, elders donning "Hard Rock Café" jackets, microbuses running every ten minutes to the nearest city, one can still hear and see the face of tradition holding a very tenuous sway against the globalizing winds of modern urban life sweeping rural Mexico. It could be seen especially in the eyes of young children as they approached an older relative and bowed to plant a ritual kiss on the uplifted hand. It is observed also in the public *fiesta* dances, where a child of eight might share the same dance platform and ritual significance with a man or woman of age forty, or even seventy. Such performances, while reduced in frequency, are still embedded in familial and public domains that give aging adults a place in their society, which transcends simple platitudes such as "show respect to your elders." These symbolic acts counter the recent claim by many elders themselves that "these days the young don't treat us like they should."

Since my research trip in 1989, I returned to Amatango every two to three years, each time focusing on how the life of the elderly was faring in the face of significant and rapid changes. Here I will explore how the elderly's place in the cultural spaces of domestic and civic life has functioned to buffer the potentially deleterious impact of rapid globalizing changes in peasant communities such as Amatango (see Rothstein 2007). The adaptations to these kinds of global transformations have been forged by more deeply embedding life within multilocal settings and establishing new cultural scripts for creating personal identity and the relations among generations.

PEASANT LIFE IN THE GLOBAL VILLAGE

Amatango is nestled in a mountain valley 8,500 feet above sea level and adjacent to the archeological remains of the residents' Aztec forbearers. Amatango is one of twenty-seven *pueblos* (rural communities) in a municipal unit politically led by the city of Texcoco, about twelve miles away. In 1972, Texcoco was a sleepy municipal capital of 25,000, but by 2007 its population had swelled to about 180,000. This urban center with its banks, supermarkets, appliance stores, movie theaters, medical clinics, film shops, Domino's Pizza delivery, computer centers, technical schools and car dealerships serves as a juncture for the diffusion of Mexican national culture and increasingly international ideas and products. It is here that inhabitants of Amatango must come to register titles to land, obtain a civil marriage, pay their electric bills or complain about an injustice that cannot be handled by their own authorities. Over the past two decades, Texcoco has become a major site of employment for Amatango's citizens, especially as bus and taxis drivers, hair stylists or workers in the stores and small factories located there.

Less than an hour west of Texcoco sits the edge of massive, vibrant Mexico City, with its 20 million inhabitants clinging improbably to a dry, extremely polluted, high-altitude valley. Since the early fifteenth century, when Amatango was founded, its fate has been connected to this national capital. While isolated in a rugged mountain region, Amatango's families managed to periodically haul valuable forest products to the city's ancient urban markets, even before the availability of cantankerous burros that the Spanish introduced during the sixteenth century.

However, it has been only within the past several decades that Mexico City has drawn families deeply into its social and cultural fabric through jobs, expanding markets for its goods and being the preferred source for machinery, consumer electronics and even ritual items such as Rosalba's wedding dress. The frequent travel from small town to megalopolis has entrenched most of Amatango's residents, especially the young, in a global cultural network of personal style, consumption and ideas. Yet, we will see that the vibrancy and strength of their culture and economy, especially in the way it connects generations, has so far resisted the worst kinds of potential social dissolution and exclusion that can result from globalization (Phillipson 2007; Fry this volume).

In the early 1970s, residents of Amatango culturally identified themselves as *indios* (Indians) and were, in fact, thought to be the most ardent followers of indigenous traditions in their region. They were bilingual in Spanish and the classic form of the Aztec language, *nahuatl*. This was the first language children learned, often while being carried around wrapped in the *rebozo* of their resident grandmother. Elders resided in house compounds of their lineage surrounded by adult sons and typically multiple generations of their extended families. Kin boundaries and connections were ritually marked every day as close relatives were always greeted by a distinctive bowing and hand-kissing respect gesture. Women used the Aztec sweat bath (*temazcal*) in many of their healing regimens and the populace kept the Aztec deity, called *nahuake,* in their spiritual pantheon. Moreover, a regular system of communal labor and a very traditional fiesta complex was continued in which families took on time-consuming and costly responsibilities for ritually celebrating the lives of various Roman Catholic saints. Along with four other nahuatl-speaking villages in the high mountain lands, Amatango remained culturally distinct from the rural communities in the lower ecological zones stretching down toward Texcoco. Inhabitants of such villages spoke only Spanish and disdained the "backward" *indios del monte* (mountain Indians), while touting themselves as *mestizos*, agrarian exemplars of a more cosmopolitan, urban style of life.

What originally drew me to study Amatango was a seeming paradox. How could these traditional cultural features coexist with a series of locally initiated, "modernizing" changes that also made the village the most rapidly transforming of the *indio* communities in its region? Some changes, such as village electrification and the building of a new elementary school, had begun a few years before I arrived. Others were transpiring during and within five years of my initial research stay. These changes included construction of a passable, flat dirt road, the creation of a potable water system and building a medical clinic building and a high school. In the early 1990s, Amatango also became the Catholic parochial center for the other nearby Indio communities and finally acquired its own resident priest. By the beginning of the twenty-first century, the community had an expanded paved road, very regular bus connections and had built a technical school and two bilingual elementary schools.

It is critical to understand that Amatango has not been a passive receptor of these changes, but has sought through its collective initiative to recast itself in terms of local concepts of a modern "civilized" place. Fortunately for the elderly, Amatango has resolved this paradox of remaining the most traditional, while also being the most changing community, by relying upon and eventually transforming its most customary aspects of belief and village organization to pursue the goal of community transformation. However, we will see that over the last decade, accelerated levels of community change and the dramatic expansion of Mexico City into the world's largest metropolis have created new challenges that are beginning to test the best of cultural intentions. In the context of such changes, the framework for the path through the life cycle are being written from a more diverse and complex script.

Amatango reached the 1970s as a highly integrated peasant enclave that depended largely on patterns traceable to Aztec ancestors, but shored up by new economic innovations. At that time, I found that almost two-thirds of extended households that included members over age sixty were producing either wooden crates for the burgeoning markets in Mexico City or decorative flowers to satisfy the ritual needs of growing urban populations. These two activities not only provided a fair amount of cash, but the work was best accomplished within a multigenerational domestic work unit. Moreover, the economic utility of the aged, especially males, was enhanced as they were more likely to continue contributing to these cash-producing endeavors long after their effectiveness in other agrarian work had diminished.

Yet the benefits of these changes were limited by an inefficient irrigation system, lack of a passable road for motor traffic and the low level of education. Fortuitously, it was in the late 1960s and early 1970s that the state government, with Mexican federal assistance, began to selectively invest in improving rural infrastructure through electrification, road building and eventually the expansion of rural health care services. As a start, the community combined its traditional communal labor system with state government-provided materials and engineers to improve their irrigation system and build a small bridge over a ravine, which had been a serious obstacle to motorized vehicles entering the community. With these initial successes in the 1960s, Amatango's leaders over the coming decades would petition for other "modernizing" changes mentioned previously. During this time, as the village's population rapidly increased and the urban zones of Texcoco and Mexico City dramatically expanded, young adults sought wage labor outside the community in transportation, service trades (e.g., hair styling), factory work, textile production and eventually in bilingual education.

AGING AND FAMILY LIFE ON THE EDGE
OF A GLOBAL MEGACITY

Mexico, like many other Third World nations, has been very slow in seeing the needs of the aged as competing with other issues. In the early twenty-first century, it was still a demographically young nation with under 5 percent of its populace age sixty-five or older. However, Mexico now has an average longevity approaching seventy-five years and has seen a drop in the fertility rate from 7.2 in 1960 to 2.2 in 2005. Like countries such as Indonesia, India and China, in another thirty years the proportion of Mexico's elderly will more than double, and by midcentury the ratio of persons aged fifteen to sixty-four years, per those sixty-five years or older, will precipitously drop from twelve to just three (Partida-Bush 2007).[3]

In Amatango, by 2005 the community's age structure still had the classic pyramidal, youth-dominated shape (Figure 16.1), although the reduction in childbirths was beginning to be seen at the youngest end of the lifespan. With just 3.4 percent over age sixty-five, this was still a young community, especially compared to other rural *pueblos* closer to Texcoco where migration and earlier limitations on fertility typically doubled or even tripled this measure of agedness.

Figure 16.1
Age Pyramid, Amantango, 2005

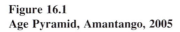

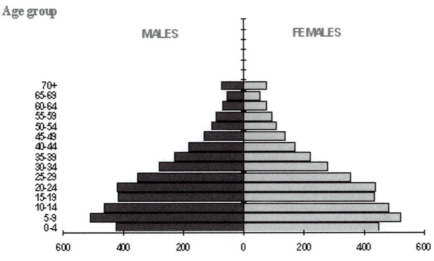

Source: Annual census completed by Amantango's community nurse, 2006.

When I began my research in the early 1970s, Mexico was undergoing economic expansion, and Amatango, like many other rural regions, witnessed a
population explosion resulting from a high rate of births, averaging 9.39 per
family (Millard 1978). Over the next several decades, with steep declines in
the mortality rate, particularly for children under age five, population more
than doubled to almost 5,000 residents in 2000.[4] Yet, by this time Amatango's
young women were also adopting new reproductive strategies and the population was increasing at a lower rate. These women were starting to use modern
birth control techniques, despite strong initial resistance from their husbands
and mothers-in-law.[5] In 1973, when I would ask young men and women what
the ideal family size was, the standard response was, "only God knows." At
that time, couples sought to have as many children as they could. By the
1990s, attitudes had changed dramatically. Almost like a Greek chorus, adults
in their twenties would repeat the maxim, "*dos hijos es mejor, pero cuatro es
el maximo!*" (two kids is ideal, but the maximum is four). Of the women who
were practicing some form of birth control, the majority would only begin after
they had given birth to three or four children. This shift in reproductive behavior was influenced by the fact that with the establishment of a medical clinic in
the community, infant mortality had plummeted to levels almost comparable
with national figures. For example, infant mortality was 390 per 1,000 in the
1960s, but by the early 1990s it had plummeted to 53.5 (Mindek 1994). Young
parents also became acutely aware of the rapidly rising costs of supporting
children, especially in the area of education. Although by 2006 the average

completed fertility for women had been reduced to about 3.5 children, the equally dramatic increased child survival and limited permanent migration meant that the population had soared to about 7,700 residents.

AGING AND THE CULTURAL SCRIPT OF THE *CAMPESINO* LIFE COURSE

When I first came to Amatango in 1972, the cultural script for just about everyone's life course centered around subsistence corn farming and animal husbandry combined with occasional wage labor, playing music in traditional fiesta bands and the sale of decorative flowers and wooden crates in Texcoco or Mexico City. When men were asked their occupation, they invariable replied, "*soy campesino*," I am a farmer. Even when men worked outside the community, it was viewed as a supplemental activity that would be easily interrupted for either work in their fields, or ritual and civil duties in the village. A woman might also state, "*soy campesina*," or sometimes just tell me in Aztec that they she was a *suwat* (wife), a proud partner in the domestic economy and the public ritual life of the household.

The attainment of adult status for both men and women comes through marriage. Couples initially live together following a ritual called "*robo de esposa*," where the young woman secretly moves into her boyfriend's family's house and then his uncles come with ritual gifts to inform the girl's family of this event. If her parents accept this, it immediately establishes a special ritual bond between the couple's parents and sets in motion a yearlong series of highly formal visits between the households.[6] For the first few years, the young couple will usually live under the roof and command of the groom's parents and any living grandparents. This provides entree into a variety of responsibilities that link the couple to broader community responsibilities. Typically, a couple will formally marry within three or five years after the girl is "robbed" and often following the birth of one or more children.

As most marriages take place within the village (about 75 percent in 2006), this imparts a particularly intense geographic density to the social networks of the aged.[7] This is especially so for men, who typically remain in their natal house compound and are surrounded by many other male-linked kin. While a women's kin group is more physically dispersed from her abode than a male's, this does not imply that females are more isolated in old age. In fact, as indicated later, women past age sixty-five will typically maintain reciprocal support networks with more personnel and have greater frequency of exchange than their male age peers.

One of the dramatic and consistently adhered to aspects of intergenerational kinship behavior is a formal system of deferential gestures. Upon seeing an older relative, a villager will, with respectful comportment, rush to that person's side, solemnly bend to ritually kiss his or her right hand and whisper the proper Nahuatl reverential term (e.g., *Nosicntzin*, my revered grandmother). Kinpersons of roughly equal age also ritually greet each other, but with simultaneous and more perfunctory bows and hand-kissing gestures. This display of "sacred respect" (*respeto*) functions to regulate the traditional lines of authority and maintain proper social distance within the kinship system. Despite the dominance of patrilineal descent, kinship ties generated through one's mother are also acknowledged by *respeto* behavior and have great practical importance. Maternal relatives comprise a significant portion of a household's total personal network of support. It is through the exchange of labor, tangible goods and money that families are able to carry out costly and time-consuming public ritual. For example, during Rosalba's wedding, almost 60 percent of the labor was provided by persons linked to the older adult women in her parent's household.

The Shift to Maturity

Individuals will attempt to retain the image of a fully functioning adult (*Tlacatl*-man, *Suwatl*-woman) as long as possible. However, it is recognized that sometime during the sixth or seventh decade of life, men and women will gradually give up total executive control of field and hearth to one of their married sons and his wife. People will begin to refer to such persons as old by generically using the term *cultzin* (grandparent) or *culi* (old person) for both males and females.[8] They will begin to be talked about as *culi* when several grandchildren have survived childhood.

However, the *culi* label is not consistently applied to a person until their early to mid-sixties when changes in strength and vitality reduce work capacity in some way. Once persons are accepted as *culi*, they will be excused from communal work groups and most public ritual sponsorship. The last stages of agedness are defined by steep declines in functional abilities, with the most obvious sign of "real" old age being the need to walk with a cane.[9] If this mobility shift is accompanied by other dramatic declines that might forecast an impending demise, people might refer to a person as *youtla moak* or "all used up."[10] This term is not used often, but sums up more precise Nahuatl words that describe the loss of real adult functioning. By the time people are labeled *yotla moak*, they have generally restricted their daily activity to their house compound and rely on nearby grandchildren and great-grandchildren to assist with their activities of daily living.

For older women, there is a noticeable lessening of social constraints on their behavior, and they are allowed greater latitude in social interaction, especially with male age peers. By the time a woman is sixty, she may be seen on occasion casually chatting with a group of men or guzzling a beer at a public festival, things forbidden to younger women. Beginning in midlife, through their forties and fifties, women may cultivate skills in nondomestic arenas. One of these is midwifery and/or some other traditional folk healing specialty such as *tepatike* (general healer), *tlamemelawa* (massage) or *tlapupua* (herbal medicine). Of the six most active midwives in 2006, four are in their mid-forties, one is fifty-five and the other two are in their mid-seventies. Each of these women practice at least one of the other healing traditions in addition to assisting with childbirth.[11]

A second area of activity for mid-age women is in the entrepreneurial realm. After menopause, women have the opportunity to venture to urban markets by themselves to sell. Most typically this will involve hawking flowers, herbs, food or animals in the crowded satellite urban areas ringing Mexico City. For example, by 1994 Doña Maria, age sixty-four, had been a widow for a decade and lived with her married son and his children on a tiny, unproductive plot of land. She began selling sheep and goats about fifteen years before. Later, she used this money to trade in flowers and put a deposit down toward the purchase of a small textile-making machine from the factory where her son was working in Chiconcaoc. They started to produce sweaters in their house and eventually used the profits for Doña Maria to set up a paper and notebook store in the late 1980s. This enterprise has done quite well, along with the completion of Amatango's own high school soon after the store opened.

As is typical in the life cycle of peasants elsewhere, women in old age show a greater continuity in the roles they play than do men (Cool and McCabe 1987; Bledsoe 2002). Most elderly women, almost to the time of their deaths, continue a familiar domestic regimen centering on food preparation, weaving, nurturance of children and the care of small livestock. Continuing this work pattern keeps old women deeply embedded in a network of both age peers and younger women from four to six households, who must cooperate to produce the huge quantities of food consumed on ritual occasions. For example, during the wedding in 2006 in *Shalali*, Doña Concha (age seventy-one) and her two resident daughters-in-law coordinated the work of ten other women from ages forty-six to seventy-five who seemed to work constantly and seamlessly over a three-day period to prepare and serve food to several hundred people. One female relative, age seventy-two, had the specialized task of rapidly dispatching seventy-five chickens that were cooked for the main celebration.

Men, even after relinquishing control of their farms, will continue to undertake arduous work alongside their sons until their mid-to-late sixties. It is after this point, when they can no longer easily plow or plant, that they switch to more sedentary tasks such as preparing cactus beer, repairing tools or collecting wild vegetables from nearby cornfields. Today, however, with so many men in the twenty to forty age bracket working out of the village on any given day, it is not unusual to see a male in his seventies planting a field by himself or with a couple of age peers. Their sons will typically help when they can, but only if it does not interfere with a wage-producing job.

Despite this, in Amatango, extended family organization is the normative form of residence that older adults hope to generate over the long run. Ideally, as male offspring get married, at least one is expected to raise children in his parent's house and provide the core basis of support in old age. More often than not these days, resident married sons and their families live in a physically independent house set within a residential compound, a moment's walk from their parents' dwelling—just across a courtyard or down a dirt path. The

Concha (far right) working with one of her two resident daughters-in-law (far left) and two older female relatives. They are preparing chickens to be cooked for Rosalba's wedding feast, 2006. Photo by Maria Vesperi.

experience of aged individuals living by themselves is still extremely rare and usually happens following the death of a spouse, where the older couple had been living alone in one of the relatively isolated mountain neighborhoods. In most such instances, there will be an attempt, as seen in the following photo, to send adolescent or teenage children to live with and help grandparents who would otherwise would be living by themselves.

Elders are in constant contact with children, if not with a resident grandchild, then with a wide range of very young kin and godchildren living within a few hundred yards from them. The child-minding aspect of grandparenting has, in fact, increased over the last decade, as in many households at least one of the parents is working in the city during the day. Relations of the very old with their grandchildren are especially important. In extended families, young children were observed sleeping in the same bed as a grandparent. This seldom seemed a matter of space, but rather a case of mutual need. The children help to warm up old bones, and the grandparent provides emotional security at night when various spirits and demons are thought to travel through the village.

While archival research indicates that the percent of elders living in extended household contexts has remained at about two-thirds over the past eighty years, important structural changes have taken place (Sokolovsky 2002). From the 1920s to the current time, a major shift has involved the significant reduction of very large extended households, where two or more married sons stayed in the house compound to work with and eventually care for their

Fifteen-year-old boy sent to live with his widowed grandmother, 1993. Photo by Jay Sokolovsky.

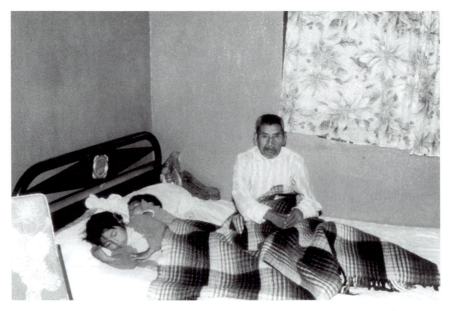

Ninety-six-year-old man sleeping with two coresident great grandchildren, 1978. Photo by Jay Sokolovsky.

parents. Such "joint" patrilineal (male-linked) households, containing twelve to twenty-five persons, were enclosed within 120- by 70-foot-long rectangular compounds protected by 15-foot-high adobe walls and at least two dogs. By the early 1970s, reductions in per capita land holdings and the rise of new money-making activities outside the village had stimulated a shift from "joint" to "stem" patrilineal groupings, where only one married son would remain with the parents. At that time, the proportion of joint, patrilineal households with more than one married son living under the parents' domain had been reduced by about half. Of more recent vintage is the formation of extended households by incorporating an adult daughter's family into her parents' residence, either by themselves or along with a married son. In most of these cases, the adult daughter has married someone from outside the village from a poor family who had little to offer the young couple. Such marriages are especially unstable and are many times more likely to break up than if the husband and wife both were born in the village. In almost all such cases of marital dissolution, the daughter will remain in her parents' house, especially if she has any young children.

GLOBALIZATION AND THE FAMILY DOMAIN FOR AGING

Over the past three decades, Mexico City has become the second largest urban area in the world. Here, families from Amatango found new, burgeoning areas in which to sell local goods produced by extended family labor. This type of work was greatly facilitated by the improved village road and more frequent bus service. A majority of families who had previously grown commercial flowers began to buy them cheaply in other communities for resale in urban markets, some even having their own little stores or stalls for this purpose. Throughout the 1980s and 1990s, increasing numbers of younger males and females sought employment in nonagricultural labor outside the village. At this time, a majority were working for wages, either part time or full time in urban factories, driving buses or taxis, selling local products in city market stalls, or making clothes in the small textile-focused city of Chiconcuac, near Texcoco. However, unlike in many other areas of Mexico, relatively few actually migrated away from the village or attempted to cross the northern border to the United States.[12] Yet, as already noted, by the twenty-first century, men in their sixties and seventies were having a hard time finding their sons around to work the fields during critical parts of the agricultural cycle. By 2006, as I walked through the village I saw that about 20 percent of former crop lands were either left fallow or were being used for the construction of new houses.[13]

Another significant change has occurred in the work pattern of young women. Up to the 1980s, the only typical wage work sought by teenage girls was to work as live-in servants for middle-class families in Mexico City or Texcoco. However, in the 1980s, the town of Chiconcuac on the outskirts of

Texcoco began to abandon its traditional, small-scale production of wool products for large-scale production of inexpensive synthetic fiber clothing. For the last 100 years, Amatango's families had provided much of the wool for Chiconcuac's once-famous serapes and sweaters. Now they began to provide their teenage daughters and some sons to help produce inexpensive dresses, shirts and other clothes for markets throughout Mexico and even the United States.

By 2000, about 200 villagers (such as my goddaughter Rosalba) still worked in Chiconcuac; however, increasing global competition began to force these factories to drastically downsize. At that time, about twenty families in Amatango decided to use their children's accumulated skills and wages to invest in sewing and weaving machines and to create clothing in their own homes for sale in regional markets. When I returned in February 2006, this pattern was becoming very popular, with about 100 households engaged in the production of clothing. Home-based textile work had become particularly attractive to young couples who could work side by side while living in the groom's parents' house and contributing monies to extended family coffers on a weekly basis. It is important to note that for the vast majority of households producing textiles, as was the case with crate-making in the 1970s, this work stabilizes multigenerational households. Typically, the capital outlays for the expensive machines are funded by the elder generation, and part of the resulting monies from this work is shared with parents or other older relatives. This has happened for my goddaughter Rosalba and her new husband Herardo, who in their case make textiles for Herardo's uncle, who following their wedding gave them land to set up a house next to his family.

A smaller core of young women were also taking advantage of growing educational opportunities, completing high school in the new local facility built in the early 1980s or in a technical school completed in 1995. Some were going on to outside technical schools, junior college and even university in Mexico City. A small core of these women were becoming hair stylists, secretaries, nurses and teachers in both regular grade schools and bilingual schools opening in the region. One such twenty-one-year-old female, a computer science major at Texcoco's junior college, opened up Amatango's first computer café, in 2003, with the financial backing of her parents. Similarly, as will be seen in the following case study, young, educated women are beginning to reshape ideas about the life course.

THE CASE OF THE RELUCTANT *CAMPESINO* AND THE EDUCATED DAUGHTER-IN-LAW

The house compound called *Shalali* (sandy soil) in 2006 contained an extended family that has taken a different path in adapting to the modern world. The eldest is the shy, widowed, very traditional, Nahuatl-speaking Concha Duran Juarez, age seventy-one, whose husband Jeronimo died at age sixty-three in 1997. Concha has four living children, two adult sons (Jose and Angel) whose families live in *Shalali*, a daughter (Lucia), wed within the village, and another daughter (Ana), who recently moved in with a man and his parents in a nearby community. Ana had been living in *Shalali* until a year ago, following the breakup of a relationship with a man she met while working in Chiconcuac.

Although Concha's husband Jeronimo had been fluent in Nahuatl and enjoyed participating in the traditional fiesta system, he was deeply conflicted about the agrarian way of life and had never liked farming. He would often intersperse tending his small fields with temporary factory jobs, or making change on buses in Texcoco. Jeronimo and his sons also made wooden crates for sale, or bought and sold flowers with Concha in the shanty towns springing up around Mexico City. At one point in the 1960s, Jeronimo moved the family to Texcoco, but Concha became depressed and threatened to kill herself, and they moved back in less than a year. In 1984, their oldest son José "robbed" his village-born wife into *Shalali*, and over a fifteen-year period they had four children, the oldest of whom is Rosalba. With population and urban congestion booming in the Texcoco region by the 1990s, the government encouraged individuals to lease buses or vans to enhance the existing intercity public transport system. By 1994, Jeronimo had leased both a large van and a small bus, which he and his two sons would drive in long shifts to support the household. They also used their collective savings to open up a small convenience store in the front of their house, which Concha managed. Following Jeronimo's death, the family gave up one of the buses, and by the late 1990s Concha's resident teenage granddaughters Rosalba and Elizabeth had both dropped out of school and were commuting daily to make sweaters in a small factory in the nearby town of Chiconcuac.

At the time of Rosalba's wedding in 2006, she, like her younger sister, had already been "robbed" into the house of her boyfriend's family and had a two-year-old son. In *Shalali*, along with Concha, was José, his wife Maria, their teenage son and adolescent daughter and José's younger brother Angel with his "robbed" girlfriend. The teenager, Miguel, while knowing some rudiments of *campesino* life, was attending the village's new technical high school and striving to become a highly skilled textile maker. While José and his wife are fluent in Nahuatl, he often tells me emphatically that this language is no longer of any use to his son, and what he needs to learn is English!

In the back of the house, Concha still maintains a garden of greens and chilies and tends a flock of chickens and turkeys as well as a handful of pigs. There was also a recently acquired small bull, but it and most of the other animals were to be slaughtered for the huge wedding feast held within the *Shalali* compound.

Two years earlier, Angel had "robbed" Anita, who grew up on the other side of the community. This woman, age twenty-four, had completed computer technical school in Texcoco and with combined financing from her parents and her new relatives in *Shalali*, quickly set up the community's newest computer café where the convenience store had once been. Angel, spending less time driving a bus, with the help of his older brother, invested in sewing and weaving machines and had begun making clothing for sale. Anita had also recently given birth to a baby boy, and it seemed that every moment he was not nursing, the child was wrapped up in a rebozo on Concha's back as she worked with the other women in the house.

Following the death of her husband, Concha, whose quiet, warm personality made relations with her daughters-in-law run smoothly, admitted she was now *culi* and let Maria know that she could take charge of the domestic scene. In fact, living in their household one could not really determine who was the boss as they just did things with and for each other with such unspoken ease that it appeared to occur via mental telepathy. Angel and Anita, however, were the edge of a new cultural script that was beginning to bind together generations in different ways and alter the work and power relations between couples.

Interesting enough, women such as Anita as a group tend to remain in the village and are among the most vocal supporters of traditional indigenous culture, especially the retention of the Nahuatl language. About a dozen of these women have found employment as bilingual, Nahuatl/Spanish teachers in Amatango, as well as in the more recently built bilingual schools in the other nearby indigenous communities.

AGING BEYOND THE FAMILY

Beyond the family, the most important source of prestige, respect and power during middle and old age derives from the carrying out of community ritual and civil responsibilities. Known in Latin American scholarship as either the cargo (literally, "burden") system or the *fiesta* system, this involves a hierarchy of ranked positions (*cargos*) occupied for short periods of time by specific households (Cancian 1992; Chick 2002).

In Amatango, community roles are loosely ranked, with the higher ones generally requiring more money and/or time, but yielding more prestige and authority. The positions are divided between *cargos* of the church and those associated with political office; the former carry out costly folk Catholic ritual (*fiestas*), while the latter form the local government.

The annual religious cycle of four *fiestas* was carried out by an annually elected set of twenty-two ritual sponsors or *mayordomos* (stewards) who are led by two *fiscals* (literally "prosecutors") who collectively are responsible for a single year of ritual.[14] The *fiscal* position is the most prestigious religious position, with election to this post usually predicated on prior service in at least one other major religious *cargo*. For the general male population, there is an expectation that over a lifetime an individual will have undertaken at least one important sacred *cargo* and thereby be worthy of public esteem.[15]

At the center of local political authority and administration is the first *delegado* (commissioner), who serves for three years as the combined mayor and head judge. The second commissioner serves as his chief assistant by recording necessary documents, while the third is in charge of collecting fines and community taxes. The first *delegado*, referred to in Nahuatl as *altepetatli* (community father), is expected to oversee the community paternally, settle most levels of internal disputes and protect local interests from any outside forces. He leads all village meetings and must solicit opinions from all present until a general consensus is reached. Other personnel in the political hierarchy distribute irrigation waters, protect community boundaries and organize the traditional system of unremunerated collective labor that carries out public works projects. It is this civil wing of community service that since the late 1960s has initiated and carried out the series of modernizing projects of which Amatango is so proud. By the time most males reach age sixty, they will have shouldered at least some local political responsibility.[16]

Besides ritual sponsorship and administrative positions, the *cargo* system affords other opportunities to enhance public esteem in old age. Some of the fiestas involve dance troops and elaborate processions. Older men, and to a lesser extent women, can volunteer to take roles as dance leaders, instructors, special musicians or simply as participants. Such activities proclaim not only moral uprightness and continuing prestige, but also that one is still actively involved in the life of the community.

Despite the emphasis on age, hierarchy and formal deference between generations in family formations, this pattern is not totally replicated in the public groupings that carry out ritual. Although the fiesta system performs an implicit age-grading function, it also provides one of the only community-wide arenas where males and females of all ages can theoretically participate as relative equals. This occurs in the large dance groups that perform at most fiestas as part of the community's "folk" version of Roman Catholic pageantry.[17] However, as will be noted later, gradually over the past two decades the number of fiestas has been reduced, especially those in which the elderly were most likely to participate.

Although women participate in the masses, processions and dancing associated with each fiesta, until 2002 they assumed no overt public leadership position in these activities. That year for the first time single women in their early twenties were elected for very minor posts in the fiesta system. Moreover, with the establishment of Amatango as a parish center, the resident priest has encouraged middle-aged and older women to become leaders of a children's catechism group. Yet, during major public ceremonies, older women generally operate behind the scenes, directing the production and serving huge quantities of the special foods required for successful ritual sponsorship. In accomplishing this they rely on, and in turn support, a wide circle of female age-peers and younger women drawn from their bilateral kin network. The reciprocal flow of assistance stimulated by the annual cycle of fiestas provides a regular source of extrahousehold engagement for all but the frailest women.

Perhaps the most important change with regard to older people and the cargo system has been the reduction in their political roles in favor of younger and better educated leaders. Prior to 1950, it was unheard of for a man to be considered for first *delegado* or senior *fiscal* before the age of fifty, and persons chosen were often at least sixty. However, since 2000, the directors of the religious hierarchy are more likely than not to be under fifty years of age. Similarly, for the last four decades, first *delegados*, holders of the most potent political position, have been forty-one years of age or younger; the youngest was thirty-one.

Despite the steady drop in age of the community mayor, the village has sought to select respected men between fifty-five and sixty-five years old as the third *delegado*. In addition, still older men are used as judicial go-betweens in difficult cases where parties initially refuse to abide by legal decisions of the *delegados*. By this pragmatic use of human resources, Amatango has put the prestige and authority accumulated over a lifetime behind political and judicial decisions.

AGING WITHIN ALTERED CULTURAL SPACES

Unlike the harping seniors of the Ju/'hoansi (Rosenberg, this volume) who complain about their own mistreatment at the hand of kin, in Amatango the only time one hears a personal narrative of neglect concerns people who are considered "strange," mentally unbalanced or who have ignored their duty to others. For example, in the mid-1990s, I documented a case where both the elder and the community defined the older person as being abandoned. This is intriguing in that the elderly man, who proclaims to all who will listen that his sons have abandoned him, actually lives with one son, while another son lives next door, and the other two reside within a few hundred yards. Why, then, was seventy-five-year-old Miguel Juarez considered to be *yamoucachiwe encaño*, that is, abandoned while living with his family? A widower for about ten years, Miguel lived with Eduardo, who is forty, mildly retarded and the only one who works with his father in the family cornfields. Eduardo has never married and is described as "a little crazy" by other people. Miguel has had a serious drinking problem since early adulthood. During his married life, he would get drunk quite often and beat his wife. Frequently in debt, he eventually sold small plots of land for money, land which he should have kept to give to his sons. None of his three married sons ever developed a very strong interest in farming. Two work in small sweater factories in Texcoco and a third makes his living by playing in the local fiesta music bands. Although in close proximity to their father, the three married sons ignore Miguel, although if he complains to them they let him know how much they resent him for having abused their mother and sold off part of their birthright.

While such cases are still exceedingly rare, since 2000, and especially from older males, I have heard an increasing litany of negative comments about changes related to young people's attitude toward work and the way older persons are publicly treated. Ask an older male what has changed the most in his lifetime and one will likely hear: "The young, they are different now. They see the land we have here and do not see the beauty or the worth in it"; "Ask anyone, the young simply do not know about hard work like we do"; "It's the young men, they don't not how to work anymore, but they sure know how to drink!" More generally, there are increasing accusations of a decrease in respect shown the elderly. Most of the talk about this is very generalized and similar to things that are heard in many cultures when a society goes through very rapid change, especially when the work goals and identity of the younger generation bears little resemblance to that of preceding ones. Listen to the comments of former first *delegado* Santiago Velazquez, age seventy-three:

The truth is, young people, some with just a little bit of training or education, say the older people don't know how to do things and we know better. And for instance, some of them have their little trucks and we don't. We go around on our donkeys. I still have mine. And it's like they exaggerate. They say that old people aren't worth anything anymore.

Such sentiments are born of the gradual shrinking of the cultural spaces in which older men gain public and even familial respect. This is seen in the decline of agriculture where previously the older males of a lineage commanded children and younger relatives in an annual reciprocal cycle of farm labor. At that time the economic futures of children were largely dependent on inheriting lands from their parents. The older generation has come to realize that reliance on the former agrarian *campesino* lifestyle, in most cases can no longer be the cornerstone of sustaining families. At best, for most males under age forty, such activities today have become an ancillary, almost ritualized activity that provides a backup to the need for a constant flow of income into the household. *Campesino* work is coming to be seen as an anachronism and treated by a majority of young men as a quaint pastime, but certainly not an identity they care to make central in their lives.

Another side of this kind of change is the shift from a very authoritarian relation between generations to one based on a more balanced, reciprocal connection. Consider these observations of similar actions, thirty years apart:

Field notes May 25, 1973:

It is pouring rain and I with my large umbrella help a frail elder, Juan Espinosa, get to his house without falling in the growing mud. As we enter, I see Juan's young grandson (about 10 years old). He had been playing in the house with a stick and laughing, but rapidly changes to a somber demeanor and carefully approaches Juan. He bends to kiss his hand and whispers *nokulkn* (my grandfather). The boy helps Juan to a small wooden chair and then proceeds, with some struggle, to pull off his grandfather's muddy boots.

Field notes June 15, 2003:

At one of the largest extended households in the community, I am talking to *Don* Edwardo, age 78 and his wife Isabela, age 74, who are working in their butcher shop attached to their house. They look up at the noisy approach of a group of young teens, I recognize one of their grandsons, age 13, who greets me with a handshake and then smiling and bobbing in a casual way skips to his grandparents, kissing first their hands and following this with a gentle affectionate kiss on their cheeks.

Ninety-two-year-old man being greeted by his forty-five-year-old nephew with a ritual hand kiss, 2000. Photo by Jay Sokolovsky.

Over the thirty years since my first fieldwork stay, indelible change has clearly occurred in generational dynamics. Most notable has been the reduced control of senior kin over the actions of junior relatives. In the early 1970s, the emotional structure of family systems was quite authoritarian, dominated by the elder couple, especially the male. Following Aztec legal tradition, parents could take disobedient children to the community judges for punishment in the form of hard labor for the community or a fine.[18] I witnessed several such cases during 1973. However, the last public trial for parental disobedience was held a decade ago.

On a more subtle level, during my earliest research in Amatango, I found that the physical gesture of *respeto* masks an underlying tension and fear that embraces the realm of kinship. A system whereby a man's access to adult roles and community status is largely predicated on inherited lands engenders not only filial conflict, but also tension between brothers and certain male cousins (the sons of a father's brother). The total acceptance of *respeto* behavior is thought to help avoid the display of angry emotions among relatives, an act that itself is thought to cause an illness called *muina*[19] or invite sorcery with its subsequent misfortune. While any adult in Amatango can be a potential witch, the quest for a suspect usually begins among one's poorer relatives.

Despite this ominous possibility, it is a person's cousins who throughout life form the core of a reciprocal work-exchange network needed for agriculture house construction and ritual sponsorship.

With the ongoing demise of the *campesino* cultural script, children are not so tied to replicating their parents' agrarian lifestyle to gain adult status. In this context, intragenerational competition and harsh dominance by the older generation has significantly decreased. Importantly, this has gone along with a steep reduction in accusations of witchcraft. When I first lived in the village, I calculated the rate at one per month.[20] By 2006, many people claimed that witchcraft no longer existed there. However, while in fact public accusations had dramatically diminished, I documented two such cases in the prior three years.

In the broader public sphere of *fiestas* and civic *cargos*, cultural spaces, especially for men, have also shrunk. Over the past two decades, the number of major fiestas has been cut in half, and those no longer performed are largely ones in which elderly men were both teachers of dances and active performance participants. This move from player to audience in these religious dramas, especially for healthy, economically active males in their sixties is generally met philosophically with such comments as, "Well, those *fiesta* dances we still perform involve very fast, hard movements for many hours and are best left to the young." However, older men are also still important ritual leaders in family ritual. For example, at Rosalba's wedding, her great uncle Julio Mendez, the oldest male lineage member at age seventy-six, received a good deal of deference from younger persons. Julio was always the first to welcome members of the groom's lineage or the family's *compadres*, and he led prayers as they entered the house compound for the festivities.

For older women, their important social spaces have been more stable and in some ways enlarged. As previously noted, go to any social event such as the wedding at *Shalali*, and one will see numerous women from other households who are sisters, cousins, aunts and comadres of Concha working happily together. They work as a well-oiled team with younger women of the lineage who have participated in mini-versions of such mega-events since their early teen years. At the public level, since Amatango became a parochial center, the resident priest has pushed to have middle-aged and older women lead informal Catholic gatherings such as catechism groups directed at teens.

THE RETIRED *CAMPESINO*—END OF A CULTURAL SCRIPT?

Some elders have already seen the cultural handwriting on the wall and are radically altering the last phases of their *campesino* lifestyle. An example is Miguel Duran, who lives halfway up the mountain from Amatango's central plaza in the house called *Tlalchichilpa* (red earth). When I first entered his house compound in 1973, I found the classic *campesino*-based lineage. Miguel, although not well-off, had just enough land to support his large family, economically supplemented by making crates and growing small amounts of flowers. In his compound was his widowed sixty-two-year-old mother, his wife

Anna, five of their children (ages one to nine) and his recently married brother Juan, age twenty-three, who was building a small new house next door. Most people considered him one of the best farmers in the village, someone who managed to feed his large family through his skill and knowledge of the land. As late as 2003, both he and his wife, then in their late fifties, seemed quite healthy and vigorously maintained the beautiful cornfields growing beyond their home. Miguel's mother had recently died at age ninety. They told me that of two coresident sons, only their married one was still interested in farming, although he also liked working textiles with his unmarried, nineteen-year-old brother. Together, with two teenage sisters, working in a newly built room, these youths made children's clothes for sale in regional street markets. Returning to visit in 2006, I saw that the cornfield was gone, replaced by two new houses, a greatly enlarged workshop and a grazing area for the few horses, goats and cows they had left.

Noting my surprise at this, Miguel proudly explained that he was *really* retired, and he would just watch the young do the work—words I had never heard uttered by a healthy, vigorous man in his early sixties. This was not the only dramatic change in his life. A year earlier his wife had succumbed to diabetes, which she did her best to ignore. Not long after this, his oldest daughter's husband left her and her two teenage daughters, and they moved in with him. His older married son decided to give up the *campesino* life and devote full time to home production of clothes in an enlarged family "factory." This work team included his wife, his now married brother and spouse, and the two sisters. Miguel had used all his resources and taken out a loan to buy the sewing and weaving equipment in Mexico City. Miguel explained with a smile, "I know Jay, you must be surprised how easily I gave up being a *campesino*. Some of my cousins and friends still cling to this path, but with my wife's death and my daughter's coming back home I realized one must adapt to things you never expected to happen."

CONCLUSION

The information I gathered over the last thirty years in Amatango seems to be at variance with some of the predicted dire consequences of modernization and globalization for the elderly (see Fry this volume). Under similar conditions of "modernizing" change, the aged of Amatango have fared better than those in many other Latin American peasant communities, studied in earlier decades. One reads, for example, that in the Colombian highland village of Aritama: "There is no room and no use for them. Old people are not respected, feared or loved. Their advice is not sought by the younger generation, nor are they thought to possess any special knowledge which might be useful" (Reichel-Dolmatoff and Reichel-Dolmatoff 1961).

Why was the situation for the aged more favorable in Amatango since the 1970s? Ironically, its isolated location and the mediocre quality of its agricultural lands protected the community from severe exploitation by a landed gentry in prerevolutionary times. Thus, substantial land and irrigation resources were retained and eventually expanded upon in the early twentieth century prior to the onset of the pressures that have caused the demise of indigenous institutions and beliefs in similar villages. This economic strength helped sustain cultural features through which the aged have maintained societal value in the light of rapid change.

In fact, it is some of those very patterns of traditional life that have been used to carry out ongoing economic development projects. When in the 1950s a rising population provoked the need for new sources of revenue and the development of village capital infrastructure, solutions were largely based on local ecological and social resources.

For Amatango, community solidarity bolstered by an economic base has enabled the community to transform itself largely on its own terms. It has modified the cultural script for the generation coming of age, with the oldest generations for the most part realizing that the changes that precipitated this alteration of the life course offer some benefits for all. So far, the local impacts of this new globalized world have been flexibly contained within key cultural spaces over which people still have some control. This is the answer to the paradox of how the village could be both the most traditional and yet the most transformed indigenous community in the region. Fortunately, Amatango is not unique within Mexico, as indicated by recent studies in the states of Chiapas (Greenfield 2004) and Tlaxcala (Rothstein 2007). When the transformation from peasant to proletariat communities is accomplished without totally abandoning an agrarian base, while developing homegrown marketable products, this can provide both a secure place for older adults and a bridge between generations.

At 1 A.M. during the third and final evening party celebrating Rosalba's wedding, my wife and I huddled within thick serapes against the bitter cold near Doña Concha and four equally elderly female relatives. Although they seemed quite content with the proceedings, from time to time I would pick up grumbling conversations about such things as their grandkids not being interested in Nahuatl or a younger relative who did not appreciate the importance of hard work. These are conversations perhaps overheard in most societies today, but here while many aged are ambivalent about the alterations they see in the society around them, they are still very much a part of the system that brought such changes about.

NOTES

1. The names for the community, people and houses have been changed to protect the anonymity of the place and people described here.

2. The Spanish words *Doña* and *Don* are titles of respect (for females and males, respectively) often used for persons older than age fifty.

3. The article is also available online at: www.un.org/esa/population/meetings/Proceedings_EGM_Mex_2005/partida.pdf and the proceedings of the meeting can be accessed at http://www.un.org/esa/population/meetings/Proceedings_EGM_Mex_2005/.

4. In the 1960s, general mortality in Amatango was 33 per thousand, but by 1989 had dropped to 6.5. In addition, a study done in the mid-1970s (Millard 1978) showed that almost three-fourths of women sampled had lost a child to disease, while at the end of the 1980s, a similar study showed that only 42 percent of women suffered such a loss.

5. Introduced slowly in 1983 by a local nurse who worked at the village clinic, a decade later some form of birth control was used by about a third of the almost 900 women still in their reproductive years.

6. Although it does happen, it is exceptionally rare that the girl's parents would not accept "robbing" of their daughter. Once this is accepted, the parents of the couple become *compadres* to each other, which further cements the bonds between the families.

7. This has changed from about 90 percent in 1973.

8. Sometimes the term *sickn* is used for older women, usually when someone is referring to themselves.

9. This went beyond saying someone was a *culi* (old man) or *sickn* (old woman). The most common specific terms linked to perceptions of extreme old age and frailty were: *akmukilnamiki* (cannot comprehend); *Yomopaltilw(he)* (is incontinent); *akmunnenemi* (cannot walk) or *aqueli itlaayi* (cannot work). A typical conversation about a very old relative considered *yotla moak* might provoke the following statement: "*noachsitntzn y kipia yosio(wk) aqueli itaayi*" (my revered great-grandmother has more than 100 years, she is very weak and cannot work). Another Nahuatl term, which is rarely used today, for a frail elder who needs a cane is *Tepikn* (nasal n).

10. This term could also be applied to sickly looking individuals who were not particularly aged.

11. To date, the local nurse and the doctors annually sent to the village medical clinic have maintained a good relationship with these midwives. Although more of Amatango's women now give birth in the clinic or even in a hospital in Texcoco, the population growth over the last twenty-five years has assured these midwives many clients.

12. In the more than thirty years since I began working in Amatango, probably not more than fifty men have made the trip to the United States. In 2006, I interviewed a forty-five-year-old man who had just returned from a year of working construction in Chicago, and he was just about to finance his twenty-two-year-old son on a similar adventure. The cost at the border would be $3,000 for a *coyote*—a handler of illegal immigration—to get him across.

13. As a slowly developing counter to this trend, since 2000 I have seen a growing number of plastic greenhouses, usually about 30 by 100 feet in size, being used by men in their sixties and early seventies to grow specialty crops such as delicate lettuces and other vegetables for sale in urban markets or directly to restaurants.

14. In 1995, the organization of the *fiesta* system was simplified with a reduction in the number of major fiestas from six to four, and the fiscal position no longer having a senior and junior member, but now are equal positions, chosen from two men from each side of the community.

15. Since 1988, the community has served as the center of a parish for the other Nahuatl villages in the area and has had its own priest living in the community since then. Over this time, the number of fiestas has been cut in half and the financial burden spread more evenly within the community.

16. Wealth will condition, to a certain degree, the extent of public prestige and power men and their families will garner as they age (Sokolovsky and Sokolovsky

1984). Nevertheless, virtually all older men from Catholic families had carried out at least once the sacred burden of ritual sponsorship, which gives them lasting honor in the eyes of the community and the saints.

17. Even in the case where teenagers introduced a new dance formation based on an urban model, middle-aged villagers eagerly volunteered to dress up and perform as *caballeros y caballeras* (cowboys and cowgirls).

18. Very little is known about preconquest village life and the actual functioning of elders in the context of rural Aztec communities. According to historical sources, the elder chief of the highest ranking clan along with a council composed of other clan elders regulated the distribution of communally owned lands, settled disputes and saw to the training of warriors and the payment of taxes by the entire community (Soustelle 1961). Aged males and females of any rank had some special roles: men made ritual speeches and prepared corpses, while women arranged marriages and served as midwives. Persons past age seventy also had the privilege of drinking alcohol in public without the severe sanctions imposed on younger individuals who imbibed.

At the household level, Aztec-era elders appeared to command filial attention and respect approaching that of the ancient Chinese. Among a child's first lessons were admonitions about showing esteem toward elders (Simmons 1945:62). Marriage seldom occurred without parental consent, and the father had the power to pawn or sell his children into slavery if his economic situation was severe enough

19. *Muina* is a culturally specific syndrom, among Latinos whose underlying cause is considered to be anger or rage. Symptoms can include tension, headache, screaming, trembling, stomach disturbances and even chronic fatigue

20. This figure was based on sitting in on many of the local legal proceedings conducted by the *delegados* and interviewing them about the ones I missed.

CHAPTER 17

Transforming the Cultural Scripts for Aging and Elder Care in Japan

Brenda R. Jenike and John W. Traphagan

Weekdays in Tokyo always begin early—too early for me (Brenda Jenike) at least. By eight o'clock in the morning it seems that everyone in my bustling, crowded neighborhood in the northwestern Tokyo working-class ward of Itabashi has long ago started their day. Breakfasts have been served and cleared. Children are off to school. Workers headed for the corporate centers of Tokyo are in the midst of their daily commuting crush, standing, pressed tightly "like sushi" against one another in unbearably steamy trains for half an hour or longer. Housewives are hard at work cleaning the home or running errands. By a lazy nine o'clock I am supposed to be at Green Hills, the local public nursing home and senior day care center, escorting residents and day care attendees to exercise class. I am, however, late as usual, madly peddling my shiny red "housewife's special" bicycle uphill and against the wind on this brisk autumn day. Once in the center doors, I am greeted by the unmistakable scent of strong detergent mingled with perspiration, a testament to both the volume of human activity within and the continuous effort to cleanse it. In the *genkan* (entranceway), I hurriedly remove my outdoor shoes and put on my indoor slippers. From my locker, I grab my light blue apron that designates me as a volunteer caregiver. My nametag says *Burenda* in the large Japanese script reserved for foreign words. Greeted by smiling nods and rounds of "*Ohayō gozaimasu!*" (Good morning!), I enter the large recreation room just in time to escort the last few participants to their seats. Exuberant music booms through the room, and I, along with three other women volunteers in aprons, two young male staff members and one elderly but robust female *sensei* (teacher), lead three consecutive sessions of physical recreation for about eighty frail seniors.

At first, the scene is surreal. Circled round me sit twenty-six or so dignified elderly Japanese women and men, some in traditional kimono (these are the oldest, or "Meiji elders"—born in the last years of the Meiji period), whose

ages range from the mid eighties through the upper nineties. In truth, I feel ri-
diculous playing "catch the balloon" with persons who should command more
respect from a young woman such as myself. We do, luckily, manage to share
some laughs. When these day care attendees leave the room for arts and crafts,
the nursing home residents, each dressed in a mix of identical pastel sweat
suits and personal articles of clothing, wheel themselves in for their turn. With
some active, some seemingly active but cognitively not quite aware, and some,
those in the "dandelion" (dementia) group not much aware of anything, the residents are divided into teams and then assembled into rows for balloon volley-
ball. Staff members essentially play the game for the residents. With large red
balloons bopping about the room, residents sometimes duck, sometimes try to
hit the balloon, but most often get hit by the balloon. No one can really play
the game, so it is declared that each side wins. With exercise time over, residents leave to be fed their lunch or bathed. Dandelion members are escorted
away by staff. Volunteers go to the tea room to chat. I spend time sitting and
talking with some residents, then chat with volunteers until it is time to help
with the afternoon *rehabiri* (physical "rehabilitation" therapy) session.

The above scene from one of the author's (Jenike) field notes is one that is
repeated at nursing homes and elder day care centers throughout Japan—
whether in rural, urban or suburban—on a daily basis.[1] Traphagan, working in
a much more rural and remote part of Japan, has also played "catch the
balloon" or other similar games with elders experiencing a range of cognitive
and physical problems, much like those Jenike describes. While the patterns of
activity and philosophy of elder care within the context of these institutions
has remained fairly consistent over the past decade and across different parts
of Japan, the approach to funding, managing and providing care has changed
dramatically since the inception of the long-term care insurance program—
known in Japanese as *kaigo hoken*—in 2000.

As of 2005, Japan had the distinction of being the most aged nation in the
world, with over 20 percent (25.76 million) of the population aged sixty-five or
over (*The Nikkei Weekly* 2006). Even more startling, Japan's National Institute
of Population and Social Security Research has now forecast a doubling of this
figure to 40 percent aged sixty-five and over by 2050 (*Kyodo News* 2006; *The
Nikkei Weekly* 2006). Japanese of all ages are well aware of the demographic
reality that they are living in a rapidly "graying society": the elderly population
in Japan is burgeoning, while the population of youth needed to support it is
shrinking.

To deal with this demographic context and its associated elder care crisis, in
the 1990s the Japanese state replaced the social welfare system that had provided elder care services with the previously mentioned national long-term care
insurance program (LTCI) in April 2000. As a mandatory program without the
stigma of welfare, over the past eight years LTCI has essentially transformed
elder care in Japan from a morally based, family-centered welfare system to a
consumer-driven entitlement system of supportive and institutional long-term
community care. A range of residential care homes, adult day care centers and

a plethora of home care and caregiver respite services, as well as some high-tech creativity, are now providing new cultural spaces for the growing numbers of Japanese seniors to experience late life. In this chapter we draw from extended participant observation in nursing homes, adult day care centers and caregiver support groups, and from in-depth interviews with caregivers and care recipients that have been conducted by the authors in separate field sites, located in Tokyo (Jenike) and about 500 km north of Tokyo in Iwate Prefecture (Traphagan), since the mid-1990s. Our purpose is to explore how a rapidly aging population and the transition to community care for frail elderly (a profound change in approach) are transforming core cultural concepts in Japan such as filial piety and respect for the elderly, as well as the meaning of old age and care itself. In considering these changes, we conclude with a discussion of what new cultural scripts future generations of Japanese might have in store for their own old age.

THE CHANGING DEMOGRAPHIC CONTEXT OF THE JAPANESE LIFE COURSE AND LATE LIFE

The life course for Japanese has lengthened considerably in only a few decades. Until quite recently, extreme old age—that is, not one, but two or three decades of life post retirement—was not a consideration for the ordinary citizen and his or her family. Up until the end of World War II, average life expectancy for Japanese males and females was around age fifty. Now sixty years later, Japanese males can expect to live an average of 78.5 years, and females 85.5 years (*Kyodo News* 2006). This longevity, highest in the world except for the small island nation of Andorra, actually exceeds prior United Nations' predictions of maximum life expectancies in human populations (Horiuchi 2000). Thus, today living into a grand old age has become a normative part of the life course for Japanese citizens.

Moreover, the proportion of the population aged eighty and over within the total senior population during this same time span has steadily increased. Just 9 percent of seniors in Japan were eighty and older in 1950; by 1970, this figure had only modestly increased to just under 13 percent. However, by 2005 this had increased to almost 25 percent.[2] Furthermore, in the past decade alone, the number of centenarians in Japan has quadrupled to over 28,000 persons, and is projected to top half a million by 2050 (Watanabe 2006; Yomiuri 2006b; Willcox et al. this volume). The rapidity with which Japan transformed to a society with an aged population has been often discussed in gerontological literature—it only took twenty-five years for Japan to move from a society with 7 percent of the population over the age of sixty-five to one with 14 percent over that age, and the trend continues to the present. This demographic transition was accomplished almost twice as fast as in any other postindustrial society (see Kinsella this volume).

The rapid growth of the elder population has been accompanied by a corresponding decline in the total fertility rate (TFR). Throughout the early 1970s, the TFR for Japan remained relatively consistent at approximately 2.13, a rate sufficient for population replacement. By the middle of the decade, the TFR began to decline, and has continued to do so since—in 2004, the TFR for Japan was 1.29, a number significantly below what is necessary for population replacement. The implications of this decreased fertility are striking. Statistics produced by the Japanese government show predictions of a decline in population throughout this century where the current population of approximately 127 million will drop to only 44 million by the first decade of the 2100s unless there are intervening factors such as increased immigration.[3]

Japan, of course, is not unusual in experiencing a low TFR combined with a rapid growth in the population of elders; South Korea and Singapore in Asia, and Sweden and Italy in Europe, are prime examples of other societies experiencing a similar set of demographic changes and associated pressures (Kinsella this volume). Perhaps what makes Japan, or any other society, particularly interesting is the manner in which those demographic changes intersect with cultural scripts about how to manage late life and how to provide care for elders who may become increasingly frail and dependent (both physically and financially). Susan O. Long, in writing about how Japanese approach end-of-life decision-making, draws on Seale's idea that people use a variety of cultural scripts, some of which may contain conflicting values, to interpret and manage the dying process (Long 2005:2; Seale 1998). This approach can be equally applied when considering the manner in which people interpret and approach the experience of aging and the process of caring for an elderly individual.

Much of the literature on elder care in Japan in recent years has painted a rather bleak picture in which fundamental changes in values related to roles and expectations within the family, as well as a shift from a stem to a nuclear family system, are forcing a movement away from family-centered support of the elderly to institutionally-centered support. Underlying these ideas is an often explicit assumption that Japanese family structure is and has been in the process of transforming from a patrilineal, patrilocal model in which coresidence of adult children and elderly parents in three-generation households forms the basis of social support for the elderly, to a bilateral, neolocal model more generally affiliated with developed societies and those that have gone through the demographic transition from high to low birth and death rates (Ogawa and Retherford 1997:59).

This assumption is usually expressed in terms not simply of change, but of a *weakening* of the family structure. In the postwar period, both within popular media and social science literature on the family in Japan, there has often been a tacit assumption that modernization and urbanization will inevitably lead to the breakdown of the traditional family form, as values of individualism encourage a stronger emphasis on the nuclear family structure in part due to the privacy gained by residence away from one's parents. Not surprisingly, this perspective tends to generate rather pessimistic opinions about the effects of population aging and the well-being of the elderly both in the present and in the future of Japanese society.

Despite these trends, throughout the postwar era, the primary cultural script that Japanese have used to cope with the process of aging and the potential need to care for an elderly individual experiencing various forms of functional decline has been one that centers upon in-home, family-based provision of care for the elderly structured around Japanese kinship ideals. This cultural script of filial obligations toward parents and filial piety continues to shape Japanese approaches to elder care, even while ideas about family structure and obligations within the family are contested and negotiated.

THE FAMILY IN JAPAN

Throughout the postwar era, structural and ideational elements of the family have occupied a major thread in the study of Japanese culture and society. Ezra Vogel's (1963) ground-breaking study of middle-class, white-collar workers in urban Japan set the stage for a long-term intellectual discussion of how Japanese conceptualize and experience family bonds, and how this is changing in response to processes of urbanization and modernization.

The term most similar in meaning to the English "family" is *kazoku*. From a sociological perspective, *kazoku* places emphasis on the conjugal bond and, thus, implies the nuclear family (*kaku kazoku*) as it is understood in the Euro-American context (Long 1987:7). While this term is routinely used in Japanese discourse about the family, another term is also employed, one that has significant implications in terms of the conceptualization of rights and responsibilities within extended families. This term, *ie*, is a complex concept that can be understood at multiple levels: as a kinship term, as a tool through which the nation-state ideology has been promulgated and as an academic concept. In common usage, the term *ie* refers to both a house or compound and its residents, hence it is normally translated into English as "household." When an individual speaks of her *ie*, the reference may be either to her house, those relatives who live with her in the same house, or inclusive of both. The term also has a nuanced meaning suggesting something that is traditional, old fashioned, and often out of date to many Japanese. As an academic concept, *ie* is understood as "a multigenerational property-owning corporate group which continues through time" (Long 1987:3). It is organized not on the basis of nuclear family structure, but on a stem family structure consisting of three generations in which there is one married couple from each adult generation who live together with the unmarried children of the younger generation. Continuity over time is essential to the structure of the *ie*. As has been frequently pointed out in scholarly work on the family, the living and the dead are linked together by the idea that family genealogy is not simply relationships based on blood inheritance and succession, but that genealogical bonds are connected to the maintenance and continuation of the family as an institution (Aruga 1954:362; Plath 1964; Traphagan 2000a).

Central to the idea of the *ie* is the idea that authority within the household is not vested in persons, but in social positions within the family unit. Each position within the household—father, mother, grandfather, grandmother, wife and eldest son—is vested with symbolic capital associated with that position, which, in turn, is associated with specific responsibilities to the household as a whole and other members of the household. In some respects, the most powerful office is that of household head, normally transferred from eldest son to eldest son, and it is the household head who forms the line of succession that characterizes the historical continuity of genealogical bonds in a given household. The household head is the representative of the household to the outside world and the final voice of authority on decisions internal to the household. The basic nature and meaning of the *ie* has been a source of ongoing debate among scholars concerned with Japanese kinship.

Although the *ie* structure has a long history in Japan, it was not until the Meiji Restoration (1868) that it became a generalized model for family organization. Prior to the Restoration, traditional norms of marriage and residence among peasants were flexible and did not necessarily include changing residence upon marriage. It was decided by the bureaucratic leadership that such a system was unsatisfactory as the basis for building a modern nation-state, or more precisely, a family-state *(kazoku kokka)*. The model that did seem appropriate was the samurai patriarchal family structure that was adopted as a basis for all family organization in Japan. Thus, who was to be included in the *koseki* (family registration) was based upon this organization (Gluck 1985:182). Indeed, the *ie* formed the primary supporting beam of society, in Meiji ideology. The emperor was the patriarch of a "family-state," his line of descent symbolically represented the ancestral ethnicity of the Japanese, and his *ie* formed the main stem family to which all other Japanese families were connected (Gluck 1985:78).[4]

What has become clear in postwar studies of the Japanese family is that it must be understood as an adaptable and dynamic social structure that incorporates elements of industrial and postindustrial proclivities towards nuclear structure while maintaining ideational elements associated with stem family structures—particularly when it comes to thinking about elder care. In short, whether people adhere to the traditional stem family approach to family organization and elder care, or whether they adhere to a nuclear approach, they continue to think about familial bonds in terms of the stem family structure and continue to conceptualize family either in line with or in contrast to that structure.

"WARM CONTACT": FILIAL CARE AND OTHER TALES FROM AN AGING SOCIETY

As stated before, throughout the postwar era, the primary cultural script that Japanese have used to cope with the process of aging and the potential need to care for an aged parent has been one that centers upon an in-home, family-based provision of care structured around Japanese stem family kinship ideals. Coresidence with one's children in old age, traditionally (and still most typically) with one's eldest son and his wife, has been a fundamental social expectation, signifying the successful maintenance of primary relationships over the life course. Whether or not a family continues to follow the inheritance and residence patterns of the patrilineal stem family system, cultural norms dictate that one adult child—the designated family successor—is still responsible for the total care of aged parents. In the minds of the current cohorts of elders and their own aging adult children, then, the physical, emotional and social support of the very old (who are not childless) are the responsibility of the child with whom they reside.

This fundamental expectation among the older cohorts is in accordance with the norms of filial piety (*oyakōkō*) upon which they were raised. According to Confucian thought, the tie between parent and child is one of the five primary human relationships, calling for the benevolent leadership of the parent and willing obedience of the child. As anthropologist David Plath explains, "devotion to one's parents in particular is the root of all virtue and the model for all human propriety" (Plath 1988:507). Furthermore, cultural ideals for old age in Japan call not only for loving indulgence by family members, but also for an accepted dependence on the part of elderly parents. A key characteristic of filial care, then, has been *amae* dependency (Doi 1973; Johnson 1993), which has been aptly termed "indulgent dependency" (Lebra 1976) and "legitimized dependency" (Hashimoto 1996). While the term *amae* is most often applied to the relationship of a dependent young child on its mother, an aging parent will likewise in turn begin to seek the indulgence and support of his or her adult child. Like a mother understanding the needs of her child, an attentive adult child (or daughter-in-law) should understand and attend to an aged parent's needs without the parent having to ask for assistance. This parent-child role set "encourages passive helplessness" by one partner and "active nurturing" by the other (Kiefer 1987:104). Jenike's caregiver respondents described this relationship, based on the feelings of *oyakōkō*, as a natural desire to care for one's parent, rather than a duty (Jenike 1997). An aged parent deserves support as part of a lifelong reciprocal relationship, in which the parent has accumulated social capital through contributions to the household and sacrifices for his or her child and grandchildren (Hashimoto 1996).

Symbolic of this idealized family-centered caregiving is the concept of "warm contact" (*fureai*) through "skinship" (physical touch by kin). While both of these ideas refer to physical assistance, such as helping an elder to stand up and walk, holding their hand or touching their arm or any bodily care such as assistance with bathing, they more importantly encompass the idea of an ongoing, emotionally warm and empathetic family relationship.

Not Enough "Silver Seats"

Cultural ideals are of course important in understanding why people (or institutions) behave (or function) the way they do. Ideals should not, however, be confused with actual practices. On trains, subways and buses in Japan, seats near the front called "silver seats" are reserved for the elderly and those with physical disabilities. Ideally, this marks seniors as special, and deserving a seat. In practice, when almost everyone on the bus, train or subway is elderly, the few "silver seats" provided become meaningless.

Likewise, cultural ideals of filial piety—coresidence (at least in late life), physical and emotional support within the household unit, indulgence and encouraged dependency—should not be confused with actual practices. Just as household units and family structure in Japan can greatly diverge from the stem family ideal, the ability of Japanese to meet the ideals and expectations for elder care that assume intergenerational coresidence and empathetic, hands-on personal care has become more and more challenging. As life expectancies have increased, and with them, added years of debilitating chronic conditions, entering into and sustaining potentially prolonged relationships of dependency are indeed fraught with much ambivalence on the part of both elderly parents and their adult children. This ambivalence is especially salient when one considers that many of these adult "children" are themselves over age sixty.

For elderly Japanese, dependency of aged parents on the younger generations is still socially encouraged. However, becoming an undue burden (*meiwaku*) on family members by outliving and exhausting the social capital accrued through reciprocal intergenerational relationships over the life course breaches the intergenerational contract, and should be avoided (Hashimoto 1996; Young and Ikeuchi 1997; Traphagan 1998a). The existence of numerous *pokkuri* ("swift" death) temples frequented by elderly Japanese who go there to pray for a peaceful and timely death and to buy amulets for the prevention of senility and other disabling conditions of old age, attests to the strong desire among elderly to avoid falling into this unilateral relationship of dependency (Wöss 1993; Young and Ikeuchi 1997). In addition, the suicide rate for Japanese aged sixty and over (35.3 per 100,000 persons for 2003) continues to be the highest for any age group (accounting for a third of all suicides) and is high when compared to that for elderly in other industrialized nations (*Asahi Shimbun Japan Almanac 2005;* Traphagan 2005a). By comparison, the U.S. suicide rate in 2003 for men over age sixty-five was 27.34 and 4.43 for women, with both figures significantly lower than in Japan.[5] These two phenomena point not only to the increased awareness among Japanese seniors of the consequences of long-term chronic illnesses in old age, but also to the long-held cultural belief that an individual has an obligation to leave this world if he or she has become burdensome (Plath 1983). In some cases, elderly Japanese have also resorted to suicide to make a strong social statement about neglectful children (Traphagan 2005a).

The main way, however, that caregiving ideals based on the stem family structure no longer fit with reality is in terms of changed residence patterns. Up until the 1990s, the majority of elderly Japanese lived in multigenerational households, and many had done so their whole lives. In the 1990s, there began an increase in delayed coresidence, that is, families were postponing forming extended households until the older generation reached advanced old age or a

Women praying at a *pokkuri* temple in Sugamo, Tokyo, an area that caters
to the elderly. Photo by Jay Sokolovsky.

health concern necessitated daily care. Delayed coresidence also often meant,
if families could afford it, living in two separate households on the same
property—a popular choice that provides some autonomy, yet still upholds the
ideal of "living at a distance where the soup (if brought from one household to
the next) won't get cold" (*sūpu no samenai kyori*). The rise in numbers of families who postpone coresidence, reside in separate households when they do,
or, most significantly, who never coreside in any form at all, has resulted in
the doubling over the past decade of the number of Japanese seniors recorded
in the national census as residing alone or with spouses only (a 10 percent
increase in total households with elderly, see Figure 17.1). In 2005, over half
of all households with elderly persons (sixty-five and over) were single elderly
and elderly couple households, with 4.05 million elderly persons recorded as
living alone, an increase of more than 1 million since the 2000 census (*Japan
Statistical Yearbook* 2008; Kan 2007).

Figure 17.1
Living Arrangements for Japanese 65 and Over, 1985–2005

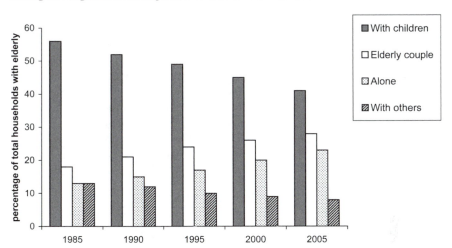

Source: Statistical Survey Department, Statistics Bureau, Ministry of Internal Affairs and Communications, in *Japan Statistical Yearbook*, accessed January 2008. [6]

Nowhere is this trend more apparent than in depopulated rural areas, where the percentage of residents age sixty-five and over can top 60 percent. Recent natural disasters and extreme weather have shed a grim light on the vulnerability of elderly Japanese living alone in rural Japan, and the consequences of adult children not wishing to leave city jobs to move back in with and care for their aged parents. In 2006, when record amounts of snow fell on rural northwestern Japan, elderly residents in mountain villages became trapped in their homes, with snow piled to second stories. Residents, many on fixed incomes, had to endure the cold and darkness within for weeks on end. Worse, with up to six feet of snow and ice weighing down their roofs, elderly in their seventies and eighties living alone climbed up to shovel. Many fell to their deaths or suffered severe injuries. Others, trying to clear piles of snow from their yards, fell or got stuck in drifts and froze to death. In all, eighty-five senior citizens across northwestern Japan died and more than 1,000 were injured (Faiola 2006). In the summer of 2004, when Japan was struck by a record twenty typhoons, the majority of those killed were elderly with dementia who lived alone and kept wandering out in the midst of the storms (personal communication with *Kyoto Shinbun* reporter).

Throughout Japan, the phenomenon of "*kodokushi*" of the elderly—"solitary death" in which a person dies alone without care or companionship and is often not discovered for a length of time—has been increasing, necessitating the formation of new companies that specialize in dealing with the deceased person's belongings at the request of family members (Kan 2007).

Yet even in the 1980s and early 1990s, when a majority of urban, rural and suburban elderly still resided in intergenerational households, the increasing pressure to continue with longer periods and more arduous care in the home had resulted in what became termed as "social hospitalization" of the disabled elderly; that is, family caregivers in need of a break admitted their chronically, but not acutely, ill elderly parents into clinics and hospitals for long in-patient stays (that were subsidized by the national health insurance system). Round-the-clock family caregivers were either unavailable (due to women working outside the home) or worn out. Elderly parents were left drugged and lying in beds in small hospitals not equipped to function as nursing homes. As costs from social hospitalization soared, government officials realized, too, that family-centered elder care alone was no longer viable.

FROM THE FAMILY TO THE COMMUNITY—
SOCIAL WELFARE AND LTCI

In 1989, the Japanese government embarked on a ten-year strategic social welfare plan, known as the Gold Plan, in order to address the long-term care needs of the growing disabled senior population, as well as to try to separate long-term care costs from those of medical care. The Gold Plan, together with the New Gold Plan implemented in 1995, was intended as a supplement to, not a replacement for, family-centered home care and thus favored respite and in-home services over institutional care.[7] The effect over the decade was a tremendous national expansion of taxpayer-funded elder care services such as part-time adult day care, home visit nurses, home care assistants, meal and bathing services and short-term and long-term stays at public nursing homes. As demand for such services always exceeded supply, elder care services during the 1990s were often rationed in areas with high populations (the case in most of Tokyo's wards and cities). This was also the case in more rural and less densely populated areas, where nursing home beds, for example, often fell well short of the need, leading to multiyear waiting lists (see Traphagan 2000b). City and district clerks based their decisions as to whom could access social welfare services not so much on the needs of the elderly family member, but on the availability of potential family caregivers. Thus, single and childless elderly, or those in elderly only households, had priority. Those residing with adult children (daughters-in-law and daughters) were put on long waiting lists (two to four years), or were told that they could not qualify for services at all. Traphagan recorded instances where women in rural areas who applied for social welfare assistance were told to quit work so they could provide the care for their bedridden in-laws themselves (2000b). Jenike heard similar accounts among frustrated daughters-in-law in Tokyo.

In April 2000, the Japanese government promulgated a new social program that was intended to reform an elder care system that was not meeting the needs of the population. This "care insurance" program (*kaigo hoken* in Japanese) is a mandatory social insurance program that provides long-term care to all people with age-related illnesses or limitations, regardless of family situation

Festival at an adult day care center in central Tokyo. Photo by Brenda Jenike.

or income. There were several reasons for the creation of this system. First, the Japanese long-term care insurance (LTCI) program was intended to meet the needs of a very rapidly aging population. As well, it sought to provide an alternative system of caring for elders as the country confronted a very low fertility rate, as well as a growing number of women who have chosen to either remain in the work force after marriage and childbirth or to opt out of marriage and child-rearing altogether (Campbell and Ikegami 2000:27–28). The new program also addressed several administrative problems, such as inadequate coverage for nonmedical services and high expenses related to long-term care being provided in hospital settings that existed under the Gold Plans. Matsuda and Yamamoto (2001) note that as of 1997, roughly 60 percent of medical expenditures in Japan were related to hospital services, and about 46 percent of hospital patients were sixty-five and older, with 43 percent of those patients having a stay of more than six months. This was partly due to a lack of skilled-nursing facilities and home care services that, hence, led to few alternatives beyond extended stays in hospitals for elderly in need of long-term care.

As stated before, the Japanese LTCI program is a national, mandatory social insurance program; everyone over the age of forty is required by law to contribute premiums and is insured by the municipal government in which they reside. The national average monthly premium is currently at 4,000 yen/month (USD 37), but varies by municipality and income level (Koyama and Yasuda 2006).[8] Insurance premiums only cover about 50 percent of the government contributions associated with the system. The remainder is covered by national (25 percent), prefectural (12.5 percent) and municipal (12.5 percent) governments through taxes and copayments required at the time of service receipt. In addition, users of services are expected to pay 10 percent of costs (up to 37,200 yen or USD 350/month) as well as costs of meals and housing associated with long-term stays in care facilities, although reductions in costs are made for low-income families. Services under the LTCI program are accessed through a care management process that involves initial assessment of the needs of the individual and formal recognition of an individual's condition by a committee consisting of health care professionals. After a person has been determined eligible for services under the program, a care manager assists the individual and family in finding either public or private services/facilities that are appropriate for that person.

Long-term care services eligibility is associated with a needs assessment that divides potential care recipients into five levels of need. The program differentiates between two distinct types of care. Those who have "care needs" or *yokaigo*, which involves continual nursing care for more than six months, normally include individuals with conditions such as dementia or who are in need of regular help in activities of daily living (ADL). The second category is for people who have "assistance needs" or *yoshien,* which includes people that do not require constant nursing care, but may need help with ADLs such as food shopping or house cleaning. Determinations about the amount of the monthly allowance assigned for LTC services is based upon the assigned level of need.

In order to obtain care through the LTCI program, a person must submit an application to the municipal office where he or she lives. The application is followed up by a home visit and an evaluation of cognitive and physical conditions by a government specialist, as well as a doctor's assessment. After all assessments have been completed, a committee for nursing care certification determines whether or not the person is eligible for care, and if the decision is positive, a care manager will work in consultation with the applicant's doctor to determine appropriate services.

With the creation of the LTCI program, there have been significant improvements over the social welfare system. Since private as well as public service providers are allowed to compete for clients, there is a greater array of choices. For example, rather than just being assigned to a facility or sent a city home helper, elderly clients and their family members can now decide which day care they want to attend, which home assistant to employ, or which type of residential facility to move into—small or large facility, a group home for Alzheimer's, an independent-living facility or a nursing home with maximum care and so on. There is now greater access to physical therapy and rehabilitative services, so elders suffering from strokes or injuries can regain an independent lifestyle. Through the visits of the care managers, LTCI also serves as a check on elder abuse. Abuse of an elderly parent, in the form of neglect, emotional or physical violence, or economic abuse, can no longer be hidden away behind the closed doors of the family home.

TOO MANY WHEELCHAIRS: CHALLENGES FACING LTCI

While implementation of the LTCI program has presented numerous hurdles, the biggest challenge for sustaining LTCI over the long run is undeniably the cost. Total spending of LTCI was 7.1 trillion yen in 2006 (USD 66 billion), up from 3.6 trillion in 2000 (USD 34 billion), with 4 million out of Japan's 25 million people aged sixty-five and older designated as beneficiaries who need LTCI's care. This is double the figure of beneficiaries compared to when the system was launched in 2000 (*The Japan Times* 2006a). Initially, the government had miscalculated the usage and cost, assuming wrongly that the will to continue with family care would stem the demand for use of community care services. The significant increase in beneficiaries, however, also means that services have been provided to elderly who do not actually need intensive care. Currently, the incentive of care managers, who are often employed by private service providers, is to oversell care services to their elderly clients. Wheelchairs and automated beds, for example, have been given to and used by people who are still mobile, and there has been a rapid growth in the number of stores that sell equipment for older people such as walkers or scooters. In some cases, service recipients have had their home helpers do all their housework, chores and prepare their meals, like personal servants, even though they could still do these activities themselves. In addition to overuse problems, there continue to be chronic staff shortages at nursing homes across Japan. The high demand for services and shortage of care personnel finally led the government to liberalize its notoriously strict immigration policy in 2007, easing licensing

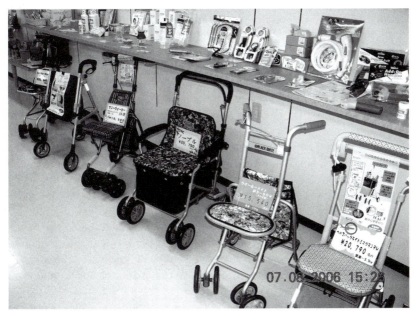

Walkers on display in a store dedicated to equipment and supplies that can be purchased or rented under the LTCI program (Iwate Prefecture). Photo by John W. Traphagan.

and allowing 400 Filipino nurses and 600 Filipino caregivers to work in Japan (*Kyodo News* 2007; *The Japan Times* 2006b).

In a move to contain ballooning costs and reduce the need for professional medical staff, the government has recently made changes in LTCI—redefining need and shifting its focus to include preventative care. The government created two new "needing support" categories, for which beneficiaries will receive preventative services (strength training and nutritional counseling), but not traditional nursing care or equipment. Household chore help for those who fall into these new categories is now limited to elderly who live alone, and those who receive it have to assist their home helper (*The Japan Times* 2006a).

Overall, through LTCI, elder care nationally in Japan has undergone a shift from the family-centered model of "warm contact" and "deserved dependency" to one of individual entitlement. Of course, for those who still wish to practice the "warm contact" family model of caregiving for their parents and parents-in-law, the greater availability of respite care services that LTCI provides has increased their ability to do so. However, with LTCI's individual-centered care model, the emphasis is now moving away from the responsibility of the family toward the responsibility of the elderly, themselves, to pursue independent, healthy aging.

CAREGIVING FOR THE TWENTY-FIRST CENTURY: HIGH-TECH CREATIVITY AND "SILVER BUSINESS" OPPORTUNITIES

One of the more interesting outcomes of the LTCI program has been the increasing commoditization of elder care services and the creation of what amounts to an elder care industry, with both new jobs, in the form of positions such as care managers, and new products. The growth of the elder population in Japan has brought with it the potential for new markets. Care technology has grown into a $1.08 billion market as of 2006 and is expected to continue growing as the population of elderly increases. Many of these new and proposed new products take advantage of Japan's abilities and fascination with high-tech solutions to problems. Recent high-tech solutions to the problem of an aging population range from wheelchairs with voice recognition to a robotic arm fitted with a spoon and fork that can be operated with the user's chin and can manipulate even soft foods such as tofu (Associated Press 2007).

While the prices of these new gadgets can be quite prohibitive for the elderly—the spoon-feeding robot arm costs $3,500—a combination of the LTCI program, labor shortages and reduced family size have stimulated the development of a variety of new technologies. Other examples of technological solutions to the problem of an aging society include some fascinating ideas, such as an automated bathing machine (basically a car wash for the human body), toy company TOMY's wide-eyed *anime*-styled robotic "grandchild" dolls for lonely elderly couples and partner robots to provide medical and nursing care (*The Nikkei Weekly* 2007). Many of these high-tech innovations have been reported in the Western news media with a combined sense of curiosity, sensationalism and suspicion. Indeed, the government has promoted research into robotics as a means of dealing with the rapid aging of the society and as an alternative, when it comes to health care, to allowing into the country significant numbers of immigrants who could fill jobs left vacant as the Japanese population declines over the remainder of this century (Hardin 2008).

The growth of the "silver business" has not been limited to high-tech. The nursing care industry itself has become a growth area as a variety of new facilities and approaches to elder care emerge. For example, in 2000, there were 369 group homes for elders suffering from conditions such as Alzheimer's disease that prevented them from living on their own. In Iwate Prefecture (where Traphagan has conducted research), there were a total of seventy such homes. By July 2006, these numbers had increased dramatically, with a total of 8,052 group homes for elders nationally and 860 within Iwate. In many cases, these homes are the result of entrepreneurs either expanding their businesses in the

In a large Tokyo bookstore, piles of how-to books for sale on "recreation games" and rehabilitation activities for the elderly, along with aisles full of manuals for LTCI and elder care. Photo by Brenda Jenike.

health care area or entering into the new industry. Not unexpectedly, the results of this rapid growth have been varied, with some group homes providing excellent care and others running afoul of the legal system for failure to provide care that meets national standards (Traphagan and Nagasawa 2008).

Beyond the health care industry, various companies have been trying to court the interest—and yen—of elderly Japanese. NTT DoCoMo has held workshops in the Tokyo area to help elders learn to use specially designed cell phones (Yomiuri 2006a). Companies such as Lawson, which has convenience stores throughout Japan, have increased the size of aisles and lowered shelves, and some major department stores have attracted older clientele by increasing areas for sitting (Associated Press 2006). This growth has not come without problems; consumer fraud against the elderly more than tripled over the first half of the decade, with over 46,000 cases in the first half of 2004 alone (UPI 2004).[9]

NEW CULTURAL SCRIPTS

Since 2000, Japan has been undergoing a major restructuring of elder care in which there has been at least the beginning of a move away from the hands-on, family-centered experience of elder care associated with the idea of "warm contact" to a more distant, institutional and technological approach to caring for the aged. In essence, what we see in Japan is the emergence of new cultural scripts that allow for a considerable expansion in the alternatives an older person and his or her family have, should that person need either minor assistance with ADLs or major, long-term nursing care. One set of cultural scripts, specifically set forward by the LTCI program, involves the ability to make use of existing and new forms of public and private institutional settings that, while providing an alternative to the traditional at-home care script, also provide means by which that script can be continued. The availability of home helpers and day care for the elderly are good examples of this; and even with the decline in the proportion of elders living in multigenerational contexts, this remains the most common pattern of living for older Japanese.

Along with the LTCI program has come, as noted already, a commoditization of elder care in which there has been a move away from simply viewing elders as deserving "respect" or "filial piety" to viewing them as significant business opportunities. Elders, and their families, have become consumers in a growing market of goods designed to help people maintain their independence as they age. Robotic and other computer technologies are at the core of a growing, if not yet highly accessible, market for devices that can take the place of traditional caregivers.

Yet, it is important to avoid drawing the conclusion that Japan is undergoing a wholesale revolution in elder care. Much of what we see with the LTCI system is consistent with existing cultural scripts—rather than replacing, new approaches to elder care augment existing approaches and established scripts. The filial child may no longer be able to coreside with his or her parents, but may set up Internet monitoring devices so the elderly living alone can be in regular touch—even if that "touch" is not as warm as it once was. Furthermore, although aged parents may readily use LTCI's community care services and spend their final years in a care residence rather than at home, this does not mean that their expectations for what constitutes an ideal, or even acceptable, old age have suddenly changed. Expectations for family care remain strong, and disappointment over perceived lack of family assistance can be profound. For the designated adult child caregiver as well, LTCI has remedied the burden of unending arduous care that was a common experience just a decade ago. But it has not alleviated the tensions associated with care decisions that must constantly be negotiated between in-laws, spouses and siblings, nor the moral responsibility to provide care. On a wider scale, there is also a general discontent among the populace that it is unjust to be forced to pay monthly premiums for future services that only an estimated 20 percent will utilize. Nonetheless, where the previous approaches to elder care under the Gold Plans used a social welfare system in an attempt to provide the same cultural script in institutional care settings that was provided in home care settings, the LTCI policy and system has shifted toward a focus on the specific needs of the elderly as individuals, and as entitled consumers rather than as dependents, providing a much broader scope of cultural scripts from which to choose than has existed in the past.

NOTES

1. The ethnographic vignette above took place ten years ago when I was conducting my doctoral fieldwork on the renegotiation of the responsibility for parent care in Japan (Jenike 2002). In summer 2005, I returned to Tokyo and to Green Hills for follow-up research. Gone were the Meiji elders in kimonos—there were now only Taishō elders, who wore their own sweat pants and shirts. Yet, to my great delight, I found some familiar faces among the residents of Green Hills. Imeda-san, a former policeman and affirmed *Edo-ko* (native of Tokyo) remembered me clearly. Still walking on his own, he told me he was now ninety-two and had been living in Green Hills for ten years. One of the younger residents when he entered, he is now one of the five or six oldest. He remarked, "When I came here, I never would have guessed I would still be living here ten years later." Imeda-san's statement is apt for many elderly Japanese today. They never expected to live so long, and never expected to spend their extended years in a care home for the elderly.

2. These data are extracted from the *Japan Statistical Yearbook* online edition http://www.stat.go.jp/English/data/nenkan/index.htm.

3. These data are extracted from the *Japan Statistical Yearbook* online edition http://www.stat.go.jp/English/data/nenkan/index.htm. For a detailed discussion of population aging and demographic change in Japan, see Traphagan and Knight (2003).

4. Vogel's work created a context to consider the Japanese family outside of the traditional emphasis on patrilineal linkages in genealogies (Brown 1966:1146) by noting the importance of the nuclear family structure among postwar urbanites. Work that followed Vogel moved alternatively between an emphasis on the nuclearization of the family to perspectives that show the continued importance, ideationally, of the stem

family structure that emphasizes patrilineal reckoning of descent with patrilocal marriage rules for eldest sons—much of the scholarly work has centered on determining whether the *ie* is fundamentally based upon economic ties or social ties among its members (cf. Brown 1966; Nakane 1967).

5. U.S. Centers for Disease Control and Prevention, http://www.cdc.gov/mmwr/preview/ mmwrhtml/mm5415a1.htm#tab.

6. *Japan Statistical Yearbook,* online edition, http://www.stat.go.jp/English/data/nen kan/1431-02.htm.

7. For example, the city-run adult day care Jenike volunteered at during 1996–1997 in Tokyo's Suginami Ward used the name *Fureai no ie,* or "house of warm contact," evoking (in name only) the image of family-centered elder care (see Thang 2001 for a discussion of the use of *fureai* and family imagery in elder care).

8. In Osaka, for instance, where the city's nursing care operations have a deficit of 2.7 billion yen (USD 25.2 million), premiums are 5,092 yen/month (USD 48) on average to cover the shortfall. In Kitakyushu, those sixty-five and over with an annual income of 4 million yen or more (USD 37,400) must pay 9,500 yen/month (USD 89; Koyama and Yasuda 2006).

9. Home renovation and improvement scams have been particularly problematic in recent years. In 2005, for example, the national police agency reported that 24,000 people had paid more than 22 billion yen (USD 205.6 million) to fraudulent renovation companies, which was about five times the number in 2004 (McCurry 2006).

CHAPTER 18

Standing Up for Others: The AMIGOS Volunteer Model for Working with Elders in Peru

Dena Shenk and Joan Mahon

Peru is an impoverished country where the increasing population of older adults has not been helped by globalization. The cultural myth remains strong that elders are cared for and receiving support within their families. Many do, in fact, live with their children and grandchildren, or have children and/or grandchildren living with them. As we will see, however, these living arrangements do not necessarily indicate that care or support are provided to meet elders' needs, and many face old age with few personal resources or government support. Despite new laws requiring local government support for older adults, and a national plan stimulated by proclamations from the United Nations' Second World Assembly on Aging of Madrid in 2002, many older adults receive no pension or medical care.

This chapter discusses an international model of volunteering in terms of the overwhelming needs of elders in and around the the Peruvian city of Arequipa. Working as a volunteer from the United States, the second author helped spearhead the development of a group of local volunteers to work with needy elders. The situation in Peru is not unlike that of many industrializing countries where the growing number of elders living in poverty have largely been set adrift to fend for themselves despite governmental laws claiming to address their needs (United Nations 2007). Over the past decade, organizations like the United Nations and HelpAge International have developed global and regional initiatives and extensive materials to help rectify these problems (www.un.org/esa/socdev/ageing; www.helpage.org/Home).

THE AGING OF PERU

Peru, until recently considered a "young country" by demographers, is faced—as are other Latin American nations—with a rapidly increasing number of older

Older woman selling prickly pears in a Peruvian regional
market. Courtesy of Dena Shenk.

adults resulting from lower birth rates and increased life expectancies (MIMDES
2002b). The latest census figures report that out of a total population of 28 million, approximately 8 percent are over the age of sixty in 2006, and this part of
the population will almost triple to 22 percent by 2050 and be only slightly less
than in the United States (INEI 2005; United Nations 2006; Spitzer 2006).

Notably, a significant portion of this rising older adult population is in dire
straits, lacking access to economic, health and social resources. Almost two-
thirds live in poverty, a similar portion lack health insurance, fewer than 40 percent have access to pensions (MCAMA 2007; Bravo 2007). While a 1997 survey
indicated that 87 percent of older persons owned their own home, significant
numbers lacked connections to public sewers, potable water or electricity.[1]
Sadly, the same report found that younger members of the family at times abuse
older relatives and take control of these dwellings (MIMDES 2002b).

In rural areas where a quarter of the nation's elders reside, extremes of
economic deprivation are found. While sixty percent of elders living in rural
highlands are poor, 80 percent of them live in extreme poverty, yet barely
10 percent of rural older adults are covered by any form of government health

care (MIMDES 2002b, 2007; Spitzer 2006). As happened through much of Latin America, tough economic restructuring measures of the 1980s and 1990s did not improve conditions of age and gender inequity; in fact, the socioeconomic gap for elders has widened, evidenced by steady increases in extreme poverty and further exclusion of older adults from access to food, shelter, and health care (Lloyd-Sherlock 2004; Bravo 2007; Gasparini et al. 2007).

PERU'S FORMAL RESPONSE TO AN AGING SOCIETY

In 2000, the Ministry for Women and Human Development (PROMUDEH) published Peru's first Policy Guidelines for Older Adults. By the end of 2002, the renamed Ministry for Women and Social Development (MIMDES) produced a report on the current situation of older adults (2002b) highlighting discrimination, high poverty rates, deficient health care, low educational levels and the generally precarious living conditions of men and women over sixty. This prompted the head of this ministry to focus her speech at the 2002 UN Second World Assembly on Ageing on addressing a secure and dignified aging for older people (United Nations 2002).

Shortly afterwards, the country's first National Plan for Older Adults for 2002–2006 took on the task of establishing a coordinated and multisectorial approach to identifying and addressing the needs of older adults. By 2005, the government had developed a revised National Plan for Older Adults covering 2006–2010. Another important step came in 2006, when Congress enacted Laws #28683 and #28735 requiring preferential treatment of older adults and other vulnerable populations, "wherever the public is served." Finally, after a four-year debate, Congress signed Law #28803, the first National Law for Older Adults, guaranteeing legal mechanisms to enable older adults an improved quality of life. More recently, a plan has been developed that focuses on the particular needs of rural older adults (MIMDES 2007).

Law #27972 outlines responsibilities of municipal governments to the older adults in their areas. While some municipalities have provided land to build a senior center, only one group in Arequipa has successfully built such a center, after fourteen years of lobbying efforts. The government view is generally that older adults should be doing more to help themselves, and that poor elders are too used to asking for help, rather than working. The lucky ones are receiving a "pension de vejez," an old-age pension, but three in five seniors nationally live without any form of social security, forcing them to work well into old age (HAI 2005). An emphasis of HelpAge International is to get governments to recognize that there should be a basic government pension, like the American Supplementary Security Income (SSI).

ORGANIZING TO MEET THE NEEDS OF OLDER ADULTS IN AREQUIPA

In 1998, this chapter's second author, an American social worker, made contact with a regional government leader in southern Arequipa, the second largest city in Peru, with a population of one million and 7.8 percent over age sixty (CTAR 1998). Motivated by a plan to disseminate United Nations and Help-Age International materials related to the UN's 1999 International Year of Older Persons, and working to connect local aging organizations, she found only a few scattered professionals (demographers, sociologists, lawyers and health providers) vaguely interested in the region's aging population or in the weakening status of older adults.

In response to the massive June 2001 earthquake that had devastated southern Peru, she called for a meeting of local colleagues to discuss elaborating plans for future disaster preparedness focused on elders. At the same time, a suggestion was made to form a voluntary organization to advocate on some of the issues related to old age, racial discrimination, and socioeconomic inequality. Meeting later that summer, a group of social workers (some unemployed, others forced to take early retirement without a pension), discussed with the second author how they had never before focused on the rights of active older persons, or the care needs of fragile older adults. Most had been employed by private and public sector institutions that were barely complying with the government's mandate to assist hourly production workers and their young families, and had no responsibility towards those who were no longer classified as "economically active." Discussions evolved to how, as they approached retirement age (or lost jobs to younger colleagues), all had been affected by daily instances of age discrimination and bias, and began to identify their coming together as an opportunity to become involved in an unknown field of social activism: aging.

Under the leadership of one of the most articulate and respected participants, university professor and retired social worker Dr. Teresa Echegaray de Ballon, the group decided to form a volunteer association of social workers, which later became known and formally registered as AMIGOS, an acronym for "Adultos Mayores Integrados Ganan Oportunidades Siempre," or "Older Integrated Adults Always Gain Opportunities." Over time, organizational objectives were defined as: (1) to contribute to a culture of healthy, active and productive aging in their region; (2) to develop and strengthen the spiritual beliefs of older adults; and (3) to promote and enable self-care and well-being of older adults. Operating expenses are covered by volunteer membership dues of less than $2 US a month, and sporadic donations are received for training materials, transportation and special celebrations.

THE AMIGOS MODEL

The authors are involved in research to study the background, development and impact of this model for working with needy older adults. Data were collected in April 2007 through interviews with senior leaders and key members in the aging network. Individual face-to-face interviews were held with each of the twelve AMIGOS volunteers active at that time to determine how they see their work and what they felt they needed to further their efforts. Finally, focus group discussions were held with each of the senior groups with which AMI-GOS volunteers worked.

Within the public advocacy role taken on by AMIGOS, a critical decision in 2002 was to bring together a regional group of policy-makers, representatives from academia, aging specialists and senior leaders to begin a systematic, multidisciplinary dialogue to listen to seniors and their leaders, prioritize needs, identify opportunities, and hold accountable government entities responsible for implementing laws cited above. The result was the formation of MCAMA ("Mesa de Concertacion del Adulto Major de la Region Arequipa") composed of over thirty working members who meet monthly, and have become the leading voice representing older persons. An Inter-Institutional Operating Plan recognizes ethnic, linguistic, gender, education and socioeconomic differences of older adults in the region and seeks to raise awareness and promote a coordinated and collaborative approach towards addressing those diverse and multiple needs. In March 2007, MCAMA invited municipal governments to the First Regional Meeting of Mayors to exhort authorities to make a commitment towards implementing both the National Plan for Older Adults and Law #27972 pertaining to local governments' responsibility towards older persons in their municipalities. Speakers included the first author, who provided an international perspective on aging issues, and the MIMDES Director of the Office of Older Adults. The participation of over 300 attendees (including 120 mayors), many traveling from the most isolated small towns of the region, surpassed all expectations and proved the timeliness and relevance of MCAMA's initiative.

Today, a cadre of sixteen AMIGOS volunteers support activities of urban, rural, and semirural associations of elders to improve the situation of, and expand opportunities for, older adults. The volunteers train senior groups in eight locations through educational programs focused on advocacy, leadership development, health and exercise, recreation, spirituality and community relations. The number of direct beneficiaries is estimated at 600, with another 200 older persons reportedly benefiting indirectly from the program (Zeballos 2007). These are conservative numbers and must be appreciated alongside the dramatic impact of AMIGOS's coalition-building efforts with various ministries, local governments, academic institutions and other aging network members.

THE CURRENT SITUATION OF ASSOCIATIONS FOR SENIORS IN AREQUIPA

Most of the senior associations' members are elders who do not receive a government pension and are not covered by health or social service insurance. Approximately 60 percent of participants are male, as domestic responsibilities and traditional cultural patterns hinder female participation. Sixty percent are bilingual (Quechua or Aymara and Spanish), and more than two-thirds are past age seventy. Most had migrated from the highlands when they were younger to seek employment opportunities in the hill towns surrounding Arequipa.

They worked in construction or in the informal economy as artisans or as farm laborers, but there is no work for them now that they are older. "They don't pick us to work and our children don't even have work" because thirty-five is even too old to be picked as daily farm laborers. The poverty is extreme, and as one focus group participant explained, "We need food here because we don't work anymore." Another group of elders had worked in a textile factory that went bankrupt and closed in 1989. Average daily income of the seniors in these groups is estimated at less than $3 US (Zeballos 2004). Many rely on the system of land-scavenging called "payapa," where landowners allow the poor, hungry and old to clear the land of whatever remaining potatoes, onions, barley or beans are left after the harvest. As one senior group participant explained:

Well, that's how it is, finding enough to live on the hills, after the bosses have harvested. After they've harvested I go behind and pick up some; whatever they leave, you know? That's how we survive. Garlic. Anything. I take it downtown and sell it, even if it's for two or three soles. At least I bring, that's what I bring back, that's how I help myself. My daughter too, when she has something she helps me, when she doesn't…

Some association members live alone or with spouses, others with children and grandchildren, but most are lonely and many are in need of medical care. "We don't have medicines, we don't have money. But when we have money the doctors see us; when we don't, they don't. When we don't have any, no one helps us." For some who live in multigenerational family groups, child care, home security or cooking are the prices paid for shelter. This is recognized as a high price for some. One tired senior leader timidly expressed the following about family members in a personal interview, "They treat us badly. We're being abused. They use us as maids to cook, clean and take care of the children."

As one women described:

I suffer a lot. All of this is dead (rubs right leg). I can't walk. I want to fall (points to leg again). I don't work for a long time. I'm eighty years old. This knee can't work but I used to work the land. Of the children, just one, they always see me.
    Researcher: How many children do you have?
    Eight, nine, ten. Two have died. Only eight remain. Sometimes they come, they give me one sole, sometimes they don't. Sometimes they come, sometimes they don't. I live with my daughter. She has children. They also have schools, notebooks, expenses.

Facing the harsh realities of poverty, many of their children and grandchildren have left in search of jobs. Whether living with family members or alone, most lack money, medicines and even food.

IMPACT OF THE AMIGOS

Arequipa's organized network of older adult associations (Red Departamental del Adulto Mayor), supported with technical assistance by AMIGOS volunteers for several years, is using its voice to demand accountability through a series of articles and press releases. These have been written by the network's president, a retired journalist and teacher, who poses hard questions on themes such as: "Poverty and Aging," "Older Adults Request Compliance with the Law" and "Elder Abuse and the Law" (Cervantes 2006, 2007).

After six years of steady advocacy work on efforts including promoting local government responses to seniors, working with the media, organizing public forums, workshops, and training programs, and providing ongoing support and technical assistance to senior organizations, AMIGOS is being recognized by Peru's government as a service model that could be expanded throughout the country, particularly as the Ministry's Department of Older Adults focuses on the needs of rural elders.

As the authors' latest field trip drew to a close in 2007, AMIGOS inaugurated their Center for Integrated Assistance for Older Adults. The property, a large charming colonial structure in downtown Arequipa, owned by the aging mother of one of the volunteers, houses the center. It is equipped to serve as an office, resource library and classroom. At last report, a group of seniors were receiving knitting instruction, a new AMIGOS income-generating project for elders (Zeballos 2007).

This effort that began as a volunteer project by a social worker from the United States has developed into a model for volunteer support by local community volunteers in Arequipa, Peru. The AMIGOS are helping to meet the needs of poor older adults in Peru, a country where the needs of the growing numbers of elders are not being met by current approaches. The AMIGOS model is being recognized as an approach that can be adapted throughout Peru to augment government programs and address the needs of the increasing numbers of needy older adults.

NOTE

1. Only 48 percent of dwellings owned by older people are connected to public sewage systems, 25 percent do not have running water, 33 percent do not have electricity and less than 18 percent have telephones (MIMDES 2002).

CHAPTER 19

Danish Home Care Policy and the Family: Implications for the United States

Mary Stuart and Eigil Boll Hansen

INTRODUCTION

Denmark has been widely recognized as a country that has implemented cost-effective community-based systems of home care for the frail elderly. In the early 1980s, with a high proportion of women in the labor force and a growing population of elderly citizens, Denmark initiated a process of reforming an institutional system of long-term care. Today, extensive service networks that integrate health, home care, and personal care can be found in nearly all of Denmark's 271 local municipalities. What impact does this system have on family relations and family care-giving? In this paper we review the basics of Danish long-term care and discuss how public services and families interact in providing assistance to the frail elderly. We then consider the implications for U.S. policy as this country seeks to meet the growing need for services for the old elderly.

OVERVIEW OF DANISH SOCIAL POLICY

To understand the Danish system of providing services for elders who need assistance with activities of daily living (ADLs), an overview of the basic principles of Danish social policy and a brief description of the developments in elder care during the last 20 years are useful. In contrast to the United States, five fundamental principles of health and social services apply to the care for older people: (1) Services are financed largely by general taxes, rather than user payment and private contributions. They are available largely without charge to consumers. (2) Service coverage is universal. All citizens are entitled to the services, and eligibility is based on an assessment of the needs of the individual and his or her household. (3) Responsibility for health and social services [is] decentralized to local counties and municipalities. Denmark has 271 local jurisdictions, known as municipalities, which range in size from

2,300 to 496,000 inhabitants. Municipal services (including personal care, home health care, nursing homes, and primary medical care) are financed through local income and property taxes as well as block grants from the central government. (4) National policy and regulations for elder care are established by the Danish Parliament and the central government. (5) Services are generally provided by the local government rather than by private or voluntary organizations. In January 2003, a new policy directed that recipients of home help should have the option of choosing a private provider for assistance financed by the local government. However, not all municipalities have a private provider, and less than 10 percent of the recipients of home help have chosen a private provider (Ankestyrelsen 2004).

BUILDING BLOCKS IN DANISH ELDER POLICY

The foundation of the contemporary Danish system of elder care dates to around 1980. At that time a national Commission on Aging completed a report, formulating principles for future policies on care and housing for older people in Denmark. One of the key recommendations was that long-term care policy should be better organized to compensate for losses that occur with aging. The Commission advocated policies and practices that would support the potential for older adults with disabilities to continue living active and independent lives, preserve self-determination, and facilitate continuity in their housing. In particular, the Commission recommended that arrangements for housing and support services for older dependent people should be organized so that they do not have to move as the need for help increases. The Commission advised that services be developed that would enable the municipalities gradually to increase help as needed in the older person's home (or in a dwelling where he or she had chosen to move).

At approximately the same time, several municipalities introduced 24-hour home-care systems. Other developments of significance followed, most notably an increase in special dwellings that were adapted to provide handicapped accessibility (and in some cases, staff) and where the residents are considered as tenants (rather than patients), a decline in nursing home beds, and an increase in the number and percentage of the elderly receiving home help from municipalities. A brief history and description of these pivotal developments follows. For a more extensive discussion of the development of the Danish system, see Stuart and Weinrich 2001a and 2001b, among other sources.

24-Hour Integrated Home Care

During the 1980s several municipalities experimented with the 24-hour/7-day per week home-care system. For evening and night shifts, personal care providers and home health nurses used a car and a wireless radio connected to a common staffed base. Elderly people needing urgent assistance could call a central number for help using the phone or an alarm system (such as those worn on wrist bands). This system made it possible to respond quickly and efficiently to the care needs of fragile elderly who were living in the community. Additional efficiency was obtained by municipalities through the *integrated care system*, in which staff from the local nursing home and home care organization were combined into a single organization to care for the frail elderly in a geographic area. With this system, the same staff could provide assistance to people living in ordinary housing, adapted special dwellings, and nursing homes. This arrangement offered flexibility; the municipality gave personal care and nursing services based on the needs of the citizen, irrespective of the type of housing. Piloted initially in Skaevinge under the direction of Lis Wagner, RN (Wagner 1997), today almost all Danish municipalities have 24-hour integrated home-care systems (Stuart and Weinrich 2001a and 2001b).

Housing for Older People

During the 1980s, municipalities also began to experiment with new types of dwellings for dependent older people as a substitute for nursing homes. The most common type of new housing had adaptations to meet the needs of older people with physical disabilities. Usually housing units were congregate, sometimes with staff, social activities, exercise equipment, or rehabilitation facilities. A typical housing unit consisted of two rooms, and a kitchen and a bathroom. The dwellings were serviced by the 24-hour home-care system. This remains the prototype of dwellings for dependent older people in Denmark (Hansen 2002). Admittance to special dwellings is granted by the local authority of a municipality and depends on an assessment of the applicant's disabilities and the possibility of receiving adequate help in his or her ordinary dwelling. Special dwellings are not institutions, and residents are similar to tenants.

In 1988, legislation was implemented that prohibited municipalities from building nursing homes. The effect of policies that encouraged construction of assisted living units and prohibited nursing home construction resulted in a dramatic increase in adapted special dwellings between 1985 and 1999 (3,207 to 32,501) and a reduction in nursing homes (49,487 to 31,244). Approximately one-third of the adapted special dwellings have 24-hour staffing. Staffed housing is generally reserved for individuals with severe dementia or those who require high levels of supervision (Hansen 2002).

A 1995 survey (Hansen and Platz 1995a) found that about 50 percent of people defined as "physically vulnerable" aged 80+ lived in ordinary dwellings or adapted dwellings cared for by the home-care system. Half of these people lived alone. People were considered "physically vulnerable" if they were not able to walk out of doors and thought they had poor health; if they needed help getting in and out of bed, washing/bathing, dressing, or using the toilet.

Home Help and Other Home Care Services

Home help, including assistance with domestic tasks such as housecleaning and personal care such as dressing and bathing, is another of the basic services that municipalities provide for the frail elderly free of charge. Home help is granted on the basis of an assessment of the household's ability to take care of various types of housework and personal care. Typically, home help personnel of the municipal provider are part of a multidisciplinary team that includes a nurse. Individuals providing these services are required to have completed a specific educational program of at least one year (Hansen and Platz 1995a).

Other home care services provided by the municipality include home nursing, which is generally short-term and prescribed by a physician to provide specified prevention or treatment. In addition, municipalities typically offer day care, night care, respite care, acute care, and rehabilitation services for the frail elderly who live at home (Hansen and Platz 1995b). Most municipalities provide transportation for health and social activities for the elderly. In many municipalities, day centers provide rehabilitation and maintenance physical therapy and occupational therapy to promote functioning and prevent deterioration. The majority of municipalities also have specialized housing for individuals with dementia (Hansen and Platz 1995b).

ATTITUDES TOWARD THE RESPONSIBILITY FOR ASSISTANCE

Only 3 percent of elders aged 70 or older in Denmark live with their children (Kahler 1992). However, the Danish policy analysts assert that Danish social legislation is based on the premise that citizens bear the primary responsibility for themselves and their families. For older people, this essentially means in practice that in addition to the responsibility for themselves, spouses also have a mutual responsibility for each other. If an elderly person in need of care lives in a household with an adult child, the child will have to contribute to the housekeeping, but not necessarily fulfill needs for personal care. Legislation puts no obligations on children or other family members not living in the same household to care for dependent elders.

A recent Danish study (Colmorten et al. 2003) concludes that the principle that one should be responsible for taking care of oneself reflects the attitudes of older people, relatives, and other parties such as municipal employees, local politicians, and volunteer and special interest organizations. If an elderly person in need of assistance has a spouse, the general attitude is that the spouse should help. Assistance from the public sector is expected only when the household is unable to take care of the housekeeping or personal care itself. However, a majority of older people think that older people who can clean their houses only with great difficulty also have the right to receive public home help.

In the study, the older people of the survey and relatives in focus groups were asked to consider who should provide assistance with different types of tasks. The answers can be summed up as follows:

• With regard to domestic tasks, they are primarily the responsibility of the spouse. The municipality should provide assistance only when an older couple is not able to handle such tasks themselves and in cases where there is no spouse. Assistance paid for privately and help from family and friends or neighbors play only minor roles in this context.

- With regard to dealing with the authorities and with money matters, it is also primarily the spouse's responsibility, and if there is no spouse who can take care of these matters, then it is, first and foremost, the family who should take on such responsibilities. The municipality is attributed only a small amount of responsibility and that is only for single older people.

- With regard to getting out of doors, it is primarily the responsibility of the spouse, followed by the municipality, according to older people and their relatives. The family is attributed more responsibility with regard to older people without spouses as opposed to older couples. Volunteer organizations are not mentioned very often by older people, while relatives think that such organizations could play greater roles.

- With regard to the need for a more suitable residence, it is primarily the municipality's responsibility, followed by the individual older person, and finally by the family.

- With regard to the need to participate in leisure-time activities or the need for someone to talk to, the older person is primarily responsible, while the municipality is not attributed any degree of responsibility worth mentioning except in cases involving older people with no spouse and with greatly reduced functional capacity (Colmorten et al. 2003:104).

ASSISTANCE TO OLDER PEOPLE

There have been several studies on assistance to older people with various types of housework and they all show the same tendencies. Table 19.1 reports findings from a survey conducted in 2002. Households with older people *mostly* take care of the housework themselves, and except for what is defined as difficult cleaning, less than 5 percent of households with people below age eighty-two have others to do most of the housework tasks. If older people do not mostly themselves take care of difficult cleaning, the public home help does, and in just a few cases family or friends mostly take care of difficult cleaning. Family and friends play a role by shopping regularly and to a lesser extent by washing clothes regularly. If older people do not prepare hot meals themselves, they usually receive meals-on-wheels or eat out in a center or in a restaurant.

Few older people pay for having the housework done. Those who do may not be eligible for publicly financed home help, or they may be unsatisfied with the quality of the help they can get from the home help system.

The ranking of the resources of help is the same for people aged eighty and above, but in this age group the households themselves take care of fewer tasks (Table 19.2).

This analysis is based on questions, including "Who mostly takes care of?" Family and friends could provide assistance with cleaning, shopping, washing clothes, etc., without doing it "mostly." In 2002, the sample population was asked whether within the latest month they had received help from family or friends with, for example, housework. Table 19.3 shows the share that

Table 19.1

People Aged 67, 72, 77, or 82 in 2002 Distributed According to Who Mostly Takes Care of Various Types of Housework (Percentages) (Excluding People in Nursing Homes)

	Difficult Cleaning[1]	Easier Cleaning[2]	Shopping	Washing Clothes	Hot Meal
Household	78	96	92	95	93
Home help (e.g., municipality)	14	2	1	3	0
Family, friends, other	2	1	6	2	1
Assistance paid for	6	1	1	1	0
Meals-on-wheels	•	•	•	•	3
Eat out	•	•	•	•	2
Do not usually eat hot meal	•	•	•	•	0
In total	100	100	100	100	99
Number of cases	*3,346*	*3,355*	*3,346*	*3,351*	*3,363*

[1]For example, vacuum-cleaning, washing the floor, washing stairs.
[2]For example, dusting, tidying up.
• = Irrelevant
Source: Special analysis on The Danish Longitudinal Database on Aging. Data are from a survey in 2002 among a representative sample of people in Denmark born in 1920, 1925, 1930, 1935, 1940, 1945, or 1950. The total number of respondents is 8,207 (response rate 81).

confirmed they had received help. It is not possible to state exactly what help older people have received from family or friends, but one can conclude that it is not common for older people in Denmark to receive help with housework from family or friends. The most common help is with maintaining the house

Table 19.2

People Aged 80+ in 1994 Distributed According to Who Mostly Takes Care of Various Types of Housework (Percentages) (Excluding People in Nursing Homes)

	Cleaning[1]	Shopping	Washing Clothes	Hot Meal
Household	40	60	60	70
Children of other family	3	12	10	3
Home help	51	21	21	1
Others	6	7	8	2
Meals-on-wheels	•	•	•	19
Eat out	•	•	•	5
Do not usually eat hot meal	•	•	•	0
In total	100	100	99	100
Number of Cases	*1,683*	*1,683*	*1,683*	*1,683*

[1]In this case it is not possible to distinguish between difficult and easier cleaning.
• = Irrelevant
Source: (Hansen et al. 2002). Data are from a survey in 1994 among a representative sample of people aged 80+ in 75 Danish municipalities. The total number of respondents is 1,845 (response rate 78).

Table 19.3
The Share of People Aged 67, 72, 77, or 82 in 2002 Who Had Received Help from Family or Friends with Housework within the Latest Month (Percentages) (Excluding People in Nursing Homes)

	Have Received Help	Number of Cases
People having difficulties in doing difficult cleaning or cannot do it	22	*961*
People having difficulties in shopping or cannot do it	25	*663*
People having difficulties in washing clothes or cannot do it	25	*476*

Source: Special analysis on The Danish Longitudinal Database on Aging. See Table 19.1.

or gardening, although only 13 percent of all the persons in the age group have received such help within the latest month (The Danish Longitudinal Database on Aging).

In Table 19.3, the share of older people having received help from family or friends is considerably higher than in Table 19.1. This can be explained by the fact that Table 19.3 includes more occasionally provided help, while Table 19.1 includes only help provided on a regular basis. Furthermore, the people included in Table 19.3 are on average more dependent on help than the people included in Table 19.1.

Studies on care for older people have not included help with personal chores such as bathing, dressing, and getting in and out of bed. This may be based on the assumption that spouses may help each other in case of disablement. In cases of disabled people living alone, help with personal chores is provided by the public home-care system, while help from children or other family members is very rare. Lewinter (1999) states that personal care is the task of the home help because this formalized intimacy is easier to handle for both older people and their families, and it supports the preserving of older people's feeling of integrity as taboo fields have not been crossed.

SOCIAL CONTACTS

Table 19.4 shows figures for how often older people in Denmark see their children. Very few older people in Denmark live with one or more of their children, but the great majority of older people usually see (one of) their children once a week, the oldest not quite as often as those in their seventies.

It is also evident from the preceding figures that despite not having the primary responsibility to provide housecleaning and personal care for the frail elderly, Danish children still visit their aging parents regularly. Do they do so more or less than children in other countries? A comparative study on selected European countries found that older people in Denmark were more likely than those in Germany to meet relatives or friends often, while the share is less

Table 19.4
People Aged 72 or 77 in 1997 and People Aged 80+ in 1995 and Having Living Children Distributed According to When They Last Saw (One of) Their Children (Percentages) (Excluding People in Nursing Homes)

When Did You Last See (One of) Your Children?	People Aged 72 or 77		People Aged 80+	
	Men	Women	Men	Women
Live with child	4	2	5	4
Today or yesterday	38	37	33	37
2–7 days ago	35	43	35	34
8–30 days ago	16	12	19	18
More than a month ago	6	6	8	7
In total	99	100	100	100
Number of cases	*707*	*1,273*	*504*	*885*

Source: (Platz 2000) and (Hansen and Platz 1996). Data on people aged 72 or 77 are from a survey in 1997 among a representative sample of people in Denmark born in 1920, 1925, 1930, 1935, 1940, or 1945. The total number of respondents is 5,864 (response rate 70). Data on people aged 80+, see Table 19.2.

when Denmark is compared with Greece, Holland, and England. There is no significant difference between Denmark and Italy on this indicator (Arendt et al. 2003). There is no clear evidence from this study that older people in Denmark have weaker or stronger social relations than older people in other countries.

DISCUSSION

Much has been written regarding the effects that race and ethnic and cultural differences play in the experiences of family caregivers within the United States (Dilworth-Anderson 2002). The potential for ethnic and cultural differences is magnified when making comparisons between countries. Given the long-standing differences between Denmark and the United States in attitudes regarding the importance of a public "safety-net," we must be cautious in generalizing from the results of Danish social policy for the United States. It is, however, because of the substantial differences in U.S. and Danish long-term care policies that the Danish experiment is worth closer examination by U.S. policymakers.

Table 19.5 enumerates some of the statistics that highlight major structural differences between the Danish and U.S. approaches to long-term care. Most notably, Denmark has a higher percentage of women in the labor force when compared to the United States (73% vs. 59%); half the number of nursing home beds per 1,000 people 65+ (26 vs. 52); and a far higher percentage of elderly receiving home help (49% of people 80+ vs. 5%).

When the frail elderly in Denmark require home help, these services are generally provided without charge by the local municipality. By contrast, when

Table 19.5
Comparative Statistics on Denmark and the United States

	Denmark[a] 2004	United States 2004
Total population	5.4 million	294 million
Percentage aged 65+	15%	12%[b]
Percentage aged 80+	4%	4%[b]
Percentage women in the labour force	73%[1]	59%[2, c]
Nursing home places per 1,000 65+	26	52[d]
Nursing home places per 1,000 80+	97	180[d]
Percentage of 65+ receiving home help	22%	3%[e]
Percentage of 80+ receiving home help	49%	5%[e]

[1] Age 16–66
[2] Age 16+

Sources:
[a] Statistics Denmark: www.statistikbanken.dk
[b] U.S. Census Bureau: http://www.census.gov/popest/national/asrh/NC-EST2004-sa.html
[c] Bureau of Labor Statistics: Women in the Labor Force: A Databook: www.bls.gov/cps/wlfdata book200r.htm
[d] National Center for Health Statistics: National Nursing Home Survey 1999: http://www.cdc.gov/nchs/data/nnhsd/NNHS99selectedchar_homes_beds_residents.pdf
[e] National Center for Health Statistics: Current Home Health Care Patients 2000: http://www.cdc.gov/nchs/data/nhhcsd/curhomecare00.pdf

home health care is purchased in the United States, 36 percent is paid for out of private funds (NHES 2004).

The amount of housekeeping and personal care services provided by family members for the frail elderly, as well as the level of out-of-pocket payments for long-term care services, are very different between the two countries. Only a small percentage of the frail elderly in Denmark lives with their families or receives help with housecleaning and personal care on a regular basis from family members outside their household. By contrast, in America, "the voluminous body of research concerning the long-term caregiving needs of frail elders ... suggests one principal conclusion: Families are their primary and most effective source of support. Family members provide 60–80% of long-term care for dependent elderly members, and formal or institutional mechanisms become activated only after family caregiving resources are expended. This is documented in extensive research reviews" (Bengtson, Rosenthal et al. 1996).

A major barrier to increasing community-based services for the elderly in the United States has been the concern that doing so would result in increases in public expenditures. However, the opposite has occurred in Denmark. During the 12-year period from 1985 to 1997, long-term care expenditures (including durable medical supplies, equipment, and nursing home expenditures for the non-elderly disabled as well as the elderly populations) for the over-80 population in the United States increased a whopping 68 percent, while comparable per capita expenditures in Denmark decreased 12 percent and declined as a percentage of gross domestic product (Stuart and Weinrich 2001a). While per capita long-term care expenditures for the population 80+ were considerably higher in Denmark than in the United States in 1985, by 1997 those expenditures were approximately the same in both countries (Stuart and Weinrich 2001a). While the average per capita costs may be roughly the same in both countries, the distribution of expenditures differs enormously. In the United States, expenditures are concentrated on a relatively small number of people who receive care in high-cost institutional settings. Conversely, the Danes are spending their resources on home care, where they serve far more people at a lower cost per person served.

Economic analysis of municipal variation in Denmark suggests that services for the frail elderly are more efficient when the reliance on nursing homes is low, relative to home care services (Hansen 1998). Thus, the need for efficiency in providing health and social services combined with a commitment to enabling people to remain in the community have led the Danes to maximize the development of efficient public home care services. Denmark has the highest level of home care among the European countries, providing nearly two times the hours of home help for the elderly as Sweden, the next closest country for this indicator (Danish Government 2000).

What is the impact of this responsibility on families? While some research has emphasized the positive benefits of intergenerational caring, including the reciprocal role that elders can play in families (Lopata 1993), reciprocity declines as the parent's health deteriorates (Spitz 1992). Depression, burden, role strain, relationship strain, and psychological distress have all been identified as negative effects associated with family caregiving. Dilworth-Anderson et al. and Lawton et al. found that greater burden was directly associated with greater depression (Dilworth-Anderson et al. 2002; Lawton et al. 1992). High levels of relationship strain have been reported using a composite measure that includes the "caregiver's feelings of being pressured, angry, depressed, manipulated, strained, resentful, depended upon, and the feeling that the relationship had a negative effect on other family members" (Cox 1993). Another study found that nearly one-third of caregivers reported that their health had deteriorated as a result of caregiving (Cox and Monk 1993). A recent study found that caregivers who experienced caregiver strain had mortality risks that were 63 percent higher than non-caregiving controls (Schulz and Beach 1999). Stress has been identified as a risk factor for elder abuse in the United States (Pillemer and Suitor 1992). "The most pervasive consequence of caregiving is the emotional strain generated by the burdens placed on the caregiver.... Competing demands, and childrearing and employment in particular, have been considered potential sources of stress" (Stone et al. 1987).

When there is no spouse to provide assistance, the caregiving role falls primarily to daughters and daughters-in-laws in the United States (Horowitz 1985). In contrast to studies in Denmark, Brody and colleagues found that housework and laundry are among the activities that daughters frequently provided, regardless of their employment status, and when these services are obtained from outside sources, they were generally privately paid for rather than subsidized by the government (Brody and Schoonover 1986).

CONCLUSION

As the United States faces continuing increases in long-term care costs, a growing percentage of old elderly, increases in life expectancy, and a high percentage of women in the labor force, the efficiency of the Danish municipal service systems should be attractive to U.S. policymakers. If the United States could import such a system, would it be good for families? There is evidence that social supports can mitigate the negative effects of caregiving stressors (Pearlin et al. 1996). There is also evidence that the types of assistance that elderly women are most willing to receive from non-family members are personal care and household help (Brody et al. 1984), two of the services the elderly are most likely to receive from the municipalities in Denmark. This same study (Brody et al. 1984) found that the types of supports the elderly preferred to receive from their children included emotional support and financial management—supports frequently provided by families in Denmark as well.

Some would argue that taking away the responsibility of caring for elderly people from the family would weaken elderly people's family network. The Danish case brings no support to this argument, since elderly people's contact with their children is just as frequent in Denmark as in other European countries with more obligations on the family. The family is still involved in practical, social, and emotional dimensions of the care for elderly people (Lewinter 1999), but the burden of caring—or at least some of it—is relieved through public assistance.

NOTE

Originally published as M. Stuart and M. Weinrich, 2001, "Home Is Where the Help Is: Community-Based Care in Denmark," *Journal of Aging and Social Policy* 12(4):81–101. Reprinted with permission of the publisher, Taylor & Francis Ltd., http://www.informaworld.com.

PART IV

The Ethnic Dimension in Aging: Culture, Context and Creativity

Jay Sokolovsky

Barbara Myerhoff in her powerful book *Number Our Days* (1978) described how a very old, ethnically Jewish population, disconnected from their kin and the surrounding ethnic community, established an unusual local variant of *Yiddishkeit* (Jewishness).[1] This did not center their lives around traditional religious behaviors, but around unique interpretations of ritual and personal performance. Surrounded by the bikini-clad youth culture of Venice Beach, California, these men and women in their eighties and nineties sought refuge in a senior center. They created within its walls and outside on boardwalk benches, an ethnic-tinged elderscape with their own transcendent sense of meaning in late life. The early cultural worlds of these elders had been largely spent in small East European *shtetls*[2] (market towns) drastically different from the large North American cities in which they spent their adulthoods. In essence, they had taken ethnic heritage, situated it in a highly changing urban landscape and lived this legacy in cultural spaces and cultural scripts of their own making. Such actions exemplify this book's prevailing themes and the emerging realities of twenty-first-century community life. Like many of the elders discussed in this section, the scripts they anticipated for late life and the spaces they expected to inhabit once they got there, had largely vanished. It was up to them to create new possibilities for their old age.

WHAT IS ETHNICITY?

Ethnicity is the manifestation of a cultural tradition in a heterogeneous societal framework. The expression of ethnic identity and the performance of ethnically rooted behaviors invariably take place under new conditions and in different locales from where the traditions originated. Ethnicity is therefore typically a creative act, meshing ancestral "native" patterns with restraints imposed by the broader society and the demands of the local environment. For example, anthropologists working in urban sub-Saharan Africa in the 1950s and 1960s found that some of the "tribal" groups they were studying in industrial cities were actually new cultural phenomena forged in the crucible of places dramatically different than their rural homelands. The topic of ethnicity opens up the question of diversity to be understood within such contextual variables as gender, economic differentiation and the migration process (Daatland and Biggs 2006). We will see that these factors play a large role in how ethnic individuals experience late life and the implications those experiences have for aging policy, especially related to health (Torres-Gil 2005). Below in Box IV.1 we have a discussion of one such effort, Project REACH, which is trying to ameliorate the impact of minority health disparity, in this case working to reduce the high incidence of diabetes among Hispanic elders in Texas. In Part VI, Carson-Henderson's chapter also focuses on this disease, this time among ethnic elders of Native American communities.

BOX IV.1. PROJECT REACH: ATTACKING HEALTH DISPARITY AMONG ETHNIC ELDERS

An underlying theme of this report is the growing problem of racial and ethnic health disparities among older adults. Two factors continue to increase the urgency of this problem—the dramatic aging of the U.S. population and the growing proportion of racial and ethnic minority groups. The health status of racial and ethnic minorities of all ages lags far behind that of nonminority populations. For a variety of reasons, older adults may experience the effects of health disparities more dramatically than any other population group. For one, older adults are more likely to have chronic illness and require frequent contact with the health care system. Also, many live in poverty, making access to health care a challenge. The care of older adults who are chronically ill, poor and members of an ethnic community is an increasingly urgent health priority.

A major effort to help address these health disparities is the Racial and Ethnic Approaches to Community Health (REACH 2010) Program, which supports community-based coalitions in the design, implementation and evaluation of innovative strategies to reduce or eliminate health disparities among racial and ethnic minorities. These groups include: African Americans, Hispanic Americans, American Indians, Alaska Natives, Asian Americans and Pacific Islanders. One example of a successful REACH 2010 Program is the Latino Education Project (LEP) in the Corpus Christi, Texas, area, which targets midlife and older Latinos—a population that suffers disproportionately from diabetes and its complications. The need for assistance in these small, rural and isolated communities is great. Approximately 80 to 95 percent of the residents are Hispanic and almost 50 percent are aged 60 or older. The depressed economy and chronic unemployment rates that characterize these communities perpetuate poverty from generation to generation.

continued

This area has been classified as medically underserved for decades and the high cost of health care, lack of access to health insurance and limited community resources contribute significantly to health disparities. LEP program activities focus on enabling and mobilizing key community institutions and organizations to respond to the diabetes crisis among midlife and older Hispanics. Community-wide health forums bring together health care providers, advocates, elected officials, radio, television and newspaper representatives and local leaders to identify the best strategies for the prevention, early diagnosis and management of diabetes. Small study circles allow for personalized attention, focusing on individual behavioral change through the selection of healthier foods, promoting and facilitating physical activity and mobilizing informal support networks. Lay health educators (*Promotores de Salud*) use their leadership skills to assist communities and individual participants to access resources on their own. The educators provide case management that leads to healthier behaviors, better health and improved management of diabetes.

As a result of these activities, LEP participants have increased their levels of physical activity and consumption of water, fruits and vegetables, as well as improved communication with their health care providers. REACH 2010 programs are fostering community commitment and active participation of seniors, stakeholders and state and local officials—two key strategies for improving health and access to health care among older adult communities of color.

Adapted from: *The State of Aging and Health in America 2007*. Whitehouse Station, NJ: Merck Company Foundation. Available at www.cdc.gov/aging/saha.htm.

McDONALDIZED—AMERICANS OR A *GLOCALIZED* NATION?

Despite a prevailing notion of the United States as a melting pot, effectively homogenizing immigrant cultures into an invariant, "alized" social soup, a highly contentious cultural plurality remains a powerful element of national life and what Roger Sanjek (1998) calls "the future of us all" (see also Aguirre and Turner 2006). The variation of *Yiddisheit* created by the elders who Myerhoff studied is related to what has been called *glocalization*, transforming a cultural pattern that traveled over global boundaries into a new variant of its original form. Within the bounds of a senior center, they altered Jewish ritual performance and modes of learning scripture to the exigencies of their lives, and when a learned Rabbi came to dissuade them from straying from "tradition," *he was asked to leave*. In this section, the chapters on Iranian and Cuban migrants will be instructive in pointing out how they are creating their own glocalized ethnic meaning in senior centers, parks and other public settings.

In the early twenty-first century, with vigilante posses guarding borders against Mexican intruders and immigrants from Islamic-centered cultures pre-emptively assumed to be potential terrorists, the issue of cultural diversity has

Figure IV.1
Population Age 65 and over, by Ethnic Grouping, 2006 and Projected for 2050

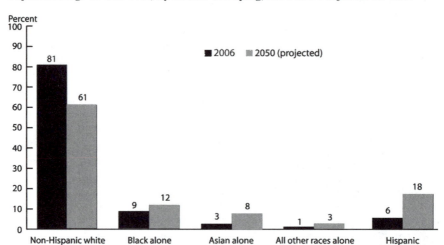

Adapted from: Older Americans Update 2008: Key Indicators of Well-Being. Federal Washington, DC: Interagency Forum on Aging Related Statistics.
www.agingstats.gov/agingstatsdotnet/Main_Site/Default.aspx

grown with special intensity. In the field of aging, this has been recognized by an explosion of new research, the establishment of national centers to study the issue (www.rcmar.ucla.edu/index.php) and as noted in this book's introduction, the invention of terms such as *ethnogerontology* and *ethnogeriatrics* to designate those with a specialized focus on ethnicity and age (American Geriatrics Society 2006). Moreover, as Torres-Gil points out, the growing diversity in our older population is beginning to impact aging policy around such issues as social security and the delivery of health care and social services (2005). In turn, such issues are emerging in the increasingly multicultural nations of Europe (Jackson, Brown, Antonucci and Daatland 2005; see also www.priae. org/publications.htm).[3]

As seen in Figure IV.1, our nation's population of older adults will get dramatically more diverse over the next several decades, essentially producing a "browning" of the graying of America (Hayes-Bautista 2002; Wilmoth 2004). While in 2004, almost 20 percent of those older than age sixty-five were classified as ethnic minorities—African American, Native American, Asian/Pacific Island American and Hispanic American—by 2050 this group of elders is projected to represent almost four out of every ten older Americans (U.S. Census Bureau 2006c). Asian and Hispanic elders will be the fastest-growing sectors of this population, reshaping the social fabric of towns and small cities across the United States (AARP 2004; Frey 2008).

ETHNIC CULTURE AND AGING

It must be noted that only a tiny number of groups in our society have maintained sociocultural systems that are not only highly variant from American cultural norms, but also stress factors that foster high status for the aged (Johnson 1995). Among the most distinct are the Amish, Hasidic Jews and Native American groups such as the Navaho and Zuni, or relatively recent arrivals such as the Hmong from Vietnam (Goodkind 2006). The long-term positive maintenance of these groups' ethnic divergence has been possible so far as they have remained economically independent of outside groups.

The Amish stand as a strong contradiction to the rule (Crist, Armer and Radina 2002). Most other immigrant groups have not been able to maintain such a close integration of ideology, social organization and economic tradition. Accordingly, the expression of ethnicity varies tremendously from encompassing communities, which can satisfy most material and spiritual needs, to having a select repertoire of subjective identity markers (food, clothes, music), or merely perceiving a vague sense of belonging to a historically felt past.

CONTEXT AND THE REALITIES OF ETHNIC COMPENSATION

A major theme in researching the cultural diversity of America's aged has been the examination of ethnicity as a positive resource for the aged—a form of compensation for the problems associated with aging (Chappell 2006). In our own societal context, a positive dimension of ethnic attachments can promote a nondenigrating component of identity to balance out potentially difficult transitions in work and family life. In a more general sense, it has been suggested that ethnicity carries with it "special resources or ethnically-inflected strategies that may be mobilized to maximize personal well-being ... in the development of long-term "careers" for successful elders and in the management of the inevitable ... crises that individuals must confront toward the end of the life cycle" (Weibel-Orlando 1987:102).

In this section's first article, Jay Sokolovsky looks at the available data to try to assess the limits of ethnic beliefs and support as a compensator for aging in our urban postindustrial society. A central point of his argument is to debunk a false policy dichotomy pitting family caring against state support of the aged. He shows that even among Asian groups, known for their attention to filial devotion, certain immigration contexts can result in a very low-perceived quality of life by the elderly. Sokolovsky, in line with Henderson's discussion (Part IV Web book) of the ethnic family's approach to Alzheimer's disease, also finds that when dealing with difficult mental health problems, the traditional ethnic response can sometimes actually exacerbate the situation. Among the more important points made in this article are that: (1) the female perspective on family support of the aged can be dramatically different from that of males; (2) elderly with social networks linking them to both kin and the broader community have better mental health profiles than those encapsulated totally in the ethnic family; (3) formal supports can be effectively used to strengthen the ability of the family to care for its elderly members (see also Antonucci and Jackson 2003). He argues that these ideas should be used as policy touchstones to counter ongoing efforts to dismantle the system of nonfamilial supports built up over the last half century. Important confirmation of the ideas in this article comes from both recent research in North America (Antonucci and Cortina 2006) and Sweden (Dunér and Nordström 2007) and the longitudinal network studies directed by Clare Wenger in rural and urban England and elsewhere in Europe (1997).

REFUGEE STATUS, CULTURAL CONTEXT AND CULTURAL SPACES

Over the last two decades, with the ending of old colonial regimes and the collapse of the Soviet Union, numerous tragic civil wars have raged and still continue in parts of the world. At the beginning of the twenty-first century, the United Nations estimated that worldwide there were already almost 20 million refugees being forced from their home areas through wars and other disasters. The next two chapters in the section deal with two such refugee groups from very different regions of the world.

The chapter by Mary Hegland gives us a very dynamic picture of Iranians fleeing the Islamic revolution in their home country and ending up highly dispersed in the San Francisco Bay area. Having largely come from the educated and secular Muslim community affiliated with the former government of the Shah of Iran, they and especially their children were able to take advantage of the booming high-tech economy of the Silicon Valley. However, these Iranian-American elders suffer a double lamentation. They have lost access to their own country, as well as to the Persian cultural fabric of easy engagement within socially enmeshed neighborhoods, in which one could build a lasting connection to an intergenerational body of meaningful relationships.

Yet, as some ethnic Iranian elders experience loss—in widowhood, the death of lifelong friends, or being distanced from their central kin network—they may also turn to a broader civic engagement and new cultural scripts. Sometimes this transpires as a personal quest, such the example of Mr. Sahed, who after his wife's death took a spiritual turn and directed his energies toward helping others in homes, hospitals and nursing facilities. This issue of activating and inspiring civic engagement of ethnic elders is being recognized as a vital, untapped community resource. It is also the focus of a national project, Project SHINE at Temple University, linking college students and older immigrants in eighteen cities, in a common effort to promote service to their surrounding community (www.projectshine.org; see also McGarvey, Petsod and Wang 2006).

In the chapter by Martinez on Cuban expatriates in Miami, we see quite a different local context for elders. Unlike the highly dispersed Iranians studied by Hegland, her sample is physically centered in a distinct ethnic community. However, the context of migration and the great reduction of immediate family have created a strong degree of social isolation and aging "*out* of place." For many, this state of aging in exile has produced a social space fraught with anxiety and, for some, even the latent manifestations of post-traumatic stress syndrome. As with the Iranians in California, these elders have sought refuge in senior centers, but also in parks where the social drama of domino play is a bittersweet connection to their Caribbean cultural roots.[4]

An important point of this chapter is the difficulty family support systems have, without external assistance, in dealing with mental health problems. The work of Neil Henderson in this section's Web book provides a unique study of a support group for Hispanic Americans (including Cubans) established in Tampa, Florida. It illustrates the impact of formal institutions, such as gerontology centers, in providing an organizational and educational role in strengthening the "natural" support systems that provide community-based care for the elderly. Yet, the effective interaction of formal institutions and ethnic families is not a matter of simply providing information and help. Henderson clearly demonstrates how an understanding of the cultural context can overcome ethnic-based problems stemming from overreliance on females as caregivers, generational differences and low "service user" patterns in the Hispanic community.

Also in this section's Web book, we see another connection to refugees from the South East Asian states of Vietnam, Laos and Cambodia. Here, social psychologist Barbara Yee uses a life span-development approach to broadly look at the dilemmas faced by the elderly in these ethnic communities, including a cultural system dramatically different from that found in their homelands. In the cases she presents, we clearly see how cultural variation can combine with personal and situational contexts, leading to dramatic success or tragic disaster. This is a valuable contribution to a growing body of recent work on Southeast Asian migrants to North America (Becker and Beyene 1999; Detzner 2004; Sung 2007; Lai and Surood 2008).

GRANDFAMILIES AND ETHNICITY

Over the past decade, a new vocabulary has emerged in social science and legislative documents talking about "grandfamilies," "skipped generation families" and the general system of "kincare" (Green 2003; Family Strengthening Policy Center 2007). In the United States, such terms are connected to the reality that over the last decade of the twentieth century the pattern of custodial care of grandchildren by elders saw a 30 percent increase (Simmons and Dye 2003) and by 2005, 4.5 million children (one in twelve) lived in grandparent-headed households (U.S. Census Bureau 2006c). At some point in their lives, more than one in ten American grandparents will have primary responsibility for raising a grandchild, typically for two or more years.[5]

Table IV.1
Percent of Grandparents Residing with Grandchildren and Percent of Those
Persons Having Custodial Care of Grandchildren, 2000

Ethnicity	% Residential Grandparents in U.S. over the Age of 30	% Custodial Grandparents of All Residential Grandparents
White	2.5	41.6
Black	8.2	51.7
Asian	6.4	20.0
Hispanic or Latino (any race)	8.4	34.7
Native American	8.0	56.7

Source: Simmons and Dye 2003.

From a broader perspective, the issue of ethnicity set in the context of rising economic disparity, increased frequency of divorce, AIDS, drug-related deaths and the dispersing of kin networks challenge our notions of how to care across generational lines (Silverstein, Giarrusso and Bengtson 2003; Carlini-Marlatt 2005; Winston 2006).[6] Increasingly, the forces of globalization are exacerbating these social fault lines on a worldwide basis (see United Nations 2005; Fry Part III this volume). Across southern Africa and parts of Southeast Asia where AIDS has become endemic, grandparents have become the mainstay of family survival, often with substantial threats to their own well-being (see Guerny 2002; Ssengonzi 2007; Knodel 2008; Bock and Johnson forthcoming).

We have already noted in Weibel-Orlando's study of Sioux Native American elders (Part II Web book) how the reemergence of their ancestral identity in old age served as a bridge to a key custodial child-care role. As seen in Table IV.1, of the United States households with both grandchildren and grandparents, large proportions in those settings have custodial responsibilities. This is especially the case within Native American and African American communities. Importantly, unexpected re-parenting in late life is one of those pivotal issues crosscutting landscapes of ethnicity, class and national boundaries. In the United States, this had spurred the formation of over 800 support groups by 1998 (AARP 2003) and in 2007 an International Alliance for Children Raised by Grandparents was created (www.grandparentsforchildren.org).

Beyond all this data lies the variable impact of ethnic and broader cultural factors on both grandparents and their grandchildren (Hayslip and Hicks-Patrick 2006). Drawing on his own psychological research and studies from a wide set of disciplines, Bert Hayslip's chapter explores the exploding literature on custodial grandparenting in varied settings. Among the factors he examines for viewing the impact of culture are: how families construct role expectations for elders, opportunities for informal and formal support and ethnic barriers to social service use.

THE CLASS CONTEXT OF MINORITY STATUS AND ETHNICITY

In the United States and other post-Industrial societies, the cultural dimension of ethnicity must also be understood within the framework of a class system that has created minority groups (Aguirre and Turner 2006). These are parts of populations that are singled out for different and inferior treatment based on characteristics such as their ethnic heritage, sex, nationality or language (Hayes-Bautista et al. 2002). While United States minority populations discussed in this book—African Americans, Hispanics, Native Americans and Southeast Asian refugees—have a considerably smaller proportion of elderly than Euro-American groups, their income, education, access to quality housing, safe communities and health care are far below that of the majority of older Americans (Kaneda and Adams 2008). These inequalities represent a "cumulative disadvantage" predicting that disparities in health and quality of life accrue over a lifetime and amplify differences in late life (Anderson, Bulatao and Cohen 2004; Bulatao and Anderson 2004; Shuey and Wilson 2008).

The most comprehensive multinational study of cumulative disadvantage took place in ten European nations. It concludes that while some nations, such as Switzerland, show a relatively low level of accumulated disadvantage in late life, overall there is a continuing negative impact of socioeconomic inequality in comparing older to middle-age samples of people (von Dem Knesebeck et al. 2007). Certainly, in the United States, as noted in Figure IV.2, we see the long-term consequences of unequal access to education, jobs and promotions mandated by the U.S. apartheid system, which effectively operated up to the 1970s. While the poverty rate for white elderly is now less than 10 percent, it is more than twice that level for African American and Hispanic older adults, by far the most numerically significant ethnic aged population (Social Security Administration 2005). The substantial decline in rates of poverty for older African Americans over the past two decades has not decreased the economic disparity between older whites and blacks and *in fact this gap has actually increased in recent years* (see Figure IV.2).

ETHNIC ELDERS AS COMMUNITY ASSETS

One historical response of African American peoples has been to establish community-based mechanisms of support that can buffer the shock of long-term discrimination on the individual (Coke and Twaite 1995). In this section, we have two chapters looking at that process in the urban areas of Chicago and Seattle. The chapter by Micki Iris takes us into the Evergreen neighborhood, one of the areas that became part of the larger "Aging in Chicago Project." Her work focuses on the way social and cultural spaces generated through an African American version of middle-class values and hard work become a bedrock and literal pillar of a community space that is both physically and economically challenged. Both within family networks and community-wide "block clubs" and church organizations, older long-term residents provided the

Figure IV.2
Median Household Net Worth, by Race of Head of Household Age 65 and Over in 2005 Dollars, Selected Years 1984–2005

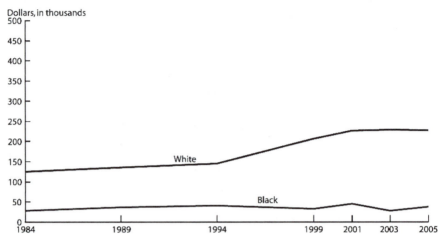

From: *Older Americans Update 2008: Key Indicators of Well-Being*
www.agingstats.gov/agingstatsdotnet/Main_Site/Default.aspx

core of stability for not only younger kin, but also for the broader neighborhood.

In another urban setting, Jane Peterson (Part IV Web book) employs her dual background as professional nurse and medical anthropologist to explore the participation of older women in two key institutions in an African American community in Seattle. Despite the ever-present specter of multiple jeopardy— being black, aged and female—a family-based role combined with the more public arena of the Pentecostal Church provide a valued context in which successful aging can take place.

Through the case of Mrs. Lottie Waters, we see that mature women in their grandparenting capacity fulfill a classic "kin-keeping role": nurturing and disciplining children; being the repository of family history; and serving as key decision makers and conveners of family ritual. Such women add to the typical characteristics of wise women a devotion to spiritual needs and some, in the role of "nurses," apply a holistic system of healing based on herbs and faith. Peterson's ethnographic work corresponds nicely with other research showing a powerful relationship in African American churches between religious participation and positive perceptions of well-being (Black 1999; Ruiz 2004; King et al. 2005).[7] The last two chapters of this section provide an important connection to classic studies such as Stack and Burton's exploration of "kinscripts" (1993), books like *All Our Kin* (Stack 1974) and more recent works like *A Different Shade of Gray* (Newman 2003), which document the dynamic contribution of African American elders to kin and community.

NOTES

1. An edited collection of Myerhoff's talks and final writings are found in Kaminsky and Weiss (2007). There is also a new Web site (http://jwa.org/exhibits/wov/myerhoff) devoted to the life and work of Barbara Myerhoff, featuring documentation of her achievements, along with audio and video clips and a comprehensive bibliography.

2. The word *shtetl* is Yiddish, meaning "little town." *Shtetls* were small market towns largely in Russia and Poland.

3. This surge in interest stems not only from the late twentieth century ethnic revival among groups long settled into North America, but by a new immigrant wave sparked initially by the 1965 immigration act that ended over forty years of restricted and ethnically skewed migration. This new stream of migration has brought more than 16 million immigrants to our shores in the last thirty decades; and during the last decade of the twentieth century, over 9 million immigrants entered the country, even more than the 8,795,000 who arrived between 1901 and 1910 (Wilmoth 2004).

4. See Treas and Mazumdar (2002) for a good discussion of the general dilemma of integration versus isolation in ethnic families.

5. For those children raised by any relative other than their parents, 75 percent are cared for by grandparents (Ruiz 2002). This trend has been affected by a rise in female substance abuse and incarcerations in America and just over half of children whose mothers are in prison are under the care of a grandmother.

6. Much of this work stands on the shoulders of pioneering work by sociologist Linda Burton (1992).

7. Important recent qualitative works on health care within African American communities include Ball et al. (2005) and Harley (2006).

CHAPTER 20

Ethnic Elders and the Limits of Family Support in a Globalizing World

Jay Sokolovsky

On February 22, 2005, a British television news program ran a story titled "Asian Elderly in Crisis—Care Lacking for Asian Elderly."[1] The story reflected a deep concern stemming from a three-year study in England showing the intersection of rapid changes in ethnic Asian family structure with a presumption by local authorities who believe that such families can readily handle the needs of their older members. As we shall see, this situation is *not* unique and is reflected in recent studies in Canada, the United States and Asian cities themselves (see especially Mackinnon, Gien and Durst 2001; Ip, Lui and Chui 2007). The news report came on the heels of initiating the Minority Elderly Care Project (MEC), Europe's largest study to date focusing on older adults from ethnic minority communities in ten European Union (EU) nations (www.priae.org/projects/mec.htm).[2] This new focus of concern in Europe matches what is also happening in North American with the recasting of diversity in cities and towns alike (Warnes, Friedrich, Kelleher and Torres 2004).

Whether in St. Petersburg, Florida, San Jose, California, or Minneapolis, Minnesota, it is hard to ignore the dramatic rise of immigrant ethnic families drawn increasingly to North America from non-Western cultures around the globe. For example, over the past two decades, in the Tampa Bay area of Florida, groups of Somalis, South-East Asians and about 15,000 indigenous people from Hidalgo, Mexico, have moved into the area. While the demographic picture of these and other such emerging ethnic communities is still quite young, it is important to understand the capacity of their family systems to support their older population. This chapter will address such issues by looking at the place of older adults in ethnic communities the United States and other postindustrial nations.

ETHNICITY AND AGING

The broadest-based view of the link between ethnicity and aging centers on the premise that varying ethnic lifestyles will alter the way old age is encountered, perceived and acted out. Describing precisely how much ethnic subcultures alter the conditions of aging is to say the very least, controversial. I will address this point by asking the basic question: Do ethnic distinctions make real differences in the experience of aging? More specifically, I will concentrate on the extent to which an idealized view of ethnic subcultures has led to a policy error that places too much emphasis on the ethnic family and informal supports as the savior of the ethnic elderly. Much is at stake as the United States Government in the first decade of the twenty-first century has strived to "remake America" by dismantling public sector support systems and most recently substituting "privatization" and "faith-based initiatives" as panaceas for our nation's ills (see Fry; Polivka this volume). This is often justified by the misguided premise that government programs reduce the incentives for families to care for their aged along with their other responsibilities (Cheung and Yuihuen 2006).

CULTURE, ETHNICITY AND AGING

To a cultural anthropologist such as myself, seeking the answers to these questions requires examining the general relationship between cultural variation and aging. The consideration of ethnicity as a factor affecting old age brings the question of sociocultural variation back home to our own doorstep. Ethnicity is commonly understood as social differentiation derived from cultural criteria such as a shared history, a common place of origin, language, dress, food preferences and values that engender a sense of exclusiveness and self-awareness of membership in a distinct social group. Viewing the variations of aging in our country within the context of ethnicity seems mandated by the continuing cultural pluralism of our nation. While at the beginning of the 1990s only about 5 percent of the elderly were foreign born, by 2006 that figure had doubled, and more than a majority of these persons now claim heritage from either Latin America or Asia (U.S. Census Bureau 2006).

CULTURE VERSUS CONTEXT

When dealing in general with ethnic segments of the United States, we almost never confront "culture in the raw," unburnished from Old World or other indigenous origins. Especially in cities, one can easily encounter such designations as "Moscow on the boardwalk" of Brighton Beach, Brooklyn, "Little Havana" in Miami or the "China towns" and "Little Asias" clinging to numerous downtown districts. However, there are precious few ethnic groups whose traditional lifestyles and values have not been altered by the reality of special immigration histories and the continuing social, economic and political constraints imposed by American class stratification and ideology. However, one cannot presume, as a given, the impact of transnational migration on growing old in a new societal setting. For example, a recent cross-national study of the black diaspora in the United States and England shows that especially for the Caribbean migrant, the place of migration and how you got there provided advantages to Afro-Caribbeans in the United States compared with counterparts in England (Nazroo, James, Karlsen and Torres 2007). While migration is often assumed to be a negative and disorienting experience, Sandra Torres points out that such changed circumstances can become the touchstone to "successful aging" (2006b).

In examining transplanted Asiatic ethnic groups, each with a strong "ideal" emphasis on filial devotion, one can see the impact of context on culture. For Chinese American elderly, migration to the United States in the early twentieth century was largely a movement of young, single males who planned to return to China. Despite living in well-defined ethnic communities, studies of these males in old age have found them to have the smallest family networks of any Asian-American group and relatively few express high satisfaction with life (Yu 1992). Although, Yu's 1992 research showed considerable "ideal" expressions of filial support by Chinese American young adults in a Midwestern university town, actual support lagged well behind good intentions. While in the last two decades new immigration patterns have evened out the gender ratio of elder Chinese Americans, continuing insecurity focuses on linguistic isolation, coupled with social distancing through what Lan refers to as "subcontracted filial piety," with sons engaging caregivers from similar ethnic backgrounds to care for their frail older kin (2002). Just recording the young as saying "we have strong family and filial devotion" does not really help one understand how such ideas translate into the lives of ethnic families. In a more recent study of Chinese immigrants to Canadian cities, it was found that while the younger generation did their best to live up to the principles of filial devotion, their elder relatives, due to their lack of resources, could not adequately fulfill their end of the cultural bargain by materially supporting success of their children (Mackinnon, Gien and Durst 2001). In this context, to prevent others perceiving them as being a burden, they avoided making demands on their children for even the simplest things such as rides to the doctor or help with buying medicine. Paralleling the findings of Zhang (this volume) for China's own cities, the authors found "Many elderly Chinese immigrants, rather than face escalating cultural conflicts and intergenerational difficulties, are showing a growing preference for independent living" (p. 11). Studying this emerging problem among Chinese immigrant families in urban Australia, Ip, Lui and Chui (2007) refer to the situation there as a "veiled entrapment." Here, while the younger Chinese adult migrants have been clear economic beneficiaries of globalization, the older parents of these new capitalists "have been trapped in dependent and isolated social situations by their lack of appropriate cultural and social capital for life in the new societal setting, and have little control of their everyday lives" (p. 734). In contrast, older Japanese

Americans, while they came to this country a few decades after the Chinese, immigrated primarily in family groups and expected to become U.S. citizens. These elders are not only more likely to be more deeply imbedded in kinship networks than the Chinese, but also exhibit higher levels of social and psychological success (Kanamoto 2006). While a majority (54 percent) of Japanese American elders in a San Diego study (Cuellar and Weeks 1980) said they were very satisfied with their lives, only 18 percent of older Chinese claimed this level of contentment. We will see later on, however, that being surrounded by relatives in an ethnic enclave does not ensure passage to a geriatric nirvana. This can also be seen by carefully reading Barbara Yee's poignant discussion of South-East Asian refugee elders (this volume Web book).

MULTIPLE JEOPARDY OR ETHNIC COMPENSATION

Understanding the context of ethnic aging also requires considering the minority aged, those who have been singled out for differential and inferior treatment (Wykle and Ford 1999). In this particular clash of culture and context, there has emerged in the ethnicity and aging literature two key themes that on the surface seem contradictory. One theme stresses how minority group membership creates "multiple jeopardies" and "cumulative disadvantage" in the context of structured inequality, and thereby intensifies the problems of growing old (Carson this volume). From this first perspective, Ron Manuel notes that "the distinction of the minority aged is not so much a function of the novel conditions of their aging as it is the dire circumstances of their existence" (1982:XV). Numerous studies have repeatedly demonstrated that in terms of income, housing quality, education and rates of chronic illness, the minority aged encounter harsher conditions than the majority of older Americans. Not only are these problems more severe, but the "aging network" set up to provide services according to uniform bureaucratic standards often creates barriers preventing the minority ethnic aged from obtaining resources to which they are entitled (Burton and Whitfield 2006).

The other theme underscores the benefits or resources accruing to those elderly who remain attached to an ethnic identity and subculture (Shenk and Sokolovsky 2001; Moriarty and Butt 2004). This second perspective, which I will refer to as "ethnic compensation," often creeps into the discussion of minority aging in an ambivalent fashion. Manuel, after making the statement quoted previously, goes on to state, "while relatively more disadvantaged because of the minority experience, the aged have often adopted distinguishable strategies for successfully coping with their problems" (1982:XV). This sentiment corresponds to the prevailing anthropological writings on aging and ethnicity, which largely echo Linda Cool's statement that, "rather than providing yet one more obstacle to be overcome in the aging process, ethnicity can furnish the elderly with a source of identity and prestige which they can manipulate to make a place for themselves in society" (1981:185).

The two themes do not logically exclude each other and in impoverished urban and rural communities, dense and locally situated ethnic networks may still provide the real balance of survival (Iris this volume). Yet, putting an undue emphasis on one or the other construct shifts policy implications toward dramatically opposed viewpoints. Ethnicity as deprivation calls for social and economic justice and strengthening federal/state resources to overcome lifelong deficits. Ethnicity as compensation or resource could be construed as a rationale to decrease, or at least to not shift, material resources toward the ethnic minority aged.

However, a major point I hope to make here is that much of the literature on ethnicity as a resource has been overly optimistic, especially in the area of informal social supports and family networks of exchange (Johnson 1995). I concentrate on the theme of ethnic compensation not because I think it is more important, but because it has been relatively ignored. By stressing this approach, one can also ask significant questions about the nonminority ethnic elderly. Moreover, it is often in this area of aging research that the ways of testing whether the "differences make a difference" have not been up to the questions asked. All too often, ethnic distinctions are measured by mass survey questionnaires, appropriate perhaps for numerically measuring variations in health complaints, the frequency of contact with friends, or the proximity of children to an elderly parent's house. However, such measures tell us little about how ethnic differences influence the way illnesses are dealt with, how they affect the perception of old age, if they lead to premature institutionalization, or how the action of social networks actually contributes to or diminishes the successful functioning of the elderly in the family and the community.

THE ETHNIC COLORS OF "WHITE"

This is especially the case in classic studies of the aged of European background, where statistical documentation can potentially mask subtle ethnic differences (Hayes, Kalish and Guttmann 1986). The work by Cohler, Lieberman and Welch (1977) is quite instructive in its study of Irish, Italian and Polish Americans in Chicago. Despite statistical similarity in levels of social contact, the authors showed how subtle differences in value orientations between the Italian and Polish communities related to the nature of support systems affecting the elderly.

In this study, the Poles were found to perceive a greater sense of isolation, and they were more likely to feel no one was available to them for aid in problematic situations. This greater degree of perceived social isolation was related to traditional Polish concerns for privacy, self-containment and formality in social relations. The authors suggest that what appears to be greater social isolation among the Polish American respondents may be a reflection of their preference for formal rather than informal relationships and a tendency to look to the community rather than to the family for support. They argue that there is a tendency here to undervalue informal relations of the family as a source of support in deference to resources through formal ties to the community.

The Italians, on the other hand, emphasized a traditional value of "family centeredness," used chain migration to link up with fellow townspeople in the same urban neighborhood and put an inordinate stress on family relationships. In contrast to Polish respondents, the Italian aged were more willing to seek out family and close friends in crisis situations. Italian women were noted as gaining higher status with age, as they were much in demand to mediate problems in the family network. As we shall see, however, there are costs attached to this "mediating Madonna" role (see also Weibel-Orlando this volume).

While ethnic differences are apparent, the ultimate question remains: Do the differences make a significant difference? In fact, Cohler, Lieberman and Welch suggest that for the groups just mentioned, ethnic saliency for explaining variant patterns of behavior decreases in old age, with middle-aged cohorts more distinct than aged ones (1977). Nonetheless, this does not mean that general cultural differences among the nonaged ethnics will not have an impact on the elderly. This can be especially important in socially patterned decisions about caring for one's aged parent. An indication of this is provided by a Baltimore study comparing Italians and Poles on attitudes toward institutionalization of the elderly (Fandeti and Gelfand 1976). As one might predict from the previous discussion, the authors note that "Italian respondents expressed a significantly stronger preference for using family arrangements than their Polish counterparts." Here is an ethnic difference that not only directly affects differential treatment of the aged, but also argues for awareness of such differences at some level of policy making.

CROSS-ETHNIC COMPARISON: DATA AND ITS DILEMMAS

The general problem of understanding the implications of statistical survey variables often occurs in the discussion of informal social interaction and exchange in family and neighborhood contexts (Sokolovsky 2006). Numerous studies now exist purporting to compare subculturally variant family caregiving and its associated "network" behavior (Pinquart and Sorenson 2005). With the predominant use of so-called sociometric techniques for gathering data, one is hard-pressed to know if statistically significant differences (or lack of variation) mean anything. A case in point is the well-known "Social and Cultural Contexts of Aging" study conducted in Los Angeles (Bengtson and Morgan 1987). Here whites were compared with blacks and Mexican Americans in terms of social interaction with children, grandchildren, other relatives, and friends. Mexican Americans were considerably more likely than white elderly to see children and grandchildren on a weekly basis, although no difference was found for contact with other relatives. The Mexican Americans were much less likely to see friends and neighbors frequently. Older blacks and whites were shown to have almost identical frequency of contact with grandchildren or other relatives, although smaller percentages of blacks reported seeing children and neighborhood friends frequently.

What use can be made of these facts with regard to the function of the aged in familial and community networks? Just because approximately 40 percent of both whites and blacks in Los Angeles see "grandchildren" and "other relatives" weekly does not mean the aged in each ethnic group fit into kinship networks and use such resources in the same way (Jett 2002; Dilworth-Anderson et al. 2005).

Various other studies, such as the classic research by Nellie Tate (1983), have given us clues to some of the significant differences. One of these distinctions is a greater flexibility in kinship boundaries among African American families, which results in the absorption of young grandchildren and "other relatives" into households headed by the elderly (see also Peterson this volume Web book). This is particularly pronounced for older black women, who are four times more likely than older white females to live with young dependent relatives under eighteen years of age. In her study of Philadelphia's black elderly, Tate has suggested how this difference makes a difference: "It appears that absorbed non-independent younger blacks are more likely to accept their aged who become functionally impaired as a result of chronic conditions" (1983:99). This is dramatically seen in the case of families caring for elders suffering from dementia. My own ongoing research on this issue in Tampa, Florida,[3] corroborates what other studies have implied, that the structure of African American families significantly reduces the perceived consequences of Alzheimer's disease on the kin caregiving unit, even though the actual disease stressors or patient functional capacity are likely worse than in Euro-American background families (Dilworth-Anderson, Gibson and Burke 2006).

An interesting parallel to this kind of analysis in North America was found in a multiethnic study of elder support in England (Moriarty and Butt 2004). The researcher's initial survey research found that not only did Asian immigrant elders have the largest density of family and co-ethnics in their local environment, but they described a regular pattern of practical help in exchange for child care. In contrast, European-heritage aged initially reported they only asked for help in a crisis. However, observing the actual functioning of elders in the community produced a different picture. The Anglo elders provided a great deal of voluntary help to kin and neighbors, while in the case of the Asian elders, "the presence of other household members or relatives nearby was no guarantee that Asian carers would receive additional help from their families" (p. 742). In other words, the Asian sample had the highest expectation, but the narrowest range of anticipated helpers to ask for practical support. The authors note that from the perspective of service providers, the "on the ground" situation for these seniors could be a barrier to support if help from the expected source did not materialize. The same study noted that Black Caribbeans had a more flexible construct of their ideal support system and incorporated non-kin friends and church members into a mutual long-term network of emotional and practical support.

Other studies have documented substantial ethnic-based variation in familial and nonfamilial support systems. One of the most comprehensive is the research of John Weeks and Jose Cuellar in San Diego comparing the elderly in nine ethnic groups to an "Anglo," nonminority sample. Variance from

"Anglo-White" norms was most prominent among "filiocentric" Asian and Pacific Island groups: Korean, Chinese, Japanese, Filipino, Samoan and Guamanian. To cite the most dramatic case, 91 percent of elderly Korean parents were found to be living with their children and over 80 percent said they would first turn to family members to satisfy all eight categories of need. By comparison, only 10 percent of the white aged surveyed were dwelling with their children and fewer than one in ten expected their family network to deal with all of their basic needs (Weeks and Cuellar 1981:391; Weeks 1984:101). Furthermore, important and substantial differences were noted in comparing the Asian groups among themselves. I could proceed with other examples showing the impact of the ethnic family on the life of the elderly, but I have already painted myself into a corner if my intent was to argue against policy makers putting too much stress on ethnic support systems and the family.

THE LIMITS OF ETHNIC COMPENSATION

From where does my pessimism spring? As I interpret studies now available, the evidence indicates that the capacity of the ethnic family in dealing with the most difficult problems of its elderly members is limited. In the context of massive globalization and the rapid shift to a postindustrial economy, rural ethnic ideals are rapidly giving way to urban realities. Even by the early 1980s, a majority of black elderly and 84 percent of Hispanic American elderly resided in urban areas. A case in point is the Hispanic American aged. Many writers have described the ideal value structure of this group as involving: (1) profound family loyalty, (2) dominance of males, and (3) subordination of younger to older persons (Cuellar, Bastida and Braccio 2004). Certain early survey studies did appear to confirm some elements of this ideal. Marjorie Cantor's tri-ethnic elderly study (whites, Hispanics and blacks) in New York showed that Hispanic elderly received the highest levels of assistance in terms of tasks of everyday living and the receiving of gifts (1979). Similarly, Vern Bengtson's Los Angeles study (mentioned earlier) showed considerably greater levels of family interactions for Mexican Americans than among whites and blacks (Bengtson and Morgan 1987).

However, other authors such as Gratton argue that much of the literature on the Chicano elderly is of limited utility due to a tendency to romanticize, distort and stereotype critical elements of the Hispanic life experience (1987). Various studies, especially in the Southern California area, describe situations where, despite the continuing ideal of intense intergenerational family concern and the actual availability of a large kin network in the respective urban environment, obligations and expectations of kin support were radically declining (Hurtado, Hayes-Bautista, Valdez and Hernandez 1992). In San Diego, even though Hispanics who lived alone had four times more extended kin in the local area than whites, they were found to be less likely to turn to family members in times of need (Weeks and Cuellar 1981:392). They preferred to "suffer in silence." The consequences of this, documented in a number of subsequent studies, can be high levels of alienation, low life satisfaction and other psychological problems (Losada et al. 2006).[4] Part of the difficulty stems from unmet expectations of family interaction. In San Antonio, Texas, results from the largest longitudinal study of Mexican Americans has shown that those aged with greatest need for a caregiver are the most likely to report that one is not available. Number of children was not associated with reported caregiver availability among barrio Mexican Americans; many identify family other than spouse or children, or nonfamily, as perceived caregivers (see Markides, Rudkin, Angel and Espino 1997; Angel and Angel 1998; Angel and Whitfield 2007).[5] Even in the previously mentioned studies in Los Angeles and New York, which showed high levels of family interaction and support for elderly Hispanic Americans, these aged were more likely to display symptoms of mental stress than either whites or blacks (see also Cuellar, Bastida and Braccio 2004). In both locales, as well as noted by Martinez for Cuban aged in Miami (this volume), the main sources of concern were children and family. Some have even argued that the intense Hispanic pattern of female adult children giving care through extremes of self-sacrifice increases in a negative way the dependence and disability of elder kin, especially women (Gonzalez, Haan and Hinton 2001; Losada et al. 2006).

This should be particularly disturbing to policy-makers, as some studies have shown Hispanic Americans families to use community-based services at a very low rate, even compared to other ethnic groups surveyed (Mui and Burnette 1994; Torres 1999a).

THE GENDER DIMENSION OF ETHNIC KIN SUPPORT

An interesting facet of research on Hispanic elderly is that the negative consequences of needs unmet through the kinship network more likely touch the lives of women than of men (Facio 1996). A study in San Antonio by Markides and Vernon (1984) corroborates this by showing that of those elder Mexican Americans who maintained a very ethnically traditional sex-role identity, only among women were there significant signs of psychological distress. They were found to have higher levels of depression than those older women who were more flexible in their gender role and were less traditionally ethnic.

This work, and another that I will now discuss, suggest the unsettling proposition that "although it has been assumed that social relations are inherently satisfying and reduce the impact of life stress it appears that, at least in some instances, such social ties may enhance rather than reduce feelings of distress" (Cohler and Lieberman 1980:462; see also Antonucci, Akiyama and Lansford 1998). Bert Cohler and Morton Lieberman base this statement on their previously mentioned study of Irish, Polish and Italian families in Chicago. These findings parallel those for the Hispanic elderly, but are even more dramatic with regard to gender, ethnicity and psychological stress. They state that among women "living in communities characterized by particularly dense social networks and complex patterns of reciprocity and obligations with adult offspring and other close relatives, there is a significant negative relationship between extent of social contact and both self-reported life satisfaction and psychological impairment (Cohler 1983:118). This relationship among a kin-keeping role, ethnic embeddedness and personal maladjustment is strongest for Italian and Polish American elderly, but did not hold in the Irish American case. Interestingly enough, for older men of Italian and Polish descent, the effect of ethnic embeddedness is opposite to that found for the women—they seem to benefit greatly in terms of adjustment to old age. In the case of the Italian American aged, where this bipolar gender effect is most notable, one sees structural, gender-based differences in the nature of the social networks by which persons are linked to the local environment. Compared to females, older adult males, even after retirement, are active in a more diverse array of community-wide social contexts outside of the family unit (see also Weibel-Orlando this volume). In this case, men's social clubs have been a long-existing traditional arena where older Italian males can gain public status, recognition, and support. This opportunity to enter old age with vital connections both to lifelong friends in ethnic neighborhood associations and to relatives is seldom obtained by women. Most of the elderly women in this Chicago study appear very much encapsulated within the sphere of kin. As one might predict, it was found that older women who exhibited the lowest levels of psychological stress were those actively involved with friends as well as family (Cohler and Lieberman 1980:454). That is, they had networks more like men in maintaining important social relations both inside and outside the realm of domestic/kin ties.

At a time when younger married women are entering the labor force, the traditional "kin-keeping" role of older women is often nervously mocked by the refrain "How is it that one girl can bring up ten kids, but ten grown-up kids cannot care for one little old lady?" Analytically, I think the evidence is quite convincing that in terms of material and emotional exchange, women are most often left holding the short end of the stick—giving considerably more through informal kin support networks than they ever receive. The implications for policy-makers are clear. Emphasizing certain ethnic family support networks as a primary service mechanism would be of likely benefit to aged males, but may be a disaster for females, who make up the majority of older ethnic citizens.

This observation is reinforced by studies of one the most family dependent of America's ethnic aged, Asian and Pacific Americans. Recall the previously mentioned Korean aged in San Diego, where nine in ten lived with children and almost that number expected to depend on their families to provide for all of their needs. Yet one is surprised to read in John Weeks's analysis of his qualitative data that "among all the groups interviewed, the Korean elders were least satisfied with their lives" (Weeks 1984:190). Being poor, primarily female, lacking strong English language skills and having been followers of their earlier migrating children, they were isolated and lonely within a small, exclusive, family life arena. Sadly, the vast majority found life hard, and one-quarter reported having contemplated suicide. In the transplanted context, generational relations ideally predicated on *hyo*, a Confucian word that means taking care of one's parents and ancestors, has become more a source of tension than a moral precept for successful aging. Studies in other urban areas have continued to corroborate the difficulty older Korean immigrants, especially women, are having, especially in terms of depression (Pang 2000; Mui 2002; Han, Kim, Lee, Pistulka and Kim 2007). Aging "out of place" as a late-life migrant has also been found to have negative consequences in other settings as noted in Jackson and Antonucci's recent work with late-life black Caribbean immigrants (2005).

CONCLUSIONS

My inspiration for writing this chapter developed from a dramatic reaction to a coauthored paper I presented in 1978 at one of the first national conventions on ethnicity and aging. As the last speaker of the conference, I was supposed to present a survey of cultural variation and growing old in the United States. Toward the end of the presentation, I told the audience that after reviewing the available data, I felt it would be a grave mistake for voluntary agencies to put too much pressure on ethnic families to take care of all of the needs of the elderly. Upon hearing this, the conference organizer, who also directed one of the types of agencies I was referring to, began to gag and actually stopped my presentation, claiming that time had run out. I knew I was on to something.

In this analysis, I am trying to be realistic about the capacity of ethnic family support systems to deal with problems of the aged (Strawbridge and Wallhagen 1992; Pinquart and Sorensen 2005). My negative attitude may seem unusual given my previously published work in the areas of gerontology and mental health (Sokolovsky and Cohen 1987; Cohen and Sokolovsky 1989). In these writings, I often sought to demonstrate the benefits derived by poor inner-city elderly and released mental patients from the social networks in which their lives were enmeshed. Having recently completed the longitudinal and applied extensions of these studies, I am certainly more pessimistic than I was in the late 1970s, when some of my publications helped feed "informal support systems" euphoria.

By following, over time, the lives of poor elderly residing in urban hotels and in analyzing an experimental intervention program, my colleagues and I readily noted the limits of informal supports. In the case of black women residents whose social networks were comparatively interconnected and contained complex exchanges, these informal structures were adequate for handling many acute health and resource problems. But longer-term difficulties could not be handled well by these intense networks. Especially in the case of alcoholism, attempts by intertwined social network members to provide support could lead to such levels of conflict that these tightly bound social matrices often disintegrated. An experimental project in one hotel to test the efficacy of interventions using informal support found that only about 20 percent of the attempts to use social networks to solve problems (such as obtaining food or getting to a hospital) were successful (Cohen, Adler and Mintz 1983).

Admittedly, SRO environments are characterized by low levels of material resources, high personal alienation and a lack of a sense of ethnic community affiliation. One should expect greater levels of success when applying network intervention techniques in strong ethnic communities. Examples include the *servidor* (community service broker) system in Southern California (Valle and Mendoza 1978) and the *Promotores de Salud* (lay health educators) system used in Texas (see Box IV.1 this volume). In these programs, Hispanic American community members informally function as a catalyst for the utilization of services by Mexican American elders.

Most studies indicate that it is those services that John Colen (1979) calls nonmechanism specific—services that can be provided in diverse settings (such as counseling, information, and referral)—that are most appropriately handled through the social organization of the ethnic community (Colen 1982). Informal coping mechanisms, which are proportionally more evident in ethnic communities, can and should be creatively used as structures in which the fulfillment of human needs in late life are realizable. These forms of ethnic compensation can be quite effective when coupled with nonfamilial systems of support such as respite and day care programs and health promotion efforts (Henderson this section Web book). Such formal systems of care have been found to greatly enhance the capacity of families who seek to care personally for their elderly (Barresi and Stull 1993).

Perhaps the best example of this is On Lok Senior Health Services, a model of community-based long-term care developed during the 1970s in San Francisco to serve the poor, frail elderly, especially Chinese Americans. Drawing on the "Day Hospitals" developed in England, On Lok (Chinese for "peaceful, happy abode") created one of the nation's first adult day health centers and later expanded to develop a complete system of medical care, social support and housing for nursing-home-eligible elderly (Kornblatt, Eng and Hansen 2003). The On Lok model, although not initially designed to be focused on ethnic groups, uses multidisciplinary teams to assess how the culture and context of the elderly's circumstances can be used to actively integrate family resources with a broad range of formal services (Ikels 2007). This system has been quite successful in assisting ethnic families in their effort to keep even quite frail aged from spending their last years in an institutional setting. Many states are now using private foundation and federal funds in an attempt to replicate the On Lok model through a program called PACE, Program of All-inclusive Care for the Elderly (Mukamel et al. 2007).

The success of On Lok in San Francisco's Chinatown indicates that when generally dealing with such needs as long-term care, too much emphasis on the ethnic family would be a grave policy mistake. As was seen in the wake of the deinstitutionalization of mental health services, unrealistic or sentimental views of the strength of informal social resources can have the most unfortunate effects. More than two decades ago, gerontologists Marjorie Cantor and Virginia Little urged the development of a single system of social care incorporating informal and formal mechanisms of support for the elderly (1985).

Although national political policy is not presently headed in that direction, it would be well worth the effort to harken to their plea. However, the assumption that public benefits for the needy aged merely supplement or displace family help continues to be used by political interest groups whose primary concern is minimizing social welfare costs and cutting programs that constitute the basis for economic well-being and care for the aged (Polivka and Longino 2006). I urge gerontologists interested in the issue of ethnicity not to become unwitting contributors to this destructive trend.

NOTES

This chapter is adapted from *Bringing Culture Back Home: Aging, Ethnicity, and Family Support. The Cultural Context of Aging*, 2nd ed. J. Sokolovsky, ed. Westport, CT: Bergin & Garvey.

1. Information about the show can be found at http://www.channel4.com/news/2005/02/week_4/22_asian.html (accessed on January 23, 2008).

2. The research objectives of this project are to draw attention to the needs of minority ethnic (ME) elders and thereby improve the provision of services for them. It will take place in the United Kingdom, Finland, France, Netherlands, Spain, Germany, Hungary, Bosnia-Herzegovina, Croatia and Switzerland.

3. This research project "Social Support of Caregivers for Dementia Patients" was supported by a National Institute on Aging Senior Research Service Award, IF33G05654-01.

4. It should be noted that other studies such as by Shurgot and Knight (2004) have not found the same kind of relation between acculturation and mental distress.

5. See www.utmb.edu/pmch/hepese/default.htm for further information on The Hispanic EPESE (Established Populations for Epidemiologic Studies of the Elderly), which is the largest epidemiologic study of the health of Mexican American elderly.

CHAPTER 21

Losing, Using and Crafting Spaces for Aging: Muslim Iranian American Seniors in California's Santa Clara Valley

Mary Elaine Hegland and Associates[1]

When Babi's American husband, Ron, opened the door in response to my ring, I walked from the dark cold outside into the light and warmth of their home. Babi had called to say she was having a party and I should come. Saying hello to everyone on the way, I went to the back, a large area set up with chairs along three walls and cushions along part of the closer wall. Several of my favorite older Iranian friends stood up from their chairs to greet me, kissing me, Iranian style, on both cheeks.

As the evening wore on, I realized that the large back room, with its smooth floor, had been arranged specifically for ballroom dancing. Babi (seventy-two) and Ron (seventy-six) performed several ballroom dances for us, giving us the artistic benefit of their years of studying and teaching ballroom dancing. Later, a bevy of belly dancers jiggled in unison, dressed in skimpy sequined tops and gauzy skirts.[2] For his special birthday gift, a renowned dance teacher led Ron to the middle chair at the other side of the room to sit between all of the women. Then, with his wife Babi in front, the whole troop performed this Middle Eastern origin dance while he appreciatively (and perhaps with a bit of embarrassment) looked on. Not satisfied with mastering ballroom dancing, Babi has been taking belly dance lessons and then teaching it for some time. I marveled at her stamina and memory as they all went through the fast moving steps, turns and quiverings.

Later, many people went out on the floor to dance. Women carried out their Persian dancing routines, dancing as individuals but often dancing to another person, eying them flirtatiously, framing their head with their hands, moving their bodies seductively, turning and then looking back in the Persian dance mode. Even a couple of the older, more reticent women flattered me by acquiescing to my pleas and getting to their feet to join the movements.[3]

For dinner, women set up a table in the formal living room area, close to the kitchen wall, with rice, several favorite Iranian meat and vegetable or fruit

stews, salad and yogurt. Dessert included *sholeh zard*, a favorite saffron fla-
vored rice pudding. Young people and teens tended to put in an appearance
later on in the evening.[4]

(Notes on the birthday party for Ron at Babi and Ron's home, December 23,
2006)

An amazing example of a successful ager, in the United States, Babi Hogue
as been able to transcend the Iranian cultural script prescribing what kind of
behavior, comportment and venues are appropriate for an older Iranian widow.
In Iran, older widows are expected to be retiring, avoid male companionship
and remain single. Sometimes the American environment can offer opportunities for self-development not available in contemporary Iran.[5] In America, with
the loss of her husband, and thus her duties and responsibilities to him, Babi
was able to construct a new life and a new identity. Mrs. Hogue developed
new types of venues and activities for aging.

As a young adult living in Iran, Babi studied and worked as a midwife and
even traveled to Germany for more education. As many middle-class Iranian
parents did back then, in the 1970s, she began coming to the United States for
a month or two to visit her children attending university here. In 1985, at age
fifty-two, she moved to the San Francisco Bay Area with her husband and
worked here for several years. Upon retirement, and after the death of her first
husband, she began constructing a new life for herself. What Babi created was
rich with Iranian traditions, culture, lifestyle, close friendships and public and
private Iranian cultural events and gatherings. She has clearly also taken
advantage of her local American environment, with opportunities to mix with
the opposite sex, take and teach classes, develop hobbies and favored activities,
meet with Americans and enjoy less gender-restricted mobility.[6]

Babi had a good command of English and this facilitated easy interaction
with community members beyond her Iranian kin and friends. After Babi's first
husband died, her son encouraged her ballroom dancing. After years of being a
dutiful wife, Babi seemed to blossomed even more as she grew older. Babi and
Ron met at a ballroom dance class. The couple stay in close contact with Ron's
two daughters and Babi's two daughters and son who live in the area.[7]

Iranian elderly come here with received, frequently reiterated scripts for aging.
As their tasks have been accomplished, often they assume older age to be a period
of waiting. They typically believe elderly cannot learn and think it useless to
become involved in new endeavors, as they are basically finished with their life
tasks. Women especially may assume that their place is within the home and
family. Transcending scripts and learned notions about appropriate spaces for
themselves can be challenging for any age. Grasping new worldviews and ideas
about their place and proper behavior can be even more difficult for the elderly.

GAINING AND LOSING IN A NEW CULTURAL SPACE

Babi Jun (Babi Dear) provides an outstanding example of an Iranian American senior crafting happy and fulfilling arenas for herself in which to thrive.

Babi and Ron perform some ballroom dance moves at his birthday party, while Babi's daughter Mina operates the video camera.

Although Babi has been unusually successful in creating an active and reward-ing life, many other Iranian American seniors have been using, modifying, discovering and crafting spaces for aging in America, even in the face of all they have lost. For some of them, not as well prepared for American life, adjustment has proven difficult. They battle loneliness, depression, lack of peo-ple with whom to speak Persian and loss of a sense of community.

For their well-educated middle-aged and younger children, the Bay Area around San Francisco and the Santa Clara Valley south of San Francisco Bay provide professional and entrepreneurial opportunities. Many had come to the United States for an education and stayed on to work. Their Iranian American children enjoy access to advancement and the rewards of successful, well-paid careers in the computer industry, engineering, medicine and health, real estate, university work, law, technology, the sciences and other professions and busi-nesses in this area.

To take advantage of these opportunities, though, the younger generations must work long hours and build up networks, and thus do not have the time for leisurely socializing with family, as had been the case for the Iranian seniors when they lived in Iran. In order to become successful in the American environment, as they and their parents want them to be, they are forced into adopting American cultural patterns of less frequent interaction and forced to give up Iranian social patterns of extensive time and care for extended family and kin, even for elderly parents.[8]

Although Iranian seniors want to be close to their children and often had religious and/or political reasons to leave Iran, the San Francisco Bay Area does not provide a user-friendly environment for them. Due to English language deficits and the less-outgoing American attitudes toward neighbors, many cannot easily find ways to engage in culturally meaningful socializing, so crucial to their well-being. Iranians in this area do not live in tight enclaves, but are scattered over dispersed residential zones. Poor public transportation prevents those who cannot drive or pass an English driver's license test from readily getting around to see friends and relatives.

The majority of Iranian American elderly have found in America the secularized, Westernized, modernized and religiously free environment that they had lost in Iran with the Iranian Revolution of February 11, 1979, and the subsequent establishment of the Islamic Republic. However, they have lost their beloved country and their Persian cultural and linguistic milieu as a space for aging. Politically and economically, their lives have been disrupted. They suffer from loss of close neighborhood ties, lack of an age-integrated social life and hardest of all to bear, loss of frequent, intimate, enmeshed interaction with children and grandchildren.

While their emigration to America results in loss in many ways, their American setting also contains new opportunities for exploration, recreation, hobbies, education, outings, travel, self-development, non-Iranian associations and friends and different kinds of relationships and interaction styles. America presents the possibility of recreating identity, self and life, which would not be accessible in Iran. In this chapter, drawing upon examples from my Iranian American friends in the Santa Clara Valley, I discuss how Iranian senior citizens, in the face of dislocation and loss, craft new spaces and new scripts for aging in America. Their senior citizens' association, "The Iranian Parents' Club of Northern California," and an Iranian American senior citizen day activity and care center, the Grace center, provide age-segregated environments for Iranian elders to meet with their peers and develop new Iranian culture and Persian language communities with people who share their experiences and thus understand.[9]

SECULARIZED AND WESTERNIZED IRANIAN AMERICAN ELDERS: LOSING MODERN LIFE IN IRAN AND FINDING IT IN THE UNITED STATES

Part of the Modernized Iranian Upper Classes

The Iranian Americans who are now senior citizens came of age during the Pahlavi reign from the 1940s to the 1970s. Enabled by the oil economy, and inspired by the example of the Westernizing ruler of Turkey, Mustafa Kemal Ataturk, Reza Shah Pahlavi and his son Mohammad Reza Shah Pahlavi (the last Shah, who was overthrown by the Iranian Revolution of February 11, 1979) wanted to modernize Iran and make it into a European-like country. Although they failed to bring about democratic political modernization,[10] they developed infrastructure, a French-influenced educational system, modern armed forces, health and medical systems and an extensive bureaucracy.[11]

Mohammad Reza Shah's government made some moves to bring literacy, health care and agricultural assistance to rural areas.[12] However, urban upper classes benefited most dramatically from his modernization efforts. By the 1960s and especially the 1970s, the elite in the armed forces, police, educational system and engineers of various sorts had Western-style homes, clothing (perhaps straight from Paris), furniture, educations and social lives.[13] For the Iranian upper class, this often included a retinue of servants, big cars and foreign travel and education for their children. Educated men and often educated women interacted with work colleagues rather than restricting their social lives to relatives and neighbors. Even middle class people, especially in urban areas, began to take on a more modern lifestyle.

Most of the Iranian American elderly who now live in the United States had been members of these emerging professional, bureaucratic, government work, police and military, service and entrepreneurial upper and middle classes. They had already become Westernized, modernized and secularized to a degree. Realizing that now in this more modern society education had become crucial for their children, many sent their offspring abroad for an education, especially if they could not pass the extremely difficult university entrance exam to study in Iran. Some young people even came to the United States for high school, perhaps accompanied by one or both parents.

Leaving the New Islamic Republic of Iran for America

During the 1970s, young Iranians formed the largest population of foreign students in the United States. Many stayed on to work and build their lives here. One of the main reasons for the presence of Iranian elderly in the United States was the wish for family reunification: they moved here to be with their children. The other main reason for their departure from Iran was the revolution, which resulted in the end of the Shah's modernizing, if dictatorial, government and the institution of an Islamic government. When the Iranian Revolution of 1978–1979 took place and the population voted for an Islamic republic to replace the fallen monarchy, these Westernized, secularized people fled the country if they could. Those especially well situated in the Shah's government often escaped across the border or faced execution. The seniors we studied are retired teachers, professors, principals, bureaucrats, engineers, executives, military people and business people. Here in the United States they have regained access to a Westernized, modernized, relatively secular society.

Religious Freedom: Lost in Iran and Found in the United States

With a Western-style education in the system developed by the Pahlavis or gained abroad, a modernized work environment and an increasingly Western-like lifestyle, this emerging class of people no longer held primarily religious worldviews. For many of these people, religion was becoming compartmentalized and a matter of individual belief and practice.[14] The Pahlavi shahs discouraged many religious practices and cut back on the power of the clergy. These people appreciate religious freedom in the United States, which is not now available in their own home country. As rituals and practices central to Islam can be carried out individually, the U.S. environment does not fail as a venue for Islamic religious practices.[15] If they are strictly practicing Muslims, which the majority of Iranians in the United States are not, people can carry out the prescribed prayers five times a day in their homes, fast during the Arabic month of Ramadan, practice alms giving and travel to Mecca on the *haj*. It is not necessary to have dedicated public spaces to perform their religion. It is not even necessary to have the services of a trained cleric for religious rituals, other than for burials and the wedding contract signing ceremony. Although anguishing over the negative attitudes of many Americans towards Islam and Muslims, in the United States, Iranian American elderly, if they wish, can carry out rituals according to their own interpretation of Shi'a Islam. Two Iranian Shi'a congregations meet regularly in the Santa Clara area. People can attend home-held rituals, mourning gatherings, death and birthday commemoration rituals for holy figures and public religious gatherings.[16] However, they are also free to *abstain* from practices, as the majority of the largely secularized Iranian American population do. In Iran, this could get them into trouble.

LOSSES

Lost Space for Aging: Iran

Mrs. Abdullahi was born in a small town in western Iran and is Kurdish. She married at age seventeen, and then went with her husband to Tehran. She worked as a teacher and raised her three daughters there. Although she and her husband divorced after fifteen years of marriage, through her work as a principal of private schools she was able to provide for her daughters without outside help. Her youngest daughter initiated the family's move to the United States when she wanted to come here to attend university. Mrs. Abdullahi came to visit her daughter, bought a house here and then moved here within a year, bringing her other two daughters who had been studying in England. With the Iranian Revolution of 1979, most of her relatives also emigrated to the United States. Mrs. Abdullahi has continued to visit Iran to see family and friends, but sold all of her property there. When asked if she was happy with her choice to move here, she answered that the move was very good for her daughters: they received good educations, obtained masters degrees and found good jobs. *Everything* here is easier for her family, she repeatedly said.[17]

Despite her daughters' success and the "easy" life she lives in the United States, I discovered that Mrs. Abdullahi is rather unhappy here. She repeatedly stated that it is "too late" for her to return to Iran; she has adapted to American life, enjoys the freedom she has acquired and feels obligated to stay because of her children. She moved for them and will always stay where they are. But Mrs. Abdullahi feels like a stranger here, although she has been in California since 1997. She notices stares from white Americans and feels that she could not join other Americans in her age group for socializing. She deeply desires to associate with Americans, but feels that her difficulties with the English language would hinder her.

Because of this discomfort, and maybe even fearing rejection from white Americans, she deeply values her relationships with other Iranian elders. She visits with her Iranian friends every Friday and Saturday in different households to share a meal and converse. However, she feels very alone: "Always I am alone inside."

When I asked Mrs. Abdullahi what she does to cope with her unhappiness here, she simply said that while she was "all the time happy" when back in Iran, she knows she appreciates the easy life here. She is taken care of by the government here, and she has her family. While she loves her granddaughter and grandson and spends as much time with them as she can, she limits her involvement with their lives. She wishes she could be with them always, but she is not in good health and knows she doesn't have the patience she needs to help raise them (Field notes from interview with Mrs. Abdullahi, Aisha Breeze Curran, December 8, 1997).[18]

The great majority of Iranian seniors in the San Jose-Santa Clara area ache with longing for their country. They idealize life under the Shah's government, which was actually quite good for them. At first, many Iranians living in the United States thought the prerevolution order would be regained, and life would return to the norms they were used to. One former general kept his packed suitcase next to the door for years, assuming things would change again and he would be able to return to his country. Now, most have lost hope of living again in Iran. They grieve for their country, for the loss of emersion in their own culture, society, interaction style and language. They have lost the comfortable sense of knowing where and who they are. They have not been able to be at "home" to age.

Disrupted Aging for Iranian American Elderly in the Santa Clara Valley

In at least three ways, the American environment fails to provide a comfortable cultural space for Iranian Americans in which to age.

Political Discomfort

Politically, Iranian Americans feel the animosity of Americans toward Iran and Iranians and do not feel comfortable in the American political milieu. Most came to the United States believing it to be a refuge from the Iranian fundamentalist Islamic Republic government that took power in 1979. Developments after 9/11 made them feel they have also lost the United States as a replacement home. They have seen the negative American attitudes towards Iranians, Muslims and people from the Middle East in general. They have watched the American attacks against Iraq with horror and outrage, and are distraught over the violence in that country, resulting in so many Shi'a deaths and destruction in places particularly holy to the Shi'a. They watch American support for Israel against the Palestinians, most of whom are Muslim, and American military attacks in Afghanistan and Iraq, and fear that Iran, located right between the two, will be the next Muslim nation targeted.

The elderly realize Iranians are regarded by other Americans as terrorists and wild-eyed fanatics or religious fundamentalists.[19] As they listen to news and American government threats, they fear an American attack against their beloved Iran, even though now, for most elderly, an alien and illegitimate government is in power there.

Loss of Close-Knit Neighborhoods

Iranian elders often do not feel comfortable in their American neighborhoods. With language barriers, the negative attitude toward Muslims and Middle Easterners in general and the very busy Silicon Valley lifestyle, Iranians cannot get to know their neighbors and form a close community as they had previously experienced in their home country. Iranians complain that Americans do not form connections with their neighbors, or even say hello, but rather interact with others at their place of work or friends elsewhere. They perceive Americans as giving less priority to social relations, as not being warm like Iranians. Women, especially, in Iran gained much satisfaction from the close relationships with neighbors. There, they were the center of a local verbal community, a group of people with whom they could talk in detail and which served almost as oxygen for their social selves. As they grow older, women in Iran may become a mainstay of the traditional neighborhood, closely familiar with the concerns of others in the neighborhood, a central node for advice, neighborhood and kin exchanges and connections.

Sharing in the lives of others in the neighborhood, as well as living among family and relatives, gave Iranian elderly a secure sense of self, a feeling of being grounded. As they reside among Americans here, in this social context many feel they cannot express themselves very well. Because they must take on complicated transportation challenges before meeting up with other Iranians, these elderly are bereft of an immediate neighborhood where people drop in and share in informal chatting, celebrations, mourning, gatherings and home-based religious rituals.

Loss of Age-Integrated and Enmeshed Family Interaction

Most painfully, the emigration to America has resulted in seriously disrupting what provided most significance for Iranian elderly: family and kinship relations. Separate residences constitute an innovation for Iranian American elderly. Their traditional cultural script about how to live as older people came from the experiences of a generation from a very different kind of society. A son may have helped his father in a merchant shop, agricultural fields or craft endeavors. The parents found a spouse for the son, who then lived with his bride and growing family in the same home with parents, at least for a period. Even just two or three decades ago, elderly parents generally did not live on their own, but shared a residence with one of more of their children.[20]

Even if an elderly couple had lived in a separate home, when the husband died, the wife went to live with a son. Similar to anthropologist Suad Joseph's analysis of Lebanese family relations, Iranians were also family "enmeshed" (Joseph 1993, 1999). People took this situation for granted and assumed it to be the natural and right way of managing family connections.[21]

In Iran, comparatively little age segregation divided family and kin ties. Typically, on Fridays, when people had the day off from work, relatives gathered in a home or an orchard or a garden owned by a kin member for a long day of eating and socializing.[22] Young people were expected to spend their time with family and relatives rather than going off with their friends in age-segregated groups to pursue their own interests. Family members often lived close to each other or on different floors in a multilevel home. Typically, daily phone calls and frequent visits brought family and kin into very close association, elderly Iranian Americans remember, which provided a sense of intimately shared lives.

In the Santa Clara Valley, the next generation works hard, putting in long hours and often time-consuming commutes. Women often work as well, and parents are busy ferrying their children around to provide them with advantages. Younger daughters-in-law, especially those who are not Iranian, like to have lives independent from in-law influence. Grandchildren have become especially Americanized in interaction with their environment. When they go to school, and other children become their peer group, they may not enjoy spending time with their old-fashioned, old-country grandparents with their strict ideas about children's behavior and their inability to speak English.

In this California context, the nuclear family comes first, no matter how much these middle-aged people love their parents. Often, though, the elderly focus their lives and selves on their children, and want to continue an enmeshed type of connection with them. Their time-stressed children try to call and drop by and perhaps share a meal with the parents on the weekend. Yet, it is not enough for the elderly. Whether they live with their children or separately, as do most, Iranian elderly often feel neglected and lonely, deprived of close-knit relationships with their children. One man talked of how his son came to get him for a meal on a weekend. But then, he remarked dismissively, he brings me back to my own rented apartment again. As student researcher Noah Levine (2006:15) points out, "(Iranian) elderly ... have been forced to contend with not only their new marginalized roles in society, but also their new marginalized roles within the family."

ALTERNATIVE, MODIFIED, DISCOVERED AND CONSTRUCTED SPACES FOR AGING

Many Iranian American elderly have turned to alternative arenas that are age segregated and/or nonfamilial in nature.

Mrs. Fakhri Aalami, a retired teacher and principal, stayed with her son and German American daughter-in-law and children for about six months after she came from Iran. Then she started to feel isolated in their outlying home. She wanted to be in an urban area where she could get out and see buses, traffic and people. Her son and daughter-in-law helped set her up in a small, one-bedroom apartment across from a park, with convenient bus service, in a more-highly populated area. As she felt lonely there, she would sit on a chair on her balcony overlooking the street, and if someone who looked as if they might be Iranian walked by, she would call out to them. In this way, she found some friends. She spent her time watching Iranian television, talking on the telephone and visiting with friends and family. She sometimes held *sofrehs,* Iranian Shi'a women's home rituals, to commemorate a holy figure and indicate thanks or request assistance. Mrs. Aalami became an important figure in the Iranian Parents' Club, calling members to remind them of upcoming meetings, serving on the board, making a monthly donation and attending the monthly meetings and holiday events. After Grace, the Iranian American senior citizen day care and activity center, opened, Mrs. Aalami eventually became a daily participant.

Iranian Parents' Club of Northern California

About ten years ago, Mrs. Mahin Roudsari, a retired math teacher, established a senior citizens' club for Iranian Americans, the "Iranian Parents' Club of Northern California" (Roudsari 1998). Particularly attuned to elderly issues and feelings because of observing and listening to her own mother displaced to California, Mrs. Roudsari, with a group of her own friends, organized outings and a monthly evening meeting where elderly people could be in an Iranian environment for several hours. During these meetings, people gathered to chat in their own language, exchange stories of heartache and difficulties, laugh and talk a blue streak and enjoy social interaction comfortably following their own familiar cultural rules. At each meeting, an Iranian American expert or medical specialist gives an informative talk and answers questions. The elderly listen to Persian musical performances, watch Persian dancing, often by young people taking classes and recite Persian poetry. They drink tea and eat pastry, fruit and Persian food. Here Iranian elderly receive respect, attention, appreciation and understanding. They can talk, brag or complain about their children, feel approval from others and gain appreciation for their Persian cultural skills and knowledge. They can even take on leadership roles or contribute to the organization in special ways, such as serving as greeter, attending planning and policy meetings or holding office. For many, the parents' club has become a social mainstay, providing a sense of belonging and community. Members of the club go on picnics and together celebrate holidays such as the Iranian (March 21) and American New Years by organizing Iranian dinners and dances at a Persian restaurant.

In summer 2006, one of the founding members and a mainstay of the parents' club, Mrs. Fakhri Aalami, died. I noticed, as I attended the various death and mourning rituals, that almost all those present, other than family, were from the Iranian Parents' Club. As club members greeted each other at the rituals, we said to each other, "I offer my condolences." Such words are offered to the relatives of the deceased, but in this case, members of the club both gave and received the expressions of sympathy. At the club meeting after the death, Mrs. Roudsari arranged a memorial table with photos and flowers in honor of Mrs. Aalami. People chatting with each other at club gatherings frequently brought up her name, saying how sad they were over the loss and how she was missed. This age-segregated group became meaningful not only as a social group, but also as a community of mourning.

Grace Adult Day Health Care

During spring 2005, students in my Anthropology of Aging class assisted me in participant observation and interviewing of Iranian American senior citizens at the day activity and care center, Grace Adult Day Health Care.[23] Student researcher Neda Behrouzi provides examples of the significance of Grace in the lives of Iranian American participants from her fieldwork there:

When I went to sit with a group of women, I asked one of them what she did outside of Grace. She said she "watches the 25 Iranian channels on my satellite TV until after midnight. I read things—books, newspapers (Persian language ones, I assume), the Qor'an. I also cook for my grandson, I walk, I shop." When I asked about America, she said, "I would rather go home. It is good we are here, but that is because our children are here. It is good to be where your children are." She told me, "Before, I had depression. I cried all the time. I was very alone. I have children, but I don't live with them. I came here (to Grace) and now I am good, happy. Before, it was hard to sleep. I never slept well."

One man with whom I spoke there told me, "Things were fine for me and my wife in the U.S. even though we lived separately from our children. But then seven years ago my wife died. I cried several times every day after that. I was desperately unhappy and lonely. Then I started coming to Grace. Now I come every day from Monday to Friday. If it were open on Saturday and Sunday I would come then too. At Grace, I go around greeting others, cheering them up and encouraging them out of their depression. When I go home in the afternoon, maybe I cry some. At night, though, I go to sleep with the hope and comfort that the next day I will be going to Grace again." (Neda Behrouzi, field notes from participant observation at Grace, April 29, 2005)

Entering the large Grace center, one is struck with the noise, chatter and laughter. People may spontaneously start clapping or dancing to Persian music. Grace offers English and poetry classes, meditation, grief and psychological groups, exercise classes, meals and snacks, a huge TV with Persian language programs, health services and board games. The center celebrates birthdays for each month and American and Iranian holidays, inviting families for the special programs. As with the Parents' Club, it offers seniors new opportunities for leadership, contributions and organizing.[24] For those elderly who go to the Iranian senior citizen center on a daily basis to sit and converse with friends, it may partially take the place of warm connections to neighborhood and kin networks.

Cultural Contributions and Community Engagement

Although this chapter's initial example of Mrs. Babi Hogue presents a dramatic case of constructing a life as an Iranian American senior, other older Iranians have also constructed satisfying lives for themselves in their Iranian American environments. For instance, since his wife's death in 1997 when he was eighty-eight years old, Mr. Saeed has devoted his life to serving God and others. He has kept improving his English and helping others with their English, calling on and phoning shut-ins and speaking at his Muslim congregation. At the Iranian Parents' Club, he has often served as greeter at the door, warmly welcoming other senior citizens. He has long served on the board. With his very good English, he also enjoys talking with non-Iranian Americans and gives them as well his warmth and delightful repartee. While Mr. Saeed was able to drive, he visited the ill at home, hospital or nursing facility. He ran errands and brought other older Iranians to the doctor, and in general devoted his time to serving others, including premarital counseling for young Iranian Americans. His deep devotion to the beliefs and practices of Islam and his love for reading, reciting and writing poetry have given him much meaning in life. Although, at age ninety-nine he is now more homebound because he cannot drive, his friends take him to the Friday evening meetings of his Muslim congregation and the Saturday morning Iranian Parents' Club English classes.[25] Facing several health challenges, Mr. Saeed sometimes spends time away from his small efficiency apartment in a hospital, recovery facility or long-term nursing establishment. An unmarried daughter who lives in the area brings food to eat lunch with him once a week. His other daughters live in Iran. Recently, he has begun going to the Iranian American Grace center. A center minibus picks him up in midmorning and delivers him home again in mid afternoon.

Avocational, Recreational and Educational Opportunities

Education for the elderly is a strange idea for Iranians. In the United States, opportunities exist for people to seek education at any time of life. In Iran, this is rarely the case. Further, elderly are commonly perceived by Iranians to have little or no ability to learn, and thus, education for them is wasted effort. Although such an attitude cuts down on the involvement of Iranian American elderly in educational endeavors, some do try to take classes. Because of their troubling language deficit, they see the significance of education for improving their American lives. Older Iranian Americans take other types of classes too, such as in flower arranging, computer and line dancing. They attend Persian poetry classes, gatherings for poetry recitation and poetry seminars. Some Iranian elderly maintain the custom of the *doreh*, a regular meeting with the same circle of friends once a week or once a month, going from home to home in turn or gathering in a public setting.

911 Ambulance, Hospitals and Long-term Care

Inevitably, even seniors who came to this country while still in relatively good health begin to develop medical problems. As they become frailer and less self-sufficient, the clash between Iranian cultural ideals and the realities of the younger generation's success and shift to North American behavioral norms is amplified. This can result in more disappointment and perhaps bitterness among the elderly and often shame among their children. Iranians consider caring for aging and ill parents to be a central aspect of Persian culture and identity. People with an Islamic outlook see devoted care for parents to be a religious duty. In Iran, separate senior housing has developed only recently. The great majority of Iranians express horror at the thought that they themselves or their parents would be cared for by strangers in a separate facility.[26] With not much room or time for care of sick parents in their children's homes, seniors' health problems present yet another challenge, the search for alternatives.

Like so many other Iranian parents, Mr. Tabrizi came with his wife to California several decades ago because their three daughters all lived in the United States, two of them in the San Jose area. The Tabrizis lived in the same apartment complex where their eldest daughter and granddaughter lived. Mrs. Tabrizi cared for her granddaughter while her daughter continued her schooling. Mr. Tabrizi loved the sun and spent most of the day out at the complex swimming pool and Jacuzzi. When Mr. Tabrizi's wife died in the late 1980s, he continued to live in the apartment and use the pool and Jacuzzi. His daughters cooked Persian food for him and brought him over to their homes. He loved nature and enjoyed hiking. Even at an advanced age, in his nineties, Mr. Tabrizi looked fit, lively and tanned.

As Mr. Tabrizi began to have health problems and grow weaker, his daughter found a roommate for him who helped out in exchange for rent. When his oldest daughter moved more than an hour's drive away for her job, caring for her father became increasingly difficult and frustrating. She tried to monitor the care and attention that his roommate was giving him, and then later, to make sure he was well cared for in hospital and long-term nursing establishments. The daughter suffered terribly at the thought of having her father in a nursing home, which was so contrary to Iranian values. As she needed to work, there was little alternative. Exhausted and stressed out from worry, the daughter drove back to the area at least once a week to spend time with Mr. Tabrizi, often bathing him and feeding him. When he died, this oldest daughter organized the large Iranian memorial service and gathering, and handled the other rituals and arrangements.

Through the course of the last decade, as I have been working with Iranian American elderly, some senior citizens whom I first knew in relatively good health have faced challenging medical problems. They may go into the hospital periodically. Some have learned about 911, so that in a medical emergency, an ambulance may transport them to the hospital. After a serious health incident, the aged may spend time in a longer-term recovery facility before being released to go home. Elderly usually do not recuperate at home with extensive care from adult children, but must be cared for by health service providers. When they recover enough to be alone or with a spouse at home, they may continue to receive home care from visiting health personnel. Their adult children usually do as much as possible to provide moral support and practical assistance if their parents are ill; however, there are limits on their ability to do so. Further, daughters-in-law, traditionally the appropriate caretaker of the elderly, may be working outside of the home or not be enthusiastic about attending to the needs of elderly in-laws, especially in the face of so many other demands on their time and attention. Often a senior having health difficulties may bounce between hospital, care facility, home of an offspring or other relative and their home setting.

When older adults with failing health must spend the last period of their lives in a nursing home, such a situation is extremely traumatic for the elderly and their children alike. It goes against deeply held values of respect and care for elderly parents, even though in the American setting there may be little alternative. The children may suffer terrible guilt, and the elderly feel horrified, humiliated and rejected.

Most Iranian elderly in the United States are secularized in that they believe mosque and state should remain separate, and that religion and spirituality should be seen as personal matters not subject to the dictates of government. The great majority of Muslim Iranian seniors living in the United States do believe in God and accept Islam. Although their levels of ritual involvement and adherence to practice vary a great deal, the majority do not regularly perform the five-times daily prayers and other rituals, or go to a mosque. However, when it comes to marriage and death, they want to follow Islamic procedures. Some modifications in preparation of the body and burial are made, due to American law and public health requirements,[27] but as much as possible, people want to follow the familiar, religiously enjoined mourning and burial procedures.[28] They wish to be buried among other Muslim dead.

Spaceless or "A Home in the Heavens"

In a few cases, if the older people do not have resources themselves and their children do not have extra in terms of space and resources, the grandparents may be in a very difficult situation.[29] This dilemma is reflected in a short story by Iranian writer Goli Taraqqi, "A House in the Heavens." It portrays a devoted mother who no longer has a place in her children's pressured and busy lives abroad. Her children live in various countries. She stays with one until the family finds they don't have space for her, and then is put on a plane to another home and so on. At one point, she begins to feel the only space she can legitimately occupy is her airline seat. It has been paid for and is hers for the duration of the flight. A seat in a metal capsule in the sky becomes her only home. Bereft of a residence on earth, she has only a "house in the heavens" (Taraqqi 1996).

The story dramatizes the perception of Iranian American grandparents that their children have developed lives in which their parents are not longer accorded a central spot or perhaps even much of a place at all. Taraqqi also conveys how scattered Iranian families may be. Among the educated, Westernized minority of Iranians who staffed the Shah's modernization and development cadres, many are now spread out in Iran, Great Britain, Europe, North America and even Australia and countries elsewhere. A mother may have children on several different continents, and thus spend time in the air traveling between her own residence and those of her children. The airplane, as well as other means of transportation, has become a common location for Iranian elderly, especially those from upper classes or whose children work in modern sectors or abroad. Some children in a family may live in Iran and others live elsewhere.

CONCLUSION

Iranian American seniors often live a very different lifestyle and hold very different world views from most other Middle Eastern, Muslim immigrant elders in the United States from Afghanistan, Egypt, India, Iraq, Lebanon, Pakistan, Syria, Yemen and other countries (Ahmed, Kaufman and Naim 1996; Omidian 1996; Ajrouch 2007a).[30] Most others did not have the same exposure to modernity, higher standards of living and Western culture, education, lifestyle and careers as did most of the older Iranians in the United States. Although they may also complain about lack of adequate respect and attention from the younger generations, immigrant Muslim elders from these other countries are more likely to live with their children and, if necessary, are more often cared for at home (Omidian 1996; Sengstock 1996; Salari 2002; Ajrouch 2005a, b, 2007a, b). Such care is typically provided by younger female kin who have less access to the American alternatives enjoyed by younger Iranian women. Among less well-off, less modernized and less secularized Muslim immigrants, extended family ties remain salient: seniors live with and share in the lives of the younger generations to a greater degree,[31] but seldom participate in peer groups activities for the elderly. They may have only occasional access to other elderly with whom they can share their troubles and feel comfortable among those who have lived through similar experiences. The possibility of going to a mosque for religious gatherings and activities may provide such seniors with opportunities for socializing, engaging in familiar and valued rituals and meaningful communication. As is common in Christian and Jewish organizations, some mosque personnel in the United States are beginning to develop activities, gatherings and services specific to particular populations, such as senior citizens (Smith 1999:123–125).

An interesting contrast can also be drawn with Iranian elders in Sweden where political refugees are more accepted and living arrangements for them are more readily provided than by the U.S. government. Iranians in Sweden tend more often to come for political asylum and are more likely to be from less privileged backgrounds. Although facing some of the same issues, they enjoy fewer of the opportunities for Persian cultural participation. Because of a much larger Iranian immigrant population, U.S. Iranian elderly enjoy many more ethnic cultural opportunities, such as TV stations, Persian language newspapers and magazines and a variety of Iranian clubs and organizations. Compared with those in America, Iranian seniors in Sweden also have a greater language challenge. Iranians had been more familiar with English and studied it as the second language if they attended high school, but Iranians had no exposure to Swedish. The higher language barrier makes it even more difficult for the Iranian elderly to socially negotiate Swedish society. However, the Swedish government provides better services for the Iranian Swedish elderly. The good public transportation system means better opportunities to get around for the Iranian seniors, and the Swedish government has funded a day activity center for them (Emami, Torres, Lipson and Ekman 2000). Further, in Sweden, Iranian elderly do not face the negative attitudes that Iranians suffer from in the United States.[32]

Much like the situation of Barbara Myerhoff's elderly Eastern European Jews in Venice, California (Myerhoff 1978), Iranian American elders' home society, the Iran that they knew, is no longer.[33] The senior Iranians in Silicon Valley, like the elderly and highly secularized Jews about which Myerhoff writes, nurtured economically successful and highly mobile children who avoided the kind of deep kin enmeshment embroidered into their parents' script for late life. Failing that, both sets of elderly sought to recreate meaningful community and relationships in ethnic, age-peer-focused organizations that serve as a replacement social circle, a home away from home, a space to age in the company of those who have similar histories, cultural values and goals.[34]

Moving to America has provided some freedom from restraints and new possibilities. Babi Jun (Babi Dear) has constructed a lively, warm, delightful home for herself, including an American husband, a dance floor, her roses and garden, the sometime presence of her children and grandchildren, her husband Ron's children and friends—both American and Iranian. She shares her gracious presence with others through her comfortable forays into many types of places—dance classes, club membership, such as in Payvand, a Persian language and cultural organization, and in the Iranian Federated women's club, both run by her close younger friend Fariba Nejat. Without the inherited cultural scripts to do so, Babi has developed new ideas of what is possible for an older Iranian widow. Dancing hand in hand with strange males,[35] a suitor and then a new husband, and performances dressed in costumes other Iranian women her age would consider too skimpy, revealing and attention grabbing—Babi has been ready for all of this. She has transgressed old boundaries and developed new scripts and spaces for herself. As one of my student researchers accurately noted, "The relative success or failure of elderly immigrants' adaptation to life in America is largely contingent on their ability to create new social networks and roles providing them with meaning, contribution and continuity" (Levine 2006:15).

NOTES

This article is dedicated to the memory of Mrs. Fakhri Aalami, teacher, principal and founding member and dedicated supporter of the Iranian Parents' Club of Northern California.

For several internal grants to fund my research about Iranian elderly both in the Santa Clara area and in Iran, I am indebted to Santa Clara University. Such financial assistance has been crucial, as for some years American government agencies have generally not been providing research funds for work in Iran. Santa Clara University also provided me with an Arrupe Scholar grant, providing funds and a course release to conduct research at the Grace senior citizen day care and activity center attended by Iranians during spring 2005. I also thank the American Institute of Iranian Studies for supporting research in Iran. I am very grateful to all of the SCU students who have been involved in this research and, of course, most of all, to the many Iranian seniors who have shared their lives with us, and to the people of "Aliabad," Iran.

1. As this article is based on collaborative research, I must give credit to a number of co-authors. Many Iranian American seniors contributed, and three provided written materials: Babi Hogue, the late Aghdas Malek Salehi and Mahin Roudsari. Tens of Santa Clara University students participated in the participant observation and in-depth interviewing, including SCU student authors Aisha Curran, Noah Levine and Elgin Schaefer; SCU student research assistants Neda Behrouzi, Jenevieve Francisco, Laura Fowler, Emily Johnson, Leslie Miller, Marisa Tsukiji and Lien Vu; and other SCU students from Anthro. 188 Peoples, Cultures, and Change in the Middle East–Winter 1998; Anthro. 3 Intro. to Soc./Cul. Anthropology–Winter 2005; and from Anthro. 172 Anthropology of Aging–Fall 1997, Winter 2004, Spring 2005 and Spring 2006.

2. The belly dancers for the evening included European Americans, Asian Americans and then Babi and her daughter, Iranian Americans. Two European Americans, perhaps sisters, jiggled, flung and thrust their well-endowed bodies as they went through the steps. In contrast, a slim Asian American looked willowy as she turned and twisted. All of them smiled continuously, exuberantly, as if they couldn't help but grin in delight from the enjoyment of dancing and sharing their expertise with the audience. I normally don't like belly dancing. However, in this home setting, in spite of the dance's erotic form, friends and relatives dancing together seemed joyful, graceful and artistic rather than lascivious.

Babi and her daughter Mina took the floor for another choreographed Middle Eastern dance. In synch, except when Babi lost a step, then with good humor took it up again, mother and daughter danced together. Mina has also been taking lessons in this Middle Eastern dancing genre. An exquisitely graceful dancer, Mina performed her dancing with smooth charm and delicate movements of her arms and hands. In her Middle Eastern dancing classes and performances, as well as in her even more active ballroom dancing participation and teaching, Babi joins with people of different ethnic groups and different ages.

3. Music and dancing are intrinsic to Iranian cultural life. Women dance at weddings, family gatherings and even when friends visit. Iranians dance as individuals, rather than as couples. In more traditional arenas, women celebrate separately from men; thus they are free to dance with only females as an audience. In tribal/ethnic areas, women commonly danced in a circle or semicircle, generally separately from the men's line. With the establishment of the Islamic Republic of Iran in 1979, the clerical authorities declared dancing un-Islamic. People either had to cease dancing—and enjoying music for a period as well—or hide it indoors. Now, however, in Iran, where unrelated men and women are legally disallowed from mixing, modern young people and adults hold mixed parties in private homes (see Moaveni 2005, for example.) During weddings and parties held in homes or public spaces, although segregated by sex as required by the government, I have seen men stray into the women's space and dance exuberantly to the women's delight.

4. Babi invited their non-Iranian friends, many of them also dancers, to Ron's birthday party. As a ballroom dance couple, they perform at various gatherings and even have served as dance instructors on cruises. Babi and Ron have business cards showing them posed in a dramatic dip. Babi seems delighted with her life—full of energy, cheer and joy.

5. Iranian American humorous essayist Firuzeh Dumas makes a similar point about new opportunities in talking about her eighty-year-old father's life in America. To celebrate his birthday, the family went on an Alaska cruise where crowds of strangers joined in singing him happy birthday (2005:34). Such experiences would not have been possible in Iran.

6. Babi seems comfortable and warmly welcoming in different atmospheres, not only in a Iranian one. When my institution, Santa Clara University, held a women's day conference a number of years ago, Babi was one of the older Iranian women who came to deliver a paper, in English, to the audience of professors, students and American women (Hogue 1998; see also Malek Salehi 1998 and Roudsari 1998). When a professor of an aging class at San Jose State University requested that I bring an older Iranian to speak to students, Babi was glad to help. Her discussion was articulate, gracious and informed.

7. For more information about immigrant Iranian seniors living in North America, see Gilani (1998); Hegland (1999a, 1999b, 2005b, 2006a); Hegland et al. (2006); Hegland, Behrouzi, Curran, Levine, Miller, Schaefer, et al. (2006); Hegland, Behrouzi, Johnson, Miller, Tsukiji, Vu et al. (2005a and 2005b); McConatha, Stolle and Oboudiat (2001); Salari (2002); Shemirani and O'Connor (2006).

8. Levine further explains, "The subsequent and successful adaptation of second and third generations into American culture minimizes (for the younger generation) the benefits of maintaining close family ties and creates intergenerational conflict. The acculturation of their children has created new hybrid ethnic identities that conflict with cultural ideals including traditional roles, attitudes and behaviors" (Levine 2006:15).

9. Fieldwork for this study has been carried out during my research trips to Iran during eighteen months in 1978–1979, shorter periods from 2003–2006 in "Aliabad" (a fictive name), Shiraz and Tehran, Iran, and by my students and myself from 1997 until the present in the Santa Clara/San Jose area of northern California. Since 1997, I have been working with Iranian American elderly in the Santa Clara Valley, south of San Francisco, also known as Silicon Valley—home to the computer industry. Unable to obtain a visa for research in Iran for some twenty-five years, I turned to Iranian Americans instead, choosing to focus on the anthropology of aging and the elderly, through participant observation at the Iranian senior citizens' organization and the Iranian day activity and care facility, gatherings in homes, Iranian cultural events and in-depth interviewing by myself and several Santa Clara University classes.

10. The American government supported Mohammad Reza Shah's rule, including military training and the presence of large numbers of American armed forces in the country, as they considered him their loyal friend. American influence in Iran became a significant source of dissatisfaction, leading to the 1979 Revolution. Many Iranians saw the Shah as a "U.S. puppet," and felt that Iran should rid itself of control by an outside country.

11. The American government encouraged Mohammad Reza Shah's White Revolution to try to bring Iran into the twentieth century. The Pahlavi shahs discouraged women's veiling, at one point even making veils illegal. Mohammad Reza Shah wanted females to be ready to serve in the workforce. In the 1960s and 1970s, females were not allowed to wear veils to teach, study at universities, provide health and medical assistance, or work in government offices. Female students did not wear veils, but rather school uniforms without a scarf. When I worked as a Peace Corps volunteer in Mahabad, Iran, during 1966–1968, I walked to school in dresses with hems just below the knee. The other female teachers of the girls' high school also wore dresses and skirts of the same length. Only one woman, from a very traditional family, wore a veil—against regulations.

12. Young people were trained and prepared to go out to rural areas as members of the Educational Corps, Health Corps or Agricultural Corps.

13. Nesta Ramazani, born in Iran in 1932, in her memoir *The Dance of the Rose and the Nightingale* (2002), for example, talks of living her early life in a medley of Iranian and Western cultures. She learned to jitterbug from watching films and studied ballet in Iran. She joined the first Iranian ballet company and accompanied by her mother, went on tour with the troupe in Turkey and Europe. Ramazani moved to the United States with her Iranian husband, who became a well-known professor and taught various types of dance here.

14. Often they left Iran because of alienation from the Islamic Republic of Iran government, which stood against all they had lived for as participants in the Shah's modernization and development agenda. The great majority of Iranian American seniors do not support a government by clerics purporting to know the one and only correct interpretation of Islam and determined to force people to live according to this perspective. Religion should be separate from government, they believe, and individuals should be free to find their own way to God. Religion should be a matter of individual choice and personal experience. They self-identify themselves as Muslims, but for most, a religious perspective colors only a small part of their lives. They believe in God, and wish to have a Muslim burial, but they compartmentalize religion, believe it has no part in politics and government and see it as an individual matter. They appreciate freedom of religion and a secular atmosphere in the United States.

15. The two Iranian Shi'a congregations in the Santa Clara Valley operate without clerics. More knowledgeable lay people speak about moral, ethical, spiritual and philosophical issues, recite passages from the Qor'an and read from other religious sources. People do not do their prayers at these gatherings, but if they are practicing, conduct their prayers at home. In one of the congregations, rather than a religious service, a wide variety of speakers are invited for the education and elucidation of the audience.

16. They are free, if they wish, to form their own congregations, form groups for study and discussion about religious and spiritual matters and raise funds for mosques. Women may gather, without possible censor and accusations of Islamically incorrect practices, in traditional home-based women's religious gatherings, providing food, companionship and religious readings, hoping in exchange to gain intermediation from the saints and assistance in their problems and goals, or to express gratitude for wishes granted. They may pursue a more spiritual and philosophical religious path, such as Sufism, try various self-help organizations or formats or even convert to Christianity, which many have done.

17. However, Mrs. Abdullahi had lost something in the area of half a million dollars upon moving to the United States, when a man, seeing she had a good deal of money, had approached her to open a business with him. She never "bothered with business" after that. (Field notes from interview with Mrs. Abdullahi, Aisha Breeze Curran, December 8, 1997.)

18. See also Schaefer 1997.

19. This was not the case before the 1979 Iranian Revolution. Many, if not most, of the now Iranian American elderly benefited from the Shah's regime and held favored or at least respected positions in the government services or bureaucracy or did well in business endeavors. They were most often on good or accommodating terms with the Shah's government. Further, U.S. government officials looked at the Shah as modernizing and a close friend in the Middle East.

20. A middle-aged friend told me, "My mother's mother lived with a son. My father's mother lived in Tabriz, also with a son. The parents lived with their sons back there. They didn't put parents in an old people's home." Personal communication, April 11, 2007. Living with a son epitomized the cultural ideal. Reality, of course, did not always live up to ideals.

21. It should be noted however, some Iranian American elders also talked realistically and sometimes negatively about the conflicts engendered by living at the home of their mother- and father-in-law, or bringing them into their own home.

22. In Iran, until relatively recently, the elderly did not have separate spaces designated for only that age group. Spaces for the elderly were situated in home, family, neighborhood, religious settings and activities shared with others of different ages, rather than age segregated. Families traveled, visited and went on excursions together. Younger people went on pilgrimages, visited shrines, took part in various calendar-year rituals, religious gatherings and life-course rituals along with the older adults. Older people did not really exist as a separate category of people. Not long ago, life expectancy was much lower than now, so fewer older adults were around. When the elderly became sick, the family did not take them to doctors or hospitals—such were rare for everyone only a few decades ago, but cared for them at home until they died. As they did not have medical attention or drugs, those who became incapacitated did not generally live much longer after a major health trauma. The elderly were not segregated into separate groups or in settings specifically for the aged. Family, gender, neighbors, relatives and coreligious practitioners were significant for identity and social interaction, rather than age.

23. I am grateful to Santa Clara University for funding and a course release to conduct this research under the SCU Arrupe Scholar fellowship. My students and I have so far presented four conference papers based on our collaborative Arrupe research project. See Hegland et al. 2006 and Hegland et al. 2005a and 2005b for more information about the Grace center and its place in the lives of the Iranian senior citizens.

24. Student researcher Noah Levine reports: "The very same challenges resulting from old age and immigration which foster the need for the Grace center also create new opportunities for members to contribute. Many of the activities and roles previously regarded as a source of self-confidence are no longer available to them as a result of their immigration. Thus, finding new roles that add meaning and significance is a crucial factor in the successful adaptation of elderly immigrants. Grace accomplishes this; it provides more than a social outlet for interaction with other Iranian immigrants. Their membership in the community gives them not only a sense of continuity, but also provides them with new roles which increase their confidence, sense of purpose and their overall satisfaction. At Grace, seniors are capable of developing a separate identity, not defined by their limitations, but rather by their service, contribution and commitment to the other members. English class grants them the opportunity to display their abilities, reaffirming their confidence and self-esteem. It is a sign of how successfully they are adapting to American society. Yet, it also provides an opportunity to help other members who are struggling. Their ability to translate English directions into Persian is a huge help in an English class. It is also common to see more physically capable seniors helping those struggling with disabilities. The simple act of walking them to the restroom or playing a game of backgammon adds meaning to the lives of both individuals. In playing backgammon with Yusef (Joseph), Mohammad found meaning through his contribution to Yusef. His interest in Yusef helps to foster Mohammad's own sense of identity and self-esteem; he is still valued and worth helping ... My experience at Grace has led me to the conclusion that, for most seniors, the Center is invaluable in the establishment of meaningful identities, interpersonal relationships and group continuity" (Levine 2006:12, 16).

25. The Saturday morning English classes eventually ended. The teacher felt he could not go on using three hours on Saturdays, and no one replaced him. Although a low price taxi for senior citizens is available through the country, it comes either an hour early or an hour late, Mr. Saeed reports. Once, after the monthly Wednesday evening meeting, he was left at the community center where club meetings are held long after everyone had left, waiting for the transportation service. His health problems are also now limiting his involvement.

26. Also see Clemetson (2006), Pulliam (2006), and Mertika (2006).

27. Iranian Americans in the San Jose/Santa Clara area do not have a cleric and attempting to follow correct Muslim burial practices may present challenges. As babies are born into the world with nothing, Muslims believe, people also return to God with nothing. Bodies should be ritually washed and then wrapped with a simple white burial shroud only, when they return to the earth. When Mrs. Roudsari's elderly mother learned about American burial practices including elaborate coffins, she decided she wanted her body to be returned to Iran. Mrs. Roudsari complied with her request. When Mrs. Aalami passed away, her son turned to Mrs. Roudsari, saying he knew nothing about correct practices. Mrs. Roudsari organized the mourning gatherings and a learned layman from Pakistan advised about burial practices and conducted prayers. Mrs. Aalami's body was wrapped in a white burial shroud (*kafan*), but to compromise with American requirements, was placed into a simple coffin before burial.

28. A useful textbook-like starting place for those service providers wishing to better understand Muslim views of death and dying is provided by Sarhill, LeGrand, Islambouli, Davis and Walsh (2001). The authors present ideal practices and expectations of practicing Muslims regarding end-of-life issues. See also Moody (1990).

29. An Iranian American friend told me of talking to an elderly Iranian woman who was sitting on a park bench and weeping. Her non-Iranian daughter-in-law had put her out, she said. Surely, this happens only extremely rarely. See also Gilani (1998).

30. For materials about other Muslim elderly living in North America, see Ahmed, Kaufman and Naim (1996); Ajrouch (2005a and b, 2007a); "Changing family structures ..." (2004); Clemetson (2006); Dossa (1994, 1999, 2002); Fakhouri (1989, 2001); Omidian and Lipson (1992); Qureshi (1996); Ross-Sheriff (1994); Salari (2002); Sengstock (1996); and Smith (1999:123–125).

31. Although it may be culturally appropriate in terms of remembered expectations from the homeland, relatively exclusive reliance of elderly on adult children in current American society may lead to problems. Based on her research among Arab Americans in the Dearborn, Michigan, area, sociologist Kristine Ajrouch concluded, "(W)hile relying on a child does occur, it may not be optimal for them to be the only source of support in times of need. It is not only the availability of support that matters, but the nature of the relationship which is key to well-being" (Ajrouch 2007b:180).

32. For other articles about Iranian seniors in Sweden, see Ahmadi (1998); Ahmadi Lewin (2000, 2001); Ahmadi Lewin and Tornstam (2000); Emami, Benner and Ekman (2001); Emami, Benner, Lipson and Ekman (2000); Emami and Ekman (1998); Emami and Torres (2000); Graham and Khosravi (1997); and Karimi (2003).

33. The Eastern European villages of Myerhoff's Jewish elderly had been wiped out, as had their Eastern European culture. It was gone and they faced the existential task of recreating meaning in the face of that void. Most Iranian elderly in the United States saw the modernized, secularized Iran of their own socioeconomic class being destroyed, to be replaced by an emerging fundamentalist, cleric-controlled government and society. Of course aspects of Iranian culture do continue in Iran. Further, some of the elderly are able to maintain connections with people in Iran, through phone calls and even visits for some. Over time, more people in Iran are becoming more secular and modern in attitude and practice, at the level of everyday lived reality, in spite of—and perhaps partly in reaction to—the government of clerics. At the informal level, signs can be seen of a society more familiar in some ways to the modernized, Westernized Iranian seniors reemerging. The elderly, usually somewhat Westernized through the former shah's infrastructural initiatives, often are not aware of these subtle modifications and often believe nothing good can come during the Islamic Republic government. They feel alienated from their own society in its transformed state, alienated from American society and cut off from their children and relatives and language and social networks.

34. Blaming the lack of attention from the young on the influence of American culture, Iranian American seniors often overlook the fact that in Iran now as well, extended family ties and intergenerational interaction have declined drastically. In Iran, too, seniors are facing the need to develop new scripts and spaces for aging, Now, widowed grandmothers in Iran often live in their own residence, separate from children. Brides are not willing to live with the in-laws and do housework under the direction of their mothers-in-law. Parents focus on their children and the resources they must provide for their children, for the sake of reputation and the children's future. Grandparents lived in a different world and their knowledge and experience are of little use to their children and grandchildren. In Iran as well, grandparents are often lonely and need to construct

lives for themselves. They cannot depend only on their children for material support and their social and emotional lives. Old people's homes are beginning to open up in Iran, too, where sometimes families feel they cannot care for incapacitated elderly themselves, although the change from family to more separate lives and pubic systems of care has changed less quickly in Iran. There, at least they are located in a community of others sharing their language, religion and culture. For some information about older Iranians and the changes in their circumstances, see Friedl (1991, 1994); Hegland (1999c, 2003a, 2003b, 2003c, 2004, 2005a, 2005c, 2007a, 2007b, 2008); Kaldi (2004); Loeffler (1988); Sheykhi (2004); and Teymoori, Dadkhah and Shirazikhah (2006). Researchers have paid little attention to aging and the elderly in Iran. This field of study stands at the threshold. As Iran is facing a rapidly growing number of elderly, and their social support through family and social networks is losing effectiveness, study of the elderly, their changing circumstances and means of replacing the older system of care and social support has become a crucial task.

35. During the anniversary party to commemorate the founding of the Iranian Parents' Club of Northern California, a small incident shouted out to me the cultural dissonance inherent in Babi's learned scripts versus those of other, less acculturated Iranian American seniors. Younger DJs and musicians played music appropriate for American couple dancing as well as for Iranian individual dancing, where perhaps people may dance to each other, but no touching is involved. Babi's husband was not present and several Iranian American males asked her to dance. As her partner took her hand and led her to the dance floor, taken-for-granted etiquette in ballroom dancing culture so much a part of Babi's life, I could not help but see this through the eyes of the other, more conservative older Iranian women: holding the hand of a man not her husband on top of the discomforting but recognizable couple dancing proximity!

CHAPTER 22

Aging in Exile: Family Support and Emotional Well-Being among Older Cuban Immigrants in the United States

Iveris L. Martinez

For to contemplate return ... is again to come face to face with the pain of exile, with a sharply refocused sense of lives, and homes, and youth, all gone forever, with the gnawing discomfort that goes with being an immigrant, no matter how privileged an immigrant, in America, and with the inexpressible, desolate sense all exiles the world over share of being at ease and at home nowhere on earth.

David Reiff, *The Exile: Cuba in the Heart of Miami*

In the shade of the palms of Maximo Gomez Park in the heart of the Little Havana neighborhood in Miami, Florida, older Cuban men can be seen playing dominos from eight in the morning to six in the evening any day of the week. Maximo Gomez was a hero of the Cuban War of Independence, otherwise known in U. S. history books as the Spanish-American War. The park is locally known as the "Domino Park." The quiet chatter of the tiles, the hushed conversation of the men and the intense concentration is only broken by brief, but fiery, verbal altercations or the delivery of a lunch meal by a wife or friend. These men are exiles. And domino playing helps them remember.

Domino playing is a popular pastime in the Caribbean and elsewhere. To many Cubans, and especially older Cubans in Miami, domino playing is an intensive, all-consuming, sometimes daily activity. Men play on the streets, with friends, at senior centers throughout the city or at family gatherings. The Domino Park is full everyday of older Cuban men (many widowed or otherwise unmarried) who pass the time in lively play, conversation and companionship. Until recently, women did not play dominos either at the park or elsewhere in public. However, older women can now be seen playing alongside men at senior centers, and city-wide tournaments.

Domino playing in this small, inconspicuous park stands as a popular local icon of "Cubanness" in exile. In fact, the park is a popular stop for tourists visiting Miami. However, digging below the surface, what emerges at the park and elsewhere throughout the city where older adults congregate, including local cafeterias and senior centers, is an intricate venue of representation, of networking and of identity formation among a displaced and isolated segment of the population—elder Cuban exiles that have recently arrived or who have aged in exile since the triumph of the Cuban Revolution in 1959. In playing dominos, these men (and increasingly women) are engaged in a process of remembering the past, maintaining a distinct identity in exile, coping with loss and establishing a sense of community, which includes "fictive" kinship in the absence of relative or blood kin. Domino playing is one way of expressing their exile identity while resisting this very same condition. This park merely opens a door to the social and cultural isolation experienced by older Cuban adults in one of the most ethnically concentrated regions of the United States. In this chapter, I will highlight how the shared experiences and the language of exile are invoked to talk about familial support and emotional stressors among older Cubans residing in Miami, Florida.

But first, to understand the cultural and social context of Cuban elders in South Florida, it is useful to understand some aspects of the history and unique demographics of this immigrant group. The great majority (nearly 90 percent) of older Cubans residing the United States fled Cuba in the 1960s due to the rapid political and economic changes occurring on the island after the Cuban Revolution of 1959 (see Condon, Dunlop and Rothman 1994). The majority consider themselves political exiles. Emotional distress in the form of

Domino tournament in downtown Miami.

depression and anxiety in this community is often attributed to their exiled condition. Portes and Rumbaut have noted that "Migration can produce profound psychological distress, even among the best prepared and most motivated and even the most receptive circumstances" (1990:144). Despite their relatively privileged legal status as refugees and the social capital brought by early waves of postrevolutionary immigrants, Cubans in South Florida experience stressors of immigration, weakening of social ties and intergenerational conflict, not unlike other immigrants. As immigrants by definition, they inhabit multiple spaces or worlds: that of their culture of origin and that of the host society. How these spaces are occupied and the ability to successfully negotiate these two worlds is crucial to everyday life.

Aging is a demographic and social phenomenon mediated by structural and phenomenological realities. In other words, the way aging is experienced socially has a much to do not only with cultural expectations, but also social context such as the availability and quality of social networks. The proportion of older Cuban immigrants in the United States to younger persons of Cuban descent is relatively large. At the turn of the century, the median age for Cubans[1] in the United States was nearly fifty years (compared to thirty-five years for the overall U.S. population), and one-third of this population is sixty-two years of age or older (U.S. Census Bureau 2000b). Over one-fifth (22.6 percent) of persons of Cuban origin in the United States are sixty-five and older, compared to 5.1 percent of overall Hispanics and 14.4 percent of the non-Hispanic white population (Ramirez and de la Cruz 2002).[2] This is due in large part to politics and resulting patterns of migration that favored older immigrants and fertility rates in Cuba that had begun to drop since the 1950s (Diaz-Briquets and Perez 1981). For example, immigration figures from the first half of the 1990s showed a continued influx of elderly Cuban immigrant population, with approximately 25 percent of incoming Cubans over fifty-five years of age (U.S. Immigration and Naturalization Service, 1990–1995).[3] But how do these figures translate to the lived social experience and stresses of older adult immigrants?

For older Cuban immigrants, the ideology of exile that imbues their everyday life is both political and affective. More than forty years after migrating, this group self-identifies primarily as Cubans and exiles. Familial and intergenerational relations, ethnic identity and politics are seen through this lens. As older generations age and die out, and younger adults assimilate, the politics of exile have become more moderate (Navarro 1997). Despite attempts to pass on the culture they were raised in and their identity as political exiles to their children, cultural values and distinct generational experiences shaping the meaning of Cubanness (*Cubanidad*) are being transformed before their eyes.

SOCIAL DRAMA AND THE ELDER CUBAN COMMUNITY

In 1998, I returned to Miami to conduct my dissertation work[4] prompted by earlier short-term research at the aforementioned Domino Park. I volunteered in a senior center, engaging in participant-observation, conducting in-depth semistructured interviews with seventy-nine older adults of Cuban descent over age sixty, as well as focus group interviews (Martinez 2001; 2002). Individual interviews were conducted in Spanish and lasted one to two hours. They covered a broad area of topics, including migration history, ethnic affiliation, familial ties, social engagement and satisfaction, as well as self-reported health. The center was located in a census tract with approximately 82 percent of the population of Cuban origin, with a high concentration of persons sixty-five and older.

I had made several initial visits in 1997 to establish what the salient issues were for older Cubans residing in South Florida. Mental health concerns were raised numerous times. The health care practitioners I spoke to in the selected region of Miami had noted a high number of cases of depression, anxiety and loneliness. In fact, this senior center was established by a local hospital as a recreational "wellness" program in order to reduce the high number of unnecessary emergency room visits due to apparent psychosomatic illness among the elderly. The senior center was using space donated by a local Catholic church.

Senior centers are useful fieldwork sites since they are oftentimes "social arenas" for constructing social networks and provide the elderly an opportunity for engaging in and acting out "social dramas" (Cuellar 1978; Myerhoff 1978; Hegland this section; Tsuji Part V Web book). The agency of older adults in creating and using "spaces for aging," including senior centers, is also described by Hegland in the case of Iranians in California (this section). In the case of the senior center where this fieldwork was carried out, it served as a place to create social networks for a majority of elders living alone, and provided a range of activities including domino playing, prayer groups, dancing, painting, crafts and theatrical skits. Many of the activities at the center were initiated and led by the seniors themselves. The social dramas of *Cubanidad* were acted out not only in their daily interactions with each other, but also were highlighted at special events, which always included exhibits of paintings, arts and crafts, as well as theatrical skits and poetry recitals.

One such event was the center's third anniversary, celebrated in February 1999 with a Valentine's Day theme. An art exhibit was set up at the entrance, as well as a table selling a cookbook and Spanish idiom book written by the club members. Almost all of the 250 members attended dressed in their best clothing. Twenty-five round tables were set up near the stage end of the church hall used for the senior center during the daytime. They were decorated with heart balloons and heart-shaped stress balls that doubled as weights and later were given away as souvenirs. The stage was decorated with white trellises and red curtains and paper hearts by Raul, one of the club members who always volunteered to decorate for such events. Rey, a former television producer in Cuba, was the master of ceremonies, announcing the speakers, who included the director of the local hospital's wellness division, the head of the senior center's advisory committee and two of the club volunteers. The advisory committee was comprised of club members elected to represent the interests and concerns of the members to the director.

The director gave a speech and showed a short professional video recorded over a year ago as a promotion of the club. Many of the members seemed to enjoy seeing themselves on screen. Awards were given to the "members of the year"—there was a tie between Maria and Evelyn. Maria, who had been a member for under a year, was very popular among the ladies who sat at the crafts table due to her sense of humor. Evelyn was an active dancer and participated in all the exercise classes, sometimes taking over for the teacher in her absence. Rey was also given "honorific mention." The volunteers (including myself) and the member of the advisory committee were given a certificate of appreciation. These signs of recognition where valued by the members and older volunteers, many of whom had no other source of validation.

Prior to a Cuban-style lunch, Raul read a poem by Gema, another club member, titled *"Generaciones"* (Generations), as well as a poem titled *"Plegaria a la Virgen María"* (Prayer to the Virgin Mary) by the deceased exiled poet Ernesto Montaner. The poem is a plea to the Virgin Mary to save the Cuban people from the tyranny of Castro, who is not mentioned by name, but described by his deplorable acts. Raul emphasized his recitation by kneeling and raising his arms and eyes.

The senior center served multiple purposes. It provided emotional and physical sustenance for the older adults in the neighborhood. Lunch was only a dollar, and was a significant help to older adults living on limited incomes. Many left immediately after lunch was served. The majority lived on incomes of less than $10,000 a year (the approximate poverty level for a household of one in 1998), relying mainly on modest incomes from social security checks. Despite the popular myth of the Cuban success story, many of the elders at the center had experienced a negative change in their occupational status after immigration. For example, many of the women had gone from being home economics teachers (a popular course of study among the older women) and/or housewives to factory workers in exile.[5] Lourdes, one of the volunteers, a childless, divorced woman in her late sixties, shared with me that while she did not get paid for volunteering, the gifts of appreciation she received from other seniors at the center helped her immensely. It meant being able to dress a little better (she often got gifts of makeup and costume jewelry), and get out of the one-room studio apartment she lived in by herself. The center therefore served as a means of social support as well.

ETHNIC CONCENTRATION AND SOCIAL ISOLATION

The median age of the group of Cuban elders interviewed at the center was seventy-five. One-third had arrived in the United States past the age of forty-five; the rest came at an age when many were raising young children. More than three-quarters had come to the United States in the period just after the Revolution of 1959, but prior to the Mariel Boatlift in 1980.[6] On average, they had arrived forty-one years before, with one-third living in Miami less than twenty years. Several had been relocated to New York, Chicago or Washington, D.C., upon arrival in Florida, and had a "return migration" to Miami in recent years (Boswell 1994). Three-quarters of this sample cited a political reason for leaving Cuba. The rest said that they had left to join family, with a minority citing economic motives for immigration.

Persons of Cuban origin are the most geographically concentrated of any Hispanic heritage ethnic group in the United States, and three-quarters of this population resides in South Florida (Ramirez and de la Cruz 2002). This continued ethnic concentration is unusual in the history of immigration in the United States and contributes to the lived experience of older Cubans, including the language they speak (Spanish), who they socialize with (mostly, though not totally, other persons of Cuban origin), and what they talk about. Cuban politics, U.S.-Cuba relations, and the shared experience of migration constitute a large part of social and public discourse.[7]

In the 1960s and 1970s, many Cuban immigrants began to settle in the densely populated area near downtown Miami known as "Little Havana." This is the site of the Domino Park, the *Calle Oche* carnival, several cigar-making shops and other symbols of Cubanness in the city of Miami. In the last three decades, the Cuban immigrant population has pushed away from the downtown areas of the city, northward, and mostly south and west into the suburbs of Miami-Dade County.[8] There are pockets of naturally occurring retirement communities (NORCs) of Cuban elders extending westward along major roads in the central part of the county, with younger populations residing in suburban southwestern reaches of the county. Thus effectively a geographical and social distance with younger generations for those not living with families has been created, and certain pockets of the older adult population have been "ghettoized."

Older Cubans in Miami also live in a linguistically isolated world. Virtually all older Cubans in Miami-Dade listed Spanish as their language of choice, and almost half did not speak English at all (Condon, Burton and Rothman 1994). While the majority were naturalized citizens, in 2000, 94 percent of Cuban-born persons residing in the United States spoke only Spanish at home, and of these 60 percent reported not speaking English very well. In my own sample, one-third reported no English language proficiency, and all but two persons reported speaking anything other than Spanish with friends, the great majority (90 percent) of whom were of Cuban-origin. For those persons with children, nine out of ten spoke to them in Spanish only, and only two out of ten with grandchildren spoke to them in English. Moreover, Spanish was the default language of information they received. This, coupled with relatively lower educational levels, can create a level of dependency on younger generations when information is not available in Spanish.

FAMILY AS SOCIAL SUPPORT OR STRESSOR?

Caregiving and the nature of social support are impacted in part by living arrangements. Intergenerational living arrangements among older Cuban immigrants have been steadily decreasing since the 1960s (see Arias 1998). The three-generation household and the economic contribution of the elderly were important in the socioeconomic reestablishment of the early waves of Cuban immigrants after the Revolution (Perez 1986; Arias 1998). However, the multigenerational household among Cuban-Americans has steadily declined in the decades since 1959 and has been replaced by nuclear family living and persons living alone. The type of households has also changed. Cuban elders, especially elderly widowed women, head more households.[9] Nonetheless, a survey in Miami-Dade County, Florida, found that of the 72 percent Cuban elders who reported living with at least one other person, 41 percent lived with children and 15 percent with grandchildren (Condon, Dunlop and Rothman 1994).

On average, the older adults I interviewed lived in households of less than two persons. One-half of those interviewed at the center were widowers. While slightly more than half lived alone, living arrangements varied greatly. Twenty-seven percent reported being currently married, but only 17 percent lived with a spouse or partner as several appeared estranged from their spouses. Of those interviewed who did not live alone or with their spouse seven lived with a daughter, three with a son, six in multigenerational households and the rest with assorted relatives and nonrelatives.[10] While intergenerational values remain important, intergenerational differences in English language proficiency and acculturation have led to a decreased role of grandchildren in the daily lives of older adults. So while there may be values of extended familial support, the reality reflects a great variety in actual support available and a continued decline in intergenerational familial arrangements.

As one might expect, the quality of social support varied in relation to complex factors, including familial histories and life course trajectories (Cattel and Albert Part II). The role of family as a supportive network is seen as central to mental health among scholars of immigrant health in the United States. While common predictors for psychological distress among Mexican, Cuban and Puerto Rican elders in the United States included poor health and unmet needs in social services, for Cubans dependence on others, familial conflict and living alone stand out as predictors for poor mental health (Mui 1996). The senior center served as a place for the development of social support beyond the family, when family support failed due to geographical distance caused by the migration of children to other counties or states, the separation from kin in Cuba, the loss of family members (spouses and siblings) due to death or dysfunctional familial relations.

Despite a certain geographic, linguistic and social isolation, family as an ideal (Martinez 2002) and intergenerational relations played an important role for the older Cubans in the center, even for those living alone and who do not have day-to-day in-person contact with family. Family is usually part of the core support system for older adults, though this varies across cultures, family structure, the availability of other supportive structures and state policies (Shenk and Christiansen 1997; Sokolovsky 2002; Lowenstein 2005). Research on social support structures of Latino elders has been conducted largely with

Mexican American samples and centered on the notion of "familism." Family is often the motivation for immigrating at older ages, and is the de facto source of social support (Angel, Angel and Markides 2000). While the perception of family as central to support does not appear to change with acculturation among Latinos, the sense of familial obligation and the family as referents do appear to decline, therefore certain familial values may be upheld in principle but may also be contradicted by their actual behavior (Sabogal et al. 1987). In this regard, research on Latinos has sometimes overlooked the structural and life course processes that impact the availability and quality of support (Miller-Martinez and Wallace 2006). The family is assumed to be the "natural" support network for the elder without considering the impact—structural, cultural, and psychosocial—of immigration on the family and declines in health (Bastida 1988; Angel et al. 2004; Gonzalez Vazquez et al. 2007).

The meanings of family and kinship are understood through a cultural interpretation of perceived structural changes, taking into consideration historical and symbolic processes from a life course approach. For older Cuban immigrants with whom I spoke, the concept of family extended beyond spouses and children to include siblings, cousins, grandchildren and nieces and nephews. The family support that Cuban elders in Miami experience was quite different from the kin context they were born into. It has been affected by several factors, including decreasing fertility, separation from kin across borders and changes in intergenerational values (see Martinez 2002). The elders that I interviewed were born before Cuba went through its demographic transition, and therefore came from relatively larger families than what they themselves had. It is not unusual to meet an older adult from a family of eight or even sixteen. For example, my Cuban grandparents on my mother's side were from families with nineteen children each! However, 18 percent of these same elders never had children, and 23 percent no longer had any children alive.[11] No one in my sample had more than three children, and on average they had only one remaining child and two grandchildren. However, siblings and extended familial relationships also play an important role in the Cuban concept of family life. While the number of siblings still alive ranged widely from none to nine, on average they had two living siblings. Therefore, the density of available kin support, be it lateral or vertical kin, is dramatically less than what their parents' generation would have experienced.

A common complaint I heard centered around changes in these elders' roles within the family. There has been an increasing trend towards Cuban elders living alone; therefore, older adults may not play such a prominent role in the day-to-day decisions of the extended family. Nevertheless, the majority expressed satisfaction with their interaction with their children and siblings. This may be because for Cubans the "functional" solidarity of the family extended beyond the household and was generally of a reciprocal nature (see Arias 1998; Bengtson, Lowenstein, Putney and Gans 2003). The majority of the elders who do not live with their children or in multigenerational households maintain regular contact through daily or regular phone calls and sometimes weekly or less frequent visits. A few paid extended visits or occasionally vacationed with their children. Elders with adult children and grandchildren may provide care for their grandchildren, especially during summer vacation or school holidays. They also helped out families financially with gifts in kind or money in return for chores. However, they acknowledged that this contact was not the same as living together, and that in the end, it is "for the best." The elders seem to perceive that older adults can be otherwise recognized as a nuisance, and therefore, they prefer to maintain their distance in terms of living arrangements. Geography and the constraints of modern life were also an explanation for decreasing contact. Children may live far away and be busy with work and raising their own children.

Contact with siblings, if they resided in the United States, usually took the form of visits and frequent phone calls. If brothers and sisters resided in Cuba or abroad, their exchange was necessarily limited to infrequent phone calls and letters, and in a few cases sending remittances in the forms of cash and goods to help their families on the island. Despite the politics of the embargo, relationships with family extended beyond the reaches of their immediate locale and across borders. Almost half had immediate close kin remaining in Cuba, including siblings, children and even some parents. Of these, 84 percent regularly sent money and goods to them despite their overall support for the embargo against Cuba. Nevertheless, contact with family in Cuba has always been a contentious issue. The ease of travel and sending money to Cuba has fluctuated with changes in U.S. law and the political climate of Miami at the time. Until the mid-1970s, travel back to the island was prohibited, and even today is only permitted for immediate family. Given this situation, "family" takes on not only its usual emotive role, but also a political one. Travel and contact with family on the island was more readily accepted by women and those who immigrated after 1980, while the subject was generally considered taboo among men and those who immigrated immediately after the Revolution. Divides between families, either due to personal politics or law, are a cause of stress and distress that older Cubans have been managing for decades.

PEQUEÑOS FIDELITOS (LITTLE FIDEL CASTROS): EXILE AND THE ROLE OF FAMILY IN EMOTIONAL WELL-BEING

At age sixty-nine, the impeccably and fashionably dressed Sylvia was independent and in very good physical health. However, her memory and emotional health were not. Sylvia exhibited a high level of depressive symptoms, took pills in order to sleep and was seeing a psychiatrist for depression. Sylvia joined the senior center (which she referred to as *El Club*) when her sister, who was like her "umbilical cord," died. Despite what some might consider an active social life, she complained of loneliness.

Sylvia came to the United States in 1961 from a small town in central Cuba via Costa Rica. After arriving in Miami, her family then relocated to New York where her sisters lived. She lived in Brooklyn for five years with her husband and daughter until she had her second child, a son, and their apartment became too small. With the encouragement of a nephew living in California, the family moved to Los Angeles. About ten years ago, her son suggested that Sylvia move closer to her sisters who had retired to Miami. At the time, she was separated from her husband and living alone. Since arriving in South Florida, Sylvia had resided alone in an apartment on Miami Beach owned by her brother. She emphatically stated that she preferred not living with either of her children (both still in Los Angeles) in order not to make them "bitter."

Sylvia was fluent in English and became a U.S. citizen in 1966. She said she realized then that Castro would be in power a long time and that she would not return to Cuba. Nevertheless, when asked her ethnic identity, she proudly stated that she considered herself "100 percent Cubana" and an exile. She got her news from Radio Mambi, one of the oldest Cuban exile "news" talk radio stations. Sylvia had a relatively good income from real estate investments and a pension, and relatively few expenses. She contributed money and time to several exile organizations, participating in their demonstrations against the Cuban government. She believed it her duty to do so. Meanwhile, her relationship with her three remaining sisters (whom she moved to Miami to be near) was strained to the point that she did not speak to them. Interestingly, she referred to one of them as a "little Fidel Castro." Sylvia concluded that life has taught her that the world is full of little Fidel Castros.

As can be seen by Sylvia's own words, the experience and language of exile colors relations with family and often overlapped with emotional well-being in the daily lives of Cuban elders. Sylvia described her difficulties with her sisters and others by generalizing and comparing these persons to Fidel Castro, the communist dictator who came into power in 1959, precipitating her exile and that of hundreds of thousands of Cubans. Sylvia's case suggests that poor mental health may be conflated with several sociocultural factors including marital disruption, strained family ties, and an adherence to the ideology of exile. Sylvia's story is but one of many. Her example provides a glimpse of the complex lives, experiences, motives, contradictory views, and emotions of the Cuban elders I interviewed at the senior center in Miami.

The challenges and stresses of family life and the experience of exile are ever present and oftentimes emerge spontaneously in everyday life. During my fieldwork in Miami, I attempted to collect life histories of a limited number of informants to record more detailed examples of the experience of aging of the Cuban elderly in Miami from a life course perspective.[12] I had proposed to lead a voluntary workshop at the senior center. However, my numerous attempts at recording life histories largely failed. The workshop was met with mixed and largely negative results. I found that among these Cuban elders, the life review was largely a spontaneous event, and not to be actively recorded or worse yet, scheduled.[13]

When asked about the importance of life review for Cuban elders in Miami-Dade, Dr. G., a local clinical psychologist working largely on

depression, said that he did not believe in "fixing what was not broken" or
what did not surface. In this context, he held that a life review is the equivalent of picking at an open wound due to the discontinuity of their life stories
caused by exile. Instead of resolve, a life review brings a painful reminder—it
opens up what in fact remains unresolved in some cases due to the vicissitudes of history and culture. Dr. G. suggested that the exercise of a life
review may bring up the fragmentation of life and family with the different
waves of exodus from Cuba.

Moreover, the life review was also associated with confronting the death of
loved ones and one's own mortality. While this was a relatively healthy group
of elders, conversations about death were generally avoided and disassociated
from the self. Despite the difficulties of a structured life review, the Cuban elders I interacted with did spontaneously reminisce. This could occur at any
given moment. Dreams, an event, or a "familiar" location might trigger it.
When they did reminisce, Cuban elders did so with great enthusiasm, even if it
was about difficult topics, such as stories of persecution and hardship during
the early years of the Revolution.

For example, on an outing with seniors from the center to a city-sponsored
event on a cruise ship docked in the port of Miami, Rey, the television producer mentioned earlier, turned to me and stated in his typical sardonic, yet
jovial, tone that that he hoped that we weren't hijacked back to Cuba. As we
made our way up the gangway, he continued to tell me the story of the harassment he suffered as he tried to leave the country shortly after the triumph of
the Revolution of 1959. Rey told me he worked at one of the local television
stations in Havana as a producer of comedy sketches and musical specials, and
was transferred to producing political segments. For eleven months, he said, he
worked without pay and with a heavily armed soldier (*miliciano*) at his back to
make sure he did not sabotage the productions. Recently married and with a
small child, he was driven to poverty and forced to move in with his parents.
His parents gave him bus fare. Ray reminisced about pacing in an insomniac
state back and forth in his room while his young wife watched him. He said it
made him *mal de los nervios* (sick from nerves). When he was finally granted
an exit permit, he was subjected to the *actos de repudio* (ritualized harassments
targeting those who were planning to leave the island).

When I interviewed Rey, over thirty-five years after he had left Cuba, the
memories were fresh enough to be spontaneously recalled. A heavy smoker
and formerly heavy drinker who had survived pancreatic cancer, Rey was generally in good spirits. At age seventy, he attended the center every day with his
wife and transferred his skills in show business to daily life at the senior center
by writing and staging theatrical skits for every party at the center, usually
associated with holidays such as Mother's Day, Valentine's Day or Christmas.
The skits, and the ones about exile in particular, followed the format of Cuban
theatrical sketches and often referred to popular characters in the pre-1959
world of entertainment, making it difficult for persons of other generations,
such as myself, to follow.

MENTAL HEALTH AMONG OLDER CUBAN IMMIGRANTS

Mental health issues among Cuban elders, including dementia, carry a degree of stigma that may affect responses to direct questioning (see Williams et al. 2001). Some of the people I interviewed in my time in Miami took a defensive attitude when asked any questions related to their mental and emotional health. Others were quick to perceive what the questions, such as the Geriatric Depression Scale (GDS),[14] were to "measure" and accordingly shifted their answers to reflect this. For example, after several responses that might indicate depression, they might switch to responding to the remaining questions to indicate the opposite. One woman said to me directly, "I know what you are getting at ... you are trying to see if I am crazy, aren't you?" During my observations at the center, the distinction between *mal de los nervios* and *mal de la cabeza* (sick in the head) and *loco* (crazy) became quite evident.[15]

Clark and Anderson argue that "mental disorder is a social judgment placed on an individual by various institutions in his society" (1980:21). It is acceptable within the Cuban immigrant community to be *mal de los nervios*, but it is less acceptable to be *mal de la cabeza*, which implies a more severe and permanent state and is a highly stigmatized category. However, to be "sick in the head" is not as severe as "to be crazy" (*estar loco*) as it does not necessarily compromise the person's ability to function on a daily basis. To be *nervioso* can refer to an anxious or depressed state, or any other acceptable, but usually temporary, emotional imbalance. Some persons may be *nervioso* as a personality trait, but this does not hinder social interactions and functioning. To see a psychiatrist may imply a more permanent, organic and stigmatized condition of madness.

The few elders with apparent cognitive deficits that attended the Center were often ostracized. Henderson observed experiences of family shame among spouses caregiving for Alzheimer's patients within a largely Cuban American population in Tampa, Florida (Henderson this section Web book). The shame of poor mental health extended onto the fictive family members of the center. In fact, Lourdes, the volunteer who took me under her wing and introduced me to many of the persons I interviewed, often tried to act as a gatekeeper, keeping me away form those persons she thought were not cognitively intact or emotionally stable enough to be interviewed. On more than one occasion, persons I had interviewed talked to me concerning information they had shared with me about their family and their mental health. Their concerns were usually relieved when they were reassured of their anonymity.

How prevalent were emotional problems in this population? Depressive symptoms, as measured by the commonly used Geriatric Depression Scale[16] (GDS), were only slightly higher (at 18 percent) to the prevalence of depression in the general older adult population, which is estimated at 15 percent (Ossip-Klein, Rothenberg and Andresen 1997) and higher than the 10 percent prevalence of depression found in a younger Cuban American population, using a similar scale in another study in the Miami area (see Narrow et al.

1990). Culture, as illustrated previously, dictates how we respond to the world around us, and therefore may influence symptom manifestation, how we measure the prevalence of mental disorders, as well as responses, including stigma associated with a disorder, whether or not treatment is sought, and what type. I therefore asked a more general question of how they would rate their present emotional health as excellent, very good, good, fair or poor. I also asked if they had ever felt depressed or sad (*deprimido o triste*) for two weeks or more in the last ten years, and whether they had sought professional treatment for these feelings. While less than one-fifth scored with depressive symptomatology, 41 percent describe their emotional health as regular or poor, and a little over half reported being depressed for two weeks or more in the past ten years. Forty-seven percent reported seeking any type of treatment, including the use of medications.[17] Medication used for sleeping was quite common and acceptable. These, along with antidepressants and sedatives, were often prescribed by a primary care physician.

Depression is clearly not the only mental health issue in this community, though it may be one of the most common. Anxiety disorders also prevail according to local psychologists. This became evident throughout the interviews about their reported of use of medication for anxiety. Fourteen percent of those surveyed reported taking medications for anxiety. Almost 18 percent take sleeping pills regularly.[18] It appeared that sleeping pills were often prescribed after the death of a spouse or other traumatic life event such as diagnosis of a major illness, such as cancer or heart disease. Though there was little mention of alternative treatments among the seniors at the center, *tilo* or tea made from linden flowers is a popular remedy for "nerves" and insomnia. It may be that depression and other mental health concerns are underestimated among older Cuban immigrants by standard scales such as the GDS.

Local psychologists I spoke to also reported Post-Traumatic Stress Disorder (PTSD) as common and always under-diagnosed among Cubans in exile. Depression and anxiety are commonly associated features with PTSD (Reid 1995:190). Symptoms for PTSD are seen following an event (whether experienced, observed, or related to a family member or other "close associate") that is extremely traumatic and experienced with intense fear, terror, and/or helplessness. These traumatic events typically involve death, serious injury or a threat to one's physical integrity. Symptoms of PTSD usually appear within the first three months and include reexperiencing the trauma, persistent avoidance and/or increased arousal, such as irritability and sleeplessness. However, PTSD among Cubans may be latent—its delayed onset is triggered by other events like the terminal illness of a spouse that may trigger feelings, such as hopelessness, similar to those experienced when arriving in the United States (Martha Corvea, personal communication, December 7, 2000). For example, a sixty-five-year-old man's wife is diagnosed with a malignant disorder that he can do nothing about. Hopelessness and a feeling of "not being safe anywhere" trigger feelings of how he felt when he came to Miami thirty years ago; symptoms show in anger, resentment or substance abuse (Ibid.). While the majority of older immigrants fled due to threats posed by the establishment of a

Marxist-Leninist dictatorship both to their way of life and their safety,[19] there has been little work on the psychological impact of violence in this population relative to other issues such as dementia.[20]

According to another psychologist who had been working in Miami on a project on long-term care for elderly Cuban dementia patients, due to language barriers, and their unfamiliarity with the concepts of dementia and formal service system, Cuban elders are lost without the help of their families. Therefore, when there are strained intergenerational relations, this can pose strong barriers for attaining needed services. "Fatalism" and notion of "destiny" may be only one of several factors deterring service use (see Abraído-Lanza et al. 2007 for summary and critique). Several older adults I interviewed at the center who complained about memory loss also expressed fear of how they would be cared for if they became ill. However, none of them had long-term care plans and were reluctant to make any. They hoped that family might take care of them, though they recognized the limits of this given the fact that even if they did have children, as one woman who lived with her son and daughter-in-law explained, they both had to work and therefore would probably not be available to care for her. Nursing homes and boarding homes where many expected they might end up were referred to as *"la casita"* (the little house).

Just recently, sitting in a waiting room at a local doctor's office, where all the clients were sixty and over, I engaged an older couple in conversation. Rosa was an elegantly attired eighty-five-year-old woman who looked at least twenty years younger, and was sitting with her husband Luis, aged eighty-three. Luis told me about his weekly domino games with his friends, held at each others' houses. They used to be held in his house until they sold their apartment because it was too large for them alone. They did not speak of any children, but Rosa did tell me that her unfortunate sister used to live with her daughter, but was asked to move out by her son-in-law, after the grandchildren had grown. During my fieldwork, I had previously heard this story of older parents living with children until they had outgrown their usefulness as babysitters for grandchildren. Luis simply stated that they would have to see what happens when they could no longer care for themselves, but that he was resigned to not expecting any help. While it is unlikely that they will not have any help, the reality is that they will probably not get the help they would expect. Families usually come together in times of crisis, but as indicated by decreased intergenerational living arrangements, help cannot be expected on a daily basis.

Immigrants, and particularly political exiles, must strike a balance in everyday life between identifying with their country and culture of origin and integrating into the host society or new place of settlement. This is not an easy thing for Cuban exiles to do when it means letting go of the dream of returning, which is tantamount to accepting defeat, especially among the more politicized and older segment of the population. This may especially be the case in Miami where the social milieu perpetuates the preoccupation of exile through media, politics and commercial endeavors. The situation may also be exacerbated by the quality of familial ties connecting people to their homeland, both within and between generations.

Changes from extended family living arrangements to living alone or with their spouse and the dwindling contact with children, and especially their grandchildren, were explained as the result of "life under a different system." There was some disagreement as to whether the perceived changes in the family were the result of a different "system" itself (i.e., the country or culture) or a change in time (through the historical evolution of things). Still others believed that the quality of intergenerational exchanges was due to the elder's responsible "upbringing" of their family. This of course perplexed those who had tried to do everything "right" and encourage intergenerational solidarity in their children and grandchildren, but who did not receive as much as they expected in return.

CHANGING INTERGENERATIONAL ENGAGEMENT WITH CUBAN CULTURE

My research took place at a particular moment in the Cuban American experience, forty years after the Revolution of 1959. Cuban popular culture's influence on American mainstream life was at an all-time high since the days of the mambo craze and Desi Arnaz belting out *"Babalu"* on television in the "I Love Lucy" show of the 1950s (see Perez-Firmat 1994). Cuban music experienced a renaissance with the release of Ry Cooder's recording of the "Buena Vista Social Club," salsa dancing classes proliferated in dance clubs across the country, and there was renewed popularity of smoking Cuban cigars (made in the Dominican Republic or Central America). However, this time around, Cuban culture in the United States is being mass consumed by Cuban Americans, the children and grandchildren of exiles.

For Cubans and their descendents, this commercialization is couched in terms of "nostalgia." The nostalgia is not simply for things Cuban, but for things Cuban pre-1959. The business potential of this market was noted in the business section of the *Miami Herald*, in an article titled "The Cuba Craze: Havana's Golden Era is Rich in Opportunity" (Whitefield 1999). The article highlighted the growing market potential for dealing in things "Cuban." What is being sold includes antiques, cigars, stamps, music and beverages, such as rum, beers and soft drinks.

Nostalgia appeals to those Cuban Americans who were not born in Cuba and who have never been there. Bill Teck, then thirty-one-year-old founder of *Generation* ñ, a magazine aimed at first-generation persons of Latino descent of Generation X, was quoted as stating, "It is the weirdest thing in the world being nostalgic for a place you've never been ... It's a longing for a weird fantasy place that doesn't exist and possibly never existed—except in the minds of our elders." It was from this article that I first learned of the Cuba Nostalgia event to be held at Coconut Grove Convention Center on May 15–16, 1999, in "commemoration" of May 20, Cuba's Independence Day. It was advertised as

"A trip through yesterday's Cuba" and an intergenerational event that claimed to "demonstrate[s] Cuban life, culture and heritage." The timing of the event is symbolic since for Cubans in exile the celebration of Cuban Independence Day is a bittersweet event. For exiles, Cuba is no longer a free country because of the long-standing Castro dictatorship. In fact, the national drink of *"Cuba Libre"* (Free Cuba) is often defiantly asked for as *"una mentirita"* (a little lie).

The event was clearly advertised as an intergenerational affair. The poster for the event, which was printed in newspaper advertisements in the local papers and was available in postcards, depicts a gray-haired grandfather dressed in a *quayabera* (typical Cuban dress shirt for men) with a little boy (presumably his grandson) on his lap. The logo—in red, blue and white with a lone star in a red triangle and a blue stripe—is reminiscent of the Cuban flag. Many of the advertisements made references to Cuba, or the past, alluded to remembering, or the continuation of tradition. The event is now in its tenth year. Yet, the relationship to Cuban culture, history and values, however commoditized, is different across the generations. As one seventy-five-year-old woman commented to me as she was having difficulty recollecting specific events while attempting to write her life history, "Cubans lost the thread of [their] history when they came over here [to the United States] ... exile has made them lose their [genealogical] line."

LA PATRIA ES LA FAMILIA (THE NATION IS ONE'S FAMILY)

While the direct link often made in the community between exile and poor emotional health is not supported by quantitative analysis, there appears to be a significant relationship between exile and poor familial relations; there is also a relationship between poor familial relations and poor emotional health. This suggests that emotional well-being is related to the quality of family relationships in the context of political immigration or exile (see Martinez 2001). Ideologies play a role in the interpretation of inevitable structural changes of the family through time (see Martinez 2002). The fact that their children and grandchildren were now Americans (*americanos*) was the "price paid for liberty." One man reflected that while the great majority of children of Cubans born and raised in the United States would not even think of going to Cuba, for they have made their lives in the United States, the definition of the homeland is the family. So while family and nation are often inextricably linked for Cuban elders, as family changes, so does the relation to the homeland.

Immigrants to the United States that are labeled as political and seen as involuntary, such as in the case of refugees and Cuban exiles, may enjoy a certain degree of acceptance in host communities than so-called "economic" immigrants. They also usually have the added benefit of relatively quick "normalization" of their legal status. However, immigration, whether political or economic, voluntary or involuntary, often entails similar difficulties of adaptation to a new and unknown environment. These difficulties include separation from kin, lower socioeconomic status vis-à-vis the larger population and discrimination, as well as changes in the quantity and quality of family social support. This was coupled by the involuntary separation of families due to the largely political nature of the immigration, and unexpected changes in the structure and quality of familial relations (see Martinez 2002).

This population provides a case example to explore the implications of aging "out of place" among immigrant elders and the multidimensional issues of migration, identity, familial relations and well-being in aging beyond the language of ethnicity and culture to that of ideological constructs of community. Migration may be experienced as a drastic change in life course and expectations. It can lead to rapid changes in familial dynamic due to changes in available social support and values. The example of Cuban immigrants may provide an opportunity for a broader understanding of aging among displaced persons and the cultural patterning of well-being among immigrant groups. This carries important implications for social as well as health care policy. Given the rapidly increasing and aging population of Latinos in the United States, mental health among immigrant elders is a subject worthy of further understanding.

NOTES

1. Refers to foreign-born Cubans, compared to Cuban-origin, which includes foreign-born and those born in the United States.

2. The median age for persons of Cuban origin (compared to Cuban-born) is lower at forty years, due in part to the demographic characteristics of immigration from Cuba.

3. Several authors have postulated that the unusually older population structure of the Cuban population in the United States is due to both low birth rates and selective immigration patterns (Perez 1992:97).

4. This research was supported by a Mellon Grant through the Department of Population Dynamics (currently the Department of Population, Family and Reproductive Health) at the Johns Hopkins Bloomberg School of Public Health and a grant from the National Institute on Aging (R03 AG16279-01A1).

5. A large proportion of Cubans leaving in the early 1960s experienced a permanent negative change in socioeconomic standing (46 percent of my sample). Several of the persons interviewed expressed a sense of being *"recogidas"* (taken in) by the United States, but not feeling a part of this country. A sense of powerlessness and alienation in aging has been precipitated in some cases by the fact of migration. Some, but not all of the women interviewed may have been considered middle class back in Cuba by our standards. However, more importantly, it seemed that regardless of class women were not expected to work outside the home. A broader network of family support, including shared household resources, may have contributed to keeping women outside the workforce.

6. Cubans have a long history of migration and exile to the United States, and particularly South Florida (see Poyo 1989). Geography, as well as economic and political interests, have inextricably linked their histories for centuries (Portes and Stepick 1993). This interconnectedness dates from the time of the Cuban struggle for independence from Spain to the present. Since the late 1800s, "Cuba gradually converted Florida into her own political backstage, where the dramas, and sometimes comedies, were

enacted" (Portes and Stepick 1993:94–95). Miami would later become the "moral community" of Cuban immigrants (Ibid. 107). The volume and flow of immigration between Cuba and the United States since the late nineteenth century has waxed and waned in relation to the political and economic environments on either side of the Florida Straights, but remained low in comparison to the migrations of the last forty years. A few of the elders I interviewed migrated in the late 1940s and 1950s as very young adults. Some were escaping rural poverty in Cuba or seeking greater job security; a few were opposed to the Batista regime. After the Revolutionary War of 1959, en masse migration to the United States by Cubans took on a different meaning and characteristic, and a new definition of exile. Cubans now entered the United States officially as refugees. The initial flow of Cuban exiles to the United States after 1959 consisted principally of upper-middle-class professionals, business owners and political rivals (primarily known sympathizers of the former Batista regime) who were hardest hit by the establishment of a communist regime in Cuba, and who thought that their exile was temporary and focused their efforts on immediate survival and deposing the new regime. The failed attempt to overthrow the Castro regime in 1961, known as the Bay of Pigs Invasion, and the Cuban Missile Crisis in 1962 ended the illusion of a temporary exile for these initial waves of migration and secured their status as political exiles. The initial exodus was then followed by a large immigration in the mid-1960s of older Cubans through the Family Reunification program via the Freedom Flights, an airlift also known as the aerial bridge (*puente aereo*) from 1965 to 1973. Approximately 451,000 Cubans immigrated to the United States between 1960 and 1967. Contrary to popular belief, by the mid-1970s the waves of "golden exiles" (i.e., upper-middle-class and professional persons) came to represent, at least economically, the spectrum of Cuban society (Aguirre 1976). Racially, "white" Cubans have been overrepresented in the migratory waves up to 1980 (over 90 percent). The flow of Cuban refugees remained relatively slow throughout the 1970s after the end of the "Freedom Flights." The next most notable influx was in 1980, during the Mariel Boatlift, at which time approximately 125,000 Cubans entered the United States (Borneman 1986). Mariel brought to the community persons who had lived under Castro's regime for over twenty years, including younger persons and those of suspected criminal backgrounds, causing many tensions in the Cuban community of Miami, but which were eventually overcome. With a rapidly rising number of boat people in 1994, the Cold War over, and the threat of another mass exodus like Mariel, Cubans were denied the special and automatic immigration status as political refugees that they had held for nearly thirty years (see Perez 1999).

7. Although the Cuban population in the United States was initially settled in the major urban centers of New York and Chicago, as well as South Florida, Miami has had a continuous pull for Cubans, even among those originally settled elsewhere in the United States. Despite the efforts of the Cuban Relocation Program, a "trickle back" was being witnessed as early as the 1970s; this phenomenon of "return" migration to Miami intensified in the next twenty years (Boswell 1994). This is contrary to the historical tendencies of immigrants in the United States to move away from their ethnic enclaves and assimilate. Among Hispanic elders, there is a greater tendency to move across state lines among other older Americans in general (Biafora and Longino 1990: S214). By 1990, 65 percent lived in the state of Florida, and 54 percent of all Cuban Americans lived in Dade County, in contrast to 1970 when 46 percent of all Cuban Americans lived in Florida, while less than 24 percent lived in Miami-Dade (Boswell 1994:11). Cubans are the most highly concentrated of Hispanic groups in the United States (Biafora and Longino 1990). Explanations for this phenomenon include the

comparable climate, proximity to Cuba and socioeconomic benefits of the ethnic enclave. Cuban elders have been even less geographically dispersed, concentrating mostly in Dade County, Florida (Queralt 1983:54). Biafora and Longino propose that "geographic concentration of Hispanics is attractive to older migrants because it facilitates a comfortable and familiar life style." (1990: S213). Forty-nine percent (thirty-nine persons) of those interviewed at the center lived in the area immediate to the senior center. Another thirty persons (38 percent) lived in the city of Miami, including Little Havana (four) and Coral Gables (twelve). Seven persons lived further west in Westchester and another three lived in neighborhoods north, south and east of the center. Length of time in current residence was fourteen years (i.e., since the mid-1980s), indicating some residential stability. Roughly half lived in houses and another half live in apartments. More than half owned the structures they lived in (53 percent), and the rest rented (38 percent) or had other living arrangements.

8. Over 50 percent of the area known as Westchester is Cuban, while Little Havana is now less than 30 percent Cuban.

9. Arias (1998) analyzed Census data from 1970, 1980 and 1990 and found that "Of all age groups within the Cuban population, individuals 65 and older experience the most pronounced changes in living arrangements. In 1970, 51 percent of the Cuban elderly population lived in complex family-households, while only 31 percent did so in 1990. No other age group experienced such a change. A good amount of extended living was replaced by single and simple family living. In 1990 elderly Cubans were twice as likely to live in single households as they were in 1970" (Arias 1998:31).

Proportionally fewer Cuban elders lived in their children's households in 1990 and more were living with siblings than in 1970 (Arias 1998:32). Nonetheless, about 21.2 percent of Cuban American children in the United States had at least one grandparent living with them (Perez 1994).

10. One person lived with a grandchild. A few others lived with other relatives (three) and nonrelatives (three).

11. The prevalence of childlessness has varied greatly through time by birth cohorts and across cultures. The reasons for childlessness are often complex and diverse. Childlessness has been related to average age of marriage, marriage rates, historical events, economic opportunities and policies. Overall childlessness for older women and men in the United States is 15 percent according to the National Survey of Families and Households (Koropeckyj-Cox, Vaugn and Call 2007).

12. Holzberg notes that "life history allows us to gain access to the conceptual world of the individual" and is a valuable source in presenting "the insider's view of the past and reflect the underlying perceptions the story tellers have of themselves and their world" (1984:262). This can help shed light on a culture from the example of individual lives, exploring the juncture of aging with lived historical time (see Myerhoff 1978 for example).

13. There is no consensus as to whether reminiscence or life review is a normative process in later life. Some believe it is beneficial in terms of adaptation, resolution, coping with loss, preservation of self-identity and continuity of the past and present (Sellers and Stork 1997). In fact, life reviews are often used in the context of mental health therapy. Some health care professionals hold that the life review is a natural part of later life and meets a need at this time of the life cycle. Others hold that the life review is a middle-age phenomena and less relevant beyond a certain age (Coleman 1986).

14. The short version of the Geriatric Depression Scale (GDS) in Spanish was administered as part of the survey (Sheikh and Yessavage 1986). A score of five or more is generally suggestive of depression.

15. There is some evidence of low rates of emotional well-being and high rates of depression among Cuban Americans in South Florida. A needs assessment conducted in Miami-Dade County, Florida, (Rothman, Dunlop and Condon 1994) found that relative to other ethnic groups, older Cubans self-report a lower degree of life satisfaction and emotional health. These findings are corroborated by earlier work of clinical family psychologists who practiced in south Florida and outlined several factors affecting the mental health of Cuban elders, including the lack of English language skills, knowledge of "American culture," social isolation and loneliness (Szapocznik, Faletti and Sopetta 1979; Hernandez 1992). However, with the exceptions of several brief articles by Bastida (1984; 1987; 1988), the mental health issues and the context of psychological distress among Cuban elders in the United States has gone unexplored.

16. While the reliability and validity of the Geriatric Depression Scale (GDS) was demonstrated for "community-dwelling" elders, one study suggested it may underestimate severe depression in older Hispanics (Ossip-Klein, Rothenberg and Andresen 1997:189–190). Others have found that the GDS may be of limited usefulness in screening for depression among Mexican American elders since there may be basic differences in how these elders present symptoms (Espino et al. 1996).

17. More recent studies have explored the prevalence of psychiatric disorders and mental health service use compared across Latino subgroups (Losada et al. 2006; Alegría et al. 2007a; Alegría et al. 2007b). While there are differences in both the lifetime and twelve-month prevalence of psychiatric disorders when examined by Latino subgroups (Puerto Ricans, Cubans, Mexicans and "other") or by nativity (U.S. born, those arriving as children and those arriving after age six), these differences are not statistically significant (Alegría et al. 2007c). However, contextual factors, such as family status and social status, were related to the risk of disorders in all Latino groups (Ibid.).

18. This, however, is not dramatically higher than the general U.S. population. The prevalence of anxiety symptoms among community dwelling elders is around 20 percent (Sheikh 1992:426). The use of benzodiazepines (a class of sedative-hypnotics) used in the treatment of anxiety and insomnia ranges from 5 to 15 percent according to surveys (Atkinson, Ganzini and Bernstein 1992:529). A recent study using data from the National Health and Nutrition Examination Survey (NHANES) found that the overall prevalence of prescription psychotropic medication use in the past month in the U.S. population was 11.1 percent in 1999–2002, up from 6.1 percent in 1988–1994. This was due largely to a three-fold increase to 8.1 percent in antidepressant drug use during the same time period. For the population aged sixty and over, the prevalence of prescription psychotropic drug use rose significantly from 10.6 percent to 14.9 percent. There was no significant increase among Mexican Americans of all ages, who reported a 4.5 percent and 4.6 percent use for each time period, respectively; the reported use of antidepressants, though relatively low, did rise significantly from 1.7 percent to 3.1 percent. Sedatives, anxiolytics and hypnotics remained low at 3.8 percent for the overall population, 6.7 percent for the sixty and over population and 1.7 percent for Mexican Americans in 1999–2002.

19. The continued imprisonments of dissidents have been documented by Amnesty International, Human Rights Watch and others (see Human Rights Watch 2008). While there is a general lack of public tolerance for moderate or any other political views other than conservative ones with regard to Cuba and U.S. politics, the ideology of exile is more than political.

20. Studies on Cuban elders have emphasized more specifically the prevalence of dementia and its impact on family caregivers compared to non-Hispanic whites and blacks

(see Henderson this volume Web book). Demirovic et al. (2003) found that Cuban ethnicity was independently associated with the prevalence of Alzheimer's disease, with prevalence rates for both Cuban women and men higher than non-Hispanic whites, but lower than African Americans. Stress experienced by Cuban wives, in particular, as caregivers was found to negatively impact family functioning (in comparison to non-Hispanic and husband caregivers); this has been attributed to the central role of women in the family (Mitrani et al. 2006). Cuban Alzheimer's patients were more likely to be living with their daughters, and daughters were more depressed than non-Hispanic white counterparts (Mintzer et al. 1992). Cuban American husband and daughter caregivers in a family therapy and technology-based intervention were found to show greater improvements in depression (Eisdorfer et al. 2003).

CHAPTER 23

Ethnic and Cross-Cultural Perspectives on Custodial Grandparenting

Bert Hayslip Jr.

DIVERSITY AMONG GRANDPARENT CAREGIVERS: A DEFINING CHARACTERISTIC

It is well documented that the numbers of grandparents drawn into the role of parents to their grandchildren has risen alarmingly in the past decade (Simmons and Dye 2003), and that this new form of caregiving, termed *custodial grandparenting* (Shore and Hayslip 1994) has been seen across all ethnic and socioeconomic boundaries (Goodman and Silverstein 2002; Hayslip and Kaminiski 2005, 2006).

In 2000, 5.8 million grandparents resided with their grandchildren, and of these, 2.4 million were providing care for such grandchildren. Thirty-nine percent of such persons had cared for a grandchild for five years or more (Simmons and Dye 2003). These numbers, which are noticeably higher than those in 1980, suggest that the phenomenon of grandparent caregiving is of societal importance: *millions* of grandchildren's and grandparents' lives are affected by the necessity to raise an adult child's child (see Hayslip and Kaminski 2005). Consequently, increasing social and health-related services, as well as their accessibility for such persons, is now viewed as an important challenge in our country. Underscoring the concern for such families, the U.S. Senate's Special Committee on Aging recently met to address the barriers impeding access to needed social and health services, housing and education for grandparent caregivers (Smith, personal communication, July 26, 2007).

Indeed, that grandparent caregivers are both ethnically and culturally diverse is perhaps what is *most notable* about them (Hicks-Patrick and Hayslip 2006). In this respect, the most recent (2000) U.S. Census data found that the incidence of grandparents living with their grandchildren varied greatly by race/ethnicity, with whites considerably less likely to do so (2 percent) than

Asians (6 percent), American Indians and Alaska Natives (8 percent), African Americans (8 percent), Hispanics (8 percent) and Pacific Islanders (10 percent). Of such persons, Asians (20 percent) were least likely to be solely responsible for their grandchildren, relative to whites (41 percent), Hispanics (35 percent), African Americans (52 percent), American Indians and Alaska Natives (56 percent) and Pacific Islanders (39 percent).

While substantial research has been conducted dealing with the incidence of custodial grandparenting, as well as exploring the role of causal factors (e.g., divorce, drug use, incarceration, abuse) accelerating this form of caregiving in middle and later life, fewer studies address the attitudes and needs of the various ethnic and cultural communities that are embedded within the grandparent's social context. Most efforts to this end have been oriented to the African American community (Ruiz 2004; Minkler and Fuller-Thomson 2005; Ross and Day 2006), especially that segment directly affected by the drug epidemic of the 1980s and 1990s and the continuing HIV/AIDS epidemic (Burton 1992; Joslin 2002; Winston, 2006; Park and Greenberg 2007). Less attention has been paid to the Hispanic community, and until recently other ethnicities have been largely overlooked (see, however, Burnette 1998; Goodman and Silverstein 2002).

WHY IS DIVERSITY IMPORTANT IN UNDERSTANDING GRANDPARENT CAREGIVERS?

Culture, as defined by a shared history, a common language, unique customs, traditions, dress or food preferences can influence grandparent caregivers in many ways (Yancura and Yee 2007; Sokolovsky Introduction, Part IV). Examples include expectations about the role of grandparents, having access to support from others and values regarding whether to ask for help at all. In a small, multiethnic study of grandparent caregivers in Hawaii, Yancura and Yee saw that in this context ethnic cultures were not sufficient in themselves to prevent negative impacts on the children they cared for. They found that custodial grandchildren were more likely to have greater physical, school-related and mental health difficulties than children not raised by their grandparents (Yancura and Yee 2007). Moreover, grandparent caregivers were less likely to seek help for themselves than for their grandchildren, making it less likely that they could deal with the problems their grandchildren were experiencing. Some of these difficulties may have preceded or followed from a change in the family structure (see also Hayslip and Shore 2000). Such factors suggest that cultural values can influence grandparent caregivers in such a way as to undermine the physical and mental health of both the grandchild and grandparent.

More generally, it is often the case that studies that investigate varying ethnic groups are undertaken to identify the needs of such persons, and not to determine the effect that cultural specificity has upon their attitudes toward raising their grandchildren (Fuller-Thomson, Minkler and Driver 1997; Strom, Buki and Strom 1997; Strom et al. 1997). In this respect, understanding cultural differences is not only important in itself, but such knowledge allows us to better comprehend the relativistic context framing the experience of raising one's grandchildren. As individuals and service providers, we ask different questions, behave differently and perhaps are more compassionate and empathic when we understand the role that culture plays in making the many choices one must make when raising a grandchild. We can communicate to the public more effectively about grandfamilies' needs, be more persuasive in changing others' attitudes and perceptions about grandparent caregivers and communicate more effectively with persons whose backgrounds are different than our own regarding this growing form of caregiving. Moreover, an appreciation of the cultural influences on custodial grandparenting helps us perceive this role in terms of its personal, social and familial antecedents. Ethnic traditions also shape role expectations and influence both limitations and opportunities for formal and informal support and predispositions to seeking help from others when necessary. Thus, some grandparent caregivers, whose cultural traditions help to define the caregiving experience by virtue of their exposure to insensitive or unskilled service providers, or as influenced by their negative feelings about seeking help from "outsiders," may be less likely to ask for assistance for themselves or their grandchildren. Thus, service providers who are sensitive to cultural traditions may not only be more effective in facilitating such grandparent caregivers' access to services, but also more sensitive in dealing with grandparent caregivers. Such interactions can go a long way toward helping grandparent caregivers feel that they are not alone in facing the challenges of raising a grandchild.

Fry (1995) points out that extending our knowledge about culture and grandparenting is valuable in many respects: it broadens the empirical base upon which theory rests, it promotes a more realistic view of human experience, and it gives us greater insight into our own social institutions (see also Ikels 1998). In these respects, custodial grandparenting research has to this point been largely atheoretical (see Hayslip and Hicks-Patrick 2003), and our knowledge of what adjustments grandparents make when they volunteer to raise their grandchildren is largely, and unfortunately, colored by a literature that has often emphasized the negative antecedents and consequences of raising a grandchild (see Hayslip and Kaminski 2005). Indeed, a recent review of the literature focuses upon the negative impact of custodial grandparenting on one's physical and mental health, relationships with others and role stress. The benefits to such persons and their grandchildren are scarcely, if not at all, mentioned (see especially Park and Greenberg 2007).

As noted previously, our attention to not only variation across cultures in custodial grandparenting, but also to that within cultures, deepens our knowledge about variations in grandparental caregiving within our own society. While cross-cultural research in this area is scarce, our understanding of the commonalities and differences between the experiences of European heritage grandparent caregivers and other grandparents raising their grandchildren has been enhanced by comparisons with African Americans (Pruchno 1999; Caputo

2000) and Hispanic grandparents (Burnette 1998; Cox, Brooks and Valcarcel 2000), as well as with both Latino and African American grandparent caregivers (Goodman and Silverstein 2002). Generally speaking, these comparisons have made us more aware of the importance of ethnic and cultural differences, in the reasons giving rise to grandparent caregiving, as well as broadening our understanding of the nature of different caregiving living arrangements, access to social services and health difficulties faced by grandparents raising their grandchildren.[1]

Ikels (1998) has pointed out that grandparenthood can be understood in terms of its primacy as a kinship relationship; that is, one becomes a grandparent through the birth of one's grandchildren. However, in the context of the distinction between bilateral (defined jointly by paternal and maternal links) and unilineal decent (defined by either paternal or maternal lines, but not both), we might characterize cross-cultural, or ethnic variations in custodial grandparenting in terms of whether one's cultural or ethnic background uniquely defines one's role as a middle-aged or older grandparent who is raising a grandchild. Key factors include: whether this role is a valued one; if it is distinct from the role of grandparent per se; and what aspects of the role influence the allocation of resources allocated to meeting the needs of such persons. Thus, studying the cultural context in which custodial grandparenting occurs can enhance our understanding of what is likely a nonnormative (idiosyncratic) life transition for most middle-aged and older adults (Baltes 1987). For example, having a child and/or caring for children in one's fifties or sixties is a developmental task that most adults assume is unique to young adulthood. Thus, many grandparents, who do not expect to be actively raising their grandchildren and caring for them on a daily basis, are taken aback physically and emotionally when confronted with the necessity of raising a child in midlife and beyond.

An appreciation for the role of such influences is brought into sharper focus in recognizing that whether one coparents a grandchild with the grandchild's parents and/or another adult child covaries with ethnicity. In this regard, Hispanic and African American grandparent caregivers are more likely to be solely responsible for a grandchild than are Euro-heritage grandparents. Within these two ethnic communities, this pattern is consistent with a broader construction of the "family" as an ongoing entity in the face of crisis and the greater expectation of intergenerational assistance (Pebley and Rudkin 1999; Caputo 2000; Cox, Brooks and Valcarcel 2000). Understandably in this context, rates of depression and distress vary between ethnic subgroups of grandparent caregivers as a function of whether they coparented or by themselves care for their grandchildren (Goodman and Silverstein, 2002; Mills, Gomez-Smith and DeLeon 2005), wherein depression is more common among those raising grandchildren by themselves. Significantly, in comparing Euro-heritage and African American families, there appear to be differences in the nature of those factors bringing about the necessity to raise one's grandchildren, for example, parental dysfunction (more common among Caucasians), unemployment, teenage pregnancy (each more common among African Americans), which may be in varying degrees, stigmatizing, stressful in themselves and unpredictable (Goodman and Silverstein 2006).

Cultural and subcultural variations may also impact the functions that accompany the grandparent role (see Thomas 1999). This can include viewing grandparents as mentors for younger parents, as transmitters of cultural values and heritage, as persons who are agents of socialization for and influence over their grandchildren or as persons who can simply enjoy their grandchildren but not be responsible for their raising (see Kopera-Frye and Wiscott 2000; Thomas, Sperry and Yarbrough 2000; Ruiz 2004). It is for this reason that over and above factors precipitating custodial grandparenthood, the individual attributes related to such caregivers— gender, health and socioeconomic status, grandchild characteristics, or access to services— interact with cultural forces to enable us to more completely understand not only cultural differences, but also variability within ethnic communities (Thomas, Sperry and Yarbrough 2000; Hayslip and Kaminski 2005; Minkler and Fuller-Thomson 2005). Indeed, while it is the cultural context that determines potential conflicts with the demands of grandparent caregiving, how such roles are defined and coped with is still influenced by the individual person's characteristics and life experiences.

EXPLAINING THE ROLE OF CULTURE IN INFLUENCING KINKEEPING

Especially relevant to custodial grandparenting is the issue of *how* such persons are influenced by cultural norms and expectations governing the extent to which one is expected to fulfill a parental role after one's own children are grown. For example, in American culture, the "empty nest" constitutes a crisis for some middle-aged persons, for whom grandparenthood may alleviate feelings of parental worthlessness (Crowley, Hayslip and Hobdy 2003). Indeed, recent discussions of the empty nest are void of references to the impact of culture (see Magai and Halpern 2001; Kennedy 2006). One might predict, however, that the strength of intergenerational connections and/or valuing one's continuing bond with adult children might mitigate the otherwise negative impact of the empty nest transition for persons varying by ethnicity.

Thomas has highlighted this conflict in role demands in discussing the "double bind" in which many grandparents find themselves (1990). They are expected to be available to help when necessary in the care of grandchildren, but are nevertheless expected to keep their opinions about how the children should be raised to themselves. Such feelings may be brought into sharp contrast from grandparents who are now raising their grandchildren. On the other hand, for traditional grandparents (those grandparents who are not raising their grandchildren on a full-time basis) or for those custodial grandparents who coreside with their grandchildren, conflicts over child rearing may emerge in light of the latter's desire to be involved in the everyday decisions about child care and discipline (Chase-Lansdale et al. 1999). In this context, Lau and

Kinoshita have pointed out that ethnic minority elders, especially those not born in the United States, who are not acculturated and who feel an obligation to adhere to role expectations and traditional values are likely to experience conflict and stress in dealing with children and grandchildren who have become acculturated and have internalized Western culture values (2006; Yee this section Web book). This is especially the case if they have not learned English and their children/grandchildren have done so or have forgotten their native language. This may indeed impact some grandparent caregivers in raising their grandchildren, undermining social support networks and lessening the chance of seeking help from others, based upon the shame of a perceived loss of authority or a loss of the ability to carry out culturally prescribed role expectations, that is, that grandparents should continue to support their children and grandchildren "no matter what."

In Hispanic and African American cultures, *familism* is a primary influence on: (1) how persons in the family define their relationships to one another; (2) the independence of roles within the family system; as well as (3) impacting both household composition and living arrangements and role boundaries associated with parenthood and grandparenthood (Ikels 1998; Thomas, Sperry and Yarbrough 2000). Each of these constructs, the empty nest and familism, consequently may represent manifestations of cultural norms that impact persons' expectations of their roles as not only traditional grandparents, but also as grandparent caregivers. Depending upon whether persons view the empty nest as a loss or see it as an opportunity to enrich a newly defined relationship with an adult child could likely influence their reaction to caring for that adult child's own child. Likewise, whether one adopts a view that emphasizes the role of the family (familism) influences whether grandparental caregiving is seen as an impediment to one's life goals, such as retirement, or as an opportunity to reinforce an already positive connection with an adult child in the context of the notion that "family comes first."

CULTURE AND GRANDFAMILIES: RECENT FINDINGS

Despite the in-depth attention given the grandparenting role in adulthood (Szinovacz 1998; Kivnick and Sinclair 2007), and in spite of the seminal research dealing with subcultural ethnic variations in the experience of grandparents raising their grandchildren, little if any *cross-cultural comparative* work has been conducted with such grandparents (see e.g., Minkler, Roe and Price 1992; Minkler and Roe 1993). As noted before, such work, at the minimum, can better inform us regarding our own culture's influence on grandparent caregivers and provide a broader basis for theory construction and intervention (see Burton 1992; Fry 1995; Ikels 1998). In this respect, Cole (2005) highlights the distinction between culture as *an independent variable,* reflected in research and practice exploring cultural differences and culture as *a medium,* wherein research and practice informs us about the processes by which culture influences persons and their individual differences. A notable exception in this respect is work of Musil and her colleagues who compared U.S.-born and Uganda grandmothers raising their grandchildren. They found the latter to be in poorer health and to report more depression, yet also that the caregiving demands and concerns over the well-being of grandchildren were similar across cultures (Musil et al. 2003).

While the processes giving rise to cross-cultural differences in custodial grandparenting have yet to be systematically investigated among custodial grandparents, likely candidates include *the degree of acculturation*, as reflected in host English language acquisition, contact with new or familiar cultural groups, and the formation and/or loss of relationships with others (Strom, Buki and Strom 1997; Safdar, Lay and Strothers 2003). Other important processes bear on the *intergenerational transmission of values* (Cox 2005) or upon *flexibility in family system boundaries*, influencing how rigid or permeable roles are defined within the family system. This last factor has a strong impact on the shift from the traditional grandparent role to that of custodial grandparenting that so many families are experiencing (see Combrinck-Graham 1990; Franks 2007).

Despite a dearth of cross-cultural research exploring not only cultural differences and cultural processes as they bear on custodial grandparenting, there are indications of recent interest in the experiences of grandparent caregivers in other cultures. One example is Poindexter's qualitative study of the stresses faced by grandmothers in Uganda caring for AIDS-orphaned children (2003). This project stresses such persons' resilience, social support and sense of spirituality in the face of the stigma attached to AIDS, poverty, death and the physical demands of raising a grandchild whose parent has died from HIV disease. More recently, Fuller-Thomson (2006) studied Canadian Indian grandparent caregivers among First Nations and Aboriginal communities and found them to be disadvantaged in many respects compared to other grandparent caregivers who were not of First Nations descent: they had fewer resources and provided the most care. The similarly negative impact of providing more care to grandchildren has also been observed among Kenyan grandmother caregivers by Oburu and Palmerus (2006).

Focusing upon differences between subgroups of grandparents within North American culture, Goodman and Silverstein (2006) found among Latina grandmother caregivers some evidence for higher well-being among Spanish-preferred versus English-preferred persons, and higher well-being among coparenting (where grandparent and parent coreside in raising the grandchild) versus skipped-generation households (where the adult child is absent, leaving the grandchild and grandparent behind). This again is consistent with the salience of family as a source of support to minority grandparent caregivers, buffering the otherwise negative impact of grandparental caregiving. In this light, it is not surprising that Watson, Randolph and Lyons (2006) and Ruiz (2004) have stressed the proactive, teaching, and mentoring role that African American grandmother caregivers play in the lives of their grandchildren. Both Ruiz (2004) and Crowther et al. (2006) have emphasized the role of spirituality in permitting African American grandmothers to cope with the demands of caregiving, while others have underscored the role of caregiver competence as a mediator of role captivity (feeling bound or constrained by the grandparent caregiver role) among such persons (Rodriguez and Crowther 2006). In this regard, Kohn and Smith (2006) found that while black grandmothers, relative to white grandmother caregivers, were less satisfied with school-related and medical services, they felt less stigmatized and more in tune with age peers.[2] The authors attributed this in large part due to the kinkeeping traditions in the African American family.

In the previously mentioned Hawaiian study of grandparent caregivers, Yancura and Lee (2007) examined grandparents' influence on their grandchildren's physical and psychosocial health in a multicultural (Caucasian, Native Hawaiian, Asian) sample. This study, while based upon a small sample of grandparent caregivers, underscores a possible relationship between kinkeeping and grandchildren's more impaired mental and physical health, though it could be that such impairments in grandchildren's functioning preceded, rather than followed the assumption of care by their grandparents (see Hayslip, Shore, Henderson and Lambert 1998).

In another study among an ethnically diverse sample of grandmother caregivers (Euro-heritage, Latino, African American), it was found that persons who varied in terms of formal access to the formal child welfare social service system experienced varying degrees of caregiver burden associated with both needs for and use of such services (Goodman, Potts and Pasztor 2006). Interestingly, among child welfare recipients, higher levels of need were linked to greater burden, while among nonrecipient caregivers, more informal support was linked to less burden. This suggests that in part, culture and ethnicity interact with service use to influence caregiver burden among grandmothers raising their grandchildren. These findings may suggest that available services were not effective, or that grandparents' needs exceeded the ability of such services to meet them.

In this light, Toledo et al. (2000) reported on a cross-cultural study of both traditional and custodial United States and native-born Mexican grandparents, utilizing self-report measures of role satisfaction, personal well-being, role meaning, social support, and quality of relationships with their grandchildren. It was found that both cultural differences (United States versus Mexico) and grandparent-type variations (traditional versus custodial) existed. While Mexican grandparents, more so than those in the United States, invested more meaning into these roles, they were more depressed, experienced less satisfying relationships with their grandchildren, and reported more financial/parental stress and less role satisfaction. This suggests that such grandparents' commitment to their roles of caregivers and the transcendent derivation of positive meaning about their roles as grandparents may have mitigated the stresses they experienced in raising them:

wherein individuals' needs are subjugated to those of the family unit. Indeed, the family in reality functions in an extended manner. As individuals' egos, privacy, and power are viewed as secondary to the integrity of the family, this may permit grandparents to retain meaning in their role as family caretakers, enabling them to tolerate disagreements with both children and grandchildren, to sustain themselves in the face of having to make ends meet financially, and to permit them to deal with the demands of raising their grandchildren. (Toledo et al. 2000, pp. 119–120)

The apparent contradiction between greater grandparental role meaning and more depression among the Mexican grandparent sample can be understood in light of the self-sacrifice and greater sense of being, defined by the caregiver role (role captivity) such persons may experience in raising their grandchildren. This interpretation would be consistent with several studies discussed by Sokolovsky (this volume Part IV), suggesting that among Hispanics and Mexican Americans, despite higher levels of family interaction, such persons were more likely to report more emotional distress. Collectively, these findings may suggest that familism, assumed to serve a protective function in making support from others more likely and thereby enhancing role satisfaction among Hispanic grandparent caregivers, comes at a personal cost of self-sacrifice and poorer mental health. This underscores the importance of separating the private versus public (role-related) dimensions of custodial grandparenting.

A subsequent qualitative analysis of these data supported the hypothesis that in Mexico, the familistic salience of the family as a culturally recognized entity would permit persons to persist in raising their grandchildren and/or value the role of grandparent despite poorer relative health, poverty, or unemployment (Hayslip et al. 2006). In essence, such individuals' needs are redefined in terms of those of the family. These dynamics may allow them to derive more personal meaning from being a grandparent caregiver. In this light, in Mexico, grandparents assume a more dominant role in the family hierarchy, leading to greater expectation of social support and a more even distribution of caregiving responsibilities among men and women, all of which would be in contrast to grandparents in the United States.

This qualitative data suggested that traditional U.S.-born grandparents emphasized the enjoyment and value of grandparental role autonomy, desired more contact with grandchildren, and yet valued the maturation of such relationships over time. In contrast, Mexican-born traditional grandparents saw their roles as extensions of earlier parenting, and viewed their grandchildren in such terms. While custodial U.S.-born grandparents emphasized the negative impact of caregiving on them, regretted having to assume an authoritative parental role, and were otherwise burdened by caregiving, Mexican-born custodial grandparents not only stressed that their lives had not changed, and that they welcomed the opportunity to parent again, but also saw their new roles as extensions of their relationships with their own adult children. For example, when queried about what was best about being a traditional grandparent, a U.S.-born grandparent stated, "It's great—I can enjoy them and send them home." Another stated that "I'm glad I'm not the primary caregiver." When asked about their new roles as caregivers, those raising grandchildren in the

United States mentioned such things as: "I have no privacy and nothing in common with my friends"; "Disciplining them takes out all the enjoyment"; and "I provide care, but I'm not appreciated." In contrast, Mexican-born traditional grandparents stressed that "My grandchildren are an extension of my children" and "I get to relive my experiences as a mother." These findings highlight differences in perceptions of the centrality of family to the lives of both traditional and custodial grandparents. U.S.-born grandparents, while they emphasized familial structure in their roles, regretted the loss of such structure when they raised their grandchildren.

In contrast, for Mexican-born grandparents, the salience of family provided continuity in their lives. Consequently, they valued and benefited from the structure that their families had provided them regardless of their custodial status. Such qualitative data further elucidate the influence of factors permitting Mexican grandparents who are raising their grandchildren to persist in deriving meaning from their roles as grandparents despite living in poverty, having less social support and experiencing less self-esteem and more depression relative to their counterparts in the United States.

HOW IMPORTANT IS CULTURE IN UNDERSTANDING GRANDPARENT CAREGIVERS?

Regardless of culture, in North America the grandparent caregiving role is likely not to be one that is anticipated and one that is assumed by necessity rather than choice (Cox 2005). This underscores the importance of the universality of the nature of the custodial role: as one that is often imposed upon grandparents, versus attending to the meaning that one assigns to such a role, which does appear to vary by (sub)culture. This distinction is consistent with a cognitive-behavioral understanding of caregiving, which distinguishes between the nature of the event with which one must cope and one's appraisal of that event (Pearlin, Mullan, Semple and Skaff 1990).

Cultural and subcultural diversity is clearly one of the many parameters differentiating grandparent caregivers. Indeed, it is important to recognize that some grandparent caregivers' (e.g., African Americans) experiences are influenced by a history of discrimination and oppression, while those of others are not (Cox 2005). Likewise, not all grandparent caregivers embrace their ethnicity, and indeed do vary in terms of whether they have completely assimilated the values of the dominant culture, or whether they have experienced conflicts with others who do not share their cultural heritage, values, beliefs, and customs (Cox 2005).[3] In this context then, it is important to point out that understanding cultural diversity enables us to learn *more* about those *individual* grandparents who have taken on the role of raising their grandchildren in middle or later life by placing them in the context of race, ethnicity and culture as forces influencing the experience of grandparent caregiving. Yet, given the dual emphasis here on culture and ethnicity in concert with individual differences among grandparent caregivers, it is clear that we have a great deal more to learn in the exploration and understanding of the complex relationship between culture and the experience of grandparent caregiving (Hayslip and Kaminski 2005; Hicks-Patrick and Hayslip 2006).

NOTES

This chapter is based upon a paper entitled *Cross Cultural Differences in Custodial Grandparenting*, presented at the Annual Family Life Electronic Seminar on Grandparents Raising Grandchildren. It can be accessed at: http://hec.osu.edu/eseminars/grg/panelist_papers/Hayslip_paper.pdf(January–February 2005).

1. While not specifically targeting grandparent caregivers, in-depth portrayals of grandparents of a variety of ethnicities can be found in Falk and Falk (2002; re: Jews, Amish, Mormons, Chinese, African Americans, Hispanics); Hunter and Taylor (1998; re: African Americans); Williams and Torrez (1998; re: Hispanics); Kamo (1998; re:Asians); and both Schweitzer (1999) and Weibel-Orlando (this volume Web book; re: American Indians).

2. This is relevant to a survey of black grandmother caregivers' attitudes toward social assistance (TANF—Temporary Assistance for Needy Families—a federally funded program to promote economic self-sufficiency), finding that despite inadequate financial support, grandmothers' commitment to their families and to their grandchildren in particular, as well as a desire to remain financially independent, characterized them (Henderson and Cook 2006),

3. It should also be noted that at present, we know virtually nothing about how culture and gender interact to influence the experience of raising a grandchild (see Hicks-Patrick and Hayslip 2006).

CHAPTER 24

African Americans Growing Older in Chicago: Living in a Time and Place of Change

Madelyn Iris

Joseph Ragsdell Sr., 83, an appliance repairman who worked two full-time jobs much of his life so he could support his children as well as the nieces and nephews he raised for a sister died Sunday. [He] taught Sunday School for more than 40 years. Mr. Ragsdell cared for his parents when they were alive and when a sister died, raised her 9 children along with his own 9, said a daughter. He would walk 3 or 4 miles to work so he could take his bus fare and buy his children candy.

Joseph Ragsdell's[1] obituary appeared in the *Chicago Tribune*, and caught my eye, both for its length, and for the story it told. The location of his church indicated that Mr. Ragsdale lived in the heart of an African American community on Chicago's south side, a still heavily segregated area of the city. Though a summary only, Mr. Ragsdell's obituary hinted at a life rich with relationships, filled with contribution and indicative of the sustaining role African American elders have played in the evolving life of the family. I did not know him, but his life exemplifies the values and characteristics of a lifestyle repeatedly encountered in life stories of the older adults who participated in my study of aging in Chicago.

BACKGROUND

In a city like Chicago, which has undergone profound demographic and economic shifts over the past decades, the older adult population represents an historical and cultural artifact of middle- and working-class life, both black and white. Although older adults represented less than 10 percent of the U.S. population only twenty to thirty years ago, conservative estimates predict that by 2050 more than 20 percent will be over age sixty-five. In urban centers, the greatest growth will likely be among African American and Spanish-speaking elders. While impressive, these numbers mask the extreme diversity found within the older population, and obscure the rich complexity of life and experience elders embody. As parents and grandparents, American elders have helped shape the values and lifestyles of today's middle- and working-class families, and in many instances still make direct and important contributions to the maintenance and functioning of their families as well as their communities.

THE AGING IN CHICAGO PROJECT

In 1990, the Chicago Community Trust, a major philanthropy, initiated a multidisciplinary project in order to generate new information about the status and needs of older adults in Chicago. The aim was to examine its funding priorities for older adult programs, shifting from a model that viewed older people as always in need to one that also took into account the contributions they make to their families and communities. Called the "Aging in Chicago Project," this three-pronged approach to understanding urban life of elders included a demographic study, a policy analysis and an ethnographic component.[2]

This last-mentioned component, "The Qualitative Study of Aging in Chicago," was a three-year, in-depth study of older adults living in five distinct communities in the greater Chicago area (Iris and Berman 1995).[3] As project director, I worked with a team of interviewers, each assigned to one community area. Using the Chicago Community Fact Book (1984) as a guide, along with other census and demographic data, we chose five distinct community areas in order to represent different ethnic and cultural groups living in Chicago. We looked for community areas with high concentrations of Hispanics; African Americans; Koreans; white Americans, including immigrants from Eastern Europe; and white middle- or working-class Americans. We also cross-matched the communities for income levels and crime statistics, and took into account their unique histories. Other selection criteria included diversity in access to resources such as grocery and retail stores, health care and other amenities; proportion of older people living in the community (categorized into high and low); and diversity in housing stock (i.e., single-family homes, apartments, condominiums and senior housing buildings). In the end, we selected one community on the southwest side of Chicago, one on the northwest side, one on the near west side, and one on the south side of the city. The fifth community area was actually a composite of several contiguous suburban communities lying to the north of the city itself.

In our initial planning, we identified five overarching themes to pursue during the interviews, as we explored our participants' life histories, social and family networks, health histories and beliefs about health and aging and their unique philosophies about aging. We probed for the effects of change over time in each of these domains, especially on the reciprocal relationships linking older adults to their communities. All interviews were tape-recorded and transcribed verbatim.[4]

In all, we collected 256 interviews from 50 participants, who ranged from fifty-five to ninety-one years of age: 56 percent were non-Hispanic white, 26 percent were African American, 10 percent were Latino (including individuals from Puerto Rico, Cuba, and Mexico), and 8 percent were Korean. These percentages correspond closely to the overall racial and ethnic distribution of older adults in Chicago at the time of the study, with Koreans representing the larger group of Asian Americans. Overall, 54 percent of the participants were married, 30 percent were widowed, and 16 percent were either divorced, separated or had never married.

THE EVERGREEN RESIDENTS

In this chapter, I focus on the lives of ten older African American men and women living in one community area of Chicago, Evergreen, and the ways in which various forces influenced their lives and as well as their values, lifestyles, and attitudes about growing older. These ten older African Americans ranged in age from fifty-five to eighty-seven; four were men and six were women. Five were married, three were widowed, and one man and one woman were separated. The average length of residence in Evergreen was 31.6 years, with a range of 15 to 40 years. Seven of the ten participants owned their own homes. Most could be described as middle or lower-middle class, by income, lifestyle and self-description. Their occupations were typical of middle- and working-class African Americans; some were retirees from governmental or school system positions, one had worked for the Chicago Public Library, and several others had held a variety of low or unskilled positions (see Patillo-McCoy 1999). One woman had never been employed, another participant who was just fifty-five years old had been unemployed for over twenty years due to various disabilities and one man was a self-ordained minister at a local store-front church, although he also worked as a chore housekeeper for a social service agency on a part-time basis. Participants' incomes came largely from social security and pensions, rental income and savings. Though none were affluent, none lived below the poverty line. Their educations ranged from third grade through high school, but none had attended college.

EVERGREEN: A COMMUNITY TRANSFORMED

The stories told by our participants recounted the history and evolution of the Evergreen community itself, framed within the context of their own personal life histories and experiences. The ties between these life experiences and the contextual spaces in which these life experiences played out are seen as deep and full of meaning. As Taylor comments, "Part of the image of self is found within the context of identification with and an attachment to the places people live" (2001:5; also see Stafford Part V). Low and Altman note that this context includes social relationships as well as physical spaces (1992). Thus, to understand the aging experience in an urban context, particularly in Evergreen, it is necessary to understand the historical, cultural, political and economic factors that have shaped both the physical as well as the social reality of the community (see Gusmano Part V).

In the remainder of this chapter, I focus on the stories of our ten African American participants who lived in Evergreen on Chicago's south side. Evergreen is located about seven to ten miles south of Chicago's downtown area and was originally settled by German and Irish workers. The economic downturn in Evergreen began in the 1940s, with a drop in real estate prices. Between 1950 and 1970, the African American population in the area rose from just 11 percent to 97 percent, as realtors engaged in "block-busting" and racial scare tactics to dislodge whites. By 1990, when this study began, only 600 residents out of almost 50,000 were of a race *other than* African American. These figures remained virtually unchanged a decade later when over 98 percent of residents were African American. Adults sixty-five and older were a small percentage of this population, just under 12 percent; although another 6.7 percent were between the ages of fifty-five and sixty-four. In addition, poverty levels increased over the next few decades, so that in 1990 median household income in Evergreen was just $17,480. By 2000, the median income had climbed to $19,348, but over 76 percent of households still reported incomes of less than $35,000 (Chicago Fact Finder 2005).

The area also suffered a significant loss of housing stock with the construction of a major expressway that cut through densely populated areas of Chicago's south side. Between 1960 and 1990, Evergreen lost over 55,000 residents, and close to 2,000 housing units were vacant (Metropolitan Chicago Information Center, 2007; Grossman, Keating, and Reiff 2004). The 2000 U.S. Census shows this trend continuing, with further decreases of over 1,700 units (http://info.mcfol.org/www/datainfo/cpol.asp[5]). In addition, the opening of two nearby suburban shopping centers had a drastic impact on the community's commercial life, and retail shopping areas were significantly degraded.

At the time of our project, Evergreen was notorious for its high levels of poverty, crime and perceived domestic instability. We chose this community specifically to interview lower-income and poverty-level elderly. Instead, we encountered elder after elder who spoke of a life committed to work, family and service to community, articulating values more usually thought of as "middle class." Our own naïveté illustrated a general lack of knowledge as well as misconceptions about the heterogeneity of the African American community held by most white Americans.

Almost all our participants represented two-parent working families, who balanced work and family responsibilities long before such a lifestyle became popularized as a distinctly middle-class phenomenon. While some worked to meet basic needs, many whom we interviewed sought to enhance their incomes to achieve a higher standard of living, including home ownership, educational opportunities for their children and recreational outlets such as travel.

LIFE AND CLASS IN A CHANGING AFRICAN AMERICAN LANDSCAPE

A remarkable picture of how older adults continue to thrive within their communities emerged from our study, illuminating the many ways elders provide a "buffer" of stability for their children and grandchildren, their neighborhoods and larger community institutions, such as schools and churches. The stories told by our African American consultants were especially enlightening. Their narratives gave depth and reality to the statistics documenting demographic shifts. They also provided an in-depth understanding of how life developed and changed in one inner-city environment, in response to social and political conflicts, economic growth and community pressures.

By today's standards, while most of these African American men and women were not what one would call "middle class" in terms of occupations or incomes, their values, lifestyles and attitudes place them solidly within a middle-class zone of aspirations. For example, while Pattillo-McCoy describes the traditional economic and demographic characteristics of the middle class, she notes that the African American middle class more likely reflects behaviors as opposed to characteristics (1999). She writes, "typical middle-class behaviors are readily apparent in Groveland [a pseudonym for the community she studied]. People mow their lawns, go to church, marry, vote ... work, own property, and so on and so on" (p. 15).

This is an apt description of our participants in Evergreen as well, where being middle class is "what you do" rather than "what you are." Most owned their own homes, and over half had sent their children through college, although they themselves generally had only eight to twelve years of education. For example, Fred Frank was a seventy-two-year-old African American man who owned his own home in the Evergreen community, where he and his wife, Roseanne, had moved in 1957, when their children were very small. Originally from Mississippi, Mr. Frank came to Chicago immediately after discharge from the army, in 1945. He had accepted a position with the Pullman Company, as a porter on their trains. In addition, during times of layoffs, he worked numerous jobs in factories around the city. Although he had only eleven years of schooling, two of his three children had college degrees, and the third, a Chicago police officer, was working on completing his as well. Mr. Frank and his wife were active in their local church, as well as the "block club" that they helped run for many years. His was clearly a life of "doing."

Various studies, dating as far back as the 1940s, have documented the fact that, until recently, distinctions between middle- and working-class African Americans in inner-city settings were blurred: professionals, white collar semi-professionals and factory workers lived side by side, restricted to particular neighborhoods and occupations by overt and covert institutionalized racial discrimination (Drake and Cayton 1945; Wilson 1987; Patillo-McCoy 1999). The highly segregated south side of Chicago, renowned as the "Black Metropolis" (Drake and Cayton 1970), provided a vibrant, yet constricted, environment within which African American residents played out their daily lives. Although within this larger geographic area more local neighborhoods may have been differentiated by socioeconomic class, racially almost all residents were African American (Patillo-McCoy 1999; Street n.d.).

This is a pattern that still continues. Patillo's recent book *Black on the Block* (2007) provides a detailed look at explicit class conflicts and clashes amongst African American residents of a south-side community in Chicago. North Kenwood/Oakdale, located just north of the Hyde Park area, home of the University of Chicago, has been undergoing "gentrification" but for the most part remains racially segregated. This "mixed homogeneity" creates both disruption to daily life experiences, as well as differentiation of residents that threatens neighborhood and community solidarity. These disruptive and destabilizing effects of class heterogeneity were also reported in Patillo's earlier study of a Chicago community she calls "Groveland." One twenty-eight-year-old male gave a litany of change on his own block:

... six houses on the block that once upon a time was full with residents that grew up and started at the same time as me. They either died or moved away. Out of that, one of those houses is knocked down, one is vacant, one is burned down, and one is empty on a Section 8 listing, and ... two are empty ... And the people who did move in two of the vacant houses were low-income-housed people. And ... they just did not take care of their property. And did not care much about the individuals surrounding them. And no, I did not know them very well. (Patillo-McCoy 1999:37)

Many of the African American men and women we interviewed in the Qualitative Study of Aging in Chicago presaged this experience. They had also watched as their community experienced an "internal" demographic shift, from middle- and working-class African American to vacant houses, high crime and higher unemployment. Fred Frank and his wife had both worked hard to purchase their own three-apartment building in Evergreen. They moved to the community in 1957, when it was a central shopping area with many conveniences. Now he lamented the deterioration of the community and the depletion of neighborhood amenities: "The area has deteriorated so much ... the major stores have moved away from me. Which I had hoped would not happen" (Interview JS2FF:981).[6] He later added,

"The neighborhood as a whole is sick. That's what I would say, my neighborhood is sick. It needs a lot of care. It needs a lot of participation from the political side as well as the people that live in the community.... It is not beyond recovery ... but I don't see it recovering in the next five years" (Interview JS2FF:1351).

Mr. Frank then spoke about a nearby residential area called Charleston, still known for its more stable middle-class milieu. He said,

"That's (Charleston) a little different now (compared to Evergreen). It's a little up, ... you have a different class of people, believe it or not, that live in that area. If I wasn't caught in down here I probably would be considered that class of peoples there.... because my ideas, my participation in church, community activities, and whatnot, I would be considered that" (Interview JS2FF:1383-1395).

Thus, despite modal images of African American life portrayed by those from outside, those African American Chicagoans who lived their day-to-day lives within the confines of what was more usually seen as an undifferentiated "south side," were sensitive to class differences, as exemplified by the community in which one lived.

URBAN PIONEERS

Our participants related their experiences as "urban pioneers," for these African American elders were among those residents who moved into Evergreen in the late 1950s through the 1960s, when it was still largely populated by white, working- and middle-class families. Despite the prejudice and harassment our participants encountered, they sought more space and a more stable neighborhood in which to raise their families. They were attracted by the tree-lined streets, solid brick bungalows, the small two- or three-apartment buildings called "two-flats" or "three-flats," and the neighborhood's safe streets, parks, schools and churches.

Lorna Richards was a seventy-five-year-old African American woman who had lived in the Evergreen area with her husband since 1951 when they bought a typical Chicago two-flat. As one of the first black families to move on the block, they exemplify the aspirations and desires of these early "pioneers." Ms. Richards said,

"I think that's why we came out to try to buy ... the block itself, the trees really did something to me ... when we first came out, that was in '51, this was when the neighborhood was changing.... I think we were about the third or fourth blacks to move in the block ... (Interview JS1LR:836).

And, "I think it was a time for things to change and actually ... I can think perhaps, that black people were able to do better, living for their families, and to own properties, whereas we had all been confined to renting apartments. And now you got a nickel, you could put down on a house and move into it ... Because a lot of the people that moved out here ... lived in the projects. And they were able to get a home for their children and their family. And this is ... a desire for better living" (Interview JS1LR:1060).

These older adults were people filled with civic pride, expressed through their neighborliness, their care for their property and larger communal spaces, and their involvement in local institutions such as churches, schools and other voluntary organizations before the idea of "civic engagement" became popularized. One particular way they engaged at the most local community level was through the "block club." Block clubs were informal associations of neighbors living on both sides of the same street, for one block length. Though no longer common, block clubs flourished in many Chicago communities; they were notable as important associations that helped maintain the quality of life for residents through social activities, joint problem-solving to address local issues and as a source of informal social controls. These clubs were dedicated to maintaining a high standard of upkeep for lawns and streets, and fostered inter-action and neighborliness amongst the residents. They often collected dues and used the money to support holiday parties or picnics, or to beautify the street. Carla Lewis was a sixty-nine-year-old woman who had been widowed more than twenty years earlier. She still lived in her own home, where she had moved in 1961. She recalled the joint efforts of her neighbors to create a posi-tive social space through the block club,

"We used to make a big party ... We all donated, we'd take out of the treas-ury and then each family still donated" (Interview JS5CL:891).

Block clubs also provided a space in which neighbors could offer mutual support, such as organizing meals when a woman was too ill to cook for her family or giving rides to those who needed assistance getting around. In addi-tion, through the block club, familiarity was maintained such that people felt comfortable keeping an eye on each other's children and property. But, as Evergreen changed, the block club and its role as a mechanism for socializa-tion and social control faded. Fred Frank stated,

"I think it, block club is about dead.... see, there's not too many peoples left in here to really call it a block club ... you've got all that torn down houses and all there, that's not here anymore" (Interview JS2FF:1509).

A second community institution that held an important place in the life of almost every Evergreen resident with whom we spoke was the church. In this way, these Evergreen residents were similar to participants in other research studies, such as Peterson's study of elderly black women living in the Pacific Northwest (see Peterson Part IV Web book). Almost all our participants were regular attendees at church services, as well as at other activities such as clubs, social events and weekly bingo. Although only a few described themselves as overtly devout, the church fulfilled a role as a site of both worship and social-ization. For many, the church was central to their social life and recreational activity, as most churches sponsored numerous clubs, trips and special events. For example, Evangeline Carson, a sixty-eight-year-old African American woman described herself as one of the first blacks on her street. She and her husband owned a home across the street from their church, and it was through her involvement there that she came to know her neighbors. She said, "I knew all the other blacks as they moved in ... you'd go over (to the church) and greet them ... and say welcome to the neighborhood. Goin' across the street to church, then I knew all the other people, ... I knew them from church" (JS3 Interview EC:1586-1601).

Fred Frank was also deeply involved in his church, and talked about how he would sometimes serve as a pall bearer at funerals, when an elderly person would pass and there were no friends or family members left to assist.

Interestingly, a number of our participants were Catholic, and several talked about the consolidation of parishes and how this affected their feelings of con-nectedness to their community. Evangeline Carson in particular spoke at length about the disruption she experienced as parishes closed. She described her experience visiting a new church for the first time,

"Well, when we went in, it's like, you usually sit in the certain pew, in your church, and when we came in over there (the new church), well, different ones had their pews, so naturally most of us from Saint R. grouped together, in the back of the church.... we didn't feel quite comfortable, because we use to say 'an how's Mary C., and how's so and so' you know, when we'd go to church. An' we'd go there, an' we'd see these people an' they'd come in, but they wouldn't smile or say anything. So, we finally, after two years I think, three years we've been there, we've gotten to know them ... by name" (Interview JS3EC:1631–61).

Thus, the degeneration of Evergreen affected residents in multiple ways, including the declining stability of their financial investments in their homes, the deterioration of their streets and sense of safety, and the disruption of social ties both in their immediate neighborhoods and in their churches.

Little sense of a stable and socially cohesive neighborhood remained at the time of our interviews. Many neighborhood streets were lined with abandoned properties, claimed by drug dealers and gangs, and parks were too dangerous to visit. A number of participants spoke about their fears of going out at night or just walking the streets doing business. Lillian Manners was sixty-eight years old at the time of our interviews. She lived with her husband in their own home, subdivided into two apartments. The second apartment was occupied by other family members. Mrs. Manners spoke about how she now stayed away from the main commercial district of the community:

"I just don't like shopping in the Evergreen area. I don't like it at all.... ain't nothing over there for to shop for, sure ain't, ain't nothing over there to shop for. And I'm gonna be honest and tell you, and you be scared to death while you're over there. Looking for somebody to be snatching your purse or something. So I just don't like shopping over there."

Many of our participants' own children had relocated to better neighborhoods, often in the suburbs, in keeping with their rising status as college-educated, middle-class professionals and white-collar workers. The elders we interviewed told us of feeling "stuck" in their communities—yet still committed to them, as they described their participation in local school councils and police district advisory committees, and churches. Mr. Frank commented on the strong sense of commitment to his community and the disappointment he feels as he sees this commitment diminishing amongst his neighbors:

"So you get to the point of saying, 'There's nothing for me.' ... one time you had community in mind. You did it for the community. You did it for the church ... But now, you don't do that anymore. Now you just stand there ... I'm on my own pedestal. You have to know your others and this is what happens ... And this where they've let the area go down, down, down down. See because ... you got away from the idea of community. Start thinking as individual" (Interview JS2FF:2193).

However, despite the fact that this theme of deterioration was echoed by almost all the Evergreen residents whom we interviewed, they also continued to commit their time and energy to community enhancement. For example, a number of our participants regularly attended meetings of the local "beat representative" steering committee, an effort by the Chicago Police Department to build closer relationships between police and residents. Ray Barry, who moved to Evergreen in 1968, and still lives with his wife in a two-apartment building that they own, has been a member of the steering committee for his local police district for a number of years. He said,

"It doesn't cost anything to join. It's real nice. I want you to see that ... something like a neighborhood watch. If you see anything's going on in the block or something, then try to protect people's property ... try to help them out as much as possible" (JS2RB:824).

The police steering committee was just one of the many community services Mr. Barry was involved with. He and his wife also were active with their block club, which his wife headed, as well as the Beat Representative program connected to the police district, and a citizen's advisory board that was working to encourage renovations of abandoned buildings in the area. He also participated in church activities and especially enjoyed doing food distribution to needy families in the community: "I enjoy doing most is really handling the food distribution, you know, I think heartily enjoy that ... It was just ... getting' it together, getting' it to the people, and I feel like it's really ... it's the help you know" (JS5RB:1142).

CONCLUSION: OLDER ADULTS AS ASSETS TO FAMILY AND COMMUNITY LIFE

Contrary to persistent mythology, many middle-class, working families are not "stand alone" systems. Parents and grandparents are considered important family members and are often direct contributors to family resources. They represent assets, not drains, on family and community life. The African American elders we interviewed fulfilled important roles within their family systems. We heard numerous stories of how these African American elders provided both material and nonmaterial support: they contributed to their children's financial and family stability, paid for the education of grandchildren and assisted with childcare.

For example, Mr. Barry frequently visited his two granddaughters, who lived on the north side of the city. When they were younger, he would pick them up from school when necessary and take care of them until their father came home from work. Being a grandparent was an especially rewarding aspect of Mr. Barry's life, as it was for most of our Evergreen participants, and his role as care provider was not unique. Carla Lewis contributed to the education of her three granddaughters, through her own entrepreneurial efforts making silk flower arrangements. As she said, you "can't call us lazy." With the money she earned, she had paid one granddaughter's tuition at a parochial school, hoping that a better quality education would enable this child to go to college. She even stated she would be willing to take a loan against her home if it was necessary.

The African American elders profiled here were indispensable to the well-being of their social networks and the larger community in which they lived. While their contributions were often unrecognized by the larger society in which they lived, they made profound differences in the lives of their families and their neighbors. Though each had a personal history and story to tell, their narratives were linked through the repeated themes of devotion to family, commitment to work, dedication to improvement and support for neighbors and community. The historical forces that brought them to Evergreen may make their stories and their places in the history of Chicago seem unique. However, to truly understand the issues and challenges faced by African American middle- and working-class families in Evergreen and similar communities, we must examine the individual lives of residents, and place these lives within the historical and social context of both the time and place. Anthropology's focus on changing social structures, household and kin relations and functions, and particularly on the meanings of these across time and space, should not neglect the place of elders in their community networks.

NOTES

1. All names used in this chapter are pseudonyms, including the community names.

2. Christine Cassell was the general principal investigator. Edward Lawlor, then at the University of Chicago, led the demographic study, a policy analysis was headed by Bernice Neugarten, also at the University of Chicago, and the ethnographic component, was led by Madelyn Iris, then at the Buehler Center on Aging, Northwestern University.

3. My thanks to my colleague and project codirector Rebecca Berman and to Jane Straker who conducted most of the interviews in Evergreen. My thanks also to Michael Marcus, who was then a program officer at the Chicago Community Trust and spearheaded the Aging in Chicago Project (Christine Cassell, principal investigator).

4. The transcripts were downloaded into The Ethnograph (Qualis Research Associates, 1990), and a comprehensive and detailed code list was developed. Coding was done by Rebecca Berman, project codirector, and myself. Interviews conducted in Spanish or Korean were translated either verbatim or as summary translations with only selected verbatim sections translated.

5. This url takes you to Metro Chicago Facts on Line, which is a page on the Metropolitan Chicago Information Center's Web site. It requires a little digging down, and you have to be a "member" of MCIC to access this—but that is free and anyone can join just by filling out the information sheet online.

6. Initials refer to interviewer and participant; line numbers refer to line number of text in each interview.

CHAPTER 25

Web Book: Age of Wisdom: Elderly Black Women in Family and Church

Jane W. Peterson

Available at www.stpt.usf.edu/~jsokolov/webbook/peterson.htm.

One historical response of African American peoples has been to establish community-based mechanisms of support that could buffer the shock of long-term discrimination on the individual. Medical anthropologist Jane Peterson draws upon her experience as a professional nurse and explores the participation of older women in both extended family and church-based care systems in an African American community in Seattle, Washington.

RELATED RESOURCES

Harvey, I. 2008. "Spiritual Beliefs and Illness Management among Older African American Men." *African American Perspectives* 10(1). Available online at: www.rcgd.isr.umich.edu/prba.

King, S., E. Burgess, M. Akinyela, M. Counts-Spriggs and N. Parker. 2005. "Your Body Is God's Temple: The Spiritualization of Health Beliefs in Multigenerational African American Families." *Research on Aging* 27(4):420–46.

Lee, O. and T. Sharpe. 2007. "Understanding Religious/Spiritual Coping and Support Resources among African American Older Adults: A Mixed-Method Approach." *Journal of Religion, Spirituality & Aging* 19(3):55–75.

Ruiz, D. 2004. *Amazing Grace: African American Grandmothers as Caregivers and Conveyers of Traditional Values*. Westport, CT: Praeger.

CHAPTER 26

Web Book: The Social and Cultural Context of Adaptive Aging by Southeast Asian Elders

Barbara W. K. Yee

Available at www.stpt.usf.edu/~jsokolov/webbook/yee.htm.

Refugees from the South East Asian states of Vietnam, Laos and Cambodia have a particular connection to the United States, which unsuccessfully, through the Vietnam War, tried to maintain the colonial domain France abandoned in this region. Since the mid-1970s, Southeast Asian refugees and immigrants have come to many different areas of America. Here, social psychologist Barbara Yee uses a life span development approach to examine how elders fare in cultural spaces and communities dramatically different from those found in their homelands.

CHAPTER 27

Web Book: Dementia in Cultural Context: Development and Decline of a Caregivers Support Group in a Latin Population

Neil Henderson

Available at: www.stpt.usf.edu/~jsokolov/webbook/henderson.htm.

Over the past several decades, there has been an explosive growth of self-help/mutual aid groups emerging as a critical resource facilitating a "health-promoting" approach to illness or psychosocial crisis as distinct from a traditional "sickness approach." These social formations that touch on the lives of the elderly tend to be of three types: life-cycle/crisis transition groups (such as widow-to-widow); affliction groups (hypertension, alcohol); and support for caregiver groups (caregivers for Alzheimer's patients).

This last type of group is the subject of Neil Henderson's chapter, which focuses on the Hispanic ethnic context of aging and the operation of a dementia caregiver support group in Tampa, Florida.

RELATED RESOURCES

Borrayo, E., G. Goldwaser, T. Vacha-Haase and K. Hepburn. 2007. "An Inquiry into Latino Caregivers' Experience Caring for Older Adults with Alzheimer's Disease and Related Dementias." *Journal of Applied Gerontology* 26:486–505.

Herrera, A., J. Lee, G. Palos and I. Torres-Vigil. 2008. "Cultural Influences in the Patterns of Long-term Care Use among Mexican American Family Caregivers." *Journal of Applied Gerontology* 27(2):141–65.

Neary, S. and D. Mahoney. 2005. "Dementia Caregiving: The Experiences of Hispanic/ Latino Caregivers." *Journal of Transcultural Nursing* 16:163–70.

PART V

Families, Communities and Elderscapes: Transforming Cultural Spaces for Aging

Jay Sokolovsky

It is not enough to talk about the bind of tradition and it's not enough to talk about its disintegration. We must find ways and means of transforming it into a modern form that will make multigenerational relationships much more viable.

Nana Apt 1998

Ghanaian sociologist and specialist on aging Nana Apt made the above remarks in a keynote address at the United Nations discussing how living arrangements and cultural traditions might be adapted to continue sustaining elders amidst the multitude of changes faced by families in industrializing nations.[1] As regional wars, genocide and pandemics such as AIDS continue to afflict parts of that world, reliance on twentieth-century models of family support are dangerously misplaced in Africa or Asia as they are in industrialized nations (Sokolovsky 2002; Mehta 2005; Lowenstein, Katz and Gur-Yaish 2007). In looking at such issues, this section's original articles traverse an Indonesian village within a woman-centered society, neighborhoods in four world cities, small Midwestern cities creating elder-friendly environments, community gardens creating urban social capital and "elderscapes" in the most senior-dense county in the United States. One approach to understanding the kinds of variation you will be reading about is to frame the information within two universal sets of social relations—the kinship systems generated by rules and practices of descent and marriage and the broader social networks that bind people within and often across communities. This applies as much to the married couple recently retired to "The Villages" in central Florida, seen on the following page, as it does to the older homeless man pushing all his worldly possessions down the streets of New York City.

A retired couple in their customized golf cart in front of their house in "The Villages," an active living older adult community in Florida, 2007. Photo by Jay Sokolovsky.

Homeless man on Fifth Avenue, Manhattan, 2007. Photo by Jay Sokolovsky.

We can begin by considering the information seen in Figure V.1. On the surface at least, the vast majority of older adults in the industrializing ("developing") world appear securely situated in multigenerational living arrangements with family, and less than 10 percent live alone. A stark contrast is seen in the so-called developed world, where a little under one-third of those past age sixty live with a relative other than their spouse and close to that percent live by themselves. There is a great deal of variation within this survey data. For instance, while only 4 percent of Denmark's older citizens live with a child or grandchild, in Bangladesh the figure is 90 percent and while the proportion living alone is less than 1 percent in Bahrain, it reaches 40 percent in Denmark (United Nations 2007c). In some developing nations, such as Ghana, we see dramatic exceptions in that during the last two decades of the twentieth century there was an almost doubling of elders residing alone, from 12 to 22 percent (see Aboderin 2006 for the implication of this change).[2] As already seen in Cattell's discussion of widowhood (Part II), gender is also a key factor here, as in all world regions; women over age sixty live by themselves two to three times more often than older men.

Such numbers, however, mask not only the inner workings of family systems, but what Stack and Burton call "kinscripts," the family centered cultural scripts that connect elders and their kin networks to the broader cultural setting in which they live (see also Sokolovsky 2002). In regions like Asia, the general

Figure V.1
Living Arrangements of Persons Over Age 60 in Developed and Developing Regions

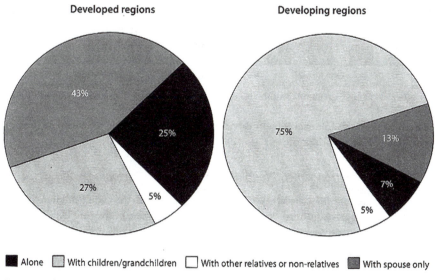

Sources: Adapted from United Nations 2007c, p. 33.

filial focus is impacted by variant kinscripts. In East Asia and the northern sector of South Asia, cultures based on either Confucian, Hindu or Moslem philosophies and an authoritarian, patrilineal system, stress coresidence and care by sons and their spouses. In Southeast Asia and the southern zone of South Asia, Buddhist spiritual orders within a less rigid, bilateral kin system push adult daughters to play equal and sometimes more important support roles in elder care than sons (Mason 1992). An important variant of this second pattern occurs in Thailand, where there is a decided preference for elder parents to reside with daughters. This example is particularly important in showing that despite steep drops in family size during the 1990s, the number of children in a family network has only a very modest impact on an elder's chances for coresidence and support. In fact, those elders with only one or two children reported that they felt as well cared for as those with five or six offspring (Knodel and Saegtienchai 2007).

The impact of kinscripts often comes into sharpest focus when things begin to change. A dramatic example is the Gwembe people of Gambia, who were studied over a ten-year period by anthropologist Lisa Cliggett (2005). The aboriginal culture was matrilineal, with the well-being of the community dependent on women's hoe-cultivation of land. The people were relocated by the building of a dam in their region and their lands thus became more suitable for tending cattle and cattle-ploughed agriculture, which was controlled by men, especially older men. This shifted social power to patrilineal groups (men and their sons) and during periodic severe droughts, old women could no longer draw on the power of their matrikin and were reduced to surviving only on grains from grass.

In looking at another matrilineal people, the Minangkabau of Indonesia, this section's lead chapter by Indrizal, Kreager and Schröder-Butterfill brings to the forefront how a women-centered kin descent system structures the life course and frames late-life cultural spaces and scripts. Through a series of expertly drawn case studies, we see a delicate interweaving of culture and context. Here ancient matrilineal customs called *Adat* place women at the center of economy, ritual and family life, but are situated within a local, devout version of Islam. Men as they age sit at the edge of most of these realms, but in a more complementary manner than experienced by women in male-centered societies. Particularly interesting contrasts are to be found in comparing the Minangkabau scripts and spaces for aging to those described for Mexico and China in Part III and in this section's chapter on India. One sees in the lives examined differing impacts of late-life vulnerabilities such as childlessness, having only sons or loss of spouse in the context of globalizing forces (Schröder-Butterfill and Marianti 2006; Wong et al. 2006a; Schröder-Butterfill forthcoming). As we saw in the chapter on Peru in Part III, what has come to be called "social protection" seldom can be accomplished exclusively within the bounds of family support systems (Lloyd-Sherlock 2004).

Another perspective on rural aging and gender is provided in this section's Web book by Dena Shenk and Kitter Christiansen who examine the support systems of older women in rural Minnesota and Denmark. While the women studied shared a strong attachment to the physical and social aspects of their locales, they also had a clear desire for personal autonomy. However, the ways by which this independence was constructed in each society were quite different. Older Danish women saw their autonomy as tied to professional service providers who could reduce their dependence on kin and close friends (also see Stuart and Hansen Part III). The women in Minnesota, in strong contrast, saw their independence as linked to an avoidance of formal services. This article also demonstrates the importance of examining how different parts of support systems fit together in varied cultural circumstances.[3]

The vulnerability of older citizens has recently emerged as a powerful issue, set against both the globalizing changes discussed in Part III and the ability of family and community systems to protect older persons in the context of demographic shifts and disasters such as the recent civil wars in Eastern Europe and Africa, the 2005 Hurricane Katrina in New Orleans or the 2003 heat wave that struck Europe and precipitated the unanticipated deaths of numerous older Parisians (Jackson and Howe 2008).[4]

These latter two disasters shift our attention to urban zones where very shortly a majority of the world's citizens will be living (United Nations 2007a).[5] Those who are not city dwellers will still feel the effects of urban cultural desires, witness the outflow of those seeking city-based jobs and experience the impact of huge portions of national resources being gobbled up by their mega-metropolises. Incredibly, only four of the top fifteen largest cities in the world are now in "developed" countries. All the rest are dispersed throughout the nations of Mexico, India, Brazil and South Korea.

In some of these countries, unexpected rapid changes in the age-related demography and social fabric of cities have developed, which are mandating shifts in planning. An example comes from the country of India, discussed in this section by Lamb. In the urban area of Chenai by 2005, fertility had dropped so rapidly that the city found itself closing ten maternity wards and retraining staff to work in new geriatric units (United Nations 2007a). In the United States, a 2006 national study, "The Maturing of America," found that just less than half of the 1,790 communities surveyed have begun preparing to deal with an aging population (www.n4a.org/pdf/MOAFinalReport.pdf). The chapter in this section by Michael Gusmano brings this issue into focus by presenting some of the core data from the ongoing World Cities Project examining aging and environment in New York City, London, Paris and Tokyo (Rodwin and Gusmano 2006; www.ilcusa.org/pages/projects/world-cities -project.php). As major global urban centers, these locales offer excellent public transportation, world-class medical facilities and concentrations of social and cultural amenities. He finds a key dividing point between the "hard" cities of London and New York, with greater risks for social isolation, inequality and concentrated poverty and their "softer" counterparts of Tokyo and Paris (see also Philipson, Scharf and Smith 2005; Cagney 2006). A critical aspect of the chapter is the differential mechanisms by which the four cities developed support systems to deal with the very high percentages of those past age eighty-five, especially women, who are living alone (see also Cornwell, Laumann and Schumm 2008; Quinn 2008). Tokyo is the exception here, with a much lower proportion of very elderly women living by themselves, but as we learned in Part III, living alone in old age is increasing substantially in that country as well.

Ironically, we will also see in Sarah Lamb's highly nuanced chapter, centered in urban Kolkata (Calcutta) India, that aloneness does not necessarily mean living by oneself (see also Van der Geest 2004). Here, set among a newly emerging middle class, she explores the transformation of *Sanyasa*, the Hindu traditional cultural script of aging, which is ideally set in the cultural space of the patrilineal joint family. It is to be enacted through *Dharma* (duty) and *Seva* (service), the mechanisms of care by young kin and reciprocal blessings they should receive in return. This ideally creates a multigenerational, kin-bounded social landscape, which is elder-male dominated and elder-female mediated. As Lamb shows, globalizing "outsourced sons" and educated young women are transforming the meaning and enactment of the scripts by which older adults connect with their younger generations (see also Lamb 2009). Aging outside of this script is culturally interpreted as "being alone" though the person might reside in an extended-family setting. Older women moving out of the traditional family setting have found refuge in a variety of cultural spaces such as in laughing clubs (see Box V.1), Hindu temples and newly forming elder residences. For many this is perceived as a failure of their societal system; for others it is a logical passage into the modern, globalized world.

BOX V.1 THE LAUGHING CLUBS OF INDIA

Ayervedic Laughter Medicine

In India where the bonds of extended family life are often considered the only culturally accepted place to experience a satisfying old age, Sarah Lamb in this section details the beginning of alternative cultural spaces harnessing age-peer power. One of these new creations is delightfully documented in the 2001 film *The Laughing Club of India*. It explores the work of Dr. Madan Kataria, who in 1995 instigated a group of mostly elderly patients and neighbors to meet daily in Mumbai's Priydarshini Park to just laugh. Drawing on yoga postures and a breathing technique called *Kapalabhati*—"cleaning out your brain"—he developed various mirth-inducing techniques, with club members learning how to produce a repertoire of different styles of laughing. Dr. Kataria found that participants experienced improved health and decreased levels of stress and he claims such behavior can alleviate hypertension, arthritis and migraines.

Subsequently, Dr. Kataria set up the School of Laughter Yoga after creating "World Laughter Day" on May 6, 1998, when at the Mumbai racetrack 10,000

continued

people turned out to laugh their heads off (www.laughteryoga.org/). This movement spread across India and now boasts over 50,000 clubs in fifty other nations. In the United States, the biggest such center for passing on Dr. Kataria's ideas is the Laughter Yoga Institute of Laguna Beach, California, where structured merriment is performed each day on sands facing the Pacific Ocean (www.joyfulb.com/laughteryoga.htm#Classes).

Health in Old Age *Is* a Laughing Matter

Dr. Kataria's creation provides a wonderful example of cultural convergence with the prior work of Dr. Norman Cousins in the United States, who stimulated research on laughter and positive immune system responses and the efforts of Dr. Patch Adams, who sought to improve hospital medical treatment through acts of clowning. Serious medical work is showing some of the health connections Dr. Kataria initially found (Houston, McKee, Carroll and Marsh 1998; Bennett and Lengacher 2008). Releasing emotions with laughter is seen as one method to the boost immune response by reducing stress hormones through the production of endorphins. Merriment healing to promote psychological well-being has now come to be practiced in senior centers and long-term care facilities (Westburg 2003; Schreiner, Yamamoto and Shiotani. 2005). After all, "A Clown is like an Aspirin," remarked Groucho Marx, "only he works twice as fast."

Related Resources: "Benefits of Laughter Yoga with John Cleese": www.youtube.com/watch?v=yXEfjVnYkqM&mode=related&search; The Dr. Patch Adams Gesundheit Institute: www.patchadams.org/campaign; The Happiness Project in Oxford, England: www.happiness.co.uk/Default2.asp.

SOCIAL NETWORKS, SUPPORT SYSTEMS AND RETHINKING COMMUNITY

Despite the proliferation of formal caregiving organizations and specialized personnel oriented toward senior citizens, growing attention has focused on the existence of "natural" support systems, or what Antonucci calls social "convoys" *generated by the elderly themselves* (Chappell 1995; Antonucci, Ajrouch and Birditt 2006). In seeking to understand the importance of informal social ties in meeting the needs of the elderly, one level of analysis has concentrated on the study of "social networks"—ego-centered sets of personal links and their interconnections generated among friends, kin and neighbors (Sokolovsky 2006). Network analysis has been particularly useful for studying urban settings where social action is not readily understood within the context of traditional social structures, such as the totemic clans of the Tiwi or East African age sets.

Ironically, while measures of informal social interaction have been viewed as crucial in gerontological theory and research, too many studies have failed to examine the qualitative characteristics and cultural meaning that social networks hold for the elderly. For example, survey studies of aged living in single room occupancy (SRO) hotels in the central core of older U.S. cities often depicted these individuals as totally isolated and incapable of replenishing an impoverished repertoire of social ties (Sokolovsky 2006). However, my own research with community psychiatrist Carl Cohen in New York City of SROs showed that elderly living there were far from true isolates—only about 5 percent fit this description. Rather, we showed that the cultural construction of their networks was different from middle-class elderly patterns and was generated through three network features: structural dispersion, highly selective intimacy and variable activation of social ties. It was found that many of these elderly identified themselves as "loners." However, this was typically a stance that enhanced local perception of their independence. It combined with their small but active social networks to connect them to their urban environment in a culturally meaningful way (Sokolovsky and Cohen 1987).[6]

In a very different cultural setting during the early 1980s, when I first developed an interest in the issue of nonfamilial environments for the elderly in Croatia's capital, Zagreb, scholars in the United States advised me not to bother. I was told that there was so little interest in homes for the aged that most of the rooms had to be rented out to students or tourists. Barely two years later, this was no longer the case, when I found that each of the nine *Dom Umirovljeni* (home for retired persons) in the city was filled to capacity with local elders, and some had waiting lists of more than one year (Sokolovsky, Sosic and Pavlekovic 1991). I found that, in general, the public was horrified at the thought of such places. Ironically, however, most of the residents themselves thought such residences situated in the heart of their lifelong neighborhoods were wonderful places where their needs were met and they felt fortunate to be living there. My research showed that the elders in these facilities typically had very few living close kin: they saw the *Dom* as a vital resource for their survival in late life.

A central issue related to social support systems among the elderly is the degree to which the development and expansion of formal supports and planned environments builds upon existing caring behaviors of kin, friends and others (Krause and Borawski-Clark 1994; Davey et al. 2005). To understand this, any student of contemporary community development for older adults has to learn a set of acronyms, blooming almost as fast as the growing crop of North American seniors. There are ACLFs, CCRCs, LCCs, LORCs and perhaps most intriguing of all, NORCs or Naturally Occurring Retirement Communities–long-standing residential areas where a high density of elders are living in the community.[7] Over the past two decades, cities like Chicago and New York were in fact developing some of the world's highest concentrations of NORCs. In the 1990s, New York City became one of the first U.S. urban areas to develop specific programs directing social services, including case managers and nurses, to where the elder concentration in apartment buildings went beyond 60 percent (Vladeck 2004).[8] In 2006, it added to this program a few elder-dense neighborhoods, or "horizontal NORCs" as they are called in suburban areas. During the same year, the federal government authorized experiments in aging in place, but did not provide any funding for implementation.

Despite the public emphasis on building totally new and separate physical environments for older adults, oriented to their changing needs, we learn in the chapter by Phil Stafford that the vast majority of older Americans consistently claim they want to stay in place. This desire is connecting with not only a growing international emphasis on promoting an active view of late life, but of conceptualizing how to construct elder friendly and life-span communities and neighborhoods (see especially Harding 2007; Matthews and Turnbull 2008; Stafford 2009).

Phil Stafford's chapter in this section draws upon the principles developed through the "AdvantAge" (www.vnsny.org/advantage) and "Aging in Place" national initiatives (www.aginginplaceinitiative.org) to center a discussion of the elder friendly community movement in Bloomington, Indiana. He uses ethnographic data from his work in that small city to explore how the local cultural construction of home and community can be directed to addresses elders' basic needs: optimizing well-being, maximizing autonomy for those with disabilities and promoting civic engagement (Rowles and Chaudhury 2008). Such work in the United States parallels global efforts to promote enabling and supportive environments such as envisioned by the World Health Organization's Healthy Cities and Active Aging Initiative (World Health Organization 2007a) or Europe's "Enable Age Project (see Iwarsson et al. 2007; www.enableage.arb.lu.se/index.html).[9]

ELDERS GREEN THE URBAN WORLD

Part of the urbanization and globalization picture that has emerged over the last two decades has been loss of farm communities and public green space (Piedmont-Palladino 2008). This is often coupled with the dumping of foul refuse in poor urban neighborhoods, dramatically altering not only the landscapes in which elders live, but also their exposure to toxic substances. One response to this that unites such disparate places as Quito, Ecuador, Kampala, Uganda and New York City is the grassroots development of urban community gardens to not only feed poor families but to reclaim and restore ruined landscapes. Just as grandmothers took to the streets to protest the genocide of their disappeared sons, daughters and grandchildren in Argentina, other countries have witnessed elders at the forefront of reclaiming communities devastated by some of the impacts of globalization. Jay Sokolovsky's chapter in this section documents elders' roles in this dramatic battle in New York City to create neighborhood-based sites of civic greening and community-building by forging ties across class, ethnicity and age (see www.gardenmosaics.cornell.edu). The model of civic greening can have many applications, from uniting generations within dangerous urban neighborhoods, improving the nutritional and health profiles of poor communities and even serving as a central part of new therapeutic environments for extremely frail elders.

The Question of Civic Engagement

This issue of civic engagement is one of the most widely written about topics in recent literature about aging (Wilson and Simson 2006; Morrow-Howell and Freedman 2006–2007).[10] Much of the impetus for this was a collaboration between the Harvard School of Public Health and MetLife Foundation, which established an Initiative on Retirement and Civic Engagement. As an outgrowth of a 2004 report, *Reinventing Aging: Baby Boomers and Civic Engagement*, a national campaign was launched to change public attitudes toward aging and motivate boomers to engage in community service. Much of this concern was driven by Robert Putnam's famous book *Bowling Alone: The Collapse and Revival of American Community* (2000), which foretold of a dramatic decline in civic life and social capital developing in the boomer and succeeding generations (see Achenbaum 2006 for an historic view). Much of the debate on this issue has been based on survey research. It has largely overlooked both qualitative information on the life of community elders, especially in poorer communities (Newman 2003) and on the growing decline in governmental support of key public resources and institutions (Minkler and Holstein 2008). In ignoring these issues, civic engagement discussions may miss much of what is emerging in elder-dense communities.

ELDERSCAPES AND ELDERS AS PIONEERS

One of the salient issues emerging from the discussion of social capital is how the variable nature of community organization relates to well-being in old age. A good example is provided in Maria Vesperi's book *City of Green Benches* (1998) about St. Petersburg, Florida. Local leaders, in an attempt to change their city's image from "God's Waiting Room," undertook a revitalization plan that included removing the numerous green benches on commercial streets and tearing down old residential hotels and small stores along downtown side streets. These were the key sites where elderly residents had generated their own very active and supportive social life. However, in partial compensation, as housing and amenities declined and the remaining population continued to age in place, congregate dining sites, adult day care and a variety of other community-based opportunities for social integration began to increase.[11]

One of the most powerful things now happening across the North American landscape is the rapid creation of alternative social spaces to accommodate the changing perception of aging itself. In this section, sociologist Stephen Katz innovatively pulls together three perspectives in aging studies: institutional ethnographies; "aging in place" debates; and community network research. He unites these streams to discuss communities based on mobility in the context of a postmodern construct of late life within the nation's oldest local zone, Charlotte County, Florida. Far from the depiction of 1960s St. Petersburg as "God's Waiting Room" or "the home of the newly wed and the soon to be dead," he creatively maps the emerging new topography of cultural spaces of retired populations, with entirely new elderscapes. One of the most important parts of the chapter is situating the "Snowbird" phenomena, especially of the large group of Canadian seasonal migrants to Florida, within the frame of globalization and the new flows of bicultural elders. This is literally redefining notions of home and community as these transnational migrants create rituals for double homecomings in both parts of North America.

The range of community spaces for experiencing aging reveals the great diversity encountered when trying to understand late adulthood in the twenty-first century. In the last three Web book chapters, readers are provided entrée into RV encampments and Papua New Guinea village life, a small town senior center and the difficult and dangerous world of older homeless women.

NOTES

1. She also chided international donor organizations, including the United Nations, for operating in a policy void, which ignores the workings of traditional welfare systems in favor of modern forms.

2. This survey data has been complemented by more qualitatively focused sociological and anthropological research that has begun to detail how family structures are adapting to dramatic global changes in Africa (Aboderin 2006); Asia (Knodel and Saengtienchai 2007; Schröder-Butterfill forthcoming); and Latin America (Lloyd-Sherlock 1998; Conceicai and Oca Zavala 2004). Many of these same issues are also dealt with by authors in this volume, particularly in Parts II, III and IV.

3. For a discussion of older men in rural areas, see Elder, Robertson and Conger (1995).

4. The Global Aging Initiative Program has developed a Vulnerability Index giving an assessment of the capacity of twelve developed countries to meet the aging challenge. See *The 2003 Aging Vulnerability Index: An Assessment of the Capacity of Twelve Developed Countries to Meet the Aging Challenge.* Available online at: http://www.csis.org/gai/index.php?option=com_csis_pubs&task=view&id=888.

5. For an important discussion of habitat and aging, see United Nations Center for Human Settlements. 1999. *Developing World: Living Conditions of Low-income Older Persons in Human Settlements.* New York: United Nations.

6. For an ethnographic perspective on older SRO dwellers in San Diego, see Eckert 1980.

7. ACLF stands for Adult Care Living Facility; CCRCs are Continuing Care Retirement Communities; LCCs are Lifecare/Continuing Care retirement communities; and LORCs are Leisure-Oriented Retirement Communities.

8. It is important to note that over the past two decades this has been increasingly difficulty for poorer elders, especially in urban cores of places like New York City where the last two decades of the twentieth century saw a massive reduction in low-cost living units and their replacement with high-priced condos (Brown et al. 2008).

9. For a special discussion of housing and elder-friendly communities, see Alley, Liebig, Pynoos and Banerjee (2007).

10. The Gerontological Society of America has an excellent Web site with links to civic engagement at: http://www.agingsociety.org/agingsociety/Civic%20Engagement/about_civic_engagement.htm.

11. For an analysis of a more disastrous impact of urban change, see Teski et al. (1983). This is a study of how the building of casinos in Atlantic City, New Jersey, affected the community life of the elderly. A more positive perspective on planned urban change can be seen in Hornum's (1987) study of the elderly in planned cities in England. For a discussion of stigma and agism is such environments, see Dobbs et al. 2008.

CHAPTER 28

The Structural Vulnerability of Older People in a Matrilineal Society: The Minangkabau of West Sumatra, Indonesia

Edi Indrizal, Philip Kreager and Elisabeth Schröder-Butterfill

Some years ago, anthropologists speculated that matrilineal principles of social organization had no future. The possibility that matriliny was "doomed," at least in Africa (Douglas 1969), owed to seemingly inevitable conflicts that arise in systems in which inheritance, personal identity, social position and various rights are determined according to female lines of descent. From an Indonesian perspective, this proposition sounds distinctly odd. The country is home to some 4.8 million Minangkabau, probably the second largest matrilineal population in the world. Matriliny has not kept the Minangkabau from actively integrating themselves into the expanding economy of Southeast Asia. To the contrary, family reputation requires young people to engage in labor migration (*rantau*), usually as independent traders. Although ever-wider involvement in the regional economy has of course brought changes, family relations continue to be interpreted within a matrilineal idiom. Migration, in other words, means that many more young couples live on their own, rather than in proximity to the presiding female head of the family, but that need not keep them from participating in important exchanges within the female-linked family networks (Benda-Beckmann 1979; Kato 1982; van Reenen 1996; Blackwood 2000; Sanday 2002).

One way of considering the viability of social systems is to examine how they cope with basic life course transitions that occur in most cultures. This chapter views Minangkabau society with respect to three potential sources of vulnerability in old age, namely childlessness, de facto childlessness and being an elderly man without a wife. As we shall see, the logic of matriliny recognizes the reality of these problems, but defines and deals with them in ways that confound what would be expected in more familiar nuclear and patrilineal family systems. The material is drawn from anthropological and demographic research in Koto Kayo, a Minangkabau community in West Sumatra that was part of the comparative longitudinal study *Ageing in Indonesia*.[1] Examples are drawn from one of the three hamlets making up the community, which represents approximately one-third of the total population of 2,300.

MATRILINY AND THE POSITION OF OLDER PEOPLE

In matrilineal societies, the succession of grandmothers, mothers and daughters defines who inherits communally held family property and guarantees the continuity of the female line. As in most complex lineage systems, the organization of descent groups is conventionally expressed as a gradation of units: the smallest unit is made up of a woman and her children and grandchildren; several such units compose the main unit owning family property and ideally occupying a *rumah gadang*, or ancestral house. The next unit up, consisting of members of several related *rumah gadang*, maintains common agricultural land and burial grounds, whereas marriages are preferably conducted among members of the matrilineal network at the next level of aggregation. This structure expresses the solidarity of the matriline, which at each level shares in one honor, one line of inheritance and one body of communal wealth.

As a political and moral structure, this collective organization has proven well-suited to communities like Koto Kayo, in which upwards of two-thirds of young people migrate, often at great distances, to Bandung, Jakarta, Surabaya and other cities on different islands in the archipelago (Kreager 2006). As a Minangkabau proverb puts it, "a young man is of no use until he has gone on *rantau* (labor migration)." Collective solidarity ensures great pressure on young men, and increasingly also on women, to prove themselves and their family's reputation by sustained and economically successful periods away from the village. The system does more than push: it provides links for young people to communities around the archipelago, structures these communities along traditional lines that ensure a steady flow of remittances and visits home, and organizes these flows to fund social welfare in the village. In time, migrant communities tend to become permanent satellites, with many children living all or most of their lives away from the village while maintaining major personal and economic ties to it. As a mechanism for organizing human capital, this system thus continues to exercise effective influence over distant members and to arrange key marriages that secure relations between lineages.

Matriliny nonetheless gives rise to important asymmetries. Although customary law, called *adat*, is commonly regarded by the Minangkabau as consistent with, and supportive of, Islamic practice, the Indonesian legal system accepts, for example, that inheritance of ancestral property passes to a sister's sons, while nonancestral property may be divided at death in a way that includes inheritance by children (Bowen 2003:142–50). A major potential source of conflict lies in the fact that husbands and wives in a matrilineal system have differing interests in their children. Both normally contribute to their material support and socialization, but only for the wife do these children represent the material and spiritual continuity of her lineage. The husband looks, rather, to his sisters' children, and as her brother carries major responsibilities to nieces and nephews who constitute the continuation of his primary group. Men thus experience a divided loyalty, their roles as fathers and brothers giving them interests in two sets of children. This tension also finds expression in the potential for conflict that arises between a husband and his wife's brother over her children and property. The Minangkabau carefully ritualize this relationship: the husband is only "an honored guest" in the household in which his wife lives and where his children grow up; the wife, in conjunction with one of her brothers, exercises primary authority in that household. The successful grandmother looks forward in later life to living in the ancestral home with one or several of her daughters, who will eventually take over household leadership from her. Successful aging for a man assumes that he has been able to balance his twin roles nicely. As the example of Nurman will show in the following discussion, he may then look forward to potential material and emotional support from two families.

As may be apparent, however, the asymmetry of male and female identities under matriliny can complicate "successful aging." What can a woman and her brothers do if no daughter is prepared to return from *rantau* to manage the family property and to live in and care for the *rumah gadang*? A man with sons and daughters, but no nieces, has no heirs. A matriline without daughters faces extinction, no matter how many sons it has. What if the man's balancing act fails, and he alienates his children and his heirs? Should a wife die before her husband, where is he to live? Minangkabau norms specify that the husband should no longer stay in the household with his daughter, but return to his own ancestral home to live with his sister's children. Yet he may feel stronger personal attachment to his own children. Vulnerabilities in later life are problems that arise from matters only partly under people's control. The question that needs to be examined is what alternative courses of action a social system makes available, and whether they are realizable.

THE PROBLEM OF CHILDLESSNESS AMONG
THE MINANGKABAU

Emblematic of the Indonesian population program is a well-known motto, which may be translated as, "A small family is a happy family! Two children are enough, boy or girl—it makes no difference!" There can be little doubt that the advantages of smaller family sizes have been embraced by Indonesians over the past thirty years (Niehof and Lubis 2003). Fertility has declined from an average of more than five children per woman in the 1960s, to around 2.5 children today. Yet equally beyond any doubt is the fact that children remain highly valued. A marriage without offspring is considered incomplete, and the practical importance of children increases with age. Given the absence of farreaching state support for older people, children are expected to provide financial and social support to their elderly parents. There is even a Minangkabau saying, "No matter how kind other people are, in old age it is your children who will make you more comfortable!" Elderly people with few or no children are widely looked upon as suffering a most unfortunate fate, facing loneliness and fearing social and physical vulnerability.

Yet how significant, one might ask, is the phenomenon of elders without children? After all, current cohorts of older Indonesians had their children well before the onset of fertility decline and the spread of family planning. On average, they have therefore been blessed with family sizes in excess of five children, making a lack of offspring seem unlikely. However, closer inspection quickly reveals that the five-child average hides considerable variation between regions and individuals. This is hardly surprising: mortality remained high in Indonesia until quite recently, and many children thus died before their parents reached old age. Migration and divorce were common and contributed to long periods spent outside of sexual union, with obvious consequences for fertility. In parts of Java, where extreme hardship during the 1940s exacerbated mortality and facilitated the spread of sexually transmitted disease, a quarter of current generations of older people were left without any surviving children (Schröder-Butterfill 2004; Schröder-Butterfill and Kreager 2005).

In Koto Kayo, the Minangkabau community studied here, levels of childlessness are more modest, but by no means negligible. Here 7 percent of older people have no surviving children, and a further 5 percent have only one child. Moreover, these figures need to be placed within their specific matrilineal context, in which not having *daughters* is tantamount to being childless. On that count, a further 17 percent of older Minangkabau perceive themselves as childless because they lack surviving female offspring. In total, almost one quarter of elders appear vulnerable, at least at first glance, because they have no daughters or no children at all.

However, vulnerability does not directly arise from a lack of children or daughters. According to the logic of the matrilineal system, one's sister's children are equivalent to one's own offspring, as they belong to the same matriline. Indeed, no terminological distinction is made between a person's own children and the children of her or his sister, both being referred to simply as *anak* (child). Children will refer to their matrilateral aunts as *mandeh ketek* ("small mother," if the aunt is junior to the mother) or *mandeh gadang* ("big mother," if the aunt is senior). A woman without children can thus take a positive and respected place in the family as classificatory mother of her sister's children (van Reenen 1996:214). It is to these children that she will look for assistance should she need it. The example of Dahlia, an elderly divorcée, illustrates the options for reputable support and well-being in old age that the matrilineal social system provides where children are lacking.

Dahlia, aged seventy, is a childless elderly woman who lives alone. She has one surviving older sister. Her husband left on labor migration immediately after their wedding, leaving Dahlia behind with her family. For ten years he rarely visited or sent news or money. When eventually he returned with a second wife, Dahlia was indignant and asked for a divorce. She never remarried and lived with her mother until the mother died. Nowadays she is the single occupant of the family's ancestral home (*rumah gadang*). She still manages to cook, shop, clean and wash her own clothes. She does not wish to be a burden on others and feels most comfortable in her own surroundings. For these reasons, she has so far declined the invitation by her older sister's daughters to join them and her sister in North Sumatra.

Although she has no children of her own, Dahlia is not worried about old-age security. She knows that her sister's children care deeply about her. One nephew, for example, visits every two weeks and gives her some money. Another nephew comes every couple of months and brings money and items for her daily needs, such as soap, sugar and cloth. Meanwhile, a niece routinely sends a generous sum every three months. Most nephews and nieces visit at least once a year, during the Muslim holiday of *Idul Fitri*, when it is customary to return to the village and pay respects to relatives, especially those who are elderly. Dahlia also harvests the fruit and vegetable crops grown on the land communally owned by her matrilineal kin group. She is also given financial support from rich villagers and successful migrants, which is distributed via the mosque.

In Dahlia's case, her matrilineal network is able to provide material and emotional support in a manner that is reliable, generous and socially acceptable. In terms of security in later life, her situation differs little from that of her peers with children. To be sure, her lack of a younger relative permanently in the vicinity entails some loneliness, but as the following example of Asnima will show, this is a fate not uncommon to Minangkabau elders, given the high levels of migration among the younger generations. At least she rests assured that her sister's daughters will on her death be able to inherit the property of the matriline—an issue that greatly troubles other childless old people in the community.

Problems arise chiefly where sisters also lack children, both in terms of support and the overriding practical and ideological issue of the absence of female heirs to inherit family property and continue the descent line. As the example of Jamain shows, elders without children, whose lineage faces extinction and who have failed to create strong bonds with more distant matrilineal kin, experience severe insecurity and loss of status in old age. They remain without the safety net of support that the Minangkabau family system normally provides.

Jamain is a man in his seventies who lives alone. Atypically for men from Koto Kayo, Jamain only briefly took part in labor migration and returned unsuccessful, settling in a small shack on the edge of the village. Both his marriages were childless and ended in divorce. The second marriage, to a woman from outside the village, earned him disapproval from fellow villagers for marrying an outsider. Jamain's older brother has four children, but their first loyalties lie with their mother's matriline. According to the structure of Minangkabau society, it is to his sister and her offspring that Jamain should turn for support. Unfortunately, the sister also remained childless and poor, and recently died. Jamain lives out his life reliant on support from a sympathetic neighbor, who gives him food, and from unsympathetic fellow villagers, who only occasionally and unwillingly give him money when he begs. By begging Jamain lowers his status and dignity and deviates from what is considered characteristic of the enterprising, successful Minangkabau.

The lack of female matrilineal descendants in the extended family network of Jamain means that his matriline is doomed to extinction. Since his sister died, Jamain can at least live in his ancestral house and benefit from the fruits of its associated rice lands. Eventually, the house with its land will fall to a distant, collateral line.[2]

Given the logic of lineal kinship organization, with its systems of ever more distant and inclusive units, relatives can usually be traced by going back several generations. In the eyes of other villagers, had Jamain conducted himself in a manner more in keeping with the ethos of the Minangkabau people, someone from such a collateral line might well have stepped in to help. Equally, money sent back to the village by successful migrants, distributed by the mosque, would have been more forthcoming.

Neither Dahlia nor Jamain started from a position of material advantage; both are childless and both have matrilineal relatives who might be expected to help out. Yet their outcomes are very different. The contrast arises primarily from the fact that Dahlia has remained within the moral norms of her network, while Jamain has not. None of Dahlia's closest matrilineal kin reside in the village, yet the support they provide is ample. Jamain is without doubt at a comparative disadvantage because his only sister is childless, too. Yet it is chiefly his behavior that has left him without recourse to the collateral kin and community institutions that would normally, in Minangkabau society, come to his rescue.

DE FACTO CHILDLESSNESS

As already noted, a lack of children need not be the result of sterility or the death of children, but may also be the outcome of lacking the "right kind" of child (in the case of the Minangkabau, daughters), or lacking access to normative support from children that exist (Kreager and Schröder-Butterfill 2004). The latter point is particularly relevant in the context of widespread outmigration of the younger generation, as is famously the case among the Minangkabau. As many as three-quarters of elderly villagers' children in Koto Kayo have moved away. Among better-off families, which can draw on strong social and material capital to assist their children in migrating, the proportion is as high as 90 percent (Kreager 2006). While regular remittances and return visits to the village ensure adequate levels of material support for most elders, the psychological insecurity arising from an absence of children locally cannot be underestimated. This is particularly felt by elderly women whose daughters are all away, as it is daughters who are expected to take over from their mothers the management and continuity of ancestral houses and property. The case of Asnima exemplifies the paradox of, on the one hand, having many successful children and on the other hand, feeling lonely, vulnerable and "childless" because none are locally available.

Asnima, aged seventy-five, is the youngest of eight siblings and the last surviving among her sisters. She is a descendant of a line of clan headmen and one of her sons currently holds this position. She has nine children, seven sons and two daughters. All of Asnima's children are married and living in their respective migration sites. The closest child, a son, lives about ten kilometers away. Both her daughters married men who are not Minangkabau. Her elder daughter, who married a Javanese, has a successful permanent job in Jakarta. The other, married to a man from Aceh (northern Sumatra), recently moved to Padang, which is still a good three hours away.

Asnima is worried that there will be no female heir living in the village to take care of the family inheritance and burial grounds and to ensure the continuity of the *rumah gadang* as the focal point of her lineage. For the time being, it is Asnima who looks after the property. She is financially secure, because her children regularly support her and she has income from the lineage rice fields. None of this, however, can allay her fears about the long-term future representation of her lineage in the village. Although Asnima frequently visits her various children, she has never considered settling permanently with one of her children. As she puts it, "Living in our own homeland, in our own house, is much better than living elsewhere, even if it is in our own child's house." In any case, living with a son is not an option, as this would violate Minangkabau tradition and reflect badly on the daughters. If she had her own way, Asnima would raise the only granddaughter she has via her daughters, because it will ultimately be that granddaughter's responsibility to continue the matriline. Asnima nowadays occupies the ancestral home on her own, although sometimes a young, unrelated woman keeps her company at night, helps her with cooking and takes care of her when she is ill.

A number of observations arise from this case study. One is that the impact of migration works in contrary ways in matrilineal societies like the Minangkabau. On the one hand, the tradition of migration continues to function as a major social guarantee of material support for elderly people in the village. The continuity of migration traditions has not caused elderly who live in the village to lose their fundamental family networks. If anything, the development of modern transport and communication infrastructure makes the maintenance of relationships much simpler. The continuity of migration traditions has not caused elderly who live in the village to lose their fundamental family networks. That said, levels of moral and material support received by elderly parents have always varied from case to case. Some young men who leave do not maintain any communication with their families in their natal villages. Among children there will be those who give support routinely and those who provide very little support. A common aphorism is that "Of all the children, one or maybe two will usually be *hampa*," that is, unsuccessful or not inclined to offer support.

On the other hand, there can be no doubt that the central importance of daughters to the continuity of descent lines and inheritance now poses problems that some families are finding almost impossible to resolve. Asnima's concern that her granddaughter will actually fulfill her responsibility and return to the *rumah gadang* in Koto Kayo is clearly genuine and reflects practical as well as psychological vulnerabilities experienced by the elderly in Minangkabau culture. Asnima is not alone in this problem: one-third of elders do not have a child in the village, and it is increasingly uncertain whether many daughters living in migration sites will eventually return. In Koto Kayo, at least, most traditional ancestral homes continue to be occupied, although some, like Asnima's, at present are rather quiet. In less prosperous communities, many *rumah gadang*, with their characteristically shaped roofs, are being abandoned and falling into disrepair. The conventional Minangkabau term *keluarga punah*, or "lost kinship," acknowledges that the lack of a daughter to carry on the matriline in the village is not an entirely new problem.

Older people whose children have all left the village may spend some time visiting them in their migration sites, although the preference for their ancestral home almost always leads them to return. Once frailty or ill health makes some form of practical assistance necessary, the choice may be between two less than perfect solutions: accepting help from a nonrelative, as in the case of Asnima, or leaving the ancestral home to be with a daughter who has moved away.

THE STRUCTURAL VULNERABILITY OF ELDERLY MINANGKABAU MEN

Most writing on aging and later life portrays older women as being in a weaker position, due to their poorer access to material resources and power. If men are portrayed as vulnerable at all, their vulnerability tends to be attributed to problems of adjustment to changes in status, dependence on women for practical tasks or smaller social networks due to poorer interpersonal investment (Rubinstein 1986; Hearn 1995; Knodel and Ofstedal 2003). The case of the Minangkabau reminds us of the fact that vulnerability can be the result of a systematic patterning of social relationships, and that this patterning can on occasion work against older men. As already noted, in the Minangkabau matrilineal system property is held by and passed down through women. While men play an important role of authority as sisters' brother, having for example the responsibility of resolving lineage conflict and brokering marriages, the ancestral house is primarily occupied by related women and their daughters. Men, therefore, are rather impermanent and marginal occupants of the domestic sphere. From an early age, boys are encouraged to spend as much time as possible away from the house, and in adolescence they often sleep in neighborhood prayer houses. Their spatial marginality is then epitomized and reinforced by long absences due to labor migration. Men's spatial position after marriage is no less tenuous. Marriage is matrilocal, thus men move in with their wife's family. As husbands, they are incessantly reminded of their status as "honored guests" in the houses of their wives and are subject to avoidance prescriptions with respect to their wife's brothers. For example, a man arriving in a coffeehouse in which his brother-in-law is already present will quickly make an excuse to leave.

None of this looms particularly large as a concern in the passage from early adulthood to late middle age, during which the vast majority of Minangkabau men are away on *rantau*, making only occasional visits back home. Problems arise once men settle back in the village for good. Their preference is then to live with their wives, although most will spend the daylight hours chatting to other men in the prayer houses or food stalls dotted around the marketplace. Structural constraints truly begin to bite if the wife dies or the couple divorce, for the options men then face are limited and strongly shaped by their past conduct and reputation. The choices comprise remaining in the house of their daughter or daughters, living alone, returning to their own ancestral home, or setting up with a new wife. As will become clear, none of these are without potential drawbacks.

Most widowed men with a daughter will initially opt to live with their daughter, especially if this is the arrangement they were already in before their wife died. Children generally feel a strong obligation to care for their elderly parents, although the bonds to fathers may sometimes be weakened by their long absences. However, it is a recognized phenomenon that widowers often begin manifesting symptoms of stress, hypertension and ill-temper when living with their daughters. This is attributed to their staying in the house of "strangers." As a man's children belong to his wife's lineage, rather than his own, it is normal for men to feel as outsiders in his children's home. The presence of a son-in-law further adds to their discomfort.

Amir, in his early seventies, was a poor farmer with several children, some of whom were away on migration. When he was younger, he had built a small house for his daughter near the house he was occupying with his wife. Once his wife died, it was an obvious step for his daughter to move into her mother's house and she urged her father to stay with her. Amir, however, insisted on moving into a small hut on his own. He felt uncomfortable living with his son-in-law. As Amir was not able to manage his daily domestic affairs by himself, his daughter sent cooked food over to his home every day. She also made sure his house was in order and that he didn't suffer from loneliness.

Amir's resolution of the structural bind he found himself in appears contrived to a non-Minangkabau observer: here is an elderly man of limited means, who has helped his daughter in the past and in exchange is invited to share his dying days with her. Instead he opts to live alone and be cared for at arm's length, a much less convenient arrangement. Yet within the logic of the matrilineal system, men are assigned to their sisters' rather than children's lineage. In this context it is perfectly understandable that older men lack a sense of belonging in their children's domestic spaces. Reorientation toward their own lineage and ancestral home is considered a most natural response. In this respect, men lacking children are not at any particular disadvantage, as the following example of Nurman shows.

Nurman is a well-respected elderly man from Koto Kayo. For several decades he held the important position of mosque elder. He married a woman from a reputable and wealthy local family, but the marriage sadly remained child-less. Nurman does, however, have several nephews and nieces via his older half-sister Fatimah, all of whom are successful. After his wife died, he main-tained cordial relations with his wife's family and, quite unusually, was encouraged to remain living in the wife's house. Nurman nevertheless opted for the more customary solution of returning to his ancestral home occupied by his sister and nieces, as according to Minangkabau culture they are now re-sponsible for him. Thanks to the high regard in which Nurman is held in the community, he continues to receive some support from his wife's relatives.

Elders like Nurman or Dahlia, who have conducted themselves in exemplary manner throughout their lives, are assured of generous support from their line-age, even if they lack children. Additionally, they have access to assistance from the wider Koto Kayo community, which controls access to charitable as-sistance. Conversely, people like Jamain, who lose the respect of their peers, find themselves with very little maneuvering room within the strict logic of the Minangkabau system.

THE ROLE OF VILLAGE INSTITUTIONS IN OLD-AGE SUPPORT

This chapter thus far may have created the impression that welfare and secu-rity in old age in Koto Kayo are almost exclusively in the hands of children and matrilineal kin. Quite the contrary. More so than among other ethnic groups in Indonesia, the Minangkabau possess well-developed and institution-alized systems of community charity and welfare. These draw on the three most important elements of Minangkabau society, namely Islam, matriliny and migration.

Throughout the Islamic world, believers of sufficient means are expected to make regular charitable donations for the benefit of the poor and unfortunate. The most important of these donations occur during the fasting month of Ram-adan and involve payments in rice or money to the local mosque. Mosque eld-ers then distribute the donations, referred to as *zakat*, among the community's needy, including the poor, widows, orphans and the elderly. In Koto Kayo, the sums available for distribution are boosted considerably by charitable remittan-ces from successful migrants during Ramadan. Moreover, migrants' generosity is not confined to the fasting month and it is the combined influences of reli-gion and lineage organization that ensure this. Proactive and well-respected mosque elders, of the kind epitomized by Nurman in the previous case study, make regular visits to the main migration destinations throughout Indonesia to see migrants from Koto Kayo. During such visits, recent misfortunes that have befallen villagers may be retold, or projects in need of funding described. When, for example, on one occasion a villager's house burned down, the money the mosque elder succeeded in raising was enough to rebuild the house in its entirety. Many Minangkabau communities similarly succeed in funding the construction and upkeep of impressive religious buildings, schools and health centers by drawing on migrant wealth channeled through the mosque.

The initiative for charity comes not only from the village, but also from migrants themselves. Minangkabau migration networks are so well-developed that they have resulted in the formation of migrants' associations in all of Indonesia's major cities with significant Minangkabau representation. These associations are organized by community of origin and so facilitate the flow of information, money and practical assistance between place of origin and place of settlement. A newly departed migrant will be entrusted to the care of the relevant migrants' association in his destination, which will organize his accommodation, access to work and start-up help. Likewise, travel assistance to the village, be it during the fasting month of Ramadan or in response to a personal or community crisis, is quickly and effectively organized through migrant associations and channeled back to the village through association members.

Although the economic success of many Minangkabau migrants and the high level of organization and generosity among them mean that charitable support in the villages is plentiful, its distribution is not uniform. Access to charity depends on social and moral status and a person's position within the lineage hierarchy of the village. For example, unless they have been "adopted" by an established village family, newcomers to Koto Kayo and their descendants are not members of the village's four dominant lineages and thus tend to be excluded from remittances channeled via these lineages. Additionally, immigrants to Koto Kayo tend to cluster in a poorer hamlet of the village, near the rice fields, because most of them work as agricultural laborers. This hamlet has its own mosque, with the result that worshippers at that mosque fail to benefit from the more generous donations sent by successful migrants to Koto Kayo's main mosque.

Among the original population, it is above all moral standing, reputation and past behavior that determine an older person's access to community charity. Elders like Dahlia, who experienced misfortune such as childlessness and divorce in their lives, but have conformed with expectations of proper conduct, are assured of generous assistance from the mosque and wealthy migrants on visits to the village. By contrast, those with moral failings and those who have violated customary norms of Minangkabau society are not looked upon kindly. While Jamain is not excluded altogether from community beneficence, the support he receives is sparse and grudgingly given. The link between appropriate conduct and access to charity is made explicit by a village elder commenting on an elderly divorcé called Abdul. To secure support in old age, Abdul had decided to remarry, sell the land belonging to his matriline and join his new wife in her village. Yet despite being the only surviving heir, he has no right to dispose of lineage land: his decision transgresses Minangkabau customary law.

"If only Abdul had a stronger feeling of loyalty to Koto Kayo, he would not think of selling his land, or moving to another village. He could instead share his property by giving it to the village. People would then not neglect him. At the end of Ramadan there is financial support from the mosque, taken from *zakat* donations and given by many migrants. On another religious festival there is the distribution of meat. Basically, people will not let elders who have helped the community go without any support. That would be an embarrassment. If Abdul feels vulnerable in his old days, that is simply on account of his own unconfident feelings. In fact, he still has a chance to improve himself and go back to the community."

These village elder's remarks capture the logic of a society in which success, faithfulness to Minangkabau values and loyalty to community have resulted in strong and well-endowed institutions of community charity, but also in little tolerance for those who fail to comply with these virtues.

CONCLUSION

The Minangkabau community of Koto Kayo presents a sophisticated adaptation of matrilineal norms in the course of active participation in the wider Indonesian economy. The perspective adopted here is based on the situation of older people in this particular rural community and might be expected to reflect a more conservative and traditional side of the culture. Matters may be different in urban or less traditional settings. However, where the majority of younger people migrate, often permanently, while their elders remain in the village, this kind of situation is likely to be creating vulnerability in old age in many different parts of the world. Yet, far from a picture of system failure, as anthropologists once proposed for matriliny, Minangkabau matrilineal and community networks are notable for the major influence and respected roles they continue to give older people in the running of society.

The logic of woman-centered kinship does, however, impose constraints, one of which is undoubtedly severe: the absence of daughters in a matriline is fatal to that social unit and inevitably lessens the status of current members. Other problems can become all but impossible to resolve happily: a husband's marginal position in his wife's household may leave him without a comfortable place to live after her death; the uncertainty that no daughter will return from *rantau* to assume responsibility for the *rumah gadang* haunts many families. In this respect, the picture of later life in Minangkabau society given in this chapter is inevitably incomplete: the story needs to be told too from the perspectives of the many Minangkabau who have chosen to live away from Koto Kayo.

NOTES

1. *Ageing in Indonesia 1999–2007* is a longitudinal anthropological and demographic study of three Indonesian communities, supported by the Wellcome Trust. We are particularly grateful for the research assistance of Tengku Syawila Fithry in the collection and analysis of data reported in this chapter.

2. There is little discussion of the exact procedure in *adat* law; collateral lines in such cases are matrilineal kin who are distant not only genealogically (e.g., female descendants of the sister of a great grandmother), but who have long lived elsewhere with no involvement in Koto Kayo. Further discussion of *adat* and its role in Koto Kayo is given in Indrizal and Fithry (2005).

CHAPTER 29

Growing Older in World Cities: Benefits and Burdens

Michael K. Gusmano

Marie lives in the Mott Haven section of the South Bronx. She is a seventy-two-year-old widow who lives alone. She has two children, but neither lives in New York City and she only sees them a few times each year. Marie knows a couple of her neighbors, but does not know them well. Her closest friends have either died or moved away from the neighborhood. Although crime rates in New York City have fallen dramatically in recent years, she is still afraid to leave her building after dark. Her arthritis makes it difficult for her to get around, and truck traffic from the Hunt's Point market and the local bridges make her nervous about crossing streets, even during the day. She feels this is the dreariest time of her life and would like to move, but says, "Where would I go? I can't afford to live anywhere else?"

John, a retired New York City police officer, is married and lives with his wife in the Bay Ridge section of Brooklyn. He is seventy years old and extraordinarily active in the community. He is on the board of directors of several local community organizations and volunteers in programs designed to assist frail older people and children at risk. He and his wife regularly take the subway into "the city" to see shows on Broadway and to visit museums and shops. In his view, Bay Ridge is "the perfect place to grow old."[1]

Marie and John illustrate the benefits and burdens associated with growing old in a world city. New York, London, Paris and Tokyo are the four largest cities among the wealthy OECD[2] nations of the world. They exercise a powerful influence in the world beyond their national boundaries. They are centers of finance, information, media, arts, education and a variety of specialized services; and they contribute disproportionate shares of gross domestic product (GDP) to their national economies. As centers of medical excellence, these world cities set a world standard for care through their medical training programs, biomedical research institutions and university hospitals. But are these

Mott Haven, Bronx. Photo by Michael Gusmano.

influential cities prepared to meet the challenges of what Dr. Robert N. Butler has called the "quiet revolution of longevity?" As life expectancy rises, birth rates decline and populations grow older, how will New York, London, Paris and Tokyo accommodate significant demographic change? These cities offer great opportunities for those who are healthy and wealthy enough to take advantage of them. But for some, these cities are threatening, lonely places. Unfortunately, we do not know enough about the degree to which older residents of these cities are living in isolation.

The aging of the world's population provokes fears of impending social security deficits, uncontrollable medical expenditures and transformations in living arrangements. Indeed, the likely causes and consequences of human longevity and population aging have been the subject of sustained study worldwide and the topic for important expert meetings of the United Nations (Vienna 1982, Malta 1986 and Madrid 2002). But there has been almost no attention to the impact of these trends on health and quality of life in cities where most of the world's population will reside in the future. In the United States, for example, a 2005 study by the National Association of Area Agencies on Aging and allied organizations, concludes that most cities are unprepared to accommodate the needs of the aging "baby boom" generation (National Association of Area Agencies on Aging 2005).[3]

In this chapter, we draw on findings from the World Cities Project to discuss what we know about the benefits and burdens of growing older in these four world cities (Rodwin and Gusmano 2006; see also http://www.ilcusa.org/pages/

projects/world-cities-project.php). In particular, we focus on the factors that influence the social connections of older people. The existence of affordable, easily accessible transportation, neighborhood shops and cultural opportunities, medical and social services that promote health and autonomy and innovative programs that encourage social interaction exist, to varying degrees, in all of these cities. At the same time, these cities are crowded, expensive places to live and older people do not always have access to affordable, appropriate housing.

What is the benefit of comparing the experience of aging in these cities? We believe that comparative analysis of urban aging is most valuable because it provides "the gift of perspective" and helps us to understand our own system "by reference to what it is like or unlike" (Marmor, Freeman and Okma 2005). Comparative analysis expands our vision of what is possible (Klein 1997). When scholars compare cities in the United States to those in other wealthy nations, it is clear that many common "urban problems"—the geographic concentration of poverty, inequality and poor health—are not inevitable attributes of modern cities. Dreier and colleagues argue that "cities in Canada, Western Europe, and Australia do not have nearly the same levels of poverty, slums, economic segregation, city-suburb disparities, or even suburban sprawl as does the United States. The question is not whether we can ever solve urban problems, but whether we can develop the political will to adopt solutions that can work" (Drier, Mollenkopf and Swanstrom 2004).

Not surprisingly, the evidence we present in this chapter suggests that, although these four cities have much in common, there are great differences among them in terms of the benefits and burdens faced by their older residents. New York and London, the "hard" world cities of the postindustrial world, have characteristics that place older residents at greater risk for social isolation than do Paris and Tokyo, their "soft" world cities counterparts. Not only do London and New York have greater income inequalities than Paris or Tokyo, they have deprived neighborhoods with a high concentration of poverty, few middle- and upper-income residents and low levels of collective efficacy. In New York, the problems faced by residents of these neighborhoods are exacerbated by poor access to medical services, to a much greater degree than they are in London.[4] When we examine indicators that are influenced by access to timely and effective health services, such as avoidable mortality and avoidable hospital conditions, we find that New Yorkers face much greater barriers to health care services than do residents of these other cities (Weisz et al. 2007).

THE GROWING IMPORTANCE OF URBAN AGING

While the general dimensions of global aging are becoming well known, the fact that the "longevity revolution" is taking place in the context of growing urbanization has not received sufficient attention. United Nations' estimates indicate that 60 percent of the population will live in cities in 2030 (United Nations 2007a). Although older people are less likely than younger people to live in urban areas, more than 70 percent of older Americans live in metropolitan areas (Kinsella and Velkoff 2001; He et al. 2005). As population aging and urbanization increase, cities will have to respond to the needs of the most rapidly growing cohort of older people—the "older old," eighty-five years of age and over who are the most vulnerable. In particular, cities must find ways to identify and respond to the needs of older people who are isolated.

Why Examine Aging in World Cities?

One reason for the increased focus among gerontologists on urban aging is that "cities are themselves undergoing radical change, notably through the process of globalization" (Phillipson 2004). Not surprisingly, the effects of globalization, both positive and negative, on life in cities are seen most acutely in world cities. The terms *world cities* and *global cities* have been used interchangeably to mean cities at the center of the global economy, or hubs in the international world of transnational corporations, financial services and information exchange (Hall 1984; Sassen 1994; Rodwin and Gusmano 2006; Gusmano et al. 2007). For thousands of years, cities have been regarded, simultaneously, as "the natural center of everything that mattered" and "the source of corruption and evil" (Zwingle 2002). When examining the characteristics of world cities and their implications for older persons, it is easy to understand why. High levels of congestion, pollution and crime rates, as well as the high cost of housing and social polarization in world cities may undermine quality of life for older people. Yet these cities offer greater access to public transportation, pharmacies and stores, world-class medical centers, museums, parks, concert halls, colleges and universities, libraries, theaters and other venues for entertainment. They are important cases to study because while they share these characteristics, they are unique examples of city life within their national borders.

As command-and-control centers in the global economy, twenty-first century world cities are marked by a growing number of wealthy and poor residents, a shrinking middle class and increasing socioeconomic inequalities (White 1998; Sassen 2001; Rodwin and Gusmano 2006). According to the predominant model of global city development, a concentration of financial, information and specialized service industries, as well as headquarters of transnational corporations, in a few cities, have accompanied the dispersion of production and distribution around the world (Friedman 1986; White 1998). As a result, they attract large numbers of highly affluent people to work in their financial, legal and information technology sectors. At the same time, globalization has created a great number of service jobs in what Tobier calls the "under the stairs" economy in the "hospitality" industry: hotels, restaurants, tourism, convention centers; in health and home care; and in small businesses of all sorts. These relatively low-skill, low-wage jobs have attracted a large and growing number of immigrants to these cities. This dichotomy has helped produce stark inequalities, particularly in New York and London (Fainstein, Gordon and Harloe 1992; Tobier 2006).

We do not know enough about the impact of this kind of urban environment on older people, yet there are reasons to believe that it may pose serious challenges to many. World cities offer tremendous cultural and entertainment opportunities, but only a small percentage of older persons have the resources to take advantage of the opportunities that these world cities provide. In New York, for example, Tobier estimates that only one out of twenty older households have "enough" money to take full advantage of New York's unique opportunities for a higher quality of life. John, from Bay Ridge, is capable of enjoying these opportunities, but Marie from Hunt's Point cannot. This is moderated, to some degree, by the range of free cultural events and subsidized transportation available to city residents, but the large and growing number of people working for low wages in service industries may have even greater need for assistance when they grow older. The substantial costs associated with long-term care, particularly assisted living, home care and other alternatives to institutionalization, make them out of reach for many of the oldest old.

We know that aging in place in cities can be risky, particularly for older people living in poor, deprived neighborhoods (Phillipson 2004). Given the expense of living in a world city, the extraordinary inequality of wealth and cultural diversity within them, there is good reason to believe that these risks may be more pronounced in such places. As Warnes puts it, "World cities are different from the generality of urban settlements ... These distinctive attributes are bound to be expressed in the activities and quality-of-life of older people. There will be positive and negative effects. Among the negative attributes may be an exceptional level of dispersion and separation of families, which in turn may generate above-average levels of social isolation and anonymity" (Warnes and Strüder 2006). These problems can be made worse if older people elect to live in a city or neighborhood, not because it is "consistent with their biographies and life histories," but because they have no choice (Phillipson 2007).

Recent findings from the English Longitudinal Study of Ageing (ELSA) appear to support these concerns, at least with regard to Greater London. Based on their analysis of ELSA, Barnes and colleagues found that "older people who live in London are most likely to suffer from neighbourhood exclusion." It is not possible to examine neighborhoods within London using the ELSA survey, but the study noted that greater degree of social exclusion among older persons in Greater London compared with the rest of the United Kingdom may be due to the fact that London has the most deprived areas in the country (Barnes et al. 2006).

Even in Tokyo, which has much lower rates of older persons living alone than the other cities we examine, there are growing concerns about the number of isolated older people. In recent years, the Japanese media has reported a growth in the number of criminals who prey on isolated older persons and attempt to swindle them out of their life savings. As one report concluded, "big cities are becoming hostile places in many ways for elderly people living alone ... These con artists know all too well that elderly people who live in isolation and suffer from a weakening sense of judgment are easy targets" (*Japan Times* 2005).

WHAT DO WE KNOW ABOUT SOCIAL ISOLATION AMONG OLDER PERSONS IN WORLD CITIES?

During the past century, sociologists and anthropologists studied the effects of urbanization on social interaction among city residents. Many studies conclude that urbanization does not lead to social isolation, but social networks in urban areas appear to be different in nature than those in rural areas (Durkheim 1893; Sokolovsky and Cohen 1981; Mookherjee 1998). According to Putnam, relationships with friends and neighbors are more important to people living in urban areas, while relationships with family are more important for those living in rural areas. He argues that "Urban settings sustain not a single tightly integrated community, but a mosaic of loosely coupled communities. As mobility, divorce and smaller families have reduced the relative importance of kinship ties, especially among the more educated, friendship may actually have gained importance in the modern metropolis" (Putnam 2000).

Much of the social network literature is focused on differences between urban and rural areas, but it is clear that the extent and nature of social networks also vary within cities. In addition to the individual characteristics that influence the scope and nature of social networks among older people in cities, neighborhoods in which older people live influence their social networks and the quality of their lives (Fischer 1982; Dreier, Mollenkopf and Swanstrom 2001; Jackson 2001). Recent studies of "productive aging," for example, highlight the importance of local institutions (Morrow-Howell 2000; Dreier, Mollenkopf and Swanstrom 2001).

Older people who live in neighborhoods with lower crime rates, more parks, fewer vacant lots and greater recreational and social opportunities are more likely to have stronger social networks, more likely to exercise and more likely to have a positive outlook on life than those who live with higher crime, less green space and fewer recreational and social opportunities (Kuo et al. 1998; Wells et al. 2006; Wen and Christakis 2006).

Our examination of growing older in New York is consistent with these findings. John, the retired police officer from Bay Ridge in Brooklyn, lives in a safe, middle-class neighborhood with ample opportunities for social interaction. This is reflected both in his feeling about his neighborhood and his interactions with his neighbors. Marie, the widow from Mott Haven in the Bronx, lives in a poorer neighborhood with a built environment that is much less conducive to social interaction. She avoids leaving her apartment at night and does not have a close relationship with many neighbors. The attitudes of these two individuals are shared by other older persons in their neighborhoods. According to the 2002 New York City Housing and Vacancy Survey, 93 percent of older persons in Bay Ridge believe that they can trust their neighbors, and 90 percent believe that neighbors are willing to help each other (U.S. Census Bureau 2002). In Mott Haven, only 45 percent of older persons believe they can trust their neighbors, and 50 percent believe neighbors are willing to help each other (U.S. Census Bureau 2002).

Indeed, a number of features of city life can limit the mobility of among older people, discourage social interaction and increase the probability of isolation. As Phillipson argues, the idea that cities threaten to "imprison" older residents has been around for centuries. Phillipson notes that "cities combine images of mobility with those of loss and abandonment" (Phillipson 2004). Moreover, "the image of confinement is still present in the city, notably with the fear of entering particular neighbourhoods, or the danger of moving around areas at certain times of the day or night, or the threats posed by natural disasters" (Phillipson 2004:964).

Fear of crime can provide a strong deterrent to social interaction. In their study of aging in Paris, for example, Joel and colleagues found that older persons in Paris were much more concerned than those who live in rural areas in France about the lack of security in their neighborhoods. Among persons aged sixty and over, 15 percent of those living in provincial cities and 22 percent in the Paris region are concerned about security, compared with less than 5 percent in the rural areas. These concerns limited mobility and interaction and feelings of "connectedness" with the neighborhood (Joël and Haas 2006). In New York, older persons in Central Harlem often expressed concerns about going out at night. One woman told us that she was not comfortable walking around the neighborhood after dusk because her eyesight was "not what it used to be." She was not worried about falling, but she could no longer recognize people who approached her on the street in the evening.

Living alone is not the same thing as being lonely or isolated (Victor et al. 2000; de Jong-Gierveld 2004). In Nordic countries, for example, surveys show high rates of living alone, but low rates of loneliness, while in southern European countries, living alone is more closely associated with feelings of loneliness (de Jong-Gierveld 2004). Nevertheless, living alone is a risk factor for social isolation. The Commonwealth Fund Commission on the Elderly Living Alone indicated, based on a national telephone survey, that one-third of older Americans live alone and one-quarter of these persons, typically older women, live in poverty and report poor health: "the elderly person living alone is often a widowed woman in her eighties who struggles alone to make ends meet on a meager income. Being older, she is more likely to be in fair or poor health. She is frequently either childless or does not have a son or daughter nearby to provide assistance when needed. Lacking social support, she is a high risk for institutionalization and for losing her independent life style" (Commonwealth Fund 1988).

Rates of living alone among all age groups are typically higher in dense urban areas, which makes world cities a prime location for all the risks associated with such household arrangements. Indeed, there are millions of people who live alone in these world cities, and the oldest old living alone is the fastest-growing segment of these populations. When the percentage of older persons living alone in the urban core of each city is compared to its first ring, there is a striking convergence. In all four cities, rates of living alone among older persons are higher in the urban cores (Table 29.1). This is true for the population

Table 29.1
Percentage of Persons Living Alone in New York City, Paris, London and Tokyo, Ages 65+ and 85+

	65 and Over		85 and Over	
	Urban Core	**First Ring**	**Urban Core**	**First Ring**
New York City (2000)	44.1	29.7	55.3	40.1
Paris and First Ring (1999)	44.0	33.6	59.8	48.5
Greater London (2001)	50.4	39.3	57.4	52.3
Central Tokyo (2000)	24.7	20.4	23.0	19.2

Sources: New York–U.S. Census 2000; Paris–INSEE 1999; Tokyo–Census 2000; London–Census 2001.

over eighty-five years old and more generally for those over sixty-five years old.

When compared across the four cities, however, Tokyo stands out as a great contrast. Its inner core has the lowest rate of persons eighty-five years and older living alone (18 percent) in comparison to London (54 percent), Manhattan (55 percent) and Paris (59 percent). The contrast is even more striking when broken down by gender. Yet, it is important to note that the rate of living alone is more than twice as high in Tokyo as it is in Japan as a whole (Kudo 2006).

In addition to gender, data on characteristics of older persons in New York and London indicate that ethnicity and race are important factors in distinguishing among older persons who live alone. In New York, rates of living alone are significantly lower among Hispanics and Asians aged sixty-five and older and slightly lower among African Americans in this cohort than among their white counterparts. Likewise, in Greater London, rates of living alone are higher among the white population than black Caribbean, Indian and Bangladeshi populations. Some groups are more likely than others to have kin in the local area, but proximity does not always translate into greater support (Moriarty and Butt 2004; Cantor 2006).

Table 29.2
Percentage of Older Persons Living Alone in New York City, Paris, London and Tokyo, by Gender, Ages 85+

	Men	**Women**
Manhattan (1999)	41.3	67.9
Paris (1999)	39.6	67.6
Inner London (2001)	45.2	62.3
Inner Tokyo (2000)	15.9	26.4

Sources: Manhattan–New York City Housing and Vacancy Survey 1999; Paris–INSEE 1999; Inner Tokyo–Tokyo Metropolitan Government 2000; Inner London–UK Census 2001.

The challenge for policy makers and service providers is to distinguish among those older persons who live alone (and not exclude those who do not) how many are vulnerable due to social isolation, poverty, disabilities, lack of access to primary care, linguistic isolation or inadequate housing (e.g., living in walk-up apartments without elevators). Recent events in these cities illustrate the importance of meeting this challenge.

In the United Kingdom, the group Age Concern has helped to push the issue of social isolation among older people onto the policy agenda by arguing that loneliness and isolation among older people is one of the contributing factors to the large number of annual winter deaths due to hypothermia (*Peterborough Evening Telegraph* 2006). In New York City, the International Longevity Center-USA emphasized the issue of isolation of older people in the wake of the September 11 terrorist attacks. They found that "within 24 hours following the 9/11 terrorist attacks, animal advocates were on the scene rescuing pets, yet abandoned older and disabled people waited for up to seven days for an ad hoc medical team to rescue them" and concluded that "currently, there is no effective way to identify vulnerable people who are not connected to a community service agency" (O'Brien 2003).

The Chicago heat wave of 1995 provides another dramatic example of the consequences of isolated older persons (Klinenberg 2002). More recently, the 2003 heat wave in France provides a window into the extent of social isolation in Paris and its consequences. The French heat wave between August 1 and 20 of 2003 had devastating effects on older people, particularly in Paris, where there were 1,254 excess deaths over the preceding three-year average, an increase of 190 percent. Excess mortality was greatest among older women living alone (Cadot, Rodwin and Spira 2007).

Unfortunately, we do not have direct, comparable measures of social isolation among older persons in these four cities. Instead, we examine the range of factors that are associated with isolation and social exclusion. These include: access to shops, amenities, transportation and medical care; innovative programs to encourage social interaction; the concentration of poverty in neighborhoods; and the cost and quality of housing.

FEATURES OF WORLD CITIES THAT PROTECT AGAINST SOCIAL ISOLATION

Neighborhood Amenities

In 1777, Samuel Johnson remarked that "When a man is tired of London he is tired of life; for there is in London all that life can afford" (as cited in Warnes and Strüder 2006:214). This assessment is, in many respects, still true today, and applies equally well to all four of our world cities. Each of these cities offers an extraordinary array of amenities, including retail shops, museums, theaters, concert halls and libraries.

Residents of these cities, and to a lesser extent, the inhabitants of nearby suburbs, enjoy an incomparable array of cultural activities. The concentration

In front of a café in Central Paris. Photo by Victor Rodwin.

of theaters, cinemas, concert halls, museums, not to mention cultural institutions, is particularly high in these world cities. As one resident of the Stuyvesant Town neighborhood in lower Manhattan exclaimed, "I have everything I could want in my neighborhood. It is a wonderful place to live and I would never want to move!"

Furthermore, retired persons in all four cities benefit from numerous cultural institutions at reduced prices, where they can enjoy events that are reserved for them. Free concerts are not rare and certain time slots are reserved for retired persons, which confer on them advantages not given to those engaged in full-time professional activities.

In Paris, holders of the Paris Emerald card enjoy free access to certain institutions managed by the Paris Administration, such as museums (permanent exhibitions), parks and gardens, pools and public baths and outdoor sporting areas. Older persons are also eligible for subsidized meals in any of the forty-four Emerald restaurants that are operated by the Paris Administration.[5] One

Woman in a wheelchair in Tokyo. Photo by Jay Sokolovsky.

can find at least one such restaurant in every arrondissement (administrative district) of Paris, and certain such areas have as many as four.

In the eastern area of London, interviews with older residents also emphasize the importance of "shops, cafes, youth clubs, sports and social facilities" (Cattell and Evans 1999). According to older persons in East London, these neighborhood institutions improve quality of life and produce a socially cohesive community, by encouraging interactions among different groups of people (Cattell and Evans 1999).

Yet, some researchers in Paris are concerned that the recent disappearance of neighborhood shops has eliminated an important venue for social interactions among neighbors. Despite their efforts, the Paris authorities have not managed to prevent this evolution, which is decidedly harmful to the quality of life and social interaction among many neighborhoods. Over the last decade, nearly a quarter of small businesses in Paris have closed for good.

The high value of land is reflected in the rents of commercial leases in the center of Paris. These high rents make it difficult for the small shops on which older people traditionally rely to remain in business. Even in the outskirts of the city, there has been a progressive disappearance of grocery stores that are now located some distance from the streets on which people live and which rent to most other shops. Likewise, banks, medical practices and real estate agencies replace butchers, fishmongers and newsagents and even cafes (de Chanay 2003). The lack of small shops is something that disturbs older persons in Paris when they assess the quality of their neighborhoods (Michaudon 2001).

Transportation

Adequate transportation is crucial to older persons and their ability to remain independent and avoid isolation. For example, one recent U.S. survey found that older persons listed a lack of transportation as one of the major barriers to seeing a physician (Fitzpatrick et al. 2004). Without adequate transportation, older persons are less likely to receive the services they need, less likely to be engaged in the community and it is more difficult for them to remain in the community.

In rural and suburban areas of the United States, and in many cities as well, there is limited public transportation and automobiles are the primary source of transportation. If older persons do not own a car or are either unable or choose not to drive, their mobility is often severely restricted. Unfortunately, 21 percent of persons sixty-five years and over do not drive. Some older persons do not drive because of poor physical or mental abilities, and others do not drive because they are concerned about safety, but some do not drive because they do not own a car (National Household Travel Survey 2001). African American, Hispanic and Asian American persons sixty-five years and over are disproportionately affected by inadequate public transportation because they are much less likely than their white counterparts to drive.

Public transportation improves the mobility of older persons in many cities, but even in New York City, with its extensive bus and subway system, older people face limitations. Few subway stations have elevators, so for many older people, subways are not a realistic form of transportation. The New York City bus system is much better for people with disabilities, but in some sections of Queens and Staten Island, the bus routes are more limited and the stops less frequent than in the dense urban core of Manhattan. As Tobier explains, "Manhattan, because of its much greater degree of residential concentration and density, is second to none among the boroughs in respect to its user-friendly public transit facilities" (Tobier 2006). When interviewing older people living in these "outer boroughs," we often heard complaints about the infrequency of bus service—or how impractical it was to use the bus system for grocery shopping. An eighty-two-year-old man living on the north shore of Staten Island told us he felt "trapped" because it was so difficult for him to visit places outside his immediate neighborhood.

Along with the problems faced by older people living in less densely population neighborhoods of the outer boroughs, older persons throughout New York complain about the adequacy of "access-a-ride," the "paratransit" service for people unable to ride regular public transit. The service is mandated by the Americans with Disabilities Act (ADA) and operated by MTA New York City Transit. The people we interviewed for our study complained that although the

"access-a-ride" vans usually show up, they are often late and this poses difficulty for older people who are frail and unable to wait on street corners for
long periods of time. The transportation system to hospitals in Inner London is
comparable to the "access-a-ride" program in New York—and seems to generate comparable complaints. According to a 2006 report by Anne Gray:

Transport to medical appointments is particularly difficult. Because hospital transport
involves a collective minibus which picks up several patients in turn from different places, the route is often very slow and roundabout and a journey of a mile or two can take
an hour and a half each way. There is a risk of appointments being missed if hospital
transport fails to arrive in time due to some delay or misunderstanding. One interviewee
had missed several appointments from this factor. (Gray 2006)

The transportation situation in Paris is similar to that in New York City.
Older Parisians are entitled to special passes for free transportation, and there
is a dense network of public transportation; free access is granted to persons
sixty years and over who are holders of specific cards (Emerald, Amethyst or
ONAC).[6] Nevertheless, it is important to note that if it is relatively easy to
travel to and from Paris, traveling from one point in the suburbs to another can
be very complicated and more time-consuming, even if the distances are
shorter. The authorities and businesses involved are doing their utmost to correct these problems, but the transportation system remains oriented primarily
towards the center of the region.

Centers of Medical Excellence

One component of the World Health Organization's definition of an "age-
friendly city" is "accessible and appropriate health services." Several studies
indicate that health and functional status influence social relations (Cerhan and
Wallace 1993; Bowling, Grundy and Farquhar 1995; Mendes et al. 1996). People in poor health are less likely to have strong social networks and interact
regularly with others—and those with poor social networks tend to have worse
health. As Lund explains, "this would mean that a vicious circle is developed
resulting in continuous deterioration in functional ability and weaker contacts
with other people" (Avlund 2004).

All four cities, particularly their urban cores—Manhattan, Inner London,
Paris and Inner Tokyo—are centers of medical excellence. They enjoy a concentration of physicians and acute hospital beds, including those among large
university teaching hospitals (Rodwin and Gusmano 2006). Do older residents
of these world cities benefit from living in close proximity to the world-class
medical care that exists within them?

With some exceptions, the answer appears to be yes for older residents of
Paris and Inner London. Residents of these urban cores are less likely than
people living in other parts of the country to suffer from "avoidable mortality,"
and die before the age of seventy-five from a treatable condition. They are also
are more likely to receive specialty medical services, like bypass surgery or

angioplasty (Gusmano, Rodwin and Weisz 2007). With regard to avoidable mortality, our city-level analysis of health and economic disparities highlights the differences across these systems with regard to the geographic distribution of access to health services that is powerful and previously not documented. We find that the lowest income neighborhoods of Manhattan have rates of avoidable mortality that are significantly higher than the rest of the city. This is not true in Inner London or Paris.[7]

When we examine the management of chronic conditions, which has significant implications for the functional status of older persons, our findings are similar. There are some geographic and racial disparities in access to primary care and the management of chronic conditions within Inner London, but these disparities are not as severe as those we observe in Manhattan (Gusmano, Rodwin and Weisz forthcoming). To document these disparities, we examine "avoidable hospital conditions" (AHCs) across and within these urban cores. Among adults, AHCs are hospitalizations for conditions like pneumonia, congestive heart failure, asthma, diabetes and chronic obstructive pulmonary disease (COPD). These conditions, if managed properly, do not usually lead to a hospital admission. As a result, high rates of hospitalizations for these conditions are recognized in the literature as an indicator of poor access to timely and effective medical care (Gusmano et al. 2007).

In Manhattan, we find a strong correlation between median household income, by zip code of residence and discharge rates for AHCs. Ethnicity and insurance status on AHCs are also significant factors. The odds of AHCs are much higher among African Americans and Hispanics than among whites, and AHCs are also significantly related to health insurance status. Moreover, the significant geographic variation in discharge rates among NYC zip codes reflects the fact that older residents of poor neighborhoods were less likely to have health insurance before they turned sixty-five and are less likely to be covered by Medicare (Parts A as well as B).[8]

In addition to these problems of insurance coverage for a portion of New York City's older population, there is also the problem of inequities in the spatial distribution of medical care resources, reflecting the unequal distribution of wealth, income and other goods and services (Politzer et al. 1991; Fossett and Perloff 1995; Andrulis 1997; Rodwin and Gusmano 2006; Gusmano et al. 2007). For example, there are high concentrations of medical and social services in areas where high-income-yielding jobs are most dense and in those neighborhoods where most residents work in these jobs, with low concentrations elsewhere. Neighborhoods in which higher-income people live also have higher rates of utilization of medical and social services compared with lower-income neighborhoods (Lantz and House 1998).

Centers of Innovation

Faced with the challenges of an aging population, each of the four world cities we examined have created programs designed to improve the health, quality of life and social interaction of older persons. Even the centralized unitary states of Japan, France and the United Kingdom have been unable to meet the needs of the oldest old without close collaboration with local government, non-profit organizations, community and neighborhood organizations and families.

National health programs address many of these needs, but not all. In particular, national health programs do not cover social services. In all of these places, the financing and delivery of social services tends to be more decentralized. Even city governments find it useful to rely on nongovernmental organizations to identify and respond to the needs of the oldest old.

Japan has the most centralized system of long-term care, but since there is an important financial contribution by prefectures and municipalities in funding this program, Tokyo Metropolitan Government and the individual wards within Tokyo, share financial risk with central government. They therefore have an incentive to plan the configuration of long-term care services and, to whatever extent possible, reduce the amount of institutional care people receive. This requires them to assess the housing, transportation and health and social service needs of older persons within their jurisdiction. Some wards can afford to provide more services than others. For example, Tokyo's Nakano, Shinagawa, Ota and Shibuya wards all provide preventive activities that are not financed by the other wards in that city (Okamoto 2006).

In France, although the financing of home help for persons with significant disabilities is more centralized than in Japan, Parisian authorities are still required to produce a local master plan for long-term care services, which includes social services, some of which are locally financed and provided. Furthermore, Paris provides cash allowances for very poor older persons, who are typically neither eligible for a pension nor for the *"allocation personnalisée d'autonomie"* (APA). APA, which was adopted in 2002, contributes toward the costs of daily home help services for people over sixty years who meet the dependency criteria.

Paris also offers a range of services for frail older persons living alone, which are more generous than those available in most other parts of France. In the aftermath of the 2003 heat wave deaths, the mayor's office developed a plan to help vulnerable older persons. By June 2006, after receiving a letter of invitation from the mayor, about 13,000 people with severe handicaps—most of whom were sixty-five years old and over—registered to be contacted and offered special services by the city's Social Services Agency in the event of a heat wave. Under the plan, a physician-led medical team conducts a preliminary screening and, if necessary, provides urgent medical services, transportation to a cooling center or other services. It is too early to evaluate this new plan, but during the 2006 heat wave in Paris, this new system appeared to increase the number of daily contacts for socially isolated older persons (Cadot, Rodwin and Spira 2007).

In the United Kingdom, the boroughs of London have responsibility for participating in the financing of, and deciding on placement of, older persons in social housing. Other examples, across all four cities, include city funding for telephone help lines, meal delivery for homebound older persons and transportation and rent subsidies.

Housing and long-term care can be strongly reinforced by such central government policies, as in Japan with preferential mortgage loans and long-term care insurance. Yet, there will always be a role for local government in implementing these policies, coordinating services and making its own policies. This is seen in London and New York for housing and residential care, in Paris for provision of nursing and residential homes, or in New York, London and Paris to manage contracts for the provision of meals to frail older persons.

In addition, each of our four cities has developed new forms of housing to meet the needs of older persons who cannot or do not wish to live alone, either because they lack the support of informal caregivers who can assist them with daily activities, or because, even with such support, they desire the company of others as opposed to individualized home care. This housing take two forms: congregate housing with common services, or individual apartments with attached and collective services (hereafter called enriched apartments). The former involves the construction of facilities for long-term care use, whereas the latter involves the grafting of services to preexisting housing stock. We find that the latter is much more readily available in the urban cores of these cities, where land is most expensive. Apartments of this kind represent an important innovative use of urban resources. However, because such units are tied in some way to the housing market, rather than being designated for a particular purpose, they are usually more expensive than are congregate facilities and are rarely fully funded through public means. Instead, various subsidies exist to pay for such housing and presume that the individual has some assets to pay for services. In the case of congregate housing, placement is means-tested in all four cities and is not readily available for the poor.[9] This type of subsidized care represents an intermediary form in an economic sense as well, somewhere between publicly funded long-term care and the private care one can procure in any of these cities.

Among the four cities, New York has the greatest variety of such intermediary forms, spanning the funding spectrum from private, for-profit facilities to government-funded residential programs. For those who can afford them, a variety of high- to middle-income apartment complexes exist with attached social and home health services. To date, twenty-eight of these complexes have become officially recognized NORCs (naturally occurring retirement communities): apartment complexes in which over 50 percent of the population is over fifty years old and which receive public funding to support their services for older persons. At the opposite extreme, there are public housing facilities set aside for older persons, some of which provide common services.

Like New York, Tokyo and Paris both provide congregate housing with collective services, or individualized apartments with collective services. In Tokyo, neither type is fully publicly funded, but subsidies do exist. In Paris, there are both residential/retirement homes, which include the *foyers-logements* (individual apartments with collective services), operated by a city agency

(CASVP), as well as the *maisons de retraite* (retirement homes). In London, there are residential care homes, but there are fewer of these places in London than in the coastal areas of the United Kingdom (Kilbey 2000). Unlike in New York and Paris, where funding exists from national sources, residential care homes in London are financed by each local authority. Residential care homes vary in terms of their size and the scope of services. Most provide room and board with congregate meals and some social services. A few also provide limited access to district nursing services. Although these homes may be appropriate for older people with mild cognitive impairment, they are designed primarily for people who do not have serious medical problems. Smaller residential care homes may only accommodate ten to fifteen older people, while others may accommodate more than one hundred older people.

In Tokyo, policy-makers face new incentives to develop more housing of this sort as a result of Japan's Long-Term Care Insurance program (LTCI). As Campbell and Campbell explain, "for a person at a given level of need, LTCI must pay at least $7–800 more per person per month for institutional care compared with the bill for community-based care. If the mayor of a Tokyo ward could arrange for 100 people to live in some sort of housing with community-based services, rather than an institution, it would save about $1 million" (Campbell and Campbell 2006). As a result, local officials in Tokyo are discussing with private developers the possibility of creating additional housing of this sort.

Paris provides the highest density of such community residential-care places, with 73.4 per 1,000 persons sixty-five and older, followed by New York City (60.8), Greater London (33.4) and Tokyo (11.9). With the exception of Tokyo, where cohabitation with children is still an important kind of living arrangement, the density of such community-based options is higher than that of institutional care settings. Even in London, nonmedicalized residential care places are more readily available than nursing home beds. Most notably, in Manhattan and Paris, the availability of enriched apartments far surpasses that of nursing home beds. Whether this is an outcome of deliberate policy or simply a reflection of market forces remains an open question; what is certain is that more care is currently provided in the community as opposed to in nursing home facilities.

Giving Voice to Older Residents

In all four world cities, municipal governments have invoked the rising importance of providing older persons with information about the multiplicity of services available to them and involving them in plans for the future. With respect to giving older persons greater voice, Paris's gerontological master plan called for a "Rights of Older People Charter," which is designed, in part, to provide older Parisians with an opportunity to voice their policy preferences. Tokyo Metropolitan Government conducted a consumer survey to evaluate the satisfaction of older persons with the implementation of LTCI. Furthermore, efforts to allow for greater voice vary within these cities. For example, in Tokyo, Nakano ward is notable for encouraging the direct participation of residents in policy-making. In this same spirit, Age Concern in the United Kingdom has advocated on behalf of "giving voice to all age groups" (Age Concern England 2000).

As for getting information to older persons, in Paris, the neighborhood coordination centers, or "Emerald Paris Points," provide information about existing services, address inquiries and assist older persons and their families and caregivers with decision making. In New York City, Department for the Aging provides a wealth of information about federal, state and local programs for older persons, including tools that help people determine their eligibility for different services. There are questions about how many older persons access this information on the Internet, but this is an important innovation that is likely to be used by an even larger portion of future cohorts of older persons.

FEATURES OF WORLD CITIES THAT PRODUCE SOCIAL ISOLATION

Just as the benefits of growing older in a world city are not shared equally among these cities, there are differences with regard to burdens associated with such places. In particular, the greater geographic concentration of poverty in New York and London distinguishes these "hard" world cities from their "soft" counterparts—Paris and Tokyo (Body-Gendrot 1996).

Previous studies of aging have often pointed to a close relationship between poverty and social isolation or loneliness (Townsend 1979; Lawton 1983). This is due, in part, to the fact that neighborhoods in which there is a high concentration of poverty, and an absence of middle- and upper-income residents, suffer from a lack of collective efficacy (Sampson, Raudenbush and Earls 1997). According to Browning and Cagney, places lacking collective efficacy are neighborhoods in which residents are less likely to trust their neighbors and are less capable of working to secure resources for the community (2003).[10]

With respect to neighborhood polarization of this kind, there are stark differences among these cities. London and New York are characterized by the largest socioeconomic disparities across neighborhoods, and both have neighborhoods in which there are high concentrations of deprivation and few affluent residents (Hamnett 1994). The "dualism" that we see in London and New York is one of the characteristics closely associated with world cities. In both cities, globalization has produced high-income jobs in the financial and technology sectors—and a host of low-income jobs in the service sector. Growing occupational polarization in these cities has led to greater income polarization and special segregation. In New York, this has reinforced existing racial and ethnic cleavages. In London, it has reinforced social class divisions (Sassen 1994; White 1998).

Yet, as White explains, this characterization of world cities does not describe Paris or Tokyo particularly well.[11] Paris has become known as a "soft" global city, in contrast to London and New York, because, reflecting national policy, it provides more income support, family services and health services to the poor (Body-Gendrot 1996). This state role goes beyond the support of an incomes policy across occupational groups. It also tempers the tendency toward spatial segregation that is more pronounced in New York and London. Although there are increasingly small neighborhoods with concentrated ethnic minorities, such as the Goutte-d'Or, Belleville or Chateau Rouge, there are still no areas the size of an *arrondissement* that can claim a spatial division along ethnic lines. This outcome is partly the result of the explicit attempt to support social heterogeneity across spatial units of Paris—the policy of *mixité social* (Rodwin 2006). The central state, as well as the Paris authorities, attempt to alleviate the harsher impacts of globalization and the general difficulties of growing older in a city characterized by increasing polarization. Likewise, Tokyo is characterized by less social and spatial polarization, not only because there is less ethnic diversity than in the other cities, but also because income distribution is more equal.

Yet, in both Paris and Tokyo, income inequality increased significantly during the 1990s. In this sense, both of these cities are, indeed, global cities with the kinds of social polarization analyzed by Saskia Sassen (Sassen 1994). It will be important to monitor the evolution of these cities and the degree to which these nations and cities remains willing and able to protect residents from the pressures of globalization.

Cost and Quality of Housing

The quality of housing is a vital component of quality of life for older persons. Without decent, affordable housing, it is impossible to gracefully "age in place" (Stafford, Part V). Generally, housing for older persons in London is better than it was in the early 1990s and, according to Warnes and Strüder (2006), "it is no longer the case that poor housing is associated with older occupants." Yet, there is still tremendous variation within the city of London. Most postwar public housing has high standards with basic amenities, but public housing in the poorer boroughs of London is often deficient, even lacking central heating. Neither the government, nor private landlords, have invested adequately in home improvement in many London boroughs.

Paris has a very old housing stock dominated by small units. In central Paris, housing is more antiquated and substandard than in its first ring. Within Paris, a slightly higher share of older persons live in housing units without bathrooms, and a slightly lower share live in housing units without toilets than their younger counterparts.

In contrast, the quality of housing in New York City is better for older persons compared with their younger counterparts. Nearly all older New Yorkers live in housing units with complete kitchen and bathroom facilities. Older persons are also more likely to own their homes (48.8 percent vs. 33 percent). Among those who rent, more than half enjoy some form of rent stabilization—either rent control or rent exemption. Another 20 percent of older persons live in public housing. Housing represents an important source of wealth, particularly for older persons in the United States (Muller et al. 2002). Despite this, housing costs are a major concern for older New Yorkers. While these expenses faced by older persons who own their homes are often lower than for the population as a whole, they tend to represent a higher percentage of income (Muller et al. 2002). The costs associated with both maintaining property and increases in property taxes represent significant financial burdens to older persons living on fixed incomes. According to the U.S. Census, ownership expenses represent more than 35 percent of income for 6 percent of New Yorkers aged sixty-five and over (U.S. Census Bureau 2000a). Older renters face an even more difficult situation. Rent increases and fluctuations in the rental market place older renters in a precarious economic situation. Although many older New Yorkers enjoy protection against rent increases through rent control and rent exemption programs, 46 percent of persons sixty-five and over pay 35 percent or more of their incomes in rent.

In London, Paris and New York, the percentage of older persons living in substandard housing is significantly higher in the poor neighborhoods of the city. For example, according to the New York City Housing and Vacancy Survey, about one-quarter of older persons living in the city's poorest neighborhoods live in quarters that are unsafe for human habitation (Knapp 2006). Although Marie from Hunts Point in the Bronx did not complain about any problems with the quality of her apartment during our interview, more than 40 percent of renters age 65 and over in the Bronx report the existence of four or more maintenance deficiencies (Knapp 2006). We do not currently have systematic data on the quality of housing among older persons in Tokyo, but John and Ruth Campbell argue that much of the housing in Tokyo is inadequate to meet the needs of frail older persons (Campbell and Campbell 2006).

CONCLUSION

The unprecedented convergence of population aging and urbanization presents great challenges and opportunities for cities and their older residents. Our project explores how the four largest cities in the wealthiest nations of the world—New York, London, Paris and Tokyo—are confronting these changes.

Many of the institutions, neighborhood characteristics and other social factors that influence the health and well-being of older people may be beyond the reach of city government and must be addressed at the national level. Cities are limited in their ability to redistribute income and address neighborhood-level poverty and inequality (Judd and Swanstrom 1994). Similarly, many environmental issues must be addressed at a regional level (Sclar 2003). Nevertheless, we should not underestimate the ability of city governments to address social issues, including the health and well-being of older residents. Nor should we overestimate the capacity of the existing national welfare states to serve those who fall through the cracks of a host of health and social welfare programs. Cities, and other local governments, address many social problems that are not addressed adequately by the national government.

Similarities and Differences

Although the cities face similar challenges, they do so within national health, social and long-term care policy contexts that are quite different. With regard to heath care, Parisians and Tokyoites are covered by systems of national health insurance (NHI). The National Health Service (NHS) covers Londoners. Medicare (Parts A and B) covers most older New Yorkers, but not all. As a result, there are greater disparities in access to health care services among older residents of New York City than of any of the other cities we examine.

There are also differences in coverage of long-term care. Japan is the only country of the four with long-term care insurance. Home help and home nursing services for older persons are covered primarily by the national Long-Term Care Insurance (LTCI) scheme, and everyone forty years old and over contributes to this program. There are two broad categories of beneficiaries for LTCI. Those aged forty to sixty-four must pay insurance premiums, but are only eligible for services if their long-term care needs are the result of one of fifteen aging-related diseases. Those sixty-five and over pay higher premiums, which are deducted from their pensions, and are eligible for home care services regardless of the level of their needs. Users are expected to pay 10 percent of the cost of services, and the other 90 percent is covered by a mix of municipal, prefectural and national funds. Premiums in 2000 were around $24 per person per month, but they vary across municipalities (including across Tokyo's wards).

Yet, despite the differences in the national policy frameworks within which world cities operate, we see a host of important similarities. First, in all four cities, even in the most centralized unitary states such as France, Japan and Great Britain, there is also an area of discretionary local policy. This is particularly important with respect to the process of determining eligibility and subsequently arranging for home nursing services and a host of social services and home help services. For example, local authorities in London have a critical role in the allocation of residential care for frail older persons; social services for older persons may vary greatly by *ku* within Tokyo, and social welfare in Paris is reputedly more generous than in most other French departments, though there appears to be considerable variation within Paris.

Furthermore, despite differences in the extent of access to health and social services among these cities, they are all struggling to find ways to cope with the challenges associated with population aging. In Manhattan, Inner London and Paris, over half of the oldest old live alone. Within this group, however, we do not know the relative share of those who are isolated and lonely versus those who have the ability to remain independent. Learning more about the location of a city's most vulnerable oldest old is crucially important. The 2003 August heat wave in France served as a dramatic example of how a city with a high concentration of older persons can be completely unprepared to cope with its aging population. In Paris, the result was thousands of deaths. But many people do not realize that a comparable event took place in Chicago in 1995. Similarly, thousands of older New Yorkers were left stranded and dangerously isolated during the days immediately after 9/11. Despite a number of striking differences in the health and social systems of these nations, neither France nor the United States were prepared to address the needs of vulnerable older persons living in their major cities. During the coming decades we will learn whether lessons from these tragedies will lead to more effective efforts to address the needs of older urban residents.

NOTES

1. In this chapter, we draw on our original pilot survey of older residents from ten neighborhoods of New York City: Mott Haven (census tract 69) in the Bronx; Bay Ridge (census tract 52.01) and Williamsburg (census tract 481) in Brooklyn; Central Harlem (census tract 236), Upper East Side (census tract 154), Peter Cooper/Stuyvesant Town (census tract 60) and Clinton/Chelsea (census tract 93) in Manhattan; Bayside (997.02) and Flushing (census tracts 1033 and 1163) in Queens; and the Rosebank section of North Shore (census tract 6) in Staten Island. During our semistructured interviews, we asked older residents a host of questions about: (1) the built environment and attitudes about the neighborhood as a place to live; (2) medical resources and neighborhood institutions; (3) social interaction, including: work and retirement; social and political activities, volunteer work; and participation in neighborhood groups and activities; (4) morale and life satisfaction; health, functional ability and physical activity. The questionnaire was based on: (1) the survey used by Marjorie Cantor for the 1970 and 1990 studies of older New Yorkers conducted by the New York City Department for the Aging and the New York Center for Policy on Aging of the New York Community Trust; (2) the survey developed for the AdvantAge Initiative; and (3) the survey of social and health indicators across King County, Washington, developed by Communities Count. We recruited participants at senior centers, religious institutions, senior housing facilities and other neighborhood institutions to produce a convenient sample of older persons living in these neighborhoods. The final sample included 216 interviews.

2. Organization of Economic Cooperation and Development

3. Fortunately, this is beginning to change (Stafford this volume). The World Health Organization began a program to promote "age friendly cities." This initiative is new and has not yet produced significant results, but the WHO's leadership in bringing attention to this issue is a welcome development. (http://www.who.int/ageing/age_friendly_cities/en/index.html)

4. Although a recent comparison of England and the United States indicates that Americans have inferior health status compared to the English (Banks et al. 2006), this study examined indicators that fail to distinguish between the determinants of population health that can be attributed to health care and those that cannot (poverty or lifestyle).

5. The Paris Emerald Card is given to Parisians sixty years and over and to certain individuals with disabilities who satisfy residency requirements (three years over the

past five) and whose income tax does not exceed a ceiling set by the Council of Paris (2028 euros in 2003). This card is given for a one-year period and is renewable. Parisians living in institutions owned by the CASVP outside the city are also eligible.

6. The Emerald card allows for free public transportation in Paris. The Amethyst card, by contrast, is purchased on a means-tested basis and allows for free public transport in Paris and the surrounding region. The eligibility conditions are similar. The ONAC card is provided for veterans and also allows for free public transportation.

7. Comparable hospital administrative data are not currently available for Japan, so we had to exclude it from this aspect of our analysis.

8. Medicare Part A is the hospital insurance component of the program. Part A helps pay for inpatient hospital care, limited inpatient care in a skilled nursing facility, home health care and hospice care. Part A has deductibles and coinsurance, but most people do not have to pay premiums for Part A. Medicare Part B helps pay for doctor's services, outpatient hospital services, durable medical equipment and a number of other medical services and supplies that are not covered by Part A. Part B has premiums, deductibles and coinsurance that an individual must pay through another insurance plan or by one of the Medicare savings programs that the state and the federal government have created to help low-income Medicare beneficiaries with their out-of-pocket expenses.

9. For example, while Medicaid does fund assisted living programs in adult homes, only around 3,000 such places were available in New York City in 2000. It is difficult to evaluate the "need" for this type of housing, but conversations with representatives of the New York City Department for the Aging and the New York City Housing Authority reinforce our view that there are not enough affordable assisted living facilities to meet the needs of older New Yorkers.

10. As Browning and Cagney explain, "collective efficacy may aid in correcting or avoiding the accumulation of neighborhood physical hazards such as decaying infrastructure and housing stock. Communities with the capacity to solicit and secure external resources to correct potentially risky conditions and monitor vulnerable residents (e.g., the elderly) are likely to enhance health" (2003). They find that "the prevalence of middle and upper middle class residents in urban communities is an important structural factor influencing health promoting conditions" (Browning and Cagney 2003).

11. This leads White to reject the "global city hypothesis" because it is too simple, overemphasizing the importance of capital mobility and globalization, while underemphasizing political variables that explain the differences among "world" or "global" cities.

CHAPTER 30

Elder Residences and Outsourced Sons: Remaking Aging in Cosmopolitan India

Sarah Lamb

One sun-drenched winter morning in 2006, I stood up to take leave from three ladies living in a modest home for elders situated amidst quiet, two-story homes in a middle-class neighborhood on the southern outskirts of Kolkata (formerly Calcutta), India. I bent down to brush the ladies' feet in the familiar gesture of *pranam* practiced by many Indians, where a junior touches an elder's feet in a sign of respect, and in turn the elder places his or her hands affectionately on the junior's head and offers blessings, such as "May you live well" or "May your children be well." The first two ladies, Uma-di and Kavika-di,[1] received the gesture and offered me blessings, but the third woman, Kalyani-di, stepped back. She was the most elegant of the three, at age eighty-one standing tall with her long, thick silvery hair tied into an attractive knot, dressed in a fresh white and taupe sari, with thin gold bangles adorning her wrists. She asked, her voice laced with chagrin, "Why are you offering so much *pranam* to us—we, who are so full of sadness, who can't give you proper blessings?"

It was as if living in an old age home had stripped Kalyani-di of the capacity to be a fruitful, potent elder. She had just been telling me of how she goes over and over in her mind, begging her son and daughter-in-law, with whom she almost never actually speaks, to give her "release" from the old age home. She had reflected, "If we had grown up with the idea that we might live separately from our children, then it might not be so hard to get used to now. But with our own eyes we had never seen or known anything like this. We never could have even dreamed that a *briddhabas* (abode for elders) existed, that we would be here, in a place like this!" Residences for elders are in fact a strikingly new phenomenon emerging quite rapidly in India's middle-class cosmopolitan centers, replacing for those who live in them the more traditional multigenerational co-residential family ties that many have long viewed as central to a proper way of aging, family and society in India.

Gopal Singh, originally from northern India, at seventy-two also lived separately from his children, but in an arrangement that he viewed sanguinely as one of his active making. He and his wife had first migrated to the United States twelve years earlier, intending to reside with their U.S.-settled children, following the elder Singh's retirement as a Government of India railroad officer. Once in the United States, however, Singh gradually ended up taking on purposefully what he saw as "American" life ways, eventually moving with his wife into a separate apartment in a government-subsidized elder housing unit. "Old age is a gift from God when spent in dignity, as in this country," he remarked one morning. "I prefer an independent life. I like to live on my own instead of living with relatives. I am happy now."

Such new trends surrounding aging and family in India and its diasporas were the focus of a multidisciplinary conference in Kolkata on "Senescence" that I participated in during spring 2006 while doing fieldwork in the city. Although the participants presented a variety of viewpoints and narratives, the most impassioned speech—impromptu closing remarks offered by a distinguished senior professor from the University of Delhi—held up the family as the unmistakable proper site of aging, and new institutions such as elder residences a modern outrage:

Some of this discussion has seemed to be advocating that we adopt old age homes. But we should *not*! ... The very data provided ... here shows that the majority of old age homes in Kolkata are *businesses*! ... They are making *money*!—they are making *money*!—by having people in old age homes. Let's not get persuaded by the idea that old age homes are the answer. They are not! *Family* is the answer. We need to strengthen the *family*!

These three brief vignettes speak vividly to the variety and intensity of meanings accruing to aging for contemporary Indians. Everyday conversations, newspaper stories, films and gerontological texts have over recent years abounded with talk about how to work out aging, and with it, a valued society. Such public narratives highlight a new cultural terrain, where family members are dispersed nationally and transnationally, and values such as materialism, consumerism and individualism (all often associated with the West and/or modernity) have taken center stage. This chapter explores such discourses, focusing on the ways older persons themselves are crafting and experiencing new forms of aging, as they confront—both embracing and critiquing—processes of "modern," "Western" and "global" living. The central social transformation examined here is a shift away from the intergenerational family as the key site of aging and elder care, to an increasing reliance on private institutions, individual selves and the state. Such emerging novel modes of aging and family are taken by Indians, at home and abroad, to represent a profound transformation—a transformation involving not only aging *per se*, but also core cultural and moral visions surrounding family, gender, personhood and the very identity of India as a nation and culture.

The focus of this chapter is on cosmopolitan middle-class Indians,[2] among whom the social-cultural changes of aging explored here are most salient. In India's rural and urban poor communities—which still make up the majority of the nation's population—elder residences and transnational living remain notably scarce. India's urban poor elderly tend to blame lack of care from their children much more on (timeless) poverty than on anything to do with modernity. And urban poor and rural Indian seniors are not participating extensively in the complex transnational mobilities and global interconnections that so engage their middle- and upper-class neighbors. Fieldwork related to this project was conducted in West Bengal, India, primarily in Kolkata, and among Indian American families in California and Massachusetts, from 1989 through 2007.[3] Kolkata is the capital of the Indian state of West Bengal in northeastern India. The city has an extended metropolitan population of over 15 million, making it the third most populous urban area in India and one of the largest in the world.

CULTURAL AND MORAL VALUES SURROUNDING "TRADITIONAL" AGING: THE JOINT FAMILY AND INTERGENERATIONAL TIES

To understand the complex of contemporary social changes surrounding aging and families in India, one must consider people's understandings of a more traditional past. Many Indians have conventionally recognized two salient life aims to be pursued in old age: (1) spiritual awareness and loosening ties to the world in preparation for the myriad leave-takings and transitions of dying; and (2) kinship and being served within an intimate multigenerational family. According to the classical Hindu[4] ethical-legal texts, the Dharmasastras, persons move through a series of four life stages or "shelters" (asramas)—as a student, a married householder, a disengaged forest dweller (vanaprastha) and finally a wandering ascetic renouncer (sannyasi) (Kane 1968–1975:vol. 2; Manu 1886, 1991). In this schema, two life phases constitute older age. When a man[5] sees the sons of his sons and white hair on his head, he knows it is time to enter the "forest-dweller" or vanaprastha phase—departing from his home to live as a hermit, either with or without his wife, or remaining in the household but with a mind focused on God. During the final life stage as a sannyasi or renouncer, a man strives to become free from all worldly attachments, through taking leave of family members, abnegating caste identity, giving up all possessions, performing his own funeral rites, begging and constantly moving from place to place so no new attachments will develop. If a person is able to free himself or herself from all binding attachments in this way, he may be able to attain ultimate "release" (moksha) from the cycle of rebirths, redeaths and reattachments to worldly life, or samsar. Few Hindus actually move to the forest or become wandering renouncers, but many do speak of late life as an appropriate and valuable time for focusing increasingly on God and spiritual awareness even while living at home, as part of preparing for the transitions of dying and grappling with the reality of human transience.[6]

Contemporary narratives of aging and social change in India do not highlight the theme of late-life spirituality as much as the theme of the family. Discourses in which the "materialist" West is encroaching into "spiritual" India—with valuable as well as injurious results—do abound; yet many feel that Western materialism exerts even more of a pull on the young than the old. Further, some of my older informants suggest that the waning family ties of modernity and globalization may in fact *facilitate* or *complement* the Hindu tradition of late-life spirituality. For some view the modern old age home as a contemporary version of the ancient Hindu "forest," a retreat away from the family, an image I will get to below.

What many view as the second major aim of a traditional old age—to be served within an intimate multigenerational family—is the theme that figures most prominently in contemporary Indian discourses of aging and social change. Indians have long seen caring for aged parents in a family home as a fundamental part of a reciprocal intergenerational cycle; and, in fact, the majority of Indian elders today, as in the past, continue to live in a multigenerational family setting.[7] There is a strong pervasive sense in India that the most "normal," culturally expected and proper way to manage aging is in the family. Both daily and media discourses widely portray living within an intergenerational "joint family"[8] as representing a quintessentially *Indian* way of life, morality and tradition.

A joint family: senior parents, two sons, their wives and children coresiding in a three-bedroom Kolkata flat.

According to visions of the proper joint family, intergenerational ties entail long-term bonds of reciprocal indebtedness extending throughout life and even after death. Children live with and care for their aging parents out of a profound sense of moral, even spiritual, duty to attempt to repay the inerasable "debts"(*rn*) they owe their parents for all the effort, expense and affection their parents expended to produce and raise them. Interestingly, it is precisely what parents once gave their children—such as a body in birth, food, material goods, money, a home, forms of love, the cleaning of urine and feces—that children are expected to reciprocate to their parents, years later in old age, and by reconstructing and venerating them as ancestors after death. Although the common discourse is that "children" provide for and coreside with their senior parents, in practice it is usually *sons* and daughters-in-law who fill this role. Upon marriage, daughters formally relinquish obligations to their own parents, taking on responsibility for their in-laws. Ironically, though, Indians commonly describe daughters as more "loving" than sons, and many married daughters offer their parents visits, gifts and practical assistance throughout life.

The providing of care for one's seniors is often termed *seva*, service to and respect for the aged. *Seva*, a key component of perceived traditional Indian ways of aging, can be offered to deities as well as elders. When provided to elders, *seva* entails acts such as serving food and tea, massaging tired limbs, combing hair, bringing warm bath water and offering loving respect.[9] As part

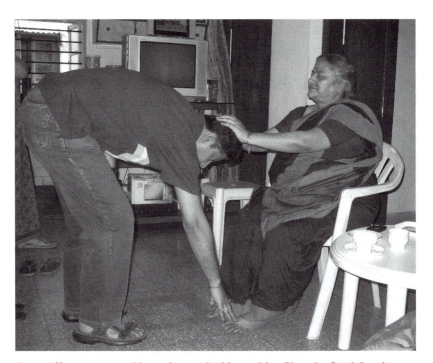

A son offers *pranam* to his mother as she blesses him. Photo by Sarah Lamb.

of intergenerational reciprocity, juniors perform *seva* not simply as a gift in the present, but in exchange for the elders' earlier tremendous labors in giving birth to and fostering them. *Pranam*, which I tried to offer old-age-home resident Kalyani-di, but was refused, is also part of serving elders properly, as well as a reciprocal action: Juniors bow down to touch their elders' feet in an act of respectful devotion, and in turn receive from their elders affectionate blessings.

Elders normally expect to gradually enter the phase of old age—when they are served more than they engage in serving—around the time that their sons are married, daughters-in-law enter the home, and (if they had been employed) retire from an active working life. "Old" or "increased" age (*buro bayas*) is thus based more on family transitions than a specific number of chronological years, although those with government jobs face a set retirement age of fifty-eight or sixty.[10] Often accompanied by years of ambivalence, arguing and competition, the senior couple in a multigenerational family will gradually hand over duties of reproduction, cooking and feeding to junior successors, usually a son or sons and their wives. Becoming widowed for a woman can plunge her rapidly into a dependent old age, as customarily property (including homes, businesses, land and bank accounts) pass from a deceased husband to his sons, even though Indian legal codes stipulate that a widow should receive a share of her husband's wealth. In practice, though, many families will simply state that a widowed woman has no need for money or property, since she can be more appropriately cared for by her sons.

The value and expectation of intergenerational reciprocity is widely described by Indians in everyday talk as a natural, expected, morally and religiously proper and rational way of doing things. For instance, one middle-aged Bengali man, whose frail mother was incontinent and bedridden, reflected to me one day while he was cleaning his mother's sheets on the shores of a pond in the village where he, his mother, wife and children lived in their family home:

Caring for parents is the children's duty; it is *dharma* [moral-religious order; right way of living]. As parents raised their children, children will also care for their parents during their sick years, when they get old. For example, if I am old and I have a bowel movement, my son will clean it and he won't ask, "Why did you do it there?" This is what we did for him when he was young. When I am old and dying, who will take me to go pee and defecate? My children will have to do it.

On their part, daughters-in-law speak of caring for parents-in-law less often in terms of reciprocity than in terms of a deeply felt social-moral duty, paired often with a real affection and respect that can develop over years of living together, along with not uncommonly a sense of tedious burden or irritation. Pratima, in her mid forties, says she cannot imagine *not* living with and caring for her widowed mother-in-law (although with her own two children settled in the United States, she does not expect the same from them). Pratima speaks unwaveringly of her commitment to, among other duties, sit with her mother-in-law for at least one hour each evening after she returns from work, hearing the details of the older woman's day. "It is so boring sometimes, I almost fall asleep. But I can't imagine not doing it."

As Pratima's comments suggest, people do now and have long recognized tensions in the intergenerational family system. Ethnographies of social-cultural life in India, for instance, have long portrayed tales of generational conflicts—particularly between mother-in-law and daughter-in-law, elders abandoned by children in the face of poverty, youth scoffing the old, small and nuclear-style families and the like.[11] Some describe the Indian joint family also as a patriarchal and restrictive institution, difficult especially for young women and even young sons.[12] So, even while frequently extolled in India, now and in the past, and widely considered the most "normal" form of aging and family, joint family living has never been perfectly harmonious, ubiquitous or revered.

Nonetheless, such a system of widely expected intergenerational reciprocity contrasts strikingly practices and outlooks in the United States, where among the white middle class in particular, the dominant expectation is that gifts will flow "down" from parent to child in a lifelong unidirectional manner. It is proper for parents to give to children (even, through gifts of money or inheritances, when their children are adults); but if an adult child gives to an aged parent, then the parent is seen as childlike.[13] Although of course many U.S. children spend much time and effort caring for senior parents (escorting to the doctor, preparing meals, offering love and companionship), most parents and children would be equally uncomfortable if the child were called upon to provide intimate bodily care or full material support for a parent. Further, it is common for both older Americans and their adult children to desire to live independently. Andrei Simic observes: "What the American elderly seem to fear most is 'demeaning dependence' on their children or other kin. Rather, the ideal is to remain 'one's own person'" (1990:94).

THE "BREAKDOWN OF THE JOINT FAMILY"[14]

At the same time that people practice and extol multigenerational family living in India, discourses in India's urban centers widely proclaim that the joint family system is fast breaking down. In its place, apparent especially within India's urban middle-class milieus, are emerging *formal institutions of nonfamily-based aging*, such as old age homes and organizations offering elder care for hire. No single cause, but rather a whole complex of social changes, explains the rise of elder homes and other forms of nonfamily living in India.

In prevailing narratives—offered by both young and old, men and women, those living in joint families and without, as well as social scientists and the media—several interrelated forces come up repeatedly as at the root of such changes in middle-class Indian family life. One of them is that today's young middle-class women, compared to those a generation earlier, are more likely to be older at marriage, to be more highly educated and to be working—meaning that, in general, daughters-in-law today have more voice, authority, and agency than their mothers-in-law did, and are often not as disposed as were their predecessors to serve, defer to and live with their husbands' parents. A second phenomenon is that many young adults are being drawn into vast national and global professional markets, moving far from aging parents and local family homes. Third, a host of interrelated ideologies and social forms is perceived to be pervading middle-class India—commonly attributed to "globalization," "Westernization" and the "modern." These include individualism, materialism, consumerism, a freedom from "traditional" rules and mores, gendered and aged egalitarianism, nuclear families, small flats, a pervasive lack of time and the institution of the old age home itself. Relatedly, with the burgeoning of a substantial economically prosperous middle class, more money is available to consider alternatives to the shared family home. That is, the "outsourcing" of elder care from the family to, for instance, old age homes requires economic resources that earlier generations did not readily possess.

Although much media and everyday discourse surrounding such processes is highly negative, it is striking that not all contemporary middle-class tales of extra-family elder care center on the "bad family" (Cohen 1998) or on modern *degeneration*. Rather, a range of other voices—from elders, junior kin, gerontologists and the media—are presenting nonfamily-based aging in quite sanguine terms, as a more practical, egalitarian, freeing, up-to-date and/or fulfilling way of organizing not only old age but also families, genders and society. Most people's perspectives are complexly ambivalent, combining positive and negative assessments. It is to such emerging forms of aging, and the richly complex and varied perspectives of those experiencing them, that this chapter now turns.

THE RISE OF OLD AGE HOMES IN INDIA

Perhaps the single most striking dimension of the emergence of a new mode of aging and family is the near flood of old age homes that has risen in India's major urban centers. Until the past two decades, old age homes scarcely existed in India, save for a handful established by Christian missionaries largely catering to the Anglo-Indian community and the very poor. Now there are hundreds across India, the vast majority founded over the last fifteen years.[15] Viewed as predominantly Western institutions, the homes are commonly referred to in English as "old age homes." Bengali alternatives include *briddhasram*—"shelter" (or ashram) for the aged or "increased" (*briddha*), and *briddhabas*—"abode" (*abas*) for the aged.

As primarily middle-class institutions, these new elder residences are possible only for those with retirement pensions, professional children and/or considerable savings.[16] Run by both nonprofit organizations and also private entrepreneurs, the rates range from about 1,000 to 5,000 Indian Rupees per month (a little over $20 to $100 USD), and often require a sizable joining fee or security deposit of anywhere from about 5,000 to 300,000 rupees (or about

$100 to $6,000). An ordinary retirement pension might range from about 3,000 to 15,000 rupees per month, so could cover the monthly expenses. However, some sell a home, or dip into their savings accounts, to come up with the deposit. In Kolkata during this fieldwork period, a full-time domestic servant's salary (six or seven days a week at about twelve hours per day) would be about 1,500 to 3,000 rupees per month, or roughly equivalent to the monthly fees of a modestly priced old age home. The poor cannot consider staying in such "pay-and-stay" homes, and to the extent they are aware of their emergence, speak of them as distinctly rich/big people's (*boro loker*) institutions.

Most of the old age homes to date require that residents be in fairly good physical and mental health, able to walk, talk and perform basic activities of daily living. Directors generally decide whom to admit based on an interview and at times a doctor's examination. Weekly or biweekly doctor visits are provided, but in the event that a resident becomes seriously ill or incapacitated, the policy of many institutions is that the resident must be sent "home." (A member of a Kolkata senior citizens club, at a gathering to discuss the new trend of old age homes, commented about this incongruous policy: "You are given an umbrella, and then just when it starts to rain, the umbrella is taken away!") Increasingly, some homes are beginning to harbor physically and/or mentally disabled elders who must, however, then pay additionally for a private nurse's care.

The homes range in size from about five to fifty residents,[17] and accommodations can come in the form of single, double or dormitory-style rooms. In some, a husband and wife (or mother and daughter, or two siblings) can opt to live together. The residents come from a range of family situations: some are childless, others have only daughters, others' children are all abroad, and others (of those I interviewed, the largest number) have sons and daughters-in-law living right nearby.[18]

The homes are arranged by and large very like the kinds of ordinary middle-class households that the residents tend to come from, with similar living, eating, sleeping, bathing, and cooking arrangements. Some of the larger homes have been established in apartment-type complexes built especially for the purpose, while others have been set up within ordinary houses and flats. All meals are provided, along with another essential ingredient of Indian social and culinary life: tea—at dawn ("bed tea"), with breakfast, and in the afternoon. Residents' clothes are washed and rooms cleaned; and in fact, one of the distinct advantages of old-age-home living, many say, is that older people no longer have to manage their own servants. Even most ordinary middle-class households in India maintain servants to help with household chores; yet peppering newspapers over recent years are stories of aged persons being tricked, robbed and even murdered by domestic workers—contributing to a widespread sense that it is inappropriate and even dangerous for elders to live on their own.

Conspicuously minimal formal activities are planned in most facilities, and residents spend their time reading, chatting, simply sitting, playing cards, knitting, writing journals and letters, having tea, watching television, going on morning walks, taking a stroll to a nearby market and (in the fancier ones) attending occasional cultural programs and functions. Female residents might also help with some light cooking, such as peeling vegetables, cleaning small stones from dried lentils or tasting a dish to see if it has turned out right. The larger homes generally house a temple, where residents can pray, make offerings to deities and sing hymns. Most women boarders and some men also maintain their own small shrines in their rooms, where they perform daily *pujas*, ritual offerings of water, flowers and sweets honoring deities as well as deceased kin such as husbands and parents. The larger, more posh homes have established one or two common areas for congregating, watching television, computer use or a library. Some more elaborate homes also maintain quite lovely gardens with flowers, fruit trees, vegetable patches sometimes a cow or dog or two, walkways, benches and perhaps a small fish and lily pond.

How do people make sense of the emergence of such residences for elders in India? One dominant position is that old age homes represent a radically new and alien—in fact, distinctly *Western*—way of life, impacting not only aging, but also core principles central to *Indian* society and culture. "Old Age Homes Against Our Culture" reads one representative newspaper headline, with the article moving on to report a government official in the southern state of Tamil Nadu proclaiming to a group of students that "the concept of old age homes reflects the impact of western culture" and asking the students to "take a vow that they would not leave their parents in old age homes" (*The Hindu* Staff Reporter 2004). Retired psychiatrist and old-age-home resident Dr. Ranjan Banerjee asserted to me: "Old age homes are not a concept of *our* country. These days, we are throwing away our culture. The U.S. is the richest nation in the world and therefore has won us over." Soumil Chowdhury, a retired engineer who had just made plans, with mixed feelings, to move into an old age home with his wife, similarly narrated:

We are experiencing a clash between the Indian era and the Western era. We [Indians] want to live jointly, amidst our relatives, not alone.... In European culture, everyone does want to live separately.... We don't want old age homes. We want joint families—sisters and brothers, daughters and sons, granddaughters and grandsons, all together.... This is Indian culture.

Yet more optimistic assessments profess that old age homes offer a valuable, welcome alternative to family based living, sustain those who have no kin readily to depend on, liberate both older and younger generations to live independently and freely, foster gendered and aged egalitarianism, and, in fact, are perhaps not so radically "new" or fundamentally "Western" after all. For instance, some expressly perceive old-age-home living as akin to the "forest-dwelling" or *vanaprastha* life phase long presented in Hindu texts as appropriate for older age, where one purposefully loosens ties to family and the world in order to pursue spiritual realization.

Female residents gathered at the temple of an elder ashram organized around the notions of "forest-dwelling" and spirituality, Hindu values appropriately pursued in late life. Photo by Sarah Lamb.

Further, elders in old age homes are often the recipients of quite a bit of sustained *seva*, or service to and respect for the aged—a key component of perceived traditional Indian ways of aging. Although offered by hired staff and proprietors rather than one's own junior kin (a not insignificant distinction), the residents of most homes nonetheless do enjoy the receipt of *seva*—in the form of the faithful arrival of daily 5 A.M. bed tea, meals served, oil massaged into hair, and bath water warmed and delivered. Several of the homes I encountered centrally figured the concept of *seva*—traditional service to and respect for the aged—in both their names and mission statements. Quite a few, in fact, are simply named *Seva*. Other similarly evocative names include *Sraddhanjali* (Offering of Reverence) and *Gurujan Kunja* (Garden Abode for Respected Elders). The manager of Gurujan Kunja explained the home's name: "It indicates the home's purpose: to serve and honor the old people living here. You see, they are all revered people living here." The motivation for establishing their elder residences, for some founders, was precisely to provide *seva*—to elders who (simply by virtue of being elder) deserve to receive it, but who are not able to find it within their families.[19]

LIVES AND DILEMMAS

I turn now to a few case studies, to illustrate the complexity and variety of ways people make sense of and choose, or are pushed into, old age homes in their own lives, as they and their kin grapple strategically with what they see as the changing conditions of their modern society.

Ashok Bose, a warm, articulate man in his early eighties, had been living in the Ramkrishna Mission Home for Aged People since its inauguration as one of the very first elder residences in Kolkata twenty-two years earlier. He was a bachelor who had long been devoted to a spiritual life, an aim in keeping with this home's mission, as described by one of its directors, to provide "a life away from the din of family, spent in solitary religious practices," a site to pursue *vanaprastha*, the "forest-dwelling" phase of the older Hindu householder's life. Ashok-da had gradually begun to lose his eyesight in his mid fifties, but he had been able to serve a full career as a Government of West Bengal Metropolitan Development Department employee, and he now drew a pension with which he could fund his expenses. But before retirement, he had worried about how to care for himself in old age, being then almost blind and having no children of his own to depend on. He tells the story: "Then one day, I came across a notice in the newspaper that the Ramkrishna Mission was planning to start an old age home! As *soon* as I read that, I went to [the Mission headquarters]." He recalls his application letter with detail and emotion: "I wrote, 'If I am accepted here, then that is very good.'" He paused and continued with a full voice: "'But if I am not selected, then please don't write that news in a letter. Because since I am blind, someone else will have to read the letter to me, and—I won't be able to bear that.'" He then narrated, brimming with pleasure and pride, "But they wrote back in a letter, saying: 'So long you have served us. Now let us serve you.'" He repeated, smiling broadly: "'So long you have served us. Now let us serve you!' And so I received admission!"

"About this ashram," Ashok-da went on, referring to the institution throughout as an ashram or spiritual shelter, "there's something you should know: We are living here *completely* without worry. *Everything* we need, we receive: the giving of food, tea, warm bath water—*whatever* we need, we receive. *Truly*, there are no worries! At *precisely* the right time, the tea comes, the food comes!" And, indeed, *just* as he was speaking, his midday meal arrived, a few minutes before noon, placed quietly on the desk-cum-eating table next to his window, as some other residents chose instead to make their way through the halls to the common dining room, several pausing in his doorway to greet him as they passed.

Mukund and Shrimayi Gangopadhyay shared a double room as a married couple in their residence for elders. The decision to move in had been his, not hers, and one he had made only after a great deal of brooding and family trouble. They had built a new house shortly before their son's marriage, and after the young man brought his bride into the multigenerational home, the father had turned the house deed over to his son. Their married daughter had advised them not to do so, lest the new daughter-in-law think, "Oh, the house is in my *husband's* name," and so not worry about her relationship with her parents-in-law at all. Such practices, however, have long been common in India: As persons move into older age, many feel it appropriate to turn over their assets to their children. Others commonly counsel, though, that this is not a good idea, as children will love their parents only as long as they have property! According to the parents and daughter, this is precisely what happened—the new daughter-in-law did not treat her parents-in-law well, and she shirked her share of cooking and other household duties. Things got so bad that finally the elder woman, the new bride's mother-in-law, tried to commit suicide, and the daughter stepped in to rescue her and take the senior couple to her own marital home.

Many Indians believe strongly that it is entirely inappropriate to live with a married daughter, however, and Mukund-da felt the same. One day, without telling anyone where he was going, he went out to look into an ashram for elders that he had seen advertised in the newspaper. He had never before encountered such an institution. He was gone for a long time, and those at home began to worry—an older man, out in the streets, where could he be? By the time he returned, he had decided to move in. His wife said, "Fine, you go live in an old age home. I am going to stay here with my daughter." But her husband insisted that she move with him.

Although Mukund-da had made the decision to move into the elder residence on his own, he felt bitter about their circumstances. Once while I was chatting with him and his coresident friend, the frequently voiced topic came up of why are there old age homes now? The friend replied matter-of-factly, "When people get old, their kids kick them out, disown them—this happens in all countries." Mukund-da interjected passionately, angrily, *"Before*, that didn't happen *here*! There was no kicking out of houses! People lived with their families—with their sons if they had them; if not, with other relatives. Everyone is saying that progress is happening," he went on. "But is this progress? or stagnation?!"

Renuka Biswas, at age eighty-four, is a lively widow of four married sons. For ten years she has resided in a forty-person ashram for elders with a lovely central Hindu temple and an expressly spiritual mission. The most gregarious of the group of five with whom she resides dormitory style, she claims with conviction to be thoroughly enjoying her independent (*svadhin*) life. Her husband had been a domineering man, and while he was alive, she had had no knowledge of money and could make no important household decisions. After he passed away and she became a widow, she decided to move to the home, although she reported that her sons all love her very much and objected to her coming. It is in fact common for elder-abode residents to emphasize to others how much their children love them and are opposed to them living in an elder residence, as there is considerable stigma, as well as pain, involved in being "thrown away" by kin.

What seems to delight Renuka-di most about living in the elder ashram is her freedom from household obligations and the ability to control the pension she receives as the widow of her husband, a former government employee. She goes out regularly to buy sweets for herself and her roommates; and she travels every few months to visit kin, including her sons in the town where she must trek to withdraw from her husband's bank her pension, which she proudly refers to as her "salary." This is the first time Renuka-di has had any financial independence. Husbands of Renuka-di's generation rarely considered teaching their wives how to manage finances, instead reasoning, "If I have a son, why should I teach my wife? My son can do it." In the Laws of Manu, widely regarded as a foundational text of Hindu law and society compiled and written about 200 CE, is found a well-known set of lines that many Indians pronounce in daily conversation: A woman should never be independent, but should be guided and controlled by her father in childhood, her husband in youth, and her sons in old age (Laws of Manu V.147–148, Manu 1886:195, 1991:115). Some who bring up this axiom in daily conversation are critical of it—that is, not all pronounce it with endorsement. However, all Indians are familiar with the adage, its lines presenting a powerful cultural model of proper female sub-servience to male kin that operates in many homes. Thus, even if a widow is nominally the one to receive a pension or other property in her husband's name, if she resides with her son/s, she will ordinarily not control the funds.

Like Renuka-di, many other pension-receiving widowed women in elder abo-des are experiencing a kind of financial freedom, autonomy and independence that they had never experienced before, finding the old age home to be a creative new cultural space not only in which to age but also to rework facets of gender. Some also speak (selflessly, it seems) of old-age-home living as a better and eas-ier option for their daughters-in-law, recalling their own difficult years of sub-missively serving mothers-in-law in a joint family home. Some, too, very much enjoy living amidst a group of peer friends for the first time in their lives, com-paring elder-abode living to what they imagine life in a college hostel to be like. Yet, although Renuka-di does not frequently give voice to such sentiments, liv-ing in a new cultural space with peers inevitably imposes a distance between her and the families of her four married sons. Most elder-abode residents do express unease and nostalgia thinking about loosening ties with kin, even when they feel they have actively chosen the alternative lifestyle of the elder abode. We see in these brief resident profiles a complex range of circumstances and attitudes, and an admixture of older and newer desires.

LIVING INDEPENDENTLY AS A MODERN LIFESTYLE

In addition to moving into old age homes, a growing number of elders among India's urban middle classes are also now living alone, in an arrange-ment that many describe as "unnatural," even "impossible" or "unthinkable" (*asambhab*), very "Western," and distinctly "modern." Those living singly form still a very small proportion of the population—in 2001, just 4 percent of persons in India aged sixty or older lived in single-person households, and 7 percent as an elderly couple.[20] Yet in public and media perceptions, living alone in India is a growing and uniquely modern phenomenon.[21]

Significantly, many in India consider that elderly persons are effectively living "alone" if they do not reside with adult children, even if they are living as a married couple or with a live-in servant. For instance, a *Times of India* article titled "Nation Leaves 11 Percent of Its Elderly Alone" moves on to explain that "about 11 percent of India's 76.4 million people aged 60 years and above *do not have a person below 60 living with them*" (Bagga 2005, emphasis added).[22] A Kolkata seniors' organization, The Dignity Foundation, offers loneliness mitigation services to older "people *who live alone either single or as a couple*" (emphasis added).[23] Elders I knew in Kolkata also frequently referred to themselves as living "alone" (*eka*), "lonely" and "independent" when they were living without adult children, even if residing with a spouse or servant.

Those who describe themselves as living *eka* (singly, alone) often present the situation as something not only uncomfortable, difficult or lonely, but also as quite unthinkable or impossible (*asambhab*), and even not fully human. One widowed math professor whose only children, both daughters, reside in the United States, described herself as living "completely alone," and yet reflected that "Human beings have always lived together; it is not part of human nature to live alone." She went on: "We couldn't have even dreamed earlier that people would be living like this! ... We had no concept at all even that a person could live alone!"

Contrast such perceptions about living alone to those prevalent in the United States, where among those sixty-five and over, 30 percent live in single-person households (a figure that has remained stable for the past twenty years), and 53 percent live with only their spouse (U.S. Census Bureau 2000).[24] Such trends are not represented in ordinary public discourse as a problem. Rather, in the United States it is widely considered normal and even desirable for older people to live alone or especially with a spouse. What many people consider to be less than ideal is to be institutionalized. Generally, in both media coverage on older Americans and in everyday talk, the possibility of living with children does not even come up, let alone become represented—when coresidence does not occur—as a modern social crisis.

To deal with what Indians are widely regarding as a modern social phenomenon, a new industry of extra-family aging is emerging to offer social, emotional and practical support for elders living apart from junior kin. Nonprofit nongovernmental organizations (NGOs), as well as private businesses, provide services such as around-the-clock telephone help lines, escorts to late-night wedding receptions and doctor appointments, visits to chat over tea, meal delivery and the promise of presence at the time of death. It is often NRI or "nonresident Indian" children who fund the services for their parents in India, able to supply money but not time or proximity. The director of one NGO, Agewell Foundation, compared their hired elder-care counselors to "surrogate sons," commenting: "A sad situation indeed when children cannot gift their parents time. But this is a contemporary reality that has to be faced."[25] Your-ManInIndia (YMI) began as an enterprise offering health care for the aged

Figure 30.1
Times of India Newspaper Story, September 1, 2004, p. 12

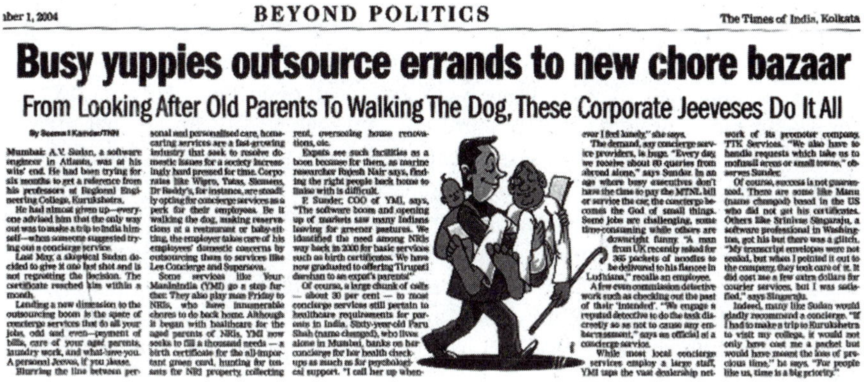

parents of busy and distant NRIs and has now expanded to offer a full range of concierge services. The *Times of India* reports: "Busy yuppies outsource errands to new chore bazaar: From Looking after Old Parents to Walking the Dog, These Corporate Jeeveses Do It All" (Kamdar 2004). Other elders living alone join the flurry of new clubs emerging in cosmopolitan centers for senior citizens, clubs that emphasize the cultivation of peer friendships, active volunteerism, fit bodies and life-long hobbies—pursuits especially appropriate for an individualistic, rather than centrally family-oriented, sense of self.

As with old age homes, both positive and negative assessments abound regarding the practice of elders living independently, and the outsourcing of care tasks from junior kin to private organizations. Much of the public and media discourse is exceedingly negative. Hearing of the emergence of hired elder care, my research assistant Hena's mother and grandmother used to beg her and other junior kin to please never let the private crevices of their bodies be touched or cared for by the hired hands of strangers or non-kin. *"Seva* (service to and respect for the aged) is *not* something that can be bought or sold," fervently remarked Papri Chowdhury, founder of a neighborhood-based group for elders living alone, one that she prefers to call a "joint family" rather than an "NGO," a term that to her connotes the "modern" and "impersonal." In Papri's "joint family" organization, elders themselves or their junior kin (often from abroad) can request such services as visits over tea, reading aloud, or escorting to the doctor or a spiritual program. But, Papri is firm that she cannot *charge* for these services, this *seva*: Instead, people who *wish to* make donations to the organization may do so at any time—but not at the same time that services are being rendered.

Papri herself, now in her fifties, grew up in a large joint family, with her father and his five brothers, their parents and children—all living together. "That was the old Indian culture. It wasn't so easy to go abroad then. No one was ever lonely.... Now families have all become nuclear and small. Among my friends, *no one* lives with their kids. Everyone is husband-wife, husband-wife." I interjected, "It's becoming like America?" "No!—it is not *becoming* like America: It has *become* like America. It is *just* like America now!" According to Papri and many others with whom I spoke, the most serious problem facing India's middle-class elderly (those with enough money but who are short on coresident kin) is loneliness. A recurrent recent media story line is that of "old person's suicide due to loneliness," such as this one: "Death from loneliness at eighty." One man's only son—an Indian Institute of Technology graduate— has settled in the United States. The old father "jumped off the landing between the 8th and 9th floors, ending a solitary existence.... Neighbors said the loneliness was probably too much for the octogenarian to bear, a condition not uncommon in a city from which the young who will take care of the old are increasingly [going abroad for better] opportunities" (*The Telegraph* Staff Reporter 2003).

However, much more optimistic perspectives are also not hard to find. For instance, among those I grew to know who were living without children in Kolkata, a regular point of discussion was the pride and sense of agency and accomplishment they felt in their children's professional success abroad. It was they, the senior parents, who had fostered this success—and thus their and their children's mutual independence—by raising their children in cosmopolitan households, sending them to elite English-speaking schools, funding higher education abroad, and encouraging their pursuit of prestigious professional careers. In many cases the senior parents benefit not only in terms of emotional pride, but also financially, from their children's success; for it is usual for Indian children living abroad to provide for their parents, if not a monthly maintenance allowance, then often large gifts such as a car or a flat in a modern apartment complex.

Further, many older persons living on their own without children are finding that they are enjoying spending much time with peers. In the modern apartment complex, Udita, where I resided in Kolkata doing fieldwork for five months in early 2006, there was an active group of senior citizens who had formed a Laughing Club, a group promoting "laughter yoga" as a means to improve health, reduce stress, and increase happiness (see Box V.2 this section). The Laughing Club in my apartment complex was a mixed-gender group of about thirty, ranging in age from their fifties to eighties. They met daily at 6 A.M. for laughter yoga, exercises, chatting and (for those who wished to attend) Bhagavad Gita[26] reading. In the afternoon, groups of men and women gathered separately for tea, snacks and conversations, rotating among each others' flats. I was welcomed into the club and became privy to lots of conversations and stories. About half of the members lived in multigenerational families with a married son and grandchildren, and about half lived alone or with a spouse. Most who lived alone had children who were working abroad. Although those who lived right with married sons and grandchildren were generally the ones considered the most fortunate, the general consensus was nonetheless that those who lived apart from children did enjoy several advantages. One of their most energetic and convivial members was a man, Viraj Ghosh, whose only son was settled as an economist in the United States. Viraj-da and his wife lived in a flat that their son had purchased for them, and Viraj spent hours each day socializing with friends, exercising at the apartment complex's gym, meditating, reading and playing music. His flat was known to be the place where friends could spontaneously congregate. He told me, "At this age, it's better to live separate.... If an old man says that he needs to have his son live with him, then the son won't advance, and the country won't advance.... I am the happiest man in the world, living in heaven! I won't live anywhere other than here, surrounded by my circle of friends." Another active member of this group, Sumant Roychowdhury, a retired engineer, highly gregarious and with a perpetual witty twinkle in his eyes, lived in a more traditional arrangement with his son, daughter-in-law and granddaughter. Although he was very close to his grandchild, he had to tiptoe around his daughter-in-law, and could not readily invite friends over.

However, the project of crafting an independent way of life in old age is not one that most Indians I have grown to know find unambiguously easy, or natural. Rather, it is a project they engage in with critical reflection, self-consciousness, effort and generally, some ambivalence. After I was invited to give a talk comparing ways of aging in India and the United States to a gathering of the Dignity Foundation senior citizens club in Kolkata, a lively and provocative discussion ensued on competing cultural models surrounding aging and

The Laughing Club of Udita. Photo by Sarah Lamb.

intergenerational relationships. The gathering consisted almost entirely of older middle- and upper-middle-class persons who were living separately from their children. Conversations were in English, signifying the elite and diverse regional backgrounds of the participants. Referring to the joint family system in which children and parents in turn reciprocally provide care for each other, one gentleman commented, "That was a very sweet relationship, but it is dying now." "We can't get rid of that expectation level, though," another member objected. "The problem is that we have grown up *expecting* our children to care for us. If you," he addressed this next comment to me, presumably as an American, or perhaps as a social scientist, "can show us how to *get rid* of this—our expectations—then there would be no problem." People smiled and nodded. A graceful dark-haired woman in about her seventies spoke up with an air of gentle, self-assured wisdom, "The main issue is: We should not demand money and love at the same time. We have to settle for one or the other. If we mistake one for the other, we will be disappointed." She went on:

We invest in our children for years. But, we should *not* do so for the interest in the bank. We should not do so expecting anything in return. From the [Bhagavad] Gita, you should know—that *disinterested* action is best. If your child gives back to you, that is a blessing. But, you should not give to the child *thinking* of the interest. *That* is the problem. It will *liberate* us to think of acting with *dis*interest!

The secretary of the group, Mr. Swaminathan, then stood up to offer a tale of an Indian doctor's experiences in Canada, which served to illustrate how the "independent aging" and "individualism" of the West can be *too* extreme, for an Indian's taste: An Indian doctor had settled in and was practicing medicine in Canada. He had an ailing elderly patient, a Canadian, residing in a nursing home. One night, shortly after midnight, the man died. The doctor phoned the man's son. After the phone rang many times, the son picked up. The doctor told him, "I'm calling from the nursing home." The son asked, "Is there a problem?" The doctor: "Yes, I'm very sorry to say: Your father has passed away." The son replied (Mr. Swaminathan mimicked an irritated, angry voice), "Why did you have to wake me up and call me in the dead of night to tell me this? I have given the name of the undertaker. They will take the dead body away, and then you could reach me in the morning—I will go over then." The doctor was so disturbed by this interchange that he decided to leave Canada and return to India.

Murmurs came from around the audience, "Could this be true? Is this really a true story?" "Yes!" Mr. Swaminathan insisted, "I met the doctor myself, who told me this story." "Surely this must be an extreme case, though." "Indeed, this would *never* happen in India." But, an elegant middle-aged woman dressed in an ash-grey *salwar kameez* suit, offered softly, "In fact, it was a very practical reaction. True, the doctor could have simply called the undertaker, and then notified the son in the morning." This led to a conversation about the merits and demerits of individualism versus collectivism, as Western and Eastern or Indian ways of being.

As we departed into the darkening summer evening, the elegant, thoughtful woman in the ash-colored *salwar* came up to me and said, "See, if you weren't an individual, then you couldn't be going out like this, pursuing your work, giving talks, writing books. You would have to be home with your children and family." I said, "Yes, that's true. Though, still, I am *worried* about them." The meeting had gone on longer than I had expected and I had just turned on my mobile phone to see eight missed calls from where my two daughters were waiting for me at our rented Kolkata flat.[27] The woman replied resolutely, "True—you can worry about them. But, still—You were able to come."

CONCLUSION

In 2006, the government of India introduced a new law, "The Senior Citizens (Maintenance, Protection and Welfare) Bill, 2006," stipulating that adult children must care for their elderly parents and grandparents, or else be fined or put in prison. Under this bill, elderly parents have the right to demand maintenance from their children. If found guilty of neglecting their parents, errant children can be fined, disinherited and jailed for a period of one month to, for severe cases of abuse, ten years. Under "Statement of Objects and Reasons," the March 3, 2006, version of the bill delineates its rationale: "Due to near disintegration of the joint family system and economic considerations by their kith and kin, the senior citizens are being ignored by their near and dear ones who are left to fend for themselves and compelled to lead a lonely and disappointed life."[28] The aim of the bill, then, is "to provide for the compulsory maintenance, protection and welfare of senior citizens so as to secure a life of dignity, peace and security for them."[29] What "used to" happen "naturally"— intimate support within the haven of the sustaining Indian joint family—must now be mandated by the state. This is the bill's clear underlying assumption. The family is the proper site of care for the aged.

However, not all agree. Some Indian gerontologists, like some of the older individuals I have grown to know through this research, advocate the development of self-sufficiency and institutional (nonfamily) means of elder support, often presenting "traditional" family centered modes of aging as "backward." S. Irudaya Rajan, U.S. Mishra and P. Sankara Sarma (1999) recommend, for instance, that the Indian government should support old age homes and pension plans, and that aging individuals should cultivate a dependence on the self— through savings, exercise and an open-mindedness about living in old age homes—as one can no longer count on, and *should* no longer count on, if one is modern and educated, depending on children in old age (cf. Lamb 2007:152). Shovana Narayana comments: "The self-sufficiency of the elderly is a very healthy trend.... The *problem* lies in the *rural mind set* where people consider their children as a support system for their old age" (in Gupta 2001, emphasis added). Some characterize joint family living, further, as a "patriarchal" and thus unenlightened way of life, in particular for younger and even older women.

The complex array of emerging nonfamily-based modes of aging in India—including elder residences, independent living and aging-focused NGOs—constitute new cultural spaces of aging, taking hold especially among a small but growing proportion of the cosmopolitan middle classes. These new cultural spaces of aging constitute vehicles through which people are practicing, conceptualizing and debating not only aging, but also gender, generation, personhood, visions of the good and the bad, and the nature of India as a society, culture and nation. Most approach such a project with complex ambivalence, endeavoring to take some from what they see as older and some from newer ways, grappling strategically with what they view as the profound changes and demands of the contemporary era.

NOTES

1. *Di* is short for *didi*, "older sister" in Bengali, the primary language spoken in the Indian state of West Bengal (of which Kolkata is the capital) and the neighboring nation of Bangladesh. Along with *da* for *dada* (older brother), *di* is used commonly as a sign of respect, and warmth, when addressing a senior person. Like other South Asians, Bengalis generally find it disrespectful to address a senior person by the first name only, so epithets such as "older sister," "older brother," "uncle" and "grandmother" are regularly used.

2. The category of *middle class*, as it is used in India, can be viewed as *middle* in relation to a *transnational* middle class—of world-traveling, English-speaking, e-mail-using persons, participating in consumption and employment within global markets. In the context of India, this so-called middle class applies actually to a quite elite group. For instance, those who can speak English well comprise only about 5 percent of the population; and just about 9 percent of households in India have a refrigerator (Derne 2005:108). Nonetheless, in cities such as Kolkata, New Delhi, Bangalore and Mumbai, the middle class has a very palpable, influential presence. The rise of this new Indian middle class is also receiving a great deal of international media attention, such as in *Time* magazine's June 26, 2006, cover story, "How wealth is uprooting tradition and transforming India's way of life" (Adiga 2006).

3. In 1989–1990, I spent eighteen months in West Bengal studying aging, gender and families, residing for most of the period in the village of Mangaldihi, while spending several weeks in Kolkata researching two of the first old age homes in the city. From 2003–2007, I made four more research trips to Kolkata, this time focusing on new modes of aging among the urban middle classes, and living in 2006 for five months in a modern apartment complex shared by many independent elders living apart from children. From 1993 on, I have also researched aging and families among Indian communities in the Boston and San Francisco regions (Lamb 2000, 2002, 2007, 2009). All names of those from my own fieldwork are pseudonyms. Most conversations with Bengalis occurred in Bengali, and those with Indians of other regions took place in English. Translations are my own.

4. About 80 percent of India's population is Hindu. Muslims are the next most prominent religious group (at about 13 percent), followed by Christians, Sikhs, Buddhists, Jains and others (including Bahais, Jews and Parsis).

5. It should be noted that these texts devote little explicit attention to defining the appropriate stages of a woman's life, which are determined by her relationships to the

men upon whom she depends for support and guidance: her father in youth, her husband in marriage, and her sons in old age (*The Laws of Manu* V.148; Manu 1886:195, 1991:115). Both women and men, especially among the more well-educated, nonetheless frequently invoke models of the four Hindu life stages when discussing the life course.

6. In Lamb 2000, I explore such perspectives in much greater detail.

7. Rajan and Kumar (2003), based on National Family Household Survey data, report that 80 percent of the elderly in India live with their adult children. See also Jamuna (2003:127–128) and Basu (2006).

8. Although a joint family technically refers to a family consisting of two or more brothers living together along with their parents, spouses and children, the phrase is more loosely and popularly used in India to refer to any multigenerational household including at least one senior parent and one married adult child (generally a son) with spouse.

9. For more on *seva* and elders, see Cohen 1998 and Lamb (2000:59–66).

10. The retirement age in the West Bengal government sector is fifty-eight and in the Government of India sector sixty. The private sector has no fixed rule.

11. For instance, see Wadley (1994, 2002) for discussions of family types in Karimpur, North India, from 1925 through 1998. Over this period, nuclear families were consistently the largest group (2002:19). Cohen (1998) explores narratives of modern "bad families" from the colonial era to contemporary times. See also the perspectives of Bengali villagers on the multiple kinds of enduring forces that interfere with successful joint family living in "Conflicting Generations: Unreciprocated Houseflows in a Modern Society" (Lamb 2000:70–111).

12. See, for instance, Dube (1988) and the short stories of influential Bengali authors translated in Bardhan 1990, notably (for portrayals of dominated and constrained sons as well as daughters-in-law), "Dhowli" by Mahasweta Devi and "Haimanti" by Rabindranath Thakur (Tagore).

13. For discussions of cultural values surrounding aging and intergenerational relationships in the United States, see, for examples, Clark (1972), Vesperi (1985), Simic (1990), Kalish (1967), Lamb (2000:52–53) and Hunt (2002:109–110).

14. The quotation marks here are meant to indicate that this prevalent narrative of the breakdown of the joint family is indeed that—a narrative or representation—rather than a quantitative measure of changing family arrangements in India.

15. From 2004–2006, I was able to locate seventy-one old age homes in the Kolkata area (visiting twenty-nine of these personally and contacting the others by phone and letters). HelpAge India's (soon-to-be-updated) 2002 guide to old age homes lists 800 across India's urban centers (HelpAge India 2002; see also Sawhney 2003).

16. Few among the very wealthy are at this point turning to old age homes, for they have other options open to them, such as the financial capacity to maintain their own private homes with plentiful servants, even in the absence of children. Across India, there are still relatively few old age homes run by charitable organizations or the government that offer accommodations to the poor.

17. The few older, free homes for the aged around India tend to be even larger. For instance, Kolkata's Little Sisters of the Poor Old Age Home currently houses 150 elders, and the West Bengal government home for "old and infirm political sufferers" and destitute women houses 68. See also Liebig (2003:170–71).

18. From 2003–2006, I interviewed one hundred old-age-home residents in the Kolkata environs (Lamb 2009). Of these, thirty-three had sons and daughters-in-law living

right in the Kolkata region, thirty had no children at all (twenty-one of these had never married), twenty-one had children all living abroad (elsewhere in India or overseas), eighteen had only daughters, and one had just a single unmarried son. It is significant to note that most Indians feel it strongly inappropriate to live in a married daughter's home (although such attitudes are changing somewhat due to various factors, probably the most significant being that more daughters are earning their own incomes).

19. A few proprietors established old age homes in their own deceased parents' names, as if continuing to honor their parents by serving other living elders now. In such cases, grand framed and flower-garlanded photographs of the parents grace the front halls of the homes.

20. Census of India 2001: "Data Highlights: HH-5: Households with number of aged persons 60 years and above by sex and household size," pp. 2–4. Of those who do live alone, a larger number are females: 2.1 million out of 38.8 million (5.5 percent) of older women aged sixty years and above lived alone in 2001.

21. "Ageing Parents Home Alone" is the cover story of the July 16, 2007, issue of *India Today*.

22. The phenomenon of living without children is occurring in both rural and urban India. According to the 2001 Indian Census, living without children is even more pronounced in rural areas, at 11.9 percent compared to 8.6 percent in urban areas (Bagga 2005). This is most likely due to the prevalence of rural-urban labor migration among younger adults.

23. The Dignity Foundation is a "Senior Citizens Life Enrichment Organization," founded in 1995, with chapters now in Mumbai, Delhi, Chennai, Jamshedpur and Kolkata. See http://www.dignityfoundation.com/. The quoted passage comes from a no longer existing "Loneliness Project" link on the foundation's Web page, viewed on April 19, 2007.

24. U.S. Census Bureau, 2000 Census: Single Person Households in 1999: 2000 Census, Tables No. 2 and No. 60: www.census.gov. In the 2000 Census, single-person households were the second most common type of household, with two-person households being the most common.

25. Founded by Himanshu Rath in 1999 in New Delhi, Agewell Foundation's mission is to "act as a catalyst of change in bridging the gap between generations and ensuring a respectful and comfortable life for old people." See http://www.agewellindia. org/about_us.htm.

26. The Bhagavad Gita is an ancient Sanskrit text that many view as a classic summary of the core beliefs of Hinduism.

27. I had taken my daughters, ages thirteen and ten, to the field with me, while they attended an international school in Kolkata.

28. http://rajyasabha.nic.in/bills-ls-rs/2006/X_2006.PDF, p. 4. "The Senior Citizens (Maintenance, Protection and Welfare) Bill, 2006," March 3, 2006. For newspaper coverage of this bill, see Gentleman (2007) and Salvadore and Mukherjee (2007).

29. Ibid., p. 1.

CHAPTER 31

Aging in the Hood: Creating and Sustaining Elder-Friendly Environments

Philip B. Stafford

From the ethnographer's journal:
One elder in the study takes great pleasure in shopping. He spends hours in the grocery store, stopping to greet children along the way who, when riding in the grocery cart, are at eye level with him from the electric cart in which he rides. He enjoys making faces at the children who try to mimic his facial tricks and expressions. He explains *"I feel babies are the closest friends I have. Everyone smiles back at me. It's a heavenly thing."* He explains that he never used to have time to talk with people and clerks in the store when he was a young parent. He says, however, that *"Now it's part of my social life. Everybody knows me and I make myself known. Without relationships I'm a dead man."*

Field notes, Bloomington, IN, March 5, 1996

When we listen deeply to the voices of elders, as anthropologists are trained to do, we get the important message that healthy aging is not merely about time and the body, but about place, and about relationships. Social scientists often refer to this as social capital—"the resources available to individuals and groups through their social connections to their communities" (Cannuscio, Block and Kawachi 2003). As the Cannuscio et al. article suggests, social connections are not just a matter of health, but, potentially, a matter of life and death, as elder Milton Figen himself attests in the quoted field note passage above. For example, in the terrible 1995 Chicago heat wave, socially connected elders experienced a 30 percent lower risk for death than isolated elders (Semenza et al. 1996, cited in Cannuscio et al., above). The shift in focus from the individual elder to the elder-in-community is significant, and good news for anthropologists for whom community and culture is their stock in trade. It moves public attention and public policy toward a new view of aging that, in Wendell Berry's words, sees "community as the smallest unit of health" (1995).

It is worthwhile to dwell on the development of this broad, worldwide policy and program shift in attention from the individual elder to the matrix of community. This movement is occurring throughout the world, under such rubrics as elder-friendly communities; communities for all ages; livable, life-span communities; and others. While the elements of an elder-friendly community are stated in various ways, one simple and comprehensive model is offered by the AdvantAge Initiative, a nationwide community planning and development project of the Center for Home Care Policy and Research (Feldman and Oberlink 2003).[1] The AdvantAge Initiative organizes the elements of an "elder-friendly" community into four domains. An elder-friendly community:

1. Addresses elders' basic needs

2. Optimizes physical and mental health and well-being

3. Maximizes independence for the frail and those with disability

4. Promotes social and civic engagement

The domains themselves were derived from a series of focus group discussions with elders and community leaders in four, diverse U.S. communities.[2] Each domain, as seen in Figure 31.1, includes several subsidiary "dimensions." In the AdvantAge Initiative, the dimensions further subsume thirty-three "indicators" of an elder-friendly community that are measured through random telephone surveys and employed as data for citizen participation planning efforts. The survey has been conducted in over twenty-five U.S. communities and with a national sample, providing a wealth of comparative data that enables communities to "benchmark" themselves against others and against their own ideals.

In the United States, major national organizations have taken up this "elder-friendly community" approach with enthusiasm. The National Association of Area Agencies on Aging (with partners) has produced the *Blueprint for Action: Developing a Livable Community for All Ages* (2007). Additionally, the American Association of Retired Persons (AARP) has identified "livable communities" as one of its five top priorities for its ten-year social-impact agenda and is developing guidebooks, walkable community assessments, and other citizen tools for creating more livable communities. Even the Environmental Protection Agency (EPA) has ramped up its efforts to help create elder-friendly communities through its initiative called "Building Healthy Communities for Active Aging."[3]

On a more global basis, the United Nations has also shifted focus to the environmental aspects of aging. It declared 1999 as International Year of Older Persons: Towards a Society for All Ages, and, since that time, has organized international conferences and research initiatives designed to increase the quality of elder environments in both rural communities and urban areas. The Madrid International Action Plan on Aging 2002 recommended "creating enabling and supportive environments" as a key focus area, and this is currently being implemented through the World Health Organization Age Friendly Cities

Figure 31.1
The AdvantAge Initiative: Four Domains of an Elder-Friendly Community

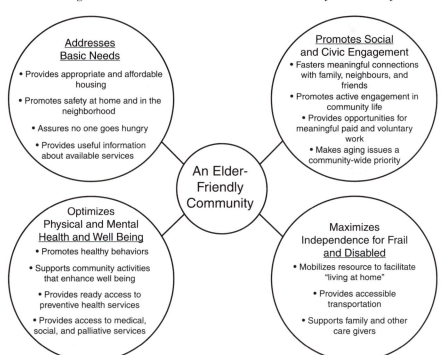

Addresses
Basic Needs

• Provides appropriate and affordable
housing

• Promotes safety at home and in the
neighborhood

• Assures no one goes hungry

• Provides useful information
about available services

Promotes Social
and Civic Engagement
• Fosters meaningful connections
with family, neighbours, and
friends
• Promotes active engagement in
community life
• Provides opportunities for
meaningful paid and voluntary
work
• Makes aging issues a
community-wide priority

An Elder-
Friendly
Community

Optimizes
Physical and Mental
Health and Well Being
• Promotes healthy behaviors

• Supports community activities
that enhance well being

• Provides ready access to
preventive health services

• Provides access to medical,
social, and palliative services

Maximizes
Independence for Frail
and Disabled
• Mobilizes resource to facilitate
"living at home"

• Provides accessible
transportation

• Supports family and other
care givers

Source: Courtesy of The Center for Home Care Policy and Research, Visiting Nurse Service of New York.

Project.[4] In Calgary, Canada, a comprehensive elder-friendly community development project has been spearheaded by a collaborative of key organizations, and its innovative "senior-empowerment" approach has been carefully evaluated.[5] Moreover, these research findings have spurred the development of a cross-national replication model being developed in Adelaide, Australia.

CREATING LIVABLE ENVIRONMENTS FOR ELDERS: A FEW EXAMPLES

So what lessons do public policy and community development initiatives provide as we begin to focus on collective solutions to the problems of elders worldwide? Whether rural, small town or urban, the proximate physical and social environment of the elder can become a key focus for public policy and program development. While public policy, especially related to health and illness, often focuses on the individual elder, a more anthropologically enlightened approach would focus on the life world, moving beyond the individual body of the older person to the body-in-place. Indeed, as noted earlier, a worldwide movement toward more age-friendly, elder-friendly, livable environments for elders is taking place. One would like to think that these developments are informed by a deep understanding of the everyday experiences of elders. In the following, I will take some examples that link everyday experience with public policy advocacy, starting with the basic needs domain of the AdvantAge model.

An Elder-Friendly Community Addresses Elders' Basic Needs

The Community Indicator: Housing is modified to accommodate mobility and safety.

The voice: "My son helped install a 'tall man's commode' in my bathroom, and it's helped a lot."

Home modification and adaptation is a growing industry that sees a vast new market in helping people adjust their living environments to meet changing needs associated with age. The National Association of Homebuilders (sic) has developed a special unit that provides education and certification to Aging in Place Specialists, in recognition of the growing market of elders who wish to stay put.[6] A similar shift in emphasis can be seen in the affordable public housing realm, as government subsidy programs are developed to shift monies from new construction to home modification.[7] As this section's introductory quote suggests, it is also important to listen deeply to language that elders find nonde-meaning, as they search for options that enable them to sustain identity and a sense of independence and agency. In South Bend, Indiana, the AdvantAge Initiative survey indicated a disturbingly high percentage of householders aged sixty-five and older resided in housing units with home modification needs. As a consequence of the survey and community process, the St. Joseph County Community Foundation provided an infusion of funding to the Agency on Aging to expand home modification services to low-income elders. In Indianapolis, the AdvantAge Initiative has organized multiple stakeholders at the neighborhood level, found new funding sources and is using home modification and repair for elders' homes as a tool to reinvigorate the entire neighborhood.[8]

An Elder-Friendly Community Optimizes Physical and Mental Health and Well Being

The Community Indicator: Opportunities for physical activity are available and used.

The voice: "My children don't want me to do that (yard) work at home, so I do it in a friend's yard."

There are many barriers to physical activity in the lives of elders—over-protective children (as above), fear of falling, fear of crime, personal physical limitations and the physical environment itself. In one AdvantAge Initiative community, Puyallup, Washington, the survey indicated fewer than 50 percent of elders engaged in regular physical activity (Hanson and Emlet 2006). As a

consequence of this research, the community established a task force that created a user-friendly guide to low-cost exercise options and a walking club that
attracted thirty members.

Many communities around the United States are implementing physical activity programs based upon new "evidence-based" research. One highly successful program called Healthy Moves, developed through the support of the
National Council on the Aging and certified by the Administration on Aging,
targets high-risk elders with home-based exercise programs delivered by
trained coaches (Wieckowski and Simmons 2006).[9]

An Elder-Friendly Community Maximizes Independence for the Frail and Those with Disabilities

The Community Indicator: There are adequate mobility options when driving is not feasible (AARP 2005).

The voice: "When I cross the street, I start to limp so the cars will pay
attention."

Planners are waking up to the value of pedestrian-friendly environments.
Aside from the value of reducing carbon emissions, promoting reliance on foot
and bicycle mobility is seen as a true environmental intervention that will
reduce levels of obesity (at all ages) and promote cardiovascular and musculoskeletal health. In the Bloomington study, 70 percent of the interactions
between elders and neighbors occurred outside—life between the buildings, as
Jan Gehl calls it (1987). Yet, 30 percent of Bloomington elders, living in a progressive and relatively affluent community, had no navigable sidewalk in front
of their home. Moreover, as the field note quote suggests, automobile (and
bicycle) traffic represent real threats to well-being, especially in more urbanized environments. The creation of "walking audits" has enabled groups of elders and advocates to measure their communities on an important indicator and
utilize participatory research for advocacy (Burden 2007).[10]

An Elder-Friendly Community Promotes Social and Civic Engagement

The Community Indicator: Residents maintain connections with friends and
neighbors.

The voice: "There are all kinds of ways of being diminished but life can
teach us how to approach the end of our lives. And how can I do that unless
you take elder people and shuffle them in like cards, a deck of cards with people of all ages. Not put them off in a corner and call it the elder place."

When it comes to the overall character of the community itself, most of the
world follows Bloomington elder Milton Figen's previous recommendation. It
is ironic that the so-called developed world is rethinking the assumption that
underlies the entire senior housing and long-term care industry —the assumption that chronological age itself is a legitimate category for segregating people
into different living environments. When Bloomington elders were asked

whether they wanted to live only with people their own age, the vast majority responded with a resounding "no" (Stafford 1996). And, while it is true that the industry and public policy remains heavily oriented to seniors-only environments, new and innovative options are popping up that in some ways replicate age-old patterns of communal living.

Following a model suggested by William Thomas, the "Green House" is a radically reengineered long-term care facility—it houses a family-sized unit of elders in need of long-term care, but places it in the traditional neighborhood setting so it communicates social connections as opposed to medical care (Kane et al. 2007; McLean this volume; Thomas this volume). Intergenerational cohousing is another senior housing option seen in Western and Northern Europe and beginning to appear more frequently in the United States. A planned, intentional community, intergenerational cohousing provides private living units for various-sized family households, along with communal space for living needs that have a more social basis—dining, recreation, laundry, child care, governance, gardening, workshops and so forth. Cohousing is based within an explicit set of values that promote well-being through our social connections (Durrett 2005).

Even colleges and universities are questioning the ghettoization of youth, and are developing or contemplating the development of shared, intergenerational environments on campus. Ithaca College has been a pioneer in the concept, in a joint venture with Longview Retirement Community, just up the road from campus, where students and elders can mutually educate and assist one another (Krout and Porgozala 2002). In another approach at Purdue University, gerontology students compete for the opportunity to reside in a local senior-housing community for an entire year, learning about old age "from the inside."[11]

In the future, community-planning organizations will more actively challenge the common development of seniors-only living environments in undeveloped areas beyond the margins of existing communities—areas that not only segregate elders from the life of the community, but contribute to urban sprawl. This approach will also connect community planning for aging with the "smart-growth" movement (cf. Howe 2001; Oberlink n.d.). Clearly, the discussion of aging is moving away from a singular emphasis on services, illness or disabilities and towards a more comprehensive, community-based emphasis on health and the strengths and contributions that elders can make to their neighborhoods and the world.

A Note on Baby Boomers

The voice: "We'd buy half a loaf of bread if someone offered it to us."

Commercial interests are becoming more aware of the economic power of elders and the now rapidly growing baby-boom population. Designers are finding the right marketing formulae to tap the growing market without playing on the age stereotypes being rejected by boomers. National chains such as Chico's, and products such as "Not Your Daughter's Jeans," are hitting the right note and reaping large profits (Earnest 2007).

Elder-friendly business certification programs and even wholesale elder-friendly business districts are cropping up around the country and helping reconfigure downtown environments as good places to grow old.[12] While the numbers of elders living in cities around the world continue to decline, there are indications that highly urbanized environments might, indeed, have unrecognized appeal to certain groups of elders, particularly those wealthy enough to take advantage of the diversity of city cultures. Eugenie Birch reports that the second largest age segment relocating to live in downtown environments is the group aged forty-five to sixty-four (2005). As Gusmano notes in this section, "world cities" have both significant challenges and significant opportunities as places in which to grow old. In many cases, the assets are in place (world-class health care, public transit, educational institutions, etc.) but not organized in such a way as to accommodate increasing dependency needs that individual citizens may develop as they reach very old age. And in some respects, important urban assets such as small owner-operated shops, are losing out to global chains that are in a position to win the battle over the increasing costs of doing business in the world city.

ETHNOGRAPHIC PERSPECTIVES ON LIVABILITY

The phrase "aging in place" has become a virtual mantra among gerontologists. Many studies have affirmed that eight out of ten elders would choose to stay put where they are if given the choice and means (AARP 2005). Knowing that the vast majority of older citizens both desire and manage to stay where they are in late life, the concept of aging in place has become a primary foundation of public policy at local, state and federal levels (Golant 2008).[13] Yet, despite the ubiquity of the phrase, little attention has gone into the deep, emic or subjective meaning of home environments-as-lived by elders (and others). Ethnographic research into the meaning of home for elders suggests that home is a rich and deep, perhaps even a core cultural concept that deserves more than a cavalier treatment by gerontologists and policy-makers (Fischer 2007). But to say that home is a core cultural concept is not to say that its meaning does not vary across cultures, nor that different cultures do not provide a variety of cultural assets that can be assembled to create a home.

Ethnographic research in Bloomington, Indiana, identified four key assets represented by home, each of which has practical implications for program and policy, as summarized later in this chapter (Stafford 2003).

Home Is a Crucible for Meaning

Home is a site of and for memory (both positive and negative). One's possessions become artifacts of a life. As an elder moves through their house, viewing and touching objects, they revisit earlier experiences, review events and relationships and the sites of former activities—a virtual reflection of selfhood. As ethnographer Joelle Bahloul notes, in a study of older female Algerian émigré's living in France and reflecting on their lives:

Domestic memory focuses not only on images of places but also on images of concrete acts ... Remembrance of socialized domestic space is thus based above all on the practice of this space as it is articulated in the repeated interactions of its agents ... Remembrance of the house is the symbolic locus for the embodiment of social practices experienced in daily life; it constitutes a system of bodily practices. (1996:136)

Among the bodily practices encoded in the memory of home might be the aesthetic process itself. As an older person looks around their rooms, casts a glance through the window, they relate to a sense of personal style, whether fulfilled by daily puttering or disappointed by the limitations of frailty. Through the practice of living, a space of occupation may be transformed into a place of beauty. Whatever it is, Martha Stewart chic or yard sale swank, it is an expression of the self. Citing a passage from *The Stone Angel*, by Margaret Laurence, the writer Kathleen Woodward describes how ninety-year-old Hagar Shipley finds himself in his objects: "My shreds and remnants of years are scattered through it (the house) visibly in lamps and vases ... If I'm not somehow contained in them and in this house, something of all change caught and fixed here, eternal enough for my purposes, then I do not know where I am to be found at all" (1991:146).

Home Is a Physically Supportive Environment

While the previous paragraphs suggest that the home is a symbolic environment, encoding memory and experience in multiple personal artifacts, one can also argue that the experience of home is more direct—not mediated by the interposition of symbols; an environment that is *felt*, not interpreted.

In the *Poetics of Space*, Gaston Bachelard describes the manner in which home becomes inscribed in our body and incorporated into our memory, an example of a more phenomenological approach to the meaning of home:

the house we were born in is physically inscribed in us. It is a group of organic habits. After twenty years, in spite of all the other anonymous stairways, we would recapture the reflexes of the "first stairway," we would not stumble on that rather high step. The house's entire being would open up, faithful to our own being. We would push that door that creaks with the same gesture, we would find our way in the dark to the distant attic. The feel of the tiniest latch has remained in our hand. (1994:15)

In the United States and elsewhere, many elders occupy the same living environment for decades. In the Bloomington study, the average duration of occupancy in the home was thirty years, with an upper range of seventy-two years! Living in one place for such a long time leads to a blending of body and place, akin to a hand in glove. From field notes, one can visualize this Bloomington elder's physical attachment to place:

Opal shuffles around her house with the help of her walker. On bad days her knee pain slows her down. As her kitchen is small, she leaves her walker at the narrow passage way and can move around to make her toast or pour her orange juice by leaning on the counters. At night Opal drags her small table that by day rests next to her easy chair, into her bedroom. With it, she takes the telephone and radio so that while she lies in bed she can keep in contact with friends and listen to the world and Christian news. (Bloomington field notes)

In interactions with another elder, ethnographers learned how Elizabeth molded and shaped her setting to adapt to her physical body and her perceived needs. She described how she unplugged her "automatic lifter" from her chair so as not to become dependent. She showed the ethnographer how she arranged her kitchen cabinets so everyday items would be just a bit out of reach, giving her some important range of motion each morning as she stretched for her cereal bowl, while taking precautions to use plastic items at this height to minimize potential breakage. Other elders interviewed discussed how they arranged their furnishings in the home so as to provide intermittent supports as they moved through the space. One elderly woman described her twice-daily routine of walking laps in her basement to stay fit.

As the home becomes an extension of the body of the elder, we can surmise that sudden removal from that environment represents an act of violence akin to amputation. Take the experience of Martha as an evocative affirmation of this fact:

With a dementia and no caregiver at home, Martha found herself being admitted to the nursing home near the Adult Day Care program. Her boisterous personality offended some but endeared her to most, as she danced her way through the day at Adult Day Care, incessantly reminding us about her many years tending switchboard at the University, taking care of the president's calls from abroad and tendering care to her beloved husband, never quite well after being gassed in the War. The loss of her strong presence was felt genuinely after her departure. While she continued to have strong days in the nursing home, she had weak ones too, and often the doldrums seemed to have left her sails flapping. Yet, through her dementia, her wisdom rose to the surface. When visited by the Day Care Coordinator a few weeks after her institutionalization, Martha's words described her fate clearly—*"They've taken the home out of me. This is a business here and I'm not used to that."* (Stafford 2003:131)

On the opposite side of the planet, among the aboriginal Walpiri of Central Australia, home is not the house but, rather, the total region, experienced through the age-old walkabout—The Trail of Dreams. Anthropologist Michael Jackson draws the connection between home and self in his ethnography *At Home in the World* (1995). He relates the true story of the negligent destruction of a tree (*watiya*) that marked, and had sprung from a Warlpiri sacred "Dreaming" site in the desert of Central Australia. Jackson remarks how he was struck by the depth of grief expressed, a year previous, by the old woman Nola Nungarrayi, who came to find a limb broken on the tree during one of their many joint excursions. Nola's daughter, Wanda, had explained to Michael that Nola's father had died against the trunk of the tree years before—"he bin pass away here, turn into this tree." Now that the tree was damaged, there was a risk that the father's *pirlirrpa* (glossed here as spirit) would leave the spot:

A year after the visit to the sacred spot, a crew of whitefellas, carelessly trying to extract a vehicle from a rut, uprooted the tree. This time, the grief over the loss of the tree was felt by all Warlpiri in the area. Anger rose as well and the Warlpiri demanded compensation from the whites—realizing that the way to hurt them would be to extract money—"the whitefella Dreaming." (1995:13)

As do Westerners, the Warlpiri make use of the tree as a metaphor for the family—the trees, as people, have limbs and trunks. Their roots descend deep into the soil, holding the branches, the offspring, in place. But, as Jackson notes, such:

Genealogical images have more force for Warlpiri, perhaps, than Westerners, as Francine and I had seen a year ago when Nola Nungarryi wept at the sight of her father's broken limb." Indeed, Jackson inferred that the tree was not simply a metaphor, a representation of ancestors, akin to our memorials and monuments. "That wasn't a tree," Clancy explained ... "it was a person. A person's Dreaming. It was the life-essence (prilirrpa) of a person. When those whitefellas knocked down that tree they hurt the Dreamings and the ceremonies there." (1995:138)

Home Is a Financial Cushion

While it is easy to romanticize the intimate relationship between body and home, there is an undeniable practical element at work as well. Home (and property) becomes a source of financial security for most elders. In the United States, rates of home ownership are higher than most other countries of the world. For elders, the rates range from 81.3 percent among ages sixty-five to seventy-five to 66.1 percent for those eighty-five and above (U.S. Census Bureau 2001). Whereas monthly income for many elders in the United States is derived from several sources, including pensions, the bottom fifth of elders rely on Social Security for 92 percent of their income (Lockhart 2004). Hence, the monetary value of the home itself is, for many elders, *the* primary financial asset. Yet, it is not a liquid asset in that, paradoxically, "cashing in" contradicts the alternative values of home cited previously. In recent years, new financial tools have enabled elders to tap into the equity of their homes to provide monthly income with deferred payments (reverse mortgages). Despite the apparent logic of utilizing existing equity to help "age in place," many elders shy away from reverse mortgages. While the demand for reverse mortgages has been increasing, only a small portion of the eligible market of existing home owners has taken reverse mortgages, even though the vast majority had taken regular mortgages on their homes earlier in life (Caplin 2001).

While reverse mortgages have not become popular, elders themselves would still maintain the view that their home is an economic asset. How can this be? Perhaps the value of this asset is not manifested in its ability to generate cash, but rather in some latent potential not quite so visible. A clue to this paradox might be found in traditional societies where wealth is not represented by cash, but by control over resources and, as a consequence, the behavior of others. For older people around the world, control over property, assured by both experience and custom, has been a, and perhaps *the*, primary source of economic security in old age (e.g., Arensberg 1988, for traditional Ireland; Nason 1981, for Micronesia).

Home as a Node in a Social Network

While casual observation leads our eyes to the physical and material elements of home as described previously, it is important to remember that a home exists within a "hood." To fully understand the at-home world of elders, we need to evaluate the network of social relations that plays such a key role in daily life. This network is the vehicle for establishing and maintaining identity, providing knowledge about the world outside, linking to practical supports available from family, neighbors, service personnel and commerce, and, often forgotten, a field to be seeded with the elder's own contributions and social capital. The appropriate model for the elder's role in a social network is not one that emphasizes the passive receipt of assistance but, rather, one that highlights the active, negotiative and managerial role of the elder in making best use of an important social resource. Even the apparently thin networks of homeless elders are "thick enough" to be actively managed to meet everyday as well as seasonal needs, as so well described by Sokolovsky and Cohen in the Web section of this volume.

The power of reciprocity in social relationships finds its manifestation in the neighborhood life of elders worldwide. In Bloomington, Opal Brown (mentioned herein), described how she noticed a young couple moving in across the street, and heard the fabulous news that the young man was an Emergency Medical Technician. Making herself visible and available for interaction on her front porch, she was able to arrange an introduction and was proud to show off her pots of flowers on the front railings. Being frail, however, Opal had difficulty bringing heavy gallons of water from her kitchen in the rear of the house to water the plants. Before long, an unspoken arrangement found Opal placing empty jugs on her railing, where they could be seen by the new neighbors. Upon seeing the empty jugs, they fulfilled the role of filling the jugs in the kitchen and returning them to be usefully employed by Opal in keeping the neighborhood beautiful. As an additional precaution, Opal explained to the paramedic that she would switch on her porch light if she needed some occasional assistance (a common way that neighbors support each other in American communities).

CONCLUSION: A ROLE FOR ANTHROPOLOGY IN THE LIVABILITY MOVEMENT

The story of Opal provides a parable for the livability movement. It starts with the tale of a feisty, inventive, and socially aware elder, places her on a front porch where she can surveil and exploit her social capital, and produces a "great good place" that both serves and preserves an entire neighborhood.[14] The story could not happen without a clever elder. But, too, in a variation on a familiar theme ... "it takes a front porch."

With its tradition of deep listening and its capacity to explore and reveal the intersection between the individual and the social-cultural matrix in which life happens, anthropology is well-positioned to add great value to the livability movement worldwide.

NOTES

1. The AdvantAge Initiative is a multicity "elder-friendly" planning project initiated in 2000. It organizes community groups to plan around thirty-three indicators of well-being. In 2006, the first statewide utilization of the planning model was implemented in Indiana. For background on the AdvantAge Initiative, visit the following Web site, accessed on November 1, 2007: http://www.vnsny.org/advantage/.

2. Chicago, IL; Allentown, PA; Long Beach, CA; Raleigh, NC.

3. Web links to these three initiatives can be found at: Blueprint for Action: Developing a Livable Community (accessed on September 20, 2007) www.aginginplaceinitiative. org/index.php?option=com_content&task=view&id=18&Itemid=47 AARP, Livable Communities Evaluation Guide (accessed on September 20, 2007) www.aarp.org/research/housing-mobility/indliving/d18311_communities.html EPA, Building Healthy Communities resources (accessed on September 20, 2007).

4. Information about the UN initiative can be found at the following Web link (accessed on September 20, 2007): www.un.org/esa/socdev/ageing/madrid_intlplanaction.html.

5. Research reports and conference papers describing the Calgary/Adelaide project can be found at: http://www.elderfriendlycommunities.org/index.php (accessed November 1, 2007).

6. Information about the Certified Aging-in-Place Specialists program (CAPS) can be found at the following Web link: www.nahb.org/generic.aspx?generic ContentID=8398 (accessed on September 20, 2007).

7. The Pennsylvania Housing Finance Agency was one of the nation's first state housing offices to organize financial supports for home modification and repair services to low-income citizens with disabilities. See a program overview at the following Web link: www.phfa.org/consumers/homeowners/renovate_repair/ (accessed on September 20, 2007).

8. For information about the AdvantAge Initiative process in South Bend and Indianapolis, see the following Web links: http://www.cfsjc.org/reports.html; www.cicoa.org/TheAdvantAgeInitiative/TheAdvantAgeInitiative.html (accessed on September 20, 2007).

9. For information on Healthy Moves, view the tool kit at the following Web link: www.ncoa.org/Downloads/ModelProgramsHealthyMoves.pdf (accessed on September 20, 2007).

10. The walkability audit can be seen at the following Web link: www.walkable.org/download/walking_audits.pdf (accessed on September 20, 2007).

11. The Ithaca College partnership has existed since 1999. See the following Web link: www.ithaca.edu/aging/longview.php (accessed on September 20, 2007).

12. Information about elder-friendly businesses and the Boston project can be found at the following Web link: www.eldersinaction.org/whatwedo/elderfriendly/ (accessed on September 20, 2007).

13. See the 2005 White House Conference on Aging Resolution #18; "Encourage Community Designs to Promote Livable Communities that Enable Aging in Place." www.whcoa.gov/index.asp (accessed on September 20, 2007).

14. The notion of the "great good place" comes from Ray Oldenburg's (1991) book of the same title. While he writes mainly of public places and hangouts such as coffeehouses, pubs, and hair salons, the point to be made concerns the fact that good places are not always the product of professional design. As W. H. Whyte put it, the meaning of a place is a product of the users and not the planners.

CHAPTER 32

Elders, Urban Community Greening and the Rise of Civic Ecology

Jay Sokolovsky

East 125th St., Harlem, New York, Jackie Robinson Garden
 It was a vision from god ... he spoke to me, one day I was walking down the street and I look over there and saw all this garbage and stuff ... and I saw they were using it for prostitution and they were shooting up over there, and I said to myself, lord I sure would like to make a big garden over there. And the voice said "You can do that, just step out on my word." But today if you see it you wouldn't believe it. We got peach trees, grape trees ... apple trees ..., you wouldn't believe it to see this dump come to paradise!

Field notes, June 14, 2002

As I sat with seventy-two-year-old Betty Gaither, munching on one of the apples from this garden in Harlem, I indeed felt like I was in a certain version of paradise. Even though this uptown green space is wedged between elevated subway tracks, apartment buildings and a lot with junked cars, spend an afternoon there with its garden members and you might believe that *urban community greening*, linking the hands of energetic urban elders with those of younger generations, might just save the world.

Betty is just one person in a score of elders who have been part of a national and even international movement to create socially enabling green spaces and community gardens in what were once abandoned urban sites left to decay, fester and erode a sense of neighborhood and local well-being (Lawson 2005; Lin 2007). What I heard from Betty was repeated in various forms, as from 1998–2007 I sought to document through ethnographic video the history of New York City's community garden movement (Sokolovsky 2008). It is an amazing story of how that city's poorest neighborhoods transformed otherwise barren and often criminally hazardous zones with plants, trees, simple structures and locally inspired art, performance and political activism. In documenting this effort, I began to see a pattern in the role of active elders. In helping to establish these green oases, they created alliances across generational, economic and ethnic lines in powerful acts, of what has come to be called "civic ecology," during one of the most troubled times in the city's turbulent history.

When community elders could not obtain adequate city help or they thought the situation required instant action, they either started these projects on their own, or strong-armed a small cadre of younger kin and immediate neighbors to get things started or protect what they had done from those who had other ideas for the space. Here I am following the lead of Tidball and Krasny in viewing such urban community greening as acts of "civic ecology," whereby local citizens by collective action, reorder a physical space into an enabling green environment, promoting and enhancing community involvement and social inclusion (2007). The impact of civic ecology is especially powerful when undertaken in the face of great social and economic inequities and rapid environmental degradation.

This chapter will look at civic ecology from two angles. First, I will examine the rise of the community gardening movement in New York City, focusing on the involvement of seniors who use the creation of such places to enhance their neighborhood's "collective efficacy." I will also very briefly discuss the connection to health and healing and the use of civic greening to create therapeutic spaces in public venues and care settings where the frail aged may one day reside. This latter perspective seeks to explore how enabling green spaces enhances social engagement of even the most disabled older adults.

URBAN DECLINE AND THE FLOWERING OF CIVIC GREENING AND COMMUNITY GARDENS

Few people would associate twenty-first-century New York City with gardening and urban agriculture, yet this most archetypical of reborn world cities is now home to one of the largest such urban community greening efforts in North America. Its five boroughs now contain over 600 locally developed and maintained community gardens and even small farms.[1] From Coney Island, Brooklyn, to Manhattan's Lower East Side and the once-devastated South Bronx, poor and often minority aged such as "Miss Betty" and their neighbors have created seeming miracles that have been a major, but unheralded part of New York City's renaissance over the past thirty years.

Citizens creating urban gardens on vacant public land has a long history in the United States, dating back to the late nineteenth century. For example, during the 1893–1897 depression, in cities like Detroit, "potato patch farms" enabled masses of the unemployed to survive by growing food in vacant lots. Since that time, a multitude of related efforts have sporadically emerged on a short-lived basis in relation to economic hard times or world wars (Lawson 2005).[2]

However, when most people think of green space in New York City, they conjure up "manicured" landscapes such as monumental public parks like

Central Park or the magnificent botanical gardens in Brooklyn and the Bronx. When Central Park was opened by the city government in 1859, it was thought of as green oasis to "civilize" the newly arrived masses of immigrants and ease the stress of urban life. Today's community gardens represent a totally different relation to place, space and power. Here, citizens from poor and neglected neighborhoods have reversed this process by reclaiming abandoned public lands to civilize city-owned spaces that they saw as totally out of control. What were once open sores on the urban landscape have become places of transcendent beauty, cultural meaning and often social and political activism. In this regard, the latest civic greening movement appears more long-lasting. It is connected to an emerging new vision of urban possibilities, whereby citizens create by their own actions and sometimes in concert with local government and other entities, more livable, more sustainable and healthier communities (Smit and Bailkey 2006).

In New York City, if there was not such good documentation on community gardens, which arose during one of its darkest periods, they might have been written off as pure urban myth. During the early 1970s, housing stock and infrastructure were crumbling, violent crime skyrocketed and the treasury was bare. As banks redlined neighborhoods and landlords abandoned their properties, the city acquired upwards of 20,000 lots. In the Lower East Side of Manhattan, 70 percent of the population was displaced as 3,400 living units were demolished and almost daily fires and a lively drug trade moved in. Uptown in the south Bronx alone, 500 acres of former housing were burned down and reverted to the city for back taxes. Many such spaces came to be used as illegal garbage dumps, drug-shooting galleries and places to abandon cars.

This is not a story about rich kids or bored elders in white gloves who form garden clubs to indulge their passion for hybrid roses or organic tomatoes. Here is a gut-wrenching, often lonely and continuing struggle for community control of neighborhoods, public space and for the very lives and well-being of neighborhood children (von Hassell 2002). As the late greening activist Adam Honigman frequently reminded people, "Land Use is a Blood Sport!" Tellingly, the importance of community voice and initiative in creating and sustaining common green space is illustrated by the early efforts of city government, which in 1976 spent 3.6 million dollars to design and build gardens throughout the city, with little or no community input on vacant land awaiting housing development. Neighborhood residents, who were expected to maintain them, were not given tools or technical assistance and as might have been expected, in short order these gardens were vandalized and abandoned. The residents knew full well that they had no real say in the construction and use of these sites and that they would be sold to developers in the future to build whatever they wished.

In 1973, an artist named Liz Christie got some friends together and began to reclaim as garden space a small abandoned lot on Manhattan's Lower East Side. In a dream, she envisioned repeating this, even in fenced lots, by tossing over balloons armed with water and seeds. Her dream also revealed a name,

A former resident of the rural south (on the right) helps a life-long urban dweller get the most from his planting in a garden on Manhattan's Upper West Side, being developed in the early 1980s. Photo by Lynn Law.

"Green Guerillas" (spelled incorrectly in her vision), which became a group she formed to teach others how to repeat her success. Two years later, she went on to develop the Open Space Greening Program for the city's Council on the Environment. These simple acts of grassroots activism were but some of the sparks that ignited New York City's current community garden movement. By the late 1970s, there were so many gardens being started on public lands that the city established "Operation Green Thumb," which initially leased plots for $1 and provided technical support to sustain greening activities (www.greenthumbnyc.org).[3] Over the ensuing three decades, additional support from the Trust for Public Land and the New York Restoration Project has facilitated the purchase of more than one hundred garden properties to prevent them from being sold to developers.[4]

ELDERS AND THE COMMUNITY GARDEN MOVEMENT

It should be made clear that whether looking at cities like New York, Seattle or Philadelphia, where strong civic greening movements emerged as part of the process of community reclamation in the late 1960s and 1970s, that persons of all ages were involved with both initiating and continuing these projects. However, I have seldom encountered a well-functioning community garden in New York City where older adults were not active participants, if not involved in leadership within that space. In many cases they were instrumental in creating such places. Visit the Clinton Garden, not far from Times Square and you might encounter a retired teacher who tends to and educates all visitors about their bee hives; most any summer day join Cynthia and Haja in Harlem's Harmony Garden to participate in a children's environmental learning program that this elder, husband-wife team has developed; stop into almost any Casita garden after work hours and listen to Puerto Rican "*Plena*" music being played by expert older adult hands.[5]

There are some obvious reasons for the strong participation of older adults in civic greening, such as their having more free time to devote to such activities, or being more likely to have been exposed to gardening in their youth. Some of the elders who became active in sustaining community gardens had spent their youth in more rural zones of South Carolina, Puerto Rico or throughout the Caribbean region where growing food, medicinal plants and even gourds for musical instruments were part of their early experiences. They were instrumental in providing the knowledge base to combine with the energy of younger residents or older neighbors who had no idea it was possible to grow tomatoes or collard greens in the middle of Manhattan.

From another perspective, in previously devastated zones such as Manhattan's Lower East Side, or the South Bronx, it was only the long-term residents who had experienced more intact, functioning communities in these areas during the 1950s and 1960s. Persons of this older generation were the ones most likely to even hope that this might again be possible (see Kweon, Sullivan and Riley 1998). This was brought home to me very powerfully when I showed my documentary "Urban Garden" in a university class in Florida. As it was ending with an upbeat message, I heard a thirty-year-old male student softly sobbing in the back of the room. I asked him what was wrong and he told the class that he had lived the first eight years of his life in the Bronx, close to one of the beautiful gardens shown in the video—the Garden of Happiness. "Much of the area was a pile of rubble and burned-out buildings, full of violent crime and junkies. I never imaged that in my lifetime, the residents themselves could create such a thing of beauty and live across from such a garden in nice town houses, this is beyond my comprehension."

As I spent more time in a wide variety of gardens, I came to realize that while nurturing organic beauty via neighborhood hands was one of the functions of such places, it usually became secondary to the social plantings and harvests occurring within. What I began to see were community-created public spaces beckoning those who entered to readily transcend the barriers of wealth, ethnicity and age. I have seldom encountered urban spaces in New York City where people of differing ages and backgrounds so readily mingle for common efforts. Here in the early mid 1970s, when the gardens were being established, elderly blacks from the rural South could be seen teaching life-long Anglo-urbanites how to plant tomatoes and greens; or Caribbean elders would grow huge squash plants and teach local kids how to turn their dried husks into musical instruments. In 2003, in a well-established garden, I observed a

Children's Education Day at "Belmont Little Farmers Garden" in the Bronx, 2002. Photo by Pedro Diez.

twelve-year-old boy who sought refuge there from a difficult foster care setting being nurtured by a small group of older garden members and tutored in math by a retired seventy-eight-year-old teacher.

Studies of community gardens have produced an impressive list of benefits such as an increased sense of community ownership and stewardship, providing a neutral space for neighborhood activities, providing inexpensive access to nutritious fruits and vegetables, exposing inner-city youth to nature, connecting people across boundaries of cultures, class and generations and even reducing crime (Malakoff 1995).[6]

Some of the best-documented impacts have been shown in the realm of neighborhood crime reduction. Large-scale studies in Chicago have found a strong association of safer environments and civic greening (Kuo and Sullivan 2001). The largest study of crime and community ever completed in that city, in fact, found that the surest indicator of impending neighborhood crime reduction was an area's ability to create and sustain a community garden (Sampson, Raudenbush and Earls 1997). Such actions, if they were successful, invariably increased the level of what the authors call "social efficacy," a measure of residents' ability to act together, especially for the interest of local children. In doing so, they build stronger relationships among themselves and create a neighborhood support system that provides alternatives to violence.

HEALTH, HEALING AND THERAPEUTIC GREEN SPACES

I am spending the day in the Bronx at a small farm and community garden with a man of Afro-Caribbean heritage in his late sixties. He was one of several key older residents who worked to reclaim this space about a decade ago with the help of their grandkids, some neighbors, and the city's support organization "Green Thumb." After helping him dig out an old bed of some spiny plants, he noticed a quickly developing rash on the back of my hand, which began to intensely itch. He led me into another part of the garden and bent down to show me a plant with green shiny leaves. Pointing to the bright red on my skin he tells me, "My grandson sometimes get that," and winking his eye, he says, "I just tell the little one to crush those leaves in his palm and put the juice on the rash." Catching on, I follow these indirect instructions and almost immediately feel relief. Over the course of the next several hours, he proceeds to describe in detail the use of dozens of medicinal herbs interspersed with the food crops of corn, several varieties of tomatoes and squashes, eggplants, greens, peaches, apples and plums. "You see, I was brought up in the Caribbean by my grandfather who was a roots medicine healer and I know everything about these plants for making people better ... but I have to be careful about claiming to be a doctor, so when people ask, I just say well, I don't know about that, but when my wife or cousin has a problem like that I just pick the so and so plant and put it in a tea for them." (Field notes July 15, 2002)

Having such an elder with this level of folk health knowledge was not common, but most gardens in ethnic minority communities maintained an assortment of medicinal plants that were regularly used for minor bodily complaints and it was the older members who people relied on for their proper use. In the broader sense of such spaces as healing places, one of the most important environmental aspects of the current community garden movement is that it rose up in marginalized, minority neighborhoods that typically had the lowest access to public green space in the city. Studies have consistently shown the ameliorative effects of civic greening in mitigating chronic urban stress among poor communities and moderating its link to negative health conditions such as hypertension, diabetes, asthma, or heart problems (Browne 1992; Lewis 1996; Thwaites, Helleur and Simkins 2005).[7]

Among the most frequently uttered and spontaneously made statements people made about their experience in community gardens referred to enhanced positive psychological moods, perceptions of stress relief and specific references to being in a peaceful, healing environment.[8] For example, in 1998, barely fifteen minutes into my first encounter with a community garden, I learned of the personal impact these spaces can have. "I came to this garden in the late 1970s, I had just gotten a divorce and did not realize I was bipolar and very depressed. This garden saved me, it healed me" (Field notes, sixty-four-year-old female, April 28, 1998). The idea of healing gardens is an old one, dating at least to the Middle Ages and is still being employed in many kinds of formal rehabilitative settings including hospitals, hospices and prisons (Winterbottom 2005).[9] For example, at Manhattan's famous Bellevue Hospital, a psychiatrist has established an art-focused "sobriety garden" where patients in addictive services can interact with this "participatory landscape" as part of their treatment.

Over the past decade especially, the notion of therapeutic landscapes has come to be applied to the most frail elderly, taking the premises of civic greening into highly restrictive long-term care environments (Hazen 1997; Predny and Relf 2004). In fact, the notion of "elder gardens" has been at the center of revolutionizing and humanizing such spaces in developing the "Eden Alternative" and "Green House" models of care. These new visions of elder-inhabited space seek to reengage the social beings hidden behind medically constructed masks of failed personhood (see Thomas 1998; McLean Part VI). As Silverman and McAllister found in their study of a specialized Alzheimer's unit:

While activities such as gardening may be important in maintaining or reactivating certain practical skills, they are equally important in the maintenance or reactivation of a sense of self and self-worth. Such activities and the practice of specialized skills also provide a context for remembering and recounting important aspects of residents' personal history. (1995:207)

Yet, Silverman and McAllister also found that without the specialized design skills of therapeutic horticultural experts, engaging elders with diverse sets of impairments through civic greening was not easily achieved. One of the important advances in this area is the work of people like Ye Jen Lin, a Taiwanese physician who was trained in horticultural therapy in the United States. She has developed a training program for medical students, which teaches them to help create and implement interactive therapeutic gardens, especially designed for highly impaired nursing home residents with a wide variety of severe physical and cognitive limitations (Linn 2007).

CONCLUSIONS: CIVIC GREENING AND ITS MANY CONNECTIONS

While today's urban community gardens began under dire circumstances that sparked greening efforts in earlier eras, they have not only persisted much longer, but for the most part have morphed into vital community-building nodes of social inclusion.[10] This stands in sharp contrast to the exclusionary impact of all too many "urban renewal" projects that may end up destroying the only kinds of housing that elder long-term residents and their interconnected kin and friends can afford. It should be noted, however, that using grassroots civic greening to center sustainable communities or care environments often requires specialized knowledge about the environment and the means of making it accessible, usable and meaningful to persons of varied ages, backgrounds and physical competence. That is why in North America the most thriving and long-lasting civic greening endeavors are actively supported by experts from urban governments. They also forge partnerships with universities, nongovernmental organizations and socially responsibly corporations (see especially www.communitygarden.org).

It is rather amazing to see the varied impact of applying civic ecology to not only restoring connections with marginalized citizens, reaching across generations or working to repair communities blown asunder by natural disasters or unnatural wars. In the United States, this is powerfully seen in programs such as Seattle's "Youth Garden Works" (www.sygw.org) or Brooklyn's "Added Value" programs (www.added-value.org). These efforts seek to empower homeless and disadvantaged youth through creating their own urban community organic farms and eventually, in the case of "Added Value," build leadership skills directed at community improvement. Moving beyond this, to the somewhat obvious strategy of using such spaces to forge strong intergenerational community ties, in reality is rather hard to achieve (Krasny and Doyle 2002; Larson and Meyer 2006). One of the most promising models for such a goal is "Garden Mosaics," which connects youth and elders through understanding the interdependence of plants, people and culture in gardens. These programs combine science learning with intergenerational mentoring, multicultural understanding and community action (http://www.gardenmosaics.cornell.edu/). There are a number of pilot projects using this model now operating throughout the United States and in South Africa.

Internationally, the idea of civic ecology and community gardens has emerged in the crucible of rapid changes that in the context of civil wars and globalization has seen the disruption of national food systems and local systems of support. In this volume, we note in Box V.1 how grandmother-centered community gardens in Africa and elsewhere are being used to not only improve the well-being of young women and their children, but to restore a vital transgenerational learning process, disrupted by globalization.[11] In Bosnia following the recent horrific civil wars, community gardens have been developed with the aid of the American Friends Committee to help begin the healing process needed after any such conflict.[12] In all this, it is important to realize that no matter how beautiful and peaceful any garden may be, it is the connection established between social beings nurturing it and the sense of inclusion and community created by their actions that have the most consequence.

NOTES

There are many people to thank for helping me in my research on community gardens, especially for the materials discussed in this chapter. These persons include: Edie Stone, Adam Honigman, Sid Glasser, Annie Chadwick, Betty Gaither, Gerard Lordahl, Dee Parisi, Jane Grundy, Donald Loggins, Abu Talib, Carolyn Radcliffe, Jackie Beach, Jane Weisman, Kate Chura, Lynn Law and Daniel Winterbottom. I would also like to thank Mari Gillogli for applying her sharp editorial eye to this chapter.

1. This figure does not include the 650 gardens being maintained, often by seniors, in the city's extensive public housing system, which housed 125,000 seniors in 2008.

2. Many people know about the "victory gardens" that were encouraged during the first two world wars, but most have forgotten about the varied attempts of cities of helping poor citizens grow food on vacant urban land during bad economic times. In Europe, a more long-lasting system called the allotment system developed in the

eighteenth and nineteenth centuries, with plots of land, usually on the outskirts of cities, given to poor families to cultivate and grow food. See http://en.wikipedia.org/wiki/ Allotment_gardens.

3. "Operation Green Thumb" was funded by federal Community Development Block Grants and continues as simply "GreenThumb"; it has been a program of the New York City Parks Department since 1995.

4. The New York Restoration Project (NYRP) is a nonprofit begun by actress Bette Midler in 1995 to reclaim and restore under-resourced parks, community gardens and open spaces in New York (see www.nyrp.org). In 1999, under the administration of Mayor Rudy Giuliani, 114 gardens were set to be auctioned off to developers. Greening activist groups such as More Gardens and Reclaim the Streets mounted strong street protests and four lawsuits were developed to prevent the sale. A day before the auction, the Brooklyn State Supreme Court issued an injunction to stop the sale. That same day the city agreed to sell the plots to NYRP and The Trust for Public Land. In 2000, the New York state attorney general secured a temporary restraining order that prevented the city not only from conveying land to a developer, but also from entering the garden to perform test borings. After Mayor Giuliani left office, in 2002, a negotiated settlement agreement preserved an additional 200 community gardens (to be transferred to parks or sold to a land trust), established a review process for 115 gardens that New York City wishes to develop and allowed the city to proceed immediately with the development of an additional 38 gardens.

5. For a good discussion of the cultural aspects of Casita gardens, see Saldivar-Tanaka and Krasny (2004).

6. A study in St. Louis also looked at the functions of community gardens in stabilizing neighborhoods. See the "Whitmire Study: Gateway Greening Community Garden Areas, Reversing Urban Decline," at www.gatewaygreening.org/WhitmireStudy.asp.

7. For a general discussion of health and urban greening, see "Health Benefits of Urban Agriculture," by Anne Bellows at: www.foodsecurity.org/UAHealthArticle.pdf. Also, as an interesting connection for Carson's chapter in Part VI, among Native Americans, where diabetes is reaching epidemic proportions, culturally appropriate community gardens are being explored as a means of at least partially restoring traditional diets under which this disease was much less common (see Lombard, Forster-Cox, Smeal and O'Neill 2006).

8. I should also note that the community garden experience also involved continuing struggle and sometimes significant conflict in maintaining and managing these spaces.

9. For an excellent new study of horticultural therapy and prisons, see Jiler 2006.

10. However, some of the intensely ethnic gardens can sometimes act counter to the notion of social inclusion and discourage persons from other backgrounds in taking advantage of the space.

11. A great Web link to international programs related to community gardens and food security is found at The Food Security Learning Center, www.worldhungeryear. org/fslc/faqs/ria_159.asp?section=3&click=6 (accessed on March 22, 2008).

12. For information on these gardens, see www.afsc.org/europe/bosnia/gardening. htm.

CHAPTER 33

Spaces of Age, Snowbirds and the Gerontology of Mobility: The Elderscapes of Charlotte County, Florida

Stephen Katz

Gerontology is a field befittingly fixed on the problems of aging-in-time and the temporal conditions of growing older. Consequently, researchers focus on *when* people retire and the social roles, economic challenges and cohort experiences associated with such a momentous life course passage. At the same time the place of retirement has become an increasingly vital dimension of later life because, as more people retire, issues of mobility, residence and community are linked to gerontologic ideals of independence and successful aging. Thus, this chapter is oriented to the questions of *where* people retire and how they create cultural spaces for retirement. Specifically, the research examines several sites or *elderscapes* unique to Charlotte County in the Gulf coastal area of southwestern Florida as evidence of the growth of new retirement and aging communities. My objective is not to produce a conventional ethnographic analysis but to sketch a social topography of spaces of age. As such, the data combine documents, photographs, personal reflections and interviews collected during a field research project conducted in Florida during 1998–99. The resulting experimental methodological weave is an attempt to represent the complexity of migrational retirement culture and the spatial dynamics that shape its regions, flows and environments.

In this chapter I use photographic materials and diary entries as the personal means by which I can include my identity and journey as a researcher within the montage of places I visited. In addition, the photographic and visual materials enrich the depiction of physical and built spaces and their relevance to cultural gerontology. Indeed, visual gerontology is a highly valuable yet surprisingly underdeveloped resource within the field. Where it has been central to the research, as in Dena Shenk and Ronald M. Schmid's work (2002) on the *Rural Older Women's Project in Minnesota* in the 1980s and 1990s, the results are innovative and edifying. As these authors note about their gerontology, "the benefits of using photography as a research tool include providing evidence that is difficult to put into words. Photography can also be viewed as a way to portray the context within which other kinds of data can be analyzed and understood" (p. 260). In another fascinating study, British cultural sociologist Andrew Blaikie demonstrates the historical influence of photographic imagery on cultural constructions of retirement, aging and old age in the United Kingdom (Blaikie 1999). In these cases visual gerontology has an inherent reflexive dimension because it not only looks to images as valuable sources of data, but it also considers the conditions under which images are used to create data. As visual ethnographer Sarah Pink reminds us, the import of photographic representations is contingent upon how they are situated and interpreted; hence, photographic research is also a reflexive exercise whereby the researchers, in part, construct the cultural environments they analyze (Pink 2001:19–21). This means that multiple narratives, ambiguous meanings and the researcher's subjective experiences can coexist in photographic imagery along with the objective goals of the research itself (p. 126). This is certainly the case with photographic research on aging, challenged as it is by our society's dominant negative images of aging and old age and the restriction of their meanings to demeaning stereotypes that prefigure other kinds of reception and interpretation.

With these methodological considerations in view, the first part of this chapter surveys gerontology's spatial inquiries and postmodern critiques of commercial retirement communities, drawing upon recent cultural theories of global processes whereby technologies, networks, and populations are identified by their movements across geo-social spaces rather than by their locations within them. The second part of the essay portrays the selected *elderscapes* of Charlotte County, Florida, with a concentration on *snowbird culture*, a migrational intercultural world where northern Americans and Canadians spend their winter months living in warm southern states.

TOWARDS A GERONTOLOGY OF MOBILITY

The Inquiries of Spatial Gerontology

If one could summarize gerontology's primary professional goal, it would be to determine the conditions and contexts in which an individual's adaptation to aging is either facilitated or limited. These include spatial and residential arrangements as key adaptational resources, which academic gerontologists investigate at three levels of inquiry: (1) institutional ethnographies, (2) "aging-in-place" debates and (3) community networks. In their combination, as the survey below indicates, these inquiries have constituted a significant literature on elder environments and their impact on an individual's health care, quality of life, independent living and functional capabilities.

Institutional ethnographies are produced by sociological researchers who have been inspired by Erving Goffman's *Asylums* and related social interactionist and ethnomethodological frameworks to tackle the internal environmental relationships and subjective conditions within institutional, residential and community-care spaces (e.g., Diamond 1992). Jaber F. Gubrium's social constructivist research is the most well-known for building this level of inquiry into a leading contribution to social gerontology (1997 [1975], 1993). For Gubrium and his associates a nursing home is not simply a building or residence; rather, it is a micro-complex of architectural, administrative, financial, clinical, familial, symbolic and emotional interactions and power relations.[1] Institutional ethnographers show how everyday existence is organized both formally, according to the structured roles, statuses and authorities of nursing home administrators, staff, residents and visitors, and informally, according to the residents' subjective experiences with meals, toileting, sleeping, bathing, activities, family visits and medical treatment. Everyday existence, as Gubrium notes, is a whole "social world" whereby "worlds are the operating frameworks that make what participants do immediately reasonable in their everyday lives" (Gubrium and Holstein 1999:295). In such worlds, within and outside institutions, even the most mundane and routine activities in the most microcosmic of spaces, such as residents meeting in the lobby of an old-age home or friends meeting in a fast-food restaurant, take on special social meaning and shape age-identities in elaborate ways (Gamliel 2000; Cheang 2002). In *Facing the Mirror* (1997), author Frida Furman discovers an entire social world of older women and their wider community of self-care and sisterhood within the confines of their local hair salon.

The second type of inquiry within spatial gerontology revolves around "aging-in-place" debates. These tend to concentrate on two issues: first, the benefits and disadvantages of people living at home or in familiar surroundings as they age; and second, the transformation of homes or familiar surroundings as people suffer physical disabilities and/or cognitive limitations. Obviously a powerful component of a person's aging is their attachment over time to their homes, neighbourhoods, parks, shopping areas, schools, religious centers, restaurants, and local points of community history. Personal identity is constantly spatialized because people narrate the things and places around them as part of their biographical development. A walk through a neighbourhood or a room-to-room tour of a house and its cherished objects are also poignant narrative experiences full of memories and stories. Therefore, the possibility of not being able to live (or die) at home can be one of the most terrifying aspects of growing older, even where home life creates its own disadvantages. Most aging-in-place research addresses this problem by measuring an individual or family's level of subjective well-being at home against the physical, accidental and financial risks home residence can generate (*Generations* 1992; Heumann and Boldy 1993). As Graham Rowles, a pioneer in spatial gerontology points out, aging-in-place thinking must neither romanticize nor exaggerate "familiarity and emotional affiliation with place" nor "overstate the negative consequences of relocation for the elderly" (Rowles 1994:122). Rather we must take into account all the pragmatic, intergenerational, income-related, situational and technical realities that go into residential decision-making (see also Rowles 1978; Rowles and Ravdal 2002; Heywood, Oldman and Means 2002).

If the first issue elucidated by aging-in-place debates is the relation between residence and the continuity of successful aging, the second issue has to do with home environment design modifications and social services that allow people to live in their homes (Lanspery and Hyde 1997; Taira and Carlson 1999). For example, simple yet effective home aids such as the installation of hand rails, non-slip floors, easy-to-reach cupboards, or volume-enhanced telephones and doorbells can make home life so much easier for older individuals who experience physical decline. In homes where stairs are a major impediment to a resident's mobility, sleeping, bathroom and kitchen areas can be relocated on the same floor. More complicated, however, are those cases where residents, despite their lifelong competencies around cleaning, gardening, cooking, travel and personal care, require professional home visits or special assisted living services in order to remain at home. Such interventions can upset the delicate domestic balance between private and public spaces, as Julia Twigg (2000) outlines in her research on home residents and visiting careworkers in Britain. In addition to cases of theft and elder-abuse (p. 85), Twigg observes that, "care, in coming into this territory [home], brings its own rationalities, and these are in many ways in conflict within those of home and domestic life" (p. 105). Another disturbing issue is that homes can become very isolating places for older residents who live alone or in secluded areas, and thus residents become house-bound and suffer further physical and psychological problems. Hence, aging-in-place debates correlate the personal circumstances surrounding privacy, identity, bodily and subjective well-being with the social, spatial and residential features of homes, homecare and home-like environments in public settings (Kontos 1998). The idea of home as a place and a resource, with its own set of risks and rewards, is also an important element of community network research, the third general inquiry within spatial gerontology.

Community network research is a more technical level of inquiry than ethnographic or aging-in-place investigations because here researchers set out to map the gerontological networks by which homes, community facilities, senior centers, geriatric clinics, hospitals and related areas are linked to the movements, visits and stays of the older individuals, caregivers, friends and families who travel between them. Of primary importance is the question of how people cope with spatial transitions, uprooting, displacement and relocations. Journals such as *Journal of Housing for the Elderly* (Haworth Press) and the social environmental research inspired by M. Powell Lawton and others (Lawton, Windley and Byerts 1982; Altman, Lawton and Wohlwill 1984; Newcomer, Lawton and Byerts 1986) examine the constant interaction between competency, adaptation, context and environment in the lives of older persons. Such interaction has also been termed the "person-environment fit" whereby "competence does not reside solely in the individual nor in the environment" but occurs "when the capabilities of the individual match the environmental demands and resources" (Schaie and Willis 1999:183). The information generated by community network and person-environment studies is vital to future health care policy because it helps to determine the conditions under which people can live *autonomously*, that is, in ways by which they negotiate control over both dependent and independent features of their aging. For example, Susan Garrett's report on poor rural communities in Virginia, *Miles to Go* (1998), illustrates how location, identity and spatial relations configure the experience of aging and determine the efficacy of professional intervention. There is still much research to do in this area, however, as Laura Strain demonstrates in her survey of Manitoba senior centers (2001). Strain found that senior center rates of participation are unpredictable, often low, or variable with very little information available as to why this is the case. This situation led her to conclude that "our research knowledge regarding senior centers, their participants, and their activities must be considered in its infancy" (p. 488).

Contemporary social policy has also contributed a different set of political meanings to "community" that profoundly affect person-environment relations. Today the institutional supports that had been built into modern Western welfare states are eroding in favour of greater political reliance upon, and often burdening of, local and community resources. One result is that social program policies coalesce around the transfer of financial state responsibilities to non-state and community social spaces and services (Aronson 2002; Broad and Antony 1999; Rose 1999; Schofield 2002). Where such spaces and services become enfolded within privatized and community-state partnerships, significant consequences for aging groups have arisen because of the fiscal limitations such partnerships entail and because their articulation within public discourses takes on a crisis-oriented tone, such as those that attempt to "oversell" the problems of population aging (Gee and Gutman 2000). Community living for aging groups is a neoliberal dilemma. On the one hand, the enhancement of familiar, local and community spaces which support older persons is desirable, especially given the largely negative and "medicalized" connotations associated with care institutions, nursing and retirement homes and other specialized environments. Good examples are where local community banks and businesses offer senior homeowners helpful reverse mortgage arrangements, tax incentives, home-sharing options, mixed-age co-op housing, reduced transportation expenses or low-cost landscaping services. There is also evidence that "naturally occurring retirement communities" (NORCs) are on the rise, whereby sizable groups of retired senior residents happen to find themselves living in a selected area by chance. As such they independently and inventively initiate community mutual aid and other supportive networks, which, in turn, evolve into new community assets (Callahan and Lansperry 1997; Pine and Pine 2002). On the other hand, the idealized sense of the "local community" and its assumed beneficence for older persons is promoted in Canada and elsewhere as a political and economic panacea to problems of dependency with little regard to the gender, ethnic, class and regional inequalities that exist in communities. In other words, as we learn from gerontological community and network research about the *local* as a genuinely creative and resourceful gerontological system of support, we must also consider its increasing role in being made to subsidize governmental fiscal policy, consumer-based health care models and market-driven retirement planning. Thus, a key challenge of this kind of research is to advance a critical analysis of both the ideals and the practices that make up gerontological communities and spatial networks.

The three areas of inquiry within spatial gerontology outlined here—institutional ethnographies, aging-in-place debates and community network mapping—create a fascinating subfield that underscores the point that any social space can be the inspiration for important commentary on the state of contemporary later life and gerontological research itself. There are many other examples than the ones offered above. However, one of the most interesting and unique spatial developments has been retirement communities. Unlike other elder spaces and networks, retirement communities call for a somewhat different kind of analysis because lifestyle and leisure values, rather than historical community and social relationships, frame their spatial characteristics and affiliated retiree identities. In particular the American "Sunbelt" or "Sun City" type of community exemplifies the new cultural connection between lifestyle and residence in retirement. As such, these communities have been accused of promoting an overly commercialized and idealized image of successful aging to the disregard of the disadvantaged living conditions faced by many older persons and their families who require sustainable support. Taking this criticism into account, the next section discusses how Sun City retirement communities, lifestyles and identities might offer spatial gerontology a fresh approach, beyond traditional and local analyses, to the larger cultural forces at work redefining age in an anti-aging culture.

Sun Cities and the Mobility of Retirement

In previous chapters I have discussed how contemporary images of timeless, ageless and "positive" cultures of aging feed into the postindustrial and postmodern blurring of conventional life course roles and transitions. Within these cultures, and despite current and popular expectations that older people will devise active, independent, self-caring and mobile lifestyles, those who lack the middle-class financial and cultural capital to do so face an even greater struggle to gain social support and recognition. In the midst of these contradictions Sun City retirement communities, built mostly in Florida, Arizona, Texas and California since the 1960s, are spatial expressions of the new social aging and its idealistic imagery. In reality, their "gated" exclusivity and predominantly white and owner-resident features tend to isolate aging groups and potentially mask the aging process itself by naturalizing retirement living as continuously active and problem-free (Kastenbaum 1993; Laws 1995b, 1996; McHugh 2000). Hence, new retirement developments that celebrate active, healthy aging can also separate it from how aging is experienced in real communities. As McHugh comments, "Sun Belt retirement communities are defined as much by the absent image—old poor folks in deteriorating neighbourhoods in cold, grey northern cities and towns—as by the image presented: handsome, healthy, comfortably middle-class 'seniors,' busily filling sunfilled days" (2000:113). From this critical perspective Sun Cities can appear as simulated lifestyle enclaves, marketed as the just rewards for a life of hard work, and where even the harsh Arizona desert can become a retirement-friendly *elderscape*. In this sense Sun Cities are little more than massive real estate ventures beckoning to well-to-do mid-lifers who are already anxious about their retirement-fit futures.

However, Sun Cities and associated retirement communities also encompass wider and non-commercial issues significant to spatial and cultural gerontological inquiries, such as mobility, migration and *transculturality*. Indeed, for those sociologists who study spatial processes at the global level the concept of *society* itself is no longer an adequate theoretical base from which to understand the contemporary movements of peoples and cultures.[2] In this regard British sociologist John Urry provides a new set of ideas stemming from his instructive examination of "mobilities for the twenty-first century" (2000). For Urry, social relations and forces now operate beyond societies due to the impact of global, social and populational *flows* (including diasporas), transcultural lifestyles, transnational economic networks, virtual connectivity webs and borderless transportation systems. Within these mobile forms, "*Scapes* are the networks of machines, technologies, organisations, texts, and actors that constitute various interconnected nodes along which the flows can be relayed" (p. 35). For example, local rapid transportation systems, informational channels, and communication satellites all compete to become connected or plugged into dominant scapes via their own "nodes." Some scapes create incredible power and prestige while others are globally ignored or bypassed altogether. "By contrast with the structured scapes, the *flows* consist of peoples, images, information, money and waste that move within, and especially across national borders and which individual societies are often unable or unwilling to control directly or indirectly" (p. 36). Inequalities in "flows" are based on the degree of their accessibility and the extent to which flows create health or environmental risks in some areas but not in others. Flows can also facilitate mobility and new nomadic lifestyles because of inexpensive travel, cheapened global consumer goods and electronic connectivity. According to Urry, therefore, places are "a set of spaces where ranges of relational networks and flows coalesce, interconnect and fragment" across distances (p. 140).

Taken together, global *scapes*, flows and places create the conditions under which global citizenries can emerge, whereby people can "migrate from one society to another," "stay at least temporarily with comparable rights as the indigenous population," and "return not as stateless and with no significant loss of rights" (Urry 2000:174). Global citizens can also expect to encounter hybrid cultures that contain some of the elements of their own culture. Most importantly, such citizens are

able to inhabit environments which are relatively free of risks to health and safety produced by both local and distant causes; to sense the quality of each environment directly rather than to have to rely on expert systems which are often untrustworthy; and to be provided with the means by which to know about those environments through multi-media sources of information, understanding and reflection. (Urry 2000:174)

The overall cultural effect of these historic global processes, as Welsch (1999) reminds us, is that cultural differences "no longer come about through a juxtaposition of clearly delineated cultures (like in a mosaic), but result between transcultural networks, which have some things in common while differing in others, showing overlaps and distinctions at the same time" (p. 201). If typical theories of globalization assume that cultures around the world are becoming homogenized or the "same," transculturality combines local and global cultures anew by merging particular cultural details with universalistic processes. In short, "transcultural identities comprehend a cosmopolitan side, but also a side of local affiliation. Transcultural people combine both" (p. 205).

Unfortunately Urry, Welsch, and other global theorists neglect to include retirement as a key contemporary "mobility" whose migrational patterns are set to become even more extensive in the years ahead. Nevertheless, their characterizations of global citizenry are appropriate to the inhabitants of retirement areas and communities framed by Sunbelt and Snowbird cultures. If we extend their ideas about social spaces (scapes, flows, places) and global transcultural citizens to migrational and mobile retirement cultures, then these, along with related spatial gerontological inquiries and postmodern Sun City critiques, can be considered part of a larger subfield we can call the *gerontology of mobility*. The gerontology of mobility would include the transculturality of both people and places as they age and change while adding a dynamic sense of retirement "flow" to the more static tradition of retirement "time." In line with these proposed defining features of the gerontology of mobility, the second part of this chapter offers a medley of sociological, visual, spatial and reflexive materials based on three elderscapes in Charlotte County, Florida: Warm Mineral Springs, the Port Charlotte Cultural Center, and Maple Leaf Estates. At the same time the study considers Canadian snowbird culture as an exemplary case of life course "flow" from which to explore the opportunities and contradictions of global life in an era of unprecedented population aging.

SPACES OF AGE IN CHARLOTTE COUNTY, FLORIDA

Diary, December 12, 1998: 9 A.M. Pearson International Airport, Toronto, waiting to depart on Canadian Airways Flight 242 to Miami. Filling the large waiting area are mostly middle-aged and older people, couples, some already with a pre-tanned skin, putting their feet up on matching "his" and "hers" luggage, migrational souls relaxed, travel-tuned and waiting for takeoff. The pre-boarding announcement for people with small children immediately inspires the elder crowd to ready themselves. Once on the plane, among the seats behind me I see a sprouting of books, bottles of water, crossword puzzles and headphones; hear the quick snapping of seat-belts, closing of overhead hand luggage doors, zipping up of seat tables and the stripping off of parkas, sweaters and other wintry wear to reveal sensible summer wear, polo shirts and short-sleeved cotton blouses. Rockport shoelaces are everywhere loosened and cell phones tucked away, grey heads that line the rows of seats lay back and smile. These folks know what they're doing. Once airborne, an elderly male cabin attendant makes his way forward with a trolley for drinks. As we descend towards the Miami Airport, I wonder if aircraft passenger cabins have become micro elderscapes and how they might change in the future accordingly.

Charlotte County, Florida was established in 1921. The story behind the county's name is that it is an Anglicized corruption of the Spanish "Carlos" which came from the original native Calusa word "Calos." What the Spanish called Carlos Bay in 1565 the English called Charlotte Harbour in 1775 in honour of Queen Charlotte Sophia, wife of King George III (*Charlotte County Statistical Prospectus* 1998–99:1). The lovely waterfront and semi-tropical area lies 50 miles south of Sarasota, 24 miles north of Fort Myers, and 160 miles northwest of Miami. The county includes the towns of Englewood, Punta Gorda and Port Charlotte. Port Charlotte, located north of the Peace River along US Highway 41, is one of the country's fastest growing areas. However, most of the growth in the county is tied to the fact that the median age of the residents is 52.1 with 32.9 percent of them aged 65 and older (*Florida Statistical Abstract* 1998). Future projections are for increased immigration and a rising median age. Put another way, 40 percent of Charlotte County is 55 or older, and in some areas 50 percent or more are 65 years or older.[3] A recent ten-year health study of Charlotte County's senior residents, according to the local newspaper, found that "they are healthier and happier than their peers across the nation" (*Charlotte Sun Herald* 1999). The Senior Community Service and Employment Program affiliated with the regional AARP (American Association of Retired Persons) Foundation office in Port Charlotte reported a 73 percent job placement success rate in 1998, making the office's success rate second in the country and winning it a bronze award. Charlotte County also hosts the popular weeklong Senior Fit for Life Games.

Hence, it is little wonder that the social landscape of the county is dominated by a large number of resident-owned retirement communities, financial and recreational organizations and health care facilities and volunteer societies. In brief, there is a five-fold grid of residential options, depending on income level, health status and individual autonomy: Home Health Care, Retirement communities, Continuing Care Retirement Communities (CCRCs), Assisted Living Facilities (ALFs) and Nursing Homes (*Senior Living Guide of South Florida* 1998:27–28). Home Health Care provides visiting professional services for residents who live at home. Retirement communities are mostly private and available to those who live independently but desire a range of leisure activities and resident conveniences. CCRCs are self-contained resident communities that also offer nursing and other care services such as housekeeping and personal assistance in one location, depending on the contractual or purchasing arrangement set out by the resident. ALFs are catered, personal care homes that range in size where recreational activities, meals, bathing and routine daily

Figure 33.1
Gulf Coast Map Showing Charlotte County

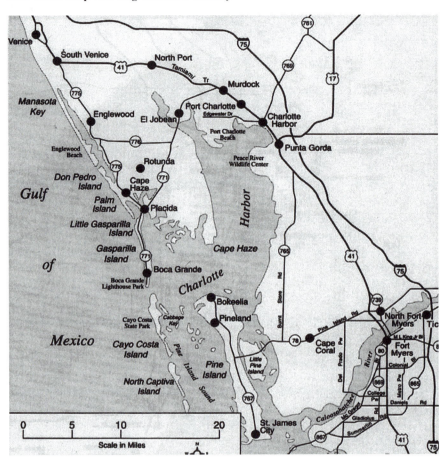

Source: The Gulf Coast of Florida: A Complete Guide. Chelle Koster Walton. Stockbridge, MA: Berkshire House Publishers, 1993, p. 42.

needs are provided. ALFs are more of a care environment than CCRCs and often include residents with Alzheimer's disease. Nursing homes are designed for those who require full-time nursing care and facilities for a complete spectrum of assistance. All these options are costly or require the resident to meet strict physical and income admission standards in order to qualify for financial assistance (where it exists). Given the size of Florida's elderly population, it is not surprising that the state's nursing home industry has recently experienced insurance, financial and labor crises which have combined to create what some critics call "a long-term-care storm" (Polivka-West et al. 2001). Meanwhile, researchers have also found that affordable government-subsidized housing for low-income residents is unequally distributed in Florida, with many people living in underserved counties (Golant 2002).

However, Charlotte County, as an area heavily populated by senior residents in Florida, is also an experimental zone where the aging demographic forces of North American populations converge to create new spatial, mobile and transcultural ways of life. This is particularly true in the case of Canadian snowbirds, semi-migrational retirees who spend their winters in Florida while maintaining their homes in Canada. It is estimated that 500,000 Canadians spend three months or more in Florida each year with another 350,000 people heading to other states such as Arizona, California and Texas. Snowbirds who come to the Gulf coastal areas of southwestern Florida are mostly Anglo-Canadians and live in a variety of residences, the most notable being retirement communities or parks.[4]

While snowbird culture is elaborated later in the essay, the point stressed here is that Charlotte County's elderscapes illustrate something of how retirement and later life are shaped both by the material struggles over health and security and by the innovative networks and flows of a unique social topography.

Warm Mineral Springs

Diary, December 16, 1998: I had been shopping in Sarasota, where most shops cater to elderly customers looking for good deals, restaurants advertise "early bird" special meals and clothing stores sell the same leisure wear and comfort clothing without extending

Elderly workers in a Port Charlotte grocery store. Photo by Stephen Katz.

Port Charlotte neighborhood. Photo by Stephen Katz.

their imagination to those shoppers who maintain a lifelong interest in fashion, elegance, sexiness and creative expressions of self. Driving back to my place in Englewood, a dark feeling surfaces as I pass identical malls, gated residences and condos, seafood "palaces," video rentals and gigantic drug-marts. The feeling is one of loneliness and desperation, a secret, fearful retirement culture that exposes the real illusion of an American Dream that not only doesn't last but may never have really existed. Along the roads connecting the towns, new buildings and communities seem to have been burned right out of the environment, in asphalted areas that separate the resorts and golf courses from the original residences that have come to appear as "quaint" or "historic" in comparison. Sometimes the alligators make an appearance as a reminder of what once was. This is a largely white world, cared for and serviced by a world of mostly non-white black or Hispanic laborers, cleaners, drivers and landscapers. But then all this is thrown into relief when I came to visit Warm Mineral Springs, Charlotte County's fountain of youth.

Warm Mineral Springs is just south of Venice and near the town of North Port in Florida. The spa opened in 1940 and is famous for its highly mineral and sulphurous 2.5-acre lake, whose waters are maintained at a luxuriously warm 87°F year-round. The lake is believed to have youth-giving and healing powers; the water is also drunk as a curative and mild laxative. The area and buildings that once housed rooms for massage, hydrotherapy, hotpacks, whirlpool and sauna now show their age, and what services are on offer look like they have had better days, although new vacation villas at the Springs are being planned along with a town center (www.warmmineralsprings.com). There are also apartments to rent or resorts nearby to accommodate people who visit the springs. Despite appearances, Warm Mineral Springs is a unique

Man sunning next to Warm Mineral Springs Lake. Photo by Stephen Katz.

and fascinating facility that joins the world's great international spas and adds to their mythical accounts about the restorative miracles of drinking and bathing in vital waters. At Warm Mineral Springs, stories and testimonials abound of people tossing away canes and walkers, even wheelchairs, after weeks of bathing or sitting on chairs in the rejuvenating lake. At the lake, mostly elderly bathers swim slowly around the perimeter of the swimming area, enjoying the mineral-rich, steamy water, and soothing their aches and pains. There is a large Eastern European clientele, and visitors to Warm Mineral Springs lean towards traditional health-management techniques involving baths, muds, minerals, massages, open air, calming views, stretching and water therapy; they appear wary of the current cultural obsession with anti-aging chemicals, surgery, diets and antioxidants. Appropriately, Warm Mineral Springs was declared a historic site in 1977. When Ponce de Leon colonized Florida in 1513 (at the age of 53), he was intent on finding the legendary Fountain of Youth but unfortunately he never made it to Warm Mineral Springs.

The Port Charlotte Cultural Center

Diary, December 17, 1998: While doing a run to the local grocery store, I discover that many of the part-time workers in drugstores and grocery stores are older and retired, but still working. Indeed older workers are everywhere: behind the counters, the cash registers, carrying out bags and stacking shelves. At the nearby Publix I talk with Joe, a retiree from the American airforce who now flies around the store aisles gathering shopping carts. He tells me how great it is that younger and older people work in the same place, since the young have so much to learn from the old. In other words, sharing a "job niche" is a great opportunity despite the different values that are placed on life at different points of the life course. Joe and the others know about the Port Charlotte Cultural Center, which they consider "their" center not because it is for seniors but because it was built by seniors for everybody in Charlotte County.

When I visited the Port Charlotte Cultural Center on December 24, 1998, I was greeted by volunteers who immediately offered me a cool drink, gave me a tour of the rooms and buildings, and left me with a sense that I had entered a special place: a temple, a micro-world operating on a different basis than the larger society. I was reminded that this was one of the largest, most successful centers of its kind and, as its brochure boasts, "There's nothing like it anywhere else in America." I can believe it. I talked with Judy Ventrella, Director of the Volunteers Office, who showed me several crowded schedules listing the hundreds of hours each month worked by volunteers and the ongoing projects that self-fund the Center. "Miracles happen all the time here," says Judy, because people come in and offer all kinds of skills and talents, creating a volunteer pool that is unrivalled elsewhere. The Center also reaches out to provide for those with special needs, such as a course for older drivers, free eye screening, legal support for those working on wills and power-of-attorney arrangements, support groups for widows and widowers and volunteer opportunities for people with disabilities or who are deaf or blind. There are intergenerational programs being developed to include younger groups so that the Center remains a broadly appealing "cultural" rather than strictly "seniors" facility.

Indeed the Port Charlotte Cultural Center is really a complex of spaces and activities, consisting of meeting and music rooms, clothing boutique, school and classrooms, library, woodworking shop, art gallery, travel agency, President's Room Museum, kitchen and cafeteria, the Trash and Treasure Shop, nurses' station, administrative and volunteer offices and a 418-seat theatre, all housed in four buildings covering five acres of land. Amazingly, along with about 30 paid employees, over 1,000 mostly retired and older volunteers, including its Board of Trustees, run the Center almost entirely. The original buildings were built in 1960 by the General Development Corporation (now called Atlantic Gulf Communities), which constructed housing estates in the area. Retired residents who moved to Port Charlotte organized an adult education school with grants from the county library and school board to build a library, theatre and classrooms. Hence, the group was referred to as PCU or "Port Charlotte University." In the 1960s PCU and the Center grew through

Residents playing cards at Port Charlotte Cultural Center. Photo by Stephen Katz.

Workers and volunteers at Port Charlotte Cultural Center. Photo by Stephen Katz.

new additions, vigorous lobbying and sizable donations until it was officially dedicated as the Cultural Center in January 1968. As local histories, such as Jim Robertson's *At the Cultural Center* (1996) demonstrate,[5] it is a case of senior power, senior resources and senior culture. Robertson's book is based on his radio series on the Cultural Center in the 1990s, and he devotes several chapters to volunteer profiles to celebrate and commemorate their ingenuity and hard work. On a deeper level, Robertson and others who write about the Center are sociologically describing a unique elderscape, one that is constantly in transition as it attracts and coordinates an expansive mutual aid society. The number of social recreation and learning opportunities is stunning; the Activities Center and the theatre offer a host of theatrical, musical, travel, health and lifestyle programs, and at The Learning Place over 140 volunteer-taught classes are available across a range of academic, lifestyle, professional and language subjects. The Cultural Center is also a social magnet that attracts regular public and media attention, public and private funding, renovation projects, partnerships and community support to Port Charlotte itself; thus, the Center extends its importance within the vibrant elder network throughout the county.

Concluding my visit to the Center I join some of the men playing cards in the club room. As we talk, most of the players tell me that they are from the northeastern part of the country where they spent most of their working lives. And while they came to Florida to retire and escape the grueling winters of the north, they found they still needed to work at something in order to maintain a rich social life and stimulate their intellectual interests. So they are fortunate to be exactly where they want to be. As I leave the Cultural Center and drive around Port Charlotte, I realize the important role the Center plays as a counter space to the commercial sites surrounding it, which announce atop their flashing billboards the seemingly endless places and services catering to eyes, muscles, hearing, rehabilitation, exercise, hair loss and teeth. Because medicine and consumerism are made to meet and mingle so well here, drugstores articulate the many malls and mini-malls around their clinical glow, absorbing into their commercial authority other opportunities for sociality, activity and collective meaning. Invisible or non-existent are computer, hardware, music, book and kitchen shops—places of doing, learning and growing. This is why the Cultural Center's members, volunteers and participants, wise in establishing themselves as an autonomous, enterprising and inclusive community, can walk outside their special elderscape and squint skeptically in the Florida sun at the age-resistant culture around them.

Snowbird Culture

"The Life of the Retired in a Trailer Park" is a short paper written by G. C. Hoyt in the *American Journal of Sociology* in 1954, but it is generally credited as one of the first sociological treatments of migrational or seasonal retirement culture. Hoyt, in his study of the historical Bradenton Trailer Park in Florida, founded in 1936, asks why the residents, whose median age is 69, "leave relatives, friends and other associations in the home community?" (p. 361). He reasons that the climate is obviously an important factor, but more so is the idea that a new kind of community is possible and desirable, one built on a sociality dedicated to retirement living and a "different code of conduct" (p. 369). Since Hoyt's study and despite the growth of migrational or snowbird retirees living in Florida during the winter months, there has been relatively little research on these retirees or the communities and spatial relations that have developed around them. In other words, we are still asking Hoyt's questions.

Charles Longino Jr., professor at Wake Forest University in North Carolina, is one of the few gerontologists who has made a career of concentrating on migrational retirement (Longino Jr. 1984, 1989, 1995, 1998 and 2001; Longino Jr., Perzynski and Stoller 2002). During the late 1980s and early 1990s Longino Jr. teamed up with Richard D. Tucker, Larry Mullins and Victor W. Marshall to write an important series of research papers on the first large-scale survey of Canadian snowbirds, whose members today form the largest group of Canadians to be in one place outside the country since the Canadian armed forces were in Europe during World War II (Tucker et al. 1988; Longino Jr. et al. 1991; Tucker et al. 1992; see also Mullins and Tucker 1988; Marshall and Tucker 1990). The team discovered three central socio-spatial components of Canadian snowbird culture. First, the relation between migration and permanence is a matter of degree or gradient rather than a binary distinction between a "here" and a "there," with seasonal migrants forming the "middleground of the continuum" between permanent migrants and vacationers (Longino Jr. and Marshall 1990). Thus, snowbirds are a kind of migrational flow in the sense of the term used by Urry above; their movements give new meaning to traditional definitions of residence, territory, distance and portability of resources. Sometimes this flow works in a reverse or "counterstream" direction whereby snowbirds move back home because of financial decline, health problems or changing family relationships, which leads Stoller and Longino Jr. to question whether in such cases people are "going home" or "leaving home" (2001).[6] Second, since most Canadian snowbirds are middle class and financially independent, they bring to their Florida communities and host economies an intercultural prosperity through their taxes, real estate and consumer purchasing. Despite concerns from American hosts that wealthier snowbirds in central, less urban areas would draw away medical resources from local needs, it has been shown that this is not the case and that snowbird medical demands on Florida geriatric services are minimal (Longino Jr. et al. 1991; Marshall and Tucker 1990). Similar findings have been reported for snowbird groups in Arizona (McHugh and Mings 1994). Third, snowbirds form their own mobile networks that attract other snowbirds. Mullins and Tucker found that Canadian snowbirds "were nomadic in the sense that their social ties were primarily with the same migrants in the communities they shared at both ends of the move. Their ties were not to places but to the migrating community itself" (Longino Jr. and Marshall 1990:234). Such networks are also symbolically fortified through the availability of Canadian TV and newspapers such as *Canada News*, *The Sun Times of Canada*, *Le Soleil de la Floride* and *RVTimes*.

This networking component of Canadian snowbird culture has been augmented by the Canadian Snowbird Association, whose clubs, activities and snowbird "extravaganza" trade show and exhibitions in Florida, California, Arizona, Texas and Toronto contribute to the social expression of a migrational citizenry.[7] Specifically, the Canadian Snowbird Association (CSA) is an advocacy organization that lobbies the government on behalf of senior travellers, provides accessible travel and health insurance packages (Medipac), and acts as a travel information service. The CSA began in March 1992 to challenge budget-slashing governmental attacks on out-of-province health care insurance and limits on travellers' prescription pharmaceutical allowances. The CSA has also inspired other businesses and agencies to focus on snowbirds and their cross-national circumstances; for example, American-Canadian banks now offer special "snowbird services" and favourable currency exchange deals. The 100,000 members to whom the CSA caters, with its images of active, healthy, independent, mobile and financially secure lifestyles, are mostly a privileged group. However, the CSA also represents the spatial dimensions of an expansive and accomplished snowbird world, a continent of *Snowbirdia*, ranging across great distances in Canada and the United States and mobilized through extensive transportation, internet, and social networks.

Outside of Canada the CSA sponsors the organization of regional snowbird clubs and retiree groups that hold special events, dinners, and golf tournaments and act to provide snowbird groups with support and community. In the Port Charlotte area when I did my fieldwork in 1998, Hazan Walters was President of the Canadian Club of Charlotte County and a very active member of the CSA. The club has been meeting since the mid-1960s and has grown in tandem with the migrational population. Like other clubs, the Port Charlotte group is more of a social network than a structured organization requiring a center or an office. When I spoke with Hazan at his condo complex near Port Charlotte on December 18, 1998, he explained that while the area has always been marketed as a kind of "dream land" for retirees, older Canadians are challenged by the fluctuating and often declining Canadian dollar, the escalating out-of-province health insurance, and American inflationary costs in health and other services. "The average Canadian is squeezed from both ends," although Charlotte Club members are mostly homeowners (85–90 percent) and therefore increases in rentals do not greatly affect them. Culturally, Hazan noted that snowbirds are quite comfortable with their bi-national identities and that travelling in both directions feels like "going home." For those who own and live in recreational vehicles, there is even the added sense of being "without an address" and living in the culturally in-between (which can also cause border-crossing problems).[8] When I asked Hazan if his work with the club and many other activities as a snowbird citizen has made him as busy as when he was working full time back in his native Newfoundland, he replied "more so." Organizing the interplay between snowbird elderscapes and migrational flows obviously takes ingenuity and work; characteristics not lost on the residents of the last place I visited, Maple Leaf Estates.

Maple Leaf Estates

Diary, December 28, 1998: When I first drove around Maple Leaf Estates, my attention was drawn to the energetic seniors on bikes or golf-carts, wearing crisp polo shirts and sensible sun hats, zooming around residential streets or trotting across the surrealistic greens of the golf course. It really had the feel of an early and eerie 1960s science fiction movie set, an elder-island inhabited by invading senior aliens. It is so interesting to observe the centrality of golf here, not only as an activity but also as a crystallizing force that bonds the social with the environmental into an accessible, international symbol of retirement life. Of course as I stopped to talk with people, I soon heard about their very real lives. These are people who raise money, help each other, mourn losses, develop networks of friendship and trust; they have fought in wars, worked hard throughout their lives and survived the upheavals and challenges of the twentieth century. Now, in the twenty-first century, they want to live well, or as best they can.

Maple Leaf Estates, also called The Maple Leaf Golf and Country Club, is a Port Charlotte resident-owned snowbird community. Sitting on 285 acres of land, the park consists of over 1,000 homes, three clubhouses, four swimming pools, five tennis courts, a library, fitness center, greenhouse, golf course and a lake stocked with fish. There are dozens of amenities, services and activities, including an internal newsletter and a CATV station that broadcasts the park's

Port Charlotte "snowbird community," Maple Leaf Estates. Photo by Stephen Katz.

many events throughout the day. Since at least 60 percent of the residents are
Canadian, the eight miles of streets boast Canadian names such as Maple Lane,
McKenzie Lane, Iroquois Trail, Huron Crescent and Nanaimo Circle. Canadian
newspapers are available, and near the entrance security gates the American
and Canadian flags fly side by side, emblematizing how the two nations are
also cultural allies in the retirement state of Florida, far from the 49th parallel.
Indeed Maple Leaf Estates is a place dedicated to Canadian snowbirds, whose
numbers swell the park's population to nearly 2,000 residents during the winter
months when the mainly Canadian Board of Directors organizes the main business and managerial meetings. And when the snowbirds pack up to return to
Canada during the summer, the park shrinks to 500 or less with about 250 permanent residents. The park was established in the late 1970s, and the residents
purchased it in 1990. They have developed their own governance and social
management according to the rights and privileges associated with several
intersecting layers of rental, leasing, purchasing, membership and ownership
arrangements. There are also strict regulations around driving, parking and cycling; use of pools and golf facilities; and treatment of property and design of
residences. The most important rule, however, is that the park exists for and is
dedicated to people 55 years and older. Children and younger people are
allowed to visit, but not to stay. For example, a note in the December 1998
issue of *Accents*, a Maple Leaf Estates Homeowners' newsletter, tries to establish generational guidelines for Christmas visitors:

We believe that as homeowners and residents of MLE we have an opportunity to deal
both creatively and proactively with the projected influx of children into our Park during
the coming Christmas Season. We are referring primarily to teenagers who are betwixt
and between adults and the young children. Younger children are constantly under the
supervision of parents or family members, and their use of Park facilities is largely limited to the kiddie's swimming pool. Our challenge is to develop some creative recreational opportunities for teenagers during their stay in MLE. (*Accents* 1998:10)

On the one hand, Maple Leaf Estates appears to conform to some of the
characteristics of Sun City retirement communities described by the postmodern
critics above: privileged, leisure-oriented, lifestyle enclaves built by property
developers who profit by fostering fantastical and protective age-segregated
communities. Dominated by promotional images that embellish healthy aging
(and anti-aging) with exhaustive regimes of activity, classes and clubs, such elderscapes create a bond between new aging identities and the consumer environments and products of postmodern capitalism. In this sense Maple Leaf Estates
may have an affinity with other Sun Cities as "a landscape to be consumed"
(Laws 1997:96), where even the children who visit must submit to sunny retirement activities as elders-in-training. On the other hand and despite its emphasis
on security and selectivity, Maple Leaf Estates is also an example of a micro-
society of migrational processes where the imagery of leisured landscapes and
lifestyles is crosscut by the movements of people across different cultures and various places. The resulting complex of interpersonal, interactional, and intercultural

Maple Leaf Estates social community. Photo by Stephen Katz.

relations is dense and delicately networked to the wider snowbird topography of Charlotte County. The earthbound features of what appears to be just another modular park of seasonal mobile bungalows built on the health/profit/lifestyle cornerstones of the Floridian economy are transcended by the communal energies and creative strategies of its inhabitants. One resident told me that when a new piano was needed for the choir, it took only a "day or less" to raise the money for it. Another resident explained how lifts were built for people in wheelchairs to get in and out of the swimming pool with money raised, again, virtually "on the spot." Flea markets, bake sales, casino days, and auctions are just the edge of a mutual aid society where volunteer labor is everywhere and part of everything. Akin to the Port Charlotte Cultural Center and other spaces of age in the area, Maple Leaf Estates is an interesting world where artless bingo coincides with the arts of sociality to create meaningful cultural resources, similar to the "definitional ceremonies" described by Barbara Myerhoff in her seminal gerontological ethnographies of aging communities in California (1978; 1986): "Definitional ceremonies deal with problems of invisibility and marginality; they are strategies that provide opportunities for being seen and in one's own terms, garnering witnesses to one's worth, vitality and being" (Myerhoff, cited in Kaminsky 1993:261).

On December 28–29, 1998, I interviewed several of the Canadian residents at Maple Leaf Estates, including Joan and Bill Charles (fictional names), both in their mid-70s, who have been staying at their park home an average of five to six months since they first bought it in 1982. Indeed, they purchased their property before they retired in 1985. Joan and Bill enjoy their time at MLE because of the social network, the volunteer opportunities for people to help each other and the freedom to feel one's age apart from the expectations of the younger society that exists back in Canada. They are also pleased to let younger members of their family "take charge" and allow the couple the time and space to withdraw on their own. To Joan and Bill their life in Canada is more constrained than it is in Florida. Besides the colder weather, work and family configure their social relations in Canada, while in Florida the mobile sense of a retirement community allows them the freedom to do things they could not do otherwise. They admit that the long-distance travel, international communications and moving between places require careful planning, organizing and fortitude. Upset with the image that snowbirds are a drain on both Canadian and American health care services, the couple is especially keen to see to their health care needs and insurance arrangements in Canada "so that they [insurance providers] will hear from us less." The decline of the Canadian dollar at that time had also required greater attention to financial resources, although since then a rising Canadian dollar has eased snowbird financial pressures somewhat. One of the most poignant realizations for Joan and Bill Charles is that "80 percent of the people that were here when we first came are no longer here," and so "it is always sad when we come back." Given the age and cohort identities of the park's population it is not surprising that the number of people who are dying is growing and the question of their replacements troubling. This issue was also raised by others whom I met, such as Ted Smith, the President at the time of the Maple Leaf Estate Homeowners Corporation. Ted, a Canadian from Ontario, patiently explained to me the economics of the park's management and the complexities of the transcultural real estate market, taxes, and rules of ownership. The park is "in transition" because, as original owners may not be physically able to continue their snowbird lifestyles, approaches to the next "coming-of-age group" are still being worked out. There is no doubt that the Port Charlotte area is experiencing tremendous retirement development, but how this will affect Maple Leaf Estates is not completely clear. Will the park become more Americanized, as was the case with neighbouring Victorian Estates, while it waits for younger cohorts to mature into retirement? Will younger cohorts make new demands on the park, look for alternative activities, and seek different residency arrangements? Will rules disallowing children to live in the park have to change? Will selectivity criteria have to become more flexible and accommodating to a future retirement culture loosened from industrial and patriarchal models of the life course?

As I left Maple Leaf Estates with these questions in mind and trying to reconcile its replication of a restrictive suburban utopia with its lively elder village atmosphere, I too wondered what will happen here. Will the next retiring generation care about such a place or care about getting old at all? Maybe retirement communities will become completely different cultural sites and re-network the spaces of age in Port Charlotte and other areas into remarkable new patterns. Future speculations aside, my visit to Maple Leaf Estates and other elderscapes gave me pause to reflect upon how a gerontology of mobility might begin with the proposition that the paradoxes of aging in time might be best understood within the contexts in which they are lived out and journeys through which they flow.

CONCLUSIONS: THE UNCHARTED TERRITORY IN A NATION OF AGE

According to Andrew Blaikie, "much of the sociology of later life remains uncharted territory.... sociology may have clarified how 'being elderly' is a learned social role, but is not particularly good at explaining what it is like to become and be old" (1999:169). Blaikie's criticism that sociologists pay scant attention to the lived experience of older individuals in favour of traditional ideas about social "role" is also relevant to the pervasive sociological portrayals of retirement and life course identities as static and bounded phenomena. Accordingly, the goal of this chapter's reviews of spatial gerontological inquiries, Sun City cultural critiques, and theories of global societies has been to illuminate that part of the "uncharted territory" of the sociology of later life related to socio-spatial dynamics. At the same time the study's excursions into the Charlotte County migrational worlds of snowbirds and other retirees have been directed to the question of lived experience as new experimental and mobile cultures challenge the definitions of what it means to grow older today. Arguably the sites selected here are shaped in part by the privileged and mobile demographic status of their occupants and participants. Nevertheless, such sites have become inventive social spaces where experiential and biographical resources culled from diverse backgrounds are summoned to counter the dominant culture's marginalization of older persons and denigration of late life transitions. Our consumer culture is one that openly subdues human values associated with continuity, memory and tradition and their means of expression despite its rhetorical promotion of "positive aging." This makes identity maintenance in time and place an arduous task of negotiation between postmodern scripts of individualistic choice and structural demands for independent lifestyles, even in the face of suffering, illness and loss. Thus, the collective strategy to redevelop roots in multiple contexts across intercultural spaces is a critical response and an indication of where the future of aging, and social gerontology, might be heading. I certainly sensed this possibility as I left Florida on January 7, 1999, from the Tampa airport where younger people were heading north and older people were arriving in the south. On the ground the terminal seemed to be a teeming traffic node where ages converged and aspirations were exchanged. And from the air, within my own mobility, I looked down at Florida and wondered how it would grow, provide leadership and resolve its contractions as it takes shape as a nation of age.

NOTES

This chapter is reprinted from *Cultural Aging: Life Course, Life Style and Senior Worlds* by Stephen Katz. Copyright © 2005 by Stephen Katz. Reprinted by permission of Broadview Press.

I would like to thank Trent University's Committee on Research for its financial support of this project and the staff at the Canadian Snowbird Association in Toronto for their help and materials. I owe much appreciation to Patricia Stamp for her photographic assistance. I am deeply grateful to the people in Florida with whom I spoke, snowbirds and others, who offered me their time and patience. I also wish to express my sympathies to all those contacts and friends who lost their homes, properties and communities due to the destruction wrought by Hurricane Charley in August 2004.

1. Although physical design problems of institutional settings invite their own critical scrutiny (see Rule, Milke, and Dobbs 1994).

2. The use of concepts and metaphors of space in sociology, due largely to the influence of Michel Foucault and Pierre Bourdieu, is generally considered a distinguishing mark of contemporary sociological theory (see Silber 1995).

3. While Charlotte County is certainly one of the "oldest" areas in the United States, the entire population of the recently created City of Laguna Woods, Orange County, California, is over 55 and the median age is 78! Dominated by the private retirement community called Leisure World, the city's residents successfully challenged the building of a nearby airport (see Ross and Liebig 2002). The city is a unique opportunity to observe what can happen when a retirement community becomes an independent polity.

4. Francophone Canadians also live in this part of Florida but have their main snowbird and holiday hubs on Florida's east coast, such as Hollywood Beach located between Fort Lauderdale and Miami. Much of this area's commerce, banks, real estate and health care facilities are geared to an estimated 100,000 Canadians that visit each year. Here restaurants offer Québec fare, stores sell Québec newspapers, Québec satellite TV is available and a seasonally transplanted Québec community lacks few of the amenities of home (Stephanie Nolen, *The Globe and Mail*, 15 March 1999).

5. Also see the Center's website for extensive information on programs, volunteers, and facilities, www.theculturalcenter.com.

6. In the United States, retirees who escape southern heat by heading north are called "sunbirds." In a study by Hogan and Steinnes (1996) of Arizona sunbirds, patterns emerged whereby snowbirds became eventual sunbirds, thus migrating in both directions.

7. These three socio-spatial elements also apply to other cases, such as Swedish snowbirds who retire in Spain (Gustafson 2001) and whose trans- and multi-local experiences of mobility and expatriate culture not only invite "further investigation of retirement migration and other forms of later life mobility" but also new knowledge "about globalisation and transnationalism" (p. 392).

8. Dorothy and David Counts capture the fascinating culture of senior recreational vehicle (RV) groups and lifestyles in their book, *Over the Next Hill: An Ethnography of RVing Seniors in North America* (2001).

CHAPTER 34

Web Book: Social Support Systems of Rural Older Women: A Comparison of the United States and Denmark

Dena Shenk and Kitter Christiansen

Available at www.stpt.usf.edu/~jsokolov/webbook/shenk.htm.

In this chapter, Dena Shenk and Kitter Christiansen contribute to our comparative understanding of aging and gender, highlighting contrasts between rural Minnesota and a similar area in Denmark. This work clearly shows the work of culture in constructing ideas of autonomy in late life and provides an important connection to Stuart and Hansen's chapter in Part III.

RELATED RESOURCES

Gerdner, L. A., T. Tripp-Reimer and H. C. Simpson. 2007. "Hard Lives, God's Help, and Struggling Through: Caregiving in Arkansas Delta." *Journal of Cross-Cultural Gerontology* 22(4):355–74.

International Rural Aging Project 1997–2001. www.hsc.wvu.edu/coa/icra/ICRA _Shepherdstown_report.pdf.

Kreager, P. and E. Schröder-Butterfill. 2007. "Gaps in the Family Networks of Older People in Three Rural Indonesian Communities." *Journal of Cross-Cultural Gerontology* 22(1):1–25.

Krout, J. and M. Kinner. 2007. "Sustaining Geriatric Rural Populations." In *Conversations in the Disciplines: Sustaining Rural Populations*. L. Morgan and P. Fahs, eds. Binghamton, NY: Global Academic Publishers.

Shenk, D. 1998. *Someone to Lend a Helping Hand: Women Growing Old in Rural America*. New York: Routledge.

CHAPTER 35

Web Book Photo Essay: Where Are the Bones in Their Noses? Community Aged in North American RV Camps and in Papua New Guinea

Dorothy Counts and David Counts

Available at www.stpt.usf.edu/~jsokolov/webbook/counts.htm.

This comparative photo essay by the husband-and-wife anthropologist team, Dorothy and David Counts, considers how elders fit into varied social configurations. As depicted in their book *Over the Next Hill* (2001), they undertook a "preretirement" research project literally on the road, in communities forged within mobile home encampments throughout North and Central America. Their chapter considers this research on the gerontology of mobility and contrasts it with their earlier, decades long, fieldwork in Papua New Guinea.

RELATED RESOURCES

Counts, D. A. and D. R. Counts. 2001. *Over the Next Hill: An Ethnography of RVing Seniors in North America*, 2nd ed. Toronto, Canada: Broadview.

Counts, D. A. and D. R. Counts. 2004. "The Good, the Bad, and the Unresolved Death in Kaliai." *Social Science & Medicine* 58(5):887–97.

CHAPTER 36

Web Book: An Organization for the Elderly, by the Elderly: A Senior Center in the United States

Yohko Tsuji

Available at: www.stpt.usf.edu/~jsokolov/webbook/tsuji.htm.

Like Great Britain, America since its inception has been known for the tendency of its citizens to join a wide variety of voluntary associations. In the United States, senior centers first developed in the 1940s, but were an outgrowth of senior clubs dating to the late nineteenth century. By 2006, an estimated 14,000–16,000 senior centers were in operation, providing a wide range of health, social, recreational and educational services for older citizens. The Older Americans Act of 1965 targeted senior centers to serve as community focal points for comprehensive service coordination and delivery at the local level. However, qualitative studies done in such environments find that it is the stimulation of informal, personal networks that is of special interest to the participants. Such is the case in this chapter on the Lake District Senior Center by Japanese anthropologist Yohko Tsuji. This work provides a nice contrast to the ethnic-based senior centers discussed in the chapters by Hegland and Martinez in Part IV.

RELATED RESOURCES

Aday, R., G. Kehoe and L. Farney. 2006. "Impact of Senior Center Friendships on Aging Women Who Live Alone." *Journal of Women & Aging* 18:157–73.

Beisgen, B. and M. Kraitchman. 2003. *Senior Centers: Opportunities for Successful Aging.* New York: Springer.

Tsuji, Y. 2005. "Time Is Not Up: Temporal Complexity of Older Americans' Lives." *Journal of Cross-Cultural Gerontology* 20(1):3–26.

CHAPTER 37

Web Book: One Thousand Points of Blight: Old, Female and Homeless in New York City

Jay Sokolovsky

Available at: www.stpt.usf.edu/~jsokolov/webbook/sokolovsky.htm.

This chapter comes from a multiyear research project with older homeless women funded by the National Institute of Mental Health. This study gathered intensive interviews with 237 females over age fifty who were homeless or near homeless. This was combined with ethnographic examination of the lifestyles of a smaller number of these individuals. Here, Jay Sokolovsky presents an edited portion of an interview conducted during early fieldwork on the "Older Homeless Women" project.

RELATED RESOURCES

Cohen, C., and J. Sokolovsky. 2001. "Homelessness and Aging." Special double issue of the *International Journal of Law and Psychiatry* on "Aging, Ethics, Law and the New Medicine." Dordrecht: Kluwer Academic Press.

Kisor, A. and L. Kendal-Wilson. 2002. "Older Homeless Women: Reframing the Stereotype of the Bag Lady." *Affilia* 17(3):354–70.

McDonald, L., J. Serafini and L. Cleghorn. 2007. "Living on the Margins: Older Homeless Adults in Toronto." *Journal of Gerontological Social Work* 49(1/2):19–46.

National Coalition for the Homeless. 2007. "Homelessness among Elderly Persons, 2007." Available at: www.nationalhomeless.org/publications/facts/Elderly.pdf.

PART VI

The Quest for Gerontopia: Culture and Health in Late Life

Jay Sokolovsky

The art of living consists of dying young, but as late as possible.

Anonymous

In those green-pastured mountains of Fotta-fa-Zee
everybody feels fine at a hundred and three
cause the air that they breathe is potassium-free
and they chew nuts from the Tutt-tutt Tree.

This gives strength to their teeth,
it gives length to their hair,
and they live without doctors, with nary a care.

Dr. Seuss—You're Only Old Once (1986)

In this book's first section, we looked globally at the general issue of population aging and its implications for human communities. Policy planners who are concerned with such things often focus on promoting the physical, mental and even social health of our eldest adults to minimize impairments, positively affect their quality of life and support those who care about them (Butler 2008). All of the chapters in this section revolve around this issue. Dr. Seuss in his lyrical verse about the land of Fotta-Fa-See mocks the ancient and diverse myths of finding a fountain of youth in some distant land, but also the more recent false claims of extraordinary long life in places like Abkhasia and the incessant commercials about youth-restoring pharmaceuticals (Vincent 2006). Ironically, while the number of geriatricians in the United States lags woefully behind other postindustrial nations, the last decade has witnessed the birth of the American Academy of Anti-Aging Physicians and has produced, as of 2008, eighty-seven board-certified specialists and a number of small chains of longevity clinics such as the Center for Healthy Living and Longevity.

THE QUEST FOR GERIATRIC UTOPIAS

It is hard to talk about aging in non-Western, "exotic" settings without inappropriately getting people's hopes up. For example, in the 1970s, print and TV media, as well as Dannon yogurt commercials, widely touted various studies of supposed "geriatric utopias"—places where the aged existed, but the hard facts of aging did not. During the 1960s and 1970s, exciting reports filtered into the gerontological literature and popular press about a small number of mountain peoples, especially in Abkhasia, who possessed *extraordinary* longevity. In this case, ages were claimed ranging from 120 to almost 168, with health profiles said to be like that of spry sixty and seventy year olds. Similar assertions were made for a peasant village in Vilacabamba, Ecuador, the Hunzakut of the Karakoram mountains in Pakistan and the inhabitants of Paros Island, Greece. It is very disquieting then, to learn that *none* of these claims for a modern fountain of youth and hyperlongevity appear to be true (Leaf 1982; Palmore 1984; Beall 1987).

Despite false claims for breaching the normal limits of the human life span, we seem to be dealing at least in Abkhasia with an exceptionally healthy group of ninety and one-hundred-year olds. Interestingly, the details of their lifestyles, when compared with those of healthy centenarians in the United States and other countries, point to a number of common factors in promoting long life. Such persons tend to have low-fat, low-calorie diets, refrain from much caffeine, tobacco and alcohol and have been physically active throughout their lives (Hadjihristev 1988; Perls and Terry 2007). In fact, a 1996 report by the MacArthur Foundation Consortium on Successful Aging noted that only about 30 percent of the features of aging are genetically based and that, by age eighty, there is little genetic influence on determining what happens after that point of time. This project identified several nongenetic factors influencing successful aging: regular physical activity and social connectedness; the ability to bounce back after suffering a loss; and having a feeling of control over one's life. On the other hand, most everyone seems to have an ancient recluse relative—what I call the "Uncle Irving Phenomenon"—who heavily smoked and imbibed and said, "oy," when the word *exercise* was mentioned. Such persons are rare exceptions to what global data teaches us about general longevity and aging. However, as is detailed in this section's first chapter, a genetic link to longevity is most associated with those who achieve exceptional long life.

THE CENTENARIANS ARE COMING!

Humans are certainly not longevity record breakers among earth's life forms. Certain giant trees live for 4,000 years, some Icelandic clam species last 400 years and when Harriet, a Galapagos tortoise, died in 2006, she was thought to be 176 years old.[1] Yet, in that same year, the U.S. Census Bureau counted 73,000 centenarians (14,000 men and 59,000 women) and by 2040 over half a million in their tenth decade of life are expected to be living.[2]

Among the most important research related to understanding why people reach one hundred years of age or more is the Okinawan Centenarian Study (www.okicent.org), which for the past twenty-five years has been following the longest-lived population on our planet. The chapter by Willcox and associates details the data on "extraordinary longevity" (living 110 years or more) and the connection to the growing number of international longevity projects that are now underway. Importantly, they show that older Okinawans have among the lowest mortality rates in the world from a multitude of chronic diseases. As a result, they and the Japanese in general enjoy the world's longest health expectancy. The growing knowledge about healthy longevity is of particular interest for women who are considerably more likely than men to survive into extreme old age (Backes, Lasch and Reimann 2006; World Health Organization 2007).[3]

Globally, the United States ranks twenty-fourth on healthy longevity and forty-second in overall longevity. Much of this difference can be accounted for in realizing that over the past thirty years Japan has substantially surpassed the level of economic equality found in the United States, while it also dramatically expanded access to health care. At the same time, the United States has downsized its portion of middle-class families and by 2008, not only were 48 million without health insurance, but the share of annual family income devoted to heath care came to exceed what was spent on either food or housing.

THE SEARCH FOR ELDERTOPIA

In 1999, Ruth Brent proposed a remaking of long-term care environments into "Gerontopias" that foster maintenance of autonomy, choice and control of the nature of one's last days (see also Charness 2005). In this section, visionary physician William Thomas builds upon the writings of Brent and lays out his related idea of "Eldertopia," offering a fundamentally different way of looking at elderhood. The practical application of these ideas were first seen in Thomas's development of the "Eden Alternative," which transformed traditional nursing facilities into socially engineered small "home"-like environments (Thomas and Johansson 2003; www.edenalt.org). More recently, Thomas has developed a "Green Houses" model that is designed to create a sense of a nurturing and interdependent community, what he calls "convivium." This short chapter is a touchstone to the discussion of a long-term care "culture change" movement analyzed later on in this section by Athena Mclean.

WHO WILL CARE FOR GRANDMA? THE MILLENNIUM'S GROWING DILEMMA

In the global arena, higher average life spans, a narrowing of localized kin networks and the increased work of women outside of households has created great challenges for those families seeking to care for elders (Martin-Matthews and Phillips 2008). As we saw in Lamb's chapter on India, this sometimes involves caring across distant international borders (see also Baldassar, Baldock and Wilding 2007). In the past decade, a series of national studies in the

United States has documented what many already know from personal experience (MetLife 1999; National Alliance for Caregiving and AARP 2004; Evercare 2007). Much of eldercare falls on the heads of mid-life and older women who on average may have spent seventeen years caring for a child and now may spend eighteen years or more helping to care for a parent. The typical caregiver is a forty-six-year-old female who has at least some college experience, provides more than twenty hours of care each week to a widowed woman aged fifty or older, usually her mother. The most recent study on the material cost of elder care found that the out-of-pocket expense of caring for an aging parent or spouse averages about $5,500 a year, more than the average American household spends annually on health care and entertainment combined (Evercare 2007).[4]

Social Viagra and the Family-Based Dynamics of Care

In 2008, the United States regained a level of fertility last seen in the 1960s—2.1 babies per woman. Virtually all other postindustrial societies and many industrializing countries, are dramatically going in the opposite direction, some already seeing populations fall, with fertility levels as low at 1.2 births per female. Of course, available kin and even strong cultural dictates are not the only factors in understanding family-based elder care. We have already seen the dilemma of social context overwhelming cultural expectations and desires among Islamic Iranian immigrants in California (Hegland Part IV; see also AARP 2001). Just north of where this research took place, a complex study of Chinese immigrant families, with both spouses working, found adult children subcontracting filial piety by engaging female caregivers from similar ethnic backgrounds to care for their frail older kin (Lan 2002). This in fact paralleled many dual-earner households working in Taiwan, Hong Kong and Singapore who hire low-wage migrant women from Southeast and South Asia to not only fulfill duties to serve parents, but also to expand autonomy from aged mothers-in-laws.

Journalist Thomas Friedman, in an article comparing the demographic futures of Europe and India in the early twenty-first century, muses that next to relatively youthful India, "Western Europe looks like an assisted-living facility with Turkish nurses" (2005). In fact, within Europe, one of the most interesting challenges for kin-based care of elders is emerging in the southern region, within traditionally family-focused cultures. In Italy, the research location for Joan Weibel-Orlando's chapter, we encounter the globe's second highest level of agedness and one of the lowest fertility rates on earth. Various attempts at what Krause calls "Social Viagra"—economic and other government incentives to produce more babies—have basically been ignored by young families (2007). This is highly problematic for countries like Italy, which are very reluctant to erect any serious support infrastructure for elder residences and care, fearing its negative impact on their strong ideology of kin support. Using metaphors of cultural action and meaning derived from the hit TV show

Sopranos, Weibel-Orlando takes readers into the heart of her ancestral homeland in rural Tuscany, to unravel the contemporary reality of community-based
and family-centered elder care. What she finds corresponds to a recent comparative study of such matters in Southern Europe: "Although it is true that most
of the care required is provided on an informal basis, it is equally evident that
informal care networks are never self-sufficient" (Simoni and Trifiletti
2004:699–700). The chapter finds a wide variety of strategies for sustaining at
least the appearance of manifesting filial devotion even at a distance. Particularly noteworthy is embedding into the process young, female migrant live-in
care workers (*badantes*), often from the poorest nations of Eastern Europe.
This extra-familial care scenario is becoming a global pattern as international
inequities interact with the new face of aging (Browne and Braun 2008).

"BIOUPGRADABILITY," DISABILITY AND THE SHIFTING
NATURE OF HEALTH IN LATE LIFE

As I recently underwent cataract operations on both eyes and am contemplating an arthroscopic shoulder tune-up to help me return to winning tennis
tournaments, I am joining the wave of baby boomers challenging the "body
inevitable" with the mindset of endless possibilities and yet another type of
makeover. In two fifteen-minute operations, this "bioupgrading" of my eyes
not only eliminated my cataracts, but also gave me clear unaided vision for the
first time in my life. It is interesting to note that even at the stage when the cataracts were just causing mild visual impairments, I was universally encouraged
by friends and family to actively undertake this frontal assault on a sure sign
of aging.

Disability, Aging and Culture

The cross-cultural study of health and disability has been the focus of the
World Health Organization since the early 1980s (Robinson et al. 2007). They
have developed a useful framework for distinguishing between impairment,
disability and handicap. Here, *impairment* means diminishment/loss of physical
function, *disability* refers to a diminishment/loss of activity and *handicap* constitutes a diminishment/loss of role performance (World Health Organization
1991).[5] As Albert and Cattell note, "while impairment involves clear physical
properties, its expression as disability and handicap depends on cultural
factors" (1994:208).[6] An excellent example is found in Albert's own work
among the Lak people of Melanesia. He found that perceptions of certain
impairments, such as cataracts, did not translate into the Western view of disability or handicap (1987). Despite a high incidence of cataracts among the
Lak elderly, this condition did not become a disabling feature of late life. Their
impaired vision seldom interfered with participation in gardening, household
assistance or ritual activities. Contrastingly, North American elders like myself
with similar levels of impairment typically experience cataracts as a disabling

condition, which limits valued activities because of the cultural emphasis on reading, driving or other tasks requiring acute vision.

GOOD NEWS ABOUT DISABILITY, BUT IN CULTURAL CONTEXT

It is clear that chronic illness and impairment tend to increase in the last decades of human life (American College of Physicians 1988). However, early on in this book, I introduced the idea that most readers will not experience a similar old age as that of their grandparents. One indication of this lies in the general trends of late-life disability rates for the United States and other postindustrial nations. Data from the U.S. National Long-Term Care Survey, stretching back to the mid 1980s, show a long-term, steady decline in the prevalence of disability, as measured by several key activities of daily living (Manton, Lamb and Gu 2007; Population Reference Bureau 2007). As noted in figure VI.1, during the twenty-year period from 1984 to 2004, drops in severe and moderate disabilities for those over age sixty-five have raised the level of persons living with no disability to over 80 percent of that population. Similar trends have been tracked for Western Europe and Japan (Äijänseppä et al. 2005); however, elsewhere in Asia, such as in China, increases in longevity have been accompanied by an upswing in levels of disability for older populations (Zimmer 2006; Zimmer and Martin 2007).[7]

While the positive trends in late-life disability have generally been observed in the United States across minority and class boundaries, health disparities linked to social and economic inequities in some cases have also increased

Figure VI.1
Declining Disability in the Elderly Population

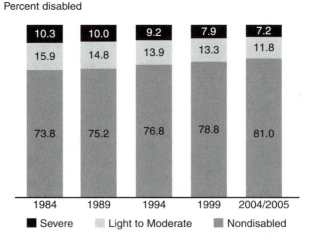

Percent disabled

1984	1989	1994	1999	2004/2005
10.3	10.0	9.2	7.9	7.2
15.9	14.8	13.9	13.3	11.8
73.8	75.2	76.8	78.8	81.0

■ Severe   Light to Moderate   ■ Nondisabled

Source: K. Manton, X. Gu and V. Lamb, 2006, "Change in Chronic Disability From 1982 to 2004/ 2005 as Measured by Long-Term Changes in Function and Health in the Elderly Population," *PNAS* 103(48):18734-9.

(Kaneda and Adams 2008). This is expressed through a dramatically increasing gap in life expectancy between whites and blacks since the 1960s and in the rise of some disabling diseases such as diabetes among disadvantaged populations.

The cultural parameters of disability in late life have received increasing attention by qualitative researchers such as Gay Becker's classic ethnography of deaf elders (1980), Sharon Kaufman's study of how stroke victims reconstruct their sense of self (1986), Luisa Margolies's (2004) book about her mother's broken hip, or Solimeo's new work on coping with Parkinson's disease (in press).[8] The articles in this section by Linda Carson Henderson and John Traphagan follow in this tradition. The chapter by Linda Carson Henderson combines her training in public health and gerontology to explore the devastating impact of soaring diabetes rates among older Native Americans in Oklahoma. Her work shows the complex interaction between a legacy of colonial oppression, indigenous health beliefs and Western models of health behavior. As seen in Box IV.1, impacting this matrix to increase positive health outcomes is never a simple matter, but must always be undertaken by first understanding the culture system from the inside. Carson Henderson's work shows how important this is for understanding how to provide a better fit between divergent cultural models of disease and the modern health care system (see also Smith et al. in press).

ABOUT THAT SENIOR MOMENT

The year 2007 marked the one-hundredth anniversary of the naming and clinical description, by Aloise Alzheimer, of a dreaded brain disorder that struck a fifty-year-old woman, severely impairing her memory and other cognitive functions. Upon autopsy, her brain was found to be shrunken and filled with strange deposits of plaques between and tangled within nerve cells. Ironically, until the 1970s, Alzheimer's disease (AD), named after the doctor who analyzed this woman's brain, was thought to be a rare, rapidly progressing disorder of mid adulthood and different from "senile" dementia caused by just plain aging.

An hereditary factor in the expression of AD has been found, associated with the Apoe-E gene. Yet, some patients with full expression of this gene and excessive brain protein deposits, called beta amyloid, *never* have dementia symptoms, just as those lacking the gene and having little protein deposits *are* diagnosed with the disease. This kind of biomedical space of uncertainty has stimulated research into both the brain's capacity for adaptation and the varied cultural responses to AD and other dementias.

In the first instance, intense studies over the past two decades indicate that some people develop "cognitive reserve," a capacity of the brain to compensate for cognitive impairment related to dementia (Scarmeas, Albert, Manly and Stern 2004). As with healthy longevity, lifestyle habits can dramatically lower the risk of getting dementia. These findings have stimulated the creation of a brain-health market, hawking vitamin supplements like coenzyme Q10, varieties of fit-brain "neurosoftware" games like "MindFit" and a series of structured physical and mental activities, called variously "MemAerobics" and "Neurobics" (see Winningham et al. 2004; www.memaerobics.net). As noted in Box VI.1, the essence of these findings is that there is no single quick fix. However, dementia's risk is diminished by increased intellectual challenges through prolonged education, brain-challenging occupations or hobbies, especially where novel learning experiences are regularly encountered (Perkinson 2008). Long-term studies in Sweden and China intriguingly suggest that complex, group-based social interactions such as community gardening or volunteering also cut the risk of serious cognitive impairment (Aamodt and Wang 2008).

BOX VI.1 NEUROBICS—TWENTY-FIRST-CENTURY GUIDE TO BRAIN HEALTH

In Homer's Odyssey, the heroic traveler Odysseus survived a series of challenges through either mental or physical prowess. Acrobatic strength vanquished the Cyclops, but the key to breaching the walls of Troy was a clever gambit—the Trojan horse—rather than direct military assault. And of course, like any hero, Odysseus met every obstacle that Homer threw at him with determination and confidence rather than fear or despair.

Decades of research in gerontology have found that the qualities that allowed Odysseus to triumph also promote general health and longevity. This counts not just for living longer, but living better: avoiding chronic depression, preserving your memory and other mental skills and functioning independently in your daily life.

Healthy Brain Aging

In recent decades, scientists have radically redefined the concept of "healthy brain aging." The ruling paradigm was once that living to a ripe old age was simply a matter of avoiding chronic disease. As for the brain, it was assumed that it would simply go along with the body for the ride—until gradual, inevitable decay transformed us all into the stereotype of the doddering, forgetful, senile elder.

There was just one problem with this: Many people make it to 100 with their mental powers virtually intact and lead physically active, interesting, satisfying lives. How did they manage to escape the "inevitable decline" that defined old age in the popular imagination?

Bulking Up Your Brain

From various longitudinal studies has come a guiding principle known as "use it or lose it." A recent brain-scanning study appeared to show this principle in action. As reported in the January 22, 2004, *Nature*, twenty-three healthy people, average age twenty-two, learned how to juggle. After three months, MRI scans showed enlargement of the gray matter in their brains—the part responsible for higher mental functions. Either existing cells had grown denser, grown more numerous connections, or the sheer number of brain cells had increased. When the study participants stopped juggling, their brains shrank. This doesn't mean we

continued

should all juggle our way to cognitive vitality. But it does strongly suggest that mental exercise has real and positive effects on brain function.

Dancing Away Dementia?

Some researchers have wondered whether mental activity might reduce the risk of Alzheimer's disease. In a study in the June 19, 2003, *New England Journal of Medicine*, researchers tracked 469 people aged seventy-five to eighty-five for up to twenty-one years. None had dementia at the start. People who participated the most in leisure activities—including reading, playing board games, playing musical instruments and dancing—were at 63 percent lower risk of being diagnosed with dementia.

It may be that the active people built up a mental bank account that helped delay the onset of dementia symptoms. "It might provide some reserve," explains Robert N. Butler, M.D., president and CEO of the International Longevity Center in New York City. "They've got enough there that even though there is decay underneath, they are still able to function pretty well." However, Dr. Butler, who in the 1950s led the first longitudinal studies of healthy older people, is reluctant to promise that a healthy-aging lifestyle can actually prevent Alzheimer's. "What I am reasonably sure of is that the various sorts of apparent cognitive impairment in the later years, as well as depression, are influenced by the level of mental activity."

Fortunately, there are no known health risks to doing crossword puzzles or reading novels. Even if lifelong mental "neurobics" doesn't prevent dementia, it may support general brain function and enhance your overall quality of life.

Social and Physical Fitness

It should be emphasized that physical fitness is also associated with lower risk of cognitive decline. Longitudinal studies also suggest that remaining socially engaged aids healthy aging. "Those individuals who had goals in life, something to get up for, actually did better and lived longer," says Butler. Butler, now in his seventies, ought to know. He has hardly slowed the pace of his career since 1982, when he left his position as the founding director of the National Institute on Aging to found the first department of geriatric medicine in the United States, at Mount Sinai School of Medicine in New York City. Perhaps, like Odysseus, we all need a quest in order to maintain our physical and mental zest.

Adapted from: "Use It or Lose It: The Key to Healthy Brain Aging," From the newsletters of the Memory Disorder Project at Rutgers University. Available at www.memorylossonline. com/use_it_or_lose_it.htm.

Dementia in Cultural Context

A second approach to studying the variable response to forms of dementia in late life is to look at the impact of culture. Over the past decade, a rapidly enlarging international and cross-cultural literature has emerged, which explores both the prevalence of dementia and the cultural response to this condition (Cohen 1995; Hinton, Franz, Yeo and Levkoff 2005; Jett 2006; Hendrie 2006; Yeo and Gallagher-Thompson 2006). Medical specialists now recognize

over seventy different causes of dementia, but in most populations, Alzheimer's disease is the most common type and evokes great fears among old and
young alike in the United States. While in the United States a little more 10
percent of all those over sixty-five suffer from some form of dementia, prevalence rates rise rapidly for persons past the eighth decade of life and up to 47
percent over age eighty-five may be afflicted with this cognitive dysfunction
(Plassman et al. 2007; Alzheimer's Association 2008).

In this section, anthropologist John Traphagan shifts attention away from the
biomedicalization of dementia to its cultural construction in the country of Japan. Here, loss of brain function is considered within the Japanese constructs
of senility and *Boke*. This latter term sets cognitive impairment within a social
and not a biomedical construct. As others have found in studying dementia in
Asian cultures (Ikels 1997; Gerdner, Xiong and Dia 2006), a key dynamic is
the perception of personhood and the factors that alter its functioning. Differing from the Western ideas about mind/body connections, Japanese are viewed
through a mind/body complex critically developed through social and moral
engagement over the life course. He finds that *Boke* is primarily a moral concept and a key to how the Japanese think about cognitive frailty in late life.

THE GLOBAL FLORIDA AND THE DILEMMAS OF LONG-TERM CARE

Imagine a country where poor elderly dressed in their hospital gowns and
with IVs still in their arms are unceremoniously dumped on skid row near a
mission, in hopes they will somehow be treated. Welcome to twenty-first century America! For those who saw this documented in Michael Moore's film
"Sicko," or read Jonathan Cohn's book *Sick: The Untold Story of America's
Health Care Crisis* (2007) this will not come as a great surprise.

Some might attribute such problems to the aging of society and the upswing
of chronic illness and disability in late adulthood. It is also to be noted that
among noninstitutionalized elderly the percentage who need help doing everyday activities doubles with each successive decade up to age eighty-four and
triples between ages eighty-five and ninety-four (German 1995). There is
indeed concern that in the period between 2006 and 2030 our population aged
sixty-five and older will double, as will be the case for persons eighty years
and older (Institute of Medicine 2008). Long-term care is certainly one of the
great challenges large postindustrial nations face. In the United States, about
1.6 million people reside in nursing homes and with an average stay of 2.4
years in such facilities, individuals would spend over $180,000 for this kind of
care (MetLife Mature Market Institute 2006).

Yet, as documented in a 2007 Congressional Research Service report to
Congress, the rate of increases in health care spending for those past age sixty-
five is in fact less than for youth eighteen years and younger (Jenson 2007:5).
Studies across a demographically grayer Europe have come up with similar
findings and show that age structure is not the key factor in controlling health

care costs (Seshamani and Grey 2002; Lesson 2004; Christensen et al., in press). In fact, the 2007 report "Accounting for the Cost of Health Care in the United States" found that despite having lower life expectancy and higher infant mortality than other postindustrial countries, the United States spends approximately $1,600 per capita more on health care (McKinsey Global Institute 2007).

As we learn in Larry Polivka's chapter in this section, the United States has not yet learned as a nation to take advantage of the innovative strategies that were pioneered during the 1970s in elder-dense Florida. In this chapter, he explores the development of community and home-based care options developed in the Sunshine State, but to date only fully implemented in a handful of states, especially Oregon. Ironically, care options pioneered in the United States have been more fully developed and available in other postindustrial nations where they are coupled with national health plans.[9]

NURSING HOMES AND THE PROMISE OF THE CULTURE CHANGE MOVEMENT

Although about 80 percent of the aged in the United States report that they can get around by themselves, it is the rapidly growing numbers of the "oldest old," those past age eighty-five, that are creating the greatest challenge for our system of long-term care. According to the U.S. Bureau of the Census, slightly over 5 percent of the sixty-five and older population occupy nursing homes, congregate care, assisted living and board-and-care homes, with only about 4.2 percent in nursing homes at any given time (U.S. Census Bureau 2007a). However, for those over age eighty-five, about one-fifth of the population resides in such care settings.

Importantly, over the past three decades, the rate of nursing home use has declined in the United States. This has corresponded with a steady and substantial decrease in the overall disability rate of older adults intersecting with more options in residential care and, in some states, better access to home care. Counterposed with the ongoing attempt to privatize long-term care in the United States is a powerful "Culture Change" movement that seeks to physically and socially transform such environments into humane and therapeutic spaces in which to encounter frail late adulthood.

The chapter by Athena McLean considers such transformations in light of her ethnographic research focusing on early attempts to create new kinds of Alzheimer's units within long-term care settings.[10] Her work draws from the long tradition of qualitative research in nursing homes and expands upon her recent book *The Person in Dementia* (2006) to consider the possibilities of dissolving the stifling institutional structure of such places (Henderson and Vesperi 1995; Stafford 2003; Eschenbruch 2006; Tinney 2008.).[11] The boundary between living "in the community" and living in an "institution" is marked by two core perceptions: the medical symbolism "you are chronically sick" and the detention symbolism "you are being supervised" (Robinson 1985).

McLean's chapter shows that breaking the bonds of "institutions" cannot be accomplished by physical changes alone, but must be accompanied by addressing the issue of personhood and how it exists within the cultural space of a long-term care environment. By focusing on this issue, she is able to examine the reality of the liberating dream suggested by the Green House model and William Thomas's conception of Eldertopia.

THE DARKER SIDE OF AGING

As Glascock points out in this book's first section, small-scale community environments are no guarantee that "death hastening" actions will not be directed toward frail elders. The complex dimensions of this issue require the kind of holistic qualitative approach that is found in this book's final chapter.

Having worked as a medical anthropologist on the Polynesian island of Niue, Judith Barker explores the paradox of how a society known for its beneficent treatment of the healthy aged and disabled young could show seemingly heartless disregard of the unfit elderly. Barker shows that understanding the neglect directed at "decrepit" older folks does not yield to simple mechanical explanations. Such disregard is neither part of a uniform way of treating all disabled persons nor an ecological expedient dictated by low surplus production. Rather, it is crucial to view how the label of "decrepit" itself is negotiated and constructed within Niuean conceptions of the life cycle, death and ancestral states. Her work provides an important link to the complex understanding of elder abuse in "traditional societies" (WHO 2002b; Daichman 2005; Malley-Morrison, Nolido and Chawla 2006; Holkup et al. 2007).

NOTES

1. This animal was reportedly brought back to England from Darwin's nineteenth-century voyage on the HMS *Bounty*.

2. In postindustrial countries, the estimated number of people aged 100 and over has doubled each decade since 1950, with the global number of centenarians projected to more than quintuple between 2005 and 2030 (National Institute on Aging 2007).

3. See Mehta (2005) for a good general discussion of aging and women in Asia.

4. Other important resources include: The National Alliance for Care Giving (www. caregiving.org); The Caregiving Project for Older Americans, http://www.ilcusa.org/pages/projects/the-caregiving-project.php; a 2004 report, Caregiving in Rural America, www.easterseals.com/site/DocServer/Caregiving_in_Rural-compressed.pdf?doc-ID=50643; and AARP, "Valuing the Invaluable: A New Look at the Economic Value of Family Caregiving" 2007.

5. For an excellent discussion of health aging and disability, see Albert and Cattell (1994):191–220.

6. They also suggest that the role of culture in the disablement process is likely to increase as people age, as the definition of disability becomes less tied to one's ability to remain fully economically active.

7. However, Lafortune et al. (2007) found a more mixed pattern. Only five countries—Denmark, Finland, Italy, the Netherlands and the United States—show clear

evidence of a decline in disability among elderly people. For Belgium, Japan and Sweden, rates of severe disability among people ages sixty-five and over have increased during the past five to ten years. Australia and Canada have a stable rate of severe disability. Data on trends in France and the United Kingdom are inconclusive. In countries like Mexico, there have been dramatic increases in disability related to rise in the incidence of chronic diseases, especially diabetes (Barquera 2003).

8. For a discussion of using qualitative methods along with other research approaches to study health and aging, see Curry, Sheild and Wetle (2006).

9. For a perspective on Asia, see Chi, Mehta and Howe (2001).

10. See also Crews and Zavotka (2006).

11. For some classic works, see Diamond (1986); Shield (1988); Savishinsky (1991).

CHAPTER 38

Exceptional Longevity and the Quest for Healthy Aging: Insights from the Okinawa Centenarian Study

D. Craig Willcox, Bradley J. Willcox, Matthew Rosenbaum, Jay Sokolovsky and Makoto Suzuki

My first impression of Tsuru when I met her at the venerable age of 104 was that of a regal older woman who appeared to be very much the center of her large extended family. Standing no more than five feet tall and weighing less than seventy pounds, she was a thin wisp of a woman. Yet she also appeared lithe and energetic, sporting a cane that she leaned on when she walked through her neighborhood or tended to her garden and carp pond. At the time that this chapter was written, she had recently turned 110 years old, joining the ranks of an elite group that gerontologists have recently termed "super-centenarians" (since they have achieved the previously unattainable age of 110 years or more). Tsuru had become the oldest living person in Okinawa. She was born the youngest of five children on June 24, 1897, in a small village where she had lived her whole life. Well-educated for the times, she passed an exam which qualified her to enter college and fulfill her dream to become a teacher, one of the few professions available to women in the beginning decades of the twentieth century.

Unfortunately, yet all too common for the times, she was not able to attend college due to objection from her parents who insisted that she find a husband as soon as possible. She married at twenty-one years of age but her husband divorced her because she was unable to conceive a child. Her second marriage was at twenty-eight years old with a man seventeen years her senior but she did not bear a child with him either. However, she brought up the child of her second husband, a likable young boy whom she loved and raised as her own. In his eighties at the time of first interview, by the time Tsuru had turned 110, both he and his wife had passed away. Losing two members, the household had shrunk to three members: Tsuru, her grandson and his wife, now in their sixties and who attended to Tsuru's daily needs for home care. Although a great-grandson and his wife were living next-door he and his wife (they were in their thirties) had yet to have a child, a point which Tsuru showed much concern about. The support of her grandchildren was supplemented by a home helper who visited five times per week and a visiting nurse who came to examine Tsuru twice a week. This was mostly paid for by

Japan's relatively new system of long-term care insurance, first implemented in 2000 (see Jenike and Traphagan Part III). Noticeably thinner and frailer since I had last seen her at age 104, I thought back on the life of this typical (as representative of her times) yet remarkable (supercentenarian) woman. Tsuru had led the life of a woman of her generation, keeping house, raising her child, working the fields of sugar cane and growing vegetables for home consumption, making her own tofu, and when time permitted, making straw hats and selling them in the market. She had been healthy throughout her incredibly long life and other than cataract surgery in her eighties, never experienced a major illness until she came down with pneumonia at age 105, which after a forty day battle, had left her practically bed-bound and in need of intensive daily support in order to carry out normal activities of daily living. What was the secret of her remarkable longevity? Was it just good fortune? Perhaps she just had a great set of genes. Maybe it was her good health habits. Her only unhealthy habit seemed to be that she had smoked a pack of cigarettes a day for forty years, a practice that she gave up in her early seventies. She drank alcohol in the form of medicinal herb liquor (garlic or plum liqueur) but only on social occasions. She practiced ancestor worship and looked after the family alter (*butsudan*) with care. Her grandson and his wife reported her character as forward-looking, someone who refused to dwell on negative thoughts. She seemed to have been conscientious

Tsuru with OCS investigator Craig Willcox and principal investigator Makoto Suzuki 2001. Photo by Kaori Higa.

about her health and exercised regularly, being an active walker. She was also careful about her meals, eating frugally, and thinking about the nutritional content of the food. (Willcox, D.C. Field notes August 8, 2001, Yomitan Village, Okinawa, Japan)

Tsuru's case is remarkable in several ways, not only for her exceptional age, but also the fact that she reached her 110th year and hence became a "supercentenarian" in relatively good health. As a participant in the Okinawa Centenarian Study (OCS), she had geriatric health assessments at various points from the time that she became a centenarian in 1997. These exams revealed no major diseases throughout this period (other than pneumonia) and that Tsuru was not taking any prescription medication—even at the incredible age of 110 years old. To put her aging achievement in perspective, when Tsuru was born in 1897, average life expectancy in Japan was only about forty-three years of age. The fact that she lived decades longer, surviving through a century fraught with tuberculosis, gastroenteritis, malaria, measles, flu epidemics, earthquakes, fires and the Second World War that ravaged Okinawa in 1945, seems miraculous. In Japan, only a handful of people of her generation achieved "exceptional longevity" (EL) and survived to the age of 100 years, and less than one in a thousand of these centenarian elite lived to reach "supercentenarian" status of age 110 years or older (Japan Ministry of Health, Labour and Welfare 2007).

In Ogimi village, a little farther north from Tsuru's home, a stone welcome marker stands near the beach. The marker displays the declaration of Ogimi village elders that reads "at seventy you are but a child, at eighty you are merely a youth, and at ninety if the ancestors invite you into heaven, ask them to wait until you are one hundred ... and then you might consider it." When this stone marker was erected in the early 1990s, it could easily have been the prefectural motto of Okinawa. Older people in this area tend to be quite healthy, and active, typically appearing youthful beyond their years. They have been the longest lived of the Japanese, who in turn are the longest-lived people in the world, for as long as records have been kept (Suzuki, Willcox and Willcox 2008). To understand the significance of this health phenomenon, it is helpful to consider a typical disease and its impact upon a typical city of 100,000 inhabitants in both Okinawa and the United States. If the city was located in Okinawa, less than twenty people would have died from coronary heart disease in a typical year. If the city was located in the United States, approximately 100 people would have died from this ailment. This is an astonishing difference.

However, despite continuing disparities in healthy longevity between Okinawa and the United States, the rise of individuals attaining EL in all postindustrial societies is dramatic. One in ten girls and one in twenty boys born today in the United States can expect to live to a hundred, and centenarians are the fastest growing age group in most postindustrialized countries today (Vaupel 2000; United Nations 2005). According to the U.S. census, the number of persons aged 100 years or over in 2000 was 50,454, and this number doubles about every ten years[1]. In Japan, the most rapidly aging society in the world, the centenarian population is now doubling at *twice* the rate found in the United States—about every five years (Willcox et al. 2008). Moreover, increasing life expectancy is not only restricted to postindustrial nations as people are also living longer in most developing societies (Kinsella this volume). How far can we go from here? What can help us to get the most out of our increased years? And what can we learn from research into the lives of people like Tsuru—who achieve EL in relatively good health? One of the research efforts to understand these issues is the Okinawa Centenarian Study (OCS), now in its thirty-second year and the world's longest continuously running research project on centenarians (www.okicent. org). Using an integrated approach combining researchers from many different fields, the OCS has sought to evaluate and investigate the exceptionally long-lived population found in the Ryukyu archipelago in southern Japan (Okinawa prefecture). The study includes interviews and examinations of more than 900 Okinawan centenarians and hundreds of younger elders in their seventies, eighties and nineties, looking for commonalities in their diets, exercise habits, genetics, psychological and spiritual practices, and social and behavioral patterns that could possibly explain their long-term vitality and exceptionally healthy longevity.

Okinawa prefecture has long been famous throughout Japan for its extraordinary health and longevity advantage, very low rates of cardiovascular diseases and cancers, the longest average life expectancy and the highest proportion of centenarians among the forty-seven prefectures. Ironically, the association of these facts with Okinawa was largely unheard of in the West until recently (Willcox, Willcox and Suzuki 2001). A major goal of the Okinawa Centenarian Study has been to gain insight into processes promoting healthy life extension and disease prevention by studying exceptionally aged individuals in social and cultural context. These "healthy-agers" are often characterized by a slow rate of decline in adaptive capacity or functional reserve and therefore are less vulnerable to age-associated disease. Throughout this chapter, we will refer to "healthy aging" as chronological aging with minimal loss of function and low prevalence rates of the diseases that usually accompany the aging process.[2]

This chapter will draw upon insights gained through four decades of study on the population widely regarded as having the world's greatest longevity. We will also look at the potential for healthy human aging by connecting this work with the growing number of centenarian (http://www.publichealth.uga.edu/geron/research/centenarian_study.html) and longitudinal healthy-aging projects now going on around the world (http://www.nia.nih.gov/ResearchInformation/ScientificResources/LongitudinalStudies.htm). First, we will examine the demography and epidemiology of healthy life expectancy, including some of the numerous false claims of extraordinary longevity.

DEMOGRAPHY AND EPIDEMIOLOGY OF HEALTHY LIFE EXPECTANCY

Exceptional Longevity Myths and the Importance of an Evidence-based Approach

Although the absolute potential for human aging is unknown, the oldest age-verified human being is Jeanne Louise Calment of France, who died aged 122 years and 5.5 months (Robine and Allard 1999; Carnes, Olshansky and Grahn 2003). No one in recorded history has ever been verified as living longer than this; in fact, only about seven people in human history have been documented as having reached the age of 116 years or more (Los Angeles Gerontology Research Group 2008).[3] However, with ever increasing numbers of healthy elderly and advancing preventive medical care, we expect that this record will be broken within the coming decades, although some gerontologists doubt that this record will ever be broken.

Myths of exceptional longevity have been around for more than two millennia and are found in many different cultures both geographically and temporally separated (Willcox, Willcox and Suzuki 2001; Hall 2003; Boia 2004). One of the earliest recorded myths of exceptional longevity came from the Chinese, who so believed in immortality that they invested significant financial resources searching for it. In the second century B.C., the first Chinese emperor, Ch'in, sent out a mission of some 2,000 individuals in search of the mythical "Eastern Sea Islands," where it was thought the "immortals" dwelled. Later on, the German painter Lucas Cranach, the Elder (1472–1553), painted at age seventy-four his famous *Fons Juventutis* (the fountain of youth) depicting a miraculous spring with withered ancient women getting in and nubile rejuvenated youths emerging from the waters. Of course this was also the age of trying to turn lead into gold.

In the 1970s, there appeared reports from several different remote parts of the world, which claimed to document a number of individuals between the ages of 120 and 168! The most notable places where this was reported included the Caucasus mountain region of the former Soviet Union, the Hunza Valley in Pakistan and the village of Vilcabamba in the Ecuadorian Andes. These all provided fascinating and hopeful media stories, but on closer examination the facts and figures just did not add up (Mazess and Forman 1979; Leaf 1982; Bennett and Garson 1983).

The case of the unfounded claims in the Caucasus (located in the former Soviet republics of Georgia, Azerbaijan and Armenia) is typical of false claims of exceptional long life in many locales. The problem with the Soviet data was that few of the so-called centenarians actually possessed birth certificates because no central birth registration system existed until after the Soviet Union was formed in 1917. Church or baptismal records were the most valued documents for confirming actual ages, but unfortunately, most churches in the region were destroyed in the early days of the Soviet Union. Some men had exaggerated their age to escape military service by assuming the identity of an older, deceased relative, others in order to gain the respect that came with being the most senior elder in the village. Shirali Mislimov, the oldest such claimant, was said to be 168 years old, and his picture even appeared on a Soviet postage stamp. In this area's Muslim villages, the link of status to elevated age was particularly important for males, and this probably explains why there were more men recorded as supercentenarians than women. If nothing else, this gender differential, dramatically opposite of any other place in the world, should have made researchers much more skeptical. For example, in January 2008, an international list of seventy-nine living supercentenarians indicated that sixty-eight were female and just eleven were male (Los Angeles Gerontology Research Group 2008). In addition, other factors such as illiteracy within a population, differing calendar systems, lack of emphasis on dates of birth or age or not having a longstanding age registration system can all contribute to age exaggeration (Willcox et al. 2008).[4] Moreover, age inflation exists in most age databases that rely on census data for their centenarian statistics, including in the United States, where a national birth registration system did not exist at the time today's centenarians were born (Kannisto 1988; Perls et al. 1999; Bourbeau and Lebel 2000).[5]

Countries that rely upon census records to estimate prevalence data for centenarians are particularly prone to inflation of actual numbers of centenarians through practices of age heaping and age rounding, where the majority of ages appear to fall at easily remembered major ages such as age 100. The 1980 U.S. Census for example, reported approximately double the actual, realistic prevalence rates of centenarians (Leaf 1982; Krach and Velkoff 1999). Therefore, in studies of exceptionally long-lived individuals, or populations that claim to have high numbers of centenarians, careful scrutiny of birth records, death records and other age-related documents is necessary in order to support longevity claims.

Japan has long been considered to have among the highest-quality data for the oldest-old (Kannisto 1994). In Japan (and Okinawa), the family registry (*koseki*) dates back to the 1870s, so age verification (equivalent of a birth certificate) is possible for all citizens, including centenarians. The *koseki* is supplemented by a regular census undertaken every five years. Life tables calculated from these data for Okinawa show one of the world's longest life expectancies, and prevalence data show the world's highest-known concentration of centenarians for any country or state (Willcox et al. 2008).

CENTENARIAN STUDIES AROUND THE WORLD

In the early 1970s, the first comprehensive attempt to scientifically study centenarians took place in Hungary (Beregi 1990); this study was soon followed by the Okinawa Centenarian Study, established in 1975, when Dr. Makoto Suzuki arrived in Okinawa to establish a Department of Community Medicine at the new medical school at University of the Ryukyus (Sanabe,

Ashitome and Suzuki 1977; Suzuki et al. 1985; Willcox, Willcox and Suzuki 2001). One important finding from these and subsequent studies with rigorous age-validation methodology is that there do seem to be areas in the world with a particularly high prevalence of centenarians, including Sardinia, Italy and Okinawa, Japan (see Figure 38.1); each such area offers a unique opportunity to assess EL from a different perspective or to validate findings from another area.

These studies have produced volumes of findings over the past several decades. The first comprehensive assessments of centenarians from a multidisciplinary perspective were reported by the OCS in the 1970s. Medical, social and family history, physical and cognitive function, ability to perform basic (e.g., eating, dressing) and instrumental (e.g., bill paying, shopping) activities of daily living and basic biological markers of health were assessed. From this work it soon became clear that common stories of cigar-smoking, whiskey-swilling centenarians who could effortlessly hike mountain ranges were a myth. When truly population-based research was conducted, and all centenarians were identified, it was clear that there was wide heterogeneity in the centenarian population. Some centenarians are remarkably well preserved, while others have high levels of disease and disability—in Okinawa about one-third were found to be functionally independent, about one-third needed major assistance with activities of daily living (ADL), and about one-third were very ill and disabled (Sanabe et al. 1977; Suzuki et al. 1995).[6]

Not surprisingly, only a minority could be characterized as "independent" in their activities of daily living (Andersen-Ranberg, Schroll and Jeune 2001). While high levels of disability are present in these exceptional survivors, an important caveat is that most centenarians seem to be healthier than the average person throughout their lives, and remain functionally independent until their mid nineties (Hitt et al. 1999; Willcox, Willcox, Shimajiri et al. 2007). A notable related finding from the Okinawa Centenarian Study was that most centenarians had good cardiovascular health over the course of their lives.

Trajectories of Health and Decline

Although studies have yet to adequately characterize the prevalence and timing of age-associated illness among exceptionally long-lived persons, the New England Centenarian Study (NECS) suggests that there may be multiple routes to achieving exceptional longevity and that there are gender differences regarding which route is taken. Initially a small population-based study of centenarians in New England, the NECS has become national in its scope by locating long-lived families and supercentenarians throughout the United States and concentrating mainly on genetic aspects of EL (Perls et al. 1999; Perls and Terry 2007). Researchers there found that centenarians fall into three morbidity profiles—survivors, delayers or escapers.[7] The survivor profile fit those who had an age-associated disease prior to the age of eighty. Delayers were those who delayed the onset of age-associated illness until at least the age of eighty. Escapers were those who made it to 100 without age-associated illness.

However, when examining only the most lethal diseases of aging (heart disease, cancer, stroke), 87 percent of male and 83 percent of female subjects escaped or delayed these diseases until the time they had reached centenarian status (Evert, Lawler, Bogan and Perls 2003).

Typically, as found in New England and almost all other areas of the world, approximately 80 to 90 percent of centenarians are female. As noted previously, despite the fact that male centenarians are fewer in number, they tend to have lower levels of disability and disease than their female counterparts. The reasons are as of yet unclear; however, women may be physiologically stronger than men when it comes to living with age-associated illness, as risk for mortality for men seems to rise quickly relative to similarly aged women, and therefore it appears that men must be relatively disease-free to make it to 100.

It was not until the late 1980s and the mid 1990s that centenarian studies came into their element with new studies being established in Georgia, Iowa, Tokyo, Sweden and Germany among other locations (Samuelsson et al. 1997; Rott et al. 2001; Frederiksen et al. 2002). New areas of inquiry in genetic, geriatric and psychosocial aspects of EL occurred. For example, in the 1990s, a massive study on French centenarians was begun by researchers Michel Allard, a medical doctor, and Jean-Marie Robine, a demographer. This study resulted in the first major association between variants of a particular gene and longevity that was replicated in numerous populations (Schachter et al. 1994; Willcox, Willcox, Hsueh et al. 2006). In addition, this study also located and verified the age of the world's oldest human, as mentioned earlier (Robine and Allard 1998).

In the United States, the Georgia Centenarian Study (begun in 1988) studied mainly psychosocial and adaptive factors related to longevity in racially diverse areas of the state of Georgia (Poon et al. 1992). This study found that personality characteristics, particularly optimism and extraversion, were part of a common centenarian personality profile, and this profile was observed in several centenarian populations. (Poon et al. 1992; Adkins, Martin and Poon 1996; Willcox, Willcox and Suzuki 2001; Martin et al. 2006).[8] By the twenty-first century, other types of centenarian studies were being founded. For example, a project on an ethnic founder population rather than a geographic area is taking place with Ashkenazi Jews in the United States at Albert Einstein Medical School (Barzilai et al. 2003). Like much of the current research, the focus here is on the genetic influence on longevity, and more and more genes have been found with suspected links to aging and longevity. There are now over a dozen active centenarian studies using various study models, and increasing collaboration is occurring between centenarian researchers and other longevity researchers. For example, the International Centenarian Consortium (ICC), based at the University of Georgia, and the Longevity Consortium, based at California Pacific Medical Center, are both bringing together researchers who study EL so large datasets can be constructed, increasing statistical power and producing results that can, hopefully, be reproduced across populations (Willcox, Willcox, Hsueh et al. 2006). Progress has been made in understanding mechanisms of longevity and healthy aging and every new discovery

Figure 38.1

Prevalence of Centenarians in Selected Countries (number of centenarians per hundred thousand persons)

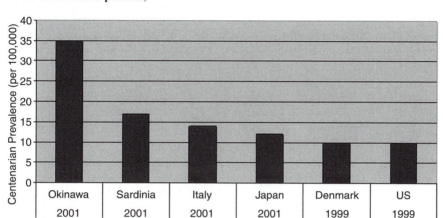

Sources: Perls et al. 1999; Poulain et al. 2004; Japan Ministry of Health, Labour and Welfare 2001.[9]

reveals another layer of complexity, demonstrating that genetic, biological, psychological and social factors, as well as their interactions, are all important for living long and living well.

LIVING LONGER IN JAPAN

In order to put the Okinawan longevity phenomenon in proper context, it is helpful to examine the dramatic increase in postwar Japanese life expectancy as a whole. In the four decades following World War II (1950–1990), two separate demographic and epidemiological transitions occurred, one affecting mainly younger age groups, and the second affecting mainly older age groups. The combined effect of these two transitions accounts for the rapid gains in average life expectancy that resulted in Japan, a longevity laggard until then, catching up and usurping Sweden as the longest-lived country in the world in the mid-to-late 1970s (Yanagishita and Guralnik 1988).

From 1955 to 1960, childhood mortality was key. The decrease in death rates under five years of age accounted for over half of the increase in average life expectancy, whereas declines in mortality among older groups (over fifty years) were negligible. However, by 1985, this trend had reversed, with declines in mortality in older groups pushing average life expectancy higher. For example, between 1985 and 1990, mortality decreases in people aged seventy-five years or older accounted for nearly one-third of life expectancy gains, and this trend has only strengthened in years since.

Numerous factors have contributed to life expectancy gains in Japan. One of the most important factors has been a decrease in stroke mortality, which came

Figure 38.2
Age-Standardized Mortality Rates in Japanese Males, 1950–2000

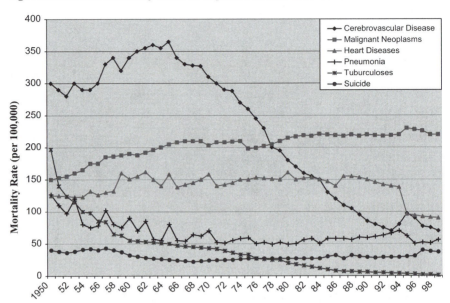

Source: Japan Ministry of Health, Labour and Welfare 2002.

about in large part due to better medical treatment of hypertension, government-mandated salt reductions in commonly consumed foods such as soy sauce, and mass screenings of the population for hypertension and other common medical conditions. These practices have resulted in Japan's dramatic decrease in (age-standardized) stroke mortality—from over 350 per 100,000 in the early 1960s to 74 per 100,000 in the year 2000 for men (see figure 38.2); for women, death rates from stroke dropped even lower—to 46 per 100,000 in 2000 (Japan Ministry of Health, Labour and Welfare 2002). There was already an extremely low death rate from the number-one killer in the West, CHD (coronary heart disease), which in Japan is only one-fourth of U.S. or Swedish levels.[10] This created the context for Japan's incredible rise in life expectancy and the emergence of a large centenarian population, which grew from 163 persons in 1963 to over 30,000 in 2007 (Japan Ministry of Health, Labour and Welfare 2007).

The Socio-economic Context for a Longevity Boom

Postwar social and economic changes contributed to reduced mortality from the various causes discussed in the previous section. First, the introduction of new antibiotics, immunizations and mass preventive-screening programs dramatically reduced mortality from infectious diseases. Second, technological innovations contributed to the decrease in mortality from particular causes. For instance, near universal access to refrigerators in the mid 1960s contributed to an increased consumption of fresh food, which is rich in vitamin C and other antioxidants and may lower risk for stomach cancer and other age-associated diseases. Refrigeration also decreases the prevalence of *Helicobacter pylori*, a bacterium that exists in poorly sanitized locales and is a principal cause of stomach cancer. In addition, refrigeration also led to a reduced consumption of sodium-rich preserved foods. Reduced sodium intake is thought to be a major contributor to the decrease in mortality due to stroke, stomach cancer and other diseases (Kobayashi et al. 2004; Nagata, Takatsuka, Shimizu and Shimizu 2004). Thus, many synergistic forces, particularly important for public health, helped drive mortality rates lower in postwar Japan.

The health professions in Japan also underwent major changes in the 1960s, resulting in a dramatic increase in both number and quality of health care facilities and health care professionals. After the establishment of a national health insurance system in 1961, screening campaigns aimed at reducing the burden of common chronic illnesses have helped in prevention and early detection of many lifestyle-related diseases. Studies have shown that populations with high participation in these screening exams suffer lower levels of mortality, and lower associated medical costs (Nara 2005; Iwasa et al. 2007; Sakihara and Yamashiro 2007).

The economic boom that followed the war resulted in a large increase in average income and greater access to education, the effects of which were felt relatively evenly across the population, resulting in less income disparity than is seen in most Western countries, especially when compared to the United States. Recent studies in Japan imply that the dramatic increase in economic equality and access to preventive health care has been a key factor to low mortality rates and soaring longevity figures (Fukuda, Nakamura and Takano 2005).[11] Less disparity in socioeconomic status indicators and universal access to quality health care would likely improve the dismal international standing of the United States in life expectancy (currently ranked forty-fifth according to the *C.I.A. World Factbook* 2007).

THE CULTURAL CONTEXT OF HEALTHY AGING IN OKINAWA

Before Okinawa was annexed by Japan in 1879, it was an independent kingdom (Ryuku Kingdom), which had close tributary ties with China for over four hundred years. Despite more than a century of cultural oppression and assimilation, major cultural differences remain, including differences in identity, language, social organization, religion, art, music and diet (Willcox, Willcox and Suzuki 2001). Franklin (1996) poetically described Okinawa as:

Japan with salsa—a hybrid culture where formal kimonos are streaked with bold geometrics, breezy palm trees grow alongside fluttering cherry, and Japanese precision and punctuality are tempered by an easygoing cadence known locally as "Okinawa time." (p. 56)

Champuru: the Food Culture of Okinawa

During the prewar period (before 1945), the traditional food culture of Okinawa was a fusion of Chinese, Japanese and Southeast Asian influences. Often referred to as *"champuru"* or *"chample"* in the Okinawan language, which means mixture, it was truly a mixed plate of Asian influences. The diet consisted largely of sweet potatoes as the staple food (>50 percent of calories), a large variety of locally grown vegetables, miso soup, tofu, some tropical fruit and fish, occasionally supplemented by small amounts of pork (Willcox B. et al. 2007). A variety of herbs and spices such as turmeric and mugwort were used to add flavor and medicinal value. A common parlance was *"nuchi gusui,"* which can best be translated as "let food be your medicine." Festival days, which provide an opportunity to eat ceremonial dishes, seem to have taken place often enough to ensure regular supplementation of a variety of other food sources such as rice, konbu seaweed, various meats and other sea-food. Noodles from wheat or buckwheat, bread and eggs were also occasionally consumed.

In the postwar period, rice completely replaced the sweet potato as the staple food, and the volume of food products imported into Okinawa, as throughout the rest of Japan, has increased rapidly in line with the progress of globalization. In modern Okinawa, people enjoy a widely varied diet, although large generational differences now stand out with elders sticking closer to the traditional diet. The traditional diet relies on low-caloric-density vegetables and legumes as staples instead of relatively high-caloric-density white rice. In addition, in the traditional dietary habits, there was a focus on small portion sizes and not eating until completely full. Even now a common saying among Okinawan elderly is *hara hachi bu* (eat until only 80 percent full).

Biocultural Benefits of the Okinawan Lifestyle

How might culture and biology have intertwined to decrease the risk of disease in Okinawa? First, the low-calorie, antioxidant and nutrient-rich food choices, the healthy eating habits and the high levels of physical activity resulted in a population that had consumed a nutrient-rich but calorie-poor diet. We estimate that Okinawans prior to the 1960s consumed 10 to 15 percent fewer calories than would normally be required per caloric guidelines. When faced with a persistent energy deficit, mammals adapt by becoming more energy efficient, producing less heat and converting a higher proportion of food into usable energy. A host of other adaptations occur, including less oxidative damage, increased DNA repair, increased resistance to stress, improved cholesterol profile and increased insulin sensitivity. These changes are commonly observed in animal studies of "caloric restriction," and this is the only consistently reproducible manner of increasing mean and maximum lifespan in experimental animals, other than select genetic manipulations (Willcox B. et al. 2007).

Second, particular food choices that resulted in lower salt intake and more varied and slightly higher protein and fat intake than for other Japanese may have had disease-specific benefits that reduced mortality risk and increased longevity. For example, a visit to any small restaurant in Okinawa that specializes in local cuisine will surprise anyone acquainted with Japanese food. Pork seems to dominate the menu, based on centuries of indigenous culinary traditions.[12] Unlike mainland Japan, the Ryukyu Islands have never had a large population of Buddhists nor any of the related social taboos against eating pork. Increased prosperity has led to pork finding its way into everyday cuisine, thanks at least in part to the import of cheap pork luncheon meats from the United States (Willcox, Willcox and Suzuki 2001).

In North America and Northern Europe, heart disease has been linked to an overconsumption of saturated fat and trans fat. However, in Japan the major problem was cerebrovascular disease (stroke). It is hypothesized that the stroke risk was elevated due in part to an insufficient intake of fat and protein, and exacerbated by high salt intake (Yamori et al. 1978; Kobayashi 1992; Matsuzaki 1992). It is hypothesized that low levels of cholesterol (caused by inadequate intake of fat) may cause a weakening of arterial walls, as cholesterol is a primary constituent (Yamori et al. 1976; Iritani, Fukuda, Nara and Yamori 1977). Animal models of stroke show that deficiency of certain amino acids in very low protein diets (or diets deficient in particular amino acids from limited protein variety) increase stroke risk in spontaneously hypertensive rats. High salt intake is another culprit, increasing the risk of hemorrhagic stroke. This combination—low blood cholesterol levels, amino acid deficiency and high salt intake—dramatically increases risk of stroke and was typical of the mainland Japanese dietary pattern before the 1960s (Yamori et al. 1978; Kagan, Popper, Rhoads and Yano 1985). The better-balanced traditional Okinawan diet (lower salt intake, more varied sources of protein and fat) has likely been contributing to the lower stroke mortality rates in Okinawa, which were about half that of the mainland from 1973 to 1992 (Okinawa Prefecture 1995). In fact, this reduced stroke mortality accounts for much of the difference in life expectancy between Okinawa and mainland Japan, with most of the remaining difference due to lower rates of certain cancers[13] and heart disease, both of which have strong connections to diet and lifestyle (Suzuki, Willcox and Willcox 2001; Willcox, Willcox, Shimajiri et al. 2007; Willcox D. et al. 2005; Willcox, Willcox, Todoriki et al. 2007).

Comparative Studies of the Elderly in Okinawa and Japan

Long-standing differences in a complex mix of culture, social organization and health practices persist between Okinawa and the rest of Japan that seem to have given the current generation of Okinawan elders a longevity edge (also see Jenike and Traphagan Part III). One of the best ways to see this is by comparing a long-lived village in Okinawa with a demographically similar mainland village in the prefecture of Akita, with one of the shortest life expectancies in Japan (Shibata et al. 1994). Upon comparison, high stroke mortality stood out in the Akita village. An examination of the diets of elderly persons in both villages revealed some major differences in the foods consumed.

The Okinawan elderly consumed higher levels of meat, green/yellow vegetables and tofu, whereas the Akita elderly consumed more white rice, fish, shellfish, seaweed and fruit. Okinawan villagers consumed higher levels of protein, calcium and mono- and polyunsaturated fats, whereas those in Akita had higher salt intake. Okinawan dietary factors, and possibly genetic factors (which may affect cholesterol levels) have contributed to population-wide low LDL ("bad" cholesterol) and high HDL ("good" cholesterol), a combination often seen in healthy centenarians (Suzuki et al. 2001). A recent study on the traditional Okinawan diet (which has been consumed by the Okinawan elderly for most of their lives) reveals that the diet is high in antioxidant-rich vegetables (mainly sweet potatoes) and soy foods containing high levels of flavonoids, which show protective effects against certain cancers, osteoporosis and hypertension (Sagara et al. 2004; Duffy, Perez and Partridge 2007; Marini et al. 2007; Willcox B. et al. 2007). The protective mechanisms are not entirely clear, but lower oxidative stress, reduced insulin signaling and stimulation of protective second-messenger pathways are among the common findings (Willcox B. et al. 2007). The Okinawan elders have a naturally nutrient-rich, calorically-poor diet, which is thought to be a major contributing factor to their longevity and good health (Todoriki, Willcox and Willcox 2004; Willcox B. et al. 2004; Willcox, Willcox, Todoriki et al. 2006; Willcox, Willcox, Todoriki et al. 2007).

Compared to the elderly in Akita, the Okinawan elders were more active with higher levels of Activities of Daily Living (ADL),[14] had more social contact, were employed longer and had lower rates of hospitalization (Shibata et al. 1994). Interestingly, nearly 40 percent of elderly women in the Okinawan sample lived alone, compared with less than 10 percent of women in the Akita sample (where most lived with children). Support networks were also different between the two villages—Akita's being mainly family-centered, whereas Okinawa's was centered around friends and neighbors (Shibata et al. 1994). The tight settlement pattern in Okinawan villages and high rates of autonomy of Okinawan elders may encourage them to stay employed longer and have greater levels of social contact. Year-round warm weather may also allow for a higher level of activity for elderly persons.[15]

OKINAWA'S HEALTHY OLDER WOMEN

Women almost everywhere outlive men (see Kinsella Part I). In Okinawa, the gender gap in life expectancy is particularly large (over eight years). Part of the longer life expectancies for women in general seems to be based in biology, but differences in this gap between societies lends weight to the importance of social and behavioral factors. Women in most postindustrialized societies are generally more health-conscious than men, with better eating habits, lower rates of smoking and drinking, more regular medical checkups, stronger social networks and less risk-taking behavior (lower rates of accidents, suicide and homicide). Okinawan women are no exception to the above, however, they also seem to possess a few other aces up their sleeves—particularly older women. Compared to older women in Western nations, women in Okinawa tend to experience menopause with less physiological complaints and fewer medical complications (Willcox, Willcox and Suzuki 2001). There is a markedly lower reported incidence of hot flashes, depression and mood changes. Medical complications such as hip fractures and coronary heart disease are much lower. Lifestyle determinants include diet, avoidance of smoking and exercise in the form of dance, soft martial arts, walking and gardening. Diet is particularly interesting. Okinawan women have a very high intake of natural estrogens through their diet, mainly from the large quantities of soy-enriched products that they consume. Legumes such as soybeans are rich in phytoestrogens, or plant estrogens, called flavonoids.[16] Recent double-blind placebo-controlled studies support the ability of isoflavones to slow the bone loss and reduce hot flashes that occur with menopause (Albertazzi et al. 1998; Alekel et al. 2000).

Okinawan women also have extremely low risk for hormone-dependent cancers including cancers of the breast, ovaries and colon. Compared to North Americans, they have approximately 80 percent less breast cancer, and less than half the ovarian and colon cancers. Some of the most important factors that may protect against these cancers include low caloric intake, high vegetable/fruit consumption, higher intake of good fats (omega-3, mono-unsaturated fat), high fiber diet, high flavonoid intake, low body fat level and high level of physical activity.

Other unique factors may be operating within this particular cultural context that have yet to be adequately explored. One such factor includes the interconnected role of religion, spirituality, aging and health in the lives of older Okinawan women. Another factor is the high level of social integration of women, especially older women, in various aspects of daily life. A good example of this is the *Basho-fu* weaving of Ogimi village in northern Okinawa. In this unique style of weaving, the time and labor-intensive process of cleaning the fibers and spooling the thread is performed mainly by groups of older women. In addition to providing social opportunities, it allows these women to be respected and active members of the local economy as well as supplement their income (Willcox, Willcox, Sokolovsky et al. 2007).

Religion and spirituality may be particularly important for women throughout the Ryukyu Island archipelago as Okinawa remains the only contemporary society in which women actually lead the mainstream, publicly funded religion (Lebra 1966; Sered 1999; Matayoshi and Trafton 2000). Numerous studies have shown benefits of positive spirituality on aging and health (Levin and Vanderpool 1989; Gesler, Arcury and Koenig 2000; Parket et al. 2003; Peterson Part IV Web book). Some researchers have questioned the current paradigm of successful aging for not explicitly including spirituality in the model (Crowther et al. 2002; Moody this volume). In Okinawa, elderly women's active engagement in religious roles may be playing a part in reducing depression and associated rates of suicide (Taguchi et al. 1999; Naka, Willcox and Todoriki 1998; Willcox and Katata 2000). Rates of suicide for elderly Okinawan women have, for many years, been among the lowest in East Asia, a region known for high

Okinawan sacred priestesses leading the community ritual (men in background). Photo by Craig Willcox.

rates of suicide among older women (Hu 1995; Yip, Callanan and Yuen 2000; Pritchard and Baldwin 2002).[17]

WHAT IS THE POTENTIAL FOR HEALTHY HUMAN AGING?

Achieving Healthy Aging

Becoming a centenarian is a rare event, occurring in only one or two persons per 10,000 in most postindustrial societies. Attaining this age does not appear to be rare because the genetic or behavioral factors that help one to reach this exceptional age are rare, but rather because having the right combination of these factors seems to be rare.

One benefits most from starting early, and recent evidence of the effects of early life environments (including the womb) point to the importance of the life course perspective when studying healthy aging, as characteristics of early childhood environments have been associated with morbidity and mortality later in life, as well as have been found to be predictive of exceptional survivorship (Kuh and Ben-Shlomo 1997; Preston, Hill and Drevenstedt 1998; Blackwell, Hayward and Crimmins 2001).

Until the 1970s, the common perception was that a person's genes ultimately determine an individual's predisposition to disease and their potential to live a long and healthy life. One of the first and most important studies that changed this view and gave support to the position that lifestyle (not genes) was the major determinant of healthy longevity was the Ni-Hon-San study (which later spawned the Honolulu Heart Program). This international collaborative project compared Japanese immigrants and their offspring in Honolulu (Hon) and San Francisco (San) to Japanese remaining in Japan (Nippon). Because the study population did not marry into other ethnic groups, the gene pool was similar to the Japanese population, forming a genetic control, and the variables of concern were environment and lifestyle (Willcox B. et al. 2004).[18] One of the important findings from the study was that the longer the Japanese-Americans lived in their adopted country, the more their life expectancy and diseases resembled that of the host country. In other words, since there was little genetic variation between the Japanese and Japanese-American populations studied, the difference in disease risk was due primarily to lifestyle factors (Trombold, Moellering and Kagan 1966; Willcox B. et al. 2004).

Many of the scientifically based recommendations for healthy aging are the most obvious, including not smoking, avoiding excessive drinking, maintaining a healthy weight and minimizing risk for accidents. In a large number of developed countries, many of the main causes of death—including coronary heart disease (CHD), cancer and stroke—are greatly influenced by lifestyle. In fact, in the United States it is estimated that about half of all "premature" deaths are due to controllable behaviors, with the majority of these being due to smoking, obesity (through lack of physical activity and poor diet), alcohol and accidents (Mokdad, Marks, Stroup and Gerberding 2004, 2005).[19] When optimal health habits are followed, at the societal level average life expectancy can increase dramatically, as exhibited by Seventh Day Adventists who, because of religious beliefs do not smoke or drink alcohol, are more active, tend to be leaner, and follow a largely vegetarian dietary regime. Not surprisingly, they live an average of ten years longer than the typical American (Fraser and Shavlik 2001).

Contrastingly, Japanese who immigrate to Brazil are also a good example of what can happen when long-lived persons are removed from their health-promoting environment. In these immigrants, we see a major change in eating habits, with Japanese-Brazilians consuming less fish and vegetables, while consuming more than three times the amount of sugar and a staggering eighteen times the amount of meat as Japanese remaining in their homeland (Moriguchi 1999). These numbers are especially pronounced when we look at Okinawan-Brazilians whose obesity ratio is 1.6 times higher, the hypertension ratio double, and the proportion of centenarians less than one-fifth that of those remaining in Okinawa. In addition, Okinawan-Brazilians also have lower levels of beneficial antioxidants and HDL cholesterol in the blood stream (Moriguchi 1999). However, just as poor diet and exercise habits and other unhealthy lifestyle choices can contribute to premature death, healthy eating habits may maximize our chances of reaching older ages in good health. In addition to reducing the incidence and prevalence of disease (morbidity) from lifestyle-related illnesses, there is substantial lab-based evidence that reduced caloric intake (a process called caloric restriction, or CR), can extend the average and maximum lifespan of various model organisms for aging studies, from bacteria to higher primates (Mattison et al. 2007; Willcox B. et al. 2007). The process by which CR works is still not well understood despite it being the only consistent, nongenetic experimental means of extending mean and maximum lifespan and markedly decreasing morbidity in a phylogenetically diverse group of species (Gredilla and Barja 2005; Ingram, Young and Mattison 2007).[20] Out of the lab, historical data on nutritional intake, recent nutritional surveys and biochemical testing all point to the oldest old in Okinawa as undergoing mild CR (10 to 15 percent fewer calories than typically required) throughout large portions of their lives, and makes a compelling argument for the role of CR and diet in healthy aging in Okinawa (Willcox B. et al. 2007).[21]

What about Those Genes?

Despite the impressive evidence for the pervasive effects of the importance of a healthy lifestyle for maximizing our chances of aging well, the importance of genes, especially in understanding exceptional healthy longevity, is gradually being understood with greater clarity. Much of the research in this area relies upon studies utilizing identical and fraternal twins. Extensive twin registries exist in the Nordic countries such as Sweden and Norway, and analyses of these data sets have suggested that environment/lifestyle accounts for about two-thirds of lifespan, while genetics accounts for one-third (Ljungquist et al. 1998). Other twin studies have also come up with estimates in the 25 to 30 percent range (McGue et al. 1993; Herskind et al. 1996). Where the line is drawn may depend on which age group one is examining, as the power of genes seems to become more apparent at advanced ages. For example, because the oldest individuals in the twin studies were in their early-to-mid eighties, those studies may provide information about the heritability of *average* life expectancy, but it is not necessarily relevant for those who reach exceptionally older ages, such as centenarians. To survive another fifteen or more years beyond the average, it appears that people may need a relatively rare, or exceptional combination of environmental, behavioral and genetic factors, and that many of these factors run in families. Ljungquist et al. (2006) have recently provided empirical support for this hypothesis when they found a larger effect from genetics in a sample population of long-lived twins compared with a sample of twins who only lived to an average life expectancy. This has led other scientists (using multiple methods) to argue that the contribution from genetics for predicting very long life is closer to one-half (Perls, Kunkel and Puca 2002).

Our work in Okinawa has shown that siblings of centenarians have cumulative survival advantages such that female centenarian siblings have a 2.58 greater likelihood and male siblings a 5.43-fold likelihood (versus their birth cohorts) of reaching the age of ninety (Willcox, Willcox, He et al. 2006). This is indicative of a strong familial component to exceptional longevity. Although shared environments may account for part of this effect, genetic epidemiological

Twin OCS investigators Craig and Bradley Willcox with Kin and Gin—Japan's oldest twins at 105 years. Photo by Makoto Suzuki.

measures, such as sibling relative recurrence risk (λ_s), which is a measure of the prevalence of a particular trait in siblings of affected individuals compared to population prevalence of the trait, show that certain traits have a strong genetic component (Risch 1990).[22]

Centenarians may live such extraordinarily long lives in large part due to genetic variations that either affect the basic rate of aging and/or have genes that result in decreased susceptibility to age-associated diseases. For example, persons who achieve EL probably *lack* genetic variations that *increase* risk for disease or "disease alleles." Some genes, like the ApoE gene (apolipoprotein E), appear to have variants that influence longevity in diverse ethnic groups and several centenarian populations. Having one or more copies of the ApoE4 allele is a disadvantage, whereas the ApoE2 allele is an advantage with regard to longevity and aging phenotypes such as cardiovascular disease (CVD) and dementia (Schachter et al. 1994; Willcox, Willcox, Hsueh et al. 2006). Others genes, like the CETP gene, may be important, but appear to have population-specific gene variants that influence longevity. For example, long-lived Japanese are more likely to possess the Int14 A variant (Koropatnick et al. 2008) of the CETP gene, whereas centenarians and their offspring of Ashkenazi Jewish descent have approximately a two- to threefold increased frequency of homozygosity for the I405V gene variant of the CETP gene (VV genotype). Both genotypes increase HDL levels leading to lower risk for CVD, and possibly lower risk for dementia. Both of these diseases strongly affect one's ability to achieve healthy longevity due to their widespread effects on physical and cognitive function.[23]

As longevity is a very complex trait, several issues challenge our ability to identify its genetic influences, such as control for environmental confounders across time, the lack of precise phenotypes of aging and longevity, statistical power, study design and availability of appropriate study populations. Genetic studies on the Okinawan population suggest that Okinawans are a genetically distinct group that has several characteristics of a founder population, including less genetic diversity, and clustering of specific gene variants, some of which may be related to longevity (Willcox, Willcox, Hsueh et al. 2006).

THE FUTURE OF HEALTHY AGING

Compressing Morbidity and Maximizing Healthy Years

Rather than an old age plagued by disease and disability, the ideal scenario as defined by most cultures around the world would seem to be maintaining a level of reasonable functionality followed by a quick decline toward death (Keith et al. 1994; Willcox, Willcox, Sokolovsky et al. 2007). This is best described by the "compression of morbidity" paradigm as first postulated by Fries et al. in 1980. As mentioned earlier, if we look back on the patterns of health and functional status of centenarians, we can see that many of them have markedly delayed or avoided clinical expression of many major diseases that have killed younger elderly people, and the majority also remain functionally independent (as defined by ability to perform basic activities of daily living) for most of their lives.

Improved medical advances in end-of-life care have resulted in "life extension," which may delay mortality from various chronic diseases, but not necessarily decrease their prevalence. This may result in a prolongation of the duration of chronic disease and possibly disability. For example, better treatment of hypertension results in longer survival with this particular "disease," and thus increases the prevalence of this disease in the population of older individuals. However, there is evidence that major diseases, such as CVD and cancer, can be delayed or avoided until late in life. Better health habits might improve the length of life and might result in the "compression of morbidity," (at least for major chronic diseases) resulting in longer, healthier and more functional lives. One oft-presumed implication of extended longevity is a rising cost of medical care for the elderly. Perhaps we should rethink this issue. It may seem counterintuitive, but living longer through promoting *healthy* longevity may actually help reduce medical costs. For example, Nakajoh et al. (1999) studied the medical records of older people who died in a small village in Japan and discovered that the medical costs incurred for those dying at an older age (average 82.2 years old) were more than one-third less than those dying at a younger age (average 76.7 years old). Similarly, in America, the cost for caring for centenarians during the last five years of their life has been estimated to be only $1,800 per year, significantly less than the approximately $6,500 per year for those dying at age seventy (Hazzard 1997). A study of cumulative Medicare costs in the United States for those living until 100 years of age were approximately equal to those living to sixty-five years of age, suggesting that those who survived to older ages were healthier over the course of their lives and had less need for acute care (Spillman and Lubitz 2000). However, lifetime costs of long-term care (not covered by Medicare) were markedly higher due mainly to the high cost of nursing home care. Long-term care occurs when people can no longer manage basic activities of daily living, and this underscores the importance of reducing disability rates in older persons and discovering how centenarians manage to avoid disability until very late in life.

From these studies we can see that longevity achieved through healthy aging can actually decrease medical expenses and lessen the burden on the health care system. Programs designed to encourage healthy aging by stressing proper diet, exercise, as well as other lifestyle choices would reduce the incidence of many diseases such as obesity, heart disease, diabetes and some cancers that are a major antecedent of disability and ultimately place major strains on the health care system (Willcox, Willcox and Suzuki 2001). There is also some evidence from long-term care surveys showing that population-wide disability rates may, in fact, be decreasing, which could potentially save the health care system billions of dollars (Manton, Corder and Stallard 1997; Manton, Lamb and Gu 2007). There will still be a need, however, for more societies to consider investing in long-term care, as the Japanese have done, since overall disability will likely increase in society due to the rapid aging of the population, even as we reduce age-adjusted disability rates.

Measuring Healthy Life Expectancy

In line with these global trends, the World Health Organization (WHO) has begun to use a measurement of healthy life expectancy referred to as "HALE" (health adjusted life expectancy) in order to better assess the quality of population health. HALE is calculated from life expectancy and adjusted for morbidity of debilitating conditions/illnesses. HALE is best thought of as a measure of disability free lifespan.[24] Although there is a correlation between life expectancy and HALE, there is still a significant amount of variation in HALE between countries with similar life expectancies. For example, within the eight countries WHO lists with a life expectancy of seventy-one or fewer years for males, HALE varies from fifty-eight to sixty-three years. Using HALE provides deeper insight into the overall health of a population than just considering life expectancy (see Figures 38.3a and 38.3b). This is particularly true in countries such as Timor-Leste and the Solomon Islands, where the life expectancy is reasonably high, but healthy life expectancy is comparatively low. In these countries, people succumb to disease or debilitating conditions relatively early and spend a disproportionate number of years in a state of disability.

Figure 38.3a
Life Expectancy and Healthy Life Expectancy (HALE) for Males in Selected Countries

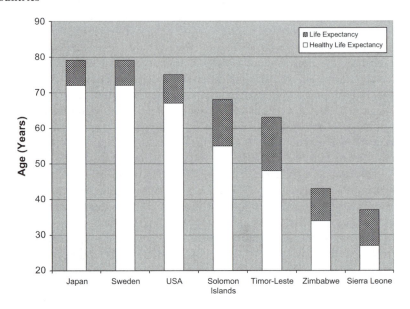

Figure 38.3b
Life Expectancy and Healthy Life Expectancy (HALE) for Females in Selected Countries

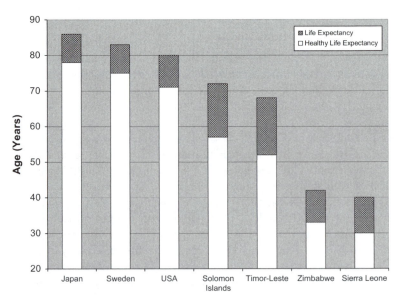

Source: WHO 2007.

According to WHO data, Japan has the highest HALE in the world at 72.3 years for men and 77.7 years for women (WHO 2007). Within Japan, Okinawans have the longest disability-free life expectancy, which arguably gives Okinawans the longest disability-free life expectancy in the world (Ministry of Health, Labour and Welfare 2000; Kurimori et al. 2006). However, even Okinawans must grapple with disability and, as mentioned earlier, only one-third of centenarians at best may be considered to be functionally independent (Willcox, Willcox, Shimajiri et al. 2007).

Healthy Aging in Peril? Two Scenarios

The longevity advantage experienced by Okinawa prefecture has been gradually eroding over the past couple of decades with life expectancy (at birth) growth rates among the slowest in Japan (Willcox D. 2005; Todoriki, Willcox and Willcox 2004). Men in particular have been experiencing slower increases in life expectancy at birth. This has led to what is called the "26 shock" in Okinawa, reflecting the fact that Okinawan men dropped from among the top five long-lived prefectures within Japan to twenty-sixth place among forty-seven prefectures according to the most recent available statistics from the year 2000. Within the past few decades, lifestyle changes that involve an uncoupling of energy intake and expenditure, along with fat intakes that are currently among the highest in the country, as well as negative health behaviors (excessive tobacco and alcohol consumption and other risk-taking behavior) and socioeconomic challenges (such as high unemployment rates, etc.) may be contributing to emerging problems of obesity, diabetes, increased cardiovascular risk factors, higher rates of lung cancer, liver disease and higher suicide rates for large subsets of the population (especially younger and middle-aged men). Looking at specific causes of death that contributed to the sudden slowing of life expectancy increases between 1985 and 2000 for Okinawan men, we can see that lifestyle-related diseases such as lung cancer, cardiovascular disease (heart diseases and stroke) and suicide are all playing a role—particularly for middle-aged Okinawan males (Willcox D. 2005).

The Road Ahead: Two Paths

What we may be seeing in the future is the emergence of two distinct groups of oldest-old. One will be marked by those who lived a healthy lifestyle—they will possess a history of eating a healthy diet, avoiding smoking and excessive alcohol consumption, exercising regularly and taking good care of their bodies and minds and engage in regular preventive health care. These individuals will live unusually long and vibrant lives, and we see evidence of their emergence already in active retirement communities around the world. The other group will be frail or disabled for much longer periods, and without medical advances would otherwise have died much earlier; they will instead be pushed into uncharted regions of survival through medical technology.

Results from studies that might shed some light on the future have been mixed. Recent studies such as the National Long Term Care Survey in the U.S. have indicated that the American elderly of today are healthier and less disabled than earlier generations (Manton, Lamb and Gu 2007). However, we have found the centenarians of present-day Okinawa to be less functional than earlier cohorts from the 1970s (Suzuki et al. 1995). Moreover, the current generation of elderly from postindustrial societies has faced different risks than younger and middle-aged persons of today.

Obesity and infectious diseases (new and reemerging) pose considerable risks to the gains that the current generation of elderly have enjoyed (Olshansky et al. 2005). In the United States, 28 percent of men and 34 percent of women are currently obese (BMI >30), and the numbers are rising. Obesity greatly increases risk of morbidity and mortality from a multitude of diseases. It is estimated that severe obesity can shorten life expectancy of men by up to thirteen years and women by up to eight years (Fontaine et al. 2003). A similar obesity trend is occurring in Japan, although not anywhere near the same degree as in the United States (Todoriki et al. 2004). Whether or not future generations of elderly continue the trend toward reduced disability and an extended health life expectancy may well depend upon the lifestyle choices that individuals make in mid-life or earlier. These gains will be coupled with the investments in preventive medicine, public health infrastructure and long-term care that societies make in the coming decades.

NOTES

1. In actuality, this number is likely lower than 50,454, as census data routinely overestimates centenarian prevalence (Krach and Velkoff 1999). For a more accurate centenarian ratio, a prevalence study is necessary. See Perls et al. (1999) for a prevalence study of centenarians in the New England area.

2. A particular challenge in these investigations is that there is no universally accepted definition of biological (or social) aging, nor easily quantifiable methods for measuring it (Butler et al. 2004). Biological aging may perhaps be best defined as "the accumulation of damage to the body's building blocks of life (DNA)." This damage is in contrast to age-related disease such as cardiovascular disease, cancer or Alzheimer's disease. Most aging research has been directed toward "curing" age-associated disease rather than dealing with the aging process itself, which is a much more daunting endeavor (Hayflick 2000). Recent work is attempting to better measure biological aging by assessing the functional ability of various organ systems and/or the accumulation of damage or dysfunction in the absence of clear clinical disease—or, when clinical disease is present, assessing the degree of disease. Some of these biological or clinical measures have been assessed across the lifespan so we have age-specific measures and can assign a biological age to the score based on average values for various ages. For example, by measuring coronary calcium, we can assign a biological age for coronary arteries based on coronary calcium score (Shaw, Raggi, Berman and Callister 2006). If someone has a higher score than their chronological age, then particularly aggressive modification of their cardiovascular risk factors may be required to slow the progression of this calcification over time. One recent study found coronary calcium to be the best

predictor of mortality in elderly persons (Abbott et al. 2007). Other tests, such as lung spirometry or grip strength, are also good predictors of mortality and good candidate markers of biological age (Willcox B. et al. 2006).

3. The *Guinness Book of World Records* stated: "No single subject is more obscured by vanity, deceit, falsehood, and deliberate fraud than the extremes of human longevity" [*Guinness World Records* 2005]. Case in point, in the 1980s, the age of 114 years was the maximum age at death that had obtained a modicum of credibility by Guinness standards. In subsequent years, the first three people to be acknowledged by Guinness as having reached age 114 have all had their claims disputed.

4. In hindsight, it should come as no surprise that claims of exceptional longevity from societies with low average life expectancy that also lack longstanding age registration systems will be less credible than claims from areas where average life expectancy is long and a good birth registration system exists. An important example of why validation of age is critical to the study of EL comes from the United States, where record keeping is generally good for most aspects of public health. Despite generally high quality demographic data, the United States Social Security Administration possesses public death records for more than a hundred citizens that lists age at death between 160 and 190 years, none of them thoroughly validated (Alter 1990; Hill and Rosenwaike 2001). Distinguishing genuine supercentenarians from alleged supercentenarians requires thorough documentation of life events, rigorous proof of birth, and is a painstaking process. It has only been within the past century or so that most countries have had age registration systems for their citizens, and in many nations around the world they still lack good data, particularly for older citizens (Kannisto 1994).

5. One of the most comprehensive databases on oldest-old mortality is the Kannisto-Thatcher Oldest-Old Database within the Odense Archive of Population Data on Aging (Kannisto 1994). The database documents ages for most countries for the oldest-old (defined as ages eighty and above) beginning in the year 1950. Numerous demographic tests of the dataset have been carried out in order to assess the quality of international data on the oldest-old. From these various analyses Kannisto (1994) categorized countries into four categories according to the quality of their data: Good—Japan and nineteen European countries; Acceptable—Australia, New Zealand non-Maori, Portugal and Singapore Chinese populations; Conditionally Acceptable—Estonia, Ireland, Latvia, Poland and Spain; and Poor—Canada, Chile, New Zealand Maori and the United States.

6. In terms of measuring autonomy of centenarians elsewhere, Andersen-Ranberg et al. (2001) defined autonomy as living at home, being relatively ADL-independent and cognitively intact, and found 12 percent of Danish centenarians to be autonomous.

7. It was found that 24 percent of male subjects and 43 percent of female subjects fit the survivor profile; 44 percent of male and 42 percent of female subjects fit the delayer profile; and 32 percent of male and 15 percent of female centenarians belonged to the escaper profile.

8. It is speculated that these personality traits contribute to longevity through health-related behavior, stress reduction and adaptation to the challenges of aging (Masui, Gondo, Inagaki and Hirose 2006).

9. It is important to note the values given in this table are for a rapidly changing statistic, thus using data from the same year is vitally important (and difficult to get) as most countries do not have accurate year-to-year national data. With a doubling time of about ten years in the United States and close to five years in Japan, these numbers are likely close to half of present values. 2007 values for Okinawa list the centenarian ratio

for Okinawa as 58 per 100,000, compared to 25 per 100,000 for Japan as a whole (Japan Ministry of Health, Labour and Welfare 2007).

10. All studies using death certificate data are dependent on the quality of those data. The results of the above analysis thus depend upon the uniform reporting of the causes of death and coding of death certificates in different countries. Secular changes in diagnostic, reporting and coding practices could influence some of the trends reported. Quality of information depends in turn upon the extent to which the person had been examined prior to death, the physicians' knowledge of the disease history of the deceased and on whether or not an autopsy was performed. Hasuo et al. (1989) maintain that differences in cerebrovascular mortality between Japan and the United States have been confirmed by many specialized studies in which no marked differences in accuracy of diagnosis with regards to stroke were found.

11. By contrast, the high level of income disparity in the United States results in differential (better) care for the wealthy and leaves the less fortunate with limited, if any, access to medical care (Weinick, Byron and Bierman 2005). These discrepancies in the United States are thought to be contributing to the significant differences in life expectancy by ethnicity (Banks, Marmot, Oldfield and Smith 2006). For example, a white male born in 2003 has an average life expectancy of about seventy-five years, compared with sixty-nine years for a black male born in the same year (United States Census Bureau 2007).

12. In the past, pork was generally reserved for ceremonial occasions and not eaten daily. Some credit Chinese influences on pig domestication gained through a tributary relationship with the old Ryukyu Kingdom beginning in the fourteenth century. But the fact that wild boars are indigenous to the islands casts doubt that pork was a recent addition to the Okinawan diet (Willcox B. et al. 2004).

13. Particularly hormone-dependent cancers, such as breast and prostate cancer, as well as stomach cancer (Willcox, Willcox and Suzuki 2001).

14. The ADL scale rates a subject's ability to perform basic daily tasks such as dressing, toileting and range of movement, among others.

15. A similar study comparing the range of mobility of Okinawan elders to elderly in rural and urban Alabama showed that Okinawan elderly had significantly better walking speed, and greater range of mobility than age-matched Alabamians (Schell et al. 2005).

16. The other important major phytoestrogens are lignans, which are derived from flax and other grains. All plants, especially legumes (beans, peas), onions and broccoli, contain these natural estrogens, but not nearly in the same quantity as soy and flax.

17. It is noteworthy that although women outlive men in all postindustrial countries with an average six more years of life expectancy, the gap in Okinawa is particularly great at 8.37 years in 2000 (compared with Japan's 6.91 years). In addition, Okinawa has the highest ratio of female centenarians to male centenarians in Japan, with 9.56 women for each man. The reason for this huge gap is that men have double the mortality rate from cancer, heart disease, stroke and pneumonia, and more than four times the mortality from suicide and accidents. Aside from possible biological factors for this difference, women in Okinawa also have a much lower rate of risk-taking behaviors such as, smoking, alcohol consumption, accidents and suicide (Willcox, Willcox, Sokolovsky et al. 2007; Willcox D. 2005).

18. The Honolulu Heart Program (formally the Honolulu branch of the Ni-Hon-San study), has become one of the longest-running prospective studies with over forty years of consistent follow-up on the same cohort of Japanese-American men. Although it began as a study on cardiovascular disease in 1965, the focus has gradually shifted

toward aging, as members of the cohort are now in their eighties or nineties or are over 100 (see Honolulu Asia Aging Study at www.kuakini.org). The study has been collecting data on genetics, blood biochemistry, medical history, diet, smoking, alcohol consumption, BMI, sociodemographic and psychological factors, among other characteristics, and has been the source for many scientific breakthroughs, including the effects of genes and lifestyle on longevity and various diseases (Willcox et al. 2004).

19. This is not surprising when one considers that three-quarters of Americans are overweight, with one-third being obese, and far too many people still smoke while far too few exercise regularly.

20. While some effects appear partly mediated by reduction of fat mass, multiple mechanisms have been proposed. Mechanisms include altered insulin signaling (better insulin sensitivity), reduced free radical damage (less damage to vital cells, tissues and DNA from unstable molecules) and hormesis (systemic beneficial reaction to a mild stressor), among others (Bordone and Guarente 2005, Rattan 2005; Kenyon 2005; Willcox B. et al. 2007). For example, lab-induced CR in mice extends lifespan up to 60 percent and makes these animals more active and more youthful appearing than non-CR mice (Masoro 2005). CR seems to work on a systematic level, and it is likely that various factors work together through multiple biological pathways to create the reported extreme increase in healthy longevity and functionality.

21. Further epidemiological evidence that suggests that CR is effective in humans comes from the Honolulu Heart Program cohort and other human populations (Fontana, Meyer, Klein and Holloszy 2004; Willcox B. et al. 2004; Willcox, Willcox, Todoriki et al. 2006).

22. Longevity is a very complex trait that is due to numerous factors, including non-biological factors, yet studies of this trait in siblings of long-lived persons in Utah who reached their mid nineties (age ninety-five for men and ninety-seven for women), showed the relative risk of recurrence ($_s$) was 2.30 (95 percent CI 2.08–2.56; Kerber, O'Brien, Smith and Cawthon 2001). The sibling relative risk for "centenarianism" (more difficult to achieve than living to age of mid nineties) in Okinawa is 6.5, which suggests that genetic factors are particularly important for achieving exceptional old age in Okinawa as well (Willcox et al. 2006).

23. As for inheritance of genetic variations that slow the basic rate of aging and/or minimize risk for life-shortening diseases, such as coronary heart disease or certain cancers ("longevity-enabling genes"), few such variants have been found, and when found they are usually not reproducible in multiple ethnic groups (Christensen, Johnson and Vaupel 2006). Centenarian studies, however, are promising populations to search for such gene variants since they are more likely to be enriched with protective variants (or to lack deleterious variants) because those less genetically fortunate are more likely to have died. Evidence for this healthy aging phenotype has been found in several studies including the OCS and NECS (New England Centenarian Study). The majority of centenarians in both the OCS and NECS appear to delay the onset of major chronic diseases until past eighty years of age (Evert, Lawler, Bogan and Perls 2003; Willcox et al. 2004; Willcox B. et al. 2007), and some candidate genes have been offered as potential contributors to this healthy-aging phenomenon. Some of the most promising candidate genes appear to be those involved in regulatory pathways such as immunoinflammatory response, stress resistance or cardiovascular function. Although gene variants with large beneficial effects have been suggested to exist, only APOE, an important regulator of lipoproteins, has been consistently associated with a longer human lifespan across numerous populations, although numerous other candidate genes show promise (Melzer, Hurst and Frayling 2007).

24. Measurements of disability-free or disability-adjusted life expectancy are still in their infancy and differ between countries. One commonly used scale from the Japan Ministry of Health, Labour and Welfare calculates disability-free life expectancy through calculating the term that one remains "self-reliant," that is, without the need for long-term nursing care (*kaigo*). The need for care or support in activities for daily living such as bathing, going to the toilet, dressing, standing, etc. is assessed at five levels ranging from "independent" to "bed-ridden."

CHAPTER 39

Eldertopia: A Vision for Old Age in a New World

William Thomas

Our longevity is both ancient and a vital contemporary presence. Human elderhood was created, protected, sustained and nurtured because it serves vital human interests. It can continue to do so if we understand it properly and provide for its continued development. We are increasingly faced with the consequences of a cruel hoax that defines old age exclusively as a useless appendage that has unfairly attached itself to our society. Public figures rage at the vast expense associated with our growing longevity but remain blind to the virtues and advantages that are also associated with aging.

Popular culture offers little or nothing that can lead us toward a deep understanding of elders and elderhood. Instead, we are tutored, day and night in the virtues of youthful vigor. Advocates for the aged work toward a society where the aged are given protection and respect equal to that accorded to the young, forgetting that the virtue of elderhood lies in how stunningly different from adulthood it is. Those who would dismiss elderhood might as well also surrender the gifts of fire-making and the idea of the wheel. Our longevity is a gift greater than either of these, it is the invention that made all other inventions possible.

Human society is a complex web of relationships that can be summarized in the form of a diagram (see Figure 39.1). The intergenerational transmission of energy, love, protection, wisdom and resources has powered human cultural advancement for tens of thousands of years. It has shaped us, served us, blunted our worst tendencies, and magnified our best. Given the terrible might of modern industrial society it would seem that we need it more than ever before. Instead, we are bombarded by claims that old age is irrelevant and possibly on the edge of its own extinction (given sufficient progress in pharmaceutical laboratories). There are many who seek refuge in treasured illusions about traditional aging. In truth, the old way of growing old was never as good as we like to remember it being and is especially ill-suited to the society in which we

Figure 39.1
A Lifespan Model of Human Society

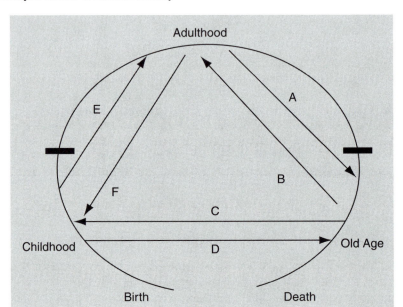

Source: Reprinted with permission from the AARP Global Aging Program, *Perspectives*, 2005. Courtesy of William Thomas.
A. Support provided to elders by adults; B. Assistance elders give to adults; C. Gentling and acculturation of children by elders; D. Assistance and affection given to elders by children; E. Participation in work of adults by children; F. Food, shelter, clothing and affection provided to children by adults.

live today. We really have no choice but to look ahead. The times demand that we create a new elderhood, one that fits the way we live now. We need this new elderhood not only for ourselves (we all deserve a better, richer, more meaningful old age) but for people of all ages.

Time is of the essence if we want to create a new elderhood for this century. Powerful forces increasingly define old age as a luxury our societies can no longer afford. Given the sums involved and the potentially devastating consequences of mismanagement, there are reasons to be concerned. What is missing from the debate, however, is a proper accounting of what elderhood can contribute to society. This side of the ledger is given scant attention by those who can see only the wealth and vigor of adults and the potentially ruinous burden imposed by the aged. What we need is a holistic perspective that appreciates and respects the contributions that people of all ages have made and are now making to the pursuit of happiness and our collective well-being. It should not come as a surprise that the English language lacks a word that describes the interdependence that joins young and old. Instead, we have "entitlements" and "cross-generational wealth transfers." The wisdom of living in a multi-generational social structure is ancient, undeniable and deserving of a word of its own. I coined the term "Eldertopia" in an effort to fill that void.

Eldertopia / ell-der-TOE-pee-uh / noun: A community that improves the quality of life for people of all ages by strengthening and improving the means by which the community protects, sustains, and nurtures its elders, and the elders contribute to the well-being and foresight of the community. An Eldertopia that is blessed with a large number of older people is acknowledged to be "elder-rich" and uses this richness to the advantage of all.

The concept of "eldertopia" is useful because it helps us illuminate the flaws inherent in the accounting systems of the "old age welfare state." Conventional practice tabulates the money spent serving the elderly to the penny even as it ignores the vital contributions that our longevity makes to society as a whole. We need a new and much more realistic set of books. Fortunately, Eldertopia can lead us to a deeper and far more accurate understanding of how longevity completes us. For a start, it can illuminate the complex and easily overlooked non-monetary intergenerational transfers that are essential to people of all ages. Becoming more conscious of the contributions that elders make to the young is a good first step. Fully developed, this more balanced approach can document in black and white why our longevity is a solid investment. Elders and elderhood are, in fact, the best investment that human beings have ever made.

NOTE

Reproduced with permission from the AARP Global Aging Program, *Perspectives*, 2005.

CHAPTER 40

La Cura Degli Nostri Cari Anziani: Family and Community Elder Care Roles in Contemporary Italy

Joan Weibel-Orlando

Yah wanna know why my mother tried to have me whacked?
Because I put her in a nursing home!
> Tony Soprano disclosing to his psychiatrist the dysfunctional
> depth of his relationship with his mother; *The Sopranos,* Episode 66

Although an obvious exaggeration (for comedic effect), of the contemporary Italo-American dictum regarding the culturally appropriate way to care for one's elderly parents, the Soprano matriarch's murderous reaction to having been involuntarily trundled off to a nursing home by her well meaning, but culturally insensitive, mobster boss son clearly underscores an enduring Italian cultural axiom. Care of the frail elderly should not be left to strangers or nonprofessionals.

For Italians, the locus of elder care should be the home and family. To care for elderly family members in any other manner would be *una vergogna* (a shameful act). And although few Italian and Italian American mothers would feel justified putting out a contract on their less than culturally exemplary and nurturing children, there certainly are emotional costs for not sufficiently revering and caring for one's parents in their frail old age. However, with very low fertility rates coupled with exceptionally high longevity of life, fewer multigenerational households and rising residential mobility; it is increasingly difficult for Italian families to adhere to long-established cultural rules regarding elder care. This chapter explores the ingenious strategies by which contemporary Italians manage to care for their frail elderly in culturally acceptable ways despite demographic, economic and geographic factors that mitigate against traditional forms of sustaining the elder generation.

Since 1992 I have conducted ethnographic research on social change and adaptation in the val di Bisenzio, an area in north central Tuscany. The val di

Bisenzio is about an hour's drive northwest of Tuscany's great cultural hub, Florence, and a half hour's drive north of Prato, one of the region's major industrial centers. The valley is flanked by ridges of the Apennine mountain range that divides Tuscany into eastern and western halves. Cavarzano, a rural village situated on a mountain ridge 2,000 feet above and to the west of the valley, is the birthplace and current residence of most of "the beloved elders" or *i cari anziani* described in this chapter.

TRADITIONAL ELDER CARE IN RURAL TUSCANY

Continuing home care for elderly parents was an organic process in nineteenth century rural and agricultural Italy. Farming families were large, often worked their rented lands as a work unit, and thereby shared the product of their collective labors with their *padroni* (landlords) and among themselves. Historically, as Kertzer has shown, Italian agriculture-based families exhibited periods of expansion and retraction (1984). Often, three generations of families shared one large farmhouse provided by their landlords on the lands they farmed (Kertzer and Saller 1991; Della Pina 1986). Occasionally, daughters or sons would marry and move out of the family household and into the homes of their new marriage partners.

Traditionally, however, at least one adult child remained in the household with the aging parents. Sometimes it was, the "sacrificial child"–that person who never married but was designated as the one child who would always remain at home to assist and, eventually, care for their aging parents.[1] Other times, the person who remained in the family household was the son designated to take over the leasehold relationship with the landowner when the parents become too frail or incapacitated to continue to perform the contractual agricultural chores. It was rarely the case that no member of a family could be found to care for its members in their frail old age.

As the oldest members of a household aged, they would move seamlessly from the heaviest farm labors (plowing, harvesting, wood cutting) to less strenuous agricultural activities (planting, preserving, shepherding and barn yard animal care; Kertzer 1984). People would continue to participate in farming activities and contribute to the corporate family enterprise in some capacity well into their eighties and nineties as their physical strength and remaining sight allowed them to do so. Since *case di reposo* (retirement homes) were almost nonexistent in Italy until the 1970s, care of the frail elderly was, out of necessity, a family affair.

This cultural dictum was as pertinent to families in Italy as it was to immigrant Italian American families. In her book, *Growing Up and Growing Old in Italian-American Families*, Colleen Johnson tells us that, traditionally, the care of the elderly has been an Italian family responsibility (1985:179). Having grown up in a Tuscan American family, my clearest model is the care my mother, her sisters and their younger brother, Albert, gave their parents in the last years of their lives. It was assumed that "the old folks" would remain at home until their death. Both *Nonno* (grandfather) and *Nonna* (grandmother) vigorously rejected any thought of going to the Danbury Hospital for "the proper care" as, in their last years, their medical needs became increasingly profound. "I want to die in my own bed," they both vehemently proclaimed. And their children, out of filial respect, exhausted themselves in their attempts to honor their parents' wishes. As their parents' health deteriorated, the five Piacenti adult children negotiated a cooperative schedule of care.[2]

I [Teresa] was working full-time at the time. But I was there every night. Marion [her younger sister] used to go down and help out a couple of times a week during the day. And Tosca [the speaker's oldest sister] was there every day. Finally Tosca said to me, "I can't do this any more. You're going to have to retire and take care of Mom." So I retired. Then your mother came down and helped out at the end. Everyone helped. Marion used to go down and cook. Albert [the speaker's younger brother] took care of Pa in the last two weeks when Pa was dying. He took time from work to do that. (Teresa Piacenti Migone, in an interview, June 22, 1991)

I asked my Aunt Teresa if she and her siblings had thought about putting their parents in a nursing home.

I did [she candidly admitted]. Toward the end I did. Because I was up day and night. And I told the doctor, "You know, I can't keep this up. I'm getting sick." I told your mother, "I think we're going to have to put her in a nursing home. I can't keep it up." [Your mother said,] "They wouldn't take care of her like you do. The minute she wets, you change her. They don't do that in a nursing home. So your mother suggested that she come down and stay with her nights and I would stay with her days. So that's how we worked it out." (In an interview, June 22, 1991)

In assuming these exhausting responsibilities, the second generation Tuscan American Piacenti children conformed to the highest standards of Italian filial duty. They, alone, cared for their parents into their last days. Only as my maternal grandparents became bedridden did Aunt Teresa, who had been living with them in "the big house" for years before their final illnesses, begin to take over the managerial reins of the household from her parents.[3] The semblance of independent living that Johnson (1985:156) says is so vital to the continuing sense of personal integrity of the elderly Italian Americans she interviewed was maintained by my mother and her siblings almost until the end of their parents' lives.

In 2006, it had been a century since the Piacenti family immigrated to the United States from the val di Bisenzio in rural, northwestern Tuscany. In 1906, this region was still largely an agrarian society. World War II, postwar reconstruction, and the industrialization of the area's textile manufacturing would radically change the economic base as well as social organization of the area. While a few farmers and landowners would continue their work contract relationships through the 1950s, the *contadino* or *mezzadria* system was essentially an anachronism by the 1960s (Santoni 1993). Rather, locals found well-paying, permanent work in the large textile mills in Prato, a city just twenty minutes by train northwest of Florence and directly south of the val di Bisenzio (Marchi 1982; di Martelli and Santoni 1997).

By the 1970s many locals also had purchased new, modern homes and apartments in and around Prato. The purchase of a town home greatly reduced their daily work commute. Families, by the hundreds, shuttered up their ancestral mountain village homesteads and moved down and into the river valley towns and cities (di Martelli and Santoni 1997:269-286). The population of the city of Prato doubled between 1950 and 1970 (Comune di Prato 1989:22).

The people who moved to urban centers continued to use their rural family homesteads as weekend and summer vacation second homes, rented them out or allowed older and/or retired family members who wished to remain in their small mountain village birthplaces to live in the vacated family homesteads during the owners' absences. Consequently, the populations of the rural towns in the val di Bisenzio dropped substantially between 1950 and 1980 (Comune di Vernio 1991).

After World War II, two other population demographic factors of the val di Bisenzio (as throughout most of contemporary Italy) changed significantly. The large, three-generation deep, corporate farming family became another anachronism. With each post-World War II generation the Italian family household configuration has decreased in size and generational depth. Italy's birth rate (1.23 children per woman) is among the lowest in the Western world, (Smith 2003) and far below the average of 2.3 children needed to keep a total population stable.

Since the 1980s, Italian couples have rarely had more than one child. Fewer children per household is coupled with a general aging of the existing Italian population. An excellent national health care system, a healthy diet and an active lifestyle have resulted in producing Italy's extremely fit population. Italians, especially Italian women, are living longer and are healthier than ever, with an average life-expectancy of 79.86 in 2005. As noted by Sokolovsky in Part I, Italy, in 2007, had 20 percent of its populace over age sixty-five and was only surpassed in this regard by Japan. Italy's current population distribution by age resembles an inverted pyramid which set the stage for becoming the globe's first nation, in 2000, to have more persons over age sixty than under age twenty. If Italians continue to value and attempt to honor the traditional cultural tenet regarding the care of frail elderly, there will be many fewer children and/or grandchildren to take on the responsibility for the in-home care of the increasing numbers of elderly parents.

The Italian dictum that children become the caretakers in their parents' old age is confounded by a second, more recently evolved, cultural dictum. The house and the kitchen have always been the Italian woman's social domains (Johnson 1985:43). A woman's personal power is expressed in the administration of her household. Having one's own house and kitchen and *not* sharing its administration with one's mother or mother-in-law is currently a cultural ideal. A second cultural ideal—the corporate, multi-generational, homestead-sharing family—has been supplanted by the privileging of personal autonomy, remaining in charge of one's own home and not turning over one's hearth authority for as long as possible. These autonomous statuses and roles provide the contemporary Italian woman with culturally valued personal agency and authority. The sharing or delegation of or removal from that valued social status can be viewed as major personal loss, even social death, by elderly Italian women.

CONTEMPORARY TUSCAN ELDERCARE STRATEGIES

Given the mixed and shifting cultural tenets with regard to successful aging, contemporary Tuscans have engineered a number of ingenious ways to both care for their elderly parents and to assure their *cari anziani*, a continuing sense of personal autonomy.

Letting Mom and Dad Stay in Their Own Home: Monitored Autonomy—The Leonettis

Elderly Tuscan *paesani* (village dwellers) are expected to live autonomously in their own homes for as long as possible. Gino and Ariana Leonetti, eighty-nine and eighty-eight respectively, in 1994, still lived alone in their family homestead across the courtyard from the house in which a younger (seventy-four in 1994) widowed cousin, her daughter-in-law and granddaughters lived. Daily, all three generations of these family members interacted with and assisted their elderly neighbors. The Leonettis' fifty-something son had moved from the family home years earlier to a valley home, six miles away. Their sixty-something son lived even further away. In the 1970s he and his wife had moved to Prato, a forty-five-minute drive south of their mountain top homestead.

Until their deaths in 1998, however, their valley-dwelling son drove up the mountain four or five times a week to visit with, but also, to tend to his parents' heavier household chores: chopping and carrying in firewood, doing the heavy garden work and performing house repairs. Their Prato-based son also routinely drove up to the village during the summer months and on weekends to visit and check on their conditions and needs. And there was always cousin Isora and her daughter-in-law and grandchildren across the courtyard, as well as dozens of other Leonetti and village residents, life-long neighbors and friends who "kept an eye on Gino and Ari" when the couple's sons were not there to do so. The elderly couple continued to live in familiar surroundings. Their social networks remained in place and accessible. The practice of their daily household activities continued as health and strength permitted. Adjustments in levels of housework responsibilities evolved organically as conditions dictated.

Three-Generation Household—The Storais

For the first twenty years of their marriage, Ernesto Storai, his wife and their only daughter had lived with his widowed mother in the mountain village homestead in which he was born. Until 2004, both Ernesto and Vittoria worked full time. His work commute was a relatively easy one—a twenty-minute drive down the mountain and along the Bisenzio River to the wool spinning factory in which he had worked since he was sixteen years old. Vittoria's commute had always been more arduous. An office manager for a textile manufacturer representative's agency, she commuted daily from their mountain village home. At first, her place of business was in Florence. Then, when the agency, in a belt-tightening move, vacated its pricey, Florence-based show rooms and reestablished their operation in more modest suburban commercial space, her daily commute became an hour or more one way, depending on traffic.

The Storai three-story, three-bedroom, mountain homestead is certainly large enough to accommodate three generations of the small family. For years, the young couple rationalized sharing the home with Ernesto's mother as an economic strategy—to save enough money to buy their own home—and a means of child care, as Nonna would always be home to care for their daughter while they worked. As the years passed and Gioia, their only child, matured and no longer needed, in fact rejected, her grandmother's monitoring of her after school activities, tensions among the three women in the home began to surface.

The Storai family's mountain home was clearly Nonna Lilliana's domain. Early on, Vittoria, exhausted from a full day's work and a two-hour roundtrip drive in heavy traffic, had been only too glad to have a home-cooked meal waiting for her at the end of her workday. As the years passed and no move to their own home seemed imminent, Vittoria began to yearn for the full autonomy of her own kitchen and privacy of her own *soggiorno* (living room, entertainment area). And, with her company's move to the relatively more isolated and distant work site, she could have shaved thirty minutes off her daily commute by relocating to a home in the valley below. Vittoria, clearly, was invested in acquiring her family's own home in the valley.

In contrast, Ernesto loved his birth home and mountain village life. An avid hunter, gardener and contributor to the village's social life, Ernesto thoroughly enjoyed and looked forward to participating in the community's ongoing weekly, seasonal and annual activities. And, since his father had died in 1973, he was the only son and his two sisters had moved to homes in the valley and Prato after their marriages, his familial duty was clear. Impelled by the cultural rule that at least one child must assume the care of aging parents, Ernesto was the logical one of the three Storai siblings to stay at home and care for his mother. For personal, as well as cultural reasons, Ernesto was, in fact, reluctant to move away from both his home town and his mother. For years he walked a fine line between assuring his mother that he would always be there for her and convincing his wife and daughter that they, shortly and indeed, would be moving to their own dream condominium in the valley. In fact, they purchased a lovely, state-of-the-art, three-bedroom condominium in the valley in 1998. For years, however, it remained uninhabited as Ernesto and his family customized the unit to their tastes and needs.

Throughout a four-year transition period, one element of the establishment of a new Storai household was constant. Although the new condominium had three bedrooms and could accommodate her presence, Lilliana (at her own insistence) was not about to move there. When I asked her about the possibility of her leaving her village home, Lilliana could not have been more adamant: "No, I will stay here. This is my home. My life is here." She was eighty-four, under a doctor's care for high blood pressure and cholesterol levels, and suffered from varicose veins and circulatory failure when she shared those feelings with me. Though at the time she was fully able to carry out her various household chores, she clearly and already needed other family members to assist her with the more arduous household maintenance tasks.

In 2002, Ernesto, Vittoria and Gioia finally moved into their valley home. However, all members of the family and even his fellow villagers agree that "Ernesto never really left the village." He seems to spend as much time in the village (and at or in the vicinity of his mother's home) as he does at his lovely, new valley condo. Daily, he drives the winding, five-kilometer road from the valley floor to the mountain village to feed his hunting dogs, check out the family gardens, enjoy the lunch or supper his mother fixes for him when he visits, go to community organization (*Pro Loco*) planning meetings, have a "coffee" at one of the town's two bars and, generally, keep a watchful eye on his community and mother.[4] At times, when his wife and daughter go to the seashore with friends and/or family to visit his wife's family for a weekend, or if he has some early morning village activity the following day (a wild boar-hunting excursion, for example), Ernesto will spend the night at his mother's home. With his retirement in 2004 and his mother's declining health, Ernesto and his two sisters found themselves driving up the mountain to "check on mamma" with increasing frequency. Of course, there are the life-long neighbors on either side of Lilliana's home as well as across the narrow and separating walkway. Daily, one or more neighbor will knock, utter a polite "*permesso?*" (a request for permission to enter a home) and then open her usually unlocked front door and enter her kitchen. At face value, the purpose of these visits seems to be to chat and perhaps to take the offered cup of coffee. In reality, and since Lilliana had had a nearly fatal fall in 2003, the casual visits are initiated, chiefly, to ensure that Lilliana is not in need of medical attention.

In February 2006, Lilliana, eighty-seven, frail and suffering from a torturous case of herpes zoster (shingles), was still living in her own home, sleeping in her own bed, fixing her own meals (and, occasionally a Sunday meal for her attentive children) and by all appearances in control of her own living situation. The care her children provided Lilliana in her old age epitomizes the Italian model of optimal exercise of family duty and responsibility toward its aging members. Her children could afford, but refused to turn the care of their mother over to professionals and they, collectively, shared monitoring her health and living conditions, acceded to her wishes for personal autonomy and accommodated their activities to allow her a sense of being "in charge of her own home and life." Yet, through frequent calls to and visits with Lilliana and reliance upon her village neighbors to "keep an eye on Mamma," they allayed their own fears that they would not be available when she really needed their assistance, and epitomized the culturally correct Italian family response to the aging of *i nostri cari anziani*.[5]

Time-Sharing Elder Care—The Torellis' *Vagabonda* Nonna

Elderly Agata Torelli had been renting out her ancestral village home for some years when I first met her and her family in 1992. Then eighty-five, over-weight and diabetic, her legs were swathed in ace bandages meant to contain the edema that usually swelled her calves to twice their normal size. As she had had no place of her own in which to live for some time, in the summer, she lived with her daughter, Patrizia, in the mountain village apartment below my rental unit. Their animated, nonstop, sunrise-to-noon conversations woke me most mornings. Every clear day, Agata and her daughter would sit out on Patrizia's terrace and shuck beans, knit, hang out clothes, greet friends and gab.

In September, my local alarm clock, the crackle of Agata and Patrizia's early morning *chiacchierate* (gab fest), abruptly ceased. When I inquired as to the possibility of Agata being under the weather, her daughter laughingly dis-missed my concerns. Agata, I was told, had packed her bags, said her goodbyes and gone off for the season to la Maremma in southern Tuscany, where her other daughter lives as, "It's always warmer there than in the mountains in winter time." Patrizia explained her mother's *vagabonda* (migratory or gypsy-like) lifestyle as "visiting family," rather than being cyclically in the care of her dispersed children. As children of elderly Italians have dispersed beyond the limits of easy and continuous physical monitoring of their elderly parents, certain accommodations have developed to maintain in-home care of the el-derly and to ensure an equitable sharing of the burden of that care by all of the children. The seasonal migration of Agata Torelli is an example of such an ad-aptation. Over each year, Agata migrated from one of three children's homes throughout Tuscany as the weather and her inclination to go elsewhere moved her. Her children were careful to have it appear as if the length of a stay in any one their homes was her decision to make. Her sense of personal agency was exquisitely preserved until the end.[6]

Caring for the Elderly Who Have No Family: Zita Borelli and *Il Paese* (the Village Community)

Among the worst circumstances of life for even contemporary Italians is that, by having lived into one's nineties, one faces the possibility of out-living all close relatives and friends. There is the correlate fear of being alone in frail old age for those who never had close and enduring family relationships. Being alone and without family support in late life is thought to be a terrible fate. Italians endeavor continuously throughout their lives to build extrafamilial relationships with their aged cohorts, community members and even members of younger generations. This is to ward off isolation and ensure some recognition of themselves as social beings and community members in late life.

What happens to individuals who are: (1) childless; (2) so elderly that their children's deaths have preceded theirs; or (3) so elderly that their siblings too (if they had had any) are deceased? Zita Borelli, fiercely independent, self-supporting and multiskilled, had never married. Both of her brothers had died in the late 1990s. By 1999, she was without close family members in her village. She, however, steadfastly refused professional in-home care and resolutely carried on her daily chores as she had all her long life.

In 2004, Zita had turned ninety-five. Since 1999, her birthday has been the catalyst for a village-wide celebration. Annually, she is venerated for being the village's oldest resident. Her health and continued safety has become the concern and responsibility of the entire village. Her neighbors regularly check her whereabouts by knocking on the door of her tiny house on the piazza whenever Zita swerves from her well-known daily round of activities. A respectful but shouted *"permesso"* (in 2004 Zita was very hard of hearing) before entering her home is calculated to ensure she is still among the living, if off her usual routine. Also nearly blind and unsteady on her feet, her neighbors make it their responsibility to offer her rides to the valley for visits to doctors, trips to the pharmacy, hair salon appointments or grocery shopping. The villagers view their efforts not as charity, but as ways in which they can preserve, protect and prolong the life of a village treasure and *la nostra cara anziana* (our beloved old one).

Professional Help in the Home: *La Badante* (Home Caretaker)

Cristina Pieratti was seventy-six years old when a massive stroke irreparably changed her quality of life. Up to that point, she had been the self-sufficient head of her household and a respected, active member of her community. In her middle age, she had, in turn and in her home, cared for her elderly mother, husband and invalid brother-in-law before their deaths. Two years after Cristina's stroke she could speak short sentences and walked only with great difficulty. Increasingly forgetful, she appeared to be slipping into senile dementia. In 2004, however, she was still living in her own home with her two oldest granddaughters.

Cristina is not without family resources. Her oldest daughter, Ciara, lives in the same mountain village. She, however, was fully occupied caring for an ailing husband at the time of her mother's stroke. Cristina's second child, Andrea, lives with his wife and two children, forty minutes away in their Prato condominium. Her third child, Desdemona, and her husband, Renzo, live forty-five minutes away in a suburb of Florence where Renzo works. Cristina's youngest child, Franco, lives with his wife and their child about forty-five minutes north of his mother's mountain village home. Franco's wife has a two-hour daily commute to her office in Bologna. Franco's work commute into Prato takes at least as much time every day. All four of Cristina's children's personal schedules, clearly, leave little time for elder care.

However, Cristina's two high school- and college-aged granddaughters had been living with her for years. They were her initial post-trauma caretakers. In 2003, her gradual descent into dementia and increasingly irrational and impulsive behavior were beginning to overwhelm them. By 2004, it was clear that the young and untrained women were no longer able to care for their grandmother and continue to attend their high school and university classes, earn a living and enjoy a modicum of social life. Cristina's distant and overly committed children could only do so much. Their modest homes and city apartments could not accommodate another person and, especially, not a physically challenged elderly woman.

With growing family, community and medical input and concern, a family counsel was held in mid 2005. The Pieratti children immediately determined that a nursing home was out of the question. Even in 2005, few could be found in the area. Those in place are very costly, have long waiting lists and are still felt to be culturally inappropriate and only to be considered as a last resort elder care solution. The Pieratti family felt compelled to put another elder care strategy in place.

Una badante, literally, is a housekeeper or caretaker who also specializes in the in-home care of the elderly. These elder care workers began to appear in major numbers in Prato and the Val di Bisenzio around 2000. *Badante* are usually women between twenty-five and forty years of age who live in the homes of their aged clients and attend to their personal needs. Preparing meals, feeding the patient when necessary, cleaning house, administering medications, bathing, dressing and grooming the patient are among the responsibilities of *una badante*. Currently, a majority of the women hired as *badante* in the Prato area are from Eastern Europe (Poland, Czechoslovakia, Romania) and Africa (South Africa, Ivory Coast, Nigeria).

The Pieratti family agreed that the soft-spoken, affectionately demonstrative, middle-aged applicant from Romania seemed the best suited of the three women they interviewed to live with and care for their aging mother. *La badante*, Monica, had been Cristina's constant companion for five months when I met her in February 2006. All family members, including Cristina, agreed that Monica was "the best thing that had happened to their mother since her stroke, and that she was the answer to their collective prayers."

Hiring *una badante* for a failing family member is an elder care strategy of last resort for only the privileged few. Of the four instances of such services in my ancestral *paese* of which I am aware, three of the *badante* were hired to care for the parents of working professionals who could afford such dedicated elder care. Only because all four of Cristina's adult children agreed to share the costs of the service could the Pieratti family manage to hire *una badante* to care for their mother.

Employing *una badante* appeals to Italian families who can afford it because it resolves a number of logistical and cultural dissonances. It allows the family to adhere to the cultural rule of in-home care of elderly parents without the custodial family members having to significantly alter their current lifestyles.

Secondly, hiring *una badante* releases the care-providing family members from the culturally induced personal guilt associated with, and social shame of, being identified as having warehoused their *cari anziani*—placing them in a nursing home. With the hiring of *una badante*, the aging parent can remain, as well as sustain, a sense of agency over one's personal space.

ELDER CARE AND TWENTY-FIRST-CENTURY ITALY

> I don't care how close you are. In the end your friends are gonna let you down. Family—they're the only ones you can depend on.
>
> Tony Soprano lecturing a family member on the
> locus of trust; *The Sopranos*, Episode 66

Tony Soprano as a cultural sage? Some readers, I feel sure, will question my valorizing, through academic reference, to such popular culture pronouncements. The genius of *The Sopranos*, to my mind, is the ability of its writing staff to appreciate and capture core Italian American values, exaggerate their expression and ability to influence dramatic behavior and, by doing so, create great, seriocomedic and ironic theater that, in important ways, reflects actual cultural attitudes at once contemporary as well as anachronistic.

Contemporarily, Italians still adhere to the long-held cultural tenet that elder care is best entrusted to other family members. To delegate that care to nonfamily members needs justification. I have been privy to a few conversations in which younger Italian family members, both in Tuscany as well as in the United States, self-consciously offered elaborate and emotional defenses of their decisions to place elderly parents in a nursing home or hospice *(casa di cura)*, when their in-home, end-of-life care experience had overwhelmed the caretakers. Cultural values are tenacious. Their adherents continue to be influenced and their actions shaped by collective notions of culturally acceptable behavior long after the social and economic rationales for such actions have shifted. Yet, with many more living into frail old age, and many fewer births per family in Italy, the pool from which possible family caretakers can be found will dramatically contract in succeeding generations. An "only child" born after 1970 can look forward to being the sole in-family caretaker option for their aging parents. How this family structure dynamic will impact individual careers, lifestyles and decisions about marriage, parenthood and personal mobility is yet to be determined. In the end, Tony Soprano's too-easily voiced cultural pronouncement—"only family can be trusted to serve"—may be the ultimate anachronism.

Based on current reportage, the Italian national government, though aware and concerned about the social, economic and ethnic consequences of its increasingly lopsided population profile, has yet to adequately address the future public health needs of its growing numbers of elders. Concerned with its falling birth rate, the Italian government has attempted to find ways to increase the future pool of traditionally acceptable persons for elder care. In 2003, Italy began offering one-child families gifts of approximately USD 1,300 at the birth of a second child (BBC News October 2, 2003).

Few Italian couples have been persuaded to increase the size of their families by such a token sum. Parents of only-children argue that the costs of raising and educating a child in Italy in the twenty-first century are such that most couples can only afford the proper care of one child.

Concerned with the increasing costs of national social and medical service provisions for a growing number of robust citizens who had been able, in the recent past, to become *pensionati* (pensioners, retirees) as early as age forty-six, the Italian national government, in 2003, was considering raising the age at which Italians can retire and receive full pension and national benefits from sixty to sixty-five (BBC News August 25, 2003).[7] This plan was meant to slow the rise of national expenditures for pensions, elder social services, and health care provision. Italy, however, has been sliding into an economic downturn and suffering from the same sort of outsourcing of manufacturing jobs and spiraling unemployment rates as in other industrialized "first world" nations. The plan, to both keep highly-paid, skilled employees in the work force for at least five more years as well as create new positions for the young adults about to enter the national work force, seems not fully practicable (BBC News August 8, 2003).

With regard to elder care, Italy seems only beginning to consider it a national issue. Increasing numbers of retirement homes have been put in place in Italy (Carpenter et al. 1999; Francesconi et al. 2006). The costs of such professionalized care, however, are beyond the reach of most Italians. Additionally, placing a parent in a retirement village, nursing home or hospice is still thought of as a strategy of last resort. Most Italians probably would agree with my mother when she refused to consider putting her parents into a nursing home because only family members would provide adequate care for *i nostri cari parenti* (our beloved parents). Italians and their government leaders seem to have not yet come to terms with the fact that the Italian cultural staple, the family, may, in the near future, not be physically configured to do its filial duty.

Eternally creative, Italians now have to devise and activate other culturally appropriate and acceptable elder care social forms. Possible strategies may include cultural acceptance of an expansion of elder responsibility from the immediate to the extended family or beyond. Immediately, the efficacy of the village community (*paese*) as an elder care social structure comes to mind. Many of the smaller hill villages, as their younger members have gone off to school and employment in urban centers, already have become, by default, senior citizen communities. Comfortable and psychologically secure (as was Lilliana Storai) in their familiar surroundings, the provision of increased instrumental social and health elder care at the village level (while keeping the elderly in their ancestral homes among friends and neighbors) may be a culturally, psychologically and economically preferable elder care strategy. Still-robust retirees, some of whom may have received "on-the-job-training" when caring for their elderly parents, could be paid stipends, in addition to their pensions, to serve as caretakers for village neighbors no longer able to live fully autonomous lives but who wish to remain at home until the end of their days.

The same sort of neighborhood elder watch could be instituted in urban residences as well. A number of former mountain villagers, since the 1960s, have purchased multiple apartments in Prato and Florence. Middle-aged children often own apartments within the same *palazzi* or apartment building in which their aging parents also have an apartment. The children (and grandchildren) move seamlessly between same-building apartments sharing chores and easily monitoring their aging parents' and grandparents' activities and states of wellness. Separate, but proximal, living space in urban settings secure each family unit a measure of personal privacy and autonomy just as proximal housing in family-based village neighborhoods do in rural towns.

As the residents of urban apartment complexes who moved, sometimes in groups, from their villages to the city in the 1960s and 1970s age, their apartment buildings, again by default, may become retirement communities. In such urban residential situations, professional services needed to sustain life and to promote well-being could be administered in place and on a regular basis. The still-robust senior residents of the apartment complexes could, by cultural fiat, assume that they have the responsibility to look after and care for their apartment building neighbors while allowing for a continuing sense of personal autonomy for *i cari aniziani*.

NOTES

1. Andrei Simic', anthropology colleague, aging and ethnicity co-researcher and co-editor with Barbara Myerhoff of the book *Life's Career Aging: Cultural Variations on Growing Old*, used the term sacrificial child in a number of conversations with me regarding our work on "successful" aging strategies and differing levels of responsibility among siblings for elderly parent care.

2. The actual names and surnames of my grandparents and their children are used in this chapter as only Marion Piacenti Fantin (ninety-seven years of age in May 2006) of the first and second generation America-based Piacenti family was still alive at the writing of this chapter. As most Tuscans about whom I have written are still alive, their privacy has been protected through the use of pseudonyms.

3. My maternal grandparents immigrated to the United States in 1906 and settled in rural, southwestern Connecticut. In 1907, my grandfather bought his first home and parcel of farmland in America. By 1927, he had purchased a total of three houses and twenty-three acres of Connecticut farming acreage and woodlands. My grandparents lived in the largest of the three houses on their property until their deaths in 1967 and 1974. Only other family members ever lived in the other two houses in their farm complex. My parents, sister and I lived in the garage apartment next-door to "the big house" from 1941 until 1948 and until my dad had completed the building of, and we moved to, our own home in town.

4. Many communities of the *paese* throughout the val di Bisenzio have formed volunteer and residential committees organized to promote general well-being and a higher quality of life in their towns. Called *Pro Loco* groups, their members plan and collect funds to finance and carry out festivals, committee suppers, picnics and entertainments for their constituents.

5. On May 15, 2006, and as I was writing this chapter, the person called Lilliana Storai in this chapter passed away. She was almost eighty-eight and still living "alone" in her own home, but was, clearly, not unassisted when she died.

6. I learned when I returned to my ancestral Apennine village in 1994, that the person I have called Agata Torelli had passed away the previous year.

7. By 2003, the official retirement ages in Italy were sixty for women and sixty-five for men. In reality, the average age at retirement in 2003 was fifty-seven due to earlier legislation that had guaranteed retirement at fifty-seven years of age or after thirty years of employment (BBC News September 30, 2003). However, some people had started working as early as age sixteen during the 1960s. By 1990, people as young as age forty-six had the option to *andare en pensione*, or retire (BBC News September 30, 2003). Many did so, but then took on second careers as boredom or reduced incomes forced them to go back to work.

CHAPTER 41

Battling a New Epidemic: American Indian Elders and Diabetes

Linda Carson Henderson

CASE 1: WHAT IT'S LIKE TO BE A DIABETIC AND AN INDIAN

Jacob is a substance abuse counselor with a southeastern American Indian tribe in Oklahoma. He is an elder and more experienced than the other counselors, a veteran of the Vietnam War. More importantly, he is the acknowledged spiritual leader of his tribe. The sweat lodge is used extensively by Jacob to help those who want to free themselves from dependency and other ills of the spirit, and for those on spiritual quests. He has had diabetes for about five years. I interviewed Jacob in his home and asked him about his illness, attitudes toward medical directives and problems he and other Indian people have encountered in adhering to these directives.

There is no support from family to stay on the diet. Family support is ... they're killing each other. They won't be very good support. They want people to be happy and eating makes people happy ... so they feed them. Education is needed in lots of areas for the family.

(For example ...) there was a sweat at Mom's house over the weekend. It was a good sweat too, it was 102° in the lodge. There were fried foods, fry bread, all kinda cakes, watermelon. Big cookouts are always a big thing. If you went and there was just peas there, it wouldn't be right.

Most of, well, we all diabetic, now, me and my brothers and sisters, and we all eat. My mom (also a diabetic), they feed her whatever she wants ... makes her happy. One thing that's hard to do is change in life. I guess I just Indian (laughs).

Jacob's testimony begins to help us understand why among American Indians and Alaska Natives (AI/AN), diabetes constitutes a devastating epidemic of monumental proportions with unacceptable levels of excess disability and death (Indian Health Service 1999; Meneilly and Tessier 2001; Lieberman 2004; American Diabetes Association 2005). The diabetes mellitus prevalence rate ranges from 17 percent among northern plains American Indians to 80 percent in Alaska.[1] In comparison, the diabetes prevalence for the general U.S. population is 6.3 percent, for African Americans 11.4 percent, and for Latinos 8.2 percent. Additionally, the degree of severity of diabetes among AI/AN is higher than the general population. AI/AN diabetics are four times more likely than their white counterparts to experience an amputation as a consequence of diabetes and six times more likely to experience kidney failure (Roubideaux and Acton 2001; American Diabetes Association 2005; Ferreira and Lang 2006).

Paradoxically, in spite of today's advanced medical treatments, prevention and health promotion strategies, prevalence rates for diabetes mellitus among American Indians are persistent, excessive and rising. In the presence of potent drugs and health education information, diabetes prevalence should be abating. Since it is not, other factors accelerating rates of diabetes must be operating. Preliminary research suggests that one possible source for persistent and increasing diabetes prevalence is that nonobvious sociocultural factors are present that impede the productive application of existing therapeutic efforts. Few projects have addressed conflicting cross-cultural models of diabetes causation, prevention and treatment as a source of persistent excess disease burden. This omission is notable because divergent culturally constructed concepts of disease are known to impede care-seeking, communication and adherence (Kleinman 1980; Henderson 2002b; Henderson, Finke and McCabe 2004). Conditions such as diabetes are the grist for health communication barriers, defensive behaviors and treatment nonadherence, leading to patients and providers losing a sense of partnership in combating this complex disease. The research presented in this chapter examines the cultural construction of disease concepts in terms of their impact upon diabetes care-seeking, self-care and adherence.

CROSS-CULTURAL HEALTH COMMUNICATIONS

Cultural factors profoundly affect ways in which symptoms are identified and given meaning, how, when and to whom these symptoms are expressed, and whether an illness episode is ignored, stigmatized or accepted (Tripp-Reimer et al. 2001). The study of patient "explanatory models" provides information about how patients make sense of illness episodes, and how they choose and evaluate medical treatments (Kleinman 1980; Henderson 2002b; Henderson, Finke and McCabe 2004). These explanatory models are heavily influenced by the culture of the patient, which serves either to facilitate or impede health care-seeking and medical adherence.

Professional and lay explanations for disease, treatment and prevention can vary radically, and nonobvious sociocultural factors operating to impede effective health care may be found in the culturally based models of diabetes held by patients and practitioners. Explanatory models held by providers and patients may be similar, and in that case facilitate health communications with resulting increased adherence to treatment recommendations and sufficient patient/provider satisfaction. However, models that are *discordant* between practitioners and patients are prone to reduce effective health communications, reduce adherence to treatment recommendations and negatively impact health outcomes.

The research delineated in this chapter was preceded by two preliminary studies in the populations of AI diabetic elders and their health providers. The pilot study findings indicated that elder diabetics held varying explanatory models of diabetes, and that tribal providers also held divergent practice models, some highly discordant with those of the elders. These models, along with the cultural identification of both elders and providers, influenced care-seeking and diabetes self-care behaviors among the elders (Henderson 2002a). The research delineated here expands upon the initial pilot studies and elaborates on the varying models of diabetes and resultant care-seeking and adherence behavior within this population of AI elders. It underscores the differences between cultural constructions of disease by patient and provider and illustrates the importance of identifying personalistic and medically inconsistent models of disease within culturally diverse patient populations.

DIVERGENT MODELS OF DIABETES

In regard to diabetes research and the cultural construction of diabetes among AI, perhaps the most directly relevant is Goforth-Parker's study of AI diabetics in rural Oklahoma. Her research provided a vivid description of the life experience of patients with the disease and underscored cross-cultural differences in the diabetes experience in terms of sociocultural factors that negatively influence adherence (Goforth-Parker 1994). In another AI context, Ferreira explores the life of a Yurok elder and writes of the cultural construction of diabetes as the perceived result of neocolonialism and oppression (2006). The graphic depictions of traumatic experiences at the hands of colonial powers illustrate the power of life events and stress on the construction of illness narratives.

Many AI and other minority elders experience "multiple jeopardy." They are members of a minority group, are often poverty-stricken and are in poor health when compared to their counterparts in the general population (Henderson 2002b). When we speak of multiple jeopardy in terms of AI elders, the term in actuality encompasses much more than is contained in a strict definition of the phrase. When we look at these elders as the descendants of a long history of structural violence at the hands of colonizing nation-states, then we expand the multiple jeopardy conceptualization exponentially. Indigenous governments and scholars attribute structural violence, with its associated social and physical suffering, traumatic memory, community destruction and nutrition trauma, to dramatically higher chronic disease morbidity and mortality exceeding that of the mainstream population (Roubideaux and Acton 2001; Ferreira 2006; Korn and Ryser 2006). While health care for American Indians is an entitlement that previously was administered by the Bureau of Indian Affairs

(BIA), it should be noted that the BIA once fell under the auspices of the Secretary of War. Because studies of Indian health status showed such extensive morbidity and mortality, the Indian health program was transferred from the BIA to the Public Health Service in 1954 (Johnson and Rhoades 2000).

A study in a nonindigenous context identified divergent explanatory models of diabetes among patients and providers in a large Midwestern university diabetes clinic (Cohen et al. 1994).The study revealed differences between patient and provider explanatory models of diabetes in terms of etiology, pathophysiology and severity. Differences were significant, even though the patients and providers in the study all were highly educated and had similar backgrounds. Within populations in which patients and providers are not of similar backgrounds, it is likely that a much greater degree of incongruence would be noted.

CASE 2: EXPERIENCES OF STRUCTURAL VIOLENCE AND COLONIALISM

Betty is eighty-one years old, has diabetes, and like Jacob, is one of the "traditional" members of her tribe. I interviewed her in her home and asked her about her diabetes management, attitudes toward providers and past experience with health care under entitlement of her tribal membership. She related a history that was horrifying in terms of the rampant prejudice against AI people that existed at the time of the episode she relates (1940s).

She talks first about her personal history. This is customary in all social interactions with others, a give and take about one's "people."

My daddy had allotment lands,[2] but my mother sold them and moved into town. Granddaddy came over from Mississippi (he was a preacher) to see if Oklahoma would be a place to be. He settled at Bethany. There is a graveyard there that he designated that Indians and whites could be buried there. So it got all filled up and you have to go to Bentley to be buried now. The Indian meetings last a week at a time. There are pots of food, a roast pig or goat, and shelters made out of grass. My uncle was a school teacher and his white wife was a school teacher.

I have a fringed shawl. I used to dance at Bethany. I remember an old lady who could barely move, could get up and dance and not stop.

In regard to the provision of diabetes education, she relates:

I learned from my mother. I learned that you didn't have feeling in your feet real good. I knew what to do and what to watch for. And what not to do. I learned all of her knowledge about diabetes from taking care of my mother. I never go to the Indian clinic. Only to get my toenails trimmed. Sometimes the nurse comes here to do foot care. I still believe in some of the old-timey remedies, sassafras tea … some herbs I stay away from.

At this point, she starts to speak of past experiences with the medical system:

I went to get my tonsils out at Talihina (the location of an Indian Health Service hospital). I only got put part to sleep. The nurse came and got me. I stayed for two weeks to guard against bleeding. I also stayed at Talihina two weeks before having a baby. My first husband ran off; he was "noholo" (white man; literal translation: person without a soul). I had to stay one month due to complications. There was a German doctor who told me when I was in pain that horses and cows don't have anything for their pain so I got no anesthesia. I tore badly. He was an awful man. The same one who took out my tonsils.

I was in a room with five other women. The woman across from me was a large Indian lady, and she didn't speak to anybody. Then one day, I looked across and she was squatting on the bed and was about to have the baby. She said, "leave me alone, I'll have this baby by myself," but I called for the nurse and they took her off, bed and all, and she was hollering at them. Her people would bring her a glass of herbs for her to drink every day. I think that had something to do with it. She didn't cry out or anything. But my granddaddy said that Indian women don't make any noise when they're in pain.

THE CULTURAL CONSTRUCTION OF DIABETES IN AMERICAN INDIAN ELDERS: THE RESEARCH

In developing this research project, I hypothesized that there would be visible, diverse and unacknowledged models of diabetes within the population of AI elders. Various culturally constructed concepts and explanatory models of diabetes would be used by AI elder patients to respond to the disease, possibly as a function of acculturation status. Furthermore, if present, and unrecognized by health care providers, these culturally constructed concepts and attendant explanatory models could constitute a communication and behavioral barrier to optimal management of diabetes. Consequently, the research identified cultural models of diabetes within a population of AI elders as a function of acculturation status, and examined how differing cultural models of diabetes among these AI elders contributed to nonadherence and delays in health care-seeking behaviors.

The Elders

Interviews were conducted with thirty AI elders with Type 2 diabetes, in a large Oklahoma American Indian tribe. Type 2 is diagnosed most often in adulthood, and is due to insulin resistance, a consequence of weight gain and dietary changes, especially increased consumption of processed sugars. Type 1 is usually diagnosed in childhood and involves the absence of insulin production. It is a sad fact, however, that children are increasingly being diagnosed with Type 2 due to the rising rates of obesity among persons in all age groups.

In this study, an eligible subject was fifty-five years of age or older,[3] had a diagnosis of Type 2 diabetes, and was American Indian as evidenced by a Certificate of Degree of Indian Blood (CDIB).[4] In this research, a nonrandom intensity sample was used. Intensity samples are composed of those who are "experiential experts" and who are "authorities about a particular experience."

All were fluent in English, but many also spoke the tribal language. Observation indicated that the majority of the subjects were subsisting at poverty level, or slightly above. Some resided in "Indian houses" (tribally sponsored) on purchased land or original allotment lands, three lived in federal housing developments and others resided in privately built homes. Participants were contacted by either tribal Community Health Representatives (CHR),[5] physicians and other health care providers, and asked if they would consent to be interviewed for the study.

The Interviews

The semistructured interview included: (1) social history, (2) medical history (self-report), (3) care-seeking assessment, (4) adherence assessments, (5) explanatory model elicitation, (6) cultural identification assessment and (7) a contact summary form used to record interviewer impressions of the subject and the affective content of the interview. The interviews were conducted face-to-face and administered in the homes of the respondents, in the tribal hospital, tribal health care clinics and other places convenient for the subjects.[6]

Cultural Identification

Due to the high degree of cultural heterogeneity in this population of AI elders, the cultural identification of participants was elicited in order to validly assess the impact of this variable on the cultural construction of diabetes, as well as care-seeking and adherence behaviors. "Cultural identification" in this research refers to acculturation status in terms of identification with either traditional indigenous life ways or identification with white mainstream life ways.[7] Cultural identity domains were based upon a review of the literature, pilot study findings, researcher observations and very importantly, lived experience with members of the tribe.

Based on these factors, subjects were placed in either an "indigenous" or "mainstream" category.[8] Cultural identification questions addressed religious affiliations and beliefs, language used in the home, attendance at traditional American Indian functions, knowledge and use of traditional medicine, including sweat lodges, knowledge of folktales, wearing of traditional dress, consumption of traditional foods and participation in communal tribal sporting events. Additionally, homes of the subjects were observed for markers of traditionalism. These included such things as decorations and personal adornments, photographs of participants in traditional dance regalia, burning rocks used for spiritual ceremonies and the presence of sweat lodges on the subject's property.

RESULTS: THE MODELS

Two divergent culturally based models of diabetes were found among the elders. One model is designated the Indigenous Model and is characterized by strong valuing of cultural insularity. Behavior is consistent with valuing a strong traditional AI cultural identity reinforced through cultural membership, friendship and kinship networks. This sometimes was accompanied by derogatory remarks about the unwanted authoritarianism of the white mainstream including "white doctors" and their directives. The Indigenous Model thus is characterized by nonadherence to biomedical dietary guidelines, medication use, delays in care-seeking and a strong identification with the more traditional life ways of the tribe.

The other AI elder diabetic model is the Mainstream Model. While there is value placed upon AI cultural ties, this model is characterized by more pronounced identification with white mainstream culture. There is more acceptance of the biomedical model of diabetes as characterized by early care-seeking, greater adherence with dietary guidelines, greater adherence with medications and greater trust in health care providers.

Indigenous Model

Indigenous Model elders postponed care-seeking in the presence of recognizable symptoms, and demonstrated considerable nonadherence with medical advice. These health behaviors were positively associated with strong identification with traditional AI culture on the cultural identification questionnaire.

Additionally, nonadherence with medical regimens was perceived in such a way that it was socially acceptable, even desirable, to ignore and/or deride medical advice. Following the recommendations of the "white" medical authority placed the elder outside of their peer group. Diabetes has become increasingly endemic among AI populations, and this has resulted in a construction of the disease as commonplace and benign. Indeed, the disease and attendant noncompliance may create a sense of solidarity with other AI diabetics within the culture.

Complicating matters further, acknowledgement of the connection between the biomechanisms of diabetes, adherence and complications was limited. Most elders had received very little diabetes education, and what was received was in many cases not culturally acceptable in terms of the way that the elders live their lives in the context of AI traditions and mistrust of white biomedicine. The traditional elder mistrusts white medical authority, and this results in an unwillingness to ask important questions about self-care. In addition to mistrust, this reticence may be due to shyness, not wanting to be a burden to the provider or not wanting to admit to lack of knowledge.

When tribal health care providers were interviewed, both AI and non-Indian, varying provider models of care delivery were elicited (Henderson, 2002a; 2002b). Interviews with providers elicited the following quotes that additionally inform us about the Indigenous Model of care-seeking and adherence:

I have to explain changes over and over. I wonder sometimes if they understand me. The patient wasn't getting what the nurse on the phone was saying. So, the patient got the CHR on the phone to interpret to her what the message was. A lot of elderly full bloods don't understand what the doctor is saying. The doctors talk fast and use big words. Even if written, the patient needs interpretation. Elderly American Indians aren't very assertive. Patients say the doctors are in too big a hurry. They're afraid to ask (questions). They don't want to offend the doctor. (Henderson 2002b:97)

The cultural construction of the elder holding the Indigenous Model is crafted from a history that includes prejudice, access to care barriers and absent or culturally inappropriate diabetes education. It is this history that engenders symptom tolerance, the normalization of the disease and its symptoms, and the devaluation of adherence. It is this context that inspires these additional quotes from providers:

They're traditional. They may want to seek alternative types of treatment. They don't understand the extent of the disease. (Henderson 2002b:100)

She would deny it at first. She's not going to give up her favorite foods. She would go to the doctor but that doesn't mean she would abide by what the doctor would say. Just the Indian way, you could say. They don't like people telling them what to do, don't like being told how to live, what to eat, what not to eat. (Henderson 2002b:100)

Mainstream Model

Within the group of elders who held the Mainstream Model of diabetes, analysis indicated the predominance of early symptom identification, early care-seeking and adherence to prescribed treatments. The elders holding this model of diabetes were more likely to be more acculturated into the white mainstream culture. The behavior of the elders in this group, in terms of the issues here, was aligned with the expectations of the white mainstream medical community. This does not suggest that they are perfect patients, but in comparison to the more traditional elders, there was trust in formal medical providers and an expressed intent to "do what the doctor says." It was considered to be socially incorrect not to comply with medical recommendations that were perceived as gifts of knowledge from health care providers. In this group of elders, as in the more traditional group, cultural identification predicted health behaviors. The elders who had received formal diabetes education were in this group of elders, and this variable would also contribute to increased adherence to treatment recommendations. Seeking out and accepting this education would also align the elder with the mainstream biomedical paradigm.

In summary, the elder holding the Mainstream Model may be likely to seek care early in the disease process, and may be likely to adhere to dietary guidelines and medication use. There is a value placed on continuing health and maximal functioning. Health care providers are seen as helpful persons, and there is no inclination to "rebel" against health care directives. The diabetes education has been instructive to this group of elders. There is a possibility that the elder who more closely identifies with the white mainstream has an increased chance of internalizing diabetes education that was crafted to meet the teaching needs of the white mainstream.

CASE 3: MUCH SUCCESS AND GOOD FORTUNE

I interviewed Jack at his home in Lukfala, Oklahoma. He was a man of eighty-seven years who closely identifies with mainstream white culture, as opposed to traditional AI culture. He has been hugely successful over time in controlling his diabetes. He was diagnosed with the disease thirty-four years ago. He states that at that time, he had numbness in his hands, as well as excessive thirst, and he sought care immediately. His blood sugar was 400 (any value over 127 is considered to be abnormal, and 400 is very high).[9] When asked if he was surprised to be diagnosed with diabetes, he said that he wasn't because it "runs in my family" and he has a "lot of cousins that have it." He does not know much about the disease because there were "no classes back then." He just knows that diet and exercise control it. He gardens and that is his exercise. At first, he was on oral medications for the diabetes, but was able to achieve control, and now takes no medications. He lives with his spouse in a privately built home in a rural area. He does not participate much in tribal activities. He states that he was "in heavy construction" before he retired, and attributes his success in controlling his diabetes to diet and exercise. He says, "There's a lot of them don't do that (what the doctor tells them to do). I say "You can live a normal life or you can die young." The day before the interview, he had just finished planting four hundred tomato plants. When I left his house, he gave me gifts of freshly picked summer squash and green peppers.

ELEMENTS OF THE AMERICAN INDIAN DIABETES MODEL

Postponement of Care-seeking

In this research, elders who held the Indigenous Model of diabetes postponed care-seeking even in the presence of recognizable symptoms, while those holding the Mainstream Model sought care early in the disease process. The "late care-seeking designation" used in this research was assigned only to those subjects who stated that they recognized symptoms of the disease, but decided to wait before seeking care. There are differences in perception between Indians and non-Indians about the physical symptoms of illness. Cultural systems vary in selecting which symptoms are considered serious enough to send the person to a health care provider, as well as the manner in which the symptoms are presented and evaluated by the provider (Weaver and Sklar 1980; Cohen et al. 1994).

Grandmother would rather get some weeds or roots to treat her. Everybody who goes (to the tribal hospital) gets cut on and dies. (Henderson 2002b:85)

As indicated in this quote, traditional AI people seek to avoid contact with the "white" medical establishment. Some relate bad experiences from the past, both their own and that of friends and relatives. The traditional elders in my research postponed care-seeking even in the presence of illness they knew could be due to diabetes. They frequently ignored symptoms, delaying diagnosis, because of lack of education (in my research, only four of the elders had had diabetes education), or attributed them to causes such as old age (Evaneshko 1994; Tom-Orme 1994; McCabe 1999; Henderson 2002b).

Due to the high prevalence of the disease within the population, and the high morbidity and mortality rates, there has been a "normalization" of diabetes and its complications within the AI population. In the group of elders that more closely identified with traditional culture, there was little alarm at both the possibility and reality of being diagnosed with diabetes:

Well, I'll have to learn to live with it. Not scary sounding. Father had diabetes. (Henderson 2002b:79)

Well, you see, I been with mama about 50 years with it and she didn't have any problem with it, except she lost a leg. (Henderson 2002b:81)

These reactions may indicate a perceived inevitability. For the traditional elders in this research, while extensive problems with vision, circulation and episodes of fainting resulted in care-seeking, earlier symptoms were minimized and/or ignored. Many elders spoke of diabetes being "caused" by life events such as loss of a spouse, or moving to another job or home location, and correlated the appearance of the disease with these perceived life stressors. This was also a feature of diabetes patients' explanatory models as indicated in the study by Cohen et al (1994). As in that study, AI elders minimized the seriousness of their disease, concentrating instead on the social and personal effects of the illness.

Adherence Issues

The elders in this study who more closely identified with the indigenous culture were less adherent to diet, exercise and medication use than culturally mainstream elders. Because of the lack of diabetes education, there was an inability among the nonadherent group to connect poor adherence to disease complications. There were also social pressures mitigating against adherence, and notable derision attached to discussion of the "white man's diet" and the "white doctor's" instructions:

I didn't know how serious it was. Then there weren't too many people who had diabetes. At first, I didn't take it serious. They wanted to put me on insulin, but I wouldn't do it. I quit taking insulin for over two years because my sugar wasn't over 200. (Henderson 2002b:79)

I know more than they do. They ain't said nothin'to me. I done lived it. I do fine as long as I take my pills. (Henderson 2002b:80)

Medication adherence was higher than dietary adherence, due in part to utilization of medications to attenuate dietary indiscretions. Ironically, among some traditional elders, use of insulin was perceived as making one "sicker." Accounts were given of family members who were placed on insulin, only to die or worsen after starting the medication. In actuality, the family member was placed on insulin only after extensive disease progression. The insulin was an attempt to halt the cascade of medical complications, but was usually unsuccessful, and was perceived as being extremely harmful.

CASE 4: WHAT NOW??

Chris Billy is sixty-five years old, and was diagnosed with diabetes mellitus twenty years ago. At the time, she thought she could "out-run it." Now, as I interview her in her home, she sits in a wheelchair. Due to her diabetes, both legs have been amputated below the knee. A dialysis bag lies at her feet, as the insulin she takes is no longer sufficient to maintain a blood sugar level that is safe for her body. Due to her diabetes, she suffered a heart attack two years ago, and has lost vision in one eye. She awaits a prosthesis, which will be delivered to her in a few days. She must learn to walk again. When she has grown used to using one artificial leg, then she will be fitted with the other leg. I asked her questions about what she thought when she was first diagnosed, the reaction of her family and what she felt about her medical care.

Commenting on when she was first diagnosed with the disease:

I didn't pay any attention to it. I just kind of ignored it, but I got so I had to pay attention to it. All the family has it.

I asked her if she had problems following the doctor's recommendations:

I do those things. They don't interfere with my life, now. In the past, taking the pills and the insulin was a problem. Sometimes I didn't take my medicine. Maybe a week would go by without insulin. It just wouldn't bother me. It just didn't matter. Then I'd get a real bad headache and crave sweets, then I'd check my sugar and take my shots. I quit partying, smoking and traveling. Sometimes I was gone a week or two weeks, then I would come back. But I stopped all that, 'cause it started affecting my eyes.

Chris pauses, looks at her friend, seated on the couch. Her friend also has diabetes. She has had the disease for four years. She is already having trouble with one foot. Chris looks over at her and says:

Look at me. Watch what you do.

Her friend just shakes her head and says:

I guess I just don't want to accept it, maybe. Sometimes I just don't feel like "diabetic," I guess. I just feel normal.

Chris shakes her head. Her niece also sits nearby, helping her aunt with tasks around the house. She has just celebrated a birthday:

When I blew out the candles, I wished that my aunt would get her new leg soon, and that she will be able to walk again.

Distrust of White Authority

Indigenous Model elders did not trust medical providers and were reluctant to ask questions of them. These elders appeared to subjugate themselves to medical authority in the clinical setting, but shed many of the medical recommendations at home. For many people who are illiterate or marginally literate, the oral discourse of the health care provider is confusing and results in the patient feeling demeaned by the experience.

The history of interaction with the white community must also be considered an important factor. Elders are a repository of memories from times past, both from their own experience and that of their parents. The history of contact with whites can be seen as one of extermination ("the only good Indian is a dead Indian"), expulsion from lands, exclusion from mainstream society through reservation internment and attempted forced assimilation through removal of children to boarding school facilities (Holmes and Holmes 1995). Within the traditional culture there is considerable distrust of white persons, and there exists within the population a history of nonadherence passed down from the preceding generation. This antecedent context has exerted influence over this cohort of elder diabetics. One subject said that she would not take her (changed) diabetes medicine because she felt the doctors were experimenting on her.

As previously mentioned, within the peer group of traditional elders, adherence to medical directives is not valued. Rebellion against white authority was cited as one reason that persons do not comply. Physicians, nurses and other health care providers are perceived by traditional elders as "white" even though they most likely are tribal members (twenty-one out of thirty providers in this study are AI/AN). Providers who are Indian might be referred to by traditional patients as "white Indians," because they have been placed in a position of authority that has been defined by the tenets of the biomedical mainstream. Such perceptions are seen in the following commentary on doctors, the first from an amputee, also on dialysis for kidney failure, both conditions consequences of uncontrolled diabetes:

It's my body. I know what I can do and what I can't do. Coming from the Indian side of the car, you're going to a white man doctor (you say) "That white man don't know it." (Henderson 2002b:84)

A Indian in the white man's way will jump right on the meds. The "real" Indian will be harder to get them to understand how diabetes works.... The "real Indian-Indian" will stay at home and say the doctor did not deal with them right. (Henderson 2002b:84)

We've done heard about this. If it wasn't for the white people, we wouldn't have all these problems. They refer to traditional cooking as good, white cooking as bad. The wild game is gone (due to whites). (Henderson 2002b:84)

Diabetes Education

For most of the AI elder subjects in this research, there was a regrettable lack of formal, culturally relevant, diabetes education in both quantity and quality. Only four AI elders interviewed had received formal diabetes education. All of the elders who had diabetes education more closely identified with mainstream culture. For these elders, then, symptom recognition and care-seeking was facilitated by this experience and the positive reception of non-Indian ideas. It is notable that many elders were diagnosed before diabetes education services were available from tribal health care. The elders, as a generational cohort, had little exposure to this knowledge at the time of diagnosis. It was possibly assumed by the health care establishment that the elders had received diabetes education, but in fact, they had not. Moreover, there was no apparent effort to convey culturally appropriate education over the years following diagnosis:

I thought it would last only one or two years and I'd be OK. Meds decrease the symptoms and then you don't take the medicine until you have a problem, and this leads to amputation. (Henderson 2002b:79)

Honey, I been with it for 50 years. I pretty well know how it works. You got blood sugar. The doctor said about her mother that her mother ate anything she wanted to. If she wanted to eat it, she ate it. (Henderson 2002b:85)

COMPARATIVE ETHNIC PERSPECTIVES ON DIABETES AND ELDERS

In the United States, as well as worldwide, diabetes is on the upswing among virtually all populations. This is due mainly to health behaviors that have diverse underlying causes strongly related to socioeconomic, political and cultural contexts (American Diabetes Association 2005; Ferreira and Lang 2006). According to the Centers for Disease Control and Prevention (CDC), the prevalence rate for the Vietnamese population living in this country is approximately 7 percent. For the African American population, it is approximately 11.3 percent (ADA 2005; CDC 2007). These prevalence rates exceed that of the non-Hispanic white population (around 5.0 percent), although all population groups have seen an escalation of the disease in recent years (CDC 2007). How do the findings of the research presented here compare with other research on diabetes in elders from other ethnic communities within the United States?

Mull, Nguyen and Mull used ethnography to examine the cultural context of diabetes in a California Vietnamese community (2001). Ideas regarding cause and treatment, as well as suggestions for improving diabetes self-care within this population, were elicited from first-generation immigrants to the United States. In contrast to the American Indian elders, among whom one-half had achieved control over their diabetes, three-fourths of the Vietnamese elders did not have good control of their diabetes.

Concepts about causation were culturally shaped, as were "proper" treatment regimens. Causation was often related to "sadness" brought on by stress, as well as perspiring less in the United States than in Vietnam. Perspiration was seen as a desirable way to rid the body of toxins. Treating diabetes included the use of Eastern herbal medicines by two-thirds of the sample to restore balance. Indeed, these persons lowered their doses of diabetes medicines while taking the herbal medicines in an effort to restore "balance."

Few AI elders spoke of using traditional medicines or consulting with practitioners of traditional medicine. Within the Vietnamese population, elders with diabetes extensively used Eastern medicines and home remedies:

Eastern medicine is much safer than doctors' medicine because it cools your body and brings it back into balance. Doctors' medicine has a lot of strong hot chemicals ... you can get really bad side effects if the dose is too high for you ..., I've been using different things from the market to bring my sugar down ... bitter gourd, guava leaf tea, and banana tree sap. If those don't work, then I'll think about taking doctors' medicine. (Mull et al. 2001:309)

Low use of professional medicine was also connected to not wanting to be a burden to adult children:

I'm old, and I don't want to bother my son with taking me to the doctor, so I just drink tea and pray I won't get any worse. (Mull et al. 2001:308)

However, if they saw a doctor, they preferred neighborhood doctors trained in Vietnam:

We go to them because they understand our language and we don't have to wait as long as in the clinic, but we can't really ask them any questions. Some of them seem to be just rushing through. (Mull et al. 2001:309)

Like their tradition-oriented AI counterparts, Vietnamese elders spoke about an aversion to insulin:

If you have to take insulin, for sure you're going to die soon. Also, they say that some people go blind because of it. (Mull et al. 2001:309)

It was apparent that within this sample, many of the Vietnamese immigrants with Type 2 diabetes lacked knowledge of this disease. This is partly because it is not common in their home country, where high levels of physical activity and low-fat diets are the norm.[10] There is also the factor of the low literacy, especially among women, found in this Vietnamese population of elders. Most were indigent, advanced in age and non-English speaking. Diabetes education for them in the United States was lacking, difficult to access, or not understandable due to language differences and low literacy.

African Americans in Florida

In an exploration of diabetes self-management techniques in an African American community in St. Petersburg, Florida, Rahim-Williams (2006) elicited behaviors and beliefs about acceptable management and treatment among women diagnosed with diabetes. As among AI elders, the cultural construction of the disease in the population of African American women encompassed both lay and biomedical perspectives. The main reasons given for lack of treatment compliance were difficulty in giving up favorite foods, the high cost of medications and supplies, weight loss, daily testing and stress. As in the AI population, there was a belief that if diabetes runs in the family, it is inevitable.

Half of the respondents thought that it was easy to manage the disease. Behaviors utilized for management included changes in diet and exercise, use of prescribed medications, and close monitoring of blood sugar by themselves and their doctors. However, many did not check their blood glucose every day. And one-fourth indicated that they did not exercise because of health problems, social factors and unsafe environments. There was the understanding that weight control was a good way to manage the disease. As in the other populations discussed previously, most reported that they struggled with the dietary changes:

I do the same thing I always have done. I eat the same things ... diabetic sugar, I'm not working with that because I don't want it. It doesn't taste good. I just eat what I like to eat. But, the only time I know that the diabetes is going to bother me is when I don't eat. I get weak and dizzy. (Rahim-Williams: 21)

As in the AI and Vietnamese populations, there was a feeling that stress reduction was important in the control of diabetes. A distinct factor that stands out in the African American community was the connection between diabetes and religious activities in terms of diabetes control:

Religion is a part of your life. Diet is a lifestyle, but your Christianity is even more than that because it's who you are and who you pattern your life after.... The connection between my religion and my belief and my health or my diet or diabetes is that I am ... going to need to have my supreme being in order for me to stay on track because I am too weak for this. I can't do it all by myself. (Rahim-Williams:13)

Whereas among the Vietnamese elders, diabetes was a relatively "new" occurrence within family systems, in the African American sample, similar to the AI sample, the majority of women studied had a family history of the disease. However, unlike the indigenous AI elders, whose families and peers devalued adherence, within this ethnic community family networks constituted a key support system for adapting to this disease:

I have 100% support from my family. They watch me like a watchdog. They ask, Momma, are you supposed to have that? I say, don't come in here with that today ... but they are only looking out for me. (Rahim-Williams:18)

In contrast, in both the Vietnamese and AI populations, all of the women in this study had attended a diabetes self-management education class. Over half, however, had not received a referral to these classes from their physicians, nor did they receive referrals to a nutritionist.[11] Rather, the women sought out diabetes education on their own.

While the women knew the self-care regimens recommended, and utilized them, the utilization was sometimes spotty and depended upon the circumstances in the person's life. Monitoring and response occurred primarily with symptom recognition and was not consistent. Mediating circumstances included barriers such as costs of medications, environmental concerns such as unsafe walking environments, and lack of insurance. Based on these identified themes, a "Model of Interruption" was delineated that explained the inconsistent use of recommended behaviors due to multiple interruptions by sociocultural, structural and/or environmental factors that lead to lack of consistent appropriate self-care.

CONCLUSION

Efforts to effectively combat diabetes by the medical community and AI tribes have been substantial in the past several years. Actions to decrease the prevalence of diabetes have thus far concentrated on disease etiology, the biology of the disease as it exists within varying segments of the population, and the infrastructure of care delivery. However, the existence of a health care delivery system is insufficient unless it is underpinned by appropriate prevention and education strategies crafted to effect changes in human behavior (Johnson and Rhoades 2000). Education regarding prevention and management of diabetes must have cultural relevance to the target population in order to be maximally effective.

The practice of medicine has two players: the patient and the physician. By focusing on both these sides of the health promotion equation, the research presented here has implications that could impact current practice. The Traditional AI patient has a stereotype of Western non-Indian providers in which the health worker is viewed suspiciously and is critiqued through the filter of the patient's culture. This stereotype may view the provider as having an insensitive nature, being greedy, arrogant, untrustworthy and intrusive (McCabe 1999; Rhoades and Rhoades 2000). It is notable that in the research presented here, to more traditional elders, the majority of medical providers were seen as symbols of "white authority," even if the providers were AI. In the research with Vietnamese elders, access to culturally relevant health care practitioners was lacking, such that Vietnamese elders sought out same-culture lay providers, rather than North American-trained physicians (Mull et al. 2001).

One of the implications of our findings for current practice is that due to the nature of the IHS directives regarding standards of care, most of the AI elders in this research receive the same general type of *ongoing* diabetes care, but that the care may not be effective because differences in cultural identification are not adequately addressed. The research also revealed that many elders had received no diabetes education (except the small amounts given during clinic visits), possibly because at the time they were diagnosed, there were no education programs. The health care system has neither recognized nor alleviated these gaps.

In the population of American Indians, as well as in other culturally diverse populations, elicitation of social and cultural histories by health care providers becomes crucial in identification of models of illness operating in patients and their families. It is necessary to evaluate each person regarding his or her inclusion within a culturally traditional support system, attitudes towards chronic illnesses such as diabetes and to what extent the family will influence decision making regarding health care. Degree of cultural immersion should be assessed along with additional factors such as literacy and socioeconomic status. In terms of optimizing health status in populations of culturally diverse elders, in whom long-standing traditions exist side-by-side with contemporary mores, the impact of efforts made to truly understand the cultural context of aging and health for individuals cannot be underestimated.

NOTES

1. The high prevalence rates noted in Alaska are due to a number of factors. Changes in the diagnostic categories for type 2 diabetes, and increases in the number of screenings conducted, may contribute to this increased prevalence. Also implicated are the changes in Alaskans' diet, from primarily subsistence hunting and fishing to a "modern" diet with its attendant high sugar, fat and sodium content.

2. Allotment lands were those parcels of land deeded to AI persons when lands that previously belonged to tribal nations were opened to white settlers by the U.S. government. A typical parcel consisted of 160 acres.

3. The age group of fifty-five years and over was chosen to designate elder status, consistent with Indian Health Service guidelines (IHS 1997). AI/AN elders experience more comorbidities at younger ages than their counterparts in the white population.

4. The Certificate of Degree of Indian Blood (CDIB) card is issued to members of American Indian and Alaska Native tribes by the Bureau of Indian Affairs (BIA). The issuance of the card is predicated on the enrollment of ancestors with the BIA, and designates the AI blood fraction of the individual. The BIA calculation of AI fraction is based on blood derived from both federally recognized and nonfederally recognized tribes. The CDIB card entitles tribal members to those trust benefits offered by the federal government that are specific to AI/AN persons, and which fulfill the trust responsibility of the federal government toward AI/AN tribal members.

5. The Community Health Representative (CHR) program is a unique community-based outreach program, staffed by a cadre of well-trained, medically guided, tribal and Native community people, who provide a variety of health services within American Indian and Alaska Native communities. A Community Health Representative (CHR) may include traditional Native concepts in his/her work and is funded with IHS-CHR appropriations.

6. Responses to questions were transcribed by the investigator and placed into the ethnograph software program in order to facilitate analysis. Utilizing the ethnograph software, codes can be defined, text data can be coded and response frequencies calculated.

7. Addressing cultural identification (CI) is crucial for contemporary AI research due to the high degree of cultural heterogeneity within tribal populations. Questionnaires assessing CI cultural identification often use an "immigrant model" for question selection. "Immigrant model" questions are relevant to persons first coming to the United States, but irrelevant to those in residence here. The "immigrant model" obviously does not apply to AI populations (c.f. Stephenson 2000). Consequently, CI life experience domains were based upon a review of the literature, pilot study findings, researcher observations and very importantly, lived experience with members of the tribe.

8. CI assessment results placed subjects in either an "indigenous" or "mainstream" category. These are terms of convenience for description and analysis. However, the technical limits of the use of these dichotomous terms must be understood. At the individual level, the existence of absolute, dichotomous designations cannot experientially exist (Hill, Fortenberry and Stein 1990). For example, the "Acculturation Continuum" has positions along a line, at one end of which is the identifier "Traditional" and at the other "Assimilated." The middle is designated "Bicultural," and movement from one pole to the other reflects processes of "acculturation" (Valle 1989). People can be said to exist at any point on the continuum based on changing social and cultural environments, and movement can be due to situational social environment variance. It is not possible in today's global cultural environment to be completely shielded from diverse cultural influences. Thus, individual experience in the sense of absolute encapsulation in one and only one cultural environment does not occur (Hill et al. 1990). The use of *indigenous* and *mainstream* to refer to the cultural identification of the elders is not perfect, but does not necessarily supersede an agreed upon "convenience usage."

9. According to the 2007 Clinical Practice Recommendations from the American Diabetes Association, a diagnosis of diabetes can be made when the fasting blood glucose level is equal to or over 126 mg/dl. A level of 400 would be considered an extremely urgent medical condition (American Diabetes Association 2007).

10. In this population, referrals to formal diabetes education classes were lacking for some of the women interviewed. The women sought information from other sources such as relatives, friends, nurses and books.

11. Regarding culturally based dietary habits, it was said to be difficult to avoid sugar, as the people liked their coffee very sweet. The admonition to cut back on the large amount of white rice in the diet also presented an adherence problem.

CHAPTER 42

Brain Failure, Late Life and Culture in Japan

John W. Traphagan

Epidemiological studies of Alzheimer's disease (AD) and other forms of dementia, such as vascular dementia (VaD), have shown a general trend toward increased prevalence in elder populations throughout many parts of the world, particularly in East Asia, over the past thirty years. Several surveys of prevalence rates of dementia in Japan have shown a rapid increase of AD from the 1970s to the late 1990s, while there has been a corresponding decline in the diagnosis of vascular dementia (Suh and Shah 2001:6). Shigeta's (2004:118) research shows a decrease from approximately 2.8 percent for VaD in 1970 to 1.0 percent, while AD increased from about 1.1 percent in 1970 to 4.0 percent by the late 1990s. Data such as these point to significant policy implications in terms of health care provision for the elderly. Indeed, in Japan, one response to these and other data related to health and population aging has been the promulgation in 2000 of a mandatory long-term care insurance program that covers all Japanese (see Jenike and Traphagan in this volume).

While such studies are important for understanding the epidemiology of dementia cross-nationally, most assume a common understanding of dementia across cultures and do not address underlying cultural factors that contribute to how various forms of dementia, such as AD, are conceptualized and, thus, diagnosed. Is the increase in AD and decrease in VaD in Japan over the past thirty years a product of changes in the prevalence of these diseases, or is it a consequence of changing conceptualizations of dementia?

Indeed, the emphasis on biomedical aspects of cognitive decline in later life, particularly on explaining and curing AD and other forms of dementia associated with the aging process, often obfuscates the manner in which these diseases are experienced and constructed within cultural contexts. Clearly, it is important to ask: What are the biological causes of brain failure in later life? But to stop here is to miss the fact that the process of brain failure is not simply a change in human physiology, but is intertwined with cultural values and meanings such as: How are illness and wellness defined by people in a particular context? What meanings are associated with loss of brain function? What are the social implications for those who experience declining brain function and for those who are charged with caring for them?

In this chapter, I am concerned with exploring questions such as these as they manifest themselves in the cultural context of contemporary Japan. While internal pathological processes influence the behavior of individuals, in order to cope with changes in behavior, it is fundamentally important to recognize that those internal processes are situated within external social and cultural processes. These influence how the individual may experience loss of brain function and how family members and others may interpret that loss (see McLean this volume). Changing patterns of behavior are not simply a pointer to physiological problems in the brain; they are also markers that can indicate what constitutes normal or abnormal behavior and how people can and should respond to that behavior.

MEDICAL MODEL (DEMENTIA) VERSUS CULTURAL MODEL (SENILITY)

In the paragraphs that follow, I will generally avoid use of the term *dementia*, in part because use of the term inherently moves the experience of loss of brain function from the realm of social interactions to that of biomedicine. This, in turn, creates an implicit assumption that loss of brain function is essentially the same for all humans, regardless of the cultural context in which it is experienced. While we may agree that the specific physiological changes associated with AD or VaD, for example, are not associated with cultural context, that is where any assumption of universality needs to end (see Henderson, this volume Web book). Instead, the process of developing a culturally sensitive understanding of loss of brain function should recognize that definitions of disease are culturally constructed and that models used to understand disease reflect epistemologies created and recreated by their users (Herskovits 1995; Traphagan 2000b; Chui and Gatz 2005). As various scholars have shown, our capacity to understand not only the physiological aspects of loss of brain function in later life, but also the manner in which those aspects are culturally constructed, requires situating the specifics of these diseases within broader cultural themes and explanatory models that are used to interpret the meanings of these conditions (Ikels 1997; Cohen 1998; Herskovits 1995; Traphagan 2000b, 2002, 2005b).[1]

By emphasizing the cultural, rather than the biomedical aspects of loss of brain function in later life, my aim is explicitly to demedicalize dementia. The benefit of doing so rests in creating a means to consider loss of brain function *not* simply as a disease or as a set of symptoms, but also as a category of differentiation, discrimination and ascription of cultural values that shapes the experience and interpretation of functional change and decline in old age.

Although the terms *senile* and *senility* have become passé in the biomedical and gerontological lexicon of aging and have been replaced by neurological disease nomenclature, senility, whether it is represented as AD, VaD or simply frailty in old age, is a social category highly susceptible to variation in interpretation among those who experience it and those who are providing care (Henderson and Traphagan 2005). In the following discussion of loss of brain function in Japan, biomedical concepts and terms for dementia are purposely suspended. In place of *dementia*, I will use two terms, *senility* and *boke*, the latter of which is a Japanese term that resists easy translation into English, but which is best understood as a concept, associated with specific symptoms related to dementia, but that is understood as a social category.

CULTURE, SENILITY AND AGING IN JAPAN

With these thoughts in mind, I now want to turn to a discussion of loss of brain function in Japan as a way of highlighting one way in which senility is culturally constructed and interpreted. The discussion here is based upon ethnographic fieldwork in northern Japan that I have conducted over the past twelve years in periods as long as 1.5 years and as short as one month. Research has involved long-term immersion within the local context and has been conducted entirely in Japanese, without the use of translators or interpreters. A variety of methods have been used, including in-depth interviews with older people about their concerns related to the onset of senility, as well as extended participant observation in two different neighborhoods (one urban and one agricultural) that had large populations of people over age sixty-five, as well as through involvement with specific activities and organizations that were limited to older people living in the region.

When considering how senility is expressed and experienced in cultural contexts outside of the Western worldview, it is necessary to give some thought to how people in a given context think about the nature of a human being. In what ways are concepts of self and person defined in the context in question? Understanding this is fundamental to understanding the manner in which senility is experienced and expressed in another culture.

For Japanese, the human person is conceptualized in ways that do not necessarily correspond to the Western emphasis on a split between mind and body, although popular renditions in the West of "Asian" concepts of mind and body tend to ignore the fact that dualism can be an important part of how people in different parts of Asia think about the human person. Elsewhere, I have shown that rather than a mind/body split, Japanese see the person in terms of a division between inner (*uchi*) and outer (*soto*) manifestations of self. The physical body is the outer aspect of the person, while the inner aspect of the person is less well-defined, but includes emotions, intellect, thought, experience and memory (Traphagan 2002). In either inner or outer elements of the person, social interaction is the basis through which people develop and grow into full-fledged human beings. Some Japanese argue that humans are not born with an inner self (the term used in this case is usually *kokoro*, which implies inner, mind, heart or center), but develop that inner self out of interaction with others. Not only is the specific person seen in terms of this inner/outer juxtaposition, but persons in general are thought of in terms of concentric rings of social embeddedness organized around inner and outer circles of relatives, friends, acquaintances and strangers. In other words, this model extends beyond the individual to describe human interconnectedness in social context. Indeed, Japanese typically see the person not in terms of a duality of mind and body, but as a mind/body complex that involves inner and outer expressions of the person and places those expressions into social contexts (Kasulis 1993). The person is not fully realized unless he or she is actively involved in social settings—it is through interactions with others that one becomes an integrated social, and thus mind/body, whole (Kondo 1990; Traphagan 2000b).

The direct relationship between senility and this concept of the person may not seem immediately evident, even if it does point out the fact that Japanese do not necessarily see the nature of human beings in the same way that Westerners do. However, before directly addressing this issue, it is necessary to take a brief diversion into Japanese moral ideas as they relate to this person embedded in social circles of innerness and outerness. Japanese moral ideas related to functional decline in old age revolve around four key concepts: activity, effort, burden avoidance and reciprocity. As Margaret Lock notes among middle-aged women facing menopause, activity and effort are closely tied together in Japanese definitions of a good person—to be active and to be making efforts to maintain an active life are inherently seen as indicating a person who is behaving well (Lock 1993). For those in later life, activity is seen as fundamentally important in conveying to others that one is making sufficient effort to avoid the onset of senility, or, in Japanese, a condition known as *boke*. Elder Japanese engage themselves in a variety of activities that are seen as being useful in possibly preventing the onset of the condition, but also are important in the sense that to be engaged is evidence that one is doing all that is possible to prevent the condition from occurring (Traphagan 2000b). Perception that one has failed to make sufficient efforts, through activities such as hobbies and learning, to delay or prevent the onset of *boke* suggests at least some degree of moral deficiency on the part of the person who develops the condition (Traphagan 1998b; 2000b).

If an individual becomes *boke*, the potential for burdening others, primarily family members, but also the society at large through use of government services, is increased. Although for Japanese, a degree of dependence is considered normal and acceptable in later life, this is balanced against ideas that limit the extent to which one should reasonably burden others with one's own needs (Hashimoto 1996). Health care for frail, demented and bed-ridden elders can easily fall into the category of over-burdening those who are charged with care provision.

How do these ideas relate to senility? In order to answer this, it is necessary to give some thought to what "senility" is in the Japanese context. The

Japanese conceptualization of senility overlaps with U.S. conceptualizations, but there are important differences between the two cultures. Japanese recognize three categories of senility: AD, known as *arutsuhaimâ*; other forms of senile dementia such as VaD, lumped together in the category known as *rôjinsei chihô*; and a third category for which there is no direct translation in English, but which is known in Japanese as *boke*. This concept is ambiguously defined in Japanese culture, but is understood in terms of symptoms that include many of those associated with AD in biomedicine such as forgetfulness or confusion. The condition, however, is clearly constructed in terms of Japanese notions of the person.

For example, in one book, the condition is divided into three areas of the person that are viewed as becoming disoriented: social, physical (outer) and inner (Kikkawa 1995). The individual faced with *boke* may exhibit symptoms in each of these areas. In terms of bodily disorientation, symptoms of *boke* may include difficulty with walking and balance problems, entanglement of words, loss of muscle strength, incontinence, loss of taste and skin sensitivity. Social symptoms of the condition include loss of interests, doubting of others, aggressiveness, jealousy, overdependence and an inability to take on one's role in society or family. In terms of inner disorientation, symptoms include forgetfulness, inability to organize ideas, reclusive behavior, emotional swings, lack of patience and an inability to persevere.

Interestingly, characteristics not normally thought of as being associated with AD, such as incontinence, are associated with *boke*. Indeed, even among Japanese, the condition is not clearly defined—its symptoms range from mild forgetfulness to complete loss of function and in some cases the term is presented as little more than a lay term for AD. What is clear when one explores the meaning and cultural construction of senility in Japan is that central in the Japanese formulation there exists an idea that *boke* involves a dis-integration of the physical, mental and social aspects of the person (Traphagan 2002).

In general, *boke* is differentiated from other forms of senility on the basis of agency or control; there is a chance, at least, that one can prevent the onset of *boke* through engaging in activities that involve the use of both mind and body, particularly those that include social involvement. Failure to be sufficiently active leads to a loss of personal integration, the possible onset of *boke* and, thus, the potential to become an undue burden on others, particularly one's family members (Traphagan 2000b). To become such a burden, without the hope of reciprocating the care one receives can be likened to a social nightmare. The Japanese mind-body complex becomes increasingly integrated as people age and interact with others socially. If an individual fails to make sufficient efforts to maintain integration through social engagement, which is the glue that holds the complex together, one becomes a burden upon others and, ultimately, socially detached. The *boke* person exists in a state of disintegration from the social world, which is the primary world through which one maintains one's individual mental/physical/social integration.

The implications for this concept are twofold. First, rather than simply being a category of disease, *boke* is a social and moral category. If effort is associated with moral behavior and also associated with the prevention or delay of *boke*, then the onset of the condition has the potential to suggest that individuals are personally and morally implicated as symptoms become increasingly apparent. Furthermore, if for the Japanese, the basis of the humanness is structured around involvement in social contexts and the interdependencies of reciprocal relations, then to become *boke* is to lose one's basic humanity. Indeed, *boke* represents a kind of antisocial behavior that is largely viewed as nonhuman in the Japanese context. To be *boke* is a profound example of a cultural disaster for Japanese (Plath 1980): To be removed from the world of social interactions and to be potentially culpable for having allowed the condition to occur through a lack of sufficient effort to prevent its onset.

In short, senility understood in terms of *boke* is fundamentally *not* a biomedical concept, even if the condition is expressed through conditions that overlap significantly with biomedical conditions such as AD. Instead, *boke* is primarily a moral concept. What is important to understand when considering this from a cross-cultural perspective is that rather than AD, for most of the past fifty years (and perhaps much longer) *boke* has been the primary concept through which people in Japan think about cognitive decline in later life. This conceptualization of senility has been changing in Japan, as the biomedical model of functional change in later life increasingly comes to dominate how people think about senility. AD and other forms of dementia are widely discussed in the media and people have come to increasingly talk about senility in terms of biomedical categories. However, many Japanese continue to think about the moral implications of becoming senile as they think about the biomedical symptoms they will face when experiencing cognitive decline in old age. In other words, the experience of "dementia" or AD or "senility" in Japan needs to be understood in terms of process—there is not a universal category that identifies the symptoms and experiences of senility. Rather, there is a matrix of symbols and meanings that include both biomedical and nonbiomedical concepts, which coalesce to create a continually shifting understanding of functional change in later life.

CROSS-CULTURAL PERSPECTIVES OF DEMENTIA

International research indicates that dementia is growing rapidly in both industrial and developing countries. Feri et al. estimate that over 24 million people had dementia as of 2005, with over 4.6 million new cases occurring annually (2005). Furthermore, most of those afflicted with dementia live in developing countries—60 percent as of 2001, with an expected rise to 71 percent by 2040 (Feri et al. 2005). This will present a tremendous challenge from not only economic perspectives, but also in terms of coping with complex and varied responses to dementia that are grounded in culture. The example of Japanese conceptualizations of loss of brain function suggest that while it may be possible to arrive at a common biomedical definition of dementia or AD, the symptoms and experiences associated with the disease are open to many interpretations. The Japanese case, however, is only one of several examples that have been identified in recent ethnographic literature on functional decline in later life. Lawrence Cohen's study of senility in India shows the intersection of culturally constructed notions of madness, old age, senility and how these are intertwined within a moral subtext about what constitutes appropriate and inappropriate behavior as families care for elder members (1998).

Other scholars have shown that within contexts such as the United States, with illness and disease discourses dominated by the perspectives of biomedicine, alternative interpretations and experiences of dementia can be profound. In their work with Hmong herbalists in Laos and Thailand, Gerdner, Xiong and Cha, for example, show that late-life cognitive changes associated with confusion and memory loss are treated there by shamans using herbal teas and medicinals and these traditional approaches often augment approaches to coping with dementia that are typical among mainstream American biomedical practitioners (2006:30). Research among Hmong immigrants in Milwaukee shows the variations in interpretations that can occur when dealing with dementia. Here Olson argues that for the Hmong, dementia is not considered a serious condition. Rather, it is viewed "as a natural part of the life cycle" (1999:92). As a result, the family or individual faced with dementia may not seek treatment, either by a biomedical professional or a shaman/healer, in part because dementia is not viewed as a form of mental illness, for which help would be sought. In cases of seeking shamanic help, this is only done where it becomes necessary to cope with the presence of evil spirits or the loss of the soul, which becomes evident when a person speaks in "tongues" (1999:92).

Henderson and Henderson's discussion of interpretations of forgetfulness and confusion among older Native Americans points out the difficulties that arise in translating ideas related to loss of brain function from one language to another (2002). Their work shows how while symptoms associated with destruction of the brain can be described in causal terms from a biomedical perspective, this is not necessarily how they will be interpreted by either the person experiencing those symptoms or others around them. Among the Native American groups they studied in Oklahoma, while forgetfulness and confusion are not seen as normal parts of the aging process (as they are in some societies, including Japan), loss of cognitive clarity is not necessarily seen as abnormal either. Rather, it represents what Henderson and Henderson describe as a "supernormal" state in which the dementia sufferers' experiences and behaviors are interpreted in terms of spiritual encounters that point to the "other side" or the afterlife. Hence, this takes on a more positive meaning, as it points to the existence of a realm of existence that is otherwise difficult to contact or unknown. As a result, their informants do not necessarily see senility as entirely pathological nor as a necessarily tragic or disastrous situation for her or the family.

Examples such as these from Japan, India, native North America and among immigrant populations in the United States are among a growing number of studies clearly indicating[2] that "dementia" is experienced within a confluence of values, social and personal histories and individual and shared experiences. In other words, dementia should not be understood simply a disease or pathological state of the brain, it should be understood as a point at which a complex of cultural values and experiences intersect and are interpreted. Understanding this point should have significant implications from a clinical perspective, because clearly, dementia is not simply a biomedically defined pathology of the brain, but is also a culturally circumscribed and shaped complex of experiences that are symbolically charged, polysemous and interpreted not only with reference to the framework of biomedicine, but also to the cultural values that operate within a particular society.

NOTES

1. See also Good (1994); Gubrium (1986); Hill, Fortenberry and Stein (1990); Manson, Shore and Bloom (1985) for earlier studies that focused on the intersection of culture and concepts of dementia.

2. See Good (1994); Gubrium (1986); Hill, Fortenberry and Stein (1990) for an earlier example of research that focused on the intersection of culture and concepts of dementia.

CHAPTER 43

The Global Florida: Long-Term Care in Postindustrial Countries

Larry Polivka

Long-term care is slowly emerging as an important public policy issue in the United States, and more rapidly in other developed countries where populations aged sixty-five and over are projected to double over the next thirty to forty years (Johnson, Toohey and Wiener 2007). The need for long-term care is greatest among those eighty and older, and this age group will increase by three-to-four fold by 2050. These demographic trends are likely to make the growing need for long-term care and its associated costs a major policy issue across the developed world over the next ten years. Several European countries and Japan have already initiated major changes in their long-term care service systems and the methods they use to finance them. We now have enough information on these initiatives to address their implications for the relative cost-effectiveness of different long-term care service delivery and financing strategies.

This chapter is divided into four sections, beginning with a comparative assessment of the divergent approaches to the provision of long-term care services in Florida and Oregon over the last twenty-five years. The second section provides a brief overview of the slow and variable development of community-based long-term care services in other states since the early 1990s. The third section is a description of recent changes in the long-term care programs of selected European countries and Japan (see Stuart and Hansen this volume; Jenike and Traphagan this volume). Most of the changes in the European countries are designed to be consistent with the social welfare traditions of the European model of social democracy, which supports a wide array of publicly funded health and social benefits. Japan's publicly funded social welfare benefits are substantially more limited, but their new long-term care system is essentially as comprehensive as those in many European countries and is largely publicly funded. The final section of the chapter discusses the many policy implications of these long-term care initiatives in the United States and other countries for the future of long-term care reform. What lessons do these experiences with systematic changes in long-term care policy hold for policy-makers looking for more cost-effective alternatives to their current long-term care systems?

THE EARLY FLORIDA MODEL AND ITS INFLUENCE ON OREGON

One of the major reasons for Florida's early initiative in long-term care reform was that the population aged sixty-five and over was growing rapidly as retirees moved to the state, especially since the 1950s. The percentage of the state's population aged sixty-five and over has exceeded all other states for over thirty years, and now stands at about 17 percent, or 5 percent above the national average of 12 percent.

Community and Home Care Programs

Florida was one of the first states to implement a statewide system of community-based, in-home long-term care services designed as an alternative to nursing home placement. The Community Care for the Elderly (CCE) program was established by the Florida Legislature in 1975 as a general revenue (GR) demonstration project, and then extended statewide at the end of that decade. The CCE program provided a wide range of services to impaired older persons at risk of requiring nursing home care such as personal care, chore services and respite for caregivers. The Home Care for the Elderly (HCE) program was also implemented statewide by the early 1980s with state GR funding. The HCE program paid a small stipend ($80 to $100 monthly) to caregivers of impaired older persons in order to help them maintain their caregiving role. The stipend could be used to purchase whatever the caregiver needed to keep the care recipient at home.

Both programs proved to be very popular with the public and policy-makers who increased funding for them by 25 percent or more annually, as the programs were extended statewide. By 1983, the percentage of state funding (Houser 2007)[1] for long-term care allocated to the two programs had risen to over 20 percent, and the percentage for Medicaid-funded nursing home care had dropped to under 80 percent from over 95 percent in the late 1970s (Wiener 1996). Florida was clearly in the process of creating an extensive home- and community-based long-term care system and reducing its dependency on expensive nursing home care, the least preferred form of long-term care among the elderly.

Oregon's Innovative Long-Term Care System

Florida's pioneering efforts to create a community-based long-term care system was based on the Older Americans Act (1966), which funded local area agencies on aging and not-for-profit service providers. This caught the eye of Oregon policy-makers and aging advocates in 1979. Richard Ladd, the Director of Senior Services in Oregon, told me in 1986, when I was director of Florida's statewide Committee on Aging,[2] that the Florida CCE and HCE programs were a major inspiration for the 1981 legislative act that established Oregon's framework for the creation of a long-term care system designed to build an extensive array of home- and community-based services (HCBS) and reduce the use of nursing home care. Between 1982 and 1990, Oregon largely achieved the kind of community-based, consumer-oriented long-term care system specified in the extraordinarily prescriptive language of the 1981 legislation. The state aging office essentially gained control of the long-term-care-related Medicaid budget that had previously been used to fund only nursing home care. It accomplished this by convincing Congress to allow the state to use Medicaid dollars, under a waiver provision, to fund adult foster homes and a new in-home services program similar to the Florida CCE program.

By making increasingly expansive use of Medicaid waiver dollars, Oregon was able to add enough home- and community-based program slots, including an assisted living program, to stop growth in the nursing home population by 1988, even though the sixty-five and older population continued to grow by 2 to 3 percent annually. Medicaid funds were used to build a case-management and service-delivery system, based on a network of area agencies on aging and local providers. This system steadily reduced the state's reliance on nursing home care by expanding less expensive in-home and community-residential programs. At the same time, the percentage of publicly supported long-term care consumers served in the community grew from less than 10 percent in 1982 to over 70 percent in 2006. During this period, Oregon also increased the percentage of funding for all long-term care going to community programs to over 70 percent, from a starting point of just 20 percent (CMS 2007). This dramatic shift in the focus of long-term care resources allowed the state to meet the long-term care needs of many more low- and moderate-income elderly than if the state had continued the nursing home-dominated policy of the pre-1982 period (Wiener 1996).

Florida also expanded its home- and community-based long-term care system over the last twenty-five years, but at a much slower rate than either Oregon and a handful of other states. In fact, Florida now spends about as much on Medicaid-funded nursing home care (85 percent), in terms of the percentage of total public long-term care funding, as it did in 1990, and more than it did in 1983 (80 percent) when the CCE and HCE programs were beginning to become statewide alternatives to nursing homes. Florida's largest Medicaid-funded ($217 million) HCBS program is a managed long-term care program largely operated by proprietary HMOs (Mitchell, Salmon, Polivka and Soberon-Ferrer 2006). The state is spending a great deal of money on long-term care, but it has failed to achieve the kind of HCBS-oriented long-term care system that seemed within reach over twenty years ago and that Oregon and a few other states, following Florida's early lead, have achieved since then.

LONG-TERM CARE IN THE UNITED STATES

Over the last twenty years, long-term care policy and practice in most states have developed in a fashion more similar to the Florida experience than to the transformational changes that occurred in Oregon. Policy-makers, advocates, researchers and the media have intermittently expressed concern about the need to create a more balanced long-term care system with many more HCBS options before the baby boomers, in large numbers, begin to require long-term care. Those individuals needing long-term care services are projected to increase from 3.4 million in 2000 to about 8 million in 2030 (Johnson et al. 2007). The intermittent, rather than sustained, nature of this attention to deficiencies in our long-term care system is one of the reasons for the slow growth in HCBS programs and the failure in most states to create balanced long-term care systems.

As of 2004, only seven states, including Oregon, were spending 50 percent or more of their Medicaid dollars on HCBS programs, and in fourteen states the figure was 40 percent or higher (Kaiser Commission on Medicaid and the Uninsured 2007). The seven states spending 50 percent on HCBS have adopted major features (e.g., consolidated administrative and budget availability for all long-term care services) of the Oregon long-term care system in the late 1980s. Yet, the current national average for most other states in terms of how they have allocated long-term care resources, standing at about 20 to 25 percent for HCBS programs for the aged, is closer to Florida than Oregon. Medicaid funding for HCBS programs has indeed grown considerably since 1990. Yet, Florida and the many other states that spend under 25 percent of these funds on HCBS programs have much ground to make up in approaching what has been achieved by Oregon for the elderly in its balanced long-term care system and in most state systems for the developmentally disabled.

Even with the declining impairment rates among the elderly and an overall improvement in health care status, the need for long-term care is projected to increase by 75 to 100 percent over the next thirty years, which will put a great deal of pressure on Medicaid budgets in many states (Johnson et al. 2007). Nationally, 20 to 30 percent of the Medicaid budget is already spent on long-term care services. Creating more balanced long-term care systems by expanding HCBS programs and containing the use of nursing home care is critical to meeting the growth in the need for long-term care services over the next two decades.

LONG-TERM CARE IN EUROPE AND JAPAN

If the projected increase in the older population and associated long-term care costs is a major motive for long-term care reform in the United States, it is an even more urgent public policy issue in most European countries and Japan. Today, persons sixty-five years and older comprise 16 percent of the population of the European Union and 20 percent in Japan, but will explode by

2050 to 30 and 35 percent, respectively, in these two places (Kinsella this volume). Over the next several decades, the very elderly, those eighty and older, in several Western European countries, will triple from about 1.5 to over 9 percent of the population. Japan will experience an even more rapid aging surge as its oldest old increase from 3.8 to 14 percent of its population. All of these countries will experience substantially greater growth in the percentage of their populations sixty-five and older and eighty and older than the United States for the next several decades. Only 20.4 percent of the U.S. population will be sixty-five and older in 2040, compared to 28 percent or more in several European countries and Japan (OECD 2005).[3] This demographic trend toward rapid population growth in most European countries is a major reason for the very substantial increases in public long-term care spending that are projected for these countries over the next forty years. The four Nordic countries now spend 2.6 percent (Denmark) to 3.3 percent (Sweden) of their GDP on long-term care. The other Western European countries are spending between 0.6 percent (Italy) and 1.7 percent (Netherlands), while Japan is at 0.9 percent, the same level as the United States. Spending on long-term care as a percentage of GDP is projected to increase by between one and two GDP percentage points across these countries by 2050, including the United States, with a projected increase of 1.4 percent. These projected increases in long-term care spending appear to be sustainable, but the combination of costs associated with population aging, especially public pensions, has caused policy-makers to consider cost-containment opportunities across the board, including long-term care (OECD 2006).[4]

Arguably, however, an even more important reason that several European countries and Japan have undertaken major long-term care reform since the early 1990s is the perception among policy-makers that the public wants substantial improvements in the quality of long-term care services and is willing to pay for improved quality on a sustained basis. These improvements include the provision of greater choice and flexibility in long-term care options by adding in-home and community-based services. The Nordic countries of Sweden, Finland, Norway and Denmark have provided a relatively generous array of long-term care services, from institutional to many in-home services, since the 1970s, when their elder population began to grow at accelerating rates. These countries also had the fiscal capacity to support the development of expansive public long-term care systems with taxation rates ranging from 40 to 60 percent of GDP and strong economic growth since World War II. Each of the Nordic countries spends a good amount on both institutional and formal in-home services, with 5 to 11 percent of those past age sixty-five receiving institutional care, and 8 to 25 percent receiving in-home services (Gibson, Gregory and Pandya 2003).[5]

All postindustrial countries, including the Nordic nations, have increasingly emphasized the expansion of in-home services and the containment of institutional care. Several European countries—Germany, Austria and the Netherlands—are using consumer-directed home care (CDC) programs as their principal means of expanding home- and community-based service alternatives to institutional care. These programs are based on the payment of cash benefits for home care, often in the form of payments to caregivers.

Japan does not yet have a consumer-directed care program, but it has rapidly increased public funding from multiple sources (national and subnational taxes and individual premium cost sharing) for HCBS programs, primarily formal in-home services like personal care and home nursing services. Japan initiated development of its public long-term care system in the early 1990s, as its older population began to increase rapidly and has modified its policy on several occasions since the late 1990s (Jenike and Traphagan this volume). Most of these modifications have involved benefit levels and funding strategies as costs exceeded original projections. These funding shortfalls have been addressed primarily by modest reductions in benefits and increases in individual fees (Gleckman 2007). Even with its new system of relatively comprehensive long-term care services and a projected growth rate in its elder population that is second only to Korea's over the next forty years, Japan's public long-term care costs are projected to increase by only 1.8 percent of GDP by 2050 (Gibson, Gregory and Pandya 2003).

The expansion of HCBS programs in most countries, especially in Europe, has contributed to a steady decline in rates of institutionalization since the 1980s. Denmark, for example, reduced the percentage of nursing home residents older than age sixty-five from 20 percent in 1982 to 9 percent in 2001. This was accomplished by freezing nursing home construction and using the savings to expand HCB services to 25 percent of all older persons, while reducing public long-term care spending (Gibson, Gregory and Pandya 2003). Such a shift in the use of long-term care resources from institutional to HCBS programs permitted Denmark, like Oregon in the United States, to meet a greater share of the need for long-term care services without increasing overall expenditures or significantly requiring family involvement in caregiving. The nature of family and home-based care may change as the need for formal care increases, as it seems to have occurred in Denmark. Stuart and Hansen (2006) found that contact between elderly parents and their children occurs as frequently in Denmark as in other European countries with greater long-term care obligations on the family. The contact, however, is more likely to occur within the social and emotional dimensions of care than physical caregiving, which is increasingly provided through public programs.

Consumer-directed programs, however, are designed to pay caregivers, most often family members, for the provision of care, including physical care. Austria and Germany have the most extensive CDC programs among the postindustrial countries, although the Netherlands, Australia, Italy, Britain and France also have substantial CDC programs, which are likely to be expanded in response to popular support and program cost-effectiveness. These are universal eligibility programs without income or asset tests and no limits on how the benefit may be used. Neither the cash payments in Austria, nor the cash payment or in-kind benefit in Germany are intended to meet the full cost of care; beneficiaries are expected to cover about half of the total cost of care at the upper end

Table 43.1
Sources of Financing for Universal Long-Term Care Programs in Four Nations, 2000

	Austria	Germany	Netherlands	Japan
Premium or special payment	No	Yes	Yes	Yes
General (income taxation)	Yes (100%)	Yes	No	Yes (50%)
Cost-sharing	Yes, for institutional care	Yes, for all institutional care	Yes, for all services	Yes, for all services
Premium amount (payroll tax)	Not relevant	1.7% of wages, shared equally by employees and employers, subject to a wage ceiling of $4,117 per month; retirees share cost with pension fund	10.25% of taxable income up to a wage threshold; with no employer contribution	0.9% of wages, shared equally between workers ages 40–64 and employers. Income-related premium for persons 65+, averages $30 per month; deducted from pension

Sources: J. Brodsky, J. Habib, I. Mizrahi, *Long-term Care Laws in Five Developed Nations: A Review.* World Health Organization 2000, p. 13; Wiener 2001.

through out-of-pocket expenditures or the means-tested public assistance program. Austria funds its program from general taxes, while Germany uses a social insurance strategy based on a payroll tax. Both programs have broad political support, even though expenditures began to exceed revenues in Germany by about 3 percent in 2005 (Gleckman 2007).

With the steady growth of its CDC program, Germany now devotes over half of its public long-term care expenditures on the elderly to noninstitutional care, compared to about 20 to 25 percent in the United States. The popularity of these programs and smaller versions of them in several other countries, the declining availability and increasing costs of formal caregivers, and their apparent capacity, if properly targeted to reduce the use of institutional care, point to the possibility that consumer-directed care will become the major source of publicly supported long-term care over the next several years—in most developed countries. Developing countries may also begin to move in this direction as their older population begins to grow over the next twenty years and in the absence of an infrastructure for formal long-term care, which they are not likely to have the resources to build.

COMPARATIVE TRENDS IN LONG-TERM CARE

Perhaps the most pressing and contentious long-term care issues confronting postindustrial countries with their large and growing populations of older people are: (1) how to finance the comprehensive, HCBS-oriented long-term care system virtually all of them are developing or plan to develop over the next twenty years; and (2) whether or not to make eligibility for the program universal or means tested and targeted to the low-income elderly with few assets. As noted in Table 43.1, several European countries and Japan have universal long-term care programs that base eligibility on the assessed need for services with no regard for income and assets. On the other hand, most English-speaking countries use income and asset levels (means test) to determine eligibility for HCBS programs (Gibson 2006). The United States also uses a means test to determine eligibility for nursing home care in the Medicaid program. The United States relies far more on private (out of pocket or private insurance) sources to pay for long-term care as well as acute care services. Unlike almost all other postindustrial nations, the United States does not provide universal, medically related home care without beneficiary cost-sharing. Most other such nations also provide nonmedical home care on a universal basis as well, though with varying levels of beneficiary cost-sharing.

A recent summary of a 2003 World Health Organization report on social health insurance in European countries noted that:

support for providing services to the broader population, rather than just to the poor, has several rationales, including the desire to provide protection through social insurance, viewing long-term care as a "normal life" risk. This rationale is reinforced by difficulties in developing private long-term care insurance, as well as the risk that broad segments of the population may become impoverished by paying for long-term care services and hence burden public programs. Another rationale is the desire to substitute long-term care services for more costly acute care (particularly hospitalization), as was the case in Japan. Finally, movement toward universal programs may also reflect a desire to reduce stress on families, with a related interest in preserving family care by providing assistance to help sustain caregiving. (Gibson, Gregory and Pandya 2003:14)

In the absence of a universal public long-term care program, a significantly greater share of the total spending on long-term care in the United States than in other developed countries comes from private sources as shown in Table 43.2. As a share of total long-term care spending, private sources contribute 42 percent in the United States, which is four times higher than in Japan, twice the level in Australia and Canada, and higher than all other postindustrial countries except New Zealand. This discrepancy reflects the fact that families in the United States are expected to provide and pay for a substantially greater share of long-term care than in other postindustrial countries where long-term care policies are better designed to support families and sustain caregiving.

Most postindustrial countries have made significant changes in their long-term care systems over the last two decades by steadily increasing the availability of home- and community-based services and reducing the use of nursing

Table 43.2
Public and Private Long-Term Care Spending, 1995 and 2000 (as percent of GDP)

% GDP US$, PPP*	Total Long-Term Care Expenditures		Public Long-Term Care Expenditures		Private Long-Term Care Expenditures	
	1995	2000	1995	2000	1995	2000
Australia	0.63%	0.80%	0.49%	0.62%	0.14%	0.18%
Canada	1.04%	1.29%	0.78%	1.03%	0.26%	0.26%
Denmark	2.02%	2.12%	NA	NA	NA	NA
France	0.31%	0.35%	0.31%	0.35%	NA	NA
Germany	1.09%	1.23%	NA	NA	NA	NA
Japan	0.26%	0.69%	0.22%	0.62%	0.03%	0.07%
Netherlands	NA	2.88%	NA	NA	NA	NA
United States	1.43%	1.29%	0.87%	0.74%	0.56%	0.54%

NA = Not available; data for these countries are derived from the OECD provider classification for Nursing and Residential Care Facilities (HP.2). Public and private spending are not reported in this classification; however, long-term care in these countries is funded primarily by public sources. Australian data for 2000 are from the Australian Department of Health and Ageing.
*PPP = Purchasing Power Parity

Source: Analysis by AARP Public Policy Institute. Gibson, Gregory and Pandya (2003). "Long-term Care in Developed Nations: A Brief Overview.

home care. Many of these countries have also undertaken initiatives to improve the quality of care and life in their institutional programs, mainly through increased staffing, improved employee pay and benefits and regulatory changes designed to achieve a more home-like and resident-oriented living environment. In the United States, these changes have been pushed with growing success by the "culture change" movement that has been inspired by the Eden Alternative and Greenhouse initiatives led by Dr. Bill Thomas, and the assisted living philosophy with its emphasis on resident rights related to autonomy, dignity and privacy (see Kane et al. 2007; Thomas this volume; McLean this volume).

These common programmatic trends, however, stand in rather sharp contrast to the differences between the United States and most other postindustrial nations in the way long-term care services are financed and the extent of individual responsibility for covering the cost of long-term care services.

Over the last two decades, several European countries and Japan have created universal long-term care programs funded by a range of social insurance strategies, mainly from payroll taxes or from general revenues. This trend is likely to continue across most of postindustrial Europe for two major reasons. First, universal long-term care coverage reflects the value that most of these nations have placed on the concept of solidarity among their citizens (a sense of mutual responsibility), social cohesion and intergenerational reciprocity. Second, universal coverage programs appear to be fiscally sustainable over the next thirty to forty years with some, mainly Scandinavian countries, experiencing very small increases in already high percentages of GDP spent on long-term care (2.5 to 3 percent) and others with relatively modest projected increases of 1 to 2 percent (Gibson, Gregory and Pandya 2003). Long-term care costs in Japan, however, may not be sustainable without significant changes in current policy, which has proven to be more expensive than originally estimated as more people than were expected have qualified for services (Gleckman 2007). Sustainable does not mean unchallenging and many countries will likely have to make a series of mid-course adjustments in response to economic changes and political developments, including the increased targeting of benefits, more beneficiary cost-sharing and an expanded role for competition and private, for-profit involvement in service delivery.

Recent efforts to reduce future Medicaid expenditures and the conservative campaign to increase the role of private insurance in paying for long-term care indicate that the United States is not likely to join the emerging trend toward universal public long-term care any time soon. The United States' outlier status in terms of long-term care and health care policy more generally could change with the aging of the population and shift in the political tide; but for the near future, it would appear that the long-term care policy gap between the United States and the rest of the postindustrial world is likely to widen. Several proposals have been made by policy-makers, health policy analysts and advocates over the last several years to create a universal long-term care program, including recommendations to add long-term care, or at least an HCBS program as a benefit under the Medicare program, which is a universal health care program for citizens sixty-five years of age or older—the only U.S. universal health care program. The failed Clinton health care reform proposal of 1994 included a very substantial long-term care program that would have greatly expanded the availability of home- and community-based services (Wiener et al. 2001).

More recently, however, the conservative opposition to universal health care, or virtually any form of publicly supported health care, has sought to pass federal legislation designed to privatize the Medicare program. The Medicare Modernization Act of 2003 includes several privatization-oriented provisions, including a new drug benefit, which, unlike any other Medicare benefit, is administered by private insurance companies. The law contains a prohibition against the federal government bargaining with drug companies to reduce drug prices, which are far higher in the United States than in any other country. The Act also includes subsidies for managed care companies to offer more benefits and potentially lower out-of-pocket costs to beneficiaries in the Medicare Advantage program in an effort to reduce the number of beneficiaries in the traditional Medicare program (Polivka 2007). Although managed care programs are 12 percent more expensive than the traditional fee-for-service Medicare, conservative supporters of privatization consider it worth the cost if it leads to a collapse of the traditional Medicare program and its absorption into the corporate health care sector, which already constitutes the largest single sector in the U.S. economy.

Conservative efforts to privatize the Medicare program, or to prevent expanding eligibility for long-term care services in the Medicaid program, are part of a larger ideological initiative. This initiative is designed to diminish the public sector and privatize as many traditional government functions as possible at the federal, state and local levels by contracting out these functions to private, usually proprietary firms, including many very large corporations like General Electric, which in 2006 bought out a nursing home chain with 186 facilities for 1.5 billion dollars.

The rationale for sweeping privatization is based on conservative economic theory, which is now often referred to as neoliberalism and the notion that market competition is the most efficient method of allocating goods, including those like health, education and social services that are often thought of as "public" goods (Harvey 2006). Contracts, however, are often awarded in the absence of any true competition and little follow-up accountability. There is very little evidence supporting the superior efficiency and cost-effectiveness of privatization compared to government-operated programs. For example, the Medicare Managed Care program, which is dominated by proprietary HMOs, has never demonstrated greater efficiency or better clinical outcomes than the traditional Medicare program (Geyman 2006). As noted earlier, the current Medicare Advantage program *actually costs more* than the traditional program.

CONCLUSION

The neoliberal privatization campaign in the United States has made substantial progress over the last twenty-five years. This has widened the ideological and public policy gulf between the United States and most other postindustrial countries, especially in Europe, where mixed economies and strong social welfare policies still prevail in most countries. This difference is clearly evident in the area of long-term care policy as many European countries move toward adding universal, publicly funded programs featuring home- and community-based services to their already relatively expansive public health care systems—more expansive, but less expensive than the U.S. health care system (Tsolova and Mortensen 2006). In the United States, on the other hand, conservative supporters of privatization have tried to undermine the expansion of long-term care coverage in the Medicaid program through budget cuts and more restrictive eligibility criteria and to weaken the Medicare program by expanding the role of for-profit HMOs, even in the face of growing evidence that many future retirees will not be able to afford health care, including long-term care, on their own (Geyman 2006). This larger political context and the fundamental conflict in political values between neoliberalism and social democracy are more likely to shape the future of long-term care policy and health care policy broadly across the postindustrial world than the combined forces of demographic changes and economic globalization (see Fry this volume).

European countries are not immune from neoliberal influences on social and health policy, including long-term care policy. The limited "marketization" of long-term care services has already emerged in several countries over the past ten years, although under the relatively tight regulatory control of the public sector. Marketization strategies have not led to much of an increase in provider competition, which is the principal rationale for these strategies, nor a significant reduction in the rate of increased public spending for long-term care services. These strategies have, however, changed the nature of the relationship between the state and provider organizations in a few countries, especially Britain and, to a lesser extent, Germany, where state agencies have introduced "contracting out" procedures like competitive bidding and a greater focus on measurable outcomes and cost-effectiveness. These procedures have created a more formal, less trust-based relationship between the public and private sectors, and limited the amount of autonomy and independent advocacy that nonprofit provider organizations have historically practiced as they have increasingly become extensions of the state (Ascoli and Ranci 2002).

The evolution of marketization procedures could lead to a slow reversal of these power relationships and the emergence of a long-term care system dominated by for-profit organizations with growing influence over the policy-making process. This has occurred with the turning towards for-profit HMOs in the U.S. Medicare Advantage program and the Medicaid Long-Term Care program, which are dominated by for-profit nursing homes in most states. Powerful private equity firms like the Carlyle and Blackstone groups are now beginning to invest in the nursing home industry and create complex ownership structures designed to frustrate regulatory efforts to ensure an adequate quality of care for nursing home residents, especially sufficient staffing levels (Duhigg

2007). The marketization (privatization) of long-term care in Europe along the lines characteristic of the U.S. model would almost certainly make long-term care more expensive and gradually less available to those dependent on publicly supported services.

NOTES

1. Public funding for long-term care includes state general revenue and federal dollars, mainly in the Medicaid program, which the federal government funds about 55 percent of on a national basis. About 35 percent of all long-term care costs are paid privately (Houser 2007).

2. The Committee on Aging was established by Governor Bob Graham to develop a comprehensive plan to shift the focus of Florida's long-term care system from nursing home care to home- and community-based care over a ten-year period.

3. This study reports on the latest trends in long-term care policies in nineteen OECD countries—trends in expenditures, financing and number of care recipients are analyzed based on new data on cross-country differences (OECD 2005).

4. The total health and long-term care spending is projected to increase on average across OECD countries in the range of 3.5 to 6 percentage points of GDP for the period 2005–2050 (OECD 2006).

5. As their populations age, all developed nations are tackling issues of access, cost and quality of long-term care services; the United States ranks twenty-ninth among the world's "oldest" countries (Gibson, Gregory and Pandya 2003).

CHAPTER 44

Beyond the Institution: Dementia Care and the Promise of the Green House Project

Athena McLean

Liberating dreams are those which keep you vigilant in a sometimes miserable existence.

They are the dreams you know when you lose yourself in a book, enjoy a piece of music, dream about falling in love. Liberating dreams hate all those things that keep us grounded in life.... and we emerge rejuvenated from any liberating dream.

.... the non-liberating dream ... is the dream which.... advertising tries to sell you.... telling you you will achieve happiness if you buy....

The nonliberating dream is everywhere today.... Everyone is selling it.

Vassilis Vassilikos 1996

The long-term care industry in the United States is facing a crisis. Not only is there increasing difficulty meeting the needs of a growing population of elders, but the very quality of existing care remains poor in many facilities in spite of two decades of efforts to correct shortcomings (see Polivka this volume, this section). The year 2007 marked the twenty-year anniversary of the federal Nursing Home Reform Act (as part of OBRA 87), which put in place historic regulations to address serious issues of neglect and abuse in nursing homes and to establish standards to promote both quality of care and quality of life.[1] Unfortunately, extensive noncompliance with those standards, chronic understaffing and turnover and ongoing confusion, even among professionals, about what actually constitutes quality have impeded the realization of OBRA 87's promise, particularly in dementia care (McLean 2007a).

During these same twenty years, the visionary work of British psychologist Thomas Kitwood (1989, 1997), and others, has led to optimistic reconceptualization of the person with dementia and her care (cf. Shomaker 1987; Sabat and Harré 1992; Hughes 2001). This has placed new emphasis on the *person* with dementia, as a dignified social being with a will and ability to meaningfully communicate even late in the illness (Killick and Allan 2001; McLean 2007b). It has also encouraged a shift from *instrumental* care, focused on custodial maintenance and medicalized *control* of the body and behaviors (as *symptoms*), to a person-centered approach to *quality of life* and understanding behaviors in the context of the person's life experience. The very locus of dementia care in a medicalized institutional setting, like a nursing home, has also been questioned since many elders with dementia lack other pressing needs for ongoing medical attention. Such settings nurture neither care receiver nor giver and may be viewed as depressing by families, who often prefer smaller homelike settings (Greene et al. 1998; Hodder 2004).

THE BIRTH OF A CULTURE CHANGE MOVEMENT

In the United States, these shifts have been promoted by advocacy organizations like the National Citizen's Coalition for Nursing Home Reform (NCCNHR) and innovative providers and other advocates of "culture change" (CC), largely through a group called the Pioneer Network.[2] More recently, the Centers for Medicare and Medicaid Services (CMS), which serve as both the federal regulatory body and the major funder for long term care, have also encouraged the adoption of CC reforms consonant with the goals of OBRA 87.

This changing climate has sparked consumer demand for new "person-centered" care, and many new "dreams" are being fashioned and marketed as person-centered approaches in long-term care (McLean 2007c). Some, like PACE (Program of All Inclusive Care for the Elderly), provide a full spectrum of long-term care directly in the home and the community. Others offer new caregiving models and training approaches for long-term care facilities, such as "dementia care mapping" (Innes 2003),[3] innovations for humanizing nursing homes like the "Eden Alternative" (Thomas 1996),[4] and new designs for creating smaller, more sociable "neighborhoods" or "households" in a larger residential unit (Shields and Norton 2006).[5] Promoting privacy, individualized care and respect for the dignity of each resident, many of these options have appealed to private-paying families, often seeking assisted living options developed for elders less physically and cognitively impaired than those now typically in nursing homes (Eckert and Morgan 2001; Ball et al. 2005). Others, like Green Houses (GH), developed by physician William Thomas, founder of the Eden Alternative, were intended to virtually replace[6] nursing homes of the future and were designed for all elders, regardless of income, as a "wonderful kind of dream idea" (Thomas 2004; Thomas this section; Kane et al. 2007).

This chapter will consider the potential of the Green House Project (GHP) as a liberating dream for persons with dementia, who constitute a majority of people in nursing homes today. I begin by briefly describing the unique problems and care needs of people with dementia. Then, I offer conclusions from my own research comparing a dementia unit dominated by a biomedical approach to one with a more holistic, person-focused one. Pulling from my case studies and other work on person-sustaining environments, I then consider the potential of Green Houses for long-term dementia care in the future (see Thomas this volume).

DEMENTIA AND THE CARE NEEDS OF AFFECTED PERSONS

Senile dementia is considered a progressive disorder of older persons (sixty-five and older) that varies in symptomatology, rate of decline and length and course of illness from three to twenty years (Richter and Richter 2002:35; see also Traphagan this section). Most common impairments occur in cognition (thought processes and organization), language, behavior, orientation to time and place and often mood. The ability to recognize and use objects may also be impaired. Taken together, these changes affect people's activities of daily living as well (ADLs and IADLs).[7] Memory (short term and, later, possibly long term) is affected, leading to distortions in the sequencing of events. This shatters the person's confidence about the past and produces a sense of fragmentation of self. Moving to an unfamiliar institutional setting often exacerbates confusion and fragmentation and promotes cognitive and social decline. Over time, persons with dementia may develop problems recognizing those who had been close to them, fracturing relational ties to loved ones as well. In very advanced dementia, incontinence, hallucinations and the inability to speak, walk and swallow often occur. This typically necessitates additional care and may involve increasing resistance from the elder, unless effective, trusting relations are established with the caregiver.

Impairments can be frightening to elders, particularly earlier in the illness when they have the most awareness and fears of what might follow; this creates a need as well for considerable emotional support. Recognizing failing abilities may lead to loss of self-confidence and self-esteem, especially as others become aware of these. Incontinence may bring shame and further erode self-esteem, and efforts to hide accidents may make the person appear even more impaired.

Elders with dementia respond in different ways to their growing dependence on others; wishes to retain independence may affect their willingness to accept help from caregivers. Those who have been independent may be especially aggressive with caregivers who come to cleanse or toilet them. Their responses have typically been interpreted as *symptoms* of their disease, not as the understandable effort to retain some control and independence. Confusion, related to memory losses and fragmentation, often leads an elder to display behaviors that appear disturbed.

Given the multiple personal and social losses that occur in dementia, its most profound impact is in shattering the person's sense of self, history and relationships—the defining elements of personhood. This is why researchers have long urged that the most pressing needs of someone with dementia are *for person work* through an enduring relationship with a supportive caregiver (Gubrium 1975; Kuhn 2002:165–66; Eggers, Norberg and Ekman 2005:343). Yet regulations, staffing levels and institutional prescripts have continued to place emphasis instead on standard physical and custodial *body work*.

My own observational research, summarized in the following discussion, found dramatic differences between residents on two identical, innovatively designed units with different approaches to care—a biomedicalized approach emphasizing *body work* and a *person-centered* approach where disturbed behaviors were viewed as more than just symptoms. I introduce this material for three reasons. First, I want to illustrate that physical models and structural designs alone are no guarantee of quality care; the underlying philosophy and values make greater difference in optimizing dementia care. Second, the unit that allowed for better care and resident outcomes adopted a philosophy of care consonant with that of the GHP. Finally, the care issues raised by the cases in both units provide serious care challenges. This offers an opportunity to consider the capacity of the GHP for handling them.

RESEARCH OF TWO SPECIAL CARE UNITS: THE HISTORIC SLEY UNITS

Setting of the Units: The First Special Care Units in the United States

In 1992–1994, I conducted research on the first two special care units in the United States designed with special environmental features to help people with mild dementia maintain their autonomy and cognitive and functional capacities. The units opened in 1974 due to pioneering efforts of Powell Lawton.[8] By the mid 1960s, Lawton and his colleagues had already envisioned an environment that challenged standard "dehumanizing" custodial care conducted "in the name of easing the effort of staff and maintaining cleanliness at all costs" (Liebowitz et al. 1979:59–61).[9] Extremely innovative for its time, this new approach was the product of a decade of research, years of planning and considerable input from international experts in gerontology, geriatrics and architecture, and of staff, families and residents.

The units were designed to compensate for deficits, while offering stimulation to help residents maintain existing capacities. Special design features, such as color-coding of rooms (to enable residents to locate them) served as visual memory aids to enable the residents to negotiate the environment (Liebowitz 1976). An open floor plan allowing visibility of activities was intended to socially cue people's memories, spark interest to engage in activities and passively stimulate residents for possible therapeutic effect (Liebowitz et al. 1979). A kitchen for cooking activities, pleasant lighting features, bright color schemes and a gazebo with safe plants were included to add meaning to elders' lives and provide cognitive stimulation (Cohen and Kirsten 1992:131). Residents dined together in one section of the floor around large tables.

By the time of my study, however, the intended use of the innovative floor plan, with all its special features, had dramatically changed, together with the level of impairment of residents who occupied the units. Many of the special design features, like the color coding of rooms and the kitchen, were either gone or in disuse. The gazebo was now used strictly by staff as a getaway, and residents were forbidden to go there. As residents became more impaired, the open design resounded with noise they produced, compounded by other institutional sounds from staff and visitors, the loudspeaker and the floor cleaners. To avoid conflict during meals, residents were now seated alone, or at the same small table with another resident. As residents became more cognitively impaired and less ambulatory, a number of demographic, fiscal and institutional factors conspired against preserving the original plan. The vision, energies, wisdom and dreams of the early planners were no longer benefiting the elders, who, like their families and most of the staff, knew little of the units' illustrious beginnings. The value of special care units themselves as superior facilities to support persons with dementia also was called into question. In one of his last published articles, Powell Lawton himself concluded that special care units could not be distinguished for offering better care (2001:158).

CASE STUDIES

Background to My Study

By the time I began studying the units, researchers were beginning to suggest that behavioral disturbances (BDs), such as fighting with caregivers, which were previously regarded as disease *symptom*s, might actually have some reasonable basis in the person's struggle to regain lost autonomy. Other BDs, such as repetition or agitation, might reflect the person's struggles both with cognitive impairment and the loss of social regard by others. Typically, confusion, evidenced by "wandering," had been seen only as a symptom. However, studies were beginning to suggest that a person did not wander aimlessly, but toward a familiar place, like "home," for example, to prepare her husband's dinner, or the bus stop to meet her children, forgetting that her husband had died or that the children were now adults. It was as if the resident found herself in a time warp.[10] So while the behavior seemed to lack sense in the present context, it clearly had some historical relevance in past contexts. Thus, behaviors that had been regarded as meaningless were beginning to gain credence as plausible efforts to *communicate* genuine needs, maintain a sense of self or revive personal stories (Sabat and Harré 1992; Hughes 2001).

One goal of my work was to study problematic behaviors in the contexts in which they had occurred—locations (the resident's room or dinner table), conditions (being pressured to wake up), persons involved (a family, nurse, NA) and time (upon waking, before dinner)—and the resolution (staff intervention, family involvement) that followed. I also tried to learn about the history of the person and more recent events that might have affected the behavior. To do so, I talked with the person (if possible), the family and staff and read their medical records.

The units each housed forty residents and were identical in design and admissions criteria: severe dementia and BDs (often verbal or physical aggressiveness). Their residents were the most severely impaired in the nursing home, whose disturbed behaviors led to their admission there. The median age on Sley 1 was 86.5 and 88.5 on Sley 2. Both units had somewhat higher than usual portions of female residents, with 80 percent females on Sley 1 and 85 percent on Sley 2.[11] Both units also enjoyed similar staffing levels: a head nurse (an RN) on the day shift, responsible for setting the philosophy and organizing the delivery of care; a nurse who served as care manager on all shifts and during weekends, responsible for supervising staff and dispensing medicine and treatments; five Nurse Assistants (NAs) during the morning and evening shifts and one or two at night; a part-time bathing assistant; and professional staff (physician and physician assistant, psychiatrist, activities specialist, nutritionist and social worker) who regularly visited the units.

However, more residents on Sley 1 were ambulatory and somewhat more behaviorally disturbed than on Sley 2, and the unit overall seemed noisier. After visiting the two units, I also discovered differences in the tenure of staff and residents and evidence of differing philosophies of care by the head nurse, who was responsible for structuring and prioritizing care. These differences, I felt, warranted a comparative study as they might contribute to differences in the residents' behaviors. I thus decided to split my time on the two units, spending nine to ten months on Sley 1 and then the same amount of time on Sley 2. I began by conducting general observations of the lives of the residents, their families and the staff. After a couple of months on each unit, the staff helped me select seven residents with severe BDs to study intensively over all shifts for one month each. The following focuses on one case study from each of the Sley units as an example for comparing the two approaches to care. In addition, I offer a second particularly challenging case from Sley 2 in considering the demands on the GH as a long-term care model.

Sley 1: Margaret—Unquieting Noise

> My greatest fear is the inability to take care of myself ever.
> They made this lovely place for the people, but it isn't though.

Margaret was the first person I came to know on Sley 1. During my first months there, she would regularly roll her wheelchair over to chat. Despite some confusion from her dementia, she was very pleasant and welcomed company. She was also socially sensitive with me, taking care not to interrupt me if I looked busy. The first time we met, she asked where she could find the trolley station, as it was getting late and her mother might worry. I explained I was new here and did not know. On later visits, she described her mother's lovely flower garden or the book club over which she had presided. At eighty-nine, she had survived two husbands and was childless. However, her brother and sister-in-law were very concerned for her and visited her frequently.

Margaret had lived in the nursing home complex for eight years, first in an apartment and, after her arthritis worsened, in a nursing unit. Previously independent, this move upset her. She lacked dementia at the time, but moving symbolized loss of autonomy and led to depression. A few years later, follow-ing hip surgery, she declined cognitively as well. During her last year on her unit, she began to call out loudly to staff when she was hungry or uncomfort-able. This disturbed other residents, and she was placed on a small dosage of an antipsychotic medication (20 mg of Mellaril®) and transferred to Sley 1 sev-eral months before I started my research.

Except for her occasional calling out, Margaret was not seen as a difficult resident. However, during baths, she would cry out loudly, and her cries were becoming more intense and generalized to other times. Her sister-in-law, who was a social worker, asked to observe her bath to see if she could find some triggers to Margaret's screaming. She found that Margaret started screaming only if she got water in her ears. To prevent this from happening, her sister-in-law brought in a rubber sunbonnet she had purchased on a trip to a tropical island specifically for Margaret. It fit snugly around Margaret's head and blocked her ears from the water. Much to her surprise, Hazel, the head nurse, could not promise it would be used.

Hazel later explained to me that locating the bonnet and using it was just too time-consuming for Rhonda, the part-time bathing assistant who bathed eight residents a day. Rhonda had to complete the eight baths within 3.75 hours or the nursing home would have to pay her benefits, which they tried to avoid. If she exceeded her allotted time, her evaluation would suffer and she could risk losing her job. Rather than let another resident delay in getting a bath, or leave bathing to the already overworked nursing assistant, Hazel encouraged Rhonda to complete her standard bathing tasks, skin checks, vital signs and dressing routines rather than to spend time with the sunbonnet, even if it improved Mar-garet's bath. Indeed, the one time that Rhonda tried it, Margaret was calmer and did not scream. Still, to Hazel, Margaret's problem was much larger than any-thing that could be solved by a "localized environmental accommodation," since to her, it stemmed directly from the dementia. It remains unclear whether the bonnet would have made a more lasting difference since Hazel no longer permit-ted Rhonda to use it.

Around this same time, a six-month psychiatric consultation, required by OBRA, led to a series of medication changes that exacerbated Margaret's symp-toms. In keeping with OBRA's mandate to use milder psychiatric medications and smaller dosages, the psychiatrist switched Margaret to Buspar®, a milder an-tipsychotic medication, which took six weeks to take effect. Almost immediately, Margaret complained about dizziness. She became intolerant of other residents and started yelling incessantly. With every medication change, her condition worsened. She became more confused and could no longer converse, recognize her family or feed herself. When other medications were added, she began to hal-lucinate. Her family insisted that she be returned to her original medication, and after twenty-nine changes and a nine-fold increase from her original dosage of Mellaril, she temporarily improved, although not to her previous level.

Then suddenly, she declined sharply. She tightly shut her eyes and just shouted or sang loudly, shutting out the world. Her brother appreciated the existential quality of her new behavior, which effectively separated her from an environment of which she would say, even in her deteriorated state, "I don't like this place; it's the *whole* thing I don't like." Hazel and her staff did not acknowledge the validity of Margaret's perceptions; to them, her decline was the predictable outcome of someone with dementia. However, for Margaret, constrained as she was, her increasingly pervasive outbursts were her only available means of articulating her existential condition.[12] Outbursts of this quality were not amenable to silencing via magic bullets.

Sley 2: Mrs. Fine—the Wicked Witch of the West

I have nothing—just this, while they have a very big house.
That is their world, and this is mine; I like it here.

When she was first entering the nursing home three years earlier, Mrs. Fine scored only four out of thirty possible points in the mini-mental status exam (MMSE) and another cognitive test.[13] Mrs. Fine stated that her husband had died a year before, when it was actually twenty years, and she seemed confused and hostile. At eighty-five, she had endured the loss of a second close male companion, six hospitalizations, a stroke and a broken hip. Left with a severe speech impediment and the inability to walk, she became depressed, more cognitively impaired and began to hallucinate. These led to brief psychiatric hospitalizations, which her daughter ended because she could not bear the artificial effects of the antidepressant on her mother: "I wanted my critical mother back!" While this endeared her to her daughter, it gained her the reputation in the nursing home as the "wicked witch of the west."

Mrs. Fine had lived on two other units before Sley 2, becoming increasingly aggressive. A tranquilizer at her previous unit disturbed her gait and she was restrained in her wheelchair. She began to disrobe in public, became incontinent and was in need of total hygienic and grooming care. At that point, she was transferred to Sley 2. Jenny, the head nurse there, determined that Mrs. Fine's anger stemmed from her awareness of her loss of control and dependence on others. She secured Mrs. Fine's cooperation for physical rehabilitation. As Mrs. Fine began walking again with the aid of a walker, her mood improved, so she was taken off the tranquilizer. An observant NA saw her remove her diaper to go to the bathroom and after additional assessment, she was deemed continent and the staff were alerted not to use diapers. They were also asked to respect Mrs. Fine's wishes to gain help with hygienic care only in the evening, the only time she wanted it. Mrs. Fine improved so markedly that staff visiting from other units could not even recognize her.

Because she had significantly improved, her family encouraged staff to transfer her to a unit with higher-functioning residents. After moving, she declined and once again was restrained in her wheelchair. She returned once again to Sley 2, this time to a highly coveted private room. With patience from the staff, she restored some autonomy, gained confidence and resumed walking independently. Her speech *aphasia* (difficulty in finding words)—brought on by a stroke—had worsened, but the staff were patient and supportive of her efforts to talk. However, following hospitalization, due to a possible stroke, she became more aggressive again and also became obsessed with photographs of family members and with fears for the safety of her daughter. She also became paranoid about others going through her belongings and seemed more deeply depressed. The psychiatrist and unit physician disagreed about how to handle this. The physician had known Mrs. Fine since her initial admission to the home and felt her behavior was only marginally more extreme than before and that the unit staff could handle it. He did not want to risk her losing functional improvement by introducing psychotropic medications.

The psychiatrist was also aware of risks in using antipsychotic medications with elderly patients, especially when dementia is involved. Tranquilizers can lead to dizziness and falls and even have disinhibiting effects, like disrobing. Antidepressants can also increase agitation or confusion. Still, the psychiatrist did not like to see Mrs. Fine suffer, so she convinced the unit physician to start Mrs. Fine on an antidepressant. In fact, Mrs. Fine's mood did improve, her depression lifted, and her paranoia diminished. She also viewed the nursing home more positively: "I like it here; I have two good doctors here." Her mini-mental status exam showed higher functioning than at any time since her admission several years earlier, and she developed a strong relationship with the psychiatrist. However, a month later, after another hospitalization for a urinary tract infection (UTI), she became irritable, so her physician withdrew the antidepressant, but her mood remained unchanged. "This," he insisted "is just Mrs. Fine."

A few weeks later, she was looking quite content, glad to be back from the hospital, but disappointed that her daughter had not yet visited her. However, this time, instead of worrying that her daughter was dead, she calmly observed that it did not really matter "as long as she's okay."

Mrs. Fine told me she had torn off a sign from her door. The sign, "Nurse in Charge," had been placed on her door because of a suspected infectious virus she might be carrying. "I just tore the 'Nurse in Charge' sign off my door," because, she confidently explained, *"I'm* in charge."

"You are protesting?" I asked.

"Yes," she firmly stated.

It appeared she was back to her old spunky self.

CONTRASTS AND IMPLICATIONS OF THE TWO APPROACHES

In contrast to the staff of Sley 1, who disregarded Margaret's complaints, those of Sley 2 not only responded to Mrs. Fine's wishes, but also were attuned to her history, personality and preferences. This led them to design and adjust her care so as to maximize her functional capacities while supporting her as a *person*, with all her foibles, including her occasionally sour disposition. Her treatment team were even willing to revisit possibilities like physical therapy, years after other clinicians had abandoned it as an option, to help her restore some independence, viewing this as vital for increasing her quality of life. This involved *working with* Mrs. Fine to help her attain greater well-being. The head nurse could look beyond the dementia and try to understand Mrs. Fine's anger as legitimate in light of the loss of her highly valued independence. This was in striking contrast to Mrs. Fine's experience at previous units, which like Margaret's, "treated" her existential protests as medical symptoms needing containment and restraint.

Rather than suppress Mrs. Fine's expressions of anger, her care team appreciated their legitimacy. To improve her functioning, they tried to determine, and then move to correct, what stimulated her disruptive behaviors. This approach served to preserve—not pathologize and suppress—the obdurate, cantankerous person, however difficult, who had always been that way. It also helped her function at a level unimaginable by staff from other units.

At Sley 1, residents' behaviors were attributed entirely to medical causes, and their *personal* needs were invalidated or relegated as secondary to the *instrumental* needs of the staff and institution to efficiently complete care tasks. What differentiated care on Sley 2 from Sley 1 was the willingness of the staff to see residents as *persons*, beyond their dementia, and to flexibly organize care to identify and correct not only medical problems, but excess disability[14] not related to the dementia, like vision problems, to optimize their life quality (McLean 2007b:23).

In yet another particularly challenging case in Sley 2, the care team expended extraordinary effort in helping Mrs. Gold, a woman who had become very unsteady and whose sleep pattern had become reversed. To protect her, staff initially restrained her in bed, but after she climbed over the bedrails and injured herself, her physician gradually withdrew her medications, which he suspected had increased her unsteadiness. Meanwhile, nursing staff gave her one-on-one attention and used less invasive protection, like a floor-level bed, and naturally tired her out by walking with her while conducting their rounds. This was time consuming, and one nurse did quit, but the situation was resolved within two months. Through experimentation and devoted personal attention, the staff restored her ambulation, sleep routine and calmness, without placing her at risk. While the demands on the staff were immense, so were the positive outcomes.

The challenge is to develop person-centered care that may be high intensity at times, but sufficiently productive that both the resident and staff are rewarded. This requires adequate staff to prevent burnout and skilled specialists to guide an optimal outcome. Any model of residential care, like the Green House, that offers skilled nursing care must be able to address such complex challenges in promoting quality of life for residents, even during difficult periods.

THE GREEN HOUSE PROJECT (GHP)

GHP is an innovative approach to long-term care that, under federal regulations, fully qualifies as skilled nursing home provision.[14] Green Houses were deliberately developed to meet regulatory and reimbursement criteria to be accessible even to the indigent elderly. Green Houses, however, were designed as intentional communities that depart radically from traditional nursing homes both structurally (in physical environment and organization of care) and philosophically. Green Houses were developed by William Thomas, founder of the Eden Alternative, a previous "culture change" (CC) approach designed to humanize nursing homes by promoting relationships and life. Eden intended to eliminate loneliness, helplessness and boredom in residents, to bring life through plants, animals and children to the home and to empower both residents and frontline staff to make everyday decisions. Despite the international popularity of the Eden Alternative, Thomas found progress to culture change slow, evaluations unimpressive, and by 1999 he became convinced of the need to fully redesign the nursing home from the beginning in order to effect the kinds of changes he had in mind.

What initially motivated Thomas to design these CC initiatives was his encounter with an elder at a nursing home where he worked in the early 1990s. As he prepared to leave her bedside, she grabbed his arm and uttered, "I'm so lonely" (Thomas 2004:180). From that haunting moment, he has been on his own CC journey, with the mission of liberating elders from institutional existence, promoting instead a new world vision of interdependence and well-being among generations, what he calls "eldertopia." This involves sustaining and protecting elders, who in turn impart wisdom and foresight to the community (see Thomas this section).

For Thomas, the GHP was one vehicle toward achieving this vision, an "opportunity ... to transform the *dream* of a warm, loving, nurturing sanctuary into a specific *innovation* that can change how we age" (Thomas 2004:222). These affect size, design, conception of residents' needs, staffing roles and delivery of expert services. Green Houses are designed as places where assistance with daily living and clinical care are available, but where the focus is not on care, but on life and relationships. Thus, by design, it redirects attention from the instrumental care task in the realm of timed work, to the person in the realm of life as nonprescriptively lived (cf. McLean 2007a).

To achieve this, he adopted a philosophy emphasizing residents' strengths and freedom to choose, used the principles of *warm* (small and nonhierarchical), *smart* (technology to foster well-being) and *green* (connection to the living world) in designing the physical environment. To create a new notion of care in this setting, Thomas evoked the mythical creature of the Shahbaz, the royal falcon who stood as protector, sustainer and nurturer of people, as the model for the *assistant* or helper of elders. He was careful, however, to distinguish *protection* (as a form of reciprocal support for those cherished) from the *restraint* and control more common in nursing home care (Thomas 2004:259–261). *Sustenance* involved friendship, homemaking and the pleasure of sharing food (what he calls *convivium*). *Nurturance* above all was relational, holding the capacity for mutual fulfillment in carrying out even the most mundane routines. Through mutual cooperation with elders, the Shabaz is invested in the enormous charge of creating a new societal understanding of elderhood.

Structurally, the GH is deliberately small[15]—a self-contained house for seven to ten residents. Ideally, it is located in a neighborhood and blends in architecturally with other homes. Up to ten private bedrooms with full bathrooms surround the heart of the home—the hearth room and kitchen. Food is cooked in the kitchen, as one would expect in one's home, and residents can participate in preparation and delight in the sensuousness of the smells of food cooking. Because of the small distance of travel to the kitchen and other places within the home, mobility is encouraged and wheelchairs are often not needed. Safety features are built in, and there is access to an outdoor garden and patio. The appearance of medical apparatuses is deliberately avoided by eliminating medication charts (keeping residents' medication cabinets in their own rooms instead), replacing a visible nurse's station with a closed-off den and using wireless call systems and silent pagers. Each bedroom has a track for a ceiling lift to assist with lifting residents from their bed to a wheel chair. The Green House may incorporate smart technology as well, to enhance communication, for example, using interactive television to connect with remote family (Rabig et al. 2006:534). But while the Green House may have the markers of a home, Thomas is clear that it is "not a family dwelling," but a particular kind of "intentional community" (2004:232).

In contrast to those in nursing homes, elders in a GH retain control over such vital daily activities as when to get up, bathe, eat and sleep, preserving the *sanctity of lived time* (McLean 2007a). Residents engage in activities whenever they want, as part of life, not as a "billable service." Elders and Shahbazim participate together in life by eating, talking, engaging in activities and even playing together (Rabig et al. 2006:534–35). They are supported physically, emotionally and spiritually. Importantly, the hope was to engage the broader community as well.

The Shahbazim are housekeepers and caregivers in the broadest sense, responsible for cooking, cleaning and laundry, as well as personal care and nurturance. Beyond CNA (certified nursing assistant) training, they receive 120 hours of training in the GH philosophy. There are two Shahbazim during the day and evening shifts and one during the night shift, accounting for forty hours for ten residents. In a typical nursing home where CNAs conduct rounds, this would amount to four hours per resident. In a Green House, it is both less and more—less, since with her other obligations, the Shahbaz is less likely to spend four hours exclusively with one resident; more, because residents can be in the presence of a Shahbaz a full twenty-four-hour period if they wish. The Shahbazim[16] are supervised by an administrator ("guide"), rather than by nurses, to avoid the traditional hierarchy in nursing relations. To break down existing professional hierarchies and organizational rigidity, Thomas made Shahbazim central to life in Green Houses and removed professionals from any nonclinical decision-making. The clinical support team (nurses, a medical director, social worker, activities specialist, dietician and other therapists) visit on a schedule dictated by regulatory mandates and needs for assessment and treatment, but are expected to "behave as guests." This further identifies the Green House as a home, not a clinical space.

PROMISES (AND CAVEATS)

Because GHP is young and little research is yet available on it, my observations will be largely speculative. Early findings from the study in Tupelo, Mississippi, of the first Green Houses, however, are promising. Self-reported quality of life measures of residents in GHs were superior to those at the two nursing homes with which they were compared.[17] On quality of care, GH residents equaled those of nursing homes and showed less decline in late-loss ADL functioning. Surprisingly, though, they showed more incontinence. Although Green Houses do not emphasize structured activities, in seven areas they equaled the comparison group (Kane et al. 2007). Anecdotal evidence is even more telling. One woman, who was viewed as too impaired and unresponsive to actually benefit from a Green House environment, was transferred there from her 140-bed nursing home at her family's request. Upon arriving at the Green House, she perked up immediately and continued to improve, talking and singing again, going from being fed pureed foods to feeding herself whole foods and gaining a spark of life (Baker 2007:88–89). Still, the original study showed that one resident was asked to leave and another returned to the nursing home (Kane et al. 2007:833). It would be worth exploring why these removals occurred in order to gain insight as to what the issues were that led the residents to leave and how well the model might be able to better address these in the future.

The GHP has succeeded in removing the medical wrappings and institutional controls that have oppressed life in nursing homes for decades. By radically reconfiguring not just the physical structure, but also the power relations between the supervisory and rank nursing staff and the pace of life within, it has enabled possibilities for elders to reconnect with their world and reinvigorate their lives. By refashioning CNAs as venerable homemakers, it has invested these women with enormous responsibility to sustain a portion of society's frail elders, to nurture relations and protect elders as those one cherishes. Yet Shahbazim begin as strangers to elders, lacking a shared history. Some will nonetheless embrace this responsibility out of sheer grace and desire for growth; others may come to this with time—or, they will not. Indeed, the success of eldertopia, as advanced within GHs, relies mainly, if not entirely, on the Shahbazim. Yet while invested with immense social responsibility for *all* of us, Shahbazim—often women of color and of modest backgrounds[18]— continue to be paid quite poorly (Baker 2007). Thus their accepting this charge is no small feat, aspiring toward what philosopher Charles Taylor has called "a new horizon of meaning," that they are part of a larger whole both socially and spiritually (1991). But how are the rest of us to be involved?

In Tupelo, GHs were integrated into regular neighborhoods, providing greater opportunity for social inclusion and intergenerational relationships within a broader community beyond strictly the Shahbazim. However, some GHs are being planned to be built on campuses of long-term care facilities, thus limiting broader social integration and perpetuating an association with a medicalized and geriatric-segregated establishment. Beyond the resident-Shahbazim relation, the GHP has not developed ways of creating the intergenerational reciprocity eldertopia seeks to promote, perhaps to avoid overly prescribing it. Nonetheless, unlike small owner-operated board and care homes, Shahbazim are less likely to gain access to informal supports (family, friends and neighbors) available to the owner-operators who live on the premises of their board and care home unless they are also part of the community (Eckert and Morgan 2001). Identifying nonprofessional staff as the core staff of the Green Houses reinforces the nonmedicalized aspects of daily life and combined resident/Shahbazim control over everyday decision-making, with help from the guide as needed. Still, some losses may result from this arrangement, such as the reduction of exposure of residents to exceptional clinicians, like Jenny, of Sley 2, whose insights helped reduce Mrs. Fine's excess disabilities and increased her autonomy. In addition, the move away from a medical model, while vital for the everyday life of residents, may lead to false dismissal of signs of genuine medical conditions (Baker 2007:77).

Implications for Dementia

Despite these potential limitations, the GHP has worked at reversing a mindset that ignores elders' needs as secondary to institutional prescripts. For elders with dementia, whose aberrant behaviors have long been pathologized as senseless symptoms of their disease and ignored, this is no less than revolutionary. Further, in redefining itself as a genuine home, not a place of shift work and rounds, the Green House frees elders and Shabahzim alike to enjoy the tempo of life as lived. Here *relationships* reign supreme and central to life quality. For the person with dementia, such relationships perpetuate meaning-making in their lives and validate both their fragile identities and their enduring need to engage meaningfully with their world (Frank 2005:177). This is therapeutic to someone whose impaired memory disrupts their sense of a unified self. Shahbazim can effectively restore that sense by continuing to acknowledge the elder. Indeed, in dementia, quality of life depends on the sense of self-esteem and belonging that derive from meaningfully relating with others (Nolan et al. 2002:200–201).

Some elders are privileged to remain in their own homes, where a sense of personal meaning and belonging has been fostered over their entire life course (Stafford Part V). For those who lack this privilege, the Green House may provide a substitute locus for home. In fact, for some people the experience of home—or of a home yearned for—is not attached to an external place at all, but to an interior space of personal security and social connectedness (Reed-Danahay 2001:60). This may be why, in the absence of these positive conditions, an elder *already* in her home may still longingly cry out for it (Frank 2005). Thus, emotional connections to the referents of home may matter even more to the elder than the actual physical site (Brent 1999:78).

How, then, might the Green House Project succeed in fostering social connectedness? It is less likely to do so by creating a generic sense of "hominess" in the environment than by providing ongoing opportunities for each elder to make meaningful connections to both past and present (Post 2006:226). These connections help to preserve a positive social identity and to fend off insecurity, social isolation and depression (cf. Williams 2002:145). As a potentially healing environment, the Green House can help maintain identity in dementia by sparking cognitive, sensorial (e.g., by smelling favorite foods cooking) and emotional experiences that recall past memories. These can be compared against experiences in other settings (Williams 2002:148), or enable the construction of new meanings through new relationships and experiences. Such experiences, together with the sense of freedom and privacy, reinforce the delicate sense of being at "home" with one's self (Frank 2005:184, 187–188), so vital to well-being in dementia (Williams 2002:145–146, 148). Finally, insofar as the Green House "shelters daydreaming" and "protects the dreamer ... to dream in peace," it reinforces meaningful continuity with the past: "it is because our memories of former home-places are relived as daydreams that these home-places of the past remain in us for all time" (Bachelard 1994:6).[19]

CONCLUSION

As the Pioneer Network gains force, many more homes are promoting person-centered care, often through remodeling to appear more homelike and appealing. While many of these homes are run by individuals or groups that have been on the forefront of change, or welcoming of it, others may see this more as a necessary marketing scheme. What is unique about the GHP is that its vision was matched with a design to reach those whose economic situations could never afford access to this kind of model. Thus, it has the makings of a broadly liberating dream. Of course, the GH is not the first to do this; Quaker facilities predated even OBRA in working to validate and dignify all elders, no matter how impaired (McLean 2007b:241–42).[20]

Dreams, though, are actualized by real people in real circumstances; they are never universally guaranteed no matter how liberating the possibilities. Thus, in the final analysis, it is people themselves (Shahbazim, guides, administrators, residents, families, policy-makers and the public) who will determine the extent to which the GH—and other CC models—will or will not be liberating and sustainable. Some will decide whether to preserve or alter the initial model to meet the needs of those who live and work there, as they strive to make the GH financially sustainable. Already, Cedars, the nonprofit owner of the four GHs in Tupelo, has built six more GHs, but with twelve beds, not the six to ten beds Thomas had in mind. To actualize his dream-idea, Thomas stayed within CMS costs. Yet to fully deliver its dream to elders with varying skilled-care needs, the GHP may need to build in additional help in exceptional circumstances, as with Mrs. Gold on Sley 2, where intensive individual staff support for two months helped her to ride out a difficult period. The challenge is to accommodate residents like her without overburdening staff and other residents; this may demand higher funding. With its call to support the human spirit, rather than to make profits, it is not surprising that GH and CC have been promoted mainly by nonprofit faith-based organizations (Baker 2007:3). One thing is for sure. The call for CC will not die, as CC agents are mobilizing internationally[21] to realize a dream of better life for elders. How this will be realized in particular contexts, both locally and internationally, will be something anthropologists will surely wish to follow and help to inform for future initiatives.

NOTES

1. The Nursing Home Reform Act, as part of the 1987 Omnibus Reconciliation Act (OBRA 87), intended to address neglect and abuse in nursing homes, but also to establish standards of care and compliance. These standards addressed quality of life by obligating nursing homes to provide "the highest practicable physical, mental, and psychosocial well-being" of residents (Turnham 2001). While heroic in intent, even with success in several areas such as restraint reduction and continual efforts to improve regulations and compliance, it has fallen short of its goals. For further elaboration on its shortcomings, see *Faces of Neglect* by NCCNHR. See www.nccnhr.org/action_center/366_1994_12825.cfm (accessed on August 15, 2008).

2. Although reformers had long complained about conditions in institutionalized homes for the aged (e.g., Henry 1963), the "culture change" movement finally gained momentum when a group of "pioneers" of nursing home reform gathered in Rochester, New York, in 1992 and again in 1997. In 2000, the group named themselves the "Pioneer Network," and have gained influence with consumers, care facilities and policy makers. For more information on its history, see www.pioneernetwork.net/who-we-are/our-history.php (accessed on August 15, 2008).

3. Dementia Care Mapping is an intensive observational method used to determine quality of dementia services on the basis of specific indicators of quality of life (Capstick 2003:11–22). It was developed by Kitwood and colleagues, the Bradford Dementia Group, UK.

4. The Eden Alternative was a new concept in nursing home care and philosophy, developed by William Thomas to tackle "loneliness, helplessness and boredom" through a habitat that engaged people in the "green" noninstitutional world of plants, animals and children. It challenged the hierarchical model of institutional organization and returned control to the direct caregivers (Thomas 1996; 2004:179–90). This model has been very successful internationally with at least 300 registered "edenized" homes. See www.edenalt.org (accessed on August 15, 2008).

5. *Neighborhoods* refer to structural divisions within nursing homes, which serve as smaller clusters of residents (about twelve per neighborhood). Each is further divided into two "houses," consisting of residents' rooms surrounding a kitchen, den and formal living room. This innovation was developed by Charlene Boyd and the staff of Providence Mount St. Vincent, in Seattle, Washington. However, in more vulgarized commercially exploitative forms, a simple door is said to divide a wing into neighborhoods, without further structural or conceptual changes.

6. By 2025, Thomas envisions a system of home and community care with 100,000 Green Houses and a few leftover nursing homes. In five years, fifty Green Houses have opened (Kane et al. 2007:839).

7. ADLs are Activities of Daily Living—personal care routines like combing one's hair; IADLs are Independent Activities of Daily Living—more complex chores like balancing a checkbook.

8. Powell Lawton was probably the most influential psychologist in reconceptualizing environmental designs for optimizing cognition and dementia care in the United States. He forged efforts to understand the impact of environment on the care and quality of life of those in nursing homes and conducted innovative research on ways to evaluate these impacts.

9. This was the type of care that Jules Henry had decried in *Culture against Man* in 1963.

10. I thank Deanna Trakas for this metaphor.

11. Most homes average around 75 percent women.

12. I thank Robert Rubinstein for this observation.

13. The difference in Mrs. Fine's performance went beyond the tests to her disposition toward being tested as well as to actual differences in her cognitive status during times of testing.

14. States have ultimate jurisdiction over classification of long-term residence. In those states where skilled nursing certification is not allowed, GHP allows them to be built as assisted living facilities. See CMS letter, December 21, 2006 from www.ncbcapitalimpact.org/default.aspx?id=414 (accessed on August 15, 2008).

15. Smaller facilities have been associated with less anxiety and depression in residents (Rabig et al. 2006:534), especially those with dementia.

16. The word *shahbaz* is Persian and a singular form of the assistant he calls the "midwife of elderhood." *Shahbazim* uses the Hebrew "im" ending to create the plural form, to capture a mixture of traditions in a novel blend, like the Green House itself (Thomas 2004:239, 255).

17. There were four Green Houses with ten residents each; two were dementia-specific. The comparison nursing homes were owned by the same nonprofit organization, and one of the homes shared their administration with the Green Houses (Kane et al. 2007).

18. Because Green Houses in many states qualify for Medicaid grants, many Green House residents may share backgrounds with the Shahbazim, in contrast to residents in private homes.

19. Cited in Brent (1999:72).

20. Quakers are a religious society that accepts the fundamental divinity in all things. This includes extremely frail and demented persons. Long before the CC movement began, Quakers had designed long-term care to support the dignity and respect of both care receiver and caregiver in demedicalized settings. Quaker-sponsored facilities such as Chandler Hall, in Newtown, Pennsylvania, have also pioneered in intergenerational programs with on-site child care and development facilities See www.chandlerhall.org (accessed on August 15, 2008). In addition, since 1973, Kendal, in Longwood, Pennsylvania, has promoted an "Untie the Elderly" movement to eliminate the use of both physical and chemical restraints. See http://ute.kendaloutreach.org/learning/learning.aspx (accessed on August 15, 2008).

21. In Ireland, on December 5–6, 2007, CC experts Steve Shields and LaVrene Norton, at workshops organized by the Health Service Executive and the National Council on Ageing and Older People, were enthusiastically received for their ideas on transforming care in the Irish context.

CHAPTER 45

Between Humans
and Ghosts: The Decrepit
Elderly in a Polynesian Society

Judith C. Barker

The distinction between decrepit and intact elders is recognized as being an important one in all societies (Foner 1985; Glascock 1982 this volume). Frequently, frail elders are seen as burdens on society and are even subject to "death-hastening" behaviors, such as neglect or abandonment by the rest of the community. Certain aspects of Polynesian life, however, lead to an expectation that the senescent old will not be abandoned or neglected, but rather will always remain a focus of attention and concern. Is this in fact the case?

Generally, Pacific ethnographies and commentaries fail to distinguish between treatment accorded the intact, mature elder and that given the frail, senescent old (e.g., Holmes 1972, 1974; Nason 1981; Rhoads 1984; Counts and Counts 1985). The following is a picture we have of old age in Polynesian societies showing that frail elders are not forgotten nor devalued, but powerful and active family and community members, much like their intact peers: "The infirm aged are cared for with matter-of-fact kindness within the family, mostly by women and older children" (R. Maxwell 1970:140). Any variation in treatment accorded the frail, elderly Polynesian is assumed to be idiosyncratic, an individual aberration having no societal or cultural basis.

Fieldwork in the early 1980s on Niue, a little-known western Polynesian island, revealed the existence of considerable differences in the treatment of very frail and of intact elders. This chapter shows not only who comprised neglected older people on Niue and how they were treated, but why this well-established and systematic variation in the treatment of the elderly makes cultural sense.

THE ELDERLY IN POLYNESIAN SOCIETY

Certain striking similarities are evident in all Polynesian societies—similarities, for example, of language, ecology, social organization and myth and history

(Holmes 1974; Ritchie and Ritchie 1979). Nonetheless, each Polynesian society is unique, different from all others. So, the case study given here describing Niuean responses to the elderly is suggestive, but not proof, of the existence of similar processes in other Polynesian societies.

Throughout this chapter, the term *elder* is used to refer to individuals who both currently or formerly held important sociopolitical positions and have reached chronological old age, that is, are sixty-five or more years old. Bear in mind, however, that the role of elder is well established before people reach numerical old age. Said to be well past the giddiness and frenzy of youth and comfortably settled into the responsibilities of marriage and family, Polynesian elders are stable and influential social figures, mature adults in the prime of life, full of vigor, with complex political, social and familial roles and responsibilities. Having acquired political and social influence by middle age, a competent person maintains that power into advanced old age. Because the role of elder is well established by midlife, before a person begins to experience significant decline in physical or mental abilities, elders suffer little life disruption as a result of mere chronological aging. While traditional roles allotted to the elderly sometimes chafe modern youth, the elderly as a group are still highly regarded; even in the face of sometimes sweeping socioeconomic and political changes, Polynesian elders sustain their high status (Holmes 1974; Maxwell 1970; Rhoads 1984).

Elders are respected not just because of family background or accomplishments, but also because they are chronologically older. Not only is attention to relative age linguistically symbolized, but it is also bolstered by the entire social, religious, economic and political organization of Polynesian life. A focus of socialization throughout Polynesian life, especially during childhood, is the inculcation of respect for those who are older (Ritchie and Ritchie 1979, 1981; Shore 1982). Older people are to be obeyed, respected, served and emulated. In return, elders will nurture, teach, love and protect. The mutuality of this form of relationship continues throughout life, younger persons always being socially obligated to care for older ones. From this comes an expectation that even in advanced old age or physical infirmity, the aged will be well cared for by children and grandchildren, because they are still important family members and because it would be shameful to neglect an elder. Most ethnographers of Polynesian societies argue that this expectation is fulfilled (e.g., Holmes 1972, 1974; Holmes and Rhoads 1987). My research, however, casts some doubts about this.

NIUE ENCAPSULATED

Relatively little is known about Niue, there being few scholarly writings or popular commentaries in either historical or contemporary times (Chapman 1976; Niue Government 1982; Ryan 1984; Scott 1993; Yarwood and Jowitt 1998; Barker 2000, 2001). Two early ethnographies exist (Smith 1983 [1902/1903] and Loeb 1926), both based on very short periods of fieldwork over seventy years ago; more recent works usually focus on specific topics, such as migration. Unlike many other Pacific islands, Niue was not colonized soon after Cook's fleeting contact in 1774 (McLachlan 1982; Ryan 1984) because it was outside regular trade routes, had little commercial potential and was not strategically or militarily important. The island was administered by New Zealand from 1900 to 1974, when independence was granted. It inherited an infrastructure for communications, roads and health and social welfare services of a standard far in excess of her nearest neighbors. New Zealand continues to provide Niueans with citizenship, protection against foreign powers, and considerable economic aid (Chapman 1976; Niue Government 1982; Scott 1993).

An isolated single island of raised coral, Niue does not fit the popular image of a tropical isle. It has no fringing reef, no sandy beaches and no lagoon. Access is difficult because steep cliffs rise directly out of deep ocean. Located some 600 km southeast of Samoa, at 19°S and 169°55'W, this large (160 square kilometers) island is covered by relatively sparse vegetation growing in shallow pockets of fertile soil between sharp pinnacles of coral rock. There are no streams or ponds, and no surface water on this drought- and hurricane-prone island.

Slash-and-burn (shifting) agriculture, arduous and labor-intensive because of the rugged terrain, supplies the populace with its basic subsistence needs and is supplemented by fishing, hunting and gathering (Barker 2001). In contrast to most other Pacific nations, the economic base of the island changed from primarily agricultural to service provision, so nearly 80 percent of employed adults on the island work for the Niuean Government (Connell 1983). This gives Niue a high standard of living compared to other Pacific nations. Money, from wages or supplemented by cash cropping of taro, passion fruit, limes or coconuts, is used to buy durable consumer goods such as motor vehicles, outboard motors and refrigerators (Pollock 1979; Yarwood and Jowitt 1998).

Niue has both a language and a social organization similar to, but somewhat different from, other western Polynesian societies (Loeb 1926; Pollock 1979; Smith 1983). Daily life and interaction on Niue, however, is much like that on any other Polynesian island, especially in relation to childrearing, family organization and central religious values (see Hanson 1970; Holmes 1974; Levy 1973; Shore 1982). In its sociopolitical forms, Niue tends to have a more rudimentary and very flexible social hierarchy, egalitarian ideals, an emphasis on individual achievement and a strong work ethic (Pollock 1979). These features influence the status of elders. For example, contemporary Niuean politics conforms to tradition by having certain elders—pastors, planters from prominent families—represent individual villages at the same time that it deviates from convention by rewarding individual achievement, with younger Western-educated people representing the entire voting public. This flexible social hierarchy, egalitarian ideals and emphasis on individual achievement, work against elders maintaining their privileged position once their competence is in any way compromised.

Though large in land area, Niue has never supported a population greater than about 5,000 (Bedford, Mitchell and Mitchell 1980). Depopulation, not overpopulation, has long been Niue's greatest worry (Niue Government 1985, 1988; Yarwood and Jowitt 1998); some 2,000 people now inhabit the island. Out-migration is permanent and consists mainly of unmarried youth and mature adult couples and their school-age children going to New Zealand to settle. Every census since 1971 shows a loss of population in the order of 20 percent, considerably affecting the island's population structure as an increasing proportion of island inhabitants comprised elderly adults. Almost twenty years ago, by 1988, life expectancy was high, approximately sixty-seven years, mortality rates were decreasing and elders aged sixty-five or more made up 8 percent of Niue's population, a proportion in excess of that usually found in the developing world (Taylor, Nemaia and Connell 1987; Barker 1994).

THE ELDERLY ON NIUE

The general ethnographic picture of the aged in Polynesian society (e.g., Holmes and Rhoads 1987) accurately portrays the intact elder on Niue: those in good health and important social functions are respected community figures, political leaders and vital family members. The frail, infirm Niuean elder, however, presents a very different picture. So, exactly how are impaired elders treated on Niue? What kinds of treatment do they receive from their kin and community? And, how is the mistreatment that I observed explainable in this cultural context?

The Treatment of Impaired Elders

I met elders with urinary or fecal incontinence, wheezing chests and runny eyes, infected sores, bleeding gums, or painful joints, none of whom had been seen recently by a doctor or nurse. One elder I saw lay semicomatose on the floor, evoking rueful smiles from visitors and kin, and comments about "going out the hard way."

Too frail to summon a physician themselves, these elders relied on their caretakers, who seemed not to bother asking for medical help. It is not difficult to get a physician to visit. A doctor visits each village on the island four times a week. A red flag hanging by the roadside brings the doctor in his van right to one's door. Public health nurses, too, can be fetched in the same way on their monthly rounds to assist in the care of patients. All medical services, including hospitalization, are free. When cases such as these do come to the attention of the medical profession, they are quickly attended to. Elders comprised a yearly average of 8 percent (N = 276) of all admissions to hospital on Niue between 1977 and 1982. Fourteen elderly patients (5 percent), most of whom remained in the hospital for over a year, were admitted solely for nursing care (Barker 1988).

Several types of old people were generally left unattended or received minimal care. These were old folk who: yelled frequently, especially at night; swore at neighbors and kin; fought all the time, hitting out at all and sundry; forgot people's names or what they were doing; wandered away at all times of day and night; talked only of events in the remote past, or conversed with absent friends and long-dead relatives; and stared vacantly about them, constantly drooled or were incontinent. Families seemed to make little effort to bathe these elders (who were generally clad in filthy rags), to clean their homes or to provide them with any material comforts; many of these elders complained of being constantly hungry.

Just as a pregnant woman is warned not to steal from others lest her unborn child be punished for the act by being born with a withered arm, so were explanations found for the causes of some degenerative processes that afflict the old. Facial tics, involuntary vocalizations and limb palsies in old age are regarded as belated punishments for evil-doing. Elders with these problems were held up as examples for children: "Old Togia makes noises like a chicken all the time now. That's because when he was young he must have stolen chickens and never confessed to doing so. If you don't want to be like that when you get old, don't steal."

Those old people who were bent over, or walked with difficulty, or tried ineffectually to fend for themselves were figures of fun. It amused everyone that an elderly man was concussed by a dry coconut falling on his head. The danger of this is constantly pointed out to young children, who quickly learn to steer clear. An old person who fails to avoid a falling nut thus demonstrates the loss of critical skills inculcated early in life. Events of the sort in which the elderly sustain injury are not unusual. Between 1977 and 1982, for example, accident or injury was a leading cause of death for Niueans over seventy years of age, accounting for 14 percent of all deaths of elders (Taylor, Nemaia and Connell 1987; Barker 1988). Old men were especially likely to die as a result of accident or injury.

People were amazed that extreme thirst late one afternoon would cause an eighty-five-year-old partially blind woman to go searching for water, only to end up falling into a disused water tank, breaking her arm, and dislocating her shoulder. Her feeble cries for help were finally heard by school children on their way home from classes. The children did call for help—amid much hilarity about the old lady's plight, and some teasing and swearing at her for creating such a situation. Anyone who gets injured on Niue is likely to be greeted with gales of laughter and ribald comment. Mocking, teasing and ridicule are common strategies of social control, of making abnormal situations appear normal. These strategies are used especially to get children to acquiesce to adult wishes or to accept painful medical treatments (Levy 1973:308–14). Giggling and laughing also hides anxiety, nervousness, fear or embarrassment. Hilarity not only covers an underlying concern for the injured, but also reinforces the fatalistic, stoic acceptance of misfortune that is expected of victims. The children's laughter over the old lady's fate was at a pitch and intensity that revealed that they were especially disturbed. Teasing her, ridiculing her and making rude jokes about her and her fate were attempts to establish control over the phenomenon, to make it conform to Niuean expectations, to normalize the unusual.

Late in 1982, a visitor from New Zealand, a nurse with many years of experience in caring for geriatric patients, made an informal inspection of elderly people on Niue. Her findings paralleled mine, echoing the things I had seen. From this evidence, I concluded that some frail elders on Niue were not receiving the kind of care and attention I had expected they would. By Western standards, some elders were clearly being neglected.

The Concept of "Neglect"

Each society has its own standards for conduct toward other persons, for conduct that is honorable, respectful, acceptable, proper, indifferent, demeaning, brutal, abusive or neglectful. The age, sex and relative social rank of the persons involved in the relationship, as well as individual characteristics of the protagonists and the history of their interactions, have a lot to do with the conduct of one to the other and how it is defined. What is deemed "neglect" by Western societies may be acceptable, expected, normal behavior elsewhere.

When I say decrepit elders on Niue were ignored or neglected by their kin or community, I do not mean they never received any attention or care. They were not completely abandoned; rather, they received minimal attention or inadequate care. Old people would be visited by kin, but not necessarily every day, and then often only by youngsters sent to check on their well-being. They would be given food, but sometimes in scant amounts and not the choice morsels they formerly enjoyed. They would be clothed, but in tattered clothes that were rarely laundered. It is this type of treatment that I refer to as neglect.

When Glascock (this volume) describes a group's behavior toward the frail elderly as "death hastening" or "neglectful," he means the outcome of the acts of behavior do not enhance the well-being of the aged individual from *our* understanding of the physical and mental processes involved. From the perspective of the people concerned, however, the outcome might be seen as helpful, if not to the individual at least to the group. In this chapter, I first describe behavior toward the elderly using Western notions of neglect, and then this behavior is related to other aspects of Niuean society to show why this apparently neglectful behavior is in fact understandable, even correct. Such behaviors cannot be understood outside their proper cultural context.

Frail and Decrepit Elders

Most elders either retain their abilities and relatively good health well into advanced age or die from acute disorders or accidents before they reach a stage of decrepitude. A survey found that less than 20 percent of the Niuean population aged sixty five or over was extremely frail or had many impairments (Barker 1989, 1994). Only about half of these frail elders are decrepit, however. Of the approximately 200 elders on the island during my fieldwork in 1982–1983, I met eleven (about 5 percent) whom I considered decrepit, while another four or five were rapidly losing their ability to maintain an independent

Table 45.1
Characteristics of Elders on Niue*

	Elders in Survey (N = 63)	Decrepit Elders (N = 11)
Average age#	under 75 years	over 80 years
Sex	30% males	64% males
Married	40%	19%
Living on own	14%	54%
Regularly attend church	71%	0%
Limited in doing work/ family activities	48%	100%
Severe mobility impairments	14%	100%
Partly or completely blind	29%	45%
Some memory problems or confusion	16%	45%

* See Barker (1989) for an extended discussion of the health and functional status of the elderly on Niue.
# Interpreting attributed age for Niuean elderly is extremely difficult. There is a tendency for chronological age attributed to the very old or the very frail, especially men, to be inflated (see Barker 1989).

existence and appeared to be on the road from frailty to decrepitude. So, I have been concerned with understanding the behavior of Niueans towards a small, but nonetheless interesting, segment of their society.

What cultural conditions make it possible for behavior radically at odds with the expected norms to become comprehensible? As a group, the characteristics of decrepit elders—those experiencing a degree of neglect—contrast sharply with the general elderly population on the island, as Table 45.1 demonstrates. A survey was performed in 1985 using a 50 percent random sample of all elders whose names appeared on the Niuean Government pension list. In general, being over seventy-five years of age, male, never married and/or having few children left on the island to care for one are all associated with impairment (Barker 1989). All these factors are even more strongly associated with decrepitude. Contributing little to their family, decrepit elders fail to maintain even minimal social roles in the general village community; in particular, the important social role of churchgoer ceases. Furthermore, decrepit elders experience more limitations in work activities, more confusion or mental deterioration, and more sensory problems (especially blindness) than do other elders on Niue.

Niuean Explanations for Neglect

Niueans themselves expressed ideas about the care of "oldies," as they commonly called all elderly people. In general, in the early 1980s, Niueans espoused respect and admiration for old folk, vehemently contrasting what they perceived as Western indifference to elders, signaled by the placement of elders in nursing homes with their own respectful concern and loving care for the aged. Within a decade of this field research, however, an "old folks' rest home" was developed on Niue, similar to nursing homes in other Pacific nations and in New Zealand, where aged care services are being delivered by the many Niuean women who now staff these facilities. The nursing home was established in an under-utilized part of the hospital facility. Destroyed by Hurricane Heta in 2004, the hospital is being rebuilt on a new site further inland along with another aged care section or nursing home. Described by the Premier as being the "home hospital of our *tupuna* (elderly) who are too old or infirmed to care for themselves" (Niue Government 2006), this is being supported with monetary aid from a group of Niueans resident overseas who "acknowledge that some of our elderly do not want to leave their ancestral homes when the rest of their families migrate elsewhere" and who are therefore "determined that they [*tupuna*] live the remainder of their lives here [on Niue] as comfortably as possible" (Niue Government 2006).

In the early 1980s, however, Niueans clearly recognized that their treatment of decrepit elders was not the same as their caring for intact elders. They gave several explanations for this. First, Niueans said some degree of decrepitude was to be expected in advanced old age and should be accepted, not complained about. Combined with a degree of fatalism, Niueans have the general Polynesian tendency to display little empathy for others (Levy 1973:312). As we have seen with respect to the old woman who fell into the disused water tank, even those experiencing severe pain or in very adverse circumstances receive little overt sympathy.

A second explanation was that in old age people receive their "just desserts." Those who had been excessively individualistic, materialistic, ill-tempered or nasty at a younger age were simply reaping in old age the harvest of unpleasant seeds they had previously sown. A further claim was that people who cared for kin and displayed their love throughout life are not neglected. People who took no time to raise a family, to help siblings and other family members through life or to establish a bond of love between themselves and younger kin have no one to call on in old age, have no one who is obligated to assist. Men were said to be more likely than women to fail to demonstrate love for kin. Generally, these would be men who failed to marry and so have no children whom they raised and obligated to provide care, or men who left the island for work and return only in old age. Biological ties that are never properly and continuously "socialized" did not suffice to ensure that an elder was adequately looked after in old age. Claims for help on the basis of biological connections alone usually induced a polite, but minimal and/or temporary response.

There is a striking parallel between this native explanation for neglect in old age and the demographic characteristics of the decrepit elderly. Males predominate in the decrepit sample, with a relatively large proportion of them (43 percent) never-married, childless or recently returned from long periods of time overseas. One of these men was an aggressive, confused seventy-year-old living on his own, next door to a niece. He had only recently been sent back to Niue from Pago Pago, American Samoa, where he had lived for most of his adult life. Another decrepit old man without children of his own had just moved to live with a nephew, having rotated from village to village, distant kin to distant kin, over the previous five years. No one was certain how long he would remain as his previous relationship with this kinsman had been very distant and tinged with hostility.

Some Niueans said old people now have a tough time because out-migration has so severely depleted the resources available to any one extended family such that there are no longer several adult women available in a household to care for both children and old people. There is undoubtedly some merit to this explanation, as the domestic workloads of individual adults, especially women, have increased. What this explanation reveals, of course, is that care of old people comes low on the list of domestic priorities, well after the care of other adults and children. Indeed, doubts can be cast about whether decrepit old folk ever received adequate care even before permanent out-migration and demographic changes disrupted family organization.

Glascock and Feinman (1981:27; Glascock this volume) note that supportive treatment of the intact aged, and nonsupportive, even death-hastening, treatment of the decrepit elderly can coexist within a society without strain as these behaviors are aimed at different populations. Niueans even signal linguistically the difference between the intact and the decrepit elderly populations. The term *ulu motua*, meaning "gray-haired one," refers to socially active, powerful, respected, intact elders. In contrast, the terms *penupenu-fonua* or *mutumutu-fonua*, "grey fish of the land," are graphic, if rather morbid, metaphors used to describe very elderly, incompetent, decrepit old men. Obviously, senescent old men are not in the same category as other old men.

Negotiation of the Label "Decrepit"

Elders do not become decrepit over night. Decrepitude is a gradual degenerative process during which negotiation constantly occurs between the elder and the rest of the community over the applicability of the label "decrepit." Becoming decrepit is a process of "fading out" (Maxwell 1986:77). It is a process in which elders begin to deploy their resources differently, often in a more self-centered fashion, while displays of deference towards them are correspondingly recast. When an old person has few remaining resources, or is unable or unwilling to use these resources to maintain even a minimal social role, the community successfully applies the decrepit label, and then the elder, albeit usually reluctantly, accepts it.

Decreases in competence are fought against, minimized in several ways. One strategy is for elders to cease doing strenuous "bush work" but to continue engaging in household chores. The very strong Niuean work ethic insists that every person—man, woman and child—assist in supporting the household.

From an early age, three to five years, children are assigned and expected to perform regularly important household tasks, including weeding gardens, feeding livestock, washing clothes and dishes or child-minding. An elder who can no longer perform any of these tasks places a greater burden on the family than does any other member except an infant. Unlike caring for a frail elder, however, caring for an infant carries the promise of future rewards; in a few years a child will be an able worker, but in a few years the elder will be no more able than at present.

A second way elders minimize the immediate impact of their increasing decrepitude is to adopt new, but valued, social roles, especially those inappropriate for younger persons, such as "storyteller" or "clown" (Holmes 1974; Holmes and Rhoads 1987). In contrast to the behavior expected of younger folk, old people, especially women, can tell lewd tales, mock high-status public figures and act generally as court jesters at important social events or ceremonies, such as weddings. This joking and ribald behavior is tolerated, even a valued new role, as commentary by elders helps delineate and uphold social norms, indirectly controlling the activities of younger persons.

An elder too frail to do any household tasks or to engage in public jesting has little to offer except perhaps being a teller of tales, a repository of lore and ceremonial knowledge. Unlike other Polynesian peoples, however, Niueans have been negligent in recording traditions and lack detailed oral histories (Ryan 1977). Thus, even a role of tale-teller or oral historian, demanding little physical skill and involving memory tasks often maintained by frail elders, is generally unavailable to *tupuna* on Niue.

One exception concerns the role of traditional healer, *taulaatua*, which is still important on Niue and is essentially reserved for elders (Barker 1985:148–53). Some healers are specialists who treat cases of major disorder from all over the island; others deal only with more minor problems within their own village. An elder in each extended family usually knows and uses the basic curative recipes and actions. Because of the secret nature of the herbal ingredients, of their proper preparation, recipes and incantations, curers who become so frail that they can no longer gather the required herbs themselves begin to lose even this role. Some elderly healers maintain power through the gradual revelation of their guarded knowledge to a grandchild or other younger relative who shows aptitude.

A third major way to demonstrate competence is to continue to raise children. As Counts and Counts put it, people "recruit a new dependent whose presence testifies to the continuing ability of an aging person to care for himself and others" (1985:5). Adoption of a child by an old person is both a demonstration of competence and an insurance against neglect in advanced old age or frailty, for adopted children are under great obligation to repay their parents by caring for them in later life. Most adoptions on Niue, especially of girls, take place through the child's mother's kin, and the driving forces behind most adoptions are closely related women, not men (Barker 1985). Elders without daughters or granddaughters will not only make fewer adoptions than others, but will be more likely to adopt children who are male and who are related only through distant or putative biological ties. This is especially true for elderly men who never married or are widowed at the time of adoption. Boys who have no close biological bond to the adoptive parent frequently feel little obligation to carry out their filial duties when the parent becomes aged. So, once more, men are more likely than women to reach advanced old age without anyone, even an adopted child, to care for them; decrepit old men are more likely to be neglected.

IS "NEGLECT" OF RECENT ORIGIN?

Thus, a picture of Niue emerges. Demographic and socioeconomic change on the island has been rampant, recent, rapid, and of monumental proportions (Barker 2000; Yarwood and Jowitt 1998). It is tempting to see these factors—modernization—as causes for the difference in treatment between the decrepit and intact elderly, a difference that would be recent in origin. Documents located in several archives dispel the notion that this distinction between decrepit and intact elders is a modern or recent phenomenon on Niue. Neglect of the elderly is not new.

In a letter written in November 1885, the European missionary on the island, Frank Lawes, quoted a Niuean *toa* or warrior thus: "It was better to have the skull broken to pieces in war, than to die in old age from neglect" (quoted in Ryan 1977:100). The first ethnographer on Niue, S. Percy Smith, had only this to say about the elderly: "In very old age, it was not infrequent that old people requested their younger relatives to strangle them to cause death" (1983:60). The veracity of this statement is unknown. In 1922, a short article about life on Niue by a visiting scholar noted that Niueans "were not thoughtful of their old folk" (Juniper 1922:612). The next ethnographer, Edwin Loeb (1926:86), wrote that the elderly were abandoned in the bush.

Reports by the New Zealand Administration's staff support these views. In 1923, the medical officer noted a "tendency for the natives to neglect their old."[1] A few years later he more bluntly reported: "At times one encounters marked cases of neglect, especially of the aged. 'Only an old person' is an expression one commonly hears. In several instances one feels that this callous indifference has been a potent factor in the cause of death."[2] Another Resident Commissioner again reported in 1945: "Old folk are left in hovels and begrudgingly fed.... I am quite convinced that neither the Church nor the people even recognize that it is a problem. It is quite taken for granted and *faka Niue* [the Niuean way]."[3]

Throughout the 1950s and into the 1960s, medical officers continued to report neglect affecting about 10 percent of the elderly population then on the island.[4] To help stem this widespread custom, a tax was levied from 1958 on to provide old people with a small pension, so they would be an economic asset to their families. Abandonment of old folk into "bush huts" had ceased by the mid 1960s, but other improvements were slow in coming about. One medical report in 1964 noted that "the elderly [living alone] fare worse than those living with relatives ... several appeared poorly clad and neglected. Nearly all had inadequate bed clothing and some none at all."[5]

The general tenor of these reports is corroborated by Niueans who migrated from the island decades ago and have become acculturated in new (Eurocentric) communities. These informants recounted the incomprehension they experienced when making return visits to Niue. Their tales of seeing how formerly influential, vital community members were neglected in old age reverberate with now familiar themes: "hunger," "filth," "smells" and "neglect." When decrepit elders died, families were genuinely distraught with grief and loudly mourned the loss of their cherished family member. My migrant Niuean informants asked: How could this be? Why did the community allow these families to neglect the elderly and not punish them for so doing? How could a family neglect an old person in life, yet so sincerely grieve their death?

CULTURAL VALUES AND "NEGLECTFUL" BEHAVIOR

By now enough evidence has been presented for it to be clear that Niuean neglect of decrepit elders is a well-established, systematic pattern of behavior and not mere idiosyncrasy or aberration. Moreover, it clearly is not a new phenomenon, or a response to massive, recent socioeconomic and demographic change. The question remains, however, given strongly espoused values about respect for the aged and a social system organized around elders, how is this variant of behavior possible?

Egalitarianism in a Fragile Ecology

Recall that Niue's agricultural system is fraught with difficulties. Periodic droughts and devastation by hurricanes, a fragile ecosystem and a harsh terrain all make food production uncertain, arduous and very time-consuming. Subsistence requires constant work from every able body, even young children, and there is little surplus available for nonproducers. A decrepit elder, too sick or frail to garden, to work around the house or even to mind infants and toddlers, creates obligations that he or she is unable to repay. Decrepit elders can easily be begrudged whatever small surplus is produced, especially in times when food is scarce.

Such sentiments combine with cultural values that stress hard work and individual achievement—looking out for oneself. The result is a system that neglects decrepit elders, leaves them to their fate, makes them cope on their own as best they can, and starts to become comprehensible. This "ecological" explanation appears rather callous, though, and very different from the sentiments accorded the healthy old. Such an explanation is also at odds with the treatment given other handicapped people.

Others with Disability

As in many Polynesian societies, babies born with physical and mental disabilities are not rejected, but rather receive special attention, and are lavished with affection. When older, these children are expected, to the best of their abilities, however minimal those might be, to aid the family in meeting its subsistence and communal obligations. A handicapped child might occasionally be mildly teased by his or her peers, but no more so than any other youngster. No child would be excluded from social gatherings or village activities just because of physical or mental "difference" (Kirkpatrick 1985:230).

Similarly, those who sustain injuries that result in permanent disabilities are not excluded from family or social activities and responsibilities. Adults with handicaps are expected to work to the extent of their abilities and to occupy whatever positions in village life are appropriate to their skills and social standing. One thirty-year-old paraplegic, for example, though confined to a wheelchair, tends his passion fruit and lime gardens by day and regularly attends village dances and other social gatherings by night. People banded together to build him a specially designed house and to pound down into level paths the coral rocks around his garden plots so that he could tend his crops unaided.

So, physically or mentally impaired children or adults are not excluded from society, and are not subjected to treatment any different from that given others of their age and status. Why then do Niueans neglect their decrepit elders? It cannot just be because of their handicaps or because of their minimal contributions to household welfare. Other cultural values must be at work.

The Origin of Misfortune and the Nature of Death

One clue is that despite this acceptance of disability, being of imposing stature, being well built and sturdy, is culturally valued in Polynesian societies. High rank and social importance are frequently associated with being tall or fat. Excessively thin individuals or those losing weight or physical robustness are suspected of illness, curse, or serious misdemeanor (Finau, Prior and Evans 1982:1542). Both literally and figuratively, decrepit elders on Niue are shadows of their former selves. Those who when younger were muscular, strong, and sturdy are now shrunken, stooped, and scrawny. Those who formerly were vital, influential figures are now ineffectual, pathetic beings with little interest in social life.

Such dramatic and obvious changes clearly raise suspicions about their origin. Degenerative changes are fundamentally different from any birth defect or disability resulting from accident and are unlike acute illnesses of rapid onset and resolution. Decrepitude is insidious, slow, and cumulative, a gradual and irreversible destruction of vitality. Very traditional ideas about the origin of such misfortunes, about the nature of death and about the proper treatment of the afflicted give us an understanding of why these degenerative processes are suspect. They explain the treatment of the decrepit elderly on Niue.

In the Polynesian cosmology, there are two parallel worlds, this world of humans and the world of the supernatural. Inhabitants of the latter keep a close watch on this world and punish those who offend. A person courts punishment by acting indecorously, by blaspheming, by transgressing the rules of proper conduct or by breaking *tapu*, rules specifying how to behave in certain localities or on special occasions. Punishment usually takes the form of sickness, especially intractable or life-threatening sickness, and is often brought about by possession by *aitu*, ghosts, the spirits of the dead.

In taking possession of a person, an *aitu*, usually a close ancestral spirit, aims to kill eventually, to take the person to the supernatural world, perhaps to avenge its own death. Once a ghost takes over, it speaks through the living in trance, delirium, or confusion, revealing secrets to the family and community at large, making salacious suggestions, and commenting generally upon the morality and correctness of the conduct of all and sundry (Goodman 1971; Shore 1978; Barker 1985:143–52).

As is common in Polynesian languages, Niuean uses the same word, *mate*, to encompass several states that we distinguish as delirium, unconsciousness, dying and death. Thus, there are no clear distinctions, linguistic or conceptual, between being incoherent, being comatose, being dying or being dead. A *mate* person is somewhere out of this world, on the way to the next.

Death in Niuean perspective is not an instantaneous, unequivocal event (Counts and Counts 1985:17). Rather, death is a process of transition, a gradual shucking of the competencies and responsibilities of this world and a simultaneous acquisition of characteristics of the new world. So death occurs over a period of time, months or even years. Death is not unexpected, as all natural living things die. Death is not always absolute, as there is no irrevocable boundary between parallel worlds, worlds occupied by humans and by supernatural beings, by ghosts.

Burial is merely a disposal of a body, a former container for the soul and animating forces. To encourage the new ghostly being to stay in the here-after with their supernatural kin and to not return to this world, Niueans bury their dead quickly, usually within twelve to twenty-four hours. Large stones or concrete slabs are placed atop the grave to discourage the new *aitu* from wanting to return to this world, from wanting to remain in the world of humans.

RELATIONS BETWEEN THE LIVING AND THE DYING

Decrepit elders, then, especially those who no longer look or behave like competent adults, who rave incoherently, who speak of long-past events or converse with long-dead kin, are being actively courted by *aitu*, are *mate*, are in transition. They are "the nearly dead." In touch with the spirit world, they are alarmingly near to becoming *aitu* themselves. Decrepit elders are in transition, inhabiting a twilight world of not-quite-human-but-not-quite-ancestor. As human beings, the decrepit elderly are obsolete, but, as inhabitants of another realm, they are incomplete.

Such near-*aitu* threaten to break the barriers between the worlds. In possession of alarming characteristics from both worlds, but not fully competent in either, this human-in-transition, this ghost-in-the-making, threatens to contaminate this world with things from beyond, things that can damage or hurt people living in this world. This threat ceases only when the dying are dead, fully dead, when they are buried and have completed the transition to the other world and stay there.

In traditional times, the intractably sick, those possessed by ghosts, by *aitu*, "were removed into the bush and placed in a temporary hut where they were left until they might recover or die. Their relatives took food to them, but no one remained with them" (Murray 1863:367). Such isolation of the sick conformed to the custom for dealing with ritually unclean objects. Imposition of a long *tapu* prevented *aitu* from spreading possession to others (Luomala 1978). Hence, we can see that abandoning or neglecting decrepit elders is not simply a rather brutal means of relieving younger people of an economic burden (though that probably plays some role), but is a ritual activity undertaken for sensible reasons. It prevents contamination by ghostly influences from beyond. Moreover, neglect is appropriate precisely because in reducing the customary ties and emotional intensity of the bonds between humans, it allows decrepit elders to complete an expected transition as smoothly as possible (Levy 1973:225–28, 291–302, 493–97):

too much concern causes difficult processes (usually social or supernatural ones) to become even more difficult and unpleasant. In regard to dying, if you are too concerned … the transformed spirit of the dead person may gain power over you … Being casual, then, frees the dying person from you, and you from him or her. (Levy 1973:229)

Men not only have greater power in life but also in death. *Aitu* of socially powerful men, particularly of traditional healers who mediate between the parallel worlds, can be especially malevolent, threatening and hard to control. This is yet another reason why it is predominantly males who experience neglect in old age. To abandon decrepit elders, or at least to limit contact even to the point of neglect, makes sense. They are not elders, but some other category of being engaged in a normal, expected, and important, but nonetheless difficult, social process—that of dying. Casualness, "neglect," with respect to decrepit elders, is a way of distancing oneself from such powerful and potentially dangerous transformations. The recently adopted practice of placing frail *tupuna* into the aged care section of the hospital is a way to be casual, a way in keeping with contemporary cosmopolitan standards, a way of distancing oneself from dying kin. Having professional nursing staff provide daily care, rather than family members, is not to disrespect older relatives, but rather to separate them from the household, to free them and their kin from each other, to transform the emotional and social bonds tying kin together from those proper in this world to those appropriate for the next.

Once the transition between the realms is complete, the cessation of life here can be noted and be grieved over. Thus, a family who apparently neglected an elder at the end of life can sincerely grieve for the person he or she once was. They had "neglected" no one whom they knew, no one who belonged in this world. Rather, they had maintained a prudent distance from a near *aitu* during the difficult process of transition between worlds. And if their actions hastened that process along, surely that cannot be thought harmful or harsh or uncaring. For Niueans to abandon or neglect their decrepit elderly, then, to engage in nonsupportive or death-hastening behaviors, makes sense. To laugh at decrepit elders, to deride their feeble endeavors at being competent humans, to ridicule them, to neglect them, to be wary of and distant during interactions with them is not to disrespect an elder but to guard against foreign intrusion. These behaviors do not involve elders, but an entirely different category of being. These behaviors are attempts to deal with "matter out of place" as Mary Douglas (1966) would put it, to persuade a nearly dead relative to go to the proper realm, to die and stay dead, to cease to be human, to leave the land of the living and become a ghost, an ancestor who can once again be revered.

NOTES

Fieldwork on which this chapter is based was supported by a project grant in 1982–1983 from the South Pacific Medical Research Committee of the Medical Research Council of New Zealand. The author gratefully acknowledges this support, and the unstinting assistance of the Niuean people.

Notes 1–5 come from files held in the National Archives, Department of Internal Affairs, Wellington, New Zealand, and from files held in the Archives, *Fale Fono*, Alofi, Niue.

1. (a) Ministerial report in Section A-3 of the *Appendix to the Journal of the House of Representatives*, New Zealand, 1923. (b) Ministerial quotation from the medical officer, Dr. Boyd, in the report in Section A3 of the *Appendix to the Journal of the House of Representatives*, New Zealand, 1926.

2. Report by Resident Commissioner Captain Bell on outbreak of influenza, April 29, 1932, in reply to a telegraph inquiry by Department of Island Territories, New Zealand.

3. Copy of report from Resident Commissioner Larsen, August 6, 1945, sent to Director General of Health, New Zealand, by Department of Island Territories, New Zealand. Memorandum by Resident Commissioner Larsen, September 3, 1945, on visit by the New Zealand Prime Minister and his reaction to the plight of old people on Niue, sent to Secretary, Department of Island Affairs, New Zealand.

4. (a) Minutes of the Island Council Meeting, October 2, 1958, and October 30, 1958. Memorandum from Resident Commissioner, dated August 9, 1946, to Secretary, Department of Island Affairs, New Zealand. (b) Minutes of the Island Council Meeting, July 31, 1958. (c) Monthly reports by Chief Medical Officer to Resident Commissioner, March and May 1967.

5. Monthly report by Chief Medical Officer to Resident Commissioner, May 1964.

Bibliography

Aamodt, S. and S. Wang. 2008. *Welcome to Your Brain: Why You Lose Your Car Keys but Never Forget How to Drive and Other Puzzles of Everyday Life*. New York: Bloomsbury USA.

AARP. 2001. "In the Middle: A Report on Multicultural Boomers Coping with Family and Aging Issues." Available at: http://assets.aarp.org/rgcenter/il/in_the_middle.pdf.

———. 2003. "Lean on Me: Support and Minority Outreach for Grandparents Raising Grandchildren." http://assets.aarp.org/rgcenter/general/gp_2003_a.pdf.

———. 2004. *Hispanic Baby Boomers Envision Retirement: A Special Analysis of the Baby Boomers Envision Retirement II Study*. Washington, DC: AARP.

———. 2005. *Reimagining America: How America Can Grow Old and Prosper*. Washington, DC: AARP.

Abbott, R., H. Ueshima, K. Masaki, B. Willcox, B. Rodriguez, A. Ikeda et al. 2007. "Coronary Artery Calcification and Total Mortality in Elderly Men." *Journal of the American Geriatrics Society* 55(12):1948–54.

Aboderin, I. 2004. "Modernization and Ageing Theory Revisited." *Ageing and Society* 24:29–50.

———. 2006. *Intergenerational Support and Old Age in Africa*. New Brunswick, NJ: Transaction.

Abraído-Lanza, A. E., A. Viladrich, K. R. Florez, A. Cespedes, A. N. Aguirre and A. A. De la Cruz. 2007. "Commentary: Fatalismo Reconsidered: A Cautionary Note for Health-Related Research and Practice with Latino Populations." *Ethnicity and Disease* 17(1, Winter):153–58.

Abramson, A. and M. Silverstein. 2006. "Images of Aging in America." Washington, DC: AARP. http://assets.aarp.org/rgcenter/general/images_aging.pdf.

Achenbaum, W. 2006. "A History of Civic Engagement of Older People." *Generation* 30(4):18–23.

Adiga, A. 2006. "My Lost World." *Time Magazine*, June 26, 167(26). http://www.time.com/time/magazine/article/0,9171,1205363,00.html.

Adinkrah, M. 2004. "Witchcraft Accusations and Female Homicide Victimization in Contemporary Ghana." *Violence Against Women* 10(4):325–56.

Adkins, G., P. Martin and L. Poon. 1996. "Personality Traits and States as Predictors of Subjective Well-Being in Centenarians, Octogenarians and Sexagenarians." *Psychology and Aging* 11:408–16.

Agarwal, B. 1994. *A Field of One's Own: Gender and Land Rights in South Asia.* New York: Cambridge University Press.

Age Concern England (ACE). 2000. *The Debate of the Age: The Agenda for the Age.* London: ACE.

Ageing International. 1994. "Caregiver Burnout." *Ageing International* 21(2):7–8.

Aguilar, M., ed. 1998. *The Politics of Age and Gerontocracy in Africa: Ethnographies of the Past and Memories of the Present.* Lawrenceville, NJ: Africa World Press.

Aguirre, A. and J. Turner. 2006. *American Ethnicity: The Dynamics and Consequences of Discrimination*, 5th ed. New York: McGraw-Hill.

Aguirre, B. E. 1976. "Differential Migration of Cuban Social Races: A Review and Interpretation of the Problem." *Latin American Research Review* 11:103–24.

Ahmadi, F. 1998. "Sufism and Gerotranscendence: The Impact of Way of Thinking, Culture and Aging on Spiritual Maturity." *Journal of Aging and Identity* 3(4):189–211.

———. 2000. "Development Towards Wisdom and Maturity: Sufi Conception of Self." *Journal of Aging and Identity* 5(3):137–49.

———. 2001. "The Meaning of Home among Elderly Immigrants: Directions for Future Research and Theoretical Development." *Housing Studies* 16(3):353–70.

Ahmadi, F. and L. Tornstam. 2000. "Elderly Iranian Immigrants in Sweden." In *Proceedings Vol. II Social and Environmental Issues of Aging.* Tehran: Goroh Banoval Nikokar Publishing.

Ahmed, N., G. Kaufman and S. Naim. 1996. "South Asian Families in the United States: Pakistani, Bangladeshi and Indian Muslims." In *Family and Gender among American Muslims: Issues Facing Middle Eastern Immigrants and Their Descendants.* B. C. Aswad and B. Bilgé, eds. Philadelphia: Temple University Press.

Äijänseppä, S., I. Notkola, M. Tijhuis, W. van Staveren, D. Kromhout and A. Nissinen. 2005. "Physical Functioning in Elderly Europeans: Ten-Year Changes in the North and South—the HALE Project." *Journal of Epidemiology and Community Health* 59:413–19.

Ajrouch, K. J. 2005a. "Arab American Elders: Network Structure, Perceptions of Relationship Quality and Discrimination." *Research in Human Development* 2(4):213–28.

———. 2005b. "Arab-American Immigrant Elders' Views about Social Support." *Ageing and Society* 25:655–73.

———. 2007a. "Health Disparities and Arab-American Elders: Does Intergenerational Support Buffer the Inequality-Health Link?" *Journal of Social Issues* 63(4): 745–58.

———. 2007b. "Resources and Well-Being among Arab-American Elders." *Journal of Cross-Cultural Gerontology* 22:167–82.

Akesode, A., J. Migeon and A. Kowarski. 1977. "Effect of Food Intake on the Metabolic Clearance Rate of Aldosterone." *Journal of Clinical Endocrinology and Metabolism* 45:849.

Alawad, A. M. E. and E. J. S. Sonugabarke. 1992. "Childhood Problems in a Sudanese City: A Comparison of Extended and Nuclear Families." *Child Development* 63:909–14.

Albert, S. M. 1987. "The Work of Marriage and of Death: Ritual and Political Process among the Lak." Unpublished dissertation, University of Chicago.

———. 2006. "Cultural and Ethnic Influences on Aging." *Encyclopedia of Gerontology*, 2nd ed. J. E. Birren, ed. San Diego: Academic Press.

Albert, S. M. and E. M. Brody. 1996. "When Elder Care Is Viewed as Child Care: Significance of Elder Cognitive Impairment and Caregiver Burden." *American Journal of Geriatric Psychiatry* 4:121–30.

Albert, S. M. and M. G. Cattell. 1994. *Old Age in Global Perspective: Cross-Cultural and Cross-National Views*. New York: G. K. Hall.

Albertazzi, P., F. Pansini, G. Bonaccorsi, L. Zanotti, E. Forini and D. De Aloysio. 1998. "The Effect of Dietary Soy Supplementation on Hot Flushes." *Obstetrics and Gynecology* 91(1):6–11.

Alegría, M., N. Mulvaney-Day, M. Torres, A. Polo, Z. Cao and G. Canino. 2007a. "Prevalence of Psychiatric Disorders across Latino Subgroups in the United States." *American Journal of Public Health* 97(1):68–75.

Alegría, M., N. Mulvaney-Day, M. Woo, M. Torres, S. Gao and V. Oddo. 2007b. "Correlates of Past-Year Mental Health Service Use among Latinos: Results from the National Latino and Asian American Study." *American Journal of Public Health* 97(1):76–83.

Alegría, M., P. E. Shrout, M. Woo, P. Guarnaccia, W. Sribney, D. Vila et al. 2007c. "Understanding Differences in Past Year Psychiatric Disorders for Latinos Living in the U.S." *Social Science and Medicine* 65(2):213–30.

Alekel, D., A. St. Germain, C. Peterson, B. Hanson, J. Stewart and T. Toda. 2000. "Isoflavone-rich Soy Protein Isolate Attenuates Bone Loss in the Lumbar Spine of Perimenopausal Women." *American Journal of Clinical Nutrition* 72:844–52.

Aliber, M., C. Walker, M. Machera, P. Kamau, C. Omondi and K. Kanyinga. 2004. *The Impact of HIV/AIDS on Land Rights: Case Studies from Kenya*. Cape Town, South Africa: HSRC Publishers.

Alley, D., P. Liebig, J. Pynoos and T. Banerjee. 2007. "Setting a Housing Context: Creating Elder Friendly Communities' Preparations for an Aging Society." *Journal of Gerontological Social Work* 49(1/2):1–18.

Almagor, U. 1978. *Pastoral Partners*. Manchester, UK: Manchester University Press.

Almeida, A. D. 1965. *Bushmen and Other Non-Bantu Peoples of Angola: Three Lectures*. Johannesburg: Witwatersrand University Press.

Aloia, J. et al. 1983. "Determinants of Bone Mass in Postmenopausal Women." *Archives of Internal Medicine* 143:1700–1704.

Alter, G. 1990. "Old Age Mortality and Age Misreporting in the United States, 1900–1940." Working Paper No. 24. Population Institute for Research and Training, Indiana University, Indiana.

Altergott, K. 1988. *Daily Life in Later Life: Personal Conditions in a Comparative Perspective*. Newbury Park, CA: Sage.

Altman, I., M. Lawton and J. Wohlwill, eds. 1984. *Elderly People and the Environment*. New York: Plenum Press.

Alzheimer's Association. 2008. "Alzheimer's Disease Facts and Figures." http://www.alz.org/national/documents/report_alzfactsfigures2008.pdf.

American College of Physicians, Health and Public Policy Committee. 1988. "Comprehensive Functional Assessment for Elderly Patients." *Annals of Internal Medicine* 109:70–72.

American Diabetes Association. 2005. "Total Prevalence of Diabetes and Pre-Diabetes." http://www.diabetes.org (accessed on May 2006).

———. 2007. "American Diabetes Association: Clinical Practice Recommendations 2007." *Diabetes Care* 30 (Supplement 1): S46.

American Geriatrics Society. 2006. "Position Statement on Ethnogeriatrics." www.americangeriatrics.org/products/positionpapers/ethno_committee.shtml.

Andersen-Ranberg, K., M. Schroll and B. Jeune. 2001. "Healthy Centenarians Do Not Exist, but Autonomous Centenarians Do: A Population-based Study of Morbidity among Danish Centenarians." *Journal of American Geriatric Society* 49:900–908.

Anderson, N., R. Bulatao and B. Cohen, eds. 2004. *Critical Perspectives on Racial and Ethnic Differences in Health in Late Life.* Washington, DC: National Academies Press. http://books.nap.edu/catalog.php?record_id=11086#toc.

Ando, K. 2005. "Grandparenthood: Crossroads between Gender and Aging." *International Journal of Japanese Sociology* 14(1)1:32–51.

Andrews, G., A. Esterman, A. Braunack-Mayer and C. Rungie. 1986. *Aging in the Western Pacific: A Four-Country Study.* Geneva: World Health Organization.

Andrulis, D. P. 1997. "The Urban Health Penalty." American College of Physicians (on-line position paper). http://www.acponline.org/ppvl/policies/e000015.pdf.

Angel, J. L. and R. J. Angel. 1998. "Aging Trends—Mexican Americans in the Southwestern United States." *Journal of Cross-Cultural Gerontology* 13:281–90.

Angel, J. L., R. J. Angel, M. P. Aranda and T. P. Miles. 2004. "Can the Family Still Cope? Social Support and Health as Determinants of Nursing Home Use in the Older Mexican-Origin Population." *Journal of Aging and Health* 16(3):338–54.

Angel, J. L., R. J. Angel and K. S. Markides. 2000. "Late-life Immigration, Changes in Living Arrangements and Headship Status among Older Mexican-Origin Individuals." *Social Science Quarterly* 81(1):389–403.

Angel, J. L., M. A. Jiménez and R. J. Angel. 2007. "The Economic Consequences of Widowhood for Older Minority Women." *The Gerontologist* 47:224–34.

Angel, J. L. and K. Whitfield., eds. 2007. *The Health of Aging Hispanics: The Mexican-Origin Population.* New York: Springer.

Ankestyrelsen. 2004. *Frit Valg i Aeldreplejen–Erfaringer fra Landets Kommuner.* Copenhagen: Ankestyrelsen.

Antonucci, T., K. Ajrouch and K. Birditt. 2006. "Social Relations in the Third Age: Assessing Strengths and Challenges Using the Convoy Model." In *Annual Review of Gerontology and Geriatrics.* K. W. Schaie, J. James and P. Wink, eds. New York: Springer.

Antonucci, T. and H. Akiyama. 1995. "Convoys of Social Relations: Family and Friendships within a Life Span Context." In *Handbook of Aging and the Family.* R. Blieszner and V. Bedford, eds. Westport, CT: Greenwood Press.

Antonucci, T., H. Akiyama and J. Lansford. 1998. "Negative Effects of Close Social Relations." *Family Relations* 47:379–84.

Antonucci, T. and K. Cortina. 2006. "Social Network Typologies of Mental Health among Older Adults." *Journal of Gerontology* 61:25–32.

Antonucci, T. and J. Jackson. 2003. "Ethnic and Cultural Differences in Intergenerational Support." In *Global Aging and Its Challenges to Families.* V. Bengtson and A. Lowenstein, eds. New York: Aldine.

Antonucci, T., C. Okorodudu and H. Akiyama. 2002. "International Perspectives on the Well-Being of Older Adults." Special issue, *Journal of Social Issues* 58(4).

Aranda, M. P. and M. R. Miranda. 1997. "Hispanic Aging, Social Support and Mental Health: Does Acculturation Make a Difference?" In *Minorities, Aging and Health.* K. Markides and M. R. Miranda, eds. Thousand Oaks, CA: Sage.

Arber, S. and C. Attias-Donfut, eds. 2000. *The Myth of Generational Conflict: Family and State in Ageing Societies, European Sociological Association Series.* London: Routledge.

Arber, S. and J. Ginn. 1995. *Connecting Gender and Ageing: A Sociological Approach.* Buckingham, UK: Open University Press.

Arendt, J., E. Hansen, H. Olsen, M. Rasmussen, J. Bentzen and B. Rimdal. 2003. *Levevilkaar Blandt Folkepensionister uden Supplerende Indkomst.* 03:15. Copenhagen: Socialforskningsinstituttet.

Arensberg, C. 1937 (1988). *The Irish Countryman: An Anthropological Study.* Prospect Heights, IL: Waveland.

Arensberg, C. and C. T. Kimball. 1940. *Family and Community in Ireland.* Cambridge, MA: Harvard University Press.

Arias, E. 1998. "The Demography of Assimilation: The Case of Cubans in the United States." Unpublished dissertation, University of Wisconsin.

———. 2006. *United States Life Tables, 2003.* Hyattsville, MD: U.S. National Center for Health Statistics.

Arnoff, F., H. Leon and I. Lorge. 1964. "Cross-Cultural Acceptance of Stereotypes Toward Aging." *Journal of Social Psychology* 5:41–58.

Aronson, J. 2002. "Frail and Disabled Users of Home Care: Confident Consumers or Disentitled Citizens?" *Canadian Journal on Aging* 21:11–25.

Aruga, K. 1954. "The Family in Japan." *Marriage and Family Living* 16:362–68.

Asahi Shimbun Japan Almanac 2005. 2004. Tokyo: Asahi Shimbunsha.

Ascoli, U. and C. Ranci. 2002. "Changes in the Welfare Mix: The European Path." In U. Ascoli and C. Ranci, eds. *Dilemmas of the Welfare Mix: The New Structure of Welfare in an Era of Privatization.* New York: Kluwer Academic/Plenum Publishers.

Asia Development Bank (ADB). 2007. "Inequality in Asia." http://www.adb.org/Documents/Books/Key_Indicators/2007/pdf/Inequality-in-Asia=Highlights.pdf.

Associated Press. 2006. "As Japan's Population Ages, Its Stores Hurry to Adapt." *International Herald Tribune,* September 4.

———. 2007. "Aging Gracefully, with Robotic Help." *Newsday,* October 5:A41.

Atkinson, P. and R. West. 1970. "Loss of Skeletal Calcium in Lactating Women." *Journal of Obstetrics and Gynaecology of the British Commonwealth* 77: 555–60.

Atkinson, R. M., L. Ganzini and M. J. Bernstein. 1992. "Alcohol and Substance-Use Disorders in the Elderly." In *Handbook of Mental Health and Aging,* 2nd ed. J. E. Birren, R. B. Sloane and G. D. Cohen, eds. New York: Academic Press.

Atzmon, G., M. Rincon, C. Schechter, A. Shuldiner, R. Lapton, A. Bergman et al. 2006. "Lipoprotein Genotype and Conserved Pathway for Exceptional Longevity in Humans." *PLoS Biology* 4:e113.

Atzmon, G., C. Schechter, W. Greiner, D. Davidson, G. Rennert and N. Barzilai. 2004. "Clinical Phenotype of Families with Longevity." *Journal of the American Geriatrics Society* 52(2):271–77.

Austad, S. 1999. *Why We Age: What Science Is Discovering about the Body's Journey through Life*. New York: John Wiley.

Avlund, K. 2004. "Disability in Old Age: Longitudinal Population-Based Studies of the Disablement Process." *Danish Medical Bulletin* 51(4):315–49.

Bachelard, G. 1964 (1994). *The Poetics of Space*. Boston: Beacon.

———. 1993. *Autonomy and Long-Term Care*. New York: Oxford University Press.

Bachmann, G. 1984. "Evaluation of the Climacteric Woman–An Overview." *Midpoint* 1(1):9–13.

Backes, G., V. Lasch and K. Reimann. 2006. *Gender, Health and Ageing: European Perspectives on Life Course, Health Issues and Social Challenges*. Hamburg: Verlag.

Bagga, C. 2005. "Nation Leaves 11% of Its Elderly Alone." *Times of India, Kolkata*. May 26.

Bahloul, J. 1996. *The Architecture of Memory: A Jewish-Muslim Household in Colonial Algeria*. London: Cambridge University Press.

Baker, B. 2007. *Old Age in a New Age: The Promise of Transformative Nursing Homes*. Nashville, TN: Vanderbilt University Press.

Balam, G. 1981. *La Migracion en el Area de lost Centros Coordinadores del I.N.I. de Yucatan: El Bracerismo Regional y sus Repercusiones Sociales*. Valladolid, Yucatan.

Baldassar, L., C. Baldock and R. Wilding. 2007. *Families Caring across Borders: Migration, Ageing and Transnational Caregiving*. London: Palgrave-Macmillan.

Ball, M. M., M. M. Perkins, F. J. Whittington, C. Hollingsworth, S. V. King and B. L. Combs. 2005. *Communities of Care: Assisted Living for African American Elders*. Baltimore: Johns Hopkins University Press.

Baltes, P. 1987. "Theoretical Propositions of Life Span Developmental Psychology: On the Dynamics of Growth and Decline." *Developmental Psychology* 23:611–26.

Banks, J., M. Marmot, Z. Oldfield and J. P. Smith. 2006. "Disease and Disadvantage in the United States and in England." *Journal of the American Medical Association* 295:2037–45.

Banner, L. 1992. *In Full Flower: Aging Women, Power and Sexuality*. New York: Knopf.

Bardhan, K., ed. and trans. 1990. *Of Women, Outcasts, Peasants and Rebels: A Selection of Bengali Short Stories*. Berkeley: University of California Press.

Barker, J. C. 1985. Social Organization and Health Services for Preschool Children on Niue Island, Western Polynesia. Ann Arbor, MI: University Microfilms.

———. 1988. "Admission of Geriatric Patients to Hospital on Niue Island, 1977–1982." *New Zealand Medical Journal* 101:638–40.

———. 1989. "Health and Functional Status of the Elderly in a Polynesian Population." *Journal of Cross-Cultural Gerontology* 4:163–94. Erratum (1994) *Journal of Cross-Cultural Gerontology* 9:419.

———. 1994. "Home Alone: The Effects of Out-Migration on Niuean Elders' Living Arrangements and Social Support." *Pacific Studies* 17(3, September):41–81.

———. 2000. "Hurricanes and Socio-Economic Development on Niue Island." *Asia Pacific Viewpoint* 41(2):191–205.

———. 2001. "Niue." In *Countries and Their Cultures*, vol. 3. M. Ember and C. R. Ember, eds. Farmington Hills, MI: Macmillan Library Reference/Gale Group.

Barnes, M., A. Blom, K. Cox, C. Lessof and A. Walker. 2006. *The Social Exclusion of Older People: Evidence from the First Wave of the English Longitudinal*

Study of Ageing (ELSA). Office of the Deputy Prime Minister, Social Exclusion Unit.

Barnicle, T. and K. Midden. 2003. "The Effects of a Horticulture Activity Program on the Psychological Well-Being of Older People in a Long-Term Care Facility." *Horticultural Technology* 13(1):81–85.

Barquera, S. 2003. "Geography of Diabetes Mellitus Mortality in Mexico: An Epidemiologic Transition Analysis." *Archives of Medical Research* 34:407–14.

Barresi, C. M. and D. Stull, eds. 1993. *Ethnic Elderly and Long-Term Care*. New York: Springer.

Bart, P. 1969. "Why Women's Status Changes in Middle Age: The Turn of the Social Ferris Wheel." *Sociological Symposium* 3:1–18.

Barzilai, N., G. Atzmon, C. Schecher, E. Schaefer, A. Cupples, R. Lipton et al. 2003. "Unique Lipoprotein Phenotype and Genotype Associated with Exceptional Longevity." *Journal of the American Medical Association* 290:2939–40.

Basch, L., N. G. Schiller and C. S. Blanc. 1994. *Nations Unbound: Transnational Projects, Postcolonial Predicaments and Deterritorialized Nation-States*. Amsterdam: Gordon Breach.

Bassen, S. and V. Baltazar. 1997. "Flowers, Flowers Everywhere: Creative Horticulture Programming at the Hebrew Home for the Aged at Riverdale." *Geriatric Nursing* 18(2):53–56.

Bastida, E. 1979. "Family Integration in Later Life among Hispanic Americans." *Journal of Minority Aging* 4:42–49.

———. 1984. "Reconstructing the Social World at 60: Older Cubans in the United States." *The Gerontologist* 24(5):465–70.

———. 1987. "Sex-Typed Age Norms among Older Hispanics." *The Gerontologist* 27:59–65.

———. 1988. "Reexamining Traditional Assumptions about Extended Familism: Older Puerto Ricans in Comparative Perspective." In *The Hispanic Elderly: A Cultural Signature*. M. Sotomayor, ed. Edinburg, TX: Pan American University Press.

Basu, A. M. 2004. "On the Prospects for Endless Fertility Decline in South Asia." Report of the United Nations Expert Group Meeting on Completing the Fertility Transition, March 11–14, 2002, New York. http://www.un.org/esa/population/publications/completingfertility/4RevisedBASUpaper.PDF (accessed on October 20, 2007).

Basu, S. 2006. "Some Social, Economic and Behavioral Problems of the Aged Inhabiting Calcutta City: An Anthropological Approach." Ph.D. diss. University of Calcutta.

Bateson, G. 1950. "Cultural Ideas about Aging." In *Research on Aging*. E. P. Jones, ed. Berkeley: University of California Press.

BBC News. 2003a. "Italians to Strike over Pensions." http://news.bbc.co.uk/2/hi/business/3152654.stm.

———. 2003b. "Italy Floats Raising Retirement Age." http://news.bbc.co.uk/2/hi/europe/3180011.stm.

———. 2003c. "Italy Slides into Recession." http://news.bbc.co.uk/2/hi/business/3134947.stm.

Beall, C. 1987. "Studies of Longevity." In *The Elderly as Modern Pioneers*. P. Silverman, ed. Bloomington: Indiana University Press.

Beard, V. and Y. Kunharibowo. 2001. "Living Arrangements and Support Relationships among Elderly Indonesians: Case Studies from Java and Sumatra International." *Journal of Population Geography* 7(1):17–33.

Becker, G. 1980. *Growing Old in Silence*. Berkeley: University of California Press.

Becker, G. and Y. Beyene. 1999. "Narratives of Age and Uprootedness among Older Cambodian Refugees." *Journal of Aging Studies* 13(3):295–314.

Bedford, R. D., G. Mitchell and M. Mitchell. 1980. "Population history." 1976 Census of Population and Housing, Niue. Volume 2: Analysis of Demographic Data. Alofi, Niue: Department of Justice. pp. 4–19.

Behrouzi, N. 2005. Student researcher field notes from participant observation at Grace, April 29. Unpublished document.

Beise, J. and E. Voland. 2002. "A Multilevel Event History Analysis of the Effects of Grandmothers on Child Mortality in a Historical German Population. Krummhörn, Ostfriesland, 1720–1874." *Demographic Research* 7:460–67.

Benda-Beckmann, F. V. 1979. *Property in Social Continuity: Continuity and Change in the Maintenance of Property Relationships through Time in Minangkabau, West Sumatra*. The Hague: Martinus Nijhoff.

Bengtson, V. 2001. "Beyond the Nuclear Family: The Increasing Importance of Multi-Generational Relationships in American Society." *Journal of Marriage and the Family* 63(1):1–16.

Bengtston, V. and A. Lowensetin. 2003. *Global Aging and Challenges to Families*. New York: Springer.

Bengtson, V., A. Lowenstein, N. M. Putney and D. Gans. 2003. "Global Aging and the Challenges to Families." In *Global Aging and Challenge to Families*. A. Lowenstein and V. Bengtson, eds. New York: Aldine.

Bengtson, V. and L. Morgan. 1987. "Ethnicity and Aging: A Comparison of Three Ethnic Groups." In *Growing Old in Different Societies: Cross-Cultural Perspectives*. J. Sokolovsky, ed. Acton, MA: Copley.

Bengtson, V., C. Rosenthal and L. Burton. 1996. "Paradoxes of Families and Aging." In *Handbook of Aging and the Social Sciences,* 4th ed. R. H. Binstock and L. K. George, eds. San Diego: Academic Press.

Bennett, M. and C. Lengacher. 2008. "Humor and Laughter May Influence Health: III. Laughter and Health Outcomes." *Evidence-based Complementary and Alternative Medicine* 5(1):37–40.

Bennett, N. and L. Garson. 1983. "The Centenarian Question and Old-Age Mortality in the Soviet Union, 1959–1970." *Demography* 20:587–606.

Bennett, R. 2007. "Nursing Homes: Shortage of Caregivers Means Shortage of Care." *Toronto Star*, August 10, AA8.

Beregi, E. 1990. "Centenarians in Hungary. A Social and Demographic Study." *Interdisciplinary Topics in Gerontology* 27:31–39.

Berglund, A.-I. 1976. *Zulu Thought-Patterns and Symbolism*. Bloomington: Indiana University Press.

Berman, H. 1986. "To Flame with a Wild Life: Florida Scott-Maxwell's Experience of Old Age." *The Gerontologist* 26(3):321–24.

Bernard, M. 2001. "Women Ageing: Old Lives, New Challenges." *Education and Ageing* 16(2):333–52.

Bernardi, B. 1985. *Age Class Systems*. London: Cambridge University Press.

Berry, W. 1995. "Health Is Membership." In *Another Turn of the Crank: Essays by Wendell Berry*. Washington, DC: Counterpoint.

Bever, E. 1982. "Old Age and Witchcraft in Early Modern Europe." In *Old Age in Pre-industrial Society*. P. Sterns, ed. New York: Holmes and Meier.

Beyene, Y. 1989. *From Menarche to Menopause: Reproductive Lives of Peasant Women in Two Cultures*. Albany: State University of New York Press.

Biafora, F. A. and C. F. Longino, Jr. 1990. "Elderly Hispanic Migration in the United States." *Journal of Gerontology: Social Sciences* 45(5):S212–19.

Biesele, M. 2007. "Digital Documentation of Ju/'hoan Narratives: Significance for Hunter-Gatherer Studies, Language Archives and Education." In *Before Farming: The Archeology and Anthropology of Hunter-Gatherers*. http://www.waspress.co.uk/journals/beforefarming/journal_20072/abstracts/index.php.

Biesele, M. and N. Howell. 1981. "The Old People Give You Life." In *Other Ways of Growing Old*. P. Amoss and S. Harrell, eds. Stanford, CA: Stanford University Press.

Biggs, S. 1993. *Understanding Ageing: Images, Attitudes and Professional Practice*. Buckingham, UK: Open University Press.

———. 2007. "Thinking about Generations: Conceptual Positions and Policy Implications." *Journal of Social Issues* 63:4.

Billings, J. and K. Leichsenring, eds. 2005. *Integrating Health and Social Care Services for Older Persons–Evidence from Nine European Countries*. Aldershot, UK: Ashgate.

Binstock, R. H. and L. K. George, eds. 2006. *Handbook of Aging and the Social Sciences*, 6th ed. Boston: Academic Press.

Birch, E. L. 2005. "Who Lives Downtown?" *Living Cities Census Series*. November. Washington, DC: Brookings Institution.

Black, H. 1999. "Life as Gift: Spiritual Narratives of Elderly African-American Women Living in Poverty." *Journal of Aging Studies* 13(4):441–55.

Blackwell, D., M. Hayward and E. Crimmins. 2001. "Does Childhood Health Affect Chronic Morbidity in Later Life?" *Social Science and Medicine* 52:1269–84.

Blackwood, E. 2000. *Webs of Power: Women, Kin and Community in a Sumatran Village*. Lanham, MD: Rowman and Littlefield.

Blaikie, A. 1999. *Ageing and Popular Culture*. Cambridge: Cambridge University Press.

Bledsoe, C. 2002. *Contingent Lives. Fertility, Time and Aging in West Africa*. Chicago: University of Chicago Press.

Bleek, D. F. 1928. *The Naron: A Bushman Tribe of the Central Kalahari*. Cambridge: Cambridge University Press.

Blieszner, R. and V. H. Bedford, eds. 1996 *Aging and the Family: Theory and Research*. Westport, CT: Greenwood Press.

Blum, R. and E. Blum. 1965. *Health and Healing in Rural Greece: A Study of Three Communities*. Stanford, CA: Stanford University Press.

Blurton Jones, N. B., K. Hawkes and J. O'Connell. 2002. "The Antiquity of Postreproductive Life: Are There Modern Impacts on Hunter-Gatherer Postreproductive Lifespans?" *Human Biology* 14:184–205.

Bock, J. and S. Johnson. Forthcoming. "Grandmothers' Productivity and the HIV/AIDS Pandemic in Sub-Saharan Africa." *Journal of Cross-Cultural Gerontology*.

Body-Gendrot, S. 1996. "Paris: A 'Soft' Global City?" *New Community* 22(4):595–605.

Bogin, B. and B. H. Smith. 1996. "Evolution of the Human Life Cycle." *American Journal of Human Biology* 8:703–16.

Boia, L. 2004. *Forever Young: A Cultural History of Longevity*. London: Reaktion Books.

Bolen, J. 1998. *Close to the Bone: Life-Threatening Illness and the Search for Meaning.* New York: Scribner.

Bongaarts, J. and Z. Zimmer. 2002. "Living Arrangements of Older Adults in the Developing World: An Analysis of DHS Household Surveys." *Journal of Gerontology* 57B:S145–57.

Bordone, L. and L. Guarente. 2005. "Calorie Restriction, SIRT1 and Metabolism: Understanding Longevity." *Nature Review of Molecular/Cellular Biology* 6(4):298–305.

Borneman, J. 1986. "Émigrés as Bullets/Immigration as Penetration: Perceptions of the Marielitos." *Journal of Popular Culture* 20(3):73–92.

Borsch-Supan, A. 1994. "Aging in Germany and the United States: International Comparisons." In *Studies in the Economics of Aging*, D. A. Wise, ed. Chicago: University of Chicago Press.

Boswell, T. D. 1994. *The Cubanization and Hispanicization of Metropolitan Miami.* Miami, FL: The Cuban American National Council.

Boswell, T. D. and J. R. Curtis. 1984. *The Cuban-American Experience: Culture, Images and Perspectives.* Towata, NJ: Rowman and Allanheld.

Bouklas, G. 1997. *Psychotherapy with the Elderly: Becoming Methuselah's Echo.* Lanham, MD: Jason Aronson.

Bourbeau, R. and A. Lebel. 2000. "Mortality Statistics for the Oldest-Old: An Evaluation of Canadian Data." *Demographic Research* 2:22–57.

Bowen, J. R. 2003. *Islam, Law and Equality in Indonesia.* Cambridge: Cambridge University Press.

Bower, B. 2001. "Healthy Aging May Depend on Past Habits." *Science News* 159(24):373.

Bowling, A. 2007. "Aspirations for Older Age in the 21st Century: What Is Successful Aging?" *International Journal of Aging and Human Development* 64:3.

Bowling, A., E. Grundy and M. Farquhar. 1995. "Changes in Network Composition among the Very Old Living in Inner London." *Journal of Cross-Cultural Gerontology* 10:331–47.

Bratter, B. and H. Dennis. 2008. *Project Renewment™: The First Retirement Model for Career Women.* New York: Scribner.

Bravo Castillo, O. 2007. *Hacia Una Universidad para Adultos Mayores Desde la Comunidad–Aprender Haciendo: Educacion en Derechos Humanos y Ciudadania.* Lima, Peru: Asociacion de Comunicacion y Educacion Comunitaria (ACECO).

Brent, R. 1999. "Gerontopia: A Place to Grow Old and Die." In *Aging, Autonomy and Architecture: Advances in Assisted Living.* B. Schwartz and R. Brent, eds. Baltimore: Johns Hopkins University Press.

Briller, S. 2000. "Crowding Out: An Anthropological Examination of an Economic Paradigm." Ph.D. diss. Case Western Reserve University.

Broad, D. and W. Antony, eds. 1999. *Citizens or Consumers? Social Policy in a Market Society.* Halifax, Canada: Fernwood Press.

Brodsky, J., J. Habib and I. Mizraha. 2000. *Long-Term Care Laws in Five Developed Countries: A Review.* Geneva, Switzerland: World Health Organization.

Brody, E. and C. Schoonover. 1986. "Patterns of Parent-Care When Adult Daughters Work and When They Do Not." *The Gerontologist* 26(4):372–81.

Brody, E. et al. 1984. "What Should Adult Children Do for Elderly Parents? Opinions and Preferences of Three Generations of Women." *Journal of Gerontology* 39(6):736–46.

Brody, H. 1992. "Assisted Death: A Compassionate Response to a Medical Failure." *New England Journal of Medicine* 327:1384–88.

Brooks, D. 2007. "The Odyssey Years." *New York Times*, October 9.

Brown, J. 1982. "Cross-Cultural Perspectives on Middle-Aged Women." *Current Anthropology* 23(2):143–48.

Brown, J., P. Subbaiah and S. Therese. 1994. "Being in Charge: Older Women and Their Younger Female Kin." *Journal of Cross-Cultural Gerontology* 9:231–54.

Brown, K. 1966. "Dozoku and the Ideology of Descent in Rural Japan." *American Anthropologist* 68(5):1129–51.

Browne, C. 1992. "The Role of Nature for the Promotion of Well-Being of the Elderly." In *The Role of Horticulture in Human Well-Being and Social Development*. D. Relf, ed., Portland, OR: Timber Press.

Browne, C. and K. Braun. 2008. "Globalization, Women's Migration and the Long-Term-Care Workforce." *The Gerontologist* 48:16–24.

Browne, D., M. Woltman, L. Tumarkin, S. Dyer and K. Mazzocchi. 2008. *Sharing Old Age: Alternative Senior Housing Options*. New York: Office of the New York City Public Advocate.

Browning, C. R. and K. A. Cagney. 2003. "Moving Beyond Poverty: Neighborhood Structure, Social Processes and Health." *Journal of Health and Social Behavior* 44(4):552–71.

Brum, S. D. and J. F. Williams. 1983. *Cities of the World: World Regional and Urban Development*. New York: Harper & Row.

Bryant, J. and A. Sonerson. 2006. "Gauging the Cost of Aging." *Finance and Development* 43(3). http://www.imf.org/external/pubs/ft/fandd/2006/09/Bryant.htm (accessed on November 6, 2007).

Buckley, C. 2007. *Boomsday*. New York: Twelve.

Bulatao, R. and N. Anderson, eds. 2004. *Understanding Racial and Ethnic Differences in Health in Late Life*. Washington, DC: National Academies Press.

Burden, D. "How Can I Find and Help Build a Walkable Community?" Orlando, FL: Walkable Communities, Inc. http://www.walkable.org/articles.htm.

Burkhauser, R. et al. 2005. "Until Death Do Us Part: An Analysis of the Economic Well-Being of Widows in Four Countries." *Journal of Gerontology* 60(B):38–46.

Burnette, D. 1998. "Grandmother Caregivers in Inner City Latino Families: A Descriptive Profile and Informal Supports." *Journal of Multicultural Social Work* 5:121–38.

Burton, L. 1992. "Black Grandparents Rearing Children of Drug-Addicted Parents: Stressors, Outcomes and Social Service Needs." *The Gerontologist* 32:744–51.

Burton, L. and K. Whitfield. 2006. "Health, Aging and America's Poor: Ethnographic Insights on Family Co-morbidity and Cumulative Disadvantage." In *Aging, Globalization and Inequality: The New Critical Gerontology*. J. Baars, D. Dannefer, C. Phillipson and A. Walker, eds. Amityville, NY: Baywood Press.

Bury, M. 1982. "Chronic Illness as Biological Disruption." *Sociology of Health and Illness* 4(2):167–95.

Buss, T. F., C. Beres, C. R. Hofstetter and A. Pomidor. 1994. "Health Status among Elderly Hungarians and Americans." *Journal of Cross-Cultural Gerontology* 9(3):301–22.

Butler, R. 2008. *The Longevity Revolution: The Benefits and Challenges of Living a Long Life*. New York: Public Affairs Books.

Butler, R., R. Sprott, H. Warner, J. Bland, R. Feuers, M. Forster et al. 2004. "Biomarkers of Aging: From Primitive Organisms to Humans." *Journals of Gerontology. Series A, Biological Sciences and Medical Sciences* 59:B560–67.

Byles, J., S. Feldman and A. Dobson. 2007. "The Art of Aging as Widowed Older Women in Australia." In *Lessons on Aging from Three Nations*, vol. 1: *The Art of Aging Well*. S. Carmel, C. Morse and F. Torres-Gil, eds. Amityville, NY: Baywood Press.

Byrne, S. 1974. "Arden, an Adult Community." In *Anthropologists in Cities*. G. Foster and R. Kemper, eds. Boston: Little, Brown.

Bytheway, B. 1995. *Ageism*. Buckingham, UK: Open University Press.

Cadot, E., V. G. Rodwin and A. Spira. 2007. "In the Heat of the Summer: Lessons from the Heat Waves in Paris." *Journal of Urban Health* 10(1007): s11524-007-9161-y.

Cagney, K. 2006. "Neighborhood Age Structure and Its Implications for Health." *Journal of Urban Health* 83(5):827–34.

Cai, F. 2003. "Rural-Urban Income Gap and Critical Point of Institutional Change." Working Paper Series, No. 37. http://iple.cass.cn/file/37.pdf.

Calasanti, T. M. and K. F. Slevin. 2001. *Gender, Social Inequalities and Aging*. New York: AltaMira.

———, eds. 2006. *Age Matters: Realigning Feminist Thinking*. New York: Taylor and Francis.

Callahan, J. 1995. *Menopause: A Midlife Passage*. Bloomington: Indiana University Press.

Callahan, J. and S. Lansperry. 1997. "Can We Tap the Power of Naturally Occurring Retirement Communities (NORCs)?" *Perspectives on Aging* 26:13–15.

Campbell, J. 1964. *Honour, Family and Patronage*. Oxford, UK: Clarendon Press.

Campbell, J. and R. Campbell. 2006. "Growing Old with Tokyo." In *Growing Older in World Cities: New York, London, Paris and Tokyo*. V. Rodwin and M. Gusmano, eds. Nashville, TN: Vanderbilt University Press.

Campbell, J. C. and N. Ikegami. 2000. "Long-Term Care Insurance Comes to Japan." *Health Affairs* 19(3):26–39.

Cancian, F. 1992. *The Decline of Community in Zinacantan*. Stanford, CA: Stanford University Press.

Canning, D. 2007. "The Impact of Aging on Asian Development." Harvard School of Public Health Seminar on Aging Asia. http://adb.org/AnnualMeeting/2007/seminars/presentations/dcanning-presentation.pdf.

Cannuscio, C., J. Block and I. Kawachi. 2003. "Social Capital and Successful Aging: The Role of Senior Housing." *Annals of Internal Medicine* 139(5):395–400.

Cantor, M. 1979. "The Informal Support System of New York's Inner City Elderly: Is Ethnicity a Factor?" In *Ethnicity and Aging*. D. Gelfand and A. Kutzik, eds. New York: Springer.

———. 2006. "The Impact of Ethnicity and Class on Older People in New York City: Lifestyle Patterns, Social Networks and Formal Services." In *Growing Older in World Cities: New York, London, Paris and Tokyo*. V. Rodwin and M. Gusmano, eds. Nashville, TN: Vanderbilt University Press.

Cantor, M. and V. Little. 1985. "Aging and Social Care." In *Handbook of Aging and the Social Sciences*, 2nd ed. R. H. Binstock and E. Shanas, eds. New York: Van Nostrand Reinhold.

Caplin, A. 2001. "The Reverse Mortgage Market: Problems and Prospects. In *Innovations in Housing Finance for the Elderly*. O. Mitchell, ed., Pension Research Council.

Capstick, A. 2003. "Theoretical Origins of Dementia Care Mapping." In *Dementia Care Mapping.* A. Innes, ed. Baltimore: Health Professions Press.

Caputo, R. 2000. "Trends and Correlates of Coresidency among Black and White Grandmothers and Their Grandchildren: A Panel Study, 1967–1992." In *Grandparents Raising Grandchildren: Theoretical, Empirical and Clinical Perspectives.* B. Hayslip and R. Goldberg-Glen, eds. New York: Springer.

Carlini-Marlatt, B. 2005. "Grandparents in Custodial Care of Their Grandchildren: A Literature Review." Loughborough, UK: Mentor Foundation UK Grandparents Project. http://www.mentorfoundation.org/uploads/UK_Grandparents_Lit_Review.pdf.

Carnes, B., S. Olshansky and D. Grahn. 2003. "Biological Evidence for Limits to the Duration of Life." *Biogerontology* 4:31–45.

Carpenter, G. I., J. P. Hirdes, A. W. Ribbe, N. Ikegami, D. Challis, K. Steel et al. 1999. "Targeting and Quality of Nursing Home Care. A Five-Nation Study." In *Aging: Clinical and Experimental Research* 11:83–89.

Carrick, P. 1985. *Ethics in Antiquity: Philosophical Perspectives on Abortion and Euthanasia.* Boston: Dordrecht.

Carstensen, L. L. and C. E. Löckenhoff. 2003. "Aging, Emotion and Evolution: The Bigger Picture." *Annals of the New York Academy of Science* 1000:152–79.

Caspari, R. and S.-H. Lee. 2004. "Older Age Becomes Common Late in Human Evolution." *Proceedings of the National Academy of Science* 101(30):10895–900.

Cattell, M. G. 1989. "Old Age in Rural Kenya: Gender, the Life Course and Social Change." Unpublished dissertation, Bryn Mawr College.

———. 1992. "Praise the Lord and Say No to Men: Older Samia Women Empowering Themselves." *Journal of Cross-Cultural Gerontology* 7:307–30.

———. 1994a. "'Nowadays It Isn't Easy to Advise the Young': Grandmothers and Granddaughters among Abaluyia of Kenya." *Journal of Cross-Cultural Gerontology* 9:157–78.

———. 1994b. "Intergenerational Relations among the Samia of Kenya: Culture and Experience." *Southern African Journal of Gerontology* 3(2):30–36.

———. 1996. "Gender, Aging and Health: A Comparative Approach." In *Gender and Health: An International Perspective.* C. F. Sargent and C. B. Brettell, eds. Englewood Cliffs, NJ: Prentice Hall.

———. 1997. "African Widows, Culture and Social Change: Case Studies from Kenya." In *The Cultural Context of Aging: Worldwide Perspectives*, 2nd ed. J. Sokolovsky, ed. Westport, CT: Bergin and Garvey.

———. 2003. "African Widows: Anthropological and Historical Perspectives." *Journal of Women and Aging* 15(2/3):49–66.

———. 2008. "Aging and Social Change in Western Kenya: Anthropological and Historical Perspectives." *Journal of Cross-Cultural Gerontology* 23(2):181–97.

Cattell, M. G. and M. M. Schweitzer. 2006. *Women in Anthropology: Autobiographical Narratives and Social History.* Walnut Creek, CA: Left Coast Press.

Cattell, V. and M. Evans. 1999. *Neighbourhood Images in East London: Social Capital and Social Networks on Two East London Estates.* York, UK: YPS in association with the Joseph Rowntree Foundation.

CeloCruz, M. 1992. "Aid in Dying: Should We Decriminalize Physician-Assisted Suicide and Physician Controlled Euthanasia?" *American Journal of Law and Medicine* 18:368–94.

Census of India. 2001. "Data Highlights: HH-5: Households with Number of Aged Persons 60 Years and above by Sex and Household Size," 2–4.

Centers for Disease Control. 2007. "Diabetes Prevalence Rates." http://www.cdc.gov (accessed on December 2007).

Central Intelligence Agency. 2007. *The CIA World Factbook.* https://www.cia.gov/library/publications/the-world-factbook (accessed on August 21, 2008).

Cerhan, J. R. and R. B. Wallace. 1993. "Predictors of Decline in Social Relationships in the Rural Elderly." *American Journal of Epidemiology* 137:870–80.

Cervantes Ticona, J. L. 2006a. "Adultos Mayores Piden Cumplimento de la Ley" (press release). Arequipa, Peru: Red Departamental de Arequipa/Red IberoAmericana de Asociacines de Adultos Mayores (RIAAAM).

———. 2006b. "Apuntes Sobre la Pobreza y la Vejez" (press release). Arequipa, Peru: Red Departamental de Arequipa/Red IberoAmericana de Asociaciondes de Adultos Mayores (RIAAAM).

———. 2007. "El Plan Nacional Para Las Personas Adultas Mayores, De Sus Actores y Sus Responsabilidades" (press release). Arequipa, Peru: Red Departamental de Arequipa/Red IberoAmericana de Asociaciones de Adultos Mayores (RIAAAM).

Chambers, P. 2005. *Older Widows and the Life Course: Multiple Narratives of Hidden Lives.* Burlington VT: Ashgate.

Chan, Y., M. Suzuki and S. Yamamoto. 1997. "Nutritional Status of Centenarians Assessed by Activity and Anthropometric, Hematological and Biochemical Characteristics." *Journal of Nutritional Science and Vitaminology* 43:73–81.

Chapman, T. M. 1976. *The Decolonization of Niue.* Wellington, New Zealand: Victoria University Press.

———. 1982. "Modern Times (Ko e magahala fakamui)." In *Niue: A History of the Island.* Niue/Suva, Fiji: Niue Government/Institute for Pacific Studies, University of the South Pacific.

Chappell, N. 1995. "Informal Social Support." In *Promoting Successful and Productive Aging.* L. Bond, S. Cutler and A. Grams, eds. Thousand Oaks, CA: Sage.

———. 2006. "Ethnicity and Quality of Life." In *Quality of Life in Old Age—International and Multi-Disciplinary Perspectives.* H. Mollenkopf and A. Walker, eds. New York: Springer.

Charness, N. 2005. "Age, Technology and Culture: Gerontopia or Dystopia?" *Public Policy and Aging Report* 15(4):20–23.

Chase-Lansdale, P. L., R. Gordon, R. L. Coley, L. S. Wakschlag and J. Brooks-Gunn. 1999. "Young African American Multigenerational Families in Poverty: The Contexts, Exchanges and Processes of Their Lives." In *Coping with Divorce, Single Parenting and Remarriage: A Risk and Resiliency Perspective.* E. M. Hetherington, ed. Mahwah, NJ: Lawrence Erlbaum.

Chavez, A. and A. Rosado. 1967. "Estudio Epidemiologico de la Pelagra en Una Communidad Rural." *Boletin del Oficina Sanitaria Panamericana* 55(4):398–404.

Chawla, M., G. Betcherman, A. Banerji, A. Bakilana, C. Feher et al. 2007. *From Red to Gray: The 'Third Transition' of Ageing Populations in Eastern Europe and the Soviet Union.* World Bank. http://siteresources.worldbank.org/ECAEXT/Resources/publications/454763-1181939083693/full_report.pdf.

Cheang, M. 2002. "Older Adults' Frequent Visits to a Fast-Food Restaurant: Nonobligatory Social Interaction and the Significance of Play in a 'Third Space.'" *Journal of Aging Studies* 16:302–21.

Chen, M. A., ed. 1998. *Widows in India: Social Neglect and Public Action.* New Delhi: Sage.

———. 2000. *Perpetual Mourning: Widowhood in Rural India.* New Delhi: Oxford University Press.

Cheng, T. and M. Seldon. 1994. "The Origins and Social Consequences of China's Hukou System." *China Quarterly* 139:644–68.

Cherlin, A. and F. Furstenberg. 1992. *The New American Grandparent: A Place in the Family, a Life Apart*. Cambridge, MA: Harvard University Press.

Cheung, C. and A. Yuihuen. 2006. "Impacts of Filial Piety on Preference for Kinship Versus Public Care." *Journal of Community Psychology* 34(5):617–34.

Chi, I., K. Mehta and A. Howe, eds. 2001. "Long-Term Care in the 21st Century: Perspectives from around the Asia-Pacific Rim." Special issue, *Journal of Aging and Social Policy* 13(2/3).

Chicago Community Fact Book Consortium. 1984. *Local Community Fact Book: Chicago Metropolitan Area*. Chicago: Department of Sociology, University of Illinois at Chicago.

Chicago Fact Finder. 2005. Institute for Latino Studies, University of Notre Dame. http://www3.nd.edu/~chifacts/communities.php?alphaorder=68&page=1&dset=1&years=1&dcat=1.

Chick, G. 2002. "Cultural and Behavioral Consonance in a Tlaxcalan Festival System." *Field Methods* 14(1):26–45.

China Daily. 2006. "Poor Rural Elderly Deserve Attention." December 3. http://www.chinadaily.com.cn/china/2006-12/03/content_749034.htm.

China National Committee on Aging. 2007. "'Zhongguo chengxiang laonian renkou zhuangkuang zhuizong diaochai' yanjiu baogao" [Research report on the investigation tracking the situations of urban and rural elderly population in China]. December 17. http://www.china.com.cn/policy/txt/2007-12/17/content_9393143.htm.

China News. 2006. "China Tries Out New Retirement Modes." June 23. http://www.chinanews.cn//news/2005/2006-06-23/24258.html.

Chopra, D. 1993. *Ageless Body, Timeless Mind: The Quantum Alternative to Growing Old*. New York: Three Rivers Press.

Choy, Y. 2006. "Transformations in Economic Security During Old Age in Korea: The Implications for Public-Pension Reform." *Ageing and Society* 26:549–65.

Christensen, K., T. Johnson and J. Vaupel. 2006. "The Quest for Genetic Determinants of Human Longevity: Challenges and Insights." *Nature Reviews Genetics* 7:436–48.

Christensen, K., M. McGue, I. Petersen, B. Jeune and J. Vaupel. Forthcoming. "Exceptional Longevity Does Not Result in Excessive Levels of Disability." *Proceedings of the National Academy of Sciences*. http://www.pnas.org/content/early/2008/08/15/0804931105.full.pdf+html.

Chui, H. C. and M. Gatz. 2005. "Cultural Diversity in Alzheimer Disease: The Interface between Biology, Belief and Behavior. *Alzheimer Disease and Associated Disorders* 19(4):250–55.

Clark, M. 1967. "The Anthropology of Aging: A New Area of Studies for Culture and Personality." *The Gerontologist* 7:55–64.

———. 1972. "Cultural Values and Dependency in Later Life." In *Aging and Modernization*. D. O. Cowgill and L. D. Holmes, eds. New York: Appleton Century Crofts.

Clark, M. and B. G. Anderson. 1967. *Culture and Aging: An Anthropological Study of Older Americans*. Springfield, IL: Charles Thomas.

———. 1980. *Culture and Aging: An Anthropological Study of Older Americans*, 2nd ed. Springfield, IL: Thomas Books.

Clemetson, L. 2006. "U.S. Muslims Confront Taboo on Nursing Homes," *New York Times*, June 13, 155(53609, A1–A18.

Cliggett, L. 2005. *Grains from Grass: Aging, Gender and Famine in Rural Africa.* Ithaca, NY: Cornell University Press.

CMS 64 Data. 2007. "Distribution of Medicaid Long-Term Care Expenditures for A/D Services: Institutional vs. Community-Based Services, FY 2006." August 10. Washington, DC: Center for Medicaid and State Operations, Division of Financial Operations.

Cohen, C., A. Alder and J. Mintz. 1983. "Assessing Social Network Interventions—Results of an Experimental Service Program Conducted in a Single-Room Occupancy Hotel." In *Rediscovering Self-Help: Professionals and Informal Care.* E. Parker and D. Pancoast, eds. Beverly Hills, CA: Sage.

Cohen, C. and J. Sokolovsky. 1989. *Old Men of the Bowery: Survival Strategies of the Homeless.* New York: Guilford Press.

Cohen, L. 1995. "Toward an Anthropology of Senility: Anger, Weakness and Alzheimer's in Banares, India." *Medical Anthropology Quarterly* 9(3):317–34.

———. 1998. *No Aging in India: Alzheimer's, the Bad Family and Other Modern Things.* Berkeley: University of California Press.

Cohen, M., T. Tripp-Reimer, C. Smith, B. Sorofman and S. Lively. 1994. "Explanatory Models of Diabetes: Patient Practitioner Variation." *Social Science and Medicine* 38(1):59–66.

Cohen, U. and K. Day. 1992. *Contemporary Environments for People with Dementia.* Baltimore: Johns Hopkins University Press.

Cohler, B. 1983. "Stress or Support: Relations between Older Women from Three European Ethnic Groups and Their Relatives." In *Minority Aging: Sociological and Social Psychological Issues.* R. Manuel, ed. Westport, CT: Greenwood Press.

Cohler, B. and M. Lieberman. 1980. "Social Relations and Mental Health." *Research on Aging* 2(4):445–69.

Cohler, B., M. Lieberman and L. Welch. 1977. "Social Relations and Interpersonal Resources among Middle-Aged and Older Irish, Italian and Polish-American Men and Women." Chicago: University of Chicago, Committee on Human Development.

Cohn, J. 2007. *Sick: The Untold Story of America's Health Care Crisis—and the People Who Pay the Price.* New York: HarperCollins.

Coke, M. and J. Twaite. 1995. *The Black Elderly: Satisfaction and Quality of Life.* Binghamton, NY: Haworth Press.

Cole, M. 2005. "Culture in Development." In *Developmental Science: An Advanced Textbook,* 5th ed. M. H. Bornstein and M. E. Lamb, eds. Mahwah, NJ: Lawrence Erlbaum.

Cole, P., J. Brown and B. MacMahon. 1976. "Estrogen Profiles of Parous and Nulliparous Women." *The Lancet* (September 18):596–99.

Cole, T. 1992. *The Journey of Life: A Cultural History of Ageing in America.* Cambridge: Cambridge University Press.

Coleman, P. 1993. "Adjustment in Later Life." In *Ageing in Society: An Introduction to Social Gerontology.* J. Bond, P. Coleman and S. Peace, eds. London: Sage.

Coleman, P. G. 1986. *Aging and Reminiscence Processes: Social and Clinical Implications.* New York: Wiley.

Colen, J. 1979. "Critical Issues in the Development of Environmental Support Systems for the Aged." *Allied Health and Behavioral Sciences* 2(1):74–90.

———. 1982. "Using Natural Helping Networks in Social Service Delivery Systems." In *Minority Aging.* R. Manuel, ed. Westport, CT: Greenwood Press.

Coles, C. 1990. "The Older Woman in Hausa Society: Power and Authority in Urban Nigeria." In *The Cultural Context of Aging: Worldwide Perspectives*. J. Sokolovsky, ed. New York: Bergin and Garvey.

Coles, L. 2004. "Demography of Human Supercentenarians." *Journals of Gerontology. Series A, Biological Sciences and Medical Sciences* 59A:579–86.

Collins, C. and A. O'Callaghan. 2007. "Healing Gardens for Assisted Living: An Interdisciplinary Approach to Health Education." *Journal of Extension* 45:6. Online only at www.joe.org/joe/2007december/iw7.shtml (accessed on March 9, 2008).

Collins, P. 2001. "'If You Got Everything, It's Good Enough': Perspectives on Successful Aging in a Canadian Inuit Community." *Journal of Cross-Cultural Gerontology* 16(2):127–55.

Colmorten, E., E. Hansen, S. Pedersen, M. Platz and B. Roenow. 2003. *Denaeldre Har Brug for Hjaelp. Hvem Boer Traede Til?* Copenhagen: AKF Forlaget.

Combrinck-Graham, L. 1990. "Developments in Family Systems Theory and Research." *Journal of the American Academy of Child and Adolescent Psychiatry* 29: 501–12.

Commission on Behavioral and Social Sciences and Education. 2001. *Preparing for an Aging World: The Case for Cross-National Research*. Washington, DC: Commission on Behavioral and Social Sciences and Education.

Commonwealth Fund Commission on the Elderly Living Alone.1988. *Aging Alone*. Baltimore: Commonwealth Fund.

Comune di Prato. 1989. "Tavolo 8: Popolazione presente e residente al Censimenti." Annuario Statistico. Firenze: Litografia, I.P.

Comune di Vernio. 1991. "Censimento di Comune di Vernio (unpublished census report)." S. Quirico: Il Archivio di Vernio.

Conceicai, C. and V. Oca Zavala. 2004. "Ageing in Mexico: Families, Informal Care and Reciprocity." In *Living Longer: Aging, Development and Social Protection*. P. Lloyd-Sherlock, ed. London: Zed Books.

Condon, K. M., B. D. Dunlop and M. B. Rothman. 1994. *Elders in Dade County, Florida: Information from the 1990 United States Census*. Miami: Florida International University, Southeast Florida Center on Aging.

Congress of Peru. 2003. *Ley No. 27972, Ley Organica de Municipalidades. Article IV, Section 6*. Lima, Peru: El Peruano.

———. 2006a. *Ley No. 28803, Ley de las Personas Adultas Mayores*. Lima, Peru: El Peruano.

———. 2006b. *Ley No. 28735, Que Regula La Atencion de las Personas Con Discapacidad, Mujeres Embarazadas y Adultos Mayores en los Aeropuertos, Aerodromos, Terminales Terrestres, Ferroviarios, Maritimos y Fluviales y Medios de Transporte*. Lima, Peru: El Peruano.

Connell, J. 1983. *Migration, Employment and Development in the South Pacific*. Country Report Number 11—Niue. Noumea, New Caledonia: South Pacific Commission.

Consejo Transitorio Regional de Arequipa (CTAR). 1998. *Datos Poblacionales del Adulto Mayor de Arequipa*. Arequipa, Peru: CTAR.

Cool, L. 1981. "Ethnic Identity: A Source of Community Esteem for the Elderly." *Anthropological Quarterly* 54:179–89.

Cool, L. and J. McCabe. 1987. "The 'Scheming Hag' and the 'Dear Old Thing': The Anthropology of Aging Women." In *Growing Old in Different Societies: Cross-Cultural Perspectives*. J. Sokolovsky, ed. Acton, MA: Copley.

Cordain, L., J. Brand Miller, S. B. Eaton, N. Mann, S. H. A. Holt and J. D. Speth. 2000. "Plant-Animal Subsistence Ratios and Macronutrient Energy Estimations in Hunter-Gatherer Diets." *American Journal of Clinical Nutrition* 71:682–92.

Cornwell, M., E. Laumann and P. Schumm. 2008. "The Social Connectedness of Older Adults: A National Profile." *American Sociological Review* 73(2):185–203.

Council of Ethical and Judicial Affairs, American Medical Association. 1992. "Decisions Near the End of Life." *Journal of the American Medical Association* 264:369–72.

Counts, D. A. and D. R. Counts, eds. 1985a. *Aging and Transformations: Moving Toward Death in Pacific Societies.* New York: University Press of America.

———. 1985b. "I'm Not Dead Yet! Aging and Death: Process and Experience in Kaliai." In *Aging and Transformations: Moving Toward Death in Pacific Societies.* New York: University Press of America.

Counts, D. A. and D. R. Counts. 1992. "They're My Family Now: Community Creation among RVers." *Anthropologica* 34:153–82.

———. 1996. *Over the Next Hill: An Ethnography of RVing Seniors in North America.* Peterborough, Canada: Broadview Press.

———. 2001. *Over the Next Hill: An Ethnography of RVing Seniors in North America,* 2nd ed. Peterborough, Canada: Broadview Press.

Cowgill, D. 1974. "The Aging of Populations and Society." *Annals of the American Academy of Political and Social Sciences* 415:1–18.

———. 1986. *Aging Around the World.* Belmont, CA: Wadsworth.

Cowgill, D. and L. Holmes, eds. 1974. *Aging and Modernization.* New York: Appleton-Century-Crofts.

Cox, C. 1993. "Service Needs and Interests: A Comparison of African American and White Caregivers Seeking Alzheimer's Assistance." *American Journal of Alzheimer's Care and Related Disorders and Research* 8(3):35.

———. 2005. "Grandparents Raising Grandchildren from a Multicultural Perspective." In *Multicultural Perspectives in Working with Families.* E. P. Congress and M. J. Gonzales, eds. New York: Springer.

Cox, C., L. Brooks, L. and C. Valcarcel. 2000. "Culture and Caregiving: A Study of Latino Grandparents." In *To Grandmothers House We Go and Stay: Perspectives on Custodial Grandparents.* C. Cox, ed. New York: Springer.

Cox, C. and A. Monk. 1993. "Hispanic Culture and Family Care of Alzheimer's Patients." *Health Social Work* 18(2):92–100.

Crary, D. 2007. "Most in U.S. Poll Back a Right to Die." *Philadelphia Inquirer,* May 30.

Cravioto, R. et al. 1945. "Nutritive Value of the Tortilla." *Science* 102:91–93.

Crewe, S. 2004. "Ethnogerontology: Preparing Culturally Competent Social Workers for the Diverse Facing of Aging." *Journal of Gerontological Social Work* 43(4):45–57.

Crews, D. 2003. *Human Senescence: Evolutionary and Biocultural Perspectives.* Cambridge: Cambridge University Press.

———. 2007. "Senescence, Aging and Disease." *Journal of Physiological Anthropology* 26:365–72.

Crews, D. and R. Garruto. 1994. *Biological Anthropology and Aging: Perspectives on Human Variation over the Life Span.* New York: Oxford University Press.

Crews, D. and S. Zavotka. 2006. "Aging, Disability and Frailty: Implications for Universal Design." *Journal of Physiological Anthropology* 25(1):113–18.

http://www.sld.cu/galerias/pdf/sitios/gericuba/aging_disability_and_frailty_implications_for_universal_design.pdf.

Crist, J., J. Armer and M. Radina. 2002. "A Study in Cultural Diversity: Caregiving for the Old Order Amish Elderly with Alzheimer's Disease." *Journal of Multicultural Nursing and Health*, 8(3):78–85.

Critser, G. 2003. *Fatland: How Americans Became the Fattest People in the World.* London: Penguin.

Crocker, J. C. 1977. "The Mirrored Self: Identity and Ritual Inversion among the Eastern Bororo." *Ethnology* 16(2):129–45.

Croker, R. and K. Dychtwald. 2007. *The Boomer Century, 1946–2046: How America's Most Influential Generation Changed Everything.* New York: Springboard Press.

Crowley, B., B. Hayslip and J. Hobdy, "Psychological Hardiness and Adjustment to Life Events in Adulthood." *Journal of Adult Development* 10:237–48.

Crowther, M., M. Parker, A. Achenbaum, W. Larimore, L. Walter and H. Koenig. 2002. "Rowe and Kahn's Model of Successful Aging Revisited: Positive Spirituality—the Forgotten Factor." *The Gerontologist* 42(5):613–20.

Crowther, M., L. M. Swanson, R. L. Rodriguez, M. Snarski and H. K. Higgerson. 2006. "Religious Beliefs and Practices among African American Custodial Grandparents." In *Custodial Grandparenting: Individual, Cultural and Ethnic Diversity.* B. Hayslip and J. Hicks-Patrick, eds. New York: Springer.

Cuellar, I., E. Bastida and S. Braccio. 2004. "Residency in the United States, Subjective Well-Being and Depression in an Older Mexican-Origin Sample." *Journal of Aging and Health* 16:447–66.

Cuellar, J. 1978. "El Senior Citizen Club: The Older Mexican-American in the Voluntary Association." In *Life's Career—Aging.* B. Myerhoff and A. Simic, eds. London: Sage.

Cuellar, J. and J. Weeks. 1980. "Minority Elderly Americans: A Prototype for Area Agencies on Aging." Executive Summary. San Diego: Allied Health Association.

Curran, A. B. 1997. Student researcher field notes on interview with Mrs. Abdullahi, December 8.

Curry, L., R. Shield and T. Wetle, eds. 2006. *Improving Aging and Public Health Research: Qualitative and Mixed Methods.* Washington, DC: American Public Health Association.

Daatland, S. and S. Biggs, eds. 2006. *Ageing and Diversity: Multiple Pathways and Cultural Migrations.* Bristol, UK: Policy Press.

Daatland, S. and A. Lowenstein. 2005. "Intergenerational Solidarity and the Family-Welfare State Balance." *European Journal of Gerontology* 2:174–82.

Daichman, L. 2005. "Elder Abuse in Developing Nations." In *The Cambridge Handbook of Age and Ageing.* M. Johnson, ed. Cambridge: Cambridge University Press.

Daniell, H. 1976. "Osteoporosis of the Slender Smoker: Vertebral Compression Fractures and Loss of Metacarpal Cortex in Relation to Postmenopausal Cigarette Smoking and Lack of Obesity." *Arch Internal Medicine* 136:298–304.

Danish Government. 2000. "Structural Monitoring–International Benchmarking of Denmark." Copenhagen: Ministry of Finance.

Dannefer, D. 2001. "Whose Life Course Is It, Anyway? Diversity and Linked Lives in Global Perspective." In *Invitation to the Life Course: New Understandings of Later Life.* R. A. Settersten, ed. Amityville, NY: Baywood Press.

———. 2003a. "Cumulative Advantage/Disadvantage and the Life Course: Cross-Fertilizing Age and Social Science Theory." *Journal of Gerontology* 58B:S327–37.

———. 2003b. "Toward a Global Geography of the Life Course." In *Handbook of the Life Course*. J. T. Mortimer and M. J. Shanahan, eds. New York: Kluwer Academic/Plenum.

Datan, N., B. Maoz, A. Antonovsky and H. Wijsenbeek. 1970. "Climacterium in Three Culture Contexts." *Tropical and Geographical Medicine* 22:77–86.

Davey, A., E. Femia, S. Zarit, D. Shea, G. Sundström, S. Berg et al. 2005. "Life on the Edge: Patterns of Formal and Informal Help to Older Adults in the United States and Sweden." *Journal of Gerontology* 60(5):S281–88.

Davey, A., L. Johansson, B. Malmberg and G. Sundström. 2006. "Unequal but Equitable: An Analysis of Variations in Old-Age Care in Sweden." *European Journal of Ageing* 3:34–40.

Davidson, K. 2006. "Flying Solo in Old Age." In *The Futures of Old Age*. J. Vincent, C. Phillipson and M. Downs, eds. London: Sage.

Davidson, K. and G. Fennell, eds. 2004. *Intimacy in Later Life*. New Brunswick, NJ: Transaction Publishers.

Davis-Friedmann, D. 1991. *Long Lives: Chinese Elderly and the Communist Revolution*, 2nd ed. Stanford, CA: Stanford University Press.

de Chenay, C. 2003. "Paris voit peu à peu disparaître ses commerces de proximité." *Le Monde*, September 16.

DeKay, W. T. 1995. "Grandparental Investment and the Uncertainty of Kinship." Seventh Annual Meeting of the Human Behavior and Evolution Society, Santa Barbara, CA.

Della Pina, M. 1986. "Gli insediamenti e la popolazione." In *Prato: Storia di una citta*. Elena Fasano Guarini, ed. Prato: Le Monnier.

Demirovic, J., R. Prineas, D. Loewenstein, J. Bean, R. Duara, S. Sevush et al. 2003. "Prevalence of Dementia in Three Ethnic Groups: The South Florida Program on Aging and Health." *Annals of Epidemiology* 13(6):472–78.

Demos, J. 1982. *Entertaining Satan: Witchcraft and Culture of Early New England*. New York: Oxford University Press.

Denzin, N. 1995. "Chan Is Missing." In *Images of Ageing: Cultural Representations of Later Life*. M. Featherstone and A. Wernick, eds. London: Sage.

Derne, S. 2005. "Globalization and the Making of a Transnational Middle Class: Implications for Class Analysis." In *Critical Globalization Studies*. W. I. Robinson and R. Applebaum, eds. New York: Routledge.

Detzner, D. 2004. *Elder Voices: Southeast Asian Families in the U.S.* Lanham, MD: AltaMira.

De Vos, S. 1990. "Extended Family Living among Older People in Six Latin American Countries." *Journal of Gerontology* 45(3):S87–S94.

Diamond, T. 1986. "Social Policy and Everyday Life in Nursing Homes: A Critical Ethnography." *Social Science and Medicine* 23(12):1287–95.

———. 1992. *Making Gray Gold: Narratives of Nursing Home Care*. Chicago: University of Chicago Press.

Diaz-Bolio, J. 1981. "El Mal de Huesos y La Chaya." *Diario de Yucatan* (September 16). Merida, Yucatan.

Diaz-Briquets, S. and L. Perez. 1981. "Cuba: The Demography of Revolution." *Population Bulletin* 36:1–43.

Dickerson-Putnam, J. 1996. "Women, Age and Power: The Politics of Age Difference among Women in Papua New Guinea and Australia." Special issue, *Pacific Studies* 19(4).

———. Forthcoming. "Cultural Contexts for Grandparent Adoption on Raivavae." *Pacific Studies.*

Dilworth-Anderson, P., B. Brummett, P. Goodwin, S. Williams, R. Wallace, R. Williams and I. Siegler. 2005. "Effect of Race on Cultural Justifications for Caregiving. *Journal of Gerontology: Social Sciences* 60B(5):S257–62.

Dilworth-Anderson, P., B. Gibson and J. Burke. 2006. "Working with African American Families." In *Ethnicity and the Dementias*, 2nd ed. G. Yeo and D. Gallagher-Thompson, eds. New York: Routledge.

Dilworth-Anderson, P., I. Williams and B. Gibson. 2002. "Issues of Race, Ethnicity and Culture in Caregiving Research: A 20-Year Review (1980–2000)." *The Gerontologist* 42(2):237–72.

di Martelli, C. and A. Santoni. 1997. "I movimenti migratora a Prato (1939–1951)." In *Prato: storia di una citta, Il distretto industriale (1943–1993), (a cura di Giacomo Becattini)* 4:269–86. Comune di Prato: Le Monnier.

Dobbs, D., J. K. Eckert, B. Rubinstein, L. Keimig, L. Clark, A. C. Frankowski and S. Zimmerman. 2008. "An Ethnographic Study of Stigma and Ageism in Residential Care or Assisted Living." *The Gerontologist* 48:517–26.

Doi, T. 1973. *The Anatomy of Dependence.* J. Bester, trans. New York: Kodansha.

Donlon, M., O. Ashman and B. Levy. 2005. "Re-Vision of Older Television Characters: A Stereotype-Awareness Intervention." *Journal of Social Issues* 61(2):307–19.

Dormandy, T. 2000. *Old Masters: Great Artists in Old Age.* London: Hambledon Press.

Dossa, P. A. 1994. "Critical Anthropology and Life Stories: Case Study of Elderly Ismaili Canadians." *Journal of Cross-Cultural Gerontology* 9(3):335–54.

———. 1999. "(Re)Imagining Aging Lives: Ethnographic Narratives of Muslim Women in Diaspora." *Journal of Cross-Cultural Gerontology* 14:245–72.

———. 2002. "Narrative Mediation of Conventional and New 'Mental Health' Paradigms: Reading the Stories of Immigrant Iranian Women." *Medical Anthropology Quarterly* 16(3):341–59.

Dougherty, M. 1978. "An Anthropological Perspective on Aging and Women in the Middle Years." In *The Anthropology of Health*. E. Bauwens, ed. St. Louis, MO: C. V. Mosby.

Douglas, M. 1966. *Purity and Danger.* London: Routledge and Kegan Paul.

———. 1969. "Is Matriliny Doomed in Africa?" In *Man in Africa*. M. Douglas and P. M. Kaberry, eds. London: Tavistock London.

Drake, St. C. and H. Cayton. 1993. *Black Metropolis: A Study of Negro Life in a Northern City.* Chicago: University of Chicago Press.

Draper, P. 1976. "Social and Economic Constraints on Child Life among the !Kung." In *Kalahari Hunter-Gatherers: Studies of the !Kung San and Their Neighbors.* R. B. Lee and I. DeVore, eds. Cambridge, MA: Harvard University Press.

———. 1992. "Room to Maneuver: !Kung Women Cope with Men." In *Sanctions and Sanctuary: Cultural Perspectives on the Beating of Wives.* D. A. Counts, J. K. Brown and J. C. Campbell, eds. Boulder: Westview Press.

Draper, P. and A. Buchanan. 1992. "If You Have a Child You Have Life: Demographic and Cultural Perspectives on Fathering in Old Age in !Kung Society." In *Father-Child Relations: Cultural and Biosocial Contexts.* B. S. Hewlett, ed. New York: Aldine de Gruyter.

Draper, P. and H. Harpending. 1994. "Cultural Considerations in the Experience of Aging: Two African Cultures." In *Functional Performance in Older Adults.* B. R. Bonder and M. B. Wagner, eds. Philadelphia: F. A. Davis.

Draper, P. and J. Keith. 1992. "Cultural Contexts of Care: Family Caregiving for Elderly in America and Africa." *Journal of Aging Studies* 6:113–34.

Dreier, P., J. Mollenkopf and T. Swanstrom. 2001. *Place Matters: Metropolitics for the Twenty-First Century.* Lawrence: University Press of Kansas.

Drèze, J. P. 1990. "Widows in Rural India." DEP Paper No. 26, Development Economics Research Program. London: London School of Economics.

Dube, L. 1988. "On the Construction of Gender: Hindu Girls in Patrilineal India." *Economic and Political Weekly* April 30:11–19.

Duffy, C., K. Perez and A. Partridge. 2007. "Implications of Phytoestrogen Intake for Breast Cancer." *CA: A Cancer Journal for Clinicians* 57(5):260–77.

Duhigg, C. 2007. "At Many Homes, More Profit and Less Nursing." *New York Times,* September 23.

Dumas, F. 2005. "Forever Young." *New York Times Magazine,* October 30. 155(53383):34.

Dunér, A. and M. Nordström. 2007. "The Roles and Functions of the Informal Support Networks of Older People Who Receive Formal Support: A Swedish Qualitative Study." *Ageing and Society* 27:67–85.

Durham, D., ed. 2006. *Generations and Globalization: Family, Youth and Age in the New World Economy.* Bloomington: Indiana University Press.

Durkheim, E. 1893. *The Division of Labor in Society.* New York: Free Press.

Durrett, C. 2005. *Senior Co-Housing: A Community Approach to Independent Living.* Berkeley, CA: Ten Speed Press.

Durrschmidt, J. 1997. "The Delinking of Locale and Milieu: On the Situatedness of Extended Milieux in a Global Environment." In *Living in the Global City.* J. Eade, ed. London: Routledge.

Du Toit, B. 1990. *Aging and Menopause among Indian South African Women.* Albany: State University of New York Press.

Dykstra, P. 1990. *Next of Non-Kin.* Amsterdam: Swets and Zetlinger.

Eagleton, T. 1983. *Literary Theory: An Introduction.* Oxford: Basil Blackwell.

Earnest, L. 2007. "A Kick in the Pants for Boomers." *Los Angeles Times,* May 2.

Eckert, J. K. and L. Morgan. 2001. "Quality in Small Residential Care Settings." In *Linking Quality of Long-Term Care and Quality of Life.* L. S. Noelker and A. Harel, eds. New York: Springer.

Eckert, K. 1980. *The Unseen Elderly: A Study of Marginally Subsistent Hotel Dwellers.* San Diego: Campanile Press.

Eggers, T., A. Norberg and S.-L. Ekman. 2005. Counteracting Fragmentation in the Care of People with Moderate and Severe Dementia. *Clinical Nursing Research* 14(4):343–69.

Eisdorfer, C., S. J. Czaja, D. A. Loewenstein, M. P. Rubert, S. Argüelles, V. B. Mitrani et al. 2003. "The Effect of Family Therapy and Technology-Based Intervention on Caregiver Depression." *The Gerontologist* 43(4):521–31.

Eisenstadt, S. N. 1956. *From Generation to Generation.* New York: Free Press.

Elder, G. H. 1999. *Children of the Great Depression: Social Change in Life Experience,* 25th anniversary ed. Boulder, CO: Westview.

Elder, G. H., Jr. and R. D. Conger. 2000. *Children of the Land: Adversity and Success in Rural America.* Chicago: University of Chicago Press.

Elder, G. H., Jr. and M. K. Johnson. 2003. "The Life Course and Aging: Challenges, Lessons and New Directions." In *Invitation to the Life Course: New Understandings of Later Life.* R. A. Settersten, ed. Amityville, NY: Baywood Press.

Elder, G. H., Jr., E. Robertson and R. Conger. 1995. "Fathers and Sons in Rural America: Occupational Choice and Intergenerational Ties across the Life Course." In *Aging and Generational Relations over the Life Course*. T. Harevan, ed. Chicago: Aldine de Gruyter.

Elderfield, J. 1978. *The Cut-outs of Henri Matisse*. New York: George Braziller.

Elias, N. 1985. *The Loneliness of the Dying*. Oxford: Basil Blackwell.

Ellickson, J. 1988. "Never the Twain Shall Meet: Aging Men and Women in Bangladesh." *Journal of Cross-Cultural Gerontology* 3(1):53–70.

Elmendorf, M. 1976. *Nine Mayan Women: A Village Faces Change*. New York: Schenkman Publishing.

Emami, A., P. Benner and S. Ekman. 2001. "A Sociocultural Health Model for Late-in-Life Immigrants." *Journal of Transcultural Nursing* 12(1):15–24.

Emami, A., P. Benner, J. Lipson and S. Ekman. 2000. "Health as Continuity and Balance in Life." *Western Journal of Nursing Research* 22(7):812–25.

Emami, A. and S. Ekman. 1998. "Living in a Foreign Country in Old Age: Elderly Iranian Immigrants' Experiences of Their Social Situation in Sweden." *Health Care in Later Life* 3:183–99.

Emami, A. and S. Torres. 2000. "The Process of Migration as a Point of Departure for Elderly Immigrants' Understandings of Illness." *The Gerontologist* 10:283.

Emami, A., S. Torres, J. Lipson and S. Ekman. 2000. "An Ethnographic Study of a Day Care Center for Iranian Immigrant Seniors. *Western Journal of Nursing Research*. 22(2):169–89.

Emanuel, E. 1994. "The History of Euthanasia in the United States and Britain." *Annals of Internal Medicine* 121:793–802.

Epel, E. S., E. H. Blackburn, J. Lin, F. S. Dhabhar, N. E. Adler, J. D. Morrow and R. M. Cawthon. 2004. "Accelerated Telomere Shortening in Response to Life Stress." *Proceedings of the National Academy of Science* 101(49):17312–15.

Eschenbruch, N. 2006. *Nursing Stories: Life and Death in a German Hospice*. New York: Berghahn Books.

Espino, D. V. and A. Miguel, M. P. Bedolla and F. M. Baker. 1996. "Validation of the Geriatric Depression Scale in an Elder Mexican American Ambulatory Population: A Pilot Study." *Clinical Gerontologist* 16(4):55–67.

Estes, C. 1979. *The Aging Enterprise*. San Francisco: Jossey-Bass.

———. 2004. "Social Security Privatization and Older Women: A Feminist Political Economy Perspective." *Journal of Aging Studies* 18(1):9–26.

Estes, C. L. and C. Phillipson. 2002. "The Globalization of Capital, the Welfare State and Old Age Policy." *International Journal of Health Services* 32(2): 279–97.

Euler, H. A. and B. Weitzel. 1996. "Discriminative Grandparental Solicitude as Reproductive Strategy." *Human Nature* 7:39–59.

European Science Foundation. 2006. "Family Support for Older People: Determinants and Consequences (FAMSUP)." In *Family Care for Older People in Thirteen European Countries*. Strasbourg: ESF.

Evaneshko, V. 1994. "Presenting Complaints in a Navajo Indian Diabetic Population." In *Diabetes as a Disease of Civilization: The Impact of Culture Change on Indigenous Peoples*. J. Joe and R. Young, eds. New York: Mouton de Gruyter.

Eveleth, P. and J. Tanner. 1976. *World Wide Variation in Human Growth*. Cambridge: Cambridge University Press.

Evercare. 2007. *Family Caregivers—What They Spend, What They Sacrifice.* http://
www.caregiving.org/data/Evercare_NAC_CaregiverCostStudyFINAL20111907.pdf.

Evers, H. 1981. "Care or Custody? The Experience of Women Patients in Long-Stay
Geriatric Wards." In *Controlling Women: The Normal and the Deviant.* B. Hut-
ter and G. Williams, eds. London: Croom Helm.

Evert, J., E. Lawler, H. Bogan and T. Perls. 2003. "Morbidity Profiles of Centenarians:
Survivors, Delayers and Escapers." *Journals of Gerontology. Series A, Biological Sciences and Medical Sciences* 58:232–37.

Eyetsemitan, F., J. Gire, O. Khaleefa and M. Satiardama. 2003. "Influence of the Cross-
Cultural Environment on the Perception of Aging and Adult Development in the
Developing World: A Study of Bahrain, Brazil and Indonesia." *Asian Journal of
Social Psychology* 6(1):51–60.

Facio, E. 1996. *Understanding Older Chicanas.* Thousand Oaks, CA: Sage.

Fainstein, S., I. Gordon and M. Harloe, eds. 1992. *Divided Cities: New York and London in the Contemporary World.* Oxford: Blackwell.

Faiola, A. 2006. "For Elderly in Japan, a Very Long Winter; Social Changes Leave
Many to Fend for Themselves." *Washington Post,* February 19.

Fairhurst, E. 1998. " 'Growing Old Gracefully' as Opposed to 'Mutton Dressed as
Lamb': The Social Construction of Recognizing Older Women." In *The Body in
Everyday Life.* S. Nettleton and J. Watson, eds. London and New York:
Routledge.

Fakhouri, H. 1989. "Ethnicity and Aging: Arab-American Elderly in Flint/Genesee
County. Project for Urban and Regional Affairs. Flint: University of Michigan–
Flint.

———. 2001. "Growing Old in an Arab American Family." In *Age through Ethnic
Lenses: Caring for the Elderly in a Multicultural Society.* L. Katz Olson, ed.
Lanham, MD: Rowman and Littlefield.

Falk, U. A. and G. Falk. 2002. *Grandparents: A New Look at the Supporting Generation.* Amherst, NY: Prometheus Books.

Family Strengthening Policy Center. 2007. "Strengthening Grandfamilies through Respite Care." Policy Brief No. 20 Washington, DC: Family Strengthening Policy
Center. http://www.nassembly.org/fspc/documents/Brief20.pdf.

Fandetti, D. and D. Gelfand. 1976. "Care of the Aged: Attitudes of White Ethnic Families." *The Gerontologist* 16(6):544–49.

Featherstone, M. 1982. "The Body in Consumer Culture." *Theory, Culture and Society*
1(2):18–33. Reprinted in M. Featherstone, M. Hepworth and B. S. Turner, eds.
The Body. London: Sage.

———. 1991. *Postmodernism and Consumer Culture.* London: Sage.

———. 2001. "Consumer Culture." In *International Encyclopedia of the Social and Behavioral Sciences.* Oxford: Elsevier.

Featherstone, M. and M. Hepworth. 1982. "Ageing and Inequality: Consumer Culture
and the New Middle Age." In *Rethinking Inequality.* D. Robins et al., eds.
Aldershot: Gower Press.

———. 1985a. "The Male Menopause: Lifestyle and Sexuality." *Maturitas* 7:235–46.

———. 1985b. "The History of the Male Menopause, 1848–1936." *Maturitas* 7:
249–57.

———. 1991. "The Mask of Ageing and the Postmodern Life Course." In *The Body:
Social Process and Cultural Theory.* M. Featherstone, M. Hepworth and B. S.
Turner, eds. London: Sage.

———. 1993. "Images of Ageing." In *Ageing in Society: An Introduction to Social Gerontology.* J. Bond, P. Coleman and S. Peace, eds. London: Sage.

———. 1995. "Images of Positive Ageing: A Case Study of Retirement Choice Magazine." In *Images of Ageing.* M. Featherstone and A. Wernick, eds. London: Sage.

Featherstone, M. and A. Wernick, eds. 1995. *Images of Ageing.* London: Sage.

Federal Interagency Forum on Aging-Related Statistics. 2004. *Older Americans 2004: Key Indicators of Well-Being.* Washington, DC: U.S. Government Printing Office.

———. 2006. *Older Americans Update 2006: Key Indicators of Well-Being.* Washington, DC: U.S. Government Printing Office.

Feldman, P. and M. Oberlink. 2003. "The AdvantAge Initiative: Developing Community Indicators to Promote the Health and Well-Being of Older People." *Family and Community Health: Community-Based Innovations in Older Populations* 26(4):268–74.

Ferguson, H. 1997. "Me and My Shadows: On the Accumulation of Body Images in Western Society, Parts 1 and 2." *Body and Society* 2(3):1–32; and 2(4):1–32.

Feri, C. P., M. Prince, C. Brayne, H. Brodaty, L. Fratiglioni, M. Ganguli et al. 2005. "Global Prevalence of Dementia: A Delphi Consensus Study. *Lancet* 366:2112–17.

Ferreira, M. 2006. "Love in Colonial Light: History of Yurok Emotions in Northern California." In *Indigenous Peoples and Diabetes.* M. Ferreira and G. Lang, eds. Durham, NC: Carolina Academic Press.

Ferreira, M. and G. Lang. 2006. "Introduction: Deconstructing Diabetes." In *Indigenous Peoples and Diabetes.* M. Ferreira and G. Lang, eds. Durham, NC: Carolina Academic Press.

Finau, S. A., I. A. M. Prior and J. G. Evans. 1982. "Ageing in the South Pacific." *Social Science and Medicine* 16:1539–49.

Finch, C. E. and S. N. Austad. 2001. "History and Prospects: Symposium on Organisms with Slow Aging." *Experimental Gerontology* 36:593–97.

Finch, J. and D. Groves, eds. 1983. *A Labour of Love: Women, Work and Caring.* London: Routledge and Kegan Paul.

Fiori, C., T. Antonucci and K. Cortina. 2006. "Social Network Typologies of Mental Health among Older Adults." *Journal of Gerontology* 61:25–32.

Fischer, C. S. 1982. "To Dwell among Friends: Personal Networks in Town and City." *Milbank Memorial Fund Quarterly* 63:350–76.

Fischer, J. D. et al. 2007. "No Place Like Home: Older Adults and Their Housing." *The Journals of Gerontology. Series B: Psychological Sciences and Social Sciences* 62:S120–28.

Fisher, B. and S. Regan. 2006. "The Extent and Frequency of Abuse in the Lives of Older Women and Their Relationship with Health Outcomes." *The Gerontologist* 46(2):200–209.

Fitzpatrick, A. L., N. R. Powe, L. S. Cooper, D. G. Ives and J. A. Robbins. 2004. "Barriers to Health Care Access among the Elderly and Who Perceives Them." *American Journal of Public Health* 94(10):1788–94.

Flint, M. 1975. "The Menopause: Reward or Punishment?" *Psychosomatics* 16(Winter):161–63.

Flint, M. and R. Samil. 1990. "Cultural and Subcultural Meanings of the Menopause." *Annals of the New York Academy of Sciences* 592:134–48.

Florida Statistical Abstract. 1998. Gainesville, FL: Bureau of Economic and Business Research, Warrington College of Business Administration.

Foner, A. and D. I. Kertzer. 1978. "Transitions over the Life Course: Lessons from Age-Set Societies." *American Journal of Sociology* 83:1081–1104.

Foner, N. 1985. "Old and Frail and Everywhere Unequal." *The Hastings Center Report* 15(2):27–31.

———. 1989. "Older Women in Nonindustrial Cultures: Consequences of Power and Privilege." *Women and Health* 14:227–37.

Fontaine, K., D. Redden, C. Wang, A. Westfall and D. Allison. 2003. "Years of Life Lost Due to Obesity." *Journal of the American Medical Association* 289:187–93.

Fontana, L., T. Meyer, S. Klein and J. Holloszy. 2004. "Long-Term Calorie Restriction Is Highly Effective in Reducing the Risk for Atherosclerosis in Humans." *Proceedings of the National Academy of Sciences of the United States of America* 101(17):6659–63.

Fortes, M. 1961. "Pietas and Ancestor Worship." *Journal of the Royal Anthropological Institute* 91:166–91.

———. 1978. "An Anthropologist's Apprenticeship." *Annual Review of Anthropology* 7:1–30.

Fossett, J. and J. Perloff. 1995, December. "The 'New' Health Reform and Access to Care: The Problem of the Inner City." Washington, DC: The Kaiser Commission on the Future of Medicaid.

Foster, G. and R. Kemper. 2002. "Anthropological Fieldwork in Cities." In *Urban Life: Readings in Urban Anthropology*. G. Gmelch and W. P. Zenner, eds. Prospect Heights, IL: Waveland Press.

Francesconi, P., E. Cantini, E. Bavazzano, F. Lauretani, S. Bandinelli, E. Buiatti et al. 2006. "Classification of Residents in Nursing Homes in Tuscany/Italy Using Resource Utilizations Groups Version III (Reg.111)." In *Aging Clinical and Experimental Research* 18(2):133–40.

Francher, J. 1973. "It's the Pepsi Generation: Accelerated Aging and the Television Commercial." *International Journal of Aging and Human Development* 4(3):245–55.

Francis, D. 1984. *Will You Still Need Me, Will You Still Feed Me, When I'm 84?* Bloomington: Indiana University Press.

Frank, J. 2005. "Semiotic Use of the Word 'Home' among People with Alzheimer's Disease: A Plea for Selfhood?" In *Home and Identity in Late Life*. G. Rowles and H. Chaudhury, eds. New York: Springer.

Franklin, D. 1996. "The Healthiest Women in the World." *Health* 9:56–64.

Franks, M. M. 2007. "What Do Aging Families Do? Developmental Stages and Tasks." Paper presented at the Annual National Clinical Geropsychology Conference, Ft. Collins, CO.

Fraser, G. and D. Shavlik. 2001. "Ten Years of Life: Is It a Matter of Choice?" *Archives of Internal Medicine* 161:1645–52.

Frederiksen, H., M. McGue, B. Jeune, D. Gaist, H. Nybo, A. Skytthe et al. 2002. "Do Children of Long-Lived Parents Age More Successfully?" *Epidemiology* 13:334–39.

Free, M. 1995. *The Private World of the Hermitage: Lifestyles of the Rich and Old in an Elite Retirement Home*. Westport, CT: Bergin and Garvey.

Freedman, M. 1999. *Prime Time: How Baby Boomers Will Revolutionize Retirement and Transform America*. New York: Public Affairs.

———. 2007. *Encore: Finding Work That Matters in the Second Half of Life*. New York: Public Affairs.

Frey, W. 2008. "America's Regional Demographics in the Early 21st Century: The Role of Seniors, Boomers and New Minorities." *Public Policy and Aging Report* 18(1).

Friedan, B. 1963. *The Feminine Mystique*. New York: Norton.

Friedl, E. 1991. *Women of Deh Koh. Lives in an Iranian Village*. New York: Penguin.

———. 1994. "Sources of Female Power in Iran." In *In the Eye of the Storm: Women in Post-Revolutionary Iran*. M. Afkhami and E. Friedl, eds. Syracuse, NY: Syracuse University Press.

Friedman, T. 2005. "A Race to the Top." Op Ed, *New York Times*. June 3.

Friedmann, J. 1986. "The World City Hypothesis." *Development and Change* 17(1):69–83.

Fries, J. 1980. "Aging, Natural Death and the Compression of Morbidity." *New England Journal of Medicine* 303:130–35.

Fries, J. and L. Crapo. 1995. *Vitality and Aging: Implications of the Rectangular Curve*. New York: W. H. Freeman.

Frisch, R. 1980. "Fatness, Puberty and Fertility." *Natural History* 89:16–27.

Frisch, R. and J. McArthur. 1974. "Menstrual Cycles: Fatness as a Determinant of Minimum Weight for Height Necessary for Their Maintenance or Onset." *Science* 185:949–50.

Fry, C. 1979. "Structural Considerations Affecting Community Formation among the Elderly." *Anthropological Quarterly* 52:19–28.

———. 1988. "Comparative Research in Aging." In *Gerontology: Perspectives and Issues*. K. Ferraro, ed. New York: Springer Publishing.

———. 1990. "The Life Course in Context: Implications of Research." In *Anthropology and Aging: Comprehensive Reviews*. R. L. Rubinstein, ed. Norwell, MA: Kluwer.

———. 1995. "Kinship and Individuation: Cross-Cultural Perspectives on Intergenerational Relations." In *Adult Intergenerational Relations: Effects of Social Change*. V. Bengtson and L. Burton, eds. New York: Springer.

———. 1999. "Anthropological Theories of Aging." In *Handbook of Theories of Aging*. V. Bengtson and K. W. Schaie, eds. New York: Springer.

———. 2003. "The Life Course as a Cultural Construct." In *Invitation to the Life Course: Toward New Understandings of Later Life*. R. A. Settersten, ed. Amityville, NY: Baywood Press.

———. 2006. "What Happened to Culture." In *Enduring Questions in Gerontology*. D. Sheets, J. Hendricks and D. Bradley, eds. New York: Springer.

———. 2008a. "Out of the Armchair and off the Verandah: Anthropological Theories and the Experiences of Aging." In *Handbook of Theories of Aging*, 3rd ed. V. Bengtson, M. Silverstein, N. Putney and D. Gans, eds. New York: Springer.

———. 2008b. "Social Anthropology and Aging." In *The International Handbook of Social Gerontology*. C. Phillipson and D. Dannefer, eds. Thousand Oaks, CA: Sage.

Fry, C. and J. Keith. 1986. *New Methods for Old Age Research*. South Hadley, MA: Bergin and Garvey.

Fukuda, Y., K. Nakamura and T. Takano. 2005. "Municipal Health Expectancy in Japan: Decreased Healthy Longevity of Older People in Socioeconomically Disadvantaged Areas." *BMC Public Health* 5:65.

Fuller-Thomson, E. 2006. "Grandparent Caregiving among First Nations Canadians." In *Custodial Grandparenting: Individual, Cultural and Ethnic Diversity*. B. Hayslip and J. Hicks-Patrick, eds. New York: Springer.

Fuller-Thomson, E., M. Minkler and D. Driver. 1997. "A Profile of Grandparents Raising Grandchildren in the United States." *The Gerontologist* 37:406–11.

Furman, F. 1997. *Facing the Mirror: Older Women and Beauty Shop Culture.* New York: Routledge.

Furstenberg, F. 2003. "Reflections on the Future of the Life Course." In *Handbook of the Life Course.* J. T. Mortimer and M. J. Shanahan, eds. New York: Kluwer Academic/Plenum.

Gamburd, M. 2000. *The Kitchen Spoon's Handle: Transnationalism and Sri Lanka's Migrant Housemaids.* Ithaca, NY: Cornell University Press.

Gamliel, T. 2000. "The Lobby as an Arena in the Confrontation between Acceptance and Denial of Old Age." *Journal of Aging Studies* 14:251–71.

Garcia Canclini, N. 1997. "Urban Cultures at the End of the Century; Anthropological Perspectives." *International Social Science Journal* 153:345–54.

Garn, S. 1970. *The Earlier Gains and Later Loss of Cortical Bone.* Springfield, IL: Charles C. Thomas Publishing.

Garrett, S. 1998. *Miles to Go: Aging in Rural Virginia.* Charlottesville: University of Virginia Press.

Gasparini, L., J. Alejo, F. Haimovich, S. Olivieri and L. Tornarolli. 2007. "Poverty among the Elderly in Latin America and the Caribbean." Centro de Estudios Distributivos, Laborales y Sociales, Special issue No. 55, *The World Ageing Situation.* http://www.un.org/esa/policy/wess/wess2007files/backgroundpapers/lac.pdf.

Gee, E. and G. Gutman, eds. 2000. *The Overselling of Population Aging: Apocalyptic Demography, Intergenerational Challenges and Social Policy.* Don Mills, Canada: Oxford University Press.

Geesaman, B., E. Benson, S. Brewster, L. Kunkel, H. Blanché, G. Thomas et al. 2003. "Haplotype-Based Identification of a Microsomal Transfer Protein Marker Associated with the Human Lifespan." *Proceedings of the National Academy of Sciences of the United States of America* 100(24): 14115–20.

Gehl, J. 1987. *Life between Buildings: Using Public Space.* New York: Van Norstrand.

Geissler, W., E. Alber and S. R. Whyte, eds. 2004. "Grandparents and Grandchildren." Special issue, *Africa* 74(1).

Generations. 1992. Vol. 16, Special issue on "Aging in Place."

Gentleman, A. 2007. "India Moving to Punish Neglect of Elderly Parents." *Boston Sunday Globe*, The World, March 4.

George, L. K. 2003. "Life Course Research: Achievements and Potential." In *Handbook of the Life Course.* J. T. Mortimer and M. J. Shanahan, eds. New York: Kluwer Academic/Plenum.

Gerdner, L. A., S. V. Xiong and D. Cha. 2006. "Chronic Confusion and Memory Impairment in Hmong Elders: Honoring Differing Cultural Beliefs in America." *Journal of Gerontological Nursing* 32(3):23–31.

Gergen, M. and K. Gergen. 2001. "Positive Aging: New Images for a New Age." *Ageing International* 27(1):3–23.

German, P. 1995. "Prevention and Chronic Disease in Older Individuals." In *Promoting Successful and Productive Aging.* L. Bond, S. Cutler and A. Grams, eds. Thousand Oaks, CA: Sage.

Gesler, W., T. Arcury and H. Koenig. 2000. "An Introduction to Three Studies of Rural Elderly People: Effects of Religion and Culture on Health." *Journal of Cross-Cultural Gerontology* 15(1):1–12.

Gessain, M. 1971. "Les Classes d'Age chez les Vassari d'Etyolo (Senegal Oriental)." In *Classes et Association d'Age en Afrique de l'Ouest*. D. Paulme, ed. Paris: Plon.

Geyman, J. 2006. "Shredding the Social Contract: The Privatization of Medicare." Monroe, ME: Common Courage Press.

Gibson, M. 2006. "European Experiences with Long-Term Care: France, the Netherlands, Norway and the United Kingdom." In AARP European Leadership Study. Washington, DC: AARP.

Gibson, M., S. Gregory and S. Pandya. 2003. "Long-Term Care in Developed Nations: A Brief Overview." Washington, DC: AARP Public Policy Institute.

Giele, J. Z. and G. H. Elder, Jr., eds. 1998. *Methods of Life Course Research: Qualitative and Quantitative Approaches*. Thousand Oaks, CA: Sage.

Gilani, B. 1998, July 31. "*Aberoo:* Troubled Iranian Families in California." *The Iranian*. http://www.iranian.com/Features/July98/Aberoo.

Giles, H. and T. Dorjee, eds. 2004. "Communicative Practices and Climates." Special issue, *Journal of Cross-Cultural Gerontology* 19(4).

Gilleard, C. and P. Higgs. 2000. *Cultures of Ageing: Self, Citizen and the Body*. London: Prentice Hall.

Giri, V. M. and M. Khanna. n.d. "Status of Widows of Vrindavan and Varanasi: A Comparative Study." http://www.griefandrenewal.com/widows_study.htm (accessed on January 24, 2007).

Gjonka, A., H. Brockmann and H. Maier. 2000. "Old-Age Mortality in Germany Prior to and after Reunification." *Demographic Research* 3. http://www.demographic-research.org/volumes/vol3/1/3-1.pdf (accessed on October 6, 2007).

Glascock, A. P. 1982. "Decrepitude and Death-Hastening: The Nature of Old Age in Third World Societies." In *Aging and the Aged in the Third World: Part I*. Studies in Third World Societies, No. 22. J. Sokolovsky, ed. Williamsburg, VA: College of William and Mary.

Glascock, A. P. and S. L. Feinman. 1980. "A Holocultural Analysis of Old Age." *Comparative Social Research* 3:311–33.

———. 1981. "Social Asset or Social Burden: Treatment of the Aged in Non-Industrial Societies." In *Dimensions: Aging, Culture and Health*. C. L. Fry, ed. South Hadley, MA: Bergin and Garvey.

Gleckman, H. 2007. "Financing Long-Term Care: Lessons from Abroad." Chestnut Hill, MA: Center for Retirement Research, Boston College.

Gluck, C. 1985. *Japan's Modern Myths: Ideology in the Late Meiji Period*. Berkeley: University of California Press.

Gluckman, P. D. and M. A. Hanson. 2006. *Developmental Origins of Health and Disease*. Cambridge: Cambridge University Press.

Goffman, E. 1991. *Asylums: Essays on the Social Situation of Mental Patients and Other Inmates*. London: Penguin Books.

Goforth-Parker, J. 1994. "The Lived Experience of Native Americans with Diabetes within a Transcultural Nursing Perspective." *Journal of Transcultural Nursing* 6(1):5–11.

Golant, S. 2002. "Geographic Inequalities in the Availability of Government-Subsidized Rental Housing for Low-Income Older Persons in Florida." *The Gerontologist* 42:100–108.

———. 2008. "Low Income Elderly Homeowners in Very Old Dwellings: The Need for Public Policy Debate." *Journal of Aging and Social Policy* 20:1.

Goldstein, L. J. 1968. "The Phenomenological and Naturalistic Approaches to the Social." In *Theory in Anthropology*, 4th ed. R. A. Manners and D. Kaplan, eds. Chicago: Aldine.

Gomez, C. and V. Zavala. 2004. "Ageing in Mexico: Families, Informal Care and Reciprocity." In *Living Longer: Aging, Development and Social Protection*. P. Lloyd-Sherlock, ed. London: Zed Books.

Gonzalez, H., M. Haan and L. Hinton. 2001. "Acculturation and the Prevalence of Depression in Older Mexican Americans: Baseline Results of the Sacramento Area Latino Study on Aging." *Journal of the American Geriatric Society* 49:948–53.

Gonzalez Vazquez, T., P. Bonilla Fernandez, B. Jauregui Ortiz, T. Yamanis, J. Salgado de Snyder and V. Nelly. 2007. "Well-Being and Family Support among Elderly Rural Mexicans in the Context of Migration to the United States." *Journal of Aging and Health* 19(2):334–55.

Good, B. J. 1994. *Medicine, Rationality and Experience*. New York: Cambridge University Press.

Goodale, J. 1971. *Tiwi Women*. Seattle: University of Washington Press.

Goodkind, J. 2006. "Promoting Hmong Refugees' Well-Being through Mutual Learning: Valuing Knowledge, Culture and Experience." *American Journal of Community Psychology* 37(1):77–93.

Goodman, C., M. K. Potts and E. P. Pasztor. 2006. "Caregiving Grandmothers with vs. without Child Welfare System Involvement: Effects of Expressed Need, Formal Services and Informal Social Support on Caregiver Burden." *Children and Youth Services Review* 29:428–41.

Goodman, C. and M. Silverstein. 2002. "Grandparents Raising Grandchildren: Family Structure and Well-Being in Culturally Diverse Families." *The Gerontologist* 42:676–89.

———. 2006a. "Grandmothers Raising Grandchildren: Ethnic and Racial Differences in Well-Being among Custodial and Coparenting Families." *Journal of Family Issues* 27:1605–26.

———. 2006b. "Latina Grandmothers Raising Grandchildren: Acculturation and Well-Being." In *Custodial Grandparenting: Individual, Cultural and Ethnic Diversity*. B. Hayslip and J. Hicks-Patrick, eds. New York: Springer.

Goodman, E. 2007. "Entering a New Stage of Life." *Lancaster Intelligencer Journal*, October 19.

Goodman, R. A. 1971. "Some Aitu Beliefs of Modern Samoans." *Journal of the Polynesian Society* 80:463–79.

Gould, K. G., M. Flint and C. E. Graham. 1981. "Chimpanzee Reproductive Senescence: A Possible Model for the Evolution of the Menopause." *Maturitis* 3:157–66.

Graham, M. and S. Khosravi. 1997. "Home Is Where You Make It: Repatriation and Diaspora Culture among Iranians in Sweden." *Journal of Refugee Studies* 10(2):115–33.

Graham, S. 2002. "Bridging Urban Digital Divides? Urban Polarization and Information and Communications Technologies." *Urban Studies* 39:33–56.

Gratton, B. 1987. "Familism among the Black and Mexican-American Elderly: Myth or Reality." *Journal of Aging Studies* 1(1):19–32.

———. 1993. "The Creation of Retirement: Families, Individuals and the Social Security Movement." In *Societal Impact on Aging: Historical Perspectives*. K. W. Schaie and A. Achenbaum, eds. New York: Springer.

Gray, A. 2006. *Growing Old in a London Borough; The Shrinking Personal Community and How Volunteers Help to Maintain It.* London: South Bank University.

Gray, G. 2007. "Kevorkian to Leave Prison, But Not Past, Behind." *Philadelphia Inquirer,* May 31.

Gredilla, R. and G. Barja. 2005. "Minireview: The Role of Oxidative Stress in Relation to Caloric Restriction and Longevity." *Endocrinology* 146(9):3713–17.

Green, L. 1999. *Fear as a Way of Life: Mayan Widows in Rural Guatemala.* New York: Columbia University Press.

Green, R., ed. 2003. *Kinship Care: Making the Most of a Valuable Resource.* Washington, DC: Urban Institute Press.

Greene, A., C. Hawes, M. Wood and C. Woodsong, 1998. How Do Family Members Define Quality in Assisted Living Facilities? *Generations* 21(4):34–36.

Greenfield, P. 2004. *Weaving Generations Together: Evolving Creativity in the Maya of Chiapas.* Santa Fe, NM: SAR Press.

Griffin, J. 1977. "A Cross-Cultural Investigation of Behavioral Changes at Menopause." *Social Science Journal* 14(2):49–55.

———. 1982. "Cultural Models for Coping with Menopause." In *Changing Perspectives on Menopause.* A. Voda, M. Dinnerstein and S. O'Donnell, eds. Austin: University of Texas Press.

Grossman, J. R., A. Durkin Keating and J. L. Reiff, eds. 2004. *The Encyclopedia of Chicago.* Chicago: University of Chicago Press.

Gruman, G. J. 2003. *A History of Ideas about the Prolongation of Life: The Evolution of Prolongevity Hypotheses to 1800.* New York: Springer.

Gubrium, J. 1975. *Living and Dying in Murray Manor.* New York: St Martin's Press.

———. 1986. *Old Timers and Alzheimer's: The Descriptive Organization of Senility.* Greenwich, CT: JAI Press.

———. 1987. "Organizational Embeddedness and Family Life." In *Aging, Health and Family: Long-Term Care.* T. Brubaker, ed. Newbury Park, NJ: Sage.

———. 1992. "Qualitative Research Comes of Age in Gerontology." *The Gerontologist* 32(5):581–82.

———. 1993. *Speaking of Life: Horizons of Meaning for Nursing Home Residents.* Hawthorne, NY: Aldine de Gruyter.

Gubrium, J. and J. Holstein. 1999. "Constructionist Perspectives on Aging." In *Handbook of Theories of Aging.* V. Bengtson and K. W. Schaie, eds. New York: Springer.

Guemple, D. L. 1969. "Human Resource Management: The Dilemma of the Aging Eskimo." *Sociological Symposium* 2:59–74.

Guenther, M. 2006. "N//ae ('talking'): The Oral and Rhetorical Base of San Culture." *Journal of Folklore Research* 43(3):241–64.

Guerny, J. 2002. "The Elderly, HIV/AIDS and Sustainable Rural Development." http://www.fao.org/sd/2002/PE0101a_en.htm.

Guinness World Records. 2005. *The Guinness Book of World Records.* New York: Time, Inc. Home Entertainment.

Gullette, M. 1985. "Creativity, Ageing, Gender: A Study of Their Intersections, 1910–1935." In *Ageing and Gender in Literature: Studies in Creativity.* A. Wyatt-Brown and J. Rossen, eds. Charlottesville: University of Virginia Press.

———. 1997. *Declining to Decline: Cultural Combat and the Politics of the Midlife.* Charlottesville: University of Virginia Press.

———. 2004. *Aged by Culture.* Chicago: University of Chicago Press.

Gulliver, P. H. 1963. *Social Control in an African Society: A Study of the Arusha, Agricultural Masai of Northern Tanganyika*. Boston: Boston University Press.

———. 1968. "Age Differentiation." In *International Encyclopedia of the Social Sciences*. New York: Free Press.

Guo, Z. L. and D. M. Zhou. 1997. "Rural Development and Social Security." In *Farewell to Peasant China*. G. Guldin, ed. Armonk, NY: M. E. Sharpe.

Gupta, A. 2001. "To Light up that Wrinkled Face." *The Asian Age*, October 2.

Gurven, M. and K. Hill. 1997. "Comment On: Offspring Provisioning and Postmenopausal Life Spans, by K. Hawkes, J. F. O'Connell, N. G. Blurton Jones." *Current Anthropology* 38(4):551–77.

Gurven, M. and H. Kaplan. 2006. "Determinants of Time Allocation to Production across the Lifespan among the Machiguenga and Piro Indians of Peru." *Human Nature* 17(1):1–49.

———. 2007. "Longevity among Hunter-Gatherers: A Cross-Cultural Comparison." *Population and Development Review* 33(2):321–65.

Gurven, M., H. Kaplan, E. Crimmins, C. Finch and J. Winking. 2008. "Lifetime Inflammation in Two Epidemiological Worlds: The Tsimane of Bolivia and the United States." *Journal of Gerontology Biological Sciences* 63A:196–99.

Gurven, M., H. Kaplan and M. Gutierrez. 2006. "How Long Does It Take to Become a Proficient Hunter? Implications for the Evolution of Delayed Growth." *Journal of Human Evolution* 51:454–70.

Gurven, M., H. Kaplan and A. Zelada Supa. 2007. "Mortality Experience of Tsimane Amerindians: Regional Variation and Temporal Trends." *American Journal of Human Biology* 19:376–98.

Gusmano, M. K., V. G. Rodwin and D. Weisz. Forthcoming. *Health Care in World Cities: A New Approach to Health Systems Analysis*. Baltimore: Johns Hopkins University Press.

Gusmano, M. K., V. G. Rodwin, D. Weisz and D. Das. 2007. "A New Approach to the Comparative Analysis of Health Systems: Invasive Treatment for Heart Disease in the U.S, France and Their Two World Cities." *Health Economics, Policy and Law* 2:73–92.

Gustafson, P. 2001. "Retirement Migration and Transnational Lifestyles." *Ageing and Society* 21:371–94.

Gutmann, D. 1987. *Reclaimed Powers: Toward a New Psychology of Men and Women in Later Life*. New York: Basic Books.

———. 1994. *Reclaimed Powers: Men and Women in Later Life*. Evanston, IL: Northwestern University Press.

Guzman, B. 2001. *Hispanic Population: Census 2000 Brief*. Washington, DC: U.S. Government Printing Office. http://www.census.gov/prod/2001pubs/c2kbr01-3.pdf.

Haber, C. 1997. "Witches, Widows, Wives and Workers: The Historiography of Elderly Women in America." In *Handbook on Women and Aging*. J. M. Coyle, ed. Westport, CT: Greenwood Press.

Hadjihristev, A. 1988. *Life-Styles for Longer Life: Longevity in Bulgaria*. G. Lesnoff-Caravaglia, trans. Springfield, IL: Charles C. Thomas.

Hagestad, G. O. 1990. "Social Perspectives on the Life Course." In *Handbook of Aging and the Social Sciences*, 3rd ed. R. H. Binstock and L. K. George, eds. San Diego: Academic Press.

———. 2002. "Interdependent Lives and Relationships in Changing Times: A Life-Course View of Families and Aging." In *Invitation to the Life Course*. R. A. Settersten, ed. Amityville, NY: Baywood Press.

Hagestad, G. O. and D. Dannefer. 2001. "Concepts and Theories of Aging: Beyond Microfication in Social Science Approaches." In *Handbook of Aging and the Social Sciences*, 5th ed. R. H. Binstock and L. K. George, eds. San Diego: Academic Press.

Hahn, T. 1870. "Die Buschmäner." *Globus* 18(5):65–153.

"Hail the Golden Years." 1999. *Charlotte Sun Herald*, May 16.

Hall, P. 1984. *The World Cities,* 3rd ed. London: Heineman.

Hall, S. 2003. *Merchants of Immortality: Chasing the Dream of Human Life Extension.* New York: Houghton Mifflin.

Hamilton, W. D. 1966. "The Molding of Senescence by Natural Selection." *Journal of Theoretical Biology* 12:12–45.

Hammer, M. and R. Foley. 1996. "Longevity, Life History and Allometry: How Long Did Hominids Live?" *Journal of Human Evolution* 11:61–66.

Hamnett, C. 1994. "Social Polarization in Global Cities: Theory and Evidence." *International Journal for Research in Urban and Regional Studies* 31(3):401–24.

Han, H.-R., M. Kim, H. Lee, G. Pistulka and K. Kim. 2007. "Correlates of Depression in the Korean American Elderly: Focusing on Personal Resources of Social Support." *Journal of Cross-Cultural Gerontology* 22:115–27.

Hannerz, U. 1992. *Cultural Complexity: Studies in the Social Organization of Meaning.* New York: Columbia University Press.

Hansen, E. 1998. "Social Protection for Dependency in Old Age in Denmark." In *Modernising and Improving EU Social Protection: Conference on Long-Term Care of Elderly Dependent People in the EU and Norway.* London: Department of Health Publications.

———. 2002. "Häusliche Versorgung fur Hilfebedürftige und Schwerkranke in Dänemark." In *Ambulant vor stationär. Perspektiven für eine integrierte ambulante Pflege Schwerkranker.* D. Schaeffer and M. Ewers, eds. Gottingen: Verlag Hans Huber.

Hansen, E., L. Milkaer, C. Swane, C. Iversen and B. Rimdal. 2002. "Mange Baekke Smaa ... Om Hjaelp til Svaekkede Aeldre." Copenhagen: FOKUS.

Hansen, E. and M. Platz. 1995a. *80–100-åriges Levekaar.* Copenhagen: AKF Forlaget.

———. 1995b. *Kommunernes Tilbud til Aeldre.* Copenhagen: AKF Forlaget.

———. 1996. *Gamle Danskere.* Copenhagen: AKF Forlaget.

Hansen, J., D. Dunn, R. Lee et al. 1993. "Hunter-Gatherer to Pastoral Way of Life: Effects of the Transition on Health, Growth and Nutritional Status." *South African Journal of Science* 89:559–64.

Hanson, A. R. 1970. *Rapan Lifeways: Society and History on a Polynesian Island.* Boston: Little, Brown.

Hanson, D. and C. Emlet. 2006. "Assessing a Community's Elder Friendliness: A Case Example of the AdvantAge Initiative." *Family and CommunityHealth* 29(4):266–78.

Hardin, B. 2008. "Demographic Crisis, Robotic Cure?" *Washington Post Foreign Service.* January 7.

Harding, E. 2007. "Towards Lifetime Neighbourhoods: Designing Sustainable Communities for All: A Discussion Paper." International Longevity Centre UK, Department for Communities and Local Government. http://www.agingsociety. org/agingsociety/publications/public_policy/ilclifetime.pdf.

Hareven, T. K. 1982. *Family Time and Industrial Time: The Relationship Between the Family and Work in a New England Industrial Community.* Cambridge: Cambridge University Press.

Harley, D. 2006. "Indigenous Healing Practices among Rural Elderly African Americans." *International Journal of Disability, Development and Education* 53(4):433–52.

Harmon, R. 2005. "Applied Anthropology and the Aged." In *Applied Anthropology: Domains of Application.* S. Kedia and J. van Willigen, eds. Westport, CT: Praeger.

Harper, S. 1997. "Constructing Later Life/Constructing the Body: Some Thoughts from Feminist Theory." In *Critical Approaches to Ageing and Later Life.* A. Jamieson, S. Harper and C. Victor, eds. Buckingham, UK: Open University Press.

———. 2005. "Grandparenthood." In *The Cambridge Handbook of Age and Ageing.* M. Johnson, ed. New York: Cambridge University Press.

———. 2006. *Aging Societies.* New York: Oxford University Press.

Harrison, A., ed. 2007. *Globalization and Poverty.* Chicago: University of Chicago Press.

Harrison, F. 2007. *Why Baby Boomers Suck! (No Offense Mom).* Seattle, WA: Code Publishing.

Hart, C. W. 1970. "Fieldwork among the Tiwi, 1928–1929." In *Being an Anthropologist: Fieldwork in Eleven Cultures.* G. Spindler, ed. New York: Holt, Rinehart & Winston.

Harvard School of Public Health. 2004. *Reinventing Aging.* Cambridge, MA: Center for Health Communication, Harvard School of Public Health.

Harvey, B. 1993. *The Fifties: A Woman's Oral History.* New York: HarperCollins.

Harvey, D. 2006. "Neo-liberalism as Creative Destruction." *2006 Swedish Society for Anthropology and Geography* 88B(2):145–58.

Harvey, P. H., R. D. Martin and T. H. Clutton-Brock. 1987. "Life Histories in Comparative Perspective." In *Primate Societies.* B. B. Smuts, D. L. Cheney, R. M. Seyfarth, R. W. Wrangham and T. T. Struthsaker, eds. Chicago: University of Chicago Press.

Hashimoto, A. 1996. *The Gift of Generations: Japanese and American Perspectives on Aging and the Social Contract.* New York: Cambridge University Press.

Hashimoto, A. and C. Ikels. 2005. "Filial Piety in Changing Asian Societies." In *The Cambridge Handbook of Age and Ageing.* M. Johnson, ed. Cambridge: Cambridge University Press.

Hasuo, Y., K. Ueda, Y. Kiyohara, J. Wada, H. Kawano, I. Kato et al. 1989. "Accuracy of Diagnosis on Death Certificates for Underlying Causes of Death in a Long-Term Autopsy-Based Population Study in Hisayama, Japan: With Special Reference to Cardiovascular Diseases." *Journal of Clinical Epidemiology* 42:577–84.

Hauser, R. M. and C. L. Rowan. 2006. *The Class of 1957 in Their Mid-Sixties: A First Look.* CDE Working Paper 2006-03. University of Wisconsin, Center for Demography and Ecology.

Hawkes, K. 2003. "Grandmothers and the Evolution of Human Longevity." *American Journal of Human Biology* 15(3):380–400.

Hawkes, K. and N. Jones. 2005. "Human Age Structures, Paleodemography and the Grandmother Hypothesis." In *Grandmotherhood: The Evolutionary Significance of the Second Half of Life.* E. Volard, A. Chasiotis and W. Schiefenhovel, eds. New Brunswick, NJ: Rutgers University Press.

Hawkes, K., J. F. O'Connell and N. Blurton Jones. 1989. "Hardworking Hadza Grandmothers." In *Comparative Socioecology of Mammals and Man.* R. Foley and V. Standen, eds. London: Basil Blackwell.

Hawkes, K., J. F. O'Connell, N. G. Blurton Jones, H. Alvarez and E. L. Charnov. 1998. "Grandmothering, Menopause and the Evolution of Human Life Histories." *Proceedings of the National Academy of Science* 95:1336–39.

Hayes, C., R. Kalish and D. Guttmann, eds. 1986. *European-American Elderly: A Guide for Practice*. New York: Springer.

Hayes-Bautista, D., P. Hsu, A. Perez and C. Gamboa. 2002. "The 'Browning' of the Graying of America: Diversity in the Elderly Population and Policy Implications." *Generations* 26(3):15–24.

Hayflick, L. 1998. "How and Why We Age." *Experimental Gerontology* 33(7/8): 639–53.

———. 2000. "The Future of Ageing." *Nature* 408(6809):267–69.

Hayslip, B., A. Baird, J. F. Toledo, C. Toledo and M. Emick. 2006. "Cross-Cultural Differences in Traditional and Custodial Grandparenting: A Qualitative Approach." In *Custodial Grandparenting: Individual, Cultural and Ethnic Diversity*. B. Hayslip and J. Hicks-Patrick, eds. New York: Springer.

Hayslip, B. and J. Hicks-Patrick, eds. 2003. "Custodial Grandparenting Viewed from within a Life Span Perspective." In *Working with Custodial Grandparents*. New York: Springer.

———, eds. 2006. *Custodial Grandparenting: Individual, Cultural and Ethnic Diversity*. New York: Springer.

Hayslip, B. and P. Kaminski. 2005. "Grandparents Raising Their Grandchildren: A Review of the Literature and Suggestions for Practice." *The Gerontologist* 45:262–69.

———. 2006. "Custodial Grandchildren." In *Children's Needs III: Understanding and Addressing the Needs of Children*. G. Bear and K. Minke, eds. Washington, DC: National Association of School Psychologists.

Hayslip, B. and R. J. Shore. 2000. "Custodial Grandparenting and Mental Health." *Journal of Mental Health and Aging* 6:367–84.

Hayslip, B., R. J. Shore, C. Henderson and P. Lambert. 1998. "Custodial Grandparenting and Grandchildren with Problems: Their Impact on Role Satisfaction and Role Meaning." *Journal of Gerontology: Social Sciences* 53B: S164–74.

Hazen, T. 1997. "Horticultural Therapy in the Skilled Nursing Facility." *Activities, Adaptation and Aging* 22(1/2):33–60.

Hazzard, W. 1997. "Ways to Make "Usual" and "Successful" Aging Synonymous." *Western Journal of Medicine* 167:206–15.

He, W., M. Sengupta, V. A. Velkoff and K. A. DeBarros. 2005. *65+ in the United States: 2005*. U.S. Census Bureau Population Report P23-209. Washington, DC: U.S. Government Printing Office.

He, Z. X. and D. Lester. 2001. "Elderly Suicide in China." *Psychological Reports* 89(3):675–76.

Hearn, J. 1995. "Imaging the Aging of Men." In *Images of Aging: Cultural Representations of Later Life*. M. Featherstone and A. Wernick, eds. London: Routledge.

Hegland, M. E. 1999a. "Iranian Women Immigrants Facing Modernity in California's Bay Area: The Courage, Creativity and Trepidation of Transformation." In *The Iranian Woman and Modernity, Proceedings of the Ninth International Conference of Iranian Women's Studies Foundation*. G. Amin, ed. Cambridge, MA: Iranian Women's Studies Foundation.

———. 1999b. "Learning Feminist Pedagogy with Students and Iranian-American Grandparents." *Association for Middle East Women's Studies Bulletin* 14(3): 1–2.

———. 1999c. "Wife Abuse and the Political System: A Middle Eastern Case Study."
In *To Have and to Hit: Cultural Perspectives on Wife Beating*. D. Counts, J.
Brown and J. Campbell, eds. Urbana: University of Illinois Press.

———. 2003a. "Talking Politics: A Village Widow in Iran." In *Personal Encounters:
A Reader in Cultural Anthropology*. L. S. Walbridge and A. K. Sievert, eds.
Boston: McGraw-Hill.

———. 2003b. "Iranians." In *Encyclopedia of Sex and Gender: Men and Women in the
World's Cultures*. C. R. Ember and M. Ember, eds. New York: Kluwer Aca-
demic/Plenum Publishers.

———. 2003c. "Iran." In *The Greenwood Encyclopedia of Women's Issues Worldwide:
The Middle East and North Africa*. B. Sherif-Trask, ed. Westport, CT: Greenwood Press.

———. 2004. "Zip In and Zip Out Fieldwork." *Journal of Iranian Studies* 37(4):
275–83.

———. 2005a. "Women, Gender and Aging as a Segment of Life Cycle: Iran/
Afghanistan." In *Encyclopedia of Women and Islamic Cultures*, vol. 3. S. Joseph,
ed. Herndon, VA: Brill Academic Publishers.

———. 2005b. "Household Forms and Composition: United States." In *Encyclopedia
of Women and Islamic Cultures*, vol. 2. S. Joseph, ed. Herndon, VA: Brill Academic Publishers.

———. 2005c. "Motherhood: Iran, Afghanistan, South Asia." In *Encyclopedia of
Women and Islamic Cultures*, vol. 2. S. Joseph, ed. Herndon, VA: Brill Academic Publishers.

———. 2006a. "Women of Karbala Moving to America." In *Women of Karbala: Ritual
Performance and Symbolic Discourses in Modern Shi'i Islam*. K. S. Aghai, ed.
Austin: University of Texas Press.

———. 2006b. "Elderly Iranians and a Transforming World: Modernization, Individu-
alization and Aging in the Islamic Republic." *DANESH Newsletter* 12:3–4,
Spring.

———. 2007a. "Großmutter lebt allein in ihrem Häuschen: Alte Frauen in einem irani-
schen Dorf" [Grandmother lives alone in her little house: old women in an Iranian village]. *Journal Ethnologie: Issue on Frauenpower, Juden und Muslime,
über den Iran*, January. http://journal-ethnologie.14art.de/?p=56.

———. 2007b. "Independent Grandmothers in an Iranian Village." *Middle-East Journal of Age and Aging* 4:1. http://www.me-jaa.com/me-jaa11June07/independent
grandmothers.htm.

———. 2008. "Esmat Khanum and a Life of Travail: 'You Yourself Help Me, God' (Iranian Village Women)." In *Muslim Voices and Lives in the Contemporary World*.
F. Trix, J. Walbridge and L. Walbridge, eds. New York: Palgrave Macmillan.

———. Forthcoming. "Aliabad of Shiraz: Transformation from Village to Suburb."
Iran Nameh [in Persian].

Hegland, M. E. et al. 2006. "Iranian-American Elderly in California's Santa Clara Valley: Crafting Selves and Composing Lives." In *Muslim Diaspora: Gender, Culture and Identity*. H. Moghissi, ed. London and New York: Routledge.

Hegland, M. E., N. Behrouzi, A. B. Curran, N. Levine et al. 2006. "Iranian Grandparents Facing Cultural Change and Making New Lives." Paper presented at the
Third International Conference on the Iranian Diaspora, April, New York.

Hegland, M. E., N. Behrouzi, E. Johnson, L. Miller et al. 2005a. "Iranian Grandparents
Displaced to Northern California: Building New Lives and Social Relations

through the Grace Senior Citizen Day Activity and Care Center." Paper presented at the Southwest Anthropological Association Conference, April, San Jose, California.

———. 2005b. "Muslims Moving to America: Iranian Elderly and Santa Clara University." Paper presented at the Symposium on Migration Studies and Jesuit Identity: Forging a Path Forward, June, Fairfield, Connecticut.

Hegland, M. E., Z. Sarraf and M. Shahbazi. Forthcoming. "Modernisation and Social Change: Impact on Iranian Elderly Social Networks and Care Systems." *Anthropology of the Middle East.*

Heikkinen, E., W. E. Waters and Z. J. Brzezinski. 1983. *The Elderly in Eleven Countries.* Copenhagen: World Health Organization, Regional Office for Europe.

Heinz, W. R. and V. W. Marshall, eds. 2003. *Social Dynamics of the Life Course: Transitions, Institutions and Interrelations.* New York: Aldine de Gruyter.

Helman, C. G. 1994. *Culture, Health and Illness,* 3rd ed. Oxford: Butterworth-Heinemann.

Help Age India. 2002. *Directory of Old Age Homes in India 2002.* New Delhi: Help Age India.

Help Age International (HAI). 2004. *Age and Security.* London: Help Age International.

———. 2005. "Respect Our Rights, Say Older People in Latin America." http://www.helpage.org/News/Latestnews/Defendingolderpeoplesrights.

———. 2007. *Help Age International en America Latina.* La Paz, Bolivia: HAI Regional Office.

Henderson, J. N., R. Crook, J. Crook, J. Hardy, L. Onstead, L. Henderson et al. 2002. "Apolipoprotein E4 and Tau Allele Frequencies among Choctaw Indians." *Neuroscience Letters* 324:77–79.

Henderson, J. N., B. Finke and M. McCabe. 2004. "Cross-Cultural Health Care for American Indians and Alaska Natives." In *Health Decisions in a Multicultural Society.* R. Adler and R. Kamel, eds. New York: American Geriatric Society.

Henderson, J. N., M. Gutierrez-Mayka, J. Garcia and S. Boyd. 1993. "A Model for Alzheimer's Disease Support Group Development in African American and Hispanic Populations." *The Gerontologist* 33:409–14.

Henderson J. N. and L. Henderson. 2002. "Cultural Construction of Disease: A 'Supernormal' Construct of Dementia in an American Indian Tribe." *Journal of Cross-Cultural Gerontology* 17:197–212.

———. 2004. "Oklahoma Choctaw Indians." In *Encyclopedia of Medical Anthropology,* vol. 2. C. R. Ember and M. Ember, eds. Netherlands: Kluwer-Plenum.

Henderson, J. N. and J. W. Traphagan. 2005. "Cultural Factors in Dementia: Perspectives from the Anthropology of Aging." *Alzheimer Disease and Associated Disorders* 19(4):272–74.

Henderson, J. N. and M. Vesperi, eds. 1995. *The Culture of Long-Term Care: Nursing Home Ethnography.* New York: Bergin and Garvey.

Henderson, L. 2002a. "The Cultural Construction of Diabetes Mellitus among Oklahoma Choctaw Elders and Health Care Providers: Discordance between Models." *Association for Anthropology and Gerontology Newsletter* 23(1): 4–6.

———. 2002b. "The Cultural Construction of Diabetes Mellitus among Oklahoma Choctaw Elders and Choctaw Nation Tribal Health Care Providers: An Examination of Concordance between Models and Implications for Care-Seeking and Compliance." Ph.D. diss. University of South Florida.

Henderson, T. L. and J. L. Cook. 2006. "The Voices of Black Grandmothers Parenting Grandchildren with TANF Assistance." In *Custodial Grandparenting: Individual, Cultural and Ethnic Diversity*. B. Hayslip and J. Hicks-Patrick, eds. New York: Springer.

Hendrie, H. 2006. "Lessons Learned from International Comparative Cross-Cultural Studies on Dementia." *American Journal of Geriatric Psychiatry* 14(6):480–88.

Henrikson, C. 2007. "Longevity's Impact on Retirement Security." In *Global Health and Global Aging*. M. Robinson et al., eds. San Francisco: Jossey-Bass.

Henry, J. 1963. *Culture against Man*. New York: Vintage Books.

Hepworth, M. 1995. "'Wrinkles of Vice' and 'Wrinkles of Virtue': The Moral Interpretation of the Ageing Body." In *Images of Ageing in Western Societies*. C. Hummel and C. Lalive D'Epinay, eds. Geneva: University of Geneva, Centre for Interdisciplinary Gerontology.

Hepworth, M. and M. Featherstone. 1982. *Surviving Middle Age*. Oxford: Basil Blackwell.

Hermalin, A., ed. 2002. *The Well-Being of the Elderly in Asia: A Four-Country Comparative Study*. Ann Arbor: University of Michigan Press.

Hernandez, G. G. 1992. "The Family and Its Aged Members: The Cuban Experience." *Clinical Gerontologist* 2(3/4):45–57.

Herskind, A. M., M. McGue, N. V. Holm, T. I. Sørensen, B. Harvald and J. W. Vaupel. 1996. "The Heritability of Human Longevity: A Population-Based Study of 2872 Danish Twin Pairs Born 1870–1900." *Human Genetics* 97(3):319–23.

Herskovits, E. 1995. "Struggling over Subjectivity: Debates about the 'Self' and Alzheimer's Disease." *Medical Anthropology Quarterly* 9:146–64.

Heumann, L. and D. Boldy, eds. 1993. *Aging in Place with Dignity: International Solutions to the Low-Income and Frail Elderly*. Westport, CT: Praeger.

Hewitt, R. 1986. *Structure, Meaning and Ritual in the Narratives of the Southern San*. Hamburg: Helmut Burke Verlag.

Heywood, F., C. Oldman and R. Robin Means. 2002. *Housing and Home in Later Life*. Buckingham, UK: Open University Press.

Hicks-Patrick, J. and B. Hayslip. 2006. "Toward an Understanding of Diversity among Grandparents Raising Their Grandchildren." In *Custodial Grandparenting: Individual, Cultural and Ethnic Diversity*. B. Hayslip and J. Hicks-Patrick, eds. New York: Springer.

Hill, K. and A. M. Hurtado. 1991. "The Evolution of Reproductive Senescence and Menopause in Human Females." *Human Nature* 2(4):315–50.

———. 1996. *Ache Life History: The Ecology and Demography of a Foraging People*. New York: Aldine de Gruyter.

Hill, M. and I. Rosenwaike. 2001. "The Social Security Administration's Death Master File: The Completeness of Death Reporting at Older Ages." *Social Security Bulletin* 64:45–51.

Hill, P. et al. 1976. "Plasma Hormone Levels in Different Ethnic Populations of Women." *Cancer Research* 36:2297–2301.

———. 1977. "Diet and Endocrine-Related Cancer." *Cancer* 39:1820–26.

———. 1980. "Diet, Lifestyle and Menstrual Activity." *American Journal of Clinical Nutrition* 33:1192–98.

Hill, R. F., D. Fortenberry and H. F. Stein. 1990. "Culture in Clinical Medicine." *Southern Medical Journal* 83:1071–80.

Hillebrant, F. 1980. "Aging among the Advantaged: A New Look at the Stereotyping of the Elderly." *The Gerontologist* 20.

The Hindu staff reporter. 2004. "Old Age Homes Against Our Culture: Vaiko." *The Hindu*, September 14. http://www.thehindu.com/2004/09/14/stories/2004091405490300. htm.

Hinterlong, J. and S. Ryan. 2008. "Creating Grander Families: Older Adults Adopting Younger Kin and Nonkin." *The Gerontologist* 48:527–36.

Hinton, L., C. Franz, G. Yeo and S. Levkoff. 2005. "Conceptions of Dementia in a Multiethnic Sample of Family Caregivers." *Journal of the American Geriatrics Society* 53(8):1405–10.

Hirsh, H. L. 1985. "Who May Eat and Who May Starve?" *Nursing Homes*, July/August, 9–10.

Hitt, R., Y. Young-Xu, M. Silver and T. Perls. 1999. "Centenarians: The Older You Get, the Healthier You Have Been." *Lancet* 354:652.

Hochschild, A. 1973. *The Unexpected Community*. New York: Prentice-Hall.

Hockey, J. and A. James. 1993. *Growing Up and Growing Old: Ageing and Dependency in the Life Course*. London: Sage.

———. 2003. *Social Identities across the Life Course*. London: Palgrave.

Hodder, R. 2004. "Connections: My Gateway to Alzheimer's World of Silence." *American Journal of Alzheimer's Disease and Other Dementias* 19(2):129–34.

Hogan, T. and D. Steinnes. 1996. "Arizona Sunbirds and Minnesota Snowbirds: Two Species of the Elderly Seasonal Migrant Genus." *Journal of Economic and Social Measurement* 22:129–39.

Hogue, B. 1998. "How to Fall in Love with Life." Paper presented at the workshop on "Elders and Immigrants in the Bay Area: Iranian Mothers Create Meaningful Lives and Share Wisdom" the Santa Clara University Women's Day 1998 Conference, Celebrating Women's Wisdom at, April 29.

Holkup, P. 2001. "20th Century." *Journal of Gerontological Nursing* 27(6):38–46.

Holkup, P., E. Salois, T. Tripp-Reimer and C. Weinert. 2007. "Drawing on Wisdom from the Past: An Elder Abuse Intervention with Tribal Communities." *The Gerontologist* 47:248–54.

Hollis, J. 2005. *Finding Meaning in the Second Half of Life: How to Finally, Really Grow Up*. New York: Gotham Books.

Holmes, E. R. and L. D. Holmes. 1995. *Other Cultures, Elder Years*. Thousand Oaks, CA: Sage.

Holmes, L. D. 1972. "The Role and Status of the Aged in a Changing Samoa." In *Aging and Modernization*. D. Cowgill and L. D. Holmes, eds. New York: Appleton-Century-Crofts.

———. 1974. *Samoan Village*. New York: Holt, Rinehart & Winston.

Holmes, L. D. and E. Rhoads. 1987. "Aging and Change in Samoa." In *Growing Old in Different Societies: Cross-Cultural Perspectives*. J. Sokolovsky, ed. Acton, MA: Copley.

Holstein, M. and M. Minkler. 2003. "Self, Society and the New Gerontology." *The Gerontologist* 43(6):787–96.

Holzberg, C. S. 1984. "Anthropology, Life Histories and the Aged: The Toronto Baycrest Centre." *International Journal of Aging and Human Development* 18(4): 255–75.

Horiuchi, S. 2000. "Greater Lifetime Expectations." *Nature* 405:744–45.

Hornum, B. 1987. "The Elderly in British New Towns: New Roles, New Networks." In *Growing Old in Different Societies: Cross-Cultural Perspectives*. J. Sokolovsky, ed. Acton, MA: Copley.

Horowitz, A. 1985. "Family Caregiving to the Frail Elderly." *Annual Review of Gerontology and Geriatrics* 5:194–246.

Houser, A. 2007. "Long-Term Care" (fact sheet). Washington, DC: AARP Public Policy Institute.

Houston, D., K. McKee, L. Carroll and H. Marsh. 1998. "Laughter and Age." *Aging and Mental Health* 2(4):328–32.

Howard, R. 1985. *Cocoon*. Hollywood, CA: Twentieth Century Fox.

Howe, D. 2001. *"Aging and Smart Growth: Building Aging-Sensitive Communities."* Funders Network for Smart Growth and Livable Communities. Translation Paper Number Seven.

Howell, N. 1979. *Demography of the Dobe Area !Kung*. New York: Academic.

Hoyt, G. 1954. "The Life of the Retired in a Trailer Park." *American Journal of Sociology* 59:361–70.

HSBC Insurance. 2007. "The Future of Retirement: The New Old Age." http://www. hsbc.com/1/PA_1_1_S5/content/assets/retirement/2007_for_report.pdf.

Hsu, F. L. K. 1943. "The Myth of Chinese Family Size." *The American Journal of Sociology* 48(5):555–62.

Hsu, H. 2007. "Exploring Elderly People's Perspectives on Successful Ageing in Taiwan." *Ageing and Society* 27:87–102.

Hu, Y-H. 1995. "Elderly Suicide Risk in Family Contexts: A Critique of the Asian Family Care Model." *Journal of Cross-Cultural Gerontology* 10(3):199–217.

Hudson, R., ed. 2008. *Boomer Bust? Economic and Political Dynamics of the Graying Society*. Westport, CT: Praeger.

Hughes, J. 2001. Views of the Person with Dementia. *Journal of Medical Ethics* 27(2):86–91.

Human Rights Watch. 2003. "Double Standards: Women's Property Rights Violations in Kenya." http://www.hrw.org/reports/2003/Kenya0303.

———. 2008. Cuba: Country Summary, January. New York: Human Rights Watch. http://hrw.org/wr2k8/pdfs/cuba.pdf.

Humes, K. 2005. "The Population 65 Years and Older: Aging in America." In *The Book of the States: 2005*. Lexington, KY: Council of State Governments.csg.org/pubs/Documents/BOS2005-AgingInAmerica.pdf (accessed on January 28, 2008).

Hummel, C., Rey, J.-C. and C. Lalive D'Epinay. 1995. "Children's Drawings of Grandparents: A Quantitative Analysis of Images." In *Images of Ageing: Cultural Representations of Later Life*. M. Featherstone and A. Wernick, eds. London and New York: Routledge.

Hunt, R. C. 2002. "Economic Transfers and Exchanges: Concepts for Describing Allocations." In *Theory in Economic Anthropology*. J. Ensminger, ed. Walnut Creek, CA: AltaMira.

Hunter, A. G. and R. J. Taylor. 1998. "Grandparenthood in African American Families." In *Handbook on Grandparenthood*. M. E. Szinovacz, ed. Westport, CT: Greenwood Press.

Hurd, H., J. Palumbo and H. Gharib. 1977. "Hypothalamic Endocrine Dysfunction in Anorexia Nervosa." *Mayo Clinic Proceedings* 52:711–16.

Hurtado, A.-D., D. Hayes-Bautista, R. Valdez and A. Hernandez. 1992. *Redefining California: Latino Social Engagement in a Multicultural Society*. Los Angeles: University of California, Chicano Studies Research Center.

Ice, G. 2006. "Biological Anthropology and Aging." Special issue, *Journal of Cross-Cultural Gerontology* 20(2).

Ikels, C. 1993. "Settling Accounts: The Intergenerational Contract in an Age of Reform." In *Chinese Families in the Post-Mao Era.* D. Davis and S. Harrell, eds. Berkeley: University of California Press.

———. 1996. *The Return of the God of Wealth: The Transition to a Market Economy in Urban China.* Stanford, CA: Stanford University Press.

———. 1997. "Long-Term Care and the Disabled Elderly in Urban China." In *The Cultural Context of Aging: Worldwide Perspectives*, 2nd ed. J. Sokolovsky, ed. Westport, CT: Bergin and Garvey.

———. 1998. "Grandparenthood in Cross-Cultural Perspective." In *Handbook on Grandparenthood.* M. E. Szinovacz, ed. Westport, CT: Greenwood Press.

———. 2004a. *Filial Piety: Practice and Discourse in Contemporary East Asia.* Stanford, CA: Stanford University Press.

———. 2004b. "The Impact of Housing Policy on China's Urban Elderly." *Journal of Urban Anthropology* 33(2–4):321–55.

———. 2007. "Older Immigrants: Cultural Issues in Access to Health Care (Commentary)." In *Social Structures: Demographic Changes and the Well-Being of Older Persons.* K. W. Schaie and P. Uhlenberg, eds. New York: Springer.

Ikels, C. and C. Beall. 2001. "Age, Aging and Anthropology." In *Handbook of Aging and the Social Sciences*, 5th ed. R. H. Binstock and L. K. George, eds. San Diego: Academic Press.

Iliffe, J. 2006. *The African AIDS Epidemic: A History.* Athens: Ohio University Press.

Indian Health Service. 1997. *Indian Health Focus: Elders.* Data Report. Rockville: U.S. Department of Health and Human Services.

———. 1999. *Regional Differences in Indian Health, 1998–1999.* Rockville: U.S. Department of Health and Human Services.

Indrizal, E. and T. S. Fithry. 2005. "Interrelasi Institusi-Institusi Islam dan Adat serta Peranannya dalam Kehidupan Masyarakat Minangkabau di Koto Kayo" (The Relationship between Islamic and Adat Institutions and their Role in the Life of Minangkabau Society in Koto Kayo), *Ageing in Indonesia Working Papers, 2005.*

Ingram, D., J. Young and J. Mattison. 2007. "Calorie Restriction in Nonhuman Primates: Assessing Effects on Brain and Behavioral Aging." *Neuroscience* 14:145(4): 1359–64.

Innes, A., ed. 2003. *Dementia Care Mapping.* Baltimore: Health Professions Press.

Institute of Medicine. 2008. *Retooling for an Aging America.* Washington, DC: National Academies Press. http://www.nap.edu/openbook.php?record_id=12089&page=R1.

Instituto Nacional de Estadistica e Informatica (INEI). 2005. *Resultados Preliminares del Censo 2005, de Poblacion y de Vivienda.* Lima, Peru: Direccion Tecnica de Demografia y Estudios Sociales.

International Labour Organization. 2006. "Action Programme on the International Migration of Health Service Workers: The Supply Side." http://www.ilo.org/public/english/dialogue/sector/sectors/health/migration.htm (accessed on October 23, 2007).

Interrante, J. 1987. "To Have without Holding: Memories of Life with a Person with AIDS." *Radical America* 2(6):55–62.

Ip, D., C. W. Lui and W. H. Chui. 2007. "Veiled Entrapment: A Study of Social Isolation of Older Chinese Migrants in Brisbane." *Ageing and Society* 27:719–38.

Iris, M. and R. Berman. 1995. *Final Report: Qualitative Study of Aging in Chicago.* Chicago: Chicago Community Trust.

Iritani, N., E. Fukuda, Y. Nara and Y. Yamori. 1977. "Lipid Metabolism in Spontane-ously Hypertensive Rats (SHR)." *Atherosclerosis* 28:217–22.

Iwarsson, S., H.-W. Wahl, C. Nygren, F. Oswald, A. Sixsmith, J. Sixsmith et al. 2007. "Importance of the Home Environment for Healthy Aging: Conceptual and Methodological Background of the European ENABLE-AGE Project. *The Gerontologist* 47(1):78–84.

Iwasa, H., H. Yoshida, H. Kim, Y. Yoshida, J. Kwon, M. Sugiura et al. 2007. "A Mortality Comparison of Participants and Non-participants in a Comprehensive Health Examination among Elderly People Living in an Urban Japanese Community." *Aging Clinical and Experimental Research* 19(3):240–45.

Jackson, J. and T. Antonucci. 2005. "Physical and Mental Health Consequences of Aging in Place and Aging Out of Place among Black Caribbean Immigrants." *Research in Human Development* 2(4):229–44.

Jackson, J., E. Brown, T. Antonucci and S. Daatland. 2005. "Ethnic Diversity in Age-ing, Multicultural Societies." In *The Cambridge Handbook of Age and Ageing*. M. Johnson, V. Bengtson, P. Coleman and T. Kirkwood, eds. Cambridge: Cambridge University Press.

Jackson, M. 1995. *At Home in the World*. Durham, NC: Duke University Press.

Jackson, R. and N. Howe. 2008. *The Graying of the Great Powers: Demography and Geopolitics in the 21st Century*. Washington, DC: Center for Strategic and International Studies.

Jackson, R. J. 2001. "What Olmsted Knew." *Western City*, March, 1–3.

Jamison, C., L. Cornell, P. Jamison and H. Nakazato. 2002. "Are All Grandmothers Equal? A Review and a Preliminary Test of the Grandmother Hypothesis in Tokugawa Japan." *American Journal of Physical Anthropology* 119:67–76.

Jamuna, D. 2003. "Issues of Elder Care and Elder Abuse in the Indian Context." In *An Aging India: Perspectives, Prospects and Policies*. P. S. Liebig and S. I. Rajan, eds. New York: Haworth Press.

Japan Ministry of Health, Labour and Welfare. 2000. *Elderly and Disabled Policy Report*. Tokyo: Statistics and Information Department.

———. 2001. *Annual Centenarian Report*. Tokyo: Statistics and Information Department.

———. 2002. *Age Adjusted Death Rates by Prefecture. Special Report on Vital Statistics 2000*. Tokyo: Health and Welfare Statistics Association.

———. 2007. *Annual Centenarian Report*. Tokyo: Statistics and Information Department.

Japan Statistical Yearbook. 2008. Table 2-18, "Private Households by Family Type, 1985–2005." Statistical Survey Department, Statistics Bureau, Ministry of Internal Affairs and Communications, Tokyo, Japan. http://www.stat.go.jp/English/data/nenkan/1431-02.htm (accessed January 25, 2008).

Japan Times. 2005. "Shutting Down Business Fraud." *Japan Economic Newswire*, July 13.

———. 2006a. "Reforms for Nursing-Care Insurance." *Japan Times*, April 21.

———. 2006b. "Japan to Accept 1,000 Filipino Nurses, Caregivers under FTA." *Japan Times*, September 12.

Jenike, B. R. 1997. "Gender and Duty in Japan's Aged Society: The Experience of Family Caregivers." In *The Cultural Context of Aging: Worldwide Perspectives*, 2nd ed. J. Sokolovsky, ed. Westport, CT: Bergin and Garvey.

———. 2002. "From the Family to the Community: Renegotiating the Responsibility for the Care of the Elderly in Japan." Ph.D. diss. University of California–Los Angeles.

Jenkins, C. L., ed. 2003. *Widows and Divorcees in Later Life: On Their Own Again.* New York: Haworth Press.

Jenson, J. 2007. "CRS Report for Congress: Health Care Spending and the Aging of the Population." Washington, DC: Congressional Research Service. http://www. globalaging.org/health/us/2007/spending.pdf.

Jett, K. 2002. "Making the Connection: Seeking and Receiving Help by Elderly African Americans." *Qualitative Health Research* 12(3):373–87.

———. 2006. "Mind-Loss in the African American Community: Dementia as a Normal Part of Aging." *Journal of Aging Studies* 20(1):1–10.

Jiler, J. 2006. *Doing Time in the Garden.* Oakland, CA: New Village Press.

Jochelson, V. 1933. *The Yakut.* New York: American Museum of Natural History.

Joël, M. and R. Haas. 2006. "Inequalities and Quality of Life among Older Persons in Paris." *Growing Older in World Cities.* V. Rodwin and M. Gusmano, eds. Nashville, TN: Vanderbilt University Press.

Johnson, C. 1985. *Growing Up and Growing Old in Italian-American Families.* New Brunswick, NJ: Rutgers University Press.

———. 1995. "Cultural Diversity in Late-Life Families." In *Handbook of Aging and the Family.* R. Blieszner and V. Bedford, eds. Westport, CT: Greenwood Press.

Johnson, E. and E. Rhoades. 2000. "The History and Organization of the Indian Health Services and Systems." In *American Indian Health: Innovations in Health Care, Promotion and Policy.* E. Rhoades, ed. Baltimore: Johns Hopkins University Press.

Johnson, F. A. 1993. *Dependency and Japanese Socialization: Psychoanalytic and Anthropological Investigations in Amae.* New York: New York University Press.

Johnson, R. and S. Schaner. 2005. "Value of Unpaid Activities by Older Americans Tops $160 Billion Per Year." *Policy Briefs/Perspectives on Productive Aging,* No. 4. Washington, DC: Urban Institute. http://www.urban.org/UploadedPDF/ 311227_older_americans.pdf.

Johnson, R., D. Toohey and J. Wiener. 2007. "Meeting the Long-Term Care Needs of the Baby Boomers: How Changing Families Will Affect Paid Helpers and Institutions." Prepared for the Robert Wood Johnson Foundation's Changes in Health Care Financing and Organization. Washington, DC: Urban Institute.

Jonas, K. 1979. "Factors in Development of Community in Age-Segregated Housing." *Anthropological Quarterly* 52:29–38.

de Jong-Gierveld, J. 2004. "Cross-National Comparisons of Social Isolation and Loneliness: Introduction and Overview." *Canadian Journal on Aging* 23(2, Summer):109–13.

Joseph, A. E. and D. R. Phillips. 1999. "Ageing in Rural China: Impacts of Increasing Diversity in Family and Community Resources." *Journal of Cross-Cultural Gerontology* 14:153–68.

Joseph, S. 1993. "Gender and Relationality among Arab Families in Lebanon." *Feminist Studies* 19(3):465–86.

———, ed. 1999. *Intimate Selfing in Arab Families: Gender, Self and Identity in Arab Families.* Syracuse, NY: Syracuse University Press.

Joslin, D. 2002. *Invisible Caregivers: Older Adults Raising Children in the Wake of HIV/AIDS.* New York: Columbia University Press.

Judd, D. R. and T. Swanstrom. 1994. *City Politics.* New York: HarperCollins College Publishers.

Judge, D. S. and J. R. Carey. 2000. "Postreproductive Life Predicted by Primate Patterns." *Journal of Gerontology: Biological Sciences* 55A(4):B201–9.

Jung-Ki, K. and F. Torres Gil. 2000. "Intergenerational and Intragenerational Equity in the United States and their Implications for Korean Society." *Journal of the Korean Gerontological Society* 20(2):91–107.

Juniper, A. B. 1922. "Native Dietary on Niue Island." *Journal of Home Economics* 14(11):612–14.

Kaati, G., L. O. Bygren and S. Edvinsson. 2002. "Cardiovascular and Diabetes Mortality Determined by Nutrition during Parents' and Grandparents' Slow Growth Period." *European Journal of Human Genetics* 10:682–88.

Kagan, A., J. Popper, G. Rhoads and K. Yano. 1985. "Dietary and Other Risk Factors for Stroke in Hawaiian Japanese Men." *Stroke* 16:390–96.

Kahler, M. 1992. "Ten Years After the Commission on Aging–Ideas and Results." *Danish Medical Bulletin* 39:216–19.

Kaid, L. and J. Garner. 2004. "The Portrayal of Older Adults in Political Advertising." In *Handbook of Communication and Ageing Research*, 2nd ed. J. Nussbaum and J. Coupland, eds. Mahwah, NJ: Lawrence Erlbaum Associates.

Kaiser Commission on Medicaid and the Uninsured. 2007. "Medicaid Home and Community-Based Service Programs: Data Update" (issue paper). Washington, DC: Kaiser Family Foundation.

Kaldi, A. R. 2004. "A Study on Physical, Social and Mental Problems of the Elderly in District 13 of Tehran." *Age and Ageing* 33(3):323.

Kalish, R. A. 1967. "Of Children and Grandfathers: A Speculative Essay on Dependency." *The Gerontologist* 7:65–69.

Kamdar, S. I. 2004. "Busy Yuppies Outsource Errands to New Chore Bazaar: From Looking after Old Parents to Walking the Dog, These Corporate Jeeveses Do It All." *The Times of India, Kolkata.* September 1.

Kaminsky, M. 1993. "Definitional Ceremonies: Depoliticizing and Reenchanting the Culture of Aging." In *Voices and Visions of Aging: Toward a Critical Gerontology.* T. Cole, W. Achenbaum, P. Jakobi and R. Kastenbaum, eds. New York: Springer.

Kaminsky, M. and M. Weiss, eds. 2007. *Stories as Equipment for Living: Last Talks and Tales of Barbara Myerhoff.* Ann Arbor: University of Michigan Press.

Kamo, Y. 1998. "Asian Grandparents." In *Handbook on Grandparenthood.* M. E. Szinovacz, ed. Westport, CT: Greenwood Press.

Kan, S. 2007. "Solitary Deaths: Groups Try to Prevent Elderly Dying Alone." *The Daily Yomiuri (Yomiuri Shimbun)*, April 22.

Kanamoto, I. 2006. *Aging among Japanese American Immigrants.* New York: Routledge.

Kane, P. V. 1968–75. *History of Dharmasastra*, 2nd ed. 5 vols. Poona Bhandarkar Oriental Research Institute.

Kane, R., T. Lum, L. Cutler, H. Degenholtz and T.-C. Yu. 2007. "Resident Outcomes in Small-House Nursing Homes: A Longitudinal Evaluation of the Initial Green House Program." *Journal of the American Geriatrics Society* 55(6): 832–39.

Kaneda, T. 2006. "China's Concern over Population Aging and Health." Population Reference Bureau. http://www.prb.org/Articles/2006/ChinasConcernOverPopulation AgingandHealth.aspx.

Kaneda, T. and D. Adams. 2008. "Race, Ethnicity and Where You Live Matters: Recent Findings on Health and Mortality of U.S. Elderly." Population Reference Bureau. http://www.prb.org/Articles/2008/racialdisparities.aspx.

Kannisto, V. 1988. "On the Survival of Centenarians and the Span of Life." *Population Studies* 42:389–406.

———. 1994. "Development of Oldest-Old Mortality, 1950–1990: Evidence from 28 Developed Countries." *Monographs on Population Aging No 1*. Odense, Denmark: Odense University Press.

Kaplan, H. S. 1997. "The Evolution of the Human Life Course." In *Between Zeus and Salmon: The Biodemography of Aging*. K. Wachter and C. Finch, eds. Washington, DC: National Academy of Sciences.

Kaplan, H. S. and M. Gurven. 2005. "The Natural History of Human Food Sharing and Cooperation: A Review and a New Multi-Individual Approach to the Negotiation of Norms." In *Moral Sentiments and Material Interests: The Foundations of Cooperation in Economic Life*. H. Gintis, S. Bowles, R. Boyd and E. Fehr, eds. Cambridge, MA: MIT Press.

Kaplan, H. S., K. Hill, J. B. Lancaster and A. M. Hurtado. 2000. "A Theory of Human Life History Evolution: Diet, Intelligence and Longevity." *Evolutionary Anthropology* 9(4):156–85.

Kaplan, H. S. and A. J. Robson. 2002. "The Emergence of Humans: The Coevolution of Intelligence and Longevity with Intergenerational Transfers." *Proceedings of the National Academy of Sciences* 99:10221–26.

Karimi, M. F. 2003. "Elderly Wellbeing: A Comparative Study between Aged Ethnic Iranians and Native Swedes." *Shiraz E-Medical Journal*, Shiraz University Medical Sciences, Department of Internal Medicine 4(4), October.

Kaskie, B., S. Imhof, J. Cavanaugh and K. Culp. 2008. "Civic Engagement as a Retirement Role for Aging Americans." *The Gerontologist* 48:368–77.

Kastenbaum, R. 1993. "Encrusted Elders: Arizona and the Political Spirit of Postmodern Aging." In *Voices and Visions of Aging: Toward a Critical Gerontology*. T. Cole, W. Achenbaum, P. Jakobi and R. Kastenbaum, eds. New York: Springer.

Kasulis, T. P. 1993. "The Body—Japanese Style." In *Self as Body in Asian Theory and Practice*. T. P. Kasulis, R. T. Ames and W. Dissanayake, eds. Albany: State University of New York Press.

Kato, T. 1982. *Matriliny and Migration: Evolving Minangkabau Traditions in Indonesia*. Ithaca, NY: Cornell University Press.

Katz, R. 1982. *Boiling Energy: Community Healing among the Kalahari Kung*. Cambridge, MA: Harvard University Press.

Katz, R. and M. Biesele. 1987. "!Kung Healing: The Symbolism of Sex Roles and Culture Change." In *The Past and Future of !Kung Ethnography: Critical Reflections and Symbolic Perspectives. Essays in Honor of Lorna Marshall*. M. Biesele with R. Gordon and R. Lee, eds. Hamburg: Helmut Buske Verlag.

Katz, R., M. Biesele and V. St. Denis. 1995. *Healing Makes Our Hearts Happy: Spirituality and Transformation among the Ju/'hoansi of the Kalahari*. Rochester VT: Inner Traditions.

Katz, S. 1995. "Imaging the Life-Span: From Premodern Miracles to Postmodern Fantasies." In *Images of Aging: Cultural Representations of Later Life.* M. Featherstone and A. Wernick, eds. London: Routledge.

———. 2001. "Growing Older without Aging? Positive Aging, Anti-ageism and Anti-aging." *Generations* 25(4):27–32.

———. 2005. *Cultural Aging: Life Course, Life Style and Senior Worlds.* Peterborough, Canada: Broadview Press.

Katz, S. and B. Marshall. 2003. "New Sex for Old: Lifestyle, Consumerism and the Ethics of Aging Well." *Journal of Aging Studies* 17(1):3–16.

Kaufert, P. and M. Lock. 1992. "What Are Women For? Cultural Construction of Menopausal Women in Japan and Canada." In *In Her Prime: New Views of Middle-Aged Women,* 2nd ed. V. Kerns and J. Brown, eds. Urbana: University of Illinois Press.

Kaufman, S. 1986. *The Ageless Self: Sources of Meaning in Late Life.* New York: Meridian.

———. 2005. *A Time to Die: How American Hospitals Shape the End of Life.* New York: Simon and Schuster.

Kearney, M. 1991. "Borders and Boundaries of State and Self at the End of Empire." *Journal of Historical Sociology* 4:48–74.

Keith, J. 1982. *Old People, New Lives: Community Creation in a Retirement Residence.* Chicago: University of Chicago Press.

———. 1988. "A Modest Little Method Whose Presumptions May Amuse You." In *Methodological Issues in Aging.* K. W. Schaie, R. Cambell, W. Meredith and J. Nesselroade, eds. New York: Springer.

Keith, J., C. Fry, A. Glascock, C. Ikels, J. Dickerson-Putnam, H. Harpending and P. Draper. 1994. *The Aging Experience: Diversity and Commonality across Cultures.* Thousand Oaks, CA: Sage.

Kendig, H., A. Hashimoto and L. Coppard, eds. 1992. *Family Support for the Elderly: An International Experience.* New York: Oxford University Press.

Kennedy, A. 2006. "Empty Nest." In *Encyclopedia of Human Development.* N. J. Salkind, ed. Thousand Oaks, CA: Sage.

Kent, S. and R. B. Lee. 1992. "A Hematological Study of !Kung Kalahari Foragers: An Eighteen-Year Comparison." In *Diet, Demography and Disease: Changing Perspectives on Anemia.* P. Stuart-Macadam and S. Kent, eds. New York: Aldine De Gruyter.

Kenyon, C. 2005. "The Plasticity of Aging: Insights from Long-Lived Mutants." *Cell* 120:449–60.

Kerber, R., E. O'Brien, K. Smith and R. Cawthon. 2001. "Familial Excess Longevity in Utah Genealogies." *Journals of Gerontology. Series A, Biological Sciences and Medical Sciences* 56:B130–39.

Kerns, V. 1983. *Woman and the Ancestors.* Urbana: University of Illinois Press.

Kerns, V. and J. K. Brown, eds. 1992. *In Her Prime: New Views of Middle-Aged Women,* 2nd ed. Urbana: University of Illinois Press.

Kertzer, D. I. 1978. "Theoretical Developments in the Study of Age-Group Systems" (review of Stewart 1977). *American Ethnologist* 5:365–74.

———. 1984. *Family Life in Central Italy, 1880–1910.* New Brunswick, NJ: Rutgers University Press.

Kertzer, D. I. and J. Keith, eds. 1984. *Age and Anthropological Theory.* Ithaca, NY: Cornell University Press.

Kertzer, D. I. and P. Laslett, eds. 1994. *Demography, Society and Old Age.* Berkeley: University of California Press.

Kertzer, D. I. and O. B. B. Madison. 1981. "Women's Age-Set Systems in Africa: The Latuka of Southern Sudan." In *Dimensions: Aging, Culture and Health.* C. L. Fry, ed. South Hadley, MA: Bergin and Garvey.

Kertzer, D. I. and R. P. Saller, eds. 1991. *The Family in Italy: from Antiquity to the Present.* New Haven, CT: Yale University Press.

Kibuga, K. F. and A. Dianga. 2000. "Victimisation and Killing of Older Women: Witchcraft in Magu District, Tanzania." *Southern African Journal of Gerontology* 9(2):29–32.

Kiefer, C. 1987. "Care of the Aged in Japan." In *Health, Illness and Medical Care in Japan: Cultural and Social Dimensions.* E. Norbeck and M. Lock, eds. Honolulu: University of Hawaii Press.

Kikkawa, T. 1995. Hito wa naze bokeru no ka: bke no genin to keâ [Why Do People Become *Boke*? The Causes and Care of *Boke*]. Tokyo: Shinseidehansha.

Kilbie, T. 2000. *Community Care Statistics 2000: Residential Personal Social Services for Adults, England.* London: Department of Health.

Killick, J. and K. Allan. 2001. *Communication and the Care of People with Dementia.* Buckingham, UK: Open University Press.

Kimble, M. and S. McFadden, eds. 2003. *Aging, Spirituality and Religion: A Handbook,* vol. 2. Minneapolis, MN: Fortress Press.

King, S., E. Burgess, M. Akinyela, M. Counts-Spriggs and N. Parker. 2005. "'Your Body Is God's Temple': The Spiritualization of Health Beliefs in Multigenerational African American Families." *Research on Aging* 27(4):420–46.

Kinsella, K. and Y. J. Gist. 1995. *Older Workers, Retirement and Pensions: A Comparative International Chartbook.* Washington, DC: U.S. Government Printing Office.

Kinsella, K. and D. R. Phillips. 2005. *Global Aging: The Challenge of Success.* Population Bulletin 60:1. Washington, DC: Population Reference Bureau.

Kinsella, K. and V. A. Velkoff. 2001. *An Aging World.* U.S. Department of Health and Human Services and U.S. Department of Commerce, International Population Report, 01-1, 95.

Kirkpatrick, J. 1985. "How Personal Differences Can Make a Difference." In *The Social Construction of the Person.* K. J. Gergen and K. E. Davis, eds. New York: Springer-Verlag.

Kitwood, T. 1997. *Dementia Reconsidered: The Person Comes First.* Buckingham, UK: Open University Press.

Kivnick, H. Q. and H. M. Sinclair. 2007. "Grandparenthood." In *Encyclopedia of Gerontology.* J. E. Birren, ed. Oxford: Elsevier.

Klein, R. 1997. "Learning from Others: Shall the Last Be the First?" *Journal of Health Politics, Policy and Law* 22(5):1267–78.

Kleinenberg, E. 2002. *Heat Wave: Social Autopsy of a Disaster.* Chicago: University of Chicago Press.

Kleinman, A. 1980. *Patients and Healers in the Context of Culture,* 1st ed., vol. 3. Berkeley: University of California Press.

Knapp, K. 2006. "Housing of Older New Yorkers." In *Growing Older in World Cities: New York, London, Paris and Tokyo.* V. Rodwin and M. Gusmano, eds. Nashville, TN: Vanderbilt University Press.

Knodel, J. 2008. "Poverty and the Impact of AIDS on Older Persons: Evidence from Cambodia and Thailand." *Economic Development and Cultural Change* 56:441–75.

Knodel, J. and M. B. Ofstedal. 2003. "Gender and Aging in the Developing World: Where Are the Men?" *Population and Development Review* 29:4:677–98.

Knodel, J. and C. Saengtienchai. 2005. "Older Aged Parents: The Final Safety Net for Adult Sons and Daughters with AIDS in Thailand." *Journal of Family Issues* 26(5):665–98.

———. 2007. "Thailand: Rural Parents with Urban Children: Social and Economic Implications of Migration on the Rural Elderly in Thailand." *Population, Space and Place* 13(3):193–210. A version of this paper is also available at: http://www.globalaging.org/ruralaging/world/2005/urban.pdf.

Kobayashi, S. 1992. "A Scientific Basis for the Longevity of Japanese in Relation to Diet and Nutrition." *Nutrition Reviews* 50:353–54.

Kobayashi, T., S. Kikuchi, Y. Lin, K. Yagyu, Y. Obata, A. Ogihara et al. 2004. "Trends in the Incidence of Gastric Cancer in Japan and Their Associations with Helicobacter Pylori Infection and Gastric Mucosal Atrophy." *Gastric Cancer* 7:233–39.

Koenig, H. 1999. *The Healing Power of Faith*. New York: Simon & Schuster.

Kohli, M. 1986. "The World We Forgot: A Historical Review of the Life Course." In *Later Life: The Social Psychology of Aging*. V. Marshall, ed. Beverly Hills, CA: Sage.

Kohn, S. J. and G. C. Smith. 2006. "Social Support among Custodial Grandparents within a Diversity of Contexts." In *Custodial Grandparenting: Individual, Cultural and Ethnic Diversity*. B. Hayslip and J. Hicks-Patrick, eds. New York: Springer.

Kondo, D. 1990. *Crafting Selves: Power, Gender and Discourses of Identity in a Japanese Workplace*. Chicago: University of Chicago Press.

Konigsberg, L. W. and N. P. Herrmann. 2006. "The Osteological Evidence for Human Longevity in the Recent Past." In *The Evolution of Human Life History*. K. Hawkes and R. R. Paine, eds. Santa Fe, NM: School of American Research Press.

Konner, M. and C. Worthman. 1980. "Nursing Frequency, Gonadal Function and Birth Spacing among !Kung Hunter-Gatherers." *Science* 207:788–91.

Kontos, P. 1998. "Resisting Institutionalization: Constructing Old Age and Negotiating Home." *Journal of Aging Studies* 12:167–84.

Kopera-Frye, K. and R. Wiscott, R. 2000. "Intergenerational Continuity: Transmission of Beliefs and Culture." In *Grandparents Raising Grandchildren: Theoretical, Empirical and Clinical Perspectives*. B. Hayslip and R. Goldberg-Glen, eds. New York: Springer.

Kopytoff, I. 1971. "Ancestors as Elders." *Africa* 41:129–42.

Korn, L. and R. Ryser. 2006. "Burying the Umbilicus: Nutrition Trauma, Diabetes and Traditional Medicine in Rural West Mexico." In *Indigenous Peoples and Diabetes*. M. Ferreira and G. Lang, eds. Durham, NC: Carolina Academic Press.

Kornblatt, S., C. Eng and J. Hansen. 2003. "Cultural Awareness in Health and Social Services: The Experience of On Lok." *Generations* 26(3):46–53.

Koropatnick, T., J. Kimbell, R. Chen, J. Grove, T. Donlon, K. Masaki et al. 2008. "A Prospective Study of High Density Lipoprotein Cholesterol, Cholesteryl Ester Transfer Protein Gene Variants and Healthy Aging in Very Old Japanese-American

Men." *Journals of Gerontology. Series A, Biological Sciences and Medical Sciences.*

Koropeckyj-Cox, T., R. Vaugn and A. Call. 2007. "Characteristics of Older Childless Persons and Parents." *Journal of Family Issues* 28(10):1362–1414.

Korton, D. 1995. *When Corporations Rule the World.* Hartford, CT: Kumarian Press.

Koyama, T. and T. Yasuda. 2006. "Nursing Insurance Costs Bite; Rising Monthly Premiums Straining Budgets, Patience." *Daily Yomiuri* (Tokyo), March 30.

Koyano, W. 1989. "Japanese Attitudes Toward the Elderly: A Review of Research Findings." *Journal of Cross-Cultural Gerontology* 4(4):335–46.

Krach, C. and V. Velkoff. 1999. *Centenarians in the United States.* U.S. Bureau of the Census, Current Population Reports, Series P23-199RV. Washington, DC: U.S. Government Printing Office.

Krasny, K. and R. Doyle. 2002. "Participatory Approaches to Program Development and Engaging Youth in Research: The Case of an Inter-generational Urban Community Gardening Program." *Journal of Extension* 40(5). http://www.joe.org/joe/2002october/a3.shtml.

Krause, K. 2007. "Fertility Politics as 'Social Viagra': Reproducing Boundaries, Social Cohesion and Modernity in Italy." *American Anthropologist* 109(2):350–62.

Krause, N. and E. Borawski-Clark. 1994. "Acculturation and Psychological Distress in Three Groups of Elderly Hispanics." *Journal of Gerontology* 47:S279–88.

Kreager, P. 2006. "Migration, Social Structure and Old-Age Support Networks: A Comparison of Three Indonesian Communities." *Ageing and Society* 26(1):37–60.

Kreager, P. and E. Schröder-Butterfill, eds. 2005. *Ageing without Children: European and Asian Perspectives.* Oxford: Berghahn.

———. 2007. "Gaps in the Family Networks of Older People in Three Rural Indonesian Communities." *Journal of Cross-Cultural Gerontology* 22(1):1–25.

Krout, J. and C. Porgozala. 2002. "An Intergenerational Partnership between a College and Congregate Housing Facility." *The Gerontologist* 42:853–58.

Kudo, Y. 2006. "Aging, Socio-Economic Status and Neighborhood Differences in Tokyo." In *Growing Older in World Cities: New York, London, Paris and Tokyo.* V. Rodwin and M. Gusmano, eds. Nashville, TN: Vanderbilt University Press.

Kuh, D. and B. Ben-Shlomo. 1997. *A Life Course Approach to Chronic Disease Epidemiology.* Oxford: Oxford University Press.

Kuhn, D. 2002. Intimacy, Sexuality and Residents with Dementia. *Alzheimer's Care Quarterly* 5(2):165–76.

Kumar, S. 2003. "Economic Security for the Elderly in India: An Overview." In *An Aging India: Perspectives, Prospects and Policies.* P. Liebig and S. Rajan, eds. New York: Haworth Press.

Kuo, F. E. and W. C. Sullivan 2001. "Environment and Crime in the Inner City: Does Vegetation Reduce Crime?" *Environment and Behavior* 33(3):343–67.

Kuo, F. E., W. C. Sullivan, R. L. Coley and L. Brunson. 1998. "Fertile Ground for Community: Inner-City Neighborhood Common Spaces." *American Journal of Community Psychology* 26(6):823–51.

Kuoppasalmi, K. et al. 1976. "Effect on Strenuous Anaerobic Running Exercise on Plasma Growth Hormone, Cortisol, Luteinizing Hormone, Testosterone Androstenedione, Estrone and Estradiol." *Journal of Steroid Biochemistry* 7(10):823–29.

Kurimori, S., Y. Fukuda, K. Nakamura, M. Watanabe and T. Takano. 2006. "Calculation of Prefectural Disability-Adjusted Life Expectancy (DALE) Using

Long-Term Care Prevalence and Its Socioeconomic Correlates in Japan." *Health Policy* 76:346–58.

Kweon, B., W. Sullivan and A. Riley. 1998. "Green Common Spaces and the Social Integration of Inner-City Older Adults." *Environment and Behavior* 30(6): 832–58.

Kyodo News. 2006. "Japan's Population Set to Fall under 90 Million by 2055." *BBC Worldwide Monitoring*, December 20.

———. 2007. "Filipino Nursing-Caregivers to See Eased Licensing." *Japan Times*, March 25.

Kyomuhendo, G. B. and M. K. McIntosh. 2006. *Women, Work and Domestic Virtue in Uganda, 1900–2003*. Athens: Ohio University Press.

Lafortune, G., G. Balestat and OECD Disability Study Expert Group Members. 2007. "Trends in Severe Disability among Elderly People: Assessing the Evidence in Twelve OECD Countries and the Future Implications." Health Working Paper No. 26. Paris: Organization for Economic Cooperation and Development. http://www.oecd.org/dataoecd/13/8/38343783.pdf.

Lai, D. and S. Surood. 2008. "Predictors of Depression in Aging South Asian Canadians." *Journal of Cross-Cultural Gerontology* 23(1):57–75.

Lamb, S. 2000. *White Saris and Sweet Mangoes: Aging, Gender and Body in North India*. Berkeley: University of California Press.

———. 2002. "Intimacy in a Transnational Era: The Remaking of Aging among Indian Americans." *Diaspora* 11(3):299–330.

———. 2007. "Aging across Worlds: Modern Seniors in an Indian Diaspora." In *Generations and Globalization: Youth, Age and Family in the New World Economy*. J. Cole and D. Durham, eds. Bloomington: Indiana University Press.

———. 2009. *Aging and the Indian Diaspora: Cosmopolitan Families in India and Abroad*. Bloomington: Indiana University Press.

Lamb, V. and G. Myers. 1999. "A Comparative Study of Successful Aging in Three Asian Countries." *Journal of Population Research and Policy Review* 18(5):433–50.

Lan, P. 2002. "Subcontracting Filial Piety: Elder Care in Ethnic Chinese Immigrant Families in California." *Journal of Family Issues* 23(7):812–35. http://pclan.social.ntu.edu.tw/html/word/Filialpiety.pdf.

Lancaster, J. B. and B. J. King. 1985. "An Evolutionary Perspective on Menopause." In *In Her Prime: A View of Middle-Aged Women*. V. Kerns and J. K. Brown, eds. Garden City, NJ: Bergen and Garvey.

Lanspery, S. and J. Hyde, eds. 1997. *Staying Put: Adapting the Places Instead of the People*. Amityville, NY: Baywood Press.

Lantz, P. M. and J. S. House et al. 1998. "Health Behaviors Don't Explain High Death Rates among Poor." *Journal of the American Medical Association* 279:1703–28.

Larson, J. and M. Meyer. 2006. *Generations Gardening Together–A Sourcebook for Intergenerational Therapeutic Horticulture*. Binghamton, NY: Haworth Press.

Laslett, P. 1976. "Societal Development and Aging." In *Handbook of Aging and the Social Sciences*. R. H. Binstock and E. Shanas, eds. New York: Van Nostrand Reinhold.

Lau, A. W. and L. M. Kinoshita. 2006. "Cognitive-Behavior Therapy with Culturally Diverse Older Adults." In *Culturally-Responsive Cognitive-Behavioral Therapy: Assessment, Practice and Supervision*. P. A. Hays and G. Y. Iwamasa, eds. Washington, DC: American Psychological Association.

Laumann, E., S. Leitsch and L. Waite. 2008. "Elder Mistreatment in the United States: Prevalence Estimates from a Nationally Representative Study." *Journal of Gerontology* 63:S248–S254.

Laws, G. 1995. "Embodiment and Emplacement: Identities, Representation and Landscape in Sun City Retirement Communities." *International Journal of Aging and Human Development* 40:253–80.

———. 1996. "'A Shot of Economic Adrenalin': Reconstructing 'The Elderly' in the Retiree-Based Economic Development Literature." *Journal of Aging Studies* 10:171–88.

———. 1997. "Spatiality and Age Relations." In *Critical Approaches to Ageing and Later Life*. A. Jamieson, S. Harper and C. Victor, eds. Buckingham, UK: Open University Press.

Lawson, L. 2005. *City Bountiful: A Century of Community Gardening in America*. San Francisco: University of California Press.

Lawton, M. 1983. *The Suprapersonal Neighborhood Context of Older People: Age Heterogeneity and Well-Being*. Philadelphia: Philadelphia Geriatric Center.

Lawton, M., P. Windley and T. Byerts. 1982. *Aging and the Environment: Theoretical Approaches*. New York: Springer.

Lawton, M. et al. 1992. "The Dynamics of Caregiving for a Demented Elder among Black and White Families." *Journal of Gerontology* 47(4):S156–64.

Lawton, P. 2001. "Quality of Care and Quality of Life in Dementia Care Units." In *Linking Quality of Long-Term Care and Quality of Life*. L. Noelker and Z. Harel, eds. New York: Springer.

Leaf, A. 1982. "Long-Lived Populations: Extreme Old Age." *Journal of the American Geriatrics Society* 38:485–87.

Lebra, T. S. 1976. *Japanese Patterns of Behavior*. Honolulu: University of Hawaii Press.

Lebra, W. 1966. *Okinawan Religion*. Honolulu: University of Hawaii Press.

Leder, D. 2000. "The Trouble with Successful Aging." http://www.evergreen.loyola.edu/~dleder/successful_aging.html (accessed January 30, 2004).

Lee, J. and F. Wang. 2001. *One Quarter of Humanity*: Malthusian Mythology and Chinese Realities, 1700–2000. Cambridge, MA: Harvard University Press.

Lee, M. 2007. "Cross-National Research on Aging." *Research Highlights in the Demography and Economics of Aging* 11:1–6.

Lee, R. B. 1968. "Sociology of !Kung Bushman Trance Performances." In *Trance and Possession States*. R. H Prince, ed. Montreal: R. M. Bucke Memorial Society.

———. 1979. *The !Kung San: Men, Women and Work in a Foraging Society*. Cambridge: Cambridge University Press.

———. 1984. *The Dobe !Kung*. New York: Holt, Rinehart & Winston.

———. 2006. "The Ju/'Hoansi at the Crossroads: Continuity and Change in the Time of AIDS." In *Globalization and Change in Fifteen Cultures: Born in One World, Living in Another*. G. Spindler and J. E. Stockard, eds. Belmont, CA: Thomson Wadsworth.

Lee, R. B. and M. Biesele. 1991. "Dependency or Self-Reliance? The !Kung San Forty Years On." Paper presented at the American Anthropological Association Annual Meeting, November, Chicago.

Lee, R. and H. G. Rosenberg. 1993. "Fragments of the Future: Aspects of Social Reproduction among the Ju/Hoansi." In *Hunters and Gatherers in the Modern Context*: *Proceedings of the Seventh International Conference on Hunting and Gathering Societies*. Moscow: Russian Academy of Sciences.

Lee, S. and A. Kleinman. 2000. "Suicide as Resistance in Chinese Society." In *Chinese Society: Change, Conflict and Resistance*. E. J. Perry and M. Selden, eds. London and New York: Routledge.

Legesse, A. 1973. *Gada*. New York: Free Press.

———. 1979. "Age Sets and Retirement Communities." *Anthropological Quarterly* 52:61–69.

Leinaweaver, J. 2008. "Aging, Relatedness and Social Abandonment in Highland Peru." *Anthropology and Aging Quarterly* 29(2):44–45.

Leith-Ross, S. 1939. *African Women: A Study of the Ibo of Nigeria*. London: Faber and Faber.

Lesson, G. 2004. *The Demographics and Economics of UK Health and Social Care for Older Adults*. Oxford: Oxford Institute on Ageing.

Levin, J. and H. Vanderpool. 1989. "Is Religion Therapeutically Significant for Hypertension?" *Social Science and Medicine* 29(1):69–78.

Levine, M. V. 1995. "Globalization and Wage Polarization in U.S. and Canadian Cities: Does Public Policy Make a Difference?" In *North American Cities and the Global Economy*. P. K. Kresl and G. Gappart, eds. Thousand Oaks, CA: Sage.

Levine, N. 2006. "Finding Their Place: Examining the Role of the Grace Center in the Successful Adaptation of Elderly Iranian Immigrants." Anthropology of Aging, Spring, Santa Clara University, unpublished. manuscript.

Levine, R. 1965. "Intergenerational Tensions and Extended Family Structures in Africa." In *Social Structure and the Family*. E. Shanas and G. Strieb, eds. Englewood Cliffs, NJ: Prentice-Hall.

Levi-Strauss, C. 1936. "Contributions a L'étude de L'organization Sociale des Indiens Bororo" [Contributions to the Study of the Social Organization of the Bororo Indians]. *Société des Americanistes de Paris* 28:269–304.

Levy, R. 1973. *Tahitians: Mind and Experience in the Society Islands*. Chicago: University of Chicago Press.

Lewinter, M. 1999. *Spreading the Burden of Gratitude–Elderly between Family and State*. Copenhagen: Sociologisk Institut.

Lewis, C. 1996. *Green Nature/Human Nature: The Meaning of Plants in Our Lives*. Urbana: University of Illinois Press.

Li, R. J. 2002. "The Life of Elderly People from Different Occupational Backgrounds and Their Choice of Eldercare Patterns." *Chinese Sociology and Anthropology* 34(2):3–12.

Lieberman, L. 2004. "Diabetes Mellitus and Anthropology." In *Encyclopedia of Medical Anthropology: Health and Illness in Today's Cultures*, vol. 2. C. R. Ember and M. Ember, eds. New York: Kluwer Academic/Plenum Publishers.

Liebig, P. S. 2003. "Old-Age Homes and Services: Old and New Approaches to Aged Care." In *An Aging India: Perspectives, Prospects and Policies*. P. S. Liebig and S. I. Rajan, eds. New York: Haworth Press. (Also published in *Journal of Aging and Social Policy* 15(2/3):159–78, 2003.)

Liebowitz, B. 1976. "Administrative and Economic Aspects of an Innovative Treatment Setting." Presented at the Symposium on the Weiss Institute, 29th Annual Scientific Meeting of the Gerontological Society, New York.

Liebowitz, B., M. P. Lawton and A. Waldman. 1979. "Evaluation: Designing for Impaired Elderly People." *American Institute of Architects Journal, 68*, 59–61.

Lin, Y. J. et al. 2007. "Connecting Elders with Stroke History, Medical Students and the Community through a 'Gardening for Health' Course in Taiwan." Presented at the 28th Annual Conference of the American Community Gardening Association, Boston.

Linn, K. 2007. *Building Commons and Community*. Oakland, CA: New Village Press.

Liu, J. Y. 2007. *Gender and Work in Urban China: Women Workers of the Unlucky Generation*. London and New York: Routledge Contemporary China Series.

Ljungquist, B., S. Berg, J. Lanke, G. McClearn and N. Pedersen. 1998. "The Effect of Genetic Factors for Longevity: A Comparison of Identical and Fraternal Twins in the Swedish Twin Registry." *Journals of Gerontology. Series A, Biological Sciences and Medical Sciences* 53:M441–46.

Lloyd-Sherlock, P. 1998. "Old Age, Migration and Poverty in the Shantytowns of São Paulo, Brazil." *Journal of Developing Areas* 32(4):491–514.

———, ed. 2004. *Living Longer: Aging, Development and Social Protection*. London: Zed Books.

Lock, M. 1993. *Encounters with Aging: Mythologies of Menopause in Japan and North America*. Berkeley: University of California Press.

Lockhart, J. B. 2004. Testimony before U.S. Congressional House Ways and Means Committee, Social Security Sub-Committee: Social Security's Future. http://www.ssa.gov/legislation/testimony_012604.htm (accessed on September 20, 2007).

Loeb, E. M. 1926. *History and Traditions of Niue*. Honolulu: Bernice P. Bishop Museum. Bulletin Number 32. New York: Kraus Reprints.

Loeffler, R. 1988. *Islam in Practice: Religious Beliefs in a Persian Village*. Albany: State University of New York Press.

Loewe, R., J. Schwartzman, J. Freeman, L. Quinn and S. Zuckerman. 1998. "Doctor Talk and Diabetes: Towards an Analysis of the Clinical Construction of Chronic Illness." *Social Science and Medicine* 47(9):1267–76.

Logan, J. R. and F. Q. Bian. 1999. "Family Values and Coresidence with Married Children in Urban China." *Social Forces* 77(4):1253–82.

Lombard K., S. Forster-Cox, D. Smeal and M. O'Neill. 2006. "Diabetes on the Navajo Nation: What Role Can Gardening and Agriculture Extension Play to Reduce It?" *Rural Remote Health* 6(4):640.

Long, S. O. 1987. *Family Change and the Life Course in Japan*. Ithaca, NY: China-Japan Program, Cornell University.

———. 2005. *Final Days: Japanese Culture and Choice at the End of Life*. Honolulu: University of Hawaii Press.

Longino, C., Jr. 1984. "Migration Winners and Losers." *American Demographics* 6:27–29, 45.

———. 1989. "Migration Demography and Aging." *Gerontology Review* 2:65–76.

———. 1995. *Retirement Migration in America*. Houston, TX: Vacation Publications.

———. 1998. "Geographic Mobility and the Baby Boom." *Generations* 22:60–64.

———. 2001. "Geographic Distribution and Migration." In *Handbook of Aging and the Social Sciences*, 5th ed. R. Binstock and L. George, eds. San Diego: Academic Press.

Longino, C., Jr. and V. Marshall. 1990. "North American Research on Seasonal Migration." *Ageing and Society* 10:229–335.

Longino, C., Jr., V. Marshall, L. Mullins and R. Tucker. 1991. "On the Nesting of Snowbirds: A Question about Seasonal and Permanent Migrants." *The Journal of Applied Gerontology* 10:157–68.

Longino, C., Jr., A. Perzynski and E. Stoller. 2002. "Pandora's Briefcase: Unpacking the Retirement Migration Decision." *Research on Aging* 24:29–49.

Lopata, H. Z. 1972. "Role Changes in Widowhood: A World Perspective." In *Aging and Modernization*. D. Cowgill and L. Holmes, eds. New York: Appleton-Century-Crofts.

———, ed. 1987a. *Widows: The Middle East, Asia and the Pacific*. Durham, NC: Duke University Press.

———, ed. 1987b. *Widows: North America*. Durham, NC: Duke University Press.

———, ed. 1988. *Widows: Other Countries, Other Places*. Durham, NC: Duke University Press.

———. 1993. "The Interweave of Public and Private: Women's Challenge to American Society." *Journal of Marriage and the Family* 55:176–90.

———. 1996. *Current Widowhood: Myths and Realities*. Thousand Oaks, CA: Sage.

Lopez, A. D., C. D. Mathers, M. Ezzati, D. T. Jamison and C. J. L. Murray, eds. 2006. *Global Burden of Disease and Risk Factors*. Washington, DC: World Bank Group.

Losada, A., G. Robinson, B. Shurgot, G. Knight, M. Marquez, I. Montorio et al. 2006. "Cross-Cultural Study Comparing the Association of Familism with Burden and Depressive Symptoms in Two Samples of Hispanic Dementia Caregivers." *Aging and Mental Health* 10(1):69–76.

Los Angeles Gerontology Research Group. 2008. "Validated Living Supercentenarians." http://www.grg.org/Adams/E.HTM.

Lovejoy, C. O. 1981. "The Origin of Man." *Science* 211:341–50.

Low, S. and I. Altman. 1992. "Place Attachments: A Conceptual Inquiry." In *Place Attachment*. I. Altman and S. Low, eds. New York: Plenum Press.

Lowenstein, A. 2005. "Global Ageing and Challenges to Families." In *Cambridge Handbook of Age and Ageing*. M. Johnson, ed. Cambridge: Cambridge University Press.

Lowenstein, A. and S. O. Daatland. 2006. "Filial Norms and Family Support in a Comparative Cross-National Context: Evidence from the OASIS Study." *Ageing and Society* 26:203–23.

Lowenstein, A., R. Katz and N. Gur-Yaish. 2007. "Reciprocity in Parent-Child Exchange and Life Satisfaction among the Elderly: A Cross-National Perspective." *Journal of Social Issues* 63(4):865–83.

Lowenthal, D. 1985. *The Past Is a Foreign Country*. Cambridge: Cambridge University Press.

Luborsky, M. R. 1994. "The Identification and Analysis of Themes and Patterns." In *Qualitative Methods in Aging Research*. J. Gubrium and A. Sankar, eds. Thousand Oaks, CA: Sage.

Luborsky, M. R. and I. LeBlanc. 2003. "Cross-Cultural Perspective on the Concept of Retirement: An Analytic Redefinition." *Journal of Cross-Cultural Gerontology* 18:251–71.

Luborsky, M. R. and R. L. Rubinstein. 1997. "The Dynamics of Ethnic Identity and Bereavement among Older Widowers." In *The Cultural Context of Aging: Worldwide Perspectives*, 2nd ed. J. Sokolovsky, ed. Westport, CT: Bergin and Garvey.

Luomala, K. 1978. "Symbolic Slaying in Niue: Post-European Changes in a Dramatic Ritual Complex." In *The Changing Pacific: Essays in Honour of H. E. Maude*. N. Gunson, ed. Melbourne: Oxford University Press.

Lustbader, W. 1991. *Counting on Kindness: The Dilemmas of Dependency*. New York: Free Press.

MacCormack, C. P. 1979. "Sande: The Public Face of a Secret Society." In *The New Religions of Africa*. B. Jules-Rosette, ed. Norwood, NJ: Ablex.

Mackinnon, M., L. Gien and D. Durst. 2001. "Silent Pain: Social Isolation and the Elderly Chinese in Canada." I. Chi, N. Chappell and J. Lubben, eds. In *Elderly Chinese in Pacific Rim Countries*. Hong Kong: Hong Kong University Press.

MacMahon, B. et al. 1974. "Urine Estrogen Profiles of Asian and North American Women." *International Journal of Cancer* 14:161–67.

Madden, J. et al. 1978. "Analysis of Secretory Patterns of Prolactin and Gonadotropins during Twenty-four Hours in a Lactating Woman before and after Resumption of Menses." *American Journal of Obstetrics and Gynecology* 132(4):436–41.

Maddigan S., S. Majumdar, L. Guirguis, R. Lewanczuk, T. Lee, E. Toth et al. 2004. "Improvements in Patient-Reported Outcomes Associated with an Intervention to Enhance Quality of Care for Rural Patients with Type 2 Diabetes." *Diabetes Care* 2(6):1306–12.

Maeda, D. and H. Ishikawa. 2000. "Ageing in Japan: Retirement, Daily Lives, Pensions and Social Security." In *Aging in the Asia-Pacific Region: Issues, Policies and Future Trends*. D. R. Phillips, ed. New York: Routledge.

Maffia, L. 1974. "Protein Quality of Two Varieties of High Lysine Maize Fed Alone and with Black Beans or Milk in Normal and Depleted Weanling Rats." *Western Hemisphere Nutrition Congress IV* August 19–22:72.

Magai, C. and B. Halpern. 2001. "Emotional Development during the Middle Years." In *Handbook of Midlife Development*. M. Lachman, ed. New York: Wiley.

Makoni, S. 2008. "Special Issue on Aging and Social Change in Africa." *Journal of Cross-Cultural Gerontology* 23(2).

Makoni, S. and K. Stroeken. 2002. *Ageing in Africa: Sociolinguistic and Anthropological Approaches*. Burlington, VT: Ashgate.

Malakoff, D. 1995. "What Good Is Community Greening?" http://7d8ca58ce9d1641c 9251f63b606b91782998fa39.gripelements.com/docs/WhatGoodisCommunity Greening.pdf.

Malek Salehi, A. 1998. "How I Found a Way to Make a Close Relationship with My Grandchildren." Paper presented at the workshop on "Elders and Immigrants in the Bay Area: Iranian Mothers Create Meaningful Lives and Share Wisdom" at the Santa Clara University Women's Day 1998 Program, Celebrating Women's Wisdom, April 29.

Malley-Morrison, K., N. Nolido and S. Chawla. 2006. "International Perspectives on Elder Abuse: Five Case Studies." *Educational Gerontology* 32(1):1–11.

Mangum, T. 1999. "Little Women: The Ageing Female Character in Nineteenth-Century British Children's Literature." In *Figuring Age: Women, Bodies, Generations*. K. Woodard, ed. Bloomington: Indiana University Press.

Manton, K. 2007. "Recent Declines in Chronic Disability in the Elderly U.S. Population: Risk Factors and Future Dynamics." *Annual Review of Public Health*. (Online publication ahead of printing.)

Manton, K., L. Corder and E. Stallard. 1997. "Chronic Disability Trends in Elderly United States Populations, 1982–1994." *Proceedings of the National Academy of Sciences of the United States of America* 18:94(6):2593–98.

Manton, K., V. Lamb and X. Gu. 2007. "Medicare Cost Effects of Recent Disability Trends in the Elderly: Future Implications." *Journal of Aging and Health* 19:359–82.

Manton, K., E. Stallard and L. Corder. 1995. "Changes in Morbidity and Chronic Disability in the U.S. Elderly Population: Evidence from the 1982, 1984 and 1989

National Long-Term Care Surveys." *Journal of Gerontology: Social Sciences* 50B(4):194–204.

Manu. 1886. *The Laws of Manu*. G. Buhler, trans. Sacred Books of the East, vol. 25. Oxford: Clarendon Press.

———. 1991. *The Laws of Manu*. W. Doniger with B. K. Smith, trans. New York: Penguin.

Manuel, R., ed. 1982. *Minority Aging: Sociological and Social Psychological Issues*. Westport, CT: Greenwood Press.

Maple Leaf Estates Homeowners. 1998. *Accents*, December. Port Charlotte, FL: Maple Leaf Golf and Country Club.

Marchi, R. 1982. *Storia Economica di Prato: Dall'Unita d'Italia ad Oggi*. Milan: Multa Paucis.

Margolies, L. 2004. *My Mother's Hip: Lessons from the World of Eldercare*. Philadelphia: Temple University Press.

Marin, M. 2001. "Successful Ageing—Dependent on Cultural and Social Capital? Reflections from Finland." *Indian Journal of Gerontology* 15(1/2):145–59.

Marini, H., L. Minutoli, F. Polito, A. Bitto, D. Altavilla, M. Atteritano et al. 2007. "Effects of the Phytoestrogen Genistein on Bone Metabolism in Osteopenic Postmenopausal Women: A Randomized Trial." *Annals of Internal Medicine* 19:146(12):839–47.

Markides, K., L. Rudkin, R. Angel and D. Espino. 1997. "Health Status of Hispanic Elderly." In *Racial and Ethnic Differences in the Health of Older Americans*. L. G. Martin and B. J. Soldo, eds. Washington, DC: National Academies Press.

Markides, K. and S. Vernon. 1984. "Aging, Sex-Role Orientation and Adjustment: A Three-Generations Study of Mexican Americans." *Journal of Gerontology* 39(5):586–91.

Marlowe, F. 2000. "The Patriarch Hypothesis: An Alternative Explanation of Menopause." *Human Nature* 11(1).

Marmor, T., R. Freeman and K. Okma. 2005. "Comparative Perspectives and Policy Learning in the World of Health Care." *Journal of Comparative Policy Analysis* 7(4):331–48.

Marshall, B. and S. Katz. 2002. "Forever Functional: Sexual Fitness and the Ageing Male Body." *Body and Society* 8:43–70.

Marshall, V. and R. Tucker. 1990. "Canadian Seasonal Migrants to the Sunbelt: Boon or Burden?" *Journal of Applied Gerontology* 9:420–32.

Martin, C. and P. Hoffman. 1983. "The Endocrinology of Pregnancy." In *Basic and Clinical Endocrinology*. F. Greenspan and P. Forsham, eds. Los Altos, CA: Lange Medical Publications.

Martin, M. A. 1987. "Widowhood as an Expectable Life Event." In *Aging in Canada*, 2nd ed. V. Marshall, ed. Markham, Canada: Fitzhenry and Whiteside.

Martin, P., G. da Rosa, I. Siegler, A. Davey, M. MacDonald and L. Poon. 2006. "Personality and Longevity: Findings from the Georgia Centenarian Study." *AGE* 28(4):343–52.

Martinez, I. 2001. "Aging in Exile: Mental Health, Family and the Meanings of History for Cuban Elders in South Florida." Ph.D. diss. Johns Hopkins University.

———. 2002. "The Elder in the Cuban-American Family: Making Sense of the Real and Ideal." *Journal of Comparative Family Studies* 33(3):359–75.

Martin-Matthews, A. and K. Davidson. 2006. "Widowhood and Widowerhood." In *The Encyclopedia of Gerontology*, 2nd ed. J. E. Birren, ed. Oxford: Elsevier.

Martin-Matthews, A. and J. Phillips. 2008. *Aging and Caring at the Intersection of Work and Home Life: Blurring the Boundaries*. New York: Psychology Press.

Martinson, M. and M. Minkler. 2006. "Civic Engagement and Older Adults: A Critical Perspective." *The Gerontologist* 46(3):318–24.

Mason, K. 1992. "Family Change and Support for the Elderly in Thailand: What Do We Know?" *Asia Pacific Population Journal* 7(3):13–32.

Masoro, E. 2005. "Overview of Caloric Restriction and Ageing." *Mechanisms of Ageing and Development* 126(9):913–22.

Masui, Y., Y. Gondo, H. Inagaki and N. Hirose. 2006. "Do Personality Characteristics Predict Longevity? Findings from the Tokyo Centenarian Study." *AGE* 28(4): 353–61.

Matayoshi, M. and J. Trafton. 2000. *Ancestors Worship: Okinawa's Indigenous Belief System*. Toronto: University of Toronto Press.

Matsuda, S. and M. Yamamoto. 2001. "Long-Term Care Insurance and Integrated Care for the Aged in Japan." *International Journal of Integrated Care* 1(3):e28.

Matsuzaki, T. 1992. "Longevity, Diet and Nutrition in Japan: Epidemiological Studies." *Nutrition Reviews* 50:355–59.

Matthews, J. and G. Turnbull. 2008. "Housing the Aging Baby Boomers: Implications for Local Policy." Andrew Young School of Policy Studies Research Paper No. 08-01. http://ssrn.com/abstract=1081305.

Mattison, J., M. Lane, G. Roth and D. Ingram. 2007. "Calorie Restriction in Rhesus Monkeys." *Experimental Gerontology* 38:1/2:35–46.

Maxwell, E. K. 1986. "Fading Out: Resource Control and Cross-Cultural Patterns of Deference." *Journal of Cross-Cultural Gerontology* 1:73–89.

Maxwell, R. 1970. "The Changing Status of Elders in a Polynesian Society." *Aging and Human Development* 1(2):137–46.

Maxwell, R., P. Silverman and E. K. Maxwell. 1982. "The Motive for Gerontocide." *Studies in Third World Societies* 22:67–84.

May, M. 1963. *The Ecology of Malnutrition in Five Countries of Eastern and Central Europe*. New York: Hafner Publishing.

May, M. and L. Donna. 1972. *The Ecology of Malnutrition in Mexico and Central America*. New York: Hafner Publishing.

Mazess, R. and S. Forman. 1979. "Longevity and Age Exaggeration in Vilcabamba, Ecuador." *Journal of Gerontology* 34:94–98.

MCAMA. 2007. *Plan Operativo*. Mesa de Concertacion del Adulto Mayor de Arequipa (MCAMA). Arequipa, Peru: Inter-Institucional de la Mesa de Concertacion del Adulto Mayor de Arequipa Periodo 2006–2007.

McArdle, J. and C. Yeracaris. 1981. "Respect for the Elderly in Preindustrial Societies as Related to Their Activity." *Behavior Science Research* 16(3/4):307–39.

McCabe, M. 1999. "Health Care of American Indian and Alaska Native Elders." In *Primary Care of Native American Patients: Diagnosis, Therapy and Epidemiology*. J. Galloway, B. Goldberg and J. Alpert, eds. Newton, MA: Butterworth-Heinemann.

McConatha, J. T., P. Stoller and F. Oboudiat. 2001. "Reflections of Older Iranian Women: Adapting to Life in the United States." *Journal of Aging Studies* 15(4): 369–81.

McCurry, J. 2006. "Building Scams Soar in Japan." *The Guardian*, February 10.

McFadden, S. 2008. "Mindfulness, Vulnerability and Love: Spiritual Lessons from Frail Elders, Earnest Young Pilgrims and Middle Aged Rockers." *Journal of Aging Studies* 22(2):132–39.

McGarvey, C., D. Petsod and T. Wang. 2006. *Investing in Our Communities: Strategies for Immigrant Integration*. Sebastopol, CA: Grantmakers Concerned with Immigrants and Refugees.

McGue, M., J. W. Vaupel, N. Holm and B. Harvald. 1993. "Longevity Is Moderately Heritable in a Sample of Danish Twins Born 1870–1880." *Journal of Gerontology* 48(6):B237–44.

McHugh, K. 2000. "The 'Ageless Self'? Emplacement of Identities in Sun Belt Retirement Communities." *Journal of Aging Studies* 14:103–15.

———. 2003. "Three Faces of Ageism: Society, Image and Place." *Ageing and Society* 23:165–85.

McHugh, K. and R. Mings. 1994. "Seasonal Migration and Health Care." *Journal of Aging and Health* 6:111–32.

McKim, E. and W. Randall. 2007. "From Psychology to Poetics: Aging as a Literary Process." *Journal of Aging, Humanities and the Arts* 1(3/4):147–58.

McKinsey Global Institute. 2004. "Italy: Aging but Saving." http://www.mckinsey.com/mgi/publications/demographics/italy.asp.

———. 2007. "Accounting for the Cost of Health Care in the United States." http://www.mckinsey.com/mgi/rp/healthcare/accounting_cost_healthcare.asp.

McLachlan, S. 1982. "Savage Island or Savage History? An Interpretation of Early European Contact with Niue." *Pacific Studies* 6:26–51.

McLean, A. 2007a. "Dementia Care as a Moral Enterprise: A Call for a Return to the Sanctity of Lived Time." *Alzheimer's Care Today* (formerly *Alzheimer's Care Quarterly*) 8(4):360–72.

———. 2007b. *The Person in Dementia: A Study of Nursing Home Care in the U.S.* Peterborough, Canada: Broadview Press.

———. 2007c. "The Therapeutic Landscape of Dementia Care: Contours of Intersubjective Spaces for Sustaining the Person." In *Therapeutic Landscapes*. A. Williams, ed. Hampshire, UK: Ashgate Publishing.

McNatty, K., R. Sawers and A. McNeilly. 1974. "A Possible Role for Prolactin in Control of Steroid Secretion by the Human Graafian Follicle." *Nature* 250(5468): 653–55.

McNeilly, A. 1979. "Effects of Lactation on Fertility." *British Medical Bulletin* 35:151–54.

Mead, M. 1951. "Cultural Contexts of Aging." In *No Time to Grow Old*, New York State Legislative Committee on Problems of Aging, Legislative Document No. 12.

———. 1967. "Ethnological Aspects of Aging." *Psychosomatics* 8(4):33–37.

Medawar, P. B. 1952. *An Unsolved Problem in Biology*. London: Lewis.

Mehta, K. 1997. "Cultural Scripts and the Social Integration of Older People." *Ageing and Society* 17:253–75.

———. 2005. *Women in Ageing Societies across Asia*, 2nd ed. Singapore: Marshall Cavendish.

Meigs, A. 1984. *Food, Sex and Pollution*. New Brunswick, NJ: Rutgers University Press.

Melzer, D., A., Hurst and T. Frayling. 2007. "Genetic Variation and Human Aging: Progress and Prospects." *Journals of Gerontology. Series A, Biological Sciences and Medical Sciences* 62(3):301–7.

Mendes de Leon, C. F., T. E. Seeman, D. I. Baker, E. D. Richardson and M. E. Tinetti. 1996. "Self-Efficacy, Physical Decline and Change in Functioning in Community-Living

Elders: A Prospective Study." *Journal of Gerontology and Social Science* 51B: S183–90.

Meneilly, G. and D. Tessier. 2001. "Diabetes in Elderly Adults." *The Journals of Gerontology. Series A: Biological Sciences* 56:M5–13.

Merimee, T. and S. Fineberge. 1974. "Growth Hormone Secretion in Starvation—a Reassessment." *Journal of Clinical Endocrinology and Metabolism* 39:385–86.

Mermin, G. B. T., R. W. Johnson and D. P. Murphy. 2007. "Why Do Boomers Plan to Work Longer?" *Journal of Gerontology: Social Sciences* 62B:S286–95.

Merrill Lynch New Retirement Study. 2006. http://askmerrill.ml.com/ask_merrill_2006/5_total_merrill/retirement_illustrator/findings/findings_working.asp.

Mesa de Concertacion del Adulto Mayor de Arequipa (MCAMA). 2007. *Plan Operativo Inter-Institucional de la Mesa de Concertacion del Adulto Mayor de Arequipa Periodo, 2006–2007*. Arequipa, Peru.

MetLife. 1999. *The MetLife Juggling Act Study: Balancing Caregiving with Work and the Costs*. http://www.caregiving.org/data/jugglingstudy.pdf.

MetLife Mature Market Institute. 2006. "Survey of Nursing Homes and Home Care Costs." Westport, CT: MetLife Mature Market Institute.

Metropolitan Chicago Information Center. 2007. http://info.mcfol.org/web/datainfo/mapreports/custommaps.asp (accessed December 20, 2007).

Michaudon, H. 2001, February. Le cadre de vie des plus de soixante ans. *INSEE Première* No. 760.

Miedema, B. and J. de Jong. 2005. "Support for Very Old People in Sweden and Canada: The Pitfalls of Cross-Cultural Studies—Same Words, Different Concepts?" *Health and Social Care in the Community* 13(3):231–38.

Miles, M. B. and A. M. Huberman. 1994. *Qualitative Data Analysis*, 2nd ed. Thousand Oaks, CA: Sage.

Millard, A. 1978. "Corn, Cash and Population Genetics: Family Demography in Rural Mexico." Ph.D. diss. University of Texas–Austin.

Miller, E. 2007. "'Living Independently Is Good': Residence Patterns in Rural North China Reconsidered." *Journal of Long-Term Home Health Care* 25(1):26–32.

Miller, F., T. Quill, H. Brody, J. Fletcher, L. Gostin and D. Meier. 1994. "Regulating Physician-Assisted Death." *New England Journal of Medicine* 331:119–23.

Miller-Martinez, D. and S. P. Wallace. 2006. "Structural Contexts and Life Course Processes in the Social Networks of Older Mexican Immigrants in the United States." *The Art of Ageing in a Global Context*. S. Carmel, C. Morse and F. Torres-Gil, eds. New York: Baywood Press.

Mills, T. L., Z. Gomez-Smith and J. M. DeLeon. 2005. "Skipped Generation Families: Sources of Psychological Distress among Grandmothers of Grandchildren Who Live in Homes Where Neither Parent Is Present." *Marriage and Family Review* 37:191–212.

Mindek, D. 1994. "'*No Nos Sobra, Pero Gracias a Dios, Tampoco Nos Falta,*' *Crecimiento Demographico y Modernizacion en San Jeronimo Amanalco*." Master's thesis. Iberoamericana University.

Ministerio de la Mujer y Desarrollo Social (MIMDES). 2000. *Lineamientos de Politica Para Las Personas Adultas Mayores*. Lima, Peru: Gerencia de Desarrollo Humano.

———. 2002a. *Plan Nacional Para Las Personas Adultas Mayores, 2002–2006*. Lima, Peru: Direccion de Personas Adultas Mayores.

———. 2002b. *Situacion Actual de las Personas Adultas Mayores*. Lima, Peru: Direccion de Personas Adultas Mayores.

———. 2006. *Plan Nacional Para las Personas Adultas Mayores, 2006–2010.* Lima, Peru: Direccion de Personas Adultas Mayores.

———. 2007. *Plan Para La Elaboracion de los Lineamientos de Politica Para las Personas Mayores Rurales del Peru: Desarrollo Rural Para Todas las Edades.* Lima, Peru: Direccion de Personas Adultas Mayores.

Minkler, M. and C. L. Estes, eds. 1999. *Critical Gerontology: Perspectives from Political and Moral Economy.* Amityville, NY: Baywood Press.

Minkler, M. and E. Fuller-Thomson. 2005. "African American Grandparents Raising Grandchildren: A National Study Using the Census 2000 American Community Survey." *Journal of Gerontology: Social Sciences* 60:S82–S92.

Minkler, M. and M. Holstein. 2008. "From Civil Rights to … Civic Engagement? Concerns of Two Older Critical Gerontologists about a 'New Social Movement' and What it Portends." *Journal of Aging Studies* 22(2):196–204.

Minkler, M. and K. Roe. 1993. *Grandmothers as Caregivers: Raising Children of the Crack Cocaine Epidemic.* Newbury Park: Sage.

Minkler, M., K. Roe and M. Price. 1992. "The Physical and Emotional Health of Grandmothers Raising Grandchildren in the Crack Cocaine Epidemic." *The Gerontologist* 32:752–61.

Mintz, S. 1998. "The Localization of Anthropological Practice: From Area Studies to Transnationalism." *Critical Anthropology* 18:117–33.

Mintzer, J. E., M. P. Rubert, D. Loewenstein, E. Gamez, A. Millor, R. Quinteros et al. 1992. "Daughters Caregiving for Hispanic and Non-Hispanic Alzheimer Patients: Does Ethnicity Make a Difference?" *Community Mental Health Journal* 28(4):293–303.

Mirowsky, J. and C. E. Ross. 2005. "Education, Cumulative Advantage and Health." *Aging International* 30(1):27–62.

Mitchell, G., J. Salmon, L. Polivka and H. Soberon-Ferrer. 2006. "The Relative Benefits and Cost of Medicaid Home- and Community-Based Services in Florida." *The Gerontologist* 46(4):483–94.

Mitrani, V. B., J. E. Lewis, D. J. Feaster, S. J. Czaja, C. Eisdorfer, R. Schulz et al. 2006. "The Role of Family Functioning in the Stress Process of Dementia Caregivers: A Structural Family Framework." *The Gerontologist* 46(1):97–105.

Moaveni, A. 2005. *Lipstick Jihad.* New York: Perseus Books Group.

Moen, P. 2001. "The Gendered Life Course." In *Handbook of Aging and the Social Sciences,* 5th ed. R. H. Binstock and L. K. George, eds. San Diego: Academic Press.

———. 2003. "Midcourse: Navigating Retirement and a New Life Stage." In *Handbook of the Life Course.* J. T. Mortimer and M. J. Shanahan, eds. New York: Kluwer Academic/Plenum.

———. 2006. "A New Life Stage: The Third Age." In *Handbook of Aging and the Social Sciences,* 6th ed. R. H. Binstock and L. K. George, eds. Boston: Academic Press.

Mokdad, A., J. Marks, D. Stroup and J. Gerberding. 2004. "Actual Causes of Death in the United States, 2000." *Journal of the American Medical Association* 291:1238–45.

———. 2005. "Correction: Actual Causes of Death in the United States, 2000." *Journal of the American Medical Association* 293:293–94.

Moody, H. 1988. *Abundance of Life: Human Development Policies for an Aging Society.* New York: Columbia University Press.

———. 1990. "The Islamic Vision of Aging and Death." *Generations, Special Issue on Spirituality and Aging*. T. Cole, ed. 14(4):15–18.

———. 2001. "Productive Aging and the Ideology of Old Age." In *Perspectives on Productive Aging*. N. Morrow-Howell, ed. Baltimore: Johns Hopkins University Press.

———. 2002. "Conscious Aging: The Future of Religion in Later Life." In *Handbook of Religion, Spirituality and Aging*, 2nd ed. M. Kimble and S. McFadden, eds. Minneapolis: Fortress Press.

Moody, H. and D. Carroll. 1998. *The Five Stages of the Soul: Charting the Spiritual Passages that Shape Our Lives*. New York: Anchor.

Mookherjee, H. N. 1998. "Perceptions of Well-Being among the Older Metropolitan and Nonmetropolitan Populations in the United States." *Journal of Social Psychology* 138(1):72–82.

Mooradian, J., S. Cross and G. Stutzky. 2007. "Across Generations: Culture, History and Policy in the Social Ecology of American Indian Grandparents Parenting Their Grandchildren." *Journal of Family Social Work* 10(4):81–101.

Moore, A. J. and D. Stratton. 2003. *Resilient Widowers: Older Men Adjusting to a New Life*. Amherst, NY: Prometheus Books.

Moore, T. J. 1993. *Lifespan*. New York: Simon and Schuster.

Moriarty, J. and J. Butt. 2004. "Inequalities in Quality of Life among Older People from Different Ethnic Groups." *Ageing and Society* 24:729–53.

Moriguchi, Y. 1999. "Japanese Centenarians Living Outside Japan." In *Japanese Centenarians*. H. Tauchi, ed. Aichi: Institute for Medical Science of Aging. 185–94.

Morrow-Howell, N. 2000. *Productive Engagement of Older Adults: Effects on Well-Being*. St. Louis, MO: Center for Social Development, Washington University.

Morrow-Howell, N. and M. Freedman. 2006–2007. Special issue, "Civic Engagement in Later Life." *Generations* 30(4).

Morrow-Howell, N., J. Hinterlong and M. Sherraden, eds. 2001. *Productive Aging: Concepts and Challenges*. Baltimore: Johns Hopkins University Press.

Mortimer, J. T. and M. J. Shanahan, eds. 2003. *Handbook of the Life Course*. New York: Kluwer Academic/Plenum.

Motel-Klingebiel, A. and S. Arber. 2006. "Population Aging, Genders and Generations." *International Journal of Ageing and Later Life* 1(2):7–9.

Mui, A. 1996. "Correlates of Psychological Distress among Mexican, Cuban and Puerto Rican Elders Living in the U.S.A." *Journal of Cross-Cultural Gerontology* 11(2):131–47.

———. 2002. "Stress, Coping and Depression among Elderly Korean Immigrants." *Journal of Human Behavior in the Social Environment* 3(3/4:281–99.

Mui, A. and D. Burnette. 1994. "Long-Term Care Service Use by Frail Elders: Is Ethnicity a Factor?" *The Gerontologist* 34:2:190–98.

Mujahid, G. 2006. "Population Ageing in East and South-East Asia: Current Situation and Emerging Challenges." Papers in Population Ageing. No.1. United Nations Population Fund Bangkok, Thailand. http://cst.bangkok.unfpa.org/docs/bkageing_asia.pdf.

Mukamel, D., D. Peterson, H. Temkin-Greener, R. Delavan, D. Gross, S. Kunitz et al. 2007. "Program Characteristics and Enrollees' Outcomes in the Program of All-Inclusive Care for the Elderly (PACE)." *The Milbank Quarterly* 85(3): 499–531.

Mull, D. S., N. Nguyen and J. D. Mull. 2001. "Vietnamese Diabetic Patients and Their Physicians: What Ethnography Can Teach Us." *Western Journal of Medicine* 175:307–11.

Muller, C., M. Honig, O. Volkov, A. Oprisiu and K. Knapp. 2002. *The Economic Status of Older Women: An International Report Prepared for the United Nations Second World Assembly on Ageing.* New York: International Longevity Center–USA.

Mullins, L. and R. Tucker, R. 1988. *Snowbirds in the Sun Belt: Older Canadians in Florida.* Tampa, FL: International Exchange Center on Gerontology, University of South Florida.

Munford, L. 1956. *Transformations of Man.* New York: Harper & Row.

Murdock, G. P. 1967. "Ethnographic Atlas: A Summary." *Ethnology* 6(2).

Murray, A. W. 1863. *Missions in Western Polynesia.* London: J. Snow.

Musil, C., J. Fitzpatrick, S. Eagan, J. Okonsky, M. Walusimbi and J. Mutabaazi et al. 2003. "Grandmothers Raisinq Grandchildren in Uganda." Paper presented at the Annual Scientific Meeting of the Gerontological Society of America, November, San Diego, California.

Mutongi, K. 2007. *Worries of the Heart: Widows, Family and Community in Kenya.* Chicago: University of Chicago Press.

Myerhoff, B. 1978. *Number Our Days: Culture and Community among Elderly Jews in an American Ghetto.* New York: Simon and Schuster.

———. 1986. "'Life Not Death in Venice': Its Second Life." In *The Anthropology of Experience.* V. Turner and E. Bruner, eds. Urbana: University of Illinois Press.

Myerhoff, B. and A. Simic, eds. 1978. *Life's Career-Aging: Cultural Variations on Growing Old.* Beverly Hills, CA: Sage.

Nadel, S. F. 1952. "Witchcraft in Four African Societies." *American Anthropologist* 54:18–29.

Nagata, C., N. Takatsuka, N. Shimizu and H. Shimizu. 2004. "Sodium Intake and Risk of Death from Stroke in Japanese Men and Women." *Stroke* 35:1543–47.

Naka, K., D. Willcox and H. Todoriki. 1998. "Suicide in Okinawa: A Consideration of Socio-Cultural Factors." *Ryukyu Medical Journal* 18:76–92.

Nakajoh, K., T. Satoh-Nakagawa, H. Arai, M. Yanai, M. Yamaya and H. Sasaki. 1999. "Longevity May Decrease Medical Costs." *Journal of the American Geriatrics Society* 47(9):1161–62.

Nakane, C. 1967. *Kinship and Economic Organization in Rural Japan.* London: Athlone Press.

Nara, M. 2005. *Journal of Japan Society of Ningen Dock* 19:1–2.

Naroll, R., G. Michik and F. Naroll. 1976. *Worldwide Theory Testing.* New Haven, CT: Human Relations Area Files Press.

Narrow, W. E., D. S. Rae, E. K. Moscicki, B. Z. Locke and D. A. Regier. 1990. "Depression among Cuban Americans: The Hispanic Health and Nutrition Examination Survey." *Social Psychiatry and Psychiatric Epidemiology* 25(5):260–68.

Nash, J. 1989. *From Tank Town to High Tech.* Albany: State University of New York Press.

Nason, J. D. 1981. "Respected Elder or Old Person: Aging in a Micronesian Community." In *Other Ways of Growing Old.* P. T. Amoss and S. Harrell, eds. Stanford, CA: Stanford University Press.

National Alliance for Caregiving and AARP. 2004. *Caregiving in the U.S.* http://www.caregiving.org/data/04finalreport.pdf.

National Association of Area Agencies on Aging. 2005. *The Maturing of America: Getting Communities on Track for an Aging Population.* In partnership with the International City/County Management Association, National Association of Counties, National League of Cities and Partners for Livable Communities. Washington, DC: National Association of Area Agencies on Aging.

———. 2007. *Blueprint for Action: Developing a Livable Community for All Ages.* http://www.aginginplaceinitiative.org/index.php?option=com_content&task= view&id=18&Itemid=47.

National Center for Education Statistics. 2002. *Findings from the Condition of Education 2002: Nontraditional Undergraduates.* http://nces.ed.gov/pubs2002/ 2002012.pdf (accessed August 28, 2005).

National Citizen's Coalition of Nursing Home Reform (NCCNHR). 2007. *Faces of Neglect: Behind the Closed Doors of Nursing Homes.* Washington, DC: NCCNHR.

National Household Travel Survey (NHTS). 2001. Washington, DC: U.S. Department of Transportation.

National Institute on Aging. 2007. "Why Population Aging Matters: A Global Perspective." Washington, DC: National Institute on Aging. http://www.state. gov/g/oes/rls/or/81537.htm.

Navarro, M. 1997. "As Older Cuban Exiles Die, Young Pragmatists Emerge," *New York Times*, December 6.

Nazroo, J., S. James, M. Karlsen and M. Torres. 2007. "The Black Diaspora and Health Inequalities in the U.S. and England: Does Where You Go and How You Get There Make a Difference? *Sociology of Health and Illness* 29(6):811–30.

Neilson, B. 2003. "Globalization and the Biopolitics of Aging." *The New Centennial Review* 3(2):161–86.

Neville, C. 1983. "Regulation of Mammary Development and Lactation." In *Lactation: Physiology, Nutrition and Breast-Feeding.* M. Neville and M. Neifert, eds. New York: Plenum Press.

Newcomer, R., J. Lawton and T. Byerts, eds. 1986. *Housing an Aging Society: Issues, Alternatives and Policy.* New York: Van Nostrand Reinhold.

Newman, K. 2003. *A Different Shade of Gray: Midlife and Beyond in the Inner City.* New York: New Press.

Newman, S. A. 1991. "Euthanasia: Orchestrating the Last Syllable of ... Time." *University of Pittsburgh Law Review* 53:153–91.

Ney, S. 2005. "Active Aging Policy in Europe: Between Path Dependency and Path Departure." *Ageing International* 30(4):325–42.

NHES. 2004. "National Health Care Expenditures Projections Tables: Table 10." Washington, DC: Centers for Medicare and Medicaid Services.

Nhongo, T. M. 2004. "The Changing Role of Older People in African Households and the Impact of Ageing on African Family Structures." Paper presented at the Ageing in Africa Conference, August, Johannesburg.

Niehof, A. and F. Lubis, eds. 2003. *Two Is Enough: Family Planning in Indonesia under the New Order (1968–1998).* Leiden, The Netherlands: KITLV Press.

Nikkei Weekly. 2006. "Japan's Population Projected to Dwindle under 90 Million in 2055." *Nihon Keizai Shimbun*, December 25.

———. 2007. "Partner Robots Good at Health Care." *Nikkei Weekly*, May 7.

Niue Government. 1982. *Niue: A History of the Island.* Alofi, Niue/Suva, Fiji: Niue Government/Institute for Pacific Studies, University of the South Pacific.

————. 1985. *Report of a 1984 Mini-Census of Population*. Alofi, Niue: Department of Economic Development.

————. 1988. *Census of Population and Dwellings, 1986*. Alofi, Niue: Statistics Unit, Administrative Department.

————. 2006. "Niue Overseas Community Continues to Offer Cyclone Relief Aid." http://www.niuegov.com/press%20release%201.htm.

Nolan, M., T. Ryan, P. Enderby and D. Reid. 2002. "Towards a More Inclusive Vision of Dementia Care Practice and Research." *Dementia* 1(2):193–211.

Nordin, C. 1982. "Bone Loss at the Menopause." *Menopause Update* 1(1):5–9.

Norwood, F. 2007. "Nothing More to Do: Euthanasia, General Practice and End-of-Life Discourse in the Netherlands." *Medical Anthropology* 26(2):139–74.

Nusberg, C. and J. Sokolovsky, eds. 1994. *The International Directory of Research and Researchers in Comparative Gerontology*. Washington, DC: AARP.

Nyambedha, E. O., S. Wandibba and J. Aagaard-Hansen. 2003. "'Retirement Lost'— the New Role of the Elderly as Caretakers for Orphans in Western Kenya." *Journal of Cross-Cultural Gerontology* 18:33–52.

Oakley, R. 1992. *Old Age and Caregiving among the !Kung San*. Master's research paper. University of Toronto.

Oberlink, M. Forthcoming. *Barriers to Developing Livable Communities*. Washington, DC: AARP.

Obermeyer, C. and L. Sievert. 2007. "Cross-Cultural Comparisons: Midlife, Aging and Menopause." *Menopause* 14(4):663–67.

O'Brien, N. 2003. *Emergency Preparedness for Older Persons* (issue brief). New York: International Longevity Center–USA.

Oburu, P. and K. Palmerus. 2006. "Stress-Related Factors among Primary and Part-time Caregiving Grandmothers of Kenyan Grandchildren." In *Custodial Grandparenting: Individual, Cultural and Ethnic Diversity*. B. Hayslip and J. Hicks-Patrick, eds. New York: Springer.

OECD. 2005. "The OECD Health Project: Long-Term Care for Older People." http://www.oecd.org (accessed on December 17, 2007).

————. 2006. "Projecting OECD Health and Long-Term Care Expenditures: What Are the Main Drivers?" Economics Department Working Papers No. 477. http://www.oecd.org/eco (accessed on December 17, 2007).

Oeppen, J. and J. W. Vaupel. 2002. "Broken Limits to Life Expectancy." *Science* 296:1029–31.

Ogawa, N. and R. D. Retherford. 1997. "Shifting Costs of Caring for the Elderly Back to Families in Japan: Will it Work?" *Population and Development Review* 23(1): 59–94.

Ogbu, J. U. 1973. "Seasonal Hunger in Tropical Africa as a Cultural Phenomenon." *Africa* 43:317–32.

Ogg, J. and S. Renaut. 2006. "The Support of Parents in Old Age by Those Born in 1945–1954: A European Perspective." *Ageing and Society* 26:723–43.

Okamoto, E. 2006. "Creativity under Uniformity: Implementation of Long-Term Care Insurance in Tokyo," In *Growing Older in World Cities: New York, London, Paris and Tokyo*. V. Rodwin and M. Gusmano, eds. Nashville, TN: Vanderbilt University Press.

Okinawa Prefecture Department of Health and Welfare. 1995. *Okinawa-ken ni okeru seijinbyou sibou no ekigakuchousa* [Epidemiological research on age associated diseases in Okinawa Prefecture]. Naha, Okinawa: Okinawa Prefecture Department of Health and Welfare.

Okonjo, K. 1976. "The Dual-Sex Political System in Operation: Igbo Women and Community Politics in Midwestern Nigeria." In *Women in Africa: Studies in Social and Economic Change*. N. J. Hafkin and E. G. Bay, eds. Stanford, CA: Stanford University Press.

Oldenburg, R. 1991. *The Great Good Place*. New York: Paragon House.

Olshansky, S., D. Passaro, R. Hershow, J. Layden, B. Carnes, J. Brody et al. 2005. "A Potential Decline in Life Expectancy in the United States in the 21st Century." *New England Journal of Medicine* 352:1138–45.

Olson, M. C. 1999. "'The Heart Still Beats, but the Brain Doesn't Answer': Perception and Experience of Old-Age Dementia in the Milwaukee Hmong Community." *Theoretical Medicine and Bioethics* 20(1):85–95.

Omidian, P. 1996. *Aging and Family in an Afghan Refugee Community: Transitions and Transformations*. New York: Garland.

Omidian, P. and J. Lipson. 1992. "Elderly Afghan Refugees: Traditions and Transitions in Northern California." In *Selected Papers on Refugee Issues*. P. DeVoe, ed. Washington, DC: AAA.

Omran, A. R. 1971. "The Epidemiologic Transition: A Theory of the Epidemiology of Population Change." *Milbank Memorial Fund Quarterly* 49(4):509–38.

O'Rand, A. M. 2003. "The Future of the Life Course: Late Modernity and Life Course Risk." In *Handbook of the Life Course*. J. T. Mortimer and M. J. Shanahan, eds. New York: Kluwer Academic/Plenum.

———. 2006. "Stratification and the Life Course." In *Handbook of Aging and the Social Sciences*, 6th ed. R. H. Binstock and L. K. George, eds. Boston: Academic Press.

O'Rand, A. M. and R. T. Campbell. 1999. "On Reestablishing the Phenomenon and Specifying Ignorance: Theory Development and Research Design in Aging." In *Handbook of Theories of Aging*. V. Bengtson and K. W. Schaie, eds. New York: Springer.

Osako, M. and Y. Watanabe. 2008. "'Kaigo Yobou'—Preventive Care Measures as a Cornerstone of Japanese Social Insurance." http://www.aarpinternational.org/usr_attach/TheJournal_summer08.pdf.

Ossip-Klein, D., B. M. Rothenberg and E. M. Andresen. 1997. "Screening for Depression." In *Assessing the Health Status of Older Adults*. E. Andresen, B. Rothenberg and J. G. Zimmer, eds. New York: Springer.

Ottenberg, S. 1971. *Leadership and Authority in an African Society: The Afikpo Village Group*. Seattle: University of Washington Press.

Palloni, A., Peláez, M. and Wong, R. 2006. "Introduction: Aging among Latin American and Caribbean Populations." *Journal of Aging and Health* 18(2): 149–56.

Palmore, E. 1984. "Longevity in Abkhazia: A Reevaluation." *The Gerontologist* 24: 95–96.

Palmore, E. and D. Maeda. 1975. *The Honorable Elders Revisited: A Revised Cross-Cultural Analysis of Aging in Japan*. Durham, NC: Duke University Press.

Pang, K. 2000. *Virtuous Transcendence: Holistic Self-Cultivation and Self-Healing in Elderly Korean Immigrants*. Binghamton, NY: Haworth Press.

Pang, L. H., A. de Brauw and S. Rozelle. 2004. "Working till You Drop: The Elderly of Rural China." *China Journal* 52:73–94.

Park, H. H. and J. S. Greenberg. 2007. "Parenting Grandchildren." In *Handbook of Ger-ontology: Evidence-Based Approaches to Theory, Practice and Policy*. J. A. Blackburn and C. N. Dulmus, eds. New York: John Wiley.

Parket, M., L. Roff, D. Klemmack, H. Koenig, P. Baker and R. Allman. 2003. "Religiosity and Mental Health in Southern, Community-Dwelling Older Adults." *Aging and Mental Health* 7(5):390–97.

Partida-Bush, V. 2007. "Demographic Transition, Demographic Donus and Ageing in Mexico." In *Proceedings of the United Nations Expert Group Meeting on Social and Economic Implications of Changing Population Age Structures. Mexico City, August 31–September 2, 2005*. New York: United Nations Population Division. http://www.un.org/esa/population/meetings/Proceedings_EGM_Mex_2005/partida.pdf (accessed on November 4, 2007).

Patillo, M. 2007. *Black on the Block: The Politics of Race and Class in the City*. Chicago: University of Chicago Press.

Patillo-McCoy, M. 1999. *Black Picket Fences: Privilege and Period among the Black Middle Class*. Chicago: University of Chicago Press.

Pearlin, L. et al. 1996. "Caregiving and Its Social Support." In *Handbook of Aging and the Social Sciences*, 4th ed. R. H. Binstock and L. K. George, eds. San Diego: Academic Press.

Pearlin, L. I., J. T. Mullan, S. J. Semple and M. M. Skaff. 1990. "Caregiving and the Stress Process: An Overview of Concepts and Their Measures." *The Gerontologist* 30:583–94.

Pebley, A. R. and L. L. Rudkin. 1999. "Grandparents Raising Grandchildren: What Do We Know?" *Journal of Family Issues* 20:218–42.

Peccei, J. S. 2001. "Menopause: Adaptation or Epiphenomenon?" *Evolutionary Anthropology* 10:43–57.

Perez, L. 1986. "Immigrant Economic Adjustment and Family Organization: The Cuban Success Story Reexamined." *International Migration Review* 20(1):4–20.

———. 1992. "Cuban Miami." In *Miami Now! Immigration, Ethnicity and Social Change*. G. J. Grenier and A. Stepick III, eds. Miami: University Press of Florida.

———. 1994. "The Household Structure of Second-Generation Children: An Exploratory Study of Extended Family Arrangements." *International Migration Review* 28(4):736–47.

———. 1999. "The End of Exile? A New Era in U.S. Immigration Policy Toward Cuba." In *Trends in International Migration and Immigration Policy in the Americas*. M. Castro, ed. Miami: University of Miami North-South Center Press.

Perez-Firmat, G. 1994. *Life on the Hypen: The Cuban-American Way*. Austin: University of Texas Press.

Peristiany, J. G., Ed. 1964. *Honour and Shame: The Values of Mediterranean Society*. Chicago: University of Chicago Press.

Perkinson, P. 2008. "Negotiating Disciplines: Developing a Dementia Exercise Program." *Practicing Anthropology* 30(3):10–14.

Perls, T. 2006. "The Different Paths to 100." *Journal of the American College of Nutrition* 83(2):484S–7S.

Perls, T., K. Bochen, M. Freeman, L. Alpert and M. Silver. 1999. "Validity of Reported Age and Centenarian Prevalence in New England." *Age and Ageing* 28:183–97.

Perls, T., L. Kunkel and A. Puca. 2002. "The Genetics of Exceptional Human Longevity." *Journal of the American Geriatric Society* 50:359–68.

Perls, T. and D. Terry. 2007. "Exceptional Longevity." In *Global Health and Global Aging*. M. Robinson, W. Novelli, C. Pearson and L. Norris, eds. San Francisco: Jossey-Bass.

Peterborough Evening Telegraph. 2006. "Age Concern: The Elderly Often Feel Cut Off from the World." *Peterborough Evening Telegraph*, January 9.

Petrie, D. 1988. *Cocoon: The Return.* Hollywood, CA: Twentieth Century Fox.

Pfeifferling, J. H. 1981. "A Cultural Prescription for Medicocentrism. In *The Relevance of Social Science for Medicine.* L. Eisenberg and A. Kleinman, eds. Boston: Reidel.

Phelan, E. and E. Larson. 2002. "Successful Aging—Where Next?" *Journal of the American Geriatrics Society* 50(7):1306–8.

Phillips, D. R. and A. C. M. Chan, eds. 2002. *Ageing and Long-Term Care. National Policies in the Asia-Pacific.* Singapore: Institute of Southeast Asian Studies and International Development Research Centre.

Phillipson, C. 2004. "Urbanisation and Ageing: Toward a New Environmental Gerontology." *Ageing and Society* 24:964.

———. 2007. "The 'Elected' and the 'Excluded': Sociological Perspectives on the Experience of Place and Community in Old Age." *Ageing and Society* 27(3): 321–42.

Phillipson, C., T. Scharf and A. Smith. 2005. "Ageing in a Difficult Place: Assessing the Impact of Urban Deprivation on Older People." In *New Dynamics in Old Age: Individual, Environmental and Societal Perspectives.* H.-W. Wahl, C. Tesch-Römer and A. Hoff, eds. Amityville, NY: Baywood Press.

Piedmont-Palladino, S. 2008. "Green Communities: Working Together to Build a Sustainable Future." *The Journal* (Summer): 76–79.

Pillemer, K. and J. Suitor. 1992. "Violence and Violent Feelings: What Causes Them among Family Caregivers?" *Journal of Gerontology* 47(4):S165–72.

Pine, P. and V. Pine. 2002. "Naturally Occurring Retirement Community-Supportive Service Program: An Example of Devolution." *Journal of Aging and Social Policy* 14:181–92.

Pink, S. 2001. *Doing Visual Ethnography: Images, Media and Representation in Research.* London: Sage.

Pinquart, M. and S. Sorensen. 2005. "Ethnic Differences in Stressors, Resources and Psychological Outcomes of Family Caregiving: A Meta-analysis. *The Gerontologist* 45:99–106.

Plakans, A. 1989. "Stepping Down in Former Times: A Comparative Assessment of Retirement in Traditional Europe." In *Age Structuring in Comparative Perspective.* D. Kertzer and K. W. Schaie, eds. Hillsdale, NJ: Lawrence Erlbaum.

Plassman, B., K. Langa, G. Fisher, S. Heeringa, D. Weir and M. Ofstedal. 2007. "Prevalence of Dementia in the United States: The Aging, Demographics and Memory Study." *Neuroepidemiology* 29:125–32.

Plath, D. 1964. "Where the Family of God Is the Family: The Role of the Dead in Japanese Households." *American Anthropologist* 66:300–317.

———. 1980. *Long Engagements: Maturity in Modern Japan.* Stanford, CA: Stanford University Press.

———. 1987. "Ecstasy Years: Old Age in Japan." In *Growing Old in Different Societies: Cross-Cultural Perspectives.* J. Sokolovsky, ed. Acton, MA: Copley.

———. 1988. "The Age of Silver: Aging in Modern Japan." *The World and I* (March):505–13.

Platz, M. 2000. *Danskere med Livserfaring–Portraetteret i Tal.* Copenhagen: Socialforskningsinstituttet.

Poindexter, C. C. 2003. "Mama Jaja (Mother-Granny): The Stress and Strength of Ugandan Grandmothers Caring for AIDS Orphans." Paper presented at the Annual Scientific Meeting of the Gerontological Society of America, November, San Diego.

Policy Research Initiative, Canada. 2004. *Views on Life-Course Flexibility and Canada's Aging Population.* https://recherchepolitique.gc.ca/doclib/Life-Course_E.pdf.

Politzer, R. et al. 1991. "Primary Care Physician Supply and the Medically Underserved." *Journal of the American Medical Association* 266:104–9.

Polivka, L. 2000. "Postmodern Aging and the Loss of Meaning." *Journal of Aging and Identity* 5(4):225–35.

———. 2007. "Medicare and the Future of Retirement Security." *The Gerontologist* 46(1):123–30.

Polivka, L. and E. Borrayo. 2002. "Globalization, Population Aging and Ethics, Part II: Toward a Just Global Society." *Journal of Aging and Identity* 7(3):195–211.

Polivka, L. and C. Longino. 2006. "The Emerging Postmodern Culture of Aging and Retirement Security." In *Aging, Globalization and Inequality: The New Critical Gerontology.* J. Baars, D. Dannefe, C. Phillipson and A. Walker, eds. Amityville, NY: Baywood Press.

Polivka-West, L., H. Tuch and K. Goldsmith. 2001. "A Perfect Storm of Unlimited Risks for Florida Nursing Home Providers." In *Liability Issues and Risk Management in Caring for Older Persons: Ethics, Law and Aging Review* 7. M. Kapp, ed. New York: Springer.

Pollock, N. J. 1979. "Work, Wages and Shifting Cultivation on Niue." *Pacific Studies* 2:132–43.

Poon, L., G. Clayton, P. Martin, M. Johnson, B. Courtenay, A. Sweaney et al. 1992. "The Georgia Centenarian Study." *International Journal of Aging and Human Development* 34:1–17.

Poon, L., S. Gueldner and B. Sprouse, eds. 2003. *Successful Aging and Adaptation with Chronic Disease.* New York: Springer Publishing.

Poon, L., Y. Jang, S. Reynolds and E. McCarthy. 2005. "Profiles of the Oldest Old." In *The Cambridge Handbook of Age and Ageing.* M. Johnson, ed. Cambridge: Cambridge University Press.

Population Reference Bureau. 2007. "Trends in Disability at Older Ages." *Today's Research on Aging* 7:1–5. http://www.prb.org/pdf07/TodaysResearchAging7.pdf.

Portes, A. and R. G. Rumbaut. 1990. *Immigrant America: A Portrait.* Berkeley: University of California Press.

Portes, A. and A. Stepick. 1993. *City on the Edge: The Transformation of Miami.* Berkeley: University of California Press.

Post, S. 2006. Respectare: Moral Respect for the Lives of the Deeply Forgetful. In *Dementia, Mind, Meaning and the Person.* J. Hughes, S. Louw and S. Sabat, eds. Oxford: Oxford University Press.

Potash, B. ed. 1986. *Widows in African Societies: Choices and Constraints.* Stanford, CA: Stanford University Press.

Poulain, M., G. Pes, C. Grasland, C. Carru, L. Ferrucci, G. Baggio et al. 2004. "Identification of a Geographic Area Characterized by Extreme Longevity in the Sardinia Island: The AKEA Study." *Experimental Gerontology* 39:1423–29.

Powell, J. and I. Cook. 2009. *Aging in Asia: Themes and Issues.* Taiwan: Casa Verde Books.

Poyo, G. E. 1989. *"With All, and for the Good of All"—The Emergence of Popular Nationalism in the Cuban Communities of the United States, 1848–1898.* Durham, NC: Duke University Press.

Predny, M. and D. Relf. 2004. "Horticulture Therapy Activities for Preschool Children, Elderly Adults and Intergenerational Groups." *Activities, Adaptation and Aging* 28(3):1–18.

Press, I. and M. McKool. 1972. "Social Structure and Status of the Aged toward Some Valid Cross-Cultural Generalizations." *Aging and Human Development* 3(4): 297–306.

Preston, S., M. Hill and G. Drevenstedt. 1998. "Childhood Conditions That Predict Survival to Advanced Ages among African Americans." *Social Science and Medicine* 47:1231–46.

Pritchard, C. and D. Baldwin. 2002. "Elderly Suicide Rates in Asian and English-speaking Countries." *Acta Psychiatrica Scandinavica* 105(4):271–75.

Pruchno, R. 1999. "Raising Grandchildren: The Experiences of Black and White Grandmothers." *The Gerontologist* 39:209–21.

Pulliam, D. 2006. "Are All Things American Inevitable?" GetReligion.org, June 19, 2006. http://www.getreligion.org/?p=1681.

Putnam, R. D. 2000. *Bowling Alone: The Collapse and Revival of American Community.* New York: Simon and Schuster.

Putnam-Dickerson, J. and J. Brown, eds. 1998. *Women among Women: Anthropological Perspectives on Female Age Hierarchies.* Champaign: University of Illinois Press.

Quadagno, J. and M. Hardy. 1996. "Work and Retirement." In *Handbook of Aging and the Social Sciences*, 4th ed. R. H. Binstock and L. K. George, eds. San Diego: Academic Press.

Queralt, M. 1983. The Elderly of Cuban Origin: Characteristics and Problems. In *Aging in Minority Groups.* R. L. McNeely and J. L. Colen, eds. Beverly Hills, CA: Sage, 50–65.

Quill, T., C. Cassel and D. Meier. 1992. "Care of the Hopelessly Ill." *New England Journal of Medicine* 327:1380–84.

Quinn, A. 2008. "Healthy Aging in Cities." *Journal of Urban Health* 85(2):51–153.

Qureshi, R. B. 1996. "Transcending Space: Recitation and Community among South Asian Muslims in Canada." In *Making Muslim Space in North America and Europe.* B. Metcalf, ed. Berkeley: University of California Press.

Rabello de Castro, L. and G. Rabello de Castro. 2001. "Coping in Old Age: Considerations from the Point of View of Case Studies from Brazil." *Indian Journal of Gerontology* 15(1/2):187–97.

Rabig, J., W. Thomas, R. Kane, L. Cutler and S. McAlilly. 2006. "Radical Redesign of Nursing Homes: Applying the Green House Concept in Tupelo, Mississippi." *The Gerontologist* 46(4):533–39.

Rahim-Williams, F. B. 2006. "Understanding the Diabetes Care Management Practices of African American Women and Diabetes Health Educators: Best Practices for Diabetes Care Education and Service Delivery." Paper presented at the Governor's Conference on Women's Health, May, Sheraton World Resort, Orlando, Florida.

Rajan, S. I. and S. Kumar. 2003. "Living Arrangements among Indian Elderly: New Evidence from National Family Health Survey." *Economic and Political Weekly* 38:75–80.

Rajan, S. I., U. S. Mishra and P. S. Sarma. 1999. *India's Elderly: Burden or Challenge?* New Delhi: Sage.

Ramazani, N. 2002. *The Dance of the Rose and the Nightingale*. Syracuse, NY: Syracuse University Press.

Ram Dass, B. 2000. *Still Here: Embracing Aging, Changing and Dying*. New York: Riverhead Books.

Ramirez, R. R. and G. P. de la Cruz. 2003. *The Hispanic Population in the United States: March 2002, Current Population Reports*. Washington, DC: U.S. Census Bureau. http://www.census.gov/prod/2003pubs/p20-545.pdf.

Randall, W. and G. Kenyon. 2004. "Time, Story and Wisdom: Emerging Themes in Narrative Gerontology." *Canadian Journal of Aging* 23(4):333–46.

Rasmussen, P. 2007. "The Danish Model of 'Flexicurity': AARP Global Aging Issues." http://www.aarp.org/research/intl/globalaging/apr_07_flexicurity.html.

Rasmussen, S. 1997. *The Poetics and Politics of Tuareg Aging: Life Course and Personal Destiny in Niger*. DeKalb: Northern Illinois University Press.

Rattan, S. 2005. "Anti-Aging Strategies: Prevention or Therapy? Slowing Aging from Within." Special issue, *EMBO Reports* S25–29.

Ratzel, F. 1894. *The History of Mankind*, vol. 2. London: Macmillan.

Rawlins, J. 2006. *Midlife and Older Women: Family Life, Work and Health in Jamaica*. Kingston, Jamaica: University of the West Indies Press.

Raymo, J. M. and Y. Xie. 2000. "Income of the Urban Elderly in Postreform China: Political Capital, Human Capital and the State." *Social Science Research* 29:1–24.

Redfield, R. 1941. *The Folk Culture of Yucatan*. Chicago: University of Chicago Press.

Reed-Danahay, D. 2001. This Is Your Home Now: Conceptualizing Location and Dislocation in a Dementia Unit." *Qualitative Research* 1(1):47–63.

Reich, R. 2007. *Supercapitalism: The Transformation of Business, Democracy and Everyday Life*. New York: Knopf.

Reichel-Dolmatoff, G. and A. Reichel-Dolmatoff. 1961. *The People of Aritama*. Chicago: University of Chicago Press.

Reid, W. H. 1995. *DSM-IV Training Guide*. New York: Bunner/Mazel.

Reiff, D. 1993. *The Exile: Cuba in the Heart of Miami*. New York: Simon and Schuster.

Reinhardt, U. E. 2003. "Does the Aging of the Population Really Drive the Demand for Health Care?" *Health Affairs* 22(6):27–39.

Rennell, T. 2001. *The Death of Queen Victoria: Last Days of Glory*. London: Penguin.

Reynolds, J. 2007. "Wifeless Future for China's Men." *BBC*, February 12. http://news.bbc.co.uk/2/hi/asia-pacific/6346931.stm.

Rhoades, E. R. and D. Rhoades. 2000. "Traditional Indian and Modern Western Medicine." In *American Indian Health: Innovations in Care, Promotion and Policy*. E. R. Rhoades, ed. Baltimore: Johns Hopkins University Press.

Rhoads, E. 1984. "The Impact of Modernization on the Aged in American Samoa." *Pacific Studies* 7:15–33.

Rhoads, E. and L. Holmes. 1995. *Other Cultures, Elder Years*, 2nd ed. Thousand Oaks, CA: Sage.

Richter, R. and Richter, B. 2002 *Alzheimer's Disease*. London: Mosby Press.

Riesco, M. 2005. "Lessons for Proposed U.S. Social Security Reform: Twenty-five Years Reveal Myths of Privatized Federal Pensions in Chile." IRC Americas Program Silver City, NM: International Relations Center. http://www.cep.cl/Cenda/Cen_Documentos/Pub_MR/Articulos/Varios/Pensiones_USA_0503.pdf.

Riley, J. C. 2001. *Rising Life Expectancy. A Global History*. Cambridge: Cambridge University Press.

Riley, M. W. and R. P. Abeles. 1982. "Introduction: Life-Course Perspectives." In *Aging from Birth to Death: Sociotemporal Perspectives*. M. W. Riley, R. P. Abeles and M. S. Teitelbaum, eds. Boulder, CO: Westview.

Risch, N. 1990. "Linkage Strategies for Genetically Complex Traits. I. Multilocus Models." *American Journal of Human Genetics* 46(2):222–28.

Ritchie, J. and J. Ritchie. 1979. *Growing Up in Polynesia*. Sydney: Allen and Unwin.

———. 1981. "Child-Rearing and Child Abuse: The Polynesian Context." In *Child Abuse and Neglect: Cross-Cultural Perspectives*. J. E. Korbin, ed. Berkeley: University of California Press.

Rivers, W. H. R. 1926. *Psychology and Ethnology*. London: Kegan Paul.

Robertson, J. 1996. *At the Cultural Center*. Charlotte Harbor, FL: Tabby House.

Robine, J. and M. Allard. 1998. "The Oldest Human." *Science* 20:279(5358):1834–35.

———. 1999. "Jeanne Calment: Validation of the Duration of Her Life." In *Validation of Exceptional Longevity*. B. Jeune, ed. Odense, Denmark: Odense University Press.

Robine, J. and C. Jagger. 2005. "The Relationship between Increasing Life Expectancy and Healthy Life Expectancy." *Ageing Horizons* 3:14–21.

Robinson, J. 1985. "Architectural Settings and the Housing of Older Developmentally Disabled Persons." In *Aging and Developmental Disabilities: Issues and Approaches*. M. Jaricki and H. Wisniewski, eds. New York: Van Nostrand Reinhold.

Robinson, J., T. Skill and J. Turner. 2004. "Media Usage Patterns and Portrayals of Seniors." In *Handbook of Communication and Ageing Research*, 2nd ed. J. Nussbaum and J. Coupland, eds. Mahwah, NJ: Lawrence Erlbaum Associates.

Robinson, M., W. Novelliet, C. Pearson and L. Norris, eds. 2007. *Global Health and Global Aging*. San Francisco: Jossey-Bass.

Rodriguez, R. and M. R. Crowther. 2006. "A Stress Process Model of Grandparent Caregiving: The Impact of Role Strain and Intrapsychic Strain on Subjective Well-Being." In *Custodial Grandparenting: Individual, Cultural and Ethnic Diversity*. B. Hayslip and J. Hicks-Patrick, eds. New York: Springer.

Rodwin, V. G. and M. K. Gusmano, eds. 2006. *Growing Older in World Cities: New York, London, Paris and Tokyo*. Nashville, TN: Vanderbilt University Press.

Rogers, A. 1993. "Why Menopause?" *Evolutionary Ecology* 7:406–20.

Rohner, R. et al. 1978. "Guidelines for Holocultural Research." *Current Anthropology* 19:128–29.

Rose, N. 1999. *Powers of Freedom: Reframing Political Thought*. Cambridge: Cambridge University Press.

Ross, A. and P. Liebig. 2002. "City of Laguna Woods: A Case of Senior Power in Local Politics." *Research on Aging* 24:87–105.

Ross, M. E. T. and L. A. Day. 2006. "Stress and Coping in African American Grandparents Who Are Raising Their Grandchildren." *Journal of Family Issues* 27:912–32.

Rossi, A. S. 1985. *Gender and the Life Course*. Chicago: Aldine Transaction.

Ross-Sheriff, F. 1994. "Elderly Muslim Immigrants' Needs and Challenges." In *Muslim Communities in North America*. Y. Y. Haddad and J. Smith, eds. Albany: State University of New York Press.

Rothman, M. B., B. D. Dunlop and K. M. Condon. 1994. *The Elders of Dade County: A Needs Assessment of Persons 60 and Over*. Miami: Southeast Florida Center on Aging of Florida International University.

Rothstein, F. 2007. *Globalization in Rural Mexico: Three Decades of Change*. Austin: University of Texas Press.

Rothstein, F. and M. Blim, eds. 1992. *Anthropology and the Global Factory*. New York: Bergin and Garvey.

Rott, C., V. d'Heureuse, M. Kliegel, P. Schonemann and G. Becker. 2001. "Heidelberg Centenarian Study; Theoretical and Methodological Principles for Social Science Research of the Oldest Old." *Gerontology and Geriatrics* 34:356–64.

Roubideaux, Y. and K. Acton. 2001. "Diabetes in American Indians." In *Promises to Keep: Public Health Policy for American Indians and Alaska Natives in the 21st Century*. M. Dixon and Y. Roubideaux, eds. Washington, DC: American Public Health Association.

Roudsari, M. 1998. "Bringing Trees to Blossom: How I Established the Iranian Parents Club." Paper presented at the workshop on "Elders and Immigrants in the Bay Area: Iranian Mothers Create Meaningful Lives and Share Wisdom" at the Santa Clara University Women's Day 1998 Program, Celebrating Women's Wisdom, April 29.

Rowe, J. 1997. "The New Gerontology." *Science* 278:367.

Rowe, J. and R. Kahn. 1998. *Successful Aging*. New York: Random House.

Rowles, G. 1978. *Prisoners of Space? Exploring the Geographical Experience of Older People*. Boulder, CO: Westview Press.

———. 1994. "Evolving Images of Place in Aging and 'Aging in Place.'" In *Changing Perceptions of Aging and the Aged*. D. Shenk and W. Achenbaum, eds. New York: Springer.

Rowles, G. and H. Chaudhury, eds. 2008. *Home and Identity in Late Life: International Perspectives*. New York: Springer.

Rowles, G. and H. Ravdal. 2002. "Aging, Place and Meaning in the Face of Changing Circumstances." In *Challenges of the Third Age: Meaning and Purpose in Later Life*. R. Weiss and S. Bass, eds. New York: Oxford University Press.

Rowles, G. and N. Schoenberg, eds. 2002. *Qualitative Gerontology: Contemporary Perspectives*. New York: Springer.

Rubinstein, R. 1986. *Singular Paths: Old Men Living Alone*. New York: Columbia University Press.

Rubinstein, R. and P. T. Johnsen. 1982. "Toward a Comparative Perspective on Filial Response to Aging Populations." In *Aging and the Aged in the Third World: Part I, Studies in Third World Societies (No. 22)*. J Sokolovsky, ed. Williamsburg, VA: College of William and Mary.

Ruggles, S. 2002. "Living Arrangements and Well-Being of Older Persons in the Past." *Population Bulletin of the United Nations*, nos. 42/43:111–61. http://www.un.org/esa/population/pubsarchive/untech/pdf/untech3.pdf.

Ruiz, D. 2002. "The Increase in Incarcerations among Women and its Impact on the Grandmother Caregiver: Some Racial Considerations." *Journal of Sociology and Social Welfare* 29:179–97.

———. 2004. *Amazing Grace: African American Grandmothers as Caregivers and Conveyers of Traditional Values*. Westport, CT: Praeger.

Rule, G., D. Milke and A. Dobbs. 1994. "Design of Institutions: Cognitive Functioning and Social Interactions of the Aged Resident." In *Aging: Canadian Perspectives*. V. Marshall and B. McPherson, eds. Peterborough, Canada: Broadview Press.

Ryan, T. F. 1977. "Prehistoric Niue: An Egalitarian Polynesian Society." Master's thesis. University of Auckland.

———. 1984. *Palagi Views of Niue: Historical Literature, 1774–1889*. Auckland, New Zealand: Auckland University Press.

Ryff, C. 1989. "Beyond Ponce de Leon and Life Satisfaction: New Directions in Quest of Successful Ageing." *International Journal of Behavior Development* 12(1): 35–55.

Sabat, S. and R. Harré. 1992. "The Construction and Deconstruction of Self in Alzheimer's Disease. *Ageing and Society* 12:443–61.

Sabogal, F., G. Marin, R. Otero-Sabogal, B. Vanoss Marin and E. J. Perez-Stable. 1987. "Hispanic Familism and Acculturation: What Changes and What Doesn't?" *Hispanic Journal of Behavior Sciences* 9(4):397–412.

Safdar, S., C. Lay and W. Strothers. 2003. "The Process of Acculturation and Basic Goals: Testing a Multidimensional Individual Difference Acculturation Model with Iranian Immigrants in Canada." *International Association for Applied Psychology* 52:555–79.

Sagara, M., T. Kanda, M. N. Jelekera, T. Teramoto, L. Armitage, N. Birt et al. 2004. "Effects of Dietary Intake of Soy Protein and Isoflavones on Cardiovascular Disease Risk Factors in High Risk, Middle-Aged Men in Scotland." *Journal of the American College of Nutrition* 23(1):85–91.

Sagner, A. 2002. "Identity Management and Old Age Construction among Xhosa Speakers in Urban South Africa: Complaint Discourse Revisited." In *Ageing in Africa: Sociolinguistic and Anthropological Approaches*. S. Makoni and K. Stroeken, eds. Burlington, VT: Ashgate.

Sakihara, S. and H. Yamashiro. 2007. "Relationship between Health Check-up Service Use and Medical Care Expenditure among Older People in Okinawa." *Okinawa International University Journal of Social Welfare and Psychology*. 1–20 [in Japanese].

Salari, S. 2002. "Invisible in Aging Research: Arab Americans, Middle Eastern Immigrants and Muslims in the United States." *The Gerontologist* 42:580–88.

Saldivar-Tanaka, L. and M. Krasny. 2004. "Culturing Community Development, Neighborhood Open Space and Civic Agriculture: The Case of Latino Community Gardens in New York City." *Agriculture and Human Values* 21(4):399–412. http://www.gardenmosaics.cornell.edu/pgs/aboutus/materials/Culturing_Community _Development.pdf.

Salvadore, S. and R. Mukherjee. 2007. "Present Tense, Future Imperfect." *Times of India*, February 28.

Sampson, R. J., S. W. Raudenbush and F. Earls. 1997. "Neighborhoods and Violent Crime: A Multilevel Study of Collective Efficacy." *Science* 227(9):18–23.

Samuelsson, S., A. Bauer, B. Hagberg, G. Samuelsson, B. Nordbeck, A. Brun et al. 1997. "The Swedish Centenarian Study: A Multidisciplinary Study of Five Consecutive Cohorts at the Age of 100." *International Journal of Aging and Human Development* 45:223–53.

Sanabe, E., I. Ashitomi and M. Suzuki. 1977. "Social and Medical Survey of Centenarians." *Okinawa Journal of Public Health* 9:98–106.

Sanday, P. R. 2002. *Women at the Center: Life in a Modern Matriarchy*. Ithaca, NY: Cornell University Press.

Sander, T. and R. Putnam. 2006. "Social Capital and Civic Engagement of Individuals over Age Fifty in the United States." In *Civic Engagement and the Baby Boomer Generations: Research, Policy and Practice Perspectives*. L. Wilson and S. Simson, eds. Binghamton, NY: Haworth Press.

Sanjek, R. 1998. *The Future of Us All: Race and Neighborhood Politics in New York City.* Ithaca, NY: Cornell University Press.

———. 2009. *Gray Panthers.* Philadelphia: University of Pennsylvania Press.

Santoni, I. 1993. *Quando Eravamo Contadini Pastore e Carbonai.* Comune di Montemurlo: Lalli Editore.

Sarhill, N., S. LeGrand, R. Islamibouli, M. Davis and D. Walsh. 2001. "The Terminally Ill Muslim: Death and Dying from the Muslim Perspective." *American Journal of Hospice and Palliative Care* 18(4):251–55.

Sassen, S. 1994. *Cities in the World Economy.* Thousand Oaks, CA: Pine Forge Press.

———. 2001. *The Global City: New York, London, Tokyo,* 2nd ed. Princeton, NJ: Princeton University Press.

Savage, M., G. Bagnall and B. Longhurst. 2005. *Globalization and Belonging.* London: Sage.

Savishinsky, J. S. 1991. *The Ends of Time: Life and Work in a Nursing Home.* New York: Bergin and Garvey.

———. 2000. *Breaking the Watch: The Meanings of Retirement in America.* Ithaca, NY: Cornell University Press.

———. 2004. "The Volunteer and the *Sannyasin*: Archtypes of Retirement in America and India." *International Journal of Aging and Human Development* 59:25–41.

———. 2006. "The Quest for Legacy in Later Life." *Journal of Intergenerational Relationships* 4(4):75–90.

Sawhney, M. 2003. "The Role of Non-Governmental Organizations for the Welfare of the Elderly: The Case of HelpAge India." In *An Aging India: Perspectives, Prospects and Policies.* P. S. Liebig and S. I. Rajan, eds. New York: Haworth Press.

Scarmeas, N., S. Albert, J. Manly and Y. Stern. 2004. "Education and Rates of Cognitive Decline in Incident Alzheimer's Disease." *Journal of Neurology, Neurosurgery and Psychiatry* 77:308–16.

Schachter, F., L. Faure-Delanef, F. Guenot, H. Rouger, P. Froguel, L. Lesueur-Ginot et al. 1994. "Genetic Associations with Human Longevity at the APOE and ACE Loci." *Nature Genetics* 6(1):29–32.

Schachter-Shalomi, Z. and R. S. Miller. 1995. *From Age-ing to Sage-ing: A Profound Vision of Growing Older.* New York: Warner Books.

Schaefer, E. 1997. Student researcher field notes from interview for Anthropology of Aging class, unpublished manuscript.

Schaie, K. W. and S. Willis. 1999. "Theories of Everyday Competence and Aging." In *Handbook of Theories of Aging.* V. Bengtson and K. W. Schaie, eds. New York: Springer.

Schapera, I. 1930. *The Khoisan People of South Africa.* London: Routledge.

Schell, J., P. Sawyer, B. Willcox, D. Willcox, E. Bodner and R. Allman. 2005. "Multiethnic Comparisons of Life-Space Mobility." *The Gerontologist.* Special issue II, 447–48.

Schiff, G. 1984. *Picasso: The Last Years, 1963–1973.* New York: George Braziller.

Schildkrout, E. 1986. "Widows in Hausa Society: Ritual Phase or Social State?" In *Widows in African Societies: Choices and Constraints.* B. Potash, ed. Stanford, CA: Stanford University Press.

Schoenberg, N. and W. McAuley. 2007. "Promoting Qualitative Research." *The Gerontologist* 47(5):576–77.

Schofield, B. 2002. "Partners in Power: Governing the Self-Sustaining Community." *Sociology* 36:663–83.

Schreiner, A., E. Yamamoto and H. Shiotani. 2005. "Positive Affect among Nursing Home Residents with Alzheimer's Dementia: The Effect of Recreational Activity." *Aging and Mental Health* 9(2):129–34.

Schröder-Butterfill, E. 2004. "Adoption, Patronage and Charity: Arrangements for the Elderly without Children in East Java." In *Ageing without Children: European and Asian Perspectives*. P. Kreager and E. Schröder-Butterfill, eds. Oxford: Berghahn.

———. Forthcoming. *Ageing, Networks and Exchange: Old-Age Support Dynamics in Indonesia*. Oxford: Oxford University Press.

Schröder-Butterfill, E. and P. Kreager. 2005. "Actual and De Facto Childlessness in Old Age: Evidence and Implications from East Java, Indonesia." *Population and Development Review* 31(1):19–55.

Schröder-Butterfill, E. and R. Marianti. 2006. "A Framework for Understanding Old-Age Vulnerabilities." *Ageing and Society* 26:9–35.

Schubel, V. 1996. "Karbala as Sacred Space among North American Shi'a: 'Every Day Is Ashura, Everywhere Is Karbala." In *Making Muslim Space in North America and Europe*. B. Metcalf, ed. Berkeley: University of California Press.

Schulz, R. and S. Beach. 1999. "Caregiving as a Risk Factor for Mortality: The Caregiver Health Effects Study." *Journal of the American Medical Association* 282: 2215–19.

Schweitzer, M. 1987. "The Elders: Cultural Dimensions of Aging in Two American Indian Communities." In *Growing Old in Different Societies: Cross-Cultural Perspectives*. J. Sokolovsky, ed. Acton, MA: Copley.

———. 1999. *Bridging Generations: American Indian Grandmothers–Traditions and Transitions*. Albuquerque: University of New Mexico Press.

Sclar, E. 2003. "Urban Planning." Conference on Health and the Built Environment, co-sponsored by the New York Academy of Medicine and the Centers for Disease Control and Prevention, March 25.

Scott, D. 1993. *Would a Good Man Die? Niue Island, New Zealand and the Late Mr. Larsen*. Auckland: Southern Cross Books.

Scott-Maxwell, F. 1968. *The Measure of My Days*. New York: Penguin.

Seabrook, J. 2004. *A World Grown Old*. London: Pluto Press.

Seale, C. 1998. *Constructing Death: The Sociology of Dying and Bereavement*. Cambridge: Cambridge University Press.

Sear, R., R. Mace and I. A. McGregor. 2000. "Maternal Grandmothers Improve the Nutritional Status and Survival of Children in Rural Gambia." *Proceedings of the Royal Society of London, Series B* 267:1641–47.

———. 2003. "The Effects of Kin on Female Fertility in Rural Gambia." *Evolution and Human Behavior* 24:25–42.

Sear, R., F. Steele, I. A. McGregor and R. Mace. 2002. "The Effects of Kin on Child Mortality in Rural Gambia." *Demography* 39:43–63.

Sedlar, J. and R. Miners. 2002. *Don't Retire, Rewire*. New York: Alpha Books.

Seedsman, T. 2007. "Developing Intergenerational Solidarity: A Global Imperative." In *Lessons on Aging from Three Nations: Volume 1: The Art of Aging Well*. S. Carmel, C. Morse and F. Torres-Gil, eds. Amityville, NY: Baywood Press.

Seefeldt, C. 1984. "Children's Attitudes Toward the Elderly: A Cross-Cultural Comparison." *International Journal of Aging and Human Development* 19(4): 321–30.

Seeman, T., T. Lusignolo, M. Albert and L. Berkman. 2001. "Social Relationships, Social Support and Patterns of Cognitive Aging in Healthy, High-Functioning

Older Adults: MacArthur Studies of Successful Aging." *Health Psychology* 20(4):243–55.

Sellers, S. C. and P. B. Stork. 1997. "Reminiscence as an Intervention: Rediscovering the Essence of Nursing." *Nursing Forum* 32(1):17–23.

Semenza, J., C. Rubin, K. Falter and J. Selanikio. "Heat-Related Deaths during the 1995 Heat Wave in Chicago." *New England Journal of Medicine* 335(2):84–90.

Sengstock, M. C. 1996. "Care of the Elderly within Muslim Families." In *Family and Gender among American Muslims: Issues Facing Middle Eastern Immigrants and Their Descendants*. B. C. Aswad and B. Bilgé, eds. Philadelphia: Temple University Press.

Senior Living Guide of South Florida. 1998. Orlando, FL: Senior Living Network.

Sered, S. 1999. *Women of the Sacred Groves: Divine Priestesses of Okinawa*. New York: Oxford University Press.

Seshamani, M. and M. Grey. 2002. "The Impact of Ageing on Expenditures in the National Health Service." *Age and Ageing* 3131:287–94.

Settersten, R. A. 1999. *Lives in Time and Place: Problems and Promises of Developmental Science*. Amityville, NY: Baywood Press.

———. 2003. "Propositions and Controversies in Life-Course Scholarship." In *Invitation to the Life Course: New Understandings of Later Life*. R. A. Settersten, ed. Amityville, NY: Baywood Press.

———. 2006. "Aging and the Life Course." In *Handbook of Aging and the Social Sciences*, 6th ed. R. H. Binstock and L. K. George, eds. Boston: Academic Press.

Shaw, L., P. Raggi, D. Berman and T. Callister. 2006. "Coronary Artery Calcium as a Measure of Biologic Age." *Atherosclerosis* 188(1):112–19.

Sheehan, T. 1976. "Senior Esteem as a Factor of Societal Economic Complexity." *The Gerontologist* 16:433–40.

Sheikh, J. I. 1992. "Anxiety Disorders in Old Age." In *Handbook of Mental Health and Aging*, 2nd ed. J. E. Birren, R. B. Sloane and G. D. Cohen, eds. New York: Academic Press.

Sheikh, J. I. and J. A. Yesavage. 1986. "Geriatric Depression Scale (GDS): Recent Evidence and Development of a Shorter Version." In *Clinical Gerontology: A Guide to Assessment and Intervention*. T. L. Brink, ed. New York: Haworth Press.

Shemirani, S. F. and D. L. O'Connor. 2006. "Aging in a Foreign Country: Voices of Iranian Women Aging in Canada." *Journal of Women and Aging* 18(2):73–90.

Shenk, D. and K. Christiansen. 1997. "Social Support Systems of Rural Older Women: A Comparison of the United States and Denmark." In *The Cultural Context of Aging: Worldwide Perspectives*, 2nd ed. J. Sokolovsky, ed. Westport, CT: Greenwood Press.

Shenk, D. and R. Schmid. 2002. "A Picture Is Worth…: The Use of Photography in Gerontological Research." In *Qualitative Gerontology: A Contemporary Perspective*. G. Rowles and N. Schoenberg, eds. New York: Springer.

Shenk, D. and J. Sokolovsky. 2001. "Positive Adaptations to Aging in Cultural Context." Special issue, *Journal of Cross-Cultural Gerontology* 16(1).

Sheykhi, M. T. 2004. "A Study of the Elderly People Living in Nursing Homes in Iran with a Special Focus on Tehran." *African and Asian Studies* 3(2):103–19.

Shibata, H., H. Haga, S. Yasumura, T. Suzuki and W. Koyano. 1994. "Possible Factors Influencing Difference in Rate of Aging in Japan." In *Facts and Research in Gerontology: Epidemiology and Aging*. B. Vellas, J. Albarede and P. Garry, eds. New York: Springer.

Shield, R. 1988. *Uneasy Endings: Daily Life in an American Nursing Home*. Ithaca, NY: Cornell University Press.

Shields, S. and L. Norton. 2006. *In Pursuit of the Sunbeam: A Practical Guide to Transformation from Institution to Household*. New York: Manhattan Retirement Foundation.

Shigeta, M. 2004. "Epidemiology: Rapid Increase in Alzheimer's Disease Prevalence in Japan." *Psychogeriatrics* 4:117–19.

Shomaker, D. 1987. "Problematic Behavior and the Alzheimer Patient: Retrospection as a Method of Understanding and Counseling." *The Gerontologist* 27(3):370–75.

Shore, B. 1978. "Ghosts and Government: A Structural Analysis of Alternative Institutions for Conflict Management in Samoa." *Man* 13:175–99.

———. 1982. *Sala'ilua: A Samoan Mystery*. New York: Columbia University Press.

Shore, R. J. and B. Hayslip. 1994. "Custodial Grandparenting: Implications for Children's Development." In *Redefining Families: Implications for Children's Development*. A. A. Gottfried and A. W. Gottfried, eds. New York: Plenum.

Short, R. 1978. "Healthy Infertility." *Uppsala Journal of Medical Science* Suppl. 22:23–26.

Shorto, R. 2008. "Childless Europe." *New York Times Magazine*, June 29. http://www.nytimes.com/2008/06/29/magazine/29Birth-t.html.

Shostak, M. 1981. *Nisa: The Life and Words of a !Kung Woman*. Cambridge, MA: Harvard University Press.

Shuey, K. and A. Wilson. 2008. "Cumulative Disadvantage and Black-White Disparities in Life-Course Health Trajectories." *Research on Aging* 30(2):200–225.

Shurgot, G. and B. Knight 2004. "Preliminary Study Investigating Acculturation, Cultural Values and Psychological Distress in Latino Caregivers of Dementia Patients." *Journal of Mental Health and Aging* 10:183–94.

Siampos, G. 1990. "Trends and Future Prospects of the Female Overlife by Regions in Europe." *Statistical Journal of the United Nations Economic Commission for Europe* 7:13–25.

Sidorenko, A. 2007. "World Policies on Aging and the United Nations." In *Global Health and Global Aging*. M. Robinson et al., eds. San Francisco: Jossey-Bass.

Sievert, L. 2006. *Menopause: A Biocultural Perspective*. New Brunswick, NJ: Rutgers University Press.

Silber, I. 1995. "Space, Fields, Boundaries: The Rise of Spatial Metaphors in Contemporary Sociological Theory." *Social Research* 62:323–55.

Silverman, M. and C. McAllister. 1995. "Continuities and Discontinuities in the Life Course: Experiences of Demented Persons in a Residential Alzheimer's Facility." In *The Culture of Long-Term Care: Nursing Home Ethnography*. J. N. Henderson and M. D. Vesperi, eds. Westport, CT: Bergin and Garvey.

Silverman, P. 1987. "Community Settings." In *The Elderly as Modern Pioneers*. P. Silverman, ed. Bloomington: Indiana University Press.

Silverman, P. and R. Maxwell. 1987. "The Significance of Information and Power in the Comparative Study of the Aged." In *Growing Old in Different Societies: Cross-Cultural Perspectives*. J. Sokolovsky, ed. Acton, MA: Copley.

Silverstein, M., R. Giarrusso and V. Bengtson. 2003. "Grandparents and Grandchildren in Family Systems: A Social-Developmental Perspective." In *Global Aging and Its Challenges to Families*. V. Bengtson and A. Lowenstein, eds. New York: Aldine.

Simic, A. 1978. "Introduction: Aging and the Aged in Cultural Perspective." *Life's Career Aging: Cultural Variations on Growing Old*. B. Myerhoff and A. Simic, eds. Beverly Hills, CA: Sage.

———. 1990. "Aging, World View and Intergenerational Relationships in America and Yugoslavia." In *The Cultural Context of Aging: Worldwide Perspectives*. J. Sokolovsky, ed. New York: Bergin and Garvey.

Simmons, L. 1945 (1970). *The Role of the Aged in Primitive Society*. New Haven, CT: Archon Books.

———. 1960. "Aging in Primitive Societies: A Comparative Survey of Family Life and Relationships." In *Handbook of Social Gerontology*. C. Tibbetts, ed. Chicago: University of Chicago Press.

Simmons, T. and J. L. Dye. 2003. *Grandparents Living with Grandchildren, 2000*. Census 2000 Brief 1-10. Washington, DC: U.S. Department of Commerce.

Simoni, S. and R. Trifiletti. 2004. "Caregiving in Transition in Southern Europe: Neither Complete Altruists nor Free-Riders." *Social Policy and Administration* 38(6):678–705.

Simpson, R. 2006. "Childbearing on Hold. Delayed Childbearing and Childlessness in Britain." Centre for Research on Families and Relationships, Research Briefing 29. http://www.crfr.ac.uk/briefingslist.htm#rb29 (accessed on December 16, 2007).

Simpson-Herbert, M. and S. Huffman. 1981. "The Contraceptive Effect of Breast-Feeding." *Studies in Family Planning* 12:125–33.

Sleebos, J. E. 2003. "Low Fertility Rates in OECD Countries: Facts and Policy Reponses." OECD Social, Employment and Migration Working Papers 15. Paris: Organization for Economic Co-operation and Development.

Smit, J. and M. Bailkey. 2006. "Building Community Capital and Social Inclusion through Urban Agriculture." In *City Farming for the Future*. R. van Veenhuizen, ed. Ottawa: IDRC Publications. http://www.idrc.ca/en/ev-103777-201-1-DO_TOPIC.html.

Smith, J. *Islam in America*. 1999. New York: Columbia University Press.

Smith, J. and A. Clurman. 2007. *Generation Ageless*. New York: HarperCollins.

Smith, J., P. Easton, B. Saylor, D. Wiedman and J. LaBelle, Sr. Forthcoming. "Harvested Food Culture and Its Influences on Valuable Functioning of Alaska Native Elders." *Alaska Journal of Anthropology*.

Smith, J. and P. Gay. 2004. *Active Ageing in Active Communities*. Bristol, UK: Policy Press.

Smith, M. P. 2001. *Transnational Urbanism*. New York: Blackwell.

Smith, R. W., Jr. 1967. "Dietary and Hormonal Factors in Bone Loss." *Fed Proc.* 26:1736–47.

Smith, S. P. 1983. *Niue: The Island and Its People*. Suva, Fiji: Institute for Pacific Studies, University of the South Pacific. (Reprinted from the *Journal of the Polynesian Society*, Vols. 11/12, 1902/1903.)

Smith, T. 2003. "Italy Baby-Cash Aims to Boost Births." *BBC News-Rome*. http://news.bbc.co.uk/2/hi/europe/3155324.stm (accessed on October 2, 2007).

Sobotka, T. and M. R. Testa. 2006. "Childlessness Intentions in Europe: A Comparison of Belgium (Flanders), Germany, Italy, Poland." Paper presented at the 2006 European Population Conference, Liverpool. http://www.oeaw.ac.at/vid/download/epc_sobotka.pdf (accessed on January 22, 2007).

Social Security Administration. 2005. "Retirement, Disability and Survivor Estimates." Washington, DC: Social Security Administration.

Society of Actuaries. 2006. *Longevity: The Underlying Driver of Retirement Risk*. Schaumberg, IL: Society of Actuaries.

Sokolovsky, J. 2001. "Ethnographic Research." In *Encyclopedia of Aging*, 2nd ed. G. Maddox et al., eds. New York: Springer.

———. 2002. "Living Arrangements of Older Persons and Family Support in Less Developed Countries." *Population Bulletin of the United Nations* 42/43: 162–92.

———. 2006. "If Not, Why Not: Synchronizing Qualitative and Quantitative Research in Studying the Elderly." In *Improving Aging and Public Health Research: Qualitative and Mixed Methods*. L. Curry, R. Shield and T. Wetle, eds. Washington, DC: American Public Health Association.

———. 2008. "Urban Garden: Fighting for Life and Beauty" (video documentary). St. Petersburg, FL: Ljudost Productions.

———. 2009. "The Maturing of an Anthropology of Aging." *IUAES Global Publications*.

Sokolovsky, J. and C. Cohen. 1981. "Being Old in the Inner City: Support Systems of the SRO Aged." In *Dimensions: Aging, Culture and Health*. C. L. Fry, ed. South Hadley, MA: Bergin and Garvey.

———. 1987. "Networks as Adaptation: The Cultural Meaning of Being a 'Loner' among the Inner City Elderly." In *Growing Old in Different Societies: Cross-Cultural Perspectives*. J. Sokolovsky, ed. Acton, MA: Copley.

Sokolovsky, J., S. Sosic and G. Pavlekovic. 1991. "Self-Help Groups for the Aged in Yugoslavia: How Effective Are They?" *Journal of Cross-Cultural Gerontology* 6(3):319–30.

Solimeo, S. Forthcoming. *With Shaking Hands: Aging with Parkinson's Disease in America's Heartland*. Piscataway, NJ: Rutgers University Press.

Solomon, M. 2003. *Late Beethoven: Music, Thought, Imagination*. Los Angeles: University of California Press.

Sontag, S. 1978. "The Double Standard of Ageing." In *An Ageing Population*. V. Carver and P. Liddiard, eds. London: Hodder and Stoughton.

Soustelle, J. 1961. *Daily Life of Aztecs on the Eve of the Spanish Conquest*. Stanford, CA: Stanford University Press.

Spencer, P. 1965. *The Samburu: A Study of Gerontocracy in a Nomadic Tribe*. Berkeley: University of California Press.

Spillman, B. and J. Lubitz. 2000. "The Effect of Longevity on Spending for Acute and Long-Term Care." *New England Journal of Medicine* 342(19):1409–15.

Spitz, G. and J. Logan. 1992. "Helping as a Component of Parent-Child Relations." *Research on Aging* 14(3):291–312.

Spitzer Chang, H. 2006. *Diagnostico de la Situacion del Adulto Mayor en el Peru y Propuestas Para el Mejoramiento de su Calidad de Vida*. Miraflores, Peru: Asociacion Adulto Feliz.

Ssengonzi, R. 2007. "The Plight of Older Persons as Caregivers to People Infected/Affected by HIV/AIDS: Evidence from Uganda." *Journal of Cross-Cultural Gerontology* 22(4):339–53.

Stack, C. 1974. *All Our Kin: Strategies for Survival in a Black Community*. New York: Harper & Row.

Stack, C. and L. Burton. 1993. "Kinscripts: Reflections of Family, Generation and Culture." *Journal of Comparative Family Studies* 24(1):157–70.

———. 1994. "Kinscripts: Reflections of Family, Generation and Culture." In *Mothering: Ideology, Experience and Agency*. E. Glenn, G. Chang and L. Forcey, eds. London: Routledge.

Stafford, P. 1996. *The Evergreen Household Survey*. Bloomington, IN: Evergreen Institute on Elder Environments.

———. 2003. "Homebodies: Voices of Place in a North American Community." In *Gray Areas: Ethnographic Encounters with Nursing Home Culture*. P. Stafford, ed. Santa Fe, NM: SAR Press.

———. 2009. *Elderburbia: Aging and a Sense of Place in America*. Westport, CT: Praeger.

Stanecki, K. A. 2004. "The AIDS Pandemic in the 21st Century." In *Global Population Profile, 2002*. Washington, DC: U.S. Government Printing Office.

State Council. 1995. "Quanmin jianshen jihua gangyao" [Outline of Nationwide Physical Fitness Program]. http://www.hnedu.cn/fagui/Law/19/law_19_1050.htm.

Steggerda, M. 1941. *Maya Indians of Yucatan*. Washington, DC: Carnegie Publication No. 531.

Stein, H. 1990. *American Medicine as Culture*. Boulder, CO: Westview.

Stephenson, M. 2000. "Development and Validation of the Stephenson Multigroup Acculturation Scale (SMAS)." *Psychological Assessment* 12:77–88.

Stewart, F. 1977. *Fundamentals of Age-Group Systems*. New York: Academic Press.

Steyn, H. P. 1994. "Role and Position of Elderly !Xu in the Schmidtsdrift Bushman Community." *South African Journal of Ethnology* 17(2):31–38.

Stilwell, B., K. Diallo, P. Zurn, M. Vujicic, O. Adams and M. Dal Poz. 2004. "Migration of Health-Care Workers from Developing Countries: Strategic Approaches to Its Management." *Bulletin of the World Health Organization* 82(8):595–600.

Stockwell, C. 2004. "Englewood." In *The Encyclopedia of Chicago*. J. Grossman, A. Keating and J. Reiff, eds. Chicago: University of Chicago Press.

Stoller, E. and C. Longino, Jr. 2001. " 'Going Home' or 'Leaving Home'? The Impact of Person and Place Ties on Anticipated Counterstream Migration." *The Gerontologist* 1:96–102.

Stone, R. et al. 1987. "Caregivers of the Frail Elderly: A National Profile." *The Gerontologist* 27(5):616–26.

Strain, L. 2001. "Senior Centres: Who Participates?" *Canadian Journal on Aging* 20:471–91.

Strassmann, B. I. and B. Gillespie. 2003. "How to Measure Reproductive Success?" *American Journal of Human Biology* 15(3):361–69.

Strathern, M. 1992. *After Nature: English Kinship in the Late Twentieth Century*. New York: Cambridge University Press.

Strawbridge, W. and M. Wallhagen. 1992. "Is All in the Family Always Best?" *Journal of Aging Studies* 4:1:81–92.

Street, P. "The Color of Community: Race and Residence in and Around Chicago at the Turn of the Millennium." http://www.thechicagourbanleague.org/723210130204959623/lib/723210130204959623/_Files/TheColorofCommunity.pdf.

Stroeken, K. 2002. "From Shrub to Log: The Ancestral Dimension of Elderhood among Sukuma in Tanzania." In *Ageing in Africa: Sociolinguistic and Anthropological Approaches*. S. Makoni and K. Stroeken, eds. Burlington, VT: Ashgate.

Strom, R., L. Buki and S. Strom. 1997. "Intergenerational Perceptions of English Speaking and Spanish Speaking Mexican American Grandparents." *International Journal of Aging and Human Development* 38:313–20.

Strom, R., S. Strom, L. Fournet, C. Wang, J. Behrens and D. Griswold. 1997. "Learning Needs of African American, Caucasian and Hispanic Grandparents." *Journal of Instructional Psychology* 28:119–34.

Stuart, M. and E. Hansen. 2006. "Danish Home Care Policy and the Family: Implications for the United States." *Journal of Aging and Social Policy* 18(3/4):27–42.

Stuart, M. and M. Weinrich. 2001a. "Home- and Community-Based Long-Term Care: Lessons from Denmark." *The Gerontologist* 41(4):474–80.

———. 2001b. "Home Is Where the Help Is: Community-Based Care in Denmark." *Journal of Aging and Social Policy* 12(4):81–101.

Stucki, B. R. 1992. "The Long Voyage Home: Return Migration among Aging Cocoa Farmers in Ghana." *Journal of Cross-Cultural Gerontology* 7:363–78.

Stuifbergen, M., J. van Delden and P. Dykstra. 2008. "The Implications of Today's Family Structures for Support Giving to Older Parents." *Ageing and Society* 28:413–34.

Suh, G.-H. and A. Shah. 2001. "A Review of the Epidemiological Transition in Dementia: Cross-National Comparisons of the Indices Related to Alzheimer's Disease and Vascular Dementia." *Acta Pyschiatrica Scandinavica* 104:4–11.

Sullivan, J. 1960. *Beethoven: His Spiritual Development*. New York: Random House.

Sundström, G., B. Malmberg, M. Castiello, É. Castejon and M. Tortosa. 2008. "Home Help Services in Sweden: Responsiveness to Changing Demographics and Needs." *European Journal of Ageing* 5(1):47–55.

Sung, K. 2007. *Respect and Care for the Elderly*. Lanham, MD: University Press of America.

Suzuki, M. 1985. *The Science of Centenarians*. Tokyo: Shinchosha [in Japanese].

Suzuki, M., M. Akisaka, I. Ashitomi, K. Higa and H. Nozaki. 1995. "Chronological Study Concerning ADL among Okinawan Centenarians." *Nippon Ronen Igakkai Zasshi* [Japanese Journal of Geriatrics] 32(6):416–23 [in Japanese].

Suzuki, M., H. Mori, T. Asato, H. Sakugawa, T. Ishii and Y. Hosoda. 1985. "Medical researches upon centenarians in Okinawa–case-controlled study of family history as hereditary influence on longevity." *Nippon Ronen Igakkai Zasshi* [Japanese Journal of Geriatrics] 22(5):457–67 [in Japanese].

Suzuki, M., B. Willcox and D. Willcox. 2001. "Implications from and for Food Cultures for Cardiovascular Disease: Longevity." *Asia Pacific Journal of Clinical Nutrition* 10:165–71.

Suzuki, M., D. Willcox and B. Willcox. 2008. "The Historical Context of Okinawan Longevity: Influence of the United States and Mainland Japan." *The Okinawan Journal of American Studies* 4:46–61.

Sverdrup, H. 1938. *Hos Tundra-folke* [With the people of the tundra]. Oslo: Gyldendal Norsk Forlag.

Szapocznik, J., M. Faletti and M. A. Sopetta. 1979. "Psychological-Social Issues of Cuban Elders in Miami." In *Cuban Americans: Acculturation, Adjustment and the Family*. J. Szapocznik and M. C. Herrera, eds. Washington, DC: National Coalition of Hispanic Mental Health and Human Services Organization.

Szinovacz, M., ed. 1998. *Handbook of Grandparenthood*. Westport CT: Greenwood.

Taguchi, M., N. Watanabe, A. Aoba, H. Nakagame, K. Naka and D. Willcox. 1999. "Jisatsu ga takai chiiki to hikui chiiki no kenjou koureisha no ikigai chousa [Research on ikigai in regions of high and low suicide]." *Ronen Shakai Kagaku* [Japanese Journal of Gerontology] 21(2):235.

Taira, E. and J. Carlson, eds. 1999. *Aging in Place: Designing, Adapting and Enhancing the Home Environment*. New York: Haworth Press.

Takagi, E. and M. Silverstein. 2006. "Intergenerational Coresidence of the Japanese Elderly." *Research in Aging* 28(4):473–92.

Takata, H., M. Suzuki, T. Ishii, S. Sekiguchi and H. Iri. 1987. "Influence of Major Histocompatibility Complex Region Genes on Human Longevity among Okinawan-Japanese Centenarians and Nonagenarians." *Lancet* 2:824–26.

Tanabe, M. 2007. "Culture Competence in the Training of Geriatric Medicine Fellows." *Educational Gerontology* 33(5):421–28.

Taraqqi, G. 1996. "A House in the Heavens." In *In a Voice of Their Own: A Collection of Stories by Iranian Women Writers since the Revolution of 1979*. F. Lewis and F. Yazdanfar, eds. and trans. Costa Mesa, CA: Mazda Press.

Tate, N. 1983. "The Black Aging Experience." In *Aging in Minority Groups*. R. McNeely and J. Colen, eds. Beverly Hills, CA: Sage.

Taylor, C. 1991. *The Ethics of Authenticity*. Cambridge: Cambridge University Press.

Taylor, R., H. T. Nemaia and J. Connell. 1987. "Mortality in Niue, 1978–1982." *New Zealand Medical Journal* 100:477–81.

Taylor, S. 2001. "Place Identification and Positive Realities of Aging." *Journal of Cross-Cultural Gerontology* 16:5–20.

Teitelbaum, M. 1987. "Old Age, Midwifery and Good Talk: Paths to Power in a West African Gerontocracy." In *Aging and Cultural Diversity: New Directions and Annotated Bibliography*. H. Strange and M. Teitlebaum, eds. South Hadley, MA: Bergin and Garvey.

———. 2000. "Long-Range Demographic Projections and Their Implications for the United States." In *United Nations Expert Group Meeting on Policy Responses to Population Ageing and Population Decline*. New York: United Nations.

Telegraph staff reporter. 2003. "Death from Loneliness at Eighty." *Telegraph*, July 22.

Teski, M., R. Helsabeck, F. Smith and C. Yeager. 1983. *A City Revitalized: The Elderly Lose at Monopoly*. Lanham, MD: University Press of America.

Teymoori, F., A. Dadkhah and M. Shirazikhah. 2006. "Social Welfare and Health (Mental, Social, Physical) Status of Aged People in Iran." *Middle East Journal of Age and Aging* 3(1):39–45.

Thang, L. L. 2001. *Generations in Touch: Linking the Old and Young in a Tokyo Neighborhood*. Ithaca, NY: Cornell University Press.

Thomas, J. 1990. "The Grandparent Role: A Double Bind." *International Journal of Aging and Human Development* 31:169–77.

Thomas, J., L. Sperry and M. S. Yarbrough. 2000. "Grandparents as Parents: Research Findings and Policy Implications." *Journal of Child Psychiatry and Human Development* 31:3–22.

Thomas, R. M. 1999. *Human Development Theories: Windows on Culture*. Thousand Oaks, CA: Sage.

Thomas, W. 1996. *Life Worth Living: How Someone You Love Can Still Enjoy Life in a Nursing Home—the Eden Alternative in Action*. Acton, MA: VanderWyk and Burnham.

———. 1998. "Long-Term Care Design: Cultural Expectations and Locale—Creating the Eldergarden." *Journal of Healthcare Design* 10:64.

———. 2004. *What Are Old People For? How Elders Can Save the World*. Acton, MA: Vanderwyk and Burnham.

Thomas, W. and C. Johansson. 2003. "Elderhood in Eden: Geriatric Rehabilitation for the Soul." *Topics in Geriatric Rehabilitation* 19(4):282–90.

Thompson, L. 1940. *Southern Lau, Fiji: An Ethnography*. Honolulu: Bernice P. Bishop Museum.

Thompson, S. 1990. "Metaphors the Chinese Age By." In *Anthropology and the Riddle of the Sphinx: Paradoxes of Change in the Life Course*. P. Spencer, ed. New York: Routledge.

Thwaites, K., E. Helleur and I. Simkins. 2005. "Restorative Urban Open Space: Exploring the Spatial Configuration of Human Emotional Fulfillment in Urban Open Space." *Landscape Research* 30(4):525–47.

Tidball, K. and M. Krasny. 2007. "From Risk to Resilience: What Role for Community Greening and Civic Ecology in Cities?" In *Social Learning Towards a More Sustainable World*. A. Wals, ed. Wageningen, Netherlands: Academic Publishers. http://krasny.dnr.cornell.edu/file/Tidball_Krasny_Urban_Resilience.pdf.

Tinney, J. 2008. "Negotiating Boundaries and Roles: Challenges Faced by the Nursing Home Ethnographer." *Journal of Contemporary Ethnography* 37(2):202–25.

Tobier, E. 2006. "Growing Old in the City that Never Sleeps." In *Growing Older in World Cities: New York, London, Paris and Tokyo*. V. Rodwin and M. Gusmano, eds. Nashville, TN: Vanderbilt University Press.

Todoriki, H., D. Willcox and B. Willcox. 2004. "The Effects of Post-war Dietary Change on Longevity and Health in Okinawa." *Okinawa Journal of American Studies* 1:52–61.

Tokarev, S. A. and I. S. Gurvich. 1964. "The Yakuts." In *The Peoples of Siberia*. M. G. Levin and L. P. Potapov, eds. Chicago: University of Chicago Press.

Toledo, R., B. Hayslip, M. Emick, C. Toledo and C. Henderson. 2000. "Cross-Cultural Differences in Custodial Grandparenting." In *Grandparents Raising Grandchildren: Theoretical, Empirical and Clinical Perspectives*. B. Hayslip and R. Goldberg-Glen, eds. New York: Springer.

Tom-Orme, L. 1994. "Traditional Beliefs and Attitudes about Diabetes among Navajos and Utes." In *Diabetes as a Disease of Civilization: The Impact of Culture Change on Indigenous Peoples*. J. R. Joe and R. S. Young, eds. New York: Mouton de Gruyter.

Tornstam, L. 1997. "Gerotranscendence: The Contemplative Dimension of Aging." *Journal of Aging Studies* 11(2):143–54.

———. 2005. *Gerotranscendence: A Developmental Theory of Positive Aging*. New York: Springer.

———. 2007. "Stereotypes of Old People Persist: A Swedish 'Facts on Aging Quiz' in a 23-Year Comparative Perspective." *International Journal of Ageing and Later Life* 2(1).

Torres, S. 1999a. "Barriers to Mental-Health-Care Access Faced by Hispanic Elderly." In *Serving Minority Elders in the 21st Century*. M. Wykle and A. Ford, eds. New York: Springer.

———. 1999b. "A Culturally-Relevant Theoretical Framework for the Study of Successful Ageing." *Ageing and Society* 19(1):33–51.

———. 2006a. "Culture, Migration, Inequality and 'Periphery' in a Globalized World: Challenges for the Study of Ethno- and Anthropo-Gerontology." In *Aging, Globalization and Inequality: The New Critical Gerontology*. J. Baars, D. Dannefer, C. Phillipson and A. Walker, eds. Amityville, NY: Baywood Press.

———. 2006b. "Making Sense of the Constructs of Successful Ageing: The Migrant Experience." In *Ageing and Diversity: Multiple Pathways and Cultural Migrations*. S. Daatland and S. Biggs, eds. Bristol, UK: Policy Press.

Torres-Gil, F. 2005. "Ageing and Public Policy in Ethnically Diverse Societies." In *Cambridge Handbook of Age and Ageing*. M. Johnson, ed. Cambridge: Cambridge University Press.

Townsend, P. 1979. *Poverty in the United Kingdom.* London: Allen Lane.

Traphagan, J. W. 1998a. "Contesting the Transition to Old Age in Japan." *Ethnology* 37(4):333–50.

———. 1998b. "Localizing Senility: Illness and Agency among Older Japanese." *Journal of Cross-Cultural Gerontology* 13:81–98.

———. 2000a. The Liminal Family: Return Migration and Intergenerational Conflict in Japan. *Journal of Anthropological Research* 56:365–85.

———. 2000b. *Taming Oblivion: Aging Bodies and the Fear of Senility in Japan.* Albany: State University of New York Press.

———. 2002. "Senility as Disintegrated Person in Japan." *Journal of Cross-Cultural Gerontology* 17:253–67.

———. 2005a. "Interpretations of Elder Suicide, Stress and Dependency among Rural Japanese." *Ethnology* 43(4):315–29.

———. 2005b. "Interpreting Senility: Cross-Cultural Perspectives." *Care Management Journals* 6(3):145–50.

———. 2007. "Aging in Asian Societies: Perspectives from Recent Qualitative Research." *Care Management Journals* 8(1):16–17.

Traphagan, J. W. and J. Knight. 2003. *Demographic Change and the Family in Japan's Aging Society.* Albany: State University of New York Press.

Traphagan, J. W. and T. Nagasawa. 2008. "Long-Term Care Entrepreneurialism in Japan: Changing Approaches to Caring for Dementia Sufferers." *Care Management Journals* 9(2):89–96.

Treas, J. and S. Mazumdar. 2002. "Older People in America's Immigrant Families: Dilemmas of Dependence Integration and Isolation." *Journal of Aging Studies* 16(3):243–58.

Treolar, A. E. 1981. "Menstrual Cyclicity and the Pre-Menopause." *Maturitis* 3:249–64.

Tripp-Reimer, T., E. Choi, L. Kelley and J. Enslein. 2001. "Cultural Barriers to Care: Inverting the Problem." *Diabetes Spectrum* 14:13–22.

Trombold, J., R. Moellering, Jr. and A. Kagan. 1966. "Epidemiological Aspects of Coronary Heart Disease and Cerebrovascular Disease: The Honolulu Heart Program." *Hawaii Medical Journal* 25:231–34.

Trusswell, A. S. and J. D. L. Hansen. 1976. "Medical Research among the !Kung." In *Kalahari Hunter-Gatherers.* R. B. Lee and I. DeVore, eds. Cambridge, MA: Harvard University Press.

Tsolova, S. and J. Mortensen. 2006. "The Cross-Atlantic Exchange to Advance Long-Term Care." Prepared for the European Commission and AARP Joint Conference on Long-Term Care. Brussels, Belgium.

Tucker, R., V. Marshall, C. Longino Jr. and L. Mullins. 1988. "Older Anglophone Canadians in Florida: A Descriptive Profile." *Canadian Journal on Aging* 7: 218–32.

Tucker, R., L. Mullins, F. Beland, C. Longino, Jr. and V. Marshall. 1992. "Older Canadians in Florida: A Comparison of Anglophone and Francophone Seasonal Migrants." *Canadian Journal on Aging* 11:281–97.

Tuljapurkar, S., C. Puleston and M. Gurven. 2007. "Why Men Matter: Mating Pattern Drives Evolution of Post-reproductive Lifespan." *PLoS ONE* 2(8):e785.

Turnham, H. 2001. Federal Nursing Home Reform Act from the Omnibus Budget Reconciliation Act of 1987, or simply OBRA '87 SUMMARY. http://www. ltcombudsman.org/ombpublic/49_346_1023.cfm (accessed on August 15, 2008).

Twigg, J. 2000. *Bathing—the Body and Community Care.* London and New York: Routledge.

UNAIDS. 2007. "Report on the Global AIDS Epidemic: December 2007." http://data. unaids.org/pub/EPISlides/2007/2007_epiupdate_en.pdf.

Unger, J. 1993. "Urban Families in the Eighties." In *Chinese Families in the Post-Mao Era.* D. Davis and S. Harrell, eds. Berkeley: University of California Press.

United Nations. 1992. "Las Naciones Unidas y la Cuestión del Envejecimiento: Principios de las Naciones Unidas en Favor de las Personas de Edad" (press release). New York: Office of Public Information.

———. 2002. "Peru at the Second World Assembly on Ageing, Madrid, Spain." http:// www.un.org/ageing/coverage/peruS.htm.

———. 2005. *Living Arrangements of Older Persons around the World.* New York: United Nations Department of Economic and Social Affairs. http://www.un.org/ esa/population/publications/livingarrangement/report.htm.

———. 2006. *United Nations Population Division Wallchart on Global Aging.* New York: United Nations Department of Economic and Social Affairs Population Division. http://www.un.org/esa/population/publications/ageing/ageing2006.htm.

———. 2007a. *State of the World Population 2007: Unleashing the Potential of Urban Growth.* New York: United Nations Population Fund.

———. 2007b. "State of the World 2007." http://www.unfpa.org/swp/2007/presskit/ pdf/sowp2007_eng.pdf.

———. 2007c. *World Economic and Social Survey 2007: Development in an Ageing World.* New York: United Nations. http://www.un.org/esa/policy/wess/wess2007files/ wess2007.pdf.

United Nations Center for Human Settlements. 1999. *Developing World: Living Conditions of Low-Income Older Persons in Human Settlements.* New York: United Nations.

United Nations Department of Economic and Social Affairs, Population Division. 2005. *World Population Prospects: The 2004 Revision.* New York: United Nations.

———. 2006. "Population Aging 2006." http://www.un.org/esa/population/publications/ ageing/ageing2006chart.pdf.

———. 2007a. *World Population Prospects: The 2006 Revision.* New York: United Nations. http://www.un.org/esa/population/publications/wpp2006/wpp2006.htm.

———. 2007b. "World Urbanization Prospects: The 2007 Revision." http://www.un. org/esa/population/publications/wup2007/2007WUP_Highlights_web.pdf.

University of Michigan–Dearborn. 2004. "Changing Family Structures Affect Health Care among Elderly Arabs and Arab Americans in Detroit Area" (press release), May 1. http://www.umd.umich.edu/univ/ur/press_releases/may04/agingstudy_pr. html.

UPI. 2004. "More Japan Elderly Conned to Buy Goods." *Washington Times,* July 12.

Urry, J. 2000. *Sociology beyond Societies: Mobilities for the Twenty-First Century.* London and New York: Routledge.

U.S. Census Bureau. 1936. *United States Life Tables.* Washington, DC: U.S. Government Printing Office.

———. 1994. *The Hispanic Population in the United States: March 1993.* Washington, DC: U.S. Government Printing Office.

———. 2000a. "Single-Person Households in 1999." 2000 Census, Tables No. 2 and No. 60. http://www.census.gov.

————. 2000b. "Table FBP-1: Profile of Selected Demographic and Social Characteristics, 2000—People Born in Cuba." Census 2000 Special Tabulations (STP-159).
  http://www.census.gov/population/cen2000/stp-159/stp159-cuba.pdf.

————. 2001. *Housing Choice: 2000.* Census Brief C2KBR/01-13. Washington, DC:
  U.S. Government Printing Office.

————. 2002. *New York City Housing and Vacancy Survey: 2002 Microdata.* Washington, DC: U.S. Census Bureau.

————. 2006a. "International Data Base." http://www.census.gov/ipc/www/idbnew.
  html.

————. 2006b. "The Older Population in the United States, 2006." http://www.census.
  gov/population/socdemo/age/2006older_table4.csv.

————. 2006c. "2006 American Community Survey S10002." Washington, DC: Bureau
  of the Census. http://factfinder.census.gov/servlet/STTable?_bm=y&-qr_name-
  ACS_2006_EST_G00_S1002&-geo_id=01000US&-ds_name=ACS_2006_EST
  _G00_&-_lang=en&-redoLog=false.

————. 2007a. *American Community Survey.* Washington, DC: U.S. Census Bureau.

————. 2007b. "Expectation of Life and Expected Deaths by Race, Sex and Age,
  2003." In *The 2007 Statistical Abstract.* Washington, DC: U.S. Government
  Printing Office.

U.S. Immigration and Naturalization Service. 1990–1995. *Statistical Yearbooks, 1989–
  1994.* Washington, DC: U.S. Government Printing Office.

Uys, J. 1982. *The Gods Must Be Crazy.* Hollywood, CA: Twentieth Century Fox.

Valle, R. 1989. "Cultural and Ethnic Issues in Alzheimer's Disease Research." In *Alzheimer's Disease Treatment and Family Stress: Directions for Research.* E. Light
  and B. D. Lebowitz, eds. Rockville, MD: National Institute of Mental Health.

Valle, R. and L. Mendoza. 1978. *The Elder Latino.* San Diego: Campanile Press.

van den Hoonard, D. K. 1994. "Paradise Lost: Widowhood in a Florida Retirement
  Community." *Journal of Aging Studies* 8:121–32.

————. 2004. "Attitudes of Older Widows and Widowers in New Brunswick, Canada
  towards New Partnerships." In *Intimacy in Later Life.* K. Davidson and G.
  Fennell, eds. New Brunswick, NJ: Transaction Publishers.

Vanderbeck, R. 2007. "Intergenerational Geographies: Age Relations, Segregation and
  Re-engagements." *Geography Compass* 1(2):200–221.

Van der Geest, S. 2002. "Wisdom to Witchcraft: Ambivalence Towards Old Age in
  Rural Ghana." *Africa* 72:437–63.

————. 2004. "'They Don't Come to Listen': The Experience of Loneliness among Older
  People in Kwahu, Ghana." *Journal of Cross-Cultural Gerontology* 19:77–96.

Van Dullemen, C. 2006. "Older People in Africa: New Engines to Society?" *NWSA
  Journal* 18(1):99–105.

van Eeuwijk, P. 2006. "Old Age Vulnerability, Ill-Health and Care Support in Urban
  Areas of Indonesia." *Ageing and Society* 26:61–80.

Van Manen, M. 1990. *Researching Lived Experience.* New York: State University of
  New York Press.

van Reenen, J. 1996. *Central Pillars of the House: Sisters, Wives and Mothers in a Rural Community in Minangkabau, West Sumatra.* Leiden, The Netherlands:
  Research School CNWS.

Van Willigen, J. and N. Chadha. 2003. "Social Networks of Old People in India:
  Research and Policy. In *An Aging India: Perspectives, Prospects and Policies.*
  P. Liebig and S. Rajan, eds. New York: Haworth Press.

Vassilikos, V. 1995. "... *And Dreams Are Dreams.*" Mary Kitroeff, trans. New York: Seven Stories Press.

Vaupel, J. 2000. "Setting the Stage: A Generation of Centenarians?" *The Washington Quarterly* 23:197–200.

Vaupel, J., A. Baudisch, M. Dolling, D. A. Roach and J. Gampe. 2004. "The Case for Negative Senescence." *Theoretical Population Biology* 65:339–51.

Vellenga, D. D. 1986. "The Widow among the Matrilineal Akan of Southern Ghana." In *Widows in African Societies: Choices and Constraints.* B. Potash, ed. Stanford, CA: Stanford University Press.

Vesperi, M. E. 1985. *City of Green Benches: Growing Old in a New Downtown.* Ithaca, NY: Cornell University Press.

———. 1998. *City of Green Benches.* Rev. ed. Ithaca, NY: Cornell University Press.

———. 2008. "Evaluating Images of Aging in Print and Broadcast Media." *Boomer Bust? Economic and Political Dynamics of the Graying Society.* R. Hudson, ed. Westport, CT: Praeger.

Victor, C., S. Scambler, J. Bond and A. Bowling. 2000. "Being Alone in Later Life: Loneliness, Social Isolation and Living Alone." *Reviews in Clinical Gerontology* 10:407–17.

Vincent, J. 2006. "Ageing Contested: Anti-Aging Science and the Cultural Construction of Old Age." *Sociology* 40:681–98.

Vincentnathan, S. and L. Vincentnathan. 1994. "Equality and Hierarchy in Untouchable Intergenerational Relations and Conflict Resolutions." *Journal of Cross-Cultural Gerontology* 9:1–19.

Vivelo, F. R. 1977. *The Herero of Western Botswana: Aspects of Change in a Group of Bantu-Speaking Cattle Herders.* St.Paul, MN: West.

Vladeck, F. 2004. *A Good Place to Grow Old: New York's Model for NORC Supportive Service Programs.* Special Report. New York: United Hospital Fund. http://www.uhfnyc.org/usr_doc/goodplace.pdf.

Vogel, E. 1963. *Japan's New Middle Class: The Salary Man and His Family in a Tokyo Suburb.* Berkeley: University of California Press.

Voland, E. and J. Beise. 2002. "Opposite Effects of Maternal and Paternal Grandmothers on Infant Survival in Historical Krummhorn." *Behavioral Ecology and Sociobiology* 52:435–43.

Voluntariado AMIGOS. 2007. "Cinco Años al Servicio de los Adultos Mayores, 21 de Agosto 2001–2006" (brochure). Arequipa, Peru.

von Dem Knesebeck, O., M. Hyde, J. Siegrist et al. 2007. "Socio-Economic Position and Quality of Life among Older People in 10 European Countries: Results of the SHARE Study." *Ageing and Society* 27:269–84.

von Hassell, M. 2002. *The Struggle for Eden: Community Gardens in New York City.* Westport, CT: Bergin and Garvey.

von Mering, O. 1957. "A Family of Elders." In *Remotivating the Mental Patient.* O. von Mering and S. King, eds. New York: Russell Sage Foundation.

Wachter, K. W. and C. Finch, eds. 1997. *Between Zeus and Salmon: The Biodemography of Longevity.* Washington, DC: National Academy Press.

Wada, S. 1995. "The Status and Image of the Elderly in Japan: Understanding the Paternalistic Ideology." In *Images of Ageing: Cultural Representations of Later Life.* M. Featherstone and A. Wernick, eds. London and New York: Routledge.

Wadley, S. S. 1994. *Struggling with Destiny in Karimpur, 1925–1984.* Berkeley: University of California Press.

———. 2002. "One Straw from a Broom Cannot Sweep: The Ideology and Practice of the Joint Family in Rural North India." In *Everyday Life in South Asia*. D. P. Mines and S. Lamb, eds. Bloomington: Indiana University Press.

Wagner, L. 1997. "Long-Term Care in the Danish Health Care System." *Health Care Management State of the Art Review* June:149–56.

Walbridge, L. S. 1997. *Without Forgetting the Imam: Lebanese Shi'ism in an American Community*. Detroit: Wayne State University Press.

Walker, A. 2002. "Strategy for Active Ageing." *International Social Security Review* 55(1):121–39.

———. 2005. Towards an International Political Economy of Ageing. *Aging and Society* 25:815–39.

Walker, R., K. Hill, H. Kaplan and G. McMillan. 2002. "Age-Dependency in Skill, Strength and Hunting Ability among the Ache of Eastern Paraguay." *Journal of Human Evolution* 42:639–57.

Wallerstein, I. 1989. *The Modern World System III: The Second Era of Great Expansion of the Capitalist World-Economy, 1730–1840s*. New York: Academic Press.

Wang, M. and C. Xia. 2001. "The Current State of the Burden of Family Support for the Elderly in China." *Chinese Sociology and Anthropology* 34(1):49–66.

Wang, Z. 2000. "Gender, Employment and Women's Resistance." In *Chinese Society: Change, Conflict and Resistance*. E. J. Perry and M. Selden, eds. London and New York: Routledge.

Wardlaw, G. and A. Pike. 1986. "The Effect of Lactation on Peak Adult Shaft and Ultradistal Forearm Bone Mass in Women." *American Journal of Clinical Nutrition* 44(August):283–86.

Warner, L. 1937. *A Black Civilization*. New York: Harper & Brothers.

Warnes, A. 1993. "Being Old People and the Burdens of Burden." *Ageing and Society* 13:297–338.

———. 2006. "Aging, Health and Social Services in London." In *Growing Older in World Cities: New York, London, Paris and Tokyo*. V. Rodwin and M. Gusmano, eds. Nashville, TN: Vanderbilt University Press.

Warnes, A., K. Friedrich, L. Kelleher and S. Torres. 2004. "The Diversity and Welfare of Older Migrants in Europe." *Ageing and Society* 24(3):307–27.

Warnes, A. and I. Strüder. 2006. "Living Arrangements and Housing among Older People in London," In *Growing Older in World Cities: New York, London, Paris and Tokyo*. V. Rodwin and M. Gusmano, eds. Nashville, TN: Vanderbilt University Press.

Washburn, S. 1981. "Longevity in Primates." In *Aging: Biology and Behavior*. J. McGaugh and S. Kiesler, eds. New York: Academic Press.

Watanabe, C. 2006. "Japan's Centenarians at Record High of 28,395." *Post Crescent*, September 17.

Watson, J. A., S. M. Randolph and J. L. Lyons. 2006. "African American Grandmothers as Health Educators in the Family." In *Custodial Grandparenting: Individual, Cultural and Ethnic Diversity*. B. Hayslip and J. Hicks-Patrick, eds. New York: Springer.

Weaver, C. and D. Sklar. 1980. "Diagnostic Dilemmas and Cultural Diversity in Emergency Rooms." *Health Care Delivery* 133:356–66.

Weaver, R. 2008. "Bridging the Social Security Divide: Lessons from Abroad." Policy Brief Series No. 166. Washington, DC: Brookings Institution. http://www.brookings.edu/papers/2008/06_social_security_weaver.aspx.

Weber, E. 1976. *Peasants into Frenchmen: The Modernization of Rural France, 1870–1914.* Stanford, CA: Stanford University Press.

Weeks, J. 1984. *Aging: Concepts and Social Issues.* Belmont, CA: Wadsworth.

Weeks, J. and J. Cuellar. 1981. "The Role of Family Members in the Helping Networks of Older People." *The Gerontologist* 21:338–94.

Weibel-Orlando, J. 1987. *Final Report: Ethnicity, Continuity and Successful Aging.* Bethesda, MD: National Institute on Aging.

Weinberger, M. 2007. "Population Aging: A Global Overview." In *Global Health and Global Aging.* M. Robinson et al., eds. San Francisco: Jossey-Bass.

Weinick, R., S. Byron and A. Bierman. 2005. "Who Can't Pay for Health Care?" *Journal of General Internal Medicine* 20(6):504–9.

Weisner, T. 1997. *African Families and the Crisis of Social Change.* Westport, CT: Greenwood.

Weisner, T., C. Bradley and P. L. Kilbride, eds. 1997. *African Families and the Crisis of Social Change.* Westport, CT: Bergin and Garvey.

Weisz, D., M. K. Gusmano, V. G. Rodwin and L. Neuberg. 2007. "Population Health and the Health System: Avoidable Mortality in Three Wealthy Nations and their World Cities." *European Journal of Public Health* (August):1–7.

Wells, W., J. A. Schafer, S. P. Varano and T. S. Bynum. 2006. "Neighborhood Residents' Production of Order: The Effects of Collective Efficacy on Responses to Neighborhood Problems." *Crime and Delinquency* 52(4):523.

Welsch, W. 1999. "Transculturality: The Puzzling Forms of Cultures Today." In *Spaces of Culture.* M. Featherstone and S. Lash, eds. London: Sage.

Wen, M. and N. A. Christakis. 2006. "Prospective Effect of Community Distress and Subcultural Orientation on Mortality Following Life-Threatening Diseases in Later Life." *Sociology of Health and Illness* 28(5):558.

Wenger, C. 1997. "Review of Findings on Social Support Networks of Older Europeans." *Journal of Cross-Cultural Gerontology* 12(1):1–21.

Wentowski, G. 1981. "Reciprocity and Coping Strategies of Older People: Cultural Dimensions of Network Building." *The Gerontologist* 21(6):600–610.

Westburg, N. 2003. "Hope, Laughter and Humor in Residents and Staff at an Assisted Living Facility." *Journal of Mental Health Counseling* 25(1):16–32.

Wex, M. 2005. *Born to Kvetch: Yiddish Language and Culture in All of Its Moods.* New York: HarperCollins.

White, J. 1998. "Old Wine, Cracked Bottle? Tokyo, Paris and the Global City Hypothesis." *Urban Affairs Review* 33(4):451–77.

White, S. V.-R., D. K. Kamanga, T. Kachika, A. L. Chiweza and F. Gomile-Chidyaonga. 2002. *Dispossessing the Widow: Gender-Based Violence in Malawi.* Blantyre, Malawi: Women and Law in Southern Africa Research and Education Trust.

Whitefield, M. 1999. "The Cuba Craze: Havana's Golden Era Is Rich in Opportunity." *Miami Herald*, January 24, 1990.

Whyte, M. K. 2003. "The Persistence of Family Obligations in Baoding." In *China's Revolutions and International Relations.* M. K. Whyte, ed. Ann Arbor: University of Michigan Press.

———. 2004. "Filial Obligations in Chinese Families: Paradoxes of Modernization." In *Filial Piety: Practice and Discourse in Contemporary East Asia.* C. Ikels, ed. Stanford, CA: Stanford University Press.

Whyte, M. K. and W. Parish. 1984. *Urban Life in Contemporary China.* Chicago: University of Chicago Press.

Wieckowski, J. and W. J. Simmons. 2006. "Translating Evidence-based Physical Activity Programs into Community-Based Programs" Special issue, *Home Health Care Services Quarterly* 25:1–2.

Wiener, J. 1996. "Can Medicaid Long-Term Care Expenditures for the Elderly Be Reduced?" *The Gerontologist* 36(6):800–811.

Wiener, J., C. Estes, S. Goldenson and S. Goldberg. 2001. "What Happened to Long-Term Care in the Reform Debate of 1993–94? Lessons for the Future." *The Milbank Quarterly* 79(2):207–52.

Wiessner, P. 1977. "Hxaro: A Regional System of Reciprocity for Reducing Risk among the !Kung San." Ph.D. diss. University of Michigan.

———. 1983. "Social and Ceremonial Aspects of Death among the !Kung San." *Botswana Notes and Records* 15:1–15.

Willcox, B., Q. He, R. Chen, K. Yano, K. Masaki, J. Grove et al. 2006. "Midlife Risk Factors and Healthy Survival in Men." *Journal of the American Medical Association* 296:2343–50.

Willcox, B., D. Willcox, Q. He, J. Curb and M. Suzuki. 2006. "Siblings of Okinawan Centenarians Share Lifelong Mortality Advantages." *Journals of Gerontology. Series A, Biological Sciences and Medical Sciences* 61(4):345–54.

Willcox, B., D. Willcox and M. Suzuki. 2001. *The Okinawa Program.* New York: Random House.

———. 2004. *The Okinawa Diet Plan.* New York: Random House.

Willcox. B., D. Willcox, H. Todoriki, A. Fujiyoshi, K. Yano, Q. He et al. 2007. "Caloric Restriction, the Traditional Okinawan Diet and Healthy Aging: The Diet of the World's Longest-Lived People and Its Potential Impact on Morbidity and Life Span." *Annals of the New York Academy of Sciences* 1114:434–55.

Willcox, B., K. Yano, R. Chen, D. Willcox, B. Rodriguez, K. Masaki et al. 2004. "How Much Should We Eat? The Association between Energy Intake and Mortality in a 36-Year Follow-up Study of Japanese-American Men." *Journals of Gerontology. Series A, Biological Sciences and Medical Sciences* 59(8):789–95.

Willcox, D. 2005. "Okinawan Longevity: Where Do We Go from Here?" *Nutrition and Dietetics* 8:9–17.

Willcox, D. and J. Katata. 2000. "Kenko Chouju to shinkoshin, shukyou, girei no kakawari [Psycho-physiology of ritual in aging and health in Okinawa]." *Ronen Igaku* [Geriatric Medicine] 389:1357–64.

Willcox, D., B. Willcox, Q. He, N. C. Wang and M. Suzuki. 2008. "They Really Are That Old: A Validation Study of Centenarian Prevalence in Okinawa." *Journals of Gerontology. Series A, Biological Sciences and Medical Sciences* 63(4):338–49.

Willcox, D., B. Willcox, W. Hsueh and M. Suzuki. 2006. "Genetic Determinants of Exceptional Human Longevity: Insights from the Okinawa Centenarian Study." *AGE* 28:313–32.

Willcox, D., B. Willcox, S. Shimajiri, S. Kurechi and M. Suzuki. 2007. "Aging Gracefully: A Retrospective Analysis of Functional Status in Okinawan Centenarians." *American Journal of Geriatric Psychiatry* 15:252–56.

Willcox, D., B. Willcox, J. Sokolovsky and S. Sakihara. 2007. "The Cultural Context of 'Successful Aging' among Older Women Weavers in a Northern Okinawan Village: The Role of Productive Activity." *Journal of Cross-Cultural Gerontology* 22(2):137–65.

Willcox, D., B. Willcox, H. Todoriki, J. Curb and M. Suzuki. 2006. "Caloric Restriction and Human Longevity: What Can We Learn from the Okinawans?" *Biogerontology* 7(3):173–77.

Williams, A. 2002. "Changing Geographies of Care: Employing the Concept of Therapeutic Landscapes as a Framework in Examining Home Space." *Social Science and Medicine* 55:141–54.

Williams, C. L., R. Tappen, C. Buscemi, R. Rivera and J. Lezcano. 2001. "Obtaining Family Consent for Participation in Alzheimer's Research in a Cuban-American Population: Strategies to Overcome the Barriers." *American Journal of Alzheimer's Disease and Other Dementias* 16(3):183–87.

Williams, G. C. 1957. "Pleitropy, Natural Selection and the Evolution of Senescence." *Evolution* 11:398–411.

Williams, N. and D. Torrez. 1998. "Grandparenthood among Hispanics." In *Handbook on Grandparenthood*. M. E. Szinovacz, ed. Westport, CT: Greenwood Press.

Wilmoth, J. 2004. "Social Integration of Older Immigrants in 21st Century America." Policy Brief, No. 29. Center for Policy Research, Maxwell School of Citizenship and Public Affairs, Syracuse University.

Wilson, L. and S. Simson, eds. 2006. *Civic Engagement and the Baby Boomer Generation: Research, Policy and Practice Perspectives*. New York: Haworth Press.

Wilson, W. 1987. *The Truly Disadvantaged: The Inner City, the Underclass and Public Policy*. Chicago: University of Chicago Press.

Winn, R. and N. Newton. 1982. "Sexuality in Aging: A Study of 106 Cultures." *Journal Archives of Sexual Behavior* 11(4):283–98.

Winningham, R. et al. 2004. "MemAerobics: A Cognitive Intervention to Improve Memory Ability and Reduce Depression in Older Adults." *Journal of Mental Health and Aging* 9(3):183–92. http://www.memaerobics.net/articles roger.htm.

Winston, C. 2006. "African American Grandmothers Parenting AIDS Orphans: Grieving and Coping." *Journal of Qualitative Social Work* 5:33–43.

Winterbottom, D. 2005. "The Healing Nature of Landscapes." *Northwest Public Health* Spring/Summer:18–20.

Wong, R. et al. 2006a. "Identifying Vulnerable Older People: Insights from Thailand." *Journal of Aging and Health* 18:157–79.

———. 2006b. "Survey Data for the Study of Aging in Latin America and the Caribbean: Selected Studies." *Journal of Aging and Health* 18:157–79.

Woodward, K. 1986. *Memory and Desire*. Bloomington: Indiana University Press.

———, ed. 1999. *Figuring Age: Women, Bodies, Generations*. Bloomington: Indiana University Press.

World Bank. 1994. *Averting the Old Age Crisis*. New York: Oxford University Press.

———. 2006. "World Economy Indicators 2006." http://devdata.worldbank.org/wdi2006/contents/Section1.htm.

World Health Organization. 1991. *World Health Statistics Annual 1990*. Geneva: World Health Organization.

———. 2002a. *Active Ageing: A Policy Framework*. Geneva: World Health Organization.

———. 2002b. *Missing Voices: Views of Older Persons on Elder Abuse, A Study from Eight Countries: Argentina, Austria, Brazil, Canada, India, Kenya, Lebanon and Sweden*. Geneva: World Health Organization.

———. 2007a. "Major Developments in Health and Ageing: Briefing Series on Major Developments and Trends in Global Aging." Briefing paper prepared for the

AARP and United Nations Programme on Ageing/DESA. New York: United Nations. http://www.globalaging.org/health/world/2007/whodevelopments.pdf.

———. 2007b. *Women, Ageing and Health: A Framework for Action.* Geneva: World Health Organization. http://www.unfpa.org/upload/lib_pub_file/684_filename _ageing.pdf.

———. 2007c. *World Health Statistics Annual.* Geneva: World Health Organization.

Wöss, F. 1993. "Pokkuri Temples and Aging: Rituals for Approaching Death." In *Religion and Society in Modern Japan.* M. Mullins, S. Susumu and P. Swanson, eds. Berkeley, CA: Asian Humanities Press.

Wray, S. 2003. "Women Growing Older: Agency, Ethnicity and Culture." *Sociology* 37(3):511–27.

Wu, D. M. W., R. Carter, T. Goins and C. R. Cheng. 2005. "Emerging Services for Community-Based Long-Term Care in Urban China: A Systemic Analysis of Shanghai's Community-Based Agencies." *Journal of Aging and Social Policy* 17(4):37–60.

Wykle, M. and A. Ford. eds. 1999. *Serving Minority Elders in the 21st Century.* New York: Springer.

Wyshak, G. 1981. "Hip Fracture in Elderly Women and Reproductive History." *Journal of Gerontology* 36:424–27.

Xiandai Jiadian. 2002. "Wo guo dianbingxiang shichang xuqiu daqushi" [The market demand trend for refrigerators in China]. http://chinese.mediachina.net/index _market_view.jsp?id=14184.

Xinhua News Agency. 2005. "China Faces Up to Aging Population." January 7. http:// www.china.org.cn/english/government/117110.htm.

———. 2006a. "China Expects Communities to Take More Care of Elderly People." August 23. http://www.china.org.cn/english/MATERIAL/178873.htm.

———. 2006b. "8000 Chinese Elderly Participate in Web Design Contest." December 8. http://news3.xinhuanet.com/english/2006-12/08/content_5452876.htm.

———. 2007. "China Vows to Halt the Sex Ratio Imbalance." January 22. http://news. xinhuanet.com/english/2007-01/22/content_5637693.htm.

Yamori, Y., R. Horie, M. Ohtaka, Y. Nara and M. Fukase. 1976. "Effect of Hypercholesterolaemic Diet on the Incidence of Cerebrovascular and Myocardial Lesions in Spontaneously Hypertensive Rats (SHR)." *Clinical and Experimental Pharmacology and Physiology* 3:S205–8.

Yamori, Y., R. Horie, M. Ohtaka, Y. Nara and K. Ikeda. 1978. "Prophylactic Trials for Stroke in Stroke-Prone SHR: Amino Acid Analysis of Various Diets and Their Prophylactic Effect." *Japanese Heart Journal* 19:624–26.

Yan, E. and C. Tang. 2003. "Proclivity to Elder Abuse: A Community Study on Hong Kong Chinese." *Journal of Interpersonal Violence* 18(9):999–1017.

Yan, Y. X. 1997. "The Triumph of Conjugality: Structural Transformation of Family Relations in a Chinese Village." *Ethnology* 36(3):191–212.

———. 2003. *Private Life under Socialism: Love, Intimacy and Family Change in a Chinese Village, 1949–1999.* Stanford, CA: Stanford University Press.

Yanagishita, M. and J. Guralnik. 1988. "Changing Mortality Patterns That Led Life Expectancy in Japan to Surpass Sweden's, 1972–1982." *Demography* 25(4):611–24.

Yancura, L. A. and B. W. K. Yee. 2007. "Grandparents Caring for Grandchildren: Health Services Implications." Paper presented at the Annual RTC Conference. University of South Florida, Tampa.

Yang, D. T. 1999. "Urban-Biased Policies and Rising Income Inequality in China." *The American Economic Review* 89(2):306–10.

Yarwood, V. and G. Jowitt. 1998. "Life on the Rock." *New Zealand Geographic* 37:56–86.

Yeo, G. and D. Gallagher-Thompson. 2006. *Ethnicity and the Dementias*, 2nd ed. New York: Routledge.

Yip, P., C. Callanan and H. Yuen. 2000. "Urban/Rural and Gender Differentials in Suicide Rates: East and West." *Journal of Affective Disorders* (1–3):99–106.

Yomiuri. 2006a. "Appliance Makers Eye Elderly Customers." *Daily Yomiuri (Yomiuri Shimbun),* March 4.

———. 2006b. "Editorial: Society Must Cherish Its Elderly Citizens." *Daily Yomiuri (Yomiuri Shimbun),* September 18.

Young, R. and F. Ikeuchi. 1997. "Religion in 'The Hateful Age': Reflections on Pokkuri and Other Geriatric Rituals in Japan's Aging Society." In *Aging: Asian Concepts and Experiences, Past and Present.* S. Formanek and S. Linhart, eds. Vienna, Austria: Verlag der Österreichischen Akademie der Wissenschaften.

Youngblood, S. M. 2005. "Widowhood: Change and Well-Being in a Florida Leisure-Oriented Community," Master's thesis. University of Florida.

Yu, L. 1992. "Intergenerational Transfer of Resources within Policy and Cultural Contexts." In *Caregiving Systems: Informal and Formal Helpers.* S. Zarit, K. Perlin and K. W. Schaie, eds. Hillsdale, NJ: Lawrence Erlbaum.

Yun, R. and M. Lachman. 2006. "Perceptions of Aging in Two Cultures: Korean and American Views on Old Age." *Journal of Cross-Cultural Gerontology* 21: 55–70.

Zarit, S. H. and L. I. Pearlin, eds. 2005. "Health Inequalities across the Life Course." *Journals of Gerontology,* Special Issue II, 60B.

Zeballos, L. 2004. "Sistematizacion del Trabajo Social Realizado con Adultos Mayores." Report to J. Mahon, September 18. Arequipa, Peru.

———. 2007. "Accomplishments of AMIGOS." E-mail to J. Mahon, July 25, Arequipa, Peru.

Zelkovitz, B. 1997. "Transforming the 'Middle Way': A Political Economy of Aging Policy in Sweden." In *The Cultural Context of Aging: Worldwide Perspectives* 2nd ed. J. Sokolovsky, ed. Westport, CT: Bergin and Garvey.

Zhan, H. J., G. Y. Liu and H. G. Bai. 2005. "Recent Development in Chinese Elder Homes: A Reconciliation of Traditional Culture." *Ageing International* 30(2): 167–87.

Zhan, H. J. and R. J. V. Montgomery. 2003. "Gender and Elder Care in China: The Influence of Filial Piety and Structural Constraints." *Gender and Society* 17(2): 209–29.

Zhang, H. 1998. "Social Transformations, Family Life and Uxorilocal Marriages in a Hubei Village, 1870–1994." Ph.D. diss. Columbia University.

———. 2004. "Living Alone and the Rural Elderly: Strategy and Agency in Post-Mao Rural China." In *Filial Piety: Practice and Discourse in Contemporary East Asia.* C. Ikels, ed. Stanford, CA: Stanford University Press.

———. 2005. "Bracing for an Uncertain Future: A Case Study of New Coping Strategies of Rural Parents Under China's Birth Control Policy." *China Journal* 54(July):53–76.

———. 2006. "Family Care or Residential Care? The Moral and Practical Dilemmas Facing the Elderly in Urban China." *Asian Anthropology* 5:57–83.

———. 2007. "Who Will Care for Our Parents? Changing Boundaries of Family and Public Roles in Providing Care for the Aged in China." *Journal of Long-Term Home Health Care* 25(1):39–46.

Zhang, L. L., B. Z. Cai, X. S. Li, X. Cheng and Y. H. Chen. 2006. "Jianqiang yu wunai: Nanjingshi duju laoren shengcun zhuangkuang yu fuwu xuqiu diaocha baogao" [Perseverance and Compromise: Research Report on the Living Conditions of the Elderly Who Live Alone in Nanjing]. *Yingdui renkou laoling hua* [Coping with the aging of the population]. Beijing, China: Social Science Document Press.

Zhang, W. G. 2007. "Marginalization of Childless Elderly Men and Welfare Provision: A Study in a North China Village." *Journal of Contemporary China* 16(51): 275–93.

Ziel, H. and W. Finkle. 1975. "Increased Risk of Endometrial Carcinoma among Users of Conjugated Estrogens." *New England Journal of Medicine* 293:1167–70.

Zimmer, Z. 2006. "Disability and Active Life Expectancy among Older Cambodians." *Asian Population Studies* 2(2):133–48.

Zimmer, Z. and L. Martin. 2007. "Key Topics in the Study of Older Adult Health in Developing Countries That Are Experiencing Population Aging." Special issue: "The Comparative Study of Health Trends and Transitions in Later Life." *Journal of Cross-Cultural Gerontology* 22(3):235–41.

Zur, J. N. 1998. *Violent Memories: Mayan War Widows in Guatemala*. Boulder, CO: Westview.

Zweifel, P., S. Felder and A. Werblow. 2004. "Population Ageing and Health Care Expenditure: New Evidence on the 'Red Herring.'" *The Geneva Papers on Risk and Insurance* 29(4):652–66.

Zweig, C. and J. Abrams. 1991. *Meeting the Shadow: The Hidden Power of the Dark Side of Human Nature*. Los Angeles: Jeremy Tarcher.

Zwingle, E. 2002. "More to Explore." *National Geographic Online*. http://www.nationalgeographic.com/ngm/0211/feature3/index.html.

Index

About the Editor and Contributors

JAY SOKOLOVSKY, Ph.D., is Professor and Chair of the Department of Anthropology, Interdisciplinary Social Sciences and Criminology at the University of South Florida St. Petersburg. He specializes in cross-cultural, comparative gerontology and has written several books and authored more than 30 articles and book chapters dealing with this subject. In his research he has studied aging in a Mexican peasant village, New York's inner-city, Tampa, Florida, the new town of Columbia, Maryland and in urban neighborhoods in Croatia and England. He has edited *Growing Old in Different Societies* and is co-author of *Old Men of the Bowery*. Dr. Sokolovsky is co-founder and former President of the Association of Anthropology and Gerontology and the founder of the International Commission on Aging of the International Union of Anthropological and Ethnological Sciences.

STEVEN M. ALBERT, Ph.D., is Professor of Behavioral and Community Health Sciences in the Graduate School of Public Health at the University of Pittsburgh. His research examines lifespan approaches to health, with a specific focus on sources of ability and disability in old age. He has conducted field research in Papua New Guinea and in a variety of U.S. health care and community settings.

JUDITH C. BARKER, Ph.D., is a Professor of medical anthropology at the University of California San Francisco in the department of Anthropology, History and Social Medicine. Her work has explored the experience and meaning of illness and its day-to-day management by those who are ill, frail or dependent in some way, such as children, the disabled and the elderly. Her research projects have examined concepts of gender and ethnic differences in health beliefs; access to health care; substance use, HIV/AIDS and oral health as well as homelessness, family, access to and delivery of informal health care and the impact of policy on health disparities.

YEWOUBDAR BEYENE, Ph.D., is Associate Adjunct Professor at the Institute for Health and Aging and Department of Social and Behavioral Sciences. She is a medical anthropologist whose areas of expertise include biocultural anthropology, women's reproductive health, human development and aging, menopause and osteoporosis, minority aging and health care beliefs and practices of traditional cultures.

LINDA CARSON HENDERSON, R.N., Ph.D., M.P.H., is an Assistant Professor of Research in the College of Public Health at the University of Oklahoma and Center Coordinator for the American Indian Diabetes Center, funded by the NIH Center for Minority Health and Health Disparities. Dr. Henderson's research has examined diverse types of disease models of diabetes in American Indian populations and health care providers.

MARIA G. CATTELL, Ph.D., is Research Associate at Bryn Mawr College and The Field Museum of Natural History and has been doing research on gender, aging and social change among Abaluyia in rural western Kenya since 1982. She has also carried out research on Zulu grandmothers in South Africa and with older white ethnics in Philadelphia. She is co-author of *Old Age in Global Perspective: Cross-Cultural and Cross-National Views*, co-editor of *Social Memory and History: Anthropological Perspectives* and co-editor of *Women in Anthropology: Autobiographical Narratives and Social History*.

MIKE FEATHERSTONE, Ph.D., is Professor of Sociology and Communications at Nottingham Trent University and Director of the Theory, Culture and Society Centre. His major research interests include: consumer culture, globalization, the body, aging and the life course, social and cultural theory, new information technologies and social change.

CHRISTINE L. FRY, Ph.D., is Professor of Anthropology Emeritus at Loyola University of Chicago. She was co-director of Project AGE. Her publications focus on the life course; the meaning of age; the meaning of a good old age (well-being); cultural transformations, globalization and old age; and anthropological theories and age. She presently lives and writes in Bisbee, Arizona.

ANTHONY GLASCOCK, Ph.D., is Professor of Anthropology at Drexel University and President of Behavioral Informatics, Inc. His current research focuses on the use of technology to improve the quality of life of at-risk older adults by allowing them to remain in their own. He has published more than 70 articles and book chapters. He has conducted research in Ireland, Somalia, Canada, England and the Netherlands.

MICHAEL GURVEN, Ph.D., is Associate Professor of Biosocial Anthropology at the University of California–Santa Barbara. He has conducted fieldwork in Paraguay and Bolivia with Ache and Tsimane forager-horticulturalists. His research interests include intragroup cooperation and problems of collective action and the application of life history theory to explaining human longevity, cognitive development, delayed maturation and high levels of sociality. Since 2002, Gurven and Kaplan have co-directed the Tsimane Health and Life History Initiative, a five-year project to develop theory and test implications of different models of human life history evolution.

MICHAEL K. GUSMANO, Ph.D., is an Assistant Professor of Health Policy and Management at the State University of New York's Downstate Medical Center in Brooklyn. He is the Co-Director of the World Cities Project, a joint project of the International Longevity Center–USA, New York University and Columbia University. He is co-author two recent books: *Growing Older in World Cities* published by Vanderbilt University Press; and *Healthy Voices, Unhealthy Silence* Georgetown University Press.

EIGIL BOLL HANSEN is an economist with the Danish Institute of Governmental Research in Denmark. He is an internationally recognized expert on Danish long-term policy.

BERT HAYSLIP JR., Ph.D. in Psychology, teaches at the University of North Texas and is Editor of *The International Journal of Aging and Human Development*. His research deals with cognitive processes in aging, grandparents who raise their grandchildren, grief and bereavement and mental health and aging. Among his varied books are: *Cultural Changes in Attitudes toward Death, Dying and Bereavement* (2005); *Diversity among Custodial Grandparents* (2006) and *Adult Development and Aging* (2007).

MARY ELAINE HEGLAND, Ph.D., teaches in Anthropology of Women and Gender Studies at Santa Clara University. Based on her field work in Iran and Pakistan, she has published about religion, ritual and politics and about women and gender in revolution, local level politics, ethnic politics and Shi'a Muslim ritual. Recently, she has been conducting ethnographic research among the elderly in California's Bay Area and in Tehran, Shiraz and Aliabad, Iran, as well as in Turkey, Tajikistan and Afghanistan.

MIKE HEPWORTH, Ph.D., taught at the University of Aberdeen as a Lecturer in Sociology and formally retired at the end of 2004 with the status of Reader. He was highly committed to the perspective of symbolic interactionism, which for him facilitated his enormous curiosity about everyday life.

EDI INDRIZAL, M.A., is Lecturer in Social Anthropology at Andalas University in Padang, Indonesia and Director of the Institute for Social and

Development Analysis in Padang. Since 1999 he has been involved in a comparative research project on aging in Indonesia. His particular interests are in kinship, gender, aging and the environment among the Minangkabau.

MADELYN IRIS, Ph.D. in Anthropology, is Director of the Leonard Schanfield Research Institute at CJE SeniorLife in Chicago Illinois, a large multiservice organization serving more than 16,000 older adults through an array of community and residential programs. Dr. Iris also holds adjunct faculty appointments at the Feinberg School of Medicine, Departments of Preventive Medicine and Psychiatry and in the Department of Anthropology, where she is Director of the Northwestern University Ethnographic Field School.

BRENDA R. JENIKE, Ph.D., is an Assistant Professor of Anthropology at Lawrence University in Wisconsin and a faculty advisor in East Asian Studies, Biomedical Ethics and Gender Studies. Her interests include contemporary Japan, culture and aging, disability and long-term care, intergenerational relations, gender ideology, social welfare and social change. Her previous publications examine the transition from family care to community care in urban Japan from the perspectives of both family caregivers and elderly care recipients.

HILLARD KAPLAN, Ph.D., is Professor of Anthropology at the University of New Mexico. He has conducted fieldwork in Paraguay, Brazil, Botswana and Bolivia. His research interests include evolutionary and economic perspectives on life course development and senescence and brain evolution. He has applied human capital theory toward explaining human life history evolution and the proximate physiological and psychological mechanisms governing fertility and parental investment in both traditional, high-fertility, subsistence economies and modern, low-fertility, industrial societies.

STEPHEN KATZ, Ph.D., is Professor of Sociology at Trent University in Peterborough, Canada. He is author of *Disciplining Old Age: The Formation of Gerontological Knowledge, Cultural Aging: Life Course, Lifestyle and Senior Worlds* and numerous book chapters and articles on critical gerontology and the aging body.

JENNIE KEITH is Centennial Professor Emeritus of Anthropology and Senior Research Associate at Swarthmore College. She co-directed Project AGE with Christine Fry. She served as Chair of the Behavioral and Social Sciences Section of the Gerontological Society of America and has written many articles and books on old age and aging from an anthropological perspective.

KEVIN KINSELLA heads the Aging Studies Branch within the Census Bureau's International Programs Center. He is the primary author of two recent publications: *Growing Older in America. The Health and Retirement Study* and *Why Population Aging Matters. A Global Perspective.* From 2001 to 2006,

Kinsella was a Special Assistant in the International Programs Center, where he led the Census Bureau contribution to the President's Emergency Plan for AIDS Relief in the areas of database development, indicator analysis and overseas field training of USG personnel.

PHILIP KREAGER, D.Phil., is Lecturer in Human Sciences, Somerville College and Senior Research Fellow, Oxford Institute of Ageing, Oxford University. From 1999 to 2007 he directed Aging in Indonesia, a multisite anthropological demography of population aging supported by the Wellcome Trust.

SARAH LAMB, Ph.D., is Associate Professor of Anthropology at Brandeis University. She is the author of *White Saris and Sweet Mangoes: Aging, Gender and Body in North India* and co-editor of *Everyday Life in South Asia*. Her forthcoming third book is entitled *On the Shores of Endless Worlds: Aging and Modernity in India and Abroad.*

JOAN MAHON, M.S.S.W., is a social worker who has been advocating for the needs of older Hispanics since 1983, providing organizational support to grassroots programs in the United States, Peru, Spain, Australia and Singapore. She is committed to self-help and mutual help programs, promoting senior volunteerism and citizen participation as keys to individual growth and empowerment.

IVERIS L. MARTINEZ, Ph.D., is an Assistant Professor and Course Director for the Medicine and Society Program at Florida International University's College of Medicine. She received a joint Ph.D. in Anthropology and Public Health from the Johns Hopkins University. Her interests and publications are in the area of immigration, cross-cultural aging, social integration and community-based approaches to health.

ATHENA McLEAN, Ph.D., is Professor of Anthropology at Central Michigan University. She is currently conducting research at the Irish Centre for Social Gerontology, NUIG and the TRILCentre and has written extensively on dementia, long-term care, mental health and the political and moral economy of health and aging. Her recent works include *The Person in Dementia: A Study of Nursing Home Care in the U.S.* and (with Annette Leibing) *The Shadow Side of Fieldwork: Exploring the Borders between Ethnography and Life.*

HARRY MOODY, Ph.D., is Director of Academic Affairs for AARP. He is the author of *Aging: Concepts and Controversies* (now in its sixth edition) and *The Five Stages of the Soul*, among other publications. Moody edits a monthly e-newsletter on positive aging, "Human Values in Aging."

LARRY POLIVKA, Ph.D., has served as Director of the Florida Policy Exchange Center on Aging at University of South Florida Tampa and as Associate Director of the USF School of Aging Studies. Dr. Polivka previously worked at the State of Florida's Health and Rehabilitative Services as Assistant Secretary for Aging. Dr. Polivka's primary research interests are in long-term care, housing, ethics and politics of care, globalization/population aging, cultures of aging and the arts/humanities and aging.

MATTHEW ROSENBAUM is currently a Fulbright Fellow at Okinawa International University and Research Associate at Okinawa Research Center for Longevity Science. After graduating from Macalester College with degrees in Japanese and Biology, he has been living in Japan and researching the ongoing dialectic between culture and biology and interactions between lifestyle and longevity in Okinawa, Japan.

HARRIET G. ROSENBERG, Ph.D., is Associate Professor at York University (Toronto, Canada) in the Health and Society Program and the Coordinator of the Foundations Program in the Social Science Division. Her research interests include social change and women and health. She is the author of *A Negotiated World: Three Centuries of Change in a French Alpine Village*, co-author of *Through the Kitchen Window: The Politics of Home and Family* and *Evidence for Caution: Women and Statin Use*.

ELISABETH SCHRÖDER-BUTTERFILL, D.Phil., is Lecturer in Gerontology at the Centre for Research on Ageing, University of Southampton, UK. She has conducted ethnographic and demographic field research on aging and social networks in Indonesia. She is co-editor of *Aging without Children: European and Asian Perspectives* and is currently completing a monograph on older people's support network dynamics in East Java.

DENA SHENK, Ph.D., is Director of the Gerontology Program and Professor of Anthropology at the University of North Carolina–Charlotte. Her primary research interests focus on diversity in the aging experience based on gender, culture and environmental contexts. She has also published on the use of visual methodologies in aging research and is currently utilizing visual methodologies in her work with people with dementia and direct care workers.

PHILIP B. STAFFORD, Ph.D., is Director of the Center on Aging and Community at the Indiana Institute on Disability and Community. He is Adjunct Professor, Dept. of Anthropology at Indiana University in Bloomington, Indiana. An applied ethnographer, Dr. Stafford incorporates participatory research methods into his community development work around aging in Indiana and in multiple communities around the United States. This approach is to be featured in his forthcoming book *Elderburbia: Aging and a Sense of Place in America* (Greenwood, 2009).

MARY STUART, Sc.D., is Professor and Director of the Health Administration and Policy Program at University of Maryland, Baltimore County. She was formerly Director of Policy for the Maryland Department of Health. Her research interests include international best practices in long-term care and the prevention and management of chronic illnesses.

MAKOTO SUZUKI, M.D., Ph.D., is a cardiologist and geriatrician. He is Professor Emeritus and former Director of the Department of Community Medicine at the University of the Ryukyus in Okinawa, Japan. Currently, he is Director, Okinawa Research Center for Longevity Science. He is the Founder and Principal Investigator of the Okinawa Centenarian Study. Dr. Suzuki has more than 700 scientific publications and was recently presented with the Nishi-Nihon News Award to recognize his lifetime contributions to health and well being in Japan.

WILLIAM THOMAS, M.D., is Professor of Aging Studies and a Distinguished Fellow at the Erickson School at the University of Maryland Baltimore County. His books include, *What Are Old People For? How Elders Will Save the World, Learning from Hannah* and *Life Worth Living*. Thomas is an international authority on geriatric medicine and founder of The Eden Alternative and Green House models of eldercare.

JOHN W. TRAPHAGAN, Ph.D., is an Associate Professor of Religious Studies and Anthropology and Faculty Affiliate of the Population Research Center at the University of Texas at Austin. He is the author or editor of numerous books and articles on Japanese culture and society, including *Taming Oblivion: Aging Bodies and the Fear of Senility in Japan* (2000) and *The Practice of Concern: Ritual, Well-Being and Aging in Rural Japan* (2004).

JOAN WEIBEL-ORLANDO, Ph.D., is Associate Professor Emeritus of the Anthropology Department at the University of Southern California. Her several research projects, publications and videos have focused on rural-to-urban migration, alcohol and drug use and intervention and aging within Native American populations. Beginning in 1992 she has worked with and written about Tuscans as well as Tuscan Americans. She is also the author of *Indian Country, L.A.* (1991).

BRADLEY J. WILLCOX, M.D., M.Sc., is an investigator in geriatrics and gerontology at Pacific Health Research Institute (PHRI) and is Clinical Assistant Professor, Department of Geriatric Medicine, John A. Burns School of Medicine, University of Hawaii. At PHRI, Dr. Willcox is the lead investigator on the Kuakini Hawaii Lifespan Study, which seeks to identify genetic and other factors that lead to a long and healthy life. He is also a co-investigator of the Okinawa Centenarian Study, one of the world's longest-running and largest studies of hundred-year-olds.

D. CRAIG WILLCOX, Ph.D., is Associate Professor of International Health/ Welfare and Gerontology at Okinawa International University. With training in medical anthropology, gerontology and public health sciences he is work focuses on public health approaches to healthy aging and cross-cultural gerontology. Dr. Willcox is Co-Principal Investigator of the Okinawa Centenarian Study, a study of the genetic and lifestyle determinants of exceptional longevity funded by the U.S. National Institutes of Health and Japan's Society for Promotion of Science.

HONG ZHANG, Ph.D., is Associate Professor of East Asian Studies, Colby College, Maine. She has published articles on changing family life, intergenerational relations and eldercare patterns in contemporary China.